EUROPEAN INTELLECTUAL PROPERTY LAW

European Intellectual Property Law

JUSTINE PILA

BA/LLB Hons, PhD (Melbourne)
Fellow of St Catherine's College, Oxford
Research Fellow of the Institute of European and Comparative Law
Faculty of Law, University of Oxford

PAUL L.C. TORREMANS

Licentiaat in de Rechten (KU Leuven)
Licentiaat in het Notariaat (Examencommissie van de Staat, Leuven) Geaggregeerde
voor het HSO en het HOKT in de Rechten (KU Leuven) LLM (Leicester) PhD (Leicester)
Professor of Intellectual Property Law, University of Nottingham

OXFORD
UNIVERSITY PRESS

OXFORD
UNIVERSITY PRESS

Great Clarendon Street, Oxford, OX2 6DP,
United Kingdom

Oxford University Press is a department of the University of Oxford.
It furthers the University's objective of excellence in research, scholarship,
and education by publishing worldwide. Oxford is a registered trade mark of
Oxford University Press in the UK and in certain other countries

© Oxford University Press 2016

The moral rights of the authors have been asserted

Impression: 1

Public sector information reproduced under Open Government Licence v2.0
(http://www.nationalarchives.gov.uk/doc/open-government-licence/open-government-licence.htm)

Published in the United States of America by Oxford University Press
198 Madison Avenue, New York, NY 10016, United States of America

British Library Cataloguing in Publication Data

Data available

Library of Congress Control Number: 2015947230

ISBN 978–0–19–872991–4

Printed in Great Britain by
Bell & Bain Ltd., Glasgow

In memory of two remarkable European women,
Elvire Henriette Sion (FitzGerald), 1897–1993, and
Bronia Landsman (Pila/Levit), 1906–2004.
And in memory of my driving force in education, Leo Torremans.

Preface

A textbook on European intellectual property (IP) law could hardly have been contemplated two decades ago. Today, by contrast, understanding IP law in Europe must begin at the European level. Hence our aim in writing *European Intellectual Property Law* (*EIPL*), which has been to produce a concise and comprehensive account of European IP law suitable for an advanced undergraduate and graduate student audience, and of value also to teachers, researchers, and professionals. To that end we consider each of the main areas of substantive EU IP law—including the law of copyright and related rights, patents and plant variety rights, trade marks, design rights, and rights in data and information—as well as the EU IP systems more generally. In addition, we present each of these areas of substantive law in the context of both the EU legal system and international IP law, including EU constitutional law, the law of the European Patent Convention 1973/2000, and private international law. While our focus on European IP law means that we do not survey the domestic IP laws of individual countries in detail, we do consider substantive differences between those laws where relevant, and draw selectively on examples from domestic IP regimes to illustrate the impact of European law on those countries. In these and other ways we go beyond a discussion of the provisions of European legal instruments and their formal statements of purpose to consider their wider context and effect. Our hope is that by doing so we will equip students with the knowledge and understanding required to think critically and self-reflectively about the Europeanization of IP law.

EIPL has three main and distinguishing aims. The first is to give readers a deep understanding of the key concepts and rules of European IP law, including their theoretical underpinnings and significance for the domestic laws of EU Member States. The second is to equip readers to analyse issues of IP law from a European perspective, and to reflect on the difference between such an analysis and one undertaken from a national or international perspective. And the third is to engage and interest readers further in the process of legal harmonization, as well as in the European IP regime. In pursuit of these aims we hope to have produced a teaching and learning resource of value in courses on European, domestic, and international IP law, European private law, and the law of the European Union. The book assumes a certain legal maturity but no prior knowledge of any area of law as such, including no prior knowledge of EU or IP law. In keeping with the book's English language authorship, and in the interests of making it accessible to as wide an audience as possible, we have limited the further references proposed at the end of each chapter to works published in English. We apologize to those scholars writing and publishing in other languages, and whose work we read and appreciate.

Authorial responsibility for the book is shared as follows: Justine Pila is the author of Parts I to III, and Paul Torremans is the author of Parts IV to VII.

Justine Pila and Paul L.C. Torremans
Oxford and Nottingham
May 2015

Acknowledgements

We are grateful to WPG Publishers Belgium, and to Eva-Maria Painer, Gered Mankowitz, and EVA & ADELE for providing the artistic works reproduced as Figures 13.4, 11.2, 11.3, and 11.4 respectively. Thank you also to Christoph Reisinger for his assistance with translation.

We would also like to join OUP in sincerely thanking the following reviewers for their close reading of chapters in draft and for their detailed and helpful comments throughout the writing process:

Mike Adcock, Durham University, UK
Lee Bygrave, University of Oslo, Norway
Janice Denoncourt, Nottingham Trent University, UK
Matthew J. Elsmore, Aarhus University, Denmark
Lucie Guibault, Institute for Information Law, The Netherlands
Marta Iljadica, University of Southampton, UK
Stavroula Karapapa, Reading University, UK
Jan Leido, Umea University, Sweden
Nicola Lucchi, Jonkoping International Business School, Sweden
Dinusha Mendis, Bournemouth University, UK
Tuomas Mylly, University of Turku, Finland
Ana Nordberg, University of Copenhagen, Denmark
Lingling Wei, Bournemouth University, UK
Ulrika Wennersten, University of Lund, Sweden

Thank you also to those reviewers who wished to remain anonymous.

Finally, we are grateful to Tom Young of OUP for proposing this project, and to him and Carol Barber for their support in bringing it to fruition.

Outline Contents

Detailed Contents

Part III The Law of Copyright and Related Rights

Table of Abbreviations

1 In General

CFR	Charter of Fundamental Rights of the European Union [2012] OJ C 326/2
CJEU	Court of Justice of the European Union
EC	European Community
ECHR	Convention for the Protection of Human Rights and Fundamental Freedoms (4 November 1950) ETS 5 (as revised)
ECSC	European Coal and Steel Community
ECtHR	European Court of Human Rights
EEA	European Economic Area
EEC	European Economic Community
EESC	European Economic and Social Committee
EFTA	European Free Trade Association
EIPR	*European Intellectual Property Review*
ETSI	European Telecommunications Standards Institute
EU	European Union
FRAND	fair, reasonable, and non-discriminatory
GATT	General Agreement on Tariffs and Trade
GDP	gross domestic product
ICT	information communications technology
IIC	*International Review of Industrial [Intellectual] Property and Competition Law*
IP	intellectual property
IPQ	*Intellectual Property Quarterly*
ISP	Internet Service Provider
NPE	non-producing entity
OJLS	*Oxford Journal of Legal Studies*
SEA	Single European Act [1987] OJ L 169/1
SME	small and medium-sized enterprises
TEC	Consolidated Version of the Treaty Establishing the European Community [2002] OJ C 325/33
TEU	Consolidated Version of the Treaty on European Union [2010] OJ C 83/13
TFEU	Consolidated Version of the Treaty on the Functioning of the European Union [2010] OJ C 83/01
Treaty of Lisbon	Treaty of Lisbon amending the Treaty on European Union and the Treaty establishing the European Community [2007] OJ C 306/1

Treaty of Rome	Treaty of Rome (25 March 1957)
TRIPS Agreement	Agreement on Trade-Related Aspects of Intellectual Property Rights, Marrakesh Agreement Establishing the World Trade Organization, Annex 1C, Legal Instruments-Results of the Uruguay Round, vol. 31 (15 April 1994) 33 ILM 81
UDHR	Universal Declaration of Human Rights UN Doc. A/810 (1948) 71
UN	United Nations
UNESCO	United Nations Educational, Scientific and Cultural Organization
WIPO	World Intellectual Property Organization
WTO	World Trade Organization

2 Patent Law and Allied Rights

Agricultural Exemption Regulation	Council Regulation (EC) No. 1768/95 of 24 July 1995 implementing rules on the agricultural exemption provided for in Article 14(3) of Council Regulation (EC) No. 2100/94 on Community plant variety rights [1995] OJ L 173/14 (as revised)
AIPPI	International Association for the Protection of Intellectual Property
Basic Regulation	Council Regulation (EC) No. 2100/94 of 27 July 1994 on Community plant variety rights [1994] OJ L 227/1 (*also* Plant Variety Rights Regulation)
Biotech Directive	Directive 98/44/EC of the European Parliament and of the Council of 6 July 1998 on the legal protection of biotechnological inventions [1998] OJ L 213/13
CPC	Community Patent Convention of 1975
CPVO	Community Plant Variety Office
CPVR	community plant variety right
DUS	distinctness, uniformity, and stability
EPC	(European Patent Convention) Convention on the Grant of European Patents (5 October 1973) 13 ILM 268 (as revised)
EPO	European Patent Office
EP Organisation	European Patent Organisation
IIB	International Patent Institute
MP Regulation	Regulation (EC) No. 469/2009 of the European Parliament and of the Council of 6 May 2009 concerning the supplementary protection certificate for medicinal products [2009] OJ L 152/1
OHIM	Office for Harmonization in the Internal Market (Trade Marks and Designs)
Paris Convention	Paris Convention for the Protection of Industrial Property (20 March 1883) 13 UST 1 (as revised)
PCT	Patent Cooperation Treaty (19 June 1970) 1160 UNTS 231 (as revised)
Plant Variety Rights Regulation	Council Regulation (EC) No. 2100/94 of 27 July 1994 on Community plant variety rights [1994] OJ L 227/1 (*also* Basic Regulation)

PPP Regulation	Regulation (EC) No. 1610/96 of the European Parliament and of the Council of 23 July 1996 concerning the creation of a supplementary protection certificate for plant protection products [1996] OJ L 198/30
PVR	plant variety right
SPC	Strasbourg Patent Convention of 1963
Supplementary Protection Certificate Regulations	Regulation (EC) No. 1610/96 of the European Parliament and of the Council of 23 July 1996 concerning the creation of a supplementary protection certificate for plant protection products [1996] OJ L 198/30; Council Regulation (EC) No. 469/2009 of the European Parliament and of the Council of 6 May 2009 concerning the supplementary protection certificate for medicinal products [2009] OJ L 152/1
Unitary Patent Regulations	Regulation (EU) No. 1257/2012 of the European Parliament and of the Council of 17 December 2012 implementing enhanced cooperation in the area of the creation of unitary patent protection [2012] OJ L 361/1; Council Regulation (EU) No. 1260/2012 of 17 December 2012 implementing enhanced cooperation in the area of the creation of unitary patent protection with regard to the applicable translation arrangements [2012] OJ L 361/89
UP Regulation	Regulation (EU) No. 1257/2012 of the European Parliament and of the Council of 17 December 2012 implementing enhanced cooperation in the area of the creation of unitary patent protection [2012] OJ L 361/1
UPC	Unified Patent Court
UPC Agreement	Agreement on a Unified Patent Court (11 January 2013) EU Doc. 16351/12
UPOV Convention	International Convention for the Protection of New Varieties of Plants (2 December 1961) 815 UNTS 89 (as revised)

3 Copyright and Related Rights

Beijing Treaty	Beijing Treaty on Audiovisual Performances (24 June 2012) WIPO Doc. AVP/DC/20
Berne Convention	Berne Convention for the Protection of Literary and Artistic Works (9 September 1886) 1161 UNTS 3 (as revised)
Collective Rights Management Directive	Directive 2014/26/EU of the European Parliament and of the Council of 26 February 2014 on collective management of copyright and related rights and multi-territorial licensing of rights in musical works for online use in the internal market [2014] OJ L 84/72
Database Directive	Directive 96/9/EC of the European Parliament and of the Council of 11 March 1996 on the legal protection of databases [1996] OJ L 77/20
E-Commerce Directive	Directive 2000/31/EC of the European Parliament and of the Council of 8 June 2000 on certain legal aspects of information society services, in particular electronic commerce, in the Internal Market [2000] OJ L 178/1

Enforcement Directive	Directive 2004/48/EC of the European Parliament and of the Council of 29 April 2004 on the enforcement of intellectual property rights [2004] OJ L 195/16
Information Society Directive	Directive 2001/29/EC of 22 May 2001 of the European Parliament and of the Council on the harmonisation of certain aspects of copyright and related rights in the information society [2002] OJ L 167/10
Orphan Works Directive	Directive 2012/28/EU of the European Parliament and of the Council of 25 October 2012 on certain permitted uses of orphan works [2012] OJ L 299/5
Rental and Lending Rights Directive	Council Directive 92/100/EEC of 19 November 1992 on rental right and lending right and on certain rights related to copyright in the field of intellectual property [1992] OJ L 346/61, replaced by Directive 2006/115/EC of the European Parliament and of the Council of 12 December 2006 on rental right and lending right and on certain rights related to copyright in the field of intellectual property [2006] OJ L 376/28 (codified version)
Resale Right Directive	Directive 2001/84/EC of the European Parliament and of the Council of 27 September 2001 on the resale right for the benefit of the author of an original work of art [2001] OJ L 272/32
Rome Convention	Convention for the Protection of Performers, Producers of Phonograms and Broadcasting Organisations (26 October 1961) 496 UNTS 43
Rome I Regulation	Regulation (EC) No. 593/2008 of the European Parliament and of the Council of 17 June 2008 on the law applicable to contractual obligations [2008] OJ L 177/6
Rome II Regulation	Regulation (EC) No. 864/2007 of the European Parliament and of the Council of 11 July 2007 on the law applicable to non-contractual obligations [2007] OJ L 199/40
Satellite and Cable Directive	Council Directive 93/83/EEC of 27 September 1993 on the coordination of certain rules concerning copyright and rights related to copyright applicable to satellite broadcasting and cable retransmission [1993] OJ L 248/15
Software Directive	Directive 91/250/EEC of 14 May 1991 on the legal protection of computer programs [1991] OJ L 122/42, replaced by Directive 2009/24/EC of the European Parliament and of the Council of 23 April 2009 on the legal protection of computer programs [2009] OJ L 111/16 (codified version)
Term Directive	Council Directive 93/98/EEC of 29 October 1993 harmonising the term of protection of copyright and certain related rights [1993] OJ L 290/9, replaced by Directive 2006/116/EC of the European Parliament and of the Council of 12 December 2006 on the term of protection of copyright and certain related rights [2006] OJ L 372/12 (codified version)
Term Amendment Directive	Directive 2011/77/EU of the European Parliament and of the Council of 27 September 2011 amending Directive 2006/116/EC on the term of protection of copyright and certain related rights [2011] OJ L 265/1

WCT	WIPO Copyright Treaty (20 December 1996) WIPO Doc. CRNR/DC/94
WPPT	WIPO Performances and Phonograms Treaty (20 December 1996) WIPO Doc. CRNR/DC/95

4 Trade Marks and Allied Rights

Aromatised Wines Regulation	Regulation (EU) No. 251/2014 of the European Parliament and of the Council on the definition, description, presentation, labelling and the protection of geographical indications of aromatised wine products [2014] OJ L 84/14
Commercial Practices Directive	Directive 2005/29/EC of the European Parliament and of the Council of 11 May 2005 concerning unfair business to consumer commercial practices in the internal market [2005] OJ L 149/22
Comparative Advertising Directive	Directive 2006/114/EC of the European Parliament and of the Council of 12 December 2006 concerning misleading and comparative advertising [2006] OJ L 376/21
Designs Directive	Directive 98/71/EC of the European Parliament and of the Council of 13 October 1998 on the legal protection of designs [1998] OJ L 289/28
Designs Regulation	Council Regulation (EC) No. 6/2002 of 12 December 2001 on Community designs [2002] OJ L 3/1
Lisbon Agreement	Lisbon Agreement for the Protection of Appellations of Origin and their International Registration (31 October 1958) 923 UNTS 205 (1974)
Madrid Agreement	The Madrid Agreement Concerning the International Registration of Marks (14 April 1891) 828 UNTS 391
Paris Convention	Paris Convention for the Protection of Industrial Property (20 March 1883) 13 UST 1 (as revised)
Quality Schemes Regulation	Regulation (EU) No. 1151/2012 of the European Parliament and of the Council of 21 November 2012 on quality schemes for agricultural products and foodstuffs [2012] OJ L 343/1
Spirits Regulation	Regulation (EC) No. 110/2008 of the European Parliament and of the Council of 15 January 2008 on the definition, description, presentation, labelling and the protection of geographical indications of spirit drinks [2008] OJ L 39/16
Trade Mark Regulation	Council Regulation (EC) No. 40/94 of 20 December 1993 on the Community trade mark [1994] OJ L 11/1, replaced by Council Regulation (EC) No. 207/2009 of 26 February 2009 on the Community trade mark [2009] OJ L 78/1 (codified version)
Trade Marks Directive	First Council Directive 89/104/EEC of 21 December 1988 to approximate the laws of the Member States relating to trade marks [1989] OJ L 40/1, replaced by Council Directive 2008/95/EC of the European Parliament and of the Council of 22 October 2008 to approximate the laws of the Member States relating to trade marks [2008] OJ L 299/25 (codified version)
Trademark Law Treaty	The Trademark Law Treaty (27 October 1994) 2037 UNTS 35

Wine Regulation	Council Regulation (EC) No. 1234/2007 of 22 October 2007 establishing a common organisation of agricultural markets and on specific provisions for certain agricultural products (Single CMO Regulation) [2007] OJ L 299/1

5 Other

Brussels I Regulation	Council Regulation (EC) No. 44/2001 of 22 December 2000 on jurisdiction and the recognition and enforcement of judgments in civil and commercial matters (16 January 2001), amended by Regulation (EU) No. 1215/2012 of the European Parliament and of the Council of 12 December 2012 on jurisdiction and the recognition and enforcement of judgments in civil and commercial matters [2012] OJ L 351/1 (recast)
Conditional Access Directive	Directive 98/84/EC of the European Parliament and of the Council of 20 November 1998 on the legal protection of services based on, or consisting of, conditional access [1998] OJ L 320/54
Convention on Biological Diversity 1992	Convention on Biological Diversity (5 June 1992) 1760 UNTS 79
Data Exclusivity Directive	Directive 2004/27/EC of the European Parliament and of the Council of 31 March 2004 amending Directive 2001/83/EC on the Community code relating to medicinal products for human use [2004] OJ L 136/34
Data Protection Directive	Directive 95/46/EC of the European Parliament and the Council of 24 October 1995 on the protection of individuals with regard to the processing of personal data and on the free movement of such data [1995] OJ L 281/31
Database Directive	Directive 96/9/EC of the European Parliament and of the Council of 11 March 1996 on the legal protection of databases [1996] OJ L 77/20
Draft Trade Secrets Directive	Proposal for a Directive of the European Parliament and of the Council on the protection of undisclosed know-how and business information (trade secrets) against their unlawful acquisition, use and disclosure COM (2013) 813 final
E-Commerce Directive	Directive 2000/31/EC of the European Parliament and of the Council of 8 June 2000 on certain legal aspects of information society services, in particular electronic commerce, in the Internal Market [2000] OJ L 178/1
EEA Agreement	Agreement on the European Economic Area [1994] OJ L 1/3
Enforcement Directive	Corrigendum to Directive 2004/48/EC of the European Parliament and of the Council of 29 April 2004 on the enforcement of intellectual property rights [2004] OJ L 195/16
Privacy Directive	Directive 2002/58/EC of the European Parliament and of the Council of 12 July 2002 concerning the processing of personal data and the protection of privacy in the electronic communications sector [2002] OJ L 201/37 (as revised)
Semiconductor Directive	Council Directive 87/54/EEC of 16 December 1986 on the legal protection of topographies of semiconductor products [1987] OJ L 24/36

Glossary of Patent Terms

Anticipation The making available to the public of an invention before the priority date.

Common general knowledge The background technical knowledge attributed to the notional skilled addressee and against which the prior art must be considered.

Euro-PCT application An application for a European patent filed with a Patent Cooperation Treaty Receiving Office and designating the European Patent Office as an Office from which protection is sought.

European patent A patent granted under the EPC and taking effect as a bundle of national patents in one or more EPC Contracting States.

Exhaustion The termination of a patent owner's rights to exclude others from the use of a patented product following the first sale of the product with the patent owner's consent.

Opposition The objection by a third party to a patent application or grant.

Patent claim construction The interpretation of patent claims.

Patent claims The formal definition of the patented invention contained in the patent specification.

Patent filing The submission to a patent office of a formal application (request) for the grant of a patent for a specified invention.

Patent specification The document representing the terms of the patent grant, and comprising the patent claims, description, and drawings in which the patented invention is defined and described.

Patent thicket A dense collection of overlapping patent rights.

Prior art Information regarding an art (field of technology) that was made available to the public before the priority date.

Priority date The date at which the novelty and inventiveness of an invention is assessed for patentability purposes, being the date of local or foreign patent filing.

Revocation The withdrawal of a patent grant.

Search report The report regarding the prior art relating to an invention.

Skilled addressee The notional reasonable person skilled in the art to which the invention relates and through whose eyes patent specifications, prior art, and other technical information is understood.

Standard essential patent A patent in relation to an invention that is essential to ensuring compliance with a technical standard.

Table of Cases

National Courts (split by jurisdiction)

Table of Legislation, Treaties, and Conventions

EU Instruments

PART I

Foundations

1

An Introduction to Domestic and International Intellectual Property Law

1.1 Introduction

In recent decades, advances in technology and a rapidly globalizing economy have made expressive and informational subject matter increasingly important, and issues surrounding their use increasingly difficult to define and resolve. Meeting these challenges is the central task of the intellectual property (IP) system. According to its supporters, IP systems and the laws on which they are based protect individual rights and interests, promote innovation, culture, creativity, and social participation, support the growth and smooth functioning of competitive markets, and are of enormous importance for business, outstripping the importance of physical (tangible) assets. Regarding their importance for trade and industry specifically, a study by the European Patent Office (EPO) and Office for Harmonization in the Internal Market (Trade Marks and Designs) (OHIM) in September 2013 found that during the three-year period from 2008 to 2010, IP-intensive industries were responsible for generating: (a) almost 26 per cent of all jobs in the EU (56.5 out of 218 million), increasing to 35.1 per cent if jobs in industries supplying goods and services to IP-intensive industries were counted; (b) almost 39 per cent of the EU's total economic activity (gross domestic product, GDP), valued at €4.7 trillion; and (c) most of the EU's trade with the rest of the world. In addition, the study reported that average weekly wages in IP-intensive industries were 41 per cent higher than in non-IP-intensive industries, at €715 compared with €507.[1] So too a study commissioned by the British Government in 2011 estimated global trade in IP licensing alone to be worth more than €819 billion a year: 'five per cent of world trade

---

[1] EPO and OHIM, 'IPR intensive industries contribution to the Economic Performance and Employment in the European Union' (Industry-Level Analysis Report, September 2013) [2.1]. See also EY, 'Creating Growth: Measuring Cultural and Creative Markets in the EU' (December 2014), estimating the creative and cultural industries specifically to account for 4.2 per cent of the EU's GDP and nearly 7 million jobs, primarily in small businesses.

and rising'.[2] When combined with the other perceived benefits of IP recognition and protection outlined above, such evidence explains the centrality of IP to European social and economic policies.

In this first chapter we commence our introduction to the European law of IP by introducing the domestic and international IP systems that preceded and continue to exist alongside it. Our starting point is the 'what, how, and why' of IP law in general: what it is, how it came to be, and why it exists. This discussion will lay the groundwork for an introduction to the EU law of IP in Chapter 2 and a more detailed study of theoretical accounts of European IP in Chapter 3. By devoting space in Part I to history and theory, our aim is to illustrate foundational aspects of the legal field studied in later parts, and to enable a fuller understanding of its substantive rules than would be possible without some awareness of their historical and normative underpinnings.

Another natural starting point for thinking about the European law of IP is with the different forms of international cooperation that preceded and continue to be developed alongside it. One reason is that international initiatives in IP share many of the aims of European initiatives, including addressing the problems created by domestic IP territoriality. Another is that the international IP system represents an explicit legal basis and framework for the European IP system. And a third is that most of the international instruments comprising this system generate legal effects within the EU legal order and may thus be counted as sources of European IP law. In this chapter we therefore follow our discussion of the what, how, and why of IP law in general with an account of the what, how, and why of the international law of IP specifically.

1.2 The What, How, and Why of Domestic Intellectual Property Law

1.2.1 What is Intellectual Property Law?

IP law is the area of law concerned with the recognition and protection of private rights in respect of expressive and informational subject matter (intellectual products), from authorial works and broadcasts to inventions, signs of commercial origin, aspects of product appearance, and confidential information. It is most commonly conceived as a mechanism for balancing competing rights and interests in respect of these subject matter, or as a tool for regulating access to their benefits. Included within the general category of IP rights are: copyright and related rights, referred to also as authors' rights and neighbouring rights respectively; patents and plant variety rights; trade marks, geographical indications, and design rights; and certain additional *sui generis* rights in respect of information and data. This is shown in Figure 1.1. In the terminology of European law, all but copyright and related rights fall within the general category of 'industrial property' rights, most of which are distinguished by their concern with industrial or commercial subject matter and activities. With a small number of exceptions, all IP rights are property rights and share the main characteristics of other property rights. Thus, they confer a set of transferable (albeit not necessarily assignable) exclusionary rights in respect of a discrete and definable object, and are enforceable by their owner or the state in civil or criminal proceedings. In this sense IP rights are negative rather than positive, since they confer only the right to prohibit others from using the object to which they attach without also

---

[2] I. Hargreaves, 'Digital Opportunity: Review of Intellectual Property and Growth' (18 May 2011) https://www.gov.uk/government/publications/digital-opportunity-review-of-intellectual-property-and-growth,3.

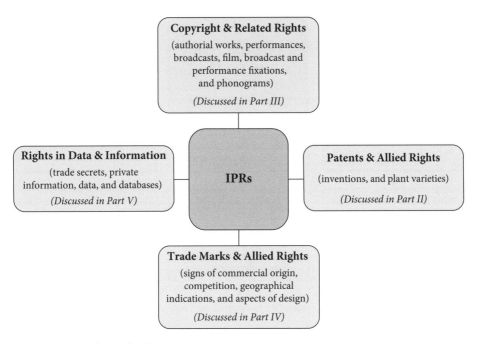

Figure 1.1 IP rights and subject matter

conferring a right to use the object itself. While this distinction may seem semantic, it is important in the case of technological products such as medicines, and plant varieties, the commercial use of which requires separate regulatory approval from the state.

When considering different species of IP right it is useful to think in terms of three things: the subject matter to which the rights attach; the uses of the subject matter which the law reserves to the holders of those rights; and the third party acts permitted notwithstanding the rights' subsistence. An overview of these aspects of copyright, patents, trade marks, and designs is given in Figure 1.2.

1.2.2 **The How and Why of Intellectual Property Law**

1.2.2.1 **Theoretical Accounts of the Existence of IP Law**

Throughout its more than 600-year history, the law of IP has been dogged by persistent disagreement over its normative foundations, and whether they are sufficient to account for the various IP regimes that exist. Particularly heated have been the debates over the classification of IP rights as property rights because of its perceived implications for their nature, scope, and enforceability, and over the capacity of IP systems to accommodate new technologies such as film, the Internet, and biotechnology.

A common starting point for these debates has been the intangible nature of the subject matter that IP rights protect. For example, as an authorial work protectable by copyright, a musical tune is a combination of sounds that exists separate from any printed score, compact disk, or other physical object on which those sounds may be recorded. Similarly, as an invention protectable by a patent, a medicine is an idea for a product that can be manufactured and used to improve human health that exists separate from any manufactured pharmaceutical substances themselves. And finally, as a sign indicating the origin of certain manufactured goods, each of the NIKE mark and its associated Swoosh design exists separate from its material instantiations on articles of clothing or sports equipment, etc.

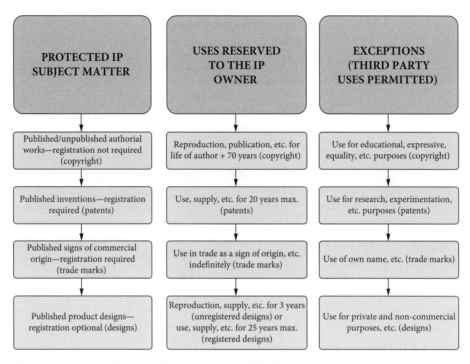

Figure 1.2 Defining features of the main types of IP right under European law

Hence the distinction between the intangible subject matter protected by IP rights and their tangible manifestations, which distinction is central to the law and practice in this field.

The intangibility of intellectual products is generally regarded as creating immediate difficulties for those seeking to justify the recognition and protection of IP rights. The reason is that property rights typically subsist in tangible objects, such as land and chairs, and are commonly explained with reference to either: (a) the natural derivation of exclusionary rights from those objects by virtue of their tangibility; or (b) the endorsement of exclusionary rights in respect of those objects by the state as a means of preventing the damage that would be caused to them, and the social conflict that would arise among members of the public, if people were free to occupy and use them simultaneously. However, the non-crowdability and non-depletability of intellectual products makes each of these explanations unconvincing in their case. Specifically, while only one person can occupy a chair at any particular time, and each use of a chair will limit its life, any number of people can simultaneously read the same poem or apply the same mark to their goods, and reading a poem or applying a mark will have no impact on its ability to be used by others. It follows that intellectual products are incapable of supporting exclusive occupation, and thus incapable of supporting exclusionary rights derived from nature. If IP rights are to exist, they must therefore be artificially created by the state.[3] However, for the state to create exclusionary rights where none exists naturally requires clear justification because of the restrictions on public freedoms which those rights entail. One possible justification could be preventing damage and social conflict, consistent with (b) above. On the other hand, the non-crowdability and non-depletability of intellectual products

---

[3] M. Lehmann, 'The Theory of Property Rights and the Protection of Intellectual and Industrial Property' (1985) 16 *IIC* 525, 531.

suggests that allowing unlimited public access to them would neither damage them nor cause social conflict. It follows that if the state is to recognize IP rights, an alternative justification must be found.

In the view of some, no such justification exists. Thus, it has been said, IP rights exist for essentially historical and pragmatic reasons, and while our investment in them is sufficient to make their abolition infeasible, they have no positive justification as such. In the frequently quoted words of Fritz Machlup:

> If we did not have a patent system, it would be irresponsible, on the basis of our present knowledge of its economic consequences, to recommend instituting one. But since we have had a patent system for a long time, it would be irresponsible, on the basis of our present knowledge, to recommend abolishing it.[4]

So too, it has been said, for other IP rights.

The argument that IP rights exist for essentially historical and pragmatic reasons alludes to the value of history in understanding them. In particular, an understanding of the origins of IP offers an empirical account of its existence in the absence of an accepted normative account. In addition, it offers an insight into the considerations and values that drove the emergence and early development of IP among European states, and in so doing allows us to identify certain themes and principles of importance for contemporary European IP law. These include themes and principles that express the values common to Member States on which European union is based, the 'spiritual and moral heritage' that European law seeks to preserve, and the 'cultures and traditions' of peoples whose diversity European law seeks to respect.[5]

1.2.2.2 Historical Accounts of the Existence of IP Law

Any discussion of the origins of IP law in the space available here will be necessarily selective. In the discussion that follows we focus on a small number of events that may be said to have especial significance for the three paradigm IP regimes: copyright, patents, and trade marks.[6] For copyright they are the themes illustrated in Figure 1.3, namely, the recognition of the idea of authorial property in the classical Roman period, the recognition of ownership rights in respect of literary reproductions in the Middle Ages, the grant of 'rights of copy' to limit the use of new technologies to reproduce and distribute information and ideas in the 16th century, and the emergence of the first common law and civil law copyright enactments in the 18th century. For patents they are the grant of privileges to reward or encourage innovation from 500 BCE, the introduction of the first general patent statute in the 15th century, the recognition of patents as exceptions to a general prohibition against 'odious monopolies' in the 17th century, the establishment of patent examination systems in the 18th century, and the so-called 'patent wars' of the 19th century. And finally, for trade marks, they are

[4] F. Machlup, *An Economic Review of the Patent System: Study of the Subcommittee on Patents, Trademarks, and Copyrights of the Committee on the Judiciary* (US Govt Printing Office, 1958) 80.

[5] See Preamble, Articles 2, 3, and 6 TEU; Preamble CFR. As we will see, the protection of intellectual property is among the fundamental rights recognized by the CFR (Article 17(2)).

[6] Compare the designs regime, which is generally regarded as a hybrid of the copyright, patents, and even trade marks regimes, consistent with the combined aesthetic and industrial (including source-indicating) character of design itself, and with its origins and early development in Europe as part of the copyright and industrial property systems respectively. See further nn 13 and 28; also Finniss (n 49) regarding the development of the designs regime in France; and R. Deazley, 'Commentary on the Calico Printers' Act 1787' in L. Bently and M. Kretschmer (eds), *Primary Sources on Copyright (1450–1900)* (1980) http://www.copyrighthistory.org, regarding the first designs regime of England.

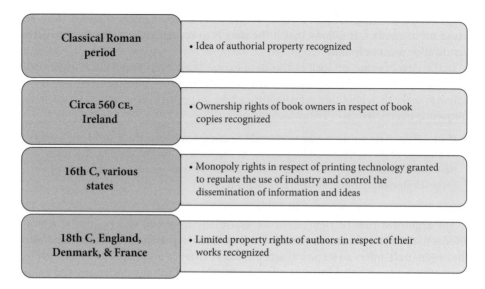

Figure 1.3 Events in the emergence of copyright

the use of marks to indicate the ownership and commercial origin of goods beginning in ancient times, and the recognition of the right of a trader to prevent others from causing deceit by applying his sign of commercial origin to their goods in the 17th century.

Before commencing our discussion of these events, it may be useful to introduce two analytical frameworks and reference points for understanding each and its significance. The first is the distinction between private and public law, and the idea of IP law as private law and IP rights as private rights. Already in this chapter we have seen two different accounts of property as rights of exclusive occupation derived from nature and as artificial regulatory instruments created by the state respectively. Whatever the normative validity of these accounts (to which we return in Sections 3.4 and 3.6), in practice the recognition and protection of IP rights have tended to follow a decision by a recognized public authority to endorse the claim of an individual in respect of a specific subject matter through the grant of limited exclusionary rights 'impressed with social obligations, and subjected to administrative interferences'.[7] Thus, while IP rights satisfy most definitions of private rights by reason of their enforceability against other individuals, they also have (and have always had) a strong public law dimension in their conferral of rights and obligations on individuals vis-à-vis society and the state. In addition, this public law dimension of IP has been accentuated at the European level by the political and constitutional orientation of European legal communities. Among other things, that orientation is reflected in the teleological, purposive, and systemic methods applied by European tribunals when interpreting substantive rules, and the emphasis given in those interpretations to the social, economic, and political—as well as the historical—context in which the rules exist and operate.

The second analytical framework connects to this idea of IP as situated at the interface of the public/private law and rights divide. Its focus is the variety of extra-legal

---

[7] F.D. Prager, 'A History of Intellectual Property From 1545 to 1787' (1944) 26 *Journal of the Patent Office Society* 711, 717.

mechanisms by which people are excluded from products, and the way in which these mechanisms work together and affect the need for intervention by the state through the recognition and protection of property. This is a key insight of Lawrence Lessig, who identifies three extra-legal mechanisms as having especial importance for IP: social norms, the market, and real-space access restrictions (architecture). According to Lessig:

> Property is protected by the sum of the different protections that law, norms, the market, and real-space code yield. . . . From the point of view of the state, we need law only when the other three modalities leave property vulnerable. From the point of view of the citizen, real-space code (such as locks) is needed when laws and norms alone do not protect enough. Understanding how property is protected means understanding how these different protections work together.[8]

Once again, the early European experience of IP is more clearly understood with this paradigm in mind. For example, the paradigm helps us to see and assess that experience in terms of the connections that exist between IP rights, the economy, technology, and the social norms of different rights-endorsing societies, and in so doing to understand the significance of that experience and those connections for the substantive rules of European IP law today.

1.2.2.2.1 The Origins of Copyright
The recognition of authorial property in the classical Roman period

While the first copyright legislation was not introduced until the 18th century, the roots of copyright can be traced to the classical Roman period, where the idea of authorial property was already recognized and accepted. According to Roman law principles of *accessio*, for example, if a person painted a picture on another person's canvas she thereby acquired ownership of the canvas.[9] Hence, from the earliest times acts of authorship have been recognized in European communities as capable of supporting property rights. So too the idea of authorial property can be seen in the social norms of plagiarism that existed during this period. Derived from the Latin word '*plagium*', meaning to steal another's slave or child, one of the earliest known uses of the term 'plagiarism' is in a charge of literary theft made by Martialis in the first century CE, reported as follows:

> It is said, Fidentinus, that in reciting my verses you always speak of them as your own. If you are willing to credit them to me, I will send them to you gratis. If, however, you wish to have them called your verses, you had better buy them, when they will no longer belong to me.[10]

Once again, the report of Martialis's words offers evidence of the early recognition of the idea of authors' rights—including here the right of authors to insist on the attribution of their works—and of the conception of those rights as objects of value capable of being traded on the market. In the use of the term 'plagiarism' itself one also sees evidence of the early conception of authorial works as metaphorical slaves or children of their authors, and of authors as harmed economically and emotionally by their unauthorized use.

---

[8] L. Lessig, *Code: Version 2* (Basic Books, 2006) 171.

[9] Cf W.W. Buckland, *A Text-Book of Roman Law: From Augustus to Justinian* (3rd edn revised by Peter Stein, CUP, 1963) 210. By contrast, if a person wrote on another person's parchment her writing ceded to the parchment.

[10] G.H. Putnam, *Authors and their Public, in Ancient Times: A Sketch of Literary Conditions and of the Relations With the Public of Literary Producers, from the Earliest Times to the Fall of the Roman Empire* (1896) 234.

*The recognition of ownership rights in respect of literary reproductions
in the Middle Ages*

The idea of authorial works as objects of both personal and property rights was also apparent in the Middle Ages, when the famous *Cathach of Columba* case was heard, resulting in the world's first reported copyright judgment. This case concerned the unauthorized copying by an Irish missionary, Columba, of a book of psalms owned by Finnian and kept in the locked library of his monastery. While visiting the monastery, Columba, an enthusiastic and prolific scribe, broke into Finnian's library and began to copy the book of psalms. He was caught and brought before King Dermot of Ireland, to whom he reportedly pleaded that as

> Finnian's book has not decreased in value because of the transcript I have made from it; also that it is not right to extinguish the divine things it contained, or to prevent me or anybody else from copying it, or reading it, or circulating it throughout the provinces. I further maintain that if I benefited by its transcription, which I desired to be for the general good, provided no injury accrued to Finnian or his book thereby, it was quite permissible for me to copy it![11]

To which King Dermot is said to have replied: 'To every cow her calf, to every book belongs its transcript. Therefore the copy you have made, O Colum Cille, belongs to Finnian.'[12]

This frequently cited exchange between Columba and King Dermot from the 6th century is of significance for four reasons. The first is its recognition of the separateness of tangible goods (the book) and intangible expression (the psalms), and of the possibility of the latter supporting property rights separate from the property rights supported by the former. Thus, while it was clear that Finnian owned the book, it was not clear that he had any rights in respect of the psalms recorded in the book, and it was this issue that the king was asked to decide. The second is its recognition of the significance of the intangible nature of authorial works for the subsistence of property rights in respect of them. Implicit in Columba's argument was that since copying the psalms would facilitate public access to them without reducing their value, preventing such copying could not be justified. In his response King Dermot did not address this argument, relying instead on Finnian's ownership of the book as giving him ownership of the unauthorized copy which Columba had made. Which leads to the third point of interest regarding the exchange, namely, the king's invocation of the paternity metaphor ('to every cow her calf . . .') to justify the recognition of Finnian's rights, consistent with the plagiary metaphor above, and supporting the idea of unauthorized copying as contrary to natural law and the values of civil society.

There remains the fourth and final reason for interest in the exchange between Columba and King Dermot, which lies in its demonstration of the variety of extra-legal mechanisms by which authorial works are protected, and the way in which those mechanisms work together and affect the need for intervention by the state. As discussed earlier, this is a key insight of Lessig, who identifies three extra-legal mechanisms as having especial importance for IP: social norms, the market, and architecture. Through this paradigm, illustrated in Figure 1.4, Lessig offers an explanation for both the absence of copyright in the Middle Ages and its emergence and development in later centuries. The explanation for its absence in the Middle Ages lies in the lack of

---

[11] L. Menzies, *Saint Columba of Iona: a study of his life, his times, & his influence* (J.M. Dent & Sons Ltd, 1920) 25.

[12] ibid.

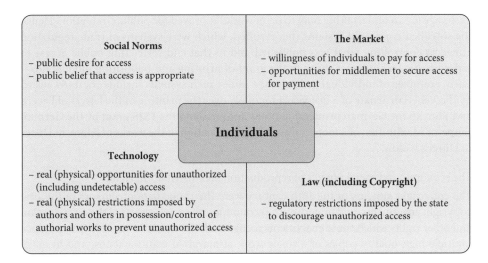

Figure 1.4 Lessig's copyright paradigm

reprographic technology and low literacy rates which then existed, and the consequential ability of authors and others to restrict access to works by keeping them in a locked room, as Finnian had done. When literacy rates increased and printing technologies became available in the 15th century, however, the situation changed, creating a perceived need for legal intervention to prevent unauthorized copying. And when digital technology was invented in the 20th century and unauthorized copying became a widespread activity for members of the public as well as commercial enterprises, the situation changed again, creating a perceived need for further legal intervention in order both to strengthen copyright, and to support owners' renewed reliance on extra-legal mechanisms to prevent unauthorized use of their protected subject matter. One such extra-legal mechanism in widespread use today is technological protection measures—so-called digital locks—which are commonly applied to protected works and subject matter in digital form so as to prevent their reproduction and distribution, and the use of which the law supports by making it an offence to circumvent them without the permission of the IP rights owner. In an era of widespread infringement and public scepticism regarding the legitimacy of copyright, this renewed reliance on extra-legal mechanisms to prevent the unauthorized use of works and subject matter—and the law's support of that reliance—can be read as reflecting the recognition that in the Internet era, 'laws and norms do not protect enough'.

The grant of rights of copy to limit the use of new technologies for the purpose of circulating ideas and information in the 16th century
The threat posed by printing technology
While the idea of authorial property was well established by the Middle Ages, it acquired a new significance with the arrival in the West of printing technology; an event that triggered profound changes in social practices and conceptions of authorial production, and that raised new issues regarding the public dissemination of information and ideas. Perceiving immediately the threat posed by such dissemination to social and political order, the Crown in England and France, following the Venetian Senate, responded by prohibiting the general public from using the new printing technology. To that end each created printing monopolies—exclusive rights of copy—and conferred them on individual printers in respect of specific works, or on companies of printers in

exchange for an undertaking only to print works approved for public circulation. Hence the so-called copy-right systems that resulted, which were systems of trade regulation aimed at controlling what was published and to that end restricting public access to reprographic technologies through the grant of printing and publishing monopolies.[13] Early examples of individual grants made under such systems include the 1469 award by the Venetian Senate of a five-year monopoly over the printing of the letters of Cicero and Pliny to the German printer, Johannes de Spira, and the 1528 grant by the German Emperor Maximilian of a monopoly over the publication of the works of Albrecht Dürer to Dürer's widow.

The economic and social aspects of reproduction and distribution rights

The copy-right systems of the 16th century were the immediate precursors of the first copyright enactments, and underline the economic and social aspects of the reproduction and other rights which those enactments recognized. For example, the ability to produce multiple high-quality copies of a single work at marginal additional cost and to make those copies available to an increasingly literate public for purchase created a new market in authorial works that was said to benefit three groups of people. The first group were the printers themselves, as the persons entitled to produce the copies and sell them to the public, who stood to benefit economically from their exclusive copy-rights. The second were the authors of the individual manuscripts that were printed, as the persons who possessed the physical objects (the manuscripts) to which the printers needed access in order to be able to produce their copies, who also stood to benefit economically from the sale of their individual manuscripts to the printers (the value of which could be expected to increase as their reputations grew with the printers' sale of copies of those manuscripts). And the third group were the members of the public, as the purchasers of the printed copies of the authors' manuscripts, who benefited personally from the increased access to information and ideas which the availability of such copies ensured, and who could also be expected to pass those benefits on to their wider community through increased engagement in its social, cultural, and political life. On the other hand, the extent of such access and its benefits depended on the price charged by the printers for the copies and on the manuscripts chosen by the printers and authorized by the Crown for printing and distribution.

Market-based censorship

A hallmark of modern copyright systems is the absence of any day-to-day role for the state in deciding which individual works and beneficiaries receive legal protection. As with the printers' systems of the 16th and 17th centuries, however, the value of such protection continues to be determined largely by the market, with publishers and other middlemen also playing an important role in deciding which works are made available to the public based on their assessment of which works are likely to be a commercial success. The result is a system that encourages the creation and publication of popular works, and that discriminates against works likely to be of interest to a small section of

---

[13] A similar system was introduced in 18th century France to accord separate IP protection for industrial designs (comprising aspects of product appearance). Thus, under a 1711 regulation enacted by the guild of Lyons, the Conseil des Prud'hommes was conferred a monopoly over the production of silk by the use of weaving looms. By the end of the 18th century the law had been amended to recognize 'new designs' as the 'property' of their 'inventor' for a term of 15 years, conditional upon the deposit of samples of the relevant design in the Conseil's archives, bringing the protection of non-authorial designs squarely within the industrial property paradigm discussed later.

the public only, or likely to have a long shelf life, i.e. to realize their commercial value over a long period. In the past this has led to criticism of the copyright system for promoting creation and publication without regard to the quality or diversity of what is created and published. As we will see in Section 3.8, one response to such criticism has been to argue for a longer term of protection to enable creators and publishers to offset the costs of creating and publishing works and subject matter less likely to offer a strong and immediate financial return with a view to increasing not merely the number, but also the diversity, of the works and subject matter created and made available to the public.

The impact of reproduction and distribution rights on public freedoms
and participation

Constructing a system that encourages the creation and dissemination of a diversity of authorial works and other expressive subject matter for the benefit of the public is an important aim of all modern copyright systems. So too ensuring that those systems do not impede creation and dissemination (and other valued activities, e.g. thought, expression, and artistic discourse) by restricting public access to protected works and subject matter more than they encourage such access is and has always been a central concern.

The impact of reproduction rights on public freedoms and democratic participation were first discussed at length in the context of the copy-right systems in the 17th century. In England the trigger for that discussion was the trade war that broke out between the Stationers' Company upon which monopoly rights of printing were conferred and provincial booksellers who took to selling copies of manuscripts without acquiring the necessary permissions. According to the Stationers, by creating a valuable market for authorial works, their monopolies ensured that authors were acknowledged and paid for their authorial efforts and that the public received access to their new and valuable manuscripts. According to the rival booksellers, by contrast, the Stationers' monopolies caused harm to the public by enabling books to be sold at inflated prices and restricting the freedom of third parties to access their contents. In these diametrically opposed positions one sees the language of 'authors' rights' and 'the public interest' so pervasive in modern copyright debates. In addition, one sees in the printers' and booksellers' positions an early allusion to different conceptions of copyright itself: the printers' case reflecting a view of authors' works as valuable products of authorial labour capable of supporting property rights, and the booksellers' case reflecting a view of authors' works as repositories of ideas and information to which the public had a right of access which the new technology of print (ought to have) facilitated. The competing conceptions were even more apparent in France, where the freedom to print and distribute ideas and information without needing first to obtain the privilege of printing from the king was won with the Revolution, and freedom of communication recognized in 1789 alongside the inviolability and sacredness of property in the Declaration of the Rights of Man and of the Citizen.[14]

The English Stationers' system collapsed under the weight of the printers' and booksellers' trade war at the end of the 17th century, with the copy-right systems of other European states following thereafter. In their place emerged the world's first civil and common law copyright enactments, starting with the English Statute of Anne 1710 and the Danish copyright ordinance of 1741.

---

[14] See P. Drahos, 'Intellectual Property and Human Rights' [1999] *IPQ* 349, 351–2. According to Drahos, during the 1750s 40 per cent of those in the Bastille were there because of offences related to the book trade.

The first common and civil law copyright enactments of the 18th century

According to its preamble, the Statute of Anne was introduced to 'encourage learned men to compose and write useful books', and to protect the 'authors or proprietors' of such books from 'ruinous' piracy. To that end it did two things of significance: first, it extended the Stationers' then existing monopolies for a further limited period; and second, it created a renewable, 14-year exclusive right to make literal or near-literal copies of books, vesting in authors on their publication, subject to their registration and deposit, and enforceable by its owner against the world.

The full title of the Statute of Anne was 'An Act for the Encouragement of Learning, by Vesting the Copies of Printed Books in the Authors or Purchasers of such Copies, during the Times therein mentioned'. Consistent with this title, the Statute is often described as reflecting a public interest or instrumentalist view of copyright, according to which authors' rights are privileges granted by a state for the purpose of encouraging the creation and dissemination of works for the benefit of its citizens. So too for the Danish ordinance of 1741, which prohibited any person from copying or selling a copy of any book or manuscript in respect of which another person from Copenhagen, whether or not the author of the book or manuscript, had acquired a lawful right and incurred 'a considerable expense'.[15]

These earliest copyright enactments of England and Denmark can be contrasted with the French *droit d'auteur* (authors' rights) decrees of the 1790s. According to Le Chapelier when reporting the first of these during the Revolution in 1791, 'the most sacred, the most legitimate, the most unassailable, and...the most personal of all properties, is the work which is the fruit of the writer's thoughts'.[16] While made with respect to unpublished works, this statement underlines key aspects of the French enactments and their difference from the English and Danish laws. For example, the 1791 decree gave authors the exclusive right to perform their dramatic and musical works in public, vesting on creation of the work and lasting for the term of the author's life plus five years. In 1792 it was replaced by a further decree, aimed expressly at strengthening the rights of authors in the face of theatre owners' failure to pay the sums demanded for permission to perform their works, and supplementing their right of public performance with a new right of publication. And in 1793, a third decree extended further the rights of authors to cover the reproduction of all authorial works, lasting for the term of the author's life plus ten years.[17]

By the 1880s, all European states had introduced legislation recognizing and protecting the rights of authors, including Spain (in 1834), Austria (in 1846), Portugal (in 1867), Denmark (in 1857), Sweden (in 1867), Germany (in 1870), and Norway (in 1876), paving the way for the conclusion of the first international copyright treaty, the Berne Convention for the Protection of Literary and Artistic Property of 1886.[18]

Conclusions

The previous discussion highlights three themes as having been especially important in the emergence and early development of copyright systems in Europe. The first is

[15] S.P. Ladas, *The International Protection of Literary and Artistic Property* (1938) vol. I, 18.

[16] G. Davies, *Copyright and The Public Interest* (Max Planck Institute for Foreign and International Patent, Copyright and Competition Law, 1994) 79 (quoting from *Archives Parlementaires de 1787 à 1860, Receuil complet des débats législatifs & politiques des Chambres françaises* (Paris, 1887) vol. xxii, 210).

[17] J.C. Ginsburg, 'Tale of Two Copyrights: Literary Property in Revolutionary France and America' (1990) 64 *Tulane Law Review* 1007–9.

[18] S. Ricketson and J.C. Ginsburg, *International Copyright and Neighbouring Rights: The Berne Convention and Beyond* (2nd edn, OUP, 2005) [1.5].

a commitment to an individuated conception of authorship, premised on a view of authors as having a personal connection with and responsibility for the works they create. The second is a recognition of informational and expressive works as objects of economic and social (including cultural) value capable of supporting property rights. And the third is a concern to balance the claims of authors to protection of their creations and of service providers (e.g. printers and publishers) to protection of their commercial interests on the one hand, with the freedom of third parties to express and access ideas and information and to exploit fully the capacities of new technologies on the other. As we will see in later chapters, these three themes are also central to European law- and policy-making in IP, with the third in particular having dominated EU copyright initiatives. Among other things, they reveal the intimate connections that have existed between conceptions of IP at particular moments in history and the prevailing social norms and state of technology and the economy. In addition, they underline the centrality to copyright historically of the concern of law- and decision-makers: (a) to recognize and protect individual creators' rights while also taking account of the impact of doing so on social and economic welfare; and (b) to regulate trade in goods and (printing and other) services in pursuit of commercial (mercantilist) and social (censorial) policies.

1.2.2.2.2 The Origins of Industrial Property Rights

Patents for inventions

The grant of privileges to reward or encourage innovation from ancient times

The practice of granting patents for inventions has its origins in the idea, often traced to Sicily (then part of Greece) in 500 BCE, of conferring exclusive manufacturing and other privileges as a reward or incentive for devising new and otherwise meritorious products and processes, including recipes for culinary dishes. This practice was also adopted by the early Romans, who reportedly rewarded their inventive citizens by exempting them from normal civic duties, such as military service.[19] Much later, European states adopted the custom of conferring monopolies over different aspects of manufacture and trade on companies of merchants and craftsmen, and then, in the 14th century, of *compromising* those guild monopolies in order to encourage the development of local industry and the exploitation of local resources. States' preferred method of doing this was to attract foreign workers with the promise of special trade privileges in exchange for a commitment to practise and train local apprentices in their trades and crafts. The English Crown reportedly made the first grant under this policy in 1331 to a wool weaver from Flanders, John Kempe.

The first general patent statute and patent specification of the 15th and 16th centuries

The early 'letters of privilege' described above tended to offer inducements other than monopoly grants. By the 15th century, however, the use of monopolies to encourage innovation was becoming common in the city-states of Italy; a frequently cited example being the 1421 grant to Filippo Brunelleschi by the Signoria of Florence of a three-year exclusive right to manufacture and use a new device for transporting heavy loads over rivers.[20] In 1474 the first general patent statute was enacted in Venice, promising anyone who built

---

[19] I. Mgbeoji, 'The Juridical Origins of the International Patent System: Towards a Historiography of the Role of Patents in Industrialization' (2003) 5 *Journal of the History of International Law* 403, 408–9.

[20] A.A. Gomme, *Patents of Invention: Origin and Growth of the Patent System in Britain* (Longmans Green and Co., 1946) 6.

a new and useful device the exclusive right to manufacture it for ten years. In full this statute provided as follows:

> WE HAVE among us men of great genius, apt to invent and discover ingenious devices; and in view of the grandeur and virtue of our City, more such men come to us from divers parts. Now if provision were made for the works and devices discovered by such persons, so that others who may see them could not build them and take the inventor's honor away, more men would then apply their genius, would discover, and would build devices of great utility and benefit to our Commonwealth.
>
> Therefore:
>
> BE IT ENACTED that, by the authority of this Council, every person who shall build any new and ingenious device in this City, not previously made in this Commonwealth, shall give notice of it to the office of our General Welfare Board when it has been reduced to perfection so that it can be used and operated. It being forbidden to every other person in any of our territories and towns to make any further device conforming with and similar to said one, without the consent and license of the author, for the term of 10 years. And if anybody builds it in violation hereof, the aforesaid author and inventor shall be entitled to have him summoned before any magistrate of this City, by which Magistrate the said infringer shall be constrained to pay him [one] hundred ducats; and the device shall be destroyed at once. It being, however, within the power and discretion of the Government, in its activities, to take and use any such device and instrument, with this condition however that no one but the author shall operate it.[21]

By the early 16th century, knowledge of the Italian practice of rewarding the introduction of new inventions with monopolies had spread to other European states, including France. In France, the first reported privilege of this type was a ten-year monopoly granted by King Henri II to Theseo Mutio of Bologna in 1551, restricted by the Parliament of Paris to five years, over a new method of manufacturing 'glass, mirrors…and other sorts of Venetian style glass'.[22] In the same year the king granted another ten-year monopoly to his mechanic, Abel Foullon, over an instrument for taking architectural measurements (a holometer) on condition that Foullon publish a description of his invention for use by the public when the patent expired. The resulting description of 1555 is generally thought to have been the first patent specification.

Patents as exceptions to a general prohibition against 'odious monopolies' in 17th century England

In England the patent policy of the 16th century remained vulnerable to abuse, and it was not long before a practice developed of granting extended monopolies as political rewards to individuals over the practice of established trades and the manufacture and sale of known devices. Well-known examples include the grant of patents for such basic and locally produced commodities as starch, salt, and vinegar. These so-called odious monopolies were devastating for trade and the public and provoked intense political opposition. This led in 1601 to a debate between the House of Commons and Crown over the scope of the latter's power that ended with a royal promise to revoke the worst of the monopolies and recognize the future jurisdiction of the common law courts to determine their legality. That jurisdiction was tested in the *Case of Monopolies* (1602) 77 ER 1260,

---

[21] G. Mandich, 'Venetian Origins of Inventors' Rights' (1960) 42 *Journal of the Patent and Trademark Office Society* 378 (translated by F.D. Prager).

[22] M. Pendergrast, *Mirror Mirror: A History of the Human Love Affair with Reflection* (Basic Books, 2003) 149; R.A. Klitze, 'Historical Background of the English Patent Law' (1959) 41 *Journal of the Patent Office* 615, 619.

in which the King's Bench established the general proposition that by reducing employment and encouraging manufacturers to raise their prices and lower their manufacturing standards, monopolies were contrary to the public interest and thus to the common law. However, the court also recognized a limited exception covering patents for new and useful trades and engines, reportedly justified with reference to the 'charge or industry' or 'wit or invention' which their introduction to the realm required. Despite this decision, the grant of odious monopolies continued, prompting further intervention by the Parliament and, finally, the introduction of the Statute of Monopolies 1623 (21 Jac. 1, c. 3). By that Act monopolies were declared 'contrary to the law' and 'utterly void and of none effect', with a limited exception in section 6 for the benefit of 'true and first Inventor[s]'. That section remained the basis for the patent laws of the UK until the introduction of the European patent system in the 1970s, and continues to be the basis for the patent laws of Australia and New Zealand.

The early patent examination systems of 17th century France

Already under the Venetian patent system of the 15th century, monopolies were granted only after some formal examination of the inventions to which they related.[23] So too in France there existed from 1632 a private organization known as the Free Academy the purpose of which was to promote discovery and the examination of inventions in support of patent grants. To give an example of its work: in 1634 the academy was asked by the then Prime Minister of France, Cardinal-Duke Richelieu, to examine the claim of a professor of mathematics, Jean-Baptiste Morin, to have invented a new, inventive, and useful method of determining the longitude of a ship. After a hearing involving expert testimony from Galileo, the academy rejected Professor Morin's claims, leading to the government's denial of a patent grant.[24]

Later in the 17th century, the role of conducting preliminary examinations of patent applications was formalized in France at the instigation of the Parliament, and delegated to a public body of scientific and technological experts, the Académie des Sciences (successor of the Free Academy). In 1699 the Académie received instructions to examine all inventions for which a privilege was sought; a role that had the further effect of publicizing the inventions before the grant of any Crown privilege was made.[25]

A contested idea: the patent wars of the 18th century

In 1791, France followed England by introducing its first general patent legislation; and by the middle of the 19th century, so had Austria (in 1810), Russia (in 1812), Prussia (in 1815), Belgium and the Netherlands (in 1817), Spain (in 1820), Bavaria (in 1825), Sardinia (in 1826), the Vatican State (in 1833), Sweden (in 1834), Württemberg (in 1836), Portugal (in 1837), and Saxony (in 1843).[26]

Of especial note regarding these early European enactments is the difference between them. At one extreme stood the 1791 French decree, which was introduced two years after property was declared an inviolable and sacred right in the Declaration of the Rights of

---

[23] Prager (n 7) 716. This contrasts with the position in England, where there was no formal examination procedure. Instead, applicants for a patent grant were required formally to attest to the merit of their invention, and risked penalties for any false statements they might make in that regard.

[24] T. Bakos and M. Nowotarski, 'A Short History of Private Patent Examination' (2009) *Insurance IP Bulletin*.

[25] L. Hilaire-Pérez, 'Invention and the State in 18th-Century France' (1991) 32 *Technology and Culture* 911, 917.

[26] I.F. Machlup and E. Penrose, 'The Patent Controversy in the Nineteenth Century' (1950) 10 *Journal of Economic History* 1, 3.

Man and of the Citizen, and which declared that 'every discovery or new invention, in all kinds of industry, is the property of its author', and that 'to assure the inventor the property and temporary enjoyment of his discovery, there shall be delivered to him a patent for five, ten or fifteen years'; the term being at the inventor's discretion. Reflecting the view of patents as natural rights of an inventor, the practice of examining inventions was dispensed with, and the task of patent offices confined to processing applications to the state for a patent grant. As the text of the French patent document stated: 'The government, in granting a patent without prior examination, does not in any manner guarantee either the priority, merit or success of an invention.'[27] In addition, while patentees were required to describe their inventions sufficiently to enable them to be performed by a person skilled in the relevant art, their descriptions were once again suppressed until after the expiry of their property.[28]

In contrast to the French system were the systems of other states, perhaps none more so than the first national German patent system of 1877. Central features of the German system included: (a) preliminary substantive examination of the relevant invention, including for inventive height; (b) policy-based exclusions from protection for medicinal, chemical, and food products; (c) restriction of entitlement to the first to file for a patent, regardless of whether he was first to devise the invention; (d) a requirement that patent applicants provide a written description of the invention for publication before the grant, and that patentees pay increasing annual renewal fees to maintain the grant over its (maximum) 15-year period; and (e) a requirement that patentees work their inventions within three years of the grant, and allow others to work them at any time for reasonable payment.[29] So demanding were these requirements that between 1877 and 1913, only 304,057 patents were granted from a total number of 765,653 applications,[30] prompting Germany to introduce a second utility model system in 1891 to protect less meritorious inventions.

Soon after the last of the patent law enactments referred to earlier was introduced, there ensued a period of intense political and public controversy as supporters of free trade in Germany and other European states sought the abolition of existing (and the rejection of proposed) domestic patent laws due to the harm they were said to cause for innovation, industry, and the general public.[31] At the height of the controversy, in 1869, the Netherlands went so far as to repeal its patent legislation. By the following decade, however, patent advocates had won the war, and by the end of the 1870s debates on the

---

[27] B.Z. Khan, *The Democratization of Invention: Patents and Copyright in American Economic Development, 1790–1920* (CUP, 2005) 43.

[28] As noted earlier (n 13) principles of the 18th century patent system of France were also extended to industrial designs. (For a description see House of Commons, *Report from Select Committee on the Silk Trade* (2 August 1832) [8849].) From 1793, the French system of design patents was supplemented by copyright for authors under the 1793 authors' rights decree; a decree later amended to confirm the availability of authorial property for works regardless of merit. The resulting system of dual (patent and copyright) protection for designs in their dual capacities as functional and expressive subject matter respectively supported the then emergent distinction between copyright and industrial property themselves, on which the Paris and Berne Conventions of the late 19th century were based. As we will see later, this distinction is preserved in European law today. With respect to designs themselves, aspects of product appearance also function as signs of use in industry, and may accordingly be protected by the law of trade marks, making them a truly hybrid form of intellectual property.

[29] See B.Z. Khan, 'An Economic History of Patent Institutions' http://eh.net/encyclopedia/an-economic-history-of-patent-institutions/; D. Guellec and B. van Pottelsberghe de la Potterie, *The Economics of the European Patent System: IP Policy for Innovation and Competition* (OUP, 2007) ch. 2.

[30] C. Burhop, *The Transfer of Patents in Imperial Germany* (Max Planck Institute for Research on Collective Goods, 2009/26) 6.

[31] For a discussion see Machlup and Penrose (n 26).

existence of the patent system had all but ended, paving the way for the conclusion of the first international patent treaty, the Paris Convention for the Protection of Industrial Property of 1883.

Signs of commercial origin (trade marks)

The use of marks to indicate the ownership and commercial origin of goods from ancient times

The practice in ancient times of applying marks of ownership and origin to goods, such as pottery and livestock, may be the earliest evidence of the idea of IP. By the Middle Ages this practice was well established in different parts of Europe, both as a voluntary measure by which merchants secured their title to goods in the event of loss or theft, and as a compulsory measure by which the state regulated trade.[32] To give an example of the voluntary use of marks: in 1332, one year after the first recorded patent grant to John Kempe, merchants from Majorca succeeded in recovering goods thrown up on the coast of Flanders by a shipwreck in the high court of Seville by proving ownership and long use of the mark appearing on the goods.[33] There followed in 1353 a statute of England (27 Edw. 3) enabling a foreign merchant who had lost his goods to rely on proof of ownership of marks appearing on them as proof of their ownership, which was applied by the courts until the end of the 18th century.[34] To give an example of the compulsory use of ownership marks: the governing charters of the merchant guilds of medieval Europe routinely required the affixing of two marks on merchants' goods—one of the guild under whose monopoly the goods were produced, and one of the individual merchant within that guild responsible for producing them—as a means of tracing their origins in the event of the goods being defective or otherwise produced in breach of guild monopoly rules.

Recognition of the right of a trader to prevent others from causing deceit by applying his mark to their goods in 17th century England

The first formal recognition of the principle of trade mark law supposedly came with the decision of the English court in *Southern v How* (1656) Pop R 144. According to the report of that case:

> [T]he action upon the case was brought in the Common Pleas by a clothier, that whereas he had gained great reputation for his making of his cloth by reason whereof he had great utterance to his benefit and profit, and that he used to set his mark on his cloth whereby it should be known to be his cloth: and another clothier, observing it, used the same mark to his ill-made cloth on purpose to deceive him, and it was resolved that the action did well lie.

While the authority and influence of this case has been contested, its report remains important evidence of the early judicial recognition of the principle of trade mark law. According to that principle in its original formulation, trade mark law applied defensively, to prevent a trader from affixing another's sign of origin to his own goods on the ground that doing so would deceive the public as to their origin. This consumer-focused and deceit-based formulation of trade mark protection is consistent with the early guild requirement that signs be affixed to goods to enable their ownership and commercial

---

[32] See E.S. Rogers, 'Some Historical Matter Concerning Trade-Marks' (1910) 9 *Michigan Law Review* 29, 43.

[33] F.I. Schechter, *The Historical Foundations of the Law Relating to Trade-Marks* (Columbia University Press, 1925) 26–7.

[34] ibid 29–31.

origin to be established, and the related guild prohibition against signs being used as a means of distinguishing and advertising the goods of individual merchants themselves.[35] It recognized an accessorial or dependent form of protection that was noticeably different from the independent protection conferred by copyright and patents. Specifically, while the economic value of a patented invention or copyright work was determined directly by the patent or copyright itself, the value of an article to which a mark had been affixed was determined by the article and not the mark; the latter operating merely as a means of communicating to the public the article's origin.[36]

Conclusions

The themes that emerge from the previous discussion of the origins of industrial property rights are similar to those identified in our discussion of the origins of copyright. For example, the view of early patentees as meriting industrial property grants by reason of their 'charge or industry' or 'wit or invention' alludes to a view of inventors as deserving such grants by reason of their intellectual endeavours and/or capacities. So too, according to Prager, the restriction of early patent grants to the inventor's life suggested a conception of patents 'as strictly personal', even as they were exploited 'in purely capitalistic ways'.[37] On the other hand, a primary motivation for granting patents in all civil and common law jurisdictions was the instrumentalist one of encouraging individuals to enhance the industrial capacity of the local community by devising or introducing from abroad new industrial and commercial ideas. Hence, even in France, where patents after 1791 were granted in vindication of inventors' natural law rights without formal examination of the invention to which they related, individual invention per se was not required to secure a grant, and patentees were obliged in all cases to introduce their inventions into practice within a specified period. So too the earliest recognition of the right of trade mark owners to exclude others from using their marks was motivated by the utilitarian concern to promote fair competition among traders, including by preventing them from deceiving the public as to the origin of their goods. Implicit was a view of industrial property rights as mechanisms for regulating trade in support of then existing economic policies focused on generating wealth and promoting industry. A central focus in that regard was restricting competition among individuals in order to encourage industrial and commercial innovation. Specifically, by restricting competition in the production of goods and services, industrial property rights were believed to promote competition at the higher innovation level, much as property rights in respect of tangible products promote competition at the production level by restricting competition in the consumption of individual goods and services.[38]

1.2.2.3 Theories and Values of Intellectual Property

The previous discussion suggests a range of social and economic values to have driven the emergence and early development of domestic IP laws and systems. These include: individual (expressive and financial) autonomy; social and political participation; fair trade and competition; freedom of expression; industrial and commercial innovation; consumer protection; and access to new technologies. It also suggests that these values were given different emphasis by different states and in the context of different IP regimes: individual autonomy having had especial importance for copyright, innovation especial importance

---

[35] ibid 47.
[36] Lehmann (n 3) 531–2; also R.A. Posner, 'The Law and Economics of Intellectual Property' (2002) *Daedalus* 5, 8.
[37] n 6, 717.   [38] Lehmann (n 3) 537 *et seq*.

for patent monopolies, and fair trade and consumer protection especial importance for trade marks. And finally, it suggests at least two foundational theories of IP focused on the protection of individuals' natural law rights and the promotion of public interests respectively, localized in different European states.

1.2.2.3.1 Deontological Theories and Values

Natural law or deontological theories of IP are best captured by the statement of Le Chapelier, when presenting the French Playwrights Decree of 1791, that '[t]he most sacred, the most legitimate, the most unassailable, and, I may say, the most personal of all properties, is the work which is the fruit of a writer's thoughts.' The implication of this statement is that the law recognizes property rights in the products of authorial (and other forms of intellectual) labour in the belief: (a) that the nature or value of such labour or of the products themselves merits such recognition; and/or (b) that such recognition is necessary or desirable, either to enable individual creators to flourish as autonomous human beings, or to protect their rights in respect of their personhood or intellectual labour.

Deontological arguments for IP depend on a belief in individual creation that many regard today with scepticism or reject as little more than a Romantic cliché. In addition, however, even those who support moral rights arguments for IP are likely to find them more compelling for some regimes than for others. For example, many would accept that a poet has a moral claim to exclude third parties from certain uses of her poems on the basis that poems are private expressions of an individual and/or have a value to society that ought to be recognized. Less obvious is whether either of these propositions supports the grant of property rights in respect of all works of poetry and, if it does, how those rights are most appropriately defined. For example, if we value the work that poets do, we might prefer to pay them a salary or lump sum for every work of poetry that they produce, and/or to offer rewards for individual works of poetry that we judge to have particular merit. In addition, if we believe that poetry ought to be protected in the manner of other private expressions of an individual, we might prefer to recognize poets as having a personal right to determine the readiness of their works for publication—perhaps with additional rights to control the presentation of their works once published—rather than the more widely cast transferrable rights of exclusion conferred by IP. And finally, even if we support the recognition and protection of IP rights in respect of poetry, we might wish to recognize the possibility of those rights coming into conflict with the expressive and other rights and interests of third parties and society, as in the case of a literary critic wishing to use the poem to illustrate a point in an article critiquing it, or a library wishing to preserve and provide public access to the cultural products of its local community.

Overall, and as we will see further in Chapter 3, while deontological arguments can help to establish a prima facie claim to legal protection in respect of certain subject matter, they offer limited assistance in defining the most appropriate form of legal protection itself. What they do offer, however, is an insight into the values protected by IP systems and their deeper normative foundations. These include several of the values that drove the emergence of copyright—such as individual (expressive and financial) autonomy, social and political participation, and freedom of expression—as well as certain others, such as privacy. As we will see in later chapters, each of these informs European copyright systems particularly.

1.2.2.3.2 Utilitarian Theories and Values

Deontological theories are also the departure point for the second set of arguments for IP, epitomized by the title of the Statute of Anne: 'An Act for the Encouragement of

Learning'. The implication of this title is that the justification for granting copyright and other forms of IP lies not in any appeal to morality or natural law rights per se, but rather in a policy commitment to encouraging certain behaviour, such as (most commonly) the production and distribution of intellectual products—including works, inventions, and signs of origin—by means of property grants. Such grants, it is said, benefit the public economically and socially. Economically, they resolve the market failure created by the intangibility of those products and, in the case of trade marks, encourage the use of signs to indicate the commercial origin of goods and services in the interests of market trans-parency. The result is more efficient and competitive markets in respect of intellectual products, and new forms of property (IP) that can be traded and otherwise deployed to generate wealth and finance activities. So too socially, property grants support a robust public domain of expressive and informational (including technical) subject matter, increasing the public's exposure to the ideas and expressions essential for innovation, crea-tivity, and cultural development. In particular, they create a false scarcity with respect to IP subject matter by excluding others from using them, and thereby enable their bene-ficiaries to exploit those subject matter in the manner of tangible objects. Provided that individual creators and innovators believe that this possibility of commercial exploita-tion will result in a reasonable financial return, utilitarian theorists claim, they will be encouraged to bring new creations and innovations to market. Hence the idea of using property rights as a mechanism for encouraging individuals to produce and disseminate expressive and informational works of value to society.

As with deontological arguments for IP, the premise of utilitarian theories is easily crit-icized. For example, the idea that authors, traders, and innovators have no deeper claim than that supported by statute to exclude third parties from the unauthorized use of their creations, signs, and innovations can seem counter-intuitive in an age in which such use is frequently described as 'plagiarism' and 'piracy'. Equally contentious are the empirical claims of utilitarianism, and in particular its assumptions: (a) that the creation of IP sub-ject matter is in all cases motivated by economic considerations rather than communica-tive, reputational, or truth-seeking ones; (b) that property rights are required (necessary) and able (effective) to cure the market failure that exists in respect of IP subject matter; and (c) that market-based systems of incentivizing creation and dissemination through the grant of property rights benefit the public more than they harm it. For example, many support the grant of IP rights as a means of encouraging people to create works or devise inventions and to make their works or inventions available to the public. However, even if we accept the social value of these acts of creation/invention and disclosure, it does not follow that the promise of property rights is necessary to encourage them. On the contrary, it is often said that in fast-moving (short shelf life) industries particularly, such as the textbook and computer industries, being the first to market with a new work or invention will in most cases create a sufficient window in which to exploit the work or invention before it is reproduced and distributed by third parties. If this is accepted, not only is there no *need* for IP rights to restrict public access to works and inventions within these industries, there is also no *justification* for them. In addition, even if we accept that there *is* a need for incentives in these and other industries, there remains the difficulty of defining what incentives are necessary, and when if ever the public interest in the long-term goals that they pursue should be recognized as outweighed by the claims of indi-viduals in particular cases. So too in respect of trade mark law, while many would accept the value of encouraging people to affix signs of origin to their goods and services, it is not clear that the promise of property is necessary to encourage this. On the contrary, many would argue that granting property rights in respect of signs of origin merely encourages them to be treated in the manner of works and inventions—i.e. as intellectual products having value in their own right, independent of their function in indicating origin—and supports their protection as such. On this view, rather than conferring a limited right to prevent unauthorized uses of a sign likely to confuse consumers as to the origin of goods or services, trade mark law should confer a right to prevent any unauthorized use of a sign likely to diminish its value as an asset and brand.

Once again, then, while utilitarian arguments can help to establish a prima facie claim to legal protection, they offer limited assistance in defining the shape that that protection should take. Still, and as with deontological arguments, they point to some of the values that IP rights protect, while also making the theoretical foundations of those values transparent. These include such commercial values as market efficiency and fair competition, as well as the range of social and economic values promoted by access to expressive and informational subject matter, including social and democratic participation, freedom of expression, and technological innovation, all of which inform the European IP regime.

1.2.2.3.3 *Pluralistic Theories*

As our earlier discussion of 18th century enactments reflects, deontological and utilitarian theories of IP have historically been aligned with civil and common law traditions respectively. In recent years, however, it has become common to downplay the differences between these traditions with a view to emphasizing both their nuances and similarities. This has coincided with a new emphasis among IP theorists on the comparative importance for the day-to-day operation of IP systems of values and corresponding mid-level principles in place of foundational, including deontological or utilitarian, theories.[39] At the supranational level especially, focusing on principles (or normative guidelines) such as the need to protect individual autonomy and (following Article 17(2) CFR) the need to protect IP itself promotes harmonization by distracting attention from foundational questions such as 'why should we protect intellectual property?' to the question 'how is the principle of intellectual property protection appropriately reconciled with other fundamental rights principles, such as freedom of expression and discrimination, in the present case?'[40] In so doing, focusing on principles also suggests a certain division of labour between supranational and domestic institutions aimed at promoting the EU legal order's objective of 'creating an ever closer union among the peoples of Europe, in which decisions are taken as closely as possible to the citizen in accordance with the principle of subsidiarity' (Preamble TEU; Section 2.4.1.3). According to that division, the role of supranational institutions, including courts particularly, is to establish the fundamental rights and other general principles of relevance for IP, and the role of their domestic counterparts is to balance those rights and principles to achieve justice in individual cases. In addition to promoting institutional cooperation and legal harmonization, such a division of labour recognizes the legal and social diversity among different IP regimes and countries, and seeks to maintain and accommodate that diversity by eschewing a 'one size fits all' model of IP in favour of one capable of accommodating a plurality of philosophies. Put differently, it is consistent with the emphasis placed by European law on 'respecting the diversity of the cultures and traditions of the peoples of Europe as well as the national identities of the Member States', and on ensuring that legal and political objectives are pursued in a manner sensitive to the 'spiritual and moral heritage' of

---

[39] See, e.g., R.P. Merges, *Justifying Intellectual Property* (Harvard University Press, 2011); also D.B. Resnik, 'A Pluralistic Account of Intellectual Property' (2003) 46 *Journal of Business Ethics* 319.

[40] A good example is Case C–201/13 *Deckmyn v Vandersteen* EU:C:2014:2132 (*Deckmyn*), considered in Section 13.4.7.2.

European communities;[41] an emphasis that gives pluralistic theories additional normative and explanatory value for the European IP regime.[42]

The question remains, what values and principles are and ought to be given priority
in that regime? And related to this, what values and principles does the European experience of IP suggest should merit priority? Based on our previous discussion we might
highlight as those ultimate and utilitarian values suggested by history to merit priority: individual (expressive and financial) autonomy; innovation; social and political
participation; fair trade and consumer protection; and access to information and new
technologies. Of immediate note regarding these is their connection to the values and
objectives of the EU. For example, Article 2 TEU describes the EU as founded on the
values of respect for freedom, democracy, the rule of law, and respect for human rights,
among others; Article 3 TEU describes its objectives to include the establishment of
an internal market based on economic growth, a competitive social market economy,
a high level of environmental protection and improvement, and the promotion of
scientific and technological advance. These provisions are underpinned and extended
by the list of CFR rights, which include, in addition to the protection of IP itself in
Article 17(2):

- civil-political (first-generation) rights to liberty (Article 6), privacy (Article 7), personal data (Article 8), freedom of thought (Article 10), expression and information
  (Article 11);

- socio-economic (second-generation) rights to education (Article 14), work (Article 15),
  and freedom to conduct a business (Article 16); and even

- collective-developmental (third-generation) rights to freedom of the arts and sciences (Article 13), respect for cultural diversity (Article 22), and a high level of consumer protection (Article 38).

Further, the connection between these rights and the values of historical importance
in IP—in combination with the explicit purpose of the CFR to support 'an ever closer
union among [the peoples of Europe] based on common values' (Preamble), and its
position in the hierarchy of European legal norms alongside the Treaties (on which see
Section 2.4.1.2)—makes the CFR, in conjunction with Articles 2 and 3 TEU, the natural
starting point for any European IP regime, especially one that takes its basic aim as being
to balance justice and order in the light of European experience and the common values
reflected therein.[43]

A final point to emerge from the connection between the values of historical importance in IP and those of the contemporary European legal order as reflected in the EU
Treaties and CFR is the tension between them. Specifically, it is at first glance difficult to
see how a commitment to protecting individual rights of liberty and equality can coexist
with a commitment to protecting collective rights of fraternity, and so too in the context
of IP, it is difficult to see how a law protecting the autonomy of individual creators with
exclusionary rights can promote the freedom of the arts and sciences. The answer to this
apparent conflict between the rights of individuals and societies lies in our earlier discussion of IP and competition.[44] Put simply, while IP rights restrict the freedom of the

---

[41] Preamble CFR; see also Preamble, Articles 2, 3, and 6 TEU. See further Section 2.4.1.2.
[42] J. Pila, 'Pluralism, Principles and Proportionality in Intellectual Property' (2014) 34 *OJLS* 181.
[43] See n 5 and accompanying text.
[44] See S.M. Twiss, 'Moral Grounds and Plural Cultures: Interpreting Human Rights in the International
Community' (1998) 26 *Journal of Religious Ethics* 271, 274.

immediate generation, their limited scope and duration ensure, in theory at least, that they promote the freedom of future generations by encouraging creators to continue creating and disseminating their creations. In this way, the idea emerges of IP as promoting individual and collective rights and interests simultaneously, consistent with the idea of first-, second-, and third-generation human rights as interdependent rather than inconsistent.[45] Again, these are ideas to which we return in Chapters 2 and 3.

1.2.3 Concluding Remarks: The Importance of IP History and Theory

In an essay concerning the limits of legal logic, the American jurist Oliver Wendell Holmes famously wrote that:

> The life of the law has not been logic: it has been experience. The felt necessities of the time, the prevalent moral and political theories, intuitions of public policy, avowed or unconscious, even the prejudices which judges share with their fellow-men, have had a good deal more to do than the syllogism in determining the rules by which men should be governed. The law embodies the story of a nation's development through many centuries, and it cannot be dealt with as if it contained only the axioms and corollaries of a book of mathematics. In order to know what it is, we must know what it has been, and what it tends to become.[46]

In *Novartis AG v Union of India* (2013) 6 SCC 1, the Supreme Court of India alluded to this passage in the context of IP when it decided that in order to understand Indian patent law particularly, 'it is essential to know the "why" and "how" of the law. Why the law is what it is and how it came to its present form' (128).

Many readers will require no persuasion to the view thus expressed that legal history and theory—the how and why of the law—promote a fuller understanding of the substantive rules of contemporary IP regimes. For others, however, it is worth pausing to consider why this is so.

There are two main reasons: the first pedagogical and the second practical. The pedagogical reason is that historical and theoretical accounts of IP offer positions of critical distance from which to view contemporary rules, and in doing so support independent engagement with and reflection on them. For example, historical accounts enable us to observe the law in action, as part of the complex web of ideas and socio-economic relations that constitute particular legal and social communities, while theoretical accounts offer a range of analytical frameworks and reference points for understanding and assessing what we observe, including its contemporary significance. Consistent with this, IP theory offers a means of connecting substantive rules *inter se* into a unified and analytically coherent whole, and a vocabulary with which to talk about those rules beyond the formal vocabulary provided by the legislature and courts. In addition, IP history offers an important reminder that while different IP laws and the ideas that underpin them embody 'the story of a nation's development through many centuries',[47] and as such ought not to be hastily dismissed in pursuit of harmonization or other political objectives,[48] they are neither inevitable nor deserving of normative priority merely on this (historical) basis or by reason of their temporal currency. While each of these points has validity for law in general, the contention surrounding the foundations of IP law specifically, including its

---

[45] ibid 275–6.

[46] O.W. Holmes, 'Lecture I: Early Forms of Liability' (Lowell Lecture, 23 November 1880).

[47] ibid.   [48] See Lehmann (n 3) 527.

appropriate conception and scope, make them especially valid for us, consistent with the Supreme Court's suggestion in the *Novartis* case.

The contention surrounding the proper conception and scope of contemporary IP also underlines the validity of the second and more practical reason for engaging with its history and theory, which is that they directly inform IP law- and decision-making. For example, lawyers often deploy history and theory in formulating legal arguments,[49] and courts often invoke history and theory to explain and justify decisions reached in individual cases.[50] In addition, within European legal orders, established rules of systemic, purposive, and teleological interpretation—according to which the meaning of laws must be derived from their object and purpose, as well as from the legal and constitutional scheme of which they form a part[51]—require courts to have regard to history and theory to the extent necessary, at least, to identify and understand the significance of the context, object, and purpose of different legislative provisions. In addition, and consistent with these interpretative obligations of European tribunals, European law- and policy-makers regularly appeal to history and theory in justification of different laws and policies, and all European institutions make decisions regarding the nature and importance of certain rights and interests when deciding IP cases that can only be fully understood and assessed with reference to their historical and normative foundations.[52] In addition, the explicit concern of European legal orders to respect the traditions and spiritual and moral heritage of their Member States[53]—also expressed in their commitment to constitutional pluralism and (related) recognition that, in the words of Harold Berman, 'the universal characteristics of legal morality and legal politics are manifested in quite different ways in different countries with different legal histories'[54]—gives them a stronger normative and historical orientation than domestic legal orders possess.[55] And given this especially, one might validly describe the process of European law- and policy-making as one of 'balancing…morality and politics in the light of history' and 'of justice and order in the light of experience,'[56] underlining again the importance of understanding the why and how of IP.

---

[49] In IP see, e.g., G. Finniss (Director of the French National Institute of Industrial Property and architect of the European industrial property system), 'The Theory of "Unity of Art" and the Protection of Designs and Models in French Law' (1964) 66 *Journal of the Patent Office Society* 615.

[50] Two recent examples from the Supreme Court of the UK are *Lucasfilm Ltd v Ainsworth* [2011] UKSC 39 and *Human Genome Sciences Inc. v Eli Lilly* [2011] UKSC 51.

[51] On the interpretative approach of the Court of Justice see, from a vast literature, K. Lenaerts (Vice-President of the Court of Justice of the European Union) and J.A. Gutiérrez-Fons (Legal Secretary at the Cabinet of the Vice-President), 'To Say What the Law of the EU Is: Methods of Interpretation and the European Court of Justice' (2014) 20 *Columbia Journal of European Law* 3. A classic EU authority remains Case C–283/81 *Srl CILFIT and Lanificio di Gavardo SpA v Ministry of Health* [1982] ECR 3415. On the interpretative approach of the Boards of Appeal of the EPO see further G2/12 and G2/13 (*Essentially Biological Processes*) (2015) EPOR 28 (supporting a similar systemic, purposive, and teleological approach with respect to the European Patent Convention (EPC)).

[52] Examples in the copyright and patents fields include *Deckmyn*, considered in Section 13.4.8, and Case C–34/10 *Brüstle v Greenpeace eV* [2011] ECR I-9821, considered in Sections 3.9 and 6.3.2.

[53] For the EU see n 5; for the EPC see G3/08 (*PRESIDENT'S REFERENCE/Computer Program Exclusion*) (2009) EPOR 9.

[54] H.J. Berman, 'The Origins of Historical Jurisprudence: Coke, Selden, Hale' (1994) 103 *Yale Law Journal* 1651, 1732.

[55] See M.P. Maduro (Advocate General of the European Court of Justice), 'Interpreting European Law: Judicial Adjudication in a Context of Constitutional Pluralism' (2007) 1 *European Journal of Legal Studies* 1, 3.

[56] n 42.

1.3 The What, How, and Why of International Intellectual Property Law

1.3.1 Preliminary Remarks

Our focus to here has been on the emergence and development of IP law in European states. As we have seen, having some awareness of domestic IP traditions within those states is important, among other reasons because of the emphasis placed by the EU and other European legal communities on developing legal rules in a way that takes account of the traditions of Member States and the common values which those traditions express. Indeed, it is precisely because of this emphasis that the aims and objectives of the European IP legal field can be expected to mirror those of European states historically.

Nonetheless, every supranational community has its own policy agendas and reasons for being separate from those of its member states, and these will inevitably influence its perspectives on and approaches to IP. Hence the need to consider European IP law with reference not only to the general law of IP as developed by (European) nation states, but also to the international IP legal field.

1.3.2 What is International Intellectual Property Law?

International IP law may be defined as the accumulated body of legislation, legal acts, and judicial decisions promulgated by the institutions of established international communities, and creating legal obligations with respect to the recognition and protection of the IP rights of those countries' citizens. Thus defined it includes a wide range of instruments focused on or relevant to IP, including several created under the aegis of the United Nations (UN), World Intellectual Property Organization (WIPO), and World Trade Organization (WTO) respectively. It also includes all IP laws promulgated or recognized by the EU and other European legal communities, and in particular,

- the collection of primary and secondary EU laws that create legal obligations with respect to the IP rights of the citizens of the 28 EU Member States, including all international agreements to which the EU is a signatory (see Article 216(2) Treaty on the Functioning of the European Union (TFEU) and Section 2.4.2.4);
- the EPC and associated decisions of the European Patent Office, which create legal obligations with respect to the IP rights of the citizens of the 38 EPC Contracting States;
- the European Economic Area (EEA) Agreement, including: (a) Protocol 28 on intellectual property, which requires Contracting Parties to adhere to a range of international IP conventions (Article 5), namely, the Paris Convention, the Berne Convention, the Rome Convention, the Madrid Agreement, the Nice Agreement, the Budapest Treaty, and the Patent Cooperation Treaty; and (b) Annex XVII, which incorporates certain EU legislative measures into EEA law (see Article 65(2) EEA Agreement), thereby extending their effect to EEA territory and creating further legal obligations with respect to the IP rights of the citizens of the 31 EEA States; and
- the European Convention on Human Rights and associated decisions of the European Court of Human Rights, which create legal obligations with respect to the IP rights of the citizens of the 47 Council of Europe Member States.

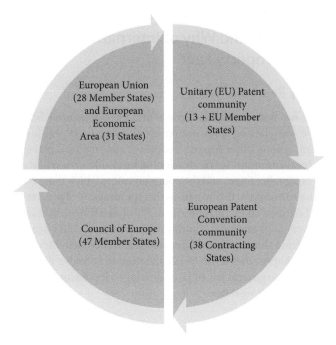

Figure 1.5 European IP communities

When the recently concluded unitary (EU) patent system is established, international IP law will also include the decisions of the Unified Patent Court, which will create legal obligations with respect to the IP rights of the citizens of the 13 or more EU Member States participating in the system. Thus, and as shown in Figure 1.5, there are several European and non-European international communities involved in the regulation of IP rights, each with its own membership, institutions, and reasons for being. As we will see in later chapters, understanding the relationship between these communities and their IP laws and policies is a central challenge presented by this field.

1.3.3 The How and Why of International Intellectual Property Law

1.3.3.1 International IP Law as a Coordinated Response to the Problems Created by Domestic IP Territoriality

Another challenge is to understand how the variety of European and other international IP laws operate. Many operate by establishing legal standards for their member states to implement within their own territories, rather than by regulating the behaviour of those states' citizens per se. Such laws are accordingly addressed to states rather than to individuals, and tend to be expressed at a higher level of abstraction than domestic IP laws, as well as being limited in their field of coverage. However, there are exceptions to this within the EU particularly, many of whose IP laws are addressed to individuals and penetrate directly into the domestic orders of EU Member States, making them more akin to the laws of a country than the laws of an international community.

Related to this is the unique concern of European and other international legal systems with replacing or supplementing the domestic laws of a given region with supranational laws and policies. In the IP context, a key reason for this concern to unify or harmonize domestic systems has been the desire to reduce or abolish their territorial restrictions in order to support peace and prosperity throughout the relevant region. In this important respect, European and other supranational initiatives differ from domestic initiatives, being a coordinated response to the problems caused by domestic IP territoriality.

1.3.3.2 **The Nature, Foundations, and Impact of Domestic IP Territoriality**

1.3.3.2.1 *IP Territoriality*

Historically, IP territoriality has denoted three things. The first is the conferral of IP rights under the national laws of individual states. The second is the restriction of the legal effects of those rights to the territory of their conferring state. And the third is the enforcement of IP rights by the courts of the conferring state applying domestic law. In addition, IP territoriality has tended to support definitions of IP rights themselves aimed at protecting the interests of the protecting state and its citizens, including at the expense of foreigners. For example, in the 18th century a citizen of Italy could only prevent a third party in Denmark from making and publishing copies of her novel if she was able to establish a sufficient connection to Danish territory to claim the protections of its domestic copyright laws and access the Danish courts to secure those laws' enforcement. She would have struggled to meet the first of these hurdles, particularly if the third party was the first person to publish the novel in Denmark, in which case he and not the novel's author would have been the beneficiary of its copyright under Danish law.

1.3.3.2.2 *The Foundations of IP Territoriality*

The territorial restrictions on IP rights can be attributed to the origin of those rights in privileges conferred on individuals by the Crown or other state authority as a means of rewarding and encouraging certain conduct of benefit to the state. When these privileges later took the form of legal entitlements, they were similarly confined to the territory over which the state's sovereign powers extended, and similarly drafted by and to benefit the conferring state. For example, and as we saw in Section 1.2, the first general patent statute of Venice from 1474 was expressed as having the purpose of encouraging men to 'apply their genius [to] discover, and…build devices of great utility and benefit to our Commonwealth', and to that end promised 'every person who shall build any new and ingenious device in this City, not previously made in this Commonwealth' a ten-year monopoly over its manufacture in 'our territories and towns', enforceable before any local magistrate. So too, as seen in Section 1.2.2.2.1, the first general copyright statute from 1710 was entitled 'An Act for the Encouragement of Learning', and promised any author who published a book in Britain, and registered and deposited it, a renewable 14-year right to prevent others from importing, printing and exploiting it, enforceable before the local courts.

As these earliest IP statutes underline, territoriality supports the sovereignty of states by recognizing their complete and exclusive authority with respect to the governance of their territory. For example, the Venetian Senate had no authority to grant monopolies that would restrict life outside Venice, and the English Government had no authority to restrict the freedom of people to copy manuscripts beyond British shores. In addition, the recognition of state sovereignty had especial importance in IP because of the different understandings of and attitudes to IP rights that existed at different times and in different countries. Hence, IP rights have been alternatively regarded as privileges granted by the government in pursuit of certain social and economic objectives, ends in themselves granted in recognition of the moral or natural property rights of their beneficiaries, and unjustifiable restraints on trade and public freedoms. Given this diversity of views, IP territoriality has been an essential means by which individual countries have been able to shape their laws to reflect their own values and interests.

Economic self-interest has always been a central determinant of domestic IP laws and policies. For countries with established creative and scientific industries and a strong export market, IP rights have tended to be viewed as a means of protecting the products of domestic manufacture when traded internationally. For countries dependent on exports from abroad to acquire their cultural and scientific products, they have tended to represent a restriction on access and a cause of inflated pricing. For example, when Switzerland introduced a patent law in the late 19th century, it restricted the law's operation to the mechanical field so as only to protect those goods in which Switzerland had an established manufacturing and export industry. By contrast, other fields in which Switzerland had no established industry and thus depended on imports from abroad—such as the chemical field—were left unprotected by patents, enabling continued free public access to chemical inventions patented abroad. Such state-supported policies of international 'piracy' in the public interest were common in 19th century Europe. Another example is provided by the French patent law of 1791, which prohibited the holding of French patents alongside patents from other countries in respect of the same invention, while also treating as inventors any person who introduced into France an invention from abroad, whether or not it was protected by a foreign patent. And finally, there is the example of the English Statute of Anne, the efforts of which to encourage the importation and circulation of foreign-language works led to its express exclusion from copyright protection of 'the Importation, Vending, or Selling of any Books in Greek, Latin, or any other Foreign Language Printed beyond the Seas.'

Whatever their motivation, by the end of the 19th century most European states had decided that IP rights ought to be recognized and protected, and that some form of international cooperation in securing such recognition and protection was necessary.

1.3.3.2.3 *The Problems Created by IP Territoriality*

In principle, IP territoriality increases the chance of IP rights being recognized and protected somewhere in the world; the non-recognition or non-enforcement of IP rights in one territory not affecting their recognition and enforcement in other territories. Overall, however, it creates more problems for individuals than benefits. From the perspective of IP rights owners, those problems arise in any situation in which IP subject matter passes (with or without the rights owner's permission) beyond the territorial boundaries of the rights-granting state. In addition, over the past 70 years, expanding economic markets combined with developing digital and other technologies have made the passage of IP subject matter across national borders commonplace. Hence the challenge for states to address the problems created by IP territoriality while preserving their freedom to define their IP laws and policies in the way that best reflects their local values and interests. Meeting this challenge has been a central aim of international initiatives since the 19th century.

1.3.3.3 The Emergence of International IP Systems in Response to IP Territoriality

1.3.3.3.1 *Mutual Recognition and Extra-Territoriality: 19th Century Bilateral Agreements*

At the international level, states have developed several strategies to help to address the problems created by IP domestic territoriality. Among the earliest were the strategies of extra-territoriality and mutual recognition, which involved: (a) declaring the state's domestic laws to have extra-territorial effect for the benefit of the citizens of other states; and (b) agreeing to recognize and enforce the IP laws or procedures of another state, subject to a requirement of formal or material reciprocity.

Mutual recognition of domestic IP laws was the basis for the bilateral IP agreements that emerged in the 19th century. These had been championed by different countries as a means of securing protection for their own citizens abroad, and by the 1890s formed an extensive and complex network of legal IP arrangements throughout Europe, including 15 with France as a party, nine with Belgium, and eight with each of Spain and Italy. While many of the agreements contained similar provisions, their separate negotiation by different pairs of states with varied IP traditions and economic interests ensured that they contained many differences, including with respect to their coverage. For most states, concerned primarily with protecting their citizens' interests (rather than the interests of individuals per se), the benefits of each bilateral agreement needed to be carefully weighed against its detriments.

In the 1850s, France boosted the political currency of bilateral IP agreements by unilaterally extending the protection of its domestic copyright laws to cover the works of foreigners, consistent with the principle of extra-territoriality. Motivated in part by its view of copyright as a natural right of individual authors, the French decree encouraged reciprocal acts of generosity by other states and helped to secure protection for the works of French and other nationals overseas.

As mechanisms for overcoming the practical effects of IP territoriality, bilateral agreements were important but ultimately insufficient in the manner of all contractual solutions. The reason was the restriction of their terms to the two contracting states, and their consequential failure to deal with the reality of interstate trade involving other countries. This was a particular difficulty in a geographical area as small as Europe, as the following excerpt from a debate in the English House of Commons from 1838 illustrates.

> *Mr. Goulburn* confessed, that he felt considerable difficulty as to the mode in which the objects of the bill [proposing a bilateral copyright agreement between France and England] were to be carried out; and one of the points which struck him the most forcibly was the question whether, in the event of England binding itself by means of a convention with France, that country was to be bound not to receive books from Belgium, the copyrights of which belonged to England, but which had been improperly printed elsewhere, and also whether England was to bind itself to receive no French books, unless from France itself. That was one of the greatest difficulties which suggested itself to his mind, for those who, for the benefit of their own trade, pirated the works of others, would take care to mark the work which they published with the name of the country from which it originally proceeded, so that the whole work would bear the strongest resemblance to the originals and the greatest difficulty would be found in distinguishing the spurious from the genuine editions.[57]

1.3.3.3.2 *The IP Conventions of the 19th and 20th Centuries*

Thus, even in the 19th century the reality of interstate trade was recognized as requiring a more comprehensive form of international cooperation in IP than a network of bilateral agreements. The obvious solution lay in a convention to establish general standards of legal protection within a wider community of states. In the 1880s two such conventions were concluded. The first was the Paris Convention for the Protection of Industrial Property 1883, which governed 'patents, utility models, industrial designs, trademarks, service marks, trade names, indications of source or appellations of origin, and the repression of unfair competition' (Article 1(2)), i.e. the collection of IP rights referred to as 'industrial property'. And the second was the Berne Convention for the Protection of Literary and

---

[57] House of Commons Debates, 20 March 1838 vol. 41 cc. 1095–108.

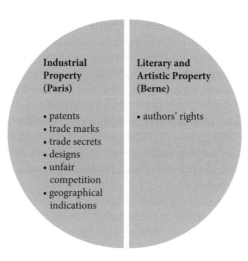

Figure 1.6 The Paris and Berne IP taxonomy

Artistic Property 1886, which governed copyright and related rights. Together these are known as the Great Conventions of the 19th century, and account for the basic distinction drawn in European IP law between industrial property rights on the one hand and copyright and related rights on the other, reflected in Figure 1.6.

Minimum standards of protection and non-discriminatory treatment: the Great (Paris and Berne) Conventions of the 19th century

The Paris and Berne Conventions are as important today as they were in the 19th century. With more than 160 members each, they remain foundational IP instruments throughout the world, and are the bases of all European IP laws and policies. In addition, their continued foundational importance for Europe is assured by at least two things. The first is the obligation of the EU and EEA States under TRIPS, the WCT and Protocol 28 EEA Agreement to comply with the substantive provisions of each. And the second is the number of continental states particularly that recognize those provisions as capable of applying directly, without the need for implementing measures, provided only that they are sufficiently clear, precise, and unconditional to satisfy domestic requirements for direct effect.[58]

Each of the Paris and Berne Conventions establishes a Union of states bound by their commitment to its principles. Hence the opening provision of the Paris Convention that '[t]he countries to which this Convention applies constitute a Union for the protection of industrial property' (Article 1(1)), and the opening provision of the Berne Convention that '[t]he countries to which this Convention applies constitute a Union for the protection of the rights of authors in their literary and artistic works' (Article 1). Two principles are central to each, and hence to the Unions they create. The first is the principle of national (non-discriminatory) treatment, which requires each Union state to accord the citizens of other Union states the same treatment under its national laws as it accords its own citizens. The result is a requirement for national treatment in a formal, rather than a material, sense: the protection offered by state A to the citizens of other Union states need not match the protection extended by those other states to the citizens of state A, but is

---

[58] See, e.g., BGHZ 141, 13, discussed in J. Bornkamm, 'The German Supreme Court: An Actor in the Global Conversation of High Courts' (2004) 39 *Texas International Law Journal* 415, 419.

rather conditional upon an agreement by those other states to extend the protections of their own laws to the citizens of state A. Hence the importance of the Conventions' second foundational principle—the principle of minimum standards of IP protection—which ensures a baseline for the recognition and protection of IP rights that is not assured by the requirement of national treatment itself. Under the Conventions' minimum standards guarantee, each Union state must recognize certain minimum standards of IP protection domestically, including those referred to in Figure 1.7, but is otherwise free to formulate its own IP laws and policies. Through these two principles of national treatment and minimum standards of protection, the Conventions affirm the domestic territoriality of IP rights while also addressing some of its negative effects through the creation of a framework for the rights' international recognition and protection.

Since the 19th century, the Paris and Berne Conventions have been revised and amended on several occasions, most recently in 1979. They have also been supplemented by several additional conventions aimed at extending the reach of the international framework they establish to take account of economic and technological developments, including by raising the minimum standards of protection required of states to reflect the increased production capacities and expanded distribution chains enabled by globalizing markets and digital technology. Those additional conventions have been concluded under the aegis of three main international institutions: the WIPO, the WTO, and the UN. The WIPO conventions include the Patent Law Treaty 2000 for patents, the Rome Convention 1961, Copyright Treaty 1996, and Performances and Phonograms Treaty 1996 for copyright, and the Madrid Agreement 1891 and Trademark Law Treaty 1994 for trade marks. The WTO and UN Conventions include the TRIPS (Trade-Related Aspects of Intellectual Property Rights) Agreement 1994, the Universal Declaration of Human Rights 1948, the United Nations Educational, Scientific and Cultural Organization (UNESCO) Universal Copyright Convention of 1952, the International Treaty on Plant Genetic Resources for Food and Agriculture of 2001, and the Convention on Biological Diversity of 1992.

Of these additional international conventions, the Universal Declaration of Human Rights (UDHR) and TRIPS Agreement may be said to have especial importance for IP in general. The UDHR follows the 1789 Declaration of the Rights of Man and of the Citizen in constitutionalizing the rights of property and IP internationally. To that end Article 27(2) UDHR recognizes the right of everyone 'to the protection of the moral and material interests resulting from any scientific, literary or artistic product of which he is the author', and Article 17 recognizes the right of individuals 'to own property' and not to be 'arbitrarily deprived' of it. In the other direction, Article 27(1) UDHR recognizes 'the right freely to participate in the cultural life of the community, to enjoy the arts and to share in scientific advancement and its benefits,' reinforcing the tension apparent throughout history between the individual and collective aspects of IP.[59]

Most favoured nation provisions: the TRIPS Agreement 1994

Of a rather different hue is the TRIPS Agreement.[60] According to conventional accounts of TRIPS, its creation was driven by the concern of the United States, supported by the European Commission, Japan, and the pharmaceutical and film industries, to bring IP rights within the framework of the WTO due to the growing manufacturing capacity of developing countries, and the increased reliance of developed countries on their comparative advantage in knowledge-based industries in order to maintain their global

---

[59] See Drahos (n 14) 358.   [60] But see Article 7 TRIPS Agreement.

Issue	Minimum Standards Required by the Paris/Berne Conventions
Protectable subject matter	Trade marks: Arts 6*ter*, 6*sexies*, and 7*bis* Paris. Literary and artistic property: Arts 2 and 2*bis* Berne.
Protection criteria	Industrial property: Arts 4, 5D, and 5*bis* Paris (formal). Patents: Art. 4*quater* Paris (substantive). Trade marks: Arts 6(2) and 6*quinquies* Paris (formal); Art. 7 Paris (substantive). Trade names: Art. 8 Paris. Literary and artistic property: Art. 5 Berne (formal); Art. 2 Berne (substantive).
Rights conferred	Industrial property: Art. 10*ter* Paris. Patents: Arts 4*bis*, 4*ter*, 5A, and 5*quarter* Paris. Trade marks: Art. 6 Paris. Industrial designs: Art. 5B Paris. Literary and artistic property: Arts 6*bis*, 8, 9, 11, 11*bis*, 11*ter*, 12, 14, and 14*ter* Berne.
Exceptions to rights	Patents: Art. 5*ter* Paris. Trade marks: Art. 6*bis* Paris. Literary and artistic property: Arts 9(2), 10, and 10*bis* Berne.
Term	Literary and artistic property: Art. 7 Berne.
Beneficiaries	Industrial property: Art. 2 Paris. Literary and artistic property: Arts 3, 4 and 14*bis* Berne.
Exploitation	Patents and utility models: Art. 5A Paris. Trade marks: Art. 6*quarter* Paris. Literary and artistic property: Arts 6*bis*, 14*ter*, 11*bis*(2), 13(1), and 14(3) Berne.
Enforcement	Trade marks and trade names: Art. 9 Paris. Literary and artistic property: Art. 16 Berne.

Figure 1.7 Key minimum standards required by the Paris and Berne Conventions

economic position and strength. By concluding the Agreement, developed countries and regions made the recognition and protection of IP rights a precondition for participation in the global market, thereby ensuring protection for their domestic IP-related assets and industries.

The overall significance of the TRIPS Agreement from a European perspective may be summarized as follows. First, it builds on and supplements the Great Conventions to establish an international framework for the recognition and protection of IP rights in a vastly different economic and technological context from that of the 19th century. To that end it requires its member states to maintain certain minimum standards of IP protection for their own nationals and for the nationals of all other member states (Article 1(1)), including the protection required by Articles 1 to 12 and 19 Paris Convention (Article 2(1)) and Articles 1 to 21 Berne Convention (except Article 6*bis* concerning authors' moral rights) (Article 9(1)), as well as a range of other provisions drawn from domestic IP systems of the mid-20th century. In addition, it reproduces the national treatment provisions of the Great Conventions, and extends them to the realm of interstate relations by

means of a 'most favoured nation' provision (Articles 3 and 4). According to the requirements of that provision, any state that confers benefits on the nationals of another state
must extend the same benefits immediately and unconditionally to the nationals of
all other member states, even if the treatment is more favourable than that which the
conferring state accords to its own nationals. Hence, in addressing the problems of IP
territory, the TRIPS Agreement deploys the same 'minimum standards' and 'national
treatment' requirements as the Paris and Berne Conventions, supplemented by a new
'most favoured nation' provision. Third, the TRIPS Agreement is subject to the WTO
dispute resolution mechanism, creating an international forum for resolving disputes
between countries regarding the meaning of its IP provisions. And finally, and as we will
see in Section 2.4.2.4.2, as an international agreement signed by the EU and falling within
its sphere of exclusive competence, the TRIPS Agreement generates legal effects within
the EU legal order and establishes a general jurisdiction for the Court of Justice with
respect to its provisions.

1.3.3.3.3 Facilitating Parallel IP Protection: International Arrangements for the Administration of IP Rights

In addition to harmonizing substantive IP law, there has been a long-standing effort to
make it easier and cheaper for people to acquire and enforce IP rights outside the territories of the states of which they are citizens. The Berne Convention was significant in
this regard because of its requirement that states grant copyright protection without the
registration or other formalities required for industrial property (Article 5(2)), and so
too for each of the Madrid Agreement 1891 and Patent Cooperation Treaty 1970, which
created an international system of trade mark registration and patent application respectively to enable people to obtain bundles of national industrial property rights via a single
administrative regime. Also, there is the EPC, referred to earlier, which created a system
for obtaining bundles of national patents from any number of its (currently 38) EU and
non-EU Contracting States.

  In these international administrative initiatives we see a further strategy that has been
developed by groups of states to reduce the negative effects of IP territoriality. That strategy involves establishing supranational procedural and other mechanisms to make it easier for people to satisfy the conditions imposed by the IP laws of different countries and
thereby acquire parallel IP protection in them. One of the earliest of these initiatives in
Europe was the creation by the Benelux countries and France of the International Patent
Institute (IIB) in The Hague in 1947 to centralize aspects of the patent-granting procedure for the benefit of people seeking patent protection in those countries.[61]

  Moving from the acquisition to the enforcement of IP rights brings us to a further
range of international initiatives aimed at establishing common rules of jurisdiction and
applicable law to facilitate the resolution of cross-border disputes. The earliest of these
was the 1968 Brussels Convention, which established the basic principle that jurisdiction
to hear a matter vests with the court of the state in which the defendant to the matter is
domiciled, regardless of where the claimant is domiciled, which state granted the right,
and where the infringing act took place (Article 2), while also recognizing exceptions
of importance for IP. According to one of those exceptions, matters involving a tort (of
which the infringement of IP rights is an example) could be brought before the courts of
the state in which the harmful act occurred (Article 5(3)). According to another, 'proceedings concerned with the registration or validity of patents, trade marks, designs, or other
similar rights required to be deposited or registered' could only be brought in the state

---

[61] Following its creation in the 1970s, the European Patent Office subsumed the IIB.

in which the deposit or registration had been applied for, taken place, or deemed to have taken place under the terms of an international convention (Article 16). These and other provisions of the Brussels Convention were aimed at supporting the enforcement of IP rights granted by different states throughout the world, and have since been reproduced and supplemented in EU legislation (see Chapter 25).

Each of these international mechanisms of administrative and judicial cooperation has been extremely successful, with the result that it is now common for individuals to hold several patents or other registrable IP rights in respect of the same invention or other subject matter from several states and to commence proceedings involving those rights in a range of domestic courts. This has also led to other legal strategies aimed at extending the benefits of parallel protection beyond IP rights owners themselves to the general public. The most important of these strategies has been the principle of exhaustion, which ensures that once a book, machine, or other good protected by IP is placed on the market with the IP rights owner's consent, the effect of the IP in respect of it is exhausted for all states in which it is protected. In this way, the principle of exhaustion prevents an IP rights owner from relying on her parallel protection in different states to restrict the movement of goods between them, and thereby limits the potential for territorially limited IP rights to be used to partition and isolate markets. Importantly, however, exhaustion is a principle of national or European law, and not of international law. Thus, to decide whether a particular IP right in respect of a product is exhausted on first sale of the product, it is necessary to have regard to the domestic or European laws governing the relevant species of right. Once again, this is a matter to which we return in later chapters, including Section 2.4.2.1.3.

1.3.3.4 Conclusions

Each of the international responses described earlier to the problems created by domestic IP territoriality has been of enormous legal and economic significance, including for European states. However, none comes close in its aims or effects to the EU's response of choice. From the earliest days of European integration, that response has been to seek to redefine the territory for which IP rights are granted and within which they take effect. Thus, instead of domestic IP rights granted by Belgium or Italy, the aim has been to create *European* IP rights to take effect throughout *European* territory and be enforceable by *European* courts, in the same manner as they would previously have taken effect throughout Belgium or Italy and been enforceable by Belgian or Italian courts. As we will see in the coming chapters, this EU solution of choice to domestic IP territoriality is consistent with wider EU social and economic policies, including the creation of an EU single market, and has been implemented widely with respect to industrial property rights, as well as being recently proposed for copyright as well.

1.4 Conclusions

The idea of IP can be traced to the ancient use of signs to distinguish the ownership and origin of goods; and in legal thought particularly, to the Roman law principle of *accessio*, according to which a person who painted a picture on a canvas thereby acquired ownership of the canvas. The first reported IP case was heard in Ireland in the 6th century, and involved a finding that literary copies of a manuscript belonged to the owner of the manuscript. And finally, the first general IP statute was enacted in Venice in 1474, and promised exclusive manufacturing rights to any person who built a new and useful device within the state. It is from such social and legal roots as these that the European IP system is derived, and in the light of their development and reflected themes, that that system is best approached. In the case of copyright, these themes include: (a) support for an individuated conception of authorship, premised on a view of authors as having a personal connection with and responsibility for the things that they create; (b) recognition of intellectual products as objects of economic and social value capable of supporting property rights; and (c) a commitment among states to using exclusionary rights as mechanisms for balancing the claims of authors and the producers and publishers of their works with the freedom of third parties to express and access ideas and information and exploit fully the capacities of new technologies. In the case of industrial property, they include: (a) a belief that inventors at least deserve property protection by reason of their intellectual endeavours and/or capacities; and (b) a commitment among states to using exclusionary rights as mechanisms for regulating trade and technology, and promoting innovation and fair competition, to the benefit of industry, consumers, and the general public. It is only by identifying these themes in historical context that one can fully understand the prior experience of European states in the light of which contemporary law- and decision-making is undertaken, as well as the values that shaped the emergence and early development of their IP systems and that continue to inform European IP law today. As we have seen, central among these values are individual (expressive and financial) autonomy, social and political participation, trade and competition, freedom of expression, industrial and commercial innovation, consumer protection, and access to new technologies.

As well as being a product of the domestic IP laws of individual European states, European IP law is part of an international network of IP laws that differ from the general IP laws of individual countries in three related aspects. First, unlike domestic IP laws, many international laws operate by establishing legal standards for states to implement within their own territories rather than by regulating the behaviour of those states' citizens per se. Second, the need for international legal communities to accommodate the diverse values and legal traditions of their member states makes their IP laws and policies less likely to reflect a single model or justificatory theory of IP than those of individual countries. And third, a central aim of international *European* IP communities is to supplement or substitute domestic laws and policies with *European* laws and policies in pursuit of *European* objectives, including some that stand in tension with domestic interests, such as the abolition of territorial restrictions on the operation of IP regimes.

Historically, all IP rights have been territorial in nature, in the sense of having been conferred by national law, confined in effect to the territory of the conferring state, and enforceable by a court with jurisdiction in respect of the laws of that state. The empirical explanation for this lies in the origins of IP rights in royal grants of privilege, and in the limits of domestic administrative and legislative authority. Normatively, its explanation lies in the support which domestic IP territoriality affords to state sovereignty, and the view of the state as the most appropriate forum for determining IP law and policy.

Today, territoriality remains a mainstay of IP systems, and a foundational aspect of European IP law. Its effects have however been mitigated by various means. These include agreements to recognize and enforce the IP laws or procedures of another state, subject to a reciprocal recognition agreement by it. Second, they also include international commitments to recognizing minimum standards of IP protection and to ensuring that the citizens of states are treated equally with respect to IP. Third, they include the creation of administrative arrangements to facilitate the acquisition of IP rights in different states simultaneously, and the formulation of the principle of exhaustion to facilitate the movement of IP-protected goods between countries. And fourth and finally, they include the introduction of unitary IP rights, which are also territorial in nature, but which are conferred by a regional authority, confined in effect of the territory of that region, and enforceable by a court with jurisdiction in respect of its laws. As we will see in later chapters, each of these four means of addressing the problems created by domestic IP territoriality is a mainstay of the current European IP field and system.

Further Reading

CORNISH, W.R., 'The International Relations of Intellectual Property' (1993) 52 *Cambridge Law Journal* 46

DREXL, J., RUSE-KHAN, H.G., AND NADDE-PHLIX, S. (eds), *EU Bilateral Trade Agreements and Intellectual Property: For Better or Worse?* (Springer, 2014)

GINSBURG, J.C., 'Proto-Property in Literary and Artistic Works: Sixteenth-Century Papal Printing Privileges' (August 2015) Columbia Public Law Research Paper No. 14-478, http://ssrn.com/abstract=2650152

GINSBURG, J.C., 'Tale of Two Copyrights: Literary Property in Revolutionary France and America' (1990) 64 *Tulane Law Review* 1007

HESSE, C., 'The Rise of Intellectual Property, 700 B.C.–A.D. 2000: An Idea in the Balance' (2002) 131 *Daedalus* 26

LADAS, S.P., *The International Protection of Industrial Property* (Harvard University Press, 1930)

MACHLUP, I.F. AND PENROSE, E., 'The Patent Controversy in the Nineteenth Century' (1950) 10 *Journal of Economic History* 1

NETANEL, N.W. (ed.), *The Development Agenda: Global Intellectual Property and Developing Countries* (OUP, 2009)

PRAGER, F.D., 'A History of Intellectual Property From 1545 to 1787' (1944) 26 *Journal of the Patent Office Society* 711

RICKETSON, S. AND GINSBURG, J.C., *International Copyright and Neighbouring Rights: The Berne Convention and Beyond* (2nd edn, OUP, 2005)

SCHECHTER, F.I., *The Historical Foundations of the Law Relating to Trade-Marks* (Columbia University Press, 1925)

TEILMANN-LOCK, S., *The Object of Copyright: A Conceptual History of Originals and Copies in Literature, Art and Design* (Routledge, 2015)

2

The Foundations of European Union Intellectual Property Law

2.1 Introduction

No area of private law has been Europeanized to the extent that IP law has been. In addition, the means by which IP law has been Europeanized differ, resulting in diverse European IP legal systems. For example, in the patent field there exists an intergovernmental system for obtaining national patents from European states, supported by centralized administrative and quasi-judicial bodies, and supplemented by EU legislation and associated case law. In the trade mark, designs, and plant variety rights fields there exist unitary (Community trade mark, designs, and plant variety rights) systems for EU territory, administered and enforced by EU institutions with the assistance of the institutions of EU Member States. And in the copyright and related rights field there exist a large number of harmonizing EU directives and associated judicial decisions with which the domestic systems of EU Member States are required, within limits, to comply.

The result of this extensive and varied European involvement in IP is a dynamic and extremely complex legal field. The EU is not the only important institutional actor in that field: some of the most important European initiatives in IP have been non-EU initiatives. Nonetheless, its role is and has always been central, both internally and externally through its negotiation and conclusion of bilateral and plurilateral agreements. As a result of this, a lot of European IP law lies at the intersection of the two specialized regimes of IP and EU law, making an understanding of the logic and terminology of each essential.

In this chapter we continue our introduction to the European law of IP by discussing the role of the EU in the IP field before and since the introduction of the Lisbon Treaty. To that end we introduce the EU legal order itself, including its founding Treaties, institutions, and authority to act (competence), with a focus on IP specifically.

2.2 From an International to a Constitutional Legal Order: The Establishment of the European Economic Community and its Development to the European Union

2.2.1 The Establishment of the European Economic Community in 1957/8

The EU began life as the European Economic Community (EEC), one of three post-war European communities created in the 1950s. It was established to exist indefinitely by a Treaty signed in Rome on 25 March 1957 by Belgium, France, Germany, Italy, Luxembourg, and the Netherlands—the same six signatories to the other two European communities established during the 1950s: the European Coal and Steel Community (ECSC) and European Atomic Energy Community—and took effect on 1 January 1958. According to the Preamble and Articles 1 to 3 of its founding Treaty, the reason for its creation was to promote peace and economic reconstruction in Europe by operating as a common market throughout which goods, persons, services, and capital would move freely, fair competition would be promoted, and other aspects of economic policy would be harmonized.[1] To that end its Treaty vested a range of legislative, executive, and judicial powers in a parliamentary Assembly and Council (political institutions), Commission (executive institution), and Court of Justice, and prohibited certain measures as between Member States inconsistent with its single market objectives.

2.2.2 The Judicial Transformation of the European Economic Community

In the more than 50 years since its creation, the EEC has grown in membership from six to 28 Member States[2] and been transformed from an economic union created by international agreement to a constitutional legal order comparable in many respects to that of a federal nation state. This transformation has been the combined result of Treaty reforms and decisions of the Community's Court of Justice from the two decades following its establishment. An early step in its judicial transformation came with the decision that the provisions of its Treaty were capable of having direct effect. This occurred in Case C–26/62 *NV Algemene Transporten Expeditie Onderneming van Gend en Loos v Nederlandse Administratis der Belastingen* [1963] ECR 1 (*Van Gend en Loos*), where the Court of Justice held as follows:

> The Community constitutes a new legal order of international law for the benefit of which the States have limited their sovereign rights, albeit within limited fields and the subjects of which comprise not only Member States but also their nationals. Independently

---

[1] See Case C–15/81 *Gaston Schul Douane Expediteur BV v Inspecteur der Invoerrechten en Accijnzen, Roosendaal* [1982] ECR 1409 [33]. Since the Treaty of Lisbon, references to the 'common market' and 'internal market' have been replaced with references to the 'internal market', defined in Article 26(2) TFEU to comprise 'an area without internal frontiers in which the free movement of goods, persons, services and capital is ensured in accordance with the provisions of the Treaties'.

[2] Austria, Belgium, Bulgaria, Croatia, Cyprus, Czech Republic, Denmark, Estonia, Finland, France, Germany, Greece, Hungary, Ireland, Italy, Latvia, Lithuania, Luxembourg, Malta, the Netherlands, Poland, Portugal, Romania, Slovakia, Slovenia, Spain, Sweden, and the UK.

of the legislation of Member States, Community law therefore not only imposes obligations on individuals but is also intended to confer upon them rights which become part of their legal heritage. These rights arise not only where they are expressly granted by the Treaty, but also by reason of obligations which the Treaty imposes in a clearly defined way upon individuals as well as upon the Member States and upon the institutions of the Community.

The effect of this decision was to recognize the capacity of Community law to confer rights on individuals capable of direct enforcement in horizontal proceedings against other individuals before the domestic courts of Member States. It was followed soon after by three further developments of importance for the Community's transformation. The first of these was the recognition in Case C–6/64 *Costa v ENEL* [1964] ECR I-1141 that Treaty provisions are supreme vis-à-vis the domestic laws of Member States. The second was the recognition in Case C–11/70 *Internationale Handelsgesellschaft mbH v Einfuhr- und Vorratsstelle für Getreide und Futtermittel* [1970] ECR 1125 (*Internationale*) of the existence of certain 'general principles' of Community law—including proportionality, legal certainty, legitimate expectations, non-discrimination, and (other) fundamental rights—derived from the common constitutional traditions of Member States, and their capacity to be drawn upon by the Court as interpretive guides and bases for reviewing the validity of Community and Member States' domestic laws. The third was the recognition in Case C–106/77 *Amministrazione delle Finanze dello Stato v Simmenthal* [1978] ECR 629 that, and as a consequence of Community law supremacy, the domestic courts of Member States must give full effect to Community law, including by disapplying any provisions of domestic law which conflict with them. According to the Court ([17]):

> [T]he relationship between provisions of the Treaty and directly applicable measures of the institutions on the one hand and the national law of the Member States on the other is such that those provisions and measures not only by their entry into force render automatically inapplicable any conflicting provision of current national law but—in so far as they are an integral part of, and take precedence in, the legal order applicable in the territory of each of the Member States—also preclude the valid adoption of new national legislative measures to the extent to which they would be incompatible with Community provisions.

None of the cases referred to here involves IP. Nonetheless, they are all of foundational importance for the EU legal order generally and for the substantive EU law of IP specifically. For example, they establish the two principles of supremacy and direct effect from which the EU legal order continues to be regarded as deriving its essential character. In addition, they mark the early accommodation within EU law of fundamental rights and other general principles derived from the common constitutional traditions of Member States.[3] And finally, they illustrate the policy-driven approach of the Court of Justice, including its concern actively to promote the effectiveness and autonomy of EU law in its decision-making. As we will see later in this chapter and in later chapters, each of these has had and continues to have important ramifications for IP. For example, it was with reference to the principles of EU law supremacy and direct effect that the Court of Justice in 2011 held the draft European and Community Patents Court Agreement to be incompatible with the EU Treaties.[4] In addition, it

---

[3] On the current status of these principles see Article 6(3) TEU.
[4] *Opinion 1/09 (Creation of a unified patent litigation system)* [2011] ECR I-1137.

was with reference to the common constitutional traditions of Member States that the Commission in 1996 sought to justify its policy commitment to ensuring a high level of copyright protection in Europe.[5] And finally, it has been due largely to the activist and policy-driven approach of the Court of Justice that there has developed such an extensive EU jurisprudence in IP.[6]

2.2.3 **Treaty Reforms**

Alongside these early judicial developments have been further changes to the Community legal order effected by revisions to its Treaty. Since 1958 four substantive revisions have been undertaken, by the Treaty on European Union signed on 7 February 1992 (Maastricht Treaty), the Treaties of Amsterdam and Nice signed on 2 October 1997 and 26 February 2001 respectively, and the Treaty of Lisbon signed on 13 December 2007, each of which has further supported the Community's development from an international to a constitutional legal order. Central again has been an expansion of the social dimension of the Community, including an expansion of its objectives from ensuring fair competition and the free movement of goods, persons, services, and capital as between Member States to recognizing and protecting the fundamental rights of European citizens and increasing the Community's democratic legitimacy. The first substantial reforms to this end came with the Maastricht Treaty in 1992, and included: a new concept of European citizenship and rights for Member States' nationals in their capacity as Community citizens; an expanded role for the European Parliament and a new co-decision procedure for passing Community legislation that involved the Council and Parliament working together; a new Title on culture; an extension of the principle of subsidiarity (now contained in Article 5(3) Treaty on European Union (TEU)) to limit the Community's authority to act in areas where Member States were also competent to act; and the creation of a European Union founded on the three pillars of the original three European Communities (the European Coal and Steel Community, the European Atomic Energy Community, and the EEC), the Common Foreign and Security Policy, and cooperation in criminal matters. In addition, the Maastricht Treaty renamed the EEC the European Community (EC), as a result of which the EEC Treaty became the EC Treaty. Two years after its introduction, the single market and other core provisions of the EC Treaty were extended to a wider geographical area and community of European (EC and EFTA) states with the introduction of the EEA Agreement.

Following Maastricht, further important reforms to the EC Treaty were made. These included (with the Amsterdam Treaty): the insertion of a new Social Chapter focused on developing the social dimensions of the Union; the insertion of a new Title on closer cooperation (now enhanced cooperation) to enable subsets of Member States to pursue further initiatives with support from Community institutions; the expansion of the Community's authority to negotiate and conclude international agreements; and an enhanced role for the Parliament in passing Community legislation. In addition, the Treaty of Nice introduced further changes to the EC institutions to prepare them for the substantial expansion of Community membership from Eastern Europe that took place in the first decade of the current century.

---

[5] Commission Communication of 20 November 1996, 'Follow-up to the Green Paper on copyright and related rights in the information society' COM (96) 568 final.

[6] See, e.g., M. McCown, 'Re-Writing the Treaties with Precedent: Intellectual Property Rights and EU Law' (2003) http://aei.pitt.edu/2894/1/133.pdf; J. Giles, 'The *Brüstle* and *Eli Lilly* Cases: Creation—God or Humankind?' (2012) 1 *Oxford Journal of Law and Religion* 518; M. Leistner, 'Europe's Copyright Law Decade: Recent Case Law of the European Court of Justice and Policy Perspectives' (2014) 51 *Common Market Law Review* 559.

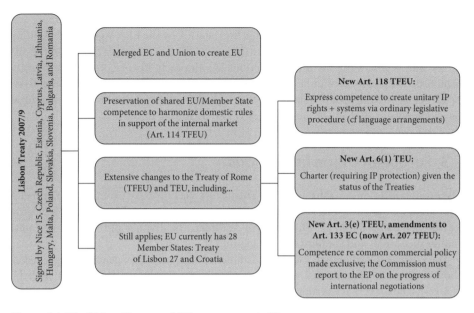

Figure 2.1 The Lisbon Treaty and EU competence in IP

This brings us to the most recent Treaty reforms, which were made by the Lisbon Treaty in 2007 and took effect on 1 December 2009. The product of a failed attempt to create a Constitution for the Union, the Lisbon Treaty made far-reaching amendments to both the Maastricht and Rome (EU and EEC) Treaties for the purpose once again of making the EU legal order more democratic, including through the greater recognition and protection of the fundamental rights of European citizens. Of greatest current relevance, its amendments included: clarification of the EU's spheres of authority (competence), including the new and amended competence provisions of relevance to IP shown in Figure 2.1; the introduction of a double majority requirement for the passage of legislation, involving support from at least 55 per cent of EU Member States and 65 per cent of EU citizens; the introduction of a new role for national parliaments in the scrutiny of draft EU legislation for compliance with the principle of subsidiarity; the enhancement of the European Parliament's (external and internal) role and powers, including via the extension of the co-decision procedure for passing EU legislation to new areas and its affirmation as the 'ordinary legislative procedure'; the elevation of the CFR to the primary law status of the Treaties, commitment to acceding to the (non-EU) European Convention on Human Rights (ECHR) 1950, and recognition of such fundamental rights as are guaranteed by the ECHR and result from the constitutional traditions common to Member States as general principles of EU law; and the introduction of a citizens' initiative, enabling citizens to ask the European Commission to propose draft laws if supported by at least one million signatures from a significant number of Member States. In addition, the Lisbon Treaty merged the EC with the Union so as to abolish the European Community as a separate entity, and renamed the EC Treaty the Treaty on the Functioning of European Union (TFEU).

2.2.4 The EU Legal Order Today

The EU legal order of today is founded upon two Treaties: the TEU, being an amended version of the Maastricht Treaty, and the TFEU, being an amended version of the EEC/

EC Treaty. In combination with the CFR and EU general principles, these represent the primary law of the EU, complemented for the EEA by the EEA Agreement. Among other things, they establish the seven institutions of the EU, empower those institutions to act, and regulate the institutions' actions. As the early history of the Community legal order's development underlines, however, they must be read alongside the jurisprudence of the European Court of Justice, which remains a primary driver of legal developments in all fields of substantive EU law, including in the field of IP.

2.3 European Union Institutions

The seven institutions established by the Treaties are the European Council, the European Commission, the European Parliament, the Council, the Court of Justice of the EU, the European Central Bank, and the Court of Auditors. The first five of these have greatest importance for IP, and are illustrated in Figure 2.2.

The European Parliament, European Council, and Council are generally regarded as the EU's political institutions, while the Commission represents its executive and the Courts its judiciary. Each is supported in its functions by a number of bodies, offices, and agencies, including (of greatest importance for IP) the European Economic and Social Committee (EESC), the Office for Harmonization in the Internal Market (Trade Marks and Designs) (OHIM), and the Community Plant Variety Office (CPVO). The EESC is a consultative body, and the OHIM and CPVO implement the EU (Community) trade mark, registered designs, and plant variety rights systems. As with the seven EU institutions themselves, the actions of all specialist bodies are founded on and subject to the provisions of the EU Treaties.

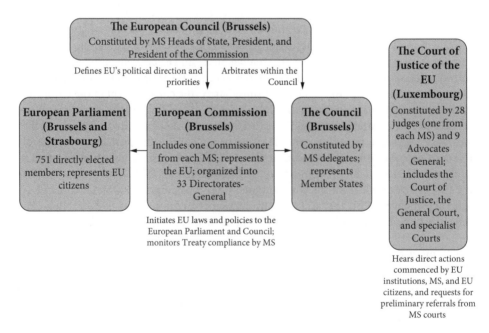

Figure 2.2 Key EU institutions

2.3.1 **The European Council**

The European Council meets approximately four times a year to discuss and define the EU's political direction and priorities under the chairmanship of its President. It is the EU's highest-level political institution and is constituted by the heads of state or government of Member States, a President, and the President of the European Commission. Of relevance for IP specifically, the European Council has endorsed and provides key oversight of the Commission's Europe 2020 Strategy, discussed later.

2.3.2 **The European Commission**

The European Commission is the executive arm of the EU. It includes a single representative (Commissioner) from each Member State, each of whom fills a five-year term, a President nominated by the European Council, and other Commissioners appointed by the European Council in agreement with the nominated President. The appointment of all Commissioners is subject to approval of the European Parliament, to which the Commissioners remain accountable while in office. Once appointed, the Commissioners' role is to promote the interests of the EU as a whole (rather than of Member States or EU citizens) by proposing and overseeing the implementation of EU policies. Central aspects of that role are the drafting of proposals for new European laws for review and passage by the European Parliament and the Council, and overseeing the application of EU laws by Member States. In these and other respects, the Commissioners are supported by a permanent staff and organized into 33 departments referred to as Directorates-General.

The activities of the EU are grouped into 15 broad categories, from agriculture, fisheries and food to transport and travel. Initiatives within these categories are proposed and drafted by the European Commission. Intellectual property arises under several of these categories, including science and technology, external relations, and foreign affairs, and the EU's so-called 'cross-cutting policies', which include the Europe 2020 growth strategy. Of the 33 Directorates-General, responsibility for internal IP matters—including those arising in connection with the Europe 2020 strategy—falls primarily to the Directorate-General for Internal Market, Industry, Entrepreneurship and SMEs (DG GROWTH).

2.3.3 **The European Parliament**

The European Parliament is the EU's democratic body: it has more than 750 members (MEPs), all of whom are elected directly by EU citizens every five years and fulfil their functions in representation of those citizens. As with the parliaments of modern states, it plays a key role in reviewing and passing European legislation, working to that end with the Council under the Treaties' ordinary legislative procedure.

2.3.4 **The Council of the European Union (Council of Ministers)**

The Council of the EU is not to be confused with the European Council or the non-EU Council of Europe. It is constituted by delegates of Member States, and acts in representation of those states rather than EU citizens or the EU itself. Its main task is to work with the European Parliament to decide the EU budget and review and pass European legislation. It also signs agreements between the EU and other countries.

2.3.5 **The Courts**

The EU Court of greatest importance for IP is the Court of Justice of the European Union (CJEU). The CJEU comprises the Court of Justice, the General Court (previously the Court of First Instance), and the EU's specialist courts. The most important of these is the Court of Justice. This Court is responsible for ensuring the consistent interpretation and application of EU law throughout the Union and for overseeing its enforcement. In addition to its 28 judges (one from each Member State), the Court of Justice includes nine Advocates General who have the same status as its judges, but who perform the different role of giving an impartial and independent but non-binding opinion on individual cases. Under the EEA Agreement, its decisions have relevance for EEA states.

All proceedings before the Court of Justice of the EU involve public hearings before a panel of three, five, or 13 sitting judges, or sometimes before the Court as a whole, depending on the complexity of the case. The Court publishes majority judgments only: dissenting opinions by minority judges are never given.

2.3.6 **Supporting Institutions of Importance for IP**

2.3.6.1 **The European Economic and Social Committee**

The EESC was established by the Treaty of Rome to involve social and economic interest groups from across the Community in EEC law- and policy-making. It has more than 350 members (councillors), all of whom are nominated to serve by the governments of Member States for a renewable five-year term. Its function is to issue opinions on matters of European interest to the Council, the Commission, and the European Parliament. In some contexts, such as during the passage of legislation, consultation with the EESC is compulsory. In the past it has played an important role in IP, most notably during the passage of the Proposal for a Directive of the European Parliament and of the Council on the patentability of computer-implemented inventions [2002] OJ C 151E/129, when its opinion was a factor in the directive's failure to win the necessary political support to be passed into legislation.[7]

2.3.6.2 **The Office for the Harmonization of the Internal Market (Trade Marks and Designs)**

OHIM was established in 1993 by the Community Trade Mark Regulation to support the registration and enforcement of Community trade marks, discussed in Part IV. Since then its founding regulation has been amended several times, and the functions of the Office extended to include the registration and enforcement of Community design rights (established by the Community Design Rights Regulation and discussed in Chapter 19), and to support the EU laws and policies concerning the enforcement of IP rights via its Observatory on Infringements of Intellectual Property Rights.

2.3.6.3 **The Community Plant Variety Office**

The CPVO was established in 1994 by the Community Plant Variety Rights Regulation to support the registration and enforcement of Community plant variety rights, discussed in Chapter 9.

---

[7] For the details see J. Pila, 'Dispute Over the Meaning of "Invention" in Art. 52(2) EPC—The Patentability of Computer-Implemented Inventions in Europe' (2005) 36 *IIC* 173.

2.4 The Legal Authority of the European Union: Competence

2.4.1 General Principles

2.4.1.1 Restrictions on EU Competence: Article 5 TEU

In pursuing their objectives, the EU institutions must act in accordance with the provisions of the Treaties. Of especial importance in this regard is Article 5 TEU, which states as follows:

1. The limits of Union competences are governed by the principle of conferral. The use of Union competences is governed by the principles of subsidiarity and proportionality.

2. Under the principle of conferral, the Union shall act only within the limits of the competences conferred upon it by the Member States in the Treaties to attain the objectives set out therein. Competences not conferred upon the Union in the Treaties remain with the Member States.

3. Under the principle of subsidiarity, in areas which do not fall within its exclusive competence, the Union shall act only if and in so far as the objectives of the proposed action cannot be sufficiently achieved by the Member States, either at central level or at regional and local level, but can rather, by reason of the scale or effects of the proposed action, be better achieved at Union level.

   The institutions of the Union shall apply the principle of subsidiarity as laid down in the Protocol on the application of the principles of subsidiarity and proportionality. National Parliaments ensure compliance with the principle of subsidiarity in accordance with the procedure set out in that Protocol.

4. Under the principle of proportionality, the content and form of Union action shall not exceed what is necessary to achieve the objectives of the Treaties.

   The institutions of the Union shall apply the principle of proportionality as laid down in the Protocol on the application of the principles of subsidiarity and proportionality.

From this provision derive the three main restrictions on the authority of EU institutions to take action in any field: the principle of conferral (Article 5(1) and (2)), the principle of subsidiarity (Article 5(3)), and the principle of proportionality (Article 5(4)) respectively.

2.4.1.2 The Principle of Conferral

It is a fundamental principle of EU law that the EU may only act within the scope of the competences conferred upon it by the Treaties. This is the principle of conferral, expressed in Article 5(1) TEU and defined in Article 5(2) TEU to mean that the EU 'shall act only within the limits of the competences conferred upon it by the Member States in the Treaties to attain the objectives set out therein.' Its effect is to deprive the EU of the inherent or general power enjoyed by nation states to make laws and policies. As a result, before any EU institution can introduce a measure or take some other form of action in a particular area, it must be satisfied that the area is one in which the EU is competent to act.

There are three general categories of EU competence: exclusive, shared, and supporting. If the EU has exclusive competence in a particular area, Member States may not act in that area unless empowered to do so by the EU or for the purpose of implementing EU acts (Article 2(1) TFEU). If the EU has shared competence in a particular area, Member States may only act in that area to the extent that the EU has either failed to act or decided not to act (Article 2(2) TFEU). And finally, if the EU has supporting competence in a particular area, it may only take action to support, coordinate, or supplement Member States' action, without thereby superseding their competence or harmonizing their own domestic laws (Article 2(5) TFEU).

As we shall see, the EU enjoys broad competence to act internally and externally in the field of IP. Important sources of its internal competence are Article 114 TFEU (authorizing the introduction of harmonizing measures to support the establishment and smooth functioning of the internal market) and 118 TFEU (authorizing the introduction of unitary IP rights and supporting arrangements), both of which are shared with Member States.[8] The main source of its external competence is Article 207 TFEU, which since the Lisbon Treaty is exclusive of the competence of Member States (Article 3(1)(e) TFEU).

The definition of the principle of conferral in Article 5(2) TEU refers expressly to the need for EU acts introduced under a competence-conferring provision of the Treaties to be aimed at attaining their objectives. Those objectives—which the Union is charged with pursuing 'by appropriate means commensurate with the competences which are conferred upon it in the Treaties' (Article 3(6))—are defined in Article 3 TEU, and include the following:

- promoting peace, its values, and the well-being of its peoples (Article 3(1));
- establishing an area of freedom, security, and justice in which the free movement of persons is ensured alongside appropriate border controls (Article 3(2));
- establishing an internal market based on economic growth, a competitive social market economy, a high level of environmental protection and improvement, and the promotion of scientific and technological advancement (Article 3(3));
- respecting the Union's rich cultural and linguistic diversity, and ensuring that Europe's cultural heritage is safeguarded and enhanced (Article 3(3)); and
- upholding and promoting the Union's values and interests externally (Article 3(5)).

The EU frequently draws on these objectives to support its law- and decision-making in IP, expressly and impliedly. For example, ensuring 'that Europe's cultural heritage is safeguarded and enhanced' was invoked by the Council in support of its decision to authorize enhanced cooperation in the area of the creation of unitary patent protection in 2011. In addition, the EU's objectives are reinforced in the Preambles to the TEU and CFR. For example, the Preamble to the CFR identifies the strengthened 'protection of fundamental rights in the light of changes in society, social progress and scientific and technological developments' as among the CFR's objectives, and purports to express through its fundamental rights provisions the 'common values' on which European integration is based. Since the Lisbon Treaty, the CFR has assumed special significance due to its elevation under Article 6(1) TEU to the primary law status of the TFEU and TEU.

Consistent with Article 5(2) TEU, Article 3 TEU objectives have been used to constrain EU competence, including in IP. An example is provided by *Opinion 1/09*, which involved a request under Article 218(11) TFEU for an opinion from the European Court regarding the compatibility of a draft agreement with the Treaties. The aim of the agreement was to establish a unified patent litigation system for greater Europe, including a court with jurisdiction to hear actions involving (non-EU) European and Community

---

[8] In the case of Article 118 TFEU, the Court of Justice expressly confirmed this in Joined Cases C–274/11 and 295/11 *Kingdom of Spain v Council of the European Union* EU:C:2013:240 (*Spain v Council*).

patents (the draft European and Community Patents Court Agreement). It was to be a mixed agreement, concluded by the EU, its Member States, and third country members of the (non-EU) EPC.

According to the Court in *Opinion 1/09*, the draft European and Community Patents Court Agreement would have changed the essential character of the EU legal order by altering the powers conferred by the Treaties on the EU and its Member States, and was therefore incompatible with the Treaties. The reason given was the Agreement's attempt to vest a court having a distinct legal personality under international law and existing outside the institutional and judicial framework of the EU with exclusive jurisdiction in relation to Community patent matters, including jurisdiction to interpret and apply primary and secondary EU law. In doing so, it was said, the draft Agreement would have deprived the EU and Member States' courts of their own powers to interpret and apply EU law, and thereby undermined: (a) the supremacy of EU law vis-à-vis the domestic laws of EU Member States; and (b) the direct applicability of many EU laws to Member States and their nationals ([65]). According to the Court, both of these were essential characteristics of the EU legal order by which the obligation of EU and Member States' courts 'to ensure the full application of European Union law in all Member States and to ensure judicial protection of an individual's rights under that law' ([68]) were supported. By undermining them, the draft Agreement would have prevented that obligation from being fulfilled.

Opinion 1/09 confirms the concern of the Court of Justice to ensure that the EU's external activities do not compromise its legal autonomy or the essential characteristics on which that autonomy is built. In this way, it underlines the importance of certain EU Treaty objectives to the Court's decision-making, and the constraints on EU competence which those objectives represent.

Having said that, and as we will also see in later chapters, the invocation of EU Treaty objectives and values by the Court of Justice frequently results in the widening and/or deepening of EU action rather than its restriction, including in IP. The potential for this is apparent from the provisions of the CFR particularly, which support many of the same values that we saw to have influenced the emergence and early development of IP in Europe in Section 1.2.2.2, including autonomy, freedom of expression, social and political participation, and ensuring 'a high level of consumer protection' (Article 38). Beyond Article 38 just cited, the CFR provisions in question include Article 17(2), recognizing the protection of IP as a fundamental right, as well as a variety of other provisions based on the same principles that underpin the existing morality- and public policy-based exclusions from IP protection, such as: the inviolability of human dignity (Article 1), the integrity of the person (Article 3), and environmental protection (Article 37) (of especial relevance for the law of patents and allied rights); respect for private and family life (Article 7), protection of personal data (Article 8), and the rights to freedom of thought, conscience, and religion (Article 10), freedom of expression and information (Article 11), freedom of the arts and sciences (Article 13), and education (Article 14) (of especial relevance for the law of copyright and related rights and in the case of freedom of expression, for the law of trade marks); and the right to engage in work and pursue a freely chosen or accepted occupation (Article 15) and freedom to conduct a business (Article 16) (of relevance for all IP rights).

The applicability of the CFR is expressly confined to existing fields of EU competence (Article 51(2) CFR), leading some to view it as having symbolic significance only. However, it seems clear from EU case law to date that this is not the case. Specifically, it seems clear that the CFR's elevation to the status of the Treaties has given both its provisions, and the role of fundamental rights in the EU legal order in general, additional prominence and weight in the decisions of the Court of Justice.[9] In addition, the effect of it doing so has been to deepen the EU's involvement in the legal orders of Member States. An example is *Seda Kücükdeveci v Swedex*, where the Court of Justice held that where the provisions of an EU directive have as their sole purpose the expression of a general principle of EU law—of which many CFR provisions will be examples—they are capable of being invoked directly by an individual in proceedings against another individual as a source of legal rights and obligations. In addition, and in the field of IP specifically, it is possible to see a new emphasis on fundamental rights in EU case law since the Lisbon Treaty. Examples include Case C–34/10 *Brüstle v Greenpeace eV* [2011] ECR I-9821 and Case C–364/13 *International Stem Cell Corporation v Comptroller General of Patents, Designs and Trade Marks* EU:C:2014:2451, supporting an expansive interpretation of a human embryo exclusion from patentability with reference to human dignity; Case C–467/08 *Padawan SL v Sociedad General de Autores y Editores de España (SGAE)* [2010] ECR I-10055, Case C–145/10 *Painer v Standard Verlags GmbH* [2011] ECR I-12533 and Case C–201/13 *Deckmyn v Vandersteen* EU:C:2014:2132, conceiving exceptions to copyright infringement as existing to strike a fair balance between the rights of copyright owners and the rights of third party users, including freedom of expression and non-discrimination; Case C–277/10 *Luksan v van der Let* EU:C:2012:65, interpreting Article 17(2) CFR as precluding the denial of copyright in a cinematographic work to its principal director in reliance on Article 14*bis* Berne Convention; and Case C–463/12 *Copydan Båndkopi v Nokia Danmark A/S* EU:C:2015:144, requiring that a private copying exception to copyright infringement be interpreted to ensure equal treatment of different media and technologies with reference to Article 20 CFR. And finally, whereas the Court of Justice has generally been sensitive to the scope for differing views among Member States regarding the meaning and requirements of fundamental rights—consistent with the approach of the European Court of Human Rights and the CJEU itself in previous years (see, e.g., Case C–36/02 *Omega Spielhallen* [2004] ECR I-9609)—recently, in the IP field at least, and with regard to certain fundamental rights especially, it has insisted on its authority to define those requirements for all EU Member States in the interests of protecting EU legal autonomy. Examples of this in IP include the *Brüstle* and *Deckmyn* cases, to which we return in Chapters 6 and 10.

In conclusion, EU action in IP and other fields is constrained by the fundamental principle that the EU may 'act only within the limits of the competences conferred upon it by the Member States in the Treaties to attain the objectives set out therein'. Identifying the competence-conferring provisions of the Treaties is comparatively easy. More difficult is understanding the relationship between Union competence and the Union's objectives, and the importance to that end of the CFR as a statement of the common values upon which European integration is based. Also difficult is determining the extent to which those objectives and values *do* constrain Union action (as Article 5(2) TEU requires) in practice.

2.4.1.3 Subsidiarity

According to the principle of subsidiarity, in any area not falling within its exclusive competence, the EU may only act if and insofar as the objectives of its proposed action cannot be sufficiently achieved by Member States, but rather can, by reason of its scale or effects, be better achieved at Union level. The role of this requirement is to protect

---

[9] For a discussion see G. de Búrca, 'After the EU Charter of Fundamental Rights: The Court of Justice as a Human Rights Adjudicator?' (2013) 20 *Maastricht Journal of European and Comparative Law* 168.

Member State sovereignty and ensure that action is taken at the level closest to those affected by it. Thus conceived, subsidiarity is a political principle, and consistent with this, it has been supported since the Lisbon Treaty by a requirement that the Commission consult with national parliaments before proposing legislative measures to the European Parliament and the Council (Protocol on the application of the principle of subsidiarity and proportionality).

In addition to being a political principle, subsidiarity is a legal principle in the sense of being subject to judicial review under Article 263 TFEU. In practice, however, it has limited legal significance, since the Court of Justice rarely enforces it. The reason generally given for this is the Court's reluctance to second-guess the policy choices of the EU legislature, which has led it to treat subsidiarity as a purely procedural requirement, satisfied by the legislature's ability to demonstrate that it considered the subsidiarity implications of a particular measure when passing the measure into law. For measures introduced in reliance on Article 114 TFEU, establishing this is easy to do, since it follows from the fact of a measure's basis in that Article that its objective is to harmonize domestic rules, and this objective is by definition better achieved at Union level. Thus, in the case of Article 114 TFEU measures—which include most EU IP measures introduced to date—subsidiarity adds nothing to the requirement for the existence of EU competence itself. This is well illustrated by the reasoning offered by the European Court in Case C–377/98 *Kingdom of the Netherlands v Parliament and Council* [2001] ECR I-7079 (*Netherlands*) in support of its decision to reject a subsidiarity-based challenge to the Biotech Directive. As the Court explained ([32] and [33]):

> The objective pursued by the Directive, to ensure smooth operation of the internal market by preventing or eliminating differences between the legislation and practice of the various Member States in the area of the protection of biotechnological inventions, could not be achieved by action taken by the Member States alone. As the scope of that protection has immediate effects on trade, and, accordingly, on intra-Community trade, it is clear that, given the scale and effects of the proposed action, the objective in question could be better achieved by the Community.

> Compliance with the principle of subsidiarity is necessarily implicit in the fifth, sixth and seventh recitals of the preamble to the Directive, which state that, in the absence of action at Community level, the development of the laws and practices of the different Member States impedes the proper functioning of the internal market. It thus appears that the Directive states sufficient reasons on that point.

2.4.1.4 Proportionality

The principle of proportionality requires that the content and form of EU action not exceed what is necessary to achieve the Treaty objective in pursuit of which the action was taken. Unlike subsidiarity, this is generally conceived as a legal principle, since it requires a legal process (review of EU actions by the Court) and is not supported by the same process of political scrutiny as the principle of subsidiarity. And consistent with this, the Court of Justice has been more willing to strike EU measures down for exceeding what is necessary to achieve their legitimate objective. To date, however, this has never occurred in the IP field.

2.4.2 European Union Competence in Intellectual Property

Having introduced the general principles regarding the EU's legal authority, we turn to consider the bases for EU competence in IP and its exercise.

2.4.2.1 Regulating the Exercise of IP Rights to Prevent Impediments to the Free Movement of Goods and Competition: Articles 34 to 36 and 101 and 102 TFEU

2.4.2.1.1 Early Tension Between Domestic IP Territoriality and the Treaties' Free Movement and Competition Policies

The territoriality of domestic IP rights created an immediate problem for the aims of the early European Communities, including the EEC particularly. One reason was that domestic IP rights included the right to restrict the free movement of IP-protected goods and services between Member States, which undermined its free movement objectives. Another was that domestic IP rights could be used to obstruct competition within it, the promotion of which was another of its central aims.

The EEC Treaty founders addressed the first of these problems explicitly, by recognizing 'the protection of industrial and commercial property' as a legitimate reason for prohibiting or restricting the free movement of goods within the Community provided the prohibition or restriction in question was neither a means of arbitrary discrimination nor a disguised restriction on trade (Article 36 EEC). In this way, the Treaty left domestic IP rights intact, consistent with its guarantee not to 'prejudice the system existing in Member States in respect of property' (Article 222), while also recognizing the Community's power to regulate the manner in which such rights were exercised in order to protect the free movement guarantees of Articles 30 to 34 EEC.

No equivalent IP exception was included in the original competition provisions of Articles 85 and 86 EEC. In the 1960s, however, the Court of Justice considered the problem and responded by confirming that, while the essence or *existence* of IP rights was a matter for the domestic laws of Member States and could not per se be questioned by the Community, the *exercise* of IP rights once existing could not be such as would breach the competition provisions of the EEC Treaty. So it was that the Court of Justice decided in Joined Cases C–56/64 and 58/64 *Consten and Grundig v Commission* [1966] ECR 429 that an agreement authorizing Consten to register Grundig's trade mark in France, on condition that Consten invoke its rights under French trade mark law to block parallel imports of Grundig products into France from other EEC Member States, was in breach of the Article 85 prohibition against 'all agreements between undertakings … which may affect trade between Member States and which have as their object or effect the prevention, restriction or distortion of competition within the common market'. The result was to confirm the distinction implicit in Articles 30 to 34 and 36 EEC between the competence of Member States to recognize IP rights on the one hand, and the competence of the EEC to ensure that the exercise of such IP rights did not infringe the provisions of the Treaty on the other (see also Case C–24/67 *Parker Davis v Probel* [1968] ECR 55).

2.4.2.1.2 Early Competence to Regulate the Exercise (But Not the Essence) of IP rights

The EEC's limited competence in respect of IP did not stop it from supporting initiatives outside that competence, such as creating new titles of IP right to have unitary and uniform effect throughout the Community. However, it did require that such initiatives be pursued as agreements between EEC Member States rather than as Community measures. An example is the Community Patent Convention of 1975, the aim of which was to establish 'a Community patent system which contributes to the attainment of the objectives of the [EEC Treaty], and in particular to the elimination within the Community of the distortion of competition which may result from the territorial aspect of national protection rights [and] the abolition of obstacles to the free movement of goods' (Preamble). As we have seen, this Convention was concluded by the then eight EEC Member States as a special agreement under Article 19 of the Paris Convention for the Protection of Industrial Property 1883, and not as a measure of the Community.

2.4.2.1.3 Reconciling IP Rights with EU Free Movement and Competition Policies: The Doctrine of Exhaustion

Throughout the 1960s and 1970s, the main situations in which Community law raised issues of IP were those in which a particular exercise of IP rights was alleged to violate the free movement or competition provisions of the Treaty. The cases regarding the second of these situations had especial importance for the later development of European IP law. According to the Court in a series of decisions in the 1970s, Article 36 EEC only permitted such IP-based restrictions to the free movement of goods as were 'justified for the purpose of safeguarding rights which constitute the specific subject-matter of such property' (Case C–78/70 *Deutsche Grammophon v Metro* [1971] ECR 487). The question that this raised was what *was* the specific subject matter of IP? In the Court's answer, it was only the right to bring products protected by IP—such as items manufactured in accordance with a patent, bearing a trade mark, or protected by copyright—into circulation, and *not* the right also to control the goods' movement thereafter between Member States. Hence the decision in *Deutsche Grammophon* that Deutsche Grammaphon could not rely on the exclusive distribution right it enjoyed as the producer of phonograms under German copyright law to prevent the resale in Germany of records that its French subsidiary had marketed in France. According to the reasoning of the Court ([12]):

> If a right related to copyright is relied upon to prevent the marketing in a member state of products distributed by the holder of the right or with his consent on the territory of another member state on the sole ground that such distribution did not take place on the national territory, such a prohibition, which would legitimize the isolation of national markets, would be repugnant to the essential purpose of the treaty, which is to unite national markets into a single market. That purpose could not be attained if, under the various legal systems of the member states, nationals of those states were able to partition the market and bring about arbitrary discrimination or disguised restrictions on trade between member states.

The result was to enable any person who had purchased an IP-protected product with the IP rights owner's consent to do as he wished with the product, uninhibited by the IP right protecting it, on the ground that his purchase of the product represented sufficient remuneration for the IP rights themselves. In the language of IP, coined by the Reichsgericht (Federal Administrative Court of Germany) in the early 20th century (see, e.g., RGZ 51, 139), his purchase of the product *exhausted* the IP rights in respect of it.

From an EEC perspective, the doctrine of exhaustion was important because it confirmed that the free movement provisions of Articles 30 to 34 EEC prevented the use of domestic IP rights to prohibit or restrict the movement from EEC Member State A to B of any product that had been put into circulation with the IP rights owner's consent, regardless of whether the product was protected by IP under the laws of Member State A. As the Court of Justice explained in Case C–187/80 *Merck & Co. v Stephar* [1981] ECR 2063 concerning patents, it was for the IP rights owner to decide 'under what conditions he will market his product, including the possibility of marketing it in a Member State where the law does not provide [IP] protection for the product in question', and if he did market it in such a Member State 'he must then bear the consequences of his choice with regard to the free movement of the product within the Common Market' ([11]). Generally speaking, the only situations in which the doctrine of exhaustion would not apply so as to enable the IP rights owner to prevent the free movement of goods in reliance on Article 36 EEC would be where the items in question were first placed on the market outside the Community, or without the consent of the IP rights owner.

Beneath this deceptively simple statement of principle there lay many uncertainties with which the European Court was required to deal in the 1970s and 1980s. One was whether the doctrine of exhaustion applied with respect to goods placed on the market by an assignee of the IP rights subsisting in the goods. In Case C–2/93 *IHT Internationale Heiztechnik v Ideal Standard* [1994] ECR I-2789, the Court held that it did not for trade marks. According to its judgment, the 'essential function' of a trade mark to indicate the commercial origin of the goods to which it applies would be undermined if the mark could be used in the same territory by undertakings with no legal or economic link beyond that created by the trade mark assignment. Given this, protection of the specific subject matter of trade mark rights—being the exclusive right of the owner to market products under his mark and thereby protect his commercial interests—required recognition of the owner's right to prevent an assignee from circulating any goods to which the mark applied throughout the Community if first placed on the market by the assignee without the owner's consent.

A second question which the Court was required to answer was when if ever the doctrine of exhaustion was excluded notwithstanding consent by the relevant IP rights owner to the first marketing of his goods on the basis that some provision of national law prevented him from receiving the reward which it was the purpose of the IP rights to secure. In Case C–19/84 *Pharmon BV v Hoechst AG* [1985] ECR 2281, the Court held that one situation in which the doctrine *was* excluded on this ground was that involving patented goods first marketed by a compulsory licensee. According to its reasoning, if a patentee is prevented by the grant of a compulsory licence from excluding a third party from doing acts which his patent would ordinarily have entitled him to prevent, he cannot be said to have consented to those acts. Given this, and that 'the substance of a patent right lies essentially in according the inventor an exclusive right of first placing the product on the market so as to allow him to obtain the reward for his creative effort' ([26]), the Court held it to be necessary to allow the patentee to prevent the compulsory licensee from importing and marketing products manufactured under the licence in other states 'in order to protect the substance of his exclusive rights under his patent' ([26]). By contrast, in Cases C–15/74 *Centrafarm v Sterling Drug* [1974] ECR 1147 and C–16/74 *Centrafarm v Winthrop* [1974] ECR 1183, the Court held that the owner of patents and trade marks in respect of pharmaceuticals could not invoke its IP rights to prevent products marketed in the UK with its consent from being imported into the Netherlands, notwithstanding that UK governmental pricing restrictions required the goods to be priced significantly lower in the UK than in the Netherlands. The message of the *Centrafarm* decisions was that the Court would be very slow to allow IP rights owners to oppose the free movement of goods first marketed in the EEC by or with their consent. That message was confirmed soon after in Joined Cases C–55 and 57/80 *Musik Vertrieb Membran v GEMA* [1981] ECR 147 and Case C–187/80 *Merck v Stephar* [1981] ECR 2063 for copyright and patents, and remains apt today.[10]

Finally, there is the question of the geographical scope of the doctrine of exhaustion supported by the free movement provisions of the Treaties, and when if ever the doctrine applies to prevent restrictions on the movement of goods within a Member State or first marketed outside EEC territory. As formulated in *Deutsche Grammophon*, the doctrine

---

[10] An invitation to revisit the decision in *Merck v Stephar* was rejected by the Court of Justice in *Merck v Primecrown* [1996] ECR I-6285.

was confined in operation to the geographical area of the EEC and cast as existing to prevent restrictions on the parallel importation of goods from one Member State into another Member State. However, it would be illogical and contrary to the principle of Community-wide exhaustion to permit IP rights to be invoked to impede the free movement of goods within a Member State, and so any principle of Community-wide exhaustion must include a principle of national exhaustion as well.[11] In the other direction, the conclusion in 1994 of the EEA Agreement, which includes in Article 2 of Protocol 28 on intellectual property a provision on IP rights exhaustion, had the effect of extending the geographical scope of the doctrine beyond the territory of the EC to that of the European Economic Area, including (currently) the territory of Iceland, Liechtenstein, and Norway. Any truly international principle of exhaustion, however, would need to be based in the domestic laws of European states.

In sum, the doctrine of exhaustion developed by the Court of Justice in the 1970s and 1980s in reliance on the free movement and competition provisions of the EEC/EC Treaty served two purposes. First, it established that IP rights could not be invoked to prevent or restrict the free movement between EEC/EC Member States of any good first placed on the market within the Community by or with the IP rights owner's consent, including that of a non-compulsory licensee. And second and relatedly, it confirmed that while the authority to create IP rights remained with Member States, this did not prevent the Community from regulating the exercise of IP rights thus created in reliance on the free movement and competition provisions of the Treaties in order to protect and promote the establishment and smooth functioning of the common market.

Since the 1980s, the doctrine of exhaustion has been affirmed repeatedly as a fundamental principle of European IP law, and given express statutory recognition for each species of IP right.[12]

2.4.2.2 Harmonizing Domestic Rules to Support the Establishment and Smooth Functioning of the Internal Market: Article 114 TFEU

2.4.2.2.1 Early Competence Regarding the Essence of IP rights

In the 1980s, the EEC abandoned its distinction between the exercise and existence of IP rights by issuing directives aimed at harmonizing all aspects of Member States' rules regarding IP in reliance on Article 100 EEC. According to that Article:

> The Council shall, acting unanimously on a proposal from the Commission, issue directives for the approximation of such provisions laid down by law, regulation or administrative action in Member States as directly affect the establishment or functioning of the common market. The Assembly and the Economic and Social Committee shall be consulted in the case of directives whose implementation would, in one or more Member States, involve the amendment of legislation.

The first IP directive to be issued in reliance on this Article was the Semiconductor Directive in 1986. According to the Directive's recitals, the fundamental importance of protecting semiconductor products for European industry (given their increasingly important role in

---

[11] D.T. Keeling, *Intellectual Property Rights in EU Law, Volume I: Free Movement and Competition Law* (OUP, 2004) 115.

[12] See Article 7(1) Trade Marks Directive, Article 13(1) Community Trade Mark Regulation, Article 15 Designs Directive, Article 21 Community Design Regulation, Article 9 Rental Right Directive, Article 4 Information Society Directive, Article 4(c) Software Directive, Article 5(c) Database Directive, Article 5(1) and (5) Semiconductor Directive, Article 16 Community Plant Variety Rights Regulation, and Article 6 Unitary Patent (UP) Regulation 1257/2012.

a range of industries), combined with differences in the protection afforded to such products under the domestic laws of Member States, created a need for harmonization in the form of the Directive, and established its legal basis in Article 100 EEC.

Implicit in the recitals of the Semiconductor Directive was a shift in Community policy regarding IP. Previously regarded primarily as an impediment to competition and free movement, in the 1980s strong and comprehensive IP rights began to be seen more positively as tools for promoting these and other European objectives. After 1987 this shift in policy was facilitated by the Single European Act [1987] OJ L 169/1 (SEA), which inserted a new Article 100a EEC to enable the Council to adopt measures for the approximation of Member States' domestic laws by qualified majority rather than unanimous action (Article 18 SEA), and set 1 January 1993 as a deadline for completing the single market.

2.4.2.2.2 Internal Market Competence as a Basis for IP Harmonizing Directives

The entry into force of the Maastricht Treaty in 1993 coincided with the beginning of a period of active Community law-making in IP following the Commission's working programme in the field of copyright and related rights of 1991.[13] Consistent with the aims of that programme, the most common form of EU law-making was the directive, introduced in reliance on Article 100a EC (ex Article 100a EEC) for the purpose of approximating different aspects of Member States' IP laws in pursuit of the two objectives of the Semiconductor Directive: recognizing and protecting IP rights (to strengthen European industry) and abolishing differences in domestic laws (to support the establishment and functioning of the internal market). This use by the Council of Article 100a EC to support directives in the field of IP was tested before and supported by the Court of Justice in *Opinion 1/94 (WTO Agreement: GATS and TRIPS)* [1994] ECR I-5267 (*Opinion 1/94*).[14]

Article 100a EC (now Article 114 TFEU, ex Article 95 EC) remains among the most commonly relied upon sources of EU competence in IP today. According to its terms post-Lisbon, and in particular to Article 114(1) TFEU:

> Save where otherwise provided in the Treaties, the following provisions shall apply for the achievement of the objectives set out in Article 26 [to establish and ensure the functioning of the internal market]. The European Parliament and the Council shall, acting in accordance with the ordinary legislative procedure and after consulting the Economic and Social Committee, adopt the measures for the approximation of the provisions laid down by law, regulation or administrative action in Member States which have as their object the establishment and functioning of the internal market.

In the case law of the Court of Justice, this provision has been interpreted expansively. According to the Court, it permits the EU to introduce any measure—including one delegating powers to implement harmonizing measures to an EU body, office, or agency—which the evidence suggests to have been introduced to improve the operation of the internal market by addressing an issue on which Member States' rules currently or might in the future come to differ. Further, the Court has confirmed that this will be the case even if:

(a) The measure in question has another public interest among its objectives, such as consumer protection or the promotion of industry and research, provided only that harmonization is not a merely incidental or subsidiary aim;

(b) A minimum of Member States have adopted or intend to adopt laws on the issue;

---

[13] Commission Communication of 17 January 1991, 'Follow-up to the Green Paper: Working programme of the commission in the field of copyright and neighbouring rights' COM (90) 584 final.

[14] See also Case C–377/98 *Kingdom of the Netherlands v Parliament and Council* [2001] ECR I-7079.

(c) The measure covers situations having no link with free movement between Member States;

(d) Another Treaty article might have also been a valid basis for the measure;

(e) The measure is directed at Member States generally and/or specific legal or natural persons; and/or

(f) The measure deals with an issue arising under international rather than national law.[15]

It was with reference to this expansive interpretation of Article 95 EC that the Court of Justice in the *Netherlands* case rejected a competence-based challenge to the validity of the Biotech Directive (harmonizing the legal protection of biotechnological inventions). In its judgment, while national patent laws were based largely on the EPC, their scope for divergent interpretation by domestic courts made different laws and practices among EC Member States likely, threatening the unity and smooth functioning of the internal market. In these circumstances, the Court held, it was appropriate for the EC to intervene directly, rather than indirectly by seeking renegotiation of the EPC. The fact that its intervention created patent rights distinct in several respects from the rights covered by existing patent law was irrelevant, and did not require the Directive's introduction in reliance on Article 308 (ex Article 235) EC, since the patents to be issued under the Directive remained national patents issued in accordance with domestic procedures and deriving their protection from domestic law. Finally, the fact that the Directive had as its chief aim to support the industrial development of the Community and scientific research in the genetic engineering field did not mean that it ought to have been adopted on the basis of Articles 157 and 163 (ex Articles 130 and 130f) EC, since the means by which it pursued that aim was removing the legal obstacles within the single market brought about by differences in national law and likely to impede and disrupt research and development activity in that field. Given this, the Court held, approximation of the legislation of the Member States could not be said to have been an incidental or subsidiary objective of the Directive, but was rather its essential purpose, notwithstanding its pursuit of an objective falling within Articles 157 and 163 EC. Hence the finding of the Court that the Directive had been correctly adopted in reliance on Article 100a of the Treaty.

2.4.2.3 Creating Unitary IP Rights: Article 118 TFEU

2.4.2.3.1 Early Competence to Establish Unitary Rights in Pursuit of Treaty Objectives

As well as introducing directives harmonizing different aspects of IP law, the Council in the period immediately after the introduction of the Maastricht Treaty relied upon its general competence under Article 235 EC (ex Article 235 EEC, after Nice, Article 308 EC) to take action necessary to attain a Treaty objective in order to introduce regulations creating three new titles of unitary (Community) IP rights: the Community Trade Mark Regulation 1993; the Community Plant Variety Rights Regulation 1994; and the Community Design Right Regulation 2001. This head of EU competence has been retained post-Lisbon as Article 352 TFEU, and provides as follows:

1. If action by the Union should prove necessary, within the framework of the policies defined in the Treaties, to attain one of the objectives set out in the Treaties, and the

---

[15] See, e.g., *Netherlands*; Case C–210/03 *Swedish Match AB v Secretary of State for Health* [2004] ECR I-11893; Joined Cases C–154/04 and 155/04 *Alliance for Natural Health* [2005] ECR I-6451; Case C–380/03 *Tobacco Advertising II: Germany v Parliament* [2006] ECR I-11573; Case C–58/08 *Vodafone* [2010] ECR I-4999; Case C–398/13 P *Inuit Tapirii Kanatami v Commission* EU:C:2015:535; Case C–270/12 *United Kingdom v Council* EU:C:2014:18.

Treaties have not provided the necessary powers, the Council, acting unanimously on a proposal from the Commission and after obtaining the consent of the European Parliament, shall adopt the appropriate measures. Where the measures in question are adopted by the Council in accordance with a special legislative procedure, it shall also act unanimously on a proposal from the Commission and after obtaining the consent of the European Parliament.

...

3. Measures based on this Article shall not entail harmonisation of Member States' laws or regulations in cases where the Treaties exclude such harmonisation.

Since the Lisbon Treaty, Article 352 has been supplemented by Declarations 41 and 42.[16] The first of these states that the reference to 'objectives of the Union' in Article 352 refers to the objectives set out in Article 3(2) and (3) TEU, as well as those set out in Article 3(5) TEU with respect to external action under Part Five of the TFEU, but *not* those of Article 3(1) TEU concerning peace, the Union's values, and the well-being of European peoples. 'It is therefore excluded', Article 41 asserts, 'that an action based on Article 352 [TFEU] would only pursue objectives set out in Article 3(1) [TEU]'. In addition, Declaration 42 reinforces the need to prevent Article 352 from undermining the principle of conferral in its statement that that Article

> cannot serve as a basis for widening the scope of Union powers beyond the general framework created by the provisions of the Treaties as a whole and, in particular, by those that define the tasks and the activities of the Union.

In practice, the need to rely on Article 352 TFEU in the field of IP has been obviated by the introduction of a new Article 118 TFEU with the Lisbon Treaty.

2.4.2.3.2 *Post-Lisbon Competence to Create Unitary IP Rights*

One problem with using the Community's residual competence under Article 235/308 EC to introduce regulations creating new titles of Community IP right was that it required unanimous action by the Council, which could be difficult to achieve, particularly with expanding Community membership. Hence the significance of Article 118 TFEU, introduced by the Lisbon Treaty, which provides as follows:

> In the context of the establishment and functioning of the internal market, the European Parliament and the Council, acting in accordance with the ordinary legislative procedure, shall establish measures for the creation of European intellectual property rights to provide uniform protection of intellectual property rights throughout the Union and for the setting up of centralised Union-wide authorisation, coordination and supervision arrangements.
>
> The Council, acting in accordance with a special legislative procedure, shall by means of regulations establish language arrangements for the European intellectual property rights. The Council shall act unanimously after consulting the European Parliament.

The introduction of Article 118 TFEU coincided with the publication of two important Commission statements regarding IP. The first was its Communication on Copyright in the Knowledge Economy,[17] focused on supporting the dissemination of knowledge in the

---

[16] Declarations annexed to the Final Act of the Intergovernmental Conference which adopted the Treaty of Lisbon, signed on 13 December 2007 [2008] OJ C 115/335.

[17] Commission Communication of 19 October 2009, 'Copyright in the Knowledge Economy' COM (2009) 532 final (2008 Green Paper Follow-up). See also Communication from the Commission to the European Parliament, the Council, the European Economic and Social Committee and the Committee of the Regions, 'A Single Market for the 21st Century Europe' COM (2007) 725 final.

context of existing copyright and related rights directives and digital technology; and the second was its Industrial Property Rights Strategy, focused on 'developing a horizontal and integrated strategy across the spectrum of industrial property rights'.[18] Both affirmed the EU's commitment to using IP law as a means of promoting European economic and social objectives, including through the creation of unitary IP rights, and explain the insertion of a new Treaty provision enabling the introduction of such rights and support-ing arrangements by means of the ordinary legislative procedure applicable in respect of harmonizing directives introduced under Article 114 TFEU. The one exception to this concerns language arrangements for European IP rights, which by express provision of Article 118 must be established by regulations introduced by '[t]he Council, acting in accordance with a special legislative procedure', involving a decision by the European Parliament or Council with participation from the other, rather than a decision by both.

Since the introduction of the Lisbon Treaty, two EU measures have been introduced in reliance on Article 118 TFEU: Regulations 1257/2012 and 1260/2012 implementing enhanced cooperation in the area of the creation of unitary patent protection and sup-porting translation arrangements. Regulation 1257/2012 establishes a new title of patent conferring unitary and uniform protection throughout the territories of 13 or more EU Member States, being those which have elected to participate in the Unitary Patent Package at the time of the patent's registration for unitary effect (Article 3). Controversially, the Regulation does not define the rights that unitary patents confer, leaving this instead to the domestic laws of participating Member States (Article 5(3)). This omission provided one ground for the applications by Spain and Italy to the Court of Justice under Article 263 TFEU to have the Regulations annulled in 2011 and 2013. Among the arguments pre-sented in the second of these annulment cases was that the Regulation does not 'establish measures for the creation of European intellectual property rights to provide uniform protection of [those] rights throughout the Union' within the meaning of Article 118 TFEU, and is thus not authorized by that Article. This argument was dismissed, along with the Member States' other contentions, and Regulations 1257/2012 and 1260/2012 confirmed by the Court to have been validly passed (Case C–146/13 *Kingdom of Spain v European Parliament* EU:C:2015:298 (*Spain v Council*)). According to the Court's 2015 decision, it is enough that Regulation 1257/2012 has as its objective the creation of unitary patent protection throughout the territories of participating Member States, and that its provisions express, through their definition of the characteristics of the patent, this objec-tive. Thus, the failure of the Regulation to harmonize completely and exhaustively all aspects of patent protection did not prevent its adoption in reliance on Article 118 TFEU.

2.4.2.4 Negotiating and Concluding International Agreements: Articles 3, 207, and 216 TFEU

2.4.2.4.1 *Early Competence to Negotiate and Conclude International IP Agreements*

The EEC/EC Treaty expressly recognized the Community as having legal personality (Article 210), thereby establishing its capacity in principle to enter agreements with non-Community states. The questions that then arose were what authority the Community had to enter such agreements, and what impact its authority had on the competence of Member States to do the same.

Two Treaty provisions authorized the Community to establish international rela-tions. The first was Article 238 EEC/EC, which recognized the Community's authority to

---

[18] Communication from the Commission to the European Parliament, the Council and the European Economic and Social Committee, 'An Industrial Property Rights Strategy for Europe' COM (2008) 465 final 2. See also 'Enhancing the patent system in Europe' COM (2007) 165 final.

'conclude with one or more States or international organisations agreements establishing an association involving reciprocal rights and obligations, common action and special procedure'. The second was Article 113 EEC/EC, which authorized the Community
to conclude tariff and trade agreements in pursuit of the common commercial policy.[19]
Supplementing these Treaty provisions was the further authority of the Community,
recognized by the European Court of Justice in the early 1970s, to engage in external
activities—including the negotiating and signing of international agreements—in support of its internal activities. This implied ('parallel') external competence was first recognized in Case C–22/70 *Commission v Council* [1971] ECR 263 (*AETR*), where the Court
of Justice held that since the adoption of a common transport policy was an objective of
the Treaty, and common rules for attaining the policy had been adopted by regulation, the
Community had the authority to enter an international agreement in the transport field.
The same reasoning supported the Community's conclusion of the TRIPS Agreement in
the 1990s. Thus, in *Opinion 1/94*, the Court held that while the connection between IP
rights and trade was not enough to bring those rights within the scope of Article 113, the
Community's entry into the TRIPS Agreement was nonetheless authorized by its implied
external competence. On the other hand, it held that the Community's competence to
enter TRIPS was shared with Member States, since:

(a) The unification or harmonization of IP rights within the Community did not
depend on its conclusion of international agreements;

(b) The Treaty bases for such unification or harmonization—Articles 100a and 235 EEC/
EC—could not of themselves confer exclusive competence on the Community; and

(c) The absence of complete harmonization of domestic rules in the areas covered by
the TRIPS Agreement, due in part to the absence of Community patent legislation, prevented the conclusion that Member States' participation in the TRIPS
Agreement would be affected by Community legislation (see [100] to [105]).

As a result of this decision, the Community was required to work closely with Member
States when negotiating IP agreements, including the WIPO Copyright and Performances
and Phonograms Treaties concluded in 1996.

Among the most important of the changes introduced by the Amsterdam Treaty for IP
was the amendment of Article 113 EC (after Nice, Article 133 EC) concerning the common commercial policy. This amendment was extremely significant. Most importantly
for us, it involved the insertion of a new paragraph 5 authorizing the Council to extend
the application of its paragraphs 'to international negotiations and agreements on services and intellectual property insofar as they are not covered by these paragraphs', and
then extending the application of its paragraphs to such negotiations and agreements
directly. In addition, the amended version of paragraph 5 replaced the usual qualified-
majority voting procedure applicable for the negotiation and conclusion of international
agreements implementing the common commercial policy with one requiring unanimity
for any IP agreement which: (a) included provisions for which unanimity was required
for the adoption of internal Community rules; or (b) related to a field in which the
Community had not yet exercised its competence under the Treaties by adopting internal

---

[19] Under the procedure of Article 113(3) EEC (after Nice, Article 133(3) EC, ex Article 113(3) EEC), negotiating agreements with third countries and, after Maastricht, with international organizations, was the
responsibility of the Commission, authorized by the Council, and acting in consultation with a special
committee appointed by the Council and within the framework of any Council-issued directives. In exercising its powers in this regard, the Council was to act by a qualified majority (Article 113(4) EEC/EC, after
Nice, Article 133(4)).

rules (Article 133(5) EC). And finally, a new paragraph 6 forbade the Council from concluding any agreements containing provisions 'which would go beyond the Community's internal powers, in particular by leading to harmonization of the laws or regulations of the Member States in an area for which this Treaty rules out such harmonisation', so as to prohibit the Community from using its external powers to harmonize IP laws internally. Under these provisions, Community competence to enter IP agreements continued to be shared with Member States, thus allowing the continued possibility of mixed agreements signed by the EU, its Member States, and third countries.

2.4.2.4.2 *Post-Lisbon Competence to Negotiate and Conclude International IP Agreements*

Under the Treaties today, Articles 216(1) and 207 TFEU authorize the EU to negotiate, enter, and interpret international agreements. While the first of these—Article 216(1) TFEU—is new since the Lisbon Treaty, it is generally understood to be a loose codification of post-*AETR* case law regarding the EU's implied external powers. By its express terms, it authorizes the Union to conclude international agreements in any case in which such conclusion:

(a) is provided for expressly by the Treaties;

(b) is necessary in order to achieve, within the framework of the Union's policies, one of the objectives referred to in the Treaties (on which see earlier); or

(c) is provided for in a legally binding Union act or likely to affect or alter the scope of common rules.

Importantly, Article 3(2) TFEU declares this external competence to be exclusive of the competence of Member States in any case in which the conclusion of the international agreement in question 'is provided for in a legislative act of the Union or is necessary to enable the Union to exercise its internal competence, or insofar as its conclusion may affect common rules or alter their scope.' The result is a very broad and exclusive authority for the EU to act externally.

Also new since the Lisbon Treaty is Article 3(1)(e) TFEU, which makes Community competence in respect of the common commercial policy under Article 207 TFEU (ex Article 133 EC)—including 'the commercial aspects of intellectual property' (Article 207(1), ex Article 133(1) EC)—exclusive, rather than shared with Member States as previously. In addition, while the procedure for the Commission's negotiation of international agreements under Article 207 remains largely unchanged, the role of the European Parliament has been enhanced by a new provision requiring that the Commission 'report regularly...to the European Parliament on the progress of negotiations' regarding agreements with third countries or international organizations, in addition to reporting to the Council-appointed committee as previously (Article 207(3) TFEU).

Since the Lisbon Treaty, the significance of Article 3(1)(e) for IP has been made clear by the Court of Justice in three cases: Case C–414/11 *Daiichi Sankyo Co. Ltd v DEMO Anonimos Viomikhaniki kai Emporiki Etairia Farmakon* EU:C:2013:520 (*Daiichi*); Case C–137/12 *Commission v Council* EU:C:2013:675; and Case C–114/12 *Commission v Council* EU:C:2014:2151. The first of these involved a preliminary referral from the Polimeles Protodikio Athinon (Multi-Member Court of First Instance of Athens) regarding the meaning of Articles 27 and 70 TRIPS Agreement concerning patentability and the scope of the Agreement's protections respectively. Among the questions referred to the Court was whether the domestic courts of EU Member States remain free post-Lisbon to give direct effect to TRIPS provisions in accordance with domestic law. In the Court's decision they do not. Specifically, while the conclusion of the TRIPS Agreement in the

1990s had involved an exercise of shared EU and Member State competence under the then EC Treaty in accordance with the principles set out in *Opinion 1/94*, subsequent EU legal developments had rendered those principles 'immaterial' ([48]). Given this, understandings of the TRIPS Agreement based on those principles were no longer valid, requiring a fresh appraisal of the EU legal status and effects of that Agreement having regard to current law, including Article 3(1)(e).

Having established this position, the issue arose as to the meaning of Articles 3(1)(e) and 207 TFEU for the division of EU/Member State responsibilities regarding TRIPS. In the Court's decision, the answer depended on the primary objective of the Agreement, and whether it 'relates specifically to international trade in the sense of being essentially intended to promote, facilitate or govern trade and has direct and immediate effects on trade' ([51]). If it does, the Court held, the Agreement must fall within the field of the common commercial policy and exclusive EU competence as distinct, for example, from the field of the internal market, where competence continues to be shared under Article 114 TFEU. Applying this test, the Court held the primary objective of the Agreement to be 'to strengthen and harmonise the protection of intellectual property on a worldwide scale'. In addition, since this objective is specifically linked to trade, all of the provisions of the Agreement that contribute to attaining it fall within the EU's exclusive competence.

The reasoning of the Court in *Daiichi* was affirmed and applied by the Court soon after in the further *Commission v Council* cases. The first of these (Case C–137/12) involved an application to the Court by the Commission to annul the Council's decision to authorize EU entry to the European Convention on the legal protection of services based on, or consisting of, conditional access (COM (2010) 753 final). In its proposal to the Council to make this decision, the Commission had suggested Article 207(4) TFEU (ex Article 133(5)) concerning the negotiation and conclusion of international agreements regarding the commercial aspects of IP, and Article 218(5) TFEU regarding the negotiation and conclusion of international agreements more generally, to be the decision's appropriate basis. (Article 218 (ex Article 300 EC) establishes the general procedure governing the EU's negotiation and conclusion of agreements with third countries or international organizations, without prejudice to the provisions of Article 207 TFEU. Paragraph 5 requires the Council, on proposal by the negotiator, to adopt a decision authorizing the signing of the agreement and, if necessary, its provisional application before entry into force.) In its decision, however, the Council cited Article 114 TFEU in place of Article 207(4). The Court agreed with the Commission that the primary objective of signing the Convention—and thus the primary objective of the decision itself—was to encourage broader ratification of the Convention by Council of Europe Member States and thereby extend the application of provisions similar to those of Directive 98/84 beyond the borders of EU territory throughout the European continent ([62] and [63]). And given that, its objective had 'a specific link' to international trade and the common commercial policy. In the words of the Court, citing *Opinion 1/94*, 'a ban on the export of illicit devices to the European Union concerns the defence of the European Union's global interests and falls, by its very nature, within the ambit of the common commercial policy' ([69]). Thus, Article 207(4) was the Convention's proper legal basis, with the result that the signing of the Convention fell within the exclusive competence of the EU, pursuant to Article 3(1)(e) TFEU. The result was to confirm the effect of the Lisbon Treaty provisions regarding EU external competence in conferring exclusive competence on the Union to enter any international agreement, the primary purpose of which can be seen from the provisions of the agreement to have a specific link to the commercial aspects of IP, and through them to the common commercial policy. These principles were reaffirmed by the Court in the second

Commission v Council case decided in 2014, resulting in the Court's annulment of a decision of the Council authorizing participation by the Union and Member States in the negotiation of a proposed Council of Europe convention on the protection of the rights of broadcasting organizations.

Through its provisions regarding the EU's external competence, the Lisbon Treaty has secured four results. First, it has revoked the prior authority of Member States to conclude or give direct effect to any provision of any IP agreement that 'relates specifically to international trade in the sense of being essentially intended to promote, facilitate or govern trade and has direct and immediate effects on trade' (*Daiichi* [51]). Second, it has revoked the prior authority of the EU itself to negotiate and enter such an agreement in reliance on Article 114 TFEU or any other Treaty provision beyond Article 207. Third, it has underlined the need for IP legislation introduced in reliance on Article 114 TFEU 'to comply with the rules concerning the availability, scope and use of intellectual property rights in the TRIPS Agreement, as those rules are still, as previously, intended to standardize certain rules on the subject at world level and thereby to facilitate international trade' (*Daiichi* [59]). And fourth, it has confirmed its exclusive interpretative jurisdiction with respect to the TRIPS Agreement. The result has been to extend the EU's external competence in IP at the expense of that of Member States.

2.4.2.5 Other Competence-Supporting Provisions

The main sources of EU competence in IP are those discussed earlier and shown in Figure 2.3, namely, Articles 34 to 36, 101, 102, 114, 118, 207, and 352 TFEU. However, and as the EU IP measures contained in Figure 2.4 show, these sources are supplemented and supported by a range of additional Treaty provisions as well. They include Article 167 TFEU (ex Article 128 EC), which requires the Union to take cultural diversity into account in its action, to contribute to the flowering of the cultures of Member States, and to bring the common cultural heritage to the fore. (Article 128 EC had been a novelty of the Maastricht Treaty. By emphasizing the role of the Community in supporting artistic and literary creation, and the dissemination and safeguarding of culture within Europe

Arts 36, 101, and 102 TFEU (competence shared with MS)	Art. 114 TFEU (competence shared with MS)	Art. 118 TFEU (i) (competence shared with MS)	Art. 118 TFEU (ii) (competence shared with MS)	Arts 3(1)(e)/207 TFEU (competence exclusive to the EU)
• *Requires* action to enforce certain uses of IP rights to impede the free movement of goods and competition within EU territory	• *Permits* harmonizing measures supporting the internal market • *Introduced by* the EP + the council via the OLP & consulting the EESC	• *Permits* regulations establishing unitary IPRs + supporting arrangements • *Introduced by* the EP + the Council via the OLP	• *Permits* regulations establishing unitary IPR language arrangements • *Introduced by* the Council via a special legislative procedure	• *Permits* the negotiation + signing of IP agreements • *Effected by* the Commision authorized & overseen by the Council & reporting to the EP

Figure 2.3 Main sources of EU competence in IP

INTELLECTUAL PROPERTY FIELD	INSTRUMENT	TREATY BASIS
Copyright and Related Rights	Collective Rights Management Directive (2014)	Arts 50(1), 53(1), and 62 TFEU, citing Art 167 TFEU
Enforcement	Enforcement Regulation (2013)	Art. 207 TFEU
Copyright and Related Rights	Orphan Works Directive (2012)	Arts 53(1), 62, and 114 TFEU
Patents	Unitary Patent Regulation (Translation Arrangements) (2012)	Art. 118 TFEU
Patents	Unitary Patent Regulation (2012)	Art. 118 TFEU
Patents	Council Decision authorising enhanced cooperation in the area of the creation of unitary patent protection (2011)	Arts 3(3) TEU and 329(1) TFEU
Copyright and Related Rights	Term Amendment Directive (2011)	Arts 53(1), 62, and 114 TFEU
Copyright and Related Rights	Software Directive (2009)	Art. 95 EC
Patents	Supplementary Protection Certificate Regulation (Medicinal Products) (2009)	Art. 95 EC
Trade Marks	Trade Mark Regulation (2009)	Art. 308 EC
Trade Marks	Trade Marks Directive (2008)	Art. 95 EC
Plant Variety Rights	Community Plant Variety Rights Regulation (2008)	Art. 308 EC
Designs	Designs Regulation (2006)	Art. 308 EC
Copyright and Related Rights	Term Directive (2006)	Arts 47(2), 55, and 95 EC
Copyright and Related Rights	Rental and Lending Rights Directive (2006)	Arts 47(2), 55, and 95 EC
Plant Variety Rights	Community Plant Variety Rights Regulation (2004)	Art. 308 EC
Trade Marks	Community Trade Mark Regulation (Madrid Agreement Accession) (2003)	Art. 308 EC
Enforcement	Enforcement Directive (2004)	Art. 95 EC
Copyright and Related Rights	Resale Rights Directive (2001)	Art. 95 EC
Copyright and Related Rights	Information Society Directive (2001)	Arts 47(2), 55, and 95 EC
Conditional Access Services	Conditional Access Directive (1998)	Arts 57(2), 66, and 100a EC
Designs	Designs Directive (1998)	Art. 100a EC

Patents	Biotech Directive (1998)	Art. 100a EC
Copyright and Related Rights	Database Directive (1996)	Arts 57(2), 66, and 100a EEC
Patents	Supplementary Protection Certificate (Plant Protection Products) (1996)	Art. 100a EC
Plant Variety Rights	Community Plant Variety Rights Regulation (1995)	Art. 235 EEC
Plant Variety Rights	Community Plant Variety Rights Regulation (1994)	Art. 235 EC
Trade Marks	Community Trade Mark Regulation (1993)	Art. 235 EC
Copyright and Related Rights	Satellite and Cable Retransmission Directive (1993)	Arts 57(2) and 66 EEC
Patents	Supplementary Protection Certificate (Medicinal Products) (1992)	Art. 100a EEC
Semiconductors	Semiconductor Directive (1986)	Art. 100 EEC

Figure 2.4 EU IP measures and their Treaty basis

and internationally, it gave further impetus to the Community's programme in copyright and related rights particularly.) In addition, Article 50(1) TFEU (ex Article 44(1) EC) empowers the European Parliament and the Council, acting in accordance with the ordinary legislative procedure and after consulting the EESC, to pursue freedom of establishment as regards a particular activity by means of directives. Third, Articles 53(1) and 62 TFEU (ex Articles 47(2) and 55 EC) authorize the issuing of directives coordinating Member States rules 'concerning the taking-up and pursuit of activities as self-employed persons', and the provision of services by Member State nationals to persons in other Member States. (A recent example of the use of these provisions in a harmonizing directive based on Article 114 TFEU is provided by the Collective Rights Management Directive: see recitals 3, 7, and 8.) And finally, reference must be made to Article 329(1) TFEU (ex Articles 43 to 45 TEU and 11 EC), first introduced with the Amsterdam Treaty, which authorizes a subset of EU Member States to seek permission from the Council to establish enhanced cooperation in accordance with the conditions laid down in Article 20 TEU and Articles 326 and 327 TFEU. It was in reliance on these provisions that a group of 12 EU Member States in 2010 sought the support of the Council to create a unitary EU patent and patent system following the failure of Member States to reach agreement regarding the language arrangements which such a system should include. (The proposed language regime involved the use of English, French, and German only, to which Spain and Italy in particular objected: see further Section 5.5.) That request was granted in Council Decision 2011/167/EU of 10 March 2011 authorizing enhanced cooperation in the area of the creation of unitary patent protection [2011] OJ L 76/53, paving the way for the introduction of the Unitary Patent Package.

As we have seen, Regulations 1257/2012 and 1260/2012 have been the object of an unsuccessful constitutional challenge to the Court of Justice by Spain and Italy. So too the decision of the Council authorizing enhanced cooperation was challenged by those Member States under Article 263 TFEU for want of legal basis in the Treaties. In the arguments advanced in support of that challenge, the decision was invalid on the grounds, among others, that the enhanced cooperation mechanism of the Treaties may only be used:

(a) in fields of shared competence—and not to address the procedural matters described in the second paragraph of Article 118 TFEU, which require unanimous action;

(b) as a last resort—and not where the possibilities of negotiation among Member States have not been exhausted, as with the unitary patent language arrangements;

(c) to promote European integration—and not to introduce a form of unitary protection for a subset of EU Member States only, which by excluding certain States would damage integration; and

(d) in a manner that respects 'the competences, rights and obligations' of the non-participating Member States—and not in a manner that will require non-participating Member States to adhere to a language regime which they have not approved.

In *Spain v Council*, the Court dismissed each of these arguments. Regarding (a), it held that the mechanism of enhanced cooperation is available in any case where agreement on a matter within the Council cannot be reached within a reasonable time period ([36] and [37]). Regarding (b), it held that provided the Council can be shown to have carefully and impartially assessed the factors leading to its decision that enhanced cooperation was necessary, and that it has given adequate reasons for that decision, the Court should accept its validity ([53] and [54]). Regarding (c), it held that 'having regard to its being impossible to reach common arrangements for the whole Union within a reasonable period', and the effect of the proposed unitary patent in conferring uniform protection throughout the territory of participating Member States, enhanced cooperation would contribute to the process of integration ([37] and [62]). And regarding (d), it held that it was permissible for participating Member States to prescribe rules with which non-participating Member States would not agree if they decided at a later date to participate, and that the prescription of such rules would not 'render ineffective the opportunity for non-participating Member States of joining in the enhanced cooperation' ([82] and [83]).

2.5 European Union Measures and Their Legal Effects

2.5.1 Types of European Union Measures

Article 288 TFEU lists the range of legislative and non-legislative measures through the adoption of which EU institutions are empowered to act ('legal acts'). These legal acts are regulations, directives, decisions, recommendations, and opinions, and are distinguished in Article 288 with reference to their legal effects, as follows.

> A regulation shall have general application. It shall be binding in its entirety and directly applicable in all Member States.
> A directive shall be binding, as to the result to be achieved, upon each Member State to which it is addressed, but shall leave to the national authorities the choice of form and methods.

A decision shall be binding in its entirety. A decision which specifies those to whom it is addressed shall be binding only on them.

Recommendations and opinions shall have no binding force.

As this Article states, only regulations, directives, and decisions are binding. For these three classes of EU legal act, a further distinction is drawn in the Treaties between legislative and non-legislative acts. This distinction flows from Article 289(3) TFEU, which states that any regulation, directive, or decision adopted by ordinary or special legislative procedure constitutes a legislative act, in contrast to any of these (or other types of) measure not so adopted, which comprise non-legislative acts.

The procedure for adopting a particular EU measure depends on the Treaty provision by which the measure is authorized. The Treaty provisions on which individual IP measures are based is shown in Figure 2.4. Most EU legislative acts—which include most EU measures in the field of IP—are subject to the ordinary legislative procedure described in Article 294 TFEU. That procedure begins with the Commission preparing a proposal for a law and distributing its proposal to Member States for review under the Subsidiarity Protocol.[20] Following such review, and depending on its outcome, the text of the Commission's proposal, including any amendments, is submitted to the European Parliament and the Council for joint adoption by those institutions following a reading and review procedure (Article 289(1)). In contrast to the ordinary legislative procedure, the special legislative procedure involves the adoption of a measure by the European Parliament with the Council's participation or vice versa in accordance with the relevant Treaty provision (Article 289(2)).

2.5.2 The Legal Effects of European Union Measures

2.5.2.1 Regulations

A defining feature of EU regulations is their direct effect. As we have seen, this means that in addition to being binding upon Member States, regulations are binding within Member States, since they penetrate automatically and directly into each Member State's legal system. They may therefore be invoked directly by individuals in proceedings before national courts—including vertical proceedings (against the state) and horizontal proceedings (against other individuals)—as a source of individual rights and obligations. The only requirement is that the provision of the regulation being relied upon is sufficiently clear and unequivocal to be enforceable by a court (justiciable).

2.5.2.2 Directives

EU directives differ from regulations in their legal effects. As Article 288 TFEU states, they are binding as to the result to be achieved, and leave Member States free to choose the form and methods by which to achieve it. Consistent with this, directives specify a time within which Member States are required to implement them domestically. In this way, they provide the EU with a means of indirect (rather than direct) law-making, and promote principles of subsidiarity and cooperation between the EU and its Member States. In addition, and as a direct consequence of this, directives do not penetrate automatically and directly into the legal orders of Member States, and cannot be invoked before domestic courts in the manner of EU regulations.

---

[20] Protocol (No. 2) on the application of the principles of subsidiarity and proportionality [2010] OJ C 83/206 creates a procedure for national parliamentary scrutiny of proposed EU legislative acts for compliance with the principle of subsidiarity contained in Article 5(3) TEU (see Section 2.4.1.1).

While this might seem clear enough, the detailed law regarding directives is extremely complex and technical. For present purposes it may be summarized as follows. As a general rule, the provisions of a directive do not have horizontal direct effect. Therefore, they may not be relied upon by an individual in domestic proceedings against another individual as a source of legal rights or obligations. However, there are exceptions to this; and more generally, directives *may* be invoked by an individual in domestic proceedings in any of the following circumstances:

- Where the proceedings involve a public authority, or a private party providing a public service under the control of the state (rather than another individual), *and* the provisions in question are sufficiently clear and unequivocal to be justiciable, *and* the time for Member States to transpose the directive has passed. In this situation, the relevant provisions may be invoked before the domestic court as a source of legal rights and obligations and must in such a case be given 'vertical direct effect'. (See, e.g., Case C–148/78 *Ratti* [1979] ECR 1629; Case C–152/84 *Marshall* [1986] ECR 723; Case C–188/89 *Foster v British Gas* [1990] ECR I-3313.)

- Where the directive is being invoked purely as an interpretive tool, to ensure that the applicable domestic law is being interpreted consistently with it (and thus consistently with EU law), and the result of that interpretation is not contrary to the relevant domestic law, legal certainty, or some other general EU legal principle. In this situation, the relevant provisions may be invoked before domestic courts and must in such a case be given 'interpretive direct effect'. (See, e.g., Case C–106/89 *Marleasing* [1990] ECR I-4135; Case C–212/04 *Adeneler* [2006] ECR I-6057.)

- Where the directive is being invoked to prevent the domestic court from (a) applying a conflicting domestic rule; or (b) acting in a way that will compromise the future transposition of the directive, *and* (in the case of (a)) the provisions in question are sufficiently clear and unequivocal to be justiciable, and aimed at protecting free movement principles *and* the time for Member States to transpose the directive has passed, *or* (in the case of (b)) the provisions in question express a general principle of EU law. In either of these situations, the relevant provisions may be invoked before domestic courts and must in such a case be given 'procedural direct effect' to prevent action which the court would otherwise take in reliance on domestic law. (In relation to (a) see, e.g., Case C–194/94 *CIA Security International SA v Signalson SA and Securitel SPRL* [1996] ECR I-2201; Case C–443/98 *Unilever Italia v Central Food* [2000] ECR I-7535. In relation to (b) see, e.g., Case C–212/04 *Adeneler* [2006] ECR I-6057; Case C–144/04 *Mangold v Helm* [2005] ECR I-9981.)

- Where the provisions in question have as their sole purpose the expression of a general principle of EU law, *and* the subject matter of the domestic proceedings falls within the scope of EU law. In this situation, the relevant provisions may be invoked before domestic courts and must in such a case be given horizontal direct effect. (See, e.g., Case C–555/07 *Seda Kücükdeveci* [2010] ECR I-365.)

The number of directives in the IP field makes an understanding of these exceptions to the general principle denying their horizontal direct effect essential. Among other things, the exceptions illustrate the potential impact of the elevation of the CFR to the status of the Treaties in having increased the scope for reading directive provisions as expressions of a general principle of EU law—such as the Article 17(2) principle that IP shall be protected—and thereby supporting their horizontal direct effect in reliance on *Seda Kücükdeveci*.

2.5.2.3 **International Agreements**

Among the decisions that the Treaties authorize the EU institutions to enter are those relating to the negotiation and conclusion of an international agreement (see the following section). According to Article 216(2) TFEU (ex Article 300(7) EC), any agreements thus entered into are 'binding upon the institutions of the Union and its Member States'.[21] This applies not only to agreements between the EU and third countries or international organizations, but also to mixed agreements between the EU, its Member States, and non-member countries or organizations. As we have seen, in the IP field such mixed agreements include the TRIPS Agreement 1994 and the WIPO Copyright and Performances and Phonograms Treaties 1996, which are accordingly binding on all EU institutions and Member States under Article 216(2) TFEU (Case C–12/86 *Demirel v Stadt Schwäbisch Gmünd* [1987] ECR 3719 (*Demirel*) [9]).

The question remains as to the consequences of international agreements being binding, and in particular as to their legal effects. In principle, the provisions of international agreements concluded by the EU are capable of having direct effect in the manner of other EU legal provisions, namely, if, 'regard being had to the wording, purpose and nature of the agreement, it may be concluded that the provision contains a clear, precise and unconditional obligation which is not subject, in its implementation or effects, to the adoption of any subsequent measure' (Joined Cases C–300/98 and 392/98 *Parfums Christian Dior SA v TUK Consultancy BV* [2000] I-11307 (*Dior*) [42]). In the case of the TRIPS Agreement, however, the European Court has made it clear that this test will never be satisfied. As a result, TRIPS provisions at least—and almost certainly the provisions of other international IP agreements as well—do not take effect immediately in EU law so as to require Member States' courts to apply them even in the absence of corresponding provisions of national law or a request for their application by the parties to the case. On the other hand, when interpreting national rules that fall with the scope of a TRIPS or other international IP agreement provision in an area covered by EU law, domestic courts must 'so far as possible' interpret them 'in the light of the wording and purpose' of that provision (ibid [47]), and so must the Court of Justice interpret secondary EU legislation, particularly where that legislation was intended to implement the international provision itself (see Case C–306/05 *SGAE v Rafael Hoteles SA* [2006] ECR I-11519 [35]).

Thus, the legal effects of international agreements concluded by the EU extend under Article 216(2) to EU Member States, which must consequently comply with them. The basis for this obligation has been the view of the EU that its conclusion of an agreement entails an assumption of responsibility for the due performance of that agreement by its Member States, and that, in consequence of this, Member States which fail to implement the agreement do so in breach of their obligations with respect to the EU (*Demirel* [11]). An example is Case C–13/00 *Commission v Ireland* [2002] ECR I-2943 (*Berne Convention*), which involved an application by the Commission under Article 226 EC for a declaration that, by failing to adhere to the Berne Convention by 1 January 1995, Ireland had breached its obligation under Article 216(2) TFEU (then Article 228(7) EC) to implement Article 5 of Protocol 28 EEA Agreement requiring such adherence. The Court of Justice allowed the application. In its decision, since the EU is a party to the EEA Agreement, and the literary and artistic property rights regulated by the Berne Convention relate to an area covered in large measure by the EU Treaties (by reason, it seems, of their capacity to affect trade in goods and services, and competitive relationships, within the Community: see Joined Cases C–92/92 and 326/92 *Collins v Imtrat Handelsgesellschaft mbH* [1993] ECR I-5171 [22]), the Community had an interest in ensuring that all Contracting Parties to the Agreement adhered to Article 5.

[21] R. Uerpmann-Wittzack, 'The Constitutional Role of International Law' in A. von Bogdandy and Jürgen Bast (eds), *Principles of European Constitutional Law* (Hart Publishing, 2009) 131, 139.

Related to the legal effects of international agreements is the scope of the CJEU's jurisdiction to interpret their provisions. In the *Berne Convention* case, the Court of Justice decided that the Commission was competent to assess compliance with the requirement of Article 5 of Protocol 28 EEA Agreement, and that the Court was in turn competent to review that assessment. So too in *Dior*, the Court agreed to decide a question of interpretation regarding Article 50 TRIPS Agreement (regarding provisional measures in IP) referred to it by the Arrondissementscrechtbank 's-Gravenhage (District Court of The Hague) and the Hoge Raad der Nederlanden (Supreme Court of the Netherlands) under Article 177 EC (now Article 267 TFEU). And finally, in *Daiichi*, the Court of Justice held its interpretative jurisdiction with respect to the TRIPS Agreement to be exclusive of that of Member States due to the agreement falling within an area of exclusive EU competence (the common commercial policy).

Our discussion so far has focused on the legal effects of agreements to which the EU is a party. However, even agreements to which the EU is *not* a party may produce EU legal effects. An example is the UDHR, consistent with the declaration in Article 3(5) TEU that the EU will promote 'the strict observance and the development of international law, including respect for the principles of the United Nations Charter'. In addition, as agreements concluded between one or more EU Member State and one or more third countries before 1 January 1958, the rights and obligations arising from the original Paris and Berne Conventions should remain unaffected by the EU Treaties as a result of Article 351 TFEU in any situation in which a relevant third country derives rights from the agreement which it can require a Member State to respect notwithstanding the effect of an EU law (see Cases C–364/95 and 365/95 *T. Port GmbH & Co. v Hauptzollamt Hamburg-Jonas* [1998] ECR I-1023 [61]). And finally, the Court of Justice has held that some agreements which have not been concluded by the EU—such as the original General Agreement on Tariffs and Trade (GATT), the Rome Convention 1961, and the Berne Convention (1971 Paris Act)—may nonetheless produce EU legal effects. In the case of the GATT, the reason given by the Court was that the agreement had been concluded before the establishment of the EEC by all Member States, and related to an area that fell within the scope of the (subsequently established) Treaties (Cases C–21/72 to 4/72 *International Fruit Company* [1972] ECR 1219). In the case of the Rome Convention, the reason given was the provision in Article 1(1) of the WIPO Performances and Phonograms Treaty 1996, to which the EU *is* a signatory, that nothing in that Treaty should impede its Contracting Parties' obligation under the Rome Convention (Case C–135/10 *Società Consortile Fonografici (SCF) v Marco Del Corso* EU:C:2012:140). And similarly in the case of the Berne Convention, the reason given was the obligation of the EU, as a signatory to the WCT, to comply with the substantive provisions of the Berne Convention (see Article 1(4) WCT; Case C–510/10 *DR, TV2 Danmark A/S v NCB–Nordisk Copyright Bureau* EU:C:2012:244).

2.6 The Court of Justice of the European Union

As we have seen, another important source of EU legal action are the decisions of the EU's Court of Justice. Generally speaking, those decisions are the product of three types of cases: direct actions, requests for preliminary rulings, and requests for opinions regarding proposed international action.

Direct actions may take any of four main forms:

(a) a complaint by a Member State or the Commission against a Member State for failing to fulfil its obligations under EU law, including by failing to implement a directive by the specified deadline (under Articles 258 and 259 TFEU);

(b) a request by the Council, Commission, or Parliament that a particular EU law be annulled on the ground of illegality (under Article 263 TFEU);

(c) a complaint by a Member State, Community institution, or individual against an EU institution for failure to act in accordance with the Treaties, including by failing to act within their conferred competences (under Article 265 TFEU); or

(d) an application to the General Court by an individual for compensation for damage suffered as a result of conduct by the EU or its staff (under Article 340 TFEU).

Requests for preliminary rulings may only be made by the courts of Member States, and are enormously important in IP. Under Article 267 TFEU, a court or tribunal may request a preliminary ruling of any question raised before it where it 'considers that a decision on the question is necessary to enable it to give judgment', and must request a preliminary ruling of any such question if 'there is no judicial remedy under national law' against its decision. In addition, the CJEU has clarified that a decision will be 'necessary' to enable a court to give judgment even if the decision is only potentially conclusive, and that a question will only be *acte clair* (so as not to require a referral) where:

(a) 'the correct application of Community law is so obvious as to leave no scope for any reasonable doubt as to the manner in which the question raised is to be resolved';

(b) the question is materially identical with a question which has already been the subject of a preliminary ruling, whether or not in a similar case; or

(c) the point of law at issue has already been dealt with by the CJEU in prior proceedings of some sort (Case C–283/81 *CILFIT v Ministry of Health* [1982] ECR 3415).

Finally, and as we saw in our earlier discussion of *Opinion 1/09*, the Court of Justice has jurisdiction under Article 218(11) to give opinions on request (from a Member State, the European Parliament, the Council, or the Commission) as to whether an international agreement is compatible with the Treaties. By further provision of that Article, '[w]here the opinion of the Court is adverse, the agreement envisaged may not enter into force unless it is amended or the Treaties are revised.'

Two distinctive characteristics of the European Court are its policy-driven approach to interpretation and its expansive view of its own interpretative jurisdiction. It has generally been accepted that each of these characteristics is motivated by the Court's concern to protect and promote European integration, including the autonomy and authority of EU institutions. Evidence in support of this view from IP is plentiful, as will be seen in later chapters.

2.7 Conclusions

The first post-war European initiative regarding IP predated the establishment of the EU and its predecessors. In 1949, French Senator Longchambon proposed that the Council of Europe—a non-EU body formed in 1949—consider the creation of a European patent and patent system. From that proposal there developed extensive work programmes by three different European institutions: the Council of Europe from 1950; the European Free Trade Association from 1964; and the EEC from 1959. The combined result of these programmes was the signing of three substantive European patent law conventions in the 1960s and 1970s: the Strasbourg Patent Convention of 1963, concluded under the umbrella of the Council of Europe; the European Patent Convention of 1973, concluded by an intergovernmental conference involving a collection of EEC and non-EEC European states; and the Community Patent Convention of 1975, concluded by the original six EEC Member States, Denmark, and the UK. The last of these Conventions never took effect, but has recently been re-enacted in modified form as the Unitary Patent Package: the two EU Regulations 1257/2012 and 1260/2012 and supranational Unified Patent Court Agreement 2013 establishing a unitary (EU) patent title and court for a subset of 13 or more participating EU Member States.

As this history of the Unitary Patent Package itself suggests, since the 1950s the EU has played a central role in the development of the European IP field. In the area of copyright and related rights, for example, it has introduced a large number of directives aimed at harmonizing the domestic laws of Member States, and signed two WIPO treaties in addition to the TRIPS Agreement (covering IP generally). In the area of industrial property rights, it has introduced three new titles of IP rights conferring protection for plant varieties, trade marks, and designs throughout EU territory, as well as supporting institutions to administer them. More recently, it has begun to consider the creation of a European Copyright Code to confer copyright protection throughout Union territory, and continued its progress on the establishment of a unitary patent right and system and the pursuit of international arrangements to ensure a high level of IP protection globally.

In its pursuit of these initiatives, the EU has been supported by increasingly expansive EU competences to introduce harmonizing and other measures in support of the establishment and functioning of the internal market, and to negotiate and sign agreements with international organizations and third countries concerning the commercial aspects of IP. It has also been supported by its increasing concern with social as well as economic policies, including the promotion of a European culture and the protection of fundamental rights and freedoms, both of which have supported deeper and more widespread involvement in the IP field.

It is perhaps inevitable given this that, since the Lisbon Treaty particularly, concerns have been expressed regarding the EU's involvement in IP. For example, it has been suggested that the elevation of the CFR's status to that of the Treaties by Article 6(1) TEU threatens the balance previously struck by EU jurisprudence between the recognition and protection of IP rights and single market policies by giving the former equal importance to the latter in the hierarchy of EU legal norms.[22] In addition, some have questioned the exclusivity of the Community's external competence in IP, and the reduced role of the Council in overseeing the negotiations of international IP agreements and treaties.[23] These concerns are significant, and connect to a wider distrust of the EU institutions and their involvement in IP, including their reliance on fundamental rights to expand the scope of EU competence and their use of trade agreements to create new enforcement and other substantive legal norms, often with the effect of increasing the level and scope of substantive IP protections internally. Such concerns connect to three of the most common and trenchant criticisms of EU law-making historically. The first focuses on its expansionist tendencies, including in areas of human rights and private law, and often following decisions of the Court of Justice. The second focuses on the perceived non-transparency of its law-making procedures and—as expressed by Joseph Weiler with characteristic force—its alleged 'democratic deficit', evidenced by its pursuit of an ambitious constitutional and legal agenda, and its failure 'to defend and protect the values it professes

---

[22] See, e.g., C. Geiger, 'Intellectual "Property" After the Treaty of Lisbon: Towards a Different Approach in the New European Legal Order?' [2010] *EIPR* 255.

[23] See, e.g., D. Matthews, 'The Lisbon Treaty, Trade Agreements and the Enforcement of Intellectual Property Rights' [2010] *EIPR* 104.

to hold most dear'.[24] And the third focuses on its perceived political messianism, namely, its reliance on the vision of European integration to justify its actions and methods.[25] These are strong criticisms which strike at the heart of the EU's formal and normative legitimacy, and go some way to explaining the frequency with which greater EU involvement in IP is met with open hostility, including from senior members of the European IP academic and judicial communities, and especially, in recent years, in connection with the establishment of a unitary EU patent system.[26]

Further Reading

ANDERMAN, A. AND EZRACHI, A. (eds), *Intellectual Property and Competition Law: New Frontiers* (OUP, 2011)

ARNULL, C. AND CHALMERS, D. (eds), *The Oxford Handbook of European Union Law* (OUP, 2015)

BARNARD, C., *The Substantive Law of the EU: The Four Freedoms* (4th edn, OUP, 2014)

CRAIG, P., *The Lisbon Treaty: Law, Politics, and Treaty Reform* (OUP, 2010)

CRAIG, P. AND DE BÚRCA, G., *The Evolution of EU Law* (2nd edn, OUP, 2011)

DIMOPOULOS, A. AND VANTSIOURI, P., 'Of TRIPS and Traps: The Interpretative Jurisdiction of the Court of Justice of the European Union Over Patent Law' [2014] *European Law Review* 210

GEIGER, C., 'Intellectual "Property" After the Treaty of Lisbon: Towards a Different Approach in the New European Legal Order?' [2010] *EIPR* 255

HARTLEY, T.C., *The Foundations of European Union Law* (8th edn, OUP, 2014)

KEELING, D.T., *Intellectual Property Rights in EU Law, Volume I: Free Movement and Competition Law* (OUP, 2004)

KLIMAS, T. AND VAICIUKAITE, J., 'The Law of Recitals in European Community Legislation' (2008) 15 *ILSA Journal of International & Comparative Law* 1

MATTHEWS, D., 'The Lisbon Treaty, Trade Agreements and the Enforcement of Intellectual Property Rights' [2010] *EIPR* 104

WILLIAMS, A.T., 'Taking Values Seriously: Towards a Philosophy of EU Law' (2009) 29 *OJLS* 549

WYATT, D., 'Community Competence to Regulate the Internal Market' in M. Dougan and S. Currie, *50 Years of European Treaties* (Hart Publishing, 2009) 93

[24] J.H.H. Weiler, 'The Political and Legal Culture of European Integration: An Exploratory Essay' (2011) 9 *I–CON* 678, 681.

[25] ibid 682 *et seq.*

[26] In that context see, e.g., J. Pagenberg (former member of the Expert Committee of judges and attorneys engaged by the European Parliament to work on the project), 'Open Letter to Herman Van Rompuy, President of the European Council' *EPLAW Patent Blog* (31 May 2012) http://www.eplawpatentblog.com/eplaw/2012/05/; J. Pagenberg, 'The EU Patent Package: Politics vs. Quality and the New Practice of Secret Legislation in Brussels' *EPLAW Patent Blog* (June 2012) http://hdl.handle.net/11858/00-001M-0000-000 E-7C60-B; D. Kitchin (Lord Justice of Appeal), 'Congress dinner—October 2012: The Rt Hon Lord Justice Kitchin' http://www.cipa.org.uk/pages/Congres-Dinner-2012-Lord-Justice-Kitchin.

3

Theoretical Accounts of European Intellectual Property

3.1 Introduction

In this chapter we complete our introduction to European IP law by offering a fuller treatment of the theoretical accounts of IP introduced in Section 1.2.2.3. To that end we focus on the most convincing explanatory and normative accounts of the existence of IP systems in general and European IP systems specifically. Thus, we ask why if at all we ought to grant property rights in respect of intellectual products, and what theories of IP best explain the European systems that exist.

At the conclusion of our discussion of the how and why of IP law, in Section 1.2.3, we offered an explanation of the importance of history and theory to understanding substantive IP rules, including substantive European IP rules particularly. For example, we suggested that theoretical accounts of IP offer positions of critical distance from which to view its substantive rules, and in doing so support independent engagement with and reflection on those rules. We also suggested that IP theory offers a range of analytical frameworks that help to elucidate different aspects of the substantive law of IP and the socio-economic values which they reflect and serve. And finally, we noted the value of IP theory in offering starting points for connecting substantive IP rules *inter se* into a unified and analytically coherent whole, and a vocabulary with which to talk about IP beyond the formal vocabulary provided by the legislature and courts. Once again, while these points are valid for law in general, they may be said to have especial importance for the law of IP due to the contention surrounding its normative foundations; and even more importance for the *European* law of IP due to the established rules of teleological, systemic and purposive interpretation which European tribunals deploy, and the explicit concern of European legal orders in general to respect and build on the cultures and traditions, spiritual and moral heritage, and common values of European peoples and states (see Sections 1.2.2.1 and 1.2.3). In this sense, and as also noted in Section 1.2.3, the European concern with promoting legal pluralism connects to the diversity of views within European society regarding the basis of IP in general.

The reference to the IP traditions, heritage and common values of European states raises a preliminary issue concerning theoretical accounts of IP, which is how convincing they ought to be before we accept them, and what if any weight should be given when assessing them:

(a) to the long-standing recognition of IP in European states, as seen in Section 1.2.2.2; and/or

(b) to the fundamental rights status of IP under Articles 27(2) and 17 UDHR (see Section 1.3.3.3.2) and, at the European level, Article 1 of Protocol 1 ECHR and Article 17(2) CFR (see Section 2.4.1.2).

On the one hand, it seems artificial and contrary to the values and objectives of the EU legal order particularly to ignore either of these things. On the other hand, contestation regarding the validity of IP could reasonably be regarded as a theme of its history, given which one might regard that history as increasing rather than decreasing the need for a convincing normative account of its existence, formulated without the assistance of positive law. In addition, the significance of the constitutional status of IP protection is equivocal for two reasons. First, and as we saw in Section 1.3.3.3.2, Article 27(2) UDHR follows the recognition in Article 27(1) UDHR of 'the right freely to participate in the cultural life of the community, to enjoy the arts and to share in scientific advancement and its benefits'. And second, each of Article 17 UDHR (recognizing the right of individuals to own property and not to be arbitrarily deprived of the property which they own), Article 1 of Protocol 1 ECHR (recognizing the right of persons to the peaceful enjoyment of their possessions), and Article 17(2) CFR (requiring that IP be protected), concerns property ownership in general and/or existing possessions and IP rights specifically, and does not confer any entitlement to acquire IP rights per se. In the case of Article 1 of Protocol 1 ECHR at least, this is clear from the case law of the European Court of Human Rights, which has interpreted that provision as conferring only a right on individuals to prevent unjustified interference by a state with an existing IP right or associated application (see *Sporrong and Lönnroth v Sweden* (1983) 5 EHRR 35), where by 'unjustified interference' is meant an interference that cannot be shown to be a proportionate means of pursuing a legitimate objective in the public or general interest, in the sense of striking a 'fair balance . . . between the demands of the general interest of the community and the requirements of the protection of the individual's fundamental rights' ([69]). In addition, when applying this standard the Court allows 'a wide margin of appreciation' to ECHR Contracting States ([69]), supporting a range of state-imposed restrictions on the freedom of individuals to exploit their IP rights. Examples of such restrictions in the patent field include the requirement to obtain regulatory approval before exploiting a patented invention, the requirement to pay renewal fees in order to maintain a patent, the provision for compulsory acquisitions and licences of patent rights by the state on public interest grounds, and the imposition of formalities as conditions for the valid licensing or transfer of patent grants.

For these reasons, in the current chapter we discount positive law in considering the normative validity of IP on the assumption that both its existence and formal legal status must be established with reference to theoretical arguments exclusively. On the other hand, we connect our discussion to existing law by considering the explanatory value of the different theories, along with two accounts of IP that depend on the CFR and EU Treaties.

If not with its prior existence or formal legal status, where should our attempt to account for the existence of IP commence? The answer must be with an understanding of that for which we are seeking to account—intellectual products and property rights—and from there, with arguments from natural law.

Put simply, a property or other right founded in natural law may be defined as a right that exists independent of statute, and that is universally and instinctively recognized.[1] In this chapter we consider two general theories in support of the recognition of IP rights as natural rights thus defined. The first casts IP as supporting the personal development and autonomy of individual creators (the argument from personhood), and the second casts it as securing creators rights they deserve by virtue of their acts of intellectual creation (the argument from desert). Included within the second of these is the well-known argument from Lockean property theory, according to which IP rights support individuals' self-ownership by recognizing the products of their labour as an extension of their bodies, and thus an extension of that in respect of which they have natural rights of ownership. If any of these natural law accounts of the existence of IP rights is accepted, it will necessarily assume a normative priority in deciding what shape those rights ought to take.

From natural law accounts of the existence of IP we move to consider three other theories. The first relies on principles of commercial justice or fairness to argue that IP is defensible as a means of preventing people either from being enriched unjustly or from harming others by unfairly reaping where they have not sown. And the second relies on principles of utility to support an instrumentalist view of IP rights as privileges conferred by the state on specific individuals in the pursuit of certain instrumentalist ends, such as encouraging socially desirable behaviour on the part of their beneficiaries or discouraging socially undesirable behaviour on the part of those whose freedoms they restrict. After considering these theories, we return to the pluralist model of IP introduced in Section 1.2.2.3.3 before concluding the chapter with a discussion of the implications of our theoretical accounts for the duration of copyright and related rights protection and the patentability of biotechnology.

3.2 Intellectual Products

Intellectual products, or products of the intellect, may be defined with reference to their possession of three essential features or qualities: an objectively discernible form; expressive or informational properties; and one or more identifiable human creators from whose intellect they can be said to have derived.

3.2.1 An Objectively Discernible Form

To exist as such an intellectual product must have an objectively discernible form. Thus, an idea in the head is not an intellectual product, in contrast to an idea that has been given an objectively discernible form through expression, including by means of literary description or visual representation.

Once expressed, the same idea may take one or more of several possible forms. Consider, for example, an idea for flying an aeroplane. Such an idea might be expressed

---

[1] W.E. Simonds, 'Natural Right of Property in Intellectual Production' (1891) 1 *Yale Law Journal* 16, 16.

as a method of manufacturing the aeroplane, i.e. as a series of steps that, if followed by a person, will result in the existence of a plane capable of being flown; or as a method of flying the aeroplane, i.e. as a series of steps that, if followed, will result in a plane being flown. Alternatively, the idea might be expressed in the form of a dramatic work, i.e. as a visual representation of a series of human actions that depict a person's operation of a plane in flight. (That representation may also be sufficient to express the method of flying adopted by the performer, in which case it will express both a dramatic work and a method of flight.) Or closely related to this, it might be expressed as a graphic representation of a person flying a plane, whether to exist and be enjoyed in its own right (as a work of expression), or for use by an airline to denote the commercial origin of its goods and services. And finally, the idea might be expressed as a statement of fact regarding a person's intention to fly a plane, i.e. as information regarding a person, in which case it will again exist as an intellectual product, albeit in the form neither of a method (of manufacture or flight), expressive (dramatic or graphic) work, nor sign of commercial origin.

3.2.2 **Expressive or Informational Properties**

Considering the form that intellectual products may take reveals two principal and closely related difficulties. The first is establishing what is and is not an intellectual product, and the second is identifying clearly the nature or constitutive features of specific intellectual products. For example, while a *method* of manufacturing or flying a plane, *the idea of a plane* produced by performing a particular method of manufacture, a dramatic or graphic *expression* of the act of flying a plane, a *sign of commercial origin* depicting a person flying a plane, and *information* regarding a person's intention to fly a plane, may all be regarded as intellectual products concerning the flight of a plane, each has different constitutive properties from the other. Given this, and depending on the nature and importance of these differences, we might expect the state's endorsement of property rights in respect of them to raise different considerations of legal theory and policy.

A central distinction in this regard is between expressive and informational subject matter. The methods of manufacture and flight, sign of commercial origin, and information regarding a person above each derive their value from and are constituted as such by the information they convey, and thus by their informational properties. More difficult is to identify the constitutive properties of the idea of a manufactured object of use, such as an aeroplane. Historically, many countries denied that such intellectual products existed independent of their methods of manufacture or intended use. However, and as we will see in Part II, since the 1970s European law has accepted that they exist independent of their methods of manufacture at least, and thus treated such products as constituted exclusively by their essential physical—and in some cases, their functional—properties, being those properties which account for their aspects of form and capacity to support a particular application in industry.

Also difficult is to define the constitutive properties of works of expression, such as the dramatic and graphic depictions of a person flying a plane. Currently in European law expressive works are defined with reference to their formal (visual or other) expressive properties. In the argument we make in Section 11.3, however, expressive works properly conceived are constituted in part by their properties of form and in part by the history of their individual production, including the view of the society in which they are created and the intention of their individual creators regarding their nature as an intellectual (expressive) product.[2] This follows the theory of art proposed by Kendall

---

[2] For a fuller account see J. Pila, 'Copyright and its Categories of Original Works' (2010) 30 *OJLS* 229.

Walton in 1970,[3] and supports an evolving conception of expressive works the boundaries of which can shift over time, creating the possibility of a subject matter being
treated as an intellectual product in one generation but not in another. It also has
strong intuitive value, as the following example illustrates.

> A pile of bricks, temporarily on display at the Tate Modern for 2 weeks, is plainly capable
> of being a sculpture. The identical pile of bricks dumped at the end of my driveway for
> 2 weeks preparatory to a building project is equally plainly not. One asks why there is
> that difference, and the answer lies, in my view, in having regard to its purpose. One is
> created by the hand of an artist, for artistic purposes, and the other is created by a builder,
> for building purposes. I appreciate that this example might be criticised for building in
> assumptions relating to what it seeks to demonstrate, and then extracting, or justifying,
> a test from that, but in the heavily subjective realms of definition in the artistic field one
> has to start somewhere.[4]

To summarize, a method of manufacturing or flying a plane derives its value and existence as such from its teaching that any person who follows its steps will cause a plane to
exist or be flown. The plane resulting from the method of manufacture derives its value
and existence as such from those of its physical and other properties that account for its
ability to support a particular use, and arguably from its method of manufacture itself.
By contrast, a dramatic or graphic representation of a person flying a plane derives its
value and existence as such from its aspects of expressive form and the history of its
individual production, supporting its recognition as a work of expressive significance. If
either type of product were to become associated with something else, then that association might support its transformation into a separate intellectual product. This is what
happens when expressive works are consistently applied to the goods of a particular
trader: they cease to exist merely as expressive works and also come to exist as 'signifiers'
of the commercial origin of the goods to which they are applied. (Their application to
those goods may also alter their expressive significance by altering the range of images
and feelings invoked in the minds of third parties upon seeing them, consistent with
their secondary role as signifier in distinguishing themselves from other traders' signs
in the marketplace. In addition, this second semiotic function of expressive works *qua*
brands may alter their commercial value to the trader using them in ways which the law
may wish to take into account when defining the trader's rights to exclude others from
using them,[5] in addition to altering their constitutive properties *qua* intellectual products.) And finally, information about a person derives its value and existence as such
from the knowledge or beliefs it creates regarding that person. The result is the understanding of intellectual products outlined in Figure 3.1.

The expressive or informational nature of intellectual products accounts for their special importance to individuals and society. That importance derives from their centrality
to knowledge creation, freedom and autonomy, innovation, cultural development, and
social and political participation, and accounts for the view of intellectual products (following theories of John Rawls) as among the range of primary goods 'that every rational
man is presumed to want'.[6]

One common feature of the intellectual (expressive and informational) products
considered in the previous section is their intangibility. As we saw in Section 1.2.2.1,

---

[3] K. Walton, 'Categories of Art' (1970) 79 *Philosophical Review* 344.
[4] *LucasFilm Ltd v Ainsworth* [2008] EWHC 1878 (Ch) [118].
[5] See B. Beebe, 'The Semiotic Analysis of Trademark Law' (2004) 51 *UCLA Law Review* 621.
[6] For a discussion see J. Rawls, *A Theory of Justice* (Harvard University Press, 1971).

Intellectual Product	Nature / Significance	Constitutive Properties
Method of achieving a result (The concern of patent law)	Informational and practical	Steps necessary for producing the result specified
Object of use (The concern of patent law)	Informational and practical	Physical and functional properties necessary for the object to exist and be used in the manner specified
Expressive work (The concern of copyright)	Expressive	Aspects of expressive form and the history of the individual work's creation
Sign of commercial origin (The concern of trade mark law)	Informational	Aspects of expressive form and its association through use to indicate the commercial origin of goods or services

Figure 3.1 Intellectual products and their constitutive properties

intangibility is generally regarded as a distinguishing feature of the subject matter protected by IP (in contrast with other property) rights, and as having special importance in accounts of those rights' existence. The reason for the perceived significance of the intangibility of intellectual products is that it deprives them of the natural or inherent scarcity of tangible products. For example, an aeroplane is a scarce resource in the sense of being rivalrous and depletable: only a limited number of people can occupy it at any particular time, and each person's occupation of it will diminish it in the literal sense of depleting its physical capacity to support future use and occupation. By contrast, it is of the essence of intellectual products such as the idea of an aeroplane, method of manufacture or flight, dramatic and graphic works, and information regarding a person that they can be 'occupied' simultaneously by any number of people, and that such occupation does not diminish in any sense their physical capacity for future use and occupation *qua* intellectual product. Thus, any number of people can simultaneously witness the dramatic depiction of a person flying an aeroplane, deploy a method of flying an aeroplane, manufacture and possess an aeroplane, apply an image of a person flying an aeroplane to their goods and services, or be aware of a person's intention to fly an aeroplane. It follows that none of these intellectual products is scarce in the manner of an aeroplane itself or other tangible product. On the contrary, it is only through the grant of property rights or the deployment of equivalent artificial exclusionary mechanisms that these intellectual products are rendered scarce.

3.2.3 **Identifiable Human Creators**

The examples of information about a person and a method of flying a plane prompt consideration of the third and final essential feature of intellectual products, which is the existence of one or more human creators from whose intellectual investment the product in question may be said to have derived. For example, a product that owes some of its essential features to the individuals who perform it—such as the method of flying a plane considered earlier, or a method of painting a sunset—may possess the formal qualities of an intellectual product, but may be too dependent on the further intellectual input of the individuals who perform it to be properly regarded as owing its existence *qua* method to one or more identifiable creators. An alternative way of expressing this might be by saying that the method lacks sufficient stability in its essential features to be regarded as having the objectively discernible form required of an intellectual product (see Section 3.2.1).

The requirement for identifiable human creators also excludes from the category of intellectual products any subject matter that owes its existence to non-human creators, such as animals. For example, as an expressive object a photograph taken by a monkey will possess the formal qualities of the category of intellectual products comprising artistic works. However, in the absence of a human directing the monkey in taking the photograph, the existence of the photograph will not be due to the intellect of a person, and will thus not be an intellectual product properly conceived. Finally, this third constitutive feature of intellectual products enables us to exclude from our discussion facts and products of nature, such as plants and animals, and chemical elements, such as hydrogen and oxygen, the discovery or use of which may be attributed to one or more individuals, but not their creation.

Lurking immediately beneath the surface of this requirement for identifiable human creators lie some of the most difficult philosophical problems with which all IP systems must engage, implicitly at least. For example, to what extent can the existence of any product be properly attributed to the mind of one or more individuals? Is a painting properly regarded as the creation of the person who applies the paint to the canvas, or of the community which has educated that person in the art of painting and inspired or conditioned him to choose the subject matter that he has chosen to paint? Similarly, do brands owe their existence as such to the trader who applies them consistently to his goods, or to the members of the public who appropriate them as objects of individual and cultural expression? If our answer is that they exist in virtue of the meaning attributed to them by members of the public, our conclusion should be that they lack the identifiable human creators (or sufficient stability in their essential features) to be regarded as intellectual products capable of supporting property rights more expansive than the rights required to protect their function of indicating the commercial origin of the goods to which they are applied in trade. And finally, if we can convincingly talk of individual human creation, and do therefore regard as meaningful the distinction between creation and discovery, at what point does a person's action upon the physical world cross the line between these two things? And what is the resulting intellectual product? Few would regard an apple growing in the wild as an intellectual product, i.e. a human creation, and few would regard that position as altered by the fact of a human seeing the apple in its natural environment. But what if the person were to pick the apple: would she thereby create a product in the form of an apple of the relevant type isolated from nature? If not, what types of action upon the environment in which the apple was grown or upon the apple itself would be sufficient to transform it from a product of nature to a product of the human intellect? And wherein lies the expressive or informational significance of the resulting product? As we will see in Chapter 9, these questions go to the heart of plant variety rights systems. Replace the apple in the example with a human gene and we also have one of the most controversial issues of contemporary patent law.

As we will also see later, the view of intellectual products as owing their existence to one or more individual creators has special importance for natural law accounts of IP systems for the simple reason that such accounts assert and proceed from the basis of a special connection between the individual beneficiaries of IP rights and the intellectual products to which those rights attach. As noted by Simonds, the essential claim of natural law arguments for IP is that 'whatever thing that is property-subject-matter which a man makes out of materials belonging to no one else, is his exclusive property by natural right'.[7] It is therefore essential to the validity of such arguments that intellectual products *can* be said to owe their existence to one or more individual creators. In the view of many, the infeasibility of this claim makes natural law theories of IP impossible to sustain.

3.3 Property Rights

3.3.1 Property Rights as Rights of Exclusion

As we saw in Section 1.2.1, property rights are exclusionary rights that attach to certain objects, i.e. rights to exclude the rest of the world from making certain uses of an object. Thus, excludability is of the essence of property.[8] This accounts for both the economic and political value of property, and for the amount of economic and political theorizing of property rights. Economically, rights of exclusion create the possibility of reserving to oneself the benefits of a protected object and charging for others' enjoyment of those benefits. If I own property rights in respect of a poem, for example, I can charge members of the public to attend a live performance of the poem or purchase copies of the poem. Of course, I can do these things even without property rights. Only with property rights, however, can I be confident when doing them that the state will reserve the opportunity to exploit the economic value of the poem to me by preventing others from reproducing or further distributing the poem without my permission. For example, while contract will enable me to impose conditions upon those wishing to access the poem, such conditions will only bind the individuals who agree to them, and will thus not be effective to restrain the activities of third parties. Thus, it is the state's willingness to exclude the entire world from using my poem, rather than merely the individuals from whom I am able to extract specific commitments, which differentiates the exclusionary rights of property from the exclusionary rights of so-called private ordering mechanisms in the form of legally enforceable contracts.

One issue arising from the definition of property with reference to excludability is how expansive if at all rights of exclusion need to be in order for them to be categorized as rights of property. According to Richard Posner, trade names and logos (i.e. signs of use in trade to distinguish the commercial origin of goods and services) are not objects of property properly defined, but rather 'merely identifiers, designed to protect consumers from being misled regarding the origin or quality of particular products or services'.[9] 'There are many interesting legal and economic issues concerning trademarks', he continues, 'but they are not centrally issues of property.'[10] The implication seems to be that for exclusionary rights to be rights of property, they must confer a general right on their beneficiaries to exclude others from the benefits of the object to which they attach *qua* object, and not merely a right to exclude others from the object in its performance of certain social or economic functions.

Two questions arise from this. The first is whether it is true that trade marks function merely as 'identifiers' of goods and services, as Posner states. And the second is whether,

---

[7] Simonds (n 1) 17.

[8] For a detailed defence of this definition see K. Gray, 'Property in Thin Air' (1991) 50 *Cambridge Law Journal* 252.

[9] R.A. Posner, 'The Law and Economics of Intellectual Property' (2002) *Daedalus* 5, 8.

[10] ibid.

if it is true, this precludes the categorization of rights to exclude others from that function as rights of property. It seems clear that the answer to both questions is no. Regarding the first: it is well established that trade marks do not exist and function merely to distinguish the commercial source of particular goods and services, but also to generate goodwill in respect of goods and services and in doing so to increase those goods' and services' commercial value.[11] Indeed, and as we see later, this additional function of trade marks is acknowledged and protected by European trade mark law. Further, even if the function of trade marks were exclusively as described by Posner, that function would still depend on the trade marks' expressive and informational properties, and thus on their existence *qua* expressive or informational (intellectual) product. Given this especially, even a limited right to exclude others from the benefits of graphic works registered as trade marks in their function as signs of commercial origin is properly categorized as a property right, underlining the elasticity in the concept of 'property'.

3.3.2 Property Rights as Rights of Income

The effect of property rights in reserving the benefits of a protected object to an individual rights holder explains the frequency with which they are conceived in economic terms, including as income rights. However, it is important to recognize that the economic value of property rights is contingent on at least three things. The first is the rights holder's desire to realize the economic value of the relevant property object; the second is the rights holder's ability to make the arrangements necessary to realize such value; and the third is the public's willingness to pay for access to that object. This means that the commercial exploitation of my property rights in the poem mentioned earlier is only a possibility, and not a certainty, since: (a) I may prefer that my poem not be placed on the market or in the public realm at all, but rather kept on my desk at home; (b) I may prefer to share my poem with the world without seeking to extract some or all of the commercial benefits potentially available for doing so; (c) I may wish to exploit my poem commercially in live performance but be unable to access a venue suitable for my performance; or (d) my attempts to exploit my poem commercially by charging third parties to witness its performance may be frustrated by a lack of interest among them to hear it, or an unpreparedness among them to pay the price for hearing it which I demand.

Let us consider the impact of any property subsisting in my poem in each of these scenarios. In the case of scenario (a), property will play an extremely important role, since, and for the reasons explained previously, it alone will enable me to protect the privacy of my poem by preventing others from reproducing or distributing it. Depending on how the property is defined, it may also enable me to prevent any person who enters my home from looking at or describing the poem, rather than merely from reproducing and distributing it in some material form. Indeed, it is in this possibility that we see property at its most powerful. On the one hand, it supports my claim 'to be let alone'[12] and to protect my personal and spiritual autonomy by writing poems that I cannot be compelled to share with the rest of the world. On the other hand, however, it enables me to control the use that third parties can make of their bodies, including potentially their eyes, minds, and faculties of speech, and thus to restrict profoundly their own freedom of action and personal autonomy.

---

[11] See F.I. Schechter, 'The Rational Basis of Trademark Protection' (1927) 40 *Harvard Law Review* 813.
[12] On the right to be let alone see S.D. Warren and L.D. Brandeis, 'The Right to Privacy' (1890) 4 *Harvard Law Review* 193.

Turning to scenario (b), another way for me to eschew the commercial benefits of a poem I create would be by uploading the poem to the Internet with an (express or implied) invitation to the world to distribute it, thereby relinquishing my claims in respect of it. An issue then arising would be whether I could reassert my property rights in the poem at a later date, or whether my initial invitation to the world to make free use of it would amount to a permanent waiver of those rights. A related issue that would arise in this case is whether one or more third parties could claim property rights in respect of my poem as an abandoned object of property, or at least rights of ownership based on their lawful occupation of it. Both invite consideration of the case of property rights in respect of a tangible object. For example, if I leave my bicycle on a street corner without a padlock, and it is still there after a month, am I free to reclaim it as my own? What if, during the month in question, local residents have developed a practice of maintaining and sharing the bike, or one local resident has claimed the bike as her own, taking it home and keeping it in her shed? In these hypotheticals we see the possibility of a range of solutions based in property, contract, or general considerations of fairness (equity). For example, it could be said that I have abandoned my property, leaving my neighbours free to acquire it by lawful occupation. Alternatively, it could be said that I have granted a revocable, non-exclusive licence to the world to use my property, permitting others to use it while asserting the right to reclaim it as my own. Or, it could be said that I have invited members of the public to deal with my bike as an object of common ownership, and that I am estopped from resiling from that invitation in circumstances in which it would be unfair for me to do so, as for example where someone has invested in maintaining the bike or given his own bike away in expectation of having the continued use of mine.

The desire of some property owners to facilitate the use of their intellectual products without reliance on property accounts for Copyleft initiatives. Broadly speaking, the aim of such initiatives is to promote non-proprietary models of exploiting and developing intellectual products, including software. For example, under the most well-known form of Copyleft licence, the GNU General Public Licence, property owners offer a protected product to the public (for a fee or free of charge) on terms guaranteeing the freedom of all persons to use, modify, and redistribute the product as well as any further products derived from it, which further products must be made available to the public on the same General Public Licence terms.[13] As the discussion above underlines, the validity of such licences depends both on the ability of contract to displace property, and on the ability of users to commit to relinquish their own future property rights and to enter agreements with third parties requiring those parties to do the same. In political economy terms, we might further note the effect of these networks of private agreements in displacing formal regulatory mechanisms of the state. According to some commentators, this act of displacement ought to be encouraged in digital environments particularly, including the Internet, where the absence of geographical boundaries is said to make traditional forms of governmental regulation obsolete and inappropriate.[14]

Moving to scenario (c), we can note the potential value of property rights in my attempts to secure a venue for the performance of my poem, either in giving me something to offer as payment for the venue (i.e. a transfer of some or all of my property rights) or, and depending on my confidence in my ability to attract an audience for my performance, in giving me a future possible source of income against which to offset that payment.

---

[13] A copy of the licence is available at https://www.gnu.org/copyleft/gpl.html.

[14] See generally W.W. Fisher III, 'Property and Contract on the Internet' (1998) 73 *Chicago-Kent Law Review* 1203, and other contributions to the symposium in which this paper is included.

Finally, if for any reason I am unable to secure a venue, or my attempts to exploit my poem commercially are otherwise unsuccessful, I may be left with no alternative but to keep the poem to myself or make it available to the public free of charge. If I keep it to myself, the chances are that it will never enter the public realm, even after my death, since its protection by property rights will prevent any person who comes across it from reproducing and distributing it to the public for the term of the property rights' subsistence at least. Hence again the potential effect of unexploited property rights in keeping the products to which they attach under metaphorical lock and key. It is partly with a view to minimizing this effect that European law makes the subsistence of property in registered trade marks and performance fixations conditional upon sufficient use of the mark/fixation, creating the concept of 'use it or lose it' IP.[15]

3.3.3 **Property Rights as Sources of Power**

As the previous discussion underlines, the exclusionary rights of property represent a form of control over an object that carries with it considerable power. This is because to recognize property rights in respect of an intellectual product is to recognize the right of the property owner to control the use that others may make of that product, which in turn entails control over the use that others may make of their physical selves and other objects. Indeed, an important feature of property rights in respect of intellectual products specifically is the breadth of the powers of control they confer in comparison with the breadth of the powers of control conferred by property rights in respect of tangible products. Put simply, the intangibility of intellectual products ensures that property rights in respect of them are more expansive in scope and thus more restrictive of public freedoms than property rights in respect of tangible products. This is because excluding others from an intangible product such as a poem requires preventing them from using certain products other than the poem itself, including personal computers and the array of other reprographic technologies that might be used to copy, modify, or distribute the poem. By contrast, property rights in respect of a tangible product, such as a chair, enable control of the chair alone: they do not also confer a right to prevent others from photographing the chair. In addition, and in contrast to intellectual products, in the case of tangible products such as a chair there will always be substitute products unaffected by the property rights, including other identical chairs, thereby limiting further the impact of individual property holdings on public freedoms.[16]

It is for these reasons that property rights are often described in political as well as economic terms, and are central to Marxist, feminist, and other political accounts of the state, as well as to accounts of international relations and development.[17] In political terms we can describe the exclusionary rights of property as creating state-sanctioned relationships between individual rights holders, objects of property, and the third parties excluded from those objects' benefits, enabling rights holders to define the rights and duties of third parties with respect to the protected objects, and thereby supporting different narratives regarding the value of those objects and the relationships between their property owners and members of the public. Among other things, seeing property rights

---

[15] See Article 10 Trade Marks Directive; Article 15 Community Trade Mark Regulation; Article 1(2a) Term Directive (regarding performance fixations).

[16] See generally T.G. Palmer, 'Are Patents and Copyright Morally Justified?' (1990) 13 *Harvard Journal of Law & Public Policy* 817, especially 830–2.

[17] Recall our account of the origins of the TRIPS Agreement in Section 1.3.3.3.2.

in political terms underlines the importance of IP ownership, including its capacity to be contractually transferred. For example, and writing now in Marxist terms, in a capitalist society we might expect, as is in fact frequently the case, that IP would be first owned not by the creators of intellectual products themselves, but rather by the persons responsible for employing or otherwise providing the conditions necessary for such creation. In addition, we might expect, as again is frequently the case, that IP would be transferable by contract, and that in situations in which it were both transferable and first owned by individual creators, it would be promptly transferred, leaving the creator with no more than a lump sum payment for her intellectual creation, and the acquirer of her property rights exclusive enjoyment of any economic benefits capable of being derived from the exploitation of that creation thereafter. In these and other ways the grant of property rights in respect of intellectual products can be said to support the capitalist enterprise by making creative labour *productive* and *alienable* labour, and intellectual products *commodities* that are dealt with separate from the social relationships in the context of which they are created. Such grant therefore supports capitalism and capitalist ideology, including by supporting the ruling classes' ownership and control of creative labour and the so-called Fetishism of Commodities.[18]

So too IP rights are readily amenable to a feminist critique focused on a different range of social structures and narratives that their construction and enforcement promote.[19] For example, in a gendered society we might expect a specifically masculine conception of culture and knowledge-production to be supported by a range of mechanisms, including individualistic (*contra* collective) notions of creation, a focus on exclusion and control rather than inclusion and interchange, and a rewarding of achievements in scientific, industrial, and creative domains from which women have historically been excluded—each of which in fact exists. We might also expect IP laws to promote a view of women as themselves constituting (intellectual) products created by others—for example, by recognizing the patentability of genes and stem cells removed from their bodies—or to use the occasion provided by biotechnology patenting as an opportunity to define the origins of life and the use that women may make of their bodies (see Section 3.9). And finally, we might expect IP laws to treat unauthorized uses of others' works to depict women in a derogatory fashion as instances of legitimate expression entitled to fundamental rights protection, as in fact occurs.[20]

Two issues of current importance in IP, that also underline the role of property rights in the construction of social and economic relations, are biopiracy and biodiversity. Biopiracy refers to the use of indigenous and developing communities' biological and other resources by European and other western firms to devise inventions the use or other benefits of which those communities are then excluded from by European and other western patent grants in combination with international patent laws. Examples of such biopiracy abound. Among the most widely publicized have involved the exploitation of plant resources such as neem tree seeds, tumeric root, and melons from India, beans from Mexico, and genetic materials from the Hagahai people of New Zealand, to produce agricultural and pharmaceutical products.

---

[18] P. Drahos, *A Philosophy of Intellectual Property* (Dartmouth, 1996) 108–14; see also K. Marx, *Capital: Critique of Political Economy* (1867) ch. 1.

[19] See generally D. Halbert, 'Feminist Interpretations of Intellectual Property' (2006) 14 *Journal of Gender, Social Policy and the Law* 431.

[20] Prominent examples include *Campbell v Acuff-Rose Music*, 510 US 569 (1994) (involving a parody of Roy Orbison's *Pretty Woman*) and *Leibovitz v Paramount Pictures Corporation*, 137 F3d 109 (1998) (US Court of Appeals for the Second Circuit) (involving a parody of a photograph by Annie Leibovitz of a heavily pregnant Demi Moore).

It was partly with a view to preventing such practices that the 1992 Convention on Biological Diversity and its 2010 Protocol on Access to Genetic Resources and the Fair and Equitable Sharing of Benefits Arising From their Utilization (Nagoya Protocol) were introduced. Most importantly for us, the Convention recognizes states' sovereign rights over their natural resources (Article 15) and obligations to: (a) 'encourage the equitable sharing of the benefits arising from the utilization of' the knowledge, innovations, and practices of indigenous and local communities (Article 8(j)); and (b) ensure that patents and other IP rights 'are supportive of and do not run counter to' the Convention's objectives of supporting the conservation and sustainable use of biological diversity and promoting the fair and equitable sharing of the benefits arising from the use of genetic resources (Article 16(5)). These obligations have been given legal force by the Nagoya Protocol, which the EU has recently implemented by means of Regulation (EU) No. 511/2014 [2014] OJ L 150/59.[21]

3.3.4 Conclusions

Property rights are state-endorsed claims of an individual to exclude others from the benefits of certain objects. Among other things, this definition explains and supports Margaret Radin's statement that 'there can be no free-standing purely "private" regime of property and contract', since both 'property and contract presuppose limits and enforcement shaped by a sovereign authority.'[22] More generally, and as we noted in Section 1.2.2.2, the impact of property rights on society has always been recognized by the state as requiring both their definition and limitation, and the regulation of their exercise, having regard to 'public law' matters such as the protection of public morality, the regulation of competition and the market more generally, and the protection of civil, political, and other human rights.[23] Hence the essential and inevitable question of what if any forms of limitation and regulation are appropriate, which question arises regardless of the basis for the private claims of individuals to exclude others from the intellectual products they create.

3.4 Accounts from Natural Law

3.4.1 Accounts from Personhood: Intellectual Products as Manifestations of their Creators' Personality

Our first account of the existence of IP is located in the natural law right of individuals to protection of their personhood and personal autonomy. This account draws on the

---

[21] For a critique of the Regulation in draft form see B. Toban, 'Biopiracy by Law: European Union Draft Law Threatens Indigenous Peoples' Rights Over Their Traditional Knowledge and Genetic Resources' [2014] *EIPR* 124.

[22] M.J. Radin and R.P. Wagner, 'The Myth of Private Ordering: Rediscovering Legal Realism in Cyberspace' (1998) 73 *Chicago-Kent Law Review* 1295, 1296.

[23] An interesting test of the public morality limits to the exercise of copyright in Europe occurred recently in Germany when Random House publishing company refused to pay the estate of Adolf Hitler's Propaganda Minister, Joseph Goebbels, for one of its author's use of copyright protected excerpts from Goebbels's diaries in a biography of him that it published (written by Peter Longerich). In July 2015 the Munich District Court ruled in favour of the estate's claim. See A. Milliken, 'Goebbels estate wins lawsuit over diaries' copyright' *Newsweek* (10 July 2015) http://europe.newsweek.com/goebbels-estate-wins-lawsuit-over-diaries-copyright-330113.

theories of Georg Wilhelm Friedrich Hegel,[24] and proceeds from a view of intellectual products as external manifestations of the personality of the individuals who create them. 'A person must give to his freedom an external sphere, in order that he may reach the completeness implied in the idea.'[25] As this suggests, the idea proposed by this account is that each act of creating an intellectual product involves the development by the creator of his personhood, and thus of his personal autonomy. Through the process of creation, a person therefore comes to occupy the product he creates as an extension of himself. It is this occupation of the product manifesting his personality that is said to be the source of his natural rights of property in respect of it. 'The reasonableness of property', Hegel wrote in *Philosophy of Right*,

> consists not in its satisfying our needs, but in its superseding and replacing the subjective phase of personality. It is in possession first of all that the person becomes rational. The first realization of my freedom in an external object is an imperfect one, it is true, but it is the only realization possible so long as the abstract personality has this firsthand relation to its object.[26]

Personhood theories of IP such as this have a certain explanatory value for European law. For example, according to EU law, copyright subsists automatically (without the need for application or registration) in and only in authorial works, defined as works that express an author's own intellectual creation and that bear her personal mark (see Section 11.3.2). This definition of the products in which copyright subsists could be said to imply a conception of copyright itself as existing in part to protect the personal autonomy of individual creators in recognition of the importance of their creations for their personal development. So too personhood theories are reflected clearly in authors' moral rights regimes, through the protection of authors' rights to be recognized as the creator of their works, to determine the readiness of their works for publication, and to prevent treatments of their works that they (or members of the public) believe to be derogatory of them. On the other hand, the capacity of personhood theories to explain copyright and moral rights regimes is limited. For example, if the purpose of those regimes were really to protect the personal autonomy of individual creators, it is difficult to see why their protections would last beyond the life of creators, why they would be capable of contractual displacement, and why they would not recognize a general exception of transformative use to enable third parties to transform existing (copyright-protected) works into their own, personality-enhancing, intellectual products. The last of these points draws attention to an important consequence of accepting personhood theories of IP, which is simply the need to recognize the claims of *all* creators, including those whose creations involve the use of existing intellectual products.

Whatever one's view of their explanatory value, there are several difficulties with personhood theories of IP. One is what Tom Palmer has described as their 'confusion regarding the ontological status of ideal objects and their relationship to their creators'.[27] Put simply, by casting intellectual products as manifestations of the personality of their creators, personhood theories fail to distinguish between the creation of an intellectual product on the one hand and its continued existence on the other. Thus, while it may be true (and we have assumed it to be true in our previous definition of intellectual products) that intellectual products can be said to owe their existence to one or more individual

---

[24] See especially G.W.F. Hegel and S.W. Dyde (transl.), *Philosophy of Right* (Batoche Books, 2001) and G.W.F. Hegel, J.N. Findlay (contr.), and A.V. Miller (transl.), *Phenomenology of Spirit* (Galaxy Books, 1979).
[25] *Philosophy of Right* (ibid) 55.   [26] ibid 56.   [27] Palmer (n 16) 843.

creators, and it may also be true for certain authorial works that those products reflect the personality of their creators, it seems far-fetched to say that they depend on those creators for their continued existence, with the result that any unauthorized interference with them involves an interference with the personality of certain individuals. If anything, intellectual products depend for their continued existence on the members of the public who read, listen to, perform, and otherwise interact with them, rather than on the persons responsible for their creation, challenging further this natural law account of IP.[28]

3.4.2 Accounts from Desert: Creators of Intellectual Products as Deserving Property Rights

A second set of arguments for the existence of IP from natural law depends on a view of those who create intellectual products as deserving property in respect of them. The basis for this view is generally said to be one or more of three things: the special kind of labour involved in creating intellectual products; the special value that intellectual products possess; and the special needs of those who create intellectual products on account of their investment in creating them.[29] Regarding the first of these: the argument is that the intellectual labour required to create an intellectual product—be it a poem, a method of manufacturing a plane, or a sign of use in industry—merits a special kind of protection for the creator in the form of property rights in the resulting product. Regarding the second: the argument is that intellectual products have a special value, on account perhaps of their nature as primary goods, which merits a special kind of payment for those who create them. And finally, regarding the third: the argument is that those who invest time, money, and energy in creating intellectual products have special financial or personal needs on account of their investment, which needs are appropriately met by the recognition of property rights in respect of the products they create. One version of this argument finds support in the writings of John Locke and notions of self-ownership. The idea here is that individuals have natural rights of ownership in respect of their bodies, which rights reach through to the products they create in exercise of their labour. On this view, when a person takes an idea or some other material from the pool of commonly owned resources (the commons) and mixes it with her labour to produce a product, she thereby acquires a natural right in respect of that product as an object that she, through her labour, has created and come to occupy. In the words of Locke:

> Whatsoever then he removes out of the state that nature hath provided, and left it in, he hath mixed his labour with, and joined it to something that is his own, and thereby he makes it his property.[30]

Once again, desert theories of IP find direct expression in European law, particularly European copyright law.[31] For example, according to recital 10 of the Information Society Directive:

> If authors or performers are to continue their creative and artistic work, they have to receive an appropriate reward for the use of their work, as must producers in order to be

---

[28]   ibid 847–8.

[29]   L.C. Becker, 'Deserving to Own Intellectual Property' (1992) 68 *Chicago-Kent Law Review* 609.

[30]   J. Locke, *Second Treatise of Government* (Hackett, 1980) 19.

[31]   While recital 46 of the Biotech Directive similarly describes 'the function of a patent' as being 'to reward the inventor for his creative efforts', it expressly describes that reward as a means of 'encourag[ing] inventive activities', suggesting an instrumentalist view of the function of patents (on which see Section 3.6).

able to finance this work. The investment required to produce products such as phonograms, films or multimedia products, and services such as 'on-demand' services, is considerable. Adequate legal protection of intellectual property rights is necessary in order to guarantee the availability of such a reward and provide the opportunity for satisfactory returns on this investment.

In comparison with personhood theories of IP, arguments from desert have a potentially broad appeal and application across the spectrum of intellectual products and property rights. A central challenge which their supporters face, however, is how to progress from the statement that creators deserve some kind of reward for their labour, products, or needs to the statement that the reward they deserve is property rights in respect of the products they create. Indeed, it would seem more in keeping with the first of the desert theories outlined earlier to reward creators with a salary for as long as they labour, independent of any intellectual products to which their labour might give rise. Similarly, and as many have argued in the context of inventors' rights especially, a more obvious type of reward than property for those who create products having special value would be prizes.[32] And finally, only if it can be convincingly established that the special needs of creators of intellectual products are appropriately met by recognition of their right to control the benefits of their products would it make sense to meet those needs with the grant of property.

One point underlined by this discussion is the intersubjectivity of notions of desert, and the consequential difficulty of establishing with any degree of confidence a means for determining the reward that individual creators merit. In addition, and as with personhood theories, any desert-based system of IP must recognize the claims of *all* creators, including those whose acts of creation involve the use of products created by others.

3.4.3 **Conclusions**

Each of the natural law theories considered in the previous sections can help to establish a preliminary or prima facie normative claim on the part of individual creators to property rights in respect of the products they create. It bears repetition, however, that while each of the theories gives normative priority to creators' claims by reason of its basis in natural law, none precludes those rights from being defined in a way that takes account of considerations of social welfare, and the impact of creators' rights on the rights and interests of others. Indeed, according to Lockean property theory, the measure of property rights derived from principles of self-ownership is appropriately defined having regard to the value of the labour invested in creating the product and 'the conveniences of life'.[33] The example illustrates well the capacity of desert-based arguments for the recognition of natural (intellectual) property rights to combine a concern with protecting the autonomy or other special interests of individual creators with ensuring that the social impact of doing so is properly accounted for in the definition of those creators' property entitlements. Determining what this might mean in practice is another matter, however, and not something that any of the natural law theories can do alone.

---

[32] See, e.g., J. Stiglitz, 'Give prizes not patents', *New Scientist* (16 September 2006) 21.
[33] Locke (n 30) 22.

3.5 Accounts from Unjust Enrichment/Unfair Competition

A quite different set of accounts for the existence of IP proceeds from a concern to prevent individuals from being unjustly enriched or unfairly harmed by their or others' acts of free riding by (to mix our metaphors) reaping where they have not sown. One example of such an account is that offered by Wendy Gordon in her work 'On Owning Information: Intellectual Property and the Restitutionary Impulse'.[34] In building her argument, Gordon compares those who use intellectual products without permission to those who undergo medical treatment while unconscious, suggesting that while there is nothing immoral in using the product or accepting the medical treatment itself, there may be something immoral in refusing to pay for such use or treatment afterwards. In the event Gordon finds the comparison inapt, since the same assumptions regarding the impact of requiring payment on the affected person's life choices cannot be made for the user of an intellectual product as for a medical patient. Nonetheless, the comparison informs her argument for the existence of IP independent of statute in recognition of a right of people not to labour under compulsion by others, and a correlative duty of any person who benefits from another's labour at the labourer's expense to disgorge such benefit by compensating the labourer for the use of her product. The challenge thus created for Gordon is to define the circumstances in which this duty is engaged, being the circumstances in which not to pay would leave the user 'unjustly enriched', i.e. and as Gordon defines that phrase, enriched at the creator's expense. According to Gordon, the answer is where the use: (a) involves knowing copying; (b) occurs in a context exhibiting asymmetrical market failure (enabling us to say that the user failed to take the opportunity which she alone had to seek the creator's permission to use the product); (c) represents a taking by the user of sales from the actual or expected market for the claimant's product (enabling us to see the user as having, through her use, entered into commercial competition with the creator); and (d) is of a type and amount not likely to be equivalently valuable to the claimant in the long term (enabling us to say that if the claimant enjoyed the freedom to use others' works in equivalent circumstances, she would enjoy no equivalent benefit).

The first thing to note about Gordon's account is its support for something other than property (as we have defined it earlier) in the form of liability rules permitting the unauthorized use of others' intellectual products for payment. And the second is its effect in protecting the freedom of individuals to use the intellectual products of others (without payment) in all circumstances except those in which the use enables the individuals to reap the commercial benefits of the product at the direct commercial expense of its creator. This requirement for a competition nexus between the user and creator suggests that Gordon's real concern lies with preventing unfair competition rather than unjust enrichment.[35] Specifically, it suggests that her theory is aimed less at disgorging the benefits acquired by a person through the unauthorized use of another's intellectual creation than preventing the commercial harm which such use may cause to the creator in circumstances in which that harm can be said to have been caused by the user's unfair competitive practices.

---

[34] W.J. Gordon, 'On Owning Information: Intellectual Property and the Restitutionary Impulse' (1992) 78 *Virginia Law Review* 149.

[35] J.L. Coleman, 'Intellectual Property and Corrective Justice' (1992) 78 *Virginia Law Review* 283.

Unfair competition accounts of IP such as that advocated by Gordon have clear explanatory value for Europe. Indeed, principles of competition and free movement are among the most consistently emphasized by the Court of Justice when interpreting substantive provisions of EU IP instruments, and are also routinely referred to in EU IP directives. To some extent this can be explained in pragmatic terms, as reflecting the need for harmonizing IP measures to be presented as supporting the establishment and smooth functioning of the internal market in order to justify their introduction in reliance on Article 114 TFEU, and thus their validity under the EU Treaties (see Section 2.4.1.2). However, the emphasis on principles of fair competition particularly goes well beyond that required to establish different instruments' formal legitimacy. An example is the limits which EU law recognizes to the freedom of patent and other IP owners to exploit their property, many of which derive from unfair competition principles. For example, under Articles 34 to 36 TFEU—and consistent with the terms of EU patent, copyright, and trade mark legislation (see Section 2.4.2.1.3)—a patentee may not rely on her patent monopoly to restrict the free movement of patented goods placed on the market with her consent in the EU. In addition, under Articles 101 and 102 TFEU, a patentee may not enter a patent licensing agreement that: (a) prohibits the licensee from exploiting (or authorizing third parties to exploit) the patented invention where doing so would impede its dissemination and prejudice competition between it and exist-ing technologies (see Case C–258/78 *Nungesser v Commission* [1982] ECR 2015);[36] or (b) limits the parallel importation of goods into different EU Member States so as to enable different prices to be charged for them where doing so would impede the dis-semination of the invention (see Joined Cases C–468/06 to 478/06 *Sot Lélos kai Sia et al. v GlaxoSmithKline* [2008] ECR I-7139). And finally, under Article 12 Biotech Directive, a patentee who obstructs competition and technological progress by preventing another person from acquiring or exploiting her own patent or plant variety rights by refusing to authorize her exploitation of the patented invention can be compelled by the relevant Member State to grant a licence in respect of the IP right.

Another aspect of IP law well explained by unfair competition principles is the range of exceptions to patent and copyright infringement that EU legislation permits Member States to recognize (see Chapters 8 and 13). These include many exceptions, such as private use and parody, that are most readily explained with reference to the absence of any competition nexus between the private user/parodist and the property owner, and the consequential inability to see the exempted use as diverting potential consum-ers of the protected intellectual product to the unauthorized user of that product. The reason for this inability in the case of parody is simply that parodies tend to be aimed at different audiences from the works they parody, and thus not to substitute for those works in the market. Thus, while a parodic use of a work may reduce the economic value of the work by making the public less interested in consuming it, such a use will gener-ally not lead potential consumers of the work to seek access to the parody in substitu-tion of it. A similar analysis applies with respect to several other copyright exceptions, including those permitting the use of a protected work for the purpose of criticizing it. So too European law's support for the treatment of copyright exceptions as having the effect of converting the property rights of copyright owners into 'income rights' is consistent with Gordon's view of liability rules as the appropriate solution to conflicting

---

[36] The EU has responded to this problem of anti-competitive licence agreements by introducing the Regulations referred to in Chapter 4 n 3 each of which defines certain categories of bilateral agreement aimed at facilitating the transfer of technology and promoting research and development respectively as falling outside the prohibition of Article 101 TFEU.

claims between creators and unauthorized users of intellectual products (see recital 36 Information Society Directive).

Finally, reference should be made to the strong connection that exists between unfair competition values and the European trade mark regime. That connection can be seen in many of the substantive rules of that regime, including the grounds for refusing registration of a mark and the definition of the protections conferred by registered marks, as well as in the harmonization of domestic trade marks laws and the creation of unitary (Community) trade marks itself. Consider as examples the following provisions of the Trade Marks Directive, mirrored by provisions of the Community Trade Mark Regulation.

- Recital 2, which describes possible impediments to the free movement of goods and services and distortions to competition arising from differences in national trade mark laws as necessitating legal harmonization 'in order to ensure the proper functioning of the internal market'.

- Article 3(1)(e), which prohibits the registration as a trade mark of signs consisting exclusively of shapes that result from the nature of or give substantial value to the goods, or that are necessary to obtain a technical result. As the Court of Justice in Case C–299/99 *Koninklijke Philips Electronics NV v Remington Consumer Products Ltd* [2002] ECR I-5475 explained, the purpose of Article 3(1)(e) is to prevent the protection conferred by trade marks from being extended beyond signs which serve to distinguish a product or service from those offered by competitors, so as to form an obstacle preventing competitors from freely offering for sale products incorporating such technical solutions or functional characteristics in competition with the proprietor of the trade mark.

- Article 5(1), which describes the protection conferred by trade marks as preventing the use by third parties in the course of trade: (a) of identical signs in relation to goods or services identical with those for which the mark is registered; and (b) of signs the use of which creates a likelihood of confusion among the public by reason of its identity with or similarity to the mark and the identity or similarity of the goods or services covered by it and the mark respectively.

- Article 7(1), which confirms the principle of exhaustion mentioned earlier by providing that the rights of a registered trade mark owner cannot be invoked to prevent the use of the registered trade mark in relation to goods which have been put on the market in the Community under that trade mark by the proprietor or with his consent. As we saw in Section 2.4.2.1.3, according to the Court of Justice in Case C–2/93 *IHT Internationale Heiztechnik v Ideal Standard* [1994] ECR I-2789, this applies to goods put on the market by the assignee of the trade mark owner on the ground that the 'essential function' of a trade mark to indicate the commercial origin of the goods to which it applies would be undermined if the mark could be used in the same territory by undertakings with no legal or economic link beyond that created by the trade mark assignment.

Each of these provisions of the Directive as interpreted by the Court of Justice suggests that unfair competition, including through diversion of a trade mark owner's actual or potential market to the alleged infringer, is a primary driver of European trade mark law. In so doing they support the statement of the Court of Justice that 'the trade mark is an essential element in the system of undistorted competition which European law seeks to establish' (Case C–323/09 *Interflora Inc. v Marks & Spencer plc* [2011] ECR I-8625 [57]).

The understanding of trade mark law as existing to prevent unfair competition is also useful in offering a framework with reference to which other aspects of that law may be criticized. For example, if the purpose of trade mark law is really to prevent unfair competition, as the EU suggests, it is not obvious that its protections should extend beyond the types of competitive use described in Article 5(1) Trade Marks Directive. And yet, under Article 5(2) its protections may extend beyond such conduct. This is because that Article enables Member States to prevent third parties from using in the course of trade any sign (identical or similar to the registered mark) in relation to goods or services which are *not* similar to those for which the mark is registered—i.e. in non-competitive contexts—where the mark has a reputation in the Member State and use of the sign 'without due cause takes unfair advantage of, or is detrimental to, the distinctive character or the repute of the trade mark'. This suggests a concern on the part of the EU legislature with something other than preventing unfair competition, be it preventing unfair business practices in general (consistent with Article 6 of the Directive) or protecting the commercial investment of trade mark owners in respect of their marks; a suggestion confirmed by the interpretation of Article 5(2) by the Court of Justice.[37]

As the discussion of Gordon's theory illustrates, a central challenge posed by restitutionary accounts of IP as existing to prevent unjust enrichment lies in establishing the injustice of reaping where one has not sown without relying on the harm caused by such reaping to the creators or third party users of the protected product.[38] However, even if causing harm (rather than unjust enrichment) *is* thought to be the justification or explanation for IP, there remains the need to identify the source of the user's obligation not to cause the harm in question. As our discussion in this section further reflects, that source is often treated as being the obligation on the part of individuals not to engage in unfair competition; an obligation that finds direct expression in the requirement of Article 10*bis* of the Paris Convention that Paris Union States protect each other's citizens against 'any act of competition contrary to honest business practices and industrial commercial matters', as well as in the EU's Unfair Competition and Misleading and Comparative Advertising Directives. Even that obligation may have different normative bases, however. For example, it might be based in a political right of individuals to participate fully and equally in the economic life of a community, or in a political commitment to use IP as a means of discouraging commercial practices that are regarded as impeding the smooth functioning of the European single market and thereby undermining the goals and values of the EU Treaties.

3.6 Accounts from Instrumentalism

Accounts of IP as existing to discourage socially undesirable behaviour or encourage socially desirable behaviour are among the most widely supported, and also afford a convincing account of all existing IP systems. Their premise is a view of IP as founded in the state's instrumentalist commitment to securing a result beyond the vindication of the rights or interests of the individual creators of intellectual products themselves, such as maximizing human happiness or the general welfare of citizens. In the case of IP, the key challenge posed by such utilitarian thinking is to demonstrate: (a) how the property rights in question are appropriately defined in order to maximize the intended benefits

---

[37] See Case C–487/07 *L'Oréal SA v Bellure NV* [2009] ECR I-5185 [50].

[38] As Coleman notes ((n 35) 285), 'the reap/sow principle and the principle of unjust enrichment, or corrective justice, are on different levels of analysis'.

to society; and (b) that such rights do benefit society more than they harm it. These are empirical questions that ultimately depend on an analysis of the economic, political, and social impact of IP rights in practice, including their impact on trade and competition, individual freedom and autonomy, research and development, and social and political participation.

As noted, instrumentalist theories of IP tend to focus on the suitability and success of IP in incentivizing certain desirable behaviour and/or disincentivizing certain undesirable behaviour. For example, we have already seen the ease with which trade mark law is explained as a means of discouraging traders from harming other traders or consumers by engaging in unfair competitive practices. So too, however, and recalling our discussion of Article 5(2) Trade Marks Directive, we might cast the purpose of trade mark law in more positive terms, as being to encourage traders to invest in the development of signs that are sufficiently distinctive to operate effectively as means of enabling consumers readily to distinguish their goods and services from the goods and services of other traders operating in the same or similar markets.

Instrumentalist accounts of the existence of IP are not confined to the trade mark realm. Indeed, copyright and patent systems are routinely justified and explained as instruments of the state. Hence the argument commonly made that the grant of property rights in respect of authorial works and technical ideas (inventions) incentivizes investment in the creation and dissemination of those works and inventions. In Europe this argument finds direct expression in the Information Society and Biotech Directives, among other copyright and patent instruments. For example, recital 4 of the Information Society Directive predicts that the establishment of a harmonized legal framework on copyright and related rights

> will foster substantial investment in creativity and innovation, including network infrastructure, and lead in turn to growth and increased competitiveness of European industry, both in the area of content provision and information technology and more generally across a wide range of industrial and cultural sectors. This will safeguard employment and encourage new job creation.

So too recital 11 of the Biotech Directive provides as follows:

> Whereas the development of biotechnology is important to developing countries, both in the field of health and combating major epidemics and endemic diseases and in that of combating hunger in the world; whereas the patent system should likewise be used to encourage research in these fields; whereas international procedures for the dissemination of such technology in the Third World and to the benefit of the population groups concerned should be promoted[.]

This is also consistent with recital 46 of the same Directive, which describes 'the function of a patent' as being simply 'to reward the inventor for his creative efforts by granting an exclusive but time-bound right, and thereby encourage inventive activities'.

As noted, those seeking to support instrumentalist arguments for IP face two main hurdles: establishing that IP does in fact create the relevant incentives or disincentives, and establishing whether (and if so, how) society benefits from the incentives or disincentives it creates, and from the existence of IP systems generally. Concerning the first of these: in the context of the copyright and patent systems, the claim is that granting property rights in respect of intellectual products creates the conditions of scarcity necessary to enable their commercial and other benefits to be exploited by the rights' beneficiaries sufficiently to recoup the costs of their investment in creating and disseminating the relevant products. In economic terms this is explained with reference to the disparity between the cost of creating and disseminating intellectual products, and of reproducing and redistributing those products once created. That disparity is most apparent in the context of resource-intensive technological and creative industries, such as the biotech, pharmaceutical, and film industries, each of which requires enormous financial investment to sustain its activities. However, the ability of most intellectual products (by virtue of their intangible and informational or expressive nature) to be perfectly reproduced and distributed throughout the world instantaneously by any member of the public with a single keystroke effected on a personal computer or other household device makes the disparity striking in almost all creative and technological industries. It accounts for the view of many that without IP to prevent such unauthorized acts of reproduction and distribution, the creators of intellectual products would have no possibility of recouping the costs of their creation, and no form of valuable consideration with which to persuade third parties to invest in the dissemination of their products.

Instrumentalist theories of IP proceed from a belief that deploying the regulatory mechanisms of the state to recognize and protect property in respect of intellectual products will advance and protect the public good. The adoption of the public good as their primary reference point accounts for their concern to ensure that the protections which IP confers are defined in a manner that takes full account of its socio-economic effects. Central in this regard are principles of distributive justice, and ensuring that IP protections do not enable the creators of expressive and informational goods to charge unreasonable prices for access to their products, or to control unreasonably either the distribution of those products within the public realm or the freedom of third parties to use other objects, including new technologies. Once again, just as digital technology increases the need for IP, so too it increases the interference of IP in the daily lives of citizens, thereby making the state's regulation of it especially important. This explains the fine balancing exercise in which IP systems are routinely said to be engaged between the provision of incentives or disincentives on the one hand and considerations of distributive justice and social welfare—including social and political participation—on the other.

The idea of IP systems as engaged in a balancing exercise is well reflected in contractarian models of IP, most prevalent in the patent field. According to one version of this model, patents represent contracts between individual inventors (and patentees) on the one hand and society (represented by the state and patent-granting offices) on the other. By disclosing his invention to the public in the text of a patent specification, the inventor offers consideration for the grant of property rights in respect of his invention. By defining the scope of those rights with reference to the invention itself, the state seeks to ensure the essential fairness or proportionality of the bargain thus concluded, and so too by insisting on substantive examination of the inventor's application for a patent, the state seeks to ensure that the invention disclosed is of sufficient merit to justify the grant of property rights and the restriction of public freedoms which that grant entails.[39]

Central in striking the right balance between the provision of incentives or disincentives through the grant of property rights and the securing to the public of the benefits of doing so is to identify the nature of those benefits. Generally speaking, encouraging the creation and dissemination of intellectual products is said to benefit the public by promoting an efficient and well-functioning market in respect of intellectual products and associated goods and services, and/or by serving the range of civil, political, economic, social, and other rights recognized by instruments such as the ECHR and CFR,

---

[39] For a discussion of the implications of this contractarian model of IP for patenting products see J. Pila, 'Chemical Products and Proportionate Patents Before and After *Generics v Lundbeck*' (2009) 20 *King's Law Journal* 489.

including human dignity and the integrity of the person, freedom of expression, privacy, and the right to education and health. As we will see throughout this book, this makes instrumentalist accounts of IP especially compelling for Europe. The reason is the support they offer for a view of IP systems as existing to serve the basic values of Europe and European citizens as expressed in the EU Treaties and CFR, building on the ECHR. These include the combination of single market and human rights values identified in Section 2.4.1.2 as having underpinned EU action in IP since the 1950s, similar to the values identified in Section 1.2.2.3 as having underpinned the emergence and development of IP systems historically. The result is a framework for understanding and a language for describing the dual focus of European IP law on promoting competition and the free movement of goods and services on the one hand, and protecting the diverse fundamental rights and interests of creators, users, and third parties on the other.

Instrumentalist theories of IP are sometimes described as offering not merely an alternative to natural law accounts of IP, but also a reversal of the damage done by those accounts and IP in general through their promotion of 'Proprietarianism'. This idea runs through the philosophical work of Peter Drahos, who defines Proprietarianism as a creed with three essential features: a tendency towards property fundamentalism (the normative prioritizing of property above other rights and interests); a dependence on a first connection thesis about property (the idea that a person first connected with an object or activity of value has a property right in respect of it); and a belief in the negative commons (suggesting that while not everything is owned, everything is capable of being owned).[40] In *A Philosophy of Intellectual Property* (published in 1996), Drahos argued that Proprietarianism was the dominant narrative in IP law, and in the ascendancy. As evidence he cited various legal developments, each of which has a counterpart in Europe, including in the extension of IP protection to basic elements of human expression and life, such as colours (registrable as trade marks), short literary phrases (protected by copyright), and isolated human genes (capable of being patented); all of which we discuss later in this chapter (for gene patents) and in later chapters.

To the extent that support for instrumentalist theories of IP is driven by a concern to restrict the scope of protections conferred by existing IP systems, and a belief that instrumentalist theories are best geared to achieving this, it may be misplaced. The reason is simply that many aspects of current law that attract controversy on account of the breadth of protections they support are commonly defended in instrumentalist terms. As we will see in Section 3.9, the availability of patents for isolated human genes has historically at least offered one example of this, along with the lowering of patentability standards to make it easier for those working in the pharmaceutical and biotech industries to obtain patent protection for their research results.[41] Typically, both of these aspects of European patent law are justified with reference to: (a) the benefits to the community of the availability of human genes in a form in which they may be put to industrial use, including for use in the development of new medicines; and (b) the special dependence of the pharmaceutical and biotech industries on property rights to secure the funding they need in order to be able to continue their research. Another is the extension of trade mark protections to cover non-competitive uses of identical or similar signs considered earlier. And finally, and as a third example, there is one of the most controversial issues in IP of recent

---

[40] Drahos (n 18) 201–2.

[41] See, e.g., *Human Genome Sciences Inc. v Eli Lilly* [2011] UKSC 51, referred to in Section 1.2.3 as an example of the courts' invocation of history and theory to explain and justify their decisions in individual cases.

years—the duration of copyright and related rights protection—to which we return in Section 3.8.

Several consequences flow from utilitarian IP theories, whether or not informed by scepticism of the type that Drahos advocates. Perhaps the most important of these is that the existence of IP is not inevitable in any given time, place, or context. As a result, nor is it static. As Arnold Weinrib has written, 'if property originated in considerations of utility...its instances from time to time should deserve constant reexamination as to their continued conformity to new wants and the new circumstances of a changing society',[42] including most obviously changes in technology and social conditions of (in)equality.

3.7 Accounts from Pluralism

Closely related to instrumentalist accounts of IP as existing to serve the basic values of the relevant property-conferring community are the pluralistic accounts introduced in Section 1.2.2.3.3. Generally speaking, pluralistic theories of IP have resulted from a dissatisfaction regarding the capacity of any one of the (instrumentalist or noninstrumentalist) theories outlined previously to account adequately for the existence of all IP systems, and a belief that an alternative account of their existence is therefore necessary.[43] One alternative account that we saw in Section 1.2.2.1 is history. Thus, it has been said that IP emerged and developed in response to a complex array of events, and that while our investment in it is now sufficient to make its abolition infeasible, it has no positive justification as such. Pluralism offers a less pessimistic alternative account. Central is a rejection of any 'one size fits all' theory in preference for a view of IP systems as existing to support a range of economic and moral values and principles in reflection of their diverse legal and social functions, and the diverse beliefs of individuals regarding their proper scope and conception.

The centrality of principles to pluralistic accounts of IP explains their normative and explanatory value for Europe. The reason is the function of principles as means by which foundational (social and legal) differences can be transcended via the pursuit of common objectives. This function accounts for the prediction by Neil MacCormick in 1993 that in the European legal order principles would come to displace the autonomous orders of individual states and the conflicting traditions which underpin them in support of a form of harmonization that accommodates legal and social diversity.[44] The prediction underlines the commonalities between the IP and EU legal fields on account of the diverse traditions and philosophies on which each is built, and helps again to explain the special value that pluralistic theories hold for European IP law.[45] With respect to their explanatory value, one can point to the diverse theoretical accounts of IP supported by the EU legislature and Court of Justice, illustrated earlier. In addition, there is the consistent emphasis by the Court of Justice on a range of EU legal principles when interpreting IP measures, from competition and free movement principles to the range of fundamental rights recognized in the CFR, building on the ECHR. This is perhaps most apparent in the

---

[42] A.S. Weinrib, 'Information and Property' (1988) 38 *University of Toronto Law Journal* 117.

[43] See, e.g., D.B. Resnik, 'A Pluralistic Account of Intellectual Property' (2003) 46 *Journal of Business Ethics* 319; R.P. Merges, *Justifying Intellectual Property* (Harvard University Press, 2011).

[44] N. MacCormick, 'Beyond the Sovereign State' (1993) 56 *Modern Law Review* 1. See further G. Itzcovich, 'Legal Order, Legal Pluralism, Fundamental Principles. Europe and Its Law in Three Concepts' (2012) 18 *European Law Journal* 358.

[45] J. Pila, 'Principles, Proportionality and Pluralism' (2014) 34 *OJLS* 181.

European law regarding the public policy exclusions from patentability which Member States must recognize, and the exceptions and limitations to copyright and related rights infringement which they may recognize. Indeed, and as we will see in our discussion of copyright exceptions and limitations particularly, in Chapter 13, IP law is increasingly cast by the EU as a means by which general legal principles, including especially those relating to fundamental rights and interests, can and are required to be balanced. These include the right to the protection of IP itself, the right to freedom of expression and education, and also other interests derived from fundamental rights such as the interest not to be associated with discriminatory messages (by means, e.g., of a racial, gendered, or religious parody). Casting copyright law in this way may be said to promote the EU's harmonization agenda by diverting attention away from the 'deep' normative question of why we give authors property rights (on which, and as we saw in Chapter 1, European states have historically disagreed) towards the mid-level principles and values on which the EU legal order is said to be based. It also establishes a division of labour between the EU and Member States, whereby the EU establishes certain ground rules for balancing the relevant competing rights and interests, and individual states proceed to balance them (within limits) as they see fit. As in all contexts, the effect is to connect and embed substantive rules of IP to and in the basic values of the European community as expressed in its constitutive legal instruments, and thereby to support a view of IP in general as serving Europe and European citizens—among other things, through the promotion and protection of fundamental rights and other EU general legal principles—and, conversely, as served by European legal harmonization and integration initiatives.

3.8 Case Study I: The Term of Copyright and Related Rights Protection

As we have seen, pluralistic accounts of IP tend to emphasize the substantive differences between regimes, suggesting the inappropriateness of any 'one size fits all' account of IP. Even in the context of specific regimes, however, foundational theories are sometimes of ambivalent utility beyond explaining or justifying a regime's existence. To some extent this is due to the limited guidance value of the theories themselves. However, it can also be a function of IP rules, and the opacity of the aims and values underpinning them. A good example is the rules governing the duration of copyright and related rights.

When calculating the term of IP protection it is always necessary to consider two things: the point at which the protection attaches to the relevant subject matter, and the period of time for which it remains attached. Under EU law, the terms of copyright and related rights are calculated differently, consistent with the different nature and purpose of the rights. As we will see in Section 11.6.1, the default position for authorial works is that they attract copyright protection automatically upon creation; though in some Member States the date of their creation is defined to mean the date of their material fixation. Nonetheless, the principle remains that the term of copyright for authorial works is calculated from the point at which the individual work is deemed to have come into existence and not, for example, from the time at which it is made available to the public, supporting a view of copyright as a right of authors rather than a privilege granted to them by the state. Under Article 1(1) Term Directive, copyright in the work then lasts 'for the life of the author and for 70 years after his death', or where there is more than one author, for 70 years after 'the death of the last surviving author' (Article 1(2))—calculated in all cases from the first day of January of the following year (recital 14). This is true even if it is the work's place of first publication which establishes the connection between it and the EU required to bring it without the scope of European copyright (see Section 11.6).

The Term Directive has been among the most controversial of EU measures in the copyright and related rights field. One reason is its effect in having revived copyright and related rights in works and subject matter that had entered the public domain but for which the new term of protection had not yet expired. That effect was confirmed by the Court of Justice in Case C–60/98 *Butterfly Music Srl v Carosello Edizioni Musicali e Discongrafiche Srl (CEMED)* [1999] ECR I-3939, subject to the obligation of Member States under the transitional provisions of the Directive 'to adopt measures to protect acquired rights of third parties' ([23] and [27]). Another reason, however, is the view of many that the Term Directive owes its existence to the lobbying efforts of corporate interests rather than matters of policy, and that it benefits such interests at the expense of individual authors and performers. This view can be seen in the Belgian response to the 2011 extension of related rights protection for performance fixations as follows (Inter-institutional File: 2008/0157 (COD)):

> Belgium believes that a term extension is not an appropriate measure to improve the situation of the performing artists. Furthermore, we believe that the negative consequences the proposal entails do not outweigh the advantages it brings. We can therefore not support this proposal.
>
> It seems that the measure will mainly benefit record producers and not performing artists, will only have a very limited effect for most of the performing artists, will have a negative impact on the accessibility of cultural material such as those contained in libraries and archives, and will create supplementary financial and administrative burdens to enterprises, broadcasting organisations and consumers. Therefore, the overall package of the proposal appears, as demonstrated by a large amount of academic studies, unbalanced.
>
> Finally, one has to observe that several initiatives which have clear links with and impact on the proposal, have recently been adopted or announced by the Commission in its Communication of 24 May 2011. These initiatives include for example a proposal for a directive on orphan works, a new initiative on collective management, and a new initiative on online distribution of audiovisual works. Taking into account this global approach of copyright issues in the internal market, we think that it would only be reasonable to re-examine the merits of this proposal in the context of this global approach.

One would expect the provisions of the Term Directive regarding the duration of copyright and related rights to reflect the justificatory basis of those rights, and the considerations that drive their recognition and protection by EU law. For example, and as noted already, if copyright existed to protect authors from personal harm, consistent with the arguments from personhood discussed previously, one would expect it to last only as long as the author's life. By contrast, if copyright were granted in recognition of the value of authorial works, the labour which their creation entails, or the special needs of authors by reason of that creation, one would expect its duration to reflect the measure of that value or labour, or the nature of authors' special needs. And finally, if the justification for copyright were the pursuit of certain public benefits—such as incentivizing the creation and dissemination of authorial works, or increasing the efficiency of the market for such works—one would expect it to last for as long as necessary to secure those public benefits. Only on the first of these understandings of copyright's justificatory basis would its duration be easy to calculate, however: copyright ought to last for the life of the author, and not one day past the author's death. Hence the question remains, if not to protect the personhood of individual creators, what is the most convincing explanation for the duration of copyright?

Aside from the lobbying efforts of corporate interests, two plausible explanations are revealed by the recitals of the Term Directive. The first is a concern to recognize and provide for authors' special needs, consistent with the third argument from desert considered earlier, and the second is a bid to encourage authors to create and third parties to invest in the production and dissemination of their creations. Support for the first of these might be read in recital 6, which provides as follows:

> The minimum term of protection laid down by the Berne Convention, namely the life of the author and 50 years after his death, was intended to provide protection for the author and the first two generations of his descendants. The average lifespan in the Community has grown longer, to the point where this term is no longer sufficient to cover two generations.

Implicit in the EU's acceptance of the Berne term of protection (adjusted to take account of increased life expectancy) is its concern to enable authors to support themselves and their families. One obvious possible explanation for this concern is a belief that authors' need to support themselves and their families is created by their authorial activities. That is not the only explanation available, however. For example, another might be that authors *believe* they need this, and that giving them what they believe they need will benefit society by encouraging them to continue their authorial activities. As an extension of this instrumentalist argument, we might further explain the effect of an extended term of copyright in encouraging third parties to invest in the production and dissemination of a greater number and wider diversity of authorial works, for example by helping publishers to balance their unsuccessful publishing ventures with their successful ones, and in doing so to ensure the publication of works unlikely to secure a strong financial return. On this view, an extended copyright term increases the diversity (rather than merely the number) of authorial works available to the public, and thereby promotes a cultured and pluralistic society of benefit to all. Support for this reading of the copyright term of life of the author plus 70 years is provided by recitals 11 and 12 of the Directive:

> The level of protection of copyright and related rights should be high, since those rights are fundamental to intellectual creation. Their protection ensures the maintenance and development of creativity in the interest of authors, cultural industries, consumers and society as a whole.
>
> In order to establish a high level of protection which at the same time meets the requirements of the internal market and the need to establish a legal environment conducive to the harmonious development of literary and artistic creation in the Community, the term of protection for copyright should be harmonized at 70 years after the death of the author or 70 years after the work is lawfully made available to the public...

Included among 'the requirements of the internal market' referred to in recital 12 are the need for consistent laws to promote the free movement of goods and services and undistorted competition (recital 2) discussed earlier and in Section 2.4.2.1, as well as—of crucial importance—'[d]ue regard for established rights', consistent with the general EU legal principle of legitimate expectations. As recital 10 of the Directive makes clear, it was at least partly with a view to maintaining 'the protection enjoyed by rightholders in the Community before the entry into force of [the] Directive'—protection which in some states had been calculated with reference to short-term economic and political factors specific to those states, such as the effects of the world wars on the exploitation of authors' works (see recital 7)—that the term of author's life plus 70 years was adopted. Given this especially, one must include general principles and pragmatism as factors in any account of the reasons for the current copyright term.

Another point of note regarding the formal explanation of the term of copyright offered in the recitals of the Term Directive is the absence of any reference to the EU legislature's consideration of the public harms that an extended period of copyright creates, and of the idea of copyright as the product of a balancing exercise informed by principles of distributive justice. Of especial importance among such public harms are the additional deadweight losses and restraints on freedoms that the public must bear as a result of copyright being extended, and the further scope for litigation due to the obscurity of the property comprising copyright and increased difficulty over time of tracing its ownership in the absence of any public register of rights. Also important is the so-called public backlash that extended copyright protection can trigger; a point first made by Lord Macaulay in response to the 19th-century proposal to extend English copyright protection beyond the life of the author (see Section 10.4.2). Given the absence of any reference to such considerations, we must assume that the term of 70 years *post mortem auctoris* was adopted by EU lawmakers without regard to any impacts on the public beyond those referred to in recitals 11 and 12. On any of the theoretical accounts of IP discussed above, this is cause for concern.

3.9 Case Study II: Biotechnology Patenting

As we saw in Section 3.8, the term of copyright and related rights protection illustrates the limited utility of foundational theories of IP due in part to the limited guidance values of those theories and in part to the opacity of substantive IP rules themselves. By contrast, a study of judicial perspectives on biotechnology patenting illustrates the analytical value of different theoretical frameworks when thinking about IP, including as a means of elucidating its substantive rules and the values underpinning and driving their development.

Biotechnology is the field of technology concerned with biological material, i.e. and as defined by Article 2(1)(a) Biotech Directive, 'material containing genetic information and capable of reproducing itself or being reproduced in a biological system'. Biotechnology patenting involves the patenting of products and processes in this field, including in particular any 'product consisting of or containing biological material or [any] process by means of which biological material is produced, processed or used' (Article 3(1) Biotech Directive). Such products might in principle include isolated human genes as well as stem cells, both of which have potential use in therapeutic treatments.

The patenting of human DNA sequences and stem cells has been among the most controversial of IP issues in recent years. Often described as the recipe of life, DNA (deoxyribonucleic acid) molecules such as that shown in Figure 3.2 contain the instructions that an organism needs to develop, live, and reproduce. They support a variety of technologies, including gene therapy, which involves the removal of a gene from one organism and its insertion (sometimes with modification) into another (genetically modified) organism where it can express the particular trait which it encodes. Of especial use in gene therapy are stem cells, which can also be removed from a human, for example, and inserted into another human in order to facilitate the process of delivering a gene, including by obviating the need for its repeated insertion. There are different types of stem cells, including neural (adult) and embryonic stem cells, each of which have their own particular therapeutic qualities and uses.

The very nature of biological material suggests two reasons that biotechnological products and processes might require special consideration in patent law. The first is

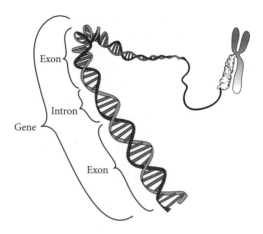

Figure 3.2 The coding region in a segment of eukaryotic DNA

uncertainty regarding their status as intellectual products, and the second is uncertainty regarding the ethical and public policy implications of recognizing property rights in respect of them. In fact, it is precisely these two issues that have occupied most of the discussion concerning biotechnology patenting to date. In this section we consider four responses to these issues offered by specialist and superior generalist tribunals. We then consider what if any insights can be gleaned from those responses regarding the nature and normative underpinnings of IP rights, the role of deontological and instrumentalist reasoning in IP cases, and the significance of appeals to fundamental rights such as human dignity in the field of IP.

3.9.1 Judicial Perspectives on Biotechnology Patenting

The four responses to biotechnology patenting that we consider in this section are: the 1969 decision of the Bundesgerichtshof (German Federal Supreme Court) in *Red Dove* [1969] *GRUR* 672, [1970] *IIC* 136; the 1994 decision of the Opposition Division of the European Patent Office (EPO) in *HOWARD FLOREY/Relaxin* [1995] EPOR 541 (*Howard Florey*); the 2011 decision of the Court of Justice of the EU in Case C–34/10 *Brüstle v Greenpeace eV* [2011] ECR I-9821; and the 2013 decision of the US Supreme Court in *Association for Molecular Pathology (AMP) v Myriad Genetics Inc.*, 133 S Ct 2107 (2013).

3.9.1.1 *Red Dove* (German Federal Supreme Court, 1969)

Red Dove involved a method of breeding 'a more beautiful dove' by a combination of breeding and selection steps.[46] According to the court, the method's ability to support a patent was to be decided as for all other methods, without any consideration being given to its biological nature. The question thus depended on whether the method was an invention (intellectual product) in the form of 'an instruction to be executed' (1 *IIC* 136, 140), namely, and as defined by the court, a 'teaching to methodically utilize controllable natural forces to achieve a causal, perceivable result' that could be repeated 'an arbitrary number of times obtaining the same result each time' (138 and 140). The court held that it was not, since repeating the method's steps could not be guaranteed to result in production of

---

[46] For a definition of the subject matter for which a patent was sought see [1970] *IIC* 136, 136.

the dove. Given this, the only advance on general knowledge represented by the method was 'the once achieved resulting product' (136 and 141). To allow a patent for the method in these circumstances would, it was held, 'produce a true monopoly on the product itself', which is a 'type of monopoly... foreign to patent law' (141).

3.9.1.2 *Howard Florey* (EPO, 1994)

The second case to be considered is *Howard Florey*, which involved an isolated human gene encoding for human H2-relaxin that involved the removal of tissue from a pregnant woman. The question was again one of patentability, which in this case was decided affirmatively. In the EPO's decision, the gene had been isolated from its natural surroundings by a developed process, giving it identifiable human creators (i.e. its isolators), and could be properly characterized by its structure, giving it an objectively discernible form. Moreover, in the EPO's assessment it was 'perfectly justified to grant broad protection' beyond the method of isolation to the isolated gene itself 'in view of the fact that H2-relaxin [had] been made available to the public for the first time' (548).

Having established its prima facie suitability for patent protection, the EPO in *Howard Florey* was required to address the opponents' arguments that to grant a patent for the isolated gene would offend morality and public policy by:

(a) making use of pregnancy for a technical process oriented towards profit;

(b) supporting the dismembering of women and their piecemeal sale to commercial enterprises throughout the world; and

(c) enabling the patenting/ownership of human life.

The EPO paid short shrift to each argument. In its decision, there could be no question of human dignity violations, since the women had consented to the removal of their tissue, and reproduction of the invention would not require further acts of removal (since it could be achieved by chemical synthesis of the existing DNA fragment). Similarly, since women ceased to be involved after providing their tissue, there could be no infringement of their human right to self-determination. And finally, since genes are chemical substances that carry genetic information and can be used as an intermediate in the production of therapeutically useful proteins, protecting them by patents could not be equated with patenting life. In the EPO's analysis, the only situation in which a morality or public policy objection to patenting could succeed would be one in which there existed an 'overwhelming consensus' among European states that the patenting of human genes—including the use to that end of consensually detached human body parts—was 'abhorrent' (550). No such consensus had been established, however. On the contrary, 'the opinion of society on the question of patenting human genes' was described as 'complex and not yet definitively formed', and the EPO 'not the right institution to decide on fundamental ethical questions' (552).

3.9.1.3 *Brüstle v Greenpeace* (CJEU, 2011)

Markedly different from the reasoning of the EPO in *Howard Florey* is that of the Court of Justice in *Brüstle v Greenpeace*. This case involved stem cell cultures that had been developed for patients suffering from Parkinson's disease and the creation of which required the destruction of a blastocyst (a human embryo in the early stage of its development). The question of law was whether the cultures fell within the scope of a patentability exception covering 'uses of human embryos for industrial or commercial purposes' (Article 6(2)(c) Biotech Directive). The Court answered the question affirmatively, following an opinion of the Advocate General in which three points had been emphasized. The first was that the pursuit of economic objectives must not be 'at the cost of sacrificing the fundamental values of the Union' ([44]). The second was that human dignity applies to existing human persons *and* to the human body from the first stage in its development. And the third was that creation of the stem cell cultures required the isolation of the stem cells from the human embryo immediately after fertilization, which isolation destroyed the embryo. Given this, the Advocate General had stated, the cultures should be denied protection as involving uses of human embryos. If they were not, he implied, prisoners of war could be killed and their organs used for scientific experiments endorsed by the state through the grant of property rights ([106] and [107]).

While less alarmist in its reasoning, the Grand Chamber's decision followed a similar pattern. Thus, it held that the legislative reference to 'human embryo' must be interpreted expansively in the light of the exclusion's basis in human dignity to include any organism that commences the process of development into a human being. The fact that the cultures here were intended for use exclusively in research was irrelevant: the mere fact of obtaining a patent indicated a use for industrial or commercial purposes.

3.9.1.4 *AMP v Myriad* (US Supreme Court, 2013)

This leads us to the fourth and final case of *AMP v Myriad*, which involved isolated breast cancer (BRCA1 and BRCA2) genes possessed by 1 to 2 per cent of women from certain ethnic groups in the United States, of whom 50 to 80 per cent can expect to develop breast cancer (and 20 to 50 per cent to develop ovarian cancer). The question of law was whether the isolated genes were inventions (in the language of US patents legislation, new compositions of matter) for which property rights might validly be granted. And according to the Supreme Court, they were not. In its decision, isolated DNA sequences are products of nature, i.e. products that differ insufficiently from their native counterparts to be regarded as new compositions of matter. The result was to reverse the decision of the Federal Circuit that isolating a gene involves 'the work of human transformation, requiring skill, knowledge, and effort' to 'reduc[e] a portion of nature to concrete form' (*Association for Molecular Pathology v US Patent & Trademark Office*, 689 F3d 1303, 1328, 1331 (Fed. Cir. 2012)).

3.9.1.5 Conclusions

Considered together, the four cases discussed in the previous section reveal different perspectives on the question whether genetic material is suitable for protection by property rights. The implication of *Red Dove* is that it is so appropriate, provided that the state declares it to be thus, and that the material in question is the product of a 'technical teaching'. The reason suggested by the court was that since living matter has the physical properties of other material phenomena and is subject to the same physical and chemical (scientific) laws, it should be subject to the same patent principles. So too *Howard Florey* supports the patenting of genetic material provided it has been isolated from its natural environment, on the ground that such material is a chemical substance of use to society the protection of which by property rights cannot be said to offend human dignity, the right to self-determination, or morality in general. Contrasting with these decisions is that of *Brüstle*, that genetic material the derivation of which involves the use or destruction of an organism capable of developing into a human being may not be protected by property in the interests of human dignity including—in the opinion of the Advocate General—the interests of discouraging the forced extraction of human organs. And finally there is the finding in *AMP v Myriad*, that isolated genetic material which is physically similar to the material in its natural environment is not a human creation and therefore incapable of supporting property rights. The question that thus arises is what if anything these different judicial perspectives on the patenting of biotechnology signify for our theoretical discussion in the earlier sections of this chapter .

3.9.2 Insights From Judicial Perspectives on Biotech Patenting

In considering this question it is useful to analyse each of the decisions in terms of three questions. The first is what was the specific intellectual product in respect of which property rights were held or alleged to subsist, and the source of its expressive or informational significance. The second is why the relevant product was held to merit or not to merit the protection of property rights. And the third is what if any account the court took in reaching its decision of the wider ethical or public policy implications of recognizing property rights in respect of the relevant product.

3.9.2.1 The Intellectual Product and its Expressive or Informational Significance

Four different views emerge from the cases regarding the intellectual product at issue and its expressive or informational significance. According to the reasoning of *Red Dove*, in the case of a method for producing a living organism, it is the method and not the resulting organism that is the intellectual product, since it is the method that signifies the technical teaching. By contrast, in *Howard Florey* the EPO accepted that the intellectual product could be the living matter itself (the isolated human gene), since it signified a teaching in the form of instructions for producing a valuable protein. This reasoning was rejected in *AMP*, which held that isolated genes are too similar to their native counterparts to be regarded as human creations, and thus as intellectual products. And finally, the basis for the *Brüstle* decision was an understanding of the stem cell cultures *qua* intellectual products as constituted in part by their history of creation, and as consequently 'remembering' and signifying the destruction of the human embryo which that creation had entailed.

3.9.2.2 Why the Intellectual Product Did or Did Not Merit Protection

Once again, different views emerge from the cases regarding the reason that the intellectual product merited or did not merit protection. According to the reasoning of *Red Dove*, consistent with a desert or instrumentalist view of IP rights, a person who offers the world a technical teaching is appropriately rewarded with a patent for that teaching, extending potentially (and in the discretion of the state) to its results. In *Howard Florey* the EPO adopted a similar position, suggesting that a person who first isolates a gene of use to society should be rewarded with a patent for the resulting gene whether on natural law or instrumentalist grounds. By contrast are the implications of *AMP*, that to recognize property rights in respect of a product of nature would represent a form of unjust enrichment, and that normative arguments for protection are inapplicable in the absence of an act of human creation. And finally there remains the suggestion of the Advocate General and the Grand Chamber in *Brüstle v Greenpeace*, that instrumentalist arguments of the type deployed in *Howard Florey* are inappropriate and/or displaced where considerations of human dignity are engaged.

3.9.2.3 The Account Taken of the Ethical and Public Policy Implications of Granting the Patent

Finally we come to the third of the issues, regarding the account taken of the ethical and public policy implications of granting the patent, where the divergence in views reflected persists. In *Red Dove*, no account of the consequences or implications of granting property rights was taken. Instead, the case was treated as raising only the question whether the dove was the product of a technical teaching so as to be capable of supporting a patent on the principles developed and applied in other technical fields. In *Howard Florey*, on the other hand, the value of the product which the applicant had made available to the public was emphasized. In addition, arguments regarding the effect of granting the patent in enabling scientists to control others' bodies and supporting certain narratives regarding the commodification of women and life were emphatically dismissed as unfounded. Different again was the approach in the *Brüstle* case, where the Advocate General and the Grand Chamber emphasized the risk that granting the patent would encourage certain undesirable behaviour (e.g. killing prisoners to extract their body parts and destroying human life in its earliest stages) and express the state's endorsement of that behaviour and its results. And finally, in *AMP*, the US Supreme Court gave no consideration to the implications of its decision beyond those implicit in the grant of a patent for a product of nature contrary to established principles of US patent law.

From this summary of the four decisions involving the patenting of biological material it is possible to gain some insight into the nature and normative basis of IP rights, the type of reasoning deployed in IP cases, and what appeals to fundamental rights might signify. To begin with the last of these: one thing clearly signified by appeals to human dignity in the patent field is a concern to take express account of (certain) ethical and public policy considerations, including the effect of granting patents in endorsing the unethical behaviour potentially involved in creating the intellectual product, as well as the use of that product as a means of generating private wealth, and thereby promoting class, ethnic, and gender inequalities. This is apparent from *Howard Florey* and *Brüstle* particularly. In addition, such appeals can be seen to signify a concern to ensure that these considerations are prioritized by decision-makers. In this regard, the style of reasoning in *Howard Florey* and *Brüstle* invites comparison. In *Howard Florey*, the EPO's belief in the value of biotechnology seemed to leave little room for arguments of the type which the opponents raised, and to be partly responsible at least for its narrow view of the morality/public policy carve-out from patent protection. Diametrically opposed to this was the view of the Court in *Brüstle* that the exception needed to be interpreted expansively, in the context of biotechnology particularly, and having regard to the principle of human dignity underpinning it. In its decision, such was the immorality of the product, and of the types of behaviour that patenting it might encourage, that their benefits to medicine were seemingly irrelevant. Different again was the view in *AMP v Myriad*, that the absence of any act of human creation left no room for the conferral of property rights; just as in *Red Dove* the existence of a technical teaching would have sufficed to justify such rights as the state had defined.

The decision in the *Brüstle* case has been described as 'a triumph of deontological reasoning'.[47] So too, however, the other decisions can be read in deontological terms. This is underlined by two remarks that were made by Jessica Giles following the *Brüstle* case. In the first she posed the rhetorical question '[i]f God created and sustains the world, how can humankind ever claim to have "invented" that creation by simply discovering how it works?'[48] And in the second she stated that '[j]ustice in any society can be measured by the ways in which it treats its weakest. Human embryos fall into the category of the weak and vulnerable, and therefore require special

---

[47] J. Giles, 'The *Brüstle* and *Eli Lilly* Cases: Creation—God or Humankind?' (2012) 1 *Oxford Journal of Law and Religion* 518, 521.

[48] ibid 523.

protection.'[49] Both remarks draw attention to the impact of *Brüstle* and *AMP* in supporting certain views regarding the origins of the world and human life, consistent with the reported origins of dignity as a human right in the values of political Catholicism.[50] This may be contrasted with the approach of *Howard Florey*, and the EPO's emphatic rejection of human dignity objections in that case as satisfied by donor consent. Implicit in that rejection is a view of dignity as at most justifying the recognition of a right of an individual to prevent others from interfering with her freedom and well-being, and as not extending to a duty not to subject human beings to instrumentalist, including profit-motivated, treatment.[51] This distinction between a rights- and duty-led conception of human dignity has been emphasized by Deryck Beyleveld and Roger Brownsword.[52] According to the first conception, associated by the authors with Kantian moral theory, dignity represents an injunction against 'instrumentalisation', translating to a duty not to treat persons as mere things rather than autonomous ends or agents. According to the second, associated with the moral theory of Alan Gewirth, dignity represents a right to prevent others from compromising our own dignity and in doing so from compromising our freedom and well-being, translating to a duty not to do anything to which a person does not freely consent that might compromise her dignity. As the authors note, the EPO's support in *Howard Florey* for a Gewirthian view of human dignity is apparent from its suggestion that no action to which a person freely consents could compromise her dignity. Thus, provided a person freely consents to donating her genetic material for use, neither such use nor the isolation of that material can violate her human rights.

Three issues are central to the cases above. The first is what (deontological and instrumentalist) considerations ought to be relevant when deciding whether to grant property in respect of biological material. The second is how much weight ought to be given to those considerations, including when if ever (and what kind of) instrumentalist considerations ought to be given normative priority vis-à-vis deontological ones. And the third and closely related issue is what if any impact the considerations raised by the opponents in *Howard Florey* and accepted by the Advocate General and the Court in *Brüstle* ought to have in decisions regarding biotechnology patenting. In their responses to these issues the courts surveyed could be said to support different understandings of the nature and purpose of IP rights, the relationship between law and ethics, and even the nature and origins of life.

3.10 Conclusions

Several conclusions may be drawn from this discussion of IP theories. One is the close connection that exists between understandings of the purpose of a law and the values that underpin and drive its development. Another is the impossibility of understanding any law in a vacuum, independent of such understandings. This is especially true for European law, which will often be drafted by committees not all the members of which speak the same native language or are versed in the same semantic conventions,

---

[49] ibid.

[50] See S. Moyn, 'The Secret History of Constitutional Dignity' (2014) 17 *Yale Human Rights and Development Journal* 2. For other perspectives see C. McCrudden, *Understanding Human Dignity* (OUP, 2013).

[51] Giles (n 47) 521.

[52] D. Beyleveld and R. Brownsword, 'Human Dignity, Human Rights and Human Genetics' (1998) 61 *Modern Law Review* 661.

and which exist in different language versions, all equally authentic. In these circumstances particularly, there is an especial need for interpretative and analytical methods focused on the underlying purpose and context of specific legal rules, including the nature and objectives of the European legal order of which they form of a part. That need has been fully recognized by the courts, including the Court of Justice.[53] Hence the fundamental questions of how to identify that purpose and context, and of how EU institutions themselves identify it and allow their understandings of it to inform the development of specific IP rules. To a large extent this book is concerned with answering these questions.

Understanding the purpose of a law and the values that underpin and drive its development is essential to understanding the law more generally. This is particularly true in the IP field, where the growing importance of IP rights to business and the economy, and their increasingly expansive scope and impact on citizens' lives due to developing technologies, have put them more and more in conflict with fundamental rights. Given this especially, it is essential that one has a framework and reference points for thinking critically about the nature and development of IP law, both as a body of interconnected rules and as a mechanism by which the lives of individuals and communities are regulated and affected. A central function and value of the various theoretical accounts of IP considered in this chapter is to provide such frameworks and reference points, and in doing so to facilitate critical reflection on different aspects of European law and decision-making and their coherence *inter se*. As the discussions of the term of copyright and related rights protection and biotechnology patenting demonstrate, this is the case notwithstanding the ambivalent guidance value of individual theories and their inability to account for substantive IP rules in all their detail.

Further Reading

BECKER, L.C., 'Deserving to Own Intellectual Property' (1993) 68 *Chicago-Kent Law Review* 609

CALABRESI, G. AND MELAMED, A.D., 'Property Rules, Liability Rules, and Inalienability: One View of the Cathedral' (1972) 85 *Harvard Law Review* 1089

DRAHOS, P., *A Philosophy of Intellectual Property* (Dartmouth, 1996)

FRANCIONI, F., *Biotechnologies and International Human Rights* (Hart Publishing, 2007)

GOLDSTEIN, P., 'Copyright' (1992) 55 *Law and Contemporary Problems* 79

GORDON, W.J., 'On Owning Information: Intellectual Property and the Restitutionary Impulse' (1992) 78 *Virginia Law Review* 149

GRAY, K., 'Property in Thin Air' (1991) 50 *Cambridge Law Journal* 252

LANDES, W.M. AND POSNER, R.A., *The Economic Structure of Intellectual Property Law* (Harvard University Press, 2003)

LEHMANN, M., 'The Theory of Property Rights and the Protection of Intellectual and Industrial Property' (1985) 16 *IIC* 525

MENELL, P.S., 'Intellectual Property: General Theories' (2000) 2 *Encyclopedia of Law and Economics* 129 http://levine.sscnet.ucla.edu/archive/ittheory.pdf

MERGES, R.P., *Justifying Intellectual Property* (Harvard University Press, 2011)

---

[53] See, e.g., Case C–283/81 *Srl CILFIT and Lanificio di Gavardo SpA v Ministry of Health* [1982] ECR 3415 [17]–[20].

PALMER, T.G., 'Are Patents and Copyright Morally Justifiable?' (1990) 13 *Harvard Journal of Law & Public Policy* 817

PLANT, A., 'The Economic Theory Concerning Patents for Inventions' (1934) 1 *Economica* 30

RADIN, M.J., 'Property and Personhood' (1982) 34 *Stanford Law Review* 957

RESNIK, D.B., 'A Pluralistic Account of Intellectual Property' (2003) 46 *Journal of Business Ethics* 319

SCHECHTER, F.I, 'The Rational Basis of Trade Mark Protection' (1926–27) 40 *Harvard Law Review* 813

PART II

The Law of Patents and Allied Rights

4

Introduction to European Patent Law

4.1 Introduction

Patents are limited-term monopoly rights granted in respect of new, inventive, and industrially applicable inventions. In Europe today they are granted by individual states to inventors, and confined in effect to the territory of the granting state. However, both the means for obtaining national patents and the law regulating national patent grants have been extensively harmonized by a combination of EU and non-EU measures. As a result, it is now easier than ever before to obtain patent protection for an invention in more than one country, and there are also comparatively few differences in the substantive patent laws of European states. Nonetheless, the territorial restrictions on domestic patent grants, combined with the absence of a European patent tribunal exercising exclusive jurisdiction with respect to European patent matters, makes the persistence of some differences in both the laws of individual states and the manner of their application in particular cases inevitable. In addition, there remain inefficiencies and costs for those seeking protection for their inventions in several countries. These facts alone explain the ongoing efforts to create a unitary patent and unified patent litigation system for Europe, culminating most recently in the so-called Unitary Patent Package of 2012/2013.

The challenges for the European patent system over the past 60 years have extended beyond harmonization and the creation of unitary rights and supporting procedural and litigation arrangements. For example, globalization and technological developments have changed the context in and range of subject matter for which patents are granted and exploited, increasing the value of patents and patent systems for business, governments, and the general public, and requiring patent offices and courts to deal with an increasing number of patent applications and cases of increasing scientific complexity. A second has been the emergence of new business practices requiring regulation, such as pharmaceutical companies seeking to extend the protection of their medicines, and companies acquiring patents for purely litigious purposes and without any intention of working the inventions to which they relate. Third, whereas historically a product or process would be protected by a single patent, the norm in some industries today is for hundreds and sometimes thousands of patents to protect different components of a single device or service, making it difficult for third parties to acquire the necessary rights in order to be able to use the underlying product or process. And finally, and as we saw in Section 3.9, the emergence of new biotechnology since the invention of genetic engineering in the 1970s has challenged the basic distinction between nature and artifice on which the patent systems of all jurisdictions depend, and given rise to a range of issues concerning the public policy implications of granting property rights in respect of subject matter incorporating biological material, including the biological material of developing countries and indigenous communities. Among other things, these effects of globalization and developing technologies have put the patent system in conflict with human rights and other public law principles, raising difficult issues regarding the relationship between IP and those principles, and increasing further the breadth and depth of expertise required of patent offices and courts.

In this chapter we begin our introduction to European patent law with a discussion of the nature of patents and the routes to obtaining patent protection in Europe. We then consider the existing European patent system established by the European Patent Convention 1973/2000, and the challenges presented to it by globalization and developing technology. Finally, we discuss the pursuit of a unitary patent system for Europe, and the features of the Unitary Patent Package currently proposed.

4.2 Patents for Inventions: An Overview

4.2.1 The Nature of Patents

The term 'patent' is an abbreviation of 'letters patent', the open form of document historically issued by the English Crown for the purpose of conferring a right or privilege or otherwise communicating the royal will. Today the term is used throughout the world to denote the species of IP right that is made by formal grant of a state or other political entity in return for the disclosure of a novel and inventive invention susceptible of industrial application. In Europe, the inventions for which a patent may be granted include any method or product that has technical character. To be patentable they must, by reason of their technical features specifically, represent an advance in the sense of something sufficiently different over what was previously available to the public (the state of the art). Applying these principles, mere discoveries, scientific theories, and business methods are not as such capable of supporting a patent. Also excluded from patentability on public policy grounds are surgical, therapeutic, and diagnostic methods, plant and animal varieties and essentially biological processes for producing plants and animals, and inventions the commercial exploitation of which would be contrary to *ordre public* (public policy) or morality.

Once granted, a patent confers a time-limited right on the patentee to prevent all others from doing certain acts in relation to the protected invention, such as making, disposing, offering, using, importing, or keeping the invention within the territory of the granting state. Patents do not confer any positive rights of use, such as the right to commercialize an invention, for which separate regulatory approval will often be required. Thus, obtaining a patent for a drug will not entitle the patentee to bring the drug to market. The grant of a patent is also no assurance of its legal validity, which can always be challenged before the courts by a defendant to an infringement action or by a third party.

The patent laws of all European states permit certain acts to be done in relation to inventions notwithstanding their protection by a patent, such as acts done privately for non-commercial purposes and certain experimental acts. The infringement of a patent can attract civil and criminal liability. Further, it is not a defence to infringement that the defendant independently devised the invention or was unaware of the existence of the patent; hence the strong monopoly-like protection that a patent confers. In certain circumstances, a person unable to obtain permission from a patentee to use a patented invention on reasonable terms may be able to obtain a compulsory licence of the patent from the patent-granting state.

As formal grants, patents for inventions must be sought from an authorized patent-granting authority. The task of such authorities is to examine the patent application to ensure that it relates to a patentable invention and that it complies with the formal requirements for a valid patent grant. Central in this regard is the requirement that a patent application contain a clear and concise definition of the invention (in the patent claims) and a description of the invention sufficient to enable a hypothetical skilled addressee to perform it. When examining patent applications, patent offices are required to search the state of the art in the field to which the claimed invention relates in order to be satisfied that it is new and sufficiently inventive to justify a monopoly grant. In fields such as biotechnology and information communications technology (ICT), determining novelty and inventiveness with confidence can be an extremely difficult task because of the technical complexity of the fields and the enormous volume of technical literature and other sources of available information regarding the art to which the invention relates (prior art). Between one and two years after they are filed, patent applications are published and the details of the invention thereby made available to the public.

The description of the invention in the patent application is the consideration for which the patent is granted, and supports a conception of patents as contracts between a state and inventor (see Section 3.6). Thinking of patents in contractual terms is useful, among other reasons because it offers an analytical framework with reference to which different aspects of law and practice can be explained and assessed. For example, it is a fundamental principle of patent law that inventors define their inventions and corresponding patent monopolies themselves. As noted earlier, that definition is contained in the patent claims, and submitted to the relevant patent office as part of the inventor's patent application. On receipt of it, the patent office is charged with reviewing the definition and notifying the applicant of any changes required to ensure its compliance with patent legislation. The result is a process of negotiation between the inventor and the public, represented by the patent office, leading to the creation of a legally enforceable document that creates rights and obligations on the part of the negotiating parties. According to the terms of that document, the inventor agrees to make a new and otherwise meritorious invention available to the public in exchange for the public's agreement not to perform that invention for a limited period. By thus undertaking to limit its freedom in the short term, the public secures the knowledge of and freedom to use the invention in the long term.

As with other contracts, therefore, patents are a means by which the law empowers individuals to create rights and obligations *inter se*. Several consequences can be said to flow from this. One is the appropriateness of interpreting patents in the same manner as other contracts are interpreted, i.e. having regard to their function of establishing legal rights and obligations as between the inventor and public. And another is the importance of ensuring that the rights derived by the inventor from the patent are proportionate having regard to the benefits which the patent confers on the public. As we will see in later chapters, these two principles are central to European patent law.

Drafting patent applications is a specialist skill of a patent agent, and is undertaken in the knowledge that the application will be read and assessed for validity adopting the perspective of a person skilled in the art to which the invention relates.

4.2.2 Routes to Obtaining Patents in Europe

In Europe currently there exist three routes by which patents may be obtained: a national route, regulated by domestic patent legislation; a European route, regulated by the supranational EPC; and an international route, regulated by the Patent Cooperation Treaty (PCT). To follow the national route, an applicant must apply to the patent office of the state in which protection is sought. To follow the European route, she must apply to the EPO or other EPC receiving office, designating in which of the currently 38 EPC Contracting States she would like protection, and thereafter seek validation of her grant in each designated state. And finally, to follow the international route, an applicant must apply to the WIPO or other PCT receiving office, designating in which of the currently 148 PCT states or regions shown in Figure 4.1 she would like protection, and thereafter pursue her application in the patent offices of each state or region.

Whichever of these national, European, or international routes is followed, the result will always be one or more national patents, conferring rights confined to the territorial boundaries of the granting state. Thus, while patents granted under the EPC are referred to as European patents, they take effect as bundles of national grants regulated by national law. Only if the unitary (EU) patent system currently proposed comes into being will it be possible to obtain a single grant that confers equal and uniform protection throughout the territories of several EU Member States (see Section 4.5).

Consistent with this overview, the European law of patents for inventions may usefully be divided into the following main aspects:

- the procedure for obtaining and maintaining (including renewing and amending) patent grants, and the persons entitled to obtain and maintain them;
- the criteria for patent protection, including the subject matter for which a patent may validly be granted; and

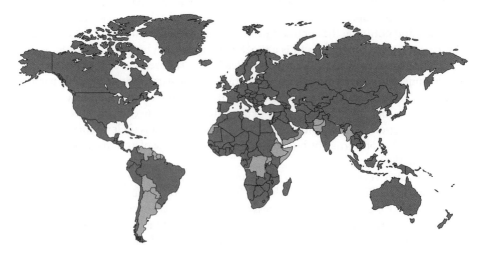

Figure 4.1 PCT Contracting States and regions

Image provided by WIPO © WIPO. The original work is in colour, and has been reproduced here in black and white.

- the nature and scope of the rights that a patent confers, including their duration, the requirements for their infringement, and the rules governing their exploitation.

In Chapters 5 to 8 we consider each of these aspects in turn. In Chapter 9 we consider certain other rights that are allied to patent rights, namely, *sui generis* plant variety rights and supplementary protection certificates. But first, we begin with an account of the emergence and development of the European patent field and some of the challenges that it currently faces.

4.3 The European Patent Convention 1973/2000

4.3.1 The Road to the European Patent Convention 1973

The earliest European initiatives in the patent field belong to the decades immediately before the Second World War, in the efforts of the Benelux countries (Belgium, the Netherlands, and Luxembourg) and France to create a supranational patent searching and examination body—the International Patent Institute in The Hague—and of Denmark, Finland, Norway, and Sweden to create a Nordic patent and patent system. Of more direct and enduring significance for Europe as a whole, however, were the post-war initiatives of the Council of Europe and EEC. The Council of Europe turned its attention to the creation of a European patent as early as 1949, the year it was established. Soon after it concluded the ECHR in 1950, recognizing the right of all natural and legal persons to the peaceful enjoyment of their possessions (Article 1 of Protocol 1), including, as the European Court of Human Rights (ECtHR) later confirmed (in *Anheuser-Busch Inc. v Portugal* [2007] ETMR 24 regarding trade mark applications), the peaceful enjoyment of their IP rights. The result of the Council's patent efforts more specifically was the conclusion of several conventions in the 1950s and 1960s, including the Strasbourg Patent Convention of 1963 (SPC). The SPC was the product of substantial work on the part of the Council's Committee of Experts on Patents, and represented an impressive agreement among represented European states on issues on which their national laws had previously diverged substantially, including the disclosure required for a valid grant, the criteria for protection (patentability), and the role of patent claims in defining the scope of the patent monopoly.

Next on the European patent scene were the EEC and its then six Member States, which in 1959 set their own sights on the creation of a European patent for the Community. Their efforts account for the second phase of work towards the EPC shown in Figure 4.2. Those efforts stalled in the 1960s, however, amidst various political controversies, including the veto by French President Charles de Gaulle of the UK's bid for EEC membership. When they resumed their work in 1969, it was with a new aim supplied by the European Free Trade Association (EFTA) of creating *two* European patents and patent systems: one for the EEC exclusively and another for a wider collection of European states. Working now with an expanded (EEC and non-EEC) membership, they concluded two conventions in the 1970s that expressed this aim: the EPC of 1973 and the Community Patent Convention (CPC) of 1975.

4.3.2 'A System of Law, Common to the Contracting States, for the Grant of Patents for Inventions'

The EPC was established as a special agreement within the meaning of Article 19 of the Paris Convention and a regional patent treaty within the meaning of Article 45(1)

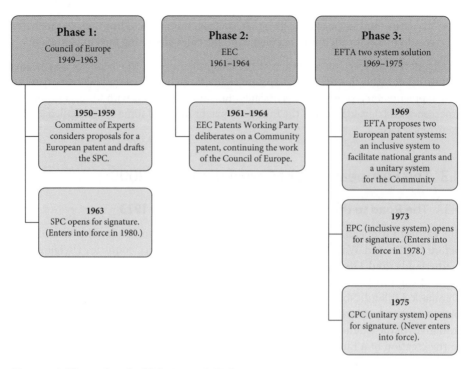

Figure 4.2 The road to the EPC 1973 and CPC 1975

of the PCT. Its Preamble describes its primary purpose as being 'to strengthen co-operation between the States of Europe in respect of the protection of inventions'. To that end it establishes 'a system of law, common to the Contracting States, for the grant of patents for inventions', and an organization—the European Patent Organisation (EP Organisation)—to administer it (Article 1). It was concluded in 1973 by 16 Contracting States and today has 38 Contracting States, including all 28 EU Member States plus (in the order of their accession) Switzerland, Liechtenstein, Monaco, Turkey, Iceland, Norway, Former Yugoslav Republic of Macedonia, San Marino, Albania, and Serbia. Two additional states—Montenegro and Bosnia and Herzegovina—have the status of so-called 'extension states', meaning that they recognize European patents on request.

The purpose of the system of law created by the EPC is to facilitate the grant of patents by its 38 Contracting States shown in Figure 4.3. Its substantive provisions build on those of the SPC, committing its Contracting States to tightened versions of the SPC provisions while also supplementing them with new provisions governing the grant of patents and method of interpreting patent claims. Given that European (EPC) patents take effect as bundles of national patents regulated domestically, provisions governing the content and exploitation of patent grants would be out of place in the EPC and are thus absent from it. The exceptions are Article 69, which establishes the role of patent claims in defining patent monopolies following Article 8(3) SPC, and Article 138, which limits the grounds on which a European patent may be revoked.

4.3.3 **The European Patent Organisation**

The structure of the EP Organisation is shown in Figure 4.4. The Organisation has its seat in Munich (Article 6), and comprises two organs: the EPO and the Administrative Council (Article 4(2)). The Council includes representatives from each of the EPC's 38

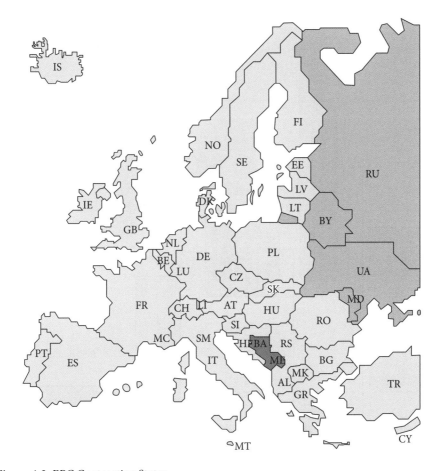

Figure 4.3 EPC Contracting States

Image provided by the EPO © EPO. The original work is in colour, and has been reproduced here in black and white.

Contracting States, and meets approximately four times a year. Its business is conducted in the three official languages of the EPO: English, French, and German (Article 16). It exercises a general supervisory power in respect of the EPO (Article 4(3)), as well as legislative powers (Article 33), and is also responsible for policy matters. It has legal personality and is represented by the President of the EPO (Article 5).

The EPO is responsible for the administration of the EPC on a day-to-day basis. It too is located in Munich, with an additional branch in The Hague (Article 6) and sub-offices in Berlin and Vienna (see Article 7). Its task is to grant European patents on behalf of the EP Organisation (Article 3(3)). To that end it has five first-tier administrative and legal arms—a Receiving Section and Search, Examining, Opposition, and Legal Divisions respectively—responsible for receiving European patent applications, conducting the background knowledge (prior art) searches necessary to examine the inventions to which those applications relate, examining the applications and inventions for compliance with the EPC, hearing third party oppositions to applications, and making decisions regarding entries in the Register of European Patents and the list of professional representatives (see Articles 16 to 20). In addition, the EPO includes Boards of Appeal responsible for hearing appeals from decisions of its first-tier arms, and constituted to that end by three legally qualified members (for appeals from decisions of the Receiving Section or Legal

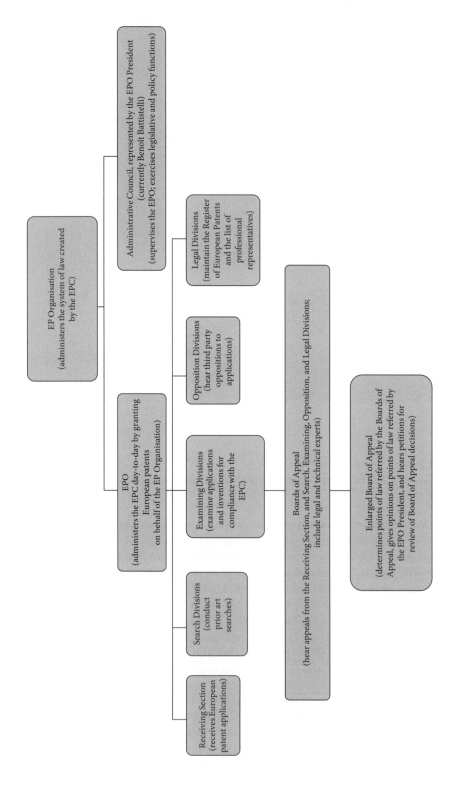

Figure 4.4 The EP Organisation

Division), a mix of three or five technically and legally qualified members and in some cases three legally qualified members (for appeals from decisions of the Examining Division), and a mix of three or five technically and legally qualified members (for appeals from decisions of the Opposition Division) (Article 21). And finally, the EPO includes an Enlarged Board of Appeal responsible for determining points of law referred by the Boards, for giving opinions on points of law referred by the EPO President, and for hearing petitions for review of a Board decision (Article 22).

4.3.4 **The Boards of Appeal**

Of especial importance among the institutions created by the EPC are the EPO's Boards of Appeal, including the Enlarged Board, which operate as European patent tribunals and which have primary responsibility for interpreting and applying the provisions of the EPC. An attempt to secure the independence of the Boards of Appeal is made in Article 23 EPC, which protects the tenure of Board members during their terms of appointment, prevents them from being members of the Receiving Section, Examining Divisions, Opposition Divisions, or Legal Division, and requires them to comply exclusively with the provisions of the EPC in reaching their decisions. Despite this, the Boards' location within the EPO deprives them of judicial independence, and for this reason represents a structural weakness of the system created by the EPC. This point has been made several times by parties appearing before the EPO's Enlarged Board of Appeal as a basis for disqualifying a Board member for conflict of interest, including successfully in R19/12 (*Ablehnung wegen Besorgnis der Befangenheit*) EP:BA:2014:R001912.20140425. It was also raised (unsuccessfully) before the CJEU by Spain in its constitutional challenge to the validity of the Unitary Patent Package in Case C–146/13 *Kingdom of Spain v European Parliament* EU:C:2015:298.

In R2/14 (*Objection to the Chairman and Members of the EBA*) [2015] EPOR 30, the Enlarged Board held that 'the inherent potential for "normative conflict"' between the administrative and judicial functions of the Chairman of the Boards of Appeal as appellate judge and EPO Vice-President under Article 11(2) and (3) EPC 'could only be resolved by institutional structural change by the European Patent Organisation' ([23]). A proposal for such change has been pending for several years. For example, in 2011 the EP Organisation published the following statement on its website.

> The *current legal position* is that the Boards of Appeal, together with their associated administrative services, are integrated into the European Patent Office as Directorate-General 3 (DG 3). However, the boards' administrative and organisational attachment to the EPO which is an administrative authority obscures their judicial nature and is not fully commensurate with their function as a judicial body.

In addition, in 2004 the President of the EPO proposed amending Article 4 EPC to give the Boards the status of a third organ of the EP Organisation (alongside the EPO and Administrative Council), and to make the Administrative Council's supervisory powers over them 'subject to judicial independence'.[1] At the same time the President proposed renaming the Boards 'the European Court of Patent Appeals' to underline their judicial character. While neither of these proposals was implemented, the EPO has recently published details of a further 'Proposal for a structural reform of the EPO Boards of Appeal' (CA/16/15) (6 March 2015)[2] by the President, aimed at

---

[1] Draft basic proposal for a revision of the EPC implementing the organisational autonomy of the Boards of Appeal of the European Patent Office within the European Patent Organisation, CA/46/04 (28 May 2004); see also CA/46/04 Corr 1 (9 June 2004).

[2] http://www.epo.org/modules/epoweb/acdocument/epoweb2/164/en/CA-16-15_en.pdf.

[increasing] the organisational and managerial autonomy of the [Boards of Appeal], the perception of their independence (enshrined in Article 23 EPC) and also their efficiency, in order to ensure the principle of effective legal protection within the current legal framework of the EPC.

This proposal follows a request by the Administrative Council of the EP Organisation triggered by the Enlarged Board's decision in R19/12, and is expected to lead to concrete proposals for institutional change following a public consultation which ended in June 2015.

4.3.5 The EPC 2000 Revisions

Since taking effect in 1978, the EPC has been revised twice: first in 1991 and again (and more substantially) in 2000. The stated aims of the 2000 revisions were: to modernize the system to take account of developments in international law (e.g. the introduction of the TRIPS Agreement); to satisfy the needs and expectations of its users, including by establishing a new centralized patent-limitation procedure before the EPO and enabling limited judicial review of Board of Appeal decisions; to introduce new procedures to help the EPO to meet its increased workload, such as the BEST (Bringing Search and Examination Together) system; to eliminate unnecessary regulatory requirements; and to move certain provisions of the EPC from the main text of the Convention to the Implementing Regulations and enable the EP Organisation to amend the Convention's substantive law provisions to avoid the need for a full diplomatic conference. The revisions took effect in December 2007, and entailed the following specific organizational, jurisdictional, and substantive changes to the Convention.

Organizational changes:

- transferring content from Articles to the Implementing Regulations and inserting Article 33(1)(b), empowering the Administrative Council to amend Parts II to VII and X of the Convention 'to bring them into line with an international treaty relating to patents or European Community legislation relating to patents';
- creating a Conference of Ministers drawn from Contracting States to meet every five years 'to discuss issues pertaining to the Organization and to the European patent system' (Article 4a);

Jurisdictional changes:

- conferring jurisdiction on the Enlarged Board of Appeal to hear petitions for review of Board of Appeal decisions on certain procedural grounds under a new Article 112a EPC.

Substantive law changes:

- amending Article 52 to confirm the availability of patents for inventions 'in all fields of technology', consistent with Article 27.1 of the TRIPS Agreement;
- transferring the medical methods exclusion from patentability from Article 52(4) to a new Article 53(c) so as to make it a stand-alone policy exclusion rather than an exclusion grounded in the requirement for susceptibility of industrial application;
- restricting the *ordre public*/morality exclusion of Article 53(a) to inventions 'the commercial exploitation of which would be contrary to *ordre public* or morality', as distinct from inventions 'the publication or exploitation of which' would be so contrary;

- inserting Article 54(5) EPC to permit protection for second and further medical uses of a known substance or composition;
- amending Article 54 to remove restrictions on the recognition of validly published European patent applications as forming part of the state of the art for subsequent European applications; and
- adding a new Article 2 to the Protocol on the Interpretation of Article 69 to require that 'due account…be taken of any element which is equivalent to an element specified in the claims' when determining the extent of protection conferred by a European patent.

These substantive law changes effected by the EPC 2000 revisions will be considered in the coming chapters.

4.4 The Challenges of Globalization and Developing Technology

4.4.1 Increasing Patent Activity Worldwide

Patent systems today remain markedly unchanged since the first (Venetian and English) patent statutes of the 15th and 17th centuries described in Section 1.2.2.2.2. By contrast, the social and economic context in which they operate has changed dramatically, including the technologies for which they are granted and the internationalism of the market. Some indication of this change can be gleaned from the workload of the EPO, including the number and nature of European (EPC) patents it grants. For example, by the end of 2005 the European Patent Office had granted 760,700 European patents, which it calculated as equivalent to 6.3 million national patents. In 2005 alone it received nearly 194,000 European patent applications, up 7.2 per cent from 2004, and made 53,300 European patent grants. In 2014, the EPO granted 64,613 European patents, 3.1 per cent less than in 2013, when it granted the highest number of patents ever in its history (66,700). Of the patents granted in 2014, the largest number (26 per cent) went to US companies, followed by 18 per cent to Japan. Next was Germany with 11 per cent, and France with 5 per cent. Of the patent applications filed with the EPO, the majority concerned medical technology (11,124 applications), followed by electrical machinery, apparatus, and energy (10,944 applications), digital communications (10,018 applications), and computer technology (9,869 applications). Biotechnology came 8th with 5,905 applications, and pharmaceuticals came 10th with 5,270 applications. The top applicants seeking protection in 2014 are shown in Figure 4.5.

4.4.2 Developing Technology and Expanding Patentability

4.4.2.1 Biotech and Pharmaceuticals: Gene Patents, Essential Medicines, and Patent Thickets

The grant of patents in the ICT, medical technology, and biotechnology fields in particular have posed significant challenges for the European patent system in recent decades. For example, the patenting of biotechnological inventions has undermined the basic distinction between nature and artifice on which the grant of patents for inventions depends. It has also raised difficult ethical issues regarding the appropriateness of granting property rights in respect of isolated genes and other human biological materials, and of encouraging the production of such things as genetically engineered animals for use in medical research. Similarly, the grant of patents for pharmaceuticals and

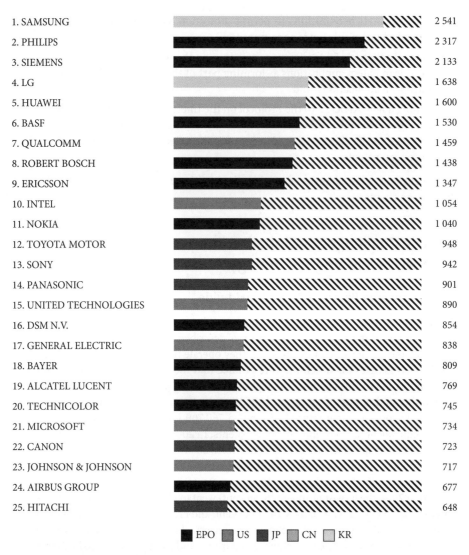

1. SAMSUNG	2 541
2. PHILIPS	2 317
3. SIEMENS	2 133
4. LG	1 638
5. HUAWEI	1 600
6. BASF	1 530
7. QUALCOMM	1 459
8. ROBERT BOSCH	1 438
9. ERICSSON	1 347
10. INTEL	1 054
11. NOKIA	1 040
12. TOYOTA MOTOR	948
13. SONY	942
14. PANASONIC	901
15. UNITED TECHNOLOGIES	890
16. DSM N.V.	854
17. GENERAL ELECTRIC	838
18. BAYER	809
19. ALCATEL LUCENT	769
20. TECHNICOLOR	745
21. MICROSOFT	734
22. CANON	723
23. JOHNSON & JOHNSON	717
24. AIRBUS GROUP	677
25. HITACHI	648

■ EPO   ■ US   ■ JP   ■ CN   □ KR

Figure 4.5 EPO patent filing table

Image provided by the EPO © EPO. The original work is in colour, and has been reproduced here in black and white.

medicines—prohibited in most European states before the introduction of the EPC—has brought patentees into conflict with individuals needing access to essential medicines protected by patent monopolies and offered at prices they cannot afford to pay. It has also created competition law issues in recent years, as several so-called 'blockbuster' medicines with annual global turnovers in excess of €0.8 billion have come to or approached the end of their patent terms at a time when, despite increasing investments in research and development, the number of new medicines reaching the market is decreasing. As noted by the European Commission in its *Pharmaceutical Sector Inquiry: Final Report* (8 July 2009), this has made originator drug companies increasingly dependent on the revenues generated by their existing products, and concerned to maintain those revenues for as long as possible. Various patenting strategies have been deployed to that end. One involves applying for several patents in respect of a single medicine, such as a product patent for the active substance comprising the medicine, a process patent for the method of producing the medicine, and a purpose-limited product patent for the medicine when used either for a different purpose or for the same purpose but via a different dosage regime. According to the Commission in its report, forming such 'patent thickets' in respect of a single product is a common practice in the pharmaceutical sector, and has as an important objective to delay or block the market entry of generic medicines, creating cost implications for the public and attracting the attention of competition authorities in Europe and elsewhere. As explained in the 'Citizens' summary of the findings' set out in [2.1.2] of the report:

> It takes too long for generic medicines to reach the market. On average, consumers wait 7 months for cheaper generic medicines to become available once patents for brand-name medicines expire. One reason is that drug companies use a variety of techniques to extend the commercial life of their medicines. When brand-names are forced to compete with generics, prices go down and more patients can be treated. The decreases can be quite substantial. For a sample of medicines we calculated that additional savings of 20% would have been possible if the generic version had become available immediately after the original patent expired.

The solution proposed by the Commission was to monitor practices in the pharmaceutical sector to obtain a fuller picture of the reason for the decline in innovation. In addition, the Commission suggested an urgent need for an EU patent and patent-litigation system to cut costs and improve efficiency for citizens and drug companies ([4.2]).

4.4.2.2 ICT Products: Patent Thickets and Trolls

Similar issues of obstructive patenting practices with a view to maximizing market exclusivity and revenues have arisen in the ICT sector, where it is not uncommon for telephones and other products to be protected by hundreds or even thousands of overlapping patents covering their various components, creating further thickets of monopoly rights through which it can be difficult for third parties to cut. In addition, there is an increasing practice in ICT and other industries of forming so-called patent trolls or non-producing entities (NPEs) to generate income by acquiring patents for the sole purpose of bringing infringement proceedings against alleged infringers without having any intention of producing or marketing the inventions to which the patents relate. In combination with the growing numbers of patent grants, the operation of these NPEs can be harmful to small and medium-sized enterprises (SMEs) particularly, for which the mere threat of litigation may be enough to persuade them to leave a market or desist from a particular line of research or development. One response to this problem in the European telecommunications industry has been the formation of the European Telecommunications Standards Institute (ETSI): an industry body that sets standards for the mobile phone industry and agrees on the specific technologies that are essential for meeting those standards. Any member that holds a patent in respect of an essential technology is then required to make it available for use by other industry participants on fair, reasonable, and non-discriminatory (FRAND) terms and conditions. These obligations are given teeth by the European Commission's monitoring of ETSI members' compliance with their commitments. For example, in 2012 the Commission announced an investigation into the series of actions brought by Samsung before EU Member State courts seeking injunctive relief for alleged infringements of patents previously declared essential for the implementation of certain European mobile telephony standards. The focus of that investigation was whether, in bringing the actions, Samsung had breached its commitment to ETSI to license any standard essential patents on FRAND terms in breach of European competition law. In December 2012, the Commission reached the preliminary view that Apple had been a willing licensee of Samsung's standard essential patents on FRAND terms and that, given this, Samsung's seeking of injunctions against Apple based on those patents in several EU Member States could constitute an abuse of a dominant position in breach of Article 102 TFEU (IP/12/1448 and MEMO/12/1021). In April 2014 it accepted commitments from Samsung not to seek further injunctive relief in Europe on the basis of its patents for smartphones and tablets against licensees who had committed to FRAND licensing terms (MEMO/14/322). In July 2015 the Commission's reading of Article 102 TFEU was supported in Case C–170/13 *Huawei Technologies Co. Ltd v ZTE Corp.* EU:C:2015:477. Citing the fundamental rights of patentees under Articles 17(2) and 47 CFR, and the need to balance them fairly with the legitimate interests of other parties, the Court affirmed that an application for injunctive and associated remedies by the owner of an SEP against a willing licensee could breach Article 102. In its decision, the owner of any SEP which has given an irrevocable undertaking to a standardization body such as ETSI to grant a licence to third parties on FRAND terms must, before bringing an action for infringement of the patent, attempt in good faith and in accordance with recognized commercial practices in the field to negotiate a licence with the alleged infringer on FRAND terms.

4.4.2.3 European Legal and Policy Commitments

As the discussion thus far illustrates, an important aspect of the context in which the challenges of developing technology and expanding patentability have been experienced in Europe is the EU and its legal and policy commitment to striking a fair balance between protecting citizens' fundamental rights to possess, use, and enjoy their property rights, including their patent monopolies in accordance with Article 17(2) CFR and Article 1 of Protocol 1 ECHR, and promoting competition and the free movement of goods and knowledge throughout EU territory in accordance with Articles 101, 102, and 34 to 36 TFEU. To this end the EU, building on the EPC, requires the recognition and protection of patents and patent applications as objects of property capable of being freely exploited throughout EU territory, while also imposing its own restrictions on that freedom, and encouraging patentees to exploit their rights in a manner that supports EU single market policies. Examples of restrictions imposed by EU law include the doctrine of exhaustion discussed in Part I, and the prohibition against licensing arrangements that impede competition and the dissemination of technology by, for example, preventing the 'ordinary orders' of customers in respect of patented medicines to be met (see Joined Cases C-468/06 to 478/06 *Sot Lélos kai Sia et al. v GlaxoSmithKline* [2008] ECR I-7139). Examples of initiatives aimed at encouraging patentees to exploit their rights in a manner supportive of the EU single market include the development of royalty-free licensing schemes, licensing policies based on FRAND terms and patent pooling arrangements to enable the aggregation of patented technologies, and the introduction of legislation to define licensing arrangements compatible with EU competition laws and policies.[3]

4.4.2.4 Practical Difficulties of Assessing New Technologies

New technologies have also created a range of practical difficulties for patent offices in Europe and elsewhere. For example, biological material cannot always be described sufficiently in writing for patent disclosure purposes, and must in such cases now be deposited physically instead (see Rule 31 EPC Implementing Regulations, reproducing Articles 13

---

[3] See, e.g., Commission Regulation (EU) No. 316/2014 of 21 March 2014 on the application of Article 101(3) of the Treaty on the Functioning of the European Union to categories of technology transfer agreements and Commission Regulation (EU) No. 1217/2010 of 14 December 2010 on the application of Article 101(3) of the Treaty on the Functioning of the European Union to certain categories of research and development agreements (defining certain categories of bilateral agreement aimed at facilitating the transfer of technology and promoting research and development respectively as falling outside the prohibition of Article 101 TFEU).

and 14 Biotech Directive). In addition, the high volume of prior art in the ICT and other fields can make it near impossible for even the best resourced patent office to determine with confidence whether a particular invention is new and inventive. So it was that in 2007, citing an increasingly globalized economy, the accumulation of backlogs in patent applications, a decreased tendency by patent applicants to comply with EPC drafting standards, a growing volume of prior art, and increasing complexity in the subject matter for which patents are sought, the EPO launched a 'raising the bar on patent quality' initiative, involving a series of reforms within the EPO itself, as well as cooperative programmes with other national European and foreign patent offices.[4]

4.4.3 Improving the Quality and Efficiency of the Patent System via the Unitary Patent Package

Improving the quality of the patents granted in Europe by reducing reliance on national patent offices with their limited jurisdiction and varied resources and expertise has been among the central motivations for establishing a unitary patent system since the 1960s. Closely related to this has been the aim of improving the quality of patent judgments themselves, and also their efficiency, by facilitating the cross-border enforcement of patent rights and the consolidation of different patent-related actions. A third motivation for establishing a unitary patent system expressed by the European Commission in its *Pharmaceutical Sector Inquiry Report* has been to reduce the cost and inefficiency of maintaining national patent systems, and to abolish the impediments that such systems are said to create for trade and competition within the internal market. To these might be added at least two other less explicit motivations. One is the intellectual interest in supranational patent systems that has existed since the war, and the challenge of using IP rights in general as a means of pursuing a 'United Europe'. And another is the fear within Europe of being left behind other jurisdictions politically, technologically, and economically—'like the less gifted child', as Swedish patent official Frederik Neumeyer expressed it to the EFTA states in 1961[5]—if it does not create a unitary patent system of sufficient strength to rival those of Japan and the United States.

4.5 The Unitary (EU) Patent System

4.5.1 The Original Unitary Patent Proposal: The Community Patent Convention 1975

4.5.1.1 Central Aspects

Two years after the conclusion of the EPC in 1973 the CPC was signed. It has, however, never been ratified, and is now accepted as a failed initiative. Nonetheless, it remains an important document for two reasons. First, its definition of patent rights and exceptions has been adopted by most European states and included in amended form in the Unified Patent Court (UPC) Agreement (see Section 8.4). And second, it represents the basis of all attempts since the 1970s to establish a unitary patent and patent system for the EC/EU. Its purpose was to fulfil the EFTA 'two convention' proposal by creating a second

---

[4] For details see https://www.epo.org/about-us/annual-reports-statistics/annual-report/2007/focus.html. For a recent report on EPO initiatives aimed at ensuring patent quality see also http://www.epo.org/about-us/annual-reports-statistics/annual-report/2014/quality.html.

[5] F. Neumeyer, 'Unification of European Patent Legislation on the Common Market' (1961) 24 *Modern Law Review* 725, 729.

and autonomous species of European patent to supplement the European bundle patent created by the EPC in the form of a Community patent. Under its provisions, Community patents were also to be granted by the EPO applying the provisions of the EPC, but were to differ from EPC patents in conferring unitary protection throughout the entire EEC territory, rather than a set of national grants for states designated for protection by the patentee and requiring separate validation, translation, renewal, and enforcement in each designated country. In addition, the CPC extended the code of substantive patent law already contained in the SPC and EPC by defining the rights conferred by Community patents, along with the exceptions to those rights. And finally, it laid the foundations for supranational patent litigation and compulsory licensing arrangements by committing EEC states to commence work on them as soon as the CPC entered into force, and to adopt certain (albeit excludable) rules on compulsory licensing in the interim. Until such arrangements were made, the enforcement of Community patents was to be left to the national courts of Member States, supported by the EPO exercising a new jurisdiction in respect of patent revocation, and by the CJEU exercising appellate jurisdiction in respect of EPO revocation decisions and hearing preliminary referrals from national courts in respect of all aspects of substantive patent law.

4.5.1.2 Why it Failed

At the time the CPC was concluded there was no suggestion that the EEC had competence to create a new patent title, and so it was that this earliest unitary patent initiative was concluded as an international agreement rather than as an EEC instrument (see Section 2.4.2.1.2). By express provision of Article 94, it depended on the ratification of all EEC Member States to take effect, which for some required a national referendum and constitutional amendment. The onerousness of this process, combined with the fact that all future Member States would have needed to enter a new agreement to accede to the Convention, explains in part why it never took effect. However, there were almost certainly other reasons for its failure as well. One was its burdensome language regime, which required that patent claims be translated into the languages of all Member States and permitted individual states also to reserve the right to demand that specifications be translated into their own language for the patent to take effect in their territory. Another was its uncertain economic impact, due in part to its bifurcation of validity and infringement proceedings, and the concerns that it would discriminate against SMEs particularly. And a third was the all-or-nothing protection it offered patentees, and the nervousness among some at the prospect of having their monopolies invalidated or enforced for the entire EEC by a single proceeding before the EPO or a national court in another country. Given that the EPC had itself only recently been introduced, and that the availability of Community patents would not have precluded the grant of European bundle patents designating one or more EEC Member States, the CPC could be said to have offered too little too soon to be worth the trouble of ratifying.

4.5.2 Intervening Developments in the European Patent Field

4.5.2.1 The Development of a European Patent Jurisprudence

Notwithstanding the failure of the CPC, the EEC and its Member States continued to pursue the goal of a unitary patent system for the European Community, with further concrete proposals for such a system published in 1985, 2000, 2003/4, 2009, and, most recently, in 2012/13. Notwithstanding their similarities, the legal context of each of these proposals has been significantly different. First, the degree of substantive harmonization in the patent field has increased progressively since the 1970s. The principal cause of this increase has been the EPO's development of a body of jurisprudence concerning patentability under the EPC. In addition, the CJEU has over the same period clarified the significance of the Treaties—including their provisions on competition and the free movement of goods and services—for the exploitation of patent rights within the internal market. Among other things, this has led to its formulation of the doctrine of exhaustion—which has diminished significantly the problems caused for the internal market by patent territoriality by preventing patentees from invoking their patent rights to prevent products from moving between Member States once placed anywhere on the market within the EU with their consent—and the other restrictions on the freedom of patentees to exploit their patent rights referred to earlier. And finally, the EU's legislative arms have tightened the degree of harmonization throughout both the EU and EPC communities by introducing the Biotech Directive of 1998.

4.5.2.2 The Biotech Directive 1998

As the only substantive EU legal instrument in the patent field, the Biotech Directive has special significance. Its provisions achieve three central legal ends. First, they reproduce the patentability provisions of the SPC and EPC, affirming the applicability of those provisions in respect of biotechnology. Second, they codify certain principles of EPO case law, including those affirming the patentability of isolated human genes and other biological material. And third, they clarify the meaning of those provisions and principles in respect of biotech subject matter generally, including the impact in that regard of EU fundamental principles, such as the principle of human dignity recognized in Article 1 CFR.

While implementation of the Directive by EU Member States has only recently been completed, its effect has already been far-reaching. For one, its operative provisions have been incorporated by the EP Organisation's Administrative Council into the Implementing Regulations of the EPC, and thereby extended beyond the 28 EU Member States to all Contracting States of the EPC (see also Rule 26(1) EPC Implementing Regulations). In addition, and as a result of such incorporation, the system of the EPC has been exposed to CJEU case law concerning biotech patenting, and also made more accountable to EU Member States as well. Two reasons may be given for this increased accountability. The first reason is the obligations of the 28 EPC Contracting States that are EU Member States with respect to CJEU decisions, which are such as to leave the EPO little choice but to respect those decisions also. And the second is the ability (and obligation) of the courts in those states to refer questions regarding the meaning of the Biotech Directive that are not *acte clair* to the Court of Justice under Article 267 TFEU, thereby giving them a direct role in the development of substantive European patent principles. Given the absence of any equivalent preliminary referral mechanism under the EPC (notwithstanding attempts by the Court of Appeal of England and Wales in *Aerotel v Telco Holdings Ltd* [2007] RPC 7 (CA) to create one), this is a development of especial significance.

As noted, the Biotech Directive remains the EU's only substantive patent legislation. While the EU proposed a second patent directive in the field of computer-related technology in 2002, that proposal proved controversial as Member States failed to agree on the appropriateness of the EPO principles which it sought to codify. After a three-year legislative passage, it was rejected by an overwhelming majority of the European Parliament in 2005.

4.5.3 **The Current Unitary Patent Proposal: The Unitary Patent Package 2012/13**

4.5.3.1 **Central Aspects**

It is in this context of increasingly harmonized substantive patent law that a subset of 25 EU Member States, with the permission of the European Council, agreed in 2012 to invoke the enhanced cooperation provisions of the EU Treaties to complete the task begun by the EEC and its Member States in 1959 and establish a unitary patent and patent system for the EU. The immediate result of that agreement was the enactment in December 2012 of two EU regulations, and the conclusion in February 2013 of the supranational UPC Agreement. If it takes effect—which it will do when 13 states, including France, Germany, and the UK, ratify the UPC Agreement[6]—the Unitary Patent Package comprising these three instruments will establish the necessary legal framework for the creation and enforcement of unitary patent protection in the territories of 13 or more participating EU Member States. In particular, it will permit the voluntary conversion of European (EPC) patents into unitary patents having 'equal effect' and providing 'uniform protection' throughout the territories of those participating states, and establish (for the same subset of EU territories) a Unified Patent Court with local, regional, and central divisions having exclusive jurisdiction (after a transitional period) in respect of all European (including EPC) patent grants, as well as supplementary protection certificates.

4.5.3.2 **Compared with the CPC**

The Unitary Patent Package clearly has much in common with the CPC from 1975. Above all, it seeks to create a new species of European patent providing uniform protection and having equal effect throughout a number of EU Member States. In addition, it builds on the existing system of the EPC, preserving its substantive law and the role of the EPO as the granter of European patents and the keeper of European patent registers. And third, it seeks to supplement rather than to displace the European bundle patent for participating EU states in order to maximize patent owners' choice regarding their preferred patent grants.

Beyond these similarities, however, and as Figure 4.6 illustrates, the Unitary Patent Package differs from the CPC in varied and significant ways. For one, while the unitary patent will have its legal basis in an EU regulation rather than a supranational agreement (as with the CPC), it will not be an autonomous right in the sense of deriving its content from its founding instrument. Instead, its content will be derived from the national laws of participating Member States, incorporating the existing provisions of the EPC and new provisions regarding patent rights and exceptions in the UPC Agreement (reproduced from the CPC). Thus, the Unitary Patent Package will not increase the scope of substantive EU law in the patent field. Consistent with this, Article 24 UPC Agreement requires the UPC to base its decisions on a variety of non-EU legal sources as well as EU law, including the UPC Agreement, the EPC, 'other international agreements applicable to patents and binding on all the Contracting Member States', and participating states' national laws; these being the diversity of sources in which the substantive law governing the new unitary patents will need to be found.

---

[6] At the time of writing eight countries had ratified the Agreement: Austria, Belgium, Denmark, France, Luxembourg, Malta, Portugal, and Sweden.

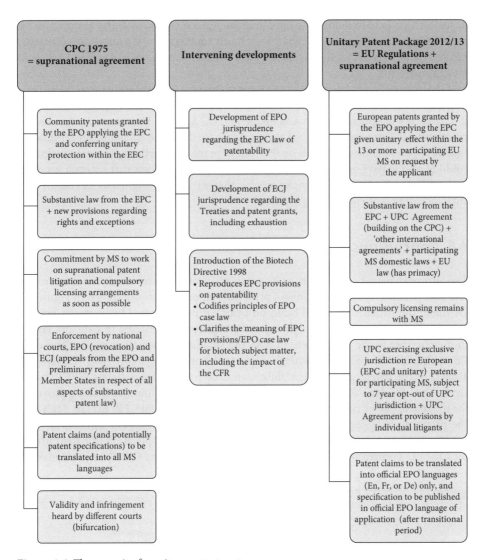

CPC 1975 = supranational agreement	Intervening developments	Unitary Patent Package 2012/13 = EU Regulations + supranational agreement
Community patents granted by the EPO applying the EPC and conferring unitary protection within the EEC	Development of EPO jurisprudence regarding the EPC law of patentability	European patents granted by the EPO applying the EPC given unitary effect within the 13 or more participating EU MS on request by the applicant
Substantive law from the EPC + new provisions regarding rights and exceptions	Development of ECJ jurisprudence regarding the Treaties and patent grants, including exhaustion	Substantive law from the EPC + UPC Agreement (building on the CPC) + 'other international agreements' + participating MS domestic laws + EU law (has primacy)
Commitment by MS to work on supranational patent litigation and compulsory licensing arrangements as soon as possible	Introduction of the Biotech Directive 1998 • Reproduces EPC provisions on patentability • Codifies principles of EPO case law • Clarifies the meaning of EPC provisions/EPO case law for biotech subject matter, including the impact of the CFR	Compulsory licensing remains with MS
Enforcement by national courts, EPO (revocation) and ECJ (appeals from the EPO and preliminary referrals from Member States in respect of all aspects of substantive patent law)		UPC exercising exclusive jurisdiction re European (EPC and unitary) patents for participating MS, subject to 7 year opt-out of UPC jurisdiction + UPC Agreement provisions by individual litigants
Patent claims (and potentially patent specifications) to be translated into all MS languages		Patent claims to be translated into official EPO languages (En, Fr, or De) only, and specification to be published in official EPO language of application (after transitional period)
Validity and infringement heard by different courts (bifurcation)		

Figure 4.6 The pursuit of a unitary patent system

4.5.3.3 Impact on the EU Legal Order

It is clear from this that the Unitary Patent Package will not support the autonomy and application of EU law to the extent envisaged by the CPC, nor indeed any of the intervening unitary patent proposals. Further, the effect of each unitary patent grant will be confined to the 13 or more participating EU Member States that have ratified the UPC Agreement and recognized the exclusive jurisdiction of the UPC at the date of the patent's registration, with the court's jurisdiction confined accordingly. As a result, neither the unitary patent nor its supporting judicial system will necessarily extend throughout EU territory. And finally, rather than covering the entire breadth of substantive patent law, the jurisdiction of the CJEU under the Unitary Patent Package will be limited to what it is currently: in effect, the Biotech Directive, and the patent-related provisions of the EU Treaties, the Brussels Regulations, and international agreements such as the TRIPS Agreement. The (non-EU) UPC will therefore be the main first and last instance court in the European patent field, though even then it will be possible for patentees to opt out of its jurisdiction (and in doing so to opt out of the Agreement's substantive law provisions) by bringing actions involving EPC patents and supplementary protection certificates before a national court for the first seven years of the system's existence at least (Article 83 UPC Agreement).

If the Unitary Patent Package seems geared to threaten EU legal autonomy and increase fragmentation and inefficiency in the European patent field, why, it might be asked, does it have such widespread support among the EU, EU Member States, and academics and practitioners? There seem to be two main reasons for this. One is a hope and expectation that its apparent deficiencies will be resolved in practice once the system takes effect, as could be said to have occurred with the EPC. Another is the view that however great the Unitary Patent Package's deficiencies may be, they will be outweighed by its various benefits, including those outlined in Section 4.4.3.

4.6 Conclusions

The European patent system derives its substantive law from several overlapping patent and non-patent sources, including (of principal importance) those shown in Figure 4.7. Of these, the patent sources all build on prior European patent instruments but differ in their basis, context, and coverage. Moving from the earliest in date and largest in membership to the most recent in date and smallest in membership: the Council of Europe's ECHR and SPC deal with the right to the protection of property (ECHR) and aspects of the patent grant, patentability, and the role of patent claims (SPC) respectively. The EPC deals with the pre-grant aspects of a patent's life, also making provision for the role of patent claims. Through the Biotech Directive and CFR, EU law deals with the patenting of biotechnological subject matter, including issues of patentability and patent scope, and the protection of human dignity in the application of patent principles; the EU Treaties and Brussels Regulations also support the CJEU's regulation of the

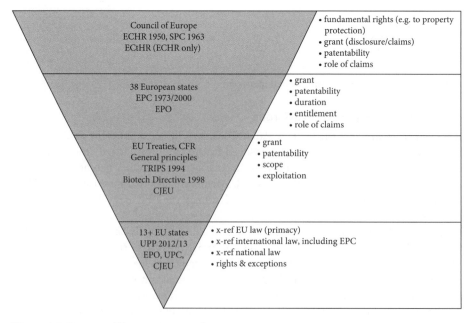

Figure 4.7 Sources of European patent law

exploitation of patents within the internal market and cross-border litigation involving patents before national courts (see Part V). And then, of course, there are international instruments such as the TRIPS Agreement, in respect of which the CJEU has exclusive competence vis-à-vis EU Member States, to say nothing of the UPC Agreement, which, if ratified, will introduce new provisions on patent rights and exceptions, reproduced from the CPC.

The complexity created by this fragmented legal system is exacerbated by the lack of clarity regarding the formal relationship between each of the instruments and their associated legal regimes. The Council of Europe, EPO, and EU are all autonomous legal communities each of which interacts with the others (and with national and international legal communities) in different and complex ways. This has been brought into relief recently by the impact of the Biotech Directive, which has led the EPO to embrace substantive fundamental rights such as human dignity in its interpretation and application of principles of patentability. It has also been made apparent in the negotiations and discussions of the Unitary Patent Package, the structure and provisions of which reflect the existing fragmentation in the European patent field even as they threaten to make it worse by creating another European patent system to sit alongside those already in existence, including another European patent court and community.

For more than 60 years, European patent law initiatives have been dominated by the largely EU goals of furthering substantive patent law harmonization, establishing a unitary patent, and creating a unified patent court. However, there have been other initiatives as well, prompted in the main by technological developments (e.g. genetic engineering) and the increased use of and dependence on the patent system by biotech, ICT, and pharmaceutical companies. Such initiatives have included: the EPO's 'raising the bar' reforms, aimed at improving the quality of European patent grants; the EU's Biotech Directive, aimed at clarifying the meaning of traditional patent principles for biotechnological subject matter and ensuring that they take sufficient account of EU fundamental rights and freedoms; the establishment of the European Telecommunications Standards Institute, aimed at facilitating access to essential mobile telephony technology; and the European Commission's commitment to scrutinizing both the pharmaceutical and ICT sectors to ensure their members' compliance with European competition law. Such initiatives underline the deep connections that exist between patent law and other legal areas, such as human rights and competition law, which we considered in Part I; connections that are also reflected in the origins of the patent system as a limited public interest-based exception to a general prohibition against monopoly grants discussed in Section 1.2.2.2.2.

Further Reading

BRINKHOF, J. AND OHLY, A., 'Towards a Unified Patent Court in Europe' in A. Ohly and J. Pila (eds), *The Europeanization of Intellectual Property Law* (OUP, 2013)

CHAPPATTE, P., 'Frand Commitments—The Case for Antitrust Intervention' (2009) 5 *European Competition Journal* 319

CULLET, P., 'Patents and Medicines: The Relationship between TRIPS and the Human Right to Health' (2003) 79 *International Affairs* 139

DREXL, J., '"Pay-for-Delay" and Blocking Patents—Targeting Pharmaceutical Companies Under European Competition Law' [2009] *IIC* 751

FISHER, M., 'Classical Economics and Philosophy of the Patent System' [2005] *IPQ* 1

GUELLEC, D. AND VAN POTTELSBERGHE DE LA POTTERIE, B., *The Economics of the Patent System: IP Policy for Innovation and Competition* (OUP, 2007)

GURRY, F., 'The Cambrian Explosion' [2007] *IIC* 255

HILTY, R., JAEGER, T., LAMPING, M., AND ULLRICH, H., 'The Unitary Patent Package: 12 Reasons for Concern' [2012] *CIPA Journal* 553

KITCH, E.W., 'The Nature and Function of the Patent System' (1977) 20 *Journal of Law and Economics* 265

MALAGA, M., 'The European Patent with Unitary Effect: Incentive to Dominate?' [2014] *IIC* 621

PILA, J., 'The European Patent: An Old and Vexing Problem' [2013] *International & Comparative Law Quarterly* 917

PILA, J. AND WADLOW, C. (eds), *The Unitary (EU) Patent System* (OUP, 2015)

SCHANKERMAN, M., 'Improving Patent Incentives and Enforcement' (2009) 4 *Journal of Intellectual Property Law and Practice* 798

STANISZEWSKI, P., 'The Interplay Between IP Rights and Competition Law in the Context of Standardization' (2007) 2 *Journal of Intellectual Property Law and Practice* 666

UNITED KINGDOM COMMISSION ON INTELLECTUAL PROPERTY RIGHTS, *Integrating Intellectual Property Rights and Development Policy* (2002) http://www.iprcommission.org/papers/pdfs/final_report/ciprfullfinal.pdf, chs 2, 4, and 6

5

The Procedure for Obtaining a European Patent

5.1 Introduction

For the most part, European law regulates the procedure for obtaining European patents only, leaving the procedure for obtaining national patents to individual states. An exception arises where the invention for which a patent is sought involves biological material, and the state in which protection is sought is an EU Member State. In such a case, the grant procedure is subject to the requirements of Chapter IV of the Biotech Directive regarding the deposit of biological material.

In this chapter we consider the procedure for obtaining a European patent. That procedure may be initiated directly with the EPO, indirectly with a competent patent office of an EPC Contracting State, or by international patent application under the Patent Cooperation Treaty 1970. Whatever route is taken, however, the result of a successful European patent application will be the same: a bundle of national patents from any number of designated EPC Contracting States. For these patents to have effect, they must be individually validated in the relevant Contracting States according to the requirements of domestic law.

Under the Unitary Patent Package, European patents having unitary effect will be granted as European (EPC) patents and later registered for unitary effect upon request by the patentee. Beyond the requirement for their registration, the procedure for granting unitary patents will remain unchanged.

From the public's perspective, the most important stages of the European patent application procedure are those involving the assessment of whether the subject matter for which a patent is claimed is a patentable invention within the meaning of the EPC, and whether the proposed text of the patent grant defines and describes that invention sufficiently. The reason is that it is the disclosure of a patentable invention via the publication of the patent text (the specification) that represents the consideration for which the patent is granted, and the definition of that invention in the patent claims with reference to which the scope of the patentee's monopoly is defined. Hence the importance not only of ensuring that the subject matter for which a patent is sought *is* a patentable invention, but also that it is clearly and completely defined and described in the patent document itself.

Throughout the European patent application procedure, the notional reasonable person of patent law—the 'person skilled in the art' to which the invention relates (the skilled addressee)—plays a central role in representing the skilled community to whom the patent is addressed and thereby protecting the interests of the public in the bargain which individual patent grants represent. Identifying the skilled addressee and her range of skills and knowledge is therefore a central preliminary step in most patent administrative and judicial enquiries, and a useful starting point for considering the procedure for obtaining a European patent grant.

5.2 The Nature and Stages of the European Patent Grant Procedure and the Role and Identity of the Skilled Addressee

5.2.1 The Nature and Stages of the European Patent Grant Procedure

The procedure for obtaining a European patent entails seven stages, illustrated in Figure 5.1:

1. the filing of an application by an inventor or other entitled person;
2. the preliminary examination of the application for compliance with formalities;
3. the preparation and transmission of a search report and non-binding assessment of the invention's patentability;
4. the publication of the application and search report;
5. the substantive examination of the application and invention for compliance with the EPC;
6. the publication of the EPO's notice of intention to grant the patent and the proposed text of the grant; and
7. the grant and publication of the patent in its final form.

Because it is initiated by an applicant without formal representation by other interested parties, obtaining a European patent is an *ex parte* administrative procedure. Having said that, from the publication of the application following the preparation of the search report at stage 4, members of the public are able to file observations with the EPO regarding the application. In addition, following the grant of the patent they are given an additional nine months within which to initiate formal opposition proceedings in respect of the patent before the EPO's Opposition Divisions on one of the grounds listed in Article 100 EPC, and are able thereafter to seek revocation of the patent on one of the grounds listed in Article 138 EPC before a domestic court in accordance with domestic law. The grounds of opposition listed in Article 100 are that:

(a) The subject-matter of the European patent is not patentable under Articles 52 to 57;

(b) The European patent does not disclose the invention in a manner sufficiently clear and complete for it to be carried out by a person skilled in the art; [or]

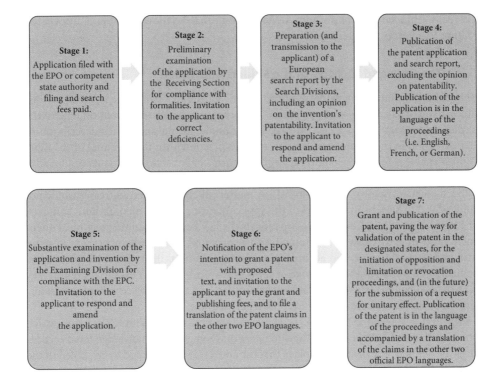

Stage 1:
Application filed with the EPO or competent state authority and filing and search fees paid.

Stage 2:
Preliminary examination of the application by the Receiving Section for compliance with formalities. Invitation to the applicant to correct deficiencies.

Stage 3:
Preparation (and transmission to the applicant) of a European search report by the Search Divisions, including an opinion on the invention's patentability. Invitation to the applicant to respond and amend the application.

Stage 4:
Publication of the patent application and search report, excluding the opinion on patentability. Publication of the application is in the language of the proceedings (i.e. English, French, or German).

Stage 5:
Substantive examination of the application and invention by the Examining Division for compliance with the EPC. Invitation to the applicant to respond and amend the application.

Stage 6:
Notification of the EPO's intention to grant a patent with proposed text, and invitation to the applicant to pay the grant and publishing fees, and to file a translation of the patent claims in the other two EPO languages.

Stage 7:
Grant and publication of the patent, paving the way for validation of the patent in the designated states, for the initiation of opposition and limitation or revocation proceedings, and (in the future) for the submission of a request for unitary effect. Publication of the patent is in the language of the proceedings and accompanied by a translation of the claims in the other two official EPO languages.

Figure 5.1 Procedure for the grant of a European patent

(c) The subject-matter of the European patent extends beyond the content of the application as filed, or, if the patent was granted on a divisional application or on a new application filed under Article 61, beyond the content of the earlier application as filed.

The grounds of revocation listed in Article 138 are the grounds of opposition above, and the further grounds:

(d) that the protection conferred by the European patent has been extended by amendment contrary to Article 123 (see Section 5.5); and

(e) that the patentee is not entitled to the patent under Article 60(1) (see Section 5.3).

Under a procedure introduced with the EPC 2000 revisions, a patent owner may also request that her patent be limited or revoked at any time after grant, provided that opposition proceedings in respect of the patent are not pending at the time of the request (Article 105a). Such requests are granted provided, in the case of a limitation request, that the requirements of Articles 84 (regarding patent claims) and 123(2) and (3) (regarding amendments) are satisfied.

One notable absence from the Article 100 grounds of opposition is breach of the Article 84 requirement that patent claims be clear and concise, and supported by the patent description. In many situations, a failure to meet this requirement will be accompanied by a failure to meet the Article 83 requirement for sufficient description, which is a basis for opposition under paragraph (b) of Article 100. However, in its Guidelines for Examination the EPO has noted the 'delicate balance' that exists between Articles 83 and 84, and warned against allowing insufficiency objections in opposition proceedings that are really 'a hidden objection' under Article 84, 'especially in the case of ambiguities in the claims' (see Part F, Chapter III 11).

5.2.2 The Role and Identity of the Skilled Addressee

Throughout the European patent application procedure and beyond, the notional reasonable person of patent law—the person skilled in the art to which the invention relates (the skilled addressee)—plays a central role. For example, for an applicant's description of her invention in the patent specification to be sufficient within the meaning of the EPC, it must enable a person skilled in the art to perform the invention across its full breadth without undue burden. In addition, for an amendment of an application or patent to be valid, it must not involve the addition of any matter which the skilled addressee would not understand to have been included in the application or patent as filed. In both contexts, the invocation of the skilled addressee reflects the law's assumption that technical documents and other disclosures are framed with a particular community of persons in mind and appropriately construed accordingly. Identifying the skilled addressee who represents that community and her range of skills and knowledge is an essential preliminary step in patent administrative and judicial enquiries, and a useful place to begin considering the procedure for obtaining a European patent grant.

The first task when identifying the skilled addressee is to determine the art in which she is skilled and with reference to which her common general knowledge must accordingly be defined. The basic principle is that the addressee is presumed to be skilled in the technical field to which the subject matter of the relevant patent or application relates. Identifying this field is made easier by the requirement of Rule 42(1) that when describing an (alleged) invention in a patent (application), a patentee (or applicant) must:

> (a) specify the technical field to which the invention relates; (b) indicate the background art which...can be regarded as useful to understand the invention...; [and] (c) disclose the invention, as claimed, in such terms that the technical problem, even if not expressly stated as such, and its solution can be understood....

Generally speaking, the field of the skilled addressee will be the field in which the technical problem solved by her invention lies. The only exception is where a specialist in that field would have been prompted to seek a solution to the problem in a different technical field, in which case the addressee will be deemed to be skilled in the field from which the solution would have been sought (see T32/81 (*FIVES-CAIL BABCOCK/Cleaning Apparatus For Conveyor Belt*) [1979–85] EPOR B377; T560/89 (*NI INDUSTRIES/Filler Mass*) [1994] EPOR 120).

Having identified the art in which the addressee is presumed to be skilled, it is necessary to determine her attributed characteristics and common general knowledge, both of which will be brought to bear on the interpretative or other task with reference to which she is invoked. The skilled addressee is generally conceived as an expert of average ability and knowledge who is cautious and entirely devoid of imagination or inventive capacities. Her common general knowledge may take any form and be evidenced by a variety of sources, including university or other formal instructional courses, and standard textbooks, scientific journal articles, and other readily available literature. In new and fast-developing fields, patent specifications and other less conventional sources of information may also be accepted as evidence of her common general knowledge (see T51/87 (*MERCK/Starting Compounds*) [1991] EPOR 329).

In addition to knowing the basic information which experts in her field would be expected to know, the skilled addressee will be assumed to know where to find such information as needed (T206/83 (*ICI/Pyridine Herbicides*) [1986] EPOR 232), and more generally to have the means and capacity for routine work, searching, and experimentation. It is when speculating as to what specific work, searching, and experimentation she would undertake in a particular context that the attributed characteristics of the skilled addressee become especially important. As stated by the Board in T455/91 (*GENENTECH/ Expression in Yeast*) [1996] EPOR 85, the caution of the skilled addressee would be presumed to stop her from challenging established prejudice, trying to enter into 'sacrosanct' or unpredictable areas, or taking incalculable risks. On the other hand (98),

> within the normal design procedures, the said expert would readily seek appropriate, manifest changes, modifications or adjustments which involve little trouble or work and no risks or only calculable risks, especially for the sake of obtaining a more handy or convenient product or of simplifying a procedure. In particular, the skilled person working in one field (e.g. expression in yeast) would regard a means conveniently adopted in a neighbouring field (e.g. the bacterial art) as being readily usable also in that field, if this transfer of technical knowledge involves nothing out of the ordinary.

In industries in which experts typically work in groups combining different fields of expertise, the skilled addressee will often be conceived as a team of people rather than as a single person.

5.3 Obtaining a European Patent

5.3.1 Filing a European Patent Application

5.3.1.1 European Patent Entitlement

5.3.1.1.1 General Principles

The procedure for obtaining a European patent begins with an entitled person initiating an application for grant. Hence the first issue that any patent applicant will need to consider is whether he is entitled to obtain a European patent.

Under the EPC, any natural or legal person or persons may apply for a European patent, regardless of whether they are citizens or residents of an EPC Contracting State. However, only the following persons may lawfully be granted a patent under the EPC (Article 60(1)):

(a) The inventor or inventors of the invention for which the patent is claimed;

(b) The successor or successors in title of the inventor or inventors under (a); or

(c) If the invention was devised by an employee, the person or persons entitled to a patent for it under the law of the state in which the employee is mainly employed or, if that state cannot be determined, the state in which the employer has the place of business to which the employee is attached.

This provision is supplemented by Article 61, which provides for the effects of a judicial declaration regarding entitlement. Both it and Article 60 EPC will continue to apply when the Unitary Patent Package takes effect, and will also govern from that date entitlement to European patents with unitary effect.

5.3.1.1.2 The Inventor as the Person Entitled to a European Patent

For the purpose of Article 60(1) EPC, the inventor is the person who devised the invention, in the sense of having been responsible for its inventive concept, regardless of whether someone else had previously devised it. This gives effect to the 'first to file' principle, whereby entitlement rests with the inventor (or other person(s) identified in Article 60(1)) who first applies for a patent for an invention. The result of this principle is that person A can obtain a patent for an invention devised by person B provided that A also devised it independently of B.

5.3.1.1.3 The Exception Concerning Employee-Devised Inventions

Of especial note regarding Article 60(1) is that it leaves the question of entitlement to European patents for employee-devised inventions to domestic law. In reality this means that in the vast majority of cases entitlement will be governed by domestic law, since most inventions are devised by employees. This will remain the case when the Unitary Patent Package takes effect, with the result that the domestic law of EU Member States will similarly govern entitlement to most European patents with unitary effect.

In fact, the EPC drafters did consider harmonizing European patent entitlement, either by including substantive provisions governing employee-devised inventions in the EPC, or by vesting jurisdiction in the EPO to determine entitlement. They decided against doing so, however, for two reasons. The first was their view that it would be 'impossible to standardise the laws on ownership of inventions for all the European States which may become Contracting parties to the Convention', and equally impossible for the EPO 'to determine which national laws would be applicable in each case' and 'apply [] twenty or so different national laws according to each individual case' (Doc. BR/144/71 [36]). And the second was the objection of some delegations that it would be inappropriate, as a matter of principle, to have 'disputes traditionally falling within the sphere of property law...dealt with by authorities other than national civil courts' (ibid). For these reasons, entitlement with respect to employee-devised inventions was left for determination by national authorities applying national law.

More than 40 years after the EPC was introduced, those laws continue to vary significantly. While most European states recognize the entitlement of employers to any patents granted for inventions devised by their employees in the course of employment, as well as the right of employee inventors to be compensated in respect of patents granted to their employers for inventions they devised, there is only limited agreement beyond these principles. The issues on which states differ are wide-ranging, and include the following:

(a) when if ever an employer is entitled to a patent granted for an employee-devised invention not devised in the course of employment, including an invention devised with the assistance of the employer's facilities;

(b) what if any notice or other formal requirements must be satisfied in order for employees or employers to assert their statutory right to obtain a patent granted for employee-devised inventions;

(c) which if any of the statutory provisions regarding employee-devised inventions may be displaced by contract;

(d) what if any distinction is drawn between inventions devised by private and public sector employees, including whether special rules exist with respect to inventions devised by academic employees; and

(e) when an employee's right to receive compensation arises, and how his compensation is assessed.

Particularly diverse are the domestic laws of European states governing the matters described in (d) and (e). For example, in Germany the employee's compensation is calculated by subtracting his salary from the profits of his employer by means of a complicated (and detailed) statutory formula, whereas in Spain it is calculated by assessing the personal contribution of the inventor and the importance of the invention which he devised. Similarly, while in the Netherlands public sector employees have fewer rights in respect of their inventions than private sector employees, in Finland the opposite position exists, and in other countries no distinction between public and private sector employees is drawn at all. Unique is the system in France, whereby public sector inventors share in the royalties that the patents for their inventions generate.

5.3.1.1.4 Entitlement Unaffected by Breach of Confidence

The terms of Article 60(1) confirm the general principle that patent entitlement is unaffected by inventor A's breach of confidence or contract in the course of devising her invention. For example, if A learns about an invention from B under a duty of confidence or equivalent contractual obligation, she will not be entitled to a patent for it, *not* because of her obligation to B, but rather because she did not herself devise the invention. If she learns about the invention from B free of any legal obligation, she will still not be entitled to a patent for it, both for the reason above (i.e. because she did not invent it) and because its disclosure to A will deprive it of the novelty required for patentability (see Section 7.2). Conversely, if A devises an invention with the mere assistance of confidential information acquired from B, she will be entitled to a patent for it if she has done enough herself to be regarded as its sole or joint inventor, though B may also have a claim to joint ownership of the patent or some other form of redress under domestic law.

5.3.1.2 International, European, and Domestic Filing Routes

There are two types of European patent applications: so-called parent applications and divisional applications. A parent application is an initiating or original application for a patent. By contrast, a divisional application is a subsequent application that relates to an already pending parent application, but that is thereafter treated independently. Divisional applications retain their parent's filing and priority dates, and designated EPC Contracting States. They are most commonly used to divide the claims of the parent application so as to ensure that it complies with Article 82, and must not claim any subject matter that goes beyond the subject matter disclosed in the parent application (see Article 76(1) EPC).

With the exception of European divisional applications (which may only be filed directly with the EPO (Article 76)), the procedure for obtaining a European patent may be initiated by any of three (international, European, or national) routes. These involve, respectively:

- filing an application under the PCT with a PCT Receiving Office and designating the EPO as an Office from which protection is sought (Euro-PCT applications: see Article 153(2) EPC);

- filing an application directly with the EPO itself, via one of its offices in Munich, The Hague, or Berlin, under the EPC (Rule 35(1)); or

- if the law of the state so permits, filing an application with a competent patent office of the state (Article 75).

Regardless of the route adopted, the EPC requires that European patent applications be filed in one of the three official languages of the EPO—English, French, or German—or, if filed in another language, translated into one of those official languages (Article 14(2)).

5.3.1.2.1 European Patent Applications Filed with a National Patent Office

European patent applications filed with a national patent office must be assigned an application number and notified without delay to the EPO, along with the details of any accompanying priority claim.[1] To remain valid, they must be forwarded to the EPO within 14 months of the filing or other priority date (Rule 37), and are thereafter treated as if they had been filed directly with the EPO under the EPC.

5.3.1.2.2 European Patent Applications Filed with the PCT (Euro-PCT Applications)

Euro-PCT applications are treated as international (PCT) applications during their international phase and as European (EPC) applications during their regional phase (see Article 150). This means that the first four of the seven stages of the grant procedure are conducted under the PCT rather than under the EPC. Thus, on receipt by a PCT Receiving Office, applications are assigned a filing or other priority date after being assessed by the Office for compliance with PCT formalities (see Article 11 PCT). They are then forwarded to a PCT International Searching Authority which searches the available knowledge regarding the art to which the invention relates (the prior art) with a view to determining whether the invention was known or obvious at the filing or other priority date (see Articles 15 and 17 PCT). The results of that search are then incorporated into an international search report, which is sent to the applicant, the EPO, and any other designated Offices, and published alongside the international patent application itself (see Article 18 PCT). Also transmitted to the applicant and designated Offices is a non-binding preliminary report on the patentability of the invention to which the application relates.

Following publication of the international search report, the applicant has a limited period within which to pursue the application by entering it into the regional phase. Under Rule 159 EPC, for Euro-PCT applications that period is 31 months from the filing or other priority date. Before entering the regional phase, the applicant has the possibility of amending the application to address any weaknesses revealed by the international search report, and of requesting its examination by an International Preliminary Examining Authority in order to obtain a more detailed report on its strength and thus a more accurate assessment of its likelihood of succeeding (Article 33 PCT). Where such an examination is requested, its results are included in a report for transmission to the applicant, the EPO, and any other designated Offices (Article 36), but otherwise treated as confidential to the applicant (Article 38 PCT).

Once the international application has entered the regional phase, it proceeds as a regular European patent application under the EPC from the point of substantive examination (see Section 5.3.5). Even before then, however, the EPO can be involved in the preliminary examination of a Euro-PCT application on account of its status as a Receiving Office, an International Searching Authority, and an International Preliminary Examining Authority under the PCT (see Articles 151 and 152 EPC).

5.3.1.3 The Content of a European Patent Application

5.3.1.3.1 The Essential Components of an Application

All European patent applications must contain certain components, in addition to satisfying the requirements of the Implementing Regulations (Article 78(1)). Those components are:

- a request for the grant of a European patent;
- a description of the invention for which the patent is claimed;

---

[1] A priority claim is a claim by the applicant to have her invention assessed for patentability at the date of an earlier patent filing for the same invention in a Paris Convention or other recognized priority country under Articles 87 to 89 EPC, rather than at the date of her current patent filing (Rule 35). See further Section 7.2.3.1.

- one or more patent claims; any drawings referred to in the description of the claims; and
- an abstract.

They must also designate the inventor and, if the applicant is not the sole inventor, explain the origin of the applicant's entitlement to the patent in accordance with Article 60 (Article 81). And finally, they must be supported by payment of the relevant filing and search fees within the time required by the Implementing Regulations (Article 78(2)), which is ordinarily one month from the date of filing (Rule 38(1)).

By provision of Article 79(1), a European patent application is deemed to designate all EPC Contracting States at the time of filing. However, an applicant has until the grant of the patent to withdraw the designation of one or more Contracting States, leaving her free to decide in which states she would like protection (Article 79(3)). The designation of a Contracting State may be subject to the payment of a further (designation) fee imposed by the relevant state (Article 79(2)).

5.3.1.3.2 The Patent Claims

The most important elements of the patent application are those comprising its specification: the claims, description, and drawings in which the invention is defined and described (Rule 73(1)).

Of these elements, the claims have special importance. Their purpose is to define the invention for which the patent is sought and the scope of the monopoly which the patent, if granted, will confer (see Articles 84 and 69). By performing these functions, patent claims enable patentees to define their own monopoly (subject to compliance with the EPC) and give notice to third parties of the subject matter they are precluded from using during the patent term. As we saw in Section 4.2.1, this is consistent with the conception of patent grants as social contracts between the inventor/patentee and the state/community by and on whose behalf the patent is granted.

European patent jurisprudence divides the class of patentable inventions, and therefore the class of valid patent claims, into two broad categories of products and processes. This division reflects the essential difference between these two categories: products being artefacts or physical entities, and processes being series of actions or steps for achieving a specific end. (See further Section 3.2, including Figure 3.1.) The division underpins all European patent law, but is especially important when determining the nature of the protection conferred by a patent. The reason is that such protection is defined differently for product and process inventions in all EPC Contracting States. So too when the Unitary Patent Package takes effect, the rights of direct use conferred by European (EPC and unitary) patents will be defined differently for product and process patents (see Section 8.4.1).

Within the two general categories of product and process inventions (and claims) there exist several further subcategories, shown in Figure 5.2. For example, a product may be a product as such (e.g. a compound) or a purpose-limited product (e.g. a compound for the purpose of treating high blood pressure); and a process may be a method (e.g. steps for manufacturing a compound), a use (e.g. steps for using a compound to treat high blood pressure), or a purpose-limited process (e.g. the use of a compound for the manufacture of a medicament for a specified therapeutic purpose).[2] A further complication in this taxonomy is the possibility in exceptional cases of defining a product as such in a

---

[2] This plurality of possible categories of invention and claim was considered by the Enlarged Board of Appeal in G2/88 (*MOBIL/Friction reducing additive*) [1990] EPOR 73.

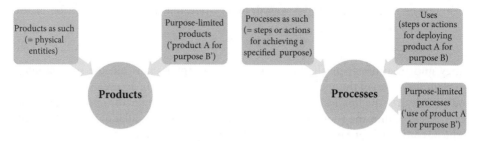

Figure 5.2 Types of inventions and valid patent claims

patent claim with reference to the method by which it is made. This form of 'product-by-process' claim was considered by the Enlarged Board of Appeal in G2/12 and G2/13 (*Essentially Biological Processes*) [2015] EPOR 28 and confirmed to be permissible if and only if '(a) it is impossible to define the claimed product other than in terms of a process of manufacture and (b) the claimed product itself meets the patentability requirements of [the] EPC' ([27]). Importantly, and as the Board emphasized in G2/12 and G2/13, the protected invention in such a case remains the product as such—i.e. the physical entity independent of the method by which it is made—and not the product when produced by the method of manufacture with reference to which it has out of necessity been defined in the patent claim.

Consistent with their importance to the public and patentees, patent claims are subject to requirements of both form and substance under the EPC. Article 82 EPC requires a new patent application for each invention by requiring that the subject matter defined in the claims be either 'one invention only' or 'a group of inventions so linked as to form a single general inventive concept'. In addition, Article 84 requires that they 'be clear and concise and be supported by the description'.

Generally speaking, a description will be regarded as supporting the claims if it discloses one way of performing the invention that the claims define. According to the Board of Appeal in T409/91 (*EXXON/Fuel Oils*) [1994] EPOR 149 (*Exxon*), this requirement of Article 84 reflects the general principle that the extent of the patent monopoly, as defined by the claims, 'should not extend to subject matter which, after reading the description, would still not be at the disposal of the person skilled in the art' (154). The result is a need for close correspondence between what the patentee claims as her invention and monopoly, and what she puts 'at the disposal' of the public (represented by the skilled addressee).

Further detailed provisions regarding the content and form of patent claims are contained in the EPC Implementing Regulations. Most importantly, Rule 43(1) requires that claims define the invention in terms of its technical features, consistent with the EPO's conception of inventions as subject matter having technical character (see Section 6.4.2.2). In addition, Rule 43(2) and (3) clarifies Article 82 in two ways. The first is by prohibiting the inclusion in a single application of more than one independent claim to an invention within the same category of product or process unless the subject matter for which the patent is sought involves a plurality of interrelated products, different uses of a product or apparatus, or alternative solutions to a particular problem that cannot appropriately be defined by a single claim. And the second is by expressly permitting the inclusion in a single application of claims describing particular embodiments of a single invention. According to the Enlarged Board in G2/10 (*SCRIPPS RESEARCH INSTITUTE/Disclaimer*) [2011] EPOR 45 (*Scripps Research Institute*), an 'embodiment' is 'a specific combination of features or a specific mode of carrying out the invention, by contrast to a more abstract definition of features which can be carried out in more than one way' ([17]).

5.3.1.3.3 The Description of the Invention

The description of the invention represents the consideration provided by the patentee for her grant. According to Article 83, and consistent with Article 84 discussed earlier, it must disclose the invention defined in the claims in a manner that is sufficiently clear and complete to enable the skilled addressee to perform it. As stated by the Board of Appeal in T435/91 (*UNILEVER/Hexagonal Liquid Crystal Gel*) [1995] EPOR 314 (*Unilever*), for this purpose 'the whole subject-matter that is defined in the claims, and not only a part of it, must be capable of being carried out by the skilled person without the burden of an undue amount of experimentation or the application of inventive ingenuity' (319). If the claim is to a principle capable of general application (e.g. one that applies generally to a class of products), the description need not prove its application in the case of every product provided the invention could reasonably be expected to work with any of them. By contrast, if the claim is to several discrete products or methods, each specific product or method must be described for the requirements of Article 83 to be met. Functionally limited product or method claims that do no more than invite the reader to perform a research programme—referred to by the EPO as 'reach-through claims'—are insufficient under Article 83 (see *Unilever* 319). Examples include patents that claim a compound for use in the treatment of a disease where the description does no more than indicate the involvement of the compound in treating the disease without, for example, specifying a method of administering the compound. As the Board stated in T1743/06 (*Amorphous silica/INEOS*) EP:BA:2009:T174306.20091127 [1.9], consistent with our earlier discussion of the attributes of the skilled addressee:

> Even though a reasonable amount of trial and error is permissible when it comes to assessing sufficiency of disclosure, there must still be adequate instructions in the specification, or on the basis of common general knowledge, leading the skilled person necessarily and directly towards success, through evaluation of initial failures.

The Implementing Regulations make detailed provision regarding the form and content of the description of the invention that is required, in Rule 42. In addition, if the invention involves biological material that is not available to the public and that cannot be described in a manner sufficient to enable the skilled addressee to perform it, Article 83 requires that a sample of the material be deposited with a recognized depositary institution in accordance with Rule 31, reproducing Articles 13 and 14 Biotech Directive.

5.3.2 **Preliminary Examination of the Application by the Receiving Section**

The second stage in the process for obtaining a European patent involves the EPO's Receiving Section examining the application to ensure that it satisfies the formal requirements for a successful filing. If it does, a date of filing is accorded (Article 90) and the Section proceeds to examine the application for compliance with the other formal requirements for a European patent, including those concerning language and translation, the content of the patent document, and the designation of the inventor (see Article 90(3)). If any deficiencies are noted in the course of its examination, the Section must give the applicant an opportunity to correct them (Article 90(4)). In some cases an oral hearing may be convened (see Rule 116).

The date of filing accorded by the Receiving Section serves three important roles. First, it is the date from which the protection conferred by a patent is deemed to run following the patent grant (see Article 63(1)). Second, unless the applicant establishes a successful priority claim under Articles 87 to 89, it is the priority date with reference to which her invention is examined for novelty and inventive step under Articles 54 to 56 EPC (see Sections 7.2 and 7.3). And third, it is the date the second anniversary of which triggers the applicant's obligation to commence paying annual renewal fees in respect of her application to the EPO (see Article 86(1)).

5.3.3 Preparation and Transmission of a European Search Report by the Search Divisions

Having examined the application for compliance with formalities, the application passes to the Search Divisions of the EPO, which conduct a prior art search before preparing and transmitting to the applicant a report on the results of its search, known as the European search report (Article 92). In most cases this report is accompanied by a non-binding opinion on whether the application and invention meet the requirements of the EPC, including those of patentability (Rule 62). The reason for this report is to give the applicant an idea of the likely success of her application and thereby enable her to make an informed decision about whether to pursue it in its current or amended form. Consistent with this aim, the Search Divisions invite the applicant to comment on the search report and, where appropriate, to correct any deficiencies noted in the accompanying opinion and to amend the proposed patent specification within a specified period (Rule 70a(1)).

5.3.4 Publication of the Application and Search Report

After transmitting it to the applicant, the EPO publishes the European search report with the application (but not the opinion) on its website (see http://www.epo.org/searching/free/documents.html). Under Article 93, publication of the application must occur as soon as possible after the expiry of 18 months from the patent filing or other priority date, or earlier if the applicant so requests. Notice of the publication of the search report is given in the European Patent Bulletin.

Applications are published in the official language in which they were filed or into which they were translated (Article 14(5)), this being the 'language of the proceedings' within the meaning of the EPC (see Article 14(3)).

Publication of the patent application communicates its existence to the world, enabling third parties to file comments with the EPO and prepare to bring opposition proceedings before the Opposition Divisions in the event of the application proceeding to grant. It also marks the date from which the applicant is entitled to provisional protection under Article 67 EPC. According to that Article, such protection shall be the same as that conferred by the patent grant itself, subject to any contrary provision by a Contracting State with respect to the application's effect in that state's territory. Even then, however, 'the protection attached to the publication of the European patent application may not be less than that which the laws of the State concerned attach to the compulsory publication of unexamined national patent applications', and must in all cases extend to a right of the applicant to 'claim compensation reasonable in the circumstances from any person who has used the invention in that State in circumstances where that person would be liable under national law for infringement of a national patent' (Article 67(2)). The only exception to this is in the case of a designated state that makes the translation of the patent claims into one of its official languages in accordance with Article 67(3) a condition of provisional protection, in which case such protection shall not be conferred until the required translation has been provided in the manner prescribed.

5.3.5 Substantive Examination of the Application and Invention by the Examining Divisions

An applicant must formally request the EPO to examine her application and invention for compliance with the EPC. That request may be filed at any time up to six months after notice of the search report's publication in the European Patent Bulletin (Rule 70(1)). However, if filed before the examination fee has been paid, it is deemed to have been filed upon such payment (Article 94(1)). If filed before the EPO's transmission of the European search report, the applicant is invited by the EPO upon such transmission to indicate within a specified period whether she wishes to proceed further with the application.

The Examining Divisions' substantive examination of an application and invention is based largely on the European search report. Its results are recorded in a further examination report for transmission to the applicant. If the Divisions conclude that the application or invention does not meet the requirements of the EPC, they invite the applicant 'as often as necessary' to respond in writing and amend the application as appropriate (Article 94(3)). If the applicant's written responses do not resolve the issues identified, either the EPO or the applicant may initiate an oral hearing in respect of the application before three Division members (see Rule 116).

5.3.6 Notice of Intention to Grant the Patent and Proposed Text

After completing the procedure above, the Examining Divisions must reach a decision regarding the application. If that decision is to allow the application, they notify the applicant of their intention to grant the patent and the proposed text of the grant, and invite her to pay the grant and publishing fees and to file translations of her patent claims into the other two official EPO languages within four months (Rule 71). During that time, the applicant may request reasoned amendments or corrections to the proposed patent text, restarting the notification or examination process as appropriate (see Rule 71(6)). If she simply pays the fees and files the translations required, she is deemed to have approved the text, paving the way for the grant of her patent in the form proposed (Rule 71(5)).

5.3.7 Grant, Publication, and Effects of the Patent

5.3.7.1 The Decision to Grant the Patent

There remains only the final stage of granting the patent and publishing a notice of the grant in the European Patent Bulletin under Article 97. According to that Article, if the Examining Divisions are of the opinion that the application and invention fulfil the requirements of the EPC and that the conditions laid down in the Implementing Regulations are met, it must grant the patent and publish the finalized text as soon as possible after the notice of grant appears in the Bulletin (Article 98). (Once again, the EPO publishes the text of all granted patents online: see http://www.epo.org/searching.html.) If the Divisions are not of this opinion, they must reject the application subject to any contrary provision of the EPC. European patent specifications are published in the language of the proceedings within the meaning of Article 14(3) EPC (see Section 5.3.1.2), and are accompanied by a translation of the claims in the other two official languages of the EPO (Article 14(6)).

With one exception, a European patent takes effect in each designated Contracting State from the date on which the mention of its grant is published in the European Patent

Bulletin, conferring on its owner from that date 'in each Contracting State in respect of which it is granted, the same rights as would be conferred by a national patent granted in that State' (see Article 64(1)). The exception arises where a Contracting State in which the patent is designated for protection requires the patentee's submission of a translation of the patent in an official language of the state as a condition for validating the patent locally. Such a requirement is expressly permitted under Article 65 EPC, as is a state's right to declare any European patent for which it is not satisfied to be void *ab initio* in that state. Once triggered, the protection conferred by a European patent is backdated to the date of the application's filing, and lasts for a maximum period of 20 years from that filing date (see Article 63(1)), without prejudice to the ability of a Contracting State to extend that protection under the same conditions as apply to national patents: (a) in order to take account of a state of war or similar emergency conditions affecting that state; or (b) if the invention is a product, a process for manufacturing a product, or a use of a product which has to undergo an administrative authorization procedure required by law before it can be put on the market in the state (Article 63(2)). The second of these paragraphs provides the basis for the grant of supplementary protection certificates in respect of previously patented inventions considered in Section 9.3.

In addition to paving the way for validation of the patent in each of the Contracting States in which it is designated for protection, the EPO's decision to grant a European patent triggers the obligation of the applicant to commence paying annual renewal fees to those states in place of the EPO (see Article 86(2); also Article 39).

5.3.7.2 National Validation of the Patent

The main condition imposed by Contracting States for validation of a European patent is that the applicant translate the patent into a local language of the validating state within three months of the Bulletin's notice of grant (see Article 65 EPC). However, since 2000 a growing number of EPC states have voluntarily waived their right to require such translation by signing the London Agreement on the application of Article 65 [2001] OJ EPO 549. That Agreement took effect in 2008, and requires an undertaking by its signatory states to waive their right to require a translation under Article 65 in any case in which: (a) the state has an official language in common with the EPO; or (b) the patent has been granted in or translated into an official EPO language prescribed by the state and supplied under the conditions of Article 65(1). Under Article 1(3) London Agreement, a state that does not have an official language in common with the EPO may still require an applicant to supply a translation of the claims into one of its own official languages (Article 1(3)). At the date of writing, 21 of the 38 EPC Contracting States are signatories of the Agreement, namely: Albania, Croatia, Denmark, Finland, France, Germany, Hungary, Iceland, Ireland, Latvia, Liechtenstein, Lithuania, Luxembourg, the Former Yugoslav Republic of Macedonia, Monaco, the Netherlands, Norway, Slovenia, Sweden, Switzerland, and the UK. Of these, France, Germany, Ireland, Liechtenstein, Luxembourg, Monaco, Switzerland and the UK have an official language in common with the EPO and have undertaken to waive the requirement for a translation entirely.

An overview of the European (EPC) patent language regime is given in Figure 5.3.

5.3.7.3 Publication of the Patent Grant

Publication of the mention of the European patent grant concludes the European application procedure, preventing the EPO from further examining the application or invention (Rule 71a). In addition, it triggers the commencement of the nine-month period in which members of the public may oppose the patent in whole or part before the EPO's Opposition Divisions under Article 100, and the time from which patentees themselves may initiate

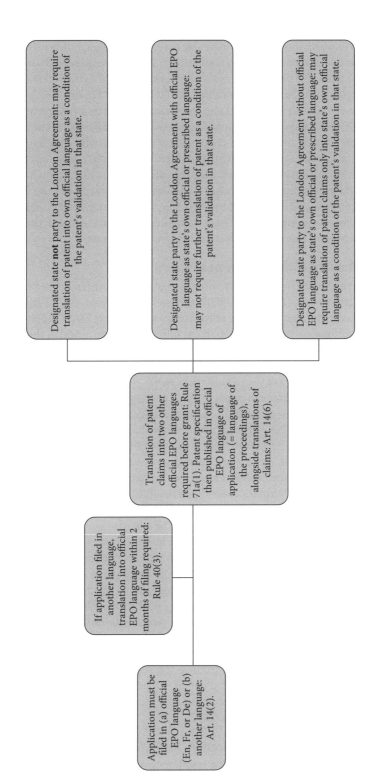

Figure 5.3 The European patent language regime

proceedings for limiting or revoking their patent under Article 105a. And finally, when the Unitary Patent Package has taken effect, it will trigger the commencement of the one-month period in which the patentee will be able to request the registration of her patent for unitary effect under Article 9(1)(g) Regulation 1257/2012. That request will need to be submitted in the language of the proceedings within the meaning of Article 14(3) EPC (Article 9(1)(g) UP Regulation). During a transitional period of at most 12 years (see Article 6(3) to (5) Regulation 1260/2012), it will need also to be accompanied by a full translation of the European (EPC) patent specification into English (where the language of the proceedings is French or German) or another official language of the Union (where the language of the proceedings is English) (Article 6(1) Regulation 1260/2012). Such translations will be published by the EPO as soon as possible after the date of submission of the request for unitary effect, but will have no legal effect, being for informational purposes only (Article 7(2) Regulation 1260/2012). To ensure uniformity in the protection they confer, 'only European patents that have been granted for all the participating Member States with the same set of claims should benefit from unitary effect' (recital 7 UP Regulation).

5.3.7.4 The Authentic Text of a European Patent

As we have seen, the EPC requires that European patent applications be filed in one of the three official languages of the EPO—English, French, or German—or, if filed in another language, translated into one of those official languages (Article 14(2)). Applications and patent specifications are then published in the official language in which they were filed or into which they were translated (Article 14(5)). In the case of a European patent itself, publication of the specification must be accompanied by a translation of the claims in the other two official languages of the EPO (Article 14(6)).

The authentic text of a European patent or application in any proceedings before the EPO or in any Contracting State is generally its text in the language of the proceedings (Article 70 EPC), namely, the official EPO language (English, French, or German) in which the application was filed or into which it was translated before the EPO (Article 14(3)). The only exceptions to this are: (a) where, in the case of a European patent application, the application was filed in a language other than English, French, or German, in which case its authentic text is the application as filed within the meaning of the EPC; or (b) where a state provides (in a manner that complies with Article 70(4)) that a translation of the application or patent into one of its official languages shall in that state be regarded as authentic, in which case its authentic text shall be as thus provided, except in revocation proceedings, in the event of the application or patent in translation conferring protection that is narrower than that conferred by the application or patent in the language of the proceedings (Article 70(3)).

The authentic text of a European patent having unitary effect will be the text in the language of the proceedings within the meaning of the EPC. However, a defendant to infringement proceedings involving a European patent with unitary effect will be entitled to request the patentee's provision of a full translation of the patent into an official language of the participating Member State in which the alleged infringement took place or in which the defendant is domiciled (Article 4(1) Regulation 1260/2012); and so too a court hearing a dispute relating to such a patent will be entitled to request the patentee's provision of a full translation of the patent into the language used in the proceedings of that court (Article 4(2) Regulation 1260/2012).

5.3.7.5 European Patents and Applications as Objects of Property

Under the domestic laws of all European states, patents and patent applications are recognized as objects of property capable of being licensed, transferred, and otherwise devolved by operation of law (including on death or in the case of bankruptcy) in the manner of other property rights. This is supported in the case of patent applications by the provision of Article 74 EPC that

> the European patent application as an object of property shall, in each designated Contracting State and with effect for such State, be subject to the law applicable in that State to national patent applications.

Consistent with this, the EPC establishes the right of a patent applicant to transfer her application in respect of one or more of its designated Contracting States (Article 71), and to license it 'in whole or in part for the whole or part of the territories' of such states (Article 73). Any assignment of a European patent application must, however, be made in writing and be signed by the contracting parties (Article 72). A copy of their contract must then be provided to the EPO with a request to register the transfer of ownership in the European Patent Register (Rule 22(1)). So too transfers of European patents themselves by the owner during the nine-month opposition period following grant or by the EPO during opposition proceedings are required to be documented in writing and submitted for recording by the EPO in the European Patent Register (Rule 85). The transfer or licensing of European patents after the opposition period has ended is subject to the national laws of the states in respect of which the patent was granted.

In terms similar to Article 74 EPC, Article 5(3) UP Regulation provides expressly for the treatment of European (EPC) patents with unitary effect as objects of property the rights of which are as defined by the national law of: (a) the participating Member State in which, according to the European Patent Register, the applicant had his residence or principal place of business on the date of filing the application for the European (EPC) patent; or, if this provision does not apply, (b) the participating Member State in which he had a place of business on that date; or, if this provision does not apply, (c) Germany (Article 7(1)). (See also Article 7(2) regarding the position in the case of joint applicants.) The practical implications of this will be considered in our discussion of patent protection in Chapter 8. For the moment, however, it is important to underline that the unitary and uniform nature of the protection conferred by European patents with unitary effect means that it will only be possible to transfer them in their entirety, i.e. with effect throughout the territory of all participating Member States in which they have unitary effect (Article 3(2) UP Regulation). By express provision of Article 3(2) UP Regulation, however, they may be licensed in respect of the whole or only part of that territory.

5.4 Amending or Correcting a European Patent or Application

5.4.1 Pre-Grant and Post-Grant Opportunities for Amendment and Correction

Amendment or correction to the text of a patent or application is common. Indeed, at several points during the grant procedure, the EPC encourages amendment and correction in order to resolve formal or substantive deficiencies in the patent application. For example, if the Receiving Section decides, following its preliminary examination of an application after filing, that the application includes deficiencies capable of correction, the EPO gives the applicant an opportunity to correct them (Article 90(3)). Further, following transmission of the European search report, the EPO invites applicants to correct any deficiencies noted in the opinion accompanying the report and to amend the description, claims, and drawings (Rule 70a). In addition, if an Examining Division following substantive examination of an application and invention decides that either does not meet the requirements of the EPC, it invites the applicant to amend the application (Article 94(3)). And so too a patentee may at any point following the grant of a European patent seek its limitation under Article 105a by amendment of the claims, provided only that opposition proceedings in respect of the patent are not pending at the time (Article 105a(2)), as may an opponent to a patent under Article 100 EPC or a defendant to a domestic infringement action. Amendments of a European patent by the EPO apply to the patent in all of the Contracting States in respect of which the patent has been granted, and take effect on the date on which the mention of the decision to amend is published in the European Patent Bulletin. As soon as possible after that date, the EPO is required to publish the amended specification, notifying the public of the new text of the patent specification. A European (EPC) patent may also be amended after grant by any state in respect of which the patent was granted, with effect in the amending state only.

The unitary effect of a European (EPC) patent will 'have an accessory nature', and will therefore 'be deemed not to have arisen to the extent that the basic European patent has been revoked or limited' (recital 9 UP Regulation). Any such amendment will take effect in respect of all the participating Member States in which the patent has unitary effect (Article 3(2) UP Regulation). The UPC may also amend a European patent with unitary effect post-grant in proceedings under Article 65 UPC Agreement. Such amendments will have effect throughout the territories of the participating Member States in which the patent has unitary effect.

5.4.2 Limits on the Amendments and Corrections That May be Made

As might be expected, there are limits on the amendments that may be made to a patent application or grant. For applications, these are contained in Article 123(2), which states that '[t]he European patent application or European patent may not be amended in such a way that it contains subject-matter which extends beyond the content of the application as filed.' For patent grants they are also contained in Article 123(3) EPC.

The purpose and meaning of Article 123(2) has been subject to extensive consideration by the EPO, including its Enlarged Board of Appeal. As a result, it is now well established that an amendment of any type to the claims, description, or drawings of a patent application—including a correction or disclaimer of subject matter—will infringe Article 123(2) if it results in the notional skilled addressee being presented with new technical information, in the sense of 'technical information which he would not derive directly and unambiguously, using common general knowledge, from the application as filed' (*Scripps Research Institute* [63]). Whether the addressee *is* presented with new information depends on how she would understand the subject matter of the amended disclosure and whether, using common general knowledge, she would regard that subject matter as explicitly or implicitly, but directly and unambiguously, disclosed in the application as filed (*Scripps Research Institute* [66]).

5.5 Conclusions

The procedure under the EPC for granting a European patent involves the scrutiny of an application drafted and submitted on behalf of the prospective patentee to ensure that it meets the Convention's formal and substantive requirements for a valid patent grant. An essential aspect of the procedure is the examination of the claimed subject matter for patentability (see Chapters 6 and 7). Equally essential is the examination of the disclosure of the subject matter in the application's claims, description, and drawings for compliance with Articles 83 and 84 EPC. The grant of a patent for a subject matter that is either not a patentable invention or insufficiently described is a basis for opposition or revocation of the patent under Article 100 or Article 138 EPC respectively.

Obtaining a European patent can be an onerous and expensive procedure requiring several years to complete. In addition, it must be remembered that the grant of a patent is no guarantee of its validity, which can only be established by a competent judicial authority. As seen in Section 4.4, reducing the burden on patentees and improving patent quality with a view to minimizing the risk of a patent's revocation post-grant are currently among the key issues of concern within the European patent community. The undertaking by signatories to the London Agreement to waive in whole or part their right to require the full translation of a European patent into their local language before validating it represents a significant development with respect to the first of these, as does the completion of the EPO/Google web-based Patent Translate service (see http://www.epo.org/searching/free/patent-translate.html). The only answer to the second is an ongoing commitment by the EPO and European states to ensuring high standards of examination by properly skilled and equipped patent officers.

When the Unitary Patent Package comes into operation, the owner of any European (EPC) patent will have one month following the patent's grant in which to request that the patent be registered for unitary effect in the territories of participating Member States. Such a request will need to be submitted in the language of the proceedings. However, if the specification of the patent has been published in accordance with the EPC, no further translation of it will be required beyond an initial transitional period. Nor will the request be subject to further substantive examination by the EPO or any other authority, making the act of converting a European (EPC) patent into one with unitary effect a purely administrative act.

The transitional period for unitary patent translation purposes will be at most 12 years. During that period, requests to register a European (EPC) patent for unitary effect will need to be accompanied by a full translation of the specification into English (where the language of the proceedings is French or German) or another official language of the EU (where the language of the proceedings is English). The inclusion of this requirement reflects the controversy caused by the Unitary Patent Package's language regime. The opposition of Spain and Italy to the use of the EPC language regime for European patents with unitary effect was the reason that EU Member States failed to reach unanimous agreement regarding the Unitary Patent Package initially, and that the EU was asked and agreed to invoke the enhanced cooperation provisions of the Treaties to enable its introduction (see Sections 2.4.2.3.2 and 4.5.3.1). It was also among the grounds relied on by those states in their challenge to the constitutionality of the Unitary Patent Package, the last of which were rejected by the CJEU on 5 May 2015.[3]

Further Reading

BRINKHOF, J.J., 'The Conflict Between Article 123(2) and (3) EPC' [1997] *IIC* 833

GALL, G., 'The Euro-PCT Route—Rights and Safeguards for Applicants' [1982] *IIC* 65

GRUBB, P.W., 'The Trilateral Cooperation' (2007) 2 *Journal of Intellectual Property Law and Practice* 397

---

[3] See Case C–146/13 *Kingdom of Spain v European Parliament* EU:C:2015:298 and Case C–147/13 *Spain v Council of the European Union* EU:C:2015:299.

HARHOFF, D. AND REITZIG, M., 'Determinants of Opposition Against EPO Patent Grants: The Case of Biotechnology and Pharmaceuticals' (2004) 22 *International Journal of Industrial Organization* 443

JANSSENS, M.-C., 'EU Perspectives on Employees' Inventions' in M. Pittard, A.L. Monotti and J. Duns (eds), *Business Innovation and the Law: Perspectives from Intellectual Property, Labour, Competition and Corporate Law* (Edward Elgar, 2013) 111

LADDIE, H., 'The Inescapable Trap—Thoughts from the United Kingdom' [1997] *IIC* 829

PFANNER, K., 'The Patent Cooperation Treaty: An Introduction' [1979] *EIPR* 98

ROGGE, R., 'The Conflict Between Article 123(2) and (3) EPC' [1997] *IIC* 842

WHEELER, W.J.L., 'The "Conflict" Between Article 123(2) and 123(3) EPC' [1997] *IIC* 822

6

Patentable Subject Matter

6.1 Introduction

A fundamental issue for any patent regime is what subject matter it will protect and what substantive criteria for protection it will impose in respect of those subject matter. Put differently, what 'essential' and 'accidental' properties should a subject matter be required to possess in order to be patentable? And as a related question, in what if any circumstances should a subject matter be excluded from protection on public policy grounds, notwithstanding its possession of the required properties?

In this and the following chapter we consider these questions. A useful starting point is with the proposition that some subject matter are inherently unsuitable for patent protection; examples being purely expressive subject matter (e.g. poems) and products of nature (e.g. chemical elements). In Europe and internationally, the explanation given for this proposition is that patents may only be granted in respect of inventions, and however new or useful to industry the subject matter above may be, they lack the essential properties of an invention properly conceived. However, and as we saw in Section 3.9, identifying those properties and the boundaries of the category of 'inventions' has proved extremely difficult for patent law- and decision-makers, particularly in the era of new biotechnology.

It is also the case that not all subject matter possessing the essential properties of an invention can support a patent. For example, the wheel may be an invention, but having long been known to and used by the public, it is not one for which a person can obtain a patent monopoly. In Europe and internationally, this is explained with reference to the restriction of patents to inventions that possess the three accidental properties of novelty, inventive step, and susceptibility of industrial application; properties we consider in Chapter 7.

Finally, even some inventions that possess these three accidental properties will be incapable of supporting a patent grant, for reasons of public policy. Once again, the European and international understandings of these classes of subject matter are the same, and include:

(a) inventions the commercial exploitation of which would be contrary to *ordre public* or morality;

(b) plant and animal varieties and essentially biological processes for the production of plants and animals; and

(c) methods of surgical, therapeutic, and diagnostic treatment.

As with inventions themselves, understanding the boundaries of these public policy exclusions and the reasons for their existence has proved increasingly difficult and controversial with the emergence of new technologies; and so too the relationship of each exclusion with the other requirements of patentability has been an issue of long-standing conceptual and practical difficulty.

6.2 The Requirements of Patentability

The basic rule of European patentability is contained in Article 52(1) EPC, according to which,

> European patents shall be granted for any inventions, in all fields of technology, provided that they are new, involve an inventive step and are susceptible of industrial application.

It follows that only inventions that have the properties of being new, inventive, and susceptible of industrial application may be patented. This rule is supplemented by Article 53 EPC, which excludes three categories of subject matter from protection regardless of whether they satisfy the requirements of Article 52(1), namely: inventions the commercial exploitation of which would be contrary to *ordre public* or morality; plant and animal varieties, and essentially biological processes for the production of plants and animals; and methods of surgical, therapeutic, and diagnostic treatment. It follows that in order to determine whether a subject matter is patentable within the meaning of European law, one must ask: (a) whether it falls within one of the Article 53 exclusions from patentability; and, if it does not, (b) whether it is an invention within the meaning of Article 52(1); and, if it is, (c) whether it is new, inventive, and susceptible of industrial application within the meaning of Article 52(1). In this chapter we focus on (a) and (b), leaving (c) for Chapter 7.

In recent years, both the Article 53 exclusions and the requirement for an invention have acquired an importance that could not have been foreseen by the drafters of the EPC, much less the expert patent committees of the Council of Europe and EEC on whose work from the 1950s and 1960s it is based. A central reason for this is that even in 1973, methods of genetic engineering were only just being discovered, 20 years after Watson and Crick had revealed the structure of DNA. Since then, the field of new biotechnology has emerged, supporting an industry that in 2012 alone was reportedly worth €3.82 billion in net revenues in the United States, Europe, Canada, and Australia.[1] That industry is supported by products such as isolated DNA (gene) sequences that encode for proteins of pharmaceutical or other industrial use, genetically modified plants that are resistant to toxins or have other beneficial properties, and genetically modified animals that are susceptible to disease and thus of use in medical research. As we saw in Section 4.4, the number of applications for European patents concerning such products increases every year, as biotech firms seek both to

---

[1] Ernst & Young Biotechnology Industry Report 2013, 'Beyond borders: Matters of evidence' http://www.ey.com/Publication/vwLUAssets/Beyond_borders/$FILE/Beyond_borders.pdf.

offset the high costs of their research and development and to exclude competitors from duplicating their research and development efforts. Such patenting also raises difficult legal and ethical issues, many of which engage the Article 53 exclusions and the requirement for an invention of Article 52(1).

At the European level, the main legal response to these issues to date has been the EU's enactment of the Biotech Directive and the EP Organisation's incorporation of its provisions into the Implementing Regulations of the EPC, as shown in Figure 6.1. The Biotech Directive restates the EPC requirements of patentability above, and clarifies their meaning and application in respect of 'biotechnological inventions', namely, product inventions consisting of or containing biological material, and process inventions by means of which biological material is produced, processed, or used (see Article 3(1) Biotech

Patentability issue	EU Biotech Directive (applies with respect to biotechnological inventions and has effect for EU Member States)	EPC (has effect for EPC Contracting States)	EPC Implementing Regulations (applies with respect to biotechnological inventions and has effect for EPC Contracting States)
The *ordre public*/morality exclusions from patentability	Article 6 and associated recitals, including 26 & 36 to 45	Article 53(a)	Rule 28
The varieties and exclusively biological process exclusions from patentability	Articles 2, 3, 4, & 12 and associated recitals, including 8 to 10, 13, 29 to 33, and 47 to 53	Article 53(b)	Rules 26(4) to (6), 27(b) and (c)
The medical methods exclusion from patentability	recital 35	Article 53(c)	–
The requirement for an invention	Articles 3, 5, and associated recitals, including 20 to 23	Article 52(1), (2), and (3)	Rule 27(a), 29(1) and (2)
The requirement for novelty	Article 3 and associated recitals, including 22	Articles 52(1), 54, 55	–
The requirement for inventive step	Article 3 and associated recitals, including 22	Articles 52(1), 56	–
The requirement for susceptibility of industrial application	Article 3 and associated recitals, including 20 to 24	Articles 52(1), 57	Rule 29(3)

Figure 6.1 Sources of European law regarding patentability

Directive), where by 'biological material' is meant 'material containing genetic information and capable of reproducing itself or being reproduced in a biological system' (Article 2(1)(a) Biotech Directive).

6.3 Public Policy Exclusions from Patentability

6.3.1 **Article 53 EPC**

The starting point for determining patentability is Article 53 EPC, which prohibits the grant of European patents in respect of:

(a) inventions the commercial exploitation of which would be contrary to 'ordre public' or morality; such exploitation shall not be deemed to be so contrary merely because it is prohibited by law or regulation in some or all of the Contracting States;

(b) plant or animal varieties or essentially biological processes for the production of plants or animals; this provision shall not apply to microbiological processes or the products thereof; [and]

(c) methods for treatment of the human or animal body by surgery or therapy and diagnostic methods practised on the human or animal body; this provision shall not apply to products, in particular substances or compositions, for use in any of these methods.

6.3.2 **The *Ordre Public*/Morality Exclusions: Article 53(a) EPC**

6.3.2.1 **Preliminary Remarks**

The current version of Article 53(a) EPC is slightly amended from the original version of 1973, which excluded 'inventions the *publication or* exploitation of which would be contrary to "ordre public" or morality...' (emphasis added). According to the EP Organisation, deleting 'publication or' entailed no change to EPO practice, and was done solely to bring Article 53(a) into line with Article 27.2 TRIPS Agreement and Article 6(1) Biotech Directive.

Perhaps surprisingly, Article 53(a) EPC received little attention from the drafters of the EPC. The only reported issue of discussion was whether '*ordre public*' was to be a European or a national concept; a European concept was agreed. Beyond this there was no attempt to define the scope of the exclusion, nor the terms '*ordre public*' or 'morality'. That was left to the EPO, which in T356/93 (*PLANT GENETIC SYSTEMS/Glutamine Synthetase Inhibitors*) [1995] EPOR 357, 366 (*PGS*) defined *ordre public* to mean 'the protection of public security and the physical integrity of individuals as part of society; as well as the protection of the environment', and morality as 'related to the belief that some behaviour is right and acceptable whereas other behaviour is wrong, this belief being founded on the totality of the accepted norms which are deeply rooted in a particular culture'; the culture for Article 53(a) purposes being that 'inherent in European society and civilisation'.

Article 53(a) is restated in Article 6(1) Biotech Directive, and supplemented in Article 6(2) (reproduced in Rule 28 EPC) by the following inclusive list of examples of subject matter that are unpatentable on *ordre public*/morality grounds:

(a) processes for cloning human beings;

(b) processes for modifying the germ line genetic identity of human beings;

(c) uses of human embryos for industrial or commercial purposes;

(d) processes for modifying the genetic identity of animals which are likely to cause them suffering without any substantial medical benefit to man or animal, and also animals resulting from such processes.

In addition, it may be inferred from recital 26 Biotech Directive that subject matter which incorporates human biological material obtained from a person without his or her free and informed consent will also be unpatentable under Article 53(a)/Article 6(1). This is consistent with international principles of medical and research ethics (e.g., Articles 6 and 7 UNESCO Declaration on Bioethics and Human Rights 2005) and the integrity of the person protected by Article 3 CFR. As discussed later, it is also consistent with the EPO's treatment of donor consent as relevant to the question whether a DNA sequence was excluded from patentability under Article 53(a) EPC in *HOWARD FLOREY/Relaxin* [1995] EPOR 541 (*Howard Florey*). However, the CJEU and EPO have rejected that Article 3 CFR or Article 53(a) EPC requires applicants for a patent in respect of human biological material to evidence consent to the material's use and/or commercialization by the person from whom it was taken (see Case C–377/98 *Kingdom of Netherlands v European Parliament* [2001] ECR I-7079 and T1213/05 (*Breast and Ovarian Cancer/UNIVERSITY OF UTAH*) EP:BA:2007:T121305.20070927). Therefore, while proof that consent was given or denied will be relevant under Article 53(a), an inability to prove that it was given will not be fatal to an application or grant.

To date, European tribunals have considered the meaning of Article 53(a)/Article 6(1) in five main cases, two of which have involved Rule 28/Article 6(2). Those cases support three approaches to the general *ordre public*/morality exclusion of Article 53(a)/Article 6(1). According to the first, supported by the CJEU in Case C–34/10 *Brüstle v Greenpeace eV* [2011] ECR I-9821 (*Brüstle*), and to a lesser extent by the Enlarged Board of Appeal in G2/06 (*WARF/Stem Cells*) [2009] EPOR 15 (*Warf*), a subject matter involving human biological material will be excluded under Article 53(a)/Article 6(1) if its commercialization might possibly offend the dignity or integrity of the person. According to the second, supported by the Technical Board of Appeal in T19/90 (*HARVARD/Onco- mouse*) [1990] EPOR 501 (*Onco-mouse*), any other subject matter will be excluded under Article 53(a)/Article 6(1) if its risks to society outweigh its benefits. And finally, the decisions of the EPO support a third view of Article 53(a)/Article 6(1) in place of that expressed in *Onco-mouse*, according to which these provisions exclude from patentability only such subject matter as would be universally regarded as outrageous or likely to breach public peace, social order, or conventionally accepted standards of European culture.

6.3.2.2 Inventions Involving Human Biological Material

The meaning of the *ordre public*/morality exclusions has been considered by the Enlarged Board of Appeal of the EPO and the CJEU in three cases to date: *Warf, Brüstle*, and Case C–364/13 *International Stem Cell Corporation v Comptroller General of Patents* EU:C:2014:2451 (*ISC*). The question of law in each of these cases was whether certain biotech inventions[2]—cell cultures comprising primate embryonic stem cells (*Warf*), isolated and purified neural precursor cells and associated methods (*Brüstle*), and human parthenotes[3] (*ISC*)—involved 'uses of human embryos for industrial or commercial purposes' so as to be excluded from patentability by Rule 28(c) EPC/Article 6(2)(c) Biotech Directive.

According to the Enlarged Board of Appeal in *Warf* and the CJEU in *Brüstle*, the inventions in those cases did. Central to the reasons given by the tribunals in reaching these decisions was their view of Rule 28(c)/Article 6(2)(c) as needing to be interpreted expansively in order to give effect to the intention of the EP Organisation and EU legislature and thereby to protect human dignity. The result was an interpretation of the human

---

[2] See further the biotechnology patenting case study in Section 3.9.

[3] Human parthenotes are stem cell lines that are produced by parthenogenesis to develop like human fertilized eggs but that are not fertilized and so, in the absence of genetic modification, are incapable of developing into a human being.

embryos exclusion as covering any invention the preparation of which involves the use of a human embryo, even if the invention itself does not include an embryo and is intended exclusively for use in research, and even if the use of the embryo in its preparation is with the donor's free and informed consent. Regarding the nature of a human embryo itself, both tribunals agreed that it should be interpreted expansively, and not limited to its conventional meaning of at least 14 days post-fertilization. While the Enlarged Board declined in *Warf* to offer a precise definition, describing its meaning as a matter for individual courts having regard to the facts of the case before them, the CJEU in *Brüstle* was not so constrained. In its decision, responding to a direct question from the referring court, 'human embryo' in the Biotech Directive designates an autonomous concept of EU law that must be interpreted in a uniform manner throughout EU territory to include 'any human ovum...as soon as fertilized' ([35]).[4] According to the Court, thus defined it potentially includes stem cells obtained from an embryo at the blastocyst stage (roughly five days after fertilization), provided they are 'capable of commencing the process of the development of a human being' ([36]), which must be determined by the referring court in the light of scientific developments.

Consistent with their approaches to defining what a human embryo is, the Enlarged Board and CJEU in *Warf* and *Brüstle* differed in their preparedness to comment generally on the meaning of Rule 28(c)/Article 6(2)(c) or Article 53(a)/Article 6(1). According to the Enlarged Board in *Warf*, offering such comments was neither necessary to resolve the legal issue before it nor appropriate in the light of that issue. Less cautious was the CJEU, which made clear its view that the patentability of any invention involving human biological material would engage the fundamental rights of human dignity and the integrity of the person, and thus require an analysis similar to that undertaken for the stem cell cultures and associated methods in *Brüstle*. This view was consistent with the Resolution adopted by the European Parliament on 30 March 2000 following the EPO's grant of the so-called Edinburgh patent (EP 0 695 351) in respect of 'animal [including by implication, human] transgenic stem cells' (and the European Commission's statement in response to it),[5] and is supported by recitals 39 and 43 Biotech Directive, which underline the importance of subjecting inventions to ethical and moral (as well as legal) scrutiny when considering their patentability, and of applying patent law having regard to the fundamental rights guaranteed by the ECHR and EU law.

The CJEU's decision in *Brüstle* may be criticized for several reasons. One is that its expansive definition of 'human embryo' as including any post-fertilization embryo conflicts with the more limited definitions supported by the (non-patent) laws of most European states. Another is the Court's refusal to allow Member States any margin of appreciation with respect either to the meaning of human embryo or the scope of Article 6(2)(c)/Rule28(c) in general, notwithstanding its basis in human dignity, which—and as the CJEU has previously recognized[6]—is a concept the meaning and requirements of which European states may reasonably have different views regarding. Third, the decision may be criticized for its potential 'chilling' effect on stem cell research; though such effect has been at least partly mitigated by new technologies enabling the creation of

---

[4] Ernst & Young Biotechnology Industry Report 2013 (n 1).

[5] At the time of the Parliament's Resolution the patent was before the Opposition Division of the EPO. On 19 April 2000 the Opposition Division approved the patent with an amendment limiting it to non-human stem cells.

[6] See Case C–36/02 *Omega Spielhallen* [2004] ECR I-9609; but cf in the context of Article 6(2) specifically, Case C–456/03 *Commission of the European Communities v Italian Republic* [2005] ECR I-5335.

embryonic stem cells without the destruction of any embryos. And finally, and recalling the discussion of Deryck Beyleveld and Roger Brownsword's analysis of human dignity in Section 3.9, the decision may be criticized for reflecting a rights-based conception of human dignity focused on preventing instrumentalist treatments of the human body, in place of a duty-based conception focused on protecting individual freedoms.

The second reference to the CJEU regarding the human embryos exclusion of Rule 28(c)/Article 6(2)(c) was made in 2013. The question referred by the court in *ISC* was whether a human embryo as defined in *Brüstle* includes unfertilized human ova the division and further development of which have been stimulated by parthenogenesis and which, in contrast to fertilized ova, contain only pluripotent cells and are therefore incapable of developing into human beings. In December 2014 the Court decided that such ova are not human embryos within the meaning of Article 6(2)(c) because of their inability to develop into human beings. In its judgment, the mere fact that an organism *commences* a process of development as a human being is not sufficient for it to be regarded as a human embryo: it must 'have the inherent capacity of developing into a human being' ([28]), including by reason of its genetic modification. Whether it does have that inherent capacity is a question for the national court to decide in the light of 'knowledge … sufficiently tried and tested by international medical science' ([36]).

One question not addressed by the Court of Justice in *ISC* is whether its decision was without prejudice to the issue of the parthenote's patentability in general, including its exclusion on *ordre public*/morality grounds under Article 6(1) Biotech Directive. In the opinion of the Advocate General in the case, it was without prejudice to the issue, with the result that the parthenote might still have been excluded from patentability, including on *ordre public*/morality grounds.

6.3.2.3 Inventions Not Involving Human Biological Material

As we have seen, *Brüstle* (as clarified in *ISC*) represents a general authority on the meaning of Article 53(a)/Article 6(1) in respect of inventions involving human biological material, and is not confined in its terms to the human embryos exclusion of Article 6(2)(c)/Rule 28(c) specifically. However, it says nothing regarding the meaning of Article 53(a)/Article 6(1) in respect of inventions not involving human biological material. That meaning must therefore be derived from the EPO's earlier Article 53(a) case law, and in particular from its decisions in *Onco-mouse, Howard Florey*, and *PGS*.

6.3.2.3.1 *Article 53(a) as a Mechanism for Balancing the Benefits and Risks of Inventions:* Onco-mouse

Onco-mouse concerned the patentability of the 'onco-mouse': a transgenic non-human mammalian animal whose cells had been modified to make the animal abnormally prone to develop tumours. When considering the application for a European patent for the animal, the EPO's Examining Divisions had declared Article 53(a) to be irrelevant, prompting an appeal to the Board of Appeal. The Board overturned the Examining Divisions' decision, deciding instead that the onco-mouse was precisely the kind of invention in respect of which Article 53(a) needed to be considered. According to the Board, when undertaking that consideration the task of the EPO was to weigh carefully the benefits and risks of the invention, including in particular 'the suffering of animals and possible risks required to the environment on one hand, and the invention's usefulness to mankind on the other' (513). It sent the application back to the Examining Divisions for reconsideration in line with this direction. The Examining Divisions began by identifying three interests as needing to be weighed (see [1991] EPOR 525): the basic interest of mankind to remedy widespread and dangerous diseases; the protection of the environment against the uncontrolled dissemination of unwanted genes; and the avoidance of cruelty to animals. It then identified the following facts as having particular relevance in weighing these interests: that the invention contributed to the development of new and improved human anti-cancer treatments; that the invention used fewer animals than other corresponding measures, and thus contributed to a reduction of the overall extent of animal suffering; that there were no equally reliable test models available; and that the risk of an uncontrolled release of the invention into the environment was limited, in effect, to intentional misuse or blatant ignorance on the part of the laboratory personnel carrying out the tests. Its conclusion was that in the overall balance, the invention could not be considered immoral or contrary to public policy, and that it was therefore not excluded from patentability under Article 53(a).[7]

Onco-mouse was decided more than 20 years ago, and before the introduction of the Biotech Directive. Nonetheless, it was expressly affirmed by the Technical Board following the enactment of the Directive, in T315/03 (*HARVARD/Transgenic Animal*) [2005] EPOR 31. In addition, the interpretation of Article 53(a) which it supports, as a mechanism for ensuring a fair balance of the competing interests of inventors and others, including in respect of public health and the protection of the environment, is consistent with EU legal understandings of the purpose of exceptions and limitations to IP rights (see e.g. Section 4.4.2 and Chapter 13). For these reasons, it should be considered strong authority on the meaning of Article 53(a) in respect of subject matter not involving human biological material.

6.3.2.3.2 *Article 53(a) as a Limited Exclusion Covering Inventions That Would Be Universally Regarded as Outrageous:* Howard Florey *and* PGS

Having said that, there exists an alternative view of Article 53(a), supported by the EPO's Opposition Divisions and Board of Appeal in *Howard Florey* and *PGS*.

Howard Florey involved a recombinant DNA sequence encoding for H2-relaxin, the patentability of which was opposed on the ground, among others, that DNA represents 'life' the patenting of which is immoral and therefore prohibited under the EPC, and that to allow a patent for the invention in question would have involved an abuse of the pregnant women from whose bodies the mRNA had been isolated, a return to slavery, and 'the piecemeal sale of women to industry' (549). As we saw in Section 3.9, these arguments were emphatically rejected by the EPO, citing four main reasons. The first was that the women from whose bodies the mRNA had been isolated had consented to donate their tissue 'within the framework of necessary gynaecological operations' (550). The second was that patents confer rights of exclusion rather than use, and are incapable of conferring 'any rights whatever to individual human beings' (ibid). The third was that DNA is not life but rather 'a chemical substance which carries genetic information and can be used as an intermediate in the production of proteins which may be medically useful' (551). And the fourth was that the *ordre public*/morality exclusions of the EPC do not permit enquiry into the intrinsic immorality or inappropriateness of gene patents, on the ground that patentability is a matter of law rather than ethics, and that ethical enquiries are beyond the proper remit of European patent tribunals. All the EPO could do, it was held, was consider whether the opponents' general assertions concerning the alleged intrinsic immorality of patenting human genes were made out. It decided they were not, as there existed

---

[7] Contrast the decision of the Supreme Court of Canada in *Commissioner of Patents v Harvard College* [2002] SCC 76.

no 'overwhelming consensus' among the EPC Contracting States that the patenting of human genes—including the use to that end of consensually detached human body parts—is 'abhorrent' (552).

The *Howard Florey* approach to Article 53(a) was supported soon after in *PGS*, involving genetically engineered plants and related methods. According to the Technical Board in that case, exclusions to patentability must be interpreted narrowly to reflect the EPC drafters' concern to maximize the scope of patentability. Applying the definitions of *ordre public* and morality discussed in Section 6.3.2.1, the Board in *PGS* rejected the opponent's argument that the exploitation of the claimed inventions would damage the environment and be contrary to both *ordre public* and morality due to their adverse environmental consequences and promotion of human dominion over the natural world for two reasons. The first was that the invention in question did not contain wild-type plant resources that could be used as starting material, and the second was that the question raised by Article 53(a) was not whether living organisms were excluded as such, but whether or not the publication or exploitation of a specific invention would be contrary to *ordre public* or morality.

The result of *Howard Florey* and *PGS* is a view of Article 53(a) as existing only to ensure 'that patents…not be granted for inventions which would universally be regarded as outrageous' such as a letter bomb (*Howard Florey* 549), or inventions the exploitation of which would be likely to breach public peace, social order, or conventionally accepted standards of European cultural standards (*PGS* 368). Thus interpreted, Article 53(a) requires an assessment of the likely adverse social effects of, and the public's attitude to, the patenting and exploitation of the invention in question, including with reference to the method by which the invention is devised.

Of immediate note regarding this approach to Article 53(a) is the difficulty of reconciling it with either the approach of *Onco-mouse* or the provisions of the Biotech Directive. It seems clear that cases involving human biological material could not be decided in the same way today; though nor would the subject matter of *Howard Florey* be excluded from patentability given the express provision in Article 5(2) Biotech Directive that isolated human genes are patentable (see Section 6.4), as the Technical Board affirmed in T272/95 (*Relaxin/HOWARD FLOREY INSTITUTE*) EP:BA:2002:T027295.20021023. However, even for inventions not involving such material, the suggestion of *Howard Florey* and *PGS* that ethical enquiries are beyond the proper remit of patentability sits uncomfortably with recitals 39 and 43 Biotech Directive discussed previously. It is also difficult to reconcile with the EU's view of Article 6(1) Biotech Directive as existing to ensure protection for 'human, animal [and] plant life [and] health' and the avoidance of 'serious prejudice to the environment' (see recital 36), particularly given the EU legal recognition of the importance of environmental protection under Article 37 CFR. For these reasons, *Onco-mouse* seems a stronger European authority regarding the meaning of Article 53(a)/Article 6(1) for inventions not involving human biological material than *Howard Florey* and/or *PGS*. On the other hand, in G2/12 and G2/13 (*Essentially Biological Processes*) [2015] EPOR 28 (*Essentially Biological Processes II*), the Enlarged Board of Appeal remarked, apparently approvingly, on the tendency of the EPO Boards of Appeal to interpret the exclusions of Article 53 EPC, including Article 53(a) specifically, 'rather restrictively' ([48]), albeit citing both *PGS* and *Onco-Mouse*. Its ambivalent treatment of the cases confirms the need for clarification by it or the CJEU regarding the appropriate interpretative approach to Article 53(a)/Article 6(1) in cases not involving human biological material post-Biotech Directive.

Figure 6.2 summarizes the different interpretations of the *ordre public*/morality exclusions of Article 53(a) EPC/Article 6(1) Biotech Directive and their current legal status.

	The purpose of the exclusion	Method of application	Status
Warf/ Brüstle	Among other things, to ensure respect for human dignity and the integrity of the person. (See further Section 3.9)	Expansively, to determine whether there is any possibility of the invention offending the dignity or integrity of the person. Regarding Rule 28(c)/Article 6(2)(c), this will be satisfied for any invention the overall teaching of which involves the destruction of human embryos.	Good law for inventions involving human biological material.
Onco-mouse	To provide a mechanism for weighing the usefulness of an invention to society with its ethical risks and consequences.	Neutrally, by identifying and weighing the benefits and risks of an invention to society.	Good law for inventions not involving human biological material: has been affirmed since the introduction of the Biotech Directive, and is consistent with general EU principles regarding the purpose of exceptions and limitations to IP rights as being to provide a site for the reconciliation of competing rights and interests.
Howard Florey/PGS	To ensure that patents are not granted for inventions that would be: universally regarded as 'outrageous', such as a letter bomb (*Howard Florey*); likely to breach public peace, social order, or conventionally accepted standards of European culture, such as through acts of terrorism (*PGS*).	Restrictively, by determining the adverse social effects of, and the European public's attitude to, the invention, including in the light of the manner in which it was devised.	Doubtful legal status: inconsistent with the Biotech Directive and EU principles regarding the reconciliation of competing rights and interest (see above).

Figure 6.2 Interpretations of the *ordre public*/morality exclusions from patentability

6.3.3 The Varieties/Essentially Biological Process Exclusions

6.3.3.1 Article 53(b) EPC

Article 53(b) EPC, reproduced in Article 4 Biotech Directive, excludes three categories of subject matter from patentability: plant varieties, animal varieties, and essentially biological processes for the production of plants and animals. By express provision of the same Article, 'microbiological processes or the products thereof' are not so excluded.

A central issue when drafting Article 53(b) EPC was the reason for the exclusions and their proper location within the EPC: are varieties and essentially biological processes unpatentable because they are not inventions within the meaning of Article 52(1) EPC, or is the reason one of public policy? As the final location of Article 53(b) suggests, public policy was the drafters' answer. Despite this, subsequent definitions of Article 53(b) have ensured that it adds little if anything to the requirement for an invention. This is because the plant and animal varieties exclusions have been restrictively interpreted so as only to cover subject matter eligible for protection by the *sui generis* plant varieties regime and their animal equivalents (G1/98 (*NOVARTIS/Transgenic Plant*) [2000] EPOR 303 (*Novartis*)) even if, in the case of a plant variety, not all of the conditions for the application of that regime are fully met (Rule 26(4) EPC). Similarly, since the introduction of the Biotech Directive, the essentially biological process exclusion has been expressly limited to non-technical processes (see Rule 27 EPC/Article 4(3) Biotech Directive). On the other hand, and as we will see, that limitation has not been strictly observed by the EPO.

6.3.3.2 Plant and Animal Varieties

6.3.3.2.1 Legislative Definitions

'Plant variety' was first defined for European patent law in Article 2(1)(3) Biotech Directive. According to that definition, it has the meaning of Article 5 Plant Variety Rights Regulation. Rather than also cross-refer to an EU instrument, the Administrative Council of the EP Organisation inserted its own definition of 'plant variety' into the EPC Implementing Regulations when it incorporated the other provisions of the Biotech Directive. That definition is based on Article 1 International Convention for the Protection of New Varieties of Plants 1991, and is consistent also with Article 5 Plant Variety Rights Regulation. Thus it defines a plant variety as any plant grouping, consisting of entire plants or parts of plants capable of producing entire plants within a single botanical taxon of the lowest known rank, and including hybrids between botanical genera or species (Rule 26(4)). By inference, the same definition applies *mutatis mutandis* for animal varieties.

Central to this definition of plant or animal variety is the reference to taxonomic rank, which restricts this exclusion of Article 53(b) to plants and animals positioned at the bottom of the taxonomic hierarchy, immediately beneath the rank of genus, as shown in Figure 6.3.

6.3.3.2.2 Plant and Animal Inventions the Technical Feasibility of Which Extends Beyond a Particular Variety

As Figure 6.3 suggests, it follows that any plant- or animal-related invention the teaching of which extends beyond a single variety will not be excluded from patentability by Article 53(b)/Article 4. That is why the Article 53(b) challenge to the 'transgenic non-human mammalian animal' in *Onco-mouse* was rejected, namely, because the invention's technical teaching extended beyond mice to other mammals, putting it in a taxon much higher than that of variety. Since *Onco-mouse*, this principle has been codified expressly in Rule 27(b) EPC/Article 4(2)(b), which state that '[i]nventions which concern plants or

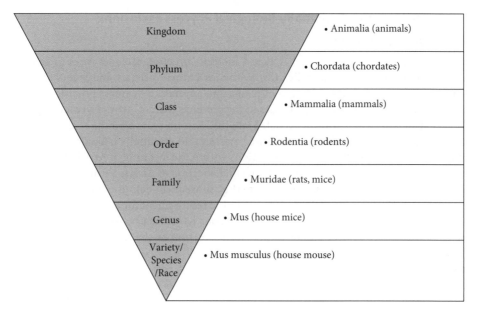

Figure 6.3 Taxonomic hierarchy for the house mouse
ITIS Report, TSN 180366

animals shall be patentable if the technical feasibility of the invention is not confined to a particular plant or animal variety'.

6.3.3.2.3 *Plants and Animals Produced by an Essentially Biological Process*

One issue more recently considered by the Enlarged Board of Appeal, in *Essentially Biological Processes II*, is whether plants or animals other than a plant or animal variety are excluded under Article 53(b) if the only known method of producing them is an essentially biological process. According to the party opposing patentability in that case, to permit patents for such products would frustrate the legislatures' aim of excluding essentially biological processes from patentability, and create the paradoxical situation whereby such processes are excluded but their products are not. However, and as the respondent pointed out, the same situation exists in the medical field, where methods of treating the human and animal body are excluded from patentability but products for use in such methods are not (see Section 6.3.4.2). The decision of the Enlarged Board of Appeal supported this argument. According to the reasoning of the Board, since products and processes are substantively different, a product cannot fall within the scope of a process exclusion. Thus, even if a product, such as a plant or plant material, 'can only be obtained by essentially biological processes with no other methods either disclosed in the patent application or otherwise known', the product will not be excluded from patentability by reason of the process exclusion of Article 53(b) EPC ([90]).

6.3.3.3 **Essentially Biological Processes**

Rule 27(c) EPC and Article 4(2)(c) Biotech Directive define a process for the production of plants or animals as 'essentially biological' if it consists entirely of natural phenomena such as crossing or selection, and a process as 'microbiological' if it involves, is performed upon, or results in microbiological material. According to the Enlarged Board, however, a process may be essentially biological within the meaning of Article 53(b) notwithstanding its use of technical means or other forms of human intervention—which use will make it an invention within the meaning of Article 52(1) EPC (see Section 6.4)—provided that the genetic traits of the plants or animals resulting from the process are determined by the underlying natural phenomenon, and not by the technical step or other human intervention itself (G2/07 and G1/08 (*Essentially Biological Processes*) [2011] EPOR 27 (*Essentially Biological Processes I*). Further, when deciding whether a process is essentially biological within the meaning of Article 53(b), it is not relevant whether a step of a technical nature is a new or known measure, whether it is trivial or a fundamental alteration of a known process, whether it does or could occur in nature or whether the essence of the invention lies in it. It follows that a process may be an invention within the meaning of Article 52(1) EPC, but nonetheless excluded from patentability for being essentially biological within the meaning of Article 53(b). As noted earlier, this would seem to contradict the provision in Rule 27 EPC/Article 4(3) Biotech Directive that the exclusions of Article 53(b) are without prejudice to the patentability of any technical process. On the other hand, it ensures that the essentially biological process exclusion does more than restate the requirement for an invention in respect of biological processes.

6.3.4 The Surgical, Therapeutic, and Diagnostic Methods Exclusions

6.3.4.1 Article 53(c) EPC

The third and last of the public policy exclusions from European patentability is contained in Article 53(c), and covers 'methods for treatment of the human or animal body by surgery or therapy and diagnostic methods practised on the human or animal body'. This exclusion was included in the original text of the EPC 1973, but was there related to the requirement for susceptibility of industrial application and expressed (in Article 52(4) EPC 1973) as follows:

> Methods for treatment of the human or animal body by surgery or therapy and diagnostic methods practised on the human or animal body shall not be regarded as inventions which are susceptible of industrial application within the meaning of paragraph 1 [Article 52(1)]. This provision shall not apply to products, in particular substances or compositions, for use in any of these methods.

As with Article 53(b), the reason for excluding surgical, therapeutic, and diagnostic methods from patentability was a persistent issue for the EPC drafters. The EEC Working Party had listed methods of therapy as among the categories of subject matter that were not to be regarded as inventions in the early 1960s. On the eve of the EPC's conclusion in 1973, however, this understanding was rejected, and the exclusion recast as Article 52(4) above. In the 2000 EPC revision it was recast again to take its current form as Article 53(c). According to the EP Organisation's Administrative Council, this was necessary since the exclusion of medical methods for lack of industrial applicability was merely a fiction; its real basis being the protection of public health (Doc. MR/2/00 e 45). In addition, it was said that moving the exclusion to Article 53(c) would bring the EPC into line with Article 27(3)(a) TRIPS Agreement, and would not involve any change to EPO practice (ibid). This understanding of Article 53(c) as aimed at protecting public health is now generally accepted.

6.3.4.2 Products For Use in a Medical (Article 53(c)) Method

6.3.4.2.1 Legislative Background

It is often said that excluding methods of medical treatment from patentability to protect public health on the one hand, while allowing patents for 'products…for use in any of these methods' such as medicines and medical implements on the other, is irrational. As one English patent judge has said: 'If one accepts that a patent monopoly is a fair price to pay for the extra research incentive, then there is no reason to suppose that that would not apply also to methods of treatment' (*Bristol-Myers Squibb Co. v Baker Norton Pharmaceuticals Inc.* [1999] RPC 253 (UK Patents Court)). In other words, if we accept that granting patents for medicines and medical implements supports research and development of benefit to human health, it is reasonable to assume that granting patents for medical methods will do the same.

In fact, the drafters of Article 53(c) considered the policy interest in encouraging investment in medical research, but concluded that it did not justify the deviation from national practice that permitting patents for medical methods would have involved. It was only later that they agreed there was a need to ensure the availability of patents for substances when used in therapeutic methods, and that this need justified an explicit provision to the effect that such treatments were actually, as distinct from potentially, patentable. Hence the last line of Article 53(c), preserved from Article 52(4) EPC 1973.

6.3.4.2.2 Medical Methods Distinguished from Uses of Products for the Manufacture of a Medicament for a Specified Therapeutic Application

This account of the history of Article 53(c) EPC is consistent with the EPO's long-standing view of that Article. According to the Enlarged Board in G5/83 (*EISAI/Second Medical Indication*) [1979–85] EPOR B241 (*Eisai*), for example, the intention behind Article 52(4) was 'only to free from restraint non-commercial and non-industrial medical and veterinary activities', with the result that it did not cover any use of a substance or composition in the manufacture of a medicament for a specified new and inventive therapeutic application ('the use of compound X for the manufacture of a medicament for a specified (new) therapeutic application Y') (248–9). After *Eisai*, patent claims of this type were allowed by the EPO and referred to as Swiss-form claims in recognition of their origin in the practice of the Swiss patent office. As the Technical Board of Appeal confirmed in T1780/12 (*BOARD OF REGENTS, UNIVERSITY OF TEXAS/Cancer Treatment*) [2014] EPOR 28 (*University of Texas*) [33], they are process rather than product claims, and in particular purpose-limited process claims. Thus, they differ from regular process claims in the restriction of their definition and scope with reference to the purpose for which the manufactured medicament is intended. Thus, they are not methods of manufacturing products as such, but rather methods of manufacturing products for a specific use: the purpose for which the product is to be used is an essential or constitutive property of the subject matter. It follows that the protection that a patent for a Swiss-form invention confers is limited to the use of compound X for the manufacture of the relevant medicinal product *for the specific purpose* defined in the claim. That is why it is no objection to the grant of a patent for such a subject matter that the method of manufacture itself is not new, namely, because the contribution to the art which the subject matter makes is only the discovery of the new purpose for which the (known) product to be manufactured may be used (see further Section 7.2).

6.3.4.2.3 Claiming a Patent for a Product for Use in a Medical (Article 53(c)) Method

Since the EPC 2000 revisions, Swiss-form claims have been rendered redundant by the express provision in Article 54(4) and (5) EPC that any known substance or composition having a previously unknown use in one of the methods excluded from patentability in Article 53(c) is itself capable of supporting a patent. The effect of this principle is to permit the patenting of purpose-limited products (rather than purpose-limited processes) in the medical field on the basis of the new and otherwise patentable therapeutic, surgical or diagnostic purpose for which the product has been discovered to have use. According to the Enlarged Board, given the express allowance of purpose-limited products by Article 54(4) and (5), the 'legal fiction' of Swiss-form claims is no long required, and also no longer valid. As it stated in G2/08 (*ABBOTT RESPIRATORY/Dosage Regime*) [2010] EPOR 26, 'under the new law the lacuna in the former provisions, which had been filled in a praetorian way by the Enlarged Board of Appeal with decision G 5/83 and the case law based on that decision, no longer exists' ([101]). Thus, when seeking a patent for the discovery of a new therapeutic indication of a known drug in Europe, an applicant must now define her invention in the patent claims as 'compound A for use in treating disease B', and not using the *Eisai*-approved wording described in Section 6.3.4.2.2. In so doing she will also obtain the more expansive protection conferred by a patent for a purpose-limited product in comparison with that conferred by a patent for a purpose-limited process (see Section 8.4.1; *University of Texas*).

In sum, products for use in a surgical, therapeutic, or diagnostic method may be patented under European law by express provision of Article 54(4) and (5), and consistent with the last line in Article 53(c) and the limited purpose of that Article to 'free from restraint non-commercial and non-industrial medical and veterinary activities' (*Eisai* 248). Methods of surgical, therapeutic, or diagnostic treatment remain excluded, however, so as not to restrain medical and veterinary activities. An alternative, and perhaps more convincing, explanation for this exclusion may be that such methods are not intellectual products, properly conceived. Put differently, they could be said to be analogous to the instructions for painting a sunset and flying an aeroplane considered in Section 3.2 in being too dependent on the discretion of those who perform them to be regarded as having the identifiable human creators or essential stability required of intellectual products. As we will see in Section 6.4.2.3, this is consistent with current European definitions of inventions as requiring sufficient repeatability.

6.3.4.3 Diagnostic Methods

A diagnostic method within the meaning of Article 52(4)/Article 53(c) has been defined by the Enlarged Board as any method that includes the four steps of: (a) examination; (b) data gathering; (c) comparison; and (d) deduction, all performed directly on the human or animal body (G1/04 (*CYGNUS/Diagnostic Methods*) [2006] EPOR 15 (*Diagnostic Methods*)). This is consistent with common language understandings of diagnosis, as the 'determination of the nature of a diseased condition; identification of a disease by careful investigation of its symptoms and history; also, the opinion (formally stated) resulting from such investigation' (*Oxford English Dictionary*). According to the Enlarged Board in *Diagnostic Methods*, however, a diagnostic method for EPC purposes does not include any diagnostic method which includes technical steps carried out by a device, consistent with the limited purpose of the exclusions described earlier.

6.3.4.4 Surgical Methods

The Enlarged Board has also considered the nature of the surgical methods excluded by Article 53(c), in G1/07 (*MEDI-PHYSICS/Treatment by Surgery*) [2010] EPOR 25 (*Medi-Physics*). That case involved an imaging method for a diagnostic purpose (the examination phase within the meaning of *Diagnostic Methods*) that involved injecting an imaging agent into the human or animal heart. The central issue for the Board was whether that method was one of surgery and thus excluded from patentability by Article 53(c). The Board held that it was, on the ground that the injection was an invasive step, involving 'a substantial physical intervention on the body which requires professional medical expertise to be carried out and which entails a health risk even when carried out with the required professional care and expertise' ([165]). Had the claim been amended to omit the injection of the contrast agent it would have avoided the Article 53(c) exclusion; the mere use of data derived directly from the imaging method in surgery—for example, to help the surgeon decide how to proceed—being insufficient in the Board's judgment to make the method one of surgery, and thus insufficient to exclude it from patentability.

The basis of the decision in *Medi-physics* is a distinction between two types of subject matter. The first are physical interventions requiring professional medical skills to be performed and involving health risks even when carried out with the requisite medical professional care and expertise; and the second are uncritical methods involving only a minor intervention and no substantial health risks when carried out with the required care and skill. According to the Enlarged Board, only subject matter of the first type are excluded from patentability by Article 53(c) EPC. Such subject matter include interventions that represent the core of the medical profession's activities, being interventions of a type for which members of that profession are specifically trained and assume a particular responsibility. By contrast are such subject matter as methods of tattooing, piercing, hair removal by optical radiation or micro abrasion of the skin, etc., which are consequently patentable.

Beyond this basic distinction the Enlarged Board in *Medi-physics* was not prepared to go. In particular, the Board declined to give an authoritative and comprehensive definition of 'treatment by surgery', explaining that 'what is to be understood by "surgery" in the medical sense is to a large extent a matter of convention', and may therefore 'change with time and with new technical developments emerging' ([162]). Nonetheless, it did emphasize the importance of ensuring that future interpretations of the surgical methods exclusion continue to reflect the purpose of Article 53(c), and in particular, that they not exclude from patentability any ([159])

> methods in respect of which the interests of public health, of protection of patients and as a counterpart to that of the freedom of the medical profession to apply the treatment of choice to their patients does not call for the exclusion from patentability.

6.3.4.5 Therapeutic Methods

Methods of therapy within the meaning of Article 53(c) have been consistently defined by the Technical Board of Appeal as including methods of preventing or curing a disease of the human or animal body. As the Board said in T24/91 (*THOMPSON/Cornea*) [1996] EPOR 19, they include 'any treatment which is designed to cure, alleviate, remove or lessen the symptoms of, or prevent or reduce the possibility of contracting any disorder or malfunction of the animal body' (23), and the same applies with respect to methods of therapeutic treatment of the human body. Thus the central issue in any case involving the therapeutic methods exclusion will be whether a given method is aimed at preventing or curing a disease of the human or animal body, and whether it is directly effective to that end. While the identity of the person performing the method may be indicative of its therapeutic nature—a method perhaps being more likely to be one of therapy if it requires professional medical or veterinarian skills to be performed—the EPO has made it clear that this not determinative (see, e.g., T116/85 (*WELLCOME/Pigs I*) [1988] EPOR 1).

It has long been accepted that as pregnancy is not a disease, methods of contraception are not excluded from patentability under Article 53(c) EPC. So too for similar reasons methods of cosmetic treatment are not excluded, though a therapeutic method (e.g. a method for removing plaque from teeth) will not escape exclusion merely because it has cosmetic effects (see T290/86 (*ICI/Cleaning Plaque*) [1991] EPOR 157).

6.4 The Requirement for an Invention

6.4.1 Preliminary Remarks

6.4.1.1 The Source of the Requirement for an Invention

We have seen that Article 52(1) EPC limits the availability of European patents to 'inventions, in all fields of technology'. For a subject matter to be patentable, it must therefore be an invention within the meaning of Article 52(1). Subject matter that satisfy this requirement are 'inherently patentable', or in the language of US patent law, 'patent eligible'.

6.4.1.2 The Role of the Requirement for an Invention

Inventions—and therefore the requirement for an invention—are central to European patent law for two reasons. First, the invention is the basic subject matter of patent protection, equivalent to the work in copyright law and the sign in trade mark law. Thus, the requirement for an invention has the essential role of filtering protectable from non-protectable subject matter. Second, the invention denotes the object of patent protection, i.e. that which must be new, inventive, susceptible of industrial application, and clearly and sufficiently defined and described in the patent specification, and that with reference to which the scope of the patent monopoly is defined under Article 69 EPC (see Section 8.3). It follows that the requirement for an invention has the further role of ensuring that a subject matter is protected *in its conception* as a protectable subject matter, i.e. *qua* invention. For these reasons, identifying the invention for which a patent is claimed or has been granted, or the patent for which has allegedly been infringed, is a step of fundamental importance, and one that depends on a clear understanding of what an invention is within the meaning of European patent law.

6.4.1.3 The Requirement for an Invention Distinguished From the Requirement for a Valid Patent Claim

Among patent practitioners and judges, the requirement for an invention is often expressed as a requirement for a valid patent claim. For example, the question whether patents may be granted for purpose-limited processes was historically expressed as depending on the validity of Swiss-form claims (see Section 6.3.4.2.2). However, while the issue of a claim's validity is related to the issue of whether the subject matter described in the claim is capable of supporting a patent, they are analytically separate and governed by different legal rules and statutory provisions. Under the EPC, for example, claim validity is governed by Articles 75 to 86, whereas the requirement for an invention is governed by Article 52(2) and (3).

6.4.1.4 The Requirement for an Invention Distinguished From the Other Patentability Requirements

More difficult is the relationship between the requirement for an invention and the secondary patentability criteria of novelty, inventive step, and susceptibility of industrial application. To use the example of purpose-limited subject matter again: we have seen that in the EPC, the inherent patentability of such products in the medical and veterinarian fields is made explicit by Article 54 EPC, defining the requirement of novelty. Once again, however, while the requirement for an invention will often overlap with the other patentability requirements—including inventive step, for example (T1329/04 (*JOHN HOPKINS/Factor-9*) [2006] EPOR 8: see Section 7.3.3), and industrial applicability (see Sections 6.3.4 and 8.3.4)—they are analytically separate and governed by different legal rules and statutory provisions. This has been frequently emphasized by the EPO Boards of Appeal, which have also made the basis for the distinction clear (see, e.g., T154/04 (*DUNS LICENSING ASSOCIATES/Estimating Sales Activity*) [2007] EPOR 38 (*Duns Licensing*)). That basis lies in the difference between the essential and accidental properties of a subject matter. Specifically, whereas the requirement for an invention is concerned with the essential properties of a subject matter, the secondary patentability requirements of novelty, inventive step, and industrial applicability are concerned with its accidental properties, being those properties that inventions may, but need not, possess in order to exist.

6.4.2 The European Definition of Inventions

6.4.2.1 The Statutory (EPC) Definition of Inventions With Reference to a Non-Exhaustive List of Non-Inventions

By Article 52(2) and (3) EPC, an 'invention' is expressly defined as not including (among other things) any subject matter that falls within one or more of the following categories, to the extent to which a patent or application relates to it 'as such':

(a) discoveries, scientific theories and mathematical methods;

(b) aesthetic creations;

(c) schemes, rules and methods for performing mental acts, playing games or doing business, and programs for computers; and

(d) presentations of information.

The origins of this inclusive, negatively cast definition of inherently patentable subject matter lie in a provision drafted by Germany and the Netherlands in the 1960s for inclusion in the then proposed Community patent law. That provision was similar to Article 52(2) and (3) with two main exceptions: it did not include computer programs, and it did include therapeutic (medical) methods. The insertion of computer programs and removal of therapeutic methods was effected by the EPC drafters with the aims of promoting international harmonization and clarifying the relationship between the requirements for an invention and susceptibility of industrial applicability respectively. The first of these aims led the drafters to include computer programs among the EPC's list of non-inventions to reflect Rules 39.1 and 67.1 PCT, which exempted the PCT International Searching and Preliminary Examining Authorities (introduced in Section 5.3.1.2.2) from searching and examining certain subject matter, including 'computer programs to the extent that the…Authority is not equipped to search prior art concerning such programs'. The second aim led the drafters to move the therapeutic methods exclusion to Article 52(4) EPC 1973 to reflect its perceived basis in the requirement for susceptibility of industrial application (see Section 6.3).

6.4.2.2 The EPO's Interpretation of the Statutory (EPC) Definition of Inventions as Denoting a Positive Requirement for a Subject Matter Having Technical Character

In the early years of the EPC, Article 52(2) and (3) and the requirement for an invention in general caused many problems for the EPO. One cause of those problems was the absence of any obvious common theme linking the paragraphs of Article 52(2) and (3), and the consequential difficulty of extracting from those paragraphs any positive understanding of what inventions for patent law purposes are. A second, closely related cause was the difficulty in practice of determining what 'discoveries' and 'programs for computers' include, and why the latter in particular are not inherently patentable.

Since then, it has been established by EPO case law that the statutory definition of inventions contained in Article 52(2) and (3) denotes a positive requirement for a technical subject matter. This means that when deciding whether a given subject matter is an invention for which a patent might be granted, the approach required by the EPC is not to ask whether the subject matter falls within any of the categories of non-inventions listed in Article 52(2) and (3), but rather to ask whether it has technical character. If and only if it does will it be an invention capable of supporting a European patent.

Also well established by EPO case law is that for a subject matter to have technical character it need only include a single technical feature, which feature need not predominate. On the other hand, when determining the novelty and inventive step of an invention, only its technical features will count. Thus, while an automated method of designing crystals or calculating the square root of a number or purchasing goods will be an invention within the meaning of Article 52(1) by reason of its technical character, its contribution (if any) will generally derive from its underlying design method, mathematical steps, or business logic, which will not be among its *technical* aspects. It follows that unless the invention also makes a contribution to a technical field—for example, by improving the processing speed of the device on which it is implemented (see T208/84 (*VICOM/Computer-Related Invention*) [1987] EPOR 74; T1616/08 (*Gift Order/ AMAZON*) EP:BA:2009:T161608.20091111)—it will not be inventive for European patentability purposes.

6.4.2.3 The Test of Whether a Subject Matter Has Technical Character So As To Be an Invention

These principles governing the requirement for an invention were summarized by the Technical Board in *Duns Licensing*, in terms affirmed by the Enlarged Board in G3/08 (*PRESIDENT'S REFERENCE/Computer Program Exclusion*) [2009] EPOR 9 (*President's Reference*). Absent from either of those cases, however, was any positive definition of the term 'technical' itself. In fact, the EPO had conspicuously avoided offering such a definition until 2010, in *Essentially Biological Processes I*. Drawing on the pre-EPC decision of the Bundesgerichtshof (German Federal Supreme Court) in *Red Dove* [1969] *GRUR* 672, [1970] *IIC* 136, the Enlarged Board in those cases for the first time defined 'technical character' to denote the requirement for some form of human action on the physical world to bring about a causal, perceivable result. In its judgment ([128]–[131]):

> Human intervention, to bring about a result by utilising the forces of nature, pertains to the core of what an invention is understood to be. Like national laws, the EPC does not define the term 'invention', but the definition that was given many years ago in the 'Red Dove' ('Rote Taube') decision of the German Federal Court of Justice ('Bundesgerichtshof')…set a standard which still holds good today and can be said to be in conformity with the concept of 'invention' within the meaning of the EPC.
>
> In that decision, in the version of the translation into English published in 1 IIC (1970), 136, the German Federal Court of Justice defined the term 'invention' as requiring a technical teaching. The term technical teaching was characterised as 'a teaching to methodically utilize controllable natural forces to achieve a causal, perceivable result' (point 3 of the Reasons)….
>
> The term 'technology' (in German 'Technik'), which is now enshrined in Article 52(1) EPC but which at all material times underlay the understanding of the term 'invention', was deliberately not defined by the legislator in order not to preclude that adequate protection would be available for the results of developments in the future in fields of research which the legislator could not foresee (see also 'Red Dove', loc. cit. point 1 of the Reasons).

Ever since then, biological forces and phenomena, to the extent that they are controllable, have been considered to pertain to the area of technologies in which patentable inventions are possible (for examples and details, see 'Red Dove', loc. cit. point 4 of the Reasons).

On the basis of this decision, it can now be said that for a subject matter to be an invention within the meaning of Article 52(1) EPC, it must represent an objectively determinable and causally determined result of some human action on or intervention in the physical world that is also repeatable.

6.4.2.4 Explaining Why the Subject Matter of Article 52(2) and (3) EPC are Not Inventions, and Why Computer Programs and Isolated Human Genes Are Inventions

Some products will clearly fail to satisfy this definition of technical character. Examples include products that lack a direct, causal connection to either the physical world (e.g. a poem or a method of calculating a number) or a human action (e.g. an animal living or a plant growing in the wild). With one exception, this confirms that—and explains why—subject matter falling within the categories described in Article 52(2) and (3) EPC are not inventions, and are therefore not capable of supporting a patent, namely, because they do not per se involve a human action on the physical world. The exception is programs for computers, which clearly *do* involve such an action, and which satisfy the EPO's definition of invention noted earlier. This is self-evident from the nature of a computer program as a set of instructions for causing a device to operate, and explains why—notwithstanding the terms of Article 52(2)(c)—computer-implemented methods (i.e. computer programs) are accepted by the EPO as being, by reason of their technical character, inventions within the meaning of Article 52(1) EPC. The EPO has reconciled this result with the express wording of Article 52(2)(c) by emphasizing its reference to 'computer programs as such' rather than 'computer programs'. In so doing it effectively asks that the reference to computer programs in Article 52(2)(c) be read as a reference to computer software, i.e. to works of source or object code comprising text generated by a programmer to enable a device to implement her program. Thus conceived, computer programs are no more inventions than recipes for baking a cake, scored instructions for performing a sonata, or other authorial works protectable by copyright. But so too when conceived as programs—i.e. as sets of instructions for causing a device to operate in a particular manner—they are no less inventions than any other technical subject matter, and so the EPO has held.

In addition to explaining why computer-implemented methods are inventions and thus capable of supporting a patent, the Enlarged Board's definition of technical character in *Essentially Biological Processes I* explains why methods of isolating a product from its natural environment, along with the resulting isolated product itself, are also inventions for which a patent may be granted. For methods of isolating a natural product, such as a gene, the reason is that they involve a human action upon the physical world to produce a result (isolation of the product) that can be reproduced by repeating the action. For isolated products, the reason is their production by a technical process (the method of isolation). Note, however, the nature of the resulting invention for which the European patent will be granted, which is not the gene or other product as such, but rather the gene or other product *in its isolated form*. Thus, a person will never infringe a patent merely on account of her genetic makeup.

For some EPC Contracting States, patents for so-called products as such, including isolated products, are an innovation of the EPC. As the previous reasoning makes clear, their validity depends on the proposition that any product of a technical process is itself technical. However, and as the EPO has again made clear (see, e.g., *Howard Florey*), it also depends on a belief that a person who first isolates a product so as to make it available to the public in an industrially applicable form deserves a monopoly over the product as such, and not merely over the method by which it was isolated or made or over the method of its industrial application.

The recognition of isolated human genes and other biological materials as protectable subject matter under European law has now been statutorily codified: first by the EU in Article 5 Biotech Directive, and later by the EP Organisation's Administrative Council in Rule 29 EPC, reproducing Article 5.

6.4.2.5 Purpose-Limited Products and Processes as Inventions

In our discussion of Article 53(c) EPC in Section 6.3.4, we saw that products for use in a surgical, diagnostic, or therapeutic method are inherently patentable; the invention in such a case being a purpose-limited product, as in the case of aspirin for the purpose of reducing blood pressure. One question that arises from the principles governing such subject matter is whether they extend beyond the medical field. For the moment at least it seems that they do not. By contrast, the Enlarged Board has confirmed the validity of purpose-limited processes outside the medical field. This occurred in G2/88 (*MOBIL/ Friction Reducing Additive*) [1990] EPOR 73 (*Mobil*), where the Board affirmed that the use of a product for a (non-medical) purpose may be patented under European law. In *Mobil*, this meant that while an engine additive previously used to inhibit rust could not per se be patented for the purpose of reducing friction, a patent could be obtained for *the use* of the additive for the purpose of reducing friction on the basis of its technical nature. Whether such a subject matter is novel and inventive are separate issues that must also be satisfied for it to be patentable.

6.4.3 Assessing the European Definition of Inventions

The EPO's definition of inventions as technical subject matter, in combination with its requirement that an invention be inventive by reason of its technical aspects specifically, supports a view of the European patent system as existing to support technological innovation. On its face at least, this is different from the stated purpose of other patent systems to support advances to the *practical* (rather than the technical) arts, and helps to explain its exclusion of certain types of potentially new, inventive, and industrially applicable subject matter, such as methods of doing business.[8]

The restriction of the European legal definition of inherent patentability to technical subject matter may be cause for criticism. In general, however, criticisms of this aspect of European patent law tend to focus on what is included more than what is excluded from protection. Particularly controversial has been the availability of patents for computer-implemented methods and isolated human genes. Insofar as isolated genes are concerned, the controversy is partly doctrinal and partly policy-based. Put simply, in the view of many, including the US Supreme Court in *Association for Molecular Pathology v Myriad Genetics Inc.*, 133 S Ct 2107 (2013), isolated genes are insufficiently different from their

---

[8] This explains why US law has historically taken a different approach to methods of doing business from that taken by European law, namely, because the purpose of the US patent system is widely accepted as being to promote the progress of the useful arts, consistent with the terms of the constitutional clause by which the US Congress is empowered to make patent laws, viz., 'To promote the Progress of Science and useful Arts, by securing for limited Times to Authors and Inventors the exclusive Right to their respective Writings and Discoveries': US Constitution Article 1 § 8 cl. 8.

native counterparts to be appropriate for protection by patent law. In the language of European patent law and policy, this amounts to the claim that they do not have technical character after all, and that the value to the public of having access to human genes in a form in which they can be used is not sufficient to justify the grant of monopoly rights in respect of parts of them. This is essentially the position adopted by the US Supreme Court in *Myriad*. According to its judgment, only synthetic cDNA sequences created in a lab by a 'technician' from mRNA, and lacking the introns of naturally occurring DNA, can support a patent.

Similar to this, objections to the patenting of computer programs rest on policy and doctrinal grounds. The main doctrinal objection is based on the terms of Article 52(2)(c) and (3), and the difficulty of reconciling the grant of patents for computer programs with the express statutory exclusion from patentability of computer programs as such. By contrast, the policy objection is based on the aim of the European patent system to encourage technological innovation, and the belief of many that since the grant of patents for computer-related inventions is neither necessary nor effective to achieve that aim, it cannot be justified. One reason it may be unnecessary is that being first to market with new computer-related inventions may be sufficient to enable inventors to make a reasonable profit (or a reasonable proportion of the profit that is likely to be made) from their inventions. One reason it may be ineffective is that the volume of prior art in the IT field may be too vast to enable even the most well-resourced patent offices to be able to conclude with confidence that individual programs are new and inventive. In fact, it was precisely this concern regarding the ability of patent offices reliably to assess the patentability of computer programs that led to their exemption from having to do so in Articles 39.1 and 67.1 PCT.

There remains a further, frequently made argument against the grant of patents for computer-related inventions, which is that they are already protected by copyright. However, the availability of copyright for computer programs is not a good reason for excluding them from patent protection, since it is often the case that subject matter are protected by more than one species of IP or other right, and provided the scope of protection conferred by the rights in question does not overlap, there should be nothing problematic about this. Indeed, the case of copyright and patent protection for computer programs is a good example of complementary IP protection since, under European law at least, copyright protects only the expressive or authorial aspects of such programs without also extending to their functionality (see Sections 11.3.5 and 12.2.6.3). Thus, and recalling our earlier distinction between computer programs and software, copyright protects computer programs *as software*, and not as computer programs as such. There should therefore be nothing problematic about the simultaneous grant of copyright and patent protection for a program, provided the protection conferred by patents is conversely limited to programs *qua* inventions and does not extend also to programs *qua* authorial works. The point underlines the importance of the second of the roles of the requirement for an invention outlined previously, namely, to ensure that patent protection is limited to individual subject matter appropriately conceived, i.e. conceived with reference to the essential technical properties that, under European law, constitute them as inventions.

6.5 Conclusions

The European law of patentability supports and is driven by a view of patents as existing to promote contributions to the technical arts. This can be seen in the EPO's conception of inventions as technical subject matter. It can also be seen in the EPO's interpretation of the medical methods exclusions of Article 53(c) as confined to the activities of doctors and veterinarians, which will almost certainly fail to satisfy the European definition of technical character. And it can be seen in the EU and EPC definitions of the varieties and essentially biological process exclusions of Article 53(b) as confined to non-technical processes and subject matter ineligible for *sui generis* plant variety protection and their animal equivalents, which will also almost certainly be lacking in technical character. In the jurisprudence of the EPO, each of these principles reflects and is supported by a view of the EPC exclusions from patentability as needing to be interpreted restrictively, having regard to their context and purpose especially (see *Essentially Biological Processes II* [48]).

The exception to the general European rule regarding the capacity of any subject matter that contributes to a technical art to support a patent concerns inventions the commercial exploitation of which would be contrary to *ordre public* or morality. These are excluded from patentability under Article 53(a) EPC and Article 6 Biotech Directive. Immediately before the introduction of the Directive, this exclusion had also been interpreted narrowly by the EPO as covering only those inventions the commercialization of which would be universally regarded as outrageous, such as a letter bomb, or likely to breach public peace, social order, or conventionally accepted standards of European culture, such as through acts of terrorism. Since the Directive, however, this has changed to some extent at least. For example, it now seems clear that patent protection will be unavailable for any invention involving human biological material the commercialization of which might offend the dignity and integrity of the person, as well as potentially for any other invention not involving such material the commercialization of which poses ethical or other risks to European society that outweigh its benefits.

The requirement for patentable subject matter has been among the aspects of substantive European patent law most affected by EU law (via the Biotech Directive) to date. The impact of the Directive has been fourfold. First, it has given the CJEU jurisdiction in respect of substantive patent law principles, thereby enabling it and individual EU Member States, charged with referring questions of EU law that are not *acte clair* to the CJEU under Article 267 TFEU, to play a more active role in the development of European patent law than previously. Second and relatedly, it has put pressure on the EPO to anticipate or abide by decisions of the Court of Justice so as to avoid any conflict between the EPC and EU law, which conflict would be disastrous for the EPC's legitimacy and authority. Third and relatedly, it has exposed the existing system of the EPC to a wider range of values and influences than those to which it has historically been exposed, including the fundamental right of human dignity, and limited the scope of patentability and, for genetic products at least, and as we will see in Chapter 8, patent scope. And fourth, it has put the previously uncodified principles of European patent law regarding the inherent patentability of human genes on a statutory footing, precluding their revision by European tribunals, even as they are revised by courts in other patent jurisdictions. For all of these reasons, we can say that the Directive, while still in its infancy, has had and looks set to continue to have a profound impact on the substantive principles of European patent law, including the European law of patentability.

Further Reading

BEYLEVELD, D. AND BROWNSWORD, R., *Mice, Morality and Patents* (Common Law Institute of Intellectual Property, 1993)

BRADSTREET, R., 'The Forbidden and the Feasible' [2013] *GRUR Int* 502

DRAHOS, P., 'Biotechnology Patents, Markets and Morality' (1999) 21 *EIPR* 441

HILTY, R.M. AND GEIGER, C., 'Patenting Software? A Judicial and Socio-Economic Analysis' [2005] *IIC* 615

LAURIE, G., 'Patenting Stem Cells of Human Origin' [2004] *EIPR* 59

MOUFANG, R., 'Patenting of Human Genes, Cells and Parts of the Body?—The Ethical Dimensions of Patent Law' [1994] *IIC* 487

ODELL-WEST, A., 'The Absence of Informed Consent to Commercial Exploitation for Inventions Developed From Human Biological Material: A Bar to Patentability?' [2009] *IPQ* 373

PLOMER, A. AND TORREMANS, P. (eds), *Embryonic Stem Cell Patents: European Patent Law and Ethics* (OUP, 2009)

SCHWARTZ, R. M. AND MINSSEN, T., 'Life After *Myriad*: The Uncertain Future of Patenting Biomedical Innovation and Personalised Medicine in an International Context' [2015] *IPQ* 189

SIMS, A., 'The Case Against Patenting Medical Treatment' [2007] *EIPR* 43

THOMAS, D.X., 'Patentability Problems in Medical Technology' [2003] *IIC* 847

7

Secondary Patentability Requirements

7.1 Introduction

In Chapter 6 we began our discussion of the European law of patentability by considering the subject matter for which European patents may validly be granted under the EPC, and the substantive legal principles governing patentable subject matter contained in European (EPC and EU) law. In this chapter we complete that discussion by considering the secondary patentability requirements of the EPC. We thus begin from the position of having established that a subject matter for which a European patent is claimed is: (a) not excluded from protection by Article 53 EPC; and (b) an invention within the meaning of Article 52(1) EPC, and move to determine whether the secondary patentability criteria of novelty, inventive step, and susceptibility of industrial application are satisfied for the invention in question. As we saw in Chapter 6, each of these three secondary patentability requirements is imposed by Article 52(1) EPC (reproduced in Article 3(1) Biotech Directive for biotechnological inventions) and defined in Articles 54 to 57 EPC. An invention that fails to possess one or more of the accidental properties of novelty, inventiveness, and susceptibility of industrial application will not be patentable within the meaning of the EPC, and may therefore be opposed under Article 100 or revoked under Article 138 EPC (see Section 5.2.1).

7.2 Novelty

7.2.1 The Statutory Framework: Articles 54 and 55 EPC

Under Article 54 EPC, an invention is new if and only if it does not form part of the state of the art at the priority date, i.e. and in the long-standing language of patent jurisprudence, if and only if it is not 'anticipated'. The specific test applied by the EPO for determining novelty/anticipation involves establishing whether, disregarding any non-prejudicial disclosures within the meaning of Article 55 EPC, the state of the art discloses

1. What is the invention and wherein lie its essential technical features?	
Requires construction of the patent claims using the principles of claim construction discussed in Section 8.3.2.	The invention's essential technical features = its physical properties (products) or steps (processes) and any essential functional features (products and processes).

2. What is the priority date, and what was the state of the art at that date?	
Priority date = the earlier of the European patent filing date and the date of any application (by the patentee) for a patent for the same invention filed in a Paris Convention/ other recognized priority country 12 months or less before the European patent filing date.	Prior art matter = all matter made available to the public anywhere in the world by description, use, or other means before the priority date + all matter contained in any European patent application published on or after the priority date but filed before it, excluding non-prejudicial disclosures.

3. Does any single prior art matter anticipate the invention by (a) disclosing its essential technical features (b) sufficiently to enable a skilled addressee to perform it?
Ask whether the skilled addressee, armed with common general knowledge, would have (a) understood the prior art matter to disclose the invention and (b) been able to perform the invention on the basis of the disclosure, as at its date.

Figure 7.1 Determining novelty

the invention sufficiently to enable a skilled addressee to perform it (G1/92 (*Availability to the Public*) [1993] EPOR 241 (*Availability to the Public*)). Applying this test requires the following three steps:

1. identifying the invention that must be new and its essential (constitutive) technical features;

2. identifying the priority date and the state of the art (prior art) at that date, excluding any non-prejudicial disclosures; and

3. determining whether any of the prior art references identified anticipates the invention by disclosing its essential technical features sufficiently to enable a skilled addressee to perform it at the relevant date.

An overview of the requirements of each of these steps is given in Figure 7.1.

7.2.2 **The Invention and its Essential Technical Features**

To identify the invention that must be new, it is necessary to construe the patent claims applying the principles of construction outlined in Section 8.3 and confirm that the subject matter which they define satisfies the legal definition of invention considered in Section 6.4. Having done that, the invention's essential technical features can be ascertained.

According to the Enlarged Board of Appeal in G2/88 (*MOBIL/Friction-reducing additive*) [1990] EPOR 73 (*Mobil*), the essential technical features of an invention will include all of the physical and functional features that are essential to it, in the sense of constituting it as a technical subject matter within the meaning of European patent law. An invention's physical features will vary according to its nature: for products they will be its physical parameters, for processes they will be its physical steps, and for uses of a product they will be both the physical parameters of the product used and the physical steps comprising the use itself. While the essential technical features of an invention will often be exclusively physical, in some cases they may be functional as well. As explained by the Technical Board in T68/85 (*CIBA-GEIGY/Synergistic Herbicides*) [1987] EPOR 302 (*Ciba-Geigy*), cited with approval in *Mobil*, functional features are characterized by their definition in terms of the result to be achieved. For example, the essential technical features of an invention comprising the use of a 'fat-dissolving solvent' or a 'compound with a reactive hydrogen atom' might be construed as including these functionally defined products (see *Ciba-Geigy* 306). In addition, the essential technical features of an invention comprising the use of an engine additive 'for the purpose B of reducing friction' might be construed as including 'the function of achieving purpose B' on the ground that 'this is the technical result' of the use, and is thus an essential technical feature of the invention comprising that use—as was held to be the case in *Mobil* (87). And finally, in the case of an isolated DNA sequence or other genetic product, the essential technical features of the invention will include the genetic function of the product as a constitutive aspect of it, consistent with recital 23 and Article 9 Biotech Directive (discussed in Section 8.3.4).

In Section 5.3 we noted that in exceptional cases, the inventor of a product may define his invention in his patent claim with reference to its underlying method of manufacture, as a product-by-process. As emphasized by the Enlarged Board of Appeal in G2/12 and G2/13 (*Essentially Biological Processes*) [2015] EPOR 28 (*Essentially Biological Processes*), however, the invention in such a case will remain the product as such, and not the product when defined by the specified process. It follows that while 'the specific process needed to obtain the claimed product should make it possible to distinguish the inevitable product of the product-by-process claim over the prior-art', nonetheless '[t]he use of the method parameter by which to define a particular product cannot in itself give the product novelty, nor can it constitute an inventive step over the prior-art' ([27]). Thus, the Board concluded ([28]):

> [T]he subject-matter of both a product claim and a product-by-process claim is the product as such, in respect of which the legal (formal and substantive) requirements for its patentability need to be fulfilled, independently of the patentability of the process by which the product can be generated or is defined. If the product in the product-by-process claim is the same as or obvious from a prior-art product, the claimed product is unpatentable even though the prior-art product was made by a different process. Conversely, if the product in the product-by-process claim is neither the same as nor obvious from a prior-art product, it is patentable even though the process applied is the same as or obvious from a prior-art process.

7.2.3 The Priority Date, the State of the Art, and Non-Prejudicial Disclosures

7.2.3.1 The Priority Date

In jurisdictions throughout the world, the priority date is the date with reference to which the state of the art is defined. Under the EPC, the priority date will be one of two possible dates: either the date on which the application for the European patent was filed (the European filing date) under Article 54(2) and (3); or, if the applicant or his predecessor in title filed a patent application claiming the same invention in a Paris Convention or other recognized priority country under Article 87 12 months or less before the European filing date, and has made a valid declaration of priority on the basis of that earlier filing, the date of the foreign filing under Article 89 EPC. For these purposes, the European filing date corresponds to the date on which the applicant filed documents with the EPO or other EPC Receiving Office containing: (a) an indication that a European patent is sought; (b) information identifying the applicant or allowing the applicant to be contacted; and (c) a description or reference to a previously filed application in accordance with Rule 40(2) and (3).

Articles 87 to 89 EPC implement the rules governing priority contained in Article 4 Paris Convention for the Protection of Industrial Property 1883. While the EP Organisation is not a member of the Paris Convention and is therefore not bound by its provisions, the Enlarged Board has recognized that since the EPC is a special agreement within the meaning of Article 19 Paris Convention (EPC Preamble), Articles 87 to 89 should be interpreted to be consistent with it (G3/93 (*Priority Interval*) [1994] EPOR 521 (*Priority Interval*); G2/98 (*X/Same Invention*) [2002] EPOR 17 (*Same Invention*)). On the other hand, the Board has also emphasized that those Articles 'provide a complete, self-contained code of rules of law on the subject of claiming priority for the purpose of filing a European patent application' (*Priority Interval* 524), and that failure to satisfy their conditions will therefore deprive a foreign filing of any effect under the EPC. In *Priority Interval* the EPO gave an example of the operation of priority rules under the EPC, an adapted form of which appears in Figure 7.2.

Of especial importance among the conditions of Articles 87 to 89 EPC is the requirement that the foreign filing relate to 'the same invention' as the European application. This condition is interpreted strictly by the EPO to require that a person skilled in the art be able to derive the invention claimed in the European patent application 'directly and unambiguously, using common general knowledge, from the previous application as a whole' (*Same Invention* [30]). '[I]f any essential element of the invention for which a European patent is sought is missing, there is no right to priority' (T81/87 (*COLLABORATIVE/Preprorennin*) [1990] EPOR 361, 365). In effect, the foreign filing must anticipate the European filing for the patentee to be able to rely on its date as the reference point for determining the validity of the later European application.

7.2.3.2 **The State of the Art**

7.2.3.2.1 *Categories of Prior Art*

The state of the art comprises two kinds of prior art described in Article 54(2) and (3) EPC respectively. The first is everything made available to the public anywhere in the world by description, use, or any other means before the priority date; and the second is the content of any European patent application published on or after the priority date but filed before it, regardless of whether it designates the same EPC Contracting States as the later application.[1] The reason for including the latter category is to prevent the

---

[1] This represents a change from the original (EPC 1973) position, which included the following Article 54(4): 'Paragraph 3 shall be applied only in so far as a Contracting State designated in respect of the later application, was also designated in respect of the earlier application as published.' This provision was deleted as part of the EPC 2000 revisions.

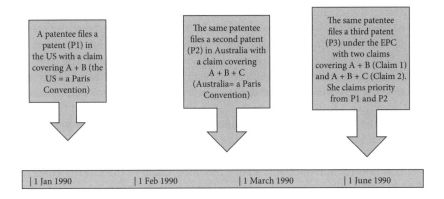

| 1 Jan 1990 | 1 Feb 1990 | 1 March 1990 | 1 June 1990 |

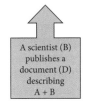

Question:

Is B's document D part of the state of the art in respect of P3?

Answer:

Yes, but in respect of Claim 2 only.

Reasons:

(i) P1 discloses the same invention as Claim 1 of P3, and P2 discloses the same invention as Claim 2 of P3. Therefore, the patentee can claim priority from them, giving Claim 1 a priority date of 1 January 1990 and Claim 2 a priority date of 1 March 1990.

(ii) B's document is made available after the priority date of Claim 1 but before the priority date of Claim 2. It is therefore part of the state of the art in respect of Claim 2 but not in respect of Claim 1.

Figure 7.2 Priority example

double patenting of inventions within Europe, and to thereby give effect to the 'first to file' principle. Specifically, if Article 54(3) did not exist, it might be possible for two people to obtain patents for the same invention within European territory: all that would be required would be for each to file a patent application before the other's application had been published. It is in order to prevent this, and to ensure that the right to patent an invention lies with the person who first files for the patent, regardless of whether she was also the first person to devise the invention, that the EPC treats the first European filing as forming part of the state of the art even before it has been made available to the public within the meaning of Article 54(2), so as to anticipate and thereby invalidate any later European filing for the same invention.[2]

Of note regarding the first category of prior art described in Article 54(2) is its breadth, and its support for a requirement of absolute novelty. Specifically, it follows from Article 54(2) that to anticipate an invention it is enough to make the invention (constituted by its essential features) available to the public by any means anywhere in

---

[2] Article 125 EPC has also been interpreted by the EPO as a basis for not allowing double patenting: see, e.g., T1423/07 (*BOEHRINGER INGELHEIM VETMEDICA GmbH/Cyclic Amine derivative*) [2007] EPOR 37 and, in the context of divisional applications, G1/05 (*ASTROPOWER/Divisional*) [2007] EPOR 17 and G1/06 (*SEIKO/Sequences of divisionals*) [2007] EPOR 47.

the world. Historically, absolute novelty in this sense was not required: for an invention to be new it needed only to be unknown within the territory of the protecting state. Such a limited definition of novelty made sense when the consideration for a patent was the applicant's undertaking to work the invention locally. However, the consideration for a European patent is the publication of information regarding the invention (see Section 5.3.1.3), which, in the digital age particularly, cannot be restricted territorially. Given this, a requirement for absolute novelty is appropriate. On the other hand, given that the world as a whole benefits from the disclosure of a patentee's first patent filing, it is right and proper having regard to the quid pro quo nature of patent monopolies that she be able to rely on that filing to obtain parallel protection for her invention in other jurisdictions. Hence the importance of the priority rules of Articles 87 to 89 EPC.

7.2.3.2.2 The Need for Prior Art to Have Been 'Made Available to the Public'

A further point of note regarding the prior art of Article 54(2) is that it must have been made available to the public. The phrase 'made available to the public' was purposefully left undefined in the EPC to avoid any risk of restrictive interpretation, and was otherwise intended to have an expansive meaning. For example, and as the *travaux préparatoires* make clear, the word 'available' was used to emphasize as key the possibility of taking note of the invention, and the word 'public' was chosen over 'generally' to express the idea that it was enough for the invention to be available to an unrestricted number of persons for it to lose its novelty.

The test applied by the EPO is consistent with this; it focuses on whether interested members of the public have been given direct and unambiguous access to the prior art in question without being constrained as to its use or dissemination. By way of example, it is well established that a single sale of an article will make the article available to the public, provided the buyer is not bound to secrecy (T482/89 (*TÉLÉMECHANIQUE/ Power Supply Unit*) [1993] EPOR 259). So too the delivery of an article to a person makes it available to the public, as does the act of placing the article on the shelves of a public library from where it may be consulted by interested parties (T381/87 (*RESEARCH CORP./Publication*) [1989] EPOR 138 (*Publication*)). The fact that it is not so consulted, and that members of the public are not aware of its availability for consultation, is irrelevant (*Publication*). Conversely, even a widely circulated document will not be prior art if the circumstances of its circulation import obligations of confidence or non-disclosure (T300/86 (*RCA/TV Receiver*) [1994] EPOR 339). By the same reasoning, a scientific article submitted in confidence to a journal for publication is not thereby made available to the public, nor an article addressed to a member of the public and placed in a post-box (*Publication*).

Especial difficulties arise in the context of information made available on the Internet. In T1553/06 (*PHILIPS/Public Availability of Documents on the World Wide Web*) [2012] EPOR 40, the Technical Board decided that the theoretical possibility of a member of the public having access to a document stored on the World Wide Web via a specific URL was insufficient to make the document available to the public within the meaning of the EPC. What was required, the Board held, was 'direct and unambiguous access', which would only be established where the document: (a) could be found with the help of a public web search engine by using one or more keywords related to the essence of its content; and (b) remained accessible at the URL for a period sufficient to enable a member of the public, under no obligation to keep its content secret, to have direct and unambiguous access to it ([11]).

An even more difficult case involves documents contained in an email transmitted via the Internet. That was the focus of T2/09 (*PHILIPS/Public Availability of an E-mail Transmitted via the Internet*) [2012] EPOR 41, where the Technical Board, without deciding the matter finally, held that 'the differences between webpages and such e-mails make a strong prima facie case against public availability of the latter' ([58]).

While each of these examples concerns documents, the same principles apply with respect to other forms of disclosure, such as oral disclosures and uses, even if proving the fact and content of these can be difficult in practice. For example, the oral disclosure of information to a single person will suffice to make it available to the public, regardless of where the disclosure took place, and provided only that the person to whom it was disclosed was not subject to any express or implied restriction regarding the information's use or dissemination. The same applies for the use of a product or method in public, which will also suffice to make the product or method available to the public, regardless of whether the public would have had any particular reason or motivation for analysing its physical properties or steps. Once again, and as confirmed by the Enlarged Board in *Availability to the Public*, 'it is the fact that direct and unambiguous access to some particular information is possible, which makes the latter available, whether or not there is any reason for looking for it' (243).

By contrast are uses that are secretive, hidden, or otherwise uninformative. As stated in *Mobil*, and in contrast to the position in some European states before the introduction of the EPC at least, 'under Article 54(2) EPC the question to be decided is what has been "made available" to the public: the question is not what may have been "inherent" in what was made available (by a prior written description, or in what has previously been used (prior use), for example)' (88). The result in *Mobil* was the Enlarged Board's decision that the prior public use of the engine additive did not make the technical effect of that use to reduce friction available to the public, notwithstanding that such effect was inherent in the use in the sense of following necessarily from it.

The decision in *Mobil* is controversial and has attracted strong criticism.[3] For one, it has been said to enable the grant of patents for subject matter already in the public realm, recalling the 'odious monopolies' of the 15th to 17th centuries (see Section 1.2.2.2.2).[4] In addition, it raises difficulties for the law of infringement by making liability dependent on the purpose for which the defendant was using the product, notwithstanding that considerations of intent are ordinarily irrelevant when establishing liability for primary patent infringement (see Section 8.4.1.1.1).

As we have mentioned, proving a non-written disclosure of information can be difficult in practice, particularly where it depends on the testimony of a small number of witnesses. In reflection of this, the EPO has tended to impose a higher standard of proof in such cases. Thus, while the question whether a prior art reference has been made available to the public is a question of fact that must generally be established on a balance of probabilities (*Publication*), an exception exists for alleged prior uses or other disclosures substantiated exclusively by witness testimony (as where a person visits another person's premises and sees the invention). In these cases, the EPO has suggested that proof of the alleged disclosure beyond any reasonable doubt, or 'up to the hilt', will be required, and not merely proof on a balance of probabilities (see, e.g., T55/01 (*SONY/Satellite Broadcast*

---

[3] See, e.g., C. Floyd, 'Novelty Under the Patents Act 1977: The State of the Art After *Merrell Dow*' [1996] *EIPR* 480.

[4] Though note that any persons who had previously used the invention will likely have a right to continue such use: see Section 8.5.4.

Recording) EP:BA:2003:T005501.20030211 and T354/05 (*Documotion RESEARCH/ Tamper-Evident Form*) [2007] EPOR 29).

7.2.3.3 Non-Prejudicial Disclosures

We have seen that matter made available to the public on terms restricting its use or dissemination is not part of the state of the art under Article 54(2) EPC. It may happen, however, that a person who receives information on such terms nonetheless uses or discloses it, and in doing so makes the information available to the public within the meaning of that Article. In such a case, the unauthorized disclosure will be capable of destroying the novelty of the invention unless it can be shown to be a non-prejudicial disclosure within the meaning of Article 55 EPC so as to be excluded from the novelty assessment. For it to be such a disclosure, it must have been made available to the public 'no earlier than six months preceding the filing of the European patent application', and be 'due to, or in consequence of:...an evident abuse in relation to the applicant or his legal predecessor' (Article 55(1)(a)). Note that the date of filing remains the reference point for identifying non-prejudicial disclosures even if it is not the priority date; a point confirmed by the Enlarged Board of Appeal in G3/98 (*UNIVERSITY PATENTS/Six-Month Period*) [2001] EPOR 33.

A second type of non-prejudicial disclosure under Article 55 EPC is one made within six months preceding the European filing date due to or in consequence of the invention's display at an official, or officially recognized, international exhibition for which the applicant has filed a notice of exhibition and a supporting certificate in accordance with the EPC Implementing Regulations (Article 55(1)(b) and (2)). This provision was originally drafted to ensure compliance with Article 11 Paris Convention, and later adopted for that reason and to ensure consistency with Article 4(4)(b) Strasbourg Patent Convention 1963.

One type of non-prejudicial disclosure for which the EPC does not provide is disclosure by the inventor herself in pursuit of research or other activities. Consider by contrast section 102(b)(1) of the America Invents Act 2011:

> A disclosure made 1 year or less before the effective filing date of a claimed invention shall not be prior art to the claimed invention [if it] was made by the inventor or joint inventor or by another who obtained the subject matter disclosed directly or indirectly from the inventor or a joint inventor.

In 2002, the European Commission reported on the issues surrounding the introduction into European law of a grace period such as that contained in the America Invents Act.[5] Those issues include the legal uncertainty created for third parties by the recognition of such a period, as against the tendency of academics in particular to publish their research before seeking patent protection, and the loss to European industry of them doing so. Perhaps the most famous example of this tendency concerns the Cohen-Boyer technique of splicing genes on which the new biotechnology industry was built in the 1970s. The inventors' prior publication of some of the research underpinning their invention in the *Proceedings of the National Academy of Science USA* made them dependent on a grace period in order to obtain protection. Since US legislation offered such a period, they were able to obtain a US patent for their technique. However, the absence of equivalent provisions in the domestic laws of European countries prevented them from obtaining corresponding protection for European territory.

---

[5] See European Commission, 'Report from the Commission to the European Parliament and Council—An assessment of the implications for basic genetic engineering research of failure to publish, or late publication of, papers on subjects which could be patentable as required under Article 16(b) of Directive 98/44/EC on the legal protection of biotechnological inventions' COM (2002) final.

7.2.4 **Anticipation by Enabling Disclosure**

When determining anticipation, prior art references may not be combined (mosaiced). Rather, anticipation depends on a single prior art reference making the invention as a whole available to the public at the date of its disclosure (for Article 54(2) references) or filing/priority (for Article 54(3) references). The test to be applied is the same test of enabling disclosure applied in other areas of European patent law, such as when determining: whether a patent application for which a priority right is asserted relates to the same invention as the European application under Article 87 EPC (see Section 7.2.3.1); whether a patentee's (or applicant's) description of her invention in a patent specification is sufficient under Article 83 EPC (see Section 5.3.1.3.3); and whether an amendment to a patent specification adds new matter under Article 123(2) EPC (see Section 5.4.2). According to the Enlarged Board of Appeal in G2/10 (*THE SCRIPPS RESEARCH INSTITUTE/ Disclaimer*) [2011] EPOR 45 [80]:

> It is vital that a uniform concept of disclosure is applied in all these respects and that the rights of an applicant are uniformly determined in all these contexts as extending to but at the same time as being limited to the disclosure made at the relevant point in time.

Hence one must ask whether the prior art in question discloses the invention sufficiently to enable a skilled addressee equipped with common general knowledge to perform it without undue burden or inventiveness (*Availability to the Public*).

There are two aspects to this test: disclosure and enablement. The test of disclosure is whether the skilled addressee, armed with common general knowledge, would have understood the prior art reference in question to disclose the invention at the relevant date (T694/91 (*TEKTRONIX/Schottky Barrier Diode*) [1995] EPOR 384), being the date on which the reference was made available to the public or, in the case of an Article 54(3) reference, its priority date. For this test to be satisfied, the prior art must be such as would have taken the skilled addressee directly to the invention as claimed.

Only if disclosure is established will the issue of enablement need to be decided. Here the question is whether the skilled addressee, armed again with common general knowledge, would have been able to perform the invention on the basis of the information which the prior art disclosed. When determining this question the focus shifts from considering what information the skilled addressee would have understood the prior art to reveal, to considering what the skilled addressee would have been able to do with the information thus revealed. Consistent with this shift, the skilled addressee is now permitted some experimentation and searching across the prior art, provided it does not involve any undue burden or inventiveness. This explains the view of the Technical Board that errors in a description of an invention will not affect its sufficiency to enable a skilled addressee to perform the invention *provided* the addressee could recognize and rectify the errors using her common general knowledge (T171/84 (*AIR PRODUCTS/Redox Catalyst*) [1986] EPOR 210). It also explains the Board's decision in T206/83 (*ICI/Pyridine Herbicides*) [1986] EPOR 232 (*ICI*) that a description of the chemical structure of (or a method for producing) a compound will not enable the skilled addressee to perform the compound if she could not be expected to prepare the required starting materials on the basis of her common general knowledge. As these decisions underline, when determining enablement the common general knowledge of the skilled addressee is critical. In the Board's analysis in *ICI* (237):

> Basically any cure of insufficiency [in the context of Article 54(3) EPC] lies with the addressee of the document, i.e. the person skilled in the art who has common general knowledge at his immediate disposal. It would be unfair to the public if more were to be

expected of him, i.e. an awareness of the whole state of the art. It is normally accepted that common general knowledge is represented by basic handbooks and textbooks on the subject in question. The skilled person could well be expected to consult these to obtain clear advice as to what to do in the circumstances, since the skills of such persons not only includes knowledge about particular basic prior art but also knowledge as to where to find such information. Such books may indeed refer him to articles describing specifically how to act or at least giving a fairly generally applicable method for the purpose, which can be used without any doubt. Normally patent specifications are not part of common general knowledge and cannot therefore cure apparent insufficiency.... The indexes of Chemical Abstracts cover virtually the whole state of the art, and represent therefore much more than what is assumed to be the common general knowledge of the addressee of the specification. Reliance on the contents of Chemical Abstracts to rectify insufficiency might be tantamount to leave the skilled reader to carry out a search in the whole state of the art, which would be an unacceptable burden on the public.

The information made available to the public by a particular prior art reference cannot be determined in the abstract, depending as it does on the reference in question and the common general knowledge of the skilled addressee at the relevant time. Nonetheless, the following principles regarding the disclosure effected by different types of prior art can be derived from the cases.

- A recipe—i.e. a description or use of a method for making a product—will disclose both the product that its performance inevitably (rather than potentially) produces and any other recipe with the same starting materials and reaction conditions (*Mobil*). The fact that the product is not per se described other than by the process of making it is irrelevant, as is the question whether a skilled addressee performing the process would be surprised at the results (T12/81 (*BAYER/Diastereomers*) [1979–85] EPOR B308).

- A product will disclose all of the information that a skilled addressee would derive by studying it 'using his normal investigation capabilities' (T953/90 (*THOMSON/Electron Tube*) [1998] EPOR 415, 420). In some cases (depending in part on the field of technology) this may extend to information obtained from reverse-engineering the product. Generally, however, the information obtained from a product will relate only to the product itself. Thus, the prior availability of product A will not necessarily disclose (or anticipate) the same product A in an isolated form, and nor will it disclose any extrinsic characteristics of the product as may be 'revealed when the product is exposed to interaction with specifically chosen outside conditions' (*Availability to the Public* 244). That is why isolated products, uses of known products, and purpose-limited products can be novel notwithstanding the prior availability of the product itself (see *Availability to the Public; Mobil*).

- A product for use for a specified medical (Article 53(c)) purpose—for example, aspirin for use to relieve pain—will disclose only the product used by the specific means and for the specific purpose, and neither: (a) the product for use for the specific purpose *by different means*; nor (b) the product used by the specific means *for a different purpose*, at least where the different means or purpose reveals a different technical effect. This is consistent with the general principle that an invention will only be anticipated if its essential technical features—including in the case of a purpose-limited product, the physical steps comprising the method of use and responsible for the end it achieves—form part of the state of the art. Hence the finding of the Enlarged

Board of Appeal in G2/08 (*ABBOTT RESPIRATORY/Dosage Regime*) [2010] EPOR 26 [123] that a medicament A for use to treat illness B was patentable notwithstanding its prior use to treat the same illness B by a different dosage regime, on the basis that its difference (i.e. its own dosage regime) was not merely 'verbal' but also 'technical'. In reasoning this decision the Board stated as follows ([120]–[123]):

> [T]here is no reason to give to a feature consisting in a new dosage regime of a known medicament a different treatment than the one given to any other specific use acknowledged in the case law...The Enlarged Board does not ignore the concerns with respect to undue prolongations of patent rights potentially resulting from patent protection for claims purporting to derive their novelty and inventive step only from a not hitherto so defined dosage regime for treatment by therapy of an illness already treated by the same drug. Therefore, it is important to stress that, beyond the legal fiction of art.54(5) EPC, for the assessment of novelty and inventive step of a claim in which the only novel feature would be the dosage regime, the whole body of jurisprudence relating to the assessment of novelty and inventive step generally also applies. In particular, the claimed definition of the dosage regime must therefore not only be verbally different from what was described in the state of the art but also reflect a different technical teaching.

- Outside the medical field, the principles above regarding purpose-limited products apply *mutatis mutandis* in respect of uses of a product for a specified purpose (i.e., purpose-limited processes). This was made clear by the Enlarged Board's decision in *Mobil*, that the use of the engine additive for the purpose of reducing friction was patentable, notwithstanding the additive's prior use by the same method to inhibit rust, on the basis that its difference in purpose (to reduce friction rather than inhibit rust) revealed a technical novelty in the form of a new technical effect (reducing friction). These cases underline again the 'intimate link' that exists in the jurisprudence of the EPO between the constitutive, technical features of an invention and its patentability (see, e.g., T939/92 (*AGREVO/Triazoles Sulphonamides*) [1996] EPOR 171 (*AgrEvo*)), and the need to identify those features with care when determining novelty.

7.3 Inventive Step

7.3.1 The Statutory Framework: Article 56 EPC

The second accidental property required of an invention under the European law of patentability is inventive step. This requirement is aimed at ensuring that the invention for which a patent is sought is not only different from what had previously been available to the public, but that it differs sufficiently from what was previously available, in the sense of representing a sufficient departure from the state of the art in the field to which it relates at the priority date. Under Article 56 EPC, an invention will involve an inventive step 'if, having regard to the state of the art, it is not obvious to a person skilled in the art', where the state of the art is comprised exclusively of the prior art described in Article 54(2), excluding once again any non-prejudicial disclosures within the meaning of Article 55 EPC (by implication of Articles 55 and 56).

As in the context of novelty, the EPO requires that an invention be inventive by reason of its essential technical features specifically. Thus, inventions that make a non-technical contribution to the prior art (e.g. by means of an inventive business or design method) are not inventive under the EPC, and nor are inventions that make no contribution to any, technical or non-technical, art.

It follows from this that determining inventiveness requires the following three steps:

(a) identifying the invention that must be inventive and its essential technical features;

(b) identifying the priority date and the state of the art (prior art) at that date, excluding any Article 54(3) references and non-prejudicial disclosures; and

(c) determining whether, having regard to the state of the art and viewed without any knowledge of the invention, the invention would have been obvious to the person skilled in the art at the priority date.

7.3.2 The Challenge of Harmonizing Approaches to Inventive Step

The origins of Article 56 EPC lie in a German proposal to the Council of Europe's Committee of Experts on Patents in the 1950s for a requirement of 'creative effort' assessed by an 'Expert of average skill' in the relevant technical art having regard to one or more disclosures as he would group them together at the date of filing. This proposal was described at the time as based on a mix of US legislation and German jurisprudence, and as consistent with the laws of several other European states as well, including Switzerland, the Scandinavian countries, Italy, the Netherlands, and the UK. It was endorsed in the early 1960s for inclusion in the then proposed Community patent law, and later adopted by the drafters of the EPC.

The result is Article 56, which remains true to the German proposal of 60 years ago. For example, the need to consider 'the state of the art as known to the average Expert' is recognized in the attribution to the skilled addressee of 'common general knowledge' regarding the field in which she is skilled (see Section 5.2.2). In addition, and unlike in the context of novelty, it is permissible to mosaic prior art disclosures when determining inventive step to the extent that the skilled addressee 'would combine them with the expectation of a desired result' (T741/98 (*NIPPON STEEL/Steel Sheet Method*) EP:BA:2002:T074198.20020222). Further, and also contrasting with the approach to novelty, inventive step is assessed at the priority date. And finally, Article 56 EPC preserves the multifactorial nature of the inventive step enquiry envisaged in the 1960s. This latter point was discussed on the eve of the EPC's conclusion in 1973 following a proposal by the Swiss delegation to insert a paragraph requiring that any evidence of technical progress furnished by the applicant be considered in determining her invention's non-obviousness. That proposal was rejected by the other delegations, citing the multifactorial nature of the inventive step enquiry, and the importance of preventing it from being eclipsed by considerations of technical progress, i.e. whether the invention represents a practical improvement on what was available previously.

The result, undoubtedly, is a somewhat vague legal standard on which examiners and judges might reasonably (and sometimes do) disagree, particularly if presented with different evidence and opinions regarding the identity and knowledge of the skilled addressee and the relevant prior art. Hence the special challenge posed by inventive step for the harmonization of European patent law. As remarked by the Dutch delegation to the Council of Europe's Committee of Experts on Patents in 1957: 'The problem is ... how to avoid a single legal text being interpreted in different ways by the national courts. A solution to the problem appears to be impossible without a European Court of Justice.'

7.3.3 The Problem/Solution Approach to Inventive Step

Enter the EPO and its so-called problem/solution approach to inventive step. According to the most recent edition of the Guidelines for Examination, this approach is to be applied in all but exceptional cases, and by means of the following three stages (Part G Chapter VII 5):

(i) determining the 'closest prior art',

(ii) establishing the 'objective technical problem' to be solved, and

(iii) considering whether or not the claimed invention, starting from the closest prior art and the objective technical problem, would have been obvious to the skilled person.

Taking these stages in turn: the closest prior art is described in the Guidelines as 'that which in one single reference discloses the combination of features which constitutes the most promising starting point for a development leading to the invention'. The 'objective technical problem' is established by identifying the difference between the technical features of the invention and the closest prior art, determining the technical effect which that difference reveals, and then inferring from that effect the technical problem which the inventor, beginning with the closest prior art, has with her invention solved. Implicit is that the specification reveals a technical problem which the invention, by virtue of its essential technical features, does in fact solve (T641/00 (*COMVIK/Two Identities*) [2004] EPOR 10 (*Comvik*)). According to the Technical Board, if no technical problem is revealed, 'an invention within the meaning of Article 52 EPC does not exist' ([21]). In addition, if the specification does not connect the invention to the objective technical problem which it reveals sufficiently that the skilled addressee would be led to contemplate solving the problem by means of the invention with a reasonable expectation of success, it will be incapable of being inventive. This was made clear by the Technical Board in a case involving a claim to a DNA sequence, GDF-9, that was speculatively described in the specification as encoding for a protein related to growth deficiency (T1329/04 (*JOHN HOPKINS/Factor-9*) [2006] EPOR 8 (*Factor-9*)), and which the applicant had sought to support with reference to documents published after the priority date. According to the Board ([22]):

> The definition of an invention as being a contribution to the art, i.e. as solving a technical problem and not merely putting forward one, requires that it is at least made plausible by the disclosure in the application that its teaching solves indeed the problem it purports to solve. Therefore, even if supplementary post-published evidence may in the proper circumstances also be taken into consideration, it may not serve as the sole basis to establish that the application solves indeed the problem it purports to solve.

Finally, having established the closest prior art and objective technical problem which the invention solves, there will remain the third and critical stage of deciding whether, starting from that prior art and problem, and avoiding any *ex post facto* analysis or hindsight, the skilled addressee would have regarded the claimed invention to be obvious at the priority date. This test is objective rather than subjective and depends on whether the invention follows logically from the closest prior art. Over the years, the EPO has attempted to render it more certain by reducing it to one or more of a number of questions. These include:

- whether the problem which the invention solved lay in an innovative industry and had been worked on by others, suggesting inventiveness (see, e.g., T90/89 (*FRISCO-FINDUS/Frozen Fish*) [1991] EPOR 42);

- whether the skilled addressee would have contemplated solving the problem by means of the invention with a reasonable expectation of succeeding, suggesting obviousness (see, e.g., T1212/01 (*PFIZER LTD/Pyrazolopyrimidinones*) (3 February 2005)) consistent with the EPO's method of determining whether an invention can be said to solve an objective technical problem above; and

- whether the skilled addressee would have been led by the prior art to devise the invention in solution to the problem, suggesting obviousness (see, e.g., T2/83 (*RIDER/Simethicone Tablet*) [1979–85] EPOR C715 (*Rider*)).

While each of these questions may be used by the Boards when deciding inventiveness, the last is given special emphasis by the EPO. According to the Guidelines for Examination (Chapter VII 5.3), it is *the* question to be answered at the third stage of the problem/solution approach. Hence the Guidelines state:

> In the third stage the question to be answered is whether there is any teaching in the prior art as a whole that *would* (not simply could, but would) have prompted the skilled person, faced with the objective technical problem, to modify or adapt the closest prior art while taking account of that teaching, thereby arriving at something falling within the terms of the claims, and thus achieving what the invention achieves.

In *Rider*, the Technical Board explained that the so-called could/would test of inventive step is not whether the skilled addressee *could* have devised the invention, 'but whether he would have done so in expectation of some improvement or advantage' ([7]). In answering this, the focus must be on the technical effect of the relevant action and invention. Thus, in *Rider*, the Board decided that as a solution to the objective technical problem, the invention would have struck the skilled addressee starting from the position of the closest prior art as 'superfluous, wasteful and devoid of any technical effect' (ibid). The Board continued that '[i]n view of the recognition that [the invention] has, after all, a substantial effect, the outcome was not predictable and the claimed modification involves an inventive step on this basis' (ibid). The reasoning of the Board underlines the EPO's assumption regarding the cautious and pedestrian character of the skilled addressee. Thus, and as the Board has elsewhere said, when considering whether an invention is obvious, the skilled addressee would at all points be conditioned by the prior art, and refrain from taking any action before carefully pondering 'any possible modification, change or adjustment against the background of the existing knowledge' (T455/91 (*GENENTECH/Expression in Yeast*) [1996] EPOR 85, 98).

Particular difficulties with the European inventive step enquiry have arisen in the context of products. In the early years of gene patenting in Europe, the EPO Opposition Division—in a decision affirmed later by the Technical Board—took a very liberal approach to the inventive step requirement in *HOWARD FLOREY/Relaxin* [1995] EPOR 541 (*Howard Florey*). As we saw in Section 6.3.3.3.2, that case involved an application for a patent for the DNA sequence encoding for H2-relaxin—a substance found in the human body and having no previously recognized existence in isolated form—characterized by its chemical structure. According to the Division, the fact of the DNA sequence's novelty was sufficient also to establish its inventiveness, since in isolating the DNA the inventor was 'providing to the public for the first time a product whose existence was previously unknown' with the result that there was no prior art to render it obvious (548).

It seems clear that this approach is no longer valid. In *AgrEvo*, for example, the Technical Board decided that for chemical compounds to be inventive, they must either include some technically useful property or, if the technical problem they solve is only to provide new chemical compounds as such, reveal 'a hitherto unknown technical effect which is caused by those structural features which distinguish the claimed compounds' from those available previously (182). More generally, and since the entrenchment of the problem/solution approach particularly, inventive step requires a determination of whether the hypothetical skilled addressee, starting from the closest prior art and seeking to solve the technical problem which the product solves, would have devised the product. This is consistent with the decisions in *Comvik* and *Factor-9*, discussed earlier. It is also the approach adopted by the Technical Board in T1213/05 (*Breast and ovarian cancer/ UNIVERSITY OF UTAH*) EP:BA:2007:T121305.20070927 when determining the inventiveness of the isolated breast cancer gene (BRCA1) at issue in *Association for Molecular Pathology v Myriad Genetics, Inc.*, 133 S Ct 2107 (2013) (see Section 3.9).

7.3.4 Pros and Cons of the Problem/Solution Approach to Inventive Step

The problem/solution approach to inventive step has definite advantages for an administrative body such as a patent office. Above all, it promotes efficiency by focusing on a single piece of prior art and thereby avoiding the cost and time of having to consider and assess a potentially large number of prior art references. In addition, by conceiving inventions as solutions to a technical problem, and focusing on whether the skilled addressee equipped with common general knowledge and starting from the position of the closest prior art would have been prompted to devise the solution herself, the EPO limits patentability to inventions that represent a technical contribution to the relevant art. As the Technical Board said in *AgrEvo*, the 'legal principle that the extent of the patent monopoly should correspond to and be justified by the technical contribution to the art…also governs the decision that is required to be made under Article 56 EPC'.

For the very same reasons, however, the problem/solution approach has been criticized, including by the Technical Board of the EPO itself. For example, in any case in which the closest prior art is not obvious, the approach will disadvantage the defendant or opponent challenging the patent's validity, increasing the risk of an invalid patent being granted or upheld. In addition, by casting inventions as solutions to pre-existing problems, and asking whether the solution they represent involves an inventive step, the approach invites something close to a requirement for technical progress,[6] and in doing so undermines the terms of the EPC and the insistence of its drafters that technical progress not be permitted to dominate enquiries under Article 56. It also forces the inventive step enquiry into a potentially artificial and distracting analytical framework; a point made by the Board in T465/92 (*ALCAN/Aluminium Alloys*) [1995] EPOR 501 as follows (514–15):

[Since] the problem and solution approach…relies on the results of a search made with actual knowledge of the invention, it is inherently based on hindsight, and therefore calls for care in its application in some circumstances. A further drawback is that it can result in complicated multi-step reasoning where the facts are clear, either for or against inventiveness. Thus, if an invention breaks entirely new ground, it may suffice to say that there is no close prior art, rather than constructing a problem based on what is tenuously regarded as the closest prior art.

The assessment of inventiveness which is required by Article 56 EPC is a matter of judgment. As reflected by some of the decisions of the Boards of Appeal, the problem and solution approach can entail the exercise of judgment in deciding what is to be treated as the so-called 'objective' problem. Once that problem has been identified, in some cases little further judgment may be needed to decide the issue of obviousness. Nevertheless, problem and solution analysis does not remove the element of judgment inherent in the assessment of inventiveness, but rather displaces it from the task set by the EPC, to another task which is inessential to Article 56 EPC. In that connection the Board sees a welcome trend in some recent unreported decisions, which have emphasised that the investigation of inventiveness should avoid formulating artificial and unrealistic technical problems, and should normally start from the technical problem identified in the patent in suit…

---

[6] Cf Part G Chapter I 3 Guidelines for Examination; see also Part G Chapter I 5.2.

Since this decision the trend referred to has ended, and the Guidelines for Examination have been amended to require that the problem/solution approach be applied in all but exceptional cases.

7.4 Susceptibility of Industrial Application

7.4.1 The Statutory Framework: Article 57 EPC

The last of the secondary patentability criteria imposed by Article 52(1) EPC requires that an invention, to be patentable, be susceptible of industrial application. According to Article 57 EPC, '[a]n invention shall be considered as susceptible of industrial application if it can be made or used in any kind of industry, including agriculture.' This definition is supplemented for biotechnological inventions by the provision in Rule 29(3) of the Implementing Regulations—reproducing Article 5(3) Biotech Directive—that '[t]he industrial application of a sequence or a partial sequence of a gene must be disclosed in the patent application.' Exactly how this relates to the further stipulation in recital 23 Biotech Directive that a 'mere DNA sequence without indication of a function does not contain any technical information and is therefore not a patentable invention' is unclear. As noted in Section 7.2, when read with Article 9 Biotech Directive, recital 23 supports a view of DNA sequences as entitled to purpose-limited product protection only, and not to product as such protection, making them analogous to purpose-limited products in the medical field. Given this especially, recital 23 is best read as analytically separate from Article 5(3), and its reference to 'function' as not being synonymous with the Article 5(3) reference to industrial applicability. The only feasible alternative would be to read DNA sequences as comprising an exceptional category of invention the protection of which is limited with reference to the requirement for susceptibility of industrial application.

7.4.2 The Requirement for a Concrete Benefit

The requirement for susceptibility of industrial application has been interpreted broadly by the EPO, consistent with the EPC drafters' intention, and with explicit regard to policy. According to that interpretation, the requirement is satisfied by the disclosure of any 'concrete benefit' in the form of a practical application and profitable use for the invention (T898/05 (*ZYMOGENETICS/Hematopoietic Cytokine Receptor*) [2007] EPOR 2 (*Zymogenetics*)). In *Zymogenetics*, after reviewing the case law on Article 57 EPC, the Board offered this understanding of the requirement and its underlying policy rationale ([15]):

> [An invention must] have such a sound and concrete technical basis that the skilled person can recognize that its contribution to the art could lead to practical exploitation in industry. It would be at odds with the purpose of the patent system to grant exclusive rights to prevent the commercial activities of others on the basis of a purely theoretical or speculative patent application. This would amount to granting a monopoly over an unexplored technical field.

Article 57 brings into relief once again the challenges posed for patent law by the field of new biotechnology. Such is the cost of biotechnological research and development that biotech companies often depend on the early grant of patents to secure the funding and security they need to continue their work. As the *Factor-9* case illustrates, this can lead applicants to seek protection in respect of proteins and other products before their technical properties and utility have been properly established. The result is pressure on patent courts and offices to define industrial applicability and the other secondary patentability requirements in a way that recognizes the special dependence of the biotech industry on patent protection without unduly stifling the research and development efforts of third parties. In the context of Article 57, the EPO has responded to this pressure by interpreting the requirement for susceptibility of industrial application as satisfied for any invention comprising a protein by the disclosure of a reasonably credible educated guess as to its role (*Zymogenetics*). Emphasizing the need to determine the matter 'in each case on its own merits, according to the particular technical circumstances (extent of disclosure, background art, post-published evidence etc)' ([30]), the Board in *Zymogenetics* nonetheless made clear its view, quoting the Examining Division, that the critical issue in any case is whether the role suggested for the invention 'is so vaguely defined that no practical application or profitable use in the sense of Article 57 EPC can be envisaged' ([36]). Merely disclosing the structure of a product—such as a nucleic acid sequence—without more than a vague indication of its function, will generally not be enough. As the Board stated ([17]), '[i]f a patent is granted therefor, it might prevent further research in that area, and/or give the patentee unjustified control over others who are actively investigating in that area and who might eventually find actual ways to exploit it'. Once again, this is consistent with the Board's decision regarding the implications of speculative patents for the inventive step requirement of Article 56 EPC in *Factor-9*. It is also consistent with the Board's decision in T870/04 (*MAX-PLANCK/BDP1 Phosphatase*) [2006] EPOR 14, that a polypeptide was not patentable for lack of industrial applicability on the ground that, while undoubtedly capable of being made and used, the patent left 'the whole burden . . . to the reader to guess or find a way to exploit it in industry by carrying out work in search for some practical application geared to financial gain, without any confidence that any practical application exists' ([35]).

7.5 Conclusions

We saw in Chapter 6 that the European law of patentability supports and is driven by a view of patents as existing to promote contributions to technology. This can also be seen in the focus of the EPO on the technical aspects of an invention when determining novelty, and in its interpretation of inventive step as requiring a sufficient contribution to the prior art of a technical field specifically.

Undoubtedly, the most conceptually difficult areas of the law of patentability are the public policy exclusions of Article 53 and the requirement for an invention of Article 52(2) and (3) that we considered in Chapter 6. As discussed in Section 4.4, the practical importance of these areas is also increasing as new technologies challenge the accepted boundaries of patentable subject matter. Nonetheless, it is the secondary requirements of novelty and inventive step particularly that tend to dominate patent examination and litigation in practice. One reason for this is simply the different requirements of establishing novelty and inventive step: unlike the requirement for a patentable subject matter, novelty and inventive step cannot be determined without establishing the state of the art, which is a costly and burdensome process that frequently requires extensive argument and expert evidence. In addition (and relatedly), while it will often be apparent from the terms of a patent specification whether or not a claimed subject matter is an invention outside the scope of Article 53, the same will rarely be true of novelty or inventive step. And finally, the vagueness of the inventive step standard particularly, and the fact-intensive nature of its associated enquiries, are such that reasonable people will often disagree about their resolution in individual cases. This is one reason that decentralized decision-making in European patent law is criticized, namely, because different courts and patent offices considering whether the same invention is inventive will sometimes reach different conclusions, even when applying the same principles of law, due in part to the different arguments and evidence presented to them. It also explains why the EPO has sought to limit the discretionary nature of the inventive step test through the adoption of the problem/solution approach, and to avoid considering directly the statutory question of whether the invention would have been obvious to a person skilled in the art.

When the unitary patent system takes effect, the European law of patentability will remain much as it is currently. The EPO will continue to be responsible for granting European patents, including those registered for unitary effect under Regulation 1257/2012, and will continue to apply the substantive law of patentability contained in the EPC when doing so. That law will also need to be applied by the Unified Patent Court (UPC) when hearing challenges to patent validity brought before it (see Article 2(1)(c) UPC Agreement 2013). The greatest change affecting it will almost certainly be an increased emphasis in its interpretation by both the UPC and the EPO on the principles and values of EU law, including the Biotech Directive, as a result of the UPC's obligation under Article 20 UPC Agreement to 'apply Union law in its entirety and [to] respect its primacy'. The area most likely to be affected by this is Article 53(a) EPC, and its application in respect of inventions not involving human biological material. In comparison, the interpretation of the secondary patentability requirements of novelty, inventive step, and susceptibility of industrial application should remain much as it is currently. Having said that, one can perhaps predict a greater focus by the UPC on the statutory question of inventive step as befits a court for which efficiency, while important, will not be so central. In addition, one can hope for an ongoing commitment to invalidating speculative patents across all fields of technology, whether for lack of inventive step, insusceptibility of industrial application, or (as discussed in Section 5.3.1.3.3) insufficiency.

Further Reading

BEIER, F.-K., 'The Inventive Step in Its Historical Development' [1986] *IIC* 301

CASALONGA, A., 'The Concept of Inventive Step in the European Patent Convention' [1979] *IIC* 412

CORNISH, W.R., 'The Essential Criteria for Patentability of European Inventions: Novelty and Inventive Step' [1983] *IIC* 765

JACOB, R., 'Novelty of Use Claims' [1996] *IIC* 170

SHERMAN, B., 'Patent Law in a Time of Change: Non-Obviousness and Biotechnology' (1990) 10 *OJLS* 278

8

Patent Protection and Exploitation

8.1 Introduction

Once a patent has been granted, the nature and scope of the protection it confers must be determined. Four issues are central to that end. The first is the effects of the patent, namely, the territories in and term for which it is valid. The second is the object of protection, namely, the subject matter which the public is excluded from using during that term. The third is the substance of protection, namely, the uses of the subject matter from which the public is excluded. And the fourth is the limitations to protection, namely, the acts which the public may undertake notwithstanding their prima facie infringement of the patent. In the current chapter we consider each of these issues under the headings 'patent effects', 'patent scope', 'patent rights', and 'patent limitations' respectively.

As we saw in Section 5.3.7, the effects of a patent depend on the species of patent grant in question. With some exceptions (provided for under the EPC), European (EPC) patents confer the same protection in each state in respect of which they are granted as the protection conferred by national patents granted in that state. As a result, they are subject to the same laws of patent scope, rights, and limitations as national patents. So too with few exceptions, European patents registered for unitary effect under Regulation 1257/2012 (UP Regulation) will be subject to the same laws of patent scope, rights, and limitations as national (and European (EPC)) patents. The main difference between them and European (EPC) (and national) patents will therefore be the unitary and uniform nature of the protection they will confer throughout the territories of the states in which they have effect.

The protection conferred by a (national or European) patent is governed by a mix of European and national law. Patent scope is regulated by the EPC, as interpreted by the EPO and domestic courts, and for EU Member States by the Biotech Directive. While these sources make only limited provision for patent rights and limitations, the Community Patent Convention of 1975 (CPC) contains a complete definition of each, and forms the basis of the national laws of European states as well as of the Unified Patent Court (UPC) Agreement of 2013. In addition, domestic courts have become increasingly concerned in recent years to interpret these definitions in a consistent and harmonized manner, reasoning comparatively from the laws of other European states when doing so, even as they continue to express their decisions in the language of their own patent traditions. Thus, while differences in national laws and jurisprudence regarding patent protection exist—for example, courts consider the patent office file when determining patent scope in some states only, and *Bolar* exceptions to patent infringement are defined differently in the legislation of different states—the area as a whole has been extensively Europeanized.

As noted earlier, the introduction of the Unitary Patent Package (UPP) will involve little if any change to the substantive European law in this field. However, the establishment of a new supranational patent court (the UPC) to interpret that law in respect of all European (EPC and unitary) patents can be expected to encourage further its harmonized interpretation and application. Even then, however, national courts and jurisprudence will continue to play an important role and to exert influence at the European level.

8.2 Patent Effects

As we saw in Section 5.3.7, European patents take effect under the EPC in each of their designated Contracting States from the date on which the mention of their grant is published in the European Patent Bulletin, subject to the patentee's fulfilment of any translation requirements imposed by the relevant Contracting State in accordance with Article 65 EPC (Article 64). Once effective, they confer on their owner the same rights as would be conferred by a national patent granted in the state for a maximum period of 20 years, subject to extension on the grounds permitted by Article 63. It follows that it is rarely necessary in practice to distinguish between European and national patents when considering the nature and scope of the protection they confer.

By contrast, and as we also saw in Section 5.3.7, the effect of European patents with unitary effect registered under the UP Regulation will differ from that of European (EPC) bundle and national patents. Specifically, European patents with unitary effect will confer unitary and uniform protection throughout the territories of the EU Member States that had ratified the UPC Agreement at the time of their registration for unitary effect (Articles 5 and 18(2) UP Regulation). The scope of that protection will however be determined in the same manner as that of European (EPC) and national patents, namely, in accordance with the principles of the EPC and Biotech Directive (see recital 9 UP Regulation). The rights they confer and the limitations to those rights will be as 'defined by the law applied to European patents with unitary effect in the participating Member State whose national law is applicable to the European patent with unitary effect as an object of property in accordance with Article 7' of the UP Regulation (Article 5(3)), meaning in practice the UPC Agreement.

8.3 Patent Scope

8.3.1 The Role of the Patent Claims: Article 69 EPC

The rights conferred by a patent grant or application must attach to a specific subject matter. In Europe that subject matter is the invention for which the patent was granted or sought, and which it is the express purpose of the patent claims to define (see Articles 84 and 69; Section 5.3.1.3.2). Hence the basic principle of patent protection, namely, that the scope of such protection is determined by the patent claims. This principle was first expressed at the European level in Article 8(3) of the Strasbourg Patent Convention 1963, and later reproduced for European patents and applications in Article 69 EPC as follows:

1. The extent of the protection conferred by a European patent or a European patent application shall be determined by the terms of the claims. Nevertheless, the description and drawings shall be used to interpret the claims.

2. For the period up to grant of the European patent, the extent of the protection conferred by the European patent application shall be determined by the claims contained in the application as published. However, the European patent as granted or as amended in opposition, limitation or revocation proceedings shall determine retroactively the protection conferred by the application, in so far as such protection is not thereby extended.

The question that arises from this provision (and Article 8(3) Strasbourg Patent Convention) is how—i.e. by what interpretative method—must one construe the claims of a patent in order to define the scope of its monopoly? Whatever method one adopts, it must be the same as the method adopted when identifying the subject matter for which a patent is claimed for the purpose of determining its patentability (see Chapters 6 and 7).

8.3.2 General Principles of Claim Construction

8.3.2.1 Contextual Interpretation From the Perspective of the Skilled Addressee

The starting point for considering this question is the Protocol on the Interpretation of Article 69 EPC (Protocol), which is an integral part of the Convention (Article 164(1) EPC). The Protocol contains two Articles, the first dealing with claim construction in general and the second with the treatment of so-called equivalents. According to Article 1:

> Article 69 should not be interpreted in the sense that the extent of the protection conferred by a European patent is to be understood as that defined by the strict, literal meaning of the wording used in the claims, the description and drawings being employed only for the purpose of resolving an ambiguity found in the claims. Neither should it be interpreted in the sense that the claims serve only as a guideline and that the actual protection conferred may extend to what, from a consideration of the description and drawings by a person skilled in the art, the patentee has contemplated. On the contrary, it is to be interpreted as defining a position between these extremes which combines a fair protection for the patentee with a reasonable degree of certainty for third parties.

It is well established that the original aim of this Article was to ensure a middle ground between the perceived extremes of the UK and German approaches to claim construction before 1973, characterized as the literal and signpost approaches respectively (see G2/88 (*MOBIL/Friction Reducing Additive*) [1990] EPOR 73 (*Mobil*) 78–9, 81–2).

As with all interpretative exercises, the construction of patent claims can be difficult in practice. In *Mobil*, the Enlarged Board construed a patent claim to the 'use of a compound A for purpose B' as including not only the compound A and the actual method by which purpose B was achieved, but also the purpose B ('the function of achieving purpose B') itself (87). In its view, this reflected an interpretation of the claim that went beyond the literal meaning of its terms without going so far as to relegate them to the status of mere guidance as to what the patentee had contemplated.

Mobil notwithstanding, most of the EPO's case law regarding the interpretation of written documents concerns prior art references under Article 54 (see Section 7.2.4), priority documents under Articles 87 to 89 (see Section 7.2.3.1), patent descriptions under Article 83 (see Section 5.3.1.3.3), and proposed amendments and corrections to patent specifications under Article 123 (see Section 5.4). In each of these contexts, however, the EPO has adopted the same approach, emphasizing the need for consistency when interpreting language-based disclosures under the EPC.

Two principles are central to the EPO's interpretative approach. The first is that the ultimate aim of interpretation is to derive meaning from the language chosen by the author of the relevant document. And the second is that while the language itself has primary importance to that end, it must be understood in its particular context, including for patent claims in the context of the patent description and drawings (following Article 69(1) EPC) and the statutory purpose of such claims to define an invention—i.e., a technical idea for a product or process—and a corresponding patent monopoly.

In the past, claim construction has been something of a poster-child for supporters of a unified European patent litigation system due to the perceived differences in the English and German approaches even after the introduction of the EPC.[1] This was especially true following *Improver Corporation v Remington Consumer Products*, in which courts in those and other countries interpreted the scope of a European patent for the Epilady shaver differently.[2] As defined in the claims of the patent, the invention was a depilatory (hair removal) device with a curved helical spring driven by a motor. When rotated, the spring gripped the hairs to be removed between its coils and pulled them from the skin. The question for the courts was whether the invention thus defined covered a depilatory device in which the hairs were gripped and removed by a rubber rod with slits in its surface. The English court held that it did not, in contrast to the German court, which held that it did on the basis of the equivalence of the use of a rubber rod and helical spring. The result was a finding of patent infringement in Germany but not in England.

Since *Improver*, however, the gap between the English and German approaches to claim construction has narrowed considerably. This has been aided in no small part by the evident concern of judges in each jurisdiction to adopt a consistent approach and take account of each other's jurisprudence when arriving at their decisions. For example, in 2004 the judge from the English *Improver* case recast the UK law of claim construction from the House of Lords in terms that mirror closely the EPO approach mentioned earlier, drawing on jurisprudence from Germany and the Netherlands in doing so (see *Kirin-Amgen Inc. v Hoechst Marion Roussel Ltd* [2004] UKHL 46, [2005] RPC 9 (*Kirin-Amgen*)). As the judge in question (Lord Hoffmann) remarked in that case, while the language deployed by different European courts when interpreting patent claims differs as a reflection of their different national patent traditions—the German courts focusing on the technical meaning that the skilled addressee would attribute to the wording of the claims, and the English courts focusing more on the meaning which the skilled addressee would understand the patentee to have intended by her claims to convey—their approaches are substantively the same. Central is what the notional skilled addressee, equipped with common general knowledge and reading the claims in their proper legal and factual context, would understand them to mean.

---

[1] See, e.g., 'Communication from the Commission to the European Parliament and the Council—Enhancing the Patent System in Europe' COM (2007) 165 final.

[2] See ibid n 17; and cf., e.g., [1990] FSR 181 (UK Patents Court) with [1993] *GRUR Int* 242, [1993] *IIC* 838 (Düsseldorf Court of Appeals). For an analysis of the English and German decisions in *Improver* as reflections of the culture and history of England and Germany see D.L. Cohen, 'Article 69 and European Patent Integration' (1998) 92 *Northwestern University Law Review* 1082.

8.3.2.2 **The Doctrine of Equivalents**

Article 2 of the Protocol was introduced as part of the EPC 2000 revisions. According to the EP Organisation's Administrative Council at the time, its introduction was required to promote the development of 'Europe-wide uniform criteria and rules for the interpretation of European patents and the assessment of their extent of protection' (Doc. MR/2/00 e 59) following the failure of Article 69 EPC, in combination with Article 1 of the Protocol, to have achieved that end. In full it provides as follows:

> For the purpose of determining the extent of protection conferred by a European patent, due account shall be taken of any element which is equivalent to an element specified in the claims.

The question is what this Article requires and permits. That is, what might taking 'due account' of equivalents when interpreting patent claims entail?

Once again, this is a question on which national courts in Europe agree substantively, even if they do not always use the same language and methodology, and reach the same outcome in a particular case. According to the predominant view, the existence of an equivalent is merely one aspect of the context in which a patent claim falls to be interpreted; something of which the notional skilled addressee is deemed to be aware when interpreting the claim. In German jurisprudence, this is reflected in the principle that a skilled addressee reading patent claims with a view to determining their technical meaning would understand them to go beyond the subject matter revealed by a literal or semantic reading of their language to include any obvious variants of that subject matter, excluding variants known or obvious as against the prior art.[3] In a later quintet of cases decided on 12 March 2002, the Bundesgerichtshof (German Federal Supreme Court) expressed this more prosaically in terms of guidelines adapted from the English *Improver* case. The effect of those guidelines is to treat any subject matter that falls outside the semantic or 'essential' meaning of a patent claim as nonetheless protected by the patent if:

(a) The subject matter is equivalent to the invention in a technical sense, namely, in the sense of solving the same objective technical problem as the invention solves by means which the skilled addressee, drawing on the essential meaning of the claims, would recognize as having the same objective technical effect as the invention has; and

(b) The skilled addressee reading the claims would not understand them to have been drafted with a view to excluding the subject matter from the scope of protection.[4]

Consistent with (b), the German Federal Supreme Court has made clear its view that any equivalent subject matter referred to in the patent specification as an alternative to the invention will fall outside the scope of the patentee's monopoly.[5]

The English approach to equivalents is similar to this. As with the German approach, its premise is a view of equivalents as one aspect of the context in which the notional skilled addressee is presumed to read the patent claims. This was made clear by Lord Hoffmann in *Kirin-Amgen*, where his Lordship endorsed an earlier decision of the House of Lords (in *Catnic Components Ltd v Hill & Smith Ltd* [1982] RPC 183) that the monopoly

---

[3] See *Formstein* [1986] *GRUR* 803, [1987] *IIC* 795 (BGH); *Ionenanalyse* [1988] *GRUR* 896, [1991] *IIC* 249 (BGH).

[4] See *Schneidmesser I* and *II* [2002] *GRUR* 515, 519; *Custodial I* and *II* [2002] *GRUR* 523, 527; *Plastic Pipe* [2002] *GRUR* 511.

[5] See, e.g., *Occlutech GmbH v AGA Medical Corporation* [2011] *GRUR* 701, [2011] *IIC* 851 (BGH) (*Occlutech*).

conferred by a patent for a 'vertical lintel' covered a lintel inclined at six degrees. The reason for his endorsement of that case was his view of the lintel inclined at six degrees as a technical approximation or equivalent of the vertical lintel and thus as substantively the same invention. In those circumstances, to limit the patentee's monopoly to the lintel inclined at zero degrees would have had the perverse result of enabling a defendant to avoid infringement by manufacturing a lintel inclined at 0.0001 degrees. It would also have required one of two things on the part of the court: either an assumption that in drafting her claim the patentee used each word in its literal sense; or a policy commitment to hold the patentee to the literal meaning of her claim whatever the context and consequences. Both are problematic, however, since people do *not* use language in a literal sense—this being the central insight of the semantic theory that underpins the contextual approach to claim construction required by the EPC—and since to hold them to their literal meaning on policy grounds is expressly prohibited by Article 1 of the Protocol. In formulating the UK position regarding equivalents, Lord Hoffmann in *Kirin-Amgen* once again considered the German courts' approach.

8.3.3 The Patent Office File

8.3.3.1 The Proposal for a European Version of the US Doctrine of File Wrapper Estoppel

Another amendment to the Article 69 Protocol proposed by the Administrative Council in 2000 was the insertion of a new Article 3 to read as follows:

> For the purpose of determining the extent of protection, due account shall be taken of any statement unambiguously limiting the extent of protection, made by the applicant or the proprietor of the patent in the European patent application or patent, or during proceedings concerning the grant or the validity of the European patent, in particular where the limitation was made in response to a citation of prior art.

Had this Article been enacted, it would have introduced into European law a version of the US doctrine of file wrapper estoppel. According to that doctrine, a patentee may not rely on the (US) doctrine of equivalents to secure protection for subject matter excluded from her patent by an amendment made during the grant procedure. Thus, the patentee is estopped against the world from denying her intention to exclude the relevant subject matter.

8.3.3.2 The Approach of Domestic Courts

The proposed Article 3 was never enacted, leaving national courts to reach their own position regarding the relevance of the patent office file when construing a patent claim. The positions thus adopted have differed among states. In the majority of European states, resort to the patent office file is supported in certain circumstances at least, such as where the scope of the claims has been narrowed during the examination procedure to secure their validity, and the aspects of the file being relied upon are open to the public. Beyond this, however, national positions diverge considerably,[6] with the courts of some states emphasizing the inequity of permitting a patentee to resile from a representation she (or someone on her behalf) has made to secure the grant of a patent in circumstances in which her doing so will increase the scope of her monopoly, and others emphasizing the requirements of Article 69 EPC, the cost of investigating the patent file, the difficulties in deciding exactly what the patentee intended by an amendment to exclude, and the

---

[6] AIPPI Committee 229, 'The Use of Prosecution History in Post-Grant Patent Proceedings' Summary report (October 2012).

legal uncertainty for the public of not being able to determine a patent's scope without having resort to its prosecution history. As these arguments for and against the recognition of some version of the doctrine of file wrapper estoppel suggest, having resort to the patent office file to determine the meaning of patent claims is directly analogous to having resort to pre-contractual negotiations to determine the meaning of a contract. On the one hand, patentees and contracting parties should not be able to profit at others' and the general public's expense from misrepresentations which they or others on their behalf make. On the other hand, patents and contracts should be able to stand on their own terms, independent of the subjective intentions of their authors, particularly given their function in defining legal rights and corresponding obligations and restrictions on public freedoms.

8.3.4 **Gene Patents Granted in Respect of EU Member States**

8.3.4.1 **Article 9 Biotech Directive**

For EU Member States, definitions of patent scope must also take account of Article 9 Biotech Directive. According to that Article, the protection conferred by a patent for a genetic product must be limited to material 'in which the product is incorporated and in which the genetic information is contained and performs its function'. This supports the patentability requirement of industrial application (restated for genetic products in Article 5(3) Biotech Directive) by ensuring that such products are only protected in situations in which they are performing the function on the basis of which they were deemed to merit patent protection. Specifically, it limits the protection available for genetic products to purpose-limited protection on the basis of a view of such products *qua* invention as constituted in part by the use for which they are intended.

8.3.4.2 **The Meaning of Article 9:** *Monsanto*

This understanding of Article 9 is consistent with that supported in European Parliament resolution P6_TA(2005)0407 [5] and Case C–428/08 *Monsanto Technology LLC v Cefetra BV et al.* [2010] ECR I-6765 (*Monsanto*). *Monsanto* involved a preliminary referral from Dutch proceedings initiated by the owner of a patent for a DNA sequence that, when inserted into a soya plant, rendered the plant resistant to a herbicide (Glyphosate). The patentee sued the importer of soya meal containing traces of the genetically modified plants for patent infringement. The Rechtbank 's-Gravenhage (District Court of The Hague) referred the following four questions to the CJEU concerning Article 9. (a) Does the Directive limit protection to situations in which the genetic information in question is performing its function at the time of the alleged infringement? (b) Does the Directive preclude absolute protection for genetic products? (c) Do the answers to (a) and (b) differ for patents granted before the Directive's adoption? And (d), when answering questions (a) to (c), is it permissible to take account of Articles 27 and 30 TRIPS Agreement?

The CJEU answered the first, second, and fourth of these questions affirmatively and the third negatively. Regarding the third, it held that Article 9 precludes the owner of a patent for a genetic product granted before the Directive's adoption from relying on domestic law according it absolute protection. Regarding the fourth, it affirmed that while the TRIPS Agreement does not have direct effect, and cannot therefore be invoked directly in horizontal proceedings by individuals in reliance on EU law, any EU legal rules within the Agreement's sphere, including Article 9 Biotech Directive, must be interpreted, as far as possible, in a manner consistent with the Agreement's provisions. Applying this principle in *Monsanto*, the CJEU held that Article 9 is consistent with TRIPS since it concerns the *scope* of patent protection, whereas Articles 27 and 30 TRIPS concern the law of patent-ability and exceptions to patent rights respectively. If limitations to a patent's protective scope count as 'exceptions', the Court decided, then the limits imposed by Article 9 do not in any case infringe Article 30 TRIPS, since they neither 'unreasonably conflict with a normal exploitation of the patent', nor 'unreasonably prejudice the legitimate interests of the patent owner, taking account of the legitimate interests of third parties', within the meaning of that Article ([76]).

8.3.4.3 The Significance of *Monsanto*

Monsanto is an important decision for two reasons of current relevance. The first is its restriction of patent protection with reference to the criteria of patentability. As we will see in Sections 8.4.2.3 and 12.2.6, this is methodologically consistent with the test of infringement-by-making supported by European domestic courts, and with the EU defi-nition of copyright scope. It is also consistent with the general principles of claim con-struction under the EPC, according to which a patent claim must be read contextually, having regard to its definition of an invention and patent monopoly.

The second reason for *Monsanto*'s importance is related to this, and derives from its sup-port for a view of a product's function as among its essential (i.e. constitutive) properties, at least in the context of genetic products.[7] This explains why a DNA sequence that is not performing its genetic function cannot infringe a patent, namely, because when it stops performing that function it ceases to exist as the invention for which the patent was granted.

The view of function as an essential (technical) property or feature of a genetic product comes through most clearly in the Advocate General's opinion in *Monsanto* (9 March 2010), with which the Grand Chamber largely agreed. While the Advocate General described his opinion as confined to the scope of protection, such scope flowed directly from his conception of the invention itself. Hence the three factors which he raised in sup-port of his approach: first, the Directive's requirement that the function performed by a DNA sequence be specified in order for the sequence to be patentable—which he regarded as evidencing the legislature's view that 'a DNA sequence has no importance in the con-text of patents if the function performed by that sequence is not indicated' ([30]); second, the importance of function in permitting 'a distinction to be drawn between "discovery" and "invention"' ([31]); and third, 'the essential nature of a patent' as a 'genuine exchange' of publication for limited property rights ([32]). The second and third of these elements were particularly important. As the Advocate General said, to allow protection for 'all the possible functions of the sequence itself, including those not identified at the time when the patent is applied for' would 'make a mere discovery patentable' ([31]), and 'confer on the patent holder a disproportionate level of protection' ([32]). The result, he suggested, would be to support a breach of the two fundamental principles of patent protection, namely, that such protection is limited to inventions properly conceived, and that it must be proportionate having regard to the nature of the same.

8.4 Patent Rights

Having established the scope of the subject matter to which the patent rights attach, it is necessary to consider the nature of those rights themselves, and the specific uses of the protected invention from which third parties are excluded during the patent term.

---

[7] On the essential features of an invention see Chapter 7.

8.4.1 **Uses Reserved to the Patentee**

8.4.1.1 **Rights of Direct and Indirect Use**

8.4.1.1.1 *Rights of Direct Use: Article 29 CPC*

The first European definition of patent rights was contained in Articles 29 and 30 CPC, corresponding to Articles 25 and 26 of the 1989 version of the Convention published as *89/695 EEC: Agreement Relating to Community Patents* [1989] OJ L 401/1. According to Article 29, a Community patent granted under the CPC would have conferred the right on its owner to prevent a third party from the following direct uses of the invention:

(a) …making, offering, putting on the market or using a product which is the subject-matter of the patent, or importing or stocking the product for these purposes;

(b) …using a process which is the subject-matter of the patent or, when the third party knows, or it is obvious in the circumstances, that the use of the process is prohibited without the consent of the proprietor of the patent, from offering the process for use within the territories of the contracting states;

(c) …offering, putting on the market, using, or importing or stocking for these purposes the product obtained directly by a process which is the subject-matter of the patent.

Of note regarding these rights is the absence from most of any requirement for actual or deemed knowledge of the patent or invention on the part of the alleged infringer, or for any intention on his part. In these respects patent infringement is a matter of strict liability. This creates difficulties in any case involving a patent for a purpose-limited product or purpose-limited process, however, where the intention to use a product for a specific purpose will be an essential and constitutive property of the protected invention (see Sections 6.3.4.2.2 and 6.3.4.2.3). As a result, it will only be possible to infringe a patent for a purpose-limited product within the meaning of the first clause of Article 29(a) CPC by making, etc., the relevant product with the intention that it be used for the purpose specified in the claim; and so too it will only be possible to infringe a patent for a purpose-limited process (i.e. for the use of a product for a specified new purpose) within the meaning of the first clause of Article 29(b) CPC by using the process with the intention that the product it involves be used for the purpose specified. In both types of case patent infringement depends on the defendant's state of mind, challenging the principle of strict liability for patent infringement, and raising difficult issues regarding the nature of the intention required (is a subjective or objective intention required?) and the evidence required to establish it (is some outward manifestation of intention in the manufacture of the product required, and if it is, may that manifestation be in the product's advertisement?).

Another result of the Article 29 CPC definition of patent rights is to prevent a defendant from avoiding liability for direct infringement of a patent by showing that the product or process that he made or used, etc., was independently devised by him. (An exception would be if the defendant were able to establish a prior user right in respect of the product or process, as discussed in Section 8.5.4.) The only exception to this is where the alleged infringement involves offering a patented process for sale without permission, which will only fall within Article 29(b) if the defendant knew or ought in the circumstances to have known that his act was prohibited.

Finally, it is worth noting the absence from Article 29 of any reference to *repairing* a product, which third parties are accordingly free to do without permission of the patentee. As discussed in Section 8.4.2.3, however, distinguishing between making and repairing a product can be difficult, and is a matter that has occupied European domestic courts recently.

8.4.1.1.2 Rights of Indirect Use: Article 30 CPC

In addition to the rights of direct use described in Article 29, a Community patent would have conferred the right on its owner to prevent a third party from the following indirect uses of the protected invention:

1. … supplying or offering to supply within the territories of the contracting states a person, other than a party entitled to exploit the patented invention, with means, relating to an essential element of that invention, for putting it into effect therein, when the third party knows, or it is obvious in the circumstances, that these means are suitable and intended for putting that invention into effect.

2. paragraph 1 shall not apply when the means are staple commercial products, except when the third party induces the person supplied to commit acts prohibited by article 29.

3. persons performing the acts referred to in article 31 (a) to (c) [acts done privately and for non-commercial purposes; acts done for experimental purposes relating to the patented invention; and the extemporaneous preparation for individual cases in a pharmacy of a medicine in accordance with a medical prescription or acts concerning the medicine so prepared] shall not be considered to be parties entitled to exploit the invention within the meaning of paragraph 1.

8.4.1.2 The Development of a European Jurisprudence of Patent Rights

8.4.1.2.1 The Adoption of Articles 29 and 30 CPC

The CPC was never ratified, with the result that Articles 29 and 30 have never taken effect. Nonetheless, the definition of patent rights that they contain has been widely adopted at the national, European, and international levels. For example, at the Munich Conference at which the EPC was signed in 1973, it was agreed to incorporate the then draft version of Article 29(c) CPC into Article 64 EPC. As a result, Article 64(2) provides that '[i]f the subject-matter of the European patent is a process, the protection conferred by the patent shall extend to the products directly obtained by such process.'

In addition to incorporating Article 29(c) into the EPC, in the 1980s the then Member States of the European Community (EC) signed a declaration regarding the adjustment of their national laws to conform, as far as possible, with the substantive provisions of the CPC. This declaration was supported by the EC Member States' preparation of a Memorandum of Understanding regarding the CPC (*Blatt für Patent-, Muster- und Zeichenwesen*, vol. 81 (1979) 325–49) and its use by domestic courts when interpreting corresponding provisions of national law. Further, when the TRIPS Agreement was concluded in 1994, it contained a definition of patent rights based on Article 29 CPC (see Article 28 TRIPS). And finally, the definition of patent rights contained in the UPC Agreement 2013 for application in respect of European (EPC and unitary) patents reproduces (and supplements) Articles 29 and 30 CPC (see Articles 25 and 26 UPC Agreement).

8.4.1.2.2 Articles 29 and 30 CPC as the Basis for a European Jurisprudence of Patent Rights

Thus, statutory definitions of patent rights are largely harmonized throughout Europe in accordance with Articles 29 and 30 CPC. As a result, such differences as exist among the laws of European states can be said to be the result of devolved judicial responsibility for interpreting and applying those definitions, and the absence of any centralized European patent court. In reality, however, the European courts' commitment to comparative reasoning and harmonized interpretations of patent law, combined with their awareness of the CPC and EPC, has limited the differences that do exist. In support of this, one can

point to the practice of the UK courts when interpreting domestic (UK) legislative provisions implementing Articles 29 and 30 CPC of referring to the patent jurisprudence of
other European courts as a matter of course. Indeed, and as the following statement by
a senior English patent judge illustrates, this has been done consciously and over many
years precisely in anticipation of the establishment of a future European patent court
(*Grimme Maschinenfabrik GmbH & Co. KG v Scott (t/a Scotts Potato Machinery)* [2010]
EWCA Civ 1110, [2011] FSR 7 [79]–[81]):

> Advocates should recognise that where a point of patent law of general importance, such as
> the construction of a provision which by Treaty (either the EPC or the Community Patent
> Convention) is to be implemented by states parties to those conventions, has been decided
> by a court, particularly a higher court, of another member state, the decision matters here.
> For, despite the fact that there is no common ultimate patent court for Europe, it is of
> obvious importance to all the countries of the European Patent Union or the parties to
> the Community Patent Convention ('the CPC'), that as far as possible the same legal rules
> apply across all the countries where the provisions of the Conventions have been imple-
> mented. An important decision in one member state may well be of strong persuasive value
> in all the others, particularly where the judgment contains clear reasoning on the point.
>
> Broadly we think the principle in our courts—and indeed that in the courts of other
> member states—should be to try to follow the reasoning of an important decision in
> another country. Only if the court of one state is convinced that the reasoning of a court
> in another member state is erroneous should it depart from a point that has been authori-
> tatively decided there. Increasingly that has become the practice in a number of countries,
> particularly in the important patent countries of France, Germany, Holland and England
> and Wales. Nowadays we refer to each other's decisions with a frequency which would
> have been hardly imaginable even twenty years ago. And we do try to be consistent where
> possible.
>
> The Judges of the patent courts of the various countries of Europe have thereby been
> able to create some degree of uniformity even though the European Commission and the
> politicians continue to struggle on the long, long road which one day will give Europe a
> common patent court.

One result of this commitment to comparative reasoning has been harmonized interpretations of the right of making a patented product under Article 29(a) CPC, considered in Section 8.4.2.3. A second has been harmonized interpretations of the right
of offering, etc., the product obtained directly from a patented process under Article
29(c) CPC/Article 64(2) EPC as supporting a 'loss of identity' test of infringement
(based on German jurisprudence since the 19th century) focused on whether the product obtained by means of the patented process retained its identity after any further
processing (see, e.g., *Pioneer Electronics Capital Inc. v Warner Music Manufacturing
Europe GmbH* [1997] RPC 757 (UK CA); *Pfizer/Pharmon (Doxycycline)* [1984] BIE 39
(Hoge Raad)). Third, there are the harmonized interpretations of the right of indirect
use under Article 30(1) CPC as infringed where, at the time of the supply or offer of supply in question, the supplier knew, or it was obvious in the circumstances, that ultimate
users of the means being supplied or offered would intend to put the invention into
effect; and of this test as generally established by showing that the supplier proposed
or recommended or even indicated the possibility in his promotional material of using
the means to put the invention into effect.[8] And finally, and related to this, there is

---

[8] See, e.g., *Grimme; Deckenheizung* [2006] *GRUR* 839 (BGH); *Haubenstretchautomat* [2007] *GRUR* 679
(BGH); *Grimme v Steenvoorden Constructie BV* Case 357005 / KG ZA 10-70 (20 April 2010) (District Court
of The Hague).

the glimmer of harmonization regarding the construction and protection of purpose-limited process patents following the decision of the Court of Appeal of England and Wales in *Warner-Lambert Company, LLC v Actavis Group Ptc EHF & Ors* [2015] EWCA Civ 556 (*Warner-Lambert*).

Warner-Lambert involved a patent held by Warner-Lambert, a member of the Pfizer group, for the use of pregabalin (or a pharmaceutically acceptable salt thereof) for the preparation of a pharmaceutical composition for treating pain, and especially neuropathic pain, marketed under the name Lyrica. The dispute arose following the application by Actavis for market authorization in respect of a generic version of pre-gabalin to be marketed as Lecaent. The Lecaent product label referred to its use for the treatment of epilepsy and generalized anxiety disorder, in respect of which all IP protection had expired, and made no reference to neuropathic pain. According to Warner-Lambert, however, the prescription and dispensing of Lecaent by doctors and pharmacists to treat neuropathic pain, and the recommendation by health-care organizations such as the English and Welsh National Health Services (NHS) that it be prescribed and dispensed to that end, involved the actual or threatened infringe-ment of its purpose-limited process patent under the UK legislative provisions mir-roring Articles 29(c) and 30(1) CPC. In the case of Article 29(c), the reason given was that the acts in question were directed to keeping, disposing of, or offering to dispose of a product (pregabalin) obtained directly by means of the patented pro-cess for the treatment of pain. In the case of Article 30(1), the reason given was that they involved the supply of means (pregabalin) relating to an essential element of the patented invention.

The High Court of England and Wales ([2015] EWHC 72 and 223) rejected Warner-Lambert's claims of direct and indirect infringement. The main reason was its view that the hypothetical skilled addressee would understand a claim to a purpose-limited process in the medical field as claiming the use of the compound in the manufac-ture of the medicament 'suitable and subjectively intended for' the patented therapeutic application ([2015] EWHC 72 [109]–[111]). It followed that in the absence of evidence establishing Actavis's subjective intention that Lecaent be prescribed and dispensed to treat neuropathic pain, there could be no direct infringement of Warner-Lambert's patent. The fact that the manufacturer knew that doctors were likely to prescribe or pharmacists were likely to dispense or patients were likely to use the product for the patented indication was not enough, it held, to show that the manufacturer intended its use for that purpose. Related to this, the High Court held that in the absence of any downstream party that used Lecaent to manufacture a medicament, the patent could not be indirectly infringed. Nonetheless, the court also recognized the potential harm that Warner-Lambert would be caused if Lecaent were dispensed for the non-indicated pur-pose of treating neuropathic pain, and agreed for that reason to order the NHS to issue guidelines to doctors stating that pregabalin should only be prescribed for the treatment of neuropathic pain under the brand name Lyrica, unless there were clinical contra-indications or other special clinical needs in which case neither Lyrica nor pregabalin should be prescribed.

On appeal this decision and analysis were not supported. For a start, the Court of Appeal believed that the skilled addressee would be more likely to understand the claimed invention as 'making pregabalin for patients to whom it will be intentionally adminis-tered for treating pain', without implying any element of subjective intent regarding such administration ([118] and [127]). Turning to the UK provisions based on Article 29 CPC, the Court of Appeal first held that the patent would be directly infringed under Article 29(b) by Actavis offering the patented process for use if and only if the manufacturer could be shown to be using the manufacturing process of the claim knowing or foreseeing that users of the resulting product would intentionally administer it for pain. In so doing, it supported a test of infringement closer to the German test of whether there existed some outward manifestation in the product's manufacture itself that could be specifically attributed to the new therapeutic indication ([81], citing the decisions of the Landgericht Düsseldorf (Regional Court of Düsseldorf) in *Chronic Hepatitis C Treatment* Case 4A O 145/12 (19 December 2006) and the Oberlandesgericht Düsseldorf (Higher Regional Court of Düsseldorf) in *Cistus* Case I-2 U 54/11 (31 January 2013)). If that were established, the court noted, dealings downstream in the product of the manufacturing process would also infringe the patent under Article 29(c). And finally, since the German and Dutch courts had both accepted the ability of purpose-limited process patents to be infringed indirectly under Article 30(1) CPC, the Court of Appeal was not prepared to preclude this as a matter of UK law in the case, for example, of a person other than the manufacturer who supplied the relevant medicament knowing or in circumstances in which it was obvious that the product was suitable and intended for use in the patented treatment.

Warner-Lambert illustrates the continued importance of the law governing purpose-limited process patents in the medical field even since the replacement of Swiss-form claims with purpose-limited product claims under the EPC 2000 due to the number of patents with Swiss-form claims that still exist. In addition, and while focused on the validity, construction, and infringement of Swiss-form claims particularly, it has relevance for other purpose-limited process and product claims as well. Third, and from a policy perspective, the case demonstrates the tensions that exist: (a) between the rights of second medical indication (and other purpose-limited product and process) patent holders and the freedom of third parties to market generic versions of previously patented drugs and other products; and (b) between the aims of patent law in promoting research and development in the medical field specifically by granting second medical indication patents, and the aims of doctors and public health-care services in prescribing and promoting access to affordable medicines. And finally, and as noted earlier, the case shows again the comparative legal methodology that is deployed by domestic courts at all levels when resolving matters of domestic patent law, and their consciousness to that end of European instruments, including the never ratified CPC, on which such domestic law is based (see, e.g., [2015] EWHC 233 [50]).

8.4.1.2.3 *Patent Rights Under the UPP*

When the UPP takes effect, even greater consistency in the approach adopted by European domestic courts to the definition of patent rights can be expected. The reason is the creation of the UPC, and the vesting in it of exclusive jurisdiction with respect to the protection conferred by all European (EPC and unitary) patents other than those EPC patents that have been opted out of the UPC system. It will then be for the UPC to develop its own 'European' jurisprudence with respect to patent protection. However, that jurisprudence will need to be based on the sources of law described in Article 24 UPC Agreement, namely, EU law, the UPC Agreement, the EPC, other international agreements applicable to patents and binding on all the Contracting Member States, and national law, with EU law having primacy under Article 20. One effect of this will be to ensure the continued relevance of cases such as *Warner-Lambert*, not only as a decision of a court of an EU Member State, but also as a product of the kind of comparative reasoning which the UPC Agreement itself envisages. Thus, while the task of the UPC to develop a European jurisprudence of patent protection might seem challenging, it is in reality a task on which domestic European courts have been working for several years.

8.4.2 **Exhaustion of Patent Rights**

8.4.2.1 **The Tension Between Intellectual Property and Personal Property Rights**

The rights of direct use conferred by a patent for a product under Article 29 CPC include the rights to prevent third parties from offering, putting on the market, or using the product, and from importing or stocking the product for those purposes. Subject to any legal provision to the contrary, this would prevent a third party purchaser of an object covered by a patent from using or reselling the item purchased, and from importing or stocking it for such purposes, thereby interfering with his enjoyment of his personal property interests.

Historically, European states have fashioned two main responses to this conflict between the intellectual property rights of a patentee and the personal property rights of a consumer of patented products. The first has been to imply a licence in respect of the patent into the contract of purchase to enable the purchaser to deal with his personal property as he sees fit. And the second has been to redefine the rights conferred by product patents themselves. Thus redefined, a patent for a product includes only the right to bring items manufactured in accordance with the patent to market, and not the right to control the products' exploitation beyond that point. Thus, any person who purchases a patented product following its entry to market with the patent owner's consent is free to do as he wishes with the purchased product, uninhibited by the patent protecting it, on the ground that his purchase of the product represents sufficient remuneration for the rights of the patentee (see Section 2.4.2.1.3).

8.4.2.2 **The Tension Between Intellectual Property Rights and Free Movement**

In the context of the EU, the tension between the private rights and interests of patentees and consumers of patented items has a further, public dimension. That dimension arises from the EU's single market policies, and the emphasis they place on free trade and competition within EU territory. A key example of that emphasis is the prohibition in Article 34 TFEU against '[q]uantitative restrictions on imports and all measures having equivalent effect…between Member States', considered in Section 2.4.2.1. On its face, this Article (as well as Article 35 TFEU) would seem to preclude Member States from granting patent rights to prevent the movement of goods between Member States. However, by separate provision of Article 36 TFEU, the prohibition of Article 34 is stated not to preclude prohibitions 'on imports…justified on grounds of…the protection of industrial and commercial property' *provided* that such prohibitions do not 'constitute a means of arbitrary discrimination or a disguised restriction on trade between Member States'. Hence the question that has arisen for the CJEU of when if ever the restrictions on imports between Member States imposed by a patent constitute such a means so as to fall outside the saving provision of Article 36 TFEU and within the prohibition of Article 34.

As we saw in Section 2.4.2.1.3, the Court answered this question in a series of decisions in the 1970s. According to its answer (see, e.g., Case C–16/74 *Centrafarm v Winthrop* [1974] ECR 1183), the specific subject matter of a product patent comprises only the right to bring items manufactured in accordance with the patent to market within EU territory, and not the right to control the products' movement thereafter between Member States. Within EU law, this is also known as the doctrine of exhaustion. However, and as we saw in Section 2.4.2.1.3, in the EU context the underlying rationale of the doctrine is based squarely on the Treaties' free movement and competition policies.

Following its development by the Court of Justice, the European doctrine of exhaustion was given statutory form in Article 32 CPC, reproduced in Article 29 UPC Agreement. As expressed in the UPC Agreement, it prohibits a patentee from invoking her right to prevent a third party from selling a patented product within the EU after the product has been placed with her consent on the market within EU territory 'unless there are legitimate grounds for the patent proprietor to oppose further commercialisation of the product'.

8.4.2.3 Limits to the Doctrine of Exhaustion: The Right of (Re-)Making

As we have seen, national and European doctrines of exhaustion operate to protect the freedom of a purchaser to deal with her personal property as she sees fit. That freedom is not unlimited, however. In particular, it only extends to dealings with a product: (a) for the term of the product's natural life; and (b) for the purposes for which it was intended. This is why, for example, the doctrine of exhaustion does not displace a patentee's right to prevent third parties from remaking a product they have purchased.

The freedom of a purchaser of a patented product to remake the product has occupied the supreme courts of different European states in recent years. Central to the resulting jurisprudence has been a distinction between repairing a product—which is not among the rights reserved to a patentee, and which can therefore never infringe a patent—and making a product within the meaning of Article 29 CPC. According to the German Federal Supreme Court in *Palettenbehälter II* [2012] *GRUR* 1118, [2013] *IIC* 351 drawing on English patent authority, the central question in a case of alleged remaking by replacing part of a product is whether one would ordinarily expect the relevant part of the product to be replaced during its lifetime, and the extent to which the part reflects the technical result of the patented invention. That case was subsequently relied on by the UK Supreme Court in 2013 to support its decision that replacing part of a product amounts to 'making' the product within the meaning of domestic patent law, interpreted in the light of the 'European patent scheme' (including the EPC and CPC), if and only if the part in question is sufficiently important to the product to be more than a subsidiary part of it (*Schütz (UK) Ltd v Werit (UK) Ltd* [2013] UKSC 16, [2013] RPC 16). As a result of these decisions, the defendant was free in each case to recondition a patented container comprising a cage and plastic bottle by replacing the container's bottle, among other reasons because the inventive concept or essential technical features of the invention were wholly embodied in the cage, and enabling its replacement protected the patentee's monopoly without stifling reasonable competition.

The definition of remaking supported by the German and UK courts reflects and supports the principle of *Monsanto* discussed in Section 8.3.4 that patent protection is limited with reference to the patentability criteria. Thus, according to the German and English courts, to make a product in breach of a patent it is neither sufficient nor necessary to produce a quantitatively substantial part of the product (e.g. the bottle in the case of the *Schütz/Palettenbehälter II* container). Rather, a defendant must produce aspects of the product that embody sufficiently its technical and inventive properties on the ground that these are the properties which merited the product its patent protection. In this reasoning one sees patent law again following the approach of European copyright law (see Section 12.2.6) in ways that challenge the EPO's insistence on a strict separation between the requirement for an invention and the secondary patentability requirements (see Section 6.4.1.4).

8.5 Patent Limitations

8.5.1 Articles 27 and 28 UPC Agreement

In Europe, statutory definitions of patent rights are supplemented by statutory definitions of limitations to those rights. Under the CPC, the relevant provision is Article 31, which again forms the basis of corresponding national laws and of the more extensively cast Article 27 UPC Agreement. Unlike the doctrine of exhaustion discussed earlier, each of the 12 acts listed in Article 27 lies entirely (rather than only partially) outside the scope of the patent monopoly, and is therefore incapable of giving rise to liability for patent infringement. According to that Article (footnotes omitted),

[t]he rights conferred by a patent shall not extend to any of the following:

(a) acts done privately and for non-commercial purposes;

(b) acts done for experimental purposes relating to the subject matter of the patented invention;

(c) the use of biological material for the purpose of breeding, or discovering and developing other plant varieties;

(d) the acts allowed pursuant to Article 13(6) of Directive 2001/82/EC or Article 10(6) of Directive 2001/83/EC in respect of any patent covering the product within the meaning of either of those Directives;

(e) the extemporaneous preparation by a pharmacy, for individual cases, of a medicine in accordance with a medical prescription or acts concerning the medicine so prepared;

(f) the use of the patented invention on board vessels of countries of the International Union for the Protection of Industrial Property (Paris Union) or members of the World Trade Organisation, other than those Contracting Member States in which that patent has effect, in the body of such vessel, in the machinery, tackle, gear and other accessories, when such vessels temporarily or accidentally enter the waters of a Contracting Member State in which that patent has effect, provided that the invention is used there exclusively for the needs of the vessel;

(g) the use of the patented invention in the construction or operation of aircraft or land vehicles or other means of transport of countries of the International Union for the Protection of Industrial Property (Paris Union) or members of the World Trade Organisation, other than those Contracting Member States in which that patent has effect, or of accessories to such aircraft or land vehicles, when these temporarily or accidentally enter the territory of a Contracting Member State in which that patent has effect;

(h) the acts specified in Article 27 of the Convention on International Civil Aviation of 7 December 1944, where these acts concern the aircraft of a country party to that Convention other than a Contracting Member State in which that patent has effect;

(i) the use by a farmer of the product of his harvest for propagation or multiplication by him on his own holding, provided that the plant propagating material was sold or otherwise commercialised to the farmer by or with the consent of the patent proprietor for agricultural use. The extent and the conditions for this use correspond to those under Article 14 of Regulation (EC) No. 2100/94;

(j) the use by a farmer of protected livestock for an agricultural purpose, provided that the breeding stock or other animal reproductive material were sold or otherwise commercialised to the farmer by or with the consent of the patent proprietor. Such use includes making the animal or other animal reproductive material available for the purposes of pursuing the farmer's agricultural activity, but not the sale thereof within the framework of, or for the purpose of, a commercial reproductive activity;

(k) the acts and the use of the obtained information as allowed under Articles 5 and 6 of Directive 2009/24/EC, in particular, by its provisions on decompilation and interoperability; and

(l) the acts allowed pursuant to Article 10 of Directive 98/44/EC.

In addition, Article 28 UPC Agreement provides for so-called prior user rights in the following manner:

> Any person, who, if a national patent had been granted in respect of an invention, would have had, in a Contracting Member State, a right based on prior use of that invention or a right of personal possession of that invention, shall enjoy, in that Contracting Member State, the same rights in respect of a patent for the same invention.

In this section we focus on three of the main limitations provided for under the UPC Agreement: the experimental acts exception of Article 27(b), the so-called *Bolar* exception of Article 27(d), and the prior user right of Article 28.

8.5.2 Experimental Acts: Article 27(b) UPC Agreement

8.5.2.1 Patents, Knowledge, and Research

As we have seen in previous chapters, the purpose of the European patent system is to promote technological innovation by rewarding and incentivizing specific contributions to the technical arts. In consideration for a patent grant, a detailed description of the contribution in question must be disclosed to the public immediately upon the application for the patent being filed, and again in final form when the grant is made. Thus, even before the public is able freely to use the invention at the end of the patent term, its details are made known and technological knowledge thereby increased.

It is in the requirement for early publication of the invention that one sees the concern of patent law with generating knowledge and (by extension) with research. That concern is also reflected in the traditional distinction drawn by patent systems between the research and development phases of innovation respectively, and in the treatment of the former as beyond the reach of patent law. For example, contributions to scientific knowledge have been regarded as incapable of supporting a patent unless and until they are turned to industrial account, in which case it is the industrial application of the knowledge rather than the knowledge per se that comprises the invention for which the patent is granted. (In the EU this restriction on protection is expressed through the patentability requirement for susceptibility of industrial application, and for genetic products at least, through Article 9 Biotech Directive. Hence the view reflected in the *Monsanto* case that the function of such a product is part of what constitutes it as an invention within the meaning of EU patent law.) Conversely, acts undertaken with a view to increasing scientific knowledge have been regarded as incapable of infringing a patent, even where they involve the use of a patented invention. Indeed, and as suggested previously, it is precisely in order to encourage such acts that patent applicants are required to publish the details of their inventions soon after filing their applications for a patent grant.

In recent decades, the commitment to keeping research beyond the reach of patent protection has been challenged by the emergence of new industries said to depend on the availability of patents at an early stage of the innovation process. In Sections 7.3 and 7.4 we saw evidence of this in our discussion of inventive step and susceptibility of industrial application. However, and as suggested in that discussion, while new technologies have led to pressure on patent systems to grant patents for the research results available at an early stage of the innovation process, it has not dulled the concern of law- and decision-makers to protect research from being impeded by the existence of patent monopolies. In Europe that concern is reflected in the development of the experimental acts exception of Article 31(b) CPC, reproduced in Article 27(b) UPC Agreement.

8.5.2.2 **Article 31(b) CPC**

The experimental acts exception of Article 31(b) CPC exists separate from the private acts exception of Article 31(a). It applies to experimental acts relating to an invention in general, and has thus been interpreted to cover experiments for any purpose, including industrial or commercial purposes, provided they are done with a view to learning (in the sense of discovering new information) about the properties, uses, or side effects of the patented invention itself. The fact that such acts might be aimed at devising a new invention and thus force the patentee into competition with the user during the patent term by requiring her to conduct her own experiments to forestall a competitive patent application at its end is no objection. According to the German Federal Supreme Court in one of two important German cases involving the exception from the 1990s—*Klinische Versuche I* and *II* [1996] *GRUR* 109 and [2001] *GRUR* 43—this interpretation of the exception is consistent with the intention behind Article 31(b), which was to prevent patent monopolies from restraining acts that promote research and technological progress regardless of the persons by whom they are undertaken.

The German interpretation of Article 31(b) CPC is consistent with that adopted in several other European states, including Belgium, Denmark, Finland, Sweden, and Switzerland, as well as the UK. Its result is an exception the terms of which were supported by Committee 202 of the International Association for the Protection of Intellectual Property (AIPPI) in 2008 following an extensive review of the scope of the experimental acts exceptions then in force in different European and non-European countries.

Nonetheless, the experimental acts exception contained in Article 31(b) CPC has been criticized and rejected in some parts of Europe. The main criticisms of it have been: (a) its alleged uncertainty, and discrimination against SMEs anxious to avoid even a threat of patent infringement proceedings; and (b) its restriction to acts focused on discovering information about the protected invention, and consequential exclusion of uses of an invention as a tool for, for example, satisfying regulatory authorities that an invention has certain previously claimed qualities, or encouraging consumers to adopt the invention. Such criticisms led Belgium in 2005 to introduce a new experimental acts exception that expressly permits acts *with* as well as *on* an invention provided they are undertaken for 'scientific purposes', where such purposes are to be defined broadly (Article 28 §1(b) Belgian Patent Act 1984).

8.5.3 **The *Bolar* Exception: Article 27(d) UPC Agreement**

8.5.3.1 **The *Bolar* Problem**

Another challenge for European law- and decision-makers arises from the interface between patent law on one hand and the separate regimes regulating the use of different kinds of technology on the other. One such regime of especial importance governed by EU legislation[9] is that concerned with obtaining regulatory approval to market a new medicinal product. The process for obtaining such approval can be time-consuming, and generally requires testing of the product to support the applicant's claims regarding its properties and effects. Where the product is a generic version of a previously approved medicine, an abridged process is required to enable the applicant to rely on information submitted in connection with the application for approval of the original (reference) product. Nonetheless, tests on the generic version of the product will often still be required,

---

[9] Directive 2001/83/EC of the European Parliament and of the Council of 6 November 2001 on the Community code relating to medicinal products for human use [2001] OJ L 311/67.

and will infringe any patent that exists for the reference product. In addition, requiring the applicant to wait until the patent term has expired before commencing the regulatory approval process for its generic version of the relevant medicine will effectively extend the term of the patentee's monopoly by delaying the ability of third parties to provide—and thus the public's ability to receive—other goods based on the patented technology.

8.5.3.2 The EU Solution to the *Bolar* Problem

The EU has responded to this problem by requiring Member States to permit generic drug manufacturers to use a patented invention before the expiry of its patent term for the purpose of undertaking the tests and fulfilling the other requirements imposed by the regulatory approval authority. This is achieved via the *Bolar* exception of Article 10(6) Directive 2001/83/EC (named after the US decision in *Roche Products Inc. v Bolar Pharmaceutical Co., Inc.*, 733 F2d 858 (Fed. Cir. 1984)), introduced by Directive 2004/27/EC and providing as follows:

> Conducting the necessary studies and trials with a view to the application of paragraphs 1, 2, 3 and 4 [regarding the obtaining of abridged regulatory approval for generic and other related versions of medicinal products] and the consequential practical requirements shall not be regarded as contrary to patent rights or to supplementary protection certificates for medicinal products.

Paragraphs 1 to 4 of Article 10 concern the regulatory approval of three classes of medicinal product: (a) generics of a previously authorized reference medicinal product; (b) products that cannot be classified as generic medicinal products (defined in Article 2(b)); and (c) biological medicinal products that are similar to a reference product but that do not meet the definition of a generic medicinal product due to differences in their raw materials or manufacturing processes. The effect of the exception is to permit an applicant for regulatory approval in respect of such products to conduct the studies and trials required in respect of each of them without infringing patent or supplementary protection certificate rights. Expressly excluded from its scope are acts done in connection with an application for regulatory approval of a 'new indication for a well-established substance', for which provision is made in paragraph 5 of Article 10.

8.5.3.3 Domestic Implementation of the *Bolar* Exception

The obligation imposed by Article 10 is a minimum-standard obligation, and therefore does not prevent an EU Member State from introducing a more expansively framed exception to fulfil its purpose of facilitating the market entry of generic and other versions of medicines as soon as the patent or supplementary protection certificate in respect of the reference medicine expires. As a result, states have implemented their obligation under the Article differently. Some states, such as Belgium, Cyprus, Greece, Ireland, Luxembourg, the Netherlands, Sweden, and the UK, have defined their domestic exceptions in the same terms as Article 10(6). By contrast, others such as Austria, Germany, and Italy, have introduced more expansive *Bolar* exceptions than required by Article 10(6), including to cover acts necessary to obtain regulatory approval for any generic or non-generic product by any abridged or non-abridged process in any EU or non-EU country.

8.5.3.4 The *Bolar* Exception under the UPP

The *Bolar* exception of Article 10(6) has no counterpart in the CPC. However, it is included among the list of exceptions to patent infringement contained in Article 27(d) UPC Agreement, thereby resolving the uncertainty regarding the capacity of the experimental acts exception of Article 27(b) to cover the acts described in Article 10(6) of the

Directive. When the UPP takes effect we can therefore expect European patents with unitary effect, and such European (EPC) patents which are not opted out of the UPC system, to be subject to the limited form of *Bolar* exception described earlier. By contrast, the rights conferred by national patents and opted out European (EPC) patents granted in respect of states recognizing a more expansive version of the exception will continue to be defined more narrowly.

8.5.3.5 The Polpharma Referral to the CJEU

A final recent development involving the *Bolar* exception concerns the preliminary referral of certain questions regarding its scope to the CJEU from the Higher Regional Court of Düsseldorf. That referral arose from proceedings involving the sale by Polpharma SA Pharmaceutical Works of active pharmaceutical ingredients (APIs) to customers requiring them for *Bolar* exception purposes, and a suit by the owner of a patent covering one of the relevant APIs for infringement of its patent. The central question for the referring court was whether Polpharma could rely on the *Bolar* purposes of its customers to avoid liability under German patent law.[10] In earlier proceedings before the Sąd Apelacyjny (Gdańsk Court of Appeal) and Sąd Najwyższy (Polish Supreme Court) (see *Astellas Pharma Inc. v Polpharma* Cases SA I ACa 320/12 and Sygn Akt IV CSK 92/13), the answer had been a resounding 'no'. So too the Regional Court of Düsseldorf was unmoved by Polpharma's argument. By contrast, the Higher Regional Court of Düsseldorf interpreted the German exception more broadly, deciding that it would cover Polpharma's acts if those acts were aimed at a purpose falling within its scope. It also agreed to refer certain questions regarding the scope of Article 10(6) Directive 2001/83/EC to the CJEU for determination. In 2014, however, those questions were withdrawn and the European Case C–661/13 was closed.

8.5.4 Prior User Rights: Article 28 UPC Agreement

As we saw in Section 7.2, for an invention to be patentable it must be new, in the sense of not having previously been made available to the public (see Articles 52(1) and 54 EPC). It follows from this definition of novelty that a patent may be granted for an invention that was previously in use by one or more individuals, provided that such use was not sufficient to make the invention available to the public. Examples are secret, hidden, or uninformative uses of a product, which are not regarded as sufficient under the EPC to make the product publicly available.

In the absence of an express provision to the contrary, the effect of a patent with respect to an invention previously in use would be to require the prior user to cease his activities on the ground that use of a patented invention is among the acts reserved to the patentee. This would conflict with the traditional principle of patent jurisprudence that a monopoly grant ought never to prevent a person from doing that which he had previously done lawfully. Hence Article 28 UPC Agreement, reproducing Article 38(1) CPC, which preserves any right granted to a person under the law of a participating Member State based on his prior use of a patented invention or rights of personal possession of a product protected by a patent in respect of that state.

---

[10] The same issue arises in other IP regimes, including in copyright, where the question is whether the exceptions to copyright infringement permitting the proportionate use of a work for certain statutory purposes, e.g. private study, cover the proportionate reproduction and distribution of works by a library, e.g. to third parties intending to use the works for their own private study purposes. See further Chapter 13.

8.6 Conclusions

The protection conferred by a European (EPC) patent is a post-grant matter that, in principle, is left to the national laws of European states. Nonetheless, national laws in this area are derived from European instruments, including the EPC (for patent scope) and the CPC (for patent rights and limitations). So too the provisions of the UPC Agreement regarding the protection conferred by European (EPC and unitary) patents are derived from and/or incorporate the same European instruments. In addition, while the interpretation and application of these provisions is a matter largely for national courts, the commitment of such courts to supporting European harmonization in this field, combined with the mutual respect and collaboration among European patent and other, appellate judges, means that they frequently take account of each others' decisions and reason comparatively when interpreting domestic legislation. Thus, while differences do exist in the jurisprudence of European states in this area, they are increasingly differences of terminology and methodology rather than of substance.

Patent protection is another area in which EU law has had a significant impact. For example, the CJEU has formulated the doctrine of exhaustion, limiting the rights conferred by European and national patents to accommodate the free movement of goods throughout the internal market. In addition, the Biotech Directive has limited the scope of protection conferred by patents for genetic products to ensure that they properly reflect the criteria for patentability, bringing patent law into line with the European law of copyright.

The greatest impact of EU law, however, has been in respect of patent exploitation. As we saw in Sections 2.4.2.1.3 and 4.4, here the same principles of free movement and competition that underpin the doctrine of exhaustion continue to result in restrictions on the freedom of patentees to exploit their patents as they see fit in order to ensure that such exploitation does not undermine the policy goals of the EU Treaties, including technological progress. In the other direction, Article 17(2) CFR supports the recognition and protection of patents as a fundamental (human) right of a patentee, consistent with Article 1 of Protocol 1 ECHR, and thereby insulating patentees from legislative and other acts of state that would interfere unreasonably and disproportionately with their exploitation of their patent rights (see Section 3.1). This conception of patents as objects of fundamental rights on one hand and threats to competition and fundamental market freedoms on the other has lent further support to calls to create a unitary patent and unified European patent litigation system to ensure strong protection for patentees while also supporting EU economic and social policies.

Further Reading

CORNISH, W.R. 'Experimental Use of Patented Inventions in European Community States' [1998] *IIC* 735

CREMERS, K. ET AL, *Patent Litigation in Europe* (ZEW Discussion Paper No. 13-072, September 2013), http://ftp.zew.de/pub/zew-docs/dp/dp13072.pdf

EISENBERG, R.S., 'Patents and the Progress of Science: Exclusive Rights and Experimental Use' (1989) 56 *University of Chicago Law Review* 1017

GRAHAM, S.J.H. AND VAN ZEEBROECK, N., 'Comparing Patent Litigation Across Europe: A First Look' (2014) 17 *Stanford Technology Law Review* 655

HEATH, C., 'Exhaustion of Patent Rights' in Okediji, R.L. and Bagley, M.A. (eds), *Patent Law in Global Perspective* (OUP, 2014)

MERGES, R.P. AND NELSON, R.R., 'On the Complex Economics of Patent Scope' (1990) 90 *Columbia Law Review* 839

PAGENBERG, J., 'The Scope of Art. 69 European Patent Convention: Should Sub-Combinations be Protected?—A Comparative Analysis on the Basis of French and German Law' [1993] *IIC* 314

PUMFREY, N. ET AL., 'The Doctrine of Equivalents in Various Patent Regimes: Does Anybody Have it Right?' (2009) 11 *Yale Journal of Law and Technology* 261

ROMANDINI, R. AND KLICZNIK, A., 'The Territoriality Principle and Transnational Use of Patented Inventions—The Wider Reach of a Unitary Patent and the Role of the CJEU' [2013] *IIC* 524

SHERMAN, B., 'Patent Claim Interpretation: The Impact of the Protocol on Interpretation' (1991) 54 *Modern Law Review* 499

STERCKX, S. AND COCKBAIN, J., 'Purpose-Limited Pharmaceutical Product Claims Under the Revised European Patent Convention: A Camouflaged Attack on Generic Substitution?' [2010] *IPQ* 88

VAN ZIMMEREN, E. AND VAN OVERWALLE, G., 'A Paper Tiger? Compulsory License Regimes for Public Health in Europe [2011] *IIC* 4

9

Plant Variety Rights and Supplementary Protection Certificates

9.1 Introduction

In this chapter we leave our discussion of the European patent system to consider two IP systems allied to it. The first of these is the plant variety rights system, which governs the recognition and protection of unitary (EU) rights in respect of plant materials. And the second is the supplementary protection certificate system, which governs the grant of domestic rights conferring follow-on protection for patented medicinal and plant protection products the commercialization of which has been delayed by the need to satisfy regulatory approval requirements.

9.2 Community Plant Variety Rights

9.2.1 The Recognition of Plant Variety Rights

Plant variety rights are *sui generis* rights conferred on application to breeders of certain strains of plant material. In Europe there exist national and Community plant variety right (PVR) systems, all of which confer exclusive rights to prevent the commercial exploitation of previously non-commercialized varieties for a limited period within the territory of the relevant state and EU respectively. This follows the arrangements under the 1991 Act of the UPOV Convention 1961, to which the EU has acceded and which the Community PVR (CPVR) system was introduced in 1994 to implement.

The idea of rewarding agricultural innovations with exclusionary rights can be traced to an 1833 Papal Edict extending the principles governing the reward and ownership of scientific and literary works in the Papal States to 'those works that relate to the progress of agriculture and its techniques'. In many European countries, however, the availability of IP protection for plant materials and breeding methods was first considered in the context of patent law. The early consensus was against the grant of patent protection for plant materials and breeding methods on two grounds. The first was that they lacked the technical, industrial, or mechanical properties of inventions, and were thus inherently unsuited to patent protection. And the second was that as sources of food, they were inappropriate for protection on public interest grounds. On the other hand, the importance of developing new plant materials, combined with a belief in the suitability of IP grants as mechanisms for encouraging such development, supported industry calls for a *sui generis* regime for their protection, and the commencement of work to that end by 13 European states at a conference convened by the French government in 1957. That work confirmed the resolve of the EEC Member States to exclude plant varieties from the scope of early drafts of the CPC, which resolve accounts for Article 53(b) EPC excluding plant varieties from European patentability, following Article 2(b) SPC 1963 (see Section 6.3.3.2).

It is fair to say that the relationship between the PVR and patent systems of Europe has been a difficult one. It has also become more so over time due to changes in the technological and economic contexts in which plant breeding is undertaken. Central among those changes have been the increasing industrialization of food production, the shift of plant breeding research from the public to the private sectors, and the increasing use of gene therapies in plant breeding.[1] In combination, these changes have increased the role of agribusiness in the field, and shifted the debate surrounding the protection of plant materials to reflect its interests.

9.2.2 **The Argument for Plant Variety Rights**

The importance of plant material to society derives from its provision of a primary food source for humans and agriculturally important animals.[2] Developing new strains of plant material involves the following five steps:[3]

(a) discovering or creating genetically stable variation for the desired plant traits, such as yield, resistance to pests and disease, stress tolerance, etc.;

(b) selecting from these variations individual plants possessing the best expression of the desired traits;

(c) incorporating the desired traits into a suitable agronomic background;

(d) testing the new variety over a range of habitats and for a number of seasons to establish its stability; and

(e) releasing the new variety.

The main difference between traditional breeding and new biotechnological breeding techniques involves the first two steps. Traditional breeding techniques focus on individual plants and populations of plants, and rely primarily on sexual reproduction to manipulate useful variability in their traits. By contrast, biotechnology focuses on the cellular and subcellular levels of plants, capitalizing on genetic engineering and other techniques to transfer genetic material from one plant to another or regenerate entire plants from single cells or plant parts, and thereby manipulate or regenerate useful variability, obviating the need for the actual breeding of plants.[4] The result in both cases is the

---

[1] The importance of new biotechnologies to plant production accounts for the timing of the EU's introduction of its CPVR system alongside its introduction of the Biotech Directive governing the patenting of biotechnological inventions. See M. Llewelyn, 'Future Prospects for Plant Breeders' Rights Within the European Community' [1989] *EIPR* 303, 304.

[2] R.G. Adler, 'Can Patents Coexist with Breeders' Rights? Developments in U.S. and International Biotechnology Law' [1986] *IIC* 195.

[3] M. Hansen et al., 'Plant Breeding and Biotechnology' (1986) 36 *BioScience* 29, 30.   [4] ibid.

same: the development of plants capable of supporting larger and more secure harvests of higher quality crops for the same investment of time, space, equipment, and other products such as fertilizers and pesticides.

The arguments for protecting plant varieties are clear: the development of new strains of plant material is of enormous benefit to farmers, consumers, and society,[5] and yet it requires substantial investment of money, time, and knowledge. In addition, the opportunities to recoup that investment are limited due to the capacity of seeds to be freely propagated at zero cost by anyone having access to them. For these reasons, plant varieties represent a paradigm example of valuable subject matter the benefits of which cannot easily be secured by extra-legal mechanisms, creating an argument for intervention by the state (see Section 1.2.2.2). In addition, if access to valuable plant materials is to be restricted by any (legal or extra-legal) means, there are third party and societal interests that need to be protected. These include the interests of farmers in remaining free to reuse seeds on their own holdings,[6] and the interests of society in maintaining genetic diversity and ensuring equality and distributive justice between countries at different stages of scientific, industrial, and social development.[7] The importance of protecting these interests in the face of proliferating IP rights, biopiracy, and commercial realities, has been frequently and widely recognized, including internationally through the Convention on Biological Diversity and Nagoya Protocol discussed in Section 3.3.3. The importance of biological diversity specifically, and of EU legal rules in protecting it, was recently underlined in Case C–59/11 *Association Kokopelli v Graines Baumaux SAS* EU:C:2012:447. There Advocate General Kokott began her opinion on the validity of EU measures governing the marketing of seed from plant varieties (in the light of fundamental rights and principles, and the International Treaty on Plant Genetic Resources for Food and Agriculture to which the EU is a party: see Council Decision 2004/869/EC of 24 February 2004 [2004] OJ L 378/1) with the following statement ([1]–[4]):

> It is well known that the number of plant varieties grown in European agriculture is on the decrease. Many traditional varieties are disappearing or are simply preserved in seed banks for future generations. Instead, the fields are dominated by a handful of varieties individual specimens of which, moreover, seem very similar to each other.
>
> For that reason, biodiversity in agriculture is in significant decline. It is possible that, as a result, certain varieties which could, for example, adapt more successfully to climate change or to new diseases than the varieties that currently predominate will, in the future, no longer exist. Today, the end-consumer's choice of agricultural products is already restricted.
>
> One would imagine that this development is primarily driven by the economic interests of farmers who, where possible, grow the most productive varieties.
>
> However, the present case demonstrates that the restriction of biodiversity in European agriculture results, at least in part, from rules of European Union ('EU') law…

Having identified a need for legal intervention, the question that arises is what form of intervention is appropriate to enable those who invest in the development of plant

---

[5] Plant breeding may be said to have especial importance for developing and least developed countries: see ibid 167.

[6] Of importance in this regard is the EU's Common Agricultural Policy, which seeks among other things to safeguard agricultural production. For details see http://ec.europa.eu/agriculture/cap-post-2013/.

[7] Of importance in this regard is the EU's commitment to promoting biodiversity through its Biodiversity Strategy and other initiatives. For details see http://ec.europa.eu/environment/nature/biodiversity/policy/index_en.htm.

materials to recover their costs and earn sufficient profit to be motivated to continue their breeding work without harming third party and wider societal (including global) interests? As noted earlier, the view has tended to be that patents are inappropriate instruments, among other reasons since plant varieties are as much products of nature as creations of individuals, and since—and relatedly—they lack the stability of intellectual products due to their propensity to spontaneous genetic variation (see Section 3.2.3).[8] The difficulty is well illustrated by the decision of the Bundesgerichtshof (German Federal Supreme Court) in *Red Dove* X ZB 15/67, [1970] *IIC* 136, on which the European legal definition of 'invention' is based (see Section 6.4.2.3). As we saw in Section 3.9, *Red Dove* involved a method of breeding a dove by a mix of breeding and selection steps, and the question whether the method (or the dove) was capable of supporting a patent. In the decision of the court, the answer depended in the case of the method on whether it represented an invention in the sense of an instruction to be executed. The court decided that it did not, since an invention comprises a teaching methodically to utilize controllable natural forces to achieve a causal, perceivable result that can be repeated an arbitrary number of times obtaining the same result each time, and the breeding method in issue could not be repeated to produce a dove. Given this, the contribution to knowledge represented by the subject matter was the once achieved product—i.e. the dove—and to grant a patent for such a contribution would be to confer a type of monopoly unknown to patent law.

It might be said that the stability of breeding methods has improved since *Red Dove* due to biotechnology, with the result that the reasoning of the court will rarely be applicable. However, even if this is true, and patents are thought to be appropriate for genetically engineered plant and animal varieties at least, they will often be ineffective. The reason is that varieties tend to lack the novelty and inventive step required for patent protection, supporting again the need, or at least the argument, for the recognition and protection of *sui generis* rights in respect of varieties instead.

9.2.3 The International (UPOV) Regime 1961/1991

The first such *sui generis* regime was established by the UPOV Convention that was signed in Paris on 2 December 1961. At the time of its introduction, the UPOV Convention followed the lead of the Netherlands and Germany by recognizing the entitlement of breeders to exclusionary rights in respect of new strains of plant material. To that end it established a Union for the Protection of New Varieties of Plants (Article 1) built on the same two principles of minimum standards and national (non-discriminatory) treatment as the Unions created by the Paris and Berne Conventions in the 19th century (see Section 1.3.3.3.2). Under its terms, UPOV States were required to recognize and protect certain rights: (a) of plant variety breeders, defined as persons who bred or discovered and developed a plant variety meeting the Convention's conditions for protection; or if the law of the state so provided, (b) her employer or the commissioner of her work; or (c) their successors in title, as appropriate (Article 1).

A central feature of the original UPOV Convention was its prohibition against dual variety and patent protection for specific plant varieties. According to Article 2(1), Union states could confer either *sui generis* plant variety protection or patent protection

---

[8] See in this regard A010/2013 *Aurora Srl v Community Plant Variety Office* (26 November 2014) (*Aurora*) [4].

in respect of 'one and the same botanical genus or species', but not both. It was not long before this ban on dual protection threatened the existence of the variety rights regime, however, as the development of genetic engineering led patent offices and courts increasingly to accept the suitability of higher and lower life forms for patent protection. This was a key motivation for amending the Convention in 1991. Among other things, the 1991 UPOV Convention Act removed the ban on double (variety and patent) protection for varieties, and strengthened the protection conferred on plant breeders under the *sui generis* regime to make it more attractive for breeders. Thus amended, the Convention requires its members to recognize certain rights in respect of all plant genera and species (Article 3) for a minimum period of 25 years (for trees and vines) and 20 years (for other species) (Article 19), subject to the variety being novel, distinct, uniform, and stable within the meaning of Articles 5 to 9. The rights in question are defined in Article 14, and include as a minimum the rights to prevent others from producing or reproducing, conditioning for the purpose of propagation, offering for sale, selling or otherwise marketing, exporting, importing, and stocking for any of these purposes the following plant materials:

(a) the seeds, grafts, bulbs, or other material from which the protected variety may be propagated (propagating material) (Article 14(1)); and

(b) the material harvested from the unauthorized use of propagating material, unless the breeder has had a reasonable opportunity to exercise his right in relation to the propagating material in question (Article 14(2)).

In addition, UPOV States have the option of extending breeders' rights beyond those outlined in Article 14(1) and (2) (Article 14(4)), including (by express provision of Article 14(3)) to ensure to breeders the right to prevent third parties from undertaking the same acts of production, etc., in respect of products made directly from harvested material within the meaning of Article 14(2) through the unauthorized use of that material, unless the breeder has had a reasonable opportunity to exercise his right in relation to the relevant products. And finally, the Convention provides for the extension of these protections beyond the variety itself to all additional varieties that are essentially derived from it, not clearly distinguishable from it, and the production of which requires the repeated use of it (Article 14(5)).

Through these provisions, the 1991 UPOV Convention Act requires the recognition of expansive rights in respect of new, distinct, uniform, and stable plant varieties, and permits the extension of those rights further still. In so doing it offers a form of *sui generis* protection for plant varieties sufficient to satisfy the requirements of Article 27(3)(b) TRIPS Agreement, which permits Member States to exclude plant varieties from patentability while requiring that they 'provide for the protection of plant varieties either by patents or by an effective *sui generis* system or by any combination thereof'. In the other direction, it requires UPOV States to exclude from the protection conferred by those rights: acts done privately and for non-commercial purposes; acts done for experimental purposes; and acts done for the purpose of breeding other varieties, including (subject to Article 14(5)) the acts referred to in Article 14(1) to (4) in respect of them (Article 15(1)). By Articles 15(2) and 17, the Convention also permits UPOV States to restrict further breeders' rights: 'within reasonable limits and subject to the safeguarding of the legitimate interests of the breeder' in order to allow farmers to use the products of their harvests for propagating purposes; and subject to the payment to breeders of equitable remuneration, to protect the public interest. Finally, Article 16 requires domestic provision for the exhaustion of breeders' rights upon the first sale or marketing within the relevant UPOV State of plant variety material or a derivate variety or material by or with the breeder's consent.

9.2.4 Community and Domestic Plant Variety Rights Systems

By the time of the EU's accession to the UPOV Convention in 2005, its own CPVR system had been operating for ten years. That system was established by the 1994 Community PVR Regulation (Basic Regulation) and took effect on 27 April 1995. The Regulation has been amended several times, most recently in 2008, and is supplemented by additional regulations governing fees, proceedings before the Community Plant Variety Office, and the agricultural exemption provided for in Article 14(3) Basic Regulation.[9] It exists without prejudice to the freedom of Member States to provide national property protection for varieties (Article 3), but expressly prohibits the protection of the same variety by national and Community PVRs (Article 92(1)). Thus, breeders must choose between Community and national PVRs for any given variety. While the domestic systems of EU Member States have not been harmonized by European legislation, the EU's accession to the UPOV Convention effectively committed its states to comply with that Convention's provisions, quite apart from the direct commitments which they and many non-EU European states assumed by virtue of their accession to the Convention in their individual capacities (see Section 2.5.2.3). Among other things, this has resulted in a high degree of harmonization between the CPVR system and the domestic PVR systems of European countries. Indeed, the main difference between the protection conferred by domestic and Community PVRs is its territorial reach and supporting administrative arrangements. Regarding the former: domestic PVRs confer protection within the territory of the conferring state, in contrast to Community PVRs, which confer unitary protection throughout the territory of the EU, and may not therefore be granted, transferred, or terminated other than for the whole EU territory (Article 2). Regarding the latter: domestic PVRs are obtained by application to the plant variety office of that state, in contrast to Community PVRs, which are obtained by application to the Community Plant Variety Office (CPVO), whether directly or indirectly through a national sub-office or agency.

Despite the high degree of harmonization that exists between the PVR systems of the EU and its Member States, there is not a single, Community-wide system of judicial enforcement for CPVRs.[10] Hence the system established by the Basic (CPVR) Regulation, whereby each CPVR is an object of the holder's property under the national law of an EU Member State (Article 22) which the domestic courts of that state are required to protect by preventing its infringement and resolving related entitlement claims. Under this system, the CPVO retains exclusive competence for determining the validity of CPVRs, and for their annulment and termination, leaving infringement and entitlement to domestic courts. It is supported in this regard by its own Boards of Appeal (similar to those of the EPO) as well as the European Court of Justice and EU General Court.

---

[9] See Commission Regulation (EC) No. 874/2009 of 17 September 2009 establishing implementing rules for the application of Council Regulation (EC) No. 2100/94 as regards proceedings before the Community Plant Variety Office [2009] OJ L 251/3 (Implementing Rules of the Basic Regulation); Commission Regulation (EC) No. 1238/95 of 31 May 1995 establishing implementing rules for the application of Council Regulation (EC) No. 2100/94 as regards the fees payable to the Community Plant Variety Office [1995] OJ L 121/37 as amended; Commission Regulation (EC) No. 1768/95 of 24 July 1995 implementing rules on the agricultural exemption provided for in Article 14(3) of Council Regulation (EC) No. 2100/94 on Community plant variety rights [1995] OJ L 173/14 as amended (Agricultural Exemption Regulation).

[10] T. Millett, 'The Community System of Plant Variety Rights' [1999] *European Law Review* 231, 254.

9.2.5 **Procedure for Grant**

9.2.5.1 Right to Apply

Any natural or legal person may apply for a CPVR (Article 12), though if she is not a national of or domiciled in an EU Member State she must designate a procedural representative who meets that criterion (Article 82). In addition, only the person who bred or discovered and developed the variety for which protection is sought, or his successor in title (the breeder), may be granted a CPVR (Article 11(1)), subject in the case of employee breeders to the provisions of national law (Article 11(4)).

9.2.5.2 Filing

The procedure for obtaining a CPVR is very similar to the procedure for obtaining a European patent under the EPC (see Section 5.2.1). It begins with the filing of an application by a breeder or other entitled person to the CPVO directly or indirectly through a sub-office or authorized national office (Articles 49 and 30(4)). Applications must be filed in an official EU language and supported by at least the following (Article 50(1)):

(a) a request for the grant of a CPVR;

(b) identification of the botanical taxon of the variety;

(c) information identifying the applicant or, where appropriate, the joint applicants for the PVR;

(d) the name of the breeder and an assurance that, to the best of the applicant's knowledge, no further persons have been involved in the breeding, or discovery and development, of the variety; or if they have, evidence regarding the applicant's entitlement to the CPVR;

(e) a provisional designation for the variety;

(f) a technical description of the variety;

(g) the geographic origin of the variety;

(h) the credentials of any procedural representative;

(i) details of any previous commercialization of the variety; and

(j) details of any other application made in respect of the variety.

In addition, applicants must propose a denomination for the variety to accompany the application (Article 50(3)), which the applicant and members of the public will then be required to use in respect of the variety, including after the CPVR's expiry (Article 17).

9.2.5.3 Designation of an Application Date

As in patent law, the date of application for a CPVR is the time at which the subject matter for which protection is sought is assessed for compliance with the statutory criteria. Assigning that date is among the first tasks of the CPVO upon receipt of an application for grant. With two exceptions, the application date is the date of receipt of the application accompanied by the information described in Article 50(1). The first exception concerns applications in respect of which the required filing fees have not been paid within the time specified (Article 52), for which any application date is void (Article 51). And the second concerns applications in respect of a variety for which the applicant or his predecessor in title has sought another property right in an EU Member State or UPOV State 12 months or less before the CPVR filing, in which case the date of that earlier filing has priority, and is thus deemed to be the date of application when assessing the distinctness and novelty of the variety, as well as the entitlement of the applicant to a CPVR in respect of it (Article 52(3)).

9.2.5.4 Examination

9.2.5.4.1 Formal Examination

Following the filing of an application and its assignment of an application date, the application and variety commence a three-stage examination procedure. The first stage involves examination of the application for compliance with the formal requirements of the Basic Regulation under Article 53, including those relating to the filing of the application and its supporting documentation.

9.2.5.4.2 Substantive Examination

The second stage involves examination of the variety for compliance with the substantive requirements of the Basic Regulation under Article 54. The purpose of this examination is specifically to ensure that the application relates to a variety within the meaning of Article 5 that is new within the meaning of Article 10 and in respect of which the applicant is entitled to file a CPVR application under Article 12. It is also at this stage that the CPVO examines whether the proposed variety denomination is suitable under Article 63.

9.2.5.4.3 Technical Examination

Finally, if the application passes the formal and substantive examination stages, it moves to the third and last stage involving assessment of the variety for compliance with the so-called DUS conditions of distinctness, uniformity, and stability under Articles 7 to 9 (Article 55). Technical examination is entrusted to a competent national testing centre in at least one Member State or, in the absence of such a centre, to another appropriate agency, known in either case as the Examination Office or Offices (Article 55(1) and (2)). Once entrusted with the technical examination of a variety, the Examination Office must decide when, where, and in what quantities and qualities the material for the technical examination and reference samples are to be submitted by the applicant (Article 55(4)). Following its receipt of the required material, it must grow the variety or undertake any other investigations required to assess its DUS (Article 56(1)).

Following the technical examination, the Examination Office will decide whether the results are adequate to evaluate the variety. If they are not it may, after consultation with or on request by the applicant, provide for complementary examination under Article 57(3). If they are, it will send the CPVO an examination report, including a description of the variety if it considers the DUS conditions to be satisfied. That report will then be communicated to the applicant with an invitation to comment on it (Article 57(1) and (2)).

9.2.5.5 Decision on the Application

The result of the examination process will be a decision by the CPVO to refuse or grant the application under Article 61 or 62. A refusal to grant the application must be made if and as soon as the Office establishes any of the failings outlined in Article 61, including a failure by the applicant to: remedy any deficiencies within the meaning of Article 53 within the time limit notified to him; comply with a rule or request under Article 55(4) or (5) within the time limit laid down; or propose a variety denomination which is suitable pursuant to Article 63 (Article 61(1)). The Office must also refuse to grant a CPVR if it establishes that the conditions required by Article 54 have not been fulfilled, or reaches the opinion on the basis of the examination reports submitted by the Examination Office under Article 57 that the variety does not meet the DUS conditions of Articles 7 to 9 (Article 61(2)). By contrast, if the Office is of the opinion that the findings of the examination are sufficient to decide on the application and that there are no impediments under Articles 59 to 61, it must grant the CPVR by a decision that includes an official description of the variety (Article 62).

9.2.5.6 Maintenance of Registers, Opposition Procedures, and Appeals

The Basic Regulation requires the maintenance by the Office of a public register of CPVR applications and grants (Article 87), including details of all CPVRs and their holders. It also provides a mechanism for third party objections to CPVR grants (under Article 59), and for rights of appeal from decisions of the Office to CPVO Boards of Appeal (Article 67). As we have seen, a key difference from the patent-granting procedure under the EPC is the ability of parties to appeal decisions of the CPVO Boards of Appeal to an independent tribunal in the form of the Court of Justice, via the General Court, on any of the grounds listed in Article 73. Direct actions may also be brought before the Court of Justice against decisions of the CPVO regarding compulsory licensing under Article 29 and the consequences of a transfer of CPVR ownership under Article 100(2) (Article 74).

9.2.5.7 Post-Grant Monitoring

Following the grant of a CPVR, the CPVO is required to 'verify the continuing existence unaltered of the protected varieties' (Article 64(1)), including by arranging for a national office to verify the technical properties of the variety pursuant to Articles 55 and 56.

9.2.6 Protectable Subject Matter

A CPVR may only be granted in respect of a plant variety. The EU legal definition of 'plant variety' is based on that of the 1991 UPOV Convention Act, and includes varieties of all botanical genera and species, including hybrids between genera and species, where by 'variety' is meant the following (Article 5(2)):

[A] plant grouping within a single botanical taxon of the lowest known rank, which grouping, irrespective of whether the conditions for the grant of a plant variety right are fully met, can be:

- defined by the expression of the characteristics that results from a given genotype or combination of genotypes,
- distinguished from any other plant grouping by the expression of at least one of the said characteristics, and
- considered as a unit with regard to its suitability for being propagated unchanged.

This definition is supplemented by Article 5(3) and (4), as follows:

3. A plant grouping consists of entire plants or parts of plants as far as such parts are capable of producing entire plants, both referred to hereinafter as 'variety constituents'.
4. The expression of the characteristics referred to in paragraph 2, first indent, may be either invariable or variable between variety constituents of the same kind provided that also the level of variation results from the genotype or combination of genotypes.

As we saw in Section 6.3.3.2, central to this definition is the reference to taxonomic rank, which restricts the subject matter for which CPVRs may be granted to plants positioned at the bottom of the taxonomic hierarchy, immediately beneath the rank of genus (see Figure 6.3). The requirement that a subject matter be capable of definition, distinction, and consideration as a unit in order to constitute a variety, independent of the requirement that it possess the additional properties of novelty and DUS, follows the basic distinction between the essential and accidental properties of an invention under European patent law (see Section 6.1). This was confirmed in A001/2002 to 003/2002 *Pieters Joseph En Luc BVBA v Community Plant Variety Office* (1 April 2003), where the Board of Appeal held that plant groupings may be a variety notwithstanding that they do not satisfy the conditions of Articles 7 to 9 CPVR, including the Article 9 requirement for sufficient stability. The result may be to confirm that plant varieties are intellectual products in the sense discussed in Section 3.2, while leaving the question whether they possess the defining properties of such products sufficiently to merit protection by property rights.

9.2.7 Secondary Criteria for CPVR Protection

As well as possessing the essential properties of a variety, a subject matter must be new, distinct, uniform, and stable in order to be the object of a CPVR.

9.2.7.1 Novelty

The CPVR definition of novelty is once again derived from the 1991 UPOV Convention Act. Under Article 10, a variety is deemed to be new if, at the date of application, constituents or harvested material of the variety have not been sold or otherwise disposed of to others by or with the consent of the breeder for the purpose of exploiting the variety:

(a) earlier than one year before the application date within EU territory; or

(b) earlier than four years (or for trees or vines, six years) before the application date outside EU territory.

It follows from this definition that novelty in the context of PVR law has a very different meaning from novelty in the context of European patent law. Rather than denoting that the subject matter for which protection is sought has not previously been made available to the public, it denotes that the subject matter has not been commercialized before the commencement of the relevant one-, four-, or six-year grace period of Article 10. Hence, a plant variety may be novel (and protected by a CPVR) notwithstanding that before the application date it had been: commercialized by a person other than the applicant and without the applicant's consent (regardless of when or where); commercialized by or with the consent of the breeder (provided this occurred up to four or six years before the application date for commercialization outside the EU or up to one year before the application date for commercialization within the EU);[11] grown (regardless of when, where, and by whom); and/or subject to acts undertaken for non-exploitative purposes (regardless of when, where, and by whom). Among other things, this definition of novelty reinforces the availability of PVRs to those who first apply for them, regardless of whether they are also the first to have bred or discovered and developed the variety, and regardless of the impact of granting them on prior use of the variety by third parties.

---

[11] For an example of a case involving a variety found to lack novelty on this basis see A004/2005 *Danziger 'Dan' Flower Farm v Shmuel Mor* (13 October 2006) (Board of Appeal).

9.2.7.2 **Distinctness, Uniformity, and Stability (DUS Conditions)**

When testing the variety for fulfilment of the DUS conditions, the Examination Office must follow the guidelines (referred to as protocols) which the Administrative Council has issued in respect of its DUS testing, as well as any instructions given by the CPVO under Article 56(2).[12]

9.2.7.2.1 *Distinctness*

Especially important among the DUS conditions is distinctness. Somewhat confusingly, this requirement corresponds more closely to the patent law requirement of novelty than the CPVR requirement of novelty itself. According to Article 7, following the 1991 UPOV Convention Act, a variety is distinct if

> it is clearly distinguishable by reference to the expression of the characteristics that results from a particular genotype or combination of genotypes, from any other variety whose existence is a matter of common knowledge on the date of application determined pursuant to Article 51.

The existence of another variety is deemed to be a matter of common knowledge if, on the date of application, a PVR for the variety had been entered in an official Community or other register of plant varieties, or an application for the granting or entering in such a register of a PVR for the variety had been filed and has since led to the PVR being granted or entered in the register (Article 7(2)). So too a variety which had been marketed or grown in a garden open to the public will be a matter of common knowledge (A023/2002 *Community Plant Variety Office v Genplant BV* (8 October 2003, Board of Appeal)), as will a variety for which a patent had been applied in Europe or elsewhere at the application date (A17/2002 *Sakata Seed Corporation v SVS Holland BV* (3 April 2003) (*Sakata*)).

Distinctness must be established with reference to characteristics of the variety previously approved as the basis for a distinctness analysis. These may include such aspects of a plant's outward appearance as leaf and stem length and colour, as well as its pest and disease resistance and time of emergence, depending always on the relevant DUS testing protocols. In A004/2007 *Brookfield New Zealand Ltd v Community Plant Variety Office* (20 September 2013), for example, the Board of Appeal invalidated a CPVR that had been granted by the Office in respect of the apple variety Gala Schnitzer on the basis that its distinctness had been found to reside entirely in its width of stripes, which was not an approved distinctness characteristic (see also A003/2007 *SNC Elaris v Schniga Srl and CPVO* (20 September 2013); Case T–135/08 *Schniga GmbH v Community Plant Variety Office* [2010] ECR II-5089 (General Court)).

To establish distinctness, the variety must be tested in direct comparison with the most similar other varieties. As the Board of Appeal has explained (*Aurora* [2]):

> Because of yearly and environmental influences on the expression of characteristics in botanic material, candidates cannot be compared with earlier collected and documented results. It is a basic rule that, in the conduction [*sic*] of DUS field trials, the direct comparison of candidates is a condition precedent for the grant of a CPVR.

---

[12] For a list of relevant protocols see, e.g., Commission Directive 2014/105/EU of 4 December 2014 amending Directives 2003/90/EC and 2003/91/EC setting out implementing measures for the purposes of Article 7 of Council Directive 2002/53/EC and Article 7 of Council Directive 2002/55/EC respectively, as regards the characteristics to be covered as a minimum by the examination and the minimum conditions for examining certain varieties of agricultural plant species and vegetable species.

Varieties for testing purposes are held by national offices in collections that the offices are required to maintain. The basis for each collection is described in the protocol governing the assessment of distinctness for the variety in question, and generally comprises varieties listed or protected at the EU level or in at least one EEA State, varieties protected in other UPOV States, and other varieties in common knowledge.

9.2.7.2.2 Uniformity

Under Article 8 CPVR, a variety is deemed to be uniform if,

> subject to the variation that may be expected from the particular features of its propagation, it is sufficiently uniform in the expression of those characteristics which are included in the examination for distinctness, as well as any others used for the variety description.

This requirement recognizes that while individual plants within a variety will not and need not be identical to each other, only certain differences may be tolerated for plant variety protection, depending on the way in which a variety is propagated.[13] Since the time for fulfilment of this criterion is the date of application, any improvements made subsequent to that date may not be taken into account (A003/2003 *Prophyl Ptd Ltd v Community Plant Variety Rights Office* (4 June 2004, Board of Appeal)).

9.2.7.2.3 Stability

The last of the DUS conditions is stability. For a variety to be stable within the meaning of Article 9, the expression of any of the characteristics used for its description must 'remain unchanged after repeated propagation or, in the case of a particular cycle of propagation, at the end of each such cycle', thus ensuring that the variety does not degenerate through reproduction.[14]

9.2.8 Entitlement

As we saw previously, only persons who have bred or discovered and developed a variety (or their successors in title) are entitled to be granted a CPVR for the variety (Article 11(1)), subject in the case of employee breeders to the provisions of national law (Article 11(4)). According to the Board of Appeal, the burden of proof when establishing entitlement rests with the applicant (A001/2004 *Keith Kirsten Horticulture International (Pty) Ltd v CPVO* (16 December 2004) (*Keith Kirsten*)).

The Board of Appeal has made it clear in *Sakata* that the concept of breeding within the meaning of Article 11 does not necessarily imply inventing something completely new, but rather includes the planting, selection, and growing of pre-existing material and its development into a finished variety. The holder in that case had carried out acts such as planting, growing, selecting atypical plants, testing the efficiency of the self-incompatibility system, and ensuring that the variety was homozygous, which was regarded by the Board to be sufficient to constitute breeding under the Basic Regulation.

Further consideration of the requirements of Article 11 was given in *Keith Kirsten*. There the Board of Appeal described the discovery of a variety to involve a person coming across the variety by search or chance, being conscious of the fact that it was a new variety unknown to her before, and believing the variety to be unknown to other persons as well. A realization that the variety may have commercial potential was said not to be relevant. The possibility of the same variety being discovered by two or more

---

[13] Millett (n 10) 237.   [14] ibid.

persons independently, at different moments in the same place or in different places, was also confirmed.

9.2.9 **Rights**

Once again, the definition of the rights conferred on breeders in respect of their plant varieties is modelled on the 1991 UPOV Convention Act provisions. Consistent with this, they include (under Article 13 Basic Regulation) the rights to prevent third parties from doing any of the following acts in respect of: constituents of the protected variety (i.e. propagating material); material harvested from the protected variety where obtained through the unauthorized use of its constituents and in circumstances in which the PVR holder did not have a reasonable opportunity to exercise his rights in relation to those constituents; and varieties which are essentially derived from the protected variety or indistinct from it or the production of which requires the repeated use of it:

(a) production or reproduction (multiplication);

(b) conditioning for the purpose of propagation;

(c) offering for sale;

(d) selling or other marketing;

(e) exporting from the Community;

(f) importing to the Community;

(g) stocking for any of the purposes mentioned in (a) to (f).

As we saw earlier, the nature and scope of the rights conferred by a CPVR fall within the jurisdiction of domestic courts. Thus, the Court of Justice will only consider these issues if asked to do so by a domestic court under the preliminary referral procedure of Article 267 TFEU (see Section 2.6). To date no preliminary referrals regarding the meaning of the rights described in Article 13 have been made.

The test of CPVR infringement has been considered in a number of cases decided by superior domestic courts. In *Lemon Symphony* X ZR 14/07, for example, the German Federal Supreme Court interpreted Article 13 as extending CPVR protection beyond the area of the protected variety's identity to an area of further tolerance covering its natural variations. This was consistent with the earlier decision of the Oberlandesgericht Düsseldorf (Higher Regional Court of Düsseldorf) in 12 U 155/02, that the infringement of a CPVR must be decided with reference to the combination of characteristics revealed in the UPOV variety description, and by asking whether any differences between the protected and used subject matter fell within the expectable natural variations of the protected variety. Of further interest is the decision of the German Federal Supreme Court again in *Melanie* X ZR 93/04 that whole plants cannot be seen as 'harvested material' within the meaning of Article 13 since their production does not require any act of harvesting.

The rights conferred by a CPVR last for 25 years or, in the case of vine and tree varieties, 30 years from the end of the calendar year in which the grant was made. They are subject to ordinary EU principles of exhaustion, expressed in Article 16, and of course to the provisions of the EU Treaties generally. According to the Court of Justice in Case C–140/10 *Greenstar-Kanzi Europe NV v Hustin* [2011] ECR I-10075, the doctrine of exhaustion does not prevent a CPVR holder from invoking her rights to prevent acts undertaken by a licensee in violation of any conditions of the licence which, in the judgment of the national court, relate directly to the essential features of the CPVR. In so deciding the Court of

Justice applied the principle from Case C–59/08 *Copad SA v Christian Dior Couture SA* [2009] ECR I-3421 (regarding trade marks) that if a licensee places goods on the market in violation of IP licence terms to which he has agreed, the rights owner cannot be said to have consented to that placement in exhaustion of her IP rights.

9.2.10 Exceptions

Following the UPOV Convention, infringement of the rights conferred by the CPVR is subject to several limitations and exceptions. These are contained in Articles 13(8) to 15 Basic Regulation, and are aimed at ensuring that the rights of breeders are appropriately balanced with the rights and interests of farmers and the wider society. To that end they include a general exception (under Article 13(5)) that prevents any exercise of the CPVR rights from violating

> any provisions adopted on the grounds of public morality, public policy or public secu-rity, the protection of health and life of humans, animals or plants, the protection of the environment, the protection of industrial or commercial property, or the safeguarding of competition, of trade or of agricultural production.

They also include the list of exceptions required by Article 15(1) of the 1991 UPOV Convention Act mentioned earlier, and an exception permitting farmers 'to use for propagating purposes in the field, on their own holding the product of the harvest which they have obtained by planting, on their own holding, propagating material of a variety other than a hybrid or synthetic variety, which is covered by a Community plant variety right' (Article 14(1)). This so-called farmers' privilege applies only in respect of certain plants, such as peas, beans, oats, rice, and rye (see Article 14(2)), and is subject to the two obligations outlined in Article 14(3). The first of these requires affected farmers (with an exception for 'small' farmers) to pay equitable remunera-tion to the CPVR holder of an amount 'sensibly lower than the amount charged for the licensed production of propagating material of the same variety in the same area' (indent 4). And the second requires affected farmers and suppliers of processing ser-vices to provide information on request by the CPVR holder concerning the use of their Article 14 privilege in certain circumstances (Article 14(3) indent 6; Agricultural Exemption Regulation).[15] Any farmer who uses the product of the harvest obtained by planting propagating material of a protected variety without paying equitable remu-neration to the CPVR holder in accordance with Article 14(3) is deemed to have under-taken such use in breach of the CPVR holder's Article 13(2) rights. In such a case the CPVR holder is therefore entitled to bring an action against the farmer for injunctive or other relief under Article 94 Basic Regulation (see *Schulin*; Case C–509/10 *Geistbeck v Saatgut-Treuhandverwaltungs GmbH* EU:C:2012:416). According to the Court of Justice in Case C–242/14 *Saatgut-Treuhandverwaltungs GmbH v Gerhard und Jürgen Vogel GbR* EU:C:2015:422, while the farmer need not pay the equitable remuneration to the holder in advance of planting the relevant farm-saved seed, nor does the period which she has for paying it continue indefinitely. Rather, in order to be able to benefit from the Article 14 privilege, the farmer must pay the remuneration before the end of the marketing year during which the relevant planting took place: i.e. no later than

---

[15] On the circumstances in which this obligation is triggered see Case C–305/00 *Schulin v Saatgu t-Treuhandverwaltungsgesellschaft mbH* [2003] ECR I-3525 (*Schulin*); Case C–336/02 *Saatgut -Treuhandverwaltungsgesellschaft mbH v Brangewitz GmbH* [2004] ECR I-9801; Case C–56/11 *Raiffeisen-Waren-Zentrale Rhein-Main eG v Saatgut-Treuhandverwaltungs GmbH* EU:C:2012:713.

30 June following the date of reseeding. Monitoring compliance with these obligations is the collective responsibility of CPVR holders, who are not entitled to any assistance in that regard from official bodies (Article 14(3) indent 5).

Finally, provision is made in Article 29 Basic Regulation for the grant of compulsory licences in respect of CPVRs by the CPVO on public interest grounds, after consulting the Administrative Council. The terms governing such licences are contained in the Implementing Rules of the Basic Regulation. Among other things, they define the public interest grounds on which a compulsory licence may be granted to mean: the protection of life or health of humans, animals, or plants; the need to supply the market with material offering specific features; and the need to maintain the incentive for continued breeding of improved varieties (Article 41(1)).

9.2.11 Naming Rights and Obligations

As we have seen, the denomination of the protected variety must be used correctly in association with the variety by the CPVR holder and third parties even after expiry of the CPVR. Hence the importance of the CPVO ensuring, during the substantive examination stage, that the denomination proposed by an application is appropriate. Under Article 63—which must be read in the light of the Guidelines adopted by the Administrative Council on variety denominations of 21 March 2007—this involves establishing that there is no impediment to its use under Article 63(3) or (4). In full the Article provides as follows:

3. There is an impediment for the designation of a variety denomination where:

   (a) its use in the territory of the Community is precluded by the prior right of a third party;

   (b) it may commonly cause its users difficulties as regards recognition or reproduction;

   (c) it is identical or may be confused with a variety denomination under which another variety of the same or of a closely related species is entered in an official register of plant varieties or under which material of another variety has been marketed in a Member State or in a Member of the International Unit for the Protection of New Varieties of Plants, unless the other variety no longer remains in existence and its denomination has acquired no special significance;

   (d) it is identical or may be confused with other designations which are commonly used for the marketing of goods or which have to be kept free under other legislation;

   (e) it is liable to give offence in one of the Member States or is contrary to public policy;

   (f) it is liable to mislead or to cause confusion concerning the characteristics, the value or the identity of the variety, or the identity of the breeder or any other party to proceedings.

4. There is another impediment where, in the case of a variety which has already been entered:

   (a) in one of the Member States; or

   (b) in a Member of the International Union for the Protection of New Varieties of Plants; or

   (c) in another State for which it has been established in a Community act that varieties are evaluated there under rules which are equivalent to those laid down in the Directives on common catalogues;

in an official register of plant varieties or material thereof and has been marketed there for commercial purposes, and the proposed variety denomination differs from that which has been registered or used there, unless the latter one is the object of an impediment pursuant to paragraph 3.

The Board of Appeal of the CPVO had occasion to consider paragraphs (c), (d), and (f) of Article 63(3) in A004/2004 *Vegetal Progress srl v Ambrogio Giovanni* (18 July 2005) (*Vegetal Progress*). That case involved an unsuccessful challenge to the CPVO's acceptance of the variety denomination 'Ginpent' on the basis of its alleged inability to be distinguished from the plant species denomination *Gynostemma pentaphyllum*, which Ginpent abbreviates, and/or the trade mark GINPENT. With respect to Article 63(3)(c), the Board held that the variety denomination Ginpent would only be properly refused if it were identical to or could be confused with another variety denomination for the same species or a closely related species. Since neither *Gynostemma pentaphyllum* nor the GINPENT trade mark was a variety denomination, neither could be the basis for refusing the Ginpent variety denomination under Article 63(3)(c). With respect to Article 63(3)(d), the Board held that the Ginpent variety denomination would only be properly refused if:

(a) It were identical to or might have been confused with the *Gynostemma pentaphyllum* plant species denomination or the GINPENT trade mark; and

(b) That species denomination or trade mark (as appropriate) was commonly used for the marketing of goods or required to be kept free under other legislation.

According to the Board, those requirements had not been satisfied for three reasons. First, only *Gynostemma pentaphyllum* was commonly used on the market to identify a particular species, and thus only *Gynostemma pentaphyllum* was required to be kept free under European law (and in particular under Article 3(1)(c) Trade Marks Directive); and since there was no evidence that Ginpent was currently being used or might in the future be used on the market as a common abbreviation for *Gynostemma pentaphyllum* to designate the species *Gynostemma pentaphyllum*, it could not be a basis for refusing the Ginpent variety denomination under Article 63(3)(d). Second, the GINPENT trade mark had not been established to be in current use on the market as a common abbreviation for *Gynostemma pentaphyllum* to designate the species *Gynostemma pentaphyllum*, and was in any case so removed from *Gynostemma pentaphyllum* in terms of its sound, written appearance, and concept that there was no risk of confusion between it and the *Gynostemma pentaphyllum* species denomination (which EU legislation required be kept free). And third, in the Board's decision an amendment to the variety denomination would not be justified on the ground that the PVR holder was marketing his variety under the GINPENT trade mark rather than the variety denomination Ginpent, since infringement of the Article 17 prohibition against offering or disposing of a protected variety (or associated material) without using the designated variety denomination is not a basis for amending that denomination itself; being rather a basis for legal action attracting more serious consequences.

This leaves the last of the Article 63(3) paragraphs considered in the *Vegetal Progress* case: Article 63(3)(f). According to the Board, for the reasons above the variety denomination Ginpent and the species denomination *Gynostemma pentaphyllum* could not be confused with one another, with the result that their respective characteristics could not be considered to be misleading within the meaning of that paragraph.

9.2.12 **The Relationship Between Plant Variety and Patent Protection**

As suggested in Section 9.1, the use of genetic engineering in plant breeding techniques underlines the potential for overlapping patent and PVR protection in respect of individual plant varieties. It is however a fundamental principle of the European (EPC and EU) patent system, and of the CPVR system as well, that such overlap be contained. Hence we saw in Section 6.3.3.2 that under the EPC and Biotech Directive, plant varieties are among the categories of subject matter excluded from protection on public policy grounds. In addition, the Basic Regulation expressly excludes national and European patent protection for any variety that is the subject of a CPVR (Article 92(1)), reinforcing Article 53(b) and Article 4(1)(a) Biotech Directive, with the latter further supporting the distinction between the two regimes by defining 'plant variety' expressly with reference to its CPVR meaning (Article 2(3)).

Of course, it does not follow from the exclusion of plant varieties from the range of subject matter capable of supporting a European patent that other subject matter which *include* varieties may not be patented. And indeed, this possibility is expressly confirmed by the provision of Article 4(2) Biotech Directive, reproduced in the EPC Implementing Regulations, that inventions 'which concern plants or animals shall be patentable if the technical feasibility of the invention is not confined to a particular plant or animal variety'. Hence the possibility for patent grants that protect plant varieties. On the other hand, the Directive goes some way to preventing this from interfering with the ability of breeders to acquire and enforce CPVRs. One way it does this is by permitting any plant breeder (or patentee) who is unable to acquire or exploit a variety (or patent) right without infringing a patent (or variety) right to seek a compulsory licence in respect of it, subject to the following four conditions (Article 12): first, the applicant must pay the rights holder an appropriate royalty; second, the applicant must be prepared to grant a cross-licence on reasonable terms to enable the licensor to use the applicant's own variety or patent, as appropriate; third, the applicant must have applied unsuccessfully to the rights holder for a contractual licence; and fourth, the right sought to be licensed must constitute 'significant technical progress of considerable economic interest compared with the invention [or] plant variety' (see Article 12(3)). In addition, under the UPC Agreement 2013, European patents will not be infringed by 'the use of biological material for the purpose of breeding, or discovering and developing, other plant varieties' (Article 27(c) UPC Agreement; see Section 8.5.1).

It may be useful to consider an example of these two systems working in practice. Imagine a biotechnology research group which isolates the gene responsible for producing a protein inhibitor that renders a certain plant (A) resistant to pest B. The group will be able to apply for a European patent for the isolated gene for the specified function of rendering plant A resistant to pest B. Since the decision of the Court of Justice in Case C–428/08 *Monsanto Technology LLC v Cefetra BV et al.* [2010] ECR I-6765 (*Monsanto*) (see Section 8.3.4.2), the protection conferred by that patent will extend only to products in which the gene is performing the specified function of rendering plant A resistant to pest B, enabling others to discover further uses for the gene and claim separate patents for them. In addition, third parties will be able in the meantime to use the patented technology to discover and develop novel and DUS varieties of plants, and seek CPVR protection for those varieties, without needing a licence from the patentee (if the UPC Agreement 2013 applies). The breeders will then be able to offer the plant varieties thus developed for sale to farmers for cultivation. One would expect the farmers to be keen to buy them, since their improved pest resistance will reduce the amount of chemical pesticides required and support crops of improved nutritional value.

9.3 Supplementary Protection Certificates

9.3.1 Preliminary Remarks

As we saw in Section 8.2, European (EPC) patents last for a maximum period of 20 years, subject to extension on the grounds permitted by Article 63 EPC. One of those grounds, described in Article 63(2)(b), permits the extension of the patent term, or the grant of corresponding protection to follow immediately on expiry of its term, under the same conditions as those applying to national patents,

> if the subject-matter of the European patent is a product or a process for manufacturing a product or a use of a product which has to undergo an administrative authorization procedure required by law before it can be put on the market in that State.

It is to this and the corresponding provisions of European domestic patent legislation that the European supplementary protection certificate regime is directed. The focus of this regime is medicinal and plant protection products that are protected by a patent in an EEA State and for which the patentee has had to acquire regulatory approval to bring the product to market. In the case of such a product, securing the necessary approval can take several years, detracting from the patentee's ability to exploit the benefits of her patent by marketing her product and thereby recouping the costs expended in devising her invention and making it available to the public. It was in order to compensate the patentee for this diminished opportunity that the EU, in 1992, followed the lead of states such as France and Italy by introducing a supplementary protection certificate regime.

In brief, the supplementary protection certificate regime operates by requiring EEA States to establish a mechanism for receiving and deciding applications by the holder of a patent for a medicinal or plant protection product for the grant of follow on protection on the same terms as the original patent where securing regulatory approval to market the product has diminished her opportunity to exploit her patent rights.[16] Its basis is the following three EU regulations, in conjunction with Article 65(2) and Annex XVII EEA Agreement:

- Regulation (EC) No. 469/2009 of the European Parliament and of the Council of 6 May 2009 concerning the supplementary protection certificate for medicinal products [2009] OJ L 152/1 (MP Regulation);
- Regulation (EC) No. 1901/2006 of the European Parliament and of the Council of 12 December 2006 on medicinal products for paediatric use [2006] OJ L 378/1; and
- Regulation (EC) No. 1610/96 of the European Parliament and of the Council of 23 July 1996 concerning the creation of a supplementary protection certificate for plant protection products [1996] OJ L 198/30 (PPP Regulation).

Supplementary protection certificates are national IP rights conferred by individual states. Nonetheless, and as with European (EPC) patent grants, when the Unitary Patent Package takes effect they will fall within the exclusive jurisdiction of the Unified Patent Court under Article 3(b) UPC Agreement 2013.

---

[16] This was explained by the Court of Justice in response to an argument made by Spain that the original Supplementary Protection Certificate Regulation was invalid under the Treaties since it created a new industrial property right in exercise of competence that the EU did not have. See Case C–350/92 *Kingdom of Spain v Council of the European Union* [1995] ECR I-1985 [15].

9.3.2 The Procedure and Conditions for Obtaining a Supplementary Protection Certificate

The supplementary protection certificate regime requires EEA States to award certificates in respect of medicinal and plant protection products protected by a domestic or European patent granted by or on the State's behalf on application by the patentee or his successor in title in any case in which the following conditions are met (Article 3 MP and PPP Regulations):

(a) the product is protected by a basic patent in force;

(b) a valid authorization to market the product as a medicinal or plant protection product has been granted in accordance with applicable EU legislation or, in the case of a non-EU EEA State (currently Iceland, Liechtenstein, and Norway), with applicable national legislation authorizing the marketing of the product in any EEA State (see Case C–617/12 *Astrazeneca AB v Comptroller General of Patents, Designs and Trade Marks* EU:C:2014:28);

(c) the product has not already been the subject of a supplementary protection certificate; and

(d) the authorization is the first authorization to place the product on the market as a medicinal or plant protection product.

The meaning of these conditions has been considered by the Court of Justice in a series of cases, including Case C–322/10 *Medeva v Comptroller-General of Patents, Designs and Trade Marks* [2011] ECR I-12051 (*Medeva*). As a result of that decision, it is now established with respect to condition (a) that a certificate may only be granted for a product the active ingredients of which are specified in the wording of the basic patent claims, including in functional terms consistent with general principles of claim construction (see Case C–493/12 *Eli Lilly and Company Ltd v Human Genome Sciences Inc.* EU:C:2013:835). If the basic patent claims a process for obtaining a product, the product for which the certificate is sought must be the product identified in the wording of the claims as that produced by the process (see Case C–630/10 *University of Queensland v Comptroller-General of Patents, Designs and Trade Marks* [2011] ECR I-12231). If the patent claims describe a product as composed of two or more active ingredients without making any claim in relation to one of the specified ingredients individually, a certificate may not be granted on the basis of such a patent for that individual ingredient in isolation. Conversely, however, if one of the specified ingredients is individually protected as such by the patent, a certificate may be obtained for it, even if the patentee has already obtained a certificate for the combination of active ingredients described in the claims (Case C–484/12 *Georgetown University v Octrooicentrum Nederland* EU:C:2013:828). With respect to condition (b), the Court has further held that a certificate may only be granted for an active ingredient the effect of which in a substance falls within the therapeutic indications covered by the wording of the marketing authorization (Case C–631/13 *Forsgren v Österreichisches Patentamt* EU:C:2015:13 (*Forsgren*)). On the other hand, a certificate will not be precluded by the fact that the product for which the marketing authorization was sought covers active ingredients not specified in the wording of the patent claims. In deciding these and other cases, the Court has emphasized the need to interpret the supplementary protection certificate regime in a way that gives effect to its fundamental purpose of ensuring 'sufficient protection to encourage pharmaceutical research, which plays a decisive role in the continuing improvement in public health' (*Medeva* [30]), and in recognition that 'the period of effective protection under the patent is insufficient to cover the investment put into pharmaceutical research' (*Medeva* [31]).

Applications for a certificate must be made directly to the patent office in the protecting state within six months of the applicant being authorized to market the relevant product or, if that date precedes the patent grant, within six months of the patent being granted (Article 7 MP and PPP Regulations). While only one certificate may ever be granted to any person in respect of a product—regardless of whether a subsequent marketing authorization is obtained (Case C–443/12 *Actavis Group PTC EHF v Sanofi* EU:C:2013:833)—if two or more people hold patents in respect of the product, a single certificate may be granted to each of them (Article 3(2) PPP Regulation).

9.3.3 The Subject Matter and Effect of Supplementary Protection Certificate Protection

The effect of a supplementary protection certificate is to confer follow-on protection in respect of the product for which authorization has been obtained and for any use of that product as a medicinal or plant protection product which has been authorized before the expiry of the certificate (Article 4 MP and PPP Regulations). It follows that the subject matter to which certificates relate is not the patented invention per se, but rather the product for which regulatory approval has been granted. In the case of a medicinal product, that product is the active ingredient or combination of active ingredients of the authorized medicinal product (Article 1(b) MP Regulation). In the case of a plant protection product, it is the active substance or combination of active substances of the authorized plant protection product (Article 1(8) PPP Regulation). For these purposes an active substance is an active ingredient in the sense of an ingredient producing in substances 'a pharmacological, immunological or metabolic action of their own' (*Forsgren* [25]), and a combination of active ingredients is understood accordingly. Hence the Court of Justice has confirmed that an adjuvant which has no therapeutic effect on its own is not an active ingredient, and the combination of such an adjuvant with a substance the therapeutic effects of which the adjuvant enhances is not a combination of active ingredients within the meaning of Article 1(b) MP Regulation (Case C–210/13 *Glaxosmithkline Biologicals SA v Comptroller-General of Patents, Designs and Trade Marks* EU:C:2013:762). In all cases, a certificate confers the same rights as are conferred by the basic patent in respect of the product, and is subject to the same limitations and obligations (Article 5 MP and PPP Regulations). It thus enables its holder to prevent the same range of acts in respect of the medicinal or plant protection product as the holder of the basic patent was entitled to prevent in respect of it.

9.3.4 Duration

The general rule is that supplementary protection certificates take effect at the end of the lawful term of the basic patent for a period equal to the period which elapsed between the date on which the patent application was filed and the date of the first authorization to place the product on the market in the territory of an EU Member State or EEA State (Article 13 MP and PPP Regulations). This is the case regardless of whether the authorization was issued by the relevant state (see Case C–617/12 *Astrazeneca AB v Comptroller General of Patents, Designs and Trade Marks* EU:C:2013:761, involving a first authorization in Switzerland that was effective in Liechtenstein). The term of the certificate is then calculated from the first authorization; though whether from the date of its grant or notification to the patentee is unclear. In some states, such as the UK, Slovenia, and Portugal, certificates are deemed to take effect from the date on which the first marketing authorization is notified, while in other states, such as Austria, they are deemed to take effect from the date of grant. The difference between these two approaches will usually be several days worth of protection. The correct approach is among the questions being considered by the Court of Justice following a referral by the Oberlandesgericht Wien (Higher Regional Court of Vienna) in Case C–471/14 *Seattle Genetics*.

In all cases, the term of a supplementary protection certificate is reduced by a period of five years, and subject to a maximum five-year cap. The result is that certificates are only available in cases where the process of obtaining market authorization has taken more than five years. As an encouragement to research into diseases affecting children, certificates for a medicinal product may be extended once by six months if the market authorization for the product includes the results of paediatric investigation studies under Article 36 Regulation 1901/2006. According to the Court of Justice in Case C–125/10 *Merck Sharp & Dohme Corp. v Deutsches Patent- und Markenamt* [2011] ECR I-12987, the effect of this provision is to enable the grant of a certificate notwithstanding that the time elapsed between lodging the patent application and obtaining the first marketing authorization is less than five years, provided it is not less than four and a half years, where this is necessary to enable the paediatric extension to apply. In such a situation, the paediatric extension commences running not from the expiry of the basic patent, but from the date determined by deducting from that expiry date the difference between five years and the duration of the period which elapsed between lodging the patent application and obtaining the first marketing authorization.

9.4 Conclusions

The protection of plant varieties by the *sui generis* CPVR regime may be said to have supported the three developments identified at the outset of this chapter as having triggered the recognition of plant variety rights initially: the industrialization of food production; the shift of plant breeding research from the public to the private sector; and the increasing use of gene therapies in plant breeding. With these developments have come many economic and humanitarian benefits, including the increased production of crops with higher yield, improved nutritional value, and enhanced resistance to pests and disease. As with all IP regimes, however, against these benefits must be weighed certain costs of the PVR regime's existence. These include centralized crop breeding and uniform environmental conditions, and reduced agro-ecological research and local breeding tailored to local conditions.[17]

Even beyond its costs and benefits, the CPVR system includes many of the same features and raises many of the same issues as the European patent and other IP systems include and raise. For example, it:

- follows the early recognition in parts of Europe that people who have applied their intelligence and industry to derive products of value to society deserve limited property rights, and builds on an international system aimed at securing such rights;

- seeks to balance strong protection for breeders with third party rights and freedoms;

- offers a form of protection which complements that offered by other IP systems, including by patents (in respect of plant technologies) and trade marks (in respect of variety denominations); and

- raises enforcement challenges for the law which rights holders have sought to meet, in part at least, by developing technological mechanisms to prevent the unauthorized reproduction of their IP subject matter (in the form of Genetic Use Restriction Technologies).

In addition, and more fundamentally, plant variety protection raises important issues regarding the appropriate reach and scope of IP. As we saw in Section 3.2, the premise of IP systems is the existence of an intellectual product, namely, a subject matter having an objectively discernible form, informational or expressive significance, and identifiable human

---

[17] E. Bonadio, 'Crop Breeding and Intellectual Property in the Global Village' [2007] *EIPR* 167, 169.

creators. The capacity of new strains of plant material to satisfy these conditions may be questioned, notwithstanding the increasing use of biotechnology to derive them, and as the definition of breeders (to include those who discover and develop a variety) reflects. Given this, it is possible to see PVR systems as reflecting the phenomenon of Proprietarianism that we considered in Section 3.6: i.e., a tendency towards property fundamentalism (the normative prioritizing of property above other rights and interests), a dependence on a 'first connection' thesis about property (the idea that a person first connected with an object or activity of value has a property right in respect of it), and a belief in the negative commons (suggesting that while not everything is owned, everything is capable of being owned).[18] It may be concerns such as these that have led some commentators to oppose the move towards increasing the protection for plant varieties by allowing patent rights to be granted in respect of subject matter including them, and to criticize the breadth of the CPVR itself, including the restrictive scope of the farmers' privilege limiting it.

Somewhat in contrast to the CPVR regime, few have questioned the appropriateness of supplementary protection certificates as a means of compensating patentees for the restriction of their patent rights effected by the demands of modern regulatory approval requirements. From a patentee's perspective, they are enormously important, coming as they do at the end of a patent's life when sales of the relevant product are likely to be at their strongest. What has caused controversy, however, is the Court of Justice's case law regarding the different provisions of the Supplementary Protection Certificate Regulations. The main reason for the controversy is its lack of clarity, due to the terseness of the Court of Justice's reasoning, and the difference in approach among domestic courts to which this has contributed. Indeed, the decision in *Medeva* regarding the meaning of Article 3 MP and PPP Regulations was invoked by one senior patent judge immediately before the conclusion of the Unitary Patent Package to support calls to remove the substantive law provisions of the then draft Unitary Patent Regulation 1257/2012 with a view to limiting the involvement of the Court of Justice with respect to European patents, and through them to supplementary protection certificates.[19]

Further Reading

BONADIO, E., 'Crop Breeding and Intellectual Property in the Global Village' [2007] *EIPR* 167

LAWSON, C., 'Plant Breeder's Rights and Essentially Derived Varieties: Still Searching for Workable Solutions' [2014] *EIPR* 499

LINARELLI, J., 'Treaty Governance, Intellectual Property and Biodiversity' [2004] *Environmental Law Review* 21

LLEWELLYN, M. AND ADCOCK, M., *European Plant Intellectual Property* (Hart Publishing, 2006)

MILLETT, T., 'The Community System of Plant Variety Rights' [1999] *European Law Review* 231

PAUNIO, E., 'Plant Variety Rights Revisited: Balancing Conflicting Interests in the Case-Law of the Court of Justice of the European Union' [2014] *EIPR* 482

SANDERSON, J., 'Reconsidering Plant Variety Rights in the European Union After *Monsanto v Cefetra BV*' [2012] *EIPR* 387

---

[18] P. Drahos, *A Philosophy of Intellectual Property* (Dartmouth, 1996) 201–2.
[19] See D. Kitchin (Lord Justice of Appeal), 'Congress dinner—October 2012: The Rt Hon Lord Justice Kitchin' http://www.cipa.org.uk/pages/Congres-Dinner-2012-Lord-Justice-Kitchin; Section 2.7.

PART III

The Law of Copyright and Related Rights

10

Introduction to the European Law of Copyright and Related Rights

10.1 Introduction

Copyright and related rights are limited-term exclusionary rights that subsist automatically in authorial works such as poems, paintings, musical tunes, and dance compositions, in addition to certain other categories of expressive subject matter such as phonograms (sound recordings), films, non-authorial databases, broadcasts, and performances.

As we saw in Section 1.2.2.2.1, the first statutory copyright and related rights systems were introduced in the 18th century. While today's systems retain the basic features of their 18th century counterparts, they operate in vastly different contexts. In Europe, a key feature of their current context is the EU (including its internal market), which has introduced several directives covering most aspects of the substantive law of copyright and related rights. Of central importance among these is the Information Society Directive 2001, which contains a basic legislative code governing the recognition and protection of copyright and related rights throughout EU territory. Its provisions, and the referring obligation of Member States' courts under Article 267 TFEU (see Section 2.6), have led the CJEU to assume a central role in this area of European IP law.

In this chapter we introduce the European law of copyright and related rights with an overview of its basic principles. We then consider the European (EU) statutory framework, and the policy agenda of the European Commission on which it is based. Finally, we look at some of the challenges posed by globalization and digital technology.

The importance of the works and subject matter protected by copyright and related rights in and for the everyday lives of European citizens and business makes the law in this area among the most complex, dynamic, and contested of all European IP laws. Perhaps the greatest challenge faced by law- and policy-makers currently is the enforcement and exploitation of copyright and related rights in the digital environment amidst widespread public scepticism regarding their legitimacy. Closely related to this challenge is that of promoting public access to protected works and subject matter, and facilitating the use of new technologies.

Balancing the rights and interests of copyright and related rights holders with the rights and interests of third parties and the public in general has always been at the heart of IP law and policy in this area. At the European level, the tension between these competing rights and interests is increasingly expressed in constitutional terms, as a tension between the fundamental rights and interests of IP protection, freedom of expression, education, social integration and participation, and freedom to conduct a business. Ensuring that Member States strike an appropriate balance between these and other fundamental rights and interests, all of which represent basic values of European society, is a central aim of EU copyright and related rights law and policy.

10.2 Copyright and Related Rights: An Overview

Copyright and related rights are types of IP right recognized and protected by all European states in respect of authorial works and certain other categories of expressive and informational subject matter. They are limited in duration and confer on their holders a range of exclusive rights, including in most cases the rights to copy and communicate to the public the protected work or subject matter. By contrast, making and using a protected work or subject matter are not among the acts reserved to the rights holder, and nor is there any rule against the subsistence of copyright or related rights in two or more identical and independently created or produced works or subject matter. In these respects, copyright and related rights confer less protection, while also being subject to less stringent subsistence requirements than registrable intellectual (industrial) property rights such as patents and trade marks. They are also subject to a larger number of exceptions and limitations, covering a range of freedom of expression and other public interest-based third party acts. As for other IP rights, their breach can give rise to both civil and criminal liability.

When studying the substantive law of copyright and related rights, it is useful to distinguish four main issues: the circumstances and subject matter in which copyright and related rights subsist, and the persons by whom they are initially owned (subsistence and ownership); the nature of the rights they confer in respect of those subject matter, including their duration and the requirements for their infringement (rights); the acts permitted in respect of protected works and subject matter notwithstanding their subsistence (exceptions and limitations); and the civil and criminal methods and consequences of enforcing them (enforcement and remedies). In this part we focus on the first three of these issues—subsistence and ownership, rights, and exceptions and limitations—leaving enforcement and remedies for discussion in Part VI.

In Europe, copyright and related rights arise and are protected under the national laws of individual states. However, they are subject to extensive EU legal regulation, the effect of which may be summarized as follows, beginning with the law of copyright. First, regarding subsistence and ownership, EU law requires the protection by copyright of all authorial works, including original computer programs, photographs, and databases, and recognizes such protection as a fundamental right under Article 17(2) CFR, consistent with the position under Article 1 of Protocol 1 ECHR, and with the result explained in Section 3.1. Second, regarding rights, EU law defines the benefits of copyright ownership as including a closed list of exclusive economic rights, including the rights to reproduce a protected work directly or indirectly and in whole or part, and to communicate a protected work to the public. It also requires that copyright in a work last until 70 years after the author's death, and that it take effect during that period according to the laws of individual Member States subject to EU principles of free movement and competition law. And finally, regarding exceptions and limitations, EU law requires

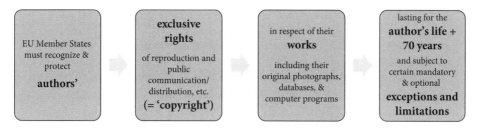

Figure 10.1 The EU copyright framework

that copyright be limited so as not to prevent third parties from making temporary and transient or incidental copies of a work necessary to a technological process, such as Internet browsing, in addition to permitting Member States to recognize certain further exceptions to copyright infringement covering such third party acts as reproducing and communicating parts of a work for the purpose of research, news reporting, criticism or review, study, instruction, quotation, or parody. A summary of these EU legal provisions is contained in Figure 10.1. Within the constraints imposed by them, Member States do retain legislative competence, as a matter of EU law, to determine the rights of authors in respect of their works, including the requirements for their subsistence and the laws governing their exploitation. However, the precise scope of that residual domestic competence is unclear, due in part to the uncertainty regarding the nature and extent of the gaps in EU copyright legislation itself, and the disagreement regarding the competence of the CJEU to fill those gaps by means of its case law. In addition, the exercise of such competence as Member States retain is further limited by their obligations under international instruments, including the Berne Convention for the Protection of Literary and Artistic Works 1886/1971, with which the EU and its Member States are required to comply.[1] Examples include authors' and performers' moral rights, and authors' and others' rights in respect of live public performances and showings of copyright works and related rights subject matter, which remain largely untouched by EU legislation notwithstanding their single market dimension.[2] On the other hand, EU legislation expressly acknowledges the requirements of international instruments regarding these rights, including in recital 19 Information Society Directive. An example of such requirements is provided by Article 6*bis* of the Berne Convention, which recognizes the rights of individuals: (a) to be identified as the authors of any works they create; and (b) to prevent others from subjecting their works to derogatory treatment, in each case for the duration of the works' copyright. These so-called rights of paternity and integrity are conceived as moral rights by reason of their non-transferability, and their conception as such in the jurisprudence of domestic European states. Also included in domestic European understandings of moral rights are the further rights, omitted from the Berne Convention: (a) to determine the readiness for public circulation of a work one has created (the right of disclosure); (b) to withdraw a work one has created from public circulation (the right of retraction); and (c) not to be identified as the author of a work one has not created (the right of non-attribution). As we will see in Chapter 13, while EU law does not regulate the recognition and protection of authors' moral rights as such, it does incorporate limited protection for the right of

---

[1] See Article 5 Protocol 28 EEA Agreement and Article 1(4) WCT; Sections 1.3.2 and 2.5.2.3.

[2] In the context of authors' moral rights see, e.g., Commission Communication of 20 November 1996, 'Follow-up to the Green Paper on copyright and related rights in the information society' COM (96) 568 final (1995 Green Paper Follow-up).

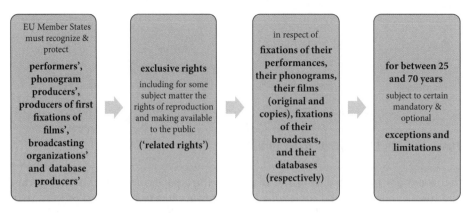

Figure 10.2 The EU related rights framework

disclosure in its definition of the exceptions and limitations which Member States may recognize to copyright and related rights infringement, as well as other forms of indirect protection for the moral rights and interests of authors to control the circumstances and manner in which their works are presented to the public.

In addition to copyright, EU law requires the recognition and protection by Member States of related rights in respect of a closed list of non-authorial expressive subject matter, including broadcasts, phonograms, fixations of films and performances, and certain databases, on terms similar to those governing copyright, as seen in Figure 10.2. The result is a two-tier system for the protection of expressive and informational subject matter involving copyright for authorial works and related rights for their non-authorial counterparts. While some subject matter, such as databases, are capable of attracting both copyright and related rights protection, the nature, scope, and beneficiaries of such protection differ, consistent with the different focus and aims of each species of right. Thus, copyright subsists in databases as authorial works, and confers the same rights as are conferred in respect of other authorial works, whereas the *sui generis* database right subsists in databases the contents of which are the product of substantial commercial investment, and confers more limited rights focused on the protection of those contents and that investment.

Throughout Europe, copyright and related rights subsist and are enforceable without the need for application or assertion by the person claiming protection, and without the need for registration or other formal action by the protecting state. In this sense they differ once again from registrable IP rights, including patents and trade marks. One consequence of this difference is the absence of any official register of rights, or of the rights holders from whom permission must be obtained in order for a work or subject matter to be lawfully reproduced or communicated to the public. This leads to the so-called orphan works problem, which arises where the holder of copyright cannot be identified by reasonably diligent search, preventing any third party from using the protected work in a manner inconsistent with its copyright. A 2010 European Commission report described the scale of this problem as follows:

- A conservative estimate of the number of orphan books as a percentage of in-copyright books across Europe puts the number at 3 million orphan books (13% of the total number of in-copyright books). The older the books the higher the percentage of orphan works.

- When handling requests for using older film material, film archives from across Europe categorized after a search for right holders 129 000 film works as orphan which could therefore not be used. Works that can be presumed to be orphan without actually search-ing for the right holders augments the figure to approximately 225 000 film works.

- A digitisation project in the UK found that 95% of newspapers from before 1912 are orphan. Also, a survey amongst museums in the UK found that the rights holders of 17 million photographs (that is 90% of the total collections of photographs of the museums) could not be traced.[3]

Unless it has already been communicated by or with the permission of its copyright holder, an orphan work can be lost to the public for the duration of the term of its protec-tion at least, and often longer. Solving this problem and facilitating access to protected material in general have been and continue to be among the central European policy initiatives in this field of IP.

10.3 The European Copyright and Related Rights System

10.3.1 The EU Copyright and Related Rights Statutory Framework

10.3.1.1 Key Copyright and Related Rights Directives

Of especial importance among the EU copyright and related rights directives are the Software, Term, Database, E-Commerce, and Information Society Directives. The Software Directive requires (and regulates) the copyright protection of original com-puter programs by Member States as authorial works. The Term Directive governs the duration of copyright and related rights in Member States, and the protection of original and unoriginal photographs by copyright and related rights. The Database Directive establishes a system for Member States' protection of original databases by copyright and of unoriginal databases by a *sui generis* database right. The E-Commerce Directive establishes a framework for electronic commerce, and limits the liability of Internet intermediaries under the laws of Member States for copyright and related rights infringement. And the Information Society Directive establishes the basic obli-gations of Member States with respect to copyright and related rights, building on the obligations imposed by the Berne and Rome Conventions, and implementing the fur-ther requirements of the two WIPO Copyright Treaties of 1996 (the WIPO Copyright Treaty (WCT) and the WIPO Performances and Phonograms Treaty (WPPT)). Of these instruments, the Information Society Directive has especial importance, repre-senting the closest thing that currently exists to a complete European copyright and related rights code. It applies ('without prejudice to any acts concluded and rights acquired before 22 December 2002') in respect of all of the works and other subject matter to which it refers that, on that date: (a) were protected by Member States' copy-right and related rights legislation; or (b) met the protection criteria of the Directive or the provisions referred to in Article 1(2) (Article 10(1)). Those criteria relate to: (a) the legal protection of computer programs; (b) the rental right, lending right, and certain rights related to copyright in the field of IP; (c) copyright and related rights applica-ble to broadcasting of programmes by satellite and cable retransmission; (d) the term of protection of copyright and certain related rights; and (e) the legal protection of databases, as amended by Article 11 Information Society Directive. Of especial note regarding them is the restriction of Member States' obligations under the Rental and Lending Rights Directive (see Article 11) to

---

[3] A. Vuopala, 'Assessment of the Orphan Works Issue and Costs for Rights Clearance' (May 2010) http://www.ace-film.eu/wp-content/uploads/2010/09/Copyright_anna_report-1.pdf.

copyright works, performances, phonograms, broadcasts and first fixations of films…
which were, on 1 July 1994, still protected by the legislation of the Member States in the
field of copyright and related rights or which met the criteria for protection under this
Directive on that date.

10.3.1.2 International Instruments in the Copyright and Related Rights Field

As we saw in Sections 1.3 and 2.5.2.3, EU law- and decision-making in the copyright
and related rights field take place within an established international legal framework
which the EU institutions recognize and strive to implement. Key aspects of that framework are the TRIPS Agreement and WIPO Treaties, each of which the EU has ratified,
and the interpretation of which lies within its exclusive competence vis-à-vis Member
States (Section 2.4.2.4.2). Two further instruments of importance to which the EU has
committed under the terms of the EEA Agreement, and which underpin its law- and
policy-making in this field, are the Berne and Rome Conventions respectively. These
Conventions have also been acceded to by all EU Member States, and are the explicit
bases of the WIPO Treaties (see Article 1(1) WPPT and Article 1(2) WCT) as well as
several of the EU's copyright and related rights directives. They are consequently treated
by the CJEU as the starting point for its interpretation of all statutory instruments in the
copyright and related rights field (see, e.g., Case C–135/10 *Societa Consortile Fonografici
(SCF) v Macro Del Corso* EU:C:2012:140 for the Rome Convention). An early justification for such treatment was offered by Advocate General Gulmann in *Magill* (Joined
Cases C–241/91 P and 242/91 P *Radio Telefis Eireann (RTE) and Independent Television
Publications Ltd (ITP) v Commission of the European Communities* [1995] ECR I-743) as
follows ([154]–[158], footnotes omitted):

> I consider that it is appropriate to interpret Article 86 [EC Treaty] in accordance with the
> Berne Convention. Many factors militate in favour of account being taken of the Berne
> Convention in interpreting the Treaty rules.
>
> The rules of the Berne Convention are designed to guarantee authors minimum pro-
> tection, and it is a Convention which enjoys broad international support.
>
> All Member States have acceded to the Berne Convention and only Ireland and
> Belgium have not yet acceded to the Paris Act of 1971. On 14 May 1992 the Council
> adopted a resolution under which the Member States of the Community, in so far as
> they have not already done so, undertake to become by 1 January 1995 parties to the
> Paris Act and to introduce national legislation to ensure effective compliance there-
> with. The Resolution further states that it is in the interests of Community copyright-
> holders that they should be ensured the minimum level of protection afforded by the
> Convention in the maximum possible number of third countries and in that connection
> the Council invites the Commission, when negotiating agreements with third coun-
> tries to pay particular attention to the ratification of or accession to the Convention by
> the third countries concerned and to the effective compliance of such countries with
> the Convention.
>
> There are several examples, as RTE has pointed out, of references in secondary leg-
> islation of the Community to the Berne Convention as an expression of a general and
> broadly accepted minimum standard, see [the Software Directive], [the Term Directive]
> and finally the Commission's [then proposed Database Directive].
>
> Finally, I would point out that in its submissions in these cases the Commission itself
> has also stressed the desirability of Community law in the field of copyright being in
> accordance with international standards.

The requirements of the key international instruments in IP are summarized in
Figure 10.3.

Instrument	Administered by...	Members	Requirements
BERNE CONVENTION 1886/1971	WIPO	168 members, including all EU Member States	Members must afford authors non-discriminatory treatment and minimum standards of economic and moral rights protection in respect of their literary and artistic works. (See further Chapter 1.)
ROME CONVENTION 1961	Jointly by WIPO, ILO & UNESCO	92 members, including all EU Member States	Members must afford performers, phonogram producers, and broadcasting organizations non-discriminatory treatment and minimum standards of economic rights protection in respect of their performances, phonograms, and broadcasts, without prejudice to copyright.
TRIPS AGREEMENT 1994	WTO	161 members, including the EU and all EU Member States	Without prejudice to their obligations under Berne, members must afford authors non-discriminatory and most favoured nation treatment, and minimum standards of economic rights protection, in respect of their literary and artistic works, including by: (a) complying with the economic rights obligations of Berne; (b) ensuring copyright protection for computer programs and databases as literary works; and (c) recognizing authors' rights of rental in respect of computer programs and cinematographic works at least. (See further Chapter 1.)
WCT 1996	WIPO	Special agreement under Berne, open to Berne members only. 93 members, including the EU and all EU Member States	Affirms and extends Berne protections in the light of economic, social, cultural, and technological developments, including by requiring members (without prejudice to their obligations under Berne and other treaties) to: (a) ensure copyright protection for computer programs and databases as literary and artistic works; (b) recognize authors' rights of distribution and rental; and (c) provide legal remedies for the circumvention of technological protection measures used by authors in connection with their rights and for the removal or altering of rights management information.

Figure 10.3 (*Continued*)

| WPPT 1996 | WIPO | 94 members, including the EU and all EU Member States | Affirms and extends Rome protections in the light of economic, social, cultural, and technological developments, including by requiring members without prejudice to their obligations under Rome and other treaties) to: (a) ensure new moral and economic rights protection for performers and phonogram producers; and (b) provide legal remedies for the circumvention of technological protection measures used by rights owners in connection with their rights and for the removal or altering of rights management information. |

Figure 10.3 Key international instruments having indirect effect under EU law

10.3.1.3 From Protecting the Single Market Against Copyright and Related Rights to Enhancing the Single Market With a European Copyright and Related Rights System

The earliest European initiatives in the IP field were focused on facilitating the grant of industrial property rights, such as patents and trade marks, by individual European states (see Part I). So too the earliest IP-related initiatives of the EEC were specifically focused on establishing industrial property rights and systems for EEC territory. Indeed, even the EEC Treaty referred to 'industrial and commercial property' rather than to copyright or intellectual property. As we saw in Section 2.4.2.1.3, that reference was contained in Article 36 EEC, in which the protection of industrial and commercial property was recognized as a justification for prohibiting or restricting 'imports, exports or goods in transit', provided the prohibition or restriction in question did not 'constitute a means of arbitrary discrimination or a disguised restriction on trade between Member States'. From the outset, the CJEU interpreted this Article as conferring competence on the Community to regulate the exercise by individuals of copyright and related rights conferred under the laws of EEC Member States. By the 1980s, it had also recognized the Community as having competence to regulate the existence or essence of copyright and related rights, including by introducing approximating (harmonizing) measures to support the establishment and smooth functioning of the single market. That recognition coincided with a change in the EEC's attitude to IP, from representing an impediment to economic integration to representing a means of supporting such integration and the pursuit of European economic and social objectives generally. There followed a period of active law- and policy-making by the (E)EC institutions in the copyright and related rights field during the 1980s, 1990s, and 2000s, including the introduction of more than ten directives which continue (in their original or reissued form) to represent the statutory basis for the accumulated EU law of copyright and related rights: the so-called *acquis communautaire* discussed in Chapters 11 to 13.[4] The most important of these are listed in Figure 10.4.

---

[4] In chronological order these are the Software Directive 1991, the Rental and Lending Rights Directive 1992, the Satellite and Cable Directive 1993, the Term Directive 1993, the Database Directive 1996, the E-Commerce Directive 2000, the Information Society Directive 2001, the Resale Right Directive 2001, the Enforcement Directive 2004, the Term Amendment Directive 2011, the Orphan Works Directive 2012, and the Collective Rights Management Directive 2014.

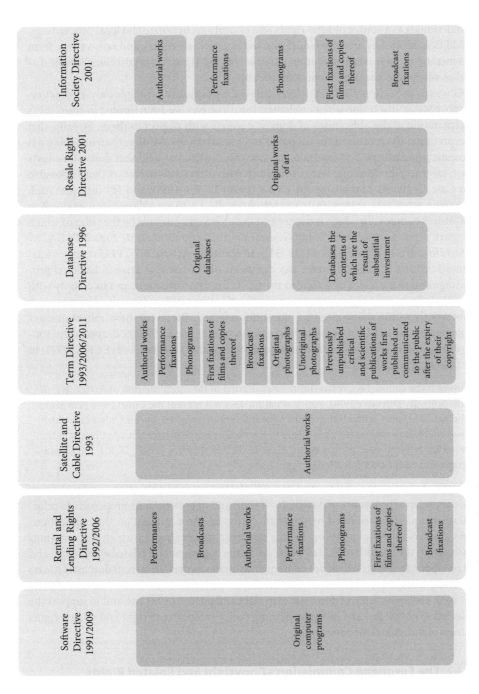

Figure 10.4 Core EU directives by subject matter

10.3.1.4 The Impact of European Copyright and Related Rights Law on Member States

As directives, each of the instruments referred to earlier is addressed to and binding on EU Member States rather than on EU citizens. They therefore cannot be invoked directly by individuals as a source of legal rights and obligations in horizontal legal proceedings. In addition, since they are only binding on states as to their effects, and not as to the form and method of their implementation (Article 288 TFEU), states retain considerable discretion when implementing them domestically.

As we saw in Section 2.5.2.2, however, this is the position in principle only. In practice, Member States' discretion when implementing directives has been limited by the CJEU's interpretation of the obligations of domestic courts with respect to them. Equally, that interpretation has increased the scope for individuals to invoke directives in horizontal domestic proceedings. For example, the Court of Justice has held that domestic courts must: (a) interpret domestic law consistently with directives insofar as that is possible (see Case C–106/89 *Marleasing SA v CIA* [1990] ECR I-4135); and (b) interpret each directive purposively, systemically and teleologically, i.e. in accordance with its wording and 'also the context in which it occurs and the objectives pursued by the rules of which it is part' (Case C–306/05 *Sociedad General de Autores y Editores de España (SGAE) v Rafael Hoteles SA* [2006] ECR I-11519 [34]). In addition, Article 267 TFEU requires final domestic courts of appeal to refer any questions of EU law that arise in national proceedings and that are not *acte clair* to the CJEU for determination, and to comply with the CJEU's answers to those questions and with all other CJEU rulings of relevance, even if not strictly within the scope of any questions referred. The last of these obligations was explained by the CJEU in a case involving copyright (Case C–393/09 *Bezpečnostní softwarová asociace—Svaz softwarové ochrany v Ministerstvo kultury* [2001] ECR I-13971) in the following terms ([43]):

> [E]ven if the national court has limited its question to the interpretation of Article 1(2) of [the Software Directive 1991], such a situation does not prevent the Court from providing the national court with all the elements of interpretation of European Union law which may enable it to rule on the case before it, whether or not reference is made thereto in the question referred (see, to that effect, Case C–392/05 *Alevizos* [2007] ECR I-3505, paragraph 64 and the case-law cited).

Also of note is the manner in which the CJEU discharges its obligations under the preliminary referral procedure of Article 267 TFEU, and in particular its propensity to reformulate the questions referred by domestic courts and to comment on the implications of its answers to those questions for the domestic proceedings in which the questions arose. Given the breadth of EU law coverage in the copyright and related rights field, and the number of referrals which are consequently made to the CJEU from domestic courts across the EU, the result is to limit further the scope for national discretion in the interpretation and application of domestic copyright and related rights law, and to support the penetration of that law and its underpinning policy into the copyright and related rights systems of individual Member States.

10.3.2 The European Commission's Copyright and Related Rights Policy Agenda

The development of the EU statutory framework in copyright and related rights can be traced to four key policy documents of the European Commission. The first is its 1991 follow-up to the Green Paper of 1988, which contained a working programme for meeting the challenge posed by technology to the pursuit of a single market by strengthening copyright and related rights protection in Europe.[5] The second is its 1996 follow-up to the Green Paper of 1995, which proposed a single market policy of maintaining and developing further the traditionally high level of copyright protection in Europe amidst a fair balance of rights and interests.[6] The third is its 2009 follow-up to the Green Paper of 2008, which announced a series of preparatory actions for achieving 'a broad dissemination of knowledge in the Single Market, notably in the online environment, ... in the context of existing copyright legislation, [and as part of] an ambitious and comprehensive intellectual property strategy' for Europe.[7] And the fourth is its 2011 strategic vision for delivering a true single market for intellectual property in Europe, which proposed the creation of a comprehensive framework for copyright in the 'Digital Single Market'[8]—defined as

> a market in which the free movement of persons, services and capital is ensured and where the individuals and businesses can seamlessly access and exercise online activities under conditions of fair competition, and a high level of consumer and personal data protection, irrespective of their nationality or place of residence[9]

—pursuant to a strategy adopted on 6 May 2015 that included 'modernising copyright rules in the light of the digital revolution and changed consumer behaviour'.[10]

10.3.2.1 Before 2009: Ensuring a High Level of Protection Amidst a Fair Balance of Rights and Interests and a Broad Dissemination of Knowledge in the Digital Single Market

The context for the first of the European Commission's policy initiatives was the January 1993 deadline that was set by the Single European Act [1987] OJ L 169/1 for completing the internal market (see Section 2.4.2.2.1). That deadline was the trigger for an ambitious harmonization programme detailed in the Commission's 1988 Green Paper Follow-up. There the Commission identified new technologies as: having increased the economic importance of copyright and related rights; internationalized questions of copyright and related rights; and led to 'profound changes in the use made of goods and services with links with copyright, neighbouring rights and the cultural sector in general' ([1.1]). In the Commission's analysis, new technologies represented an opportunity for individuals to increase their quality of life, and a challenge due to their facilitation of 'large-scale and uncontrolled copying of works' ([1.2]). It concluded that, in the face of these considerations, and given the imminent establishment of the

---

[5] Commission Communication of 17 January 1991, 'Follow-up to the Green Paper: Working programme of the commission in the field of copyright and neighbouring rights' COM (90) 584 final (1988 Green Paper Follow-up).

[6] n 2.

[7] Commission Communication of 19 October 2009, 'Copyright in the Knowledge Economy' COM (2009) 532 final (2008 Green Paper Follow-up) 3.

[8] Communication from the Commission to the European Parliament, the Council, the Economic and Society Committee and the Committee of the Regions, 'A Single Market for intellectual property rights boosting creativity and innovation to provide economic growth, high quality jobs and first class products and services in Europe' COM (2011) 287 final.

[9] http://ec.europa.eu/digital-agenda/en/digital-single-market.

[10] Communication from the Commission to the European Parliament, the Council, the European Economic and Society Committee and the Committee of the Regions, 'A Digital Single Market Strategy for Europe' COM (2015) 192 final [2.4].

single market, the Community had 'a duty to act' ([1.3]). It thus committed itself to a harmonization programme guided by two principles: first, the need to strengthen the protection of copyright and related rights throughout the Community; and second, the need for EC action to be comprehensive.

The result of the Commission's 1988 Green Paper Follow-up was an ambitious legislative programme that included proposals for EU directives on rental and lending rights, home copying, database protection, the duration of protection, and satellite and cable transmission rights. With the exception of home copying (on which no action was taken), that programme was implemented with the introduction of the following six copyright and related rights directives between 1991 and 2004:

- the 1991 Software Directive, providing a framework for the protection of original computer programs by literary copyright;

- the 1993 Satellite Broadcasting and Cable Retransmission Directive, establishing an internal market for broadcasting services and a scheme of collective rights management for cable retransmissions;

- the 1993 Term Directive, harmonizing the term of copyright and related rights protection to 70 years from the death of the author and 50 years respectively;

- the 1996 Database Directive, providing a framework for the protection of original databases by literary copyright and database contents by a *sui generis* (database) right;

- the 2001 Resale Right Directive, providing for an author's right to receive a royalty for any resale of her works of graphic or plastic art, subsequent to the works' first transfer by the author; and

- the 2004 Enforcement Directive, providing for harmonized mechanisms for enforcing copyright and related rights, including remedies.

In its 1995 Green Paper Follow-up, the European Commission affirmed its commitment to maintaining and further developing 'the traditionally high level of copyright protection in Europe', citing the nature of copyright as property 'guaranteed by the constitution in many countries', and the need to ensure a favourable environment for creativity and investment ([1.3]). On the other hand, it also recognized the importance of safeguarding 'a fair balance of rights and interests between the different categories of rightholders, as well as between rightholders and rightusers' (ibid). The result was its support for harmonizing further the protection conferred by copyright and related rights at the European and international levels, and addressing questions of enforcement, moral rights, and collective and individual rights management within the internal market. This led directly to the EC's signing of the 1996 WIPO Copyright Treaties (adapting copyright and related rights to the digital environment), and to its passage of the 2001 Information Society Directive (harmonizing the nature and scope of copyright and related rights protection) and the 2007 Rome II Regulation (providing a 'choice of law' exception for IP right infringements to ensure their governance by the law of the protecting state). In 2004, the Commission also issued a communication on the issue of copyright and related rights management.[11] Regarding the contractual licensing of rights by individuals, it decided there was sufficient similarity in the domestic laws of Member States to obviate the need for Community action. By contrast, it called for the introduction of a

---

[11] Communication from the Commission to the Council, the European Parliament and the European Economic and Social Committee, 'The Management of Copyright and Related Rights in the Internal Market' COM (2004) 261 final.

common legal framework governing the management of rights by collecting societies,[12] citing the benefits of Community licensing for the exploitation of rights and completion of the internal market. In the same communication, the Commission also recommended legislative action to promote the cross-border collective management of rights of relevance for online music services.

10.3.2.2 Since 2009: The Movement of Knowledge and Innovation as a Fifth Freedom of the Internal Market

In 2009 the Commission published a follow-up to its 2008 Green Paper on Copyright in the Knowledge Economy. This came two years after it had declared the free movement of knowledge and innovation to be the 'fifth freedom' of the internal market, alongside the free movement of goods, services, labour, and capital.[13] Consistent with that declaration, the Commission's 2008 Green Paper Follow-up focused on ways to achieve a broad dissemination of knowledge in the context of the Information Society Directive and digital technology. In it the Commission identified a tension between the interests and views of rights holders (seeking strong protection mediated via licensing agreements) and society (seeking more limited protection informed by the public interest) respectively, and cast itself the challenge of reconciling those interests through a series of preliminary actions focused on libraries and archives (including e-libraries), orphan works, teaching and research (including open access to publicly funded research and university licensing), access to protected works and subject matter for disabled persons, and licensing measures to support new 'user-created' content.

Since 2009 the European Commission has published several further communications and other policy documents reinforcing its commitment to establishing a copyright and related rights system geared to promoting the free movement of knowledge and innovation throughout EU territory.[14] It has also launched its Europe 2020 initiative, in which it proposed modernizing the framework of copyright as a means of supporting its development of an 'innovation union' to 'improve framework conditions and access to finance for research and innovation so as to ensure that innovative ideas can be turned into products and services that create growth and jobs.'[15] Together, these two objectives account for its most recent initiatives in this area. Of especial

---

[12] A collecting society is an organization that manages the IP rights on behalf of multiple rights owners (the society's members) by negotiating the terms on which the rights may be licensed and collecting the resulting licence fees.

[13] Communication from the Commission to the European Parliament, the Council, the European Economic and Social Committee and the Committee of the Regions, 'A Single Market for the 21st Century Europe' COM (2007) 725 final.

[14] See, e.g., Communication from the Commission, 'Europe 2020: A European strategy for smart, sustainable and inclusive growth' COM (2010) 2020 final (Europe 2020 Strategy); Communication from the Commission to the European Parliament, the Council, the Economic and Society Committee and the Committee of the Regions, 'Towards a Single Market Act—For a highly competitive social market economy—50 proposals for improving our work, business and exchanges with one another' COM (2010) 608 final; Communication from the Commission to the European Parliament, the Council, the Economic and Society Committee and the Committee of the Regions, 'Single Market Act—Twelve levers to boost growth and strengthen confidence—Working together to create new growth' COM (2011) 206 final; Communication from the Commission to the European Parliament, the Council, the Economic and Society Committee and the Committee of the Regions, 'A coherent framework for building trust in the Digital Single Market for e-commerce and online services' COM (2011) 942; Communication from the Commission, 'On content in the Digital Single Market' COM (2012) 789 final.

[15] Europe 2020 Strategy 3.

importance among those initiatives has been the introduction of three new directives since 2011: the Term Amendment Directive, increasing the protection for performers and phonogram producers by extending the term of related rights for phonograms and providing for a reversion of those rights to performers if under-exploited (a so-called use it or lose it requirement); the 2012 Orphan Works Directive, permitting printed, cinematographic, and audiovisual works and phonograms that are 'orphan' to be made available to the public and reproduced for digitization and related purposes by certain public organizations, including publicly accessible libraries; and the 2014 Collective Rights Management Directive, establishing a European framework for the management of copyright and related rights by collecting societies and the licensing of musical copyright for online use. Further actions of importance, such as establishing a legal framework to facilitate the exploitation of protected works and subject matter being stored over the Internet (i.e. in 'the cloud'),[16] and reviewing the Satellite and Cable Directive,[17] are currently pending.

10.3.2.3 Conclusions

The EU statutory framework in copyright and related rights has been driven by the commitment of the European Commission over the past three decades to two things: first, ensuring a high level of protection for authors and other rights holders 'fairly balanced' against protection for third party rights and interests; and second, securing a broad dissemination of knowledge throughout the EU, especially via the Internet. At the legislative level, this commitment has been translated into strong statutory rights for authors and related rights holders offset by a large number of finely tuned exceptions and limitations, and supplemented by rules aimed at facilitating the exploitation of rights in pursuit of social and economic objectives. A particular focus in recent years has been modernizing the copyright and related rights framework in the light of globalization and developing technology, including particularly the Internet. This focus is reflected in the Digital Single Market Strategy of May 2015, where the Commission emphasized the role of copyright to creativity and the European cultural industry, the increasing importance of digital content to the growth of the economy, and the barriers to accessing copyright content across territorial borders that are caused by IP territoriality, contractual arrangements and business practices, and unclear and un-harmonized laws. Its conclusion was that 'Europe needs a more harmonized copyright regime which provides incentives to create and invest while allowing transmission and consumption of content across borders, building on our rich cultural diversity', to which end it committed to undertake the following reform ([2.4]):

> The Commission will make legislative proposals before the end of 2015 to reduce the differences between national copyright regimes and allow for wider online access to works by users across the EU, including through further harmonisation measures. The proposals will include: (i) portability of legally acquired content, (ii) ensuring cross-border access to legally purchased online services while respecting the value of rights in the audiovisual sector, (iii) greater legal certainty for the cross-border use of content for specific purposes (e.g. research, education, text and data mining, etc.) through harmonised exceptions, (iv) clarifying the rules on the activities of intermediaries in relation to copyright-protected content and, in 2016, (v) modernising enforcement of intellectual property rights,

---

[16] See EP resolution of 10 December 2013 on unleashing the potential of cloud computing in Europe (2013/2063(INI)).
[17] (n 8) 7.

focusing on commercial-scale infringements (the 'follow the money' approach) as well as its cross-border applicability.

10.4 The Challenges of Globalization and Developing Technology

In 2012 the European Parliament asserted that 'copyright should be fit for the internet environment and based on social legitimacy, with due respect for fundamental rights'.[18] Aside from reinforcing the policy agenda of the European Commission discussed earlier, this statement points to some of the most enduring themes in this area of IP. These include the ideas of copyright as being 'at war' with technology, as lacking social legitimacy, and as failing to respect fundamental rights. Of central importance to the last of these ideas is the extent to which European law preserves individual freedoms to contract out of copyright and related rights protection.

10.4.1 Copyright's War with Technology

As we saw in Part I, the development of copyright and related rights has been closely connected throughout history to the development of technology. Before the 14th century, the absence of reprographic technology made it possible for authors and others to exclude third parties from using their works sufficiently to protect their commercial and other interests without the need for legal intervention in the form of property rights. Even when unauthorized copying did occur, it was a low-level activity of non-professional users that caused little harm to authors. In the 14th century, printing technology made it more difficult for authors and printers/publishers to exclude third parties from using their works. In addition, when unauthorized copying occurred, it was a high-level activity of professional users. The result was a perceived need for legal intervention to enable the creators and printers/publishers of authorial works to protect their interests; a need met by the introduction of statutory laws of copyright. Finally, in our current era the widespread availability of digital reprographic and communication technologies makes the exclusion of third parties from the unauthorized use of authorial works and related rights subject matter even more difficult. In addition, when unauthorized copying occurs it is a high-level activity of both professional (commercial) and non-professional (individual) users. The result, once again, has been an increasingly perceived need for greater legal intervention to protect authorial and related interests, and a growing conflict between rights holders and the individual 'end users' of protected works and subject matter.

10.4.2 Copyright's Struggle to Maintain Social Legitimacy

One effect of this conflict has been to fuel a view among sections of the public that the impact of copyright on individual rights and freedoms is excessive and unjustified. Regardless of its validity, this view undermines the social legitimacy of copyright, and in doing so makes its enforcement difficult. Lord Macaulay famously expressed the problem in the 18th century when he argued against extending copyright beyond the

---

[18] EP legislative resolution of 11 September 2012 on the Commission Work Programme for 2013 (2012/2688(RSP)) [20].

life of the author on the ground that doing so would cause a public backlash against copyright, which would harm the very authors whose interests it seeks to protect. He wrote:

> At present the holder of copyright has the public feeling on his side. Those who invade copyright are regarded as knaves who take the bread out of the mouths of deserving men. Everybody is well pleased to see them restrained by the law, and compelled to refund their ill-gotten gains. No tradesman of good repute will have anything to do with such dis-graceful transactions. Pass this law: and that feeling is at an end. Men very different from the present race of piratical booksellers will soon infringe this intolerable monopoly. Great masses of capital will be constantly employed in the violation of the law. Every art will be employed to evade legal pursuit; and the whole nation will be in the plot. On which side indeed should the public sympathy be when the question is whether some book as popular as Robinson Crusoe, or the Pilgrim's Progress, shall be in every cot-tage, or whether it shall be confined to the libraries of the rich for the advantage of the great-grandson of a bookseller who, a hundred years before, drove a hard bargain for the copyright with the author when in great distress? Remember too that, when once it ceases to be considered as wrong and discreditable to invade literary property, no person can say where the invasion will stop. The public seldom makes nice distinctions. The wholesome copyright which now exists will share in the disgrace and danger of the new copyright which you are about to create. And you will find that, in attempting to impose unreasonable restraints on the reprinting of the works of the dead, you have, to a great extent, annulled those restraints which now prevent men from pillaging and defrauding the living.[19]

This argument—'that, when once it ceases to be considered as wrong and discreditable to invade literary property, no person can say where the invasion will stop'—offers a possible explanation for the frequently alarming statistics regarding the intentional illegal down-loading of music and films from the Internet,[20] as well as the emphasis placed on the role of education alongside enforcement as a way of reducing the incidence of copyright and related rights infringement.[21]

10.4.3 **Technological Determinism**

Digital technology increases substantially the demand and opportunities for unau-thorized copying and distribution. In addition, however, it makes preventing such acts difficult, among other things by making it easy for infringers to conceal their acts and identities. As we noted in Section 1.2.2.2.1, it was with a view to addressing this difficulty that provisions requiring the protection of rights holders' technological protection meas-ures (and rights management information systems) were included in the Information Society Directive. By helping rights holders to take their own steps to exclude third par-ties from using their works, such provisions relieve the burden on the state of protecting their property interests.

---

[19] T.B. Macaulay, 'A Speech Delivered in the House of Commons on the 5th of February 1841' in *The Miscellaneous Writings, Speeches and Poems of Lord Macaulay* (1880) vol. 3, 149 http://www.yarchive.net/macaulay/copyright.html.

[20] According to one statistic supplied by UK music industry group BPI's Digital Music Nation, 65 per cent of music downloads from the Internet in the UK in 2010 were illegal: I. Hargreaves, 'Digital Opportunity: A Review of Intellectual Property and Growth' (2011) http://www.gov.uk/government/publications/digital-opportunity-review-of-intellectual-property-and-growth [8.11].

[21] See, e.g., L.E. Harris, 'Understanding Copyright—A Life Skill', *WIPO Magazine* (April 2012) http://www.wipo.int/wipo_magazine/en/2012/02/article_0002.html.

The creation of new forms of legal protection for rights holders in response to the challenges of digital technology alludes to a wider phenomenon which may be said to exist in this field. This is the phenomenon of technological determinism, whereby the specific demands of technology are allowed to drive the development of general legal principles. An example is the law's expanding conception of authorial works to include subject matter previously regarded as too insubstantial to support copyright (*de minimis non curat lex*). Specifically, the Internet has spawned a range of media monitoring and other commercial services involving the reproduction and communication to the public of short extracts from newspaper articles and other authorial works, such as films and music. In so doing it has made previously 'trivial' subject matter commercially valuable, increasing the pressure on the law to protect them by copyright in their own right. As we will see in Section 11.3.7.2, this has occurred in Europe with the Court of Justice's recognition that any part of an authorial work is itself an authorial work protected by copyright, independent of the work of which it is a part; a finding first made in a case involving a media monitoring service.[22]

Another example of technological determinism may be provided by the idea/expression distinction, according to which the copyright subsisting in a work protects its expression but not its ideas. As we will see in Chapters 11 and 12, at the European level the idea/expression distinction is given direct statutory expression in the context of computer programs only, in Article 1 Software Directive. In that context it plays the important role of ensuring that the protection conferred on the author of a program is confined to the program's authorial aspects and does not extend to its functional or technical aspects as well. Once given legislative expression, however, the principle risks taking on a life of its own by being applied beyond computer programs to protected subject matter in general, without proper consideration of the consequences of such general application for the conception of authorial works and the coherence of copyright systems in general. In fact, this tendency can be seen in the history of Article 9(2) TRIPS Agreement, according to which copyright protection 'shall extend to expressions and not to ideas, procedures, methods of operation or mathematical concepts as such', which was initially proposed as an exception to the requirement for the recognition of literary copyright in respect of computer programs under Article 10(1) only.[23]

As the reference to Article 9(2) TRIPS Agreement suggests, technological determinism can affect both the courts and the legislature. At the legislative level it may be said to represent a particular risk in Europe currently due to the EU focus on modernizing copyright for the digital environment.[24]

10.4.4 **Replacing Copyright with Ethics and Technology**

Encouraging and facilitating the use of authorial works and related rights subject matter is not the only way in which digital technology threatens copyright. Another way is by disconnecting copyright and related rights from the subject matter they exist to

---

[22] Case C–5/08 *Infopaq International A/S v Danske Dagblades Forening* [2009] ECR I-6569.

[23] See D. Gervais, *The TRIPS Agreement: Drafting History and Analysis* (2nd edn, Sweet & Maxwell, 2003) [2.98]–[2.99].

[24] Jane Ginsburg has criticized the European Copyright Code drafted by the so-called Wittem Group of academics for technological determinism. See J.C. Ginsburg, 'European Copyright Code—Back to First Principles (with Some Additional Detail)' (2011) 58 *Journal of the Copyright Society of the USA* 265.

protect. As John Perry Barlow argued more than ten years ago,[25] the reason for this disconnect is the effect of digitization in undermining the distinction on which copyright rests between the content of an authorial work or other expressive subject matter and its form, and the ability to reproduce and distribute works and subject matter without the need for material packaging, relying instead on patterns of zeros and ones. In Barlow's argument, this requires a fundamental reconception of copyright subject matter from packaged information (authorial works and related rights subject matter) to unpackageable information (communicative activity, life form, and relationship), and an acceptance that such unpackageable information is best protected not by the state through property rights, but by the public through ethics and technology. In calling for greater reliance on the extra-legal mechanisms (social norms and real-space access restrictions) by which objects of value are protected so as to obviate the need for law, this argument brings to mind the copyright paradigm of Lawrence Lessig that we saw in Section 1.2.2.2.[26]

Barlow's argument draws attention to some of the difficulties that face copyright and related rights in the digital environment. Nonetheless, and as others have pointed out,[27] abolishing copyright and related rights as he suggests would almost certainly leave public access to expressive and informational subject matter in the control of wealthy corporations able to afford the most sophisticated technological protection mechanisms. Therefore, to the extent that his proposal is driven by a concern to promote individual freedoms and access to protected material, it would almost certainly fail.

10.4.5 Negotiating the Private and Public Domains: Copyright's Respect for Fundamental Rights

Closely related to accounts of copyright and related rights as being at war with technology are accounts of their negative impact on the public domain. According to Europeana, the European Commission-funded digital library, museum, and music archive, the public domain:

> comprises all the knowledge and information—including books, pictures and audiovisual works—which does not have copyright protection and can be used without restriction, subject in some European countries to the author's perpetual moral rights. The Public Domain provides a historically developed balance to the rights of creators protected by copyright and it is essential to the cultural memory and knowledge base of our societies. The Public Domain covers two categories of material: 1. Works on which copyright protection has expired....2. The essential commons of information that is not covered by copyright.[28]

As an organizing mechanism for copyright, the distinction between the public and private domains is not particularly helpful, since—and as the Europeana definition illustrates—it depends on a definition of copyright. Nonetheless, the distinction has value in focusing attention on the regulatory function of copyright and related rights and their impact on '[t]he cultural memory and knowledge base of our societies.' In

---

[25] J.P. Barlow, 'The Economy of Ideas: Selling Wine Without Bottles on the Global Net' (1992/3) https://homes.eff.org/~barlow/EconomyOfIdeas.html.

[26] See L. Lessig, *Code Version 2* (Basic Books, 2006) 171.

[27] e.g., H. Wiese, 'The Justification of the Copyright System in the Digital Age' [2002] *EIPR* 387.

[28] The Europeana Public Domain Charter http://pro.europeana.eu/files/Europeana_Professional/Publications/Public%20Domain%20Charter%20-%20EN.pdf.

so doing it connects to the wider question of whether the law in this field reflects 'due respect for fundamental rights'.

An initial issue in answering this question is what fundamental rights copyright and related rights engage and should therefore pay 'due respect' to. A natural starting point for considering this issue is with the two fundamental rights instruments that purport to express the European community's basic values: the ECHR and the CFR. Of especial relevance among the provisions of the second of these instruments in particular are the rights of authors and others to protection of their subsisting IP rights (Article 17(2)),[29] and the rights of individuals and the public in general to respect for private and family life, home, and communications (Article 7), freedom of expression (Article 11), education (Article 14), respect for cultural, religious, and linguistic diversity (Article 22), and measures to ensure the independence, social and occupational integration and participation in community life of disabled persons (Article 26).

As the previous discussion illustrates, the European law of copyright and related rights is frequently cast as existing to ensure a fair balance between competing rights and interests. At the legislative level, this can be said to explain the scope of rights conferred on authors and related rights holders, the large number of finely tuned exceptions and limitations to those rights, and the additional rules aimed at facilitating their commercial exploitation in pursuit of general social and economic objectives, such as disseminating knowledge and creating a favourable environment for creativity and investment. In addition, and as we will see in Chapter 13, the view of European law in this area as existing to balance competing rights and interests is the starting point for the CJEU's interpretation of the exceptions and limitations to copyright and related rights. One effect of this has been the Court's view that *all* fundamental rights and interests engaged by a defendant's use of a protected work or subject matter must be considered before deciding whether the use falls within a statutory exception or limitation permitted by EU law, and not merely those fundamental rights and interests which underpin the exception or limitation in question. Thus, under European law, the purpose of copyright and related rights exceptions and limitations is not merely to protect third party interests and rights, such as freedom of expression, but also to provide a site for ensuring sufficient protection for the rights and interests of owners themselves, including rights and interests other than IP protection. This was made clear in Case C–201/13 *Deckmyn v Vandersteen* EU:C:2014:2132, where the CJEU held that when deciding whether a parody involving the unauthorized use of a copyright work avoids liability for copyright infringement under a domestic exception permitted by Article 5(2)(k) Information Society Directive, domestic courts must consider any effect which the parody might have in associating the author of the protected work with a discriminatory message within the meaning of Article 21 CFR.[30] The decision underlines the ease with which the concept of 'balance' can be used as a rhetorical device to justify limiting or expanding authors' rights.[31]

Central to the question whether the European law in this area reflects due respect for fundamental rights is the extent to which it enables those statutory provisions most protective of such rights—such as the exceptions and limitations provided for by Article 5

---

[29] On the scope of corresponding Article 1 of Protocol 1 ECHR, see Section 3.1.

[30] Article 21(1) prohibits 'discrimination based on any ground such as sex, race, colour, ethnic or social origin, genetic features, language, religion or belief, political or any other opinion, membership of a national minority, property, birth, disability, age or sexual orientation'.

[31] Once again, Jane Ginsburg made this point in her critique of the Wittem Group's European Copyright Code (n 24), albeit this time drawing attention to the invocation of notions of 'balance' to support restrictions on authors' rights.

Information Society Directive—to remain unimplemented by Member States and/or overridden by contract.

10.4.6 Preserving Individuals' Freedom to Contract Out of Copyright and Related Rights

As we saw in Chapter 3, copyright and related rights—like other IP rights—are exclusionary rights that operate by creating a false scarcity with respect to the authorial works and subject matter they protect so as to enable those works and subject matter to be exploited in the manner of tangible goods. And as for tangible goods, the primary mechanism for effecting such exploitation is contract. Indeed, contract plays an even greater role in the context of copyright and related rights than in the context of tangible goods because of the traditional dependence of authors and related rights holders on third parties, such as publishers, galleries, producers, and other middlemen, to make their works and subject matter available to the public. This means that in addition to contractual arrangements between the rights holder and individual end users of the protected work or subject matter, there are also typically contractual arrangements between the rights holder on the one hand and the publisher or other producer or distributor of the work or subject matter on the other.

Territorial restrictions on domestic copyright and related rights, combined with EU competition and free movement principles, increase further the importance of contractual arrangements for ensuring the establishment and smooth functioning of a market in those rights and the subject matter to which they attach. This is recognized explicitly by European legislation. For example, recital 9 Satellite and Cable Directive states:

> Whereas the development of the acquisition of rights on a contractual basis by authorization is already making a vigorous contribution to the creation of the desired European audiovisual area; whereas the continuation of such contractual agreements should be ensured and their smooth application in practice should be promoted wherever possible[.]

So too the Information Society Directive explicitly envisages the possibility of copyright and related rights being exploitable by contract in its statements that '[t]he rights referred to in this Directive may be transferred, assigned or subject to the granting of contractual licences, without prejudice to the relevant national legislation on copyright and related rights' (recital 30), and that '[t]he exceptions and limitations [to copyright and related rights] referred to in Article 5(2), (3) and (4) should not...prevent the definition of contractual relations designed to ensure fair compensation for the rightholders insofar as permitted by national law' (recital 45).

Consistent with the position envisaged by EU law, most European (EU and non-EU) states conceive copyright and related rights as property rights capable of being dealt with in the manner of other (personal) property rights. Above all, this means that their ownership may be transferred by assignment to a third party, approximating the sale of tangible goods, and that it devolves on death as part of the rights owner's estate. There are however exceptions to this. One arises under the laws of Germany and Austria, which prohibit outright assignments of copyright in reflection of their conception of it as a species of (inalienable) personal right. Another is authors' moral rights and artists' resale right, which may not be assigned under the laws of any European (EU or non-EU) state for similar reasons, consistent with Articles 6*bis* and 14*ter* Berne Convention and, for EU Member States, Article 1(1) Resale Right Directive. By contrast, all European states—including Germany and Austria—permit the licensing of copyright and of all related rights other than moral rights and the resale right. Instead of transferring ownership of the IP right as such, a licence confers a contractual interest with respect to that right that is enforceable between the licensing parties and that enables the licensee to do one or more of the acts with respect to the protected work or subject matter from which he is ordinarily excluded by the copyright or related rights. A licence may be exclusive to the licensee, in which case it will resemble an assignment, or non-exclusive.

To a large extent, domestic law recognizes the freedom of parties to determine their own contractual arrangements with respect to copyright and related rights. The premise of that recognition is that each contracting party can be expected to have sufficient bargaining power vis-à-vis the other to negotiate terms that reflect and protect his own commercial and other interests. The reality, however, will often be different, with authors frequently the weaker party in negotiations with publishers and other middlemen, and end users frequently the weaker party in negotiations with rights holders. Indeed, publishing and other exploitation contracts will often be offered to authors and other rights holders on a 'take it or leave it' basis, as will access by end users to protected works and subject matter. This creates two types of risk. The first is that authors and end users will be unable to negotiate a fair price for the assignment or licensing of copyright or related rights or, in the case of end users, for securing access to a protected work or subject matter. And the second is that authors and end users will be denied the protections of copyright and related rights legislation itself, including those regarding moral rights (for authors) and exceptions and limitations (for end users). It is in contexts such as this that one sees the importance of understanding the purpose of those moral rights and exceptions and limitations, and the values and interests that they exist to protect. For example, if their purpose is to protect fundamental rights such as human dignity and freedom of expression, it is not obvious that the law should permit their alienation and abandonment by contract. Indeed, even requiring members of the public to pay for access to works and subject matter could be said to undermine copyright and related rights legislation by preventing individuals from exercising their freedom to make such use of works and subject matter as that legislation permits, including their freedom to read literary works and listen to music.

In fact, all states go to some lengths to protect individuals from submitting to unfair contractual arrangements. While the mechanisms deployed to that end vary considerably, they include the following:

- requiring that assignments and/or certain licences of copyright and related rights be concluded in writing;
- restricting the freedom of authors and others to effect a future transfer of copyright or related rights in works or other subject matter not yet created or produced;
- prohibiting transfers of certain rights, such as (most commonly) authors' moral rights;
- providing for a reversion of assigned or licensed rights to their initial beneficiary in the event that they are insufficiently exploited by their assignee or licensee;
- providing for a restrictive interpretation of contractual assignments and licences, and for the implication into such assignments and licences of certain terms protective of the initial rights owners' interests; and
- prohibiting certain standard form end user agreements.

Some of these mechanisms are also required by European (EU) copyright and related rights legislation itself. For example, the Database Directive expressly prohibits the overriding of exceptions to database copyright by declaring '[a]ny contractual provision contrary to [those exceptions] null and void' (Article 15), as does the Software Directive for exceptions to software copyright (Article 8; see also Article 5(2)). In addition, the Term Amendment Directive 2011 provides for the reversion of related rights subsisting in the fixation of a performance to the performer if the phonogram producer to whom they have been transferred fails to make the phonogram sufficiently available to the public after 50 years. And finally, the Resale Right Directive prevents the author of a work to which the resale right applies from transferring or waiving in advance that right (Article 1(1)). For the most part, however, and these exceptions aside, European copyright and related rights legislation is expressed as being 'without prejudice to . . . the law of contract' (see, e.g., Article 8 Software Directive; Article 9 Information Society Directive; Article 13 Database Directive). The possibility that this creates for the exceptions and limitations to copyright and related rights recognized by the Information Society Directive to be overridden by private agreement has been widely criticized, as has the ability of authors in some EU Member States to waive their moral rights. In the context of an EU legal order increasingly concerned with the protection of fundamental rights, and long willing to regulate the exercise of copyright and related rights with a view to protecting free movement and competition principles, these criticisms are compelling. In the case of contractual overrides at least, the problem has also been long recognized by the Commission. Indeed, and as we saw earlier, addressing contract-based impediments to the cross-border use of copyright content for research, education, and other purposes is among the reforms to which the Commission has committed in its 2015 Digital Single Market strategy.

10.5 Conclusions

In Europe and elsewhere, copyright and related rights confer a time-limited right to exclude others from doing certain acts in respect of authorial works and other expressive subject matter, subject to various public interest exceptions and limitations. In Europe they are domestic rights conferred under the laws of individual states and confined in their effects to the territorial boundaries of the conferring state. There thus exist 28 national copyright and related rights systems in the EU currently, each with its own governing legislation and case law. Nonetheless, the substantive differences between these systems have been significantly reduced as a result of nearly 30 years of active EU law- and policy-making. The products of that activity to date include several communications by the European Commission, more than 12 harmonizing directives by the Parliament and Council, ratification of several international agreements, and a substantial body of case law from the CJEU. Together these legal and policy sources cover almost all aspects of the law of copyright and related rights, making it among the most Europeanized of IP fields.

While the EU law of copyright and related rights is extensive in coverage, it is not exhaustive. On the other hand, the extent of Member States' residual competence (legal authority) in this field is unclear, due in part to the uncertainty regarding the nature and extent of the gaps in the EU legislative framework itself, and in part to the disagreement regarding the competence of the Court of Justice to fill those gaps by means of its case law. Three areas that EU law does leave largely untouched are the recognition and protection of rights in respect of live public performances of copyright works and showings of related rights subject matter, the recognition and protection of authors' moral rights, and the contractual licensing of copyright and related rights by individuals. On the other hand, all European states are subject to international obligations regarding the recognition and protection of authors' and performers' moral rights, and general EU legal principles of exhaustion and competition go some distance in regulating the exploitation of IP rights by contract.

The EU's policy agenda in the copyright and related rights field has remained largely unchanged since the 1980s. Four concerns can be seen to have driven that agenda. The first is to ensure a high level of protection for copyright and related rights, consistent with their nature as property rights and associated constitutional protections, and with the perceived link between such protection and other European social and economic policy objectives such as promoting creativity and innovation. The second is to support EU autonomy by ensuring that legislative action in this field is comprehensive and consistent with existing European concepts and policies. The third is to adapt copyright and related rights to meet the challenges and exploit the economic and social opportunities presented by digital technology. And the fourth is to ensure a fair balance of competing rights and interests—including particularly fundamental rights and freedoms—in respect of authorial works and related rights subject matter. In addressing these concerns, the EU has also been mindful of the need to ensure that copyright and related rights are based on social legitimacy.

The legal complexity created by the existence of a large number of piecemeal directives in the European copyright and related rights field, combined with the impediments posed by the territorial restrictions on their scope to individuals' ability to access products and services online, has led to calls for the creation of a single copyright and related rights title in Europe.[32] The European Commission is currently considering these calls as part of its review and modernization of the EU copyright and related rights framework in connection with the Europe 2020 initiative. Among other things, the introduction of a copyright and related rights regulation would put the existing statutory and case law on a firmer legislative basis, reduce the fragmentation in the current EU statutory regime, and perhaps abolish once and for all copyright and related rights territoriality. It would also reduce further the role of domestic legislatures and courts in this area of IP, including by regulating the exploitation of copyright and related rights and, in doing so, clarifying the extent to which the provisions of copyright and related rights legislation may be overridden by private agreement between rights holders and other parties.

Further Reading

AREZZO, E., 'Competition and Intellectual Property Protection in the Market for the Provision of Multi-Territorial Licensing of Online Rights in Musical Works—Lights and Shadows of the New European Directive 2014/26/EU' [2015] *IIC* 534

CASO, R. AND GIOVANELLA, F. (eds), *Balancing Copyright Law in the Digital Age: Comparative Perspectives* (Springer, 2015)

COOK, T. AND DERCLAYE, A., 'An EU Copyright Code: What and How, if Ever?' [2011] *IPQ* 259

ELKIN-KOREN, N., 'Copyrights in Cyberspace—Rights Without Laws?' (1998) 73 *Chicago-Kent Law Review* 1155

FARRAND, B., 'The Digital Agenda for Europe, the Economy and its Impact Upon the Development of EU Copyright Policy' in I. Stamatoudi and P. Torremans (eds), *EU Copyright Law: A Commentary* (Edward Elgar, 2014) 988

---

[32] Directorate General for Internal Market and Services of the European Commission, 'Report on the responses to the Public Consultation on the Review of the EU Copyright Rules' (July 2014) http://ec.europa. eu/internal_market/consultations/2013/copyright-rules/docs/contributions/consultation-report_en.pdf.

GRIFFITHS, J., 'Constitutionalising or Harmonising? The Court of Justice, the Right to Property and European Copyright Law' [2013] *European Law Review* 65

GUIBAULT, L.M.C.R., *Copyright Limitations and Contracts: An Analysis of the Contractual Overridability of Limitations on Copyright* (Kluwer International Law, 2002)

HILTY, R.M., 'Intellectual Property and the European Community's Internal Market Legislation—Copyright in the Internal Market—Harmonisation vs. Community Copyright Law' [2004] *IIC* 760

KLASS, N. AND RUPP, H., 'Europeana, ARROW and Orphan Works: Bringing Europe's Cultural Heritage Online' in I. Stamatoudi and P. Torremans (eds), *EU Copyright Law: A Commentary* (Edward Elgar, 2014) 946

KOELMAN, K.J., 'Copyright Law and Economics in the Directive: Is the Droit d'Auteur Passé?' [2004] *IIC* 603

MATULIONYTE, R., 'The Upcoming EU Copyright Review: A Central-Eastern European Perspective' [2015] *IIC* 439

RAMALHO, A., 'Conceptualising the European Union's Competence in Copyright—What Can the EU Do?' [2014] *IIC* 178

11

The Subsistence and Ownership of Copyright and Related Rights

11.1 Introduction

Under the domestic laws of European and other states, the subsistence of copyright and related rights requires three things: (a) the existence of a subject matter of protectable type; (b) that is sufficiently connected to the territory of the protecting state; and (c) that satisfies any applicable formalities. For EU Member States, the principles governing each of these requirements have been largely harmonized by a combination of international and EU instruments and associated case law. The result is a body of accumulated EU law (*acquis communautaire*) requiring the recognition and protection of authorial works by copyright and of certain other categories of expressive subject matter by related rights provided they are sufficiently connected to EU territory.

In this chapter we consider the European legal requirements for copyright and related rights subsistence and the beneficiaries of the resulting protection. Central in this regard is the definition of copyright-protectable subject matter. To some extent this definition aims at restricting the availability of copyright to intellectual products. However, it also aims at ensuring that the intellectual products in question are appropriate for protection by copyright specifically, rather than (or in addition to) some other species of IP right, such as a patent, registered trade mark or design right, or *sui generis* database right. As we saw in Section 3.2, distinguishing features of the subject matter protected by copyright and related rights are their objectively discernible form, their origination from one or more identifiable human creators, and their expressive value and significance. Even with this understanding, however, identifying the essential properties or constitutive features of authorial works is difficult, and so too it follows from this difficulty is identifying the essential properties of subject matter suitable for copyright.

11.2 The Requirements for Subsistence

11.2.1 Preliminary Remarks

Under the domestic laws of EU and non-EU European states, copyright and related rights subsist in any subject matter that: (a) is of a protectable type; (b) is sufficiently connected to the territory of the protecting state; and (c) satisfies any applicable formalities. For EU Member States, each of these requirements is subject to EU law provision. For example, the Software, Database, Term, and Information Society Directives require that Member States recognize and protect:

- authorial works—including original computer programs, databases, and photographs—by copyright; and

- phonograms, first fixations of films (and copies thereof), performances and fixations of performances, broadcasts and fixations of broadcasts, certain databases, and previously unpublished works first published or communicated to the public after their copyright has expired, by related rights,

and limit the formalities that may be imposed as a precondition to such protection. In addition, Article 18 TFEU provides that '[w]ithin the scope of application of the Treaties', which scope includes the recognition and protection of EU citizens' copyright and related rights, 'and without prejudice to any special provisions contained therein, any discrimination on grounds of nationality shall be prohibited'. In the current chapter, each of these EU legal provisions is considered. Before embarking on that consideration, however, a note is required regarding the distinction between the authorial works protectable by copyright and the other categories of subject matter protectable by related rights.

11.2.2 The Distinction Between Copyright Works and Related Rights Subject Matter

This distinction is foundational to the European copyright and related rights regime, and reflects the substantively different nature of each type of subject matter and the rights they attract. Broadly speaking, authorial works are intangible creations of a person meriting the title 'author', such as poems, dances, and musical tunes, while most related rights subject matter are recordings or communications of expressive content produced or otherwise brought into existence by persons other than authors. While authors receive the 'deep' protection of copyright, including the right to prevent non-mechanical and non-literal reproductions of their protected works, related rights owners receive the 'shallower' protection of related rights, confined in most cases to the tangible form of their subject matter and not extending to the content which those subject matter record. The difference may be illustrated by the examples of a sonata and a phonogram recording it. As an authorial work, a sonata will be protected by copyright, in contrast to a phonogram, which will be protected by related rights. Copyright in the sonata will entitle the copyright holder to prevent both mechanical reproductions—for example, digital recordings of it being performed or photocopies of the score on which it is recorded—as well as non-mechanical reproductions—for example, recreations of it by a pianist which are then recorded. By contrast, related rights in the phonogram will entitle the rights holder to prevent only mechanical reproductions of the phonogram itself, and not recreations of the sonata which it records.

It is not always clear from the nature of a subject matter which species of right subsists in it. An example is photographs, which share the materiality of phonograms and other related rights subject matter, but which are nonetheless protected by copyright as authorial works. It follows that the creator of a photograph will be able to prevent third parties from recreating its image, either by reconstructing the scene and retaking the photograph, or by depicting it in another artistic medium such as pastel or paint, in addition to preventing third parties from reproducing the image by mechanical (including digital) means, such as by scanning it. Further, some subject matter are protected by both species of right, i.e. by copyright as well as related rights. An example is databases, which attract copyright as authorial works and related rights as products of substantial investment in the obtaining, verification, and presentation of their contents.

11.2.3 The Importance of Identifying Clearly the Work or Subject Matter in Question

Regardless of the species of right in question, it is important to begin all copyright and related rights analyses by identifying clearly the individual work or subject matter in which copyright or related rights is alleged to subsist, and to be clear about how the work or subject matter is conceived, and what it does and does not include for copyright and related rights purposes. For example, if a novel for copyright purposes is merely a form of expression and does not include its underlying plot, then the intellectual investment in conceiving that plot for expression will neither count when determining the novel's entitlement to protection nor support a claim of joint authorship of the novel and ownership of its copyright; and reproducing the plot will not infringe the copyright owner's rights. As will be seen in Section 12.2.6.2, novels do include their plots and other non-literal elements for copyright purposes, in some European states at least, with the result that the unauthorized reproduction of such elements may infringe their copyright. Not all authorial works are so expansively conceived, however. Examples of works which are not so conceived are databases and computer programs, which do not include their contents (for databases) or underlying ideas and principles (for computer programs), with the result that such elements must be excluded from copyright subsistence and infringement analyses involving those categories of authorial work. This reflects the fundamental principle of EU law that works and subject matter are protected only in their capacity as such. Thus, a computer program is protected by copyright in its capacity as an authorial work, as distinct from a technical or functional object, and its protection by copyright is defined accordingly; and so too for databases, as seen above. In this respect, European copyright law follows European patent law in only protecting subject matter in its particular conception as a work of protectable (here, copyrightable) type (see Section 6.4.1.2).

11.3 Authorial Works Protectable by Copyright

11.3.1 The Statutory Framework

11.3.1.1 The International Framework

All European states have international obligations to ensure copyright and moral rights protection for authorial works. Of especial importance is the Berne Convention, which requires Berne Union states to recognize and protect copyright in the following categories of 'protected works' (see Article 2):

- literary or artistic works, including any literary, dramatic, musical, artistic, or other original expressive subject matter, and in particular any literary work ('writing'), dramatic work, musical work, cinematographic work, artistic work (including photographs and works of applied art), informational/utilitarian work (e.g. maps and sketches), and 'other production in the literary, scientific, and artistic domain, whatever may be the mode or form of its expression';
- alterations of such (literary or artistic) works; and
- collections of such (literary or artistic) works that constitute 'intellectual creation'.

In addition, Berne Union states must exclude 'news of the day [and] miscellaneous facts having the character of mere items of press information' from copyright protection on the ground that they lack the authorial character of a protectable (authorial) work (Article 2(8)).

The TRIPS Agreement 1994 and WCT reinforce and supplement these obligations. Specifically, their provisions require that contracting parties:

(a) comply with Articles 1 to 21 Berne Convention (with an exception under TRIPS for Article 6*bis* regarding authors' moral rights);

(b) exclude 'ideas, procedures, methods of operation [and] mathematical concepts as such' from copyright protection; and

(c) protect 'computer programs...as literary works under the Berne Convention' and 'compilations of data or other materials...which by reason of the selection or arrangement of their contents constitute intellectual creations'. (See Articles 9 and 10 TRIPS Agreement and Articles 1(4), 2, 4, and 5 WCT.)

The result is an expansive definition of the subject matter which European (and other) states must protect by copyright, extending to all authorial works, or intellectual creations, 'whatever may be the mode or form of [their] expression'.

11.3.1.2 The European (EU) Framework

At the European level, too, this definition is entrenched by legislation requiring EU Member States to ensure copyright protection for all protected works within the meaning of Article 2 Berne Convention, including (by express provision) all databases, photographs, and computer programs that are original in the sense of expressing the intellectual creation of an author, as 'authorial works'. This requirement is consistent with the aim of EU copyright law to ensure a high level of protection *for authors*, and is expressed in Articles 2 to 4 Information Society Directive, as well as in a number of other EU directives. For example:

- the Term Directive requires Member States to ensure that '[t]he rights of an author of a literary or artistic work within the meaning of Article 2 Berne Convention shall run for the life of the author and for 70 years after his death' (Article 1(1)), and that '[p]hotographs which are original in the sense that they are the author's own intellectual creation shall be protected in accordance with Article 1';
- the Software Directive requires Member States to 'protect computer programs, by copyright, as literary works within the meaning of the Berne Convention', provided they are 'original in the sense that [they are] the author's own intellectual creation' (Article 1); and

- the Database Directive requires that collections of independent works, data, and other materials (databases) 'which, by reason of the selection or arrangement of their contents, constitute the author's own intellectual creation...be protected as such by copyright' (Article 3(3)), mirroring Article 2(5) Berne Convention.

The result once again is an expansive definition of the subject matter protectable by copyright that includes any and all authorial works, where by 'authorial works' is meant *original* works, i.e. works that express an author's own intellectual creation, including those protected by other IP rights, such as unregistered designs (see Case C–168/09 *Flos SpS v Semeraro Casa e Famiglia SpA* [2011] ECR I-181 [34]; Chapter 19). In contrast is the position under Article 17 Designs Directive, which requires that a design protected by a design right registered in or in respect of a Member State in accordance with the Directive be eligible for protection by copyright under the laws of that state to the extent and on the conditions determined by the Member State.

11.3.2 Distinguishing Authorial (Original) From Non-Authorial (Unoriginal) Works Protectable by Copyright

The interpretation of the EU statutory provisions outlined in the preceding section as requiring the protection by copyright of any and all works that express an author's own intellectual creation has been repeatedly affirmed by the Court of Justice in a series of decisions since 2009, beginning with Case C–5/08 *Infopaq International A/S v Danske Dagblades Forening* [2009] ECR I-6569 (*Infopaq*). According to those decisions, for a subject matter to satisfy this description it must be a bounded expressive object (a work) that can be said to have resulted from an author's free and creative choices and to bear her personal mark. Determining whether a subject matter satisfies this test is a two-stage process that involves deciding whether it is of a type the creation of which leaves scope for free and creative choices, and if it is, the extent if any to which that scope has been exploited by the alleged author of the work in the course of creating it such that the work bears her personal mark. As shown in Figure 11.1, the first of these stages establishes whether the subject matter is of a type capable of supporting copyright, and the second establishes whether it and the manner of its creation are such as to trigger its protection by copyright. As the CJEU has confirmed, this is an expansive definition of 'authorial work' that is capable of including any type of expression the origination (bringing into existence) of which leaves scope for the exercise of free and creative choices.

Few subject matter will fail to satisfy this test so as to be unprotectable by copyright. One obvious example of a subject matter that will fail to satisfy it is ideas, including ideas for an authorial work, such as the plot of a novel or the theme for a television series. The reason is that unless and until they are expressed, ideas are not bounded expressive objects (works) (see Section 3.2). It is therefore only through its authorial expression that an idea can be protected by copyright. This offers one explanation for the principle of Article 9(2) TRIPS Agreement, that '[c]opyright protection shall extend to expressions and not to ideas...as such'.

Aside from ideas, only two categories of subject matter have been held by the Court of Justice to be incapable of satisfying the requirement for an authorial work: individual words (and other building blocks of expression) and sporting events. According to its decision in Joined Cases C–403/08 *Football Association Premier League Ltd v QC Leisure* and 429/08 *Karen Murphy v Media Protection Services Ltd* [2011] ECR I-9083 (*FAPL*), for example, football games and other sporting events are so constrained by the rules of the game as to leave 'no room for creative freedom for the purposes of copyright' ([98]).

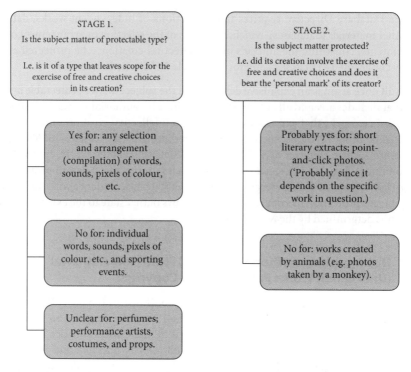

Figure 11.1 The CJEU's two-stage test for identifying an authorial work

Thus, they fail the CJEU's test for the existence of an authorial work at its first stage. So too the Court held in *Infopaq* that words 'are not as such an intellectual creation of the author who employs them', since '[i]t is only through the choice, sequence and combination of…words that the author may express his creativity in an original manner and achieve a result which is an intellectual creation' ([45]). Thus, and like sporting events, individual words are not protectable by copyright. By contrast are short literary phrases, which the Court held in *Infopaq* to be capable of expressing an author's own intellectual creation and thus to be works of authorship. It seems clear that this applies equally in respect of other expressive elements and selections and combinations of them, such as individual sounds and short musical phrases respectively. For example, in *FAPL* the Advocate General expressed the opinion, referring to *Infopaq*, that the individual pixels of colour that make up a digital image are not themselves protectable by copyright, since it is the act of bringing them together into the image that represents the author's own intellectual creation, and not the individual pixels themselves. It follows that such pixels are not authorial works protectable by copyright, in contrast to the photographic image or film frame in which they are combined, which can be.

In conclusion, the CJEU in *Infopaq* and *FAPL* identified certain subject matter which are not protectable by copyright. Nonetheless, the premise of the Court's decision in each case was an expansive definition of authorial work as potentially including *any* selection and arrangement of any words, sounds or other expressive elements that leave scope for the exercise of free and creative choices. It was with reference to this definition that the Court of Justice in Case C–145/10 *Painer v Standard VerlagsGmbH* [2011] ECR I-12533 (*Painer*) confirmed that simplicity is no bar to protection by copyright. That case involved a preliminary referral from the Handelsgericht Wien (Commercial Court of Vienna) in domestic proceedings involving the photographic portrait of Natascha Kampusch

Figure 11.2 The work at issue in *Painer*

Photograph by Eva-Maria Painer, © Eva-Maria Painer. The original work is in colour, and has been reproduced here in black and white.

reproduced in Figure 11.2. One of the issues referred to the Court was whether such a portrait was too simple to support copyright. According to the Court it was not, since the creator of a photographic portrait 'can make free and creative choices in several ways and at various points in its production' so as to 'stamp the work created with his "personal touch"' ([92]). Given this, and consistent with the definition of authorial works outlined earlier, photographic portraits were held to be capable of protection by copyright. In addition, the Court of Justice confirmed in *Painer* that where a photograph *is* an authorial work protected by copyright, the simplicity or realism of its subject matter will not in any way limit the scope or depth of its resulting copyright protection, since copyright protects all authorial works equally. This is consistent with the general EU legal principle of equal treatment—also enshrined in Article 20 CFR—which requires that comparable situations not be treated differently unless the difference is objectively justified. While not referred to expressly by the Court in *Painer*, this principle has recently been invoked in Case C–463/12 *Copydan Båndkopi v Nokia Danmark A/S* EU:C:2015:144 to support an interpretation of the Information Society Directive as requiring that different technological components be treated comparably for the purpose of domestic private copying levies, and supports the Court's reasoning in the *Painer* case. Specifically, it explains the Court's rejection of the argument presented to it that the Information Society Directive, in the light of the constitutional protection afforded to IP by Article 1 of Protocol 1 ECHR and

Article 17(2) CFR, should be interpreted to mean that portrait photographs in particular 'are afforded "weaker" copyright protection or no copyright protection at all against adaptation because, in view of their "realistic image", the degree of formative freedom is too minor' ([43]).

11.3.3 Photographs and Films (Cinematographic or Audiovisual Works) Can Be Authorial Works

11.3.3.1 Photographs as Authorial Works

The decision of the Court of Justice in *Painer* is consistent with Article 6 Term Directive, which requires Member States to ensure copyright for photographs 'which are original in the sense that they are the author's own intellectual creation' as literary or artistic works within the meaning of Article 2 Berne Convention. It suggests that even 'point-and-click' photographs will be protectable by copyright provided their creator exploited the scope which such photography offers for making free and creative choices to produce an image that bears her personal mark. This test will almost certainly be satisfied in any situation in which a person has consciously influenced the final visual form of the photographic image by means of her decision-making in the course of creating it. Consistent with this, the fact that she did not herself press the shutter button on the camera should not prevent her from being regarded as the sole or joint author of the photograph, and nor conversely should pressing the shutter button automatically make her the author of the image entitled to photographic copyright.

Since the Court's decision in the *Painer* case, the Paris Tribunal de Grande Instance (High Court of First Instance of Paris), in a surprising and surely incorrect decision of 21 May 2015, has held the well-known photograph of Jimi Hendrix by Gered Mankowitz reproduced in Figure 11.3 not to be an authorial work within the meaning of EU law

Figure 11.3 The work at issue in the *Hendrix* case

Photograph by Gered Mankowitz, © Bowstir Ltd. 2015/Mankowitz.com.

protected by French copyright. According to the Court, when applying the EU test of copyright subsistence a distinction must be drawn between the aesthetic characteristics of the relevant work and its originality. For a photograph to be an authorial work following *Painer*, the Court held, its visual aspects—including in the case of the Mankowitz photograph, the pose, costume, and demeanour of the subject, as well as the framing, use of black and white, and the picture's lighting—must be due to choices made by the alleged author specifically, and thus reflect his personal imprint, rather than being due to choices made by (and reflecting the imprint of) Jimi Hendrix himself.

11.3.3.2 Films as Authorial Works

It seems clear that the same principles as apply for photographs apply for films within the meaning of Article 2(c) Rental and Lending Rights Directive, namely, any 'cinematographic or audiovisual work or moving images, whether or not accompanied by sound'. The reason is Article 2 Term Directive, which defines the authors of cinematographic or audiovisual works and the term of copyright in such works as lasting for the same period as copyright in other authorial works. Further, the Berne Convention includes 'cinematographic works to which are assimilated works expressed by a process analogous to cinematography' within its definition of literary or artistic work (Article 2(1)), and expressly requires that 'a cinematographic work be protected by copyright as an original work', and that the owner of such copyright 'enjoy the same rights as the author of an original work' (Article 14*bis*(1)).

11.3.3.3 Photographic and Film Scenes as Authorial Works

One issue that the European provisions regarding photographic and film copyright raises is whether the recorded content of a film or photograph might itself attract copyright as an authorial work separate from any copyright subsisting in the film or photograph itself. While this has not yet been considered by the Court of Justice, a photographic or film scene plainly leaves scope for free and creative choices in the course of its creation, and would thus seem to be capable of satisfying the CJEU's definition of authorial works discussed earlier, provided it is sufficiently contained to be regarded as a bounded expressive object (i.e. a work). (Once again, this is a restatement of the idea in Section 3.2 that a defining feature of an intellectual product is its possession of an objectively discernible form.) In addition, while it is true that the protection conferred by copyright in a photograph or film will extend to the scenes depicted in the work as part of the photograph or film, and that the creators of such scenes will be among the initial owners of the works' copyright, this did not prevent the CJEU from deciding in *Infopaq* that short sequences of words contained in a longer literary work are themselves authorial works protectable by copyright, and should therefore not be relevant. While the question might seem an academic one, it will be important where a person reproduces a scene without also reproducing the photograph or film itself. An example is where copying takes place before the photograph or film has itself been created, as occurred in the UK case of *Creation Records v News Group Newspapers* [1977] EMLR 444 (Ch).

11.3.3.4 Non-Authorial Photographs and Films as Protectable by Related Rights

In addition to the copyright subsisting in films and original photographs, EU law expressly permits Member States to protect unoriginal photographs by related rights (Article 6 Term Directive), and requires that Member States protect first fixations of films and copies thereof by such rights as well (Articles 2 and 3 Information Society Directive). Implicit is a two-tier scheme for the protection of films and photographs that mirrors the scheme for databases described earlier, namely, copyright for films and photographs as authorial works, and related rights for first fixations of films and non-authorial photographs.

11.3.4 Perfumes Can Be Authorial Works

11.3.4.1 Perfumes as an Author's Own Intellectual Creation

While the CJEU is yet to consider this issue, perfumes are clearly capable of satisfying its definition of authorial works. The reasons are that a perfume is a bounded expressive object—a product with an objectively discernible form—and that the technical considerations which constrain a perfume's creation nonetheless leave scope for the exercise of free and creative choices. Thus, provided that scope is exploited in a particular case to produce a perfume that bears its creator's personal mark, the perfume ought to be protected by copyright in accordance with the principles of EU law outlined in Section 11.3.2.

11.3.4.2 The Divergent Treatment of Perfumes by European States

In the absence of EU case law on this issue, it is interesting to consider the divergent position that exists regarding the status of perfumes as authorial works in different European states. According to the Hoge Raad (Supreme Court of the Netherlands) in *Kecofa v Lâncome* [2006] ECDR 26, a perfume may be an original creation which reflects the personality of its creator and can be perceived by others, and will in such cases be appropriate for protection by copyright. The bases for this decision were Articles 1 and 10 Dutch Copyright Act 1912, which define copyright as 'the exclusive right of the author of a literary, scientific or artistic work…', and 'a literary, scientific or artistic work' to include 'any creation in the literary, scientific or artistic areas, whatever the mode or form of its expression', consistent with Article 2 Berne Convention. A similar view was expressed by the Cour d'Appel de Paris (Court of Appeal of Paris) in *L'Oréal SA v Bellure* [2006] ECDR 16, applying the rather differently worded Article L-111-1 and L-111-2 of the French Intellectual Property Code as follows:

> The author of a work of the mind shall enjoy in that work, by the mere fact of its creation, an exclusive incorporeal property right which shall be enforceable against all persons…. A work shall be deemed to have been created, irrespective of any public disclosure, by the mere fact of realization of the author's concept, even if incomplete.

By contrast was the decision of the Cour de Cassation (Supreme Court of France) in *Bsiri–Barbir v Haarmann* [2006] ECDR 28, applying the same provisions of French legislation, that a perfume is a mere product of know-how rather than a work of the mind, and is thus not entitled to protection by copyright. That view is consistent with the acceptance of the parties in the UK case of *Special Effects Ltd v L'Oréal SA* [2006] EWHC 481 (Ch) that 'it is not an infringement of copyright in the United Kingdom to manufacture a perfume that mimics the smell of a successful fragrance' ([13]).

11.3.4.3 Objections to the Treatment of Perfumes as Authorial Works

At least five objections may be raised to the protection of perfumes by copyright. The first is that perfumes and other olfactory subject matter lack the expressive features of an intellectual creation: they have no literary, dramatic, or musical form, and lack the visual qualities of works of art. On the other hand, there is no reason in principle to restrict the category of authorial works on purely formal grounds, and the Berne Convention prohibits such restriction by defining its category of 'literary or artistic work' to include 'every...production in the literary, scientific and artistic domain, whatever may be the mode or form of its expression'. As the decision in *Kecofa* suggests, this definition would seem to include olfactory subject matter.

A second objection emerges from considering the implications of such an outcome: if a fragrant liquid can be an authorial work in the form of a perfume, why not a cake or other fragrant or tasty foodstuff? Among other things, this analogy between perfumes and food draws attention to the fact that the creator of a perfume will almost certainly have copyright in her formula, just as the creator of a cake will have copyright in her recipe, which protection will potentially prevent reproduction of the perfume or cake itself as a three-dimensional version of the two-dimensional (and copyright-protected) formula or recipe (see Section 12.2.4). On the other hand, it is widely accepted that the subsistence of copyright in the written description of a subject matter does not affect the subsistence of copyright in the subject matter itself, and vice versa. Thus, one can have copyright in a description of a sculpture as well as copyright in the sculpture itself, with each right triggered by a separate authorial act (and potentially owned by a different person).

A third objection which might be raised against the recognition of copyright in perfumes is that they are too unstable to support property rights, and a fourth objection is that they are more appropriately protected as inventions (synthetic compositions) under patent law than as authorial works under the law of copyright. The first of these objections receives some support at the EU level from the Court of Justice's decision in Case C–273/00 *Sieckmann v Deutsches Patent- und Markenamt* [2002] ECR I-11737, that olfactory works are insufficiently clear and precise to be registered as trade marks. However, it does not follow from this that they are too unstable to support protection by copyright, for the requirements of copyright and trade mark protection differ, consistent with their different rationales and conceptions of protectable subject matter. In addition, the possibility of recording copyright works is generally accepted as sufficient to establish their expressive content and boundaries for the purposes of copyright, so as to make them 'works'.

The same analysis also dispels the fourth objection, regarding the possibility of patenting perfumes. Specifically, the mere fact that perfumes are capable of supporting a patent ought not to preclude them from attracting copyright, for patents and copyright confer different rights consistent with their different aims and conceptions of their respective subject matter. Provided the distinction between those rights is properly maintained so that copyright does not come to protect the technical or other non-authorial aspects of a subject matter, there should be nothing inconsistent or otherwise problematic in recognizing that perfumes may be protected in different capacities by different IP regimes, as indeed is the case for computer programs and databases, among other categories of subject matter (see further Chapter 12).

There remains a fifth and final objection, which may be the strongest one. That objection is simply that however worthy of IP protection perfumes may be, they ought not to be protected by copyright since they are not among the diversity of subject matter which society recognizes as works of authorship. Specifically, it might be objected that, if the concern of copyright law is to ensure protection *for authors*, perfumes should be excluded from its reach. This objection points to a possible deficiency in the CJEU's conception of authorial works due to the failure of that conception to take account of the history of a particular subject matter's creation, including (as part of that history) the view of society regarding its authorial or non-authorial nature. This possible deficiency is consistent with our definition of intellectual products in Section 3.2, and is considered further in Section 11.3.7.3.

11.3.5 **Computer Programs Can Be Authorial Works**

Similar to a perfume formula or food recipe is a set of instructions for causing a computer apparatus to operate in a particular manner, i.e. a computer program. And as for perfume formulae and food recipes, computer programs are protectable by copyright (as literary works within the meaning of the Berne Convention) provided they express the intellectual creation of an author, and without regard to any other subsistence criterion, including any test as to their qualitative or aesthetic merits. In the case of computer programs, this is made explicit in recital 8 and Article 1(1) and 1(3) Software Directive, which confirm that computer programs satisfy the first step of the European test for identifying an authorial work discussed earlier. Thus, provided the creator of a program is able to establish that she exploited the scope which programs in general offer for free and creative choices in their creation so as to produce a program which bears her personal mark, she should be entitled to copyright protection for the program, consistent with EU principles of copyright. In effect, her program is protected as a work of computer software, rather than a computer program. This is consistent with the distinction between methods and expressive works drawn in our discussion of different types of intellectual products in Section 3.2. In addition (and relatedly), it is also consistent with the distinction we drew in Section 6.4.2.4 when discussing the exclusion of 'computer programs as such' from the scope of European patent law between a work of source or object code comprising text generated by a programmer to enable a device to implement her program (an authorial work of software protectable by copyright) and a set of instructions for causing a device to operate in a particular manner (a computer program protectable by a patent).

An important aspect of Article 1 Software Directive is its exclusion from the protection conferred by copyright in a computer program of the program's underlying ideas and principles. That exclusion is consistent with the restriction of copyright in a work to the authorial aspects of the work, as distinct from its non-authorial (including technical and functional) aspects, as discussed in Section 11.3.2.

In other respects, the Software Directive defines the category of computer programs broadly. According to Article 1 and recital 7, for example, a program may take 'any form', and include programs which are incorporated into hardware (recital 7), as well as preparatory design material created during a program's development and from which a program might result at a later stage (Article 1(1), recital 7). On the other hand, as a set of instructions a program does not include any works or other subject matter created in the course of its implementation. This was confirmed in Case C–393/09 *Bezpečnostní softwarová asociace—Svaz softwarové ochrany v Ministerstvo kultury* [2010] ECR I-13971 (*BSA*), where the Court held that a graphic user interface is not a computer program within the meaning of the Directive, notwithstanding the ambivalent reference to program interfaces in Article 1(2). However, and as the Court also made clear in *BSA*, this is without prejudice to whether a graphic user interface can support copyright independent of the Software Directive, as an authorial work in its own right. The same principle was applied in Case C–406/10 *SAS Institute Inc. v World Programming Inc.* EU:C:2012:259, where the Court of Justice held that the exclusion from a computer program of the program's functionality, language, and data files for the purpose of its protection under the Software Directive is without prejudice to the status of those subject matter as authorial works in their own right. This decision is plainly correct, and is consistent with the principle discussed earlier that copyright may subsist in descriptions of a subject matter as well as in the subject matter itself. Having said that, it is difficult to see how any subject matter excluded from the legal definition of a computer program in order to ensure the restriction of copyright to authorial works could nonetheless be regarded as an authorial work protected by copyright in its own right.

Video games include computer programs within the meaning of Article 1 Software Directive. However, and as the Court of Justice held in Case C–355/12 *Nintendo Co. Ltd v PC Box Srl* EU:C:2014:25 (*Nintendo*), as authorial works video games are much more than the computer programs which drive them; they also include other subject matter, such as graphic and sound elements, and 'have a unique creative value which cannot be reduced' to their underlying program as such ([23]). EU law recognizes this by protecting video games in their entirety as authorial works within the meaning of the Information Society Directive. This is in addition to the protection which their underlying programs might receive as authorial works within the meaning of the Software Directive, and is significant because of the different nature and scope of the protection which copyright confers in respect of programs under the Software Directive vis-à-vis other categories of authorial work under the Information Society Directive.

11.3.6 **Databases Can be Authorial Works**

We have seen that collections of literary or artistic works which, by reason of the selection and arrangement of their contents, constitute intellectual creations, are recognized in the Berne Convention as a category of protected work separate from the category of literary or artistic work itself. Two examples of such collections are given in the Convention: encyclopedias and anthologies, the originality of each of which derives (as for all original collections) from their creators' choices as to which contents to include and how to arrange them in the resulting work.

The principle of copyright subsistence in original collections as authorial works is expressly confirmed for EU Member States in the Database Directive. According to Article 3(1) of that Directive, any 'collection of independent works, data or other materials arranged in a systematic or methodical way and individually accessible by electronic or other means'—as Article 1(2) defines a 'database' to be—'shall be protected as such by copyright', if and only if 'by reason of the selection or arrangement of [its] contents' it 'constitute[s] the author's own intellectual creation'. The only exception to this is for 'computer programs used in the making or operation of [a database] accessible by electronic means', which is defined not to be a database in Article 1(2). In addition, and by provision of Article 3(2) of the Directive (mirroring Article 1(2) Software Directive), the copyright protection of a database does not extend to and is without prejudice to any rights subsisting in its contents.

Implicit in the EU principles governing database copyright is that the act of creating works or deriving information for inclusion in a database is not part of the act of authoring the database itself. However, while this is obviously true for anthologies and other collections of authorial works, it is less obviously true for encyclopedias and other collections of information, where the act of deriving the information might conceivably be regarded as part of the act of selecting it, and thus as part of the act of authoring the database itself.

The legitimacy of this view was among the central issues considered by the Court of Justice in Case C–604/10 *Football Dataco Ltd v Yahoo! UK Ltd* EU:C:2012:115 (*Football Dataco*). That case involved a referral from the Court of Appeal of England and Wales in proceedings concerning annual fixture lists produced and published for the purposes of the English and Scottish football leagues. The lists had been admitted by the parties to be databases within the meaning of the Database Directive (as systematically arranged, individually accessible collections of independent data), leaving the question whether they were, by reason of the selection and arrangement of their data, the intellectual creation of their producers so as to be original (i.e. authorial) for the purpose of European copyright law. It had been held in the domestic proceedings that they were original, on the ground that the selection and arrangement of the data which they contained—including particularly the choice of dates and decisions as to the scheduling of the games—required the exercise of judgement and discretion and resulted in a fixture that reflected creativity. Central to this reasoning was a broad interpretation of the concepts of selection and arrangement as including acts undertaken while the fixture data were being generated. That interpretation was based on long-standing UK authority rejecting the distinction between the expressive and pre-expressive stages of authorship, and affirming the principle that in some cases at least, deriving material for compilation is part of the process of selecting and arranging it. In the domestic proceedings in *Football Dataco*, this had been affirmed as surviving the introduction of the Database Directive, and held to support copyright subsistence in the football fixture lists at issue in that case.

In 2012 the CJEU rejected this understanding of database copyright in a decision that involved four central findings. First, when determining whether copyright subsists in a database, the intellectual effort and skill of creating the data must be excluded. The only relevant effort and skill, the Court held, is that which expresses 'originality in the selection or arrangement' of the data which that database contains' ([46]). Second, 'selection or arrangement' for these purposes does not include adding important significance to a pre-existing item of data, by, for example, fixing the date of a football match. Third, the test of 'author's own intellectual creation' does require more than significant labour and skill from the author. In particular, it requires that the author, 'through the selection or arrangement of the data which [the database] contains...expresses his creative ability in an original manner by making free and creative choices' ([38]). In addition, the CJEU held, and consistent with its approach to identifying an authorial work above, this test 'is not satisfied when the setting up of the database is dictated by technical considerations, rules or constraints which leave no room for creative freedom' ([39]). And finally, the Court of Justice held that the Directive does cover the field of database copyright, with the result that Member States are unable to grant copyright protection in respect of any subject matter satisfying the European definition of 'database' other than as provided for by the Database Directive. It seems reasonable to extrapolate from this decision the wider principle that Member States may not protect any authorial work other than as provided for by EU law, consistent with the EU legal principle of subsidiarity (see Section 2.4.1.3).

When considered in its wider legal and policy context, the decision in *Football Dataco* makes sense. The reason is that in addition to their protection as authorial works by copyright, the investment in obtaining, verifying, and presenting database contents is protected by related rights, and in particular by the *sui generis* database right considered in Section 11.4.5. It follows that if generating information for inclusion in a database were part of the authorial act protected by copyright in the database, such copyright would confer a stronger form of the very protection which it is the purpose of the *sui generis* database right to confer, and in so doing undermine (and render redundant) that *sui generis* right. The point underlines once again the principle of EU law that the protection conferred by different IP rights is defined having regard to the reason for conferring it and to the nature of the protected subject matter properly conceived in the light of that reason and the wider legislative scheme of which it is a part.

11.3.7 Assessing the EU Definition of Authorial Work

11.3.7.1 'Pros' and 'Cons' of the Definition

The EU definition of authorial work reflects an amalgam of traditional French and German domestic definitions and has certain clearly positive aspects. One such aspect is its sensitivity to the differences that exist between different categories of expressive subject matter. In particular, by dividing the test into two stages and asking, first, whether subject matter of the relevant type leave scope for the exercise of free and creative choices in their creation and, second, whether the creator of the specific subject matter in question has exploited that scope sufficiently to produce a work that bears her personal mark, the Court of Justice ensures that different categories of subject matter are taken on their own terms, subject only to the parameters set by their protection as authorial works. Another positive aspect is the definition's approximation of non-legal understandings of authorship and authorial works. In particular, by defining a work of authorship as an author's own intellectual creation, EU law eschews an explicitly policy-driven definition designed to capture any and all subject matter that is considered appropriate for copyright-like protection on policy grounds, consistent with the aim of EU copyright law to recognize and protect the rights of *authors* in respect of their *works*.

Despite these positive features, the EU definition of authorial works may be criticized in at least two respects. One is the definition's failure sufficiently to distinguish authorial works from their individual parts, and its treatment of every part of an authorial work as an authorial work in its own right. And a second, related criticism, is its failure to reflect the most convincing non-legal definition of authorial work, and thus to ensure that copyright does protect authors (and only authors) properly defined. In combination, these aspects of the law raise doubts regarding the appropriateness of the current definition of authorial work supported by European law.

11.3.7.2 Conflating Authorial Works and Their Parts

As we have seen, an important case regarding the nature of authorial works is *Infopaq*. That case involved a preliminary referral from the Højesteret (Danish Supreme Court) in proceedings involving the unauthorized copying of 11-word extracts from newspaper articles. Among the questions referred by the domestic court was whether the reproduction of such extracts could be regarded as acts of reproduction protected in accordance with Article 2(a) Information Society Directive on the basis that they were part of the authorial works comprising the newspaper articles. (Article 2(a) Information Society Directive requires Member States to 'provide for the exclusive right to authorise or prohibit direct or indirect, temporary or permanent reproduction by any means and in any form, in whole or in part: (a) for authors, of their works'.) According to the CJEU in reply, they could be so regarded, provided each of the extracts in question expressed the intellectual creation of an author. Hence the principle resulting from *Infopaq*, that the Information Society Directive requires the protection by copyright of any part of any authorial work, defined as any subject matter that expresses the intellectual creation of an author. In addition, the explicit basis for that principle was the view of the Court that every part of an authorial work receives the same copyright protection as the work itself; where by 'part' the Court understood any element of the work that 'shares' its originality (*Infopaq* [38]; see also *Nintendo*). In effect, the result was to collapse the distinction between an authorial work and its parts by defining them in the same manner, i.e. as the expression of an author's own intellectual creation, and in so doing to increase substantially the range of subject matter protected by copyright. Among other things, this means that a literary work such as a novel or newspaper article will potentially comprise thousands of authorial works and thus support thousands of property rights. It also means that in order for a claimant to establish infringement of her copyright, she will not need to show, first, that there exists a work protected by copyright and, second, that the defendant has reproduced (or made some other unauthorized use of) a part of that work, as the Information Society Directive suggests. Rather, she will need to show that the defendant has reproduced an authorial work.

11.3.7.3 Failing to Reflect the Most Convincing Non-Legal Definition of Authorial Work

In order to consider the second criticism of the EU definition of authorial work identified in Section 11.3.7.1 it is necessary to define an author and authorial work independent of copyright. One definition that has widespread support among non-legal theorists states that an author is a natural person who creates (or contributes substantially to the creation of) a work: (a) that has a certain (literary, artistic, dramatic, musical, or other) expressive form; and (b) the history of the creation of which is not inconsistent with its recognition as an authorial work. The premise of this definition is a conception of authorial works as constituted in part by their expressive form and—of especial importance in this context—in part by the history of their individual creation, including the intention of their creator and view of society with respect to their nature as a work of authorship or otherwise. (See further Section 3.2.)

A central difference between the EU legal conception of authorial works and this non-legal definition is the former's disregard of the history of a work's creation when deciding whether it is a work of authorship. This inattention brings into relief certain aspects of the current law which are unconvincing, and helps to explain *why* they are unconvincing. For example, it is difficult to accept the CJEU's decision in *FAPL* that the rules of football so constrain the players' movements as to leave no scope for their making of free and creative choices. The reason is that they represent no more of a constraint on expressive freedom and creativity than the technological constraints of computer programming or the physical constraints of painting, and yet neither computer programs nor paintings are excluded from copyright. A more convincing explanation for the CJEU's denial of copyright to sporting events is that, while possessing the dramatic form of other authorial works, such events are neither created (i.e. played) with the intent, nor regarded by society, to exist as authorial works. The same also seems true of the 11-word extracts considered in *Infopaq*. Specifically, while such extracts certainly share the literary expressive form of authorial works, and could also be said to be the intellectual expression of an author, they will generally not have been intended to exist, nor regarded by society to exist, as authorial works in their own right, separate from the larger works of which they form part. Finally, and as we saw above, while perfumes would seem to satisfy the EU law test for an authorial work, they are generally not created to exist, nor regarded by society to exist, as *works of authorship*.

The analytical value of history in helping to resolve the authorial (and hence, the copyright) status of borderline subject matter can be further demonstrated with reference to the subject matter from two domestic cases, *Eva and Adele* [1999] ZUM 658 and *Lucasfilm Ltd v Ainsworth* [2011] UKSC 39, involving people (performance artists) and film costumes respectively.

11.3.7.3.1 *People as Authorial Works:* Eva and Adele

Eva and Adele involved the two performance artists shown in Figure 11.4 who claimed unsuccessfully to be intellectual creations entitled to copyright protection under German

Figure 11.4 *EVA & ADELE*, Daily Selfportrait, 18.04.2015, 15:47 h

Photograph supplied by Eva & Adele, © *EVA & ADELE*, VG Bild-Kunst, Bonn. The original work is in colour, and has been reproduced here in black and white.

law. In their claim, 'we are an artwork'; 'wherever we are is museum'.[1] According to the Amtsgericht Hamburg (Hamburg District Court), by contrast, the absence of any distinction between the women as people and the women as forms of expression meant that there could not be said to exist any expression *of* a person, and thus nothing that could be regarded as an authorial work. Once again, this reasoning seems artificial. A more convincing explanation for the court's finding may be fundamental rights, and the inability of people to be the object of property rights on human dignity/integrity of the person grounds (see Articles 1 and 3 CFR). In addition, however, it may be said that while performance artists such as EVA & ADELE share the visual expressive form of other authorial (artistic) works, their history of creation is not consistent with their recognition as such, since society does not generally regard people as works of art, and thus they should not receive the protection of copyright. To accept this analysis is to accept that the EU definition of authorial work should be amended to include an historical aspect better to reflect the non-legal definition of authorial work outlined earlier.

11.3.7.3.2 *Film Props as Authorial Works:* Lucasfilm

Lucasfilm involved the reproduction for sale of objects created for use in the Star Wars films. The focus of the appeal was the Stormtrooper helmet shown in Figure 11.5: part of the 'fascist white-armoured suits' for which (among other things) the films' costume designer won an Oscar. Conceived by George Lucas, the helmet was given visual expression by various people, including the defendant in *Lucasfilm*, who was engaged by Lucas to make vacuum-moulded prototypes of it in 1976. In 2004 the defendant used his original tools to make versions of the helmet, which he offered for sale to the public over the Internet. Lucasfilm sued him for infringement of copyright in the United States and England.

---

[1] H. Pidd, 'EVA & ADELE: "We invented our own sex"', *The Guardian* (1 November 2011) http://www.theguardian.com/artanddesign/2011/nov/01/eva-and-adele-interview.

Figure 11.5 The Stormtrooper helmet at issue in *Lucasfilm*

Photograph by Crosa, © Crosa. The photograph is reproduced here under the terms of the Creative Commons Attribution 2.0 Generic licence https://creativecommons.org/licenses/by/2.0/legalcode.

In the English proceedings, Lucasfilm's case turned on the issue of copyright subsistence in the helmet as a sculpture within the meaning of UK copyright legislation. That issue went to the Supreme Court, which agreed with the lower court's decision that the helmet was not a sculpture, and was therefore not protected by UK copyright.[2] The reason given by the court was that sculptures are constituted in part by their artistic form (as three-dimensional objects carved or shaped by hand) and in part by the intent of their creator. It followed that for the helmet to be a sculpture, it would have needed to have been created with the intent that it exist as such, rather than merely as a step in the process of creating the film. By treating authorial intent as part of what constitutes an authorial work, the court deviated from EU law by supporting something close to the non-legal definition above, and in doing so explained why certain categories of subject matter that share the expressive form of authorial works are nonetheless *not* authorial works, and thus not protectable by copyright.

11.4 Subject Matter Protectable by Related Rights

11.4.1 Preliminary Remarks

Supplementing European states' domestic laws regarding copyright in authorial works are separate provisions regarding the protection by related rights of other categories of expressive subject matter, including those shown in Figure 11.6, namely, performances and fixations of performances, phonograms (sound recordings), first fixations

---

[2] For a fuller discussion of the Supreme Court's decision, see J. Pila, 'The *Star Wars* Copyright Claim: An Ambivalent View of the Empire' (2012) 128 *Law Quarterly Review* 534.

Authorial/Original Works
(protectable by copyright)

= works that express an author's own intellectual creation, in the sense of resulting from her free and creative choices and bearing her personal mark.

Such works may include:

Any combination of words, sounds, movement, colour, etc. even if part of a larger work.

(Information Society Directive; *Infopaq*)

Photographs, however simple or realistic, including portraits.

(Term Directive; *Painer*)

Databases, i.e. collections of independent works, data, or other materials arranged in a systematic or methodical way and individually accessible by electronic or other means.

(Database Directive)

Computer programs, *contra* graphic user interfaces, programming languages, computer functionality, computer data files (though these may be authorial works in their own right).

(Software Directive; *BSA; SAS Institute*)

Films, i.e. cinematographic or audiovisual works or moving images, whether or not accompanied by sound.

(Term Directive; Rental and Lending Rights Directive)

Non-Authorial Subject Matter
(protectable by related rights)

Performances.

(Rental and Lending Rights Directive)

Fixations of (live or other) performances, whether or not published.

(Information Society Directive; Term Directive)

Phonograms (sound recordings), i.e. fixations of the sounds of a performance or of other sounds, or of a representation of sounds, other than in the form of a fixation incorporated in a cinematographic or other audiovisual work, whether or not published.

(Information Society Directive; Term Directive; WPPT)

Fixations of films, i.e. fixations of a cinematographic or audiovisual work or moving images, whether or not accompanied by sound, whether or not published.

(Information Society Directive; Term Directive; Rental and Lending Rights Directive)

Broadcasts, whether transmitted by wire or over the air, including by cable or satellite.

(Rental and Lending Rights Directive)

Fixations of broadcasts, whether or not published.

(Information Society Directive; Term Directive)

Databases (defined as for copyright), the maker of which can show a qualitatively and/or quantitatively substantial investment in either the obtaining, verification, or presentation of the works, data, or other materials which it contains.

(Database Directive)

Previously unpublished works first published or communicated to the public after the expiry of their copyright.

(Term Directive)

Figure 11.6 Copyright and related rights subject matter

of films and copies thereof, broadcasts and fixations of broadcasts, certain databases, and previously unpublished works first published or communicated to the public after the expiry of their copyright. As for the subsistence of copyright, the subsistence of these related rights has been extensively harmonized at the international and European

(EU) levels. At the EU level, the relevant provisions are contained primarily in the Information Society Directive, supported and supplemented by the Term Directive, the Rental and Lending Rights Directive, and the Satellite and Cable Directive, each of which builds on the Rome Convention and other international instruments. Among other things, the Rome Convention requires the recognition and enforcement of certain minimum standards of protection in respect of: (a) performances by a person of a literary or artistic work; (b) 'transmission[s] by wireless means for public reception of sounds or of images and sounds' (i.e. broadcasts); and (c) 'exclusively aural fixation[s] of sounds of a performance or of other sounds' (i.e. phonograms). These requirements are supported, clarified, and extended by Article 14 TRIPS Agreement and Article 14 WPPT.

11.4.2 Performances and Fixations of Performances

Under the domestic laws of European states, the exclusive rights of a copyright owner can be expected to include the right to exclude others from performing the protected work in public; albeit this being among the rights of authors not governed by EU law (see Section 12.3.1). In addition to being a right conferred by copyright, performances (and fixations of a performance) are categories of subject matter which Member States must protect by related rights. For performances that obligation finds expression in Article 7(1) Rental and Lending Rights Directive; and for fixations of a performance it finds expression in Articles 2(b) and 3(2)(a) Information Society Directive. The EU treatment of such subject matter differs from that of other countries, such as the United States, where performances are protected by copyright.

The initial question that arises under EU law is how a performance or fixation of a performance is identified, i.e. what exactly do these categories contain? EU legislation does not define either a performance or a fixation of a performance, and generally provides little detail regarding the obligations of Member States in respect of their protection beyond making it clear, in Article 3(1) Term Directive, that fixations need not be published to be protected. By contrast, Article 2 of both the WPPT and the WIPO Beijing Treaty on Audiovisual Performances 2012 defines 'performers' to mean 'actors, singers, musicians, dancers, and other persons who act, sing, deliver, declaim, play in, interpret, or otherwise perform literary or artistic works or expressions of folklore', supporting a broad understanding of performance itself. Article 2(c) WPPT also defines a 'fixation' to mean 'the embodiment of sounds, or of the representations thereof, from which they can be perceived, reproduced or communicated through a device', with the same Article of the Beijing Treaty offering a similar definition of 'audiovisual fixation', as 'the embodiment of moving images, whether or not accompanied by sounds or by the representations thereof, from which they can be perceived, reproduced or communicated through a device'. Finally, agreed statements appended to the Beijing definitions clarify that performers include 'those who perform a literary or artistic work that is created or first fixed in the course of a performance', and that the Treaty's definition of 'audiovisual performance' is 'without prejudice to Article 2(c) of the WPPT'.

This, then, is the international guidance regarding the subject matter to which performers' rights attach, and on which the relevant EU legal principles in this area are based. One point that the international provisions do not make explicit is whether a performance must be live in order for its fixation to be protected. On the other hand, it is implicit in the provisions of the Rental and Lending Rights Directive (following the WPPT)—and in particular from the reference to 'broadcast performances' in Article 8 of that Directive—that no such restriction applies, and that the definition covers all performances, whether or not they take place in a live concert.

The distinction between the performance and creation of a musical work in particular can be difficult in practice. For example, in some cases a performer will, through his performance of a work, create both a performance and a new authorial work. This is more likely to occur in some genres than others; the obvious example being jazz, musical scores for which often omit all the sounds which it is assumed will be made when performing the work. The result may be to make it more difficult for the creator of the work recorded on the score to establish that the improvised performance was derived from it.

11.4.3 Phonograms and Fixations of Films

Articles 2(c) and 3(2)(b) Information Society Directive, supported by Article 3(2) Term Directive, require EU Member States to recognize and protect certain rights of phonogram producers in respect of their published and unpublished phonograms. In the absence of a definition of 'phonogram' for such purposes it is necessary once again to look to the international instruments on which the EU law in this area is based. Doing so takes one to Article 3 Rome Convention, which defines a phonogram to mean 'any exclusively aural fixation of sounds of a performance or of other sounds'. A more expansive version of this definition is contained in Article 2(b) WPPT. In addition, an agreed statement appended to the WPPT definition clarifies that it is not to be read as suggesting 'that rights in the phonogram are in any way affected through their incorporation into a cinematographic or other audiovisual work'. It follows that while a film may include sounds (as seen earlier), creating the possibility of a phonogram protected within and as part of a film, such inclusion will not extinguish any prior rights subsisting in the sound track itself as a phonogram.

As we saw above, EU law establishes a two-tier system for the protection of films, involving copyright for the authors of a film (extending to its expressive content) and related rights for the producers of first fixations of a film and copies thereof (confined to the material form of the fixation itself). The second of these species of protection arises under Articles 2(d) and 3(2)(c) Information Society Directive, and applies to any fixation of a film as defined in Article 2(c) Rental and Lending Rights Directive, namely, of a 'cinematographic or audiovisual work or moving images, whether or not accompanied by sound', whether or not the fixation has been published (see Article 3(3) Term Directive).

11.4.4 Broadcasts and Fixations of Broadcasts

The fourth category of related rights subject matter which EU law requires Member States to recognize and protect is broadcasts and fixations of broadcasts. For broadcasts this obligation is expressed in Article 7(2) Rental and Lending Rights Directive, and for fixations of broadcasts it is expressed in Articles 2(e) and 3(2)(d) Information Society Directive.

Broadcast is similar to performance in being both an act reserved to the owner of copyright in a work and a subject matter entitled to protection in its own right. The provisions for the protection of each subject matter are also similar. Thus, protection under the Rental and Lending Rights, Information Society, and Term Directives attaches to both broadcasts and (published and unpublished) fixations of broadcasts, whether transmitted by wire or over the air, including by cable or satellite. And rather than a definition of 'broadcast' as such, related rights instruments contain only a definition of 'broadcasting'. According to the Rome Convention, for example, '"broadcasting" means the transmission by wireless means for public reception of sounds [e.g. radio] or of images and sounds [e.g. television]'. While narrower than the EU conception in its restriction to transmissions by wire, this definition captures the essence of a broadcast as a digital or analogue communication by a broadcasting organization of signals intended for audio and/or visual reception. In this sense broadcasts are again similar in nature to performances.

11.4.5 **Databases**

As we have seen, databases are similar to films and computer programs in their capacity to attract simultaneous protection by different IP rights. In the case of databases, the rights in question are copyright (see Section 11.3.6) and the *sui generis* database right defined in Article 7 Database Directive (see Chapter 21). For copyright to subsist in a database, the database must, by reason of the selection and arrangement of its contents, represent an author's own intellectual creation. By contrast, for the *sui generis* database right to subsist, there must be shown to have been a qualitatively and/or quantitatively substantial invest-ment in either the obtaining, verification, or presentation of the works, data, or other materials contained in the database. Hence again, and as with the two species of right subsisting in films and computer programs, copyright and the *sui generis* database right are complementary rather than overlapping rights often vesting in different people and always protecting different aspects of a database consistent with their different aims of protecting authors (for copyright) and encouraging the investment required to produce accurate, exhaustive, and otherwise useful collections of materials and preventing unfair competition (for the *sui generis* right) respectively. As will be seen in later chapters, the nature and scope of the protection conferred by each species of right is similarly defined in a way that reflects these aims.

11.4.6 **Previously Unpublished Works First Published or Communicated to the Public After the Expiry of Their Copyright**

Article 4 Term Directive requires Member States to recognize related rights in respect of any previously unpublished work following its first publication or communication to the public after the expiry of the work's copyright. While the subject matter of these rights is an authorial work (protectable by copyright), the act which triggers their subsistence is not the act of authoring the work, but rather the act of first publishing or communicating the work to the public. Consistent with this, the beneficiary of the related rights is the person responsible for that act of first publication or communication, whether or not she is also the work's author.

11.4.7 **Other Subject Matter which Member States May Protect by Related Rights**

In addition to requiring Member States to recognize and protect related rights in respect of the categories of non-authorial subject matter considered above, EU legislation expressly permits Member States to recognize and protect such rights in respect of two further categories of subject matter: critical and scientific publications of public domain works (see Article 5 Term Directive), and unoriginal (non-authorial) photographs (see Article 6 Term Directive). The express provision for such protection supports the previous suggestion that Member States may not recognize and protect copyright or related rights other than as provided for by EU law.

11.5 The Requirement for a Sufficient Territorial Connection

After establishing the existence of a work or subject matter of a protectable type, it is necessary to determine whether it is sufficiently connected to the territory of the protecting state.

11.5.1 Copyright

This requirement for a sufficient territorial connection has been extensively harmonized at the international and European (EU) levels. Internationally, the Berne and Rome Conventions require their contracting parties to ensure non-discriminatory and minimum standards of protection for the nationals of other contracting parties. In the Berne Convention this is expressed in Article 5(1), as follows:

> Authors shall enjoy, in respect of works for which they are protected under this Convention, in countries of the Union other than the country of origin, the rights which their respective laws do now or may hereafter grant to their nationals, as well as the rights specially granted by this Convention.

It is in fulfilment of this Article that (EU and non-EU) European states extend the protections of their domestic copyright systems to any work first published in or authored by a person who was, at the time of its creation or of the alleged infringement, a national or habitual resident of the protecting state or another Berne Convention country (following Article 3 Berne Convention), with an exception (following Article 4 Berne Convention) for films, works of architecture, and artistic works incorporated in a building or other structure as follows:

(a) the authors of films must, at the time of the film's creation or of the alleged infringement, have had their headquarters or habitual residence in the protecting state or another Berne Convention country;

(b) works of architecture must have been constructed in the protecting state or another Berne Convention country; and

(c) the building or other structure in which the artistic works are incorporated must have been located in the protecting state or another Berne Convention country.

11.5.2 Related Rights: Articles 4 to 6 Rome Convention

Similarly for phonograms, performances, and broadcasts, the territorial connections required by European states can be expected to follow Articles 4, 5, and 6 Rome Convention, and thus to require:

(a) for performances, that the performance (i) took place in the protecting state or another Rome Convention country, or (ii) was incorporated in a phonogram or, for performances not so incorporated, carried by a broadcast, protected under the Rome Convention;

(b) for phonograms, that (i) the producer is a national of the protecting state or another Rome Convention country, (ii) the sounds were first fixed in the protecting state or another Rome Convention country, or (iii) the phonogram was first published in the protecting state or another Rome Convention country, including simultaneously with its publication (i.e. within 30 days of being published) outside such territory; and

(c) for broadcasts, that the broadcast was transmitted either by a broadcasting organization with headquarters, or from a transmitter situated, in the protecting state or another Rome Convention country.

11.5.3 EU Member States' Obligations of Non-Discrimination: Article 18 TFEU

The obligations of non-discriminatory and minimum standards of protection imposed by the Berne and Rome Conventions are further strengthened for EU Member States by the prohibition in Article 18 TFEU against 'any discrimination on grounds of nationality' within the scope of application of the EU Treaties. The effect of this prohibition may be illustrated by three decisions. The first is Case C–326/92 *Phil Collins v Imtrat* [1993] ECR I-5145, where a German law restricting related rights protection for non-German performers in respect of performances given in Germany was held by the CJEU to be discriminatory on grounds of nationality. The second is C–28/04 *Tod's SpA v Heyraud SA* [2005] ECR I-5781, where a French law conferring copyright in designs was held by the CJEU to extend to an Italian company notwithstanding the absence of copyright for designs in Italy and the provision in Article 2(7) Berne Convention that '[w]orks protected in the country of origin solely as designs and models shall be entitled in another country of the Union only to such special protection as is granted in that country to designs and models…' And the third is *Experience Hendrix LLC v Purple Haze Records Ltd* [2007] EWCA Civ 501, where an English law conferring related rights protection for performances given by a qualifying individual or in a qualifying country was held by the Court of Appeal of England and Wales to include performances given by an individual or in a country which, at the date of the alleged infringement, was a qualifying individual or country on the ground that any other interpretation would contravene (what is now) Article 18 TFEU.

11.6 The Requirement for Satisfaction of Applicable Formalities

The third and final requirement for copyright or related rights to subsist under the national laws of European states is the satisfaction of any applicable formalities.

11.6.1 Copyright

It is a fundamental principle of the Berne Convention, and of the body of EU law that builds upon it, that copyright subsists in and is enforceable automatically upon the creation of a protected work. Thus, Article 5(2) of the Convention provides that '[t]he enjoyment and the exercise of [authors'] rights shall not be subject to any formality' other than, at the discretion of individual countries, a requirement that a work be 'fixed in some material form' before being protected by copyright. This position is supported for EU Member States by the general absence in EU law of any formal preconditions for the subsistence or enforcement of copyright, and is consistent with the aim of that law to ensure a high level of protection for authors' rights (see Section 10.3.2). The only exception is for anonymous works, truly pseudonymous works (i.e. works the pseudonym of which leaves some doubt as to the author's identity) and certain collective works, all of which must have been lawfully made available to the public in order to be protected by copyright under Article 1(3) and (4) Term Directive. By way of contrast, US law precludes the enforcement of copyright unless and until the copyright holder has registered her rights. At a policy level, this facilitates the exploitation of copyright, including through the grant of licences, by creating a central register of rights holders and their protected works.

Several European states exploit the freedom granted by the Berne Convention to require the material fixation of a work before protecting it by copyright. The most extreme example is the UK, which recognizes copyright as subsisting upon the creation of a protectable work, defined in the case of non-artistic works as the date on which the work is first recorded in writing or otherwise (see section 3(2) Copyright, Designs and Patents Act 1988). More common is the recognition of a requirement of fixation for certain categories of work only, such as choreographic works. An example is Article L112-2 French Intellectual Property Code, which provides for the subsistence of copyright in 'choreographic works, circus acts and feats and dumb-show works, the acting form of which is set down in writing or in other manner'. Finally, some European states, such as Germany and Austria, do not require fixation even for choreographic works.

In all European states in which material fixation is required as a precondition for protection by copyright, the requirement has the purely evidentiary purpose of establishing the existence of the protected work and its nature. Because it is not a substantive requirement it may be satisfied by any person (whether or not she is the author of the work), is without prejudice to any rights subsisting in the recording of the work (e.g. a phonogram), and in no way affects the principle that copyright subsists in the work, separate from and independent of its material fixation. As a practical matter, the last of these points means that a work's protection will be unaffected by the destruction of its material fixation, and that where the work as created differs from the work as recorded (e.g. in the case of a prematurely ended or otherwise imperfect recording of a speech), it should be the former and not the latter which is protected by copyright.

In reality, any person wishing to assert copyright must establish the existence and nature of the authorial work in respect of which she alleges protection, and to that end a material recording of the work will always be the most effective evidence.

11.6.2 **Related Rights**

The position regarding formalities is very similar in respect of related rights as in respect of copyright. For example, Article 11 Rome Convention restricts the formalities that may be imposed as preconditions for protecting the rights of either phonogram producers or performers in relation to phonograms by providing that any such formalities as Rome Convention countries may recognize will be

> considered as fulfilled if all the copies in commerce of the published phonogram or their
> containers bear a notice consisting of the symbol (P), accompanied by the year date of the

first publication, placed in such a manner as to give reasonable notice of claim of protection; and if the copies or their containers do not identify the producer or the licensee of the producer (by carrying his name, trade mark or other appropriate designation), the notice shall also include the name of the owner of the rights of the producer; and, furthermore, if the copies or their containers do not identify the principal performers, the notice shall also include the name of the person who, in the country in which the fixation was effected, owns the rights of such performers.

More extensive is the provision of Article 20 WPPT that the enjoyment and exercise of the related rights provided for in that Treaty (concerning performances, phonograms, and broadcasts) 'shall not be subject to any formality'. While EU law is silent on this issue, the EU is a contracting party of the WPPT and must therefore respect its provisions on formalities.

11.7 Ownership

11.7.1 Copyright

11.7.1.1 The General Rule: Copyright for Authors

As we have seen, the Information Society Directive requires EU Member States to recognize and protect copyright for 'authors, in respect of their works'. The implication of this requirement is that copyright vests initially in the author or authors of the relevant protected work. Once again, this is consistent with the aim of EU copyright law to ensure protection *for authors*, and with the definition of the term of copyright protection with reference to the author's life (see Section 12.4). It is also consistent with the provision in Article 3(1) Berne Convention that '[t]he protection of this Convention shall apply to…authors'.

Establishing that authors own copyright means little without defining who an author is. While neither EU nor international instruments contain a general definition of 'author', it is a well-established principle that the author of a work is the person whose intellectual creation it expresses, i.e. and to use the language of the CJEU that we considered earlier, the person who has made free and creative choices in creating the work and whose personal mark the work consequently bears. It is therefore in this person that initial ownership of copyright should vest. As made clear in Article 14 Term Directive, determining who this is in a particular case will be a question of fact that national courts may need to decide.

EU directives contain three exceptions to this general definition of the author of a work. The first concerns databases, the authors of which are defined in Article 4(1) Database Directive to 'be the natural person or group of natural persons who created the base or, where the legislation of the Member States so permits, the legal person designated as the rightholder by that legislation'. The second concerns computer programs, the authors of which are defined in Article 3(1) Software Directive to be 'all natural or legal persons eligible under national copyright legislation as applied to literary works'. And the third concerns cinematographic or audiovisual works, the authors of which are defined in Article 2(1) Term Directive to be the principal director of the work and such co-authors as the protecting state may designate. The effect of the last of these provisions was considered by the CJEU in Case C–277/10 *Luksan v Petrus van der Let* EU:C:2012:65, involving the referral of a question from the Handelsgericht Wien

(Commercial Court in Vienna) regarding the validity of paragraph 38(1) Austrian Law on Copyright. As amended, that paragraph vested the copyright subsisting in commercially produced cinematographic works in the works' producer. According to the Court of Justice, this contravened Article 2(1) Term Directive. In addition, the Court held, by depriving principal directors of copyright in their films, Austrian legislation subverted the objective of EU copyright law to ensure a high level of protection for authors, and breached the rights of principal directors (as authors) to the protection of their IP under Article 17(2) CFR. The fact that the Berne Convention expressly permits Member States to designate the authors of copyright in such works was held to be irrelevant.

11.7.1.2 The Exception: Copyright for Employers

An exception to the initial vesting of copyright in the author(s) of a work arises in the case of a computer program 'created by an employee in the execution of his duties or following the instructions given by his employer', copyright in which is owned by the author's employer, subject to any contractual provision between the parties to the contrary (see Article 2(3) Software Directive). For employee created databases, recital 29 Database Directive expressly leaves the ownership of copyright to the discretion of the protecting Member State. No equivalent provision exists in respect of employee authored works in general, however, perhaps implying that Member States do not have the same freedom regarding their copyright ownership. On the other hand, this seems unlikely, particularly given the CJEU's decision in Case C–518/08 *Fundación Gala-Salvador Dalí and Visual Entidad de Gestión de Artistas Plásticos (VEGAP) v Société des auteurs dans les arts graphiques et plastiques (ADAGP)* [2010] ECR I-3091. There the Court of Justice held that Article L123-7 French Intellectual Property Code—which vests the resale right of authors of original works of graphic or plastic art on the death of the author in the author's heirs 'to the exclusion of any legatees and successors in title'—was not inconsistent with EU law, and in particular with Article 6(1) Resale Right Directive, which vests the resale right in 'the author of the work and, subject to Article 8(2), after his death to those entitled under him/her'. The reason given was that Article 6(1) offers no guidance as to 'those entitled' following the author's death, and that the French provision in no way compromised the Directive's two objectives of: (a) ensuring that authors of graphic and plastic works of art share in the economic success of their original works; and (b) ending the distortions of competition on the market in art. The implication is that any provision of domestic law vesting the ownership of copyright in someone other than the author of a work will be permitted if and only if it can be reconciled with the wording and purpose of EU statutory law. While a blanket provision vesting copyright in someone other than the author would be unlikely to satisfy this test, the same provision for works created in the course of an author's employment would very likely do so.

This interpretation of EU law as protecting Member States' discretion with respect to the ownership of copyright in employee authored works is consistent with the variety of national laws on this issue that currently exist. For example, some states (such as the UK) do vest copyright in works created by an author in the course of her employment in her employer, while others (e.g. France and Belgium) vest it in the employee author subject to contract. Different again is the position of Germany, which vests copyright in the employee author, without any possibility either of transfer of ownership or *ex ante* licences in favour of her employer.

11.7.2 **Related Rights**

EU legislation is also explicit regarding the beneficiaries of related rights protection. For performances and fixations thereof they are the performers themselves, defined in the international instruments considered earlier; for phonograms they are the producers of the phonogram; for broadcasts they are the broadcasting organizations responsible for fixing or transmitting the broadcasts; for first fixations of films and copies thereof they are the producers of the first fixation; for databases they are the maker of the database; and for previously unpublished works first published or communicated to the public after the expiry of copyright, they are the persons responsible for the works' first publication or communication.

11.8 **Conclusions**

Throughout Europe, copyright and related rights subsistence is governed by domestic legislation and associated case law. For EU and non-EU European states, however, the law governing such subsistence has been extensively harmonized in accordance with the Berne and Rome Conventions. For EU Member States specifically, there is even greater harmonization as a result of the far-reaching and increasingly prescriptive EU copyright and related rights *acquis*. The legislative basis of that *acquis* comprises several EU directives, including the Information Society, Term, Database, Software, and Rental and Lending Rights Directives, each of which interacts with the others and international instruments, including the Berne and Rome Conventions and WIPO Treaties particularly. The result is a complex and highly fragmented body of statutory law governing the subsistence of copyright and related rights under the domestic laws of EU Member States, the principles of which are summarized in Figure 11.7.

In recent years, the CJEU has done much to fill the gaps in this body of law, thereby lessening the degree of fragmentation and complexity. Its most important contribution to date has been to define the authorial works in respect of which copyright must be recognized and protected by Member States. That definition is yet to be adopted fully at the domestic level, creating uncertainty and a certain tension between the CJEU and some domestic courts and commentators. The reason for that tension is the view of some that the purpose of the Information Society Directive was only to harmonize the rights conferred by copyright (and the limitations and exceptions to them), without providing a basis for the harmonization of the law of copyright subsistence as well, and that in deciding to the contrary the CJEU has exceeded its competence at the expense of subsidiarity.

Despite this, all EU Member States accept and comply with the basic principles of copyright and related rights subsistence contained in the Berne and Rome Conventions, and in the EU directives that build on them. Central to those principles is a commitment to recognizing and protecting the rights: of authors, in respect of their works, without the need for application, registration, or the satisfaction of any other formalities beyond perhaps the work's material fixation; and of performers, broadcasting organizations, producers of first fixations of films and phonograms, database makers, and first publishers or communicators to the public of previously unpublished authorial works, in respect of the non-authorial subject matter that they create or in respect of which they are regarded to have an interest worth protecting by a species of IP right approximating copyright.

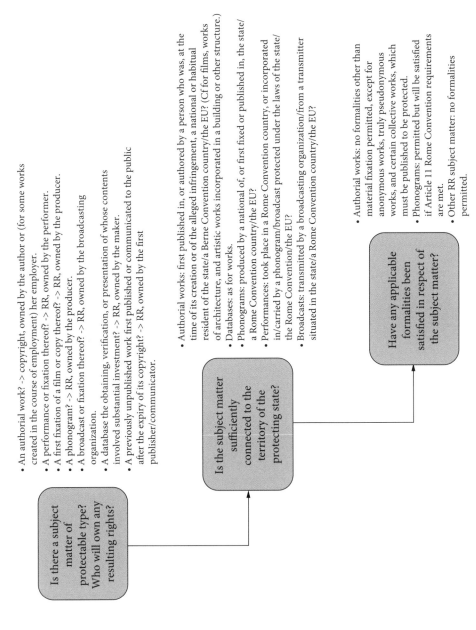

Figure 11.7 The subsistence and ownership of copyright and related rights

Is there a subject matter of protectable type? Who will own any resulting rights?

- An authorial work? -> copyright, owned by the author or (for some works created in the course of employment) her employer.
- A performance or fixation thereof? -> RR, owned by the performer.
- A first fixation of a film or copy thereof? -> RR, owned by the producer.
- A phonogram? -> RR, owned by the producer.
- A broadcast or fixation thereof? -> RR, owned by the broadcasting organization.
- A database the obtaining, verification, or presentation of whose contents involved substantial investment? -> RR, owned by the maker.
- A previously unpublished work first published or communicated to the public after the expiry of its copyright? -> RR, owned by the first publisher/communicator.

Is the subject matter sufficiently connected to the territory of the protecting state?

- Authorial works: first published in, or authored by a person who was, at the time of its creation or of the alleged infringement, a national or habitual resident of the state/a Berne Convention country/the EU? (Cf for films, works of architecture, and artistic works incorporated in a building or other structure.)
- Databases: as for works.
- Phonograms: produced by a national of, or first fixed or published in, the state/ a Rome Convention country/the EU?
- Performances: took place in a Rome Convention country, or incorporated in/carried by a phonogram/broadcast protected under the laws of the state/ the Rome Convention/the EU?
- Broadcasts: transmitted by a broadcasting organization/from a transmitter situated in the state/a Rome Convention country/the EU?

Have any applicable formalities been satisfied in respect of the subject matter?

- Authorial works: no formalities other than material fixation permitted, except for anonymous works, truly pseudonymous works, and certain collective works, which must be published to be protected.
- Phonograms: permitted but will be satisfied if Article 11 Rome Convention requirements are met.
- Other RR subject matter: no formalities permitted.

Further Reading

KAMINA, P., 'The Subject-Matter for Film Protection in Europe' in E. Derclaye (ed.), *Research Handbook on the Future of EU Copyright* (Edward Elgar, 2009) 77

KARNELL, G.W.G., 'European Originality: A Copyright Chimera' in J.J.C. Kabel and G.J.H.M. Mom (eds), *Intellectual Property and Information Law: Essays in Honour of Herman Cohen Jehoram* (Kluwer Law International, 1999) 39

KLINK, J., 'Titles in Europe: Trade Names, Copyright Works or Title Marks?' [2004] *EIPR* 291

LATREILLE, A., 'From Idea to Fixation: A View of Protected Works' in E. Derclaye (ed.), *Research Handbook on the Future of EU Copyright* (Edward Elgar, 2009) 133

ROSATI, E., *Originality in EU Copyright: Full Harmonization Through Case Law* (Edward Elgar, 2013)

TORREMANS, P.L.C., 'Authorship, Ownership of Right and Works Created by Employees: Which Law Applies?' [2005] *EIPR* 220

VAN GOMPEL, S., *Formalities in Copyright Law: An Analysis of their History, Rationales and Possible Future* (Kluwer Law International, 2011)

12

The Rights Conferred by Copyright and Related Rights

12.1 Introduction

Having established that copyright or related rights subsist in a particular work or subject matter, it is necessary to determine the consequences of its subsistence. This involves establishing the rights enjoyed by the copyright or related rights holder(s), and the uses of the work or subject matter from which third parties are excluded without the permission of the holder(s) for the term of the copyright or related rights subsistence.

In this chapter we consider these matters. Specifically, we consider the nature and scope of the rights conferred by copyright and related rights, and the corresponding uses from which third parties are excluded during the term of those rights' subsistence. Our starting point in doing so is the territoriality of copyright and related rights (see Section 1.3.3.2.1), and the freedom and responsibility of individual states to define the protections which they confer. In the exercise of that freedom and responsibility, the domestic laws of individual European (EU and non-EU) states define copyright and related rights as conferring a range of economic and moral rights on authors and related rights holders to authorize or prohibit certain acts in relation to the protected work or subject matter within the territory of the protecting state, subject to the availability of a limitation or exception. The most important of these rights are the rights of authors to prevent third parties from reproducing the work or subject matter, and from communicating and distributing copies of the work or subject matter to the public. For EU Member States, the precise nature and scope of these and the other rights conferred by copyright and related rights have been extensively harmonized by the EU directives identified in Figure 12.1 and an associated body of Court of Justice case law, with the result that there remain few aspects of this area of copyright and related rights untouched by European law.

Software Directive 1991/2009	Rental and Lending Rights Directive 1992/2006	Satellite and Cable Directive 1993	Term Directive 1993/2006/2011	Database Directive 1996	Resale Right Directive 2001	Information Society Directive 2001
Reproduction (original computer programs)	Fixation (performances and broadcasts)		Term of authors' rights (authorial works)	Reproduction (original databases)		Reproduction (authorial works, performance fixations, phonograms, first fixations of films and copies thereof, broadcast fixations)
Translation, adaptation, arrangement, and other alteration (original computer programs)	Broadcasting (performances, phonograms, broadcasts)		Term of related rights (performance fixations, phonograms, first fixations of films and copies thereof, broadcast fixations, previously unpublished critical and scientific publications of works first published or communicated to the public after the expiry of their copyright)	Translation, adaptation, arrangement, and other alteration (original databases)		Communication to the public (authorial works)
Distribution (original computer programs)	Rental and lending (authorial works other than buildings and works of applied art, performance fixations, phonograms, first film fixations and copies thereof)			Distribution (original databases)		Making available (authorial works, performance fixations, phonograms, first fixations of films and copies thereof, broadcast fixations)
Loading, displaying, running, transmission, or storage necessitating reproduction (original computer programs)		Satellite broadcasting (authorial works)		Communication, display, or performance (original databases)	Resale (original works of art)	
	Distribution to the public (performance fixations, phonograms, first film fixations and copies thereof, broadcast fixations)		Copyright (original photographs)	Reproduction, distribution, communication, display, or performance of the results of the acts of translation, adaptation, arrangement, and other alteration (original databases)		Distribution (authorial works, performance fixations, phonograms, first fixations of films and copies thereof, broadcast fixations)
Re-production, distribution, communication, display, or performance of the results of the acts of translation, adapation, arrangement, and other alteration (original computer programs)			Related rights (unoriginal photographs, critical scientific publications)			
			Rights reversion (performance fixations)	Extraction and reutilization rights (databases the contents of which are the result of substantial investment)		Remuneration (works and subject matter to which the reproduction right applies)
	Remuneration (works and subject matter above)		Remuneration (performance fixations)			

Figure 12.1 EU directives by rights

12.2. The Reproduction Right

12.2.1 Article 2 Information Society Directive

The centrepiece of the first copyright legislation of 1710 was the right of reproduction, accounting for the term 'copyright' (see Section 1.2.2.2.1). Today the right of reproduction remains among the central rights conferred by copyright and related rights systems throughout the world, albeit conferring significantly expanded protection in comparison with that conferred by the right of 300 years ago. At EU level, too, the right of reproduction has been described as 'the core of copyright and related rights'.[1] It is defined in Article 2 Information Society Directive—supplemented for original computer programs and databases by Articles 4(1)(a) and 5(1) Software and Database Directives—and applies with respect to all authorial works, as well as performance fixations, phonograms, first film fixations and copies thereof, and broadcast fixations. It is complemented by a further right (for performers and broadcasting organizations) to authorize or prohibit the fixation of performances and broadcasts under Article 7 Rental and Lending Rights Directive, and (for the makers of databases the contents of which are the result of substantial investment) to authorize or prohibit the extraction and reutilization of database contents under Article 7 Database Directive (see Chapter 21). In combination, these provisions aim at achieving close to full harmonization of the right of reproduction for EU Member States, and may thus not be deviated from or treated as setting minimum standards of protection, except to the extent that the directives provide otherwise. Two examples of such provision are Articles 5 and 6 Term Directive, which permit (without requiring) Member States to protect critical and scientific publications of works that enter the public domain only after the expiry of their copyright (for a maximum period of 30 years from the date of such entry) and non-original photographs.

The recitals of the Information Society Directive make it clear that the right of reproduction provided for by Article 2 of that Directive is to be interpreted expansively in the interests of legal certainty and ensuring that 'proper support for the dissemination of culture [is not] achieved by sacrificing strict protection of rights' (recitals 21 and 22). This is also consistent with the definition of the reproduction right itself—following Article 9 Berne Convention, and consistent with Articles 4(1)(a) and 5(1) Software and Database Directives—as covering any (a) direct or indirect act (b) of temporary or permanent reproduction (c) by any means and in any form (d) of any authorial work or related rights subject matter (e) in whole or in part (f) that is not exempted by Article 5(1) Information Society Directive.

12.2.2 Direct versus Indirect Reproduction

By 'direct or indirect' acts of reproduction are meant reproductions of a work that have been made by a person having direct or indirect access to the work. For example, photographing a painting and copying out the lines of a poem as they are spoken are acts of direct reproduction of the painting and poem respectively. By contrast, producing a sculpture according to a person's description of an existing sculpture (and without ever seeing it) is an act of indirect reproduction. Under Article 2 Information Society

---

[1] Green Paper on Copyright and Related Rights in the Information Society, COM (95) 382 final (19 July 1995) 49.

Directive, both types of reproduction are reserved to the holders of copyright and related rights.

12.2.3 Temporary versus Permanent Reproduction

A reproduction of a work or subject matter is 'permanent' if it requires a human act to be destroyed, and 'temporary' if it is destroyed automatically without the need for human intervention (see Section 12.2.7). An example of a permanent reproduction is a reproduction on paper of a newspaper article, which will exist unless and until a person destroys the paper. An example of a temporary reproduction is a reproduction in quick succession of the individual frames of a film on a television screen in the course of showing it. Under Article 2 Information Society Directive, both types of reproduction are reserved to the holders of copyright and related rights.

12.2.4 Reproduction by Any Means and in Any Form

The definition of the reproduction right as including reproductions of a work or subject matter by any means and in any form makes it clear that copyright and related rights can be infringed by reproducing a work or subject matter in different media and/or different dimensions (e.g. by making a two-dimensional drawing or photograph of a three-dimensional sculpture, or by transferring an image from paper to canvas: see Case C–419/13 *Art & Allposters International BV v Stickting Pictoright* EU:C:2015:27 (*Art & Allposters*) considered in Section 12.3.3.2), and in material or immaterial form. Thus defined, the right is sufficiently wide to encompass translations and adaptations of authorial works, including transformative uses of a work such as parodies and photographic reconstructions of a person based on an existing photographic image (photofits) (see Case C–145/10 *Painer v Standard VerlagsGmbH* [2011] ECR I-12533 (*Painer*)). This is wider than the corresponding definitions of the reproduction right contained in the domestic laws of most European states, which are confined to copying in *material* form, thereby excluding such acts of immaterial reproduction as performing a musical work or reciting a literary work. On the other hand, such laws tend to make separate provision for the rights of authors and others to authorize or prohibit both the adaptation and the public performance, showing and playing of their works and subject matter, consistent with the requirements of Articles 12 and 11 Berne Convention. Exactly how far the Court of Justice will interpret the reproduction right of Article 2 Information Society Directive to cover these acts of adaptation and public performance, etc., remains to be seen.

12.2.5 Protected Works and Subject Matter

The reproduction right of Article 2 Information Society Directive applies in respect of all authorial works, fixations of performances, phonograms, first film fixations and copies thereof, and fixations of broadcasts, as defined in Sections 11.3 and 11.4. As noted earlier, separate but similar rights of fixation, and of reutilization and extraction, are also provided for by the Rental and Lending Rights Directive and the Database Directive for performances and broadcasts (fixation) and databases the contents of which are the product of substantial investment (reutilization and extraction), as shown in Figure 12.2.

Subject Matter	Act Reserved to the Rights Owner	EU Instrument
Authorial works	Direct and indirect acts of temporary or permanent reproduction by any means and in any form of any part of the authorial work as such—i.e. of any element of the work that expresses the intellectual creation of its author—unless Article 5(1) applies.	Article 2(a) Information Society Directive
Authorial works: computer programs	As for authorial works, with the program's underlying ideas and principles expressly excluded (as elements not expressing the intellectual creation of its author).	Article 2(a) Information Society Directive, subject to Article 1(2) Software Directive
Authorial works: databases	As for authorial works, with the database's contents expressly excluded (as elements not expressing the intellectual creation of its author).	Article 2(a) Information Society Directive, subject to Article 3(2) Database Directive
Performance fixations	Direct and indirect acts of temporary or permanent reproduction by any means and in any form of any part of the subject matter unless Article 5(1) applies.	Article 2(b) Information Society Directive
Phonograms	As for performance fixations.	Article 2(c) Information Society Directive
Film fixations and copies thereof	As for performance fixations.	Article 2(d) Information Society Directive
Broadcast fixations	As for performance fixations.	Article 2(e) Information Society Directive
Performances	Fixation.	Article 7(a) Rental and Lending Rights Directive
Broadcasts	Fixation.	Article 7(c) Rental and Lending Rights Directive
Databases the contents of which are the result of substantial investment	Re-utilization and extraction.	Article 7 Database Directive (see Chapter 21)

Figure 12.2 Reproduction and related rights

12.2.6 Reproduction in Whole versus Reproduction in Part

12.2.6.1 Copyright Protection For (and Only For) a Work's Authorial Aspects

For EU legal purposes, the right of reproduction covers the reproduction of any 'part' of a protected work or subject matter. A key issue in this area is therefore what constitutes such a part. That issue has been the focus of several preliminary referrals to the CJEU from the domestic courts of Member States. According to its decisions, elements of an authorial work will be part of the work for copyright infringement purposes if they express the intellectual creation of its author (Case C–5/08 *Infopaq International A/S v Danske Dagblades Forening* [2009] ECR I-6569 (*Infopaq*)). As we saw in Section 11.3.1, the phrase 'express the intellectual creation of an author' has its origins in the EU statutory and Berne Convention definitions of originality and authorship. Thus, for elements of a work to be part of the work they must be original in the sense of contributing to the work's authorial character. Applying this definition, the Court has held 11-word extracts from newspaper articles to be part of the articles, and four audio or video fragments of a protected film (reproduced for up to 160 milliseconds each in the course of transmitting the film) to be part of the film (Joined Cases C–403/08 *Football Association Premier League Ltd v QC Leisure* and 429/08 *Karen Murphy v Media Protection Services Ltd* [2011] ECR I-9083 (*FAPL*)).

One effect of the EU law in this area is to exclude from the definition of reproduction, and from the scope of copyright protection, the copying of any non-authorial aspects of a work. The policy justification for this distinction between infringing reproductions of the authorial aspects of a work and non-infringing reproductions of its non-authorial aspects lies in the purpose of copyright to ensure a high level of protection for *authors*, in respect of their *works*. On this view of copyright's purpose, which the EU has supported with reference to Article 17(2) CFR, any protection by copyright of the non-authorial aspects of a work would be inappropriate and unjustified.

While the Court of Justice has not yet considered what constitutes 'part' of a phonogram or other related rights subject matter, it is clear from its decisions regarding authorial works above, and in particular from *FAPL*, that an expansive interpretation will be adopted.

12.2.6.2 Copyright Protection for the Non-Literal Elements of a Work: The Idea/Expression Distinction

Few aspects of copyright law generate more controversy than the so-called idea/expression distinction, according to which copyright protects the expressive aspects of a work to the exclusion of its underlying ideas and other non-literal aspects. The reason for the controversy is the risk that permitting copyright holders to prevent third parties from reproducing a work's ideas—whether they be the plot of a novel, the artistic technique of a painting, or the editing style of a film—will offend the public interest and infringe third party freedom of expression rights.

According to Article 9(2) TRIPS Agreement, '[c]opyright protection shall extend to expressions and not to ideas, procedures, methods of operation or mathematical concepts as such'. In Section 11.3.2 we noted the support which this Article provides for the denial of copyright subsistence in respect of 'ideas . . . as such', independent of works. The question remains, however, what if any meaning it has beyond the subsistence test, and in particular, what if any impact it has on the definition of the protection conferred by copyright.

The first thing to note in this regard is that, as a general principle of copyright, the idea/expression distinction finds limited support in EU legislation and case law.

Its strongest support derives from decisions such as *Infopaq* that copyright subsists in and only in selections and arrangements of words or other expressive elements. As suggested in Section 11.3.7.3, the result of these decisions is a formalistic conception of authorial works that sits uncomfortably with non-legal conceptions and is therefore difficult to reconcile with the aim of European copyright law to ensure a high level of protection for and only for the works of authors. The same reason might be invoked against the recognition of a general idea/expression distinction in copyright. Specifically, it might be said that the ideas of a work—the plot of a novel, for example, or the brush technique of a painting—are part of what gives the work its literary or artistic originality, and thus part of what constitutes it as an authorial work. If this is accepted, it should follow that such ideas are also part of what the copyright subsisting in the work protects. This is consistent with the decisions of superior domestic European courts that the unauthorized reproduction of a novel's characters and aspects of plot is capable of infringing its literary copyright (see, e.g., *Lara's Daughter* [1999] *GRUR* 984, [2000] *IIC* 1050 (BGH)), just as the unauthorized reproduction of a painting's brush-stroke and other aspects of artistic technique can contribute to a finding of artistic copyright infringement (see, e.g., *Designers Guild Ltd v Russell Williams (Textiles) Ltd* [2000] UKHL 58). At the same time, however, it bears emphasis that these jurisdictions have not traditionally supported the expansive test of infringement which European copyright law supports, according to which the reproduction of any part of a work can infringe its copyright. Even *with* the recognition of an idea/expression distinction, such a test of infringement threatens freedom of expression rights and interests by preventing third parties from reproducing banal arrangements of words and other basic elements of human expression, as the facts and finding of *Infopaq* itself suggest, supporting the phenomenon of Proprietarianism discussed in Section 3.6. In addition, and importantly, the conception of copyright as an author's right *requires* the recognition of an idea/expression distinction in the context of certain categories of technical and informational works, such as computer programs and databases. This is particularly so given the availability of other forms of IP protection for the non-authorial aspects of such works, including patent protection for the technical aspects of computer programs (i.e. for programs as inventions) and *sui generis* database protection for the contents of databases (i.e. for databases as products of substantial investment), and the importance that the protection conferred by copyright not overlap with the protection conferred by such other, complementary, IP regimes.

12.2.6.3 Copyright Protection for Computer Programs

By express provision of the Software Directive, the object of copyright protection in the case of a computer program is 'the expression in any form' of the program, in contrast to its underlying ideas and principles, which represent its non-authorial or technical elements, and which are accordingly excluded from the scope of its protection (Article 1(2)). In Case C–406/10 *SAS Institute Inc. v World Programming Inc.* EU:C:2012:259, the CJEU held that this exclusion also extends to the programming language, functionality, and data file structure of a computer program. In the Court's decision, '[t]o accept that the functionality of a computer program can be protected by copyright would amount to making it possible to monopolize ideas, to the detriment of technological progress and industrial development' ([40]). As a result of this decision and Article 1(2) Software Directive, any IP protection for these non-authorial elements of a program will need to be established on the basis either of their claim to be authorial works in their own right, or of their entitlement to another form of IP protection, such as that provided by patent law.

12.2.6.4 **Copyright Protection for Databases**

Similar to computer programs, databases may be the product of authorial and/or non-authorial contributions, so as to be appropriately conceived as authorial and/or non-authorial works. Whatever the case, however, they receive copyright protection in and only as authorial works. This explains the definition of 'database' in the Database Directive as a selection and arrangement of works, data, or other materials (see Article 1(2), discussed in Section 11.3.6), and the restriction of the copyright protection which they attract to those aspects of the database that, by reason specifically of their selection and arrangement, 'constitute the author's own intellectual creation' (Article 3(2)). Expressly excluded from such protection are the contents of a database. For those contents to be protected, they must either be authorial works in their own right—as in the case, for example, of the poems included in an anthology—so as to qualify for their own copyright protection, independent of the copyright in the database, or satisfy the criteria for protection by the *sui generis* database right of Article 7 Database Directive (see Chapter 21).

12.2.7 **Reproductions Exempted by Article 5(1) Information Society Directive**

12.2.7.1 **The Purpose and Meaning of Article 5(1)**

As we have seen, the reproduction right of Article 2 Information Society Directive is defined widely, and covers both permanent and temporary reproductions. It therefore has the potential to cover the act of reproducing content from an Internet site in the memory and on the screen of a computer in the course of Internet browsing. It was with a view to excluding these and similar acts from the scope of the right that Article 5(1) Information Society Directive was introduced. According to that Article, any temporary act of reproduction within the meaning of Article 2 that is:

(a) transient or incidental,

(b) an integral and essential part of a technological process,

(c) and the sole purpose of which is to enable (i) a transmission in a network between third parties by an intermediary, or (ii) a lawful use of a work or subject matter to be made, and

(d) which has no independent economic significance,

is excluded from Article 2 and may therefore be undertaken without infringing copyright or related rights. By express provision of recital 33 of the Directive, '[t]o the extent that they meet these conditions…acts which enable browsing as well as acts of caching to take place, including those which enable transmission systems to function effectively' may be undertaken notwithstanding the subsistence of copyright or related rights.

The majority of cases involving Article 5(1) relate to acts of reproduction the sole purpose of which is alleged to be to enable a lawful use of the work or subject matter that has been reproduced. In such cases, identifying both the lawful use at issue and the technological process of which the act of reproduction is said to be an integral and essential part is key. This is clear from the cases involving Article 5(1) to date, including *Infopaq*, Case C–302/10 *Infopaq International A/S v Danske Dagblades Forening* EU:C:2012:16 (*Infopaq II*), *FAPL*, and Case C–360/13 *Public Relations Consultants Association Ltd v Newspaper Licensing Agency Ltd* EU:C:2014:1195 (*PRC*), summarized in Figure 12.3. According to the CJEU in these cases, the Article 5(1) exemption must be interpreted strictly, having regard to legal certainty, while also allowing and ensuring the development and

Case	Facts	Issue
Infopaq and *Infopaq II*	Infopaq offered a media monitoring service that used an automated data capture process involving several acts of reproduction: generating TIFF and text files, storing result data, and printing/emailing result data to subscribers.	Did Infopaq need permission to process the articles via its data capture process?
FAPL (Karen Murphy case)	FAPL filmed football matches and licensed the right to broadcast them and other works (anthem and logo). UK pubs/restaurants accessed them lawfully from Greek licensee and showed them on TVs to their customers, which involved several acts of reproduction: making copies of the works within the decoder box and on the TV screen during transmission.	Did the pubs, etc. need permission to reproduce the works in the course of transmitting them to customers?
PRC	Subscribers to a media monitoring service which used a process similar to that in *Infopaq* accessed the results on the service provider's website, requiring acts of reproduction: making copies of the works in the computer's cache and on its screen to view them.	Did the subscribers need permission to access the results on the service provider's website?

Figure 12.3 The Article 5(1) cases

operation of new technologies, and safeguarding 'a fair balance between the rights and interests of rights holders and of users of protected works who wish to avail themselves of those technologies' (*PRC* [24]). Adopting this approach, the Court has interpreted the Article 5(1) requirement for a 'transient or incidental' act as requiring an act that is limited in duration to what is necessary for completion of the relevant technological process and deleted automatically (without the need for human intervention) once its function in that process is complete (*Infopaq*). It has also held that for an act to have no independent economic significance within the meaning of Article 5(1), the act must not generate any economic advantage beyond that derived from the transmission or lawful use in question.

Article 5(1) is a technical provision the meaning and significance of which is best illustrated with reference to the facts and reasoning of the four cases above.

12.2.7.2 *Infopaq* and *Infopaq II*: Providing Media Monitoring Services

Infopaq and *Infopaq II* originated from proceedings in the Netherlands involving a media monitoring service (offered by Infopaq) that involved identifying and summarizing articles from a range of Danish newspapers and other periodicals on topics of interest to the service's individual subscribers. The service operated by means of a data capture process that involved the following five acts:

(a) Scanning the pages of the monitored articles and generating a TIFF file for each page;

(b) Transferring the TIFF files to an Optical Character Recognition (OCR) server and translating them into text files;

(c) Searching the text files for search words provided by subscribers, and generating for each match result data comprising the details of the article in which the words were found and an 11-word extract from the article comprising the search word and five words on either side of it;

(d) deleting all TIFF and text files except the extracts; and

(e) printing a cover sheet containing the result data and sending those data to the relevant subscriber by email.

The issue for the Højesteret (Supreme Court of Denmark) was whether this procedure required the consent of the holders of copyright subsisting in the articles, which depended on whether it involved any acts of reproduction within the meaning of Article 2 Information Society Directive not exempted by Article 5(1). According to the CJEU, the service involved several acts of reproduction, namely, generating the TIFF and text files, storing the result data, and printing and emailing the result data to Infopaq's subscribers. In addition, the last of these did not satisfy the Article 5(1) criteria, since it involved the creation of a material record that could only be destroyed with human intervention, making it permanent rather than temporary or transient (see Figure 12.3). This meant that the Infopaq service could not be offered without the permission of the holders of copyright in the monitored articles. Implicit in the Court's decision, however, is that the situation would have been different had Infopaq used a means of communicating the result data to its subscribers that did not involve print or email.

12.2.7.3 *FAPL*: Showing TV Broadcasts in Pubs and Restaurants

FAPL originated from proceedings in England involving films of Premier League football matches and certain authorial works (e.g. the Premier League anthem and logo) that were embedded within the films. The holder of the copyright in those works was Football Association Premier League (FAPL), which had authorized the works' TV broadcast by a single licensee in each EU Member State. In Greece the licensee was NetMed Hellas, and in the UK it was BSkyB, which charged third parties more than NetMed Hellas charged for access to the broadcasts.

To avoid paying the BSkyB access fees, Karen Murphy and other UK publicans and restaurateurs used foreign decoding devices to enable them to receive the broadcasts from other states, including Greece. They then showed the broadcasts to customers in their pubs and restaurants in the UK. They were convicted of criminal offences under domestic copyright legislation associated with the dishonest receipt of a broadcast programme, and appealed with the following two arguments:

(a) that Article 54 TFEU (requiring the abolition of restrictions on the freedom to provide services) prevented FAPL from restricting their access to broadcasts transmitted in other parts of the EU; and

(b) that the Information Society Directive permitted them to show the broadcasts in their pubs and restaurants without first obtaining the permission of the copyright holder.

The CJEU agreed with the first of these arguments, leaving the question of copyright infringement. That question turned on two further issues: first, whether showing the broadcast works involved acts (of reproduction or another type) reserved to the holders of their copyright; and second, if showing the broadcasts did involve acts of reproduction, whether those acts fell within the scope of Article 5(1). According to the CJEU, showing the broadcasts involved two acts of reproduction within the meaning of Article 2—namely, creating transient copies of the works within the decoder box and on the TV screen linked to that box—as well as the communication of the works to the public within the meaning of Article 3(1) Information Society Directive (see Section 12.3.2). Insofar as the acts of reproduction were concerned, however, Article 5(1) was held to apply (see Figure 12.4), thus excluding the acts from the scope of the EU reproduction right. Central to the Court's reasoning in this regard was its view that the acts in question had as their sole purpose to facilitate the broadcasts' reception, which was not prohibited by UK or EU law. Nonetheless, the decision did not free the defendants from liability, since they still needed the permission of FAPL to communicate the works to the public in accordance with Article 3(1).

Article 5(1) criteria: Was each temporary act of reproduction…	*Infopaq* and *Infopaq II*	*FAPL*	*PRC* (UKSC and CJEU)
(a) transient or incidental? – i.e. limited to what was necessary to complete the technological process and deleted automatically once its function was spent? [Note the importance of identifying clearly the technological process.]	Yes, *except* the acts of printing and emailing the results, which created a material record that could only be destroyed with human intervention. 'Once the reproduction has been affixed onto [a paper] medium, it disappears only when the paper itself is destroyed.' The technological process was conducting automated research to facilitate the efficient drafting of summaries of newspaper articles. Note that the parties to the domestic proceedings had agreed that (a) press monitoring and (b) manually selecting articles and 'genuinely independent summary writing per se is lawful and does not require consent from the rightholders.'	Yes. The technological process was transmitting the broadcasts.	UKSC: Yes, on the reasoning of *Infopaq*. The technological process was Internet browsing. 'Transient' means the same as 'temporary', and includes reproductions of cached material when browsing, notwithstanding the possibility of intervening to ensure that material remains in the cache for longer/ indefinitely, since (a) 'it is not enough that forensic ingenuity can devise a method of extending to some extent the life of copies which are by their nature temporary', and (b) human intervention is not in any case required to delete the material.

Figure 12.4 (*Continued*)

(b) an integral and essential part of the technological process? – i.e. carried out entirely in the context of implementing a technological process and necessary for the correct/efficient functioning of that process?	Yes, even though they required human intervention to begin and end (inserting the articles into a scanner).	Yes.	Yes.
(c) aimed solely at enabling (i) a transmission in a network between third parties by an intermediary or (ii) a lawful use of a work or protected subject matter? – i.e. re (ii), was its sole purpose to facilitate a use of a work authorized by the rights owner or not restricted by legislation? [Note the importance of identifying clearly the lawful use.]	Yes. Their sole purpose was to enable the efficient preparation of summaries of articles, which was not restricted by EU or Danish legislation.	Yes. Their sole purpose was to facilitate the reception of the broadcasts, which was not prohibited by UK or EU legislation. 'Mere reception as such of those broadcasts–that is to say, the picking up of the broadcasts and their visual display–in private circles does not reveal an act restricted by [EU or UK] legislation…and that act is therefore lawful'. The EU law against restricting the importation/sale/use of foreign decoders also meant that receiving broadcasts from another Member State via such a decoder was lawful. Note the Court's description of the lawful use permitted by the act of reproduction as the *reception*, rather than the transmission or *communication*, of the broadcasts.	UKSC: Yes. Their sole purpose was to enable the copyright material to be viewed. 'The software puts a web-page on screen and into the cache for the purpose of enabling a lawful use of the copyright material, i.e. viewing it.'

| (d) lacking independent economic significance? – i.e. did it generate any economic advantage beyond that derived from the transmission / lawful use? | Yes. The economic advantages generated by the acts only materialized during the lawful use (summarizing) of the articles, and were therefore neither distinct nor separable from the advantages derived from such use. However, the acts would acquire independent economic significance if their author were able to profit from the economic exploitation of the temporary reproductions themselves, or if they led to a change in the protected articles (in which case they would no longer facilitate its use, but rather the use of a different subject matter). | No. They had *value*, but generated no advantage beyond enabling the broadcasts to be transmitted. '[They] formed an inseparable and non-autonomous part of the process of reception and of the broadcasts. Furthermore, they were performed without influence, or even awareness, on the part of the persons thereby having access to the protected works. Consequently, they were not capable of generating an additional economic advantage beyond the advantage derived from mere reception of the broadcasts.' | UKSC: Yes, 'because unless they download or print out the material (in which case it is not disputed that they require a licence), the sole economic value which they derive from accessing information on Meltwater's website is derived from the mere fact of reading it on screen.' |

Figure 12.4 The reasoning in the Article 5(1) (transient or incidental copying) cases

12.2.7.4 *PRC*: Using Media Monitoring Services

PRC also originated in UK proceedings, and involved a media monitoring service similar to that at issue in *Infopaq* and *Infopaq II*. A key difference with this service, however, was that the result data were made available to subscribers on the service provider's website rather than by email. Also different was the issue before the Court, which was not whether the service provider itself needed the permission of the relevant rights holders to offer the service, but whether the individual subscribers needed such permission themselves. The High Court of Justice and the Court of Appeal of England and Wales decided that they did. The case progressed to the UK Supreme Court, which disagreed with that decision (*Public Relations Consultants Ltd v Newspaper Licensing Agency Ltd* [2013] UKSC 18 (*PRC* (UKSC)); see Figure 12.4). Central to the Supreme Court's reasoning was its view that the acts of reproduction in question—namely, creating transient copies of the result data in the memory and on the screen of the subscriber's computer when accessing those data from the service provider's website—had as their sole purpose to enable the works to be viewed, which is not among the acts restricted by copyright. In addition, the court held, while the works in question could be saved indefinitely in the computer's memory cache, the acts of reproduction nonetheless remained temporary and transient in nature, since human intervention was not required to delete the works. As Lord Sumption expressed it, 'it is not enough that forensic ingenuity can devise a method of extending to some extent the life of copies which are by their nature temporary' ([32]). In response to a referral from the court, the CJEU agreed with the Supreme Court's decision. In its judgment ([26]):

> As regards the first condition, under which the act of reproduction must be temporary, it is apparent from the documents before the Court, first, that the on-screen copies are deleted when the internet user moves away from the website viewed. Secondly, the cached copies are normally automatically replaced by other content after a certain time, which depends on the capacity of the cache and on the extent and frequency of internet usage by the internet user concerned. It follows that those copies are temporary in nature.

12.2.7.5 The CJEU's Interpretation of Article 5(1)

Regardless of one's view of the outcome in each of the cases considered in the preceding sections, there are difficulties with the reasoning by which those outcomes were reached. For example, central to *Infopaq* and *Infopaq II* was the parties' agreement (and the CJEU's acceptance) that summarizing the monitored articles by extracting the subscriber's search terms and their surrounding ten words was a lawful use of the works. However, this will only be the case if the summary can be brought within the scope of a valid defence to copyright infringement. The reason is the CJEU's decision in *Infopaq* that 11-word extracts from a larger literary work are themselves authorial works protected by copyright, with the result that any person who copies such an extract will thereby reproduce 100 per cent of a protected work. As we will see when we consider the defences to copyright infringement in Chapter 13, 100 per cent copying supports a strong presumption of copyright infringement, since reproductions of a work in its entirety are far less likely to fall within the scope of a defence to copyright infringement than reproductions of *part* of a work.

A similar difficulty can be seen in the CJEU's decision in *FAPL* that reproducing the works in the course of showing the broadcasts in restaurants and pubs had as its sole purpose to enable the reception of those broadcasts, which was a lawful act. The reason is that it seems truer to characterize the purpose of the acts of reproduction in *FAPL* as having been to enable the communication of the broadcasts and works to the public, which is among the acts reserved to the relevant rights holders, as the Court in *FAPL* itself confirmed (see Section 12.3.2.2). However, and as the distinction between the rights of reproduction and communication suggests, it is important to distinguish between the act of reproducing the films and works (by turning the TV on) and the act of communicating the films and works to the public (by adjusting the TV's position and volume to enable the broadcasts to be received by those present in the pub or restaurant). When that distinction is kept in mind, the CJEU's characterization of the lawful use in *FAPL* as the reception of the broadcasts is easier to understand.

The final difficulty with the Article 5(1) cases is the Court's decision that the temporary reproductions involved in offering the Infopaq and Meltwater media monitoring services had no independent economic significance, notwithstanding that those reproductions were—as the High Court of Justice in *PRC* remarked—the very product for which the subscribers to the service were paying.

When reading the cases in this area, it is difficult to ignore the importance of policy to each court's decision and reasoning. For example, according to the High Court of Justice in the domestic proceedings that led to *PRC* ([2010] EWHC 3099 (Ch) [109]–[110]):

> [A]ny copy which is 'consumption of the work', whether temporary or not, requires the permission of the copyright holder... The exception cannot have been intended to

legitimise all copies made in the course of browsing or users would be permitted to watch pirated films and listen to pirated music.

In stark contrast to this is the view expressed by the UK Supreme Court in the same domestic proceedings, that a finding of infringement 'would make infringers of many millions of ordinary users of the internet across the EU' ([36]). According to Lord Sumption, it would be better for copyright holders to seek a single, higher licensing fee from Meltwater than many small licensing fees from end users, and to seek relief for copyright infringement from parties more obviously at fault than users of the Internet. Different again was the policy emphasis of the CJEU in *FAPL*, which was on supporting access to new technologies consistent with recital 31 Information Society Directive. In the Court's decision ([179]):

> If the acts at issue were not considered to comply with the conditions set by Article 5(1) …all television viewers using modern sets which, in order to work, need those acts of reproduction to be carried out would be prevented from receiving broadcasts containing broadcast works, in the absence of an authorisation from copyright holders. That would impede, and even paralyse, the actual spread and contribution of new technologies, in disregard of the will of the EU legislature as expressed in recital 31 in the preamble to the Copyright [Information Society] Directive.

12.3 Rights of Communication, Distribution, Rental and Lending, and Resale

12.3.1 Preliminary Remarks

Since the invention of broadcasting and the Internet especially, controlling the transmission of protected works and subject matter to the public has been essential to the ability of copyright and related rights holders to exploit fully the commercial value of their works and subject matter. European states had recognized this by making separate provision for the exclusive right of those holders to prohibit or authorize a range of communicative acts, consistent with the requirements of the Berne and Rome Conventions.[2] Insofar as authorial works are concerned, the WIPO Copyright Treaty of 1996 (WCT) sought to rationalize and update the Berne Convention provisions by introducing a single 'communication to the public' right in Article 8 and a new 'making available to the public' (distribution) right in Article 6. Corresponding rights for performers, phonogram producers, and broadcasting organizations were introduced by the WIPO Performances and Phonograms Treaty of 1996 (WPPT), building on Articles 7 and 13 Rome Convention.

EU law implements these international provisions by requiring Member States to ensure to authors, performers, phonogram producers, producers of first fixations of films, and broadcasting organizations the following exclusive rights, summarized also in Figure 12.5.

- The right to authorize or prohibit the communication of their works and subject matter to the public: see Article 3(1) Information Society Directive for works other than databases; Article 5(d) Database Directive for databases; Article 2 Satellite and

---

[2] See, e.g., Articles 11 (public performance and communication), 11*bis* (broadcasting and wireless communication), and 11*ter* (public recitation) Berne Convention, and Articles 7 (broadcasting and communication of performances) and 13 (rebroadcasting and communication of broadcasts) Rome Convention.

Act	Right Engaged	EU Instrument
Transmitting (from the protecting state) a work via terrestrial/satellite/cable broadcast or Internet-based streaming of such a broadcast	Communication to the public	Article 3 Information Society Directive For databases: Article 5(d) Database Directive For computer programs: Article 4(1)(a) Software Directive For works transmitted via satellite broadcasting: Article 2 Satellite and Cable Directive
Transmitting (from the protecting state) a performance via terrestrial/satellite/cable broadcast or Internet-based streaming of such a broadcast	Broadcast; communication to the public, provided the performance is not already a broadcast performance or made from a fixation	Article 8(1) Rental and Lending Rights Directive
Retransmitting (from the protecting state) a terrestrial/satellite/cable broadcast by wireless means, or transmitting (from the protecting state) a broadcast in any place accessible to the public against payment of an entrance fee	Broadcast retransmission; communication to the public	Article 8(3) Rental and Lending Rights Directive
Displaying or performing a database in public	Communication to the public	Article 5(d) Database Directive
Intervening in the transmission via broadcast (from the protecting state) of a work, performance, or broadcast to the public	Communication to the public	For works: Article 3 Information Society Directive and Article 1 Satellite and Cable Directive For performances and broadcasts: Article 8 Rental and Lending Rights Directive
Showing a work (in the protecting state) to members of the public (e.g. customers of a pub, hotel, or restaurant) not present at the place where the communication originated	Communication to the public	Article 3 Information Society Directive
Making a work or subject matter available on the Internet (from the protecting state) to be viewed or listened to at a place and time chosen by members of the public	Making available to the public	Article 3 Information Society Directive

Making a work or subject matter available on the Internet (from the protecting state) to be downloaded by members of the public	Making available to the public	Article 3 Information Society Directive
Sharing a work or subject matter on a peer-to-peer computer network (in the protecting state)	Making available to the public	Article 3 Information Society Directive
Emailing a work or subject matter (from the protecting state) to a large number of people	Making available to the public	Article 3 Information Society Directive
Transferring ownership by sale, gift, or otherwise (in the protecting state) of (a) a physical product incorporating a work, (b) a database, computer program, or copy thereof, or (c) a subject matter or copy thereof, which had not already been placed on the EU market by or with the rights owner's consent, including (in the case of a computer program at least) by provision of a copy for download from the Internet under an exclusive licence	Distribution to the public	For works: Article 4 Information Society Directive For databases: Article 5(c) Database Directive For computer programs: Article 4(1)(c) Software Directive For subject matter and copies thereof: Article 9 Rental and Lending Rights Directive For computer programs provided for download under licence: *UsedSoft*
Renting a work (other than a building or work of applied art) or subject matter	Rental	Article 3 Rental and Lending Rights Directive Computer programs: Article 4(c) Software Directive
Failing to remunerate an author or performer following the rental of a phonogram or original/copy of a film in respect of which the author or performer has transferred or assigned his rental right	Right to remuneration	Article 5 Rental and Lending Rights Directive
Lending a work through an establishment accessible to the public or failing to remunerate the rights owner after lending a work through such an establishment without a valid exemption	Lending; right to remuneration	Articles 3 and 6 Rental and Lending Rights Directive
Failing to remunerate the author of an original work of art following the work's resale	Resale/*Droit de suite*	Article 1 Resale Right Directive

Figure 12.5 Communication, distribution and related rights

Cable Directive for satellite broadcasts of works; and Article 8 Rental and Lending Rights Directive for unfixed performances and broadcasts.

- The right to authorize or prohibit the making available of their works and subject matter to the public 'in such a way that members of the public may access them from a place and at a time individually chosen by them': see Article 3(1) and (2) Information Society Directive for works, performance fixations, broadcast fixations, phonograms, and first film fixations and copies thereof.

- The right to authorize or prohibit the distribution of their works and subject matter to the public: see Article 4 Information Society Directive for works other than computer programs and databases; Article 4(1)(c) Software Directive for computer programs; Article 5(c) Database Directive for databases; and Article 9 Rental and Lending Rights Directive for performance fixations, broadcast fixations, phonograms, and first film fixations and copies thereof.

- The right to authorize or prohibit the rental of originals and copies of their works and subject matter: see Article 3 Rental and Lending Rights Directive for works (other than computer programs, buildings, and works of applied art), performance fixations, phonograms, first film fixations and copies thereof; and Article 4(1)(c) Software Directive for computer programs.

- At the discretion of Member States, the right *either* to authorize or prohibit the public lending of originals and copies of their works and subject matter *or* to be remunerated for such public lending (other than lending by an exempt establishment): see Article 3 Rental and Lending Rights Directive for works (other than buildings and works of applied art), performance fixations, phonograms, and first film fixations and copies thereof.

- For performers and phonogram producers only, the right to receive a single fee, which must be shared between them, by way of remuneration from any person who communicates a commercially published phonogram or reproduction thereof to the public: see Article 8(2) Rental and Lending Rights Directive.

- For graphic and plastic artists only, the right to be remunerated for resales of their original works: see Article 1 Resale Right Directive.

- For performers who have transferred their rights to a phonogram producer, the rights: (a) to terminate the transfer after 50 years if the phonogram fails to make sufficient quantities of the phonogram containing the performance available to the public; or (b) if the transfer was made for a non-recurring remuneration, the right to receive a further annual remuneration from the phonogram producer after 50 years: see Articles 3(2a) to 3(2e) Term Directive.

As with the EU provisions governing the reproduction right, these provisions aim at full harmonization of the rights of authors and others to control the public communication and distribution of their works and subject matter, and thus may not be deviated from or treated as setting minimum standards of protection only, except to the extent that the relevant directives expressly provide to the contrary or make it clear that certain acts were not intended to be caught within their sphere of regulation. One example of the second type of provision is recital 23 Information Society Directive, which makes it clear that live public performances of works and showings of subject matter were not intended to be governed by the Directive, leaving them for protection by Member States in accordance with their obligations under the Berne Convention (see Section 12.3.2.1). An example of the first kind of provision is recital 16 Rental and Lending Rights Directive, which permits

Member States 'to provide for more far-reaching protection' for related rights holders in respect of broadcasting and communication to the public than is provided for by that Directive—subject now to Article 3 Information Society Directive (establishing a making available right for rights holders as part of the communication to the public right; see Section 12.3.2.5). The significance of this recital was considered by the Court of Justice in Case C–279/13 *C More Entertainment AB v Sandberg* EU:C:2015:199, involving Swedish legislation that conferred wider related rights on broadcasting organizations than those contained in Article 3(2)(d) Information Society Directive, in the form of rights to make works available other than on-demand. In the judgment of the Court, recital 16 enabled the legislation in question. Specifically, it was held to enable Member States to provide for more protective provisions with regard to the broadcasting and communication to the public of transmissions made by broadcasting organizations than those required by Article 8(3) Rental and Lending Rights Directive. In addition, it followed from this that Article 3(2) Information Society Directive also did not affect ([36])

> the option open to the Member States…to grant broadcasting organisations the exclusive right to authorize or prohibit acts of communication to the public of their transmissions provided that such protection does not undermine that of copyright.

In addition to preserving Member States' freedom to make their own provisions for certain types of acts, EU legislation leaves certain matters expressly for determination by individual states. Examples are whether to include public lending among the acts reserved to copyright and related rights holders, how to calculate the remuneration which must be paid to rights holders in states that do not include public lending among such acts, and which if any public lending establishments to exempt from the obligation to pay such remuneration (see Section 12.3.4.2). In determining these matters, Member States are bound by the provisions of the Rental and Lending Rights Directive and other applicable sources of EU law.

12.3.2 **Communication to the Public**

12.3.2.1 **Distinguished from Live Performance**

In many European states historically, the right of public communication was defined broadly to include any transmission of a work or subject matter to members of the public, regardless of whether the members of the public were present at the time and place where the communication originated (e.g. in the case of a live performance of a song or the TV broadcast/cinema screening of a film). This expansive definition has been retained in EU law for databases only; Article 5(d) Database Directive giving the author of a database the exclusive right to 'carry out or authorize…any communication, *display or performance* to the public' (emphasis added). For all other works and subject matter, however, the communication right of Article 3 Information Society Directive is restricted to transmissions (or retransmissions) of the work or subject matter to members of the public not present at the place where the communication originated (recital 23). This was confirmed by the Court of Justice in Case C–283/10 *Circul Globus București (Circ & Variete Globus București) v Uniunea Compozitorilor și Muzicologilor din România—Asociația pentru Drepturi de Autor (UCMR—ADA)* [2011] ECR I-12031: a preliminary referral by the Înalta Curte de Casație și Justiție (Romanian Supreme Court of Cassation and Justice) arising from proceedings involving the communication of musical works to the public during circus and cabaret shows. According to the Court, since the communication of the works involved their live performance before a public

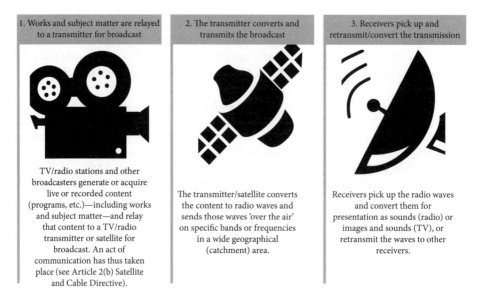

1. Works and subject matter are relayed to a transmitter for broadcast	2. The transmitter converts and transmits the broadcast	3. Receivers pick up and retransmit/convert the transmission
TV/radio stations and other broadcasters generate or acquire live or recorded content (programs, etc.)—including works and subject matter—and relay that content to a TV/radio transmitter or satellite for broadcast. An act of communication has thus taken place (see Article 2(b) Satellite and Cable Directive).	The transmitter/satellite converts the content to radio waves and sends those waves 'over the air' on specific bands or frequencies in a wide geographical (catchment) area.	Receivers pick up the radio waves and convert them for presentation as sounds (radio) or images and sounds (TV), or retransmit the waves to other receivers.

Figure 12.6 Communicating works via TV/radio or satellite broadcast transmission

that was in direct physical contact with the performers, it fell outside the scope of the right of communication which it was the purpose of the Information Society Directive to regulate, and was therefore not governed by that Directive. As the Court said, the right of communication regulated by Article 3 Information Society Directive 'does not cover any activity which does not involve a "transmission" or a "retransmission" of a work, such as live presentations or performances of a work' ([40]), which accordingly remain governed by each state's domestic laws.

12.3.2.2 **Communication by Broadcast and Interactive On-Demand Transmissions**

Within its sphere of application, the communication right of Article 3 Information Society Directive is to be construed broadly (recital 23), and as including all broadcasts of a work by wire and wireless means, including over the air (terrestrial), satellite, and cable broadcasting, by means of the technology summarized in Figure 12.6.

This has been confirmed by the Court of Justice in a series of cases involving the following acts:

(a) the retransmission by a hotel of TV broadcasts to its residents' rooms by means of cable (Case C–306/05 *SGAE v Rafael Hoteles* [2006] ECR I-11519 (*SGAE*));

(b) the installation by a hotel of TV sets in its residents' rooms to enable their direct receipt of TV broadcasts via the hotel's TV antenna (Case C–136/09 *Organismos Sillogikis Diacheirisis Dimiourgon Theatrikon kai Optikoakoustikon Ergon v Divani Acropolis Hotel and Rousim AE* [2010] ECR I-37 (*Organismos*));[3]

(c) the showing by a pub or restaurant of TV broadcasts to its customers (*FAPL*), and the playing by a bar of radio broadcasts to its customers (Case C–151/15 *Sociedade Portuguesa de Autores CRL v Ministério Público* EU:C:2015:468);

---

[3] See also Case C–162/10 *Phonographic Performance (Ireland) v Ireland* (15 March 2012), where the Court of Justice reached a similar decision under Article 8(2) Rental and Lending Rights Directive.

(d) the encryption by a broadcast organization of TV broadcasts and provision to a third party's subscribers of encryption technology to enable their receipt of the encrypted broadcasts (Joined Cases C–431/09 and 432/09 *Airfield and Canal Digitaal v Sabam* and *Airfield NV v Agicoa Belgium BVBA* [2011] ECR I-9363);[4] and

(e) offering Internet-based streaming of TV broadcasts within the original broadcaster's catchment area (Case C–607/11 *ITV Broadcasting Ltd v TV Catchup Ltd* EU:C:2013:147).

According to the Court of Justice in these cases, each of the acts described involves a communication to the public so as to require permission from the relevant rights holders. The reason is that each involves the for profit retransmission or intervention in the transmission of a work or subject matter to ensure its receipt by a 'new public'—i.e. an indeterminate and fairly large number of people not contemplated by the rights holder when authorizing the original communication of the work or subject matter. Consistent with this reasoning, in Case C–135/10 *Societa Consortile Fonograhici (SCF) v Marco Del Corso* EU:C:2012:140 the Court held that the playing of phonograms by a dental practice to its clients did not involve their communication to the public within the meaning of Article 8(2) Rental and Lending Rights Directive, so as to require the payment of a single equitable remuneration by the user in accordance with that Article, since the number of people was small, they did not choose to listen to the phonograms, and playing the phonograms was not part of the service for which the dental practice charged. The Court's emphasis on the for profit nature of the transmissions in *SCF* is consistent with the restriction of the Article 8(2) remuneration right to 'phonograms published for commercial purposes', and of the communication right enjoyed by broadcasting organizations under Article 8(3) Rental and Lending Rights Directive to transmissions of their broadcasts in 'places accessible to the public against payment of an entrance fee'. While it is also consistent with the reasoning in the cases above concerning the communication to the public right of Article 3 Information Society Directive, in the context of that (Article 3) right it has recently been relaxed. This is clear from *Svennson*, discussed in Section 12.3.2.3, as well as from Case C–351/12 *OSA—Ochranný svaz autorský pro práva k dílům hudebním os v Léčebné lázně Mariánské Lázně as* EU:C:2014:110. In *OSA*, the Court of Justice held that the playing by a spa of works to its residents' rooms by means of intentionally distributed TV or radio signals involved a communication of the works to the public within the meaning of Article 3(1) Information Society Directive. The basis for its decision was an expansive interpretation of the Article 3(1) right as covering any transmission of works, irrespective of the technical means or process used, to a new public in the sense defined above, namely, an indeterminate but fairly large number of people not accounted for by the rights holder when authorizing the works' communication to the original public. In reaching its decision the Court distinguished *SCF* as based on principles specific to Article 8(2) Rental and Lending Rights Directive, and not relevant to Article 3(1).

12.3.2.2.1 FAPL *on the communication to the public right*
In *FAPL* (for the facts see Section 11.3.7.3), the referring national court asked the CJEU whether showing TV broadcasts of films of football matches incorporating certain authorial works in a pub or restaurant involved their communication to

---

[4] While this case was decided under the Satellite and Cable Directive, the Court made clear its view that the communication right provided for by Article 1(2)(a) of that Directive must be interpreted consistently with the communication right provided for by Article 3 Information Society Directive.

the public within the meaning of Article 3 Information Society Directive. The Court decided that it did for three reasons. The first was that the customers of the pub and restaurant were a new public not contemplated by the relevant rights holder (FAPL) when authorizing the broadcast transmissions by NetMed Hellas and the other FAPL licensees. The second was that the customers to whom the broadcasts were shown were not present at the place where the relevant act of communication originated (see recital 23), which were held to be the places where the football matches had been played and the works incorporated into the films, and not the pubs and restaurants in which the broadcasts were received. And the third was that the acts in question were carried out for profit, and affected the pubs' and restaurants' number of customers and financial results. The Court's reasoning built on *SGAE* and *Organismos* in emphasizing the effect of the defendants' acts in making the works available to a new public not authorized by FAPL, while also considering their commercial value to the pubs and restaurants. It involved a rejection of the opinion of the Advocate General that the defendants' acts did not fall within the scope of Article 3 since (the Advocate General had reasoned) live TV broadcasts originate on the screen and not at the place where the representation or performance that is broadcast originates, and the EU legislature did not intend rights holders to be able to prevent free public showings of TV broadcasts. (In the Advocate General's opinion, the hotel cases were distinguishable from *FAPL* in having involved a retransmission of the broadcasts by the hotel to the TV receivers in its guests' rooms. This was significant, the Advocate General suggested, since in cases of retransmission the retransmitting receiver could be regarded as the place where the retransmissions originated, and that was a different place from where the viewing public were present.)

12.3.2.3 Communication by Hyperlinking

In 2014 the Court of Justice handed down its much awaited decision regarding the provision of hyperlinks to works and subject matter hosted on a third party's website in Case C–466/12 *Svennson v Retriever Sverige AB* EU:C:2014:76 (*Svennson*). According to its decision, such an act will involve the communication of the relevant works and subject matter to the public if the hyperlink enables the circumvention of restrictions on their accessibility. Central to the Court's reasoning was its interpretation of the Article 3 communication right as covering any transmission or retransmission of a work or subject matter to the public—i.e. to an indeterminate and fairly large number of people—in circumstances in which *either* the public *or* the technical means of transmission was not contemplated by the rights holders. This definition is broadly consistent with that supported in the broadcasting cases considered in Section 12.3.2.2, with two exceptions. First, the transmission or retransmission need not be to a *new* public if it involves new technical means. And second, the transmission or retransmission need not be for profit.

12.3.2.4 Communication as Involving Reproduction

The communication of a work within the meaning of EU law will generally involve a reproduction of the work as well. This follows the decision of the Court of Justice that the temporary storage of video and/or audio fragments of a work in the memory or on the screen of a device involves their reproduction within the meaning of Article 2 (see Section 12.2.3). Nonetheless, and as the decision in *FAPL* makes clear, such acts of reproduction are merely facilitative of and secondary to the act of communicating the work, and as such are removed from the scope of the Article 2 reproduction right by Article 5(1) (see Section

12.2.7). Thus, while playing a TV broadcast in public involves the two separate acts of turning the TV set on (thereby reproducing the broadcast works and subject matter) and adjusting the TV set's position and volume (thereby enabling the transmission of those works and subject matter to be received by members of the public), only the second act requires the permission of the rights holders.

It seems clear that making a work available on the Internet for download is an act of communication within the meaning of Article 3. This is contrary to the position in other jurisdictions, such as Canada, since the decision of its Supreme Court in *Entertainment Software Association v SOCAM* [2012] 2 SCR 231. According to that decision, to treat the making of works available for download as involving their communication to the public would be inconsistent with the principle of technological neutrality. That principle, the court said, supports a view of the Internet as a technological taxi by which durable copies of a work can be delivered to third parties, and the preservation in the digital environment of the traditional balance in Canadian copyright law between promoting the public interest in the encouragement and dissemination of works and obtaining a just reward for the creators of those works.

12.3.2.5 Communication by Making Available to the Public

By express provision of Article 3 Information Society Directive, to make a work or subject matter available to the public is to communicate it 'in such a way that members of the public may access [it] from a place and at a time individually chosen by them'. This plainly covers the act of making a work or subject matter available over the Internet for download (see Section 12.3.2.4), as well as the provision of a hyperlink to a work or subject matter hosted on a third party's website for download from that site in the circumstances outlined in *Svensson* (see Section 12.3.2.3). It also almost certainly covers the sharing of works and subject matter in peer-to-peer (P2P) computer networks.[5] By contrast, recital 27 expresses the EU legislature's intention to exclude the mere provision of software or hardware facilities to enable such sharing to take place from the scope of Article 3, leaving Member States to determine the circumstances in which such provision gives rise to secondary (accessory) liability for copyright and related rights infringement by Internet Service Providers (ISPs) and other third parties. In so determining, Member States are bound by the provisions of the E-Commerce Directive. Among other things, those provisions restrict the liability of ISPs for the mere conduit of Internet transmissions, and for their caching or hosting of information for the purpose of facilitating such transmissions. According to the Court of Justice, when transposing and interpreting these provisions, and the related provisions governing the enforcement of copyright and related rights protection contained in the Enforcement Directive, Member States must ensure that a 'fair balance' is struck between the various rights protected by the CFR, including the right of rights holders to the protection of their IP (see Article 17(2) CFR), the right of third parties to the protection of their privacy, personal data, and freedom of expression (see Articles 7, 8, and 11 CFR), and the freedom of ISPs to conduct a business (see Article 16 CFR).[6] This is discussed further in Part VI.

---

[5] Peer-to-peer (P2P) transmissions are transmissions between networked computers that do not need to be stored or otherwise depend on a central server. Computers in a P2P network can share access to files and other resources, including protected works and subject matter.

[6] See, e.g., Case C–275/06 *Productores de Música de España (Promusicae) v Telefónica de España SAU* [2008] ECR I-271; Case C–70/10 *Scarlet Extended v SABAM* [2011] ECR I-11959; Case C–360/10 *SABAM v Netlog NV* EU:C:2012:85; Case C–461/10 *Bonnier Audio AB v Perfect Communication Sweden AB* EU:C:2012:219.

12.3.3 **Distribution to the Public**

12.3.3.1 **The Meaning of Distribution to the Public**

Separate from the communication and making available rights is the right of authors, performers, phonogram producers, producers of first film fixations, and broadcasting organizations to authorize or prohibit any form of distribution to the public 'by sale or otherwise' of the original or copies of their works, performance fixations, phonograms, first film fixations and copies thereof, and broadcast fixations. This right is regulated for works other than computer programs and databases by Article 4 Information Society Directive, for computer programs and databases by Article 4(1)(c) Software Directive and Article 5(c) Database Directive, and for performance fixations, phonograms, first film fixations and copies thereof, and broadcast fixations by Article 9 Rental and Lending Rights Directive.

As defined in the Information Society Directive, the distribution right covers only the distribution of works incorporated in a 'tangible article', such as books and compact disks (CDs) (recital 28), and exists without prejudice to the separate rights of authors to prohibit or authorize the rental and public lending of originals and copies of their works (see Section 12.3.4). By contrast, the distribution rights of Articles 5(c) Database Directive and 4(1)(c) Software Directive cover all forms of distribution of the original work and copies of it, including for software their distribution by rental.

Until recently an act of distribution within the meaning of EU law had been held by the Court of Justice to require a transfer of ownership in respect of the relevant work, subject matter, or product incorporating the work, whether by means of sale, gift, or otherwise. This was made clear by the Court of Justice in Case C–456/06 *Peek & Coppenburg v Cassina* [2008] ECR I-2731: a preliminary referral by the Bundesgerichtshof (German Federal Supreme Court) arising from proceedings involving the use in Germany of armchairs and sofas manufactured according to copyright designs of Le Corbusier. In the decision of the CJEU, interpreting Article 4 to be consistent with Article 6 WCT, making the chairs available to the public in Germany to use or see without actually transferring ownership in them did not involve their distribution within the meaning of EU law, and was thus not an infringement of copyright. For a distribution of the armchairs and sofas to have occurred, the Court held, there would have needed to be a contract of sale and performance of that contract by delivery of the goods to the purchaser. That decision was confirmed by the Court of Justice in Case C–5/11 *Donner* EU:C:2012:370, where it was held that the series of acts commencing with the advertisement from Italy of copies of a work protected by copyright in Germany to the German public and ending with the shipment of the copies to the purchasers entailed a distribution of the copies in Germany by the person responsible for advertising their sale and arranging for their delivery.

More recently, in Case C–516/13 *Dimensione Direct Sales Srl v Knoll International SpA* EU:C:2015:315, the Court of Justice relied on the 'series of acts' definition of the distribution right to abolish the earlier requirement for a transfer of ownership. In *Dimensione* the issue arose from a dispute in Germany concerning the offering for sale over the Internet of pieces of furniture alleged to be infringing of copyright. The question referred to the Court of Justice was whether the distribution right of Article 4(1) included the right merely to offer the original or copies of the work to the public for sale, and if it did, whether the right to offer included binding (contractual) offers as well as non-binding offers by advertisement. The Court answered both questions in the affirmative, relying on the need for the harmonization of copyright to take 'as a basis a high level of protection', to ensure that authors receive an appropriate reward for the use of their works, and that the copyright system 'be rigorous and effective' ([34]). It followed in its judgment ([33]) that

> an infringement of the distribution right can be observed where consumers located in the territory of the Member State in which that work is protected are invited, by targeted advertising, to acquire ownership of the original or a copy of that work.

12.3.3.2 Exhaustion

As in other IP regimes, the territoriality of copyright and related rights protection threatens the prohibition under Articles 34 and 35 TFEU against the imposition of restrictions on the free movement of tangible goods throughout EU territory. And as in other IP regimes, this threat has been addressed in part by recognizing an exception for restrictions deriving from the enforcement of copyright in Article 36 TFEU, and in part by recognizing a principle of exhaustion limiting the right of authors and others to control the distribution of originals and copies of their works and subject matter throughout the EU. As a result of that limitation, a CD or book which has been placed on the market in an EU Member State by or with the consent of the rights holder may be resold anywhere in the EU without obtaining further permission. The reason is that the initial marketing of the product incorporating the protected work or subject matter has the effect of exhausting the right of distribution insofar as that product is concerned. By contrast, it has no impact on the rights holder's other rights, including her other rights of reproduction, communication, making available, rental, public lending, and broadcast.

In EU law currently, the principle of exhaustion is asserted expressly in Article 4(2) Information Society Directive (for works), Article 4(2) Software Directive (for computer programs), Article 5(c) Database Directive (for databases), and Article 9(2) Rental and Lending Rights Directive (for performance fixations, phonograms, first film fixations and copies thereof, and broadcast fixations). Its inapplicability beyond the right of distribution is confirmed (for rental and lending rights) by Article 1(2) Rental and Lending Rights Directive (see also Case C–61/97 *Foreningen af danske Videogramdistributorer v Laserdisken* [1998] ECR I-5171). As seen in Part I, its rationale lies in the view that the payment or other consideration received by the rights holder for the transfer of ownership of a product represents sufficient consideration for any IP right attaching to that product insofar as that specific product is concerned. In those circumstances, allowing the rights holder to rely on her IP right to restrict the further exploitation of the product would involve an arbitrary restriction on the free movement of that product in breach of Articles 34 and 35 TFEU. It follows that a copyright or related rights holder may only invoke the distribution right to prevent the redistribution within the EU of a product incorporating a work or subject matter if that product was placed on the market without her consent. An example of such a case was considered in Case C–342/87 *EMI Electrola v Patricia Im- und Export* [1989] ECR 79, where the Court of Justice held that phonograms manufactured lawfully in one EU Member State by reason of the expiry of their related rights protection in that state could not be sold in another Member State in which protection continued to subsist. Another is *Donner*, involving the advertising from Italy of copies of a work not protected by copyright in Italy to members of the public located in Germany, where the work was protected. As the seller of the copies was not the owner of the work's copyright, his sale of them could not exhaust the copyright owner's right of distribution so as to permit their resale.

An important recent decision involving the principle of exhaustion expressed in Article 4(2) Information Society Directive is *Art & Allposters*. This case arose from domestic proceedings in the Netherlands involving two parties: the copyright collecting society, Pictoright, responsible for managing the copyright of certain Dutch and (by agreement with foreign collecting societies) foreign artists; and a company, Allposters, that markets posters and other reproductions, including reproductions on canvas, depicting the works of painters covered by the copyright managed by Pictoright. In order to produce each reproduction on canvas, Allposters applied a chemical process to transfer the image from a paper poster to the canvas. According to the Gerechtshof te 's-Hertogenbosch (Regional Court of Appeal, 's-Hertogenbosch), the sale of the resulting canvas was a new publication of the protected work that infringed Dutch copyright law. On appeal the Hoge Raad (Supreme Court of the Netherlands) stayed the proceedings and referred the following question to the Court of Justice: is the distribution right of Article 4 Information Society exhausted in respect of a copy of an artistic work (here, the canvas) that was previously marketed in the EU with the copyright holder's consent before its medium was changed via transfer of the work from a different medium (paper to canvas)? According to the Court of Justice, it is not. In its judgment ([43]):

> [A] replacement of the medium... results in the creation of a new object incorporating the image of the protected work, whereas the poster itself ceases to exist. Such an alteration of the copy of the protected work... is actually sufficient to constitute a new reproduction of the work, within the meaning of Article 2(a) of Directive 2001/29, which is covered by the exclusive right of the author and requires his authorisation.

In these circumstances, the distribution right enjoyed by the copyright holder in respect of the canvas incorporating the work was only exhausted upon the first sale or transfer of ownership of that new object itself with the rights holder's consent.

An important consequence of the restriction of the principle of exhaustion to the redistribution of products is to exclude its operation in the context of services, including cloud computing and other online services by which works and subject matter stored on a central server are made available to individual end users with the consent of the rights holder. This is made explicit in recital 29 Information Society Directive, which excludes material copies of a work or other subject matter made by the user of such a service from the scope of exhaustion. In Case C–128/11 *UsedSoft v Oracle International* EU:C:2012:407, however, the Court of Justice held that the act of downloading a copy of a computer program from the Internet under licence permitting unlimited use of the program involves a transfer of ownership in that copy, which exhausts the copyright holder's right of distribution in respect of it. According to the Court, such a user is therefore free to resell the copy in reliance on Article 4(2) Software Directive, and notwithstanding recital 29 Information Society Directive. Whether this decision will be confined to computer programs or also extended to other digital copies of a work acquired under licence, such as e-books, remains to be seen.

12.3.4 Rental and Public Lending

12.3.4.1 Rental

Before the introduction of the Rental and Lending Rights Directive, European states treated the rental of works and subject matter, such as copies of films and phonograms, in different ways. In some states rental was a form of distribution covered by the distribution right, while in others it was treated as a separate type of act and made the subject of a separate right. One result of this different treatment was inconsistent application throughout the EU of the principle of exhaustion. In states that treated rental as an act of distribution, the authorized sale of a copy of a film or other work was regarded as exhausting the rights holder's right to control its rental, whereas in others (e.g. France), the relevant rights holder retained control of such rental even after sale. By harmonizing the rental right in accordance with the Rental and Lending Rights Directive (see Article 3), and specifying that the principle of exhaustion does not apply with respect to rentals (see Article 1(2)), the EU secured to copyright and related rights holders the ability to control the rental of originals and copies of their works and subject matter even after their distribution to the public, thereby ensuring to them a potentially significant source of income.

Under Article 3 Rental and Lending Rights Directive, the rental right applies with respect to works (other than buildings and works of applied art), performance fixations, phonograms, and first film fixations and copies thereof. By express provision of Article 4, this is without prejudice to Article 4(c) Software Directive, under which the rental of originals and copies of a computer program is an act of distribution to the public. To rent a work or subject matter is defined in Article 2(1)(a) Rental and Lending Rights Directive as meaning 'to make it available for use, for a limited period of time and for direct or indirect economic or commercial advantage'.

12.3.4.2 Public Lending

The commercial significance of rental makes its reservation to the owner of copyright and related rights relatively uncontentious. By contrast, enabling rights holders to control the public lending of their works and subject matter, notwithstanding the non-remunerative nature of public lending, is controversial. This is particularly true in jurisdictions such as the UK that have traditionally required the deposit of works in a public library as a condition of their protection by copyright to ensure public access to the works during the copyright term and beyond. To recognize lending as among the acts reserved exclusively to copyright and related rights holders is to forego this 'right' of public access, on the basis that while non-remunerative, lending can be expected to diminish the public's willingness to pay for access to a work or subject matter and thereby to reduce the rights holder's potential income.

Thus it is that the Rental and Lending Rights Directive recognizes lending—defined as 'making available for use, for a limited period of time and not for direct or indirect economic or commercial advantage, when it is made through establishments which are accessible to the public' (Article 2(1)(b))—as among the exclusive rights of the beneficiaries of the rental right above. In recognition of its controversy, however, the Directive also permits Member States to derogate from this requirement by recognizing (in place of an exclusionary right) a right for such beneficiaries to be remunerated for public lending of their works and subject matter (see Article 6). Thus, Member States may replace rights holders' exclusionary rights (preventing unauthorized public lending) with a liability rule (permitting unauthorized public lending subject to remuneration of the rights holder). By further exception in Article 6(3), Member States are also authorized to 'exempt certain categories of establishments from the payment of [this] remuneration'; a provision which the Court of Justice has interpreted—drawing on the objective of the Directive 'to guarantee that authors and performers receive appropriate income and recoup the especially high and risky investments required particularly for the production of phonograms and films' (see recital 5)—as not enabling a blanket exemption by a Member State of all public lending establishments from the Directive's liability obligations (see Case C–175/05 *Commission v Ireland* [2007] ECR I-3).

12.3.5 **Resale (*Droit de Suite*)**

Different types of works and subject matter lend themselves to different types of exploitation, giving the rights enjoyed by copyright and related rights holders different value according to the nature of the protected work or subject matter in issue. For most authors, the right of reproduction remains the most valuable right, since the intangible nature of authorial works means that they can be fully enjoyed in reproduced form. The exception to this is visual artists, whose works are best enjoyed in their original (non-reproduced) state. This creates a problem for those artists, however, since the principle of exhaustion prevents them from being remunerated for each resale of their original works. The difficulties that this presents for artists, combined with the tendency for artistic works to increase in value as an author's reputation increases, explains the long-standing recognition by several European states of a *droit de suite* for authors of original works of art. In 2006 the EU introduced the Resale Right Directive to harmonize this right for the benefit of authors of works of graphic or plastic art, including pictures, collages, paintings, drawings, engravings, prints, lithographs, sculptures, tapestries, ceramics, glassware, and photographs (Article 2(1)), and limited reproductions of them (Article 2(2)). The result is the recognition by all EU Member States of an inalienable (non-transferable) and non-waivable right for such artists, lasting for the duration of copyright in their works, to receive a royalty for each resale of those works according to a scale capped at €12,500 (see Article 4). By express provision of the Directive, Member States may make the application of this resale right conditional upon a specified resale price of €3,000 or less (Article 3), and may also exclude from its scope the resale for €10,000 or less of a work of art acquired directly from the author in the previous three years (Article 1(3)). According to a decision of the Court of Justice in February 2015 (Case C–41/14 *Christie's France SNC v Syndicat national des antiquaries* EU:C:2015:119), the Directive does not preclude the person by whom the resale royalty is payable under Article 1(4)—namely, the seller of the work and/or an art market professional involved in the sale who has been designated to pay the royalty in whole or part by the Member State—from agreeing with any other person, including the buyer, that that other person will bear in whole or part the cost of the royalty, provided that the agreement in question does not affect the obligations and liability which the person(s) by whom the royalty is payable has towards the author.

The introduction of the Resale Right Directive caused little difficulty for the majority of EU Member States, all but four of which (Austria, Ireland, the Netherlands, and the UK) already recognized the *droit de suite*. Those four states and certain later joining EU Member States that did not recognize the resale right had until January 2012 to do so by implementing their obligations under the Directive.

According to a 2011 European Commission report into the impact of the Directive,[7] in the year 2010 works subject to the resale right accounted for approximately €2.1 billion in global auction sales of art and 50 per cent of the value of fine art auction sales in the EU, compared with 35 per cent of sales in the United States, 25 per cent in Switzerland, and 3 per cent of sales in the rest of the world. According to the same report, between 2005 and 2010 the EU market share in the sale of works of living EU artists decreased from 27 per cent to 30 per cent, as it also did from 2008 to 2010, in contrast to the market share of the United States and China, which increased over the same periods. The Commission expressly declined in its report to attribute this loss of EU market share to the Resale Right Directive, however. Nonetheless, it did note the varying quality of the

---

[7] COM (2011) 878 final (14 December 2011).

resale right's administration across the EU, and the 'particularly high' burden that the cost of such administration places on those at the lower end of the art market. Given this overall picture, it committed to keeping the market developments in this area under review. More recently, in February 2014, collecting management organizations, authors, and art market professionals signed up to certain 'Key Principles and Recommendations on the management of the Author Resale Right' aimed at improving the right's administration, including through increased transparency.[8]

12.4 The Term of Copyright and Related Rights Protection

In addition to the definition of the rights they confer, the scope of the protections conferred by copyright and related rights depends on their duration, which in turn depends on two things: the point at which the protection attaches to the relevant work or subject matter, and the period of time for which it remains attached. Under EU law, and as we saw in Section 3.8, the terms of copyright and related rights are calculated differently, consistent with the different nature and purpose of the rights. The default position for authorial works is that they attract copyright protection automatically upon their creation; though in some Member States the date of their creation is defined to mean the date of their material fixation (see Section 11.6.1). Nonetheless, the principle remains that the term of copyright for authorial works is calculated from the point at which the individual work is deemed to have come into existence and not, for example, from the time at which it is made available to the public. Under Article 1(1) Term Directive, copyright in the work then lasts 'for the life of the author and for 70 years after his death', or where there is more than one author, for 70 years after 'the death of the last surviving author' (Article 1(2))—calculated in all cases from the first day of January of the following year (recital 14). This is true even if it is the work's place of first publication which establishes the connection between it and the EU required to bring it within the scope of European copyright.

Five main exceptions exist to this general rule of copyright duration, as shown in Figure 12.7. The first is for works first lawfully published or communicated to the public *after* the expiry of copyright protection, which 'shall benefit from a protection equivalent to the economic rights of the author' lasting for 25 years from the time of such publication or communication (Article 4). The second is for critical and scientific publications of works in the public domain, which Member States are permitted to protect for a maximum term of 30 years from the date of the publication's first lawful publication (Article 5). The third is for works comprising musical and lyrical contributions created specifically for the work, copyright in which lasts for 70 years after the death of the last to survive of the author of the lyrics and music (Article 1(7) Term Directive). The fourth is for anonymous and pseudonymous works, and certain collective works, copyright in which lasts for 70 years after the work has been made lawfully available to the public unless, in the case of a pseudonymous work, the author's identity is obvious or revealed during the copyright term, in which case the general term of copyright applies (Article 1(3) to (6) Term Directive). And the fifth is for films, copyright in which lasts for 70 years after the death of the last to survive of the principal director, the author of the screenplay, the author of the dialogue, and the composer of any music specifically created for use in the film (Article 2(2) Term Directive).

---

[8] http://ec.europa.eu/internal_market/copyright/docs/resale/140214-resale-right-key-principles-and-recommendations_en.pdf.

Subject matter	Duration, calculated from the start of the calendar year following the relevant event	Term Directive provision
Authorial works (other than those listed below)	From creation until 70 years after the death of the author	Article 1(1)
Pseudonymous/anonymous authorial works	70 years from lawfully making available	Article 1(3) to (6)
Works first lawfully published or communicated to the public after the expiry of their copyright	25 years from publication/communication	Article 4
Musical compositions with specially created lyrics	70 years from death of last to survive of authors of lyrics and music	Article 1(7)
Critical and scientific publications of works in the public domain	30 years or less from the date of publication	Article 5
Films	70 years from death of last to survive of principal director and authors of the screenplay, dialogue, and any specially created music	Article 2(2)
First fixations of films	70 years after death of last to die of principal director, screenplay author, dialogue author, or composer of (specially created) music	Article 3(3)
Phonograms	50 years after making *or* 70 years after first publication/making available (if within first 50 years)	Article 3(2)
Broadcasts	50 years after first transmission	Article 3(4)
Performances	50 years from performance *or* 50 years from first lawful publication/ communication to the public of non-phonogram fixation of performance (if within first 50 years) *or* 70 years from first lawful publication/ communication to the public of phonogram fixation of performance (if within first 50 years)	Article 3(1)

Figure 12.7 Copyright and related rights duration

In addition to providing for the duration of copyright protection, the Term Directive provides for related rights to persist as follows:

(a) in performances, for 50 years from the date of the performance, or if a fixation of the performance otherwise than in a phonogram is lawfully published or communicated to the public within this period, from the earlier of the dates of such publication or communication (Article 3(1) Term Directive);

(b) in performances fixed in a phonogram lawfully published or communicated to the public within 50 years from the date of the performance, for 70 years from the earlier of the dates of such publication or communication (Article 3(1) Term Directive);

(c) in phonograms, for 50 years from the date the phonogram is made, or if the phonogram is lawfully published or communicated to the public during this period, for 70 years from the earlier of the dates of such publication or communication (Article 3(2) Term Directive);

(d) in first fixations of films and their copies, from the date the fixation is made, or if the film is lawfully published or communicated to the public during this period, from the earlier of the dates of such publication or communication (Article 3(3) Term Directive); and

(e) in broadcasts, for 50 years from the date of its first transmission, whether by wire or over the air, and including by cable or satellite (Article 3(4) Term Directive).

The provisions regarding the 70 year term of protection for published or publicly communicated phonograms and performances fixed in such phonograms were introduced by Directive 2011/77/EU of the European Parliament and of the Council amending Directive 2006/116/EC on the term of protection of copyright and certain related rights, extending the original term for their protection of 50 years. That Directive also created two new performers' rights: the first being the right to terminate a transfer or assignment of rights in a performance to a phonogram producer should the producer make insufficient quantities of the phonogram containing the fixation of her performance available to the public after 50 years (Article 3(2a) Term Directive); and the second being the right to receive, under any transfer or assignment of rights in her performance to a phonogram producer for a non-recurring remuneration, an annual supplementary remuneration from the producer after 50 years (Article 3(2b) to 3(2e) Term Directive).

As we saw in our case study involving the term of copyright and related rights protection in Section 3.8, the Term Directive has been among the most controversial of EU measures in the copyright and related rights field, including for its effect in having revived copyright and related rights in works and subject matter that had entered the public domain but for which the new term of protection had not yet expired. That effect was confirmed by the Court of Justice in Case C–60/98 *Butterfly Music Srl v Carosello Edizioni Musicali e Discongrafiche Srl (CEMED)* [1999] ECR I-3939, subject to the obligation of Member States under the transitional provisions of the Directive 'to adopt measures to protect acquired rights of third parties', and more recently for designs entitled to cumulative (registered designs and copyright) protection under Article 17 Designs Directive in Case C–168/09 *Flos SpS v Semeraro Casa e Famiglia SpA* [2011] ECR I-181.

12.5 Conclusions

Throughout Europe, the rights of copyright and related rights holders have been extensively harmonized. This is particularly true for EU Member States, the domestic laws of which have been variously adapted to comply with the requirements of the several EU directives introduced since the early 1990s for the explicit purpose of minimizing the differences in the nature and scope of copyright and related rights protection within EU territory. The initial focus of those directives was on harmonizing the protection conferred in respect of specific subject matter (e.g. computer programs, photographs, and databases) and/or specific aspects of copyright and related rights protection (e.g. its term or inclusion of satellite broadcasting, rental, and public lending rights). More ambitious was the Information Society Directive of 2001, which required EU Member States to harmonize their domestic legal recognition and protection of the rights of authors and others to reproduce, communicate, and distribute authorial works and related rights subject matter.

In combination with the other EU measures in the copyright and related rights field, the effect of the Information Society Directive has been to establish a near-exhaustive code of copyright and related rights, and to provide the Court of Justice with a legislative basis for developing its own jurisprudence regarding the nature and scope of those rights. The Court's guiding considerations to that end have been the stated policy aims of the Information Society Directive to ensure a high level of protection for rights holders in recognition of the proprietary nature of their rights and the asserted link between such protection and investment in creativity and innovation, growth, and increased industrial competitiveness (see, e.g., recitals 3 and 4).

A recurring theme in academic commentaries regarding this area of European law is the fragmentation and complexity of its legislative framework due to the large number of overlapping directives. Another is the extent of the involvement of the Court of Justice in defining the obligations of Member States on account of the sparsely worded provisions of those directives. Once again, these criticisms have supported calls for the introduction of a single and consolidating EU Copyright Regulation to put this area of the *acquis communautaire* on a firmer and clearer legislative basis.

There is merit to the criticisms of the EU law in this area for being fragmented and over-reliant on judicial law-making. Nonetheless, there is also a high degree of coherence in the European law regarding the rights conferred by copyright and related rights, due to the consistency in the Court of Justice's decisions and their grounding in the primary law and values of the EU Treaties. It is largely for this reason that there exist few substantive differences between the domestic laws of European (EU and non-EU) states in relation to the economic rights of copyright and related rights holders at least. Very different is the position regarding authors' moral rights, which remain largely unharmonized.

Further Reading

ASSOCIATION LITTÉRAIRE ET ARTISTIQUE INTERNATIONALE (ALAI), 'Opinion on the Criterion "New Public", Developed by the Court of Justice of the European Union (CJEU), Put in the Context of Making Available and Communication to the Public' (adopted by the Executive Committee on 17 September 2014) http://www.alai.org/en/assets/files/resolutions/201 4-opinion-new-public.pdf

ANGELOPOULOS, C., 'The Myth of European Term Harmonisation: 27 Public Domains for the 27 Member States' [2012] *IIC* 567

AREZZO, E., 'Hyperlinks and Making Available Right in the European Union—What Future for the Internet After *Svensson*?' [2014] *IIC* 524

GAUBIAC, Y., LINDNER, B., AND ADAMS, J.N., 'Duration of Copyright' in E. Derclaye (ed.), *Research Handbook on the Future of EU Copyright* (Edward Elgar, 2009) 148

GROSHEIDE, W., 'Moral Rights' in E. Derclaye (ed.), *Research Handbook on the Future of EU Copyright* (Edward Elgar, 2009) 242

HELBERGER, N., ET AL., 'Never Forever: Why Extending the Term of Protection for Sound Recordings is a Bad Idea' [2008] *EIPR* 174

HILTY, R.M., KÖKLÜ, K., AND HAFENBRÄDL, F., 'Software Agreements: Stocktaking and Outlook—Lessons from the *UsedSoft v. Oracle* Case From a Comparative Law Perspective' [2013] *IIC* 263

SEVILLE, C., 'Copyright's Bargain—Defining our Terms' [2003] *IPQ* 312

TEILMANN-LOCK, S., 'False Friends and Moral Rights: A Comparative Study' [2010] *Revue Internationale du Droit d'Auteur* 3

VOUSDEN, S., '*Infopaq* and the Europeanisation of Copyright Law' [2010] *WIPO Journal* 197

13

Copyright and Related Rights Exceptions and Limitations

13.1 Introduction

As we saw in Chapter 12, throughout Europe the nature and scope of the rights conferred by copyright and related rights continue to be governed by the domestic laws of individual states. So too the exceptions and limitations to those rights are matters for domestic law. Once again, however, the domestic laws of EU Member States have been extensively harmonized, including by Article 5 Information Society Directive and corresponding provisions of the Software, Database, and Rental and Lending Rights Directives.

In this chapter we complete the discussion of copyright and related rights protection begun in Chapter 12 by considering the meaning and requirements of these EU legislative provisions. Of particular importance is Article 5 Information Society Directive. As we saw in Section 12.2.7, Article 5(1) requires EU Member States to exclude certain temporary acts of reproduction effected during a technological process from the reproduction right required by Article 2 of the Directive. In addition, Article 5(2) to (4) contains an exhaustive list of the further exceptions that EU Member States may, in their discretion, recognize to the reproduction, communication/making available, and distribution rights required by Articles 2 to 4 of the Directive. They include several exceptions permitting the use of a protected work or subject matter for a specific purpose, such as private use, criticism or review, the reporting of a current topic or event, illustration for teaching or scientific research, and parody. Taken together, these purpose-limited exceptions can be read as comprising an EU 'proportionate use' exception, corresponding to the 'fair use' exception of other jurisdictions, including the United States. In combination with the other exceptions and limitations permitted by Article 5, the proportionate use exception of EU law performs the important function of ensuring that the rights of authors and producers of related rights subject matter take account of the rights and interests of third parties and society to freedom of expression and education. It is therefore an essential means by which copyright and related rights are prevented from encroaching too far on the use that individuals may make of their bodies, minds, and faculties of speech (see Section 3.3.2), and are made 'fit for the internet environment and based on social legitimacy, with due respect for fundamental rights' (see Section 10.4). Related to this, it is also an essential means by which the EU law of copyright and related rights is anchored to the objectives of EU law and the common values on which European union is based, as expressed in the CFR and EU Treaties (see Sections 1.2.2.3.3, 2.4.1.2, and 3.7).

On its face, Article 5 Information Society Directive preserves considerable freedom for EU Member States to define the scope of copyright and related rights protection according to their legal traditions and policies by leaving it to each state to decide which of the exceptions and limitations permitted by Article 5(2) to (4) to recognize. However, domestic law- and decision-making in this area is increasingly being challenged and tested for inconsistency with Article 5, resulting in a growing body of EU case law concerning the meaning of each exception and limitation it permits.[1] This, combined with the CJEU's confirmation that once implemented by a Member State each exception and limitation to copyright and related rights must be interpreted as the EU Court directs, has resulted and can be expected to continue to result in the gradual diminution of Member States' legislative and interpretative freedoms in this area of IP.

13.2 The European (EU) Legislative Scheme

Having established, first, that there exists a work or subject matter in which copyright or related rights subsist (see Chapter 11) and, second, that a person has done or authorized an act reserved to the copyright or related rights holder with respect to that work or subject matter without the owner's permission (see Chapter 12), it is necessary to determine whether the act falls within the scope of a valid exception and, if it does, the consequence of it so doing.

13.2.1 The General Exceptions of Article 5 Information Society Directive

13.2.1.1 Mandatory and Non-Mandatory Exceptions

Throughout Europe the domestic laws of individual states govern the nature and scope of the exceptions to copyright and related rights. For EU Member States, however, those laws are subject to regulation by EU law. Of central importance is Article 5 Information Society Directive, which contains an exhaustive list of the exceptions (referred to as 'exceptions and limitations') for which each Member State must (Article 5(1)) and may in its discretion (Article 5(2) and (3)) provide to the reproduction (Article 5(1) to (3)) and communication/making available to the public (Article 5(3) only) rights. By further provision of Article 5(4), a Member State that does provide for one of the exceptions permitted by paragraph 2 or 3 may extend its operation to the right of distribution 'to the extent justified by the purpose of the authorized act'. And finally, by provision of the three-step test of Article 5(5), reproduced from Article 9(2) Berne Convention, any mandatory or non-mandatory exception recognized by a Member State 'shall only be applied in certain special cases which do not conflict with a normal exploitation of the work or other subject-matter and do not unreasonably prejudice the legitimate interests of the rightholder'. A summary of the resulting legislative scheme is contained in Figure 13.1.

---

[1] And of domestic case law: see, e.g., the recent challenge to the validity of the UK private copying exception considered in *British Academy of Songwriters, Composers and Authors v Secretary of State for Business, Innovation and Skills* [2015] EWHC 1723 (Admin).

Subject Matter	Right	Mandatory Exceptions	Non-Mandatory Exceptions
Authorial works other than computer programs and databases	Reproduction (as defined in Article 2 Information Society Directive)	Article 5(1) Information Society Directive	Article 5(2) Information Society Directive
Authorial works other than computer programs and databases	Communication, making available, and distribution (as defined in Articles 3 and 4 Information Society Directive)	None	Article 5(3) and (4) Information Society Directive
Authorial works other than computer programs and databases	Rental (as defined in Articles 2 and 3 Rental and Lending Rights Directive)	None	None
Authorial works other than computer programs and databases	Public lending (as defined in Articles 2 and 3 Rental and Lending Rights Directive)	None	Article 6 Rental and Lending Rights Directive
Computer programs	Reproduction, alteration, and distribution (as defined in Article 4(1) Software Directive)	Articles 5 and 6 Software Directive	None
Databases	Reproduction, alteration, communication, display, performance, and distribution (as defined in Article 5 Database Directive)	Article 6(1) Database Directive	Article 6(2) Database Directive
Databases	Reproduction, alteration, communication, display, performance, and distribution (as defined in Article 5 Database Directive)	Article 6(1) Database Directive	Article 6(2) Database Directive
Print, cinematographic and audiovisual works, and phonograms, that are orphan	Reproduction and making available (as defined in Articles 2 and 3 Information Society Directive)	Article 6 Orphan Works Directive	None
Performance fixations, phonograms, first film fixations, and broadcast fixations	Reproduction (as defined in Article 2 Information Society Directive)	Article 5(1) Information Society Directive	Article 5(2) Information Society Directive
Performance fixations, phonograms, first film fixations, and broadcast fixations	Communication, making available and distribution (as defined in Articles 3 and 4 Information Society Directive)	None	Article 5(3) and (4) Information Society Directive

Figure 13.1 The European (EU) legislative scheme governing copyright and related rights exceptions

Article 5(1) Information Society Directive covers temporary acts of reproduction during a technological process, and was considered in Section 12.2.7 when discussing the scope of the reproduction right. In this chapter our focus is on the remaining, non-mandatory exceptions of Article 5(2) and (3), which are of two general types. The first enables the use of protected works and subject matter by specific methods or institutions, and the second enables the use of protected works and subject matter for specific purposes. In combination they are as follows:

2. Member States may provide for exceptions or limitations to the reproduction right provided for in Article 2 in the following cases:
   (a) in respect of reproductions on paper or any similar medium, effected by the use of any kind of photographic technique or by some other process having similar effects, with the exception of sheet music, provided that the rightholders receive fair compensation;
   (b) in respect of reproductions on any medium made by a natural person for private use and for ends that are neither directly nor indirectly commercial, on condition that the rightholders receive fair compensation which takes account of the application or non-application of technological measures referred to in Article 6 to the work or subject-matter concerned;
   (c) in respect of specific acts of reproduction made by publicly accessible libraries, educational establishments or museums, or by archives, which are not for direct or indirect economic or commercial advantage;
   (d) in respect of ephemeral recordings of works made by broadcasting organisations by means of their own facilities and for their own broadcasts; the preservation of these recordings in official archives may, on the grounds of their exceptional documentary character, be permitted;
   (e) in respect of reproductions of broadcasts made by social institutions pursuing non-commercial purposes, such as hospitals or prisons, on condition that the rightholders receive fair compensation.

3. Member States may provide for exceptions or limitations to the rights provided for in Articles 2 and 3 in the following cases:
   (a) use for the sole purpose of illustration for teaching or scientific research, as long as the source, including the author's name, is indicated, unless this turns out to be impossible and to the extent justified by the non-commercial purpose to be achieved;
   (b) uses, for the benefit of people with a disability, which are directly related to the disability and of a non-commercial nature, to the extent required by the specific disability;
   (c) reproduction by the press, communication to the public or making available of published articles on current economic, political or religious topics or of broadcast works or other subject-matter of the same character, in cases where such use is not expressly reserved, and as long as the source, including the author's name, is indicated, or use of works or other subject-matter in connection with the reporting of current events, to the extent justified by the informatory purpose and as long as the source, including the author's name, is indicated, unless this turns out to be impossible;
   (d) quotations for purposes such as criticism or review, provided that they relate to a work or other subject-matter which has already been lawfully made available to the public, that, unless this turns out to be impossible, the source, including the author's name, is indicated, and that their use is in accordance with fair practice, and to the extent required by the specific purpose;

(e)   use for the purposes of public security or to ensure the proper performance or reporting of administrative, parliamentary or judicial proceedings;

(f)   use of political speeches as well as extracts of public lectures or similar works or subject-matter to the extent justified by the informatory purpose and provided that the source, including the author's name, is indicated, except where this turns out to be impossible;

(g)   use during religious celebrations or official celebrations organised by a public authority;

(h)   use of works, such as works of architecture or sculpture, made to be located permanently in public places;

(i)   incidental inclusion of a work or other subject-matter in other material;

(j)   use for the purpose of advertising the public exhibition or sale of artistic works, to the extent necessary to promote the event, excluding any other commercial use;

(k)   use for the purpose of caricature, parody or pastiche;

(l)   use in connection with the demonstration or repair of equipment;

(m)   use of an artistic work in the form of a building or a drawing or plan of a building for the purposes of reconstructing the building;

(n)   use by communication or making available, for the purpose of research or private study, to individual members of the public by dedicated terminals on the premises of establishments referred to in paragraph 2(c) of works and other subject-matter not subject to purchase or licensing terms which are contained in their collections;

(o)   use in certain other cases of minor importance where exceptions or limitations already exist under national law, provided that they only concern analogue uses and do not affect the free circulation of goods and services within the Community, without prejudice to the other exceptions and limitations contained in this Article.

13.2.1.2 The Purpose-Limited Exceptions: An EU Proportionate Use Exception?

The second category of exceptions permitted by Article 5(2) and (3) Information Society Directive, enabling the use of protected works and subject matter for specific purposes, can be read as corresponding broadly to international conceptions of fair use or dealing, and as therefore supporting an EU fair—or in European language and conception, *proportionate*—use exception. The purpose-limited exceptions in question are those contained in Article 5(2)(b), (3)(a)–(e), and (3)(j)–(n) of the Directive, and permit the following uses of any protected work or subject matter by any natural or legal person, unless otherwise stated, subject to certain conditions:

- reproduction by a natural person for private use and non-commercial ends (Article 5(2)(b));

- use for the sole purpose of illustration for teaching or scientific research (Article 5(3)(a));

- uses for the benefit of disabled persons (Article 5(3)(b));

- use of published articles or broadcast works or subject matter on current economic, political, or religious topics, and use in connection with the reporting of a current event (Article 5(3)(c));

- quotations for such purposes as criticism or review (Article 5(3)(d));

- use for the purposes of public security or to ensure the proper performance or reporting of administrative, parliamentary, or judicial proceedings (Article 5(3)(e));

- use for the purpose of advertising the public exhibition or sale of artistic works (Article 5(3)(j));

- use for the purpose of caricature, parody, or pastiche (Article 5(3)(k));

- use in connection with the demonstration or repair of equipment (Article 5(3)(l)); and

- communication/making available for the purpose of research or private study by means of dedicated terminals on the premises of establishments referred to in Article 5(2)(c).

For ease of reference we will refer to these purpose-limited exceptions collectively as the EU proportionate use exception. Those relating to private copying, illustration in teaching or research, reporting a current topic or event, criticism or review, and parody, are considered further in Section 13.4.

13.2.2 The Specific Exceptions of the Computer Programs, Database, Rental and Lending Rights, and Orphan Works Directives

13.2.2.1 Limits and Additions to the Applicability of Article 5 Information Society Directive

Article 5 Information Society Directive applies generally (horizontally) with respect to the rights of reproduction, communication/making available, and distribution governed by Articles 2 to 4. As with all other provisions of the Directive, however, its application is without prejudice to the more specific provisions of the Rental and Lending Rights, Software, Satellite and Cable, and Database Directives (recital 20), as well as the 2012 Orphan Works Directive. This has the result that Article 5 does not apply with respect to the copyright or related rights subsisting in a computer program or database, or with respect to the fixation, broadcasting, communication and distribution rights of performers, producers of phonograms and first film fixations, and broadcasting organizations, since the exceptions to each are regulated exclusively by the Software Directive, Database Directive, and Rental and Lending Rights Directive respectively. By contrast, the Satellite and Cable Directive makes no provision for copyright or related rights exceptions, and is best read as not displacing Article 5 Information Society Directive. While the Rental and Lending Rights Directive is similarly silent as to any exceptions to the rental right of authors, the Directive's provision for exceptions to the related rights of fixation, broadcasting, communication, and distribution provided for in Articles 7 to 9 supports the view that no equivalent exceptions for the former were intended. Finally, while Article 5 Information Society Directive does apply (to the extent that it is capable of doing so) with respect to the copyright and related rights subsisting in orphan works within the meaning of the Orphan Works Directive, it is supplemented for those works by the additional exceptions and limitations required by the Orphan Works Directive.

13.2.2.2 Exceptions to Database Copyright: Article 6 Database Directive

The copyright subsisting in a database is subject to the exceptions (referred to as 'limitations') provided for in Article 6 Database Directive. These include a mandatory exception (which Member States must recognize) permitting the doing by a lawful user of a database or copy thereof of any acts reserved to the copyright holder to the extent that such acts are necessary to access or make normal use of the database's contents (Article 6(1)). They also include non-mandatory exceptions (which each Member State may in its discretion recognize) corresponding to Article 5(2)(b), (3)(a), (3)(e), and (3)(o) Information Society Directive, and permitting respectively:

- reproduction for private use and non-commercial ends;
- use for the purpose of illustration for non-commercial teaching or scientific research;
- use for the purpose of public security or to ensure the proper performance or reporting of administrative, parliamentary, or judicial proceedings; and
- use authorized under any existing domestic exceptions covering 'other cases of minor importance'.

As with all the exceptions provided for in the Information Society Directive, each of these mandatory and non-mandatory exceptions is subject to the three-step test of the Berne Convention, reproduced in Article 6(3) Database Directive.

13.2.2.3 Exceptions to Computer Program Copyright: Articles 5 and 6 Software Directive

More limited is the scope for Member States to recognize exceptions to the copyright subsisting in computer programs. Under the Software Directive, the only exceptions to such copyright for which Member States may provide are the three contained in Articles 5 and 6 Software Directive, each of which is mandatory. The first of these permits such acts of reproduction and alteration as are necessary for the lawful acquirer of the program to use it in accordance with its intended purpose, including for the purpose of error correction (Article 5(1)). By express provision of Article 5(2), this exception may be excluded by contract except to prevent the making of a back-up copy 'in so far as it is necessary' for use of the program.

The second mandatory exception required by the Software Directive is to permit the use of a program (by any authorized user of a copy of it) to observe, study, or test its functioning in order to determine the ideas and principles that underlie any aspect of it. However, such use is only permitted when undertaken while performing an act of loading, displaying, running, transmitting, or storing the program which the user is authorized to perform (Article 5(3)).

Finally, Article 6 Software Directive requires Member States to recognize acts of reproduction and alteration that are 'indispensable' to obtaining the information necessary to ensure the interoperability of an independently created computer program with other programs, subject to certain conditions and limitations which Article 6 specifies, including compliance with the three-step test of the Berne Convention (Article 6(3)).

Overall, the exceptions provided for in the Software Directive are limited in number and scope, and have as their aim to ensure that the copyright subsisting in a program does not in practice extend beyond its expression, in accordance with Article 1(2) of the Directive.

13.2.2.4 Exceptions to Rental and Public Lending Rights: Articles 6 and 10 Rental and Lending Rights Directive

As we saw in Section 12.3.4.2, Article 6 of the Rental and Lending Rights Directive permits Member States to derogate from the obligation which that Directive imposes to recognize and protect a public lending right of authors and others in certain circumstances. In addition, Article 10 permits Member States to recognize certain exceptions (referred to as 'limitations') to the related rights of fixation, communication/broadcast, and distribution which Articles 7 to 9 require them to recognize and protect in terms corresponding to the exceptions of Article 5(2)(b), (3)(a), (3)(c), and (3)(b) Information Society Directive and any exceptions to literary and artistic copyright which the Member State recognizes, subject in each case to compliance with the three-step test of the Berne Convention reproduced in Article 10(3).

13.2.2.5 Exceptions for Orphan Works: Article 6 Orphan Works Directive

The 2012 Orphan Works Directive postdates the Information Society Directive, and supplements its exceptions and limitations for certain categories of work and subject matter that are 'orphan works'. Its stated purpose is to facilitate the large-scale digitization of public institutional collections of works and phonograms in order to create European digital libraries (e-libraries) and thereby to promote the free movement of knowledge and innovation throughout the EU. To that end it requires Member States to permit certain public organizations to make limited uses of these works and subject matter in pursuit of their public interest objectives. In deciding whether the Directive applies, one must first establish whether the work or subject matter to be used is of a relevant type and satisfies the definition of an orphan work.

By provision of Article 1, the Directive applies to the following categories of work and subject matter:

(a) printed works ('works published in the form of books, journals, newspapers, magazines or other writings'), cinematographic or audiovisual works, and phonograms contained in the collections of certain public organizations, namely, publicly accessible libraries, educational establishments, and museums, archives, film, or audio heritage institutions; and

(b) cinematographic or audiovisual works and phonograms produced by public-service organizations up to and including 31 December 2002 and contained in their archives;

provided in each case that the work or phonogram is protected by copyright or related rights, and that it (i) was first published in a Member State, or (ii) if unpublished, was first broadcast in a Member State, or (iii) if never published or broadcast, has been made publicly accessible by the relevant organization with the consent of the rights holder, and it is reasonable to assume that the rights holder would not oppose the uses of the work or phonogram permitted by the Directive.

For a work or phonogram falling within these categories to be an orphan work, it must satisfy Articles 2 and 5. According to those Articles, an orphan work is any work or phonogram within the meaning of Article 1 for which none of the rights holders is identified or, if one or more of the rights holders is identified, for which none has been located despite a diligent search having been carried out and recorded in accordance with Article 3 of the Directive, and whose orphan works status has not been ended by a rights holder.

Having established the existence of an orphan work, it remains to determine who may make what particular use of it. The sole beneficiaries of the Orphan Works Directive are public organizations within the meaning of Article 1 established in EU territory. By Article 6 of the Directive, Member States are required to permit these organizations to:

- make orphan works available to the public within the meaning of Article 3 Information Society Directive; and

- reproduce orphan works within the meaning of Article 2 Information Society Directive for the purposes of digitization, making available, indexing, cataloguing, preservation, or restoration;

for the specific purpose of enabling the relevant organizations 'to achieve aims related to their public-interest missions, in particular the preservation of, the restoration of, and the provision of cultural and educational access to, works and phonograms contained in their collection'. Finally, Article 6(2) of the Directive permits the relevant organizations to 'generate revenues in the course of such uses', but only for the purpose of covering their costs of digitizing and making available the orphan works.

13.3 The Purpose of the Exceptions and Other Interpretative Principles

13.3.1 Ensuring a High Level of IP Protection

From the outset, the CJEU has emphasized the need to interpret the various exceptions to copyright and related rights 'strictly', as derogations from the primary rights of copyright and related rights holders (see, e.g., Case C–5/08 *Infopaq International A/S v Danske Dagblades Forening* [2009] ECR I-6569 (*Infopaq*)). This interpretation has been supported with reference to the three-step test of the Berne Convention (reproduced in the Information Society, Software, Database, and Rental and Lending Rights Directives), the need to ensure legal certainty for rights holders, and the aim of EU copyright and related rights law to ensure a high level of protection for rights holders in recognition of the proprietary nature of their IP rights and their protection under domestic and European fundamental rights instruments (see Section 10.3.2.1). Among other things, this explains the provision in recital 22 of the Information Society Directive that promoting learning and culture, including by application of the Article 5 exceptions, 'must not be achieved by sacrificing strict protection of rights or by tolerating illegal forms of distribution of counterfeited or pirated works'.

13.3.2 Ensuring a Fair Balance of Competing (Fundamental) Rights and Interests

The interpretative principles outlined in Section 13.3.1 continue to be valid, and to inform the European Court's interpretation of the exceptions provided for in the Information Society and other directives noted earlier. More recently, however, they have been supplemented by a judicial emphasis on the purpose of such exceptions to ensure that EU copyright and related rights law achieves a fair balance of competing rights and interests overall, consistent with the emphasis of the European Commission in its copyright policy documents (see Section 10.3.2.1). That conception finds direct expression in recital 31 Information Society Directive, on which the CJEU places special emphasis in its decisions involving Article 5(2) to (4) particularly. According to recital 31, '[a] fair balance of rights and interests between the different categories of rightholders, as well as between the different categories of rightholders and users of protected subject-matter must be safeguarded.' Also made clear in the Court's decisions is the nature of the third party rights and public interests that must be balanced, which include those deriving from the CFR. Of especial importance are the Article 11 right to freedom of expression (including the freedom and pluralism of the media) which underpins the exceptions of Article 5(3)(c) (use by the press and for reporting a current event), (3)(d) (quotation), and (3)(k) (caricature, pastiche, or parody) (see Case C–467/08 *Padawan SL v Sociedad General de Autores y Editores de España (SGAE)* [2010] ECR I-10055 (*Padawan*); Case C–145/10 *Painer v Standard VerlagsgmbH* [2011] ECR I-12533 (*Painer*); and Case C–201/13 *Deckmyn v Vandersteen* EU:C:2014:2132 (*Deckmyn*)), and the Article 14 right to education, which underpins the exceptions of Article 5(2)(c), (3)(a), and (3)(n) (see recital 14). Also important are the other provisions listed in Figure 13.2, and in particular the Article 7 right to respect for one's private and family life, home, and communications, the Article 10 right to freedom of thought, conscience, and religion, the Article 13 right to freedom from constraint of the arts and scientific research, the Article 26 right of persons with disabilities to benefit from measures designed to ensure their independence, social and occupational integration, and participation in the life of the community, and the range of rights of citizenship and justice recognized in Chapters V and VI, each of which can be seen to underpin one or more of the non-mandatory exceptions of Article 5(2) to (4) Information Society Directive.

Respect for private life	• Reproductions by a natural person for private use and non-commercial ends: Art. 5(2)(b)
Education	• Specific (non-commercial) acts of reproduction by publicly accessible libraries, educational establishments, or museums, or by archives: Art. 5(2)(c) • Uses by communication/making available, for the purpose of research or private study, to individual members of the public by dedicated terminals in para. 2(c) establishments of certain works/other subject matter: Art. 5(3)(n) • Proportionate uses for the sole purpose of illustration for non-commercial teaching or scientific research: Art. 5(3)(a)
Freedom of thought, conscience, and religion; citizenship and justice	• Reproductions of broadcasts made by non-commercial social institutions (e.g. hospitals or prisons): Art. 5(2)(e) • Uses for the purposes of public security or to ensure the proper performance or reporting of administrative, parliamentary, or judicial proceedings: Art. 5(3)(e) • Uses during religious celebrations or official celebrations organized by a public authority: Art. 5(3)(g) • Use of works, such as works of architecture or sculpture, made to be located permanently in public places: Art. 5(3)(h)
Freedom of expression, including press freedom and pluralism	• Reproduction by the press, and communication/making available of published articles on current economic, political, or religious topics, or of broadcast works/other subject matter of the same character, where such use is not expressly reserved, subject to sufficient acknowledgement of the work/subject matter: Art. 5(3)(c) • Proportionate uses of works/other subject matter in connection with the reporting of current events, subject to sufficient acknowledgement of the work/subject matter: Art. 5(3)(c) • Proportionate quotations for purposes such as criticism or review of a work or other subject matter which has already been lawfully made available to the public, subject to sufficient acknowledgement of the work/subject matter: Art. 5(3)(d) • Proportionate uses of political speeches as well as extracts of public lectures or similar works or subject matter for informatory purposes, subject to sufficient acknowledgement of the work/subject matter: Art. 5(3)(f) • Uses for the purpose of caricature, parody, or pastiche: Art. 5(3)(k)
Independence, integration, and participation of persons with disabilities	• Proportionate (non-commercial) uses, for the benefit of people with a disability, which are directly related to the disability: Art. 5(3)(b)

Figure 13.2 The fundamental rights underpinnings of Article 5(2) to (4) Information Society Directive

13.3.3 **Promoting the Internal Market while Respecting Subsidiarity**

13.3.3.1 **Promoting the Internal Market**

As legislative measures introduced under the precursors to Article 114 TFEU to support the establishment and functioning of the internal market, the Information Society Directive and other copyright and related rights directives have the harmonization of EU Member States' laws among their primary aims (see Sections 2.4.2.2.2 and 10.3). Given this, it is no surprise that promoting such harmonization and supporting the smooth functioning of the internal market in general are among the principles that govern interpretation of the exceptions to copyright and related rights which those directives recognize. This is made clear in recital 32 Information Society Directive, which describes the list of exceptions contained in Article 5 as 'aiming to ensure a functioning internal market'. It is also made clear in the case law, and the CJEU's requirement that Member States interpret even the non-mandatory exceptions of the Information Society Directive consistently in the interests of the internal market (see, e.g., *Deckmyn*). Thus, while the decision to implement one or more of the exceptions defined in Article 5(2) to (4) rests with individual states, once implemented those exceptions must be interpreted in line with CJEU authority. The same will apply with respect to the non-mandatory exceptions of the Database and Rental and Lending Rights Directives.

13.3.3.2 **Respecting Subsidiarity and the Legal Traditions of Member States**

As we saw in Section 2.4.1.3, Article 5(1) TEU makes the use of EU competences subject to the general EU law principle of subsidiarity with a view to ensuring that action is taken as close as possible to the people it affects. As a result, any Union action in areas not falling within its exclusive competence, which will include most action in the IP field, must be confined to action the objectives of which cannot be sufficiently achieved by Member States. In addition, and as discussed in Sections 1.2.3 and 2.4.1.2, both the TEU and CFR emphasize the importance for European union of building on and respecting the 'common values' and diversity of 'cultures and traditions' of European peoples and states; an aim supported by the principle of subsidiarity.

Recital 32 Information Society Directive expresses these principles and aims in the context of exceptions to copyright and related rights by describing the list of exceptions contained in Article 5 as 'tak[ing] due account of the different legal traditions in Member States', and requiring that Member States 'arrive at a coherent application of these exceptions and limitations'; use of the term 'coherent' alluding to states' margin of appreciation to that end. This concern with subsidiarity and respecting the different legal traditions of Member States accounts for the non-mandatory nature of the Article 5(2) to (4) exceptions, and for the preservation by Article 5(3)(o) of existing domestic exceptions covering 'cases of minor importance'. It also accounts for the considerable variation in the nature and scope of the individual exceptions which Member States currently recognize, and for the emphasis placed by the Court of Justice on the discretion of domestic courts when interpreting and applying them. Having said that, such variation can be expected to decrease now that all states have implemented the Information Society Directive, and even more so since the Court of Justice has made clear its view that once implemented, the core concepts of each exception permitted by the Directive must be interpreted consistently throughout the EU (as autonomous concepts of EU law) to ensure the proper functioning of the internal market, and applied to the facts of individual cases having regard to the same basic EU legal values and methodologies. In this view one sees the function of CFR and other general EU legal principles as a basis for harmonizing domestic copyright laws, including by supporting a certain division of labour and responsibility between European and domestic courts (see Section 1.2.2.3.3).

13.3.4 Applying these Interpretative Principles: Proportionality

The concern to respect the different legal traditions of Member States and promote harmonization around general principles of EU law and the CFR is further reflected in the centrality to this area of copyright and related rights jurisprudence of proportionality. By provision of Article 5(4) TEU, which we saw in Section 2.4.1.1, the principle of proportionality, with which all Union institutions must comply, requires that 'the content and form of Union action shall not exceed what is necessary to achieve the objectives of the Treaties'. Thus expressed, proportionality limits the valid exercise of EU competence to actions necessary and effective to achieve their legitimate (statutory) objective. According to the CJEU, however, it also limits the valid exercise by Member States of the discretion reserved to them by EU law in this area. Hence the Court's decision in the *Painer* case that when adopting measures to implement Article 5 Information Society Directive, Member States 'must exercise their discretion in compliance with the general principles of EU law, which include the principle of proportionality', including by ensuring that any such measures adopted are 'appropriate for attaining their objective and [do] not go beyond what is necessary to achieve it' (*Painer* [106]). The result is a view of each of the non-mandatory exceptions permitted by Article 5 as only covering such uses of a work or subject matter as are proportionate in the Article 5(4) TEU sense of not exceeding what is necessary to achieve the legitimate purpose which they serve. Article 5(3)(a), (3)(b), (3)(c), (3)(d), and (3)(f) Information Society Directive makes this restriction explicit for each of the exceptions contained therein, as does Article 5(4) of the Directive.

An initial question that arises from the restriction of the non-mandatory exceptions to proportionate uses of a protected work or subject matter is how to define the legitimate purpose which the use serves. For example, is the purpose of an Article 5(3)(c) use of a work to report a current event to be defined locally, as reporting a current event, or at a higher level of generality, as protecting freedom of expression? It seems clear that in the case of the purpose-limited (proportionate use) exceptions at least, the former, local definition of the purpose of the use is correct. One reason is the express terms of Article 5(3)(a), (3)(b), (3)(c), (3)(d), and (3)(f), which define the scope of each exception with reference to the relevant 'non-commercial purpose', 'specific disability', 'informatory purpose', 'specific purpose', and 'informatory purpose' respectively. In addition, however, a local definition of the legitimate purpose of the use better supports the interpretative principles outlined in Section 13.3.1, including the need to interpret the exceptions strictly to ensure a high level of IP protection, legal certainty, and compliance with the three-step test of Article 5(5). We can therefore say that in order for the use of a work or subject matter to fall within the scope of Article 5(3)(c), it must be limited to what is necessary to report the current event in question, and that the same interpretative approach should be adopted *mutatis mutandis* with respect to the other purpose-limited exceptions of Article 5(2) to (4). On the other hand, when deciding what exactly *is* necessary to report the event in question, the starting presumption must be that speaking and hearing of the relevant event is an exercise of freedom of expression. In this way, the basis of the current reporting exception in freedom of expression is recognized, consistent with the purposive, systemic, and teleological approach to legislative interpretation which EU law requires (see Section 1.2.3).

This proportionality-based approach to copyright and related rights exceptions might be said fully to satisfy the interpretative principles of Section 13.3.1 to 13.3.3. It seems clear from recent case law, however, that that is not the view of the EU Court. Specifically, it seems clear from the Court's decision in the *Deckmyn* case that having established that a use of a work or subject matter is not excessive having regard to the purpose that it serves, domestic courts must go on to consider whether, having regard to all the facts of the case, the application of the exception would ensure a fair balance of the competing rights and interests which the use engages. In addition, when doing this the courts must look beyond the particular freedom of expression or other general right or interest that motivates the exception itself to identify any other fundamental rights and interests engaged by the unauthorized use of the work or subject matter. Only in this way, *Deckmyn* suggests, can they decide whether permitting the unauthorized use in question would be consistent with the fair balance that Article 5 requires. Hence the finding in *Deckmyn* that in determining whether a parodic use of a work is permitted under a domestic exception implementing Article 5(3)(k) (based on the Article 11 CFR right to freedom of expression), a national court must consider whether the use has the effect of associating the work with a discriminatory message so as to engage also Article 21 CFR and, if it does, weigh that consideration on the side of the copyright owner when deciding what a fair balance of competing rights and interests requires. The case supports a three-stage test of proportionality that requires explicit judicial engagement with a wider range of rights and interests than those which it is the purpose of copyright and the relevant exception to protect. Put differently, it supports replacing the two-stage necessity-focused test of proportionality supported by Article 5(4) TEU with a more traditional proportionality test that requires, as a further step in the analysis, that the overall disadvantages of allowing the dealing not be disproportionate to the aims pursued. Hence, when deciding proportionate use in European copyright law, one must determine whether the use in question: (a) was for a legitimate (statutory) purpose; (b) exceeded what was necessary to achieve that purpose; and (c) engaged any other fundamental rights and interests such that permitting it would fail to reflect a fair balance of competing rights and interests overall.

In supporting this three-stage test of proportionate use, the Court of Justice may be criticized on at least three closely related grounds. The first is for reducing the scope of freedom of expression and other fundamental rights protections afforded by EU copyright law to third parties and society by turning provisions designed specifically to protect them from undue encroachment by copyright and related rights into general sites for balancing all parties' rights and interests. The second is for rejecting the view of the EU legislature as to the social importance of the object to be achieved by each exception and the burdens imposed by the means used to achieve it, and thereby usurping the legislature's law-making role.[2] And the third is for reducing legal certainty, and the benefits which it confers in enabling: (a) individuals to organize their lives and businesses; and (b) the EU Court and domestic courts to apply EU legislation in a way that gives effect to the legislature's legal policy choices. Indeed, when cast as a general site for balancing competing rights and interests, the proportionate use exception of EU copyright law begins to resemble the US fair use defence, albeit informed by the values of the CFR and EU Treaties rather than those of US copyright law (see Section 13.4.1).

13.3.5 **Exceptions versus Limitations**

A final interpretative issue of relevance concerns the nature and significance of the Directive's distinction between 'exceptions' and 'limitations' to copyright and related rights (see, e.g., Article 5 Information Society Directive). According to the Court of

---

[2] See in this regard L. Hoffmann, 'The Influence of the European Principle of Proportionality upon UK Law' in E. Ellis (ed.), *The Principle of Proportionality in the Laws of Europe* (Hart Publishing, 1999) 107, 109.

Justice in Joined Cases C–457/11 to 460/11 *VG Wort v Kyocera* EU:C:2013:426 (*VG Wort*), a provision is an exception if it excludes particular uses of a work or subject matter from those reserved to the rights holder and a limitation if it merely restricts the holder's rights in relation to the relevant uses without necessarily excluding them from the uses reserved to the rights holder as such. The consequence of this interpretation would seem to be that only provisions guaranteeing complete third party freedom to use a work or subject matter will be appropriately classified as exceptions, while provisions permitting such use subject to payment or satisfaction of some other condition will be classified as limitations. If this were true, however, one would expect domestic provisions introduced in reliance on Article 5(2)(a), (b), or (e) Information Society Directive to be limitations, since those paragraphs only allow Member States to permit third party uses of a work or subject matter for the purpose specified on condition that the third parties compensate the relevant rights holder for the use. Thus, rather than protecting third parties' freedom of use as such, Article 5(2)(a), (b), and (e) turns the exclusionary rights of copyright and related rights into liability rules by allowing use subject to payment.

This, however, is not consistent with the reasoning and decision in *VG Wort*. On the contrary, according to the Court in that case, any domestic provision that permits a reproduction or other reserved use without first obtaining the rights holder's authorization—including a provision introduced in reliance on Article 5(2)(b)—is an exception. Given this, the Court held, any purported authorization by a rights holder of an Article 5(2)(b) act will be invalid and irrelevant for the purpose of considering the 'fair compensation' to which the holder is entitled under the Information Society Directive. This analysis is difficult to accept, since it seems to leave no scope for the existence of a limitation that is not also an exception within the meaning of Article 5, and therefore to undermine the Court's insistence that the distinction between exceptions and limitations 'be given effect' ([35]).

13.4 Determining Proportionate Use in Practice

13.4.1 Limits of the EU Proportionate Use Exception

It was suggested earlier that the purpose-limited exceptions permitted by Article 5(2) and (3) Information Society Directive correspond broadly to international conceptions of fair use, and can therefore be read as supporting an EU proportionate use exception. An important difference between the EU proportionate use exception thus defined and the fair use exceptions of other jurisdictions, such as the United States, is the restriction of the former to uses of a work or subject matter for one or more statutorily defined purposes. In addition, in the United States the fairness of an unauthorized use must be determined having regard to the following inclusive list of factors (17 USC § 107):

> 1. The purpose and character of the use, including whether such use is of a commercial nature or is for non-profit educational purposes; 2. The nature of the copyrighted work; 3. The amount and substantiality of the portion used in relation to the copyrighted work as a whole; and 4. The effect of the use upon the potential market for or value of the copyrighted work.

The result on its face is a spectrum of unauthorized uses, ranging from non-commercial uses of non-expressive works that do not substitute for the protected work in the market (which are presumptively fair and therefore non-infringing) to commercial uses of expressive works that do substitute for the protected work in the market (which are presumptively unfair and therefore infringing). In practice, however, and as the US case law on parody illustrates, the courts exercise a wide discretion, allowing any unauthorized use of a protected work the allowance of which they believe to be consistent with the constitutionally inscribed purpose of US copyright law (to promote the progress of science and the useful arts) and a 'sensitive balancing of interests' (*Campbell v Acuff-Rose Music*, 510 US 569 (1994) 584–5).

In the discussion that follows we consider five of the specific uses which the EU proportionate use exception permits, covering private copying (Article 5(2)(b)), use for illustration in teaching or research (Article 5(3)(a)), use in connection with the reporting of a current topic or event (Article 5(3)(c)), quotations for such purposes as criticism or review (Article 5(3)(d)), and use for the purpose of parody (Article 5(3)(k)). Before doing so, however, it is important to note some restrictions on the scope of these provisions. First, neither the current topic exception of Article 5(3)(c) first part, nor the quotation exception of Article 5(3)(d), permits uses of a previously unpublished work or subject matter. In addition, all but the private use and caricature, parody, or pastiche exceptions require the user to indicate the source of the work or subject matter used, including the author's name, unless, in the case of certain exceptions, doing so turns out to be impossible. Third, it seems clear that none of the exceptions permits any use of a work or subject matter or a copy thereof acquired by the user unlawfully. And finally, and as seen in Section 13.3.4, all exceptions are subject to a three-stage proportionality requirement, and thus do not permit any use that is not for a legitimate (statutory) purpose, that goes beyond what is necessary having regard to its legitimate purpose, or that fails to reflect a fair balance of competing (fundamental) rights and interests more generally.

The policy rationale for each of these four restrictions is clear. First, confining the current topic and quotation exceptions to previously published works protects the moral rights and interests of authors and others to determine the readiness of their works and subject matter for public dissemination. For example, there would seem to be no public interest justification for permitting third parties to reproduce parts of an unfinished novel for the purpose of criticizing or reviewing it. By contrast, there may be a public interest justification for permitting such reproduction where necessary to report an event in which the public has an inherent interest. Hence the absence of an equivalent restriction to the exception contained in Article 5(3)(c) second part, which signals the EU legislature's view that a fair balance of competing rights and interests might sometimes require the use of a previously unpublished work or subject matter in connection with the reporting of a current event.

So too requiring users to indicate the source of the work or subject matter they have used protects the moral rights or interests of persons to be identified as the author or maker of their works and subject matter, in addition to facilitating the exploitation of their rights by making it easier for members of the public to identify them. Third, confining the exceptions to uses of a (copy of a) work or subject matter that the user has lawfully acquired conforms with the principle of justice that a person ought not to benefit from his own wrongdoing. And finally, confining the exceptions to proportionate uses of a work or subject matter via the methodology described in Section 13.3.4 (see also Section 13.4.3.1) helps to ensure that their application reflects a fair balance between ensuring a high level of IP protection and (other) fundamental rights and interests.

13.4.2 Determining Proportionate Use in Practice

13.4.2.1 A Test of Purpose and Proportionality

In order to establish proportionate use in practice it is necessary to identify the use in question and establish, first, that it was for a protected purpose and, second, that it was proportionate. It is important to keep these two steps separate, since there is no point considering the proportionality of a use if it is not of a type recognized as capable of supporting an exception. On the other hand, the two steps are plainly related, since the proportionality of a use depends on the legitimate purpose that it serves.

The test of a use's purpose must be an objective rather than a subjective one in the sense of depending on its impact on its intended audience rather than the subjective intention of the user of the work or subject matter as such. On this view, a use should be regarded as having the purpose that a reasonable person would assume it to have been intended to have.

As we have seen, the requirement that a use be proportionate having regard to its purpose derives from the express terms of Article 5(3)(a), (3)(c), (3)(d), and (3)(f) for the exceptions contained therein and, for the Article 5(2)(b), (3)(k), and other proportionate use exceptions, from Article 5(4) and the CJEU's interpretation of the Directive's recitals and general requirements of EU law. In determining whether it is satisfied, it is important to bear in mind the purpose of Article 5 to ensure a fair balance between the competing rights and interests of rights holders and users, including the rights and interests of rights holders to a high level of IP protection. The result in practice is the approach outlined in Section 13.3.4, involving the determination of proportionality in three parts. The first part requires the court to decide whether the use was for a legitimate (statutory) purpose. If it was, the second part requires the court to decide whether the use exceeded what was necessary to achieve that purpose. And if it did not, the third part requires the court to consider all the facts of the case and decide whether the use engages any other fundamental rights and interests beyond those underpinning the protection of IP and exception in question and, if it does, whether a finding of proportionate use would nonetheless reflect a fair balance of the competing rights and interests engaged by the use overall. The result is the test described in Figure 13.3.

13.4.2.2 Proportionate Use Distinguished from Defamation and Breach of Confidence

When considering the availability of a proportionate use exception, a distinction must be drawn between proportionate use of a work or subject matter on the one hand and malicious or unjustified criticism of a person on the other. While a claim of copyright or related rights infringement will sometimes be motivated by a claimant's objection to

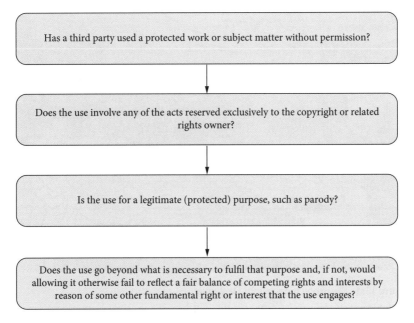

Figure 13.3 Determining proportionate use in practice

the critical content of a defendant's work, particularly in the case of an unauthorized use for the purpose of criticism or parody under Article 5(3)(d) or (3)(k), ensuring that such use is substantively justified is not the concern of copyright or related rights. Thus, for example, neither Article 5(3)(d) nor Article 5(3)(k) requires that a criticism or parody be substantively justified. The only situation in which such considerations will be relevant is if the criticism or parody has the effect of associating the author of a work with a discriminatory message so as to engage Article 21 CFR. This was made clear by the CJEU in the *Deckmyn* case, which involved a parody of a picture depicting a crowd of white, unveiled people collecting coins as they were thrown to the ground by a figure flying above (see Figure 13.4). The parodist had replaced the people collecting the coins with people of colour wearing veils and, in so doing the Court of Justice said, had potentially

Figure 13.4 The protected work in *Deckmyn*

Image by Willy Vandersteen, © WPG Publishers Belgium.

engaged Article 21 by associating the protected work with a discriminatory message. If that were the case (which was for the national court to decide), the balancing exercise required by Article 5(3)(k) would have needed to take account of the copyright holder's 'legitimate interest in ensuring that the work protected by copyright is not associated with such a message' (*Deckmyn* [31]).

So too when considering the availability of a proportionate use exception, one must distinguish the issue of copyright or related rights infringement from the issue of breach of confidence. Once again, while a claim of copyright or related rights infringement will sometimes be motivated by a claimant's objection to the effect of a defendant's use of a work or subject matter in making the work or subject matter available to the public, protecting the confidentiality of information is not the purpose of copyright or related rights. Thus, only where the exception is expressly limited to previously published works or subject matter, or where the unauthorized use engages the fundamental rights or interests of authors or others to privacy, should such considerations be relevant.

13.4.3 Private Copying: Article 5(2)(b) Information Society Directive

For many, copying works, sound recordings, and films included on a lawfully acquired CD or DVD to enable them to be played on another device and/or shared with immediate family members would likely be regarded as a paradigmatic example of proportionate use. Having purchased a copy of the work or subject matter, we ought surely to be able to enjoy it on our devices of choice, and to effect any acts of technological conversion (format shifting) required to enable this.

In some European countries, the issues surrounding the private copying of protected works and subject matter first arose in the context of the authorization right of copyright and related rights holders (see Sections 12.2.1 and 12.3.1). This followed the claims of rights holders that manufacturing and selling blank tapes, tape recorders, and other products commonly used to reproduce protected works and subject matter involved an authorization to engage in acts of unauthorized copying itself. A well-known example is the claim that was made against the manufacturers and sellers of tape recorders in *CBS Songs Ltd v Amstrad Consumer Electronics Plc* [1988] UKHL 15, [1987] RPC 104 (*CBS*). The claim was rejected by the English House of Lords, with Lord Templeman offering the following analysis of some of the issues raised by private copying for copyright and related rights (610–12).

> From the point of view of society the present position is lamentable. Millions of breaches of the law must be committed by home copiers every year. Some home copiers may break the law in ignorance, despite extensive publicity and warning notices on records, tapes and films. Some home copiers may break the law because they estimate that the chances of detection are nonexistent. Some home copiers may consider that the entertainment and recording industry already exhibit all the characteristics of undesirable monopoly—lavish expenses, extravagant earnings and exorbitant profits—and that the blank tape is the only restraint on further increases in the prices of records. Whatever the reason for home copying, the beat of Sergeant Pepper and the soaring sounds of the Miserere from unlawful copies are more powerful than law-abiding instincts or twinges of conscience. A law which is treated with such contempt should be amended or repealed.
>
> In these proceedings the court is being asked to forbid the sale to the public of all or some selected types of tape recorder or to ensure that advertisements for tape recorders shall be censored by the court on behalf of copyright owners. The court has no power to make such orders and judges are not qualified to decide whether a restraint should be placed on the manufacture of electronic equipment or on the contents of advertising.

No one is to blame for the present situation. Copyright law could not envisage and now cannot cope with mass-production techniques and inventions which create a vast market for the works of a copyright owner but also provide opportunities for his rights to be infringed. Parliament could place limitations on the manufacture or sale of certain types of tape recorder and could prescribe notices and warnings to be included in advertisements. Parliament might take the view that any such restraints and prescriptions would constitute an unwarrantable interference with the development of the electronic industry and be ineffective.

Parliament could legalise home copying just as the copying of sound broadcasts was expressly authorised for 'private purposes.' . . . Since 1977 . . . a levy on blank tapes has met with more favourable consideration. In face of the difficulties inherent in the problem generated by the mass-production of electronic equipment capable of infringing copyright Parliament has not yet determined on any course of action. These proceedings will have served a useful purpose if they remind Parliament of the grievances of the recording companies and other owners of copyright and if at the same time they draw the attention of Parliament to the fact that home copying cannot be prevented, is widely practised and brings the law into disrepute.

Among other things, this passage is notable for its view of private copying as evidence of the difficulties created for the copyright and related rights regime by the emergence of new technologies, and the struggle of that regime to maintain social legitimacy in the face of such new technologies particularly (see Section 10.4). It also highlights the demands on courts to address new problems as they arise, rather than waiting for the legislature to intervene. In the private copying context specifically, several domestic European parliaments have intervened to address the problem highlighted in *CBS* by means of a private copying exception, accompanied in countries such as Germany by a levy (payment obligation) attached to copying devices and products. The provision of the Information Society Directive that enables such intervention is Article 5(2)(b), which expressly allows Member States to permit natural persons to make a reproduction of a protected work or subject matter on any medium for private use and for ends that are neither directly nor indirectly commercial. However, and recalling our previous discussion of the distinction between exceptions and limitations, Article 5(2)(b) also requires that any such permission be made conditional upon the copyright or related rights holder's receipt of fair compensation for the unauthorized use. In addition, it states that such compensation must be calculated to take account of the application or otherwise of technical measures within the meaning of Article 6 of the Directive. This provision has triggered more preliminary referrals to the Court of Justice than any other paragraph of Article 5 to date, including several focused on the obligation to pay fair compensation, which obligation arises under Article 5(2)(a) and (e) as well.

13.4.3.1 Private Copying of Lawfully Acquired Published or Unpublished Works or Subject Matter: *ACI Adam, Portrait Art*, and *Technische Universität Darmstadt*

The CJEU and superior domestic courts of EU Member States have considered the scope of the private copying exception permitted by Article 5(2)(b) on several occasions. In Case C–435/12 *ACI Adam BV v Stichting de Thuiskopie* EU:C:2014:254 (*ACI Adam*), for example, the Court of Justice confirmed that the exception only permits reproductions of a work or subject matter made from a lawfully acquired source. As justification for this decision it invoked the three-step test of Article 5(5) and the interpretative principles outlined in Section 13.3, including the aim of Article 5(2)(b) to ensure a fair balance between the competing rights and interests of rights holders and users, the need to respect the different legal traditions of Member States while also protecting the proper functioning of the internal market, and the importance of ensuring that the dissemination of culture is not achieved by sacrificing the strict protection of rights or tolerating the illegal distribution of counterfeited or pirated works.

In its further decision in Case C–117/13 *Technische Universität Darmstadt v Eugen Ulmer KG* EU:C:2014:2196, the CJEU considered whether Article 5(2)(b) permits the authorization by a Member State of the use of dedicated terminals under Article 5(3) (n) Information Society Directive that enable works and subject matter to be printed out or stored on a USB stick. That question arose because of the restriction of Article 5(3) (n) to acts of communication/making available within the meaning of Article 3 of the Directive, which precluded the Article from being relied upon by the referring Member State to authorize the acts of printing and storing in question. According to the EU Court, however, such acts could nonetheless be authorized under national legislation transposing the private copying exception of Article 5(2)(b) (or the separate exception of Article 5(2)(a)) provided its conditions were met.

A final decision of note from 2014 is that of the Bundesgerichtshof (German Federal Supreme Court) in *Porträtkunst* BGH, I ZR 35/13 (19 March 2014) (*Portrait Art* (2014) 45 *IIC* 981) concerning the private copying exception of Section 53(1) German Copyright Act. The issue for the German court was whether a person could rely on Section 53(1) to avoid liability for scanning and storing on his computer digital copies of unpublished photographs which depicted him. The court held that he could, since the conditions for the exception had been satisfied: the defendant was a natural person who had acquired the copies of the images by lawful means, and whose reproduction of them served no commercial purpose. In reaching its decision the court affirmed the decision of the appeal court that the Section 53(1) exception was not to be construed restrictively, and in particular was not to be read as applying only to published works. In its view, such a restrictive reading of the exception was supported by neither the restriction of other copyright and related rights exceptions to published works, the German constitutional right of freedom of art, nor Article 5(2)(a) Information Society Directive. This must be right since, and as the German court explained, the restriction of an exception to previously published works and subject matter is aimed at protecting the moral rights or interests of authors or others to determine the readiness of their works and subject matter for publication. It follows that where the exception in question permits the reproduction of a work or subject matter only, without also permitting its communication/making available or distribution to the public, this moral right or interest is not engaged, and thus the justification for the restriction does not apply.

13.4.3.2 The Obligation to Pay Fair Compensation: *Padawan*, *Opus Supplies*, *Amazon.com*, *ACI Adam*, *VG Wort*, and *Copydan*

The CJEU has also had occasion in several cases to consider the obligation of third parties to pay fair compensation for any private copying permitted under Article 5(2)(b). That obligation also arises under Article 5(2)(a) and (e) (see *VG Wort* [32]), and is described in recital 35 of the Directive as follows:

> In certain cases of exceptions or limitations, rightholders should receive fair compensation to compensate them adequately for the use made of their protected works or other subject-matter. When determining the form, detailed arrangements and possible level of such fair compensation, account should be taken of the particular circumstances of each case. When evaluating these circumstances, a valuable criterion would be the possible harm to the rightholders resulting from the act in question. In cases where rightholders

have already received payment in some other form, for instance as part of a licence fee, no specific or separate payment may be due. The level of fair compensation should take full account of the degree of use of technological protection measures referred to in this Directive. In certain situations where the prejudice to the rightholder would be minimal, no obligation for payment may arise.

The first fair compensation decision of the CJEU was *Padawan*, where the Court held that since 'fair compensation' is an autonomous concept of EU law, it is subject to EU regulation. Thus, and as with the other non-mandatory exceptions of Article 5(2) to (4), while it is open to Member States to introduce a private copying exception in reliance on Article 5(2)(b), any such exception must be implemented in accordance with the requirements of that Article, and defined and developed in a consistent and harmonized manner.

In *Padawan* the Court also established several other principles regarding the obligation to pay fair compensation under Article 5(2)(b). First, it affirmed that the aim of such payment is to make good the harm that is or might be caused to a rights holder by the unauthorized use of her work or subject matter within the scope of that Article; albeit proof of actual harm to a rights holder not being required, consistent with the reference to 'possible harm' in recital 35. In addition, while it is in principle for the user herself to make good such harm, the practical difficulties of enforcing this obligation, and the fact that the harm caused by each separate private use may be too minimal to give rise to an obligation for payment at all (see again recital 35), led the Court to interpret the fair compensation requirement as capable of being satisfied by a Member State's establishment of a private copying levy of the type referred to by Lord Templeman in *CBS* discussed earlier. Such a levy requires the fair compensation to be paid not by the users of works and subject matter themselves, but rather by the third parties who supply them with the equipment or copying services needed to reproduce the works and subject matter. Those third parties are then able if they choose to pass the costs of paying such compensation on to the users by charging more for the equipment or copying services supplied. According to the CJEU, these features of a private copying levy ensure the fair balance required between the interests and rights of rights holders and users of protected works and subject matter in the application of Article 5(2)(b). The only qualification imposed by the Court was to require that the levy be confined to equipment and services liable to be used for private copying, and not applied indiscriminately with respect to equipment and services not made available to private users and clearly reserved for uses other than private copying. If that qualification is satisfied, the Court in *Padawan* held, it is not necessary to show that those acquiring the equipment or services have in fact used them to copy a protected work or subject matter. In addition, according to the Court in the *ACI Adam* case, since Article 5(2)(b) only permits reproductions made from lawfully acquired copies of a work or subject matter, any private copying levy must distinguish between reproductions made from lawful and unlawful sources in order to ensure respect for the fair balance required by Article 5. This is because, in the absence of such a distinction, all the users of equipment and copying services subject to the levy will be indirectly penalized for the unauthorized acts of those who reproduce works and subject matter from unlawful sources, which would be unfair.

Further issues regarding the obligation to pay fair compensation for private copying arose for the Court in Case C–462/09 *Stichting de Thuiskopie v Opus Supplies Deutschland GmbH* [2011] ECR I-5331 (*Opus Supplies*), Case C–521/11 *Amazon.com International Sales Inc. v Austro-Mechana Gesellschaft zur Wahrnehmung mechanisch-musikalischer Urheberrechte Gesellschaft mbH* EU:C:2013:515 (*Amazon.com*), and Case C–463/12 *Copydan Båndkopi v Nokia Danmark A/S* EU:C:2015:144. In *Opus Supplies*, the Court confirmed that the obligation to pay fair compensation—or more particularly, the obligation of a Member State to secure fair compensation for rights holders whose works or subject matter have been reproduced for private ends under a domestic exception introduced in reliance on Article 5(2)(b)—arises even where the persons responsible for paying the compensation under national law are established outside the territorial borders of the state. In *Opus Supplies* itself, the issue arose in the context of a dispute involving a German-based company that offered reproduction equipment and media for sale online to consumers in the Netherlands. The goods were ordered and paid for over the Internet, after which the supplier arranged for the goods to be delivered from Germany to the individual purchasers. The question arose as to who was responsible under the Dutch private copying levy for paying the compensation due to the rights holders: the German company that supplied the reproduction equipment and media, or the Dutch individuals who purchased them? According to the Court of Justice, while that question was for the national authorities to decide, the Netherlands remained under an obligation to ensure, in accordance with its territorial competence, that the harm suffered by authors as a result of Dutch residents copying their works for private ends was fairly compensated. The fact that the suppliers of the reproduction equipment and media were based in another EU Member State had 'no bearing' on that obligation. So too, the Court confirmed in *Amazon.com*, the fact that a levy intended to finance that compensation has already been paid in another Member State has no bearing on the obligation of the first Member State.

The premise of *Padawan*, confirmed in *Opus Supplies*, is that Member States enjoy broad discretion when deciding who must discharge the obligation to pay compensation required by Article 5(2)(b). In *Amazon.com*, the Court affirmed that the same broad discretion exists with respect to 'the form, detailed arrangements and possible level of such compensation' ([20]), subject to the state taking account of all the relevant circumstances in each case (see recital 35 of the Directive). In addition, this discretion extends to enabling a state to require or permit part or all of the compensation to be paid indirectly, rather than directly, to those entitled to it, including to social and cultural institutions established for their benefit. However, where compensation is paid indirectly to a social or cultural institution, the institution must actually benefit the relevant rights holders, and must not operate in a discriminatory manner—as, for example, by excluding nationals of other Member States. According to the Court, this interpretation of Article 5(2)(b) is supported by recitals 10 and 11 of the Directive, which establish as one of the objectives of IP protection,

> to ensure that European cultural creativity and production receive the necessary resources to continue their creative and artistic work and to safeguard the independence and dignity of artistic creators and performers.

The extent of Member States' discretion when deciding who should pay the compensation required by Article 5(2)(b) was considered again by the CJEU in *Copydan*. That case arose from a domestic dispute between Copydan—the copyright collecting society authorized to collect, administer, and distribute payments made under a private copying levy system—and Nokia, a company marketing mobile telephones to business customers in that state. Several issues were referred to the Court, and answered as follows:

(a) All equipment, devices, and media that are able to make copies and that are made available to natural persons as private users can be subject to a private copying levy. This includes detachable and non-detachable memory cards contained in mobile telephones that are capable of storing copyright works, notwithstanding their other functions and the ancillary nature of their copying functionality.

(b) The principle of (a) also applies where the equipment, etc., is made available to business customers rather than individuals, provided: (i) that the persons responsible for paying the levy are aware that the cards will be sold on by those business customers, but do not know to whom they will be sold; (ii) the introduction of the system is justified by practical difficulties; (iii) the persons responsible for paying the levy are exempt from doing so if they can establish that they have supplied the equipment, etc., to persons other than natural persons for purposes clearly unrelated to copying for private use; and (iv) the system provides for an effective right exclusive to any final purchaser of the equipment, etc., to reimbursement of the levy.

(c) Notwithstanding (a), the multi-functionality of the relevant medium or ancillary nature of its copying function may be treated by a Member State as affecting the amount of fair compensation payable. This may be significant, for example, in a state that has exercised the discretion conferred by recital 35 to limit the obligation to pay fair compensation to uses that cause more than minimal prejudice to the rights holder. In such a state, if all users of a medium can be shown rarely to use its copying function in practice, the making available of that function may produce minimal prejudice to the rights holder and thereby prevent the obligation to pay fair compensation from arising under domestic law.

(d) Since the general EU legal principle of equal treatment—enshrined also in Article 20 CFR—requires that comparable situations not be treated differently unless the difference is objectively justified, Member States cannot (for example) treat mobile telephone memory cards differently from the internal memories of MP3 players unless, in the view of the state's domestic courts: (i) the components in question are not comparable from the point of view of the requirements relating to fair compensation; or, if the components are comparable, (ii) the differential treatment is justified. With respect to (i), an example of non-comparable components may be components that are detachable and non-detachable from a device. With respect to (ii), one basis for justifying the differential treatment of components may be the rights holders' receipt of fair compensation with respect to one component in another form.

(e) In contrast to other paragraphs of Article 5, such as Article 5(2)(a), Article 5(2) (b) is not limited to reproductions made on specific types of media. Given this, Member States may provide for fair compensation in respect of reproductions of protected works made by a natural person by or with the aid of a device belonging to a third party.

Finally, and as we noted earlier, in *VG Wort* the Court of Justice held that where national legislation implementing a private copying exception in reliance on Article 5(2)(b) is properly characterized as an 'exception' rather than a 'limitation' within the meaning of the Information Society Directive, it will not be possible for the rights holder expressly or impliedly to discharge the unauthorized user of her obligation to pay fair compensation within the meaning of that Article due to the effect of the exception in excluding her right to prevent or authorize the relevant private copying act.

13.4.3.3 The Relevance of Technological Protection Measures: *VG Wort* and *Copydan*

As we have seen, Article 5(2)(b) requires that the fair compensation which must be paid to rights holders in any Member State in which a private copying exception exists is calculated to take account of the application or otherwise of any technical measures within the meaning of Article 6 of the Directive, being technical measures designed to prohibit or restrict unauthorized use of the relevant work or subject matter. In *VG Wort* the issue arose as to the impact if any on the obligation of Member States recognizing a private copying exception to ensure that fair compensation to rights holders is paid of a failure by such rights holders to apply the relevant technical measures. According to the Court, it is for Member States and not rights holders to ensure that the private copying exception of Article 5(2)(b) is properly implemented, among other things by ensuring that acts not falling with its scope remain prohibited. Given this, the Court held, a failure by rights holders to apply technical measures to prevent or restrict such acts does not deprive them of their right to receive fair compensation in accordance with Article 5(2)(b). On the other hand, the adoption by rights holders of technical measures is, the Court held, something that Member States should encourage, since it facilitates the proper application of the private copying exception, and adjusting the compensation owed to rights holders is one legitimate means of encouraging it.

13.4.4 Use of a work or Subject Matter for Illustration in Teaching or Scientific Research: Article 5(3)(a)

Article 5(3)(a) permits Member States to recognize exceptions to the reproduction and communication/making available to the public rights 'for the sole purpose of illustration for teaching or scientific research … to the extent justified by the non-commercial purpose to be achieved' and subject to the user's indication of the source, including the author's name, unless this turns out to be impossible. As we saw earlier, in the case of orphan works within the meaning of the Orphan Works Directive, Member States must also recognize exceptions to the reproduction and making available to the public rights of Articles 2 and 3 Information Society Directive to permit educational establishments (among other public organizations) to 'achieve aims related to their public-interest missions' (see Section 13.2.2).

13.4.4.1 Illustration for Teaching

The teaching exception permitted by Article 5(3)(a) follows that permitted by Article 10 Berne Convention (see also Article 15(1)(d) Rome Convention), and seems to have been intended to have the same meaning. Hence its restriction to proportionate uses accompanied by an acknowledgement of the work or subject matter used, and its inclusion of uses of works and subject matter in both face-to-face and distance teaching (see recital 42). The exception is also wide enough to cover a variety of acts by and on behalf of teachers and students at primary, secondary, and tertiary levels, provided only that such acts are directly linked to the clarification or exemplification of a point made in the delivery or examination of a formal educational programme. Such acts can be expected to include the proportionate reproduction, communication, or distribution of protected materials to students as part of a lecture or PowerPoint presentation, or in an informal, online discussion of some aspect of the curriculum being taught. They can also be expected to include the proportionate reproduction, communication, or distribution to the public of the original or copies of a musical or dramatic work in the course of studying music or drama. By contrast, the performance of a play by students to members of the public is unlikely to be considered a use for the sole purpose of illustration for teaching within the meaning of Article 5(3)(a).

13.4.4.2 Scientific Research

As with the illustration for teaching exception, there is no CJEU case law concerning the meaning of the scientific research exception of Article 5(3)(b). It seems likely, however, that the Court would interpret that exception as extending to any proportionate use of a work or subject matter for the purpose of testing a hypothesis or reaching a conclusion in the course of undertaking a systematic investigation of some topic of theoretical or practical interest. Such an interpretation reflects common language understandings of 'research' as well as the interpretative principles outlined in Section 13.3. The result would be a more restrictive reading of the exception than that supported in other jurisdictions, including Canada, where the Supreme Court in *SOCAN v Bell Canada*, 2012 SCC 36 supported its own 'ordinary meaning' definition of 'research' to find that making excerpts of musical works available for download on the Internet to enable members of the public to decide whether to purchase a full copy of the work was fair dealing with the works for the purpose of research. According to that definition ([22]), 'research' includes

> many activities that do not demand the establishment of new facts or conclusions. It can be piecemeal, informal, exploratory, or confirmatory. It can in fact be undertaken for no purpose except personal interest. It is true that research can be for the purpose of reaching new conclusions, but this should be seen as only one, not the primary component of the definitional framework.

Important to the court's analysis in *SOCAN v Bell Canada* was its understanding of the purpose of Canadian copyright law to encourage the dissemination of musical and other works, and its view that the concept of research should be analysed from the perspective of the actual end users of works, and not from the perspective of those who facilitate their use. In *SOCAN* this led 'research' to be defined from the perspective of the prospective purchaser of the musical works and not the online service providers themselves. As we have seen, however, the purpose of EU copyright law is very different from this: instead of encouraging the dissemination of authorial works, its purpose is to ensure a high level of protection for authors in respect of their works, balanced in certain specific contexts against competing fundamental interests and rights. Also unclear is whether EU law permits or requires the exceptions of Article 5(2) to (4) to be interpreted from the perspective of the end users of works rather than, in all cases, the perspective of the defendant himself. As we saw in Section 8.5.3.5, the same issue has recently arisen in the context of the *Bolar* exception to patent infringement required by European law.

13.4.4.3 Non-Commercial Purpose

An important restriction on the scope of the Article 5(3)(a) exceptions derives from their exclusion of uses having a commercial purpose. This restriction is not without its difficulties, since most teaching and research-related activities can be said to be commercially motivated, if only in the sense of being undertaken in exchange for payment. To interpret the restriction as excluding even these activities would clearly deprive Article 5(3)(a) of meaningful operation. A more plausible reading of the restriction would result in the exclusion from that Article of uses of a work or subject matter in support of teaching or research undertaken for obviously commercial ends. Examples might include teaching on vocational courses offered to practising professionals at commercial rates, and the in-house research undertaken to devise new products for a company to commercialize.

13.4.5 Use to Report a Current Topic or in Connection with the Reporting of a Current Event: Article 5(3)(c) Information Society Directive

Article 5(3)(c) permits Member States to recognize two exceptions. The first covers reproductions by the press and communications/the making available to the public of published articles or broadcast works or subject matter on current economic, political, or religious topics, provided that such use is not expressly reserved and that the source of the work or subject matter used, including the author's name, is indicated. And the second covers uses of works and subject matter in connection with the reporting of current events, to the extent justified by the informatory purpose and provided that the source of the work or subject matter used, including the author's name, is indicated, unless this turns out to be impossible.

It is clear, as the CJEU has confirmed, that the Article 5(3)(c) exceptions exist to protect the rights and interests of users to freedom of expression, including the freedom and pluralism of the press (see Section 13.3.2). Aside from the requirements of proportionality and source acknowledgement, the main restriction on their scope derives from the need for the published articles or broadcast works/subject matter falling within the first exception to be on 'current economic, political or religious topics', and for the uses falling within the second exception to be connected to 'the reporting of current events'. The effect of both expressions is to restrict the exceptions to uses of a work or subject matter that serve the public interest by facilitating the dissemination of information of real and current interest to it, as distinct from uses that facilitate the dissemination of information that some members of the public might find interesting. In the case of the second (reporting) exception, the fact that the event being reported is not recent in time should be irrelevant, provided it raises issues having currency at the time of the use in question. In addition, it is clear from the wording of the reporting exception that when determining the first and second stages of the proportionality test, the questions to be asked are whether the use was for the purpose of reporting a specific event and did not go beyond what was necessary having regard to the informatory purpose to be served by reporting it. As we saw earlier, this provides support for the view that the purpose of any unauthorized use must be defined as locally as possible when determining this aspect of its proportionality at least (see Section 13.3.4).

13.4.6 Use for Purposes Such as Criticism or Review: Article 5(3)(d) Information Society Directive

Article 5(3)(d) is another of the non-mandatory copyright and related rights exceptions which the CJEU has recognized as having a freedom of expression basis (see Section 13.3.2). It permits Member States to recognize an exception to the rights of reproduction and communication/making available in respect of 'quotations for purposes such as criticism or review', provided: (a) that the work or subject matter quoted from has previously been made available to the public; (b) that its source, including the author's name, is indicated, unless this turns out to be impossible; and (c) that the use is proportionate and 'in accordance with fair practice'.

The terms 'criticism' and 'review' in Article 5(3)(d) are illustrative only, being used to demonstrate the types of use capable of falling within the scope of the Article's exception. In combination they imply a requirement for some critical engagement with a specific object, be it the work or subject matter quoted from or something else. Among other things, this suggests that merely reproducing part of a work to enable consumers to decide whether to purchase it would not fall within the exception's scope.

13.4.7 **Use for the Purpose of Caricature, Parody, or Pastiche: Article 5(3)(k) Information Society Directive**

Article 5(3)(k) permits Member States to allow uses of a work or subject matter for the purpose of caricature, parody, or pastiche without infringing the rights of reproduction or communication/making available to the public.

13.4.7.1 **The Problem of Parody**

Parody in particular has long raised difficulties for copyright. By its nature, a parody imitates and appropriates an existing work in order to comment on it or something else, often (but not always) humorously. Its success depends on its ability to recall the parodied work in the audience's mind to ensure that the critical point of the parody is understood. Given this, a parody will invariably need to reproduce the most distinctive aspects of a work in order to succeed. That is why parody is frequently defined as a genre inherently infringing of copyright.

It is in this context that the question perennially arises as to whether there should exist a special exception for parody. A complicating factor in considering this question is the fact that most parodies will be authorial works, and thus most parodists authors with their own claims to copyright.

Several policy arguments may be advanced for and against a parody exception to copyright, including arguments from authorship, unfair competition, market failure, legal certainty, and freedom of expression respectively. The first (argument from authorship) asserts that authorial rights ought not to prevent further acts of authorship, of which parody as a type of transformative use is an example. As we saw in Section 3.4, this argument follows naturally from natural rights theories of copyright, whether derived from Hegelian ideas of personhood or from Lockean and other arguments from desert. In the case of EU law, however, it is made unconvincing by the absence of a general exception covering transformative uses. The second (argument from unfair competition) asserts that the types of non-competitive and psychological harm caused by parody are not types of harm which copyright ought to prevent. Implicit is that the only harm which copyright ought to prevent is that which results from the use of a copyright work to divert the copyright owner's market to the user. Generally speaking parodic use will never have this effect, since parodies are almost always aimed at a different audience from that of the parodied work. In addition, to accept it as the basis of Article 5(3)(k), one would need to accept an unfair competition theory of copyright that finds little support in EU copyright jurisprudence (see Section 3.5). This leads us to the third commonly advanced argument for parody. This is the argument from market failure, which asserts that in a rational world authors would license third parties to parody their works, and that their refusal in practice to do so creates a market failure which the law ought to correct by means of a parody exception. Again, however, the EU legal emphasis on the proprietary nature of copyright and its purpose in ensuring a high level of protection for authors makes this theory unconvincing, for why should the law compel authors to exploit their property rationally when it does not require such behaviour of other rights holders, including other property owners? A similar difficulty exists with the fourth argument *against* the recognition of a parody exception, which states that the difficulties of defining parody make its protection via a stand-alone exception harmful to legal certainty and thus to the public. Specifically, the difficulty here is that the law in general, and EU law in particular, protects many things that are difficult to define, including authorial works themselves.

There remains the fifth and final argument, which the CJEU has accepted as the basis of Article 5(3)(k). This argument casts parody as an exercise of expressive freedom, and as meriting protection on that (freedom of expression) basis, and is consistent with the well-established purpose of EU copyright to ensure a high level of protection for authors amidst a fair balance of third party and societal rights and interests (see Section 10.3). Any assessment of it in theory must proceed from a conception of the nature and purpose of copyright as well as of freedom of expression itself. For example, and as we saw in Section 1.2.2.3.3, while copyright and IP in general tend to be seen as supporting individual rights that conflict with collective freedoms, including collective freedoms of expression, it is perfectly possible to see them as interdependent. This is because while IP rights restrict the expressive freedom of the immediate generation, their limited scope and duration ensures that they promote the expressive freedom of future generations by encouraging creators to continue creating and disseminating their creations to the public. On the other hand, even those who believe copyright to be an 'engine of free speech' might still support an exception from copyright infringement for parody as a form of social commentary of the type protected by several of the other proportionate use exceptions to copyright. In addition, while protection for parody on freedom of expression grounds does not in theory require a stand-alone exception, each of the other freedom of expression exceptions permitted by Article 5 within which parody might be brought is subject to limitations that make it unsuited to that end. For example, Article 5(3)(d) is restricted to quotations, and requires that the source of the work or subject matter used be indicated, which a parody would be unlikely ever to satisfy. Given this, it might be said that a stand alone exception for parody not subject to the limitations of the other freedom of expression exceptions is necessary, supporting freedom of expression as the most convincing explanation for Article 5(3)(k) Information Society Directive.

13.4.7.2 *Deckmyn* and Parody

In September 2014 the Court of Justice delivered its only decision to date concerning the parody exception of Article 5(3)(k) in the *Deckmyn* case. That case involved the drawing from the Belgian comic book series *Suske en Wiske* reproduced in Figure 13.4 (see Section 13.4.2.2), an altered version of which Mr Deckmyn had reproduced in a calendar, giving rise to domestic proceedings for copyright infringement. According to the defendant to those proceedings, by replacing the main character in the image with the mayor of Ghent and darkening the skin colour of the people collecting the coins, he had created a parody protected from infringement under domestic legislation based on Article 5(3)(k). The proceedings were stayed pending a preliminary referral to the Court of Justice regarding the meaning and scope of that Article.

According to the Court of Justice's decision in the *Deckmyn* case, parody—like most other concepts of EU IP legislation—is an autonomous concept of EU law that must be given a single meaning for all Member States. According to the meaning offered by the Court, for a use of a work to be a parody within the meaning of Article 5(3)(k) it must evoke an existing work while being noticeably different from it and constitute an expression of humour or mockery.

In addition to stating what a parody requires, the Court in *Deckmyn* made clear what a parody does not require. This came with its finding that a parody need not be original (so as to be entitled to copyright protection in its own right), attributable to someone other than the author of the original work (so as to breach the author's moral right of paternity), or related to the protected work or subject matter itself (so as to be a so-called 'target' parody that comments on the reproduced work or subject matter, as distinct from a 'weapon' parody that comments on something else). Nor in the Court's decision need the parody acknowledge the source of the work parodied, as the Directive expressly requires for the Article 5(3)(a), (3)(c), and (3)(d) exceptions. Indeed, it seems that the only restriction on the parody exception of Article 5(3)(k) beyond the need for the existence of a parody itself derives from the proportionality requirement. Hence the Court's decision in *Deckmyn* that in deciding whether the application of the parody exception in a particular case strikes a fair balance between the interests and rights of copyright and related rights holders on one hand and of parodists on the other, a domestic court must take 'all the circumstances of the case…into account', including the impact of the parody on the legitimate interest of rights holders not to be associated with a message that is discriminatory within the meaning of Article 21 CFR.

The definition of parody offered by the Court in *Deckmyn* is consistent with the definition offered by other superior courts in Europe and elsewhere and for this reason alone seems uncontroversial.[3] More difficult is to assess the Court's treatment of the issue of discrimination. For a start, there are the three issues outlined in Section 13.3.4 concerning the interpretation of what appears to be, and has been acknowledged by the Court to be, a freedom of expression exception into a general site for balancing rights and interests by means of a three-stage proportionality test in place of the two-stage necessity-focused test of Article 5(4) TEU. In addition, there is the suggestion that any parody alluding to an issue of race, religion, gender, or one of the other grounds of discrimination listed in Article 21 CFR—of which most litigated parodies are examples[4]—may be regarded as failing for that reason to reflect the fair balance of rights and interests required by the Information Society Directive as a whole, and thus as falling outside the scope of Article 5(3)(k). At a substantive level it is difficult to know what to make of this concern by the Court to protect copyright owners from association with potentially discriminatory speech. To the extent that such association represents a legally recognized harm, there seems nothing controversial in the suggestion that it ought not to be allowed on the basis of a parody exception that exists to protect free speech. This is because freedom of expression is not an absolute right, but rather takes effect subject to the rights of others, including the rights of others to prevent third parties from defaming them. Given this, it seems appropriate to limit the availability of the freedom of expression-based defence to forms of speech that do not infringe the non-copyright rights of others. However, if the effect of *Deckmyn* is to enable a court to deny the benefit of the exception to parodies which the court regards as being discriminatory even in the absence of a legally recognized form of harm—for example, on the ground that the parody causes offence within the community or undermines the community's values by supporting a certain narrative or promoting social inequality; which religious, racial, and gendered parodies will often be said to do—it is more difficult to justify from a freedom of expression perspective.[5] Only time and further case law by the Court of Justice will tell which of these interpretations of the decision is correct.

Overall, the Court's decision in *Deckmyn* supports the restriction of the Article 5(3)(k) exception to proportionate uses of a protected work or subject matter, where by proportionate use is meant any use of a protected work or subject matter that: (a) is for the legitimate statutory purpose of parody, caricature, or pastiche; (b) does not exceed what

---

[3] See e.g. *Laugh it Off Promotions CC v South African Breweries International (Finance) BV t/a Sabmark International* [2005] ZACC 7 [77] (Sachs J).

[4] Gendered and racial parodies in particular account for some of the most prominent parody cases in Europe and elsewhere. See, e.g., Chapter 3 n 20.

[5] See in this regard D. van Mill, 'Freedom of Speech' in *The Stanford Encyclopedia of Philosophy* (2012) http://plato.stanford.edu/entries/freedom-speech/.

is necessary to achieve that purpose; and (c) does not engage any other fundamental right or interest, including the interest of the copyright or related rights holder not to be associated with discriminatory speech, such that permitting it would fail to reflect a fair balance of competing rights and interests overall. Setting the test out in full like this draws attention to another challenge for courts when deciding the availability of a parody, caricature, or pastiche defence, which arises from the difficulty of deciding whether the use of a work or subject matter exceeds what is necessary to achieve the purpose of parody, caricature, or pastiche. Indeed, the question seems akin to asking whether the author of a novel needed to include its final chapter to achieve her particular, expressive objectives. Given this difficulty, the proportionality enquiry in parody cases can be expected to focus on a more general balancing of competing rights and interests, with particular attention being paid to whether the use in question is for one of the legitimate statutory purposes of Article 5(3)(k) and, if it is, whether the effect of allowing it would be to associate the rights holders with a discriminatory message in the minds of the public.

13.5 Conclusions

Implementation of the Information Society Directive by EU Member States has only recently been completed, with the result that there remains limited case law regarding the meaning of each of the Article 5 exceptions. On the other hand, the general interpretative principles applicable to each are now well established. They include, first, the need to interpret the exceptions strictly, with a view to ensuring legal certainty and a high level of protection for copyright and related rights holders and, second, the need to ensure that the application of each exception reflects a fair balance of the interests and rights of copyright and related rights holders on one hand, and of users of their protected works and subject matter on the other. Of especial importance among the competing interests and rights to be balanced are those given recognition in the CFR, including those concerning the protection of IP (Article 17(2)), privacy (Article 7), freedom of expression, including the freedom and pluralism of the media (Article 11), education (Article 14), non-discrimination (Article 21), and the integration of persons with disabilities (Article 26 CFR). Third and finally, the CJEU has confirmed that the interpretation and application of exceptions to copyright and related rights must promote the internal market, while also respecting the different legal traditions of Member States and the general EU principles of subsidiarity and proportionality.

   In practice, determining whether a use falls within the scope of one of the exceptions permitted by Article 5(2) to (4) requires three enquiries. The first is whether the use was for one of the purposes identified in that Article, such as reporting a current event or parody. Assuming it was, the second is whether the use exceeded what was necessary to achieve that legitimate (statutory) purpose. Assuming it did not, the third is whether the use engaged any other fundamental rights and interests such that applying the exception would fail to ensure a fair balance of the competing rights and interests at stake. This enquiry can be understood as involving the application of a three-stage proportionality test. While the precise significance of the third stage is yet to be determined, its existence would seem to threaten the degree of protection secured by the EU proportionate use exception for the free speech and other rights and interests of third parties and the public which underpin them by requiring courts to take account of other rights and interests when deciding whether the exceptions are established in each case. In this sense its addition brings the EU proportionate use exception closer to the open-ended fair use defence of other copyright jurisdictions, such as the United States. Having said that, the values informing its application remain those of the CFR and EU Treaties, rather than for example the values of US copyright law.

The EU regime governing the exceptions to copyright and related rights has been criticized for not going far enough in its harmonization of Member States' laws. According to its critics, the non-mandatory nature of Article 5(2) to (4) and corresponding provisions of other directives stands in contrast to the mandatory nature of Member States' obligations to recognize and protect the copyright and related rights of authors and others, and reflects a failure by the EU to ensure the fair balance which it is the stated purpose of that Article to ensure. Introducing an EU Copyright Code would provide the EU legislature with an opportunity to redress this by enacting an exhaustive list of exceptions which all EU citizens could invoke directly in disputes before domestic courts.

In the meantime, several important issues regarding the exceptions remain unresolved, including their relationship to contract law. For example, can a copyright owner exclude the operation of copyright exceptions as a condition of making her protected work available to the public, or are those exceptions available to third parties as a matter of right? The issue might not arise but for the express provision of Article 9 Information Society Directive, which describes the Directive as being 'without prejudice to ... the law of contract', and is among the issues identified by the Commission as requiring action in its Digital Single Market strategy of 2015.[6]

Further Reading

GRIFFITHS, J., 'The "Three-Step Test" in European Copyright Law: Problems and Solutions' [2009] *IPQ* 428

HELBERGER, N. AND HUGENHOLTZ, P.B., 'No Place Like Home for Making a Copy: Private Copying in European Copyright Law and Consumer Law' (2007) 22 *Berkeley Technology Law Journal* 1061

QUINTAIS, J.P., 'Private Copying and Downloading from Unlawful Sources' [2015] *IIC* 66

SENFTLEBEN, M., 'Towards a Horizontal Standard for Limiting Intellectual Property Rights?— WTO Panel Reports Shed Light on the Three-Step Test in Copyright Law and Related Tests in Patent Law and Trademark Law' [2006] *IIC* 407

SPENCE, M.J., 'Intellectual Property and the Problem of Parody' [1998] *Law Quarterly Review* 594

TORREMANS, P.L.C. (ed.) *Copyright and Human Rights* (Kluwer Law International, 2004)

---

[6] Communication from the Commission to the European Parliament, the Council, the European Economic and Society Committee and the Committee of the Regions, 'A Digital Single Market Strategy for Europe' COM (2015) 192 final [2.4].

PART IV

The Law of Trade Marks and Allied Rights

14

Registration and Use
of the Trade Mark

14.1 Introduction

In the previous parts of this book we have dealt with the two weightiest IP rights. Patents reward the inventor for new inventions that take our technological development further and copyright encourages literature and the arts. Suffice it to refer to the constitutional references in the United States. In comparison trade marks are mere instruments of commerce that do not seem to protect important elements for the development of our society. Labels on products and services appear to be less important, but such appearances can be misleading. Today, the trade mark industry is such a vital component of the whole structure of the advertising and marketing that is a key feature of the commercial scene. Logos, catchphrases, and images all fall within the ambit of the trade mark and form a valuable part of the goodwill of the business with which they are associated.

The earliest form of a trade mark is both the most obvious and the type that is still at the heart of the law of trade marks today. Even in Roman times, pottery was made (and has survived) bearing the name of the potter responsible for it. Then, as now, the trade mark was an important badge of origin for the product; the origin, of course, also being indicative of the quality of the associated product. Many major brand names are the names of the founder of the brand: Ford for cars or Kellogg's for breakfast cereals are obvious examples. Exceptionally, the name may even become synonymous with the product itself: people will often refer to any brand of vacuum cleaner as a 'Hoover', for example.

But throughout history, with only a couple of minor exceptions, trade marks were essentially part of the private sector, attracting legal protection by use, rather than by formal grant by the state. This was unacceptable in a society that was rapidly changing and industrializing, and it became clear both that a more formal system was required and that the central authority of the state should form a central feature of that system. Across Europe trade mark laws that rely on a registration system have therefore emerged. One needs to add immediately though that, in line with the general trend in IP, the rights that result from the registration are private rights, that will need to be enforced by the rights holder. Public authorities, such as trading standards officers or customs officers, may assist with the enforcement of trade mark rights, but the rights holder bears the main responsibility on this point and should take the initiative. With the arrival of the EU and the single market, the combination of that single market with 26 national trade marks (not 28, as the single Benelux TM covers Belgium, the Netherlands, and Luxembourg) became increasingly problematic. Small and medium-sized businesses that operate essentially within the confines of a single Member State are still well served by a national trade mark and, when they expand a bit, they can register the same trade mark in one or more additional Member States. But for those businesses that operate on the whole or a major part of the single market the upkeep of 26 national trade marks increasingly became a hurdle to trade, especially as the same mark may not have been available to them in a number of Member States. A single trade mark system, with a single registration for the whole of the EU became necessary. And national trade marks for a number of Member States are much easier to manage if they are based on harmonized provisions.

The influence of the EU on trade mark law takes therefore two separate, but related, forms. First, a directive was passed as far back as 1988 (Council Directive 89/104/EEC to approximate the laws of the member states relating to trade marks [1989] OJ L 40/1, now codified as Directive 2008/95/EC of the European Parliament and of the Council of 22 October 2008 to approximate the laws of the Member States relating to trade marks [2008] OJ L 299/25) that sought to harmonize the national laws relating to trade marks so as to remove potential barriers to freer trade. The terms of the Directive required compliance with its terms by the end of 1991 (later extended by a year). The second aspect of EU activity that has had a significant impact on the reform process is the establishment of a Community-wide trade mark, distinct from the individual national marks. After interminable discussion and the traditional haggling, the Regulation approving the creation of such a mark was finalized in 1994 (Council Regulation (EC) No. 40/94 on the Community trade mark [1994] OJ L 11/1, now codified as Council Regulation (EC) No. 207/2009 on the Community trade mark [2009] OJ L 78/1). The Community Trade Marks Office or Office for the Harmonization of the Internal Market (Trade Marks and Designs) (OHIM), is sited in Alicante in Spain and it has been confronted with an (unexpected) flood of applications ever since opening its doors to the public. This new mark is, of course, not subject to amendment by domestic legislation, but, conversely, has represented a sensible opportunity to try to match the domestic and European procedures so as to minimize any conflict or duplication between the two systems.[1] In 2011 a study on ways to reform and improve the system was completed, but the law reform that was supposed to follow relatively swiftly has not yet been finalized.[2]

But the integration of markets is of course not limited to the EU. Trade has taken on an increasingly international dimension and, thus, the international protectability of trade mark rights takes on an even greater importance. For over a century, an international

---

[1] See A. von Muhlendahl, 'Community Trade Mark Riddles: Territoriality and Unitary Character' [2008] *EIPR* 66.

[2] See Max Planck Institute for Innovation and Competition, 'Study on the Overall Functioning of the European Trade Mark System' http://www.ip.mpg.de/de/pub/aktuelles/trade_mark_study.cfm or http://ec.europa.eu/internal_market/indprop/tm/index_en.htm.

register of trade marks has been maintained under the provisions of the Madrid Agreement (Madrid Agreement Concerning the International Registration of Marks of 14 April 1891) with an International Register maintained by the World Intellectual Property Organization (WIPO) in Geneva. This system was not entirely successful, because it reflected continental rather than common law approaches to the topic thus making it difficult for common law countries with a full examination system to join, but the era of harmonization meant that change was not only appropriate, but also necessary. In consequence, a protocol (Protocol Relating to the Madrid Agreement Concerning the International Registration of Marks of 28 June 1989) was added to the Madrid Agreement enabling the UK and many other countries to fall within its scope. The combination of the Madrid Agreement and its Protocol is known as the Madrid system. The EU adhered to the Madrid Protocol on 1 October 2004. With that adhesion the Community trade mark also entered the Madrid system and can be applied for internationally, rather than merely directly at OHIM. One should indeed remember that the Madrid system does not harmonize substantive trade mark law or put in place a single international trade mark; it merely provides a single application procedure. The outcome of the procedure is the grant of the equivalents of national trade marks. In terms of substantive trade mark law minimal harmonization is achieved through the combination of the Paris Convention 1883 and the TRIPS Agreement 1994.

It is against this historical, European, and international background that we will examine the EU law on trade marks, i.e. the law that applies at national level as a result of the Directive and the law governing the Community trade mark on the basis of the Regulation. We will see that these provisions run parallel to one another. In this chapter in Part IV we will look at the conditions that apply to the registration of a trade mark, the absolute grounds for the refusal of such a registration, as well as certain aspects of the use of the trade mark.

Before examining the detail of EU trade mark law, it is appropriate to investigate the rationale behind a system of trade marks. It is clear that trade mark law has to achieve a balance between various potentially competing interests: the trader seeks to protect the image and reputation of his or her goods, but the rival trader—in a society based on free competition—has every reason to wish to compete on level terms within the same market and will, at the very least, hope that the monopoly conferred by the grant of a trade mark is confined to reasonable limits so as not to inhibit legitimate competition. The consumer also has an interest: he associates the product or service and its quality with its associated brand name or logo, and will not wish to be confused by similar names or logos placed on different—particularly inferior—products.

As has been seen, the trade mark originally evolved in the private sector at the behest of the traders themselves and this has generally been the principal interest to which protection has been given by the trade marks system. The protection afforded has centred on the origin of the goods and, while this has also been of benefit to consumer interests, it has, first and foremost, been in the interests of the proprietor of the trade mark. In indicating origin, the mark, being distinctive, differentiates that product from another and by doing so, in turn, guides the consumer in the exercise of choice. This, it is suggested, may now be seen as the 'core' function of trade marks and it will be pertinent to bear this view in mind, particularly when considering the direction taken by the law of trade marks.[3]

---

[3] See F. Schechter, 'The Rational Basis for Trade Mark Protection' (1926–7) 40 *Harvard Law Review* 813 and W. Landes and R. Posner, 'Trademark Law: An Economic Perspective' (1987) 30 *Journal of Law and Economics* 265.

There can be no doubt as to the commercial significance of trade marks in modern society. Brand names or product identities, such as that of Guinness or Coca-Cola, are hugely valuable assets to their owners and as such are vigorously protected. Trade marks are essentially pro-competitive, because they allow the origin of goods to be distinguished. A producer of goods can therefore distinguish his or her goods from those of other producers of the same goods. That allows each to set itself apart and to compete with one another. At least in theory, each can always pick another trade mark. Exclusive rights in one or other mark do not therefore restrict the opportunity for competitors to pick their own mark and compete.

A mark therefore allows one to create goodwill in a brand; that goodwill necessarily exists in the relationship with the consumer. The mark allows the consumer to get information about the goods or services and the consumer should be able to rely on that information. Trade marks operate in the relationship between rights holder and consumers, and the interests of both sides to the relationship are necessarily reflected in trade mark law.

14.2 Applying for Classes of Goods or Services

A trade mark can be applied for at the national trade mark offices, or in Belgium, the Netherlands, and Luxembourg at the Benelux trade mark office that administers their single trade mark system. Alternatively a Community trade mark can be applied for at OHIM. There is no restriction on who can apply. The Regulation makes it clear that any natural or legal person, including authorities established by public law, can be the proprietor of a Community trade mark and to get to this stage they must first have applied for one (Article 5 Regulation 207/2009).

A trade mark is not, however, granted for all purposes, only for those classes of goods and services for which an application has been made. The classification of goods and services is carried out in accordance with the Nice Classification,[4] an international agreement that splits goods and services into, respectively, 34 and 8 classes. There is also the 1985 Vienna Agreement Establishing an International Classification of the Figurative Elements of Marks. The Nice Classification is designed to be comprehensive and, by definition, covers the whole range of manufacturing and service industries. Thus, as a random example, Class 12 of the classification comprises all vehicles, while firearms, ammunition, explosives, and fireworks comprise Class 13. Inevitably, there are anomalies: beers and soft drinks form Class 32, while all alcoholic drinks other than beers form Class 33. It is important to add that the statement of the goods or services for which the trade mark is sought does not have to use the class headings in the Nice Classification. It may specify certain goods or services only. What is important is that there is a sufficient degree of clarity and precision for the authorities and other traders to be able to determine the extent of protection. If the general indications of the class headings are used there is no problem as far as it results in a clear and precise identification of the goods or services concerned and any limitation must also be clearly expressed (Case C–307/10 *Chartered Institute of Patent Attorneys v Registrar of Trade Marks* [2012] ETMR 42).

When a Community trade mark is applied for, either directly with OHIM or indirectly through the national trade mark office, there will only be a check regarding the

---

[4] 10th edn, WIPO Nice Agreement concerning the International Classification of Goods and Services for the Purposes of the Registration of Marks of 1957 http://www.wipo.int/treaties/en/classification/nice/index.html.

absolute grounds for refusal and other parties will have three months to enter an opposition after publication of the application. OHIM itself deals with these oppositions, as well as an appeal to one of its Boards of Appeal. Further Appeals can be brought before the General Court and finally before the Court of Justice. National offices run similar procedures. The main difference in terms of outcome is that national offices will continue to grant national trade marks (or Benelux trade marks in the case of the Benelux trade mark office), whereas the Community trade mark has a unitary character. This means that it shall have equal effect throughout the Community and cannot be transferred or revoked in part only (Article 1 Regulation 207/2009).

But clearly, the requirements for registration lie at the heart of this process and it is to these and, first and foremost, to the key question of what is a trade mark that we now turn. We will look at these requirements from the combined perspective of the Directive and the Regulation.

14.3 Requirements for Registration: A Definition of a Trade Mark

The basic definition of a 'trade mark' is given by Article 2 Directive 2008/95/EC/ Article 4 Regulation 207/2009 and appears alarmingly straightforward. The Articles state that a 'trade mark' consists of 'any signs capable of being represented graphically, [particularly words, including personal names, designs, letters, numerals, the shape of goods, or of their packaging,] provided that such signs are capable of distinguishing the goods or services of one undertaking from those of other undertakings'. It should immediately be stated that certain marks that fall within this broad definition are nevertheless refused registration in accordance with the rules on the grounds for refusal, considered subsequently. Be that as it may, there are three essential requirements. First, there needs to be a sign. Second, that sign needs to be capable of being represented graphically. And third, the sign needs to be distinctive. In addition the Article contains a list of potential signs, but the use of the term 'particularly' means that these are merely examples and that the list is by no means exhaustive. These requirements are shown in Figure 14.1.

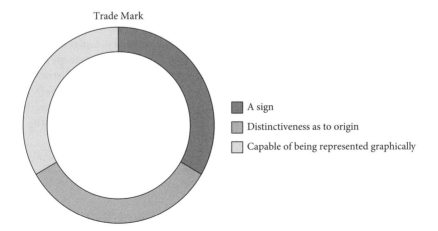

Figure 14.1 Requirements for trade mark registration

14.3.1 **A Sign**

Let us therefore look at each of the three requirements for a trade mark. The graphical representation point and the distinctiveness point will be discussed in more detail later, but it is important to mention the third element at this stage: a trade mark is described as 'any sign'. This term is very wide in scope and could, on the basis of the list of examples, be taken to mean 'anything which can convey information' (*Philips Electronics BV v Remington Consumer Products* [1998] RPC 283 (Jacob J)). There are nevertheless limits to what can be a sign. Dyson attempted to register two trade marks consisting of a transparent bin or collection chamber forming part of the external surface of a vacuum cleaner. It tried to register the marks as a concept, which could then be applied in a specific way to each of its vacuum cleaners. The European Court of Justice refused to allow the registration, because, in the Court's view, the requirement that there needs first to be a sign was not fulfilled. Abstract concepts are not signs; the latter need to take a specific format. The Court clearly gave consent to the concept of 'a sign' in order to avoid an unduly broad trade mark being granted, which would have damaged the unfair competition avoidance function of the trade mark system (Case C–321/03 *Dyson Ltd v Registrar of Trade Marks* [2007] ECR I-687, [2007] 2 CMLR 14, [2007] RPC 27).

One should also bear in mind that this broad requirement that a sign needs to take a specific format does not stand alone. Such a sign may still fall foul of the inherent bars to registration found in the absolute grounds for refusal and problems may also arise relating to the existence of other marks that may present a difficulty for registration, as per Article 4 of the Directive/Article 8 of the Regulation. Meanwhile, the initial definition of a trade mark continues: 'particularly words, including personal names, designs, letters, numerals, the shape of goods or of their packaging'.

In other words, to be registrable a mark can consist of anything, with the items listed here clearly being no more than illustrations. It is apparent, however, that no mark can be registered unless it satisfies the two vital, but related, factors of being capable of being represented graphically and also capable of distinguishing one trader's products from those of others.

14.3.2 **Capable of Being Represented Graphically**

The concept of distinctiveness will, in due course, warrant further examination, but the requirement of capability of graphical representation may, in certain cases, create more of a problem than was initially thought. At first the provision merely gave the impression that in both the application and the register figured a box into which the trade mark should be put. Especially in the days of paper filings that seemed to equal the possibility of representing the trade mark graphically. One could expand the concept slightly by arguing that what was represented in the box also had to enable both the registrar and any competitor consulting the register to understand the mark precisely without reference to samples of the goods or any additional information. That was necessary to allow the register to fulfil its function. But the focus of the provision is much broader than the single idea of it being able to fit on the register. That much would soon become clear.

In recent years, the issue of graphical representation has become the focus of attention in relation to olfactory (smell), sound, and colour marks.

14.3.2.1 **Olfactory Marks**

A first question mark arises from the fact that all of the examples of registrable signs that are listed in the Directive and the Regulation are, in themselves, capable of being perceived visually, whereas an olfactory sign is not and relies on an indirect route in this respect. But when confronted with this question for the first time in Case 273/00 *Ralf Sieckmann v Deutsches Patent- und Markenamt* [2002] ECR I-11737, [2003] Ch 487, [2003] RPC 685, the CJEU brushed the suggestion aside, confirming that there is no fourth requirement in this respect and that the list should be considered as containing nothing more than random examples. In the words of the Court:

> The Directive must be interpreted as meaning that a trade mark may consist of a sign which is not in itself capable of being perceived visually, provided that it can be represented graphically.[5]

This quotation draws attention to what has become the major issue—that is, is the olfactory mark capable of being represented graphically? Looking back at olfactory marks that were granted at an early stage, it cannot be denied, on the one hand, that the Sumitomo mark (the smell of roses for tyres and wheels) and marks such as 'the smell of freshly cut grass' are not defined very precisely. Both roses and freshly cut grass can mean many different things in different circumstances and to different persons. On the other hand, any third party should be able to find out exactly what the trade mark is from consulting the register, not only to avoid infringement, but also to find out whether another mark can still be registered. The Registrar of Trade Marks or OHIM must also know exactly what the mark is in order to carry out its examination and publication. And all of this must be done on the basis of the register—that is, the graphic representation only—because that is the material that is in the public domain and therefore accessible to third parties. In the *Sieckmann* case, the Court drew from this the conclusion that:

> If the users of that register are to be able to determine the precise nature of a mark on the basis of its registration, its graphic representation in the register must be self-contained, easily accessible and intelligible.
>
> Furthermore, in order to fulfil its role as a registered trade mark a sign must always be perceived unambiguously and in the same way so that the mark is guaranteed as an indication of origin. In the light of the duration of a mark's registration and the fact that, as the Directive provides, it can be renewed for varying periods, the representation must be durable.
>
> Finally, the object of the representation is specifically to avoid any element of subjectivity in the process of identifying and perceiving the sign. Consequently, the means of graphic representation must be unequivocal and objective.
>
> In the light of the foregoing observations, the answer to the first question must be that…the Directive must be interpreted as meaning that a trade mark may consist of a sign which is not in itself capable of being perceived visually, provided that it can be represented graphically, particularly by means of images, lines or characters, and that the representation is clear, precise, self-contained, easily accessible, intelligible, durable and objective.[6]

But what did that mean in practice? Mr Sieckmann had described, and represented graphically, the olfactory trade mark he applied for as follows:

> Trade mark protection is sought for the olfactory mark deposited with the Deutsches Patent- und Markenamt of the pure chemical substance methyl cinnamate (= cinnamic

---

[5] Case 273/00 *Ralf Sieckmann v Deutsches Patent- und Markenamt* [2002] ECR I-11737, [2003] Ch 487, 509.

[6] Ibid 509.

acid methyl ester), whose structural formula is set out below. Samples of this olfactory mark can also be obtained via local laboratories listed in the Gelbe Seiten (Yellow Pages) of Deutsche Telekom AG or, for example, via the firm E. Merck in Darmstadt.

C6H5–CH = CHCOOCH3.

Mr Sieckmann also submitted, with his application, an odour sample of the sign in a container and stated that the scent was usually described as 'balsamically fruity with a slight hint of cinnamon'.

The question was therefore whether, in relation to an olfactory mark, a chemical formula, a description in words, the deposit of an odour sample, or any combination of these elements could satisfy the requirements concerning the mark's capability of being represented graphically, as set out by the Court. The Court came to the conclusion that it could not and gave the following reasons for reaching that conclusion:

> As regards a chemical formula...few people would recognise in such a formula the odour in question. Such a formula is not sufficiently intelligible. In addition...a chemical formula does not represent the odour of a substance, but the substance as such, and nor is it sufficiently clear and precise. It is therefore not a representation for the purposes of...the Directive.
>
> In respect of the description of an odour, although it is graphic, it is not sufficiently clear, precise and objective.
>
> As to the deposit of an odour sample, it does not constitute a graphic representation for the purposes of...the Directive. Moreover, an odour sample is not sufficiently stable or durable...
>
> In the light of the foregoing considerations, the answer to the second question must be that, in respect of an olfactory sign, the requirements of graphic representability are not satisfied by a chemical formula, by a description in written words, by the deposit of an odour sample or by a combination of those elements.[7]

This seems to leave very little room indeed for olfactory marks, at least in the current state of technology, and most of the marks already granted do not meet these stringent requirements. The latter are therefore liable to be declared invalid on the basis of Article 3(1)(a) Directive 2008/95/EC/Article 52(1)(a) Regulation 207/2009.

14.3.2.2 Sound Marks

Let us now move on to sound marks, as did the CJEU 11 months after the *Sieckmann* case, when it delivered its judgment in Case C–283/01 *Shield Mark BV v Joost Kist hodn Memex* [2003] ECR I-14313, [2004] Ch 97. Shield Mark had registered various signature tunes or jingles as sound trade marks with the Benelux Trade Marks Office. Let us consider the following Shield Mark marks as an example:

> Four of those trade marks consist of a musical stave with the first nine notes of the musical composition *Für Elise*, by Ludwig von Beethoven. Two of them also state: Sound mark. The trade mark consists of the representation of the melody formed by the notes (graphically) transcribed on the stave, plus, in one case, played on a piano...
>
> Three further marks consist of the sequence of musical notes E, D#, E, D#, E, B, D, C, A. Two of them also state: Sound mark. The trade mark consists of the reproduction of the melody formed by the sequence of notes as described, plus, in one case, played on a piano.
>
> Two of the trade marks registered by Shield Mark consist of the denomination Kukelekuuuuu (an onomatopoeia suggesting, in Dutch, a cockcrow). One of them states: Sound mark, the trade mark consists of an onomatopoeia imitating a cockcrow.

---

[7] Ibid 511.

As a preliminary matter, the issue raised was whether sound marks could, by their nature, be distinctive. Having disposed of that issue by ruling that sound signs are not, by nature, incapable of distinguishing the goods or services of one undertaking from those of other undertakings, the Court returned to the key issue of graphical representation and applied its *Sieckmann* approach to sound marks. The written description of a sound, the onomatopoeia, and the musical notes all failed to pass the *Sieckmann* test: they were neither clear, nor precise, nor objective enough.

But whereas the Court did not have a suggestion as to how olfactory marks could pass the test, it did come up with a solution for sound marks:

> a stave divided into bars and showing, in particular, a clef (a treble clef, bass clef or alto or tenor clef), musical notes and rests whose form (for the notes: semibreve, minim, crotchet, quaver, semiquaver, etc.; for the rests: semibreve rest, minim rest, crotchet rest, quaver rest, etc.) indicates the relative value and, where appropriate, accidentals (sharp, flat, natural)—all of this notation determining the pitch and duration of the sounds—may constitute a faithful representation of the sequence of sounds forming the melody in respect of which registration is sought. This mode of graphical representation of the sounds meets the requirements of the case-law of the Court that such representation must be clear, precise, self-contained, easily accessible, intelligible, durable and objective.
>
> Even if such a representation is not immediately intelligible, the fact remains that it may be easily intelligible, thus allowing the competent authorities and the public, in particular traders, to know precisely the sign whose registration as a trade mark is sought.[8]

Or should one add that full musical notation graphically represents the sound itself, whereas a chemical formula, which arguably can also be read by a large number of people and therefore become easily intelligible, merely represents the chemical substance, rather than its smell?

14.3.2.3 Colour Marks

That leaves us with the question of whether the door also remains open—even if not wide open—for the registration of a single colour as a trade mark. This extreme scenario was put before the CJEU in May 2003 in Case C–104/01 *Libertel Groep BV v Benelux-Merkenbureau* [2003] ECR I-3793, [2004] FSR 65. Libertel had applied for the registration of the colour orange, per se, and, in the box for reproducing the trade mark, the application form contained an orange rectangle and in the space for describing the mark it contained the word 'orange' without reference to any colour code. The Court once more put the focus on graphical representation and the need for it to be clear, precise, self-contained, easily accessible, intelligible, durable, and objective, along the lines of the approach set out in the *Sieckmann* case.

The Court held that a mere sample of a colour is not durable enough, because it may fade; it may also change slightly depending on the background on which it is printed or against which it is put. The mere sample therefore fails the *Sieckmann* test, but, in the view of the Court, a verbal description of a colour could pass the test, depending on the circumstances of the case, as may the combination of a sample and a verbal description. The Court also deemed an internationally recognized colour identification code to be precise and stable enough to pass the test. *Libertel* therefore failed—but the addition of a colour code to the sample and the (maybe somewhat fuller) verbal description might have seen the colour orange being registered successfully.

---

[8] Case C–283/01 *Shield Mark BV v Joost Kist hodn Memex* [2003] ECR I-14313, [2004] Ch 97, 118.

But even in those cases, the mark will still have to pass the distinctiveness test. And passing the graphical representation hurdle does not make the distinctiveness hurdle less daunting, so much had already become clear in Case T–173/00 *KWS Saat v OHIM* [2002] ECR II-3843. Without wishing to anticipate the discussion of this requirement that is to follow, it is important to note that in *Libertel* itself the Court admitted that this will be a difficult hurdle for a colour mark to pass, as colours possess little inherent capacity for communicating specific information. But as the Court went on to say:

> that factual finding would not justify the conclusion that colours per se cannot, as a matter of principle, be considered to be capable of distinguishing the goods or services of one undertaking from those of other undertakings. The possibility that a colour per se may in some circumstances serve as a badge of origin…cannot be ruled out.[9]

What is clear though is that the Court will systematically apply the *Sieckmann* test to check whether a sign is capable of being represented graphically.

At the European level the discussion has remained restricted to applications where the applicant registers a single colour as such and puts that colour, with or without a colour code, in the box. A further complication could arise if the applicant wants to register the 'predominant' colour applied to the whole visible surface of the packaging of the goods, leaving it free to add features and vary the amount of surface covered by the colour. The Court of Appeal in the UK ruled in the Cadbury case (*Société des Produits Nestlé SA v Cadbury UK Ltd* [2013] EWCA Civ 1174, reversing [2012] EWHC 2637 (Ch)) that this did not satisfy the requirement of a sign being capable of being represented graphically, as set out in *Sieckmann* and *Libertel*. The court argued that the mark lacked the required clarity, precision, self-containment, durability, and objectivity to qualify for registration. Obiter one of the members of the court suggested that a formula such as 'covering more than 50%' would on the other hand pass the test. Whether the CJEU and other national courts will agree with this approach remains to be seen. The debate surrounding colour trade marks has clearly not yet been exhausted.

14.3.3 **Distinctiveness in Trade**

In order for a sign to be registered as a trade mark it has to be capable of distinguishing the goods or services of one undertaking from those of other undertakings. This is a fundamental requirement, but it is defined in much more detail through the application of the absolute grounds for refusal of registration. Distinctiveness is to be tested through the experience of the relevant public. If we take the example of banking services offered to all consumers, the relevant public for a Community trade mark application will be the consumers in the EU. If the name applied for is then allegedly descriptive in one language, for example German, the relevant public becomes in practice the German-speaking consumers in the EU. The CJEU has repeatedly held that members of the relevant public are to be seen as reasonably well informed and reasonably observant and circumspect (see, e.g., Case C–304/06 P *Eurohypo v OHIM* [2008] ECR I-3291). And their level of attention varies in relation to the importance and value of the transaction (e.g. one pays more attention when buying a car than when buying a bottle of water).

From its very concept it is clear that distinctiveness operates in a commercial or trade context. We are concerned here with distinctiveness in trade. But there does not appear to be any need for the trade in question to be for valuable consideration. Use in

---

[9] Case C–104/01 *Libertel Groep BV v Benelux-Merkenbureau* [2003] ECR I-3793, [2004] FSR 65 [41].

announcements, advertising, and on badges by a non-profit-making association was after all held to be use of the trade mark and therefore use in trade by the CJEU in Case C–442/07 *Verein Radetzky-Orden v Bundesvereinigung Kameradschaft, Feldmarschall Radetzky* [2009] ETMR 14. But private individuals may not be able to register their names or signatures as such; they must at least trade on the back of them, by endorsing products, by character merchandising, or otherwise.

Overall, the distinctiveness requirement means that the main purpose of a trade mark is to convey a message about the source of, and responsibility for, or quality of the goods or services that are labelled with the mark. This does not exclude the option that the goods are made for the trade mark owner by a third party using the trade mark owner's specification or that the services are provided by a third party according to the trade mark owner's specification, but the trade mark owner must adopt the goods or services as his own in those cases after having checked that they match his specification. And the relevant public must perceive it that way.

The *Elvis Presley* case in the UK provides a negative example to illustrate this (*Re Elvis Presley Trade Marks* [1997] RPC 543). In that case, a cursive rendition of the singer's name was held not to be distinctive. Laddie J ruled that the public bought memorabilia carrying the Elvis name, because it referred to the singer; the public did not assume that these goods came from one source that was linked to the singer. The proposed mark was therefore not capable of distinguishing memorabilia marketed by the applicant from those marketed by other traders. The famous name referred to the person and, as such, it did not possess the distinctiveness required to distinguish goods from one source from those of another.

This once more illustrates that certain signs are less inherently capable of being distinguished, but the approach set out in the previous paragraph has now been endorsed by the CJEU. The question whether a common surname could be a trade mark arose in Case C–404/02 *Nichols plc v Registrar of Trade Marks* [2004] ECR I-8499. The Court held that the distinctive character of such a mark needed to be assessed in the same way as that of any other mark. No special criteria applied and such an assessment should therefore focus, first, on the products or services in respect of which registration is applied for and, second, on the perception of the relevant consumers. In other words, one needs to determine whether, in relation to the relevant product or service, the relevant consumers would see the name as a mark distinguishing the goods or services of one source from the goods or services of another, or whether they would see it as nothing more than a surname. *Nichols* was a case about names, but in dealing with the matter the Court of Justice made it clear that in analysing distinctiveness any kind of mark is subject to exactly the same rule. No special criteria should be applied and the analysis should therefore simply focus, first, on the products or services in respect of which registration is applied for and, second, on the perception of the relevant consumers. These are the consumers to which the product is directed. In other words, one needs to determine whether, in relation to the relevant product or service, the relevant consumers would see the name as a mark distinguishing the goods or services of one source from the goods or services of another. There are now several CJEU cases that confirm the approach, such as Case C–144/06 P *Henkel v OHIM* [2007] ECR I-8109 [34]; Case C–304/06 P *Eurohypo v OHIM* [2008] ECR I-3291 [66]; Joined Cases C–473/01 P and 474/01 P *Procter & Gamble v OHIM* [2004] ECR I-5173 [51]; and Case C–64/02 P *OHIM v Erpo Möbelwerk* [2004] ECR I-10031 [36].

Laudatory epithets and advertising slogans are a nice example to illustrate the general rule, as the relevant public does not necessarily see them as (inherently) distinctive. The CJEU has on a number of occasions dealt with laudatory epithets and advertising slogans that applicants wanted to register as a trade mark (Case C–64/02 P *OHIM v Erpo Möbelwerk* [2004] ECR I-10031 and Case C–517/99 *Merz & Krell* [2001] ECR I-6959). The starting point is that one applies the general rule for distinctiveness. The fact that the mark can also be seen as and used as a laudatory epithet or as an advertising slogan (or indications of quality or incitements to purchase) does not therefore exclude the marks from registration (Case C–517/99 *Merz & Krell* [2001] ECR I-6959 [40]). Use as a mark and other use can go together and does not warrant the application of a stricter rule on distinctiveness (e.g. that the advertising slogan should be imaginative). However, when applying the general rule one needs to take into account that the relevant public's perception is not necessarily the same for each kind of mark and each use. It could therefore be more difficult to establish distinctiveness in relation to certain kinds of marks (Case C–64/02 P *OHIM v Erpo Möbelwerk* [2004] ECR I-10031). All that is required though is that apart from being seen by the relevant public as a laudatory epithet, an advertising slogan, etc., the mark is also seen ('also' means here 'as well' and not 'immediately' or 'in the first place') by the relevant public as an indication of the commercial origin of the goods or services. On this basis registration of Audi's slogan 'Vorsprung durch Technik' (Advance or advantage through technology) as a trade mark was ultimately allowed by the CJEU for cars and other goods, as the public would also see it as distinctive for goods coming from Audi (Case C–398/08 P *Audi v OHIM* [2010] ETMR 18), but the term 'Real People, Real Solutions' was refused registration as a trade mark for technical support services in the computer industry (Case T–130/01 *Sykes Enterprises Inc. v OHIM* [2002] ECR II-5179), as the relevant public would only see it as a promotional message, without a hint of distinctiveness as to commercial origin.

14.4 Unregistrable Marks

Fulfilling the basic requirements of trade mark registration does not guarantee that a trade mark will be obtained. The Directive and the Regulation make clear that certain marks are either never registrable or are unregistrable in the light of market conditions. It is the first category that we now examine.

14.5 Absolute Grounds for Refusal of Registration

Article 3 of the Directive establishes the principal rules relating to absolute unregistrability. It lists a range of different grounds and states that the following marks shall not be registered:

1. ...

    (a) signs which cannot constitute a trade mark;

    (b) trade marks which are devoid of any distinctive character;

    (c) trade marks which consist exclusively of signs or indications which may serve, in trade, to designate the kind, quality, quantity, intended purpose, value, geographical origin, or the time of production of the goods or of rendering of the service, or other characteristics of the goods or services;

    (d) trade marks which consist exclusively of signs or indications which have become customary in the current language or in the bona fide and established practices of the trade;

  (e)   signs which consist exclusively of:

     (i)   the shape which results from the nature of the goods themselves;

     (ii) the shape of goods which is necessary to obtain a technical result;

     (iii) the shape which gives substantial value to the goods;

  (f)   trade marks which are contrary to public policy or to accepted principles of morality;

  (g)   trade marks which are of such a nature as to deceive the public, for instance as to the nature, quality or geographical origin of the goods or service;

  (h)   trade marks which have not been authorised by the competent authorities and are to be refused or invalidated pursuant to Article 6 ter of the Paris Convention for the Protection of Industrial Property, hereinafter referred to as the 'Paris Convention'.

2.   …

3.   A trade mark shall not be refused registration or be declared invalid in accordance with paragraph 1(b), (c) or (d) if, before the date of application for registration and following the use which has been made of it, it has acquired a distinctive character. Any Member State may in addition provide that this provision shall also apply where the distinctive character was acquired after the date of application for registration or after the date of registration. Article 3 also stipulates that the same grounds can be used as grounds for invalidity in case a trade mark that offends against any of these grounds has nevertheless been registered.[10]

Article 7 of the Regulation contains the same absolute grounds for refusal of registration and adds in a paragraph 2 that registration shall be refused even if the ground for refusal applies only to part of the EU. In other words any application needs to steer clear of the absolute grounds for refusal in the entire EU.

   These complex provisions go to the heart of the issue of distinctiveness already flagged up previously as crucial. They help to define the requirement of distinctiveness and each of them reflects (different) public policy considerations (Case C–104/01 *Libertel Groep BV* [2003] ECR I-3793 [50] and Cases C–456/01 P and 457/01 P *Henkel v OHIM* [2004] ECR I-5089 [46]). The first four paragraphs of Article 3(1) are by no means mutually exclusive and may apply in combination in any given case. Nevertheless, each of the grounds and paragraphs is independent from the others and calls for a separate examination (Case C–53/01 *Linde AG* [2003] ECR I-3161 [67]). Overcoming one of the grounds does not therefore also guarantee the same result for the other grounds (Case C–363/99 *Koninklijke KPN Nederland NV* [2004] ECR I-1619 [70]).

14.5.1 **Article 3(1)(a)**

This provision restates the principle that signs that are not capable of being represented graphically and that are not distinctive as to commercial origin cannot be registered as a trade mark and that this is an absolute ground for refusal of registration. It is clear from the wording of Article 3(1)(a) and the structure of the Directive that that provision is intended essentially to exclude from registration signs which are not generally capable of being a trade mark and thus cannot be represented graphically and/or are not capable of distinguishing the goods or services of one undertaking from those of other undertakings. Signs or indications which do not meet one of the two conditions imposed by

---

[10] See also Article 52 of the Trade Mark Regulation.

Article 2 of the Directive, that is to say, the condition requiring such signs to be capable of distinguishing the goods or services of one undertaking from those of other undertakings, shall not be registered. It follows, according to the CJEU in Case C–299/99 *Philips Electronics NV v Remington Consumer Products Ltd* [2002] ECR I-5475, that there is no class of marks having a distinctive character by their nature or by the use made of them which is not capable of distinguishing goods or services within the meaning of Article 2 of the Directive.

The second half of the definition of a trade mark in Article 2 does not in turn impose any requirement of distinctiveness separate from that imposed by Article 3(1)(b)–(d), and there is no requirement that a mark be both 'capable of distinguishing' and 'not devoid of distinctive character'. There is therefore, as the CJEU said in *Philips*, no category of marks that is not excluded under paragraphs (b)–(d) that then goes on to be excluded under paragraph (a). One cannot reverse that statement though. Even if a sign is in general capable of constituting a trade mark it may still face problems under paragraphs (b)–(d) (Cases C–456/01 P and 457/01 P *Henkel v OHIM* [2004] ECR I-5089).

Taken on its own though, the effect of paragraph (a) seems to be limited. The CJEU used it to hold that there is no reason to find that the mark 'Postkantoor' is not capable of fulfilling the essential function of a trade mark for certain goods (Case C–363/99 *Koninklijke KPN Nederland NV* [2004] ECR I-1619). As such paragraph (a) was therefore not a problem in that case. That was more the case when the distinctiveness of a colour was at issue. The CJEU doubted whether a colour would, in most circumstances, have the distinctive character that is required:

> Save in exceptional case, colours do not initially have a distinctive character, but may be capable of acquiring such character as a result of the use made of them in relation to the goods or services claimed.
>
> Subject to the above, it must be accepted that…colours and combinations of colours, designated in the abstract and without contours, may be capable of distinguishing the goods or services from one undertaking from those of other undertakings.[11]

14.5.2 Article 3(1)(b)

Article 3(1)(b) denies trade mark registration to trade marks that are devoid of any distinctive character. A trade mark must, at the very least, be able to serve as a guarantee of trade origin—that is, it must be capable of distinguishing the goods that originate with one trader from similar goods that originate with another. A mark that is devoid of any distinctive character can never convey the message 'these are the goods of a particular trader' (see Joined Cases C–468/01 P to 472/01 P *Procter & Gamble v OHIM* [2004] ECR I-5141 [32]; Case C–64/02 P *OHIM v Erpo Möbelwerk* [2004] ECR I-10031 [42]; and Case C–304/06 P *Eurohypo v OHIM* [2008] ECR I-3297); that conclusion is reached by considering the mark on its own, taking into account no use, but looking at it with reference to the goods or services for which it is registered as well as the relevant public. When Philips tried to register its three-headed rotary shaver as a trade mark, it was held that the shaver as a 'sign can never only denote shavers made by Philips and no one else because it primarily says "here is a three-headed rotary shaver"' and that the sign 'is not "capable" of denoting only Philips goods' (*Philips Electronics NV v Remington Consumer Products Ltd* [1998] RPC 283 (Jacob J) in the underlying UK case). The mark was therefore invalid. It is important to note that the Philips sign did not include the name 'Philips' and that any other three-headed rotary shaver design would have infringed the mark if it had been

---

[11]   Case C–49/02 *Heidelberger Bauchemie GmbH* [2004] ECR I-6129 [39] and [40].

granted. It was also irrelevant that no other manufacturer had hitherto made such shavers. The CJEU confirmed these finding in the *Philips* case (Case C–299/99 *Philips Electronics NV v Remington Consumer Products Ltd* [2002] ECR I-5475). The Court agreed that the shape of a three-headed rotary shaver as such could not be a trade mark, because it only conveyed the message that the item was a three-headed rotary shaver and could therefore not distinguish one such shaver from one manufacturer from another such shaver from another manufacturer.

Similarly, the General Court held that the rectangular shape of washing powder tablets in two colours could not be registered as a trade mark, because it indicated the product, and did not allow the consumer to distinguish between the product and another tablet from another manufacturer, because the shape was commonly used (see Case T–335/99 *Henkel v OHIM* [2001] ECR II-2581). And the cylindrical shape of a torch was not registrable, because it referred to the product rather than to a specific manufacturer; again, the distinctive character of the mark was lacking (see Case T–88/00 *Mag Instrument v OHIM* [2002] ECR II-467).

This does not mean that trade mark protection for shapes of goods is to be ruled out altogether: the distinctive Coca-Cola bottle is probably a good example of a successful case. In relation to word marks, the meaning of a word can depend on its usage, and it is permissible and necessary to determine the meaning of a word as used at the time of the application for registration. 'Usage' means usage by those engaged in the relevant trade and includes the average consumer, as well as manufacturers, wholesalers, and retailers. Through usage, a word could acquire—but also lose—a distinctive character. It was therefore necessary to determine the meaning of the word on the basis of the usage before deciding whether, under Article 3(1)(b), the mark was, or had become, devoid of distinctive character, or whether instead distinctive character had been acquired.

The UK case *West (t/a Eastenders) v Fuller Smith & Turner plc* [2003] FSR 816 raised interesting questions concerning Article 3(1). The trade mark concerned was 'E.S.B.', an acronym for Extra Strong Bitter, and its revocation was sought on the basis that it was devoid of distinctive character and that is was merely descriptive. In the Court of Appeal, it was held that if, at the date of registration, the mark served as a trade mark to the interested public (as the judge had held it did in fact), it could not be regarded as being devoid of distinctive character. The mark would offend against section 3(1)(b) Trade Marks Act 1994 (the domestic equivalent of Article 3(1)(b)) only if the average consumer knew that the sign 'E.S.B.' was used exclusively as an indication or the kind or quality of the goods or was in common use. The word 'devoid' had to be construed strictly and the concession that the mark possessed distinctiveness *in vacuo* was fatal to the objection under this subsection. The court followed the guidance of the CJEU in Case C–383/99 P *Procter & Gamble v OHIM* [2001] ECR I-6251 on this point, but the example is illustrative.

Acronyms and abbreviations can also be used in conjunction with the descriptive terms they stand for in an attempt to take away the merely descriptive nature of the latter. Attempts were made, for example, to register 'Multi Market Fund MMF' and 'NAI - Der Natur-Aktien-Index'. The Court of Justice held that these signs were still caught by Article 3(1)(b) if the public understand the abbreviation as another way to describe the descriptive content (Joined Cases C–90/11 and 91/11 *Alfred Strigl v Deutsches Patent- und Markenamt* and *Securvita Gesellschaft zur Entwicklung alternativer Versicherungskonzepte mbH v Öko-Invest Verlagsgesellschaft mbH* EU:C:2012:147).

Article 3(1)(b) is therefore particularly concerned with those marks that, from the point of view of the relevant public, are commonly used, in trade, for the presentation of the goods or services concerned, or in connection with which there exists, at the very least, concrete evidence justifying the conclusion that they are capable of being used in that manner (see Case T–305/02 *Nestlé Waters France v OHIM* [2004] ETMR 566 [28]; Joined Cases T–79/01 and 86/01 *Bosch v OHIM (Kit Pro & Kit Super Pro)* [2002] ECR II-4881 [19]). Moreover, these marks are incapable of performing the essential function of a trade mark—namely, that of identifying the origin of the goods or services—thus enabling the consumer who acquired them to repeat or avoid the experience on a subsequent occasion (see Case T–79/00 *Rewe Zentral v OHIM (LITE)* [2002] ECR II-705 [26]; Case T–305/02 *Nestlé Waters France v OHIM* [2004] ETMR 566 [28]). The emphasis is placed on the fact that they are completely devoid of distinctive character and incapable of being distinguished as to commercial origin (see Case C–398/08 P *Audi v OHIM* [2010] ECR I-535). Another example that makes this clear is the refusal of the General Court to register an exclamation mark (!) in a standard font as a trade mark in its own right. Despite the fact that for years it had successfully been used in the combination mark 'JOOP!', the exclamation mark as such remained devoid of distinctive character (Case T–75/08 *JOOP! GmbH v OHIM* [2009] ECR II-191).

It is important to note that, for the purposes of Article 3(1)(b), no distinction should be made between different categories of mark. It is not therefore appropriate to apply more stringent criteria when assessing the distinctiveness of three-dimensional marks comprising the shape of the goods themselves or the shape of the packaging of those goods than in the case of other categories of mark, even if, in practice, fewer three-dimensional marks will pass the test (see Joined Cases C–53/01 and 55/01 *Linde AG and ors v Deutsches Patent- und Markenamt* [2003] ECR I-3161 [49]; see also Case T–88/00 *Mag Instrument v OHIM* [2002] ECR II-467 [32]; Case T–305/02 *Nestlé Waters France v OHIM* [2004] ETMR 566 [35]). The same applies to laudatory epithets and advertising slogans as can be seen in Case C–64/02 P *OHIM v Erpo Möbelwerk* [2004] ECR I-10031 and Case C–398/08 P *Audi v OHIM* [2010] FSR 24. Finally, in Case C–311/11 P *Smart Technologies ULC v OHIM* EU:C:2012:460, the refusal to register 'WIR MACHEN DAS BESONDERE EINFACH' (we make special things simple) for computerized systems was upheld.

One needs to examine each case on its facts, and types of marks such as single letters cannot be excluded as such on the basis of Article 3(1)(b), as became clear in Case C–265/09 P *OHIM v BORCO-Marken-Import-Matthiesen* [2011] ETMR 4 which dealt with the sign α. But nonetheless one needs to keep in mind, when applying those criteria in each case, that the relevant public perception is not necessarily the same in the case of a three-dimensional mark that consists of the appearance of a product itself as it is in case of word or figurative marks that consist of signs that are unrelated to the appearance of the product. Consumers are simply not used to making assumptions about the origin of products on the basis of their shape, or of the shape of their packaging, without reference to any word or graphic element. It must therefore be more difficult to establish distinctiveness for three-dimensional marks (see recently Case C–96/11 P *August Storck KG v OHIM* EU:C:2012:537). The practical outcome is therefore that only a mark that departs significantly from the norm of the sector can fulfil its essential function of indicating origin and can therefore potentially escape being devoid of distinctive character (Case C–24/05 *Storck KG v OHIM* [2006] ECR I-5677; Case C–173/04 *Deutsche SiSi-Werke GmbH & Co. Betriebs KG v OHIM* [2006] ECR I-551, [2006] ETMR 41 [31]). But even in those cases, the fact that they now fulfil the essential function of indicating origin on their own is not a foregone conclusion and needs to be demonstrated. Lindt's application for a three-dimensional sign consisting of the shape of a chocolate rabbit with a red ribbon and golden wrapping paper is a good example of an application that failed to pass this hurdle, as the shape, the ribbon, and the golden wrapping paper were in use by plenty of other manufacturers and failed to refer the consumer exclusively to Lindt (Case C–98/11 P *Chocoladefabriken Lindt & Sprüngli AG v OHIM* EU:C:2012:307).

A minimum degree of distinctive character is, on the other hand, sufficient to render inapplicable the ground for refusal set out in Article 3(1)(b). In a case involving bottles for mineral water, Case T–305/02 *Nestlé Waters France v OHIM* [2004] ETMR 566, the sign claimed consisted of the shape of the packaging of the product, rather than the product itself, because beverages, such as mineral water, cannot be sold without packaging. That three-dimensional mark was composed of commonly used elements, but they were combined in a particular way that made the combination stand out. The mark therefore had the minimum degree of distinctiveness required.

Language issues can also arise: is a descriptive word in one language necessarily devoid of distinctiveness when it is used as a trade mark in another language? In Case C–421/04 *Matratzen Concord AG v Hulka SA* [2006] ECR I-2303, [2006] ETMR 48, the mark concerned was '*Matratzen*' ('mattresses' in German). The mark was, however, registered and used in Spain. In Spanish, the word has no meaning and the CJEU therefore ruled that it could be distinctive for mattresses, unless the relevant parties in the Member State in relation to which registration was sought were capable of identifying the meaning of the term. Unless the latter situation arises, the mark is not caught by Article 3(1). French case law has become increasingly strict on this point. The trade mark Argane was invalidated as it referred to argan oil (*huile d'argan* in French) and, despite being a foreign term not known to the general public at the time of registration, it was known to a more limited and specialized public at that time as a generic name for a vegetal substance. The fact that only a limited section of the public understood the term was sufficient for the exclusion to apply (*Sté Pierre Fabre v Sté Clairjoie*, Supreme Court, Cass. Com., case no. 13-16470, 6 May 2014 [2014] 53 Propriétés Intellectuelles 408).

Specific problems arise in relation to compound signs, namely signs that are composed of several elements. In assessing distinctiveness, looking at each of the parts separately is unavoidable but the final decision needs to be taken on the basis of the whole compound sign. When SAT.2 was applied for in relation to satellite broadcasts it was clear that on its own the element SAT was a mere abbreviation of satellite and that was exactly what it meant to the relevant public (merely descriptive), whilst the element 2 was equally devoid of distinctive character. The CJEU decided nevertheless that the same conclusion did not apply to the compound mark (Case C–329/02 P *SAT.1 Satellitenfernsehen GmbH v OHIM* [2004] ECR I-8317). SAT.2 is not merely descriptive and can be distinguished, as consumers could identify the channel on the basis of it. As such it was not devoid of distinctive character. Or to quote the Court:

> Finally, as regards a trade mark comprising words or a word and a digit, such as that which forms the subject-matter of the dispute, the distinctiveness of each of those terms or elements, taken separately, may be assessed, in part, but must, in any event, depend on an appraisal of the whole which they comprise. Indeed, the mere fact that each of those elements, considered separately, is devoid of distinctive character does not mean that their combination cannot present a distinctive character.[12]

On the other hand, BioID® as a trade mark for the computer-aided identification and/ or verification of live organisms based on one or more specific biometric characteristics was held to be devoid of distinctive character as it was merely descriptive and unable to be distinctive in relation to commercial origin (Case C–37/03 P *BioIDAG v OHIM* [2005] ECR I-7975).

---

[12] *SAT.1* [28].

Finally, it should be noted that the CJEU has held that the distinctiveness of a trade mark must be assessed by reference to, first, the goods or services in respect of which registration is sought and, second, the perception of the relevant persons—namely, the consumers of the goods or services. According to the Court, that means the presumed expectations of an average consumer of the category of goods or services in question, who is reasonably well informed, and reasonably observant and circumspect (see Case C–210/96 *Gut Springenheide & Tusky* [1998] ECR I-4657 [31]; Joined Cases C–53/01 and 55/01 *Linde AG and ors v Deutsches Patent- und Markenamt* [2003] ECR I-3161 [41]).

14.5.3 Article 3(1)(d)

A similar approach applies to Article 3(1)(d) of the Directive. That much was made clear by the CJEU in Case C–210/96 *Gut Springenheide & Tusky* [1998] ECR I-4657. The starting point for subsection (d) is that, for it to apply, the mark must consist exclusively of signs or indications that have become customary in the current language or in the established practices of the trade in the products or services in respect of which the mark is to be registered. This should not be taken to mean, however, that the signs or indications must have become a direct description of the goods or services concerned and that they describe their essential elements or characteristics; it is sufficient that the signs or indications bring the goods or services to mind to the average consumer (see the conclusion of Advocate General Damaso Ruiz-Jarabo Colomer in Case C–517/99 *Merz & Krell & Co.*, delivered on 18 January 2001 [2001] ETMR 48). Whether or not the sign describes the properties or characteristics of the goods or services is irrelevant. Subsection (d) does not exclude signs on the basis that they are descriptive, but on the basis that they have become customary as a term for the goods or services, for example as a result of persistent advertising (Case C–517/99 *Merz & Krell & Co.* [2000] ECR I-6959).

14.5.4 Article 3(1)(c)

Article 3(1)(c) is designed to deny trade mark registration to descriptive marks that, as such, are not likely to be distinctive. Philips' shaver head fell foul of this provision insofar as the public took it as a picture of the goods and not as a trade mark (Case C–299/99 *Philips Electronics NV v Remington Consumer Products Ltd* [2002] ECR I-5475). It is important to note that the bar on registration applies only if the mark is exclusively composed of these types of descriptive matter and marks can be registered that, among other elements, include matters of this sort, whether or not the subject of a disclaimer. A trade mark can therefore include descriptive matter, as long as it does so in combination with other matter that adds a distinctive character to the combination. For a mark to be caught there must be a direct and specific relationship with the goods or services in question to enable the public to immediately perceive, without further thought, a description of the category of goods and services or one of their characteristics.

One can draw a broader conclusion on this basis. Paragraphs (b), (c), and (d) of Article 3(1) were not designed to exclude from registration marks that merely possess an indirect descriptive connotation. The words 'devoid of any' in paragraph (b) and 'exclusively' in paragraph (c) are to be given effect.

The fact that some mental activity is necessary to discern a reference to the quality, or characteristic, of the goods can assist in its registrability, as can uncertainty as to the precise nature of the reference to the quality or character of the goods. And marks that can only refer to the quality or character of the goods are on the other hand to be refused registration, because such a mark does not differ from the usual way of designating the

goods or their characteristics and because it might serve in normal usage, from a cus-
tomer's point of view, to designate the relevant goods either directly or indirectly, or
by reference to one of their essential characteristics (see also Case T–426/11 *Maharishi
Foundation v OHIM* EU:T:2013:63). A good example on this point is the failed application to register the sign TDI for cars and their engines, as in the car world it is generally
known that the sign consists merely of the first letters of the words contained in the
expressions 'turbo direct injection' or 'turbo diesel injection' (Case T–318/09 *Audi and
Volkswagen v OHIM* [2011] ETMR 61). The consumer will not see TDI as referring to a
single brand of cars.

14.5.4.1 Common Words

The distinctive character of trade marks that consist of common words has also taken up
a lot of time in the courts. The CJEU held, in Case C–383/99 P *Procter & Gamble Co. v
OHIM* [2001] ECR I-6251 (the *Baby-Dry* case), that the combination of the words 'baby'
and 'dry' was not simply descriptive, and that the distinctive character of the mark could
be established. In order to do so, the Court held that the descriptive character does not
solely relate to the individual words, but also to the sign of which they form part. The
distinctive character can, in other words, be shown by any difference in use and expression between the combination of words and the normal terminology, and the normal
use of the words in everyday language. In the *Baby-Dry* case, the distinctive character
was derived from the fact that the words 'baby' and 'dry' are not normally used in that
particular combination in relation to nappies. Such a difference should be in relation to
important aspects of form or meaning of the sign. It is submitted that the key element in
the *Baby-Dry* case was, indeed, the fact that, while common words were used, they were
used in an unusual combination that, on its own, is not a common word and that is not
part of normal everyday language.

The debate surrounding trade marks that consist of common words continued though
and came to a climax in the *Doublemint* case (Case C–191/01 P *OHIM v Wm Wrigley Jr Co.*
[2004] RPC 327, [2004] ETMR 121). Wrigley wanted to register 'Doublemint' as a trade
mark for mint-flavoured chewing gum. The CJEU was eventually called upon to sort out
the *Doublemint* saga. The key question was whether the absolute ground for refusal of
marks that are descriptive under Article 3(1)(c) of the Directive applies only if the mark
is exclusively descriptive. The General Court had held that the word 'Doublemint' was
not exclusively descriptive in this case (Case T–193/99 *Wm Wrigley Jr Co. v OHIM* [2001]
ECR II-417). It found that the adjective 'double' was unusual when compared with other
English words, such as 'much', 'strong', 'extra', 'best', or 'finest', and that, when combined
with the word 'mint', it had two distinct meanings for the potential consumer: twice the
usual amount of mint or flavoured with two varieties of mint. Furthermore, it found that
mint is a generic term that includes spearmint, peppermint, and other culinary herbs,
and that there are several possible ways of combining two sorts of mint and, in addition,
various strengths of flavour are possible in the case of each combination. The registration
had therefore been allowed.

On appeal, the CJEU overturned that decision.[13] According to the Court, Article 3(1)
(c) pursues an aim that is in the public interest—namely, that descriptive signs or indications relating to the characteristics of goods or services in respect of which registration is
sought may be freely used by all. That provision accordingly prevents such signs and indications from being reserved to one undertaking alone, because they have been registered
as trade marks. In order for the registration to be refused, it is not therefore necessary

---

[13] Case C–191/01 P *OHIM v Wm Wrigley Jr Co.* [2004] RPC 327, [2004] ETMR 121.

that the signs and indications composing the mark that are referred to in that provision actually be in use at the time of the application for registration in a way that is descriptive of goods or services such as those in relation to which the application is filed, or of characteristics of those goods or services. It is sufficient, as the wording of that provision itself indicates, that such signs and indications could be used for such purposes (see Case C–51/10 P *Agencja Wydawnicza Technopol v OHIM* [2011] ETMR 34 [38]). The rule that has been established is therefore clearly that a sign must be refused registration under that provision if at least one of its possible meanings designates a characteristic of the goods or services concerned. Because, at least in one sense, 'Doublemint' was descriptive, its registration as a trade mark therefore had to be refused (*Wrigley*). It is also not required that the sign is the most common or usual way to describe the goods or services (*Agencja Wydawnicza Technopol*).

Slightly different issues arise, as we saw earlier in relation to distinctiveness, when a descriptive word from another language is used as a mark. In Case C–421/04 *Matratzen Concord AG v Hulka SA* [2006] ECR I-2303, [2006] ETMR 48, the mark concerned was 'Matratzen', which means 'mattresses' in German. The mark was, however, registered and used in Spain. In Spanish, the word has no meaning and the CJEU ruled therefore that it could be distinctive for mattresses, unless the relevant parties in the Member State in relation to which registration was sought were capable of identifying the meaning of the term. Unless the latter situation arises, the mark is not caught by Article 3(1); if, however, the word is descriptive and understood as such by the public, any particular representation of the word will remain caught by the exclusion.

In the UK Arnold J had such a case before him with the 'Now' trade mark. Six fine lines arranged in a star or sun shape emanating from the central letter 'o' had been added. But in relation to telecommunication services and broadcasting over the Internet the word 'now' could be held to describe the instantaneous nature of the goods and services. The additions could not change that conclusion. Or in the words of Arnold J:

> Taking all of the evidence into account, I conclude that the CTM is precluded from registration by [Article 3(1)(c)] in relation to the services in issue because NOW would be understood by the average consumer as a description of a characteristic of the service, namely the instant, immediate nature of the service. The figurative elements of the CTM do not affect this conclusion.[14]

There is also an obvious overlap between Article 3(1)(b) and (c). A sign that fails to clear one hurdle also often stumbles at the other hurdle. Or, as the CJEU put it:

> [I]t should be noted, first of all, that, although each of the grounds for refusal to register listed in Article 3(1) of the directive is independent of the others and calls for separate examination, there is none the less a clear overlap between the scope of each of the grounds for refusal set out in Article 3(1)(b) and (c)...
>
> Thus, a sign which, in relation to the goods or services in respect of which its registration as a mark is applied for, has descriptive character for the purposes of Article 3(1)(c) of the directive is therefore necessarily devoid of any distinctive character as regards those goods or services, within the meaning of Article 3(1)(b) of that directive.[15]

---

[14] *Starbucks (HK) Ltd, PCCW Media Ltd and UK Broadband Ltd v British Sky Broadcasting Group plc, British Sky Broadcasting Ltd and Sky IP International Ltd* [2012] EWHC 3074 (Ch) [116].

[15] Joined Cases C–90/11 and 91/11 *Alfred Strigl v Deutsches Patent- und Markenamt and Securvita Gesellschaft zur Entwicklung alternativer Versicherungskonzepte mbH v Öko-Invest Verlagsgesellschaft mbH* EU:C:2012:147 [20] and [21]. See also Case C–363/99 *Koninklijke KPN Nederland* [2004] ECR I-1619 [85] and [86]; and Case C–51/10 P *Agencja Wydawnicza Technopol v OHIM* [2011] ETMR 34 [33].

14.5.4.2 A Need to Look at All of the Circumstances

The same approach was used by Advocate General Ruiz-Jarabo Colomer in his conclusions in Case C–265/00 *Campina Melkunie BV v Benelux-Merkenbureau* [2004] ETMR 821 (the *Biomild* case) and in Case C–363/99 *Koninklijke KPN Nederland NV v Benelux-Merkenbureau* [2004] ETMR 771 (the *Postkantoor* case). He added that, in examining whether a sign is suitable for registration as a trade mark, the trade mark office should not limit its analysis to the sign as it appears in the application; attention should also be paid to all other relevant circumstances and these include the acquisition of distinctive character through use that has been made of the sign, as well as the danger that the average consumer will be confused or misled by the use of the mark for the goods or services in relation of which registration is sought.

The CJEU confirmed the approach in the *KPN Postkantoor* case in the following terms:

> Article 3(1)(c) of Directive 89/104 must be interpreted as meaning that a mark consisting of a word composed of elements, each of which is descriptive of characteristics of the goods or services in respect of which registration is sought, is itself descriptive of the characteristics of those goods or services for the purposes of that provision, unless there is a perceptible difference between the word and the mere sum of its parts: that assumes either that because of the unusual nature of the combination in relation to the goods or services the word creates an impression which is sufficiently far removed from that produced by the mere combination of meanings lent by the elements of which it is composed, with the result that the word is more than the sum of its parts, or that the word has become part of everyday language and has acquired its own meaning, with the result that it is now independent of its components. In the latter case, it is necessary to ascertain whether a word which has acquired its own meaning is not itself descriptive for the purposes of the same provision.
>
> For the purposes of determining whether Art.3(1)(c) of Directive 89/104 applies to such a mark, it is irrelevant whether or not there are synonyms capable of designating the same characteristics of the goods or services mentioned in the application for registration or that the characteristics of the goods or services which may be the subject of the description are commercially essential or merely ancillary.[16]

14.5.4.3 Three-Dimensional Marks

It has also been argued that Article 3(1)(c) of the Directive has no relevance for the three-dimensional shape of product trade marks. The CJEU has rejected that argument and has added that:

> When examining the ground for refusing registration in Article 3(1)(c) of the Directive in a concrete case, regard must be had to the public interest underlying that provision, which is that all three-dimensional shape of product trade marks which consist exclusively of signs or indications which may serve to designate the characteristics of the goods or service within the meaning of that provision should be freely available to all and, subject always to Article 3(3) of the Directive, cannot be registered.[17]

This policy consideration is of crucial importance in relation to the application of Article 3(1)(c) in practice and applies across the board.

---

[16] Case C–363/99 *Koninklijke KPN Nederland NV v Benelux-Merkenbureau* [2004] ETMR 771. See also Case C–265/00 *Campina Melkunie BV v Benelux-Merkenbureau* [2004] ETMR 821

[17] Joined Cases C–53/01 and 55/01 *Linde AG and ors v Deutsches Patent- und Markenamt* [2003] ECR I-3161 [76]–[77].

14.5.5 **The Proviso**

Obviously, certain—but not all—marks can become distinctive and capable of being distinguished through use, and through educating the public that the sign is a trade mark. The Coca-Cola bottle may be seen as an example. The shape of the bottle clearly became a sign that refers uniquely to the Coca-Cola Company. If there is evidence that this has happened before an application is made to register the marks, then there is no problem. Indeed, in such a case, the position of the applicant is further enhanced by the proviso to Article 3(1)(b)–(d) found in Article 3(3), which provides that, in such a case, registration of the trade mark shall not be refused. The parallel provision in the Regulation is found in Article 7(3).

The CJEU has held that this proviso constitutes a major exception to the rules laid down in Article 3(1)(b)–(d) in Cases C–108/97 *Windsurfing Chiemsee Produktions und Vertriebs GmbH v Boots- und Segelzubehör Walter Huber* and C–109/97 *Windsurfing Chiemsee Produktions und Vertriebs GmbH v Attenberger* [1999] ECR I-2779. The distinctive character that can be obtained through use must therefore 'serve to identify the product…as originating from a particular undertaking and thus to distinguish that product from goods of another undertaking' (*Windsurfing*). Only then will the geographical indication or any of the other items listed in Article 3(1)(c)—have gained a new significance as will its connotation, which is no longer purely descriptive, justify its registration as a trade mark.[18] In making the assessment of whether the mark has acquired such a distinctive character, the court may take account of points such as the market share held by the mark; how intensive, geographically widespread, and long-standing the use of the mark has been; the amount that the applicant has invested in promoting the mark; the proportion of the relevant class of persons who identify the goods as originating from a particular undertaking as a result of the use of the mark; and statements from trade and professional associations. The final test in this respect is that at least a significant section of the relevant class of persons must identify goods as originating from a particular undertaking because they are labelled with the mark (see Case T–399/02 *Eurocermex v OHIM* (*Shape of a beer bottle*) [2004] ECR II-1391 [42] and Case T–262/04 *BIC v OHIM* (*Shape of a lighter*) [2005] ECR II-5959 [61]). If this is the case, the distinctive character will have been acquired. It is not therefore required that the goods are also manufactured in the desired location. In cases in which a real link between the location and the goods or services is absent, in principle nothing stands in the way of registering a geographical location as a trade mark for those goods or services,[19] as long as that location does not evoke any connotation in the mind of the consumer (Cases C–108/97 *Windsurfing Chiemsee Produktions und Vertriebs GmbH v Boots- und Segelzubehör Walter Huber*; C–109/97 *Windsurfing Chiemsee Produktions und Vertriebs GmbH v Attenberger* [1999] ECR I-2779).

A somewhat complex set of facts arose in Case C–108/05 *Bovemij v Benelux-Merkenbureau* [2006] ECR I-7605, in which the mark involved was 'Europolis'. In Dutch

---

[18] The French courts have applied this approach to allow under the proviso the mark SeLoger.com, which had become a reference to a single undertaking despite its humble descriptive beginnings as 'to acquire housing', see *Janny B. v Pressimmo On Line and SA SeLoger.com*, Court of Appeal Paris, CA Paris pôle 5-1, 14 October 2014, [2014] 54 Propriétés Intellectuelles 81.

[19] For a French example see *Commune de Laguiole v Lunettes Folomi SAS, Simco Cash Sarl, Polyflame Europe SA and others*, Court of Appeal Paris, CA Paris pôle 5-2, 2 April 2014, RG no. 12/20559 [2014] 52 Propriétés Intellectuelles 295. Registration of the name Laguiole for glasses could not be stopped by the village of Laguiole as, despite its fame and reputation in relation to knives, the village has no link with glasses and the consumer would not link Laguiole glasses to the village.

(one of the languages spoken in the Benelux), this is a contraction of 'euro' and 'polis', the latter word meaning policy, as in insurance policy. The mark was indeed to be used in relation to insurance. At first glance, the mark therefore failed the test in Article 3(1). The Court ruled that the proviso could only save the application if the sign has acquired distinctive character throughout the Member State concerned. For the Benelux, this means the part of the territory for which the ground of refusal exists. When the ground for refusal is based on the use of a language in part of a Member State or in the Benelux, evidence of acquired distinctiveness in that part of the Member State or the Benelux will suffice.

As such, there is nothing special about the judgment: it is a logical application of the provision concerned. It is, however, interesting to contrast the decision with the decision of the ECJ on Article 3(1) in Case C–421/04 *Matratzen Concord AG v Hulka SA* [2006] ECR I-2303, [2006] ETMR 48). It is important to see, though, that the second decision is not concerned with the proviso, but with Article 3(1)(b) and (c) itself. The mark concerned was 'Matratzen', and as that German word is not understood in Spain it is not caught by Article 3(1) in the first place and there is therefore no need to turn to the proviso. On that basis the mark could be distinctive for mattresses.

The use that is required to acquire distinctiveness through use may be the result of the use of the mark in conjunction with, or as part of, another registered trade mark. The Court of Justice held so in Case C–353/03 *Societe des Produits Nestlé SA v Mars UK Ltd* [2005] ECR I-6135, [2005] 3 CMLR 12. The case turned around Nestlé's attempt to register 'Have a Break' as a trade mark, while they already had trade marks in the name KIT KAT and in the slogan 'Have a break…have a KIT KAT'.

14.5.6 **Article 3(1)(e)**

Article 3(1)(e) creates further instances of unregistrability arising directly from the extension of trade mark protection to shapes of items, as does the parallel provision in Article 7(1)(e) of the Regulation. This is the first set of absolute grounds for refusal of registration to which the proviso does not apply. Distinctiveness through use is therefore no longer a means to overcome these absolute grounds for refusal of registration. We will now look in turn at each of the provisions of Article 3(1)(e)/Article 7(1)(e).

14.5.6.1 Shapes Resulting From the Nature of the Goods and Shapes Necessary to Achieve a Technical Result

Clearly, there is a risk of overlap between trade marks and other IP rights, and this is addressed by the provision that shapes (in each case exclusively) resulting from the nature of the goods themselves and shapes necessary to achieve a technical result shall not be registered. But how does one determine whether a sign consists exclusively of a shape that results from the nature of the goods themselves? French case law helpfully provides guidance by excluding shapes that are regularly used in the relevant trade, such as the shape of a Kit Kat chocolate bar. These do not result from the nature of the goods themselves (*Sté des produits Nestlé SA v Directeur général de l'INPI*, Court of Appeal Paris, CA Paris pôle 5-2, 13 December 2013, RG no. 13/09001, [2014] 51 Propriétés Intellectuelles 183). But, by contrast, the shape of an apple results exclusively from the nature of the good and is therefore covered by the exclusion.

The definition that is given to the concept of the goods themselves is vital in this respect. If the goods are defined narrowly—for example, as three-headed rotary shavers in the *Philips* case—any shape mark would be rendered invalid. It could, of course, be argued that the goods should be taken to mean the specification of goods for which the mark is intended to be registered.

Jacob J rejected that argument in the *Philips* case before it went to the CJEU and called the whole issue *'a practical business matter'* (*Philips Electronics BV v Remington Consumer Products Ltd* [1998] RPC 283, 305). He arrived at his ruling that the goods in the case at issue were electric shavers on the basis of the criterion that this was how things were in practice, as articles of commerce.

The CJEU turned its attention to this particular absolute ground for refusal in Case C–205/13 *Hauck GmbH & Co. KG v Stokke A/S, Stokke Nederland BV, Peter Opsvik, Peter Opsvik A/S* EU:C:2014:2233. This case was concerned with the well-known Tripp Trapp chair for children. The functional design features of the chair had been incorporated in the shape mark. The question that arose was whether the ground for refusal of registration may apply only to a sign which consists exclusively of the shape which is indispensable to the function of the product in question or whether it may also apply to a sign which consists exclusively of a shape with one or more characteristics which are essential to the function of that product and which consumers may be looking for in the products of competitors. That is, are functional features which consumers like to see in any such product, also those of other manufacturers, part of a shape that results from the nature of the goods? The CJEU based its analysis on the single policy consideration underlying Article 3(1)(e), which is to prevent trade mark protection from granting its proprietor a monopoly on technical solutions or functional characteristics of a product which a user is likely to seek in the products of competitors. Consequently, in order to apply the first indent of Article 3(1)(e) of the Trade Marks Directive correctly, it is necessary to identify the essential characteristics—that is, the most important elements—of the sign concerned on a case-by-case basis, that assessment being based either on the overall impression produced by the sign or on an examination of each the components of that sign in turn.

The Court emphasized that the ground for refusal of registration set out in the first indent of Article 3(1)(e) cannot be applicable where the trade mark application relates to a shape of goods in which another element, such as a decorative or imaginative element, which is not inherent to the generic function of the goods, plays an important or essential role. The condition of a shape consisting 'exclusively' of a shape resulting from the nature of the goods would not then be satisfied.

But, an interpretation whereby the provision is to apply only to signs which consist exclusively of shapes which are indispensable to the function of the goods in question, leaving the producer of those goods no leeway to make a personal essential contribution, would not allow the objective of the ground for refusal set out therein to be fully realized. Indeed, an interpretation to that effect would result in limiting the products to which that ground for refusal could apply to: (a) 'natural' products (which have no substitute); and (b) 'regulated' products (the shape of which is prescribed by legal standards), even though signs consisting of the shapes formed by such products could not be registered in any event because of their lack of distinctive character. Account should be taken of the fact that the concept of a 'shape which results from the nature of the goods themselves' means that shapes with essential characteristics which are inherent to the generic function or functions of such goods must, in principle, also be denied registration. These characteristics cannot and should not be reserved to one operator.

As a result, the ground for refusal of registration may apply to a sign which consists exclusively of the shape of a product with one or more essential characteristics which are inherent to the generic function or functions of that product and which consumers may be looking for in the products of competitors.

Alternatively, the problem under Article 3(1)(e) may lie in the fact that the shape of the goods is necessary to achieve a technical result. This was held not to mean that there was no other route to that result by Advocate General Damaso Ruiz-Jarabo Colomer in his conclusion in Case C–299/99 *Philips Electronics BV v Remington Consumer Products Ltd* (delivered on 23 January 2001 [2001] ETMR 48); rather it means that, in substance, the shape is motivated by function. The test was established as whether, in substance, the shape solely achieves a technical result. The Philips three-headed rotary shaver shape was held to have been chosen to achieve a technical result and it therefore fell foul of Article 3(1)(e)(ii) when the CJEU confirmed this approach. The Court additionally explained in the *Philips* case, that the exclusion from trade mark registrability of a shape that is necessary to achieve a technical result still applies if other shapes could allow the same or a similar result to be reached, as long as the essential features of the shape were chosen to achieve the result (Case C–299/99 *Philips Electronics NV v Remington Consumer Products Ltd* [2002] ECR I-5475).

When Lego attempted to register the shape of their toy bricks as a trade mark and took the case all the way up to the Grand Chamber, the CJEU was given the opportunity to restate the law on this absolute ground for refusal (Case C–48/09 P *Lego Juris v OHIM* [2010] ECR I-8403). Building on the *Philips* case, the Court started its analysis by stating that this absolute ground for refusal to register must be interpreted in the light of the public interest underlying it, which is to prevent trade mark law granting an undertaking a monopoly on technical solutions or functional characteristics of a product (see Case C–173/04 P *Deutsche SiSi-Werke v OHIM* [2006] ECR I-551 [59]; Case C–299/99 *Philips Electronics NV v Remington Consumer Products Ltd* [2002] ECR I-5475, [2003] Ch 159, [2003] RPC 14 [78]; and Joined Cases C–53/01 to 55/01 *Linde and ors* [2003] ECR I-3161 [72]). The rule balances two elements, both of which are likely to help to establish a healthy and fair system of competition. On the one hand, the prohibition on registration as a trade mark of any sign consisting of the shape of goods which is necessary to obtain a technical result ensures that undertakings may not use trade mark law in order to perpetuate, indefinitely, exclusive rights relating to technical solutions. On the other hand, is the recognition that any shape of goods is to an extent functional and that it would therefore be inappropriate to refuse to register a shape of goods as a trade mark solely on the ground that it has functional characteristics. That explains the appearance of the terms 'exclusively' and 'necessary' to ensure that only shapes of goods which exclusively incorporate a technical solution, and the registration of which as a trade mark would therefore actually impede the use of that technical solution by other undertakings, are not to be registered. Putting that into practice it was held that the ground for refusal precludes registration of any shape consisting exclusively, in its essential characteristics, of the shape of the goods which is technically causal of, and sufficient to obtain, the intended technical result, even if that result can be achieved by other shapes using the same or another technical solution. One starts by looking at the essential characteristic of the shape, here for example the two rows of studs to connect the toy bricks, and these are excluded from registration if they only incorporate a technical solution in the sense that all essential characteristics of the shape perform a technical function. It is irrelevant that the result can also be achieved by another shape and that non-essential characteristics of the shape perform other non-technical functions (Case C–48/09 P *Lego Juris v OHIM* [2010] ECR I-8403; see also Case T–164/11 *Reddig GmbH v OHIM—Morleys Ltd* EU:T:2012:443). On that basis the shape of the toy bricks could not be registered.

Patent and design law may offer alternative routes to IP protection in appropriate cases that are excluded from trade mark law through the operation of Article 3(1)(e). This is also the clear steer given by the CJEU in the Tripp Trapp case (Case C–205/13 *Hauck GmbH & Co. KG v Stokke A/S, Stokke Nederland BV, Peter Opsvik, Peter Opsvik A/S* EU:C:2014:2233).

14.5.6.2 **Shapes That Give Substantial Value to the Goods**

More difficulty is encountered with the third exclusion in this group—namely, the exclusion under Article 3(1)(e)(iii) of a shape 'which (exclusively) gives substantial value to the goods'. This is an entirely new provision in the law and has its origins in the trade mark law of the Benelux countries. Taken at face value, it appears to exclude a significant range of products from trade mark protection, because those involved in marketing will obviously seek to attract customers to a product by, among other things, its distinctive shape and, if this ploy succeeds, they will have enhanced the value of the product.

Examples are manifold. The success of the film *Jurassic Park* caused many manufacturers of such foodstuffs as fish fingers and burgers to shape their products to resemble dinosaurs. It would be reasonable to assume that this helped the sales of the products and thus the shape gave added value (although there is a query as to whether it gave substantial added value) to the product. Many items of designer clothing or jewellery also seem to fall within this exception, and significant litigation has occurred in the Benelux countries from where this new provision is derived. The key cases in the Benelux emphasize on the one hand the need for the value conferred by the shape to be substantial (*Adidas v De Laet*, Benelux Court, 23 December 1985, [1985] Jun 38), and on the other hand that it must be the shape itself, rather than the overall image of the product, that must be responsible for the extra value (*Superconfex v Burberrys*, Benelux Court, 14 April 1989, [1989] Jun 19).

The easy scenario is the one where the shape exclusively adds value and does not on its own allow for source identification. Here the absolute ground for refusal clearly applies and by way of example one could think of the facts of the *Philips* case.

A case in which the shape does allow source identification, but nevertheless gives substantive value to the goods, presents more of a dilemma. Trade mark protection will necessarily apply to both aspects, comprised in a single shape, and not just to the trade mark function. One needs to keep in mind that the CJEU's emphasis on the public interest underlying the ground for refusal, as set out in the *Lego Juris* case in relation to technical effect (Case C–48/09 P *Lego Juris v OHIM* [2010] ECR I-8403), applies to this absolute ground for refusal too. In other words, a trade mark will not be granted for a shape that gives substantial value to the goods in order to prevent trade mark law granting an undertaking a monopoly on the functional characteristics of a product (see Case C–173/04 P *Deutsche SiSi-Werke v OHIM* [2006] ECR I-551 [59]; Case C–299/99 *Philips Electronics NV v Remington Consumer Products Ltd* [2002] ECR I-5475, [2003] Ch 159, [2003] RPC 14 [78]; and Joined Cases C–53/01 to 55/01 *Linde and ors* [2003] ECR I-3161 [72]). Moreover, such a monopoly in a shape that gives substantial value to the product would potentially be of unlimited duration. Other traders have a legitimate right to use the same shape for their competing products. The rule balances two elements, both of which are likely to help to establish a healthy and fair system of competition. On the one hand, the prohibition on registration as a trade mark of any sign consisting of the shape of goods which gives substantial value to the goods ensures that undertakings may not use trade mark law in order to perpetuate, indefinitely, exclusive rights that go beyond the essential distinctiveness function of a trade marks. On the other hand, is the recognition that any shape of goods is to an extent functional and it would therefore be inappropriate to refuse to register a shape of goods as a trade mark solely on the ground that it has functional characteristics. That explains the appearance of the term 'exclusively'. The General Court therefore held in the *Bang & Olufsen* case (Case T–508/08 *Bang & Olufsen A/S v OHIM* [2012] ETMR 10) that all essential elements of the shape of a rather peculiar design of loudspeaker had been chosen merely as a function of the peculiar design, as the latter would give additional and substantive value to the product. The consumer would buy the loudspeaker for its design and would be prepared to pay a substantially higher price for it. The shape therefore added substantive value to the goods and registration was denied. The General Court added that the fact that there were other characteristics of the goods, such as the sound quality it produced, that also give substantial value to them was irrelevant. This case is a good example of a shape that gives substantial value to the goods, but it is important to recognize that this case comes at the end of a long story. In an earlier decision the General Court had held that the shape was not devoid of distinctive character. In other words, contrary to what happened in the *Philips* case (Case C–299/99 *Philips Electronics NV v Remington Consumer Products Ltd* [2002] ECR I-5475), the shape was distinctive. Distinctiveness does not seem to stop the application of this absolute ground for refusal to register the shape as a trade mark, but it is important to note that the shape in all its essential characteristics has primarily been chosen for the value it adds to the product and that its distinctiveness is merely a side effect. That seems to be the effect of the insertion in the legislation of the term 'exclusively'. The same logic seems to underpin the CJEU's decision in the *G-Star* case. This case dealt with an application for the registration of sloping stitching, contrasting colour bands, seams, and further stitching for trousers (G-Star trousers) (Case C–371/06 *Benetton Group SpA v G-Star International BV* [2008] ETMR 5). The national court had accepted that such a sign added substantial value to the goods: the shape of the trousers that resulted from it had indeed become the example par excellence of a style or fashion. That added substantial value, but also made it necessary, from a policy point of view, that other traders could compete with goods of the same style or fashion. The CJEU accepted that the emphasis on the stitching had given that particular shape substantial added value. It had become a style wanted by consumers and other traders should be able to offer goods in that style too. But important for our purposes is also that all courts involved seem to accept that the shape was distinctive, as consumers recognize the products of the brand on the basis of it.

14.5.7 Article 3(1)(f) and (g)

The next parts of Article 3(1) of the Directive, paragraphs (f) and (g), and the equivalent paragraphs (f) and (g) of Article 7(1) of the Regulation, add further restrictions. No mark may be registered if, first, it is contrary to public policy or accepted principles of morality or, second, if it would have the effect of deceiving the public.

14.5.7.1 Morality

The first category will, of course, be one that will be hard to predict given the inherent changeability of such issues as public policy and morality. And a certain degree of vagueness is also no doubt intended, as these provisions hand registrars and OHIM an emergency tool to stop inappropriate trade marks from being registered. Examples can probably be found in terms that would offend religious communities if used in relation to certain goods of services or terms that are derogatory and would stigmatize a community of a certain descent.

The logic behind this provision seems to be that one needs to look at the intrinsic qualities of the mark. These intrinsic qualities need to contravene generally accepted moral principles for the prohibition to apply (Case T–140/02 *Sportwetten GmbH Gera v OHIM* [2005] ECR II-3247). It is not sufficient that the mark is seen as distasteful. Morality demands a stronger reaction and an application to offend against morality is more likely to be one that was calculated to cause outrage amongst a large section of the population. The test applies with the public at large in mind, rather than the specific professional community at which the mark is targeted (Case T–526/09 *Paki Logistics GmbH v OHIM* EU:T:2011:564 [18]). Common ground on morality is of course notoriously difficult to find in our modern pluralist and multicultural society. Marks that need to be used in a certain context to become objectionable are not covered by the prohibition. An example of the latter scenario was the mark 'FCUK', which was capable of being seen as a swear word, but whether and to what extent this would be the case depended on the circumstances of its use (see in the UK *Woodman v French Connection Ltd* [2007] RPC 1). It escaped the prohibition. An example of the former scenario was the mark 'Jesus' for clothing. Any commercial use or appropriation of that name would be an anathema to Christians (see the UK case *Basic Trademark SA's Trade Mark Application* [2005] RPC 25, religious significance on its own is not sufficient though). The General Court also refused to register the verbal sign 'PAKI', on an application from a German transport company, as an English-speaking audience would necessarily interpret that as a derogatory term for people of Pakistani descent (Case T–526/09 *Paki Logistics GmbH v OHIM* EU:T:2011:564).

14.5.7.2 Deceiving the Public

Trade marks are there to distinguish origin. Without distinctiveness there will be no trade mark registered. But one should not forget what is being distinguished. The pro-competitive function of trade marks is that they enable the consumer to distinguish between identical goods of different origin. It logically follows that trade marks should not be descriptive (of the product or service), as that would mean they cannot distinguish as to origin between identical products or services. Any random non-descriptive sign can therefore at least in theory be used as a trade mark. But trade marks operate in the relationship between the rights holder (producer of the goods or renderer of the service) and the consumer. The consumer relies on the trade mark for information and to enable repeat purchases. That means that the bottom line of the freedom to choose a non-descriptive trade mark is that the trade mark should not deceive the product, for example as to the nature of the goods, as that would destroy the essential relationship between the rights holder and the consumer. Deceiving the public is therefore an absolute ground for refusal and in terms of its function in the wider framework it fits with morality and public policy.

The provision itself points out, inter alia, that the deception may arise in connection with the nature of the goods or services, their quality, or their geographical origin. In the old English case *Re Royal Worcester Corset Co.'s Application* (1909) 26 RPC 185, a nice factual example arose when trade mark registration was refused for the use of the company's name as a trade mark on corsets, because the application did not distinguish between corsets made by the company in Worcester, Massachusetts, and other corsets, and, in any event, no royal patronage had been conferred on the goods. Thus the proposed mark was doubly deceptive.

Case C–259/04 *Elizabeth Florence Emanuel v Continental Shelf 128 Ltd* [2006] ECR I-3089, [2006] ETMR 56 provided the CJEU with an opportunity to explain the provision. Ms Emanuel is a well-known designer of wedding attire. She registered the trade mark 'Elizabeth Emanuel' for her company. Later, the business, goodwill, and the registered trade mark were assigned to Frostprint Ltd, which immediately changed its name to Elizabeth Emanuel International. Soon afterwards, Ms Emanuel left the business. After another assignment, the new company, with which Ms Emanuel has no links, applied to register another trade mark, 'ELIZABETH EMANUEL'. Ms Emanuel filed a notice of opposition to that application and, in September 1999, she lodged an application to revoke the registered trade mark 'ELIZABETH EMANUEL'. In her view, the registration of her name by a company with which she had no links was likely to deceive the public that still associated her name with wedding attire, but she had no involvement whatsoever in that company's garments.

The Court refused to establish the narrow link between the use of a name and deception, simply because the person whose name is used is no longer involved. In the view of the Court:

(i) A trade mark corresponding to the name of the designer and first manufacturer of the goods bearing that mark may not, by reason of that particular feature alone, be refused registration on the ground that it would deceive the public,... in particular where the goodwill associated with that trade mark, previously registered in a different graphic form, has been assigned together with the business making the goods to which the mark relates.

(ii) A trade mark corresponding to the name of the designer and first manufacturer of the goods bearing that mark is not, by reason of that particular feature alone, liable to revocation on the ground that that mark would mislead the public,... in particular where the goodwill associated with that mark has been assigned together with the business making the goods to which the mark relates.[20]

The applicant is therefore required to prove actual deception. In the absence of that proof, the rights holder that has acquired the trade mark in a bona fide way as a tradable commodity in its own right can continue to use it. Or, having obtained the business, nothing will stand in the way of additional trade mark registrations.

Clearly, the combination of paragraphs (f) and (g) of Article 3 of the Directive/Article 7 of the Regulation represents a sensible and necessary set of controls.

14.5.8 **Further Absolute Grounds for Refusal**

Article 6*ter* of the Paris Convention protects the flags and emblems of states that are party to the Paris Convention, as well as the names and emblems of international intergovernmental organizations (IGOs), of which any Paris Convention state is a member, against unauthorized registration and use as trade marks. Apart from national flaws, the best example of this is the impossibility of being able to register red crosses or red crescents for any purpose apart from the humanitarian activities of the Red Cross and related organizations. The Directive and the Regulation deal with this ground for refusal in paragraph (h) of Articles 3 and 7 respectively. Member States are also given the opportunity to adopt in their national laws a provision making it impossible to register any mark use of which is forbidden by other laws, according to Article 2(a) of the Directive. This provision is often used in the same context to achieve similar aims.

When the maple leaf symbol that appears on the Canadian flag became the subject of a trade mark application the CJEU seized the opportunity to clarify the meaning of this exclusion (Joined Cases C–202/08 P and 208/08 P *American Clothing Associates SA v OHIM, OHIM v American Clothing Associates SA* [2010] ETMR 3). State emblems are protected irrespective of whether there is in the mind of the consumer a connection between the mark that is applied for and the emblem. And the protection extends to cases where the emblem was not the whole mark, but only an element of the trade mark applied for. Exact copies of emblems as well as imitations are protected. It is, however, required that the reproduction or imitation does not refer to the image as such (i.e. any maple leaf), but to its heraldic expression. The public had to perceive the mark as an imitation of the heraldic expression of the emblem. Thus the unauthorized use of a wide range of insignia is controlled as a matter of law, rather than as one of discretion.

---

[20] *Elizabeth Florence Emanuel* [51] and [53].

14.5.9 **Bad Faith**

Finally, the Directive (Article 2(d)) gives the Member States the option to introduce a provision according to which a trade mark shall not be registered if the application is made in bad faith. The Regulation has a bad faith provision as an absolute ground for invalidity in Article 52(1)(b).

The CJEU was confronted with the definition of the concept of the bad faith issue in Case C–529/07 *Chocoladefabriken Lindt & Sprüngli AG v Franz Hauswirth GmbH* [2009] ETMR 56. In this case a number of competing undertakings had for years been selling chocolate Easter bunnies in similar shapes and presentations. One of them then registered its version and tried to use it to stop the other from making the Easter bunnies with a similar shape and presentation. The question arose whether the application for the trade mark had been made in bad faith. The Court argued that an overall assessment that takes account of all the relevant factors in a specific case needs to be made at the time of the application. Bad faith requires that an intention is shown and that intention needs to be demonstrated on the basis of objective elements arising from the facts of the case. In this case the commercial reality was such that the applicant must have known about the use of the shape by its competitors. That knowledge alone though does not prove an intention of bad faith. That element is rather found in the intention to stop others from making the products in that shape. Long undisturbed use by competitors also points towards the idea that registration is sought to gain an unfair advantage. The fact that technical and commercial constraints limit the competitors' freedom to choose another shape also point in the direction of bad faith. Other factors such as the reputation earned by the sign may however point in the opposite direction and need to be taken into account too. On the facts of the case though there were strong indications of bad faith. Thus the 'bad faith' exception has potential for considerable use; it may best be regarded as a general catch-all provision.

14.6 Relative Grounds for Refusal of Registration

It is now necessary to turn to the second group of unregistrable marks—namely, those that cannot be registered not because of their own inherent problems, but because of the pre-existing presence in the market of other similar or identical marks on other similar or identical goods or services. Because of the involvement of other marks and because the ground for refusal results from the relationship between the marks, these grounds are known as relative grounds for refusal and apply to marks that have already overcome the absolute grounds for refusal of registration. The relevant provisions are Article 4 of the Directive and Article 8 of the Regulation.

14.6.1 **An Earlier Mark**

The first thing to establish is that, in looking at the pre-existing marks that may affect the registrability of a new mark, it is necessary to cast the net widely and look beyond merely what trade marks have been registered in the Member State concerned when one looks from the perspective of the Directive and beyond which Community trade marks have been registered when one looks from the perspective of the Regulation. The relevant provisions refer to an 'earlier trade mark' and this key phrase is explained as including all national marks, the Community trade mark, and trade marks registered through the provisions of the Madrid Protocol, and also applications for trade marks in each case in which that mark has, in effect, an earlier priority date. The phrase also covers well-known trade marks—that is, those marks being well known for the purposes of the Paris Convention—namely, a mark of a person or business from any signatory country who, although not in business or even in possession of business goodwill in the relevant territory, nevertheless has a mark that is well known.

14.6.2 **The Relative Grounds**

Having ascertained the requirements of an 'earlier trade mark', it is now necessary to consider the ways in which such a mark will intervene to prevent a subsequent registration. The Directive and Regulation offer a three-tier system of protection. This system is, in essence, the same as that used for infringement cases. We therefore refer the reader to Chapter 15 for a more in-depth analysis.

First, and most simply, no trade mark can ever be registered if it is identical to an earlier mark and is used on identical goods or services, this being perhaps a relatively unlikely scenario. The more likely situation is that in which either, or both, the mark, or the goods or services, are not identical but merely similar. So, second, a mark must also not be registered if it is *either* identical to an earlier mark and to be used on similar goods and services, *or* similar to an earlier mark and to be used on identical *or* similar goods and services. This is, however, subject to a proviso—namely, that the overlap must cause confusion on the part of the public. So the essential question to ask is whether the similarities in question are likely to confuse.

Article 8(1) of the Regulation sets these rules out as follows:

1. Upon opposition by the proprietor of an earlier trade mark, the trade mark applied for shall not be registered:

    (a) if it is identical with the earlier trade mark and the goods or services for which registration is applied for are identical with the goods or services for which the earlier trade mark is protected;

    (b) if because of its identity with, or similarity to, the earlier trade mark and the identity or similarity of the goods or services covered by the trade marks there exists a likelihood of confusion on the part of the public in the territory in which the earlier trade mark is protected; the likelihood of confusion includes the likelihood of association with the earlier trade mark.

The parallel provision in the Directive is found in Article 4(1).

There is a third level though. In certain circumstances, prior use of a mark, whether similar or identical, will prevent a subsequent registration even for totally dissimilar goods or services. This arises in cases in which the earlier mark has gained a reputation and the subsequent use of the same mark in a different context would either take unfair advantage of, or be detrimental to, the distinctive character or repute of the earlier trade mark. For a recent example see Case T–301/09 *IG Communications Ltd v OHIM, Citigroup and Citibank NA* [2013] ETMR 17, where the CITIGATE mark was held to take unfair advantage of Citibank's CITIBANK trade mark with a reputation (and other CITI…marks).

Article 8(5) of the Regulation sets this rule out as follows:

5. Furthermore, upon opposition by the proprietor of an earlier trade mark within the meaning of paragraph 2, the trade mark applied for shall not be registered where it is identical with, or similar to, the earlier trade mark and is to be registered for goods or services which are not similar to those for which the earlier trade mark is registered, where, in the case of an earlier Community trade mark, the trade mark has a

reputation in the Community and, in the case of an earlier national trade mark, the trade mark has a reputation in the Member State concerned and where the use without due cause of the trade mark applied for would take unfair advantage of, or be detrimental to, the distinctive character or the repute of the earlier trade mark.

The Directive has a slightly different approach on this point. Article 4(3) imposes the same approach in a mandatory way when there is an earlier Community trade mark, whereas in relation to earlier national trade marks, etc. the approach is optional and left to the discretion of the Member States according to paragraph 4(a) of Article 4.

In all cases, the consent of the proprietor of the earlier mark negates the operation of these provisions. Article 4(5) of the Directive explicitly provides so, whereas Article 8 of the Regulation achieves the same result by subjecting the operation of these provisions to the proprietor of the mark bringing opposition proceedings.

14.7 Applying for a Community Trade Mark

The reference to opposition proceedings brought by the proprietor of an earlier mark as the way to rely on relative grounds for refusal in the context of a Community trade mark application provides a lead-in to more procedural issues. It is worth looking in a bit more detail at the application procedure for a Community trade mark and placing the absolute and relative grounds for refusal of registration in that context.

Article 26 of the Regulation sets out the conditions with which any application must comply and upon receipt of the application the office will first of all conduct an examination of the conditions of filing. This examination is mainly concerned with the formal aspect of the application (Article 36). The first substantial examination concerns the absolute grounds for refusal. The examiner will check whether any of the absolute grounds applies and if this is the case the application will be refused. Non-distinctive elements can be disclaimed though and the examiner can request that the applicant disclaims these non-distinctive elements (Article 37).

In a second phase OHIM will conduct a search (Article 38). In practice this means that a report is drawn up listing all potentially conflicting marks or applications. That list is relayed to the applicant and at least one month later the application is published by OHIM. The proprietors of all earlier Community trade marks or Community trade mark applications that are cited in the search report are also informed by OHIM of the publication, thus giving them a right to defend their rights (Article 39).

Third parties then have the opportunity to make observations to OHIM, primarily in relation to absolute grounds for refusal which they think apply to the application (Article 40). Contrary to what occurs in relation to these absolute grounds, OHIM itself will not examine and decide on the relative grounds for refusal of the registration. Upon publication of the application, proprietors of earlier marks have three months in which to bring opposition proceedings before the Opposition Division. Such an opposition is based on any of the relative grounds and is decided upon by the Opposition Division (Articles 41 and 42).

The applicant can of course withdraw the application at any time, but the application can also be amended, restricted, or divided (Articles 43 and 44). Registration of the trade mark will follow once the opposition has been rejected, or of course once the three-month term for opposition proceedings to be brought has expired without any party doing so (Article 45). The registration will be published on the register and is valid for ten years (and can subsequently be renewed) (Articles 46 and 47).

Parties that are adversely affected by any decision of OHIM, be they applicants or third parties, can bring an appeal against such a decision. This therefore includes, amongst others, both decisions on absolute and on relative grounds for refusal of registration. Appeals are brought before the Boards of Appeal at OHIM and they need to be brought within two months of the decision that is appealed having been notified (Articles 58 to 60). Further appeals can be brought before the General Court and the CJEU (Article 65).

The Cancellation Division of OHIM is in charge of applications for the revocation of Community trade marks and of applications for their invalidity (Article 134).

14.8 Uses of Trade Marks

If a trade mark is registered in accordance with the foregoing rules, it confers on the proprietor of the mark exclusive rights in the mark and the right to bring actions for infringement of the mark. The mark becomes an item of personal property. The effect of the registration is to confer these exclusive rights for a period of ten years, which is renewable for further periods of ten years. Given that a trade mark is an item of property, naturally, proprietors of trade marks will wish to trade with them. Clear provisions exist permitting (relatively) unrestricted dealing with trade marks.

14.8.1 Assignment

The first major provision is found in Article 17 of the Regulation, which permits assignment or other disposition of a Community trade mark in just the same way as any other items of personal property. The standard rule is that a Community trade mark can be transferred and that this can be done in respect of all or some of the goods or services for which it is registered. If desired, this can be done separately from any transfer of the undertaking. The transfer of the Community trade mark is not necessarily linked to that of its undertaking. It is, however, normally the case that the Community trade mark is dealt with or transferred for the whole area of the EU, according to Article 16 of the Regulation. Assignments of Community trade marks need to be signed and they have to be made in writing. They can also be noted on the register at the request of any of the parties and until that is done the successor in title cannot exercise the rights granted by the Community trade mark (Article 17 paragraphs (3), (5) and (6)).

A Community trade mark can also be used as security or be subject to rights in rem. These details can again be entered onto the register at the request of any of the parties involved (Article 19).

The Directive does not contain specific provisions on the assignment of national trade marks, but similar provisions to those in the Regulation exist in the national laws of the Member States.

14.8.2 Licensing

Licensing of trade marks is permitted and regulated by Article 8 of the Directive and Article 22 of the Regulation respectively. A licence is essentially a permit to carry out all or some of the acts that trade mark law comprises in the exclusive right it grants to the proprietor of the trade mark. A licence may be granted in whole, or in part, both in terms of the goods or services for which the trade mark was registered and in terms of the Member State concerned in the case of national trade marks or the EU in the case of Community trade marks. Most licences are non-exclusive in nature. Such a licence does not therefore stop the proprietor of the trade mark from granting further licences. But a licence can also be exclusive in nature and then it excludes the grant of further licences for the activity and the territory that it covers. It may also exclude activities by the proprietor itself. The proprietor in any case retains the right to invoke the rights granted by the trade mark in case the licensee contravenes the provisions of the licence contract.

The Regulation deals with licensing in the following terms in Article 22:

Licensing

1. A Community trade mark may be licensed for some or all of the goods or services for which it is registered and for the whole or part of the Community. A licence may be exclusive or nonexclusive.

2. The proprietor of a Community trade mark may invoke the rights conferred by that trade mark against a licensee who contravenes any provision in his licensing contract with regard to:

   (a) its duration;

   (b) the form covered by the registration in which the trade mark may be used;

   (c) the scope of the goods or services for which the licence is granted;

   (d) the territory in which the trade mark may be affixed; or

   (e) the quality of the goods manufactured or of the services provided by the licensee.

3. Without prejudice to the provisions of the licensing contract, the licensee may bring proceedings for infringement of a Community trade mark only if its proprietor consents thereto. However, the holder of an exclusive licence may bring such proceedings if the proprietor of the trade mark, after formal notice, does not himself bring infringement proceedings within an appropriate period.

4. A licensee shall, for the purpose of obtaining compensation for damage suffered by him, be entitled to intervene in infringement proceedings brought by the proprietor of the Community trade mark.

5. On request of one of the parties the grant or transfer of a licence in respect of a Community trade mark shall be entered in the Register and published.

It is interesting to note that paragraphs (3) to (5) have no equivalent in the Directive, even if national law can of course deal with the matter in a similar way in respect of national trade marks. The Regulation deals in these paragraphs with the right of the licensee to bring infringement actions, with or without the support of the proprietor of the Community trade mark, with its entitlement to compensation and the way to handle that and with the option to have the licence entered onto the register.

In many cases, the parties will wish to restrict the number of licences so that the licensee gains the monopoly benefits normally enjoyed by the proprietor of a mark. This can be done in the form of an exclusive licence, under which the licensee has the sole right to use a trade mark, excluding even exploitation by the proprietor of the mark herself.

There is, of course, a problem that arises in relation to exclusive licences. Any such licence has the effect of moving the monopoly right from the originator of the trade mark, who may, in broad terms, be regarded as having deserved such a privilege, to another. Such extensions of monopoly rights have naturally attracted the interest of the EU.

14.9 Conclusions

The obvious starting point in this chapter is the definition of a trade mark, be it a national trade mark or a Community trade mark. Both the Directive and the Regulation begin by making the distinction between the product or service to which the trade mark is applied on the one hand and the trade mark on the other hand. One needs first of all to be in the presence of a sign, something that can be applied to the product or service and that can convey information. Second, the sign needs to be capable of being represented graphically. The CJEU laid down detailed guidance on this point in the *Sieckmann* case and its guidance and criteria on this point should be to the benefit of both the consumer and third parties/potential competitors. But of course, the cornerstone of the matter is that the sign should be distinctive as to origin. The main aim of trade mark law is to enable rights holders and consumers to distinguish the source of identical goods or services with a different origin.

A second main element is formed by the absolute grounds for refusal of registration. Marks that are descriptive and that refer to any characteristic of the goods or services cannot be registered as trade marks. And neither can shapes that are needed for a technical effect or that give substantial value to the goods. Only a limited number of these absolute grounds can be overcome through use, because distinctiveness is acquired through use.

Third, a mark never stands alone. On the contrary it operates alongside other marks. Out of that relationship may arise relative grounds for refusal of registration. There is obviously no place in the context of distinction as to origin for marks that are identical to an earlier mark and that are applied to identical goods or services. But problems can arise even if either the marks or the goods or services are merely similar. Confusion can then damage the essential relationship between the rights holder and the consumer and stop the trade mark from taking up its pro-competitive role. And trade marks with a reputation may even be affected when similar signs are used in relation to dissimilar goods or services.

Finally, we looked at the use of trade marks. Trade marks, as items of property, can be assigned or licensed.

Further Reading

HANDLER, M., 'The Distinctive Problem of European Trade Mark Law' (2005) 27 *EIPR* 306

MANIATIS, S. and BOTIS, D., *Trade Marks in Europe: A Practical Jurisprudence* (2nd edn, Sweet & Maxwell, 2010) ch. 4

MOSCONA, R., 'Bad Faith as Ground for Invalidation under the Community Trade Mark Regulation: The ECJ Decision in *Chocoladefabriken Lindt & Sprüngli AG v. Franz Hauswirth GmbH*' (2010) 32 *EIPR* 48–50

15

Infringement and Revocation of the Trade Mark

15.1 Introduction

In the previous chapter we looked at the acquisition of a trade mark. Now that we have an insight into which sign can be registered as a trade mark, what the absolute and relative grounds for refusal of registration are, and how a rights holder can assign or license a trade mark as an item of property, the time has come to turn our attention to the exercise of the trade mark rights. Like most IP rights the exclusive right granted by a trade mark registration is in essence a negative right. Its proprietor can stop others who do not have his consent from making use of the trade mark under certain circumstances. Looking at the rights conferred by the trade mark means in practice looking at trade mark infringement.

In trade mark law, just as in patent law, the issues of infringement and revocation, although separate, are inevitably interlocked in many examples of litigation. It is typical for a claim that a trade mark has been infringed to be countered by the argument that the trade mark has been wrongly registered in the first place; similarly, a revocation claim may be met by the counter-threat of an infringement allegation. In this context revocation is closely linked to and based on invalidity. As such it links back to the discussion in the previous chapter.

Trade marks are there to distinguish, which presupposes use in the relationship between the proprietor and the consumer. Non-use is therefore a problem. Here again revocation will be the sanction, but in these circumstances it stands on its own and does not refer to invalidity. In terms of litigation this form of revocation is often used to clear the way for the use or the registration of a similar sign.

We argued in the previous chapter that the origin function is the core function of the trade mark. Distinctiveness as to origin is indeed the key requirement for the grant of a trade mark. A sign that cannot fulfil the origin function cannot be registered as a trade mark, irrespective of its other qualities or the functions it can fulfil. That origin function plays out in the relationship between the rights holder on the one hand and the consumer on the other hand. The rights holder can use the registered trade mark on an exclusive basis to communicate the origin of the goods or services to the consumer and the consumer can rely on the trade mark to determine the origin of the goods or services when confronted with identical or similar goods from different sources.

Once the trade mark is in place it plays a somewhat wider role. The consumer is in part, or even to a large extent, made aware of the rights owner's goods or services through the use of the trade mark in advertising. This way the trade mark becomes in practice an indication of the source of the goods or services for the consumer. And once the consumer is aware of the trade mark and purchases the goods or services that are labelled with it, the consumer will also link the trade mark with a certain level of quality. Whatever the level of that quality, the consumer can rely on it staying the same when making repeat purchases and the latter are in turn what the rights holder is aiming at. Once the trade mark is in place one can therefore distinguish between the various roles it plays and the functions it fulfils:[1]

- the origin function;
- the advertising function;
- the guarantee of quality function or if one wishes the investment function from the perspective of the rights holder.

Historically, trade mark law was merely protecting the origin function directly. The other functions were protected indirectly through the origin function. Gradually this has changed and the other functions found their way directly into trade mark law.[2] We will see the traces of this process as we discuss the key cases in this chapter. Looking at the trade mark as a property right clearly assists in completing this process of change. The various functions then neatly fold into the property right. That does not mean though that each of these functions has the same value in all circumstances.

Let us for now leave the details for the remainder of the chapter. What is clear is that all these functions play out in the relationship between the rights holder and the consumer. The infringement provisions which we are about to discuss will therefore serve to protect these functions and to preserve the relationship between the rights holder and the consumer. When the functions of the trade mark can no longer function adequately in that relationship the trade mark loses its value for both parties and the infringement provisions are there to prevent that from happening.

A final introductory point to which we will need to return is the balance that needs to be struck in this context between the various interests involved. From the previous discussions it has already become clear that the rights holder and the consumer have interests in this context and that, whilst these interests to an extent run parallel to one another, they are different. And the competitors of the rights holder have their interests too. Trade mark law is, as we saw, in essence pro-competitive, but this means that competitors should be given their space, without being hindered by unduly broad rights and the accompanying threats of infringement. The infringement provisions will need to strike a balance between these various and sometimes conflicting interests. That balancing act

---

[1] See R. Callmann, 'Trade-Mark Infringement and Unfair Competition' (Spring 1949) 14 *Law and Contemporary Problems* 185, available at http://scholarship.law.duke.edu/lcp/vol14/iss2/2.

[2] See F. Schechter, 'The Rational Basis of Trade Mark Protection' (1927) 40 *Harvard Law Review* 812.

has similarities to the one discussed in relation to the requirement of capability of graphical representation in the sense that the same three parties' interests were also involved at that stage.

15.2 Infringement: The Starting Point

Despite their title 'rights conferred', Article 5 of the Trade Mark Directive and Article 9 of the Trade Mark Regulation respectively establish the basic criteria for an infringement action. This is logical, as the proprietor of a trade mark is given the exclusive right to prevent certain activities of third parties not having his consent. If a mark is already on the register, it is an infringement to use the same mark for the same goods or services. If either, or both, of the two marks and the product in question are similar rather than identical, there will be an infringement if the later use of the earlier mark is likely to cause confusion to the public. Finally, unauthorized use of an identical or a similar mark, even on totally different goods, will also be an infringement if the repute of the original mark would be harmed by such a use.

The crucial provision is worded as follows in the Regulation:

1. A Community trade mark shall confer on the proprietor exclusive rights therein. The proprietor shall be entitled to prevent all third parties not having his consent from using in the course of trade:

   (a) any sign which is identical with the Community trade mark in relation to goods or services which are identical with those for which the Community trade mark is registered;

   (b) any sign where, because of its identity with, or similarity to, the Community trade mark and the identity or similarity of the goods or services covered by the Community trade mark and the sign, there exists a likelihood of confusion on the part of the public; the likelihood of confusion includes the likelihood of association between the sign and the trade mark;

   (c) any sign which is identical with, or similar to, the Community trade mark in relation to goods or services which are not similar to those for which the Community trade mark is registered, where the latter has a reputation in the Community and where use of that sign without due cause takes unfair advantage of, or is detrimental to, the distinctive character or the repute of the Community trade mark.[3]

Article 5(1) of the Directive refers of course to a registered trade mark, rather than to a Community trade mark, but, more importantly, the Directive leaves paragraph (c) as an option to the Member States. Article 9 of the Regulation has an additional paragraph 3, where it is specified that the rights of the proprietor will prevail from the date of publication of the registration of the Community trade mark. From that same moment courts will, however, also be able to award reasonable compensation for the defendant's activities during the period between the publication of the application for the trade mark and the publication of the registration of the trade mark.

The application of each of these three paragraphs involves an assessment that is carried out through the eyes of the 'average consumer', who is deemed to be reasonably well informed and reasonably observant and circumspect (Case C–342/97 *Lloyd*

---

[3] Article 9(1).

Schuhfabrik Meyer & Co. GmbH v Klijsen Handel BV [1999] ECR I-3819 [26]). The 'average consumer' is a legal construct rather than a real member of the public (Case T–6/01 *Matratzen Concord v OHIM—Hukla Germany* [2002] ECR II-4335). In practice this means that the judge can often put herself in the position of the average consumer (Case C–201/96 *Gut Springerheide GmbH v Oberkreisdirektor des Kreises Steinfurt—Amt für Lebensmitterüberwachung* [1998] ECR I-4657).

Even so, the application of each of the three subsections gives rise to a number of issues. Before turning to these issues, however, one preliminary matter is worth highlighting: a trade mark is often used as a shorthand term to describe the goods—but might this be an infringement of the mark? In other words, exactly how far do the rights of the trade mark owner go to stop its use in the course of trade?

The judgment of the CJEU in Case C–2/00 *Holterhoff v Freiesleben* [2002] ECR I-4187 sheds some light on this. Mr Freiesleben had registered the marks 'Spirit Sun' and 'Context Cut' in relation to diamonds and precious stones. Both marks correspond to a particular cut of precious stone and Mr Holterhoff had used the names to describe the type of cut to his clients. Did this amount to trade mark infringement? The Court held that it did not, on the basis that the proprietor of a trade mark cannot rely on her exclusive right if a third party, in the course of commercial negotiations, reveals the origin of goods that she has produced herself and uses the sign in question solely to denote the particular characteristics of the goods on offer for sale, in such a way that there can be no question of the trade mark used being perceived as a sign indicative of the undertaking of origin.

Trade mark infringement requires the 'use in the course of trade' of the goods labelled with the trade mark. Filling cans that carry an infringing sign was therefore not use of the mark if the cans were delivered with the marks on them by the company awarding the contract to fill the cans (Case C–119/10 *Frisdranken Industrie Winters BV v Red Bull GmbH* [2012] ETMR 16). It is generally accepted that 'use' includes importation (see, e.g., Article 5(2)(c) of the Directive), even if the territorial scope of national laws implementing the Directive is restricted to the Member State concerned. So what exactly are the meanings of the concepts of 'use' and 'importation'? This is the question that the judgment of the CJEU in Case C–405/03 *Class International BV v Colgate-Palmolive Co. and ors* [2006] 1 CMLR 14 addressed.

In this case, the goods—branded toothpaste—were lawfully under the external transit procedure or the customs warehousing procedure. There was no evidence that a purchaser had already been found. The Court had to define what was meant by the concept of 'importation' and whether it also covered the external transit procedure or the customs warehousing procedure. The Court held that interference with the exclusive right of the rights holder needed to be shown. That exclusive right is necessarily limited to the Member State concerned, or to the Community, in the case of a Community trade mark. The interference that may be pleaded consists, in the Court's view, either in the release for free circulation of the goods or an offering or sale of those goods that necessarily entails putting them on the market in the Community. In the absence of such interference, the goods have not been imported and the rights holder cannot invoke infringement of its trade mark. In this case, such interference had not been shown, because only warehousing under the customs procedure and the use of the external transit procedure had been demonstrated. The infringement claim was therefore bound to fail.

We now turn to the three main paragraphs on infringement, Articles 5(1)(a), (b) and (2) in the Directive and Article 9(1)(a), (b) and (c) of the Regulation respectively, which each deal with a different form of trade mark infringement.

15.3 Article 5(1)(a) Directive/Article 9(1)(a) Regulation

Here we are concerned with the use of a sign that is identical to the trade mark in relation to identical good or services. For the purposes of brevity we will refer to the relevant provisions merely as Article 5(1)(a).

15.3.1 A Sign Used in the Course of Trade

The provision refers first of all to a 'sign' that is allegedly infringing and that is used by the alleged infringer. It is initially necessary to define what is a 'sign' in any particular case. One turns to the register to identify the trade mark, but that is not an option for an allegedly infringing sign. In many cases it is clear in practice what the sign is. For example, if the trade mark for a product is 'Alpha' and the alleged infringer labels its identical product 'ALPHA' the latter will be the sign. But the sign can also be combined with other elements on the packaging. One can think of a company called Robertson using 'Robertson's Toffee Treat' for a product that contains toffee and that is arguably identical to a product for which the rights holder has registered 'Treat' as a trade mark. It is then at least arguable that the first two words are added matter to describe the goods and that the alleged infringer uses 'Treat' as a sign. The identification of the sign will therefore be a matter of fact, to be determined in each case.[4] One is in practice looking for the element that is used to distinguish the particular product or service.

Additionally, the sign must be used in the course of trade. The Directive and the Regulation refer in this context to the affixing of the sign to the goods or their packaging, to offering the goods, selling or stocking them under the sign, to importing the goods labelled with the sign, and to using the sign on business paper and in advertising. Arguably, this use in the course of trade goes beyond mere use to distinguish, as the latter example shows. On the other hand, there must be use in the jurisdiction. This can be illustrated with the following example. The use of the sign 'Crate & barrel', which was identical to the 'Crate & Barrel' mark registered in the UK, on the website of a shop in the Irish capital Dublin was not use in the course of trade in the UK, because the advertisement was merely intended to address a local Irish clientele on the shop premises and because no trade was taking place on the Internet through the website (*Euromarket Designs Inc. v Peters* [2001] FSR 20).

One should not be carried away too easily by this 'use in the course of trade' argument, however, and one should, in any case, not rush too easily to the conclusion that there was no use in the course of trade as a way out of the alleged infringement—as the *Arsenal v Reed* saga clearly demonstrates. Arsenal had registered a series of trade marks in relation to memorabilia. Reed sold Arsenal memorabilia bearing these or similar marks without having obtained a licence from Arsenal Football Club. When sued for trade mark infringement, Reed ran as a defence the argument that there was no use in the course of trade, because he was only using the marks to express loyalty towards the club. In the UK High Court (*Arsenal v Reed* [2001] 2 CMLR 481, [2001] RPC 922), Laddie J had accepted Reed's defence, and ruled that such use to express loyalty was not use in the course of trade and did not therefore amount to infringement. Nevertheless, he referred the matter to the CJEU for a preliminary opinion.

---

[4] The 'Treat' example has been borrowed from the English case *British Sugar plc v James Robertson & Sons Ltd* [1996] RPC 281.

That Court disagreed with Laddie J's view and ruled (Case C–206/01 *Arsenal v Reed* [2002] ECR I-7945) that, in cases such as this, there would be infringement and that it is immaterial that, in the context of the use of the mark, the sign is perceived as a badge of support for, or loyalty or affiliation to, the trade mark proprietor. Laddie J, in his second judgment (*Arsenal v Reed* [2003] 1 All ER 137, [2003] 1 CMLR 382), argued that, in coming to this conclusion, the CJEU had reached a different conclusion on the facts and had therefore gone beyond its powers. He did not feel bound by the judgment and ruled again in favour of Matthew Reed.

On appeal, the Court of Appeal (*Arsenal v Reed* [2003] RPC 696, [2003] 2 CMLR 800) rejected Laddie J's approach to the interpretation and application of the CJEU's opinion. The Court of Appeal's judgment highlights a couple of important points. First, the reference to the CJEU started from the point of view that any decision on infringement hinged on whether or not the use of the mark was use in the course of trade—that is, on trade mark use and an indication of origin in the somewhat wider sense described earlier. That issue was a separate point and a prerequisite for Article 5(1)(a). If the prerequisite was not met, there was no need to continue the infringement examination under Article 5(1)(a). The Court of Appeal, as well as the CJEU, disagreed. In its view, the mark has to be considered as a property right and the question that needs to be asked is whether the use of the sign causes damage to the trade mark as a property right. In other words, would there be damage to the essential function of the trade mark as a badge of origin? There is therefore no prerequisite, but rather one substantial test that includes the trade issue. There is an inextricable link between the property-essential function issues and the use in the course of trade issue. The French courts have, for example, derived from this link that the mere registration of a similar or an identical mark amounts to use in the course of trade (and can lead to a finding of infringement) even if no exploitation of the later mark follows (*SAS Free v Vanessa M*, Court of Appeal Paris, CA Paris pôle 5-1, 9 September 2014, RG no. 13/05804, [2015] 54 Propriétés Intellectuelles 82, where reference is also made to judgments of the Supreme Court and the same Court of Appeal in Paris, Cass. Com., 26 November 2003, no. 01-11.784, [2004] PIBD III 98 and CA Paris, 25 May 2005, [2005] PIBD III 509, respectively).

In the *Arsenal* case, once Mr Reed's memorabilia left his stand, it was no longer possible to determine whether they originated from him or from Arsenal. The origin function of the mark was therefore affected. That confusion element is vital in this context. The case is also remarkable because, in this way, it represents the first application of the after-sale confusion doctrine: the confusion only arose when the consumers and the goods had left Mr Reed's stand.

Use in the course of trade also plays a pivotal role when it comes to the use of trade marks for the purpose of parody and criticism. Such use will in a sense be made against the rights holder and may give rise to an infringement claim. On the other hand, parody and criticism rely on the fundamental right of freedom of expression. In a number of cases national courts have been able to allow the use of the trade mark for the purposes of parody and criticism by ruling that such use was not use in the course of trade. Examples include the use of the Marlboro trade mark in a grotesquely altered form and context in a calendar that promoted non-smoking (German Supreme Court, *Marlboro/Mordoro*, BGHZ 91, 117, 121 [1984] Neue Juristische Wochenschrift 1956 and [1986] ECC 1) and the use by Greenpeace of the slogans 'STOP ESSO' and 'STOP E\$\$O, E££O' on its website to denounce Esso's attacks on the environment and the risks to human health causes by certain of its industrial activities (*Esso Plc v Greenpeace France*, Court of Appeal Paris, CA Paris, 4th Chamber, section A, case 04/12417, [2006] ETMR 53). But courts are also prepared to strike a balance with the right to freedom of expression in cases where the alleged infringer engages in commercial activity. The fact that the use is satirical in nature and for products that are not directly in competition with those of the rights holder does assist in these circumstances (German Supreme Court, *Lila Postkarte* (*Milka*), BGH I ZR 159/02, 5 February 2005, [2007] *GRUR* 65). However, the approach in the *Arsenal* case, which viewed the trade mark as an item of property and its infringement as the equivalent of stepping on the property right, only makes this balancing exercise more difficult. A similar broadening of the right happens in the context of Article 5(2) for marks with a reputation and the *Milka* case already shows this as a further complicating factor. Dilution protection as such, to which we will return later, increases the risk of a conflict with the right of freedom of expression.[5]

15.3.2 **The Comparison**

The main point in Article 5(1)(a), and the test for infringement, is the comparison that needs to be made between the use of the claimant's trade mark in a normal and fair manner in relation to the goods for which it has been registered, and the way in which the defendant actually used its allegedly infringing sign, discounting added or surrounding matter or circumstances. For example, the use by the defendant of the surrounding words 'independent' and 'specialist' in combination with the claimant's 'Volvo' trade mark in a style similar to that of the registered trade mark has to be discounted, because the defendant effectively uses the 'Volvo' trade mark in the same style (font, etc.) as Volvo AB. Simply verbally describing oneself as an 'independent Volvo specialist' is a different matter, as shown by Case C–63/97 *BMW AG v Ronald Deenik* [1999] ECR I-905. In our example the defendant still uses an identical word in the course of trade and that constituted prima facie infringement under Article 5(1)(a).

This brings us back to the test in relation to Article 5(1)(a).

15.3.2.1 **Identical Signs**

First, this test will have to determine whether the sign and the trade mark can be considered to be identical. Case C–291/00 *LTJ Diffusion SA v Sadas Vertbaudet SA* [2003] ECR I-2799 clarifies the application in relation to this issue. When confronted with the question of whether the sign ARTHUR ET FÉLICIE was identical to the mark ARTHUR (mark and sign written in the same way, but in the sign additional material has been added), the CJEU ruled that a sign is identical with the trade mark if it reproduces, without any modification or addition, all of the elements constituting the trade mark or if, viewed as a whole, it contains differences so insignificant that they may go unnoticed by the average consumer. In that sense, both aural and visual identity may be required. Additions and modification bring the case outside the scope of Article 5(1)(a), which seems to be restricted merely to cases of blatant piracy. To take another example, this time from national case law, in the same way that ARTHUR ET FÉLICIE was not identical to ARTHUR, COMPASS LOGISTICS was held not to be identical to COMPASS (*Compass Publishing BV v Compass Logistics Ltd* [2004] RPC 809). The criterion of identity is therefore a very strict one, even if the use of the average consumer somewhat blurs the test.

---

[5] See A. Rahmatian, 'Trade Marks and Human Rights' in P. Torremans (ed.), *Intellectual Property and Human Rights* (2nd edn, Kluwer Law International, 2008) 335, 348–51.

15.3.2.2 Use in Relation to Identical Goods or Services

Second, because the provision requires use of the sign in relation to goods or services that are identical to those for which the mark has been registered, one must also determine whether the goods or services in relation to which the allegedly infringing sign is used fall within the specification contained in the trade mark registration.

In the *Treat* case mentioned earlier, that meant answering the question whether Robertson's product was a dessert sauce or a syrup (the trade mark that was allegedly infringed was registered for these). Courts tend to adopt a pragmatic approach on this point. They often argue that the words in a trade mark specification should be construed in a practical manner, taking into account how the product is regarded for the purposes of trade. A trade mark specification is, after all, concerned with use in trade. In the example, Robertson's spread would hardly be used on desserts, despite the comments on the label putting that forward as a typical use. It was marketed in a jam jar and supermarkets regarded it as a spread. The pragmatic conclusion had indeed to be that, for the purposes of trade, it was neither a dessert sauce nor a syrup. Isolated and rare use of the product as a dessert sauce could not change that conclusion. The product was not identical to the goods in relation to which the trade mark was registered and the infringement claim based on Article 5(1)(a) failed.

15.3.2.3 A Special Example

Article 5(1)(a) can have consequences that may be surprising at first glance. The trade mark badge is also reproduced faithfully when a scale model of a car is produced. In Case C–48/05 *Adam Opel AG v Autec AG* [2007] ETMR 33, Opel had also registered its trade mark for toys. When Autec affixed the mark to the scale model, it was held to be a straightforward infringement under Article (5)(1)(a), despite the fact that it was not used at all on the typical product: cars. AdWords, on the other hand, proved to be less straightforward.

15.3.3 AdWords

AdWords are a service provided by Internet Service Providers, such as Google, whereby a trader buys a term as an AdWord, which means in practice that the website of the trader and his little advert will show up on the screen as a promotional link whenever the user searches for that particular term. For the purposes of trade mark infringements matters become interesting when the term that is bought is the trade mark of a competitor. Will the use of the AdWord amount to trade mark infringement? The CJEU addressed this question for the first time in Case C–236/08 *Google France Sarl v Louis Vuitton Malletier SA* [2011] All ER (EC) 411, [2010] ETMR 30. Vuitton's trade marks had been used as AdWords by third parties and the goods advertised had not necessarily been genuine goods. The Court held as a matter of principle that Article 5(1)(a) must be interpreted as meaning that:

> the proprietor of a trade mark is entitled to prohibit an advertiser from advertising, on the basis of a keyword identical with that trade mark which that advertiser has, without the consent of the proprietor, selected in connection with an internet referencing service, goods or services identical with those for which that mark is registered, in the case where that advertisement does not enable an average internet user, or enables that user only with difficulty, to ascertain whether the goods or services referred to therein originate from the

proprietor of the trade mark or an undertaking economically connected to it or, on the contrary, originate from a third party.[6]

A typical example of an Article 5(1)(a) scenario is where a company selling erotic products owns the trade mark 'Bananabay' and finds out that a competitor has bought 'Bananabay' as an AdWord to advertise its own sales of erotic products. A sign that is identical to the trade mark is then used for identical goods (Case C–91/09 *Eis.de GmbH v BBY Vertriebsgesellschaft mbH* EU:C:2010:174). And there is use in the course of trade even if the sign selected as an AdWord does not appear in the advertisement itself (Case C–278/08 *Die BergSpechte Outdoor Reisen und Alpinschule Edi Koblmuller GmbH v Guni* [2010] ETMR 33 [19]).

The fundamental point behind this which is made by the Court is that in this situation the use of the AdWord amounts to an infringement because the origin function of the trade mark is affected (Case C–236/08 *Google France Sarl v Louis Vuitton Malletier SA* [2011] All ER (EC) 411, [2010] ETMR 30, [2010] RPC 19 [81]–[84]). The trade mark's investment function may also be adversely affected if there is a substantial interference with the owner's use of its trade mark to acquire or preserve a reputation that is capable of attracting consumers and retaining their loyalty (Case C–323/09 *Interflora Inc. v Marks & Spencer Plc* [2012] CEC 755, [2012] ETMR 1, [2012] FSR 3). On the other hand, the use of an identical sign by way of an AdWord does not have an adverse effect on the advertising function of the trade mark (*Louis Vuitton* [98]). It is therefore clear that the Court once more starts its infringement analysis from the point of view that the functions of the trade mark must be affected negatively and that that starting point is also the key element in this context. It is to be regretted that the Court fails to take account at this central stage of the balance between the functions of the trade mark, representing the interests of the rights holder, on the one hand, and countervailing interests, such as those of the consumer, on the other hand. This balance is considered by many to be at the very heart of trade mark law. The Court however seems to stick to the functions of the trade mark and then afterwards in the implementation of the rule there is some elasticity to accommodate elements of the balance in order to achieve the desired result.

But by focusing on the functions of the trade mark it does not come as a surprise that the Court held that the origin function is affected and that there is infringement of the trade mark if the packaging of the goods has been removed and if the consequence of the removal is that essential information, such as the information relating to the identity of the manufacturer or the person responsible for the marketing of the product, is missing.

That means that in certain circumstances one can sue the advertiser who buys the AdWords from Google, but on the other hand Google itself cannot be sued for its automated service. According to the Court 'an internet referencing service provider which stores, as a keyword, a sign identical with trade mark and organises the display of advertisements on the basis of that keyword does not use that sign' within the meaning of Article 5 (Case C–236/08 *Google France Sarl v Louis Vuitton Malletier SA* [2011] All ER (EC) 411, [2010] ETMR 30, [2010] RPC 19). The same conclusion applies to the operator of an online marketplace when marks appear in offers for sale displayed on its site (Case C–324/09 *L'Oréal SA v eBay International AG* [2012] All ER (EC) 501, [2011] ETMR 52, [2011] RPC 27). That changes radically when the online marketplace operator, such as

---

[6] *Google France Sarl* [121]. See also Case C–558/08 *Portakabin Ltd v Primakabin* [2010] ETMR 52 and Case C–278/08 *Die BergSpechte Outdoor Reisen und Alpinschule Edi Koblmuller GmbH v Guni* [2010] ETMR 33.

eBay, buys on behalf of the traders using its service AdWords on Google to advertise. eBay's liability was then based on the negative impact on the origin function on the condition that:

> the advertising does not enable reasonably well-informed and reasonably observant internet users, or enables them only with difficulty, to ascertain whether the goods concerned originate from the proprietor of the trade mark or from an undertaking economically linked to that proprietor or, on the contrary, originate from a third party.

And the safe haven provision of the E-Commerce Directive will not provide shelter if the operator of the website provides assistance, in particular, in optimizing the presentation of the offers for sale or their promotion.[7]

The *eBay* case also clarifies that use of the trade mark in advertisements on an online marketplace that are targeted at an audience in a country where the trade mark is protected will as such amount to infringing use in the course of trade of the trade mark, even if the goods are located in a third state when the advertising takes place.

It is remarkable that the Court of Justice is not prepared to transpose its strict approach to signs being (absolutely) identical to the mark to its approach to the question whether the goods or services are identical. On the latter point a much more flexible approach is taken. The *eBay* case was after all decided on the basis of Article 5(1)(a). eBay's liability is therefore based on the finding that advertising cosmetics sold by other parties and reserving AdWords is using the trade mark for identical goods or services, despite the fact that it is not eBay but the vendors using its platform that use the trade mark in relation to the cosmetics and their sale. One could argue that this is an improper use of Article 5(1)(a) that empties Article 5(1)(b) and its need to prove similarity and confusion from its scope in this context, but one has to agree that in practice the outcome is convenient.

15.3.4 **The Summary**

For a rights holder to succeed under Article 5(1)(a), six conditions need to be met, according to the case law:

(a) there must have been use of a sign by a third party;

(b) that use must have been in the course of trade;

(c) the use was without the consent of the trade mark owner;

(d) the sign was identical to the trade mark;

(e) the use was in relation to goods or services that are identical to those for which the trade mark was registered;

(f) the use affected or was liable to affect the functions of the trade mark, in particular its essential function of guaranteeing the origin of the goods or services to consumers.

The use is normally in relation to a third party's goods, but that is not required. The use can also be infringing if the third party uses the sign in relation to the rights holder's goods, for example in an advertising context, as long as the functions of the trade mark are affected (Case C–48/05 *Adam Opel AG v Autec AG* [2007] ETMR 33 and Case C–533/06 *O2 Holdings Ltd v Hutchinson 3G UK Ltd* [2008] ECR I-4231).

---

[7] See Article 14(1) Directive 2000/31/EC of the European Parliament and of the Council of 8 June 2000 on certain legal aspects of information society services, in particular electronic commerce, in the Internal Market (E-Commerce Directive) [2000] OJ L 178/1.

15.4 Article 5(1)(b) Directive/Article 9(1)(b) Regulation

As both provisions are identically worded, we will refer to them as Article 5(1)(b) for purposes of brevity. In addition, Article 5(1)(b) resembles Article 5(1)(a). The term 'sign' and the concept of 'use in the course of trade' are used in the same way here as they were in relation to Article 5(1)(a). Once more, the comparison that needs to be made is between the use of the claimant's trade mark in a normal and fair manner in relation to the goods for which it has been registered, and the way in which the defendant actually used its allegedly infringing sign, discounting added or surrounding matter or circumstances. The essential difference is that Article 5(1)(b) deals either with a similar, rather than identical, sign that is used in relation to identical or similar goods or services, or with an identical sign, but this time in relation to similar, rather than identical, goods or services. And the use of the allegedly infringing sign must give rise to a likelihood of confusion, because of the similarity.

If we restrict the analysis to the scenario where the sign is identical to the trade mark in a first stage, it might be said that the provision involves a three-point test.

- Is the sign used in the course of trade?
- Are the goods or services for which the sign is used similar to those in relation to which the trade mark has been registered?
- Is there a likelihood of confusion because of that similarity?

This is also shown in Figure 15.1

15.4.1 Similarity

The first point of the test requires no further comment. The question of similarity, however, needs some further analysis. That question is wholly independent of the particular mark or of the defendant's sign and similarity constitutes a separate issue that needs to be established independently before considering the third point of likelihood of confusion. The category of similar goods needs to be defined narrowly, because the trade mark owner should, as a starting point, be encouraged to register the mark for all classes of goods for which he wants to use the mark. A comparison of the use, users, and the physical nature of the claimant's and the defendant's goods or services, the way in which they were sold

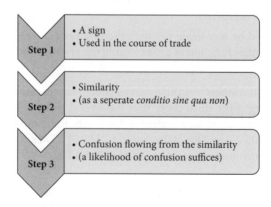

Figure 15.1 TM infringement: similarity and confusion

or offered, and the extent to which they were competitive were the relevant factors in considering similarity.

When applying these criteria in the *Treat* example mentioned earlier, one can arrive at the conclusion that Robertson's spread is not similar to dessert sauces and syrups, because it is different in physical nature (hardly pourable and in need of spooning out, as opposed to pourable), because market research puts it in a different sector, and because it is sold in another location in the supermarket. In another example, also taken from a real case, it was held that television programmes with an adult content were not similar to videotapes and video discs, which were the products in relation to which the claimant had registered his trade mark (*Baywatch Production Co. Inc. v The Home Video Channel* [1997] FSR 22). In that case, the products were distributed in a different way.

Overall, in assessing similarity, account must be taken of all the relevant factors that characterize the relationship between the goods or services. One can derive from the guidance provided by the CJEU that among these factors one finds the nature, intended purpose, method of use of the goods or services, and whether they are in competition with each other or whether instead they are complementary (Case C–39/97 *Canon Kabushiki Kaisha v Metro-Goldwyn-Mayer Inc.* [1998] ECR I-5507 [23]; Case T–169/03 *Sergio Rossi v OHIM—Sissi Rossi* [2005] ECR II-685 [54]).

One should not forget, however, that, as a minimum, similarity between the goods or services must be established. Absence of similarity cannot be overcome for the purposes of Article 5(1)(b), even if the mark is virtually identical to a mark that is distinctive to a very high level. The similarity requirement applies cumulatively, both between the sign and the mark on the one hand and between goods and services on the other hand (Case C–39/97 *Canon Kabushiki Kaisha v Metro-Goldwyn-Mayer Inc.* [1998] ECR I-5507; Case C–106/03 P *Vedial SA v OHIM* [2004] ECR I-9573 [51]). By way of example, glassware and wine were held not to be similar, and that meant that there could not be infringement, even if the mark 'Waterford' was used for both (Case T–105/05 *Assembled Investments (Proprietary) Ltd v OHIM—Waterford Wedgwood plc* [2007] ECR 1160, upheld on appeal in Case C–398/07 P [2009] ECR I-75).

15.4.2 **Confusion**

The third point, that of confusion, has created grave difficulties. What is clear is that it can only be treated separately from similarity and once the latter has been established. Otherwise, stronger marks would get protection for a greater range of goods or services than weaker marks, because the use of a strong mark in relation to dissimilar goods might create confusion in the mind of the consumer. It is equally clear though that similarity as such is not sufficient. Confusion will also need to be demonstrated (separately) (Case C–533/06 *O2 Holdings Ltd v Hutchinson 3G UK Ltd* [2008] ECR I-4231).

'Confusion' requires simply that the average consumer will be confused. Traditionally, this has been interpreted as meaning that the consumer, when confronted with the similar goods or services that are labelled with the sign, is confused about the origin of these goods or services and thinks that they originate from the trade mark owner. Traditionally, confusion meant confusion as to origin. The major problem that arises in relation to this traditional link between confusion and origin is created by the Benelux law-based addition in the Directive that confusion must now include the likelihood of association with the trade mark. Association means in its broadest sense that the sign makes one think of the trade mark. If one sticks to confusion as to origin that would mean squeezing the

Figure 15.2 The signs at issue

broader concept into the narrower one.[8] The word 'origin' is also conspicuously absent from the text of the Directive. Arguably therefore the Directive operates a different concept of confusion, one that reconciles confusion and association. The CJEU was asked to rule on the confusion–association point in *Sabel v Puma*. That case concerned two bounding feline trade marks, shown in Figure 15.2, and the German Bundesgerichtshof (Supreme Court) asked the ECJ to explain the relevant provisions of the Directive.

15.4.3 *Sabel v Puma*

A careful analysis of the *Sabel* case is required in an attempt to clarify the situation.

15.4.3.1 The New Concept of Confusion

Two views were put to the Court. First, the Benelux countries argued that their concept of association had been incorporated into the wording of the Directive and should be followed (Case 251/95 *Sabel BV v Puma AG* [1997] ECR I-6191, [1998] 1 CMLR 445 [14] and [15]). That meant that, in an extreme case, the likelihood of association may arise 'where the public considers the sign to be similar to the mark and perception of the sign calls to mind the memory of the mark, although the two are not confused' ([16]). For example, the 'Sabel' mark would infringe if, when confronted with that mark, the public would associate it with the 'Puma' mark in the sense that the Puma mark would come to mind, without leading the public to confuse the two marks and think that it saw the Puma mark.

Sabel, the Commission, and the UK strongly opposed this view. They argued that the wording of the Directive excluded this interpretation. The Court agreed and argued that:

> it follows from th[e] wording that the concept of likelihood of association is not an alternative to that of likelihood of confusion, but serves to define its scope[; t]he terms of the provision itself exclude its application where there is no likelihood of confusion on the part of the public.[9]

The Directive only uses the concept of 'association' to define the scope of the concept of 'confusion'. For the purposes of the Directive, there can be no likelihood of association if there is not at least a certain form of confusion. Likelihood of association is not an alternative to, but a way to define the meaning of, likelihood of confusion (Case C–425/98 *Marca Mode CV v Adidas AG* [2000] All ER (EC) 694, [2000] 2 CMLR 1061; Case C–39/97 *Canon Kabushiki Kaisha v Metro-Goldwyn-Mayer Inc.* [1998] ECR I-5507, [1998] All ER (EC) 934).

---

[8] See in the UK *Wagamama Ltd v City Centre Restaurants* [1995] FSR 713. The practical outcome of the case can be approved of, but not its reasoning.

[9] *Sabel v Puma* [18].

The Court backs up its view with a reference to the 'tenth recital in the preamble of the Directive, according to which "the likelihood of confusion…constitutes the specific condition for such protection"' (*Marca Mode CV* [19]). But two types of likelihood of confusion need to be distinguished (*Marca Mode CV* [16] and [17]). First, the straightforward type of direct consumer confusion—that is, confusion as to origin—arises in the situation in which the public sees the sign and links the goods labelled with it to the trade mark and its owner. In the *Sabel v Puma* example, such a situation would arise if the public was confronted with the Sabel mark, thought that it saw the Puma mark, and assumed that the Sabel goods originated from Puma.

The second type of likelihood of confusion is somewhat more sophisticated. In this situation, the public is not directly confused, but it makes a connection between the proprietors of the sign and those of the mark, and confuses them. This type of confusion can be described as indirect confusion or association, and it is here that the inclusion of the concept of association in the concept of confusion plays its widening role. An example would be a situation where the public connects the Sabel mark with the Puma mark due to the similarity between the two marks and assumes that there is a link between the two trade mark owners. The public might unjustifiably suspect the existence of a licence or any other kind of business link between the two companies involved (Case C–39/97 *Canon Kabushiki Kaisha v Metro-Goldwyn-Mayer Inc.* [1998] ECR I-5507).

A likelihood of confusion needs, however, to be demonstrated.[10] There is no ground for presuming the existence of confusion merely because a likelihood of pure association existed, even for highly distinctive marks. Neither is it sufficient that the mere fact that a risk or possibility that an association may give rise to confusion could not be excluded (Case C–425/98 *Marca Mode CV v Adidas AG* [2000] All ER (EC) 694, [2000] 2 CMLR 1061).

It is submitted that both types of confusion are now covered by the Directive, because, whereas the prerequisite of the likelihood of confusion needs to be adhered to, the limitation of the concept of confusion to confusion in relation to the origin of the product or service can no longer be sustained; to do so would be to empty the concept of association of its content. The argument that European trade mark law must now include a finding of infringement in cases in which there is, strictly speaking, no confusion in relation to origin and therefore offers an increased level of protection to the trade mark owner, is supported by a number of factors. First, at no point does the Court's judgment refer to the notion of confusion in relation to origin, even if the Advocate General had made such a reference in his conclusion. Second, in some more recent cases (Cases C–427/93, C–429/93, and C–436/93 *Bristol Myers Squibb v Paranova* [1996] ECR I-3457, [1997] 1 CMLR 1151; Case C–337/95 *Parfums Christian Dior v Evora* [1997] ECR I-6013, [1998] 1 CMLR 737), the Court has given the trade mark owner a right under the trade mark to oppose shoddy advertising of his product or shoddy repackaging of it, even if no doubt is created in relation to origin. That must mean that trade mark law must protect more than the original function of the trade mark and that the quality guarantee function of the trade mark is now also protected. In turn, that means that the trade mark must be infringed by confusing associations that affect that guarantee of a certain level of quality.

---

[10] Mere aural similarity between marks ('Lloyd' and 'Loint's'), e.g., can create a likelihood of confusion: Case C–342/97 *Lloyd Schuhfabrik Meyer & Co. GmbH v Klijsen Handel BV* [1999] ECR I-3819, [1999] All ER (EC) 587.

15.4.3.2 Assessing the Likelihood of Confusion

A number of elements can be taken into account when determining whether or not there exists a likelihood of confusion. In *Sabel v Puma*, the CJEU elaborated on this point (Case 251/95 *Sabel v Puma* [1997] ECR I-6191, [1998] 1 CMLR 445 [22]–[25]). The Court lists, in a non-exhaustive way, a number of factors that are to be taken into account by the national courts in arriving at their decision on the point of likelihood of confusion, but adds that account must be taken of all factors that are relevant in the circumstances of each individual case. The degree of recognition of the trade mark on the market (see also Case C–39/97 *Canon Kabushiki Kaisha v Metro-Goldwyn-Mayer Inc.* [1998] ECR I-5507), the degree of similarity between the sign and the trade mark, and between the goods and services that are labelled, as well as the possibilities of making associations with the registered trade mark are factors that the Court borrows from the Preamble to the Directive. Likelihood of confusion is to be assessed globally, taking into account all factors relevant to the circumstances of the case (Case 251/95 *Sabel v Puma* [1997] ECR I-6191, [1998] 1 CMLR 445 [22]):

> The assessment is carried out through the eyes of the average consumer: For the purposes of that global appreciation, the average consumer of the category of products concerned is deemed to be reasonably well-informed and reasonably observant and circumspect. However, account should be taken of the fact that the average consumer only rarely has the chance to make a direct comparison between the different marks but must place his trust in an imperfect picture of them that he has kept in his mind. It should also be borne in mind that the average consumer's level of attention is likely to vary according to the category of goods or services in question.[11]

It is important to note that the assessment needs to take place at the moment at which the allegedly infringing sign starts to be used. The perception of the public at that stage, as a group of reasonably circumspect individuals, is the starting point (Case C–145/05 *Levi Strauss & Co. v Casucci SpA* [2006] ECR I-3703). What is assessed is whether there is a likelihood of confusion in that the public might believe that the goods or services originate from the same undertaking or from economically linked undertakings. That assessment must be undertaken in a comprehensive way, by reference to the perception of the relevant public of the goods or services and taking into account all relevant factors of the case that arise from the contact of the public with the sign, the mark, and the goods or services. Particular attention needs to be paid to the interdependence between the similarity of the sign and the mark, and that of the goods or services (Case T–162/01 *Laboratorios RTB v OHIM—Giorgio Beverly Hills* [2003] ECR II-2821 [29]–[33]). Accordingly, a lesser degree of similarity between the goods or services may be offset by a greater degree of similarity between the sign and the mark (Case C–171/06 P *T.I.M.E. Art Uluslararasi Saat Ticareti ve dis Ticaret AS* [2007] ETMR 38 [13]). Or, to put it in the words of the Court:

> A global assessment of the likelihood of confusion implies some interdependence between the relevant factors, and in particular a similarity between the trade marks and between these goods or services. Accordingly, a lesser degree of similarity between these goods or services may be offset by a greater degree of similarity between the marks, and vice versa. The interdependence of these factors is expressly mentioned in the tenth recital of the preamble to the Directive, which states that it is indispensable to give an interpretation of the concept of similarity in relation to the likelihood of confusion, the appreciation of which depends, in particular, on the recognition of the trade mark on

---

[11] Case C–342/97 *Lloyd Schuhfabrik Meyer & Co. GmbH v Klijsen Handel BV* [1999] ECR I-3819 [26].

the market and the degree of similarity between the mark and the sign and between the goods or services identified.[12]

One must also take into account the distinctive character of the earlier mark. In particular, its reputation must be taken into account when determining whether there is a likelihood of confusion (*Canon Kabushiki Kaisha* [24]). The more distinctive the earlier mark, the higher will be the likelihood of confusion (Case C–342/97 *Lloyd Schuhfabrik Meyer & Co. GmbH v Klijsen Handel BV* [1999] ECR I-3819, [1999] All ER (EC) 587 [20]). Therefore, highly distinctive marks enjoy broader protection. A good example is a case in which both the sign and the mark involved a cowhide and were used for milk goods (Case T–153/03 *Inex SA v OHIM* [2006] ECR II-1677). There were, of course, conceptual similarities between the sign and the mark, but there were also strong visual differences. The goods were, of course, entirely similar. It was held that the cow-related nature of the sign and the mark made the similarity not very distinctive—that is, that the consumer expects something of that nature in that line of business. The mark was, however, not particularly distinctive. This led to the conclusion that there was no likelihood of confusion.

Another interesting scenario arises when a mark is combined by a third party with its company name in practice: for example, 'Life' and 'Thomson Life' respectively. If the mark still plays an independent distinctive role in the composite mark, and if the goods and services are identical, there can be a likelihood of confusion, even if the mark only has normal distinctiveness (Case C–120/04 *Medion AG v Thomson Multimedia Sales Germany & Austria GmbH* [2005] ECR I-8551).

It is indeed the case in this respect that the more similar the goods or services covered and the more distinctive the earlier mark, the greater the likelihood of confusion. And in determining the distinctive character of a mark and, accordingly, in assessing whether it is highly distinctive, it is necessary to make a global assessment of the greater or lesser capacity of the mark to identify the goods or services for which it has been registered as coming from a particular undertaking, and thus to distinguish those goods or services from those of other undertakings. In making that assessment, account is to be taken of all relevant factors and, in particular, of the inherent characteristics of the mark, including the fact that it does or does not contain an element that is descriptive of the goods or services for which it has been registered (Case C–342/97 *Lloyd Schuhfabrik Meyer & Co. GmbH v Klijsen Handel BV* [1999] ECR I-3819). It is indeed recognized that, in the case of a largely descriptive mark, small differences may suffice to avoid confusion, because the consumer realizes that other traders are likely to rely on the same descriptive content. The Court added in *Sabel* that the national court is to adopt the perspective of the average reasonably circumspect consumer and that the mark must be considered as a whole. It is clear that, from this perspective, a more distinctive mark will more easily give rise to a likelihood of confusion (Case C–39/97 *Canon Kabushiki Kaisha v Metro-Goldwyn-Mayer Inc.* [1998] ECR I-5507). The Court specifically cited the German Bundesgerichtshof with approval on the point that the overall impression of a mark as a whole, while giving proper weight to special distinctive characteristics, must be the starting point of the analysis.

It is arguable that confusion also covers 'initial interest confusion' whereby the consumer is initially confused, despite the fact that that confusion is resolved by the time the transaction or purchase takes place (Case C–278/08 *Die BergSpechte Outdoor Reisen under Alpinschule Edi Koblmüller GmbH v Guni* [2010] ETMR 33 and Case C–558/08 *Portakabin Ltd v Primakabin BV* [2010] ETMR 52). And the concept of a family of marks

---

[12] Case C–39/97 *Canon Kabushiki Kaisha v Metro-Goldwyn-Mayer Inc.* [1998] ECR I-5507 [17].

has also been recognized in the context of confusion. A family of marks consists of a series of similar marks registered by the same owner, for example Citibank has registered 'Citi', 'Citicorp', 'Citigold', 'Citicard', 'Citibank', etc. Confusion can then arise when another sign is associated with the family of marks by the average consumer, who may believe the sign is part of the family. That can then result, for example, in confusion as to origin, but only if the earlier trade marks in the family are effectively present on the market (Cases C–553/11 *Bernhard Rintisch v Klaus Eder* [2013] CEC 845, [2013] ETMR 5 and T–301/09 *IG Communications Ltd v OHIM—Citigroup Inc. and Citibank NA* [2013] ETMR 17).

15.4.4 Similar Signs

Article 5(1)(a) applies not only in the case where the goods or services are not merely similar but also where the sign and the trade mark are similar. Some of the cases we looked at previously already fall into this category, but similarity between sign and trade mark warrants some additional comments. Similarity in relation to the sign (when compared to the trade mark) was held to be a question of degree; a degree of similarity is tolerable, provided that the mark and the sign are not confusingly similar. The mark and the sign will be similar when, from the point of view of the relevant public, they are at least partially identical in one or more relevant aspects. A naive representation of an elephant could be an example, even if it is a single elephant in one case and multiple elephants in a frame in the other, as can be seen in Case T–424/10 *Dosenbach-Ochsner AG Schuhe und Sport v OHIM—Sisma SpA* EU:T:2012:58, see also Case T–6/01 *Matratzen Concord v OHIM—Hukla Germany* [2002] ECR II-4335 [30]). Once more, all surrounding matter needs to be disregarded, both in relation to the mark and to the sign. The assessment of similarity is to be carried out on a global basis, with reference to the degree of similarity between the mark and the sign. The specific nature of the mark and the sign and of their similarity is relevant on this point (Case C–252/07 *Intel Corp. Inc. v CPM United Kingdom Ltd* [2008] ECR I-8823). For example, the fact that the mark is the shape of the product itself, without the addition of a fanciful element is relevant. That narrows it down to a rule that a sign and a mark are similar when in the eyes of the relevant public there is between them at least a partial identity in relation to one or more essential aspects of the sign (Case T–06/01 *Matratzen Concord v OHIM—Hukla Germany* [2002] ECR II-4335 [30]; Case T–363/04 *Koipe v OHIM—Aceites del Sur* [2007] ECR II-3355 [98]; and Case T–273/08 *X-Technology R&D Swiss GmbH v OHIM—Ipko-Amcor BV* EU:T:2009:418 [29]). It is therefore clear that a sign that is composed of the mark, with the addition of another word, is likely to be similar to the earlier mark (Case T–22/04 *Reemark v OHIM* [2005] ECR II-1559 [40]).

There may also be cases where the mark and the sign are visually different, but phonetically similar. The aural effect of the mark is particularly relevant to the comparison in those cases, but nevertheless the claimant cannot rely on such an aural effect to disregard those distinctive features of its mark that can be seen, but not heard. The assessment of the visual, aural, or conceptual similarity between the sign and the mark is to be based on the overall impression that is made by them on the average consumer. In making that assessment, the distinctive and dominant component of the sign and the mark should be kept in mind (Case T–292/01 *Phillips-Van Heusen v OHIM–Pash Textilvertrieb und Einzelhandel (BASS)* [2003] ECR II-4335 [47]).

One also needs to remember that consumers only rarely have the chance to make a direct comparison with both the sign and the mark in front of them (Case C–342/97 *Lloyd Schuhfabrik Meyer* [1999] ECR I-3819 [26]). Instead, consumers rely on an imperfect recollection of them, and the reality is then that the dominant and distinctive features are most easily remembered (Case T–104/01 *Oberhauser v OHIM—Petit Libero (Fifties)* [2002] ECR II-4359 [47] and [48]). In assessing the overall impression, there is therefore no bar to prevent assessing each of its components in order to identify the dominant features. That has led the CJEU to decide, for example, that, in principle, there will be similarity between a sign and a mark if one consists of a word that has no conceptual meaning to the public and the second copies that word in combination with another word, which again has no conceptual meaning either alone or in combination, as long as the word found in both is identical, both visually and aurally (Case C–120/04 *Medion AG v Thomson Multimedia Sales Germany & Austria GmbH* [2005] ECR I-8551; Case T–286/02 *Oriental Kitchen v OHIM—Mou Dybfrost (KIAP MOU)* [2003] ECR II-4953 [39]; Case T–22/04 *Reemark Gesellschaft für Markenkooperation mbH v OHIM—Bluenet Ltd (Westlife)* [2005] ECR II-1559 [37]). But conceptual differences between sign and mark can be such as to counteract, to a large extent, the visual and aural similarities between them (Case C–171/06 P *T.I.M.E. Art Uluslararasi Saat Ticareti ve dis Ticaret AS* [2007] ETMR 38 [13], approving of the Court of First Instance decision in the case and copying the reference to Case T–292/01 *Phillips-Van Heusen v OHIM—Pash Textilvertrieb und Einzelhandel (BASS)* [2003] ECR II-4335 [54]).

15.4.5 **AdWords**

The CJEU's case law on AdWords which we discussed in relation to Article 5(1)(a) in Section 15.3.3 also applies to Article 5(1)(b) cases (Case C–278/08 *Die BergSpechte Outdoor Reisen und Alpinschule Edi Koblmuller GmbH v Guni* [2010] ETMR 33 and Case C–558/08 *Portakabin Ltd v Primakabin* [2010] ETMR 52). Once more the starting point will be that the functions of the trade mark must be affected by use of the trade mark in the course of trade. How the typical Article 5(1)(b) scenario with similarity and confusion, and in the appropriate cases the suggestion that there is an economic link, works out was explained as follows by the CJEU:

> In respect of the function of indicating origin, the Court held that the question whether that function is adversely affected when internet users are shown, on the basis of a keyword identical with a mark, a third party's ad depends in particular on the manner in which that ad is presented. The function of indicating the origin of the mark is adversely affected if the ad does not enable normally informed and reasonably attentive internet users, or enables them only with difficulty, to ascertain whether the goods or services referred to by the ad originate from the proprietor of the trade mark or an undertaking economically connected to it or, on the contrary, originate from a third party.
>
> On that point the Court also stated that, in the case where a third party's ad suggests that there is an economic link between that third party and the proprietor of the trade mark, the conclusion must be that there is an adverse effect on the function of indicating origin. Similarly, in the case where the ad, while not suggesting the existence of an economic link, is vague to such an extent on the origin of the goods or services at issue that normally informed and reasonably attentive internet users are unable to determine, on the basis of the advertising link and the commercial message attached thereto, whether the advertiser is a third party vis-à-vis the proprietor of the trade mark or, on the contrary, economically linked to that proprietor, the conclusion must also be that there is an adverse effect on that function of the trade mark.[13]

---

[13] Case C–278/08 *Die BergSpechte Outdoor Reisen und Alpinschule Edi Koblmuller GmbH v Guni* [2010] ETMR 33 [35]–[36].

15.4.6 **An Attempt at Summarizing**

The courts in the UK have helpfully attempted to summarize the approach to Article 5(1)(b) as follows:

(a) The likelihood of confusion must be appreciated globally, taking account of all relevant factors.

(b) The matter must be judged through the eyes of the average consumer of the goods or services in question, who is deemed to be reasonably well informed and reasonably circumspect and observant, but who rarely has the chance to make direct comparisons between marks and must instead rely upon the imperfect picture of them he has kept in his mind, and whose attention varies according to the category of goods or services in question.

(c) The average consumer normally perceives a mark as a whole and does not proceed to analyse its various details.

(d) The visual, aural and conceptual similarities of the marks must normally be assessed by reference to the overall impressions created by the marks bearing in mind their distinctive and dominant components, but it is only when all other components of a complex mark are negligible that it is permissible to make the comparison solely on the basis of the dominant elements.

(e) Nevertheless, the overall impression conveyed to the public by a composite trade mark may, in certain circumstances, be dominated by one or more of its components.

(f) Beyond the usual case, where the overall impression created by a mark depends heavily on the dominant features of the mark, it is quite possible that in a particular case an element corresponding to an earlier trade mark may retain an independent distinctive role in a composite mark, without necessarily constituting a dominant element of that mark.

(g) A lesser degree of similarity between the goods or services may be offset by a greater degree of similarity between the marks, and vice versa.

(h) There is a greater likelihood of confusion where the earlier mark has a highly distinctive character, either per se or because of the use that has been made of it.

(i) Mere association, in the strict sense that the later mark brings the earlier mark to mind, is not sufficient.

(j) The reputation of a mark does not give grounds for presuming a likelihood of confusion simply because of a likelihood of association in the strict sense.

(k) If the association between the marks causes the public to wrongly believe that the respective goods [or services] come from the same or economically linked undertakings, there is a likelihood of confusion.[14]

15.5 Article 5(2) Directive/Article 9(1)(c) Regulation

Finally, we turn to Article 5(2) of the Directive (to which we will refer for reasons of brevity), which deals with infringement of trade marks with a reputation. The Directive has this as an optional provision, but little turns on this, whereas it is part and parcel of the Regulation. The text of the provision in both the Directive and the Regulation also

---

[14] *WHG (International) Ltd, WHG Trading Ltd and William Hill plc v 32ed plc* [2012] EWCA Civ 19, [2012] RPC 19 [79] and *Och-Ziff Management Europe Ltd and Oz Management LP v Och Capital LLP, Union Investment Management Ltd and Ochocki* [2010] EWHC 2599 (Ch), [2011] ETMR 1 [73].

requires use in relation to dissimilar goods or services, but as will be seen this is no longer the case as a result of the case law of the CJEU. The provisions also apply even if the goods or services are merely similar. There are a number of requirements, shown in Figure 15.3 at the end of the next section, that need to be met for there to be infringement of the trade mark under this provision.

15.5.1 **Requirements**

First, the sign that is used in relation to the other goods or services must at least be similar to the trade mark. Obviously, the use of an identical sign will also be covered. It can be argued that the similarity of the mark must give rise to a likelihood of confusion on the part of the public; otherwise, the arguably illogical result would be reached that greater protection is granted in relation to dissimilar goods or services if, in comparison to Article 5(1)(b), the confusion requirement were dropped. But the requirement that likelihood of confusion is required has now effectively been ruled out by the CJEU in the *Adidas* case (Case C–408/01 *Adidas-Salomon & Adidas Benelux BV v Fitnessworld Trading Ltd* [2004] Ch 120, [2004] FSR 401, [2004] 1 CMLR 448). Second, the mark must also have a reputation, meaning that not all marks can benefit under this provision. The mark must be a strong mark—and this may also explain why likelihood of confusion is not required and why it is not that illogical after all. Strong or famous marks may be entitled to a stronger protective regime. In order to enjoy this stronger protection extending to non-similar goods or services, the CJEU has imposed the requirement that the registered mark must be known to a significant section of the public concerned by the products or services covered by the mark (Case C–375/97 *General Motors Corp. v Yplon SA* [1999] ECR I-5421). That significant section of the public can obviously be a significant section of the public in the country concerned, but it can also be a significant section of the public in a substantial part of the country concerned if the goods or services bearing the mark are specifically marketed (only) in that part of the country (*General Motors v Yplon*). Apart from that exceptional scenario though there is an expectation that the reputation applies throughout the country concerned. A strictly local reputation in a town and the surrounding area has been explicitly rejected (Case C–328/06 *Alfredo Nieto Nuño v Leonci Monlleó Franquet (Fincas Tarragona)* [2007] ECR I-40093). Despite that, the Court's case law can hardly be set to impose a high threshold. And whereas arguably this category should be restricted to relatively few really strong and exceptional trade marks, it applies in practice to many trade marks as it is easy to pass the threshold. In relation to the Community trade mark the standard case will be that of a reputation throughout the EU but, depending on the strength of the reputation, one that exists only in a certain Member State can also be acceptable. The minimum requirement is that the reputation must exist in a substantial part of the EU (Case C–301/07 *PAGO International GmbH v Tirolmilch registrierte Genossenschaft mbH* [2010] ETMR 5).

Third, the use of the sign must be without due cause. An example of use that is not without due cause can be found in the car repair business. An independent repairer may be entitled to use a sign that corresponds to the trade mark of a car manufacturer to indicate to the public that he specializes in repair work in relation to cars of that particular make. The repairer may, for example, wish to describe himself as an 'independent Mercedes specialist' (Case C–63/97 *Bayerische Motorenwerke AG & BMW Nederland BV v Ronald Karel Deenik* [1999] ECR I-905).

Fourth, that use of the sign must take advantage of, or must be detrimental to, the distinctive character or repute of the mark. This requirement effectively adds to the similarity requirement and can be seen as a more flexible alternative to the likelihood of confusion requirement. On the one hand, a negative example by means of which unfair advantage might be demonstrated arose when DaimlerChrysler sued a clothing retailer who used the name 'Merc' for his clothing (this is an example taken from the UK case *DaimlerChrysler AG v Alavi (t/a Merc)* [2001] RPC 813). The court acknowledged that the mark 'Merc' was commonly used as an abbreviation of the mark 'Mercedes', which had been registered by the claimant, but, in the light of the defendant's long-standing use of the mark and the claimant's recent entry in the clothing market, no unfair advantage or damage to reputation could be established. On the other hand, by way of a positive example, it was held, when cyberpirates registered domain names comprising the trade marks of well-known companies, that this use of a similar sign—for example, 'sainsburys.com'—did come under Article 5(2) and the use was held to be detrimental to the marks by damaging the claimant's exclusivity (see the UK case *Tesco Stores Ltd v Elogicom Ltd and anor* [2006] ETMR 91). It was accepted that the domain names were registered to take advantage of the distinctive character and reputation of the mark, and that this was unfair and detrimental. The territorial nature of trade marks and the global scope of domain names often lead to clashes between trade marks and domain names. The World Intellectual Property Organization (WIPO) has established guidelines in this respect, and its Arbitration and Mediation Centre is very active in resolving these conflicts. In cybersquatting cases mere registration of the domain name without permission amounts to use in the course of trade. The use of a trade mark in the course of the business of a professional dealer for the purposes of making domain names more valuable through registration and extracting money from the trade mark owner before handing over the registration is clearly use in the course of trade.

The requirements are shown diagrammatically in Figure 15.3.

15.5.2 A Wide Approach in the Courts: A Contrast with TM Theory?

Another example of a case that would fit in well under Article 5(2) is the controversial Benelux case *Claeryn/Klarein* (Benelux Court of Justice, 1 March 1975, [1975] NJ 472). Because of their phonetic similarity in Dutch, these were similar signs and they were used in relation to gin and a toilet cleaner, respectively. That means that there was use in relation to dissimilar products. The finding of infringement in the case was primarily based on the fact that the strong mark was diluted and suffered detriment, because a sign once exclusively associated with gin would now also be

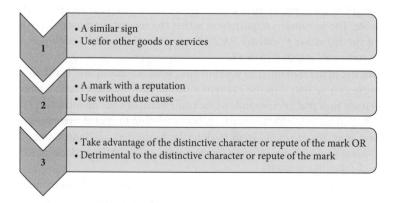

1
- A similar sign
- Use for other goods or services

2
- A mark with a reputation
- Use without due cause

3
- Take advantage of the distinctive character or repute of the mark OR
- Detrimental to the distinctive character or repute of the mark

Figure 15.3 The requirements for infringement of Art. 5(2)

associated with a toilet cleaner. Also, no due cause for the use of the sign could be established in this case.

The CJEU has rendered a series of wide-ranging and remarkable judgments in this area. We will turn to these shortly, but in order to understand them, as well as the new interpretation of the law in this area, a brief return to basics is warranted. Article 5(2) of the Directive contains an additional ground for infringement and Member States were left to decide whether or not to implement that ground. Trade marks that have a reputation will get additional protection and they will also be infringed through the use of an identical or similar sign in relation to goods or services that are not similar to those in respect of which the mark has been registered. That additional protection is conditional upon the use of the sign being without due cause and taking unfair advantage of, or being detrimental to, the distinctive character or repute of the trade mark.

When the Directive was implemented in the Member States, it seemed clear that this was not an overall third layer of rights, but a special rule that dealt with an exceptional situation. First of all, it did not apply to all trade marks, only to those trade marks with a reputation. The approach seemed to have many similarities with the approach to famous trade marks in the historical Paris Convention for the Protection of Industrial Property 1883: it seemed to represent an equally narrow category. Additionally, there needed to be use of the similar or identical sign without due cause and that use needed to be detrimental to the distinctive character or repute of the trade mark, or it needed to take unfair advantage of that distinctive character or repute, which could be described as the dilution scenario. And, most importantly, the additional protection would only apply when the sign was used in relation to goods or services that were not similar to those for which the trade mark had been registered. Or would it? There is, of course, also the argument that the fact that a trade mark has a reputation—that is, that it is not your ordinary trade mark—entitles it to stronger protection. Its reputation gives it a special kind of goodwill, which is both important for the trade mark owner and for the public. Trade mark law should therefore not allow that goodwill to be diluted without due cause as a result of the use of an identical or similar sign over which the trade mark owner has no control. After all, the third party using the sign is free to pick another sign and does not necessarily lose out. Article 5(2) seems to support this argument. If that is the case, then, why should there be a distinction between use in relation to goods or services that are not similar to those for which the trade mark has been registered, on the one hand, and goods or services that are identical or similar, on the other? The negative impact of dilution is indeed even more likely to be felt, or to be felt more strongly, as a result of use of the sign in relation to identical or similar goods.

15.5.3 *Davidoff*

The potential problem could, of course, be defused or would not even exist if the concept of taking unfair advantage of, or of being detrimental to, the distinctive character of the repute of the trade mark were to be, in fact, based on the public being confused. The latter would then cover the use in relation to identical or similar goods or services, and Article 5(2) would simply expand that same kind of protection for marks with a reputation to use in relation to goods or services that are not similar.

The CJEU was confronted with this issue for the first time when it rendered its judgment in Case C–292/00 *Davidoff & Cie SA & Zino Davidoff SA v Gofkid Ltd* [2003] ECR I-389. Davidoff objected to the use of the sign 'Durffee' by Gofkid for goods that were

Davidoff v Gofkid

Figure 15.4 The trade marks concerned

similar (see Figure 15.4). It alleged that the use of the similar sign, while not causing confusion, caused its 'Davidoff' mark to be diluted, without there being a good cause for Gofkid to use that sign.

The Court made it clear, first of all, that Article 5(2) is not based on the concept of confusion, but on a wider concept. In the words of the Court:

> where there is no likelihood of confusion, Article 5(1)(b) of the Directive could not be relied upon by the proprietor of a mark with a reputation to protect himself against impairment of the distinctive character or repute of the mark.

But Article 5(2) can apply according to the Court's analysis and confusion is therefore not required. But to the surprise of many, the Court went on to hold that:

> In those circumstances, ... Articles 4(4)(a) and 5(2) of the Directive are to be interpreted as entitling the Member States to provide specific protection for registered trade marks with a reputation in cases where a later mark or sign, which is identical with or similar to the registered mark, is intended to be used for goods or services identical with or similar to those covered by the registered mark.

The Court accepted therefore that marks with a reputation deserve wider protection and that that logic exists not only in a case of use of the identical or similar sign in relation to goods or services that are not similar, but also in relation to similar or identical goods or services.

In *Davidoff*, however, the Court seemed only to say that Member States are entitled to provide such a protection. Some of the points were barely spelled out and the exact width of the judgment was not clear, especially because questions could be asked about how this freedom for Member States that seemed to go against the specific wording used in Article 5(2)—'not similar' can hardly be said to mean 'identical, similar or not similar'— could be reconciled with the idea that the Directive would provide complete harmonization on certain points such as this.

15.5.4 *Adidas v Fitnessworld*

Of course, that sparked much debate and there were far more questions than answers in terms of how far the Court really wanted to go—but the debate was fairly short-lived. Nine months after starting the debate in *Davidoff*, the Court handed down a much more robust judgment in Case C–408/01 *Adidas-Salomon & Adidas Benelux BV v Fitnessworld Trading Ltd* [2003] ECR I-12537, [2004] 1 CMLR 448. The case dealt with the use by Fitnessworld of a motif composed of two parallel stripes of equal width that contrast with the main colour of the item of clothing and which is applied to the side seams of the clothing. The clothing was sold under the name 'Perfetto'. Adidas considered this to amount to the use of a sign that was similar to its trade mark, which consisted of three, very striking, vertical stripes of equal width that run parallel to each other. In the presence of a mark with a reputation and in the absence of confusion in the sense of Article 5(1)(b), this was another case about the use of Article 5(2) in relation to similar goods or services.

15.5.4.1 Use in Relation to Identical, Similar, or Non-Similar Goods or Services

First of all, the Court made it clear that, as a result of its decision in *Davidoff*, Article 5(2) could be used to offer anti-dilution-style protection in cases in which the goods or services were identical or similar, not merely in cases in which the goods or services were not similar. It went on to add that:

> where the sign is used for identical or similar goods or services, a mark with a reputation must enjoy protection which is at least as extensive as where a sign is used for non-similar goods or services.

It then concluded that:

> In the light of those findings, the Member State, if it transposes Article 5(2) of the Directive, must therefore grant protection which is at least as extensive for identical or similar goods or services as for non-similar goods or services. The Member State's option thus relates to the principle itself of granting greater protection to marks with a reputation, but not to the situations covered by that protection when the Member State grants it.

In other words, the Court opts for a full purposive interpretation of Article 5(2) even if it goes against the explicit language of the provision. In the Court's view, the logic of the overall scheme of trade mark protection prevails: what had seemed to be an option nine months earlier had now become an obligation for the Member States.

15.5.4.2 Dilution Instead of Confusion

Once the principle was established, the Court went on to clarify some of the concepts used—which was, indeed, much needed, because many questions had remained unanswered in the aftermath of *Davidoff*.

First, the idea that confusion might be involved as a requirement was buried once and for all when the Court ruled that:

> it must be noted at the outset that, unlike Article 5(1)(b) of the Directive, which is designed to apply only if there exists a likelihood of confusion on the part of the public, Article 5(2) of the Directive establishes, for the benefit of trade marks with a reputation, a form of protection whose implementation does not require the existence of such a likelihood. Article 5(2) applies to situations in which the specific condition of the protection consists of a use of the sign in question without due cause which takes unfair advantage of, or is detrimental to, the distinctive character or the repute of the trade mark.

A key point of difference with confusion is that the risk that the use without due cause of the mark will take unfair advantage of the distinctive character or repute of the trade mark continues to exist when the consumer, without necessarily confusing the commercial origin of the product or service, is attracted by the mark for itself and will buy the product or service on the ground that it bears the mark, which is identical or similar to an earlier mark with a reputation (Case T–215/03 *Sigla SA v OHIM* [2007] ETMR 79, [2007] Bus LR D 53 [42]). There must, however, be an unfair advantage or detriment to the distinctive character or the repute of the trade mark; that is the essence of the dilution.

The owner of the earlier trade mark, meanwhile, is not required to demonstrate actual or present harm to his mark: all that needs to be shown is prima facie evidence of a future risk, which is not hypothetical, of unfair advantage or detriment (Case T–67/04 *Spa Monopole v OHIM & Spa-Finders Travel Arrangements* [2005] ECR II-1825, [2005] ETMR 9; see also *Sigla SA* [46]). The CJEU has left it to the national courts to determine whether or not an unfair advantage or detriment will exist, but the burden does not seem to be unduly high, because it was not ruled out that detriment could arise through the use of a trade mark for cars on scale models of those cars (Case C–48/05 *Adam Opel AG v Autec AG* [2007] ETMR 33 [36]).

15.5.4.3 A Link

The crucial concept is, of course, that of 'dilution' and the interpretation that 'dilution' is to be given to the final part of Article 5(2).

This is the definition put forward by the Court:

> The infringements referred to in Article 5(2) of the Directive, where they occur, are the consequence of a certain degree of similarity between the mark and the sign, by virtue of which the relevant section of the public makes a connection between the sign and the mark, that is to say, establishes a link between them even though it does not confuse them. The existence of such a link must, just like a likelihood of confusion in the context of Article 5(1)(b) of the Directive, be appreciated globally, taking into account all factors relevant to the circumstances of the case.[15]

One needs to be slightly careful with this typical association–dilution requirement in terms of there being a link. It needs to be proved that the public makes the link between the sign and the trade mark, and while, until that point, the case seemed to be going Adidas's way, this proved to be its difficulty, because there was evidence that the public saw the Fitnessworld motif as an embellishment rather than as a mark, and did not make the link with the Adidas trade mark. Or, as the Court put it:

> The fact that a sign is viewed as an embellishment by the relevant section of the public is not, in itself, an obstacle to the protection conferred by Article 5(2) of the Directive where the degree of similarity is none the less such that the relevant section of the public establishes a link between the sign and the mark.
>
> By contrast, where, according to a finding of fact by the national court, the relevant section of the public views the sign purely as an embellishment, it necessarily does not establish any link with a registered mark. That therefore means that the degree of similarity between the sign and the mark is not sufficient for such a link to be established.

The establishment of such a link with the trade mark[16] will then make the unfair advantage or the detriment possible.

---

[15] Case C–408/01 *Adidas-Salomon & Adidas Benelux BV v Fitnessworld Trading Ltd* [2004] Ch 120, 139.

[16] The existence of a family of trade marks is a factor to be taken into account, but nothing more, in this respect if the trade mark is part of a family of trade marks. Case T–301/09 *IG Communications Ltd v OHIM—Citigroup Inc. and Citibank NA* EU:T:2012:473.

15.5.4.4 **Due Cause**

The one point that the Court did not address was the concept of 'due cause'. Even if all other requirements are met, Article 5(2) will only lead to a finding of infringement if the use of the sign was without due cause. There was clearly no due cause in *Adidas v Fitnessworld*, but it is not always such a clear-cut case. In other words, it is important to know how strictly the requirement needs to be interpreted. It is submitted that the concept of 'due cause' should be used as a balancing tool to avoid unduly strong protection for marks with a reputation. Arguably there will be a 'due cause' whenever a market operator needs to use the trade mark to communicate effectively with the market, for example to indicate the product for which there is not yet a commonly accepted name, such as the Segway, or to indicate a specific expertise in relation to goods made by a manufacturer whose trade mark is used. One can of course then argue that the word can be used, but not the surrounding matter, for instance a colour scheme. But 'due cause' defined in such a way goes beyond a mere necessity to use the mark. The CJEU has, for example, held that the earlier use, i.e. before the registration of the trade mark, of a similar sign (The Bulldog, Red Bull being the trade mark) for the same class of goods amounts to use with due cause if the earlier sign is used for identical goods (within the class of registration) in good faith (Case C–65/12 *Leidseplein Beheer BV and Hendrikus de Vries v Red Bull GmbH and Red Bull Nederland BV* [2014] ETMR 24).

This is all the more important as a result of the relative ease with which a link can be demonstrated, which may bring rather a lot of cases within the scope of Article 5(2) when coupled with the low threshold for marks with a reputation that was set out by the Court in the *BMW* case (Case C–63/97 *Bayerische Motorenwerke AG & BMW Nederland BV v Ronald Karel Deenik* [1999] ECR I-905). The fact that the mark must be known to a significant section of the public concerned with the product or service to which the mark is applied, is not going to be a major hurdle; the future will reveal whether this broad interpretation of Article 5(2) will effectively do away, in practice, with the careful approach and the restrictions that seemed to have been put in place in relation to association under Article 5(1)(b). It will also make clear whether Article 5(2) will set the norm or whether the courts will tighten up the requirements for reputation, while widening the scope of the due cause exception.

15.5.5 *Intel*

After *Adidas v Fitnessworld* the question remained open whether the presence of the link will automatically result in dilution and damage. And the establishment of a link seemed relatively easy as long as the link proved to be a link with the mark. Such a wide approach risked making Article 5(2) the norm and limiting Article 5(1)(b) to a small number of cases, whereas in origin the opposite scenario seemed to be the reasonable expectation of almost everyone. The *Intel* case offered the CJEU the opportunity to clarify whether this scenario would indeed unfold (Case C–252/07 *Intel Corp. Inc. v CPM United Kingdom Ltd* [2008] ECR I-8823, [2009] RPC 15). Intel is of course the world-famous manufacturer of computer chips and it objected on the basis of its Intel trade mark to the use of 'INTELMARK' for marketing and telemarketing services. The fact that the Intel trade mark has a reputation was beyond doubt.

Turning to the link one could summarize the Intel argument by saying that the term Intelmark called to mind the mark Intel. That was allegedly obvious and beyond doubt due to the massive reputation enjoyed by the Intel mark. The CJEU rejected that argument.

A link between the sign and the mark could not be implied and has to be demonstrated (*Intel*, the link requirement was again emphasized in Case C–320/07 P *Antartica Srl v OHIM* [2009] ETMR 47).[17] That should be done on the basis of a global assessment that takes account of the similarity between the mark and the sign, the nature of the goods and services for which the mark is registered (including the similarity or dissimilarity of the respective goods or services concerned and the relevant section of the public), the strength of the earlier mark's reputation, the degree of the earlier mark's distinctive character, and the likelihood of confusion on the part of the public. A link was held to be likely to exist if the sign called the mark to mind for the average, reasonably well-informed, observer, and circumspect consumer. Nevertheless, a huge reputation for certain types of goods or services was not enough to imply a link (Case C–252/07 *Intel Corp. Inc. v CPM United Kingdom Ltd* [2008] ECR I-8823, [2009] RPC 15).

Such a huge reputation was not enough to imply that the sign would take unfair advantage of or be detrimental to the mark. Focusing on detriment, the Court argued that harm, or at least a serious likelihood of it (see also Case C–197/07 P *Aktieselskabet af 21 November 2001 v OHIM* [2009] ETMR 36), should be proven.[18] The existence of a link will not automatically mean the requirement of detriment has been met. Again a global assessment that takes account of all relevant factors is called for. The bottom line is, though, that the trade mark owner must demonstrate actual harm in the sense that there is a change in the economic behaviour of the average consumer or a serious likelihood that such a change will occur in the future (*Intel*).

When we return to the facts of the case it becomes clear that Intel failed on this point. There was no evidence whatsoever that consumers would buy fewer Intel chips (or computers containing them) as a result of the use of the sign INTELMARK for marketing and telemarketing services. *Intel* therefore places important limits to the potentially broad application of the link doctrine and of Article 5(2). The link needs to be demonstrated and most importantly detriment needs to be proven through positive evidence of a change in the economic behaviour of the consumer (Case C–252/07 *Intel Corp. Inc. v CPM United Kingdom Ltd* [2008] ECR I-8823, [2009] RPC 15. For another case where lack of detriment was the main issue see *G-Star International BV v Pepsico Inc.* (Arrondissementsrechtbank The Hague) [2009] ETMR 18).

15.5.6 *L'Oréal*

Whilst *Intel* provided much clarification it left at least one point rather vague. The emphasis on the need to prove detriment makes one wonder how all this applies to situations where unfair advantage is being taken. Surely one cannot insist on proof of detriment in those cases. *L'Oréal* was all about unfair advantage and it allowed the Court the opportunity to express itself on that point (Case C–487/07 *L'Oréal SA v Bellure NV* [2009] ECR I-5185, [2009] ETMR 55). In this case the defendant made and sold imitation perfumes. The smells, names, and packaging of the perfumes were similar to the originals made by L'Oréal. It also produced a table of comparison which included both the original perfumes and the imitation perfumes.

---

[17] The Court of First Instance held in Case T–438/07 *SPA MONOPOLE v OHIM* EU:T:2009:434, that the similarity between 'Spago' for alcoholic drinks and 'SPA' for mineral water was not sufficient for a link to be demonstrated in practice.

[18] There must be a serious risk that the injury will occur in the future. Case C–100/11 P *Helena Rubinstein SNC and L'Oréal SA v OHIM—Allergan Inc.* [2012] ETMR 40 [93].

The Court held that there was no requirement for there to be detriment to the distinctive character of the mark. Taking advantage of the reputation of the mark was sufficient. And in the view of the Court there was an unfair advantage where the third party sought to ride on the coat-tails of the mark with a reputation in order to benefit from its power of attraction, its reputation, and its prestige and to exploit, without paying any financial compensation, the marketing effort expanded by the rights holder.

That later allowed the Court of Appeal in the UK to argue that no unfair advantage had been taken and that an Article 5(2) action failed where Kenwood entered the market for kitchen robots with a model that resembled the iconic KitchenAid kitchen robot that is protected by a shape trade mark. Kenwood had after all established its own goodwill in kitchen appliances and it did not ride on the coat-tails of the rights holder. In order to compete in a niche market where the rights holder and its shape had had a monopoly for years, it did need to offer the same basic shape. That was due to the commercial circumstances and the case was in that sense very different from *L'Oréal* (*Whirlpool Corp. v Kenwood Ltd* [2010] ETMR 7 (CA)).

Perhaps more controversially, *L'Oréal* also confirms the line started in *Arsenal* which signals, at least for marks with a reputation, a move away from pure distinctiveness. It has long been said that trade mark law only protected the distinctiveness function of the mark. The Court of Justice now clearly goes beyond that and states that as a property right the mark is also offering the rights holder protection for the advertising, investment, and communication functions of the mark. The list is not exhaustive and further case law will have to show how far the Court is prepared to venture down this path.[19]

15.5.7 **AdWords**

The CJEU was also asked if and how the use of AdWords could have a detrimental effect on trade marks with a reputation. As expected, the outcome was that there could indeed be a detrimental effect on the functions of such a trade mark, for example by riding on its coat-tails, and that as a result:

> the proprietor of a trade mark with a reputation is entitled to prevent a competitor from advertising on the basis of a keyword corresponding to that trade mark, which the competitor has, without the proprietor's consent, selected in an internet referencing service, where the competitor thereby takes unfair advantage of the distinctive character or repute of the trade mark (free-riding) or where the advertising is detrimental to that distinctive character (dilution) or to that repute (tarnishment).
>
> Advertising on the basis of such a keyword is detrimental to the distinctive character of a trade mark with a reputation (dilution) if, for example, it contributes to turning that trade mark into a generic term.
>
> By contrast, the proprietor of a trade mark with a reputation is not entitled to prevent, inter alia, advertisements displayed by competitors on the basis of keywords corresponding to that trade mark, which put forward—without offering a mere imitation of the goods or services of the proprietor of that trade mark, without causing dilution or tarnishment and without, moreover, adversely affecting the functions of the trade

---

[19] Case C–487/07 *L'Oréal SA v Bellure NV* [2009] ECR I-5185, [2009] ETMR 55. An automated AdWord service created by Google did not, however, constitute an infringement under Article 5(2). See Case C–236/08 *Google France Sarl v Louis Vuitton Malletier SA* [2011] All ER (EC) 411, [2010] ETMR 30, [2010] RPC 19.

mark with a reputation—an alternative to the goods or services of the proprietor of that mark.[20]

15.6 Exceptions to Infringement

There are, of course, some exceptions to the foregoing in respect of which what would otherwise be an infringement is exempted. One might think that an alleged infringer who has obtained a (later) registered trade mark for the allegedly infringing sign should not be treated as an infringer, as she has obtained a registered right at the same level. One could argue that in such a case the later trade mark should be revoked first. This is indeed the strategy adopted by a number of national trade mark laws, but at least in terms of Community trade marks the CJEU held that this strategy does not apply. The strategy hinges on the definition of the term 'third party' in the infringement provisions. One needs to exclude the proprietor of another trade mark (for the same goods or services) from this definition, but the CJEU refused to do so and specifically ruled out the need for a revocation action. The Court argued in Case C–561/11 *FCI v FCIPPR* [2013] ETMR 23 that a later registered Community trade mark does not have to be declared invalid before the owner of an earlier registered Community trade mark is allowed to bring an infringement action. The equivalent provision in the Directive uses identical terms, so arguably the same interpretation should apply in relation to national trade marks and the alternative approach adopted by a number of Member States may be in breach of the Directive.

Leaving this false start behind, we turn to Article 6 of the Directive and Article 12 of the Regulation, both of which remove the threat of an infringement action from a range of situations, in each case subject to a proviso that the use that would otherwise be an infringement is a use that is, once again, 'in accordance with honest practices in industrial or commercial matters'. The test for honesty is to be judged by an objective standard. This fits in well with the provisions on bad faith and absolute grounds. These will stop registration in some of the cases we will discuss in a moment, whereas the exception regulates the use without registration in similar cases. The honest practices standard then shows a similar approach is being taken to these issues.

15.6.1 Article 6(1)(a) Directive/Article 12(a) Regulation

The activities exempted by Articles 6(1) and 12 respectively, include, first in paragraph (a), the use by a person of his own name or address. Arguably, this includes the use by a company of its own registered name or even its trading name. The exception also covers trade mark use of the name. The CJEU held that the provision applied to a scenario where soft drinks and mineral water were produced under the trade mark Kerry Spring using water from an Irish spring called Kerry spring. In terms of honest practices the Court refused to rely merely on aural similarity, but it left the final assessment to the national court (Case C–100/02 *Gerolsteiner Brunnen GmbH & Co. v Putsch GmbH* [2004] ETMR 40). Although this exception seems obvious and only fair, the use in trade of a sign including name and address is not an essential feature of many trades and may well therefore not be honest. If a Mr Ronald McDonald of Leicester were to want to open a burger bar, there are many burger-related names that would be more appropriate than his own name and the only reason for using it would be the less-than-honest desire to steal trade from

---

[20] Case C–323/09 *Interflora Inc. v Marks & Spencer Plc* [2012] CEC 755, [2012] ETMR 1, [2012] FSR 3.

his better known namesake; if a Mr Herbert Smith of Leicester wants to set up a solicitor's firm in his own name, this may be honest, given that a solicitor normally trades under his own name if a sole practitioner, despite the global presence of the law firm Herbert Smith Freehills.

According to the CJEU, the condition of 'honest practices' to which this exception is subject constitutes, in substance, the expression of a duty to act fairly in relation to the legitimate interests of the trade mark owner (Case C–100/02 *Gerolsteiner Brunnen GmbH & Co. v Putsch GmbH* [2004] ECR I-691 [24]). There must also be some degree of coexistence and some degree of confusion must therefore be tolerated. The extent of confusion that is to be tolerated is a matter of degree and infringement is only to be found if, objectively, the use of her name or address by the person concerned amounted to unfair competition. No doubt the Court will, in future, be called upon again to clarify this test further (see also Case C–63/97 *BMW AG v Ronald Deenik* [1999] ECR I-905).

15.6.2 Article (6)(1)(b) Directive/Article 12(b) Regulation

A second exception in paragraph (b) covers the honest use of all the descriptive matter that cannot be registered as a trade mark unless it has become distinctive through use. It is the purpose of this exception to permit the fair use of the claimant's mark to indicate the characteristics of goods or services of the user of the sign. That purpose does not extend to performing the dual function of indicating both the characteristics and the trade origin of the goods. Use of a sign as a trade mark can, indeed, never constitute descriptive use that is authorized under the exception.

A somewhat exceptional set of facts arose in Case C–48/05 *Adam Opel AG v Autec AG* [2007] ETMR 33. This case deals with a trade mark, 'Opel', that had been registered both for motor vehicles and for toys. The question then arose whether the use of the trade mark on scale reproductions of these motor vehicles constituted trade mark infringement. The CJEU held that if a trade mark is registered, inter alia, in respect of motor vehicles, the affixing by a third party of a sign identical to that mark to scale models of that make of vehicle, without the authorization of the proprietor of the trade mark, in order faithfully to reproduce those vehicles and the marketing of those scale models does not constitute use of an indication concerning a characteristic of those scale models, within the meaning of the exception.

15.6.3 Article 6(1)(c) Directive/Article 12(c) Regulation

The third exception relates to the use of a mark to indicate the purpose of goods or services: for example, as spare parts or accessories. Thus if I am free to make spare parts for Ford cars, it will not be an infringement to use—as ever, honestly—the name, or even the mark, of Ford to indicate the suitability of my parts for Ford cars.

The CJEU dealt with the lawfulness of use of the trade mark by a third party in Case C–228/03 *The Gillette Company & Gillette Group Finland Oy v LA-Laboratories Ltd Oy* [2005] ECR I-2337, [2005] 2 CMLR 62. In this case, the defendant made replacement shaving knives that were compatible with Gillette's originals. The Court held that, in these circumstances, the legitimacy of the use of the trade mark depended on whether that use was necessary to indicate the intended purpose of the product. This is the case, for example, if such use is the only means of providing the public with comprehensible and complete information on that intended purpose in order to preserve the undistorted system of competition in the market for that product; any other conclusion would lead to the use of the trade mark for anti-competitive purposes. The fact that the product involved is not a spare part or accessory, but could be described as the product itself—or, at the very least, the essential part of it—does not affect these findings. The use by the third party must, however, be honest use. The third party is therefore obliged to act fairly in relation to the legitimate interests of the trade mark owner. One should therefore not use the mark in such a way as to suggest a connection between the third party and the trade mark owner, or present one's own product as an imitation or replica of the original product. Neither should one discredit or denigrate the mark, or affect its value by taking unfair advantage of its distinctive character or repute.

15.6.4 Article 6(2) Directive

A further area covered by these provisions that permit what would otherwise be infringements is created by Article 6(2) of the Directive. There is no equivalent exception in the Regulation in relation to Community trade marks.

This is a somewhat odd provision that protects the use in a particular locality of an earlier right applicable only in that locality. Such a right must be enjoyed continuously prior to the first use of the registration of the mark by its user. No assistance is given as to the definition of a 'locality' and, once again, the use of this provision should be infrequent, given that the earlier local mark should, in an effective system of examination, be unearthed and thus deprive the later mark of the necessary distinctiveness. Because of this, it is far from easy to think of an example of the operation of the provision, but a possible example may be if a trade mark is granted in respect of a Scotch named after an island and it is then discovered that a small local firm on the island has been brewing whisky for the locals using the island's name as part of the brand name.

15.6.5 Exhaustion

Article 7 of the Directive creates an important and different restriction of the right to bring infringement actions. It brings into this area of the law the 'exhaustion of rights' principle that is familiar from other areas of IP. In brief, this is the principle whereby goods that bear, in this case, a trade mark go beyond the control of the proprietor of the mark once they are put on the market—his rights in them are exhausted once the goods are in circulation and he cannot object to any use of them. This has a particular relevance in the European context, where the principle of the single market has obliged EU law to assert that the circulation of goods in any one Member State equates to their circulation in all such states, unless any of the standard objections to free movement principles apply, as exemplified by the *Hag II* case (Case C–10/89 *CNL-Sucal NV SA v HAG GF AG* [1990] ECR I-3711, [1990] 3 CMLR 571).

The problem arises primarily in the context of parallel imports, in which case a company makes goods bearing a mark in both Germany, for example, and, more cheaply, through a subsidiary in Portugal. Ideally, such a company would prevent goods from Portugal being imported cheaply into Germany, thus undermining its home market, but the two principles of exhaustion and single market now combine to make this impossible.

This situation is given effect by Article 7. This removes the right to bring an infringement action in relation to goods put on the market anywhere in the European Economic Area (EEA) by the proprietor with her consent. But Article 7(2) goes on to remove this if the proprietor has legitimate reasons to oppose further dealings, such as a change in the conditions of the product, again reflecting the jurisprudence of the CJEU (Case C–3/78

Centrafarm BV v American Home Products Corp. [1978] ECR 1823, [1979] 1 CMLR 326). Clearly, however, national trade mark law can still be used to stop parallel imports from countries elsewhere in the world. Article 13 of the Regulation is the equivalent provision for Community trade marks, in respect of which the same rule applies.

15.7 Revocation and Invalidity

The grant of a trade mark lasts initially for ten years from the date of its registration (see Article 46 of the Regulation) and this may be renewed for a seemingly indefinite number of further periods of ten years thereafter on payment of the appropriate fee.

As ever, however, there is a problem: such rights may be lost in two ways—either by way of a successful application for the revocation of the trade mark or, alternatively, by way of a claim that the initial registration was invalid. Either of these routes will, if pursued successfully, lead to the sudden end of the trade mark and the rights therein.

15.7.1 Revocation

There are three grounds listed in the parallel provisions of Article 12 of the Directive and Article 51 of the Regulation as being reasons for revocation. First, five years' lack of genuine use of the mark[21] without cause can lead to revocation of the registration and it is for the proprietor to prove that there has been use. A suspension for the same period (after initial use) is also a ground for revocation (Article 12(1) Directive/Article 51(1)(a) Regulation). Article 10(1) of the Directive provides further clarification on this point.

A second ground is that, whether due to the acts or the inactivity of the proprietor, the mark has become the common name for the product in question in the trade (Article 12(2)(a) Directive/Article 51(1)(b) Regulation). The main difficulty here is to determine the scope of the trade—that is, of the relevant circles in which the mark is now used as a common name for the product. This is a particularly difficult issue in those cases in which the product is not directly sold to the end user, but in which intermediaries are also involved. The CJEU has provided the following guidance on that point:

> in cases where intermediaries participate in the distribution to the consumer or the end user of a product which is the subject of a registered trade mark, the relevant circles whose views fall to be taken into account in determining whether that trade mark has become the common name in the trade for the product in question comprise all consumers and end users and, depending on the features of the market concerned, all those in the trade who deal with that product commercially.[22]

Finally, revocation of a mark is also appropriate if it has been used in a misleading manner, especially as to the nature, quality, or origin of the goods or services in question (Article 12(2)(b) Directive/Article 51(1)(c) Regulation).

In effect, the first two grounds penalize non-use, while the latter two grounds are aimed at confusing use of a mark. For a while it was not clear whether the courts had the option to revoke the mark only for part of the goods or services for which it was registered, for example in cases on non-use for that part of the goods or services. It is now clear that that is possible and that where grounds for revocation or invalidity exist in respect of only some of the goods or services for which the trade mark has been registered (or has been

---

[21] See *United Biscuits (UK) Ltd v Asda Stores Ltd* [1997] RPC 513.
[22] Case C–371/02 *Björnekulla Fruktindustrier AB v Procordia Food AB* [2004] ETMR 977 [26].

applied for) revocation or invalidity shall cover those goods or services only (Article 13 Directive/Article 51(2) Regulation).

15.7.2 Genuine Use

'Use' seems to be generously defined. Use by someone other than the proprietor—although with his consent—will suffice, which is an obvious corollary of the more relaxed approach to the licensing of trade marks. The grant of a trade mark licence on its own, however, was held not to be sufficient evidence of use of the trade mark; real genuine use by the licensee was also required. Similarly use of a mark that is not identical, but equally not different, in its essential character will count as use of the mark.

A good example from before the Directive of the first type of revocation is provided by the facts of *Imperial Group Ltd v Philip Morris & Co. Ltd* [1982] FSR 72, in which the word 'Nerit' was registered for cigarettes by the defendants, who were hoping in due course to launch the 'Merit' brand of cigarettes, which was, of course, unregistrable as a laudatory epithet, but the use of which by others could be blocked by the 'Nerit' mark. A tiny number of cigarettes were sold under the name, but the UK Court of Appeal saw through the subterfuge. There was no genuine use of the mark and it was accordingly expunged from the register. This case would appear to be one that would be decided similarly under the Directive. But there will be genuine use of the mark if another (registered) mark is used if the differences between the marks, for example 'Proti' and 'Protiplus' or 'Proti Power' respectively, do not alter the distinctive character of the trade mark. Use of the distinctive aspect 'Proti' as a component of the two other marks was sufficient to demonstrate genuine use of the mark 'Proti', even if the registration could be considered to be a defensive one (Case C–553/11 *Bernhard Rintisch v Klaus Eder* [2013] ETMR 5).

The question of what amounts to genuine use of the trade mark in this context was examined by the CJEU in Case C–40/01 *Ansul v Ajax* [2003] ECR I-2349. The Court ruled that there is 'genuine use' of a trade mark if the mark is used in accordance with its essential function—that is, to guarantee the identity of the origin of the goods or services for which it is registered[23]—in order to create or preserve an outlet for those goods or services. The use has to be sufficient to maintain or to create market share for the goods or services covered by the mark (conclusion of Advocate General Sharpston in Case C–149/11 *Leno Merken BV v Hagelkruis Beheer BV* EU:C:2012:422). Genuine use does not include token use for the sole purpose of preserving the rights conferred by the mark. When assessing whether use of the trade mark is genuine, regard must be had to all the facts and circumstances that are relevant to establishing whether the commercial exploitation of the mark is real, particularly whether such use is viewed as warranted in the economic sector concerned to maintain or create a share in the market for the goods or services protected by the mark, the nature of the goods or services at issue, the characteristics of the market, and the scale and frequency of use of the mark. Genuine use will normally be use across borders, but market conditions may limit such use to a single Member State. There is no *de minimis* rule (for use in a single Member State see Case C–149/11 *Leno Merken BV v Hagelkruis Beheer BV* [2013] ETMR 16). The fact that a mark that is not used for goods that are newly available on the market, but for goods that were sold in the past, does not mean that its use is not genuine if the proprietor makes actual use of the same mark for component parts that

---

[23] See also the judgment of the French Supreme Court in *Sté Doubrère Chausseur v Doubrère Chaussure*, Cass. Com., case no. 11-14317, 31 January 2012 [2013] 46 Propriétés Intellectuelles 106, where mere use in an Internet address and as a sign on the shopfront was held not to amount to genuine use.

are integral to the make-up or structure of such goods, or for goods or services directly connected with the goods previously sold and intended to meet the needs of customers of those goods.

Genuine use does not have to be use for profit. In the words of the Court of Justice:

> a trade mark is put to genuine use where a non-profit-making association uses the trade mark, in its relations with the public, in announcements of forthcoming events, on business papers and on advertising material and where the association's members wear badges featuring that trade mark when collecting and distributing donations.[24]

Use only on promotional items that are handed out for free as a reward to purchasers of other goods or to encourage the sale of those other goods did not, on the other hand, amount to genuine use (Case C–495/07 *Silberquelle GmbH v Maselli-Strickmode mbH* [2009] ETMR 28).

In the absence of genuine use, revocation can only be averted if there is a proper reason for the non-use. A proper reason must arise independently of the will of the trade mark owner, because any inference from the owner would enter into conflict with the basic premise that a trade mark registration carries with it a desire to exploit, rather than to block, opportunities for other competitors. The hurdle must also have a direct relationship with the mark. The potential to use the mark must depend on the hurdle being overcome successfully. Hurdles that are only indirectly related to the mark, but that, for example, make exploitation of the mark less profitable or more cumbersome than foreseen in the initial business plan will not be sufficient. On top of that, a hurdle that simply makes it more difficult to use the mark is not sufficient: the use must have become impossible or at least unreasonable. The appropriate use of the mark must have been seriously jeopardized. For example, a trade mark owner cannot seriously be required to sell its goods in the outlets of its competitors. In such a case, the use of the mark is not impossible, but it has become unreasonable. Or as the CJEU summarized it:

> only obstacles having a sufficiently direct relationship with a trade mark making its use impossible or unreasonable, and which arise independently of the will of the proprietor of that mark, may be described as 'proper reasons for non-use' of that mark.[25]

15.7.3 Confusing Use

The 'confusing use' grounds for revocation pose separate issues. The fact that the acts, in particular, of a proprietor lead to his trade mark becoming a household or generic name may be thought to be grounds for acclaim, rather than for the revocation of the mark. But the fact that this ground for revocation only arises from the acts or omissions of the proprietor is the explanation for the provision, the scope of which is quite narrow, and justifies its presence. If the public habitually refers to all vacuum cleaners as 'Hoovers', no ground for revocation arises; it is only if the proprietors cause the confusion—perhaps by failing to make clear that their use of 'Hoover' is as a trade mark—that this ground arises.

Misleading use is the most obvious ground for revocation, given that, if the intention was present at the time of registration, such a mark would never be allowed in the first place. Inactivity when a mark turns into a common name is also a risk: the mark 'spambuster', for example, turned into a common name for computer programming services to prevent or combat spam. The rights holder's inactivity then exposed it to the possibility of revocation.

[24] Case C–442/07 *Verein Radetzky-Orden v Bundesvereinigung Kameradschaft, Feldmarschall Radetzky* [2009] ETMR 14 [24].
[25] Case C–246/05 *Armin Häupl v Lidl Stiftung & Co. KG* [2007] ETMR 61 [54].

Case C–409/12 *Backaldrin Österreich The Kornspitz Company GmbH v Pfahnl Backmittel GmbH* [2014] ETMR 30 provides a typical example (see also the Dutch Shiso (RB. Den Haag, 2 April 2014, *Cresco v Koppert Cress.*, IEF 13711, ECLI:NL:RBDHA:2014:5266) and Turbo (Vrz. Rb. Den Haag, 9 September 2014, *BNP Paribas v Binckbank* IEF 14181) cases). Backaldrin has an Austrian trade mark for the word KORNSPITZ and it supplies a bread mix to bakeries. The latter then bake typical breads and Backaldrin allows them to sell these under the name Kornspitz. The bakeries are aware of the trade mark, but end users and consumers see the term as a descriptive term for the bakery product (irrespective of the source of the bread mix). Bakeries do not draw the attention of their customers to the fact that Kornspitz is a registered trade mark. And Backaldrin does not oblige the bakeries to use the trade mark when selling products made on the basis of the bread mix. The CJEU drew harsh consequences on this basis. The Court ruled that the fact that the proprietor of a trade mark does not encourage sellers to make more use of that mark in marketing a product in respect of which the mark is registered amounts to 'inactivity' in the sense of the revocation provision and that revocation will follow and that a trade mark is liable to revocation in respect of a product for which it is registered if, in consequence of acts or inactivity of the proprietor, that trade mark has become the common name for that product from the point of view solely of end users of the product.

15.7.4 Invalidity

Turning to removal of a trade mark from the register on the grounds of its invalidity, it is Articles 3 and 4 of the Directive and Articles 52 and 53 of the Regulation that provide the relevant rules. It is important to note that a finding of invalidity means that the registration is deemed to have never been made and thus amounts to a complete legal nullity, except in relation to transactions that are past and closed.

The grounds for claiming invalidity are straightforward and refer back to the rules on unregistrable marks. In the Directive the same Articles cover both and in the Regulation the invalidity Articles cover absolute and relative grounds, which once again hints at the parallel approach. Any mark gained in contradiction of those provisions is an invalid mark. The sole exception to this is in relation to marks that should not have been registered on the grounds of non-distinctiveness, descriptiveness, or customary or generic use. These will not lose their validity if, after registration, they acquire by their use the necessary distinctive character that, had it been present at the time of registration, would have, in any event, justified their valid registration at that time.

A case dealing with chocolate Easter bunnies which both parties had produced in a similar shape for a number of years before one of them registered the shape as a trade mark, gave the CJEU the chance to look at the issue of bad faith. The Court ruled that in order to determine whether an applicant was acting in bad faith one has to consider whether, at the time of filing the application for registration: (a) the applicant knew or must have known that the third party was using an identical or similar sign for an identical or similar product capable of being confused with the sign for which registration was sought; (b) the applicant intended to prevent that third party from continuing to use such a sign; and (c) the third party's and the applicant's signs enjoyed a degree of legal protection (Case C–529/07 *Chocoladefabriken Lindt & Sprungli AG v Franz Hauswirth GmbH* [2009] ECR I-4893, [2009] ETMR 56).

In general, it is clear that the symbiotic relationship of infringement and invalidity arguments has been well understood by the authors of the new trade mark legislation. The same basic ideas stemming from the basic notion of trade mark registrability run through both infringement and invalidity provisions. One should not wait too long if one wants to rely on an earlier trade mark in support of an invalidation action. Acquiescence for a five-year period will take away the right to rely on the earlier mark, according to Article 9 of the Directive and Article 54 of the Regulation, respectively (see Case C–263/09 P *Edwin Co. Ltd v OHIM—Elio Fiorucci* [2011] ETMR 45). This takes away prolonged uncertainty and increases the degree of legal certainty. However, the proprietor of an earlier trade mark cannot be held to have acquiesced in the long and well-established honest use, of which he has long been aware, by a third party of a later trade mark which is identical with that of the proprietor if that proprietor was not in any position to oppose that use, for example because both parties have been authorized by the court to register the mark 'Budweiser'. The five-year limitation period will start to run from the registration of the later mark (Case C–482/09 *Budějovický Budvar, národní podnik v Anheuser-Busch Inc.* [2012] ETMR 2).

15.8 Conclusions

That the old law needed reform was undoubted: its convolutions and complexities were considerable, and became worse as amendment after amendment was made.

The Directive and the Regulation introduced changes that were for most Member State radical in nature in relation to trade mark infringement and the scope of trade mark protection. In these areas, the legal system now extends its protection beyond the origin function of the trade mark, even if the latter is still its primary function. The contours of the new system clearly emerge from the case law of the CJEU. Case C–251/95 *Sabel v Puma* [1997] ECR I-6191, [1998] 1 CMLR 445 provided a first indication in this respect and this has now been followed up by a ruling that confusion can exist if the public perceives the goods or services as being produced in different places and by economically linked undertakings, rather than necessarily by the same undertaking (Case C–39/97 *Canon Kabushiki Kaisha v Metro-Goldwyn-Mayer Inc.* [1998] ECR I-5507). This clearly goes beyond the protection of the function of origin. The trade mark owner also gets protection for some of the non-origin uses of its trade mark.

At one stage, one had the impression that things would stop there and that Article 5(2) of the Directive would really remain reserved for exceptional cases. That has now all changed, and it seems easy for a mark to acquire a reputation and bring itself under the scope of that provision. On top of that, the requirements contained in the provision have been interpreted liberally and the impression was created that Article 5(2) would become the norm, and that Article 5(1)(b) and its stricter norms would only apply to a limited number of cases. Such a move could not be welcomed unreservedly and would have represented a massive expansion of the rights of the owners of trade marks. With *Intel* the tide seems to have turned and proper limitations are being put in place, such as the need actually to prove detriment or the taking of unfair advantage (Case C–252/07 *Intel Corp. Inc. v CPM United Kingdom Ltd* [2008] ECR I-8823).

Clearly, the legal debate has not yet reached a final conclusion in this area. But whatever the final outcome turns out to be, the changes in this area will have been far more revolutionary than the initial cases would have us believe. And of course, whilst a clear line is now emerging the CJEU has not always made it easy. Some cases went in different directions and a straight line did not always emerge (immediately).

Further Reading

CARBONI, A., 'Two Stripes and You're Out! Added Protection for Trade Marks with a Reputation' (2004) 26 *EIPR* 229

CHEUNG, A.S.Y. AND PUN, K.K.H., 'Comparative Study on the Liability for Trade Mark Infringement of Online Auction Providers' (2009) 31 *EIPR* 559

DAVIS, J., 'The European Court of Justice Considers Trade Mark Dilution' (2009) 68 *Cambridge Law Journal* 290

MORCOM, C., '*L'Oréal v. Bellure*: Who Has Won?' (2009) 31 *EIPR* 627

MORCOM, C., 'Trade Marks and the Internet: Where Are We Now?' (2012) 34 *EIPR* 40

SIMON, I., 'Embellishment: Trade Mark Use Triumph or Decorative Disaster' (2006) 28 *EIPR* 321

WÜRTENBERGER, G., 'Community Trade Mark Law Astray or Back to the Roots!' (2006) 28 *EIPR* 549

16

Trade Marks and the Free Movement Aspects of EU Law

16.1 Introduction

The internationalization of the trade mark scene is an inevitable reflection of multinational companies and multinational trade. Clearly, such interests need protection as a reflection of their commercial value—but there must be a slight note of caution. The promotion of image through trade marks is not an abstract exercise, but one that interacts with the citizen, who is being persuaded to buy a product or use a service. Individual perceptions vary from state to state and are nurtured in different ways by different languages. International cooperation may be essential, but international conformity is not and may even be unwise. The permissive Madrid approach may be thought to reflect this more satisfactorily than the single Community trade mark, but more and more companies do business across the EU and treat it as a single market in which they market their goods or services under a single trade mark. For them, the Community trade mark may be the ideal tool and they may use the Madrid system only to expand protection to certain non-EU Member States.

Community trade marks may not necessarily raise questions in this respect, but in parallel the EU still operates a harmonized system of 26 national trade marks. Their territorial nature potentially raises problems of compartmentalization of the single market on the basis of trade mark law. Hence the need to look in detail at the interaction between trade mark law and the principles of free movement of goods in the EU. We discussed, in relation to patents, how the provisions on free movement and competition law in the Treaty of Rome apply to IP rights. The principles we set out there obviously also apply to trade marks and this section will only be concerned with the specific application of these principles.

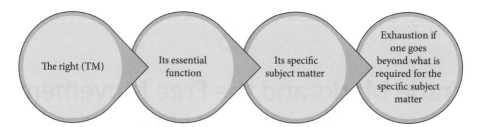

Figure 16.1 Essential function and specific subject matter

We will turn next to the concepts of essential function and specific subject matter, shown schematically in Figure 16.1. Arguably, the CJEU uses these concepts to distinguish between what amounts to pro-competitive use of the trade mark, which the Treaty encourages (as an exception to the free movement provisions) and anti-competitive abuse of the trade mark rights which the Treaty prohibits (as an exception to the exception, amounting to an arbitrary restriction of trade). The essential function looks at this from a theoretical perspective, whilst the specific subject matter translates this in more practical guidelines. In its early version the distinction between essential function and specific subject matter was also a tool to distinguish the EU's competence for the operation of the single market and the free movement of goods from the Member States' competence for the IP rights as such. IP rights in those days were national rights and the EU stayed away from touching these rights as such. Their exercise had to comply with the free movement rules though. In its later version of the essential function/specific subject matter approach, once the Community rights have appeared and the EU's competence has been enlarged, the focus shifts to a way for the EU to promote a competitive European single market. This shift in focus is clearly visible as an undercurrent in the cases that shaped this area of law and to which we now turn.

16.2 Towards a Definition of Specific Subject Matter and the Essential Function

16.2.1 *Centrafarm v Winthrop*

The first case decided by the CJEU is a parallel case to that of Case 15/74 *Centrafarm v Sterling Drug* [1974] ECR 1147, [1974] 2 CMLR 480, in relation to patents and is, in relation to trade marks, Case 16/74 *Centrafarm v Winthrop* [1974] ECR 1183. As in the patent case, Centrafarm was buying drugs in the UK and importing them into the Netherlands for resale. In both countries, the drug was marketed under the trade mark 'Negram'. Winthrop, the Dutch subsidiary of Sterling, owned the trade mark in the Netherlands, and tried to exercise its rights under that right to block the importation into, and resale operation in, the Netherlands. Unfortunately, the Court did not spell out fully the essential function of a trade mark in this case, although it is fair to say that the approach taken is identical to that taken in relation to patents, because the Court went on to define the specific subject matter, which included a reference to the exhaustion doctrine.

The specific subject matter of a trade mark is:

the guarantee that the owner of the trade mark has the exclusive right to use that mark, for the purpose of putting products protected by the trade mark into circulation for the first time, and is therefore intended to protect him against competitors wishing to take advantage of the status and reputation of the trade mark by selling products illegally bearing that mark.

The owner of the trade mark has the exclusive right to use the trade mark for commercial purposes and can oppose infringement. She can exercise the right by putting products (or services) labelled with the trade mark on the market for the first time, but, afterwards, her rights are exhausted.

These are all rights available under parallel trade marks in the Community. The comments that we made in relation to the similar specific subject matter of a patent apply here as well. Any exercise of the trade mark that goes further will fall foul of Articles 34 and 36 Treaty on the Functioning of the European Union (TFEU). Obviously, the trade mark owner can put the products on the market himself, or can allow a third party to exploit the trade mark with his consent. The option taken does not influence the application of the exhaustion doctrine: Winthrop could thus not be allowed to exercise its Dutch trade mark rights to block the importation and resale operation that Centrafarm was setting up for Negram, because the marketing in the UK had been done by the Sterling group, meeting the consent requirement, and had exhausted all rights under parallel trade marks in the Community. Such exercise of its trade mark rights by Winthrop would go beyond the specific subject matter of a trade mark, and it therefore falls foul of Articles 34 and 36. In the words of the Court:

> the exercise, by the owner of a trade mark, of the right which he enjoys under the legislation of a Member State to prohibit the sale, in that State, of a product which has been marketed under the trade mark in another Member State by the trade mark owner or with his consent is incompatible with the rules of the EEC Treaty concerning the free movement of goods within the Common Market.[1]

The fact that the product has been manufactured outside the EU, before it was put on the market inside the EU, is irrelevant as long as the product was put into circulation in the EU by, or with the consent of, the trade mark owner (Case C–352/95 *Phytheron International SA v Jean Bourdon* [1997] ECR I-1729).

The consent for the marketing within the EU is the crucial element. In its decision in Case C–16/03 *Peak Holding AB v Axolin-Elinor AB* [2005] ECR I-11313, the CJEU clarified the concept of putting the goods on the market with the consent of the proprietor. In this case, the proprietor had imported the goods into the EEA and had offered them for sale in its own shops, but it had not actually sold them. The Court held that the goods had not been put on the market with the consent of the proprietor of the mark in the absence of a first sale of the goods; such a first sale would take place were the goods to be sold to another operator in the EEA even if the contract were to prohibit resale in the EEA. The onus to prove the consent—whether express or implied (Case C–127/09 *Coty Prestige Lancaster Group GmbH v Simex Trading AG* [2010] FSR 48, [2010] ETMR 41)—of the proprietor of the trade mark lies with the parallel importer, but the standard of proof is the usual one in civil litigation—that is, the balance of probabilities. The Court has used the term 'unequivocal consent' simply to indicate that the consent must be clear and that proven acts that can be consistent with consent, but also with its absence, are not sufficient to demonstrate consent. That does not change the standard of proof. The parallel importer can however demonstrate that the

---

[1] *Centrafarm BV v Winthrop BV.*

goods were put on the EEA market by a third party which has no economic link with the rights holder with the implied consent of the latter. In that case the consent must be inferred from facts and circumstances prior to, simultaneous with, or subsequent to the placing on the market of the goods, but they must unequivocally demonstrate that the proprietor has renounced his exclusive rights. This is a tall order (Case C–324/08 *Makro Zelfbedieningsgroothandel CV, Metro Cash & Carry BV and Remo Zaandam BV v Diesel SpA* [2010] ETMR 2).

Whereas consent is the key component, one should also not forget the requirement that the goods must have been put on the market. The CJEU has held that that requirement is not satisfied when the goods that are parallel imported started life as 'testers', 'demonstrators', or 'samples' (e.g. for perfumes) which the rights holder/manufacturer puts at the disposal of shops inside its distribution chain and that are clearly labelled as such. These have not been put on the market and the trade mark cannot therefore be exhausted in relation to them (Case C–127/09 *Coty Prestige Lancaster Group GmbH v Simex Trading AG* [2010] FSR 48, [2010] ETMR 41; Case C–324/09 *L'Oréal v eBay* [2011] ETMR 52, [2011] RPC 27).

16.2.2 *Hoffmann-La Roche v Centrafarm*

The essential function of the trade mark was spelled out in the next trade mark case to reach the CJEU. In *Hoffmann-La Roche v Centrafarm*, the Court said that the essential function of a trade mark was:

> to guarantee the identity of the trade marked product to the consumer or ultimate user, by enabling him without any possibility of confusion to distinguish that product from products which have another origin.[2]

This has to be read in conjunction with the partial statement on the subject in Case 16/74 *Centrafarm BV v Winthrop BV* [1974] ECR 1183, [1974] 2 CMLR 480, in which the protection of the goodwill of the owner of the trade mark was emphasized—but why this seemingly odd combination?

It is submitted that, in relation to trade marks, it is impossible to say that one function is more essential than the other as was the case in relation to patents. Goodwill is an essential element of a trade mark for its owner, but it will only exist if the consumer distinguishes the product or service labelled with the trade mark from other products or services. The guarantee for consumers or users that the product or service labelled with the trade mark is of a standard quality is essential in order for the goodwill—whether negative or positive—to be created. The combination of these two elements forms the essential function of a trade mark, which is fulfilled by the exercise of the rights within its specific subject matter.

It should also be remembered that this whole area of law is concerned with putting goods on the single market. The rights holder can, in respect of lawfully manufactured goods, only act if the goods are to be put on the market. Lawfully manufactured goods that are in transit in order to be placed on a market outside the EU cannot be stopped and detained by customs authorities without infringing Article 34 of the Treaty (Case C–115/02 *Administration des Douanes et Droits Indirects v Rioglass SA & Transremar SL* [2004] ETMR 519).

---

[2] Case 102/77 *Hoffmann-La Roche & Co. AG v Centrafarm* [1978] ECR 1139, 1164 [1978] 3 CMLR 217, 241.

16.3 The Repackaging and Relabelling Saga

16.3.1 The Starting Point: Repackaging in *Hoffmann-La Roche*

Further complications arose when certain trade marked drugs were sold in different pack-ing formats in various Member States. In the *Hoffmann-La Roche* case, the drug Valium was sold in packs containing a different number of pills in the UK and in Germany. Centrafarm bought the drugs in the UK, removed the outer packing and repacked the drug for the German market in packs containing the number of pills that was normal on the German market. It applied the Valium trade mark, which Hoffmann-La Roche owned all over Europe, to the packs destined for the German market. Hoffmann-La Roche wanted to rely on its German Valium trade mark to stop Centrafarm. It argued that it had not exhausted its rights in the trade mark, because it had not applied it to the repacked goods.

The CJEU rejected the argument. Hoffmann-La Roche had marketed the drugs in the UK under the Valium trade mark and thereby exhausted its rights in all parallel trade marks. The way in which Hoffmann-La Roche wanted to use its trade mark went beyond its specific subject matter and fell foul of Articles 34 and 36. The interesting element in this case relates to the essential function of trade marks, because this needs to be ful-filled by the exercise of the rights under the specific subject matter of the trade mark. The goodwill of Hoffmann-La Roche and the interest of the consumers had therefore to be protected. This is the reason why the Court laid down additional requirements. It specified that there needs to be a guarantee that the repacking has no adverse effect on the original condition of the goods, because tampering with the goods would affect the goodwill of the owner of the trade mark and undermine the identity guarantee to which the consumer is entitled. The fact that the goods have been repacked means that the identity of the repacker should also figure on the repacked goods for the information of the consumer; the owner of the trade mark should be informed of the intention to repack the goods so that it can keep an eye on the market to safeguard its goodwill and act when that is threatened. The key element in mentioning the name of the entity repack-ing the goods is that of liability. It is therefore acceptable to mention merely the name of the entity assuming responsibility and liability for the operation, even if the actual act of repackaging is carried out by another entity in the same group of companies or by a third party (Joined Cases C–400/09 *Orifarm A/S v Merck, Sharp & Dohme Corp.* and C–207/10 *Paranova Denmark A/S and Paranova Pack A/S v Merck, Sharp & Dohme Corp.* [2012] 1 CMLR 10, [2011] ETMR 59). If these conditions are met, the essential function of the trade mark is fulfilled and every exercise that goes beyond the specific subject matter of the trade mark will fall foul of Articles 34 and 36 (Case 102/77 *Hoffmann-La Roche & Co. AG v Centrafarm* [1978] ECR 1139).

The Court confirmed this approach in Case 1/81 *Pfizer Inc. v Eurim-Pharm GmbH* [1981] ECR 2913, [1982] 1 CMLR 406.

16.3.2 The Starting Point: Relabelling in *American Home Products*

It is not only repackaging that caused problems: a company could also use different trade marks for one product in different Member States. This can, of course, be done for legiti-mate reasons, because it may not be possible to register the same trade mark in certain Member States if a similar mark already exists or if the trade mark has a negative con-notation in the language of that Member State. The trade mark owner can, however, have less legitimate reasons. One trade mark per Member State effectively partitions the single market: the owner of the trade marks can operate freely in each of the national markets from a dominant position. A challenger should be entitled to use the trade mark that the owner uses in that market in order to mount an effective challenge, and the owner will try to prevent this by relying on the trade mark and by alleging infringement.

This is what happened in Case 3/78 *Centrafarm BV v American Home Products Corp.* [1978] ECR 1823 where American Home Products marketed the same drug in the UK under the trade mark 'Serenid', while using the trade mark 'Seresta' in the Benelux countries and Germany. Centrafarm bought the drug in the UK and sold it in the Netherlands, after changing the trade mark to Seresta, because Dutch consumers were familiar with this trade mark. American Home Products objected to this practice and argued that it infringed its Dutch Seresta trade mark. In this case, there was no legitimate reason to use a different trade mark in the Netherlands. For an example of a case in which there was such a legitimate reason one can refer to Case C–313/94 *Fratelli Graffione SNC v Ditta Fransa* [1996] ECR I-6039. Returning to *American Home Products*, the goodwill of American Home Products was not affected and the interests of the consumers were unharmed, safeguarding the essential function of the trade mark. The rights conferred by the trade mark were exercised to serve one function—that is, to restrict the free movement of goods and to partition the single market. Therefore this exercise of trade marks should fall foul of Articles 34 and 36, because it constitutes a disguised restriction of trade, and this was indeed what the Court decided (Case 3/78 *Centrafarm BV v American Home Products Corp.* [1978] ECR 1823). To be precise, the specific subject matter of the trade mark as a description of what is allowed was preserved, because the trade mark owner still put all products concerned on the market for the first time.

This case has been criticized, because it seemed to introduce a subjective criterion by relying on the intent of the owner of the trade marks.[3] Subsequent developments in the case law of the CJEU have shown that it never intended to introduce a subjective element: the parallel importer does not have to prove that the rights holder set out to partition the market deliberately.

We now turn to the detailed analysis of these subsequent developments, which have clarified a number of points.

16.3.3 **Article 7 of the Directive: Mere Codification?**

This, then, was the position before the harmonization of national trade mark laws. The Court's case law dealt with the apparent clash between the national trade mark laws of the Member States and Articles 34 and 36 TFEU. The First Harmonization Directive changed that picture. It dealt with exhaustion in its Article 7, which has been retained in the codified version (Directive 2008/95/EC [2008] OJ L 299/25 (the Trade Marks Directive)). On the basis of that Article, the pharmaceutical industry challenged the validity of the Court's case law.[4] The issue of whether Case 102/77 *Hoffmann-La Roche v Centrafarm* [1978] ECR

---

[3] C.H. Baden Fuller, 'Economic Issues Relating to Property Rights in Trade Marks' (1981) 6 *European Law Review* 162.

[4] The real reason why parallel imports of pharmaceutical products are such a problem in the Community—and especially in the eyes of the main pharmaceutical companies—is the difference in prices between the different Member States. This would not be such a problem if the different prices were determined entirely freely by the pharmaceutical companies that produce the drugs, but, in practice, there is also a lot of government regulation in the area. The circumvention of the absence of a harmonization in the national rules regulating the prices of pharmaceutical products and the perceived lack of political will to achieve it by breaching the rules on free movement is not, however, allowed. National trade mark law

1139 was still good law was brought before the Court as a preliminary question on the interpretation of Article 7 of the Directive after a series of cases had been brought in the national courts by pharmaceutical companies that objected to the repackaging activity of parallel importers (Joined Cases C–427, 429, and 436/93 *Bristol-Meyers Squibb, CH Boehringer Sohn, Boehringer Ingelheim KG, Boehringer Ingelheim A/S & Bayer AG, Bayer Danmark A/S v Paranova A/S* [1996] ECR I-3457, [1997] 1 CMLR 1151; Cases C–71, 72, and 73/94 *Eurim-Pharm Arzneimittel GmbH v Beiersdorf AG; Boehringer Ingelheim KG & Farmitalia Carlo Erba GmbH* [1996] ECR I-3603, [1997] 1 CMLR 1222; Case C–232/94 *MPA Pharma GmbH v Rhone-Poulenc Pharma GmbH* [1996] ECR I-3671).

The Directive grants the trade mark owner the exclusive right to affix the trade mark to the product or its packaging (Article 5(3)(a) of the Directive), subject to the impact of the exhaustion principle. That principle is said, in Article 7(1), not to 'entitle the proprietor to prohibit [the trade mark's] use in relation to goods which have been put on the market within the Community under that trade mark by the proprietor or with his consent'. Article 7(2) adds that Article 7(1) will not stop the trade mark owner from opposing the continued marketing of the goods if she does so on reasonable grounds. Obvious examples of such grounds are cases in which the goods have been impaired or altered after having been put on the market by the trade mark owner, or with her consent.

The pharmaceutical companies argued that Article 7(1) should be interpreted in such a way that the goods are the goods in the format and the unit in which they have been put on the market. This would mean, for example, 20 tablets of the pharmaceutical product in a box with certain dimensions, colours, etc. The parallel importer would be free to buy these boxes in another Member State and resell them as they are, but any repackaging and reaffixing of the trade mark would constitute an infringement of the trade mark. Article 7(2) would only operate, for example, to allow the trade mark owner to stop the marketing of damaged products. The same result is achieved if one admits that Article 7(1) results in the exhaustion of the trade mark as soon as the trade marked product has been put on the market in any form, while giving a broad interpretation to Article 7(2) by including any change of the brand presentation—that is, any form of repackaging and/or reaffixing of the trade mark—as a reasonable ground on which to exclude the operation of the exhaustion principle in Article 7(1).[5]

This would, of course, involve a radical change in the definition of the exhaustion principle and it would reverse the Court's case law. Can the Directive be interpreted in this way? Or should one stick to the interpretation that Article 7(1) results in the exhaustion of the trade mark as soon as the trade marked product has been put on the market in any form, while the only reasonable ground on the basis of which the trade mark owner can object involves a change to the product that is actually consumed—that is, the tablets in our earlier example?

16.3.4 Article 7 of the Directive: A Return to Basics

Before jumping to any conclusion, one should start with the basics. The starting point of all Community law in this area is Articles 34 and 36 TFEU. Any secondary Community legislation can only apply and not change the Treaty, and should therefore be interpreted

---

cannot be allowed to disregard Community law in this area: the purpose of trade marks is not to remedy the market distortions caused by the national price-regulating regimes; what needs to be done is to harmonize those different national regimes.

5 See K. Dyekjaer-Hansen, 'The Trade Mark Directive and the Protection of Brands and Branding' [1996] 1 *EIPR* 62.

in a way that is in line and compatible with its provisions (see Case C–47/90 *Etablissements Delhaize Frères v Promalvin* [1992] ECR I-3669 [26]; Case C–315/92 *Verband Sozialer Wettbewerb* [1994] ECR I-317 [12], referred to in Joined Cases C–427, 429, and 436/93 *Bristol-Meyers Squibb v Paranova A/S* [1996] ECR I-3457 [27]). The provisions of the Directive must thus be interpreted in the light of Articles 34 and 36 TFEU. What is not under discussion is that Article 36 only provides for a partial exemption of trade mark rights from the application of Article 34 and its free movement rule; what is exempted is the specific subject matter of the trade mark. The Court explicitly recognized that trade mark rights (within the constraints of their specific subject matter) form an essential element of the system of free competition on the single market that the Treaty set out to establish in Joined Cases C–427, 429, and 436/93 *Bristol-Meyers Squibb v Paranova A/S* [1996] ECR I-3457 [43].The trade mark can play its competition-enhancing role in the economy, but any other use is caught by Article 34.

What, then, is the essence of a trade mark? A trade mark is essentially an indication of origin. The trade mark guarantees the consumer that a certain product has been manufactured by, or under the control of, a certain company that bears responsibility for the fact that the product meets certain standards or expectations of quality. The trade mark is the means by which the product is identified. That identification by customers leads to the establishment of goodwill for the company that is able to bind the customers to itself (*Bristol-Meyers Squibb* [43], with reference to Case C–10/89 *CNL-SUCAL NV SA v HAG GF AG (Hag II)* [1990] ECR I-3711 [13] and Case C–9/93 *IHT Internationaler Heiztechnik GmbH & Danziger v Ideal Standard GmbH* [1994] ECR I-2789 [37] and [45]).

The next question that needs to be answered therefore is the origin of what is indicated by the trade mark. The obvious answer is that of the goods that are labelled with the trade mark—but this does not solve our problem if one considers that marketing experts might suggest that the whole trade dress of a carefully marketed product forms part of the goods. A return to the basic principles of trade mark law provides the solution to this problem: a trade mark is a sign to distinguish goods that is registered in relation to a certain category or certain categories of goods. This means that a trade mark is, for example, registered in relation to pharmaceutical products; no one will pretend that anything other than the product that is actually used for medicinal purposes is covered by this category.

The trade dress, meanwhile, is not part of the goods. The goods or products are, for example, the tablets, but they do not include the box in which they are packed by the manufacturer. This is the maximum coverage of trade mark law before the Treaty provisions interfere with it, which interference can only reduce the level of protection and the options offered to the trade mark owner due to the fact that Article 34 rules out restrictions to free movement and Article 36 only partially alleviates that ban. The outcome of the process cannot therefore be that trade dress is now included in the definition of the goods to which a trade mark is applied and in relation to which it creates certain exclusive rights.

Let us now turn to the Directive: it must be clear that the Directive, or any other piece of secondary Community legislation, cannot introduce quantitative restrictions if it can only apply the provisions of the Treaty. Any other conclusion would involve a violation of Articles 34 and 36—and only a new Treaty can change these Articles (see Case C-51/93 *Meyhui NV v Schott Zwiesel Glaswerke AG* [1994] ECR I-3879 [11], referred to in *Bristol-Meyers Squibb* [35]).

The final step brings us to the national trade mark laws. These must obviously be interpreted along the lines of the Directive. Because the Directive was supposed to harmonize the trade mark laws of the Member States and the protection of trade marks as allowed in the context of Article 36, one should, first of all, turn to the Directive when the compatibility of a provision of national trade mark law with Community law is at issue (see Case 5/77 *Tedeschi v Denkavit Commerciale srl* [1977] ECR 1555 [35]; Case 227/82 *Van Bennekom* [1983] ECR 3883 [35]; Case C–37/92 *Vanacker & Lesage* [1993] ECR I-4947 [9]; Case C–323/93 *Société Civile Agricole du Centre d'insémination de la Crespelle* [1994] ECR I-5077 [31]; referred to in *Bristol-Meyers Squibb* [25]). The Directive is supposed to offer more detailed rules and guidance, which is fully in line with the provisions of the Treaty.

16.3.5 Article 7 of the Directive: Practical Implications

Where does all this theory lead us in practical terms? The question of whether or not national trade mark law can allow a trade mark owner to oppose the repackaging of pharmaceutical products and/or the reaffixing of the trade mark needs to be answered on the basis of the provisions of the Directive (*Bristol-Meyers Squibb* [26]).

Article 7 deals with the exhaustion issue in a complete way. The trade mark owner can oppose the activities of the parallel importer if that Article does not exhaust his right to object to those activities. On the basis of the text of Article 7(1), it could be suggested that the term 'goods' can be said to include the goods as packed. It has been shown, however, that this would involve an unjustifiable expansion of trade mark protection and that such an interpretation of the Directive would not be in line with the Treaty provisions—which leaves us with the question of whether a change of packaging can be a reasonable ground under Article 7(2) of the Directive. If so, no exhaustion would take place. Once more, the text of the Directive does not provide a conclusive answer. We have to turn to the provisions of the Treaty (see *Bristol-Meyers Squibb* [40]) and analyse whether such a wide interpretation of the reasonable ground concept is required to guarantee that the trade mark can fulfil its essential role.

It is submitted that the CJEU rightly decided that this was not the case. The trade mark should function as an indication of origin. For the consumer, this means she needs to be sure that, when buying the trade marked product, she is buying the original pharmaceutical product—for example, the tablets—produced by the trade mark owner or under his control. No other products should be marketed under the trade mark to achieve this aim. In the cases under discussion, there was no evidence that the pharmaceutical products had been tampered with or that any product was passed off as the product of the trade mark owner. Indeed, in the one instance in which a vaporizer was added by the parallel importer (*Bristol-Meyers Squibb* [61]), that item did not bear the trade mark and it was made clear that the item had been added by, and under the sole responsibility of, the parallel importer.

The consumer should also be able to rely on the trade mark to be sure that the pharmaceutical product he buys is of a certain quality, which requirement is met as long as the original product is not tampered with. The trade mark owner should also be allowed to preserve the goodwill created by the trade mark. The indication of origin points indeed towards certain goods, of a certain quality, coming from one source, or at least with one party—the trade mark owner—controlling the system. This requirement is met as long as no other goods are labelled with the trade mark and as long as the goods are not tampered with (*Bristol-Meyers Squibb* [59]–[64]).

To guarantee this, further additional rules have been added. The packaging should clearly indicate who produced the goods, so as not to create the impression that the parallel importer or any third party has any right to the trade mark (Joined Cases C–71,

72, and 73/94 *Eurim-Pharm v Beiersdorf* [1996] ECR I-3603 [64], with reference to Case 1/81 *Pfizer v Eurim-Pharm* [1981] ECR 2913 [11]). The parallel importer responsible for the repackaging also needs to be identified clearly on the packaging, in order to show that the third party, and not the trade mark owner, is responsible for the packaging. The straightforward way to do so is to print on the new packaging in a prominent way a message that 'X' manufactured the product, while 'Y', the parallel importer, imported and repacked the product (*Bristol-Meyers Squibb* [70]). Even so, the packaging should not be of a low standard, because that association with materials of a low quality would damage the high-quality standard that is associated with pharmaceutical products (*Bristol-Meyers Squibb* [65]–[66] and [75]–[76]; see also Case C–348/04 *Boehringer Ingelheim KG and ors v Swingward Ltd and ors (No. 2)* [2007] 2 CMLR 52). The key element in mentioning the name of the entity repacking the goods is that of liability. It is therefore acceptable to mention merely the name of the entity assuming responsibility and liability for the operation, even if the actual act of repackaging is carried out by another entity in the same group of companies or by a third party (Joined Cases C–400/09 *Orifarm A/S v Merck, Sharp & Dohme Corp.* and C–207/10 *Paranova Denmark A/S and Paranova Pack A/S v Merck, Sharp & Dohme Corp.* [2012] 1 CMLR 10, [2011] ETMR 59).

The trade mark owner should also be allowed to control the use of the trade mark and to prevent any damage to the goodwill associated with the trade mark that any inappropriate use of the trade mark could cause. This means that the trade mark owner should be advised in advance of any repackaging activity and should be given the opportunity to request a sample copy of the repacked product for inspection (*Bristol-Meyers Squibb* [78]). It is the responsibility of the parallel importer to give that notice and the rights holder should at least be given 15 days in which to object (Case C–143/00 *Boehringer Ingelheim AG v Swingward Ltd* [2002] ECR I-3759).

Under these conditions, the trade mark can fulfil its role as an indication of origin. Any further requirement goes beyond that role and would therefore be out of line with Article 36 EC Treaty. A requirement, for example, that the fact that the repackaging took place without the consent of the trade mark owner should be mentioned explicitly on the packaging would create the impression that there might be something wrong with the product (*Bristol-Meyers Squibb* [72]).

16.3.6 **Article 7 of the Directive: A Mere Codification!**

Article 7(2) of the Directive is really only a way of restating the rule contained in Article 36 TFEU (*Bristol-Meyers Squibb* [40]; for an application of Article 7(2) in the context of AdWords see Case C–558/08 *Portakabin Ltd v Primakabin* [2010] ETMR 52). The interpretation that the Court had previously given to that Article in a repackaging context remains good law; all that these new cases have added is the fact that the Court seized the opportunity to clarify the rule and to provide the national court with more detailed guidance.

The parallel importer of pharmaceutical products is not free to repack them in any circumstances. Repackaging only becomes an option if the product is de facto marketed in different quantities in different Member States. The right of the trade mark owner to oppose repackaging is only exhausted if the repackaging is necessary for the product to be marketable in the country of importation, for example because health insurance legislation prescribes a standard size. This can be seen as a prerequisite for any repackaging and reaffixing of trade mark operation. The fact that the product is, apart from the size in which it is bought by the parallel importer, also available in the country of exportation in the size in which it is repacked does not alter this conclusion (see *Bristol-Meyers Squibb* [54]).

There is, however, no need for the parallel importer to prove that the trade mark owner set out to partition the market deliberately by marketing the product in different quantities in different Member States. It was therefore also held in a relabelling case that one has to assess whether all the circumstances at the time of the marketing in the import state made it objectively necessary to use another mark to make marketing possible. In the absence of such objective necessity, there will be no artificial partitioning of the market, which is required to allow relabelling. By requiring an artificial partitioning of the market to be demonstrated before allowing the repackaging of products, the Court left open only the option of opposing the marketing of parallel imported products by the trade mark owner in those cases in which this is necessary to preserve the specific subject matter of the trade mark. A de facto use of different packaging sizes is all that the parallel importer needs to demonstrate initially to justify its activity (Case C–379/97 *Pharmacia & Upjohn SA v Paranova A/S* [2000] 1 CMLR 51).

16.3.7 **Necessity**

This set of cases could create the false impression that the parallel importer has an almost absolute freedom to repack and relabel the products. The analysis has shown that this is not the case, and that the parallel importer's activity is restricted to what is required and necessary to allow parallel imports.

The necessity point has become a vital one. The CJEU summarized it as follows:

> a trade mark proprietor may rely on its trade mark rights in order to prevent a parallel importer from repackaging pharmaceutical products unless the exercise of those rights contributes to artificial partitioning of the markets between Member States.[6]

It continued, vitally, to state that:

> replacement packaging of pharmaceutical products is objectively necessary within the meaning of the Court's case-law if, without such repackaging, effective access to the market concerned, or to a substantial part of that market, must be considered to be hindered as the result of strong resistance from a significant proportion of consumers to re-labelled pharmaceutical products.[7]

It is therefore clear that the necessity test applies to the act of repackaging, but the question whether it also applies to the presentation of the repackaged product—that is, should the parallel importer also show that it had done nothing more than what was necessary in the terms of the manner of repackaging?—needed to be answered. How broad exactly is the concept of necessity?

The Court clarified the point by holding that the condition that the repackaging of the pharmaceutical product—either by re-boxing the product and reapplying the trade mark, or by applying a label to the packaging containing the product—be necessary for its further commercialization in the importing Member State is directed solely at the fact of repackaging, and not at the manner and style of the repackaging. There is therefore no need to show that a particular manner and style of repackaging or relabelling were required (Case C–348/04 *Boehringer Ingelheim KG and ors v Swingward Ltd and*

---

[6] Case C–143/00 *Boehringer Ingelheim AG v Swingward Ltd* [2002] ECR I-3759.
[7] Case C–443/99 *Merck, Sharp & Dohme GmbH v Paranova Pharmazeutika Handels GmbH* [2003] Ch 327, [2002] ETMR 923.

ors (No. 2) [2007] 2 CMLR 52 and Case C–276/05 *Wellcome Foundation Ltd v Paranova Pharmazeutika Handels GmbH* [2009] ETMR 20). The style of repackaging and the exact presentation that results from it are not therefore to be assessed against the condition of necessity and a minimum change only requirement is to be ruled out, but the condition that the presentation should not be liable to damage the reputation of the trade mark or its proprietor remains applicable (Case C–276/05 *Wellcome Foundation Ltd v Paranova Pharmazeutika Handels GmbH* [2009] ETMR 20).

Case C–349/95 *Frits Loendersloot v George Ballantine & Son Ltd* [1997] ECR I-6227, [1998] 1 CMLR 1015 also illustrates the necessity point. The parallel importer was given a certain freedom to bring the labelling of the bottles of whisky in line with the requirements of each Member State and to identify itself, but the Court did not approve of the removal of the identification numbers from the bottles. The latter was not required to allow parallel import to take place. It has been held, along the same lines, by Belgian courts that trade mark law allowed the trade mark owner to oppose acts of the parallel importer such as deletion of bar codes, deletion of the mention that the product can only be sold through recommended distributors, and cutting the seal on boxes of perfume. It was held that these measures were not necessary to allow parallel import and that less invasive measures that did not affect the goodwill of the trade mark owner (e.g. mention on the shop window or shelves that, despite the impression created by the products, the parallel importer is not a recommended distributor) would have been sufficient. The cutting of the seals specifically could create the impression or the suspicion that the bottle in the box had been tampered with or had been replaced and this could seriously affect the goodwill of the trade mark owner (*Delhaize v Dior*, Court of Appeal Liège, 13 April 1995, [1995] Ing-Cons 379; *SA Parfums Nina Ricci v SA Best Sellers Belgium*, Commercial Court Liège, 18 October 1999, [2000] TBH 386).

Obviously, the presence of these numbers would also allow the producer of the whisky to trace the suppliers of the parallel importer. The Court argued that competition law would provide a remedy if the producer decided to take action against the supplier of the parallel importer in an attempt to stop the parallel importation. This is, however, not necessarily a straightforward conclusion and the decision of the General Court to annul a Commission decision on this point is a stark reminder of the difficulties of applying competition law successfully on this point (Case T–41/96 *Bayer AG and EFPIA v Commission & Bundesverband der Arneimittel-Importeure eV* [2000] ECR II-3383, [2001] All ER (EC) 1, [2001] 4 CMLR 4; upheld by the CJEU on appeal (Cases C–2/01 P and C–3/01P [2004] 4 CMLR 13)).

16.3.8 **Marketing Authorization**

It should also not be forgotten that the marketing of pharmaceutical products is subject to a marketing authorization and that the parallel import licence of the parallel importer makes reference to the marketing authorization of the original product. Deliberately revoking the marketing authorization for the original product when bringing a newer version of the product on the market might therefore be a means for the producer to block parallel imports of the original product. The CJEU held therefore that Articles 28 and 30 EC Treaty (now Articles 34 and 36 TFEU) preclude national legislation under which the withdrawal, at the request of its holder, of the marketing authorization of reference automatically entails the withdrawal of the parallel import licence granted for the medicinal product in question. Restrictions on parallel imports of products are only allowed in such cases if there is, in fact, a risk to human health as a result of the continued existence of that medicinal product on the market of the importing Member State (Cases C–15/01 *Paranova v Läkemedelsverket* [2003] 2 CMLR 856; C–175/00 *Ferring Arzneimittel GmbH v Eurim-Pharm Arzneimittel GmbH* [2002] ECR I-6891).

16.3.9 Article 7 and Licence Agreements

A somewhat peculiar set of facts arises when the trade mark proprietor enters into an agreement with a seller that includes a clause stipulating that the latter shall not sell to discount stores with the consent of the proprietor. What happens if the seller neverthe-less does so? Can the third party rely on exhaustion? The CJEU argued that the seller who breaches the agreement must be held to have acted without the consent of the proprietor. The breach must refer to the essential clauses and aspects of the trade mark that are found in Article 8(2) of the Directive. The Court accepted that in the case of luxury goods that quality not only resulted from the material characteristics of the goods, but also from the allure and the prestigious image conferred by the aura of luxury. The outlets in which they were sold were part of this picture. And in cases where the seller must be considered to have sold to the discount stores with consent, the proprietor may nevertheless rely on Article 7(2) to avoid exhaustion on the condition that the sale damages the reputation of the trade mark. The Court accepted in this case that impairing the aura of luxury effec-tively affected the actual quality of the goods. Hence the need to be able to rely on Article 7 to stop exhaustion. This is a far-reaching interpretation though which uses Article 7 in a wide sense (Case C–59/08 *Copad SA v Christian Dior Couture SA* [2009] ECR I-3421, [2009] ETMR 40).

16.3.10 A Summary

The second *Boehringer Ingelheim v Swingward* case (Case C–348/04 *Boehringer Ingelheim KG and ors v Swingward Ltd and ors (No. 2)* [2007] ECR I-3391, [2007] 2 CMLR 52) gave the CJEU the opportunity to summarize the position on parallel imports of trade marked goods. The Court highlighted the following key points. The trade mark owner may legiti-mately oppose further commercialization of a pharmaceutical product imported from another Member State in its original internal and external packaging with an additional external label (over-sticker) applied by the importer, unless:

- it is established that reliance on trade mark rights by the proprietor in order to oppose the marketing of the over-stickered product under that trade mark would contribute to the artificial partitioning of the markets between Member States;

- the repackaging of the pharmaceutical product—either by re-boxing the product and reapplying the trade mark, or by applying a label to the packaging contain-ing the product—is necessary for its further commercialization in the importing Member State, albeit that this condition is directed solely at the fact of repackaging, and not at the manner and style of the repackaging;

- it is shown that the new label cannot affect the original condition of the product inside the packaging;

- the packaging clearly states who over-stickered the product and the name of the manufacturer;

- the presentation of the over-stickered product is not likely to damage the reputation of the trade mark and of its proprietor—that is, the label must not be defective, of poor quality, or untidy;

- the importer gives notice to the trade mark proprietor before the over-stickered product is put on sale and, on demand, supplies the proprietor with a specimen of that product;

- the presentation of the pharmaceutical product after repackaging or relabelling is not such as to be liable to damage the reputation of the trade mark and of its proprietor. This condition is not limited to cases in which the repackaging is defective, of poor quality, or untidy. The standard usually applied in the trade is to be adhered to.

The question whether the fact that a parallel importer responsible for any of the following is likely to damage the trade mark's reputation is a question of fact for the national court to decide in the light of the circumstances of each case:

- failure to affix the trade mark to the new exterior carton—that is, 'de-branding';

- application of either his own logo, house style, get-up, or a get-up used for a number of different products—that is, 'co-branding';

- positioning of the additional label so as wholly or partially to obscure the proprietor's trade mark;

- failure to state on the additional label that the trade mark in question belongs to the proprietor;

- printing of the name of the parallel importer in capital letters.

In terms of burden of proof, it is for the parallel importer to prove the existence of the conditions that:

- reliance on trade mark rights by the proprietor in order to oppose the marketing of repackaged products under that trade mark would contribute to the artificial partitioning of the markets between Member States;

- the repackaging cannot affect the original condition of the product inside the packaging;

- the new packaging clearly states who repackaged the product and the name of the manufacturer;

- the presentation of the repackaged product is not such as to be liable to damage the reputation of the trade mark and of its proprietor;

- he has given notice to the trade mark proprietor before the repackaged product is put on sale and, on demand, supplied him or her with a specimen of the repackaged product. If a parallel importer has failed to give prior notice to the trade mark proprietor concerning a repackaged pharmaceutical product, he infringes that proprietor's rights on the occasion of any subsequent importation of that product, as long as he has not given the proprietor such notice.

As regards the condition that it must be shown that the repackaging cannot affect the original condition of the product inside the packaging, it is sufficient, however, that the parallel importer furnishes evidence that leads to the reasonable presumption that the condition has been fulfilled. This applies *a fortiori* also to the condition that the presentation of the repackaged product must not be such as to be liable to damage the reputation of the trade mark and of its proprietor. If the importer furnishes such initial evidence that the latter condition has been fulfilled, it will then be for the proprietor of the trade mark, who is best placed to assess whether the repackaging is liable to damage her reputation and that of the trade mark, to prove that they have been so damaged (*Boehringer Ingelheim KG and ors*).

16.4 Exhaustion Without Parallel Import

Most exhaustion cases involve an element of parallel importation, but that is not necessarily the case. Article 7(1) of the Directive does not require parallel importation. A good example is found in the *Viking Gas* case. Bottled gas was put on the market in design bottles, rather than in the standard ones. These design bottles were later refilled by an independent trader. The bottles were unchanged and still sported the original trade mark and the refilling company added its own identification as re-filler by means of a large sticker. The CJEU held that the re-filler was not liable for trade mark infringement, as the first sale of the design bottle had exhausted the trade mark. The Court rejected the argument that the bottle was mere packaging and that as a result exhaustion only applied to the resale of the original bottle filled with the original gas. The design bottle had its own economic value, reflected in a higher price than the standard one, which had been realized when it was first sold. The refilling operation did not therefore in the circumstances fall foul of Article 7(2) of the Directive either. The bottle still carried the original trade mark and was in its original condition, whilst the re-filler clearly identified itself as such and took responsibility for the new gas in the bottle and for the refilling activity. Exhaustion therefore applied (Case C–46/10 *Viking Gas A/S v Kosan Gas A/S* [2011] ETMR 58).

16.5 Exhaustion Covers Publicity

Parallel importation can only work in practice if the parallel importer can sell the goods successfully. This requires that he can advertise the fact that the original product is now also available through his outlets and that his prices are lower. Can the parallel importer reproduce the trade mark for the purposes of this advertising?

The answer to this question can only be affirmative if the exhaustion of the trade mark by putting it on the market in the Member State from which it was imported by the parallel importer also covered the trade mark's reproduction for advertising purposes. This should indeed be the case, because normal advertising practices will not damage the goodwill of the trade mark owner, if they only inform the public about the availability of the product. The consumer is not misled either, because the original product is advertised, rather than any similar product. The advertising does not normally create the impression that the parallel importer manufactures the product; on the contrary, the importer will try to emphasize she is selling the 'real thing'—that is, the original product, from the original producer—but only at a lower price. That is her best strategy by which to maximize sales. This means that the essential function of the trade mark is fulfilled and that there is no need to allow the trade mark owner to use her trade mark to stop the advertising, because the goods concerned have been marketed with her consent.

The CJEU approved this approach in Case C–337/95 *Parfums Christian Dior SA & Parfums Christian Dior BV v Evora BV* [1997] ECR I-6013, when it stopped Dior from relying on its trade marks to stop the parallel importer from advertising its goods by reproducing in its publicity the boxes in which the perfumes were sold. These boxes obviously carried the trade marks. The advertising took place in the format that was normally used by the parallel importer and others in the same type of trade. Dior argued that the form of advertising did not meet its high standards and could therefore affect the reputation of its trade marks in a negative way. The Court ruled that any form of advertising in the way and quality in which the parallel importer normally advertised its goods could not damage the goodwill of Dior.

The Court expressed this ruling as follows:

> The proprietor of a trade mark may not rely on Article 7(2) of Directive 89/104 to oppose the use of the trade mark, by a reseller who habitually markets articles of the same kind, but not necessarily of the same quality, as the trade-marked goods, in ways customary in the reseller's sector of trade, for the purpose of bringing to the public's attention the further commercialisation of those goods, unless it is established that, given the specific circumstances of the case, the use of the trade mark for this purpose seriously damages the reputation of the trade mark.[8]

The only reason why Dior could stop the use of its trade marks was the fact that its goodwill would be affected. This had to be demonstrated on the basis of the facts of the case. Advertising of a very low and sloppy quality, far below the normal standards of the type of business concerned, could be an example of such an exceptional case. In that case, the essential function of the trade mark could no longer be fulfilled, which justifies the use of the trade mark to stop such a practice.

16.6 International Exhaustion

16.6.1 The Concept of International Exhaustion

The EEA Agreement expanded the area in which exhaustion applies to the whole of the EEA, which means that, apart from the EU, it applies to Iceland, Liechtenstein, and Norway [1994] OJ L 1/3. Until recently, however, it was unclear whether or not the EU would opt for the principle of international exhaustion.

In very simple terms, 'international exhaustion' means that all trade mark rights are exhausted once the product labelled with the trade mark has been put on the market anywhere in the world by, or with the consent of, the trade mark owner. Trade mark owners in the EU would no longer be able to stop parallel importation of their products from outside the EEA by relying on their parallel trade marks in the Member States if the principle of international exhaustion were to apply.

Traditionally, certain Member States—such as Austria—had incorporated the principle of international exhaustion into their domestic trade mark system, but, recently, the majority of the Member States and the Commission seemed to have abandoned the principle of international exhaustion. One could take a cynical view and argue that this was a symptom of the 'Fortress Europe' mentality and that they only wanted to protect themselves from cheap imports. The crucial issue was whether or not the Trade Marks Directive had decided the issue.

Article 7 of the Directive deals with the issue of exhaustion and refers to goods that have been put on the market in the EEA. It is clear that this provision does not oblige the Member States to operate an international exhaustion rule. Insofar as it imposes a system of exhaustion, the provision restricts its scope to the EEA. Two conclusions seemed possible on this basis: first, it could be left to the Member States to decide whether or not they wanted to adopt an international exhaustion rule, which argument sees Article 7 as the minimum, but a minimum to which additions can be made; second, one could argue that Article 7 is a restriction on the rights of trade mark owners and that the Directive does not

---

[8] *Parfums Christian Dior.*

allow the Member States to add the further restrictions that an international exhaustion rule would necessarily carry with it.

16.6.2 *Silhouette*

The *Silhouette* case (Case C–355/96 *Silhouette International Schmied GmbH & Co. KG v Hartlauer Handelsgesellschaft mbH* [1998] ECR I-4799, [1998] 2 CMLR 953) gave the CJEU the opportunity to decide the issue. Silhouette had sold a large number of its spectacle frames in Bulgaria and these had been reimported into the EEA by Hartlauer, a parallel importer, for sale in the latter's outlets in Austria. Silhouette sued for infringement of its Austrian trade mark and the Austrian court asked the Court whether it could still operate an international exhaustion rule.

The Court argued that the Trade Marks Directive set out to harmonize fully all those elements of trade mark law that may distort competition within, and the functioning in general of, the common market. The Court derives, from this starting point, the rule that 'Article 5 to 7 of the Directive must be construed as embodying a complete harmonization of the rules relating to the rights conferred by a trade mark' (*Silhouette* [25]) and that Member States can add only those rules that are included as optional provisions in this Article. Any other additions would destroy the aim of the Directive. Member States are therefore no longer free to operate a rule of international exhaustion, because such a rule was not included in the Directive as an option. The Court effectively declared international exhaustion dead under the existing legislation and it confirmed that position in Case C–173/98 *Sebago & Maison Dubois* [1999] ECR I-4103.

16.6.3 **Evaluation**

This decision is, however, highly political and regrettable. There is nothing in the essential function of a trade mark that can justify the fact that exhaustion needs to stop at the borders of the EEA; on the contrary, the logic of the system is that the system of exhaustion should operate on all occasions when the original product is concerned and when that product has been marketed by, or with the consent of, the trade mark owner, irrespective of the place of first marketing. Exhaustion should only be put aside in exceptional cases, for example if the product has been tampered with or if the quality of the parallel imported product is inferior to the product marketed under the same name by the original producer in the area into which parallel importation takes place. In those examples, the operation of the exhaustion rule would impinge on the goodwill of the producer and the interests of consumers would be harmed. The essential function of the trade mark would be affected in these exceptional cases.

It is submitted that neither does the Directive rule out this radically different conclusion: the full harmonization in Article 7 could be restricted to the operation of an EEA-wide exhaustion rule. All points that have not been decided by what is, after all, called a 'First' Harmonization Directive should be left to the discretion of the Member States. Any such state would then be free to introduce an international exhaustion rule—and, arguably, any use of a trade mark to block parallel importation under the laws of a Member State that had opted against international exhaustion would amount to an abusive use of the rights granted by a trade mark, because it would obstruct the operation of the common market.

Alternatively, the free circulation of the parallel imported goods that were first marketed outside the EEA could be restricted to the Member State under the international exhaustion rule of which their importation took place, because they were not put on the market in the EEA by, or with the consent of, the trade mark owner. In either case, this solution would have fitted in much better with the current climate of worldwide free trade and the expectation for the latter that was created by the WTO Agreement signed in Marrakesh.

One can also look at the *Silhouette* case from another angle. If one separates the requirement of consent from the determination of the geographical scope one can argue that Article 7 is merely concerned with the geographical scope of European exhaustion. Consent is then a separate requirement that can refer to marketing anywhere in the world with the consent of the rights holder. International exhaustion could then be based outside the scope of European law and would be based on first marketing with consent. The main mistake in the CJEU's approach would then be to conflate both requirements and to try and construe international exhaustion inside EU law.

16.6.4 *Davidoff* to No Avail

The CJEU was yet again given an opportunity to reconsider its approach to the issue of international exhaustion when requests for a preliminary ruling were forwarded to the Court by the courts in the UK. Laddie J had ruled, in the *Davidoff* case (*Zino Davidoff SA v A&G Imports Ltd (No. 1)* [2000] Ch 127, [1999] 3 All ER 711), that contract law had a role to play in this area and that, as a result, goods that had been put on the market outside the EEA with the consent of the trade mark owner could be parallel imported into the EEA if the trade mark owner had not used his right to include a reservation of title in the contract and to prohibit certain forms of re-exportation. In the absence of effective constraints, UK contract law allowed the conclusion that the trade mark owner had impliedly consented to the goods being re-exported and parallel imported into the EEA. It was argued that this approach could be adopted in parallel with the Court's ruling in *Silhouette* and that the latter remained unaffected.

The Court rejected this approach and ruled that the consent of a trade mark proprietor to the marketing within the EEA of products bearing that mark that have previously been placed on the market outside the EEA by that proprietor, or with her consent, may be implied—if that implied consent follows from facts and circumstances prior to, simultaneous with, or subsequent to the placing of the goods on the market outside the EEA that, in the view of the national court, unequivocally demonstrates that the proprietor has renounced her right to oppose placing of the goods on the market within the EEA (Joined Cases C–414/99 *Zino Davidoff SA v A&G Imports Ltd*; C–415/99 *Levi Straus & Co. v Tesco plc*; and C–416/99 *Levi Strauss & Co. v Costco Wholesale UK Ltd* [2001] ECR I-1891, [2002] RPC 403, 414).

The need to demonstrate unequivocally that the rights holder renounces his right to oppose marketing of the goods in the EEA had already slammed the brakes on Laddie J's approach, but the Court went on to really shut the door almost entirely when it added that:

Implied consent cannot be inferred:

- from the fact that the proprietor of the trade mark has not communicated to all subsequent purchasers of the goods placed on the market outside the European Economic Area his opposition to marketing within the European Economic Area;

- from the fact that the goods carry no warning of a prohibition of their being placed on the market within the European Economic Area;

- from the fact that the trade mark proprietor has transferred the ownership of the products bearing the trade mark without imposing any contractual reservations and that, according to the law governing the contract, the property right transferred includes, in the absence of such reservations, an unlimited right of resale or, at the very least, a right to market the goods subsequently within the European Economic Area.[9]

Ignorance on the side of the importer or failure by authorized retailers to reimpose the restrictions imposed originally by the rights holder have also been excluded as grounds that could allow the parallel importation. The Court held in this respect that:

With regard to exhaustion of the trade mark proprietor's exclusive right, it is not relevant:

- that the importer of goods bearing the trade mark is not aware that the proprietor objects to their being placed on the market in the European Economic Area or sold there by traders other than authorised retailers;

- or that the authorized retailers and wholesalers have not imposed on their own purchasers contractual reservations setting out such opposition, even though they have been informed of it by the trade mark proprietor.[10]

This amounts to a very stringent approach that effectively blocks the door to parallel importation based on international exhaustion. The Court has squarely put the ball back in the camp of the legislator, but the latter is, at present, unable to reach any kind of agreement on this point.

The only slight comfort for the parallel importer in this context is to be derived from the fact that, where they would normally have to prove that they acquired the goods from a source that allows them to rely on Community exhaustion, they can argue that revealing their sources would bring with it a real risk of partitioning the market. This would, for example, be the case if the rights holder were to use an exclusive distribution system. The burden of proof then shifts to the rights holder, who should demonstrate that the goods were originally marketed outside the EU. Proof of that point would require the parallel importer to prove the consent of the rights holder to subsequent marketing of the goods in the EEA. Small as it may be, this is a welcome concession to the parallel importer, because revealing its sources may well get it off the hook, but it would, at the same time, make sure that the sources dried up quickly afterwards (Case C–244/00 *Van Doren+Q. GmbH v Lifestyle sports + sportswear Handelsgesellschaft mbH & Michael Orth* [2003] ECR I-3051).

16.7 **The Real Context**

Although the impression might be created that the interference of the Court and of European law in relation to trade marks is enormous, this is not correct and the whole issue must be seen in its real context. Generally, the grant of trade marks and the right to take action against infringement are national (harmonized) competences. The Court will only interfere when these provisions are applied in a discriminatory manner.[11]

This was emphasized in Case C–317/91 *AG Deutsche Renault v Audi AG* [1993] ECR I-6227, [1995] 1 CMLR 461, in which the Court verified whether the German requirements for trade mark protection were equally applied to trade marks of national and foreign origin, while leaving it to the German courts to decide whether, under German trade mark law, the use of the name 'Quadra' by Renault created confusion with Audi's 'Quattro' trade mark. The Court merely focuses on the abusive exercise of trade mark rights.

---

[9] *Davidoff and Strauss* 416.   [10] Ibid 417.
[11] See G. Würtenberger, 'Determination of Risk of Confusion in Trade Mark Infringement Proceedings in the European Union: The *Quattro* Decision' [1994] 7 *EIPR* 302.

16.8 Conclusions

Trade mark law has a substantial interaction with the Treaty provisions on the free movement of goods. Parallel importation has given rise to a constant supply of challenging cases and heated debate. That debate focuses essentially on the relabelling and repackaging of parallel-traded goods. In Case C–348/04 *Boehringer Ingelheim v Swingward* [2007] ECR I-3391, [2007] 2 CMLR 1445, 1488–90, the CJEU summarized the main points as follows.

The trade mark owner may legitimately oppose further commercialization of a pharmaceutical product imported from another Member State in its original internal and external packaging with an additional external label applied by the importer, unless:

- it is established that reliance on trade mark rights by the proprietor in order to oppose the marketing of the over-stickered product under that trade mark would contribute to the artificial partitioning of the markets between Member States;

- the repackaging of the pharmaceutical product, either by re-boxing the product and reapplying the trade mark or by applying a label to the packaging containing the product, is necessary for its further commercialization in the importing Member State, albeit that this condition is directed solely at the fact of repackaging and not at the manner and style of the repackaging;

- it is shown that the new label cannot affect the original condition of the product inside the packaging;

- the packaging clearly states who over-stickered the product and the name of the manufacturer;

- the presentation of the over-stickered product is not such as to be liable to damage the reputation of the trade mark and of its proprietor; thus, the label must not be defective, of poor quality, or untidy;

- the importer gives notice to the trade mark proprietor before the over-stickered product is put on sale, and, on demand, supplies him or her with a specimen of that product;

- the presentation of the pharmaceutical product after repackaging or relabelling cannot be such as to be liable to damage the reputation of the trade mark and of its proprietor. This condition is not limited to cases where the repackaging is defective, of poor quality, or untidy. The standard usually applied in the trade is to be adhered to.

The EU does however limit exhaustion to the EEA sphere, and international exhaustion has been ruled out.

Further Reading

DYRBERG, P., 'For EEA Exhaustion to Apply, Who Has to Prove the Marketing of the Trade Marked Goods: The Trade Mark Owner or the Defendant?' [2004] *EIPR* 81

MURPHY, G., 'Who's Wearing the Sunglasses Now?' (2000) 21 *European Competition Law Review* 1

STAMATOUDI, I., 'From Drugs to Spirits and from Boxes to Publicity: Decided and Undecided Issues in Relation to Trade Mark and Copyright Exhaustion' [1999] *IPQ* 95

STAMATOUDI, I. AND TORREMANS, P., 'International Exhaustion in the European Union in the Light of *Zino Davidoff*: Contract Versus Trade Mark Law?' (2000) 31 *IIC* 123

STOTHERS, C., 'Political Exhaustion: The EU Commission's Working Paper on Possible Abuses of Trade Mark Rights within the EU in the Context of Community Exhaustion' [2003] *EIPR* 457

17

Unfair Competition Law

17.1 Introduction

Trade marks with a reputation can be infringed if an identical or similar sign is used in a way that takes unfair advantage of the mark and its reputation. Here the concept of unfairness and unfair competition by taking advantage (in an unfair way) appears in the narrow context of trade mark law and trade mark infringement. That concept does however also play a broader role in IP law in the context of unfair competition law. And that will be the topic of this chapter.

A market economy does not merely allow competition. It positively encourages competition between industrial and commercial actors. Suffice it to refer to the example of trade mark law. Trade marks as signs that allow producers of identical goods or services to distinguish their goods or services from those of other competitors enable competition between the various producers of those identical goods or services. The trade mark is then a pro-competitive tool to say to the consumer 'buy my product or service, rather than the identical product or service from my competitor'. But as competitors are out to win, they may sometimes be tempted to use malicious means to gain an unfair advantage, such as making a direct attack against a competitor or misleading the public to the detriment of a competitor. There are, in other words, fair means of competition, for example price, quality, and special characteristics, and there are unfair means of competition. Whilst a free market economy needs the former, the latter can have a negative impact and needs to be regulated.

Regulation does not necessarily means legislative intervention, especially in a broad field such as unfair competition. Self-regulation, via associations of organizations, can play an important role. Businesses as a group have an interest in fair competition and keeping unfair competitive practices by a few (rogue) individual competitors in check. Self-regulation can then assist by controlling practices if the association or organization has a certain regulatory power or by setting up a code of conduct. However, self-regulatory efforts often fail to be respected by participants. It is often also unable to cover the whole potential spectrum of unfair competition and judicial authorities are not necessarily always prepared to back up self-regulatory efforts.

This is where unfair competition law fits in. Unfair competition law is concerned with fair play in commerce. It normally acts in tandem with its more powerful, but much more narrowly focused, counterpart competition law. Together they are generally regarded as necessary in order to steer competition along an orderly course. And they thereby contribute to promoting an efficient market system that serves the interests of all participants.

17.2 Diversity at National Level

Despite all the differences, national laws in Europe tend to be based on common concepts of copyright law, patent law, and trade mark law. The situation is very different in relation to unfair competition law. There is no set of common concepts. Suffice it to illustrate the diversity on the basis of the fact that in the absence of a right most civil law countries have fitted unfair competition in with tort law and created in the process a tort of unfair competition. In common law there is no tort of unfair competition. There is merely a much more narrowly construed and focused tort of passing-off. Admittedly, the latter has been interpreted widely in recent years and now covers a range of unfair competition issues. The significance of unfair competition law also varies from one country to another. Whereas in some countries, such as Germany, it is seen as one of the most effective commercial laws, in other countries, such as the UK, it leads rather a shadowy existence.

What, then, against that background of diversity, is unfair competition? A broad concept that is accepted and shared by most legal systems is that of honest commercial practices. Unfair competition can then be defined by contrasting it with this concept and that results in any act or practice carried out in the course of industrial or commercial activities contrary to honest practices constituting an act of unfair competition. In Belgium and Luxembourg honest practices are sometimes referred to as 'honest trade practices', in Switzerland and Spain as 'the principle of good faith', and in Italy as 'professional correctness'.

The more one moves towards the detail of the definition, the more difficult matters therefore become. Diversity takes over once more and it is not easy to find a clear-cut and globally accepted definition of what constitutes an act contrary to honest practices. Standards of 'honesty' and 'fairness' tend to differ from country to country to reflect the economic, sociological, and moral concepts of a given society. British judges disagreed, for example, very strongly with the CJEU finding that Bellure engaged in unfair practices by copying L'Oréal's perfumes and riding on the coat-tails of their publicity campaign. They saw the practice as a normal trade practice, making money by selling to clients that could not afford the original perfume or that did not want to spend the money on it (Case C–487/07 *L'Oréal SA v Bellure NV* [2009] ETMR 55). Therefore, the notion of 'honesty' has to be interpreted by the judicial bodies of the country concerned. Conceptions of honest practices established by international trade should also be taken into consideration, especially in cases of competition between organizations in different countries.

Despite that diversity, when it comes to defining honesty and fairness in detail, the concept of 'an act contrary to' can be defined widely. It can also be held to include an omission to act. The WIPO Model Provisions on Protection Against Unfair Competition show this quite clearly when they define the 'failure to correct or supplement information concerning a product test published in a consumer magazine, thereby giving a wrong impression of the quality of the product offered on the market, or failure to give sufficient information concerning the correct operation of a product or concerning possible side-effects of a product', as an act of unfair competition.

The same model provisions also propose that a failure to comply with honest practices should arise 'in the course of industrial or commercial activities'. But this is really merely saying that the issue arises in a competitive market context and this can therefore be broadly understood as being activities of organizations providing goods or services. In other words, not only trading companies selling or buying products or services are included, but also professional and therefore commercial activities of professionals such as medical doctors or lawyers.

The roots of the law of unfair competition are found in the regulation of the market, i.e. in the need to protect an honest business person against the unfair practices of his less scrupulous counterparts. Hence also the link with and operation in tandem with competition law. But the law of unfair competition has evolved from there and the consumer and the need to protect the consumer against unfair trading practices have entered the picture, in tandem with the evolution of trade. Having moved away from what one would call now a strict business-to-business model to include also the business-to-consumer model it is fair to say that nowadays laws against unfair competition aim to ensure fair competition in the interests of all concerned.

17.3 International Treaties and the Link with IP

At the Brussels Diplomatic Conference for the Revision of the Paris Convention in 1900, Article 10*bis* was added to the Convention to try and prevent unfair competition. This insertion also brought the law of unfair competition within the traditional ambit of IP law.

Article 10*bis* reads as follows:

(1) The countries of the Union are bound to assure to nationals of such countries effective protection against unfair competition.

(2) Any act of competition contrary to honest practices in industrial or commercial matters constitutes an act of unfair competition.

(3) The following in particular shall be prohibited:

   (i)   all acts of such a nature as to create confusion by any means whatever with the establishment, the goods, or the industrial or commercial activities, of a competitor;

   (ii) false allegations in the course of trade of such a nature as to discredit the establishment, the goods, or the industrial or commercial activities, of a competitor;

   (iii) indications or allegations the use of which in the course of trade is liable to mislead the public as to the nature, the manufacturing process, the characteristics, the suitability for their purpose, or the quantity, of the goods.

The Paris Convention, with which Article 2 TRIPS Agreement requires all WTO Member States to comply, therefore imposes a general obligation to offer protection against unfair competition and it does so on the basis of the broad concept of honest practices in industrial or commercial matters. It does however offer a bit more detail and classifies three types of behaviour as unfair competition. The first type of behaviour revolves around acts that cause confusion. An act or practice, in the course of industrial or commercial activities, that causes, or is likely to cause, confusion with respect to another's enterprise or its activities, in particular the products or services offered by such an enterprise, constitutes an act of unfair competition. The inclusion of the likelihood of confusion strengthens this provision enormously.

Acts damaging goodwill or reputation are a second type of act of unfair competition. By reducing the distinctive character, appearance, value, or reputation attached to a product one could damage another's goodwill or reputation. Other acts that could be classified as causing unfair competition include discrediting another's enterprise or its activities, industrial or commercial espionage, and acting unfairly with respect to confidential information such as breach of contract or breach of confidence.

And then third, there are misleading acts. These can create a false impression of a competitor's product or services leading to the consumer, acting on false information, suffering financial damage. Misleading acts can take the form of a statement giving incorrect indications or allegations about an enterprise or its products or services. For example, misleading statements concerning the manufacturing process of a product may relate to a product's safety and create a false impression.

17.4 **EU Unfair Competition Law**

All in all, Article 10*bis* is a broad provision that leaves a great deal of freedom to national legislators. The link with IP is firmly established and one can clearly see a lot of trade mark-related scenarios that would fit in with each of the types of behaviour covered by Article 10*bis*. With that we turn to the EU level. There is no single EU instrument that deals with unfair competition law as a whole. But there is a significant level of EU legislative intervention in relation to advertising and in relation to unfair business-to-consumer commercial practices. In the limited space available in this chapter we will now look in a bit more detail at each of these. Schematically they can be summarized as shown in Figure 17.1.

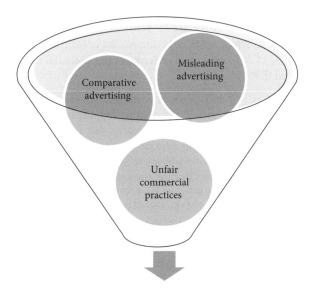

A comprehensive approach?

Figure 17.1 EU unfair competition law

17.4.1 **Comparative and Misleading Advertising**

The context of comparative and misleading advertising is predominantly one of business-to-business. As an appendix to the modernization of trade mark law over recent decades we have seen a liberalization of the approach to comparative advertising—that is, the practice of promoting one's own product with reference to its rivals and the alleged lack of quality in their goods—in the EU. The primary objective is to allow comparative advertising and as a minimum to allow the use of a mark by anyone to take place without there being an infringement if the use is to identify any goods or services as being those of the proprietor of the mark. So the use, as in the old English News Group case (*News Group Ltd v Mirror Group Ltd* [1989] FSR 126), of a rival paper's logo so as to emphasize the difference between the papers would now seem, as such, to be legitimate. But one often also sees the emergence of a proviso that is all but unfamiliar in an unfair competition context and according to which such use will continue to be an infringement if it is not 'in accordance with honest practices in industrial or commercial matters'.

The EU has taken an interest in the issue of comparative advertising in an attempt to harmonize the approach taken to it EU-wide. The specialist EU Directive (Parliament and Council Directive 2006/114/EC concerning misleading and comparative advertising [2006] OJ L 376/21 (the Comparative Advertising Directive)) accepts the principle that comparative advertising should be allowed in principle. It defines comparative advertising as 'any advertising which explicitly or by implication identifies a competitor or goods or services offered by a competitor' (Article 2(c)).

As this definition already indicates, the European approach is wider in scope than only the use of a competitor's trade mark: for example, the use of an equipment manufacturer's identification numbers by a producer of alternative toner cartridges for the manufacturer's equipment in a catalogue of products can be a form of comparative advertising that objectively compares one or more material, relevant, verifiable, and representative features of the goods, and can thus be a permissible form of comparative advertising under the Directive's rules (Case C–112/99 *Toshiba Europe GmbH v Katun Germany GmbH* [2001] ECR I-7945; see also Case C–44/01 *Pippig Augenoptik GmbH & Co. KG v Hartlauer Handelsgesellschaft mbH & Verlassenschaft Nach Dem Verstorbenen Franz Josef Hartlauer* [2003] ECR I-3095). And in terms of the potential to take unfair advantage, the CJEU added that:

> where product numbers…of an equipment manufacturer are, as such, distinguishing marks…their use in the catalogues of a competing supplier enables him to take unfair advantage of the reputation attached to those marks only if the effect of the reference to them is to create, in the mind of the persons at whom the advertising is directed, an association between the manufacturer whose products are identified and the competing supplier, in that those persons associate the reputation of the manufacturer's products with the products of the competing supplier. In order to determine whether that condition is satisfied, account should be taken of the overall presentation of the advertising at issue and the type of persons for whom the advertising is intended.[1]

The Directive lays down the conditions under which comparative advertising is permitted and, in particular, it requires traders to make sure that their advertisements:

- are not misleading;
- compare 'like with like'—goods and services meeting the same needs or intended for the same purpose;

---

[1] *Toshiba* [60].

- objectively compare important features of the products or services concerned;
- do not discredit other companies' trademarks;
- do not create confusion among traders (Article 4 of the Directive).

The interaction between the Directives concerning trade marks and comparative advertising is not straightforward. The Court of Appeal in the UK has held that advertising that complies with the Comparative Advertising Directive must be covered by the exception in the trade mark rules and must meet the standard of 'honest practices' (*O2 Holding Ltd v Hutchinson 3G Ltd* [2007] ETMR 19 (CA)). What is not clear, however, is whether use of the mark must be indispensable: must there be a necessity of using the mark? Case C–112/99 *Toshiba Europe GmbH v Katun Germany GmbH* [2001] ECR I-7945 does not seem to require necessity. And if one uses the mark, does that also cover use of the mark not exactly as registered? For example, could one use the 'O2' trade mark of static images in a modified form as a background for a television advert for a competitor?

That was the question in the *O2* case, in which all these questions were referred to the CJEU. The CJEU focused on the interaction between the two Directives and the cornerstone of its analysis is that both operate a concept of confusion and that that must be the same concept of confusion (Case C–533/06 *O2 Holdings Ltd v Hutchinson 3G UK Ltd* [2008] ECR I-4231, [2008] 3 CMLR 14). That leads the Court to start its analysis with Article 3(a)(1) Comparative Advertising Directive. That Article only permits comparative advertising if it is not misleading, does not create confusion between the advertiser's trade mark and those of competitors, does not take unfair advantage of the reputation of the trade mark, and does not present the goods or services as imitations or replicas of the goods or services bearing a protected trade mark (the latter two requirements were not respected by the use of the comparative perfume table in Case C–487/07 *L'Oréal SA v Bellure NV* [2009] ETMR 55). In order to let this provision play its role, trade mark law should not overrule it by holding the comparative advertising use of a mark to be an infringement in those cases where the requirements of Article 3(a)(1) Comparative Advertising Directive have been met (Case C–533/06 *O2 Holdings Ltd v Hutchinson 3G UK Ltd* [2008] ECR I-4231, [2008] 3 CMLR 14). That is not such a strange approach after all, as confusion is then ruled out and that is a fundamental requirement in trade mark infringement cases. Confusion is the key and needs to be looked at in the exact circumstances of the advertising use, but the emphasis on confusion must also mean there is no obligation to use an identical mark. A sign that is similar to the mark must also be allowed under these circumstances (insofar as it meets the definition of a comparative advertisement). There is also no need to prove that the use is indispensable. On the other hand, the CJEU found it unnecessary to provide a definition of honest practices.

The England and Wales Court of Appeal asked that question again in the *L'Oréal* case. The CJEU responded by ruling that the rights holder could rely on damage not just to the distinctiveness function of the trade mark, but also on damage to other functions of the trade mark such as the advertising, communication, and investment function in those cases where the requirements of Article 3(a)(1) Comparative Advertising Directive had not been met. The comparison lists in that case constituted comparative advertising and did do damage to those functions. The rights holder could therefore successfully rely on its trade mark, even if there was still no general definition of honest practices (Case C–487/07 *L'Oréal SA v Bellure NV* [2009] ETMR 55).

With that we return to the *O2* case, where the CJEU added that trade mark infringement rules will also not be of any use to stop comparative advertisements

that do not meet the standards of the Comparative Advertising Directive in circumstances such as *O2* where the domestic court had found that there was no confusion
(Case C–533/06 *O2 Holdings Ltd v Hutchinson 3G UK Ltd* [2008] ECR I-4231, [2008]
3 CMLR 14). That may sound like an awkward conclusion, but it is logical and it says
more about the need for enforcement of the comparative advertising standards than
about trade mark law.

The same Directive also deals with misleading advertising and obliges Member States
to provide effective remedies against it. Article 2 defines misleading advertising as

> any advertising which in any way, including its presentation, deceives or is likely to deceive
> the persons to whom it is addressed or whom it reaches and which, by reason of its decep-
> tive nature, is likely to affect their economic behaviour or which, for those reasons, injures
> or is likely to injure a competitor.

The emphasis is therefore placed on the capacity:

- to deceive the persons to whom it is addressed;
- to distort their economic behaviour; or
- as a consequence, to harm the interests of competitors.

When determining whether advertising is misleading, several factors shall be taken into
account. These are listed in Article 3:

> In determining whether advertising is misleading, account shall be taken of all its fea-
> tures, and in particular of any information it contains concerning:
>
> (a) the characteristics of goods or services, such as their availability, nature, execution,
>   composition, method and date of manufacture or provision, fitness for purpose,
>   uses, quantity, specification, geographical or commercial origin or the results to be
>   expected from their use, or the results and material features of tests or checks carried
>   out on the goods or services;
>
> (b) the price or the manner in which the price is calculated, and the conditions on which
>   the goods are supplied or the services provided;
>
> (c) the nature, attributes and rights of the advertiser, such as his identity and assets,
>   his qualifications and ownership of industrial, commercial or intellectual property
>   rights or his awards and distinctions.

17.4.2 Unfair Commercial Practices

As highlighted earlier, unfair competition law has moved away from its origins as a
mere business-to-business tool and has entered the business-to-consumer sphere too.
At the EU level the main instrument in this area is Directive 2005/29/EC concerning
unfair business to consumer commercial practices in the internal market [2005] OJ
L 149/22 (the Commercial Practices Directive). That Directive has a very broad scope
of application, as its title already seems to indicate. This is emphasized by the definition of (business-to-consumer) commercial practices in its Article 2(d) which reads
as follows:

> any act, omission, course of conduct or representation, commercial communication
> including advertising and marketing, by a trader, directly connected with the promotion,
> sale or supply of a product to consumers.

In turn the term product is described widely as 'any goods or service including
immovable property, rights and obligations'. The Directive applies to virtually all

business-to-consumer ('B2C') transactions and in all sectors. In addition, it applies not only at the advertising/marketing stage of a transaction but also 'during and after a commercial transaction in relation to a product' (Article 3). It is, however, only concerned with protection of the economic interests of consumers in relation to measures aiming at or resulting in the classification of a commercial practice as unfair, to the exclusion of other interests such as health and safety or the environment. The Member States remain free to extend the scope of the Commercial Practices Directive or to regulate, in conformity with other EU legislation, other types of relations. They are also free to determine the effect of unfair practices on the validity, formation, or effect of a contract, given that the Directive does not harmonize contract law. This Directive is also wider in scope than that discussed earlier, as it is not restricted to specific products, specific media, or specific types of market behaviour, such as advertising. It only applies though if there exists no specific EU law provisions that deal with the particular issue at hand.

The Directive is built up around a key provision, which is followed by a number of subsequent provisions that each deal with specific practices. Article 5(2) is that key provision or, if one wishes to use that term, the 'general clause', as it generally prohibits unfair commercial practices. It does so on the basis of two cumulative criteria for assessing whether a commercial practice should be deemed unfair. These are, first, whether the commercial practice is contrary to the requirements of 'professional diligence' and, second, is then found materially to distort or likely materially to distort the economic behaviour of the average consumer. This provision refers back to Article 2(h) where professional diligence is defined as the

> standard of special skill and care which a trader may reasonably be expected to exercise towards consumers, commensurate with honest market practice and/or the general principle of good faith in the trader's field of activity.

This notion encompasses principles which were already well established in the laws of the Member States, such as 'honest market practice' and 'good faith', with additional relevance being given to the normative values specifically applying in a given field of business activity. And of course the implementation and the enforcement of the prohibition of certain practices is left to the Member States and their national laws.

Articles 6 and 7 follow up by dealing specifically with provisions addressing the problem of misleading commercial practices, both as misleading actions and as misleading omissions. Practices are misleading because they contain false information and are untruthful. And the idea is that the action or omission is likely to cause the average consumer to take a transactional decision that she would not have otherwise taken.

Article 8 and 9 in turn address the issue of aggressive commercial practices. The definition offered in Article 8 is that:

> A commercial practice shall be regarded as aggressive if, in its factual context, taking account of all its features and circumstances, by *harassment, coercion, including the use of physical force, or undue influence, it significantly impairs or is likely to significantly impair the average consumer's freedom of choice or conduct with regard to the product* and thereby causes him or is likely to cause him to take a transactional decision that he would not have taken otherwise.[2]

---

[2] Emphasis added.

17.5 **Conclusions**

The transition from trade mark law and the protection of trade marks with a reputation to the law of unfair competition is a logical one, as very similar concepts are involved. But we have not seen the same involvement of the EU legislator in the area of unfair competition as in trade mark law. The initiative is still very much with the Member States and that has resulted in a certain degree of diversity in terms of solutions.

Two areas have however received detailed attention from the EU legislator. At a business-to-business level detailed provisions deal with comparative and misleading advertising. And at a business-to-consumer level there is a broad-ranging Directive on unfair commercial practices.

Further Reading

HENNING-BODEWIG, F., *International Handbook on Unfair Competition Law* (Hart Publishing, 2013)

HILTY, R. AND HENNING-BODEWIG, F. (eds), *Law Against Unfair Competition: Towards a New Paradigm in Europe?* (Springer, 2007)

HOWELL, C., 'O2 v Hutchinson 3G Comparative Advertising: European Trade Mark Law Beyond Compare?' [2008] *Communications Law* 155

18

Indications of Geographical Origin

18.1 Introduction

In the first three chapters of this part of the book we discussed trade marks in detail. Trade marks are in essence indications of source or origin, i.e. indications that the goods are produced by or under the responsibility of a particular producer. And they operate in the relationship between rights holder and consumer, allowing the rights holder to communicate the source (and quality...) of the product to the consumer, with the consumer in turn being able to distinguish the product from the rights holder from identical products from other sources.

In this chapter we are once more looking at that relationship between rights holder and consumer and at the indications of origin. Only this time we are looking at geographical origin and almost as an inevitable consequence there will not be an individual rights holder, as several producers are likely to be based in a certain geographical location. The indication of geographical origin establishes a link between a geographical location and the goods (of a particular type) which originate in that location. And that link is communicated to the consumer by the geographical indication, allowing the consumer to distinguish between identical or similar goods on the basis of their geographical origin.

Indications of geographical origin are by no means a new phenomenon. For centuries producers of certain products have developed designations to distinguish their products from similar products produced elsewhere and operated these as a form of collective mark. Brandy producers in various regions of France, for example, put designations such as 'Cognac' or 'Armagnac' on their products to indicate their geographical origin and distinguish them from each other and from brandy produced in other regions. Champagne and Cava for sparkling wines from a particular geographical location form another example. As with anything in the relationship between the rights holder and the consumer, its needs to be built up over time. This means that the rights holder will need to invest in the promotion of the indication of geographical origin and educate the consumer in this respect. Being enabled to distinguish on this geographical basis, the consumer will develop—in the successful cases where the consumer values and likes the distinction—a special appreciation for the product that comes with a particular indication of geographical origin.

Indications of geographical origin often go beyond the mere indication of the geographical origin of a product and can include indications of quality of reputation which emanate from the geographical location covered by the indication of origin. A first element is the human factor, which is based on the identification and development of characteristics that can in essence be attributed to a specific geographical location. People working in these particular or unusual circumstances have come up with innovative solutions and ways to produce the product. A second element can be described as the natural resources factor. A specific location and the soil and climate in that location have an impact on the products produced there. Certain characteristics of the goods are due to the characteristics of the geographical location of the production. This already hints at the justification for the exclusive right in the indication of geographical location; whilst it is possible to copy the innovative solution, it is not possible to copy the location and its characteristics elsewhere to make the very same product with the very same characteristics that are due to the influence of the geographical location. In a sense, indications of origin protect a form of traditional knowledge, due to their unique combination of the human and natural resources of a particular geographical location.

In this chapter we will first look at the position given to indications of geographical origin in the global and European IP systems. How did a historical practice develop into an exclusive right? And how is that exclusive right shaped and protected? We will then in the next phase focus in more depth on the European system for the protection of indications of geographical origin.

18.2 An Exclusive Right in the Global IP System

18.2.1 From Paris to Lisbon

The Paris Convention for the Protection of Industrial Property 1883 sets up an international system for the protection of industrial property and it does so on the basis of exclusive rights granted country by country on the basis of the national treatment rule. Article 1 Paris Convention defines the object of the protection of industrial property as follows:

> The protection of industrial property has as its object patents, utility models, industrial designs, trademarks, service marks, trade names, *indications of source or appellations of origin*, and the repression of unfair competition.[1]

Indications of geographical origin are therefore included in the scope of the Paris Convention and will receive protection by means of exclusive rights granted on a national basis. It is fair to say though that the Paris Convention gives no further indication of what such a national system of exclusive rights should look like. The matter is almost entirely left to the Member States. The Madrid Agreement, which is mainly concerned with trade marks, similarly touches on the topic of the protection of indications of geographical origin. This is not surprising in the light of the similarity with collective marks, but again no comprehensive set of rules emerges.

The Lisbon Agreement for the Protection of Appellations of Origin and their International Registration 1958 is the first international instrument that deals in detail

---

[1] Emphasis added.

with indications of geographical origin. It is fair to say though that its impact is limited, as relatively few countries have signed up to the Agreement. And inside the EU, the EU's proper system which we will discuss later has now taken over, including at the international level through the conclusion of bilateral trade agreements that include provisions on indications of geographical origin. The Lisbon Agreement is a special Agreement under Article 19 Paris Convention. Any country party to the Convention may accede to the Agreement. From that perspective the Agreement puts in place the detailed rules that were missing from the Paris Convention whilst building on the general principles of the Convention, such as the national treatment principle.

Before the appearance of the Lisbon Agreement, WIPO Member States had adopted very diverse approaches. Many of them had put in place unfair competition or consumer protection laws containing general provisions dealing with the misappropriation of indications serving to designate products that originate in a particular geographical area. There were also multiple examples of special systems aimed at identifying the specific features for which such indications are known to designate the products in question and for which they deserve special protection. But at a cross-border level it was exactly that diversity in legal concepts and the differences from country to country, based on different national legal traditions within a framework of specific historical and economic conditions, that caused problems. Often these national solutions were barely compatible and this made securing protection for indications of geographical indications in other countries complicated. The main objective of the Lisbon Agreement was therefore to overcome that hurdle and to satisfy the need for an international system that would facilitate the protection of a special category of such geographical indications, i.e. 'appellations of origin', in countries other than the country of origin, by means of their registration at the International Bureau of WIPO.

It is therefore important to define first of all this limited category of indications of origin which the international registration system covers. Article 2(1) Lisbon Agreement defines an 'appellation of origin' as

> the geographical denomination of a country, region, or locality, which serves to designate a product originating therein, the quality or characteristics of which are due exclusively or essentially to the geographical environment, including natural and human factors.

We are therefore dealing with a narrower category than that highlighted in the introduction to this chapter. Article 2(2) adds to this by defining the 'country of origin', which will in Paris Convention-style be the starting point for international protection, as

> the country whose name, or the country in which is situated the region or locality whose name, constitutes the appellation of origin that has given the product its reputation.

The cornerstone of the Lisbon Agreement is then protection and recognition of the indication of origin in the country of origin. Only if that is in place can there be registration at the International Bureau of WIPO, according to the rule in Article 1(2). The double requirement of protection and recognition means that the appellation of origin must be constituted by a geographical denomination that is protected in the country of origin as the denomination of a geographical area (country, region, or locality) and that is recognized as serving to designate a product that originates therein and meets certain qualifications. It is essential that the recognition of the denomination is based on the reputation of the product, but the way this is done is left to the national law of each Member State and the law of the country of origin will apply. And the protection of the appellation of origin must have been formalized either by means of legislation, by administrative provisions, by a judicial decision, or by any form of registration.

When it comes to the protection to be afforded, the Lisbon Agreement adopts the approach that was already applied to trade marks and designs, by the Madrid system and the Hague system respectively. This approach to the international registration of trade marks and industrial designs respectively is anchored on the facilitation of the registration of industrial property rights at the international level on the basis of provisions laying down the procedural rules governing the international registration procedure. The Lisbon Agreement does the same for denominations of origin. But in the absence at the international level of the equivalent of the substantive rules for the protection of trade marks and industrial designs, the Lisbon Agreement goes beyond the procedural aspect of according protection for denominations of origin. The Lisbon Agreement also contains a number of provisions on the substantive protection to be accorded to internationally registered appellations of origin. Article 3, for example, obliges Member States to protect appellations of origin registered at the International Bureau against any usurpation or imitation of the appellation of origin, even if the true origin of the product is stated or if the appellation is used in translated form or accompanied by terms such as 'kind', 'type', 'make', 'imitation', or the like. The international registration of an appellation of origin assures it of protection, without any need for renewal, for as long as the appellation is protected in the country of origin.

The Member States of the Agreement also have to put in place in their national legal systems a means of defence against any usurpation or imitation of an appellation of origin in their territory. This involves an action before the competent authorities of each of the countries of the Union in which the appellation is protected, according to the procedural rules laid down in the national legislation of those countries.

18.2.2 **The TRIPS Agreement**

The TRIPS Agreement deals with what it calls geographical indications in its Articles 22 to 24. Article 22 is the main provision and Articles 23 and 24 put in place additional protection for geographical indications for wines and spirits, coupled with a pledge of further negotiations on that point. Article 22 builds on the foundations of the Paris Convention and the Lisbon Agreement, but it goes further and the main strength of the TRIPS Agreement is that it expands the geographical cover of the system massively. The number of states bound by TRIPS is much higher than the number of states signed up to the Lisbon Agreement.

The definition of geographical indications in paragraph 1 of Article 22 sounds very familiar in the sense that it refers to:

> indications which identify a good as originating in the territory of a Member, or a region or locality in that territory, where a given quality, reputation or other characteristic of the good is essentially attributable to its geographical origin.

But paragraph 2 adds a clearly defined level of protection. Member States are to provide interested parties under their national laws with the legal means to prevent:

> the use of any means in the designation or presentation of a good that indicates or suggests that the good in question originates in a geographical area other than the true place of origin in a manner which misleads the public as to the geographical origin of the good.

In addition, they should also provide the legal means to prevent any use of a geographical indication that constitutes an act of unfair competition within the meaning of

Article 10*bis* Paris Convention. Any false attribution is therefore actionable, as is any unfair competition based on the invocation of a geographical indication.

One could of course try to circumvent the provisions on geographical indications by registering a sign identical to a geographical indication as a trade mark. The latter could then be used on any goods, even those that do not originate in the territory of the geographical indication. Paragraph 3 of Article 22 deals with this problem by instructing Member States to set up a system to refuse or invalidate the registration of a trade mark which contains or consists of a geographical indication. The system applies if the trade mark is used for goods not originating in the territory indicated and if use of the indication in the trade mark for such goods in that Member State is of such a nature as to mislead the public as to the true place of origin.

And finally, the protection provided in the first three paragraphs of Article 22 shall also be applicable against a geographical indication which, although literally true as to the territory, region, or locality in which the goods originate, falsely represents to the public that the goods originate in another territory.

All in all, even after the implementation of the TRIPS Agreement the international IP system contains very few substantive rules, especially when compared to other IP rights. As long as the basic principles are respected the international rules leave a lot of freedom to national legislation to shape its own system for the protection of indications of geographical origin. And national legislations show as a result a great deal of variety. Some go down the path of using the existing trade mark regime, often by including in it concepts of collective and certification marks. The former can be held by organizations representing producers of certain products in a certain area and the latter can be opened up for use by any producer meeting the requirements of producing the product in a certain geographical area. Countries that do not use trade mark law tend to use a *sui generis* system for the protection of indications of geographical origin. In this category one finds registration systems and recognition systems. Registration systems require that in order to be created an indication of geographical origin is formally registered, often on the basis of legislation adopted specifically for that purpose. Recognition systems on the other hand do not require formalities. From the moment a geographical designation fulfils the function of an indication of geographical origin this is recognized by national law. This can be done on the basis of existing legislation, such as trade practices law that turns making use of any false, misleading, or unreasonably incomplete information (here on the geographical origin of the goods) that can affect the demand or the supply of the product into an offence, but it can also be done by making an action available in the courts along the lines of principles developed by the case law. One could in this respect think of the action of passing-off in the common law legal systems.

18.2.3 **The European Union**

From this broad overview of possible approaches we move to one particular approach, that adopted by the EU. Based on the previous analysis it is logical that national protection systems for indications of geographical origin are found in each of the Member States. These national systems may of course enter into conflict with the Treaty provisions on the free movement of goods (and those on competition law) in the same way as national trade marks. We discussed the latter in detail in Chapter 16. Suffice it to state here that the CJEU has recognized national indications of geographical origin as IP rights that are covered by the (limited) exception to the free movement of goods principles. In other words, there can be restrictions to the free movement of goods on the basis of these national indications of origin, but these rights should not be abused and lead to arbitrary restrictions on the free movement of goods. It is not our intention to go into great detail concerning this distinction. The approach along the lines of the trade can be illustrated on the basis of a couple of key cases. In the *Sekt* case the CJEU ruled that indications of geographical origin:

> only fulfil their specific purpose if the product which they describe does in fact possess qualities and characteristics which are due to the fact that it originated in a specific geographical area. As regards indications of origin in particular, the geographical area of origin of a product must confer on it a specific quality and specific characteristics of such a nature as to distinguish it from all other products.[2]

This then led to the logical conclusion that:

> the protection accorded by the indication of origin is only justifiable if the product concerned actually possesses characteristics which are capable of distinguishing it from the point of view of its geographical origin, in the absence of such a condition this protection cannot be justified.[3]

The CJEU returned to the specific function of indications of geographical origin in the *Rioja I* case and ruled that:

> the specific function of a registered designation of origin is to guarantee that the product bearing it comes from a specified geographical area and displays certain particular characteristics.[4]

The *Rioja I* case was concerned with Spanish rules concerning the indication of origin Rioja for wines that required that the wine should be bottled at the bodega. The Belgian supermarket chain Delhaize bought the wine in bulk and bottled it in Belgium and the question arose whether it was in breach of the rules by applying the indication of origin Rioja to the bottles in Belgium. The CJEU applied the principle it set out above as follows:

> the requirement that the wine be bottled in the region of production, in so far as it constitutes a condition for the use of the name of that region as a registered designation of origin, would be justified by the concern to ensure that that designation of origin fulfilled its specific function if bottling in the region of production endowed the wine originating in that region with particular characteristics, of such a kind as to give it individual character, or if bottling in the region of production were essential in order to preserve essential characteristics acquired by that wine.[5]

On that basis the supermarket won and the Spanish bottling at source rule was held to be in breach of the free movement provisions. In the view of the CJEU it led to an abuse.[6]

---

[2] Case 12/74 *Commission of the European Communities v the Federal Republic of Germany—Indirect appellation of origin—Sekt* [1975] ECR 181 [7].

[3] Ibid [12].

[4] Case C–47/90 *Établissements Delhaize frères and Compagnie Le Lion SA v Promalvin SA and AGE Bodegas Unidas SA* [1992] ECR I-3669 [17].

[5] Ibid [18].

[6] See also Case 16/83 *Criminal proceedings against Karl Prantl* [1984] ECR 1299 and Joined Cases C–321/94, 322/94, 323/94, and 324/94 *Criminal proceedings against Jacques Pistre, Michèle Barthes, Yves Milhau and Didier Oberti* [1997] ECR I-2343.

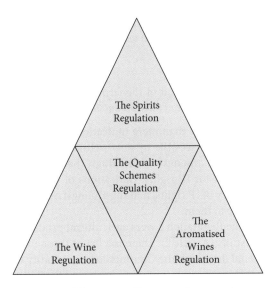

Figure 18.1 The current European framework

It would lead too far to analyse each of the national systems for the protection of indications of origin, or to look at the history of developments in the EU. Instead we will move on to the rather comprehensive set of rules that has emerged at the European level. The current legal framework is composed of (see Figure 18.1):

- the *Quality Schemes Regulation*, covering agricultural products and foodstuffs (with the exception of wines and spirits)—Regulation (EU) No. 1151/2012 of the European Parliament and of the Council of 21 November 2012 on quality schemes for agricultural products and foodstuffs [2012] OJ L 343/1;

- the *Spirits Regulation*—Regulation (EC) No. 110/2008 on the definition, description, presentation, labelling and the protection of geographical indications of spirit drinks [2008] OJ L 39/16;

- the *Wine Regulation*—Council Regulation (EC) No. 1234/2007 establishing a common organisation of agricultural markets and on specific provisions for certain agricultural products (Single CMO Regulation) [2007] OJ L 299/1;

- the *Aromatised Wines Regulation*—Regulation (EU) No. 251/2014 of the European Parliament and of the Council on the definition, description, presentation, labelling and the protection of geographical indications of aromatised wine products [2014] OJ L 84/14.

18.3 The Quality Schemes Regulation

18.3.1 Scope and Objectives

The Quality Schemes Regulation sets up a structure for quality schemes, as its name already suggests. Indications of geographical origin easily fit in with such an approach. This becomes immediately clear when one looks at the objectives of the Regulation in Article 1. Paragraph 2 states that the

Regulation establishes quality schemes which provide the basis for the identification and, where appropriate, protection of names and terms that, in particular, indicate or describe agricultural products with:

(a) value-adding characteristics; or

(b) value-adding attributes as a result of the farming or processing methods used in their production, or of the *place of their production* or marketing.[7]

Whilst this is potentially broader than mere indications of geographical origin the latter are clearly covered and one sees the by now well-known characteristics appearing once more. Paragraph 1 adds, amongst other things, that it is also the objective of the Regulation to ensure respect for IP rights. Indications of geographical origin are thus clearly placed in the category of IP rights, making amongst other things the enforcement tools for IP rights available to them.

The system set up by the Regulation covers agricultural products intended for human consumption and foodstuffs (Article 2). There is a list of those in Annex I to the Treaty and there is an additional list which the Commission can modify that is attached to the Regulation as Annex I. This approach combines clarity and flexibility. Title II then specifically deals with protected designations of origin and protected geographical indications for these agricultural products and foodstuffs.

The indications of geographical origin scheme of Title II starts from the link to a certain geographical area and has the specific aim if ensuring uniform EU-wide protection for the relevant names as IP rights. In terms of objectives this is coupled with a fair return for the qualities of their products for the producers and clear information for consumers on the value-added attributes of the product.

18.3.2 Designations of Origin and Geographical Indications

The Regulation then introduces a critical distinction between designations of origin and geographical indications in its Article 5. The requirements for designations of origin are a bit tighter.

A designation of origin is defined (Article 5(1)) as a name that identifies a product:

(a) originating in a specific place, region, or, in exceptional cases, a country;

(b) the quality or characteristics of which are essentially or exclusively due to a particular geographical environment with its inherent natural and human factors; and

(c) the production steps of which all take place in the defined geographical area.

The concept is clearly that of a link in terms of origin with a specific geographical location, coupled with quality or characteristics that result from that geographical location. And the whole production process needs to take place locally.

A 'mere' geographical indication is again a name that identifies a product, but the second and third requirements are weakened. The link with the area may be merely in terms of reputation and as a minimum only one step in the production process needs to take place locally. That results in the following definition in paragraph 2:

a name which identifies a product:

(a) originating in a specific place, region or country;

---

[7] Emphasis added.

(b) whose given quality, reputation or other characteristic is essentially attributable to its geographical origin; and

(c) at least one of the production steps of which take place in the defined geographical area.

It is of course not the case that just any name can be registered as a designation of origin or a geographical indication once the conditions set out above are met. Generic names cannot distinguish, cannot indicate a link with a specific geographical area, and should remain available to all producers to identify the product. They are therefore excluded from registration. Similarly, names of plant varieties and animal breeds should remain available to breeders and producers in all locations. To achieve this the Regulation excludes from registration all names that conflict with names of plant varieties and animal breeds. This includes not only names that are identical to the names of plant varieties or animal breeds, but all similar names that are likely to mislead the consumer as to the true origin of the product. The consumer may also be misled about the true identity of the product if a proposed name is similar to a trade mark with a reputation. No registration will occur if there is a conflict with such a trade mark and the criterion used to establish the existence of such a conflict is whether the consumer is likely to be misled about the true origin of the product (Article 6).

18.3.3 **The Application**

Any application needs to be based on a product specification (Article 7). Such a product specification is the basic document on the basis of which the Commission will examine the application. But it also provides the conditions under which the indication of geographical origin can be used and it determines the scope of the indication of geographical origin.

The starting point of any product specification is the name that will be protected as a designation of origin or geographical indication. That name needs to be authentic and it therefore needs to be stated as it is used, whether in trade or in common language, and only in the languages which are or were historically used to describe the specific product in the defined geographical area. The freedom of the applicant on this point is clearly much more restricted than the freedom enjoyed by an applicant for a trade mark. Next, the application needs to contain a description of the product. This description includes the raw materials and the principal physical, chemical, microbiological, or organoleptic characteristics of the product. In addition to the name and the product one also needs of course a description of the relevant geographical area, coupled with evidence that the product originates in that geographical area. But as a mere link to the geographical area is not sufficient, the product specification will also need to provide evidence of the link between the quality or characteristics of the product and the geographical environment or, where appropriate, of the link between a given quality, the reputation, or other characteristic of the product and the geographical origin.

Having established the three key components of product, name, and geographical area the product specification needs in addition to provide a description of the method of obtaining the product and, where appropriate, the authentic and unvarying local methods as well as information concerning packaging, if the applicant group so determines and gives sufficient product-specific justification for why the packaging must take place in the defined geographical area to safeguard quality, to ensure the origin, or to ensure control, taking into account Union law, in particular that on the free movement of goods and the free provision of services. Any specific labelling rule for the product in question also needs to be included. This second group of details is vital if the indication of geographical origin is to work as a standard for all producers in the geographical area. The idea is indeed that all producers in the area can use the indication of geographical origin, but to do so they need to know the standards with which they have to comply (which will, in turn, match with the expectations of the consumer when the latter is confronted with the indication of geographical origin).

Finally, such an open standard needs to be policed, especially as there is no single owner of the right as in the case of a trade mark. This can either be done by a body specifically set up to verify compliance with the provisions of the product specification, or to whom such a task is entrusted, or by the public authorities. The product specification will therefore need to describe the task at issue and provide details of the party carrying it out.

The product specification may be the cornerstone of any application, but more is needed to complete the application to the Commission for the grant of an EU-wide indication of geographical origin, be it a designation of origin or a geographical indication. The group (of producers) making the application needs to identify itself, as well as the body or authority that will verify compliance. And there will need to be a summary of the main points of the product specification: the name, a description of the product, including, where appropriate, specific rules concerning packaging and labelling, and a concise definition of the geographical area, coupled with a description of the link between the product and the geographical environment or geographical origin. The latter includes, where appropriate, the specific elements of the product description or production method justifying the link.

From a procedural point of view the application process starts with a group that works with the products carrying the name the registration of which is proposed. Exceptionally single persons can also apply. In a first stage the application needs to be addressed to the Member State in which the relevant geographical area is situated. That Member State will scrutinize the application and check whether it meets the conditions of the Regulation, either under the designation of origin scheme or under the geographical indication scheme. This process includes an opposition procedure at the national level that allows all interested parties to lodge their opposition to the registration of the name, either because the application does not satisfy the legal requirement or because it conflicts with existing rights of the party opposing it. Only if the Member State concludes at the end of this phase of the procedure that the application meets the requirements of the Regulation, will the application be forwarded to the Commission (Article 49).

The Commission will in turn examine the application in the light of the conditions of the relevant scheme, normally within a six-month period. It will also publish, in a first stage, the name applied for and the date of application and, in a second stage, when it considers that the requirements have been met, the complete summary of the application (Article 50). Once publication in the Official Journal has taken place, a three-month period follows during which an opposition procedure can be launched by national authorities and any person having a legitimate interest (Article 51). As part of the opposition procedure the Commission will invite the parties to engage in consultations with the aim of working out a solution that is acceptable to all parties. At the end of the procedure the Commission will take a decision on the application. It can refuse to register the name, grant the registration in the absence of any opposition, grant the registration on the basis of the agreement reached by the parties in the consultation procedure, or make a decision in the absence of such an agreement in the consultation period. Any such decision shall again be published in the Official Journal. And the Commission will keep a publicly accessible register of all registrations (Article 11).

18.3.4 **The Right**

Once on the register, protected designations of origin and protected geographical indications may be used by any operator that markets a product that conforms to the product specification. The right is open to all who comply with the requirements of the specification. The products concerned can be labelled with the sign PDA or PGI respectively, according to Article 12. Member States are obliged to put in place authorities that will take the appropriate administrative and judicial steps under their national laws and procedures to prevent or stop the unlawful use of protected designations of origin or protected geographical indications. Registered names will in particular be protected against (Article 13):

(a) any direct or indirect commercial use of a registered name in respect of products not covered by the registration where those products are comparable to the products registered under that name or where using the name exploits the reputation of the protected name, including when those products are used as an ingredient;

(b) any misuse, imitation, or evocation, even if the true origin of the products or services is indicated or if the protected name is translated or accompanied by an expression such as 'style', 'type', 'method', 'as produced in', 'imitation', or similar, including when those products are used as an ingredient;

(c) any other false or misleading indication as to the provenance, origin, nature, or essential qualities of the product that is used on the inner or outer packaging, advertising material, or documents relating to the product concerned, and the packing of the product in a container liable to convey a false impression as to its origin;

(d) any other practice liable to mislead the consumer as to the true origin of the product.

The protection granted by Article 13 is rather broad and the key concept is that the consumer should not be misled, emphasizing once more that indications of geographical origin function in the relationship between those using them legitimately and the consumer and that both parties should be able to rely on the information they convey. The similarity with trade mark law on this point is striking. Paragraph (a) logically prohibits commercial use in respect of similar products that are not covered by the registration or where the reputation of the protected name is exploited. One recognizes elements of trade mark law, both in terms of similarity and in terms of the use of trade marks with a reputation. Paragraph (b) adds to that obvious examples of misuse, imitation, or evocation. And paragraphs (c) and (d) return fully to the theme of misleading the consumer. One should add though that protected designations of origin and protected geographical indications are protected in the way in which they are registered and within the limits of their product specification.

Later registration of trade marks that would conflict with Article 13 will no longer be possible. One cannot get around the Regulation by registering a trade mark. Trade marks that are already in existence can continue to coexist with the indication of geographical origin, as long as there is no ground for invalidity (Article 14).

It is also important to note that paragraph 2 of Article 13 puts down the simple rule that once registered, protected designations of origin and protected indications of origin can no longer become generic, by operation of law and irrespective of the circumstances (exception made for the cancellation procedure to which we will turn shortly).

The one exception to the rules on protection is that where a protected designation of origin or a protected geographical indication contains within it the name of a product which is considered to be generic, the use of that generic name (alone) shall not be considered to infringe. This is entirely logical as other parties have a legitimate interest in continuing the use of a generic name. To make up a simplistic example, if 'Red Leicester Cheese' were to be registered as a designation of origin the use of the generic name 'cheese' would remain free.

18.3.5 **Cancellation**

There are two obvious reasons for the cancellation of a registration. First, the relationship between the user of the name and the consumer can be damaged. That is clearly so when compliance with the conditions of the specification is not ensured. That clearly amounts to a ground for cancellation and on the other hand the clear aim of a registration is that it will be used. It is therefore also a ground for cancellation if for at least seven years no product is placed on the market bearing the protected designation of origin or the protected geographical indication. These are strong grounds for cancellation and Article 54 therefore logically imposes few restrictions as to who can apply for such cancellation. The Commission can act on its own initiative, but it can also act at the request of any natural or legal person. The latter merely needs to show a legitimate interest. There is also a third ground for cancellation in the sense that the producers of products marketed under the protected designation of origin or under the protected geographical indication can request its cancellation.

18.4 **The Spirits Regulation**

As its name suggests, the Spirits Regulation covers spirit drinks and these must be of agricultural origin (Regulation (EC) No. 110/2008 on the definition, description, presentation, labelling and the protection of geographical indications of spirit drinks [2008] OJ L 39/16). They must fall within the category of agricultural products and foodstuffs. The relevant provisions for our current purposes are found in Chapter III of the Regulation that deals with geographical indications. Applications that pass the requirements lead to registration of the relevant geographical indication and that is then added to the list of geographical indications in Annex III to the Regulation that forms the relevant register.

18.4.1 **Scope**

It is striking that the Spirits Regulation only uses one concept, that of a geographical indication. The definition of that concept is aligned strongly to the definition found in Article 22(1) TRIPS Agreement. More in detail Article 15 stipulates that

> [f]or the purpose of this Regulation a geographical indication shall be an indication which identifies a spirit drink as originating in the territory of a country, or a region or locality in that territory, where a given quality, reputation or other characteristic of that spirit drink is essentially attributable to its geographical origin.

The emphasis is on the spirit originating in a certain geographical area and that link being responsible for a given quality, reputation, or other characteristic of the spirit drink. Generic names cannot meet this criterion and should not therefore be registered and registered geographical indications may not become generic.

In terms of the protection of geographical indications that have successfully been registered one finds in Article 16 a provision that shows strong similarities with its counterpart in the Quality Schemes Regulation. The emphasis is once more on the prohibition to use the registered geographical indication on similar products not covered by it, the prohibition to exploit its reputation, misuse, imitation, or evocation, and the misleading of the consumer. Article 16 puts that as follows:

> The geographical indications registered…shall be protected against:
>
> (a) any direct or indirect commercial use in respect of products not covered by the registration in so far as those products are comparable to the spirit drink registered under that geographical indication or insofar as such use exploits the reputation of the registered geographical indication;
>
> (b) any misuse, imitation or evocation, even if the true origin of the product is indicated or the geographical indication is used in translation or accompanied by an expression such as 'like', 'type', 'style', 'made', 'flavour' or any other similar term;
>
> (c) any other false or misleading indication as to the provenance, origin, nature or essential qualities on the description, presentation or labelling of the product, liable to convey a false impression as to its origin;
>
> (d) any other practice liable to mislead the consumer as to the true origin of the product.

Once registered a geographical indication will also imply that the registration of a trade mark containing it will be refused or invalidated if it would lead to any of the situations described above. This rule does not apply to existing trade marks though that can continue to coexist with the geographical indication (Article 23).

18.4.2 **Procedure**

The application for a geographical indication is in essence based on a technical file that sets out the specification with which the spirit drink must comply (Article 17). That technical file must include the name and category of the spirit drink including the geographical indication, a description of the spirit drink including the principal physical, chemical, and/or organoleptic characteristics of the product as well as the specific characteristics of the spirit drink as compared to the relevant category, the definition of the geographical area concerned, a description of the method for obtaining the spirit drink, and, if appropriate, the authentic and unvarying local methods, the details bearing out the link with the geographical environment or the geographical origin, any requirements laid down by Community and/or national and/or regional provisions, the name and contact address of the applicant, and any supplement to the geographical indication and/or any specific labelling rule, according to the relevant technical file.

  The application to the Commission is also in this system made by the Member State and the Commission has 12 months to examine it and reach a decision. Once the details of the application have been published in the Official Journal anyone with a legitimate interest can object to the registration within a six-month period. At the end of the procedure it is the Commission which decides and its decision is published in the Official Journal. An eventual cancellation of the registration is also left to the Commission and it can be decided if compliance with the specifications in the technical file is no longer ensured (Article 18).

18.5 The Wine–Single CMO–Regulation

The EU has a special indication of geographical origin regime for wines. It is contained in Council Regulation (EC) No. 1234/2007 establishing a common organisation of agricultural markets and on specific provisions for certain agricultural products (the Single CMO Regulation [2007] OJ L 299/1). There exist however strong similarities between this special system and that contained in the Quality Schemes Regulation.

18.5.1 **Substance**

As is the case under the quality schemes approach, the Regulation has two levels of indications of geographical origin. Article 118b defines these as follows:

(a) 'designation of origin' means the name of a region, a specific place or, in exceptional cases, a country used to describe a product…that complies with the following requirements:

    (i) its quality and characteristics are essentially or exclusively due to a particular geographical environment with its inherent natural and human factors;

    (ii) the grapes from which it is produced come exclusively from this geographical area;

    (iii) its production takes place in this geographical area; and

    (iv) it is obtained from vine varieties belonging to Vitis vinifera;

(b) 'geographical indication' means an indication referring to a region, a specific place or, in exceptional cases, a country, used to describe a product…which complies with the following requirements:

    (i) it possesses a specific quality, reputation or other characteristics attributable to that geographical origin;

    (ii) at least 85% of the grapes used for its production come exclusively from this geographical area;

    (iii) its production takes place in this geographical area; and

    (iv) it is obtained from vine varieties belonging to Vitis vinifera or a cross between the Vitis vinifera species and other species of the genus Vitis.

A designation of origin is clearly subject to more stringent requirements. All the grapes have to be specific wine grapes and have to come exclusively from the relevant geographical area, in which the whole winemaking process also needs to take place. And, as a key requirement, the product must possess a specific quality and characteristics that are essentially or exclusively due to a particular geographical environment with its inherent natural and human factors. There is a combination of natural (the soil concept) and human (a particular know-how) factors and the characteristics or quality must be due essentially or exclusively to the geographical environment. For a geographical indication, that is watered down to a specific quality, a reputation, or other characteristics attributable to that geographical origin. And only 85 per cent of the grapes need to come from the area and a wider variety of grapes can be used. Overall though these are tighter requirements than the ones found in the Quality Schemes Regulation.

Generic names are excluded from registration as they cannot distinguish as the geographical origin and protected designations of origin or protected geographical indications shall not become generic. Article 118m then stipulates that protected designations of origins and protected geographical indications may be used by any operator marketing a wine which has been produced in conformity with the corresponding product specification. In other words the same main principle applies, the names are open to anyone who produces the product, here the wine, in the relevant geographical area and who complies with the requirements of the scheme. In terms of protection, the protected designations of origins and protected geographical indications and the wines using those protected names in conformity with the product specification shall be protected first of all against any direct or indirect commercial use of a protected name. This covers both use for comparable products that do not comply with the product specification of the protected name and use that exploits the reputation of a designation of origin or a geographical indication, even if the products are not similar. There is also protection against any misuse, imitation, or evocation, even if the true origin of the product or service is indicated or if the protected name is translated or accompanied by an expression such as 'style', 'type', 'method', 'as produced in', 'imitation', 'flavour', 'like', or similar. The first level of protection specifically focuses on the use of the name, whilst this second level of protection extends that to any misuse, in essence use of similar names or use implying a link with the name. In a third stage, protection is offered against misleading activity. This covers first of all any other false or misleading indication as to the provenance, origin, nature, or essential qualities of the product, on the inner or outer packaging, advertising material or documents relating to the wine product concerned, and the packing of the product in a container liable to convey a false impression as to its origin, but it further includes any other practice liable to mislead the consumer as to the true origin of the product. This is clearly a very broad range and level of protection with the clear aim of safeguarding the role of the name in the relationship between user and consumer. Both parties must be able to rely without reservation on the communicative value of the name and the reputation that goes with it.

Once registration has taken place one sees the by now familiar approach to the interaction with trade marks. Later registration of protected designations of origins and protected geographical indications as trade marks will not be possible, but existing trade marks will be allowed to coexist with the protected designations of origins and protected geographical indications (Article 118l).

18.5.2 **Procedure**

Each application starts with a technical file, consisting of the name that is to be protected, the name and address of the applicant, and, crucially, a product specification (and a single document summarizing it). The aim of the product specification is to enable interested parties to verify the relevant conditions of production of the designation of origin or geographical indication. To do that, it shall consist at least of:

(a) the name to be protected;

(b) a description of the wine(s);

(c) where applicable, the specific oenological practices used to make the wine(s) as well as the relevant restrictions on making the wine(s);

(d) the demarcation of the geographical area concerned;

(e) the maximum yields per hectare;

(f) an indication of the wine grape variety or varieties from which the wine(s) is obtained;

(g) the details bearing out the link between geographical area and quality;

(h) applicable requirements laid down in Community or national legislation or, where foreseen by Member States, by an organization which manages the protected designation of origin or the protected geographical indication, having regard to the fact that such requirements shall be objective, and non-discriminatory and compatible with Community law;

(i)   the name and address of the authorities or bodies verifying compliance with the provisions of the product specification and their specific tasks.

The final two elements also provide a further insight into the scheme. There is often an organization that is set up specifically to manage the protected designation of origin or the protected geographical indication, i.e. a kind of trade organization, but there is on the other hand also an authority or body to verify compliance with the provisions of the product specification. The latter is vital to ensure that the consumer can trust the name and that the users can continue to rely on it, as in comparison with trade marks there is no single rights holder who can privately and individually enforce the right (Article 118c).

Such an application can be filed by any interested group of producers (single applicants being the exception) and the application necessarily covers wines they produce (Article 118d). In a sense what is envisaged is a form of self-regulation and standard setting that will result in an identifier and a quality label.

The application is first of all dealt with at national level in the Member State where the applicants are based. The Regulation describes this stage in Article 118f as a preliminary national procedure. During it, the requirements for an application are checked and all interested parties are given at least two months to bring an opposition against the application. If the Member State forms the view that the requirements are not met it can refuse the application, otherwise the single document and the product specification will be published and the Member State will forward an application for protection to the Commission. The Commission will first of all acknowledge publicly that it has received the application, but it will then in turn examine the application in the light of the requirements of the scheme (Article 118g). If it decides that the application does not need to be turned down, the single document will be published in the Official Journal. The first publication by the Commission also forms the starting point for another, this time EU-wide opposition procedure of two months (Article 118h). In the end it will be up to the Commission to take the final decision (Article 118i) and eventually to add the name to its register of protected designations of origin or protected geographical indications (Article 118n).

The Commission may also cancel the registration if compliance with the product specification is no longer ensured. The Commission can take action on its own initiative or at the motivated request of a Member State, a third country, or a natural or legal person that can show a legitimate interest.

18.6 The Aromatised Wine Regulation

Aromatised wine products are products obtained from products of the wine sector that have been flavoured. Vermouth and Glühwein are typical examples. In European law these aromatized wine products have always been dealt with in a separate regulation. The most recent version is Regulation (EU) No. 251/2014 of the European Parliament and of the Council on the definition, description, presentation, labelling and the protection of geographical indications of aromatised wine products [2014] OJ L 84/14. This new Regulation deals for the first time in a specific section, Chapter III, with indications of geographical origin. Article 2, paragraph 3 defines the concept as a 'geographical indication'. Rather than two concepts in the Wine Regulation there is only one in relation to aromatized wines and a 'geographical indication' means an indication which identifies an aromatised wine product as originating in a region, a specific place, or a country, where a given quality, reputation, or other characteristic of that product is essentially attributable to its geographical origin. That link with a territory and the fact that a quality, reputation, or other characteristic is attributable to that territory sounds by now familiar. 'Essentially attributable' does not, however, point to a very stringent requirement.

Our further analysis of the provisions in Chapter III can be very brief, as the Regulation has merely copied the approach taken with wines. The only difference is found in the provision dealing with the content of applications for protection and the product specification. There is an additional reference to the raw material used for the drink and on the other hand no management body is envisaged. Article 10 puts it as follows:

Content of applications for protection

1. Applications for the protection of names as geographical indications shall include a technical file containing:

    (a) the name to be protected;

    (b) the name and address of the applicant;

    (c) a product specification as referred to in paragraph 2; and

    (d) a single document summarising the product specification referred to in paragraph 2.

2. To be eligible for a geographical indication protected under this Regulation a product shall comply with the corresponding product specification which shall include at least:

    (a) the name to be protected;

    (b) a description of the product, in particular its principal analytical characteristics as well as an indication of its organoleptic characteristics;

    (c) where applicable, the particular production processes and specifications as well as the relevant restrictions on making the product;

    (d) the demarcation of the geographical area concerned;

    (e) the details bearing out the link referred to in point (3) of Article 2;

    (f) the applicable requirements laid down in Union or national law or, where provided for by Member States, by an organisation which manages the protected geographical indication, having regard to the fact that such requirements shall be objective, and non-discriminatory and compatible with Union law;

    (g) an indication of the main raw material from which the aromatised wine product is obtained;

    (h) the name and address of the authorities or bodies verifying compliance with the provisions of the product specification and their specific tasks.

Finally, one should not forget that the aromatized wine scheme is merely the little brother or sister. Under the previous regulation (Regulation 1601/91) the list was effectively limited to Nürnberger Glühwein, Samoborski Bermet, Thüringer Glühwein, Vermouth de Chambéry, and Vermouth di Torino. And whilst the new system is more attractive and modern, a massive number of additional registrations is not exactly expected.

18.7 Conclusions

Indications of geographical origin are quite important in practice, but they have attracted little by way of in-depth theoretical analysis. The key element is that they involve a link between a product and a certain territory, with the product deriving some quality, reputation, or other characteristic from that link. The strength of the link varies between the different schemes and involves both human and natural elements. It is also important to realize that whilst similar to (collective) trade marks, indications of geographical origin are radically different as they are open standards. Anyone adhering to the relevant standards can use the indication of geographical origin if they make the relevant product in the territory concerned.

Further Reading

BLAKENEY, M., *The Protection of Geographical Indications: Law and Practice* (Edward Elgar, 2014)

GANGJEE, D., *Relocating the Law of Geographical Indications* (CUP, 2012)

MANTROV, V., *EU Law on Indications of Geographical Origin: Theory and Practice* (Springer, 2014)

19

Designs

19.1 Introduction

Designs have something to do with shape and they are closely linked with the concept of a trade mark for a three-dimensional shape. It should from that perspective not be surprising that this chapter is in Part IV of the book, the first three chapters of which dealt with trade marks. But let us leave that link to one side and look in more detail at design law in the EU. This is another area where there has been a directive harmonizing national laws on designs (European Parliament and Council Directive 98/71/EC on the legal protection of designs [1998] OJ L 289/28) that runs in parallel with a regulation creating a community design (Council Regulation (EC) No. 6/2002 of 12 December 2001 on community designs [2002] OJ L 3/1, as amended by Council Regulation 1891/2006 [2006] OJ L 386/14). The substantive provisions of both instruments are identical. Both instruments put in place a system of registered designs, that grant its owner exclusive rights. But the Regulation also has an unregistered design component, to which we will return later. Under the Community Designs Regulation, a single registered design right is granted in essence and this is done for the whole of the EU. That system is administered by the Office for Harmonization in the Internal Market (OHIM), which is based in Alicante, Spain, and which also administers the Community trade mark (Article 2 of the Regulation). As with the Community trade mark, the Community design right has a unitary character (Article 1(3) of the Regulation).

One could be forgiven for thinking that a design is a plan or blueprint that shows how an item is to be constructed or how the elements of the item are arranged. IP law, however, has never accepted that simple definition. For our purposes, a design is concerned with aspects of an item or with features applied to it, and is never concerned with the item itself.

19.2 Requirements for the Grant of a Registered Design

Whereas many traditional design systems required the registration of a design for each product separately, the essence of the new system is that it protects a design for a product. The emphasis is on the design, even if it has to be a design for a product. The object of protection is the design. This can be better understood if we compare the design with a trade mark. Just like the trade mark, the design is the object of protection, but like the trade mark the design is registered for certain goods. This gives the protection a potentially very wide scope indeed and it is therefore of capital importance to consider carefully how the concepts involved are defined.

19.2.1 A Design

The concept of a 'design' is defined as

> the appearance of the whole or a part of a product resulting from the features of, in particular, the lines, contours, colours, shape, texture and/or materials of the product itself and/or its ornamentation.[1]

A design is therefore an element of appearance in products.

This definition is much wider than 'eye appeal'. The Directive emphasizes this by indicating, in its recital 14, that no aesthetic quality is required, meaning that arbitrary, but non-appealing, features can also be covered by the definition. But this has to be read in conjunction with the reference in recital 11 to 'features which are shown visibly'. This has to be combined with the use of the word 'appearance' in the definition of a design and, as such, the definition clearly points primarily to aesthetic elements and to an aesthetic impression being created in the mind of the consumer on seeing the design. We are mainly concerned, in this respect, with the 'look and feel' of the product.

19.2.2 A Design for a Product

What is protected is a 'design for a product'. That concept of a 'product' is defined, in turn, and is said to mean

> any industrial or handicraft item, including inter alia parts intended to be assembled into a complex product, packaging, get-up, graphic symbols and typographic typefaces, but excluding computer programs

while a complex product is, in turn, defined as

> a product which is composed of multiple components which can be replaced permitting disassembly and re-assembly of the product.

In reality, in relation to the latter, the legislator had primarily costly, complex, and long-lasting products, such as cars or computers, in mind.

The only restrictive element in this definition is the exclusion of computer programs, but this is a logical exclusion, because a special regime of protection has already been

---

[1] Article 1(a) of the Directive/Article 3(a) of the Regulation.

established for computer programs. Apart from that, the definition is very wide. There is no need for the design to be applied to a product by an industrial process, as is evidenced by the inclusion of handicrafts in the definition. Another consequence of this wide definition will be a substantial weakening of the link between the design and the item or product to which it is applied. The inclusion of 'get-up' in the definition will increasingly make it possible to register the design almost as such, or at least to see its scope of protection against infringement widened in practice. In general, there is no need to register the design in respect of every specific item or group of items. The use of the word 'item' in the definition leads to a degree of uncertainty. The word 'item' seems to suggest some physical form, which is easy to understand in relation to packaging and get-up, because bottle shapes and distinctive labels come to mind, but what is meant by items that consist of graphic symbols or typefaces?

It is likely that the legislator wanted to indicate that the design could be on any kind of surface. Things printed on paper, stamps, and posters are therefore, for example, also covered, as are the more traditional designs for curtains and wallpaper. This clearly expands the traditional scope of design law and some even argue that the carrying medium or product does not need to be permanent.[2] Designs can also be for a part of an item; there is no need for the product to which the design refers to be sold separately.

These are obviously important matters, but in a sense they are preliminary matters. We now turn to what Article 3 of the Directive and Article 4 of the Regulation call the requirements for protection. This is the heart of EU design law.

19.2.3 **Requirements for Protection**

It is worth setting out the starting point for these requirements for protection *expressis verbis*:

1. A design shall be protected by a Community design to the extent that it is new and has individual character.

2. A design applied to or incorporated in a product which constitutes a component part of a complex product shall only be considered to be new and to have individual character:

   (a) if the component part, once it has been incorporated into the complex product, remains visible during normal use of the latter; and

   (b) to the extent that those visible features of the component part fulfil in themselves the requirements as to novelty and individual character.

3. 'Normal use' within the meaning of paragraph (2)(a) shall mean use by the end user, excluding maintenance, servicing or repair work.[3]

The latter part of the Article repeats the requirement that the design must remain visible, which we have already referred to earlier as having been highlighted in the recitals of the Directive.

In both instruments this starting point is followed up by two Articles dealing explicitly with the requirements of novelty and individual character respectively. We will discuss these in detail first, and they are set out in Figure 19.1, before returning to the special situation for complex products.

---

[2] See A. Kur, 'Protection of Graphical User Interfaces under European Design Legislation' (2003) 34 *IIC* 50.

[3] Article 4 of the Regulation.

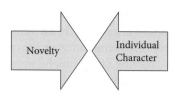

Figure 19.1 Key requirements for registered designs

19.2.4 **Novelty**

In order to be registrable, a design must first of all be new (Article 4 of the Directive/ Article 5 of the Regulation). Novelty is defined in a far less strict way than in patent law: 'a design shall be considered to be new if no identical design has been made available to the public', but 'designs shall be deemed to be identical if their features differ only in immaterial details'.

The first point in this definition of novelty that needs to be clarified is the concept of the 'relevant date'. Normally, this will be the date on which the application for protection is filed. In international cases, however, the applicant may be able to take advantage of the rule in the Paris Convention for the Protection of Industrial Property 1883 that allows an applicant to rely on the date of her first application in a Contracting State during a six-month period whenever an application in another Contracting State is filed within that period and to claim priority on that basis (see Article 5 (1) of the Regulation).

On that relevant date, the test that should be applied is whether the same design—or one with a similar character—is already available to the public through publication, whether following registration or otherwise, through exhibition, through use in trade, or through any other form of disclosure. Any design that is already available to the public in this way will no longer be new and cannot be registered, because it is part of the prior art (see Case T–450/08 *Coverpla v OHIM—Heinz-Glas* EU:T:2012:117). That prior art is composed of designs. In other words, only designs are to be taken into account. Even if that is now a wide definition, which will include many artistic works of copyright and general designs for any kind of item, there are still limitations: for example, human beings are excluded even if they have become icons and are used as such in publicity campaigns.[4]

Certain disclosures will, however, be disregarded when novelty is examined. This flows from the way a disclosure is defined in Article 6 of the Directive and in Article 7 of the Regulation. The same concept of availability to the public will also apply in relation to the requirement of individual character. First of all, any disclosure that is made in confidence to outsiders is not taken into account. Second, in a certain sense, novelty, unlike in patent law, is limited to novelty within Europe, by disregarding any disclosures that could not reasonably have become known in the normal course of business to persons carrying out business in the Community and who specialize in the relevant design area. Third, there is a set of exclusions that are based on the same 12-month grace period principle. On the basis of this principle, disclosures made in that period by the designer or a successor in title, disclosures made by the recipient of information from the designer or such a successor, or disclosures made by anyone in abuse of a relation with the designer or such a successor are to be disregarded. This latter limitation may be an advantage, as well as a disadvantage. On the positive side, it allows a designer to show, that is, disclose, the design at a trade exhibition to assess its success before filing an application for protection. This

---

[4] See *Spice Girls' Application* [2000] ECDR 148.

will only trigger the start of the grace period and the designer will still be able to claim novelty during that grace period. The negative consequences, that is, the destruction of the novelty of the design, will surface if another designer picks up the design at the exhibition, copies it, and brings the product on the market within the Community before the designer files its application. Such behaviour is, on top of anything else, not at all uncommon in the relevant trade circles.

Not only an identical design, but also a design that differs only in immaterial details can destroy novelty. A good example is an application for a design for a bottle carrier. An existing design for a bottle carrier had many features in common with the new design, but the two differed in that:

- they had a different ratio between width and height;
- the handle part in the design applied for encompassed its top half, while that in the existing design comprised only its top third;
- the hole in the handle was circular in shape in the design applied for, while it was oval in the existing design;
- the body part in the design applied for encompassed its bottom half, while in the existing design it encompassed its bottom two-thirds.[5]

These were held by OHIM's Invalidity Division to be more than immaterial differences and the design that had been applied for satisfied the novelty requirement. One should also keep in mind that in assessing novelty (and for that purpose individual character) one cannot exclude from the comparison a prior design just because the design was for a product used for a different purpose from the one the subject of the registration (for an example see the UK case *Gimex International Groupe Import Export v The Chill Bag Company Ltd, Kiki's Import & Export Ltd, David Samuel Turner, Colin David Brand and David Frederick Brand* [2012] EWPCC 31 [41]). Let us turn from this example where the difference fell narrowly on the material side of the spectrum to a case where the difference fell on the immaterial side of the spectrum.

A design for a heater radiator that shared the same pattern of arrangement of features, shapes, and contours with an existing design for radiators was, indeed, held not to be new, despite the fact that the ratio between width and height had been changed from 1:2.5 to 1:2. In this case, these differences were held to be immaterial details. All other aspects of the design were the same (*Pitacs Ltd v Kamil Korhan Karagülle*, decision of 26 April 2006, OHIM Invalidity Division).

19.2.5 **Individual Character**

In addition to being new, the new registered design system requires the design to have 'individual character', which is defined as follows:

> A design shall be considered to have individual character if the overall impression it produces on the informed user differs from the overall impression produced on such a user by any design which has been made available to the public before the date of filing the application for registration or, if a priority is claimed, the date of priority.[6]

The background against which this criterion will be evaluated is that of a design that has at an earlier date been made available to the public. The latter concept is the same as the one

---

[5] *Built NY Inc. v I-Feng Kao*, decision of 8 May 2006, OHIM Invalidity Division.
[6] Article 5 of the Directive, cf Article 6 of the Regulation.

used in relation to novelty and Article 6 of the Directive and Article 7 of the Regulation emphasize that that means in the first place that the earlier design has been published following registration or otherwise (see the decision of OHIM's third Board of Appeal on 15 April 2013 in Case 442/2011-3 *Profile Vox Sp z.o.o. Spolka Komandytowa v Cezar Przedsiebiorstwo Produkcyjne Dariusz Bogdan Niewinski*), but that a design can also be made available to the public by being exhibited, used in trade, or by being disclosed otherwise. In other words, the concept is much broader than publication as a registered design by the competent office. This was demonstrated clearly by the General Court in a case involving the Puma bounding feline trade mark. The General Court saw no problem in the fact that Puma never registered its bounding feline sign as a design. Registration as a trade mark was held to be sufficient to make it available to the public and it could be used to demonstrate that the later design did not have an individual character (Case T–666/11 *Danuta Budziewska v OHIM (Puma SE intervening)* EU:T:2013:584). The Directive and the Regulation do not impose a particular standard of proof when it comes to showing prior availability to the public (see Case T–450/08 *Coverpla v OHIM—Heinz-Glas* EU:T:2012:117).

Whereas novelty essentially looks at whether the design is, save for immaterial details, identical to a pre-existing design, the requirement of individual character is much more in the eye of the particular beholder. The question that is asked is whether the overall impression that the design produces on the informed user differs from the overall impression that a prior design produced on that person. The emphasis is on the overall impression, so bringing together existing features that exist in different products may suffice. And it is the informed user who decides on the issue of the individual character of a design (Case T–246/10 *Industrias Francisco Ivars v OHIM* EU:T:2011:578). There should be no feeling of déjà vu. Small differences that do not alter the overall impression should be disregarded, even if they are by no means insignificant details (Case T–666/11 *Danuta Budziewska v OHIM (Puma SE intervening)* EU:T:2013:584 and Case T–153/08 *Shenzen Taiden v OHIM (Bosch Security Systems)* [2010] ECR II-2517). One should look out for differences that are sufficiently pronounced so that they alter the overall impression (*Danuta Budziewska* and Case T–513/09 *Baena Grupo v OHIM (Neuman and Galdeano del Sel)* (16 December 2010)). The exercise is one with a synthetic nature. Merely listing differences and similarities is not sufficient. The comparison is also limited to the aspects that are protected or will be protected by the registered design. And it is carried out on the basis of the design. The products to which the design will be applied in trade can only be taken into account by way of illustration (Case C–281/10 P *Pepsico Inc. v Grupo Promer Mon Graphic SA and OHIM* [2011] ECR I-10153, [2012] FSR 5 [73]). But the overall impression which the design produces must be compared with and must be different from the one produced by an individual earlier design. It is not permissible to combine features taken from a range of earlier designs for this purpose (Case C–345/13 *Karen Millen Fashions Ltd v Dunnes Stores and Dunnes Stores (Limerick) Ltd* [2014] Bus LR 756 [35]).

This should not obscure the fact, however, that this is a tough test. In many cases, a design will show differences when compared with prior designs, but that by no means guarantees that the informed user will judge that a different overall impression is created. The new law offers no definition of the concept of the 'informed user'. But the fact that the words 'user' and 'informed' are combined suggests that we are dealing with someone who has a certain level of knowledge of the design area concerned, either as a professional working in that field, or as a consumer. That, yet again, makes the test harder, because such users will be particularly aware of the design features that already exist in the field. The CJEU was given the opportunity to define the concept of the informed user in the *Pepsico v Grupo Promer* case. It held that the concept must be understood as lying somewhere between that of the average consumer, applicable in trade mark matters, who need not have any specific knowledge and who, as a rule, makes no direct comparison between the trade marks at issue, and the sectoral expert, who is an expert with detailed technical expertise (see at the national level, e.g., *Normandie Structure Sarl v Cathérine Dalo and Dalo Frères SAS*, Court of Appeal Paris, CA Paris pôle 5-2, 11 January 2013, case no. 2012/013045 and *SA Caroline Diffusion v Sarl Ida 2000*, Supreme Court, Cass. Com., 3 April 2013, case no. 12-13356, [2013] 49 Propriétés Intellectuelles 437). The 'informed user' refers therefore, not to a user of average attention, but to a particularly observant one, either because of his personal experience or his extensive knowledge of the sector in question (Case C–281/10 P *Pepsico Inc. v Grupo Promer Mon Graphic SA and OHIM* [2011] ECR I-10153, [2012] FSR 5 [53] and Joined Cases C–101/11 P and 102/11 P *Herbert Neuman and Andoni Galdeano de Sel v OHIM and José Manuel Baena Grupo SA* [2013] ECDR 76 [53]). The informed user compares the proposed design with what is already available in the field and according to the Court he does so with a particular level of attention:

> [A]s regards the informed user's level of attention, it should be noted that, although the informed user is not the well-informed and reasonably observant and circumspect average consumer who normally perceives a design as a whole and does not proceed to analyse its various details (see, by analogy, *Lloyd Schuhfabrik Meyer & Co GmbH v Klijsen Handel BV* (C-342/97) [1999] E.C.R. I-3819; [1999] 2 C.M.L.R. 1343; [2000] F.S.R. 77 at [25] and [26]), he is also not an expert or specialist capable of observing in detail the minimal differences that may exist between the designs in conflict. *Thus, the qualifier 'informed' suggests that, without being a designer or a technical expert, the user knows the various designs which exist in the sector concerned, possesses a certain degree of knowledge with regard to the features which those designs normally include, and, as a result of his interest in the products concerned, shows a relatively high degree of attention when he uses them.*[7]

The concept of the observant user who is not a technical expert reinforces the idea that designs that do not present significant differences produce the same overall impression on such an informed user and will therefore not lead to a finding of individual character (Case T–11/08 *Kwang Yang Motor v OHIM (Honda Giken Kogyo)* EU:T:2011:447 [13] and *Danuta Budziewska* [32]).

The comparison is normally a direct comparison, i.e. with both designs being present in front of the informed user. That may however be impracticable or uncommon in certain sectors and then an indirect comparison is acceptable. In the latter case the Court accepts that the informed user may have an imperfect recollection of the overall impression produced by both designs. But those features for which the designer had more design freedom and where there were no or fewer technical constraints are more likely to be remembered (Joined Cases C–101/11 P and 102/11 P *Herbert Neuman and Andoni Galdeano de Sel v OHIM and José Manuel Baena Grupo SA* [2013] ECDR 76 [56]–[57] and Case C–281/10 P *Pepsico Inc. v Grupo Promer Mon Graphic SA and OHIM* [2011] ECR I-10153 and [2012] FSR 5 [57]).

The only flexibility that has been built into the system is the sensible approach by which the degree of freedom that was available to the author of the design in creating it should be taken into account when assessing individual character (Case T–9/07 *Grupo Promer Mon Graphic SA v OHIM* [2010] ECDR 7, confirmed on appeal Case C–281/10 P *Pepsico Inc. v Grupo Promer Mon Graphic SA and OHIM* [2011] ECR I-10153 and [2012] FSR 5).

---

[7] Case C–281/10 P *Pepsico Inc. v Grupo Promer Mon Graphic SA and OHIM* [2012] FSR 5 [59] (emphasis added).

Indeed, if there is little room for manoeuvre, maybe for technical reasons, small differences between a new design and existing designs may be particularly telling, and may therefore confer individual character.

A first good example concerned designs for bicycle wheels (*Rodi Comercial SA v Vuelta International SpA*, decision of 20 December 2005, OHIM Invalidity Division). The individual character of an application was challenged on the basis of a 2002 international patent application that contained a bicycle wheel. The informed user was obviously aware of the functional requirements of such wheels and of the prior art known to those who specialize in this area. The informed user would also be aware of the fact that design freedom was limited by the need to lace the wheel with spokes between the hub and the rim. That would focus attention on areas in relation to which design freedom remained, such as the pattern of distribution of spokes around the hub. In this case, the number of spokes was the same, and the same symmetrical, orderly arrangement and pattern had been used. This consequently produced the same overall impression on the user and the design failed the individual character test.

Another example concerned dolls (*Aktiebolaget Design Rubens Sweden v Marie Ekman Bäcklund*, decision of 20 December 2005, OHIM Invalidity Division). The dolls in question were very similar, but the addition of features such as the shape of the nose or belly button, which made the dolls appear more human, meant that the design passed the novelty test. Despite that finding, however, the dolls still produced the same overall impression on the informed user and they therefore failed the individual character test.

The General Court did derive from all this that the question whether or not a design possesses individual character is best approached in four stages. In stage 1 one identifies the sector of the goods to which the design is to be applied. In stage 2 one puts in place the theoretical concept of the informed user of such goods, and with it the level of attention that will be paid by the informed user during the (direct) comparison. In stage 3 one considers the design freedom that was available to the creator of the design under consideration. And in stage 4 the comparison is made and one decides whether the design possesses individual character. Before embarking on this test one obviously has to establish the existence and the anteriority of any design with which the design, the individual character of which is examined, is to be compared. That is, which designs are already out there that may deny the design applied for its individual character (*Danuta Budziewska* [21]).

19.2.6 Component Parts of Complex Products

Additionally, novelty and individual character are said to require that a design that is applied to a component part of a complex product remains visible during the normal use of the complex product, and the novelty and individual character requirements obviously have to be met by the visual features of the component part (Article 3(3) of the Directive/Article 4(2) of the Regulation). This additional rule applies to separate removable parts of a product, rather than to the inside surface of the product. Consumables, such as staples in a staple gun, are also not component parts of the product, that is, the staple gun.

Normal use is defined as use by the end user (Article 3(4) of the Directive/Article 4(3) of the Regulation), with the exclusion of maintenance, servicing, or repair work in relation to the product. The requirement that the design must remain visible in normal use applies therefore in relation to use by the user, rather than by a maintenance technician. Components of an engine that are only visible when the latter is carrying out maintenance work on the engine of a car, for example, are therefore excluded.

19.3 Grounds for Refusal of Registration

19.3.1 Technical Function

As we have already indicated, registered designs are not available to grant rights in merely technical effects. They are rather oriented towards aesthetic designs, at least in the sense of a personal approach by the creator to the visual appearance of the product. While this works well as a starting point, its implementation, in practice, is not entirely straightforward. The legislator has decided that no registered design right shall subsist in features of the appearance of a product that are solely dictated by the product's technical function (Article 7(1) of the Directive/Article 8(1) of the Regulation). Much will depend on the interpretation of this provision. A narrow interpretation will exclude virtually nothing and might allow a designer to monopolize the product by registering a few designs for all of the practical ways of giving effect to a clever technical idea, while a wide interpretation may unduly limit design registrations.

What seems relatively clear from the wording of the provision is that the exclusion will only operate if the features concerned are solely dictated by the product's technical function. This must mean that the main idea is to cover those cases in which the designer had no choice, due to technical constraints linked to the technical function of the product. The exclusion will not apply if the designer can show that there is sufficient design freedom for the product at issue to enable others to create a product that performs the same technical function, while being designed differently. It may be that the exact line separating both options might be drawn along the line of which features are essential to obtain a technical result—that is, to allow the product to fulfil its technical function to the same standard; those features that are not essential in this sense can be the subject of design registration, while essential features, in the sense that they are dictated by technical necessity, cannot.[8]

It is important, however, to add that the exception does not directly exclude designs. All that it excludes are features of appearance that are solely dictated by the product's technical function; all features that are not solely dictated by the product's technical function remain open for design protection. A design for the appearance of a product is therefore still possible if there are enough non-technical features left to meet the criteria for design registration. It is not the case that the presence of one or more technical features excludes the whole appearance of the product from design registration. This makes a lot of business sense, because competitors need those technical features in order to compete, but there is no need for them to copy the non-technical features.

Overall, this interpretation of the provision does, it is submitted, strike a correct competition-friendly balance between adequate design protection and the risk of competition excluding technical designs.

Matters were neatly summarized by OHIM's third Board of Appeal:

> It follows from the above that art. 8(1) CDR denies protection to those features of a product's appearance that were chosen exclusively for the purpose of designing a product that performs its function, as opposed to features that were chosen, at least to some degree, for the purpose of enhancing the product's visual appearance. It goes without saying that these matters must be assessed objectively: it is not necessary to determine what actually went on in the designer's mind when the design was being developed. The matter must be

---

[8] Cf the decision of the CJEU on trade marks for shapes that are necessary to obtain a technical result in Case C–299/99 *Koninklijke Philips v Remington* [2002] ECR I-5475, [2003] RPC 14.

assessed from the standpoint of a reasonable observer who looks at the design and asks himself whether anything other than purely functional considerations could have been relevant when a specific feature was chosen.[9]

19.3.2 The 'Must Fit' Exception: Designs of Interconnection

The other important exception from the scope of registered designs is the 'must fit' exception, which deals with a type of functional design feature that can be characterized as a feature of interconnection. Article 7(2) of the Directive and Article 8(2) of the Regulation define the scope of the exception for what are called designs of interconnections in the following way:

> A design right/Community design shall not subsist in features of appearance of a product which must necessarily be reproduced in their exact form and dimensions in order to permit the product in which the design is incorporated or to which it is applied to be mechanically connected to or placed in, around or against, another product so that either product may perform its function.

Clear examples in practice are electrical plugs and sockets, connectors for lamps to fit into sockets, and batteries to fit into watches. In all these cases, there is a need for the features of appearance to be reproduced in their exact form and dimensions, and this necessity for exact reproduction is therefore the key element in the exception.

This exception is clearly very similar to the technical function exception and there could arguably be an overlap. In fairness to the drafters of the legislation, it can be said that the technical function exception primarily deals with a product that works on its own and in relation to which the design features are dictated by the technical function of that product, whereas the 'must fit' exception deals with two products that need to be connected, etc., in order for them to work. Rather than a technical, this is more a functional, exception. But it is clear that the exception is vital to make sure that no single designer or trader monopolizes a connector system due to the fact that interoperability of products is a vital element to enhance competition. The technical function exception on its own may not have been able to achieve this result, because the shape of the connector is not dictated solely by the product's technical function. Indeed, as the electrical plug and socket example shows, for instance, different plugs and sockets can be devised, and are in use in the UK and in continental Europe. A narrowly defined technical function exception would not therefore cover this example, because the design features of one system are not essential for any product to carry out its technical function.

There is one exception to the 'must fit' exception: designs that serve 'the purpose of allowing multiple assembly or connection of mutually interchangeable products within a modular system' (Article 7(3) of the Directive/Article 8(3) of the Regulation) will still be registrable. Lego toy bricks or stackable chairs come to mind by way of examples. This exception is not based on any particular logic or argument, but is the result of effective lobbying by the toy industry and others.

19.3.3 Public Policy and Morality

Designs that are contrary to public policy or to accepted principles of morality will not be registered (Article 8 of the Directive/Article 9 of the Regulation). Morality can only

---

[9] Case R 690/2007-3 *Lindner Recyclingtech GmbH v Franssons Verkstäder AB* [2010] ECRD 1, approved in the national courts in the UK by *Dyson v Vax* [2010] FSR 39 (Arnold J) and *Samsung Electronics (UK) Ltd v Apple Inc.* [2012] EWHC 1882 (Pat) (HH Judge Birss QC).

be invoked, however, if the design would offend against the moral principles of right-thinking members of society; the fact that some people might find the design distasteful is not sufficient.

This is a standard prohibition. The theoretical reason for its existence is clear, but its application, in practice, is often problematic, because public policy and public morality are hard to define.

19.4 Rights of the Owner and Infringement

19.4.1 Rights and Their Infringement

The next question which obviously arises is the question as to which rights will be conferred by a design that is new and has individual character. Article 12 of the Directive and Article 19 of the Regulation provide a seemingly simple answer to that question, but in reality they cover only half of the answer. The principle they provide reads as follows:

> The registration of a design/A registered Community design shall confer on its holder the exclusive right to use it and to prevent any third party not having its consent from using it. The aforementioned use shall cover, in particular, the making, offering, putting on the market, importing, exporting or using of a product in which the design is incorporated or to which it is applied, or stocking such a product for those purposes.

It seems easy enough to understand the traditional IP approach. An exclusive right is granted and the design cannot be used without the consent of its owner. And that is coupled with a list of examples of activities that amount to use, such as the making, offering, putting on the market, importing, exporting, or using of a product in which the design is incorporated or to which it is applied, or stocking such a product for those purposes. The answer thus provided to the question which rights are granted is however only easy if one assumes that any alleged infringer makes an exact copy of the design and uses it for similar or identical products. That is, of course, not necessarily the case. A slightly different and merely similar design may be used and then the question arises how one defines use of 'the design'. How broadly or how narrowly does one construe this question and therefore also the scope of protection for the rights holder? The Directive and the Regulation provide guidance on this point in a separate Article, Article 9 of the Directive and Article 10 of the Regulation respectively. Under the heading 'scope of protection' these Articles provide that:

(1) The scope of the protection conferred by a design right shall include any design which does not produce on the informed user a different overall impression.

(2) In assessing the scope of the protection, the degree of freedom of the designer in developing his design shall be taken into consideration.

One does in other words go back to the question and standard of individual character. A similar design that provides a different overall impression will not infringe … and may be entitled to registration in its own right. This creates a neat line between entitlement to protection and infringement. And it gives the rights owner a fair degree of protection, i.e. any design that is not different enough to be entitled to its own protection will lead to a finding of infringement. So maybe the better way to put it is that a similar design that provides a different overall impression will not infringe, because it may be entitled to registration in its own right. And logically the design freedom of the creator of the design shall also play a role in shaping the scope of protection. The influence this factor has in terms of individual character and therefore on what can amount to a design obviously translates in a parallel way to the scope of the right once it is protected.

But this does not solve another key problem: how does one deal with the relationship between the design, on the one hand, and the item, on the other? The design will still be registered for a product, or a class of products, and any infringement case is almost bound to compare design as applied to products, rather than design in isolation, but infringement is, in this system, no longer confined to use on the product for which the design is registered. The design may be infringed if no different overall impression is created, irrespective of the type of product to which it is applied. But is it not reasonable to assume that in practice a similar design applied to a very different product is far more likely to create a different overall impression than the same similar design on the exact products for which the design is registered and used? It is not clear in detail what role will be played by the fact that the design is registered for certain goods. The design may also only affect a part of a product. This may make it rather difficult to apply the negative test of not creating a different impression to the design. How, in practice, is one going to make abstraction of the product to assess the overall impression created by the allegedly infringing design? On top of that, the negative formulation of the test does nothing to alleviate the problem (which is fairly inevitable in relation to designs). Does 'different' mean that the design must not create the same identical impression or will some (strong) form of similarity infringe in practice? It will be up to the courts, and, eventually, the CJEU, to determine the exact boundaries in this respect.

In the UK, the Court of Appeal of England and Wales made a start in *Procter & Gamble Co. v Reckitt Benckiser (UK) Ltd* [2008] ECDR 3, [2008] FSR 8. This is also a nice example from the national courts, as the parties also litigated the case in Austria (Higher Provisional Court in Vienna 4Ob 239/04g). This case was concerned with a design applied to sprayers for air-freshener products. The canister for the defendant's 'Air-Wick' product was inspired by the claimant's design for its 'Febreze' canister. The question arose whether there was more than inspiration and whether an infringement had occurred.

The Court of Appeal, first of all, turned its attention to the concept of the 'informed user'. Similar characters in both patent and trade mark law were held not to be of assistance. What we are dealing with here is a user who is aware of the existing design corpus in the area. Such a user has experience of other similar items and designs, and will therefore be reasonably discriminatory. She will be able to appreciate enough detail to decide whether a design creates an allegedly infringing design or produces a different overall impression. In doing so, there is no decisive role for the idea that the user must have an imperfect recollection. She would view things carefully and, as such, remember more details. What matters in making the decision is what strikes the mind of the informed user when the designs are viewed carefully. The informed user therefore has more extensive knowledge than an average consumer in possession of average information, awareness, and understanding. In particular, the informed user is open to design issues and is fairly familiar with them.[10] This includes the knowledge of the fact that, by reason of function, shapes can be, to a certain extent, required to conform to a certain standard.

The court then turned its attention to the concept of 'a different overall impression'. A difference that allows the informed user to discriminate between the two designs is

---

[10] The Court of Appeal in *Procter & Gamble Co. v Reckitt Benckiser (UK) Ltd* [2008] ECDR 3, [2008] FSR 8 cited, with approval, the conclusion reached in a case between the same parties by the Higher Provisional Court in Vienna 4Ob 239/04g: *Procter & Gamble Co. v Reckitt Benckiser (UK) Ltd* [2007] EWCA Civ 936 [26].

required, but it is not required that the allegedly infringing design 'clearly differs' from the registered design. What one has in mind is the question of whether or not the designs are substantially different. The court offered the following guidelines for the application of the test:

i) ...the test is 'different' not 'clearly different.'

ii) The notional informed user is 'fairly familiar' with design issues...

iii) Next [it] is not a proposition of law but a statement about the way people (and thus the notional informed user) perceive things. It is simply that if a new design is markedly different from anything that has gone before, it is likely to have a greater overall visual impact than if it is 'surrounded by kindred prior art.'... It follows that the 'overall impression' created by such a design will be more significant and the room for differences which do not create a substantially different overall impression is greater. So protection for a striking novel product will be correspondingly greater than for a product which is incrementally different from the prior art, though different enough to have its own individual character and thus be validly registered.

iv) On the other hand it does not follow, in a case of markedly new design (or indeed any design) that it is sufficient to ask 'is the alleged infringement closer to the registered design or to the prior art', if the former infringement, if the latter not. The test remains 'is the overall impression different?'

v) It is legitimate to compare the registered design and the alleged infringement with a reasonable degree of care. The court must 'don the spectacles of the informed user' to adapt the hackneyed but convenient metaphor of patent law. The possibility of imperfect recollection has a limited part to play in this exercise.

vi) The court must identify the 'overall impression' of the registered design with care. True it is that it is difficult to put into language, and it is helpful to use pictures as part of the identification, but the exercise must be done.

vii) In this exercise the level of generality to which the court must descend is important. Here, for instance, it would be too general to say that the overall impression of the registered design is 'a canister fitted with a trigger spray device on the top.' The appropriate level of generality is that which would be taken by the notional informed user.

viii) The court should then do the same exercise for the alleged infringement.

ix) Finally the court should ask whether the overall impression of each is different. This is almost the equivalent to asking whether they are the same—the difference is nuanced, probably, involving a question of onus and no more.[11]

When the court applied these guidelines to the case at issue, it again agreed with the Austrian court's decision that:

In reality, even though the same features are found in both, there are clear differences between the two sprayers resulting from the different mode of their execution: the Febreze sprayer is smaller, has a slightly larger diameter and so looks more compact. The head of this sprayer is shallower but also broader, so that the Febreze sprayer fits the hand differently than the Airwick sprayer (with the Airwick sprayer, which has the considerably narrower head, there is a feeling that it could slip out of the user's hand). In contrast to the Airwick sprayer, the metal can of the Febreze sprayer tapers upwards, so that the waist

---

[11] *Procter & Gamble Co. v Reckitt Benckiser (UK) Ltd* [2008] ECDR 3, [2008] FSR 8, [2007] EWCA Civ 936 [35].

begins lower down than in the Airwick sprayer. The 'train' goes down much further in the Febreze sprayer, so that the lower boundary of the plastic part echoes the angle of the head part far more markedly than in the Airwick sprayer. The shape of head too is different: while the head of the Febreze sprayer—to draw a comparison from the animal kingdom—is reminiscent of a snake's head, the shape of the Airwick sprayer head is like a lizard's head.[12]

The similarities are clearly only found at a general level and it was therefore held that a different overall impression was produced on the informed user. On that basis, the infringement case failed (*Procter & Gamble Co.* [62]–[63]).

One should also keep in mind that this is a visual exercise. What counts is what the court can see with its own eyes. So when Apple sued Samsung arguing that the design of Samsung's tablet computer infringed the design of Apple's iPad the UK court put the emphasis on the fact that one design was markedly thinner and that the back of the devices was very different. The similarities of the screen and the front of the tablets were less important as they were down to functionality and offered very little design freedom. On that basis the court held that a different overall impression was created and the infringement case failed (*Samsung Electronics (UK) Ltd v Apple Inc.* [2012] EWHC 1882 (Pat), confirmed on appeal *Samsung Electronics (UK) Ltd v Apple Inc.* [2012] EWCA Civ 1339. See also *Dyson v Vax* [2010] EWHC 1923 (Pat), [2010] FSR 39, confirmed on appeal *Dyson v Vax* [2011] EWCA Civ 1206, [2012] FSR 4).

A defendant who has received a cease and desist letter may of course try to register its own design before being sued for infringement, but the fact that the defendant has its own design registered has no influence on the infringement assessment. There is no need to invalidate the later design before an infringement case can be brought (Case C–488/10 *Celaya Emparanza y Galdos Internacional SA (Cegasa) v Proyectos Integrales de Balizamiento SL* [2012] ECDR 17).

19.4.2 Exclusion from Protection: Defences to Infringement

The exclusive rights of the rights holder are subject to certain limitations and exclusions (Article 13 of the Directive/Article 20 of the Regulation). For an alleged infringer, these turn into a series of defences:

(a) acts done privately and for non-commercial purposes will not constitute an infringement;

(b) acts done for experimental purposes are exempted;

(c) acts of reproduction for the purposes of making citations or of teaching are also exempted provided that the act of reproduction is compatible with fair trade practices and does not unduly prejudice the normal exploitation of the design, on the one hand, and that the source is mentioned, on the other;

(d) there are specific exceptions in relation to foreign-registered ships and aircraft, which are temporarily in the country, the repairing of these, and the importation of spare parts for that purpose.

Spare parts are a particularly thorny issue and no final agreement could be reached when the Regulation was put in place. It therefore contains the following transitional provision:

> Until such time as amendments to this Regulation enter into force on a proposal from the Commission on this subject, protection as a Community design shall not exist for a

---

[12] Ibid [61].

design which constitutes a component part of a complex product used within the meaning of Article 19(1) for the purpose of the repair of that complex product so as to restore its original appearance.[13]

The exhaustion rule will also apply at the EEA level (see already Case 144/81 *Keurkoop BV v Nancy Kean Gifts BV* [1982] ECR 2853, [1983] 2 CMLR 47). The usual rule applies in this respect. Accordingly, Article 15 of the Directive and Article 21 of the Regulation respectively stipulate that:

> The rights conferred by a design right upon registration/a Community design shall not extend to acts relating to a product in which a design included within the scope of protection of the Community design is incorporated or to which it is applied, when the product has been put on the market in the Community by the holder of the Community design or with his consent.

19.5 Ownership of and Entitlement to a Registered Design

The questions who is entitled to a registered design and who will be its owner are left to the national laws of the Member States by the Directive, which does not contain specific provisions on this point. The Regulation on the other hand contains detailed rules on these points. According to Article 14 'the right to the Community design shall vest in the designer or his successor in title'. The starting point is therefore that the author of a design, i.e. the designer, as the person who creates the design, will be entitled to the Community design (see the *Bolero* case, German Bundesgerichtshof I ZR 23/12 [2014] *IIC* 239). The logical consequence is then of course that joint developers of a design will jointly be entitled to the Community design. But the provision also mentions an eventual successor in title. This might not merely be the heir of a deceased designer, since the Regulation clearly envisages that the entitlement to the Community design can in advance be transferred by contract, for example to the person commissioning the design. The latter will then be entitled to register the Community design directly in its name. There is only one exception to this rule. The employer of the employee who creates a design will be the first owner of the registered design if the design is created in the course of employment, unless the parties (or the applicable national law) agree otherwise (Article 14(3) of the Regulation). There is, however, no presumptive transfer of ownership to the commissioner of the design (see Case C–32/08 *Fundación Española para la Innovación de la Artesanía (FEIA) v Cul de Sac Espacio Creativo SL and Acierta Product & Position SA* [2009] ECDR 19). But the designer shall in any case retain the right to be cited as such in the register (Article 18). It is of course possible that the Community design has either been applied for or registered in the name of a person who it not entitled to it. Article 15 gives in those circumstances the person entitled to the Community design a claim to be recognized as the legitimate owner of the Community design.

Ownership of a registered Community design can change and the right can be transferred. Article 27 clearly envisages that, but puts forward the principle that the Community design shall be dealt with in its entirety and for the whole of the Community. Licences, as well as assignments, can therefore be envisaged. Any transfer can at the request of one of the parties to it be registered in the register and will then be published. Until the transfer has been entered into the register it cannot be invoked against third parties, which means that the successor in title cannot invoke the rights that arise from the registration of the

---

[13] Article 110 of the Regulation.

Community design (Article 28). This means that, in practice, it is advisable that assignments and licences are in writing, although this is, in theory, not an express requirement.

19.6 Invalidity

A registered design can be declared invalid (Article 11 of the Directive/Article 24 of the Regulation). This can always be done in court, for a Community design this will be in a Community design court on the basis of a counterclaim in infringement proceedings. For a Community design an application for a declaration can also be made to OHIM's Invalidity Division and a similar option exists in many national laws.

The first and obvious grounds for invalidity arise where the design does not meet the definition of a design or the requirements of novelty and individual character that are set out in the Directive and the Regulation (see Cases T–666/11 *Danuta Budziewska v OHIM (Puma SE intervening)* EU:T:2013:584; T–10/08 *Kwang Yang Motor Co. Ltd v OHIM* [2012] ECDR 2; T–68/10 *Sphere Time v OHIM* [2011] ECDR 20; and T–153/08 *Shenzhen Taiden v OHIM* T:2010:248), or where there are problems with disclosure, morality, or public policy.

A person who is entitled to the design may also apply for its invalidity if the applicant or holder is not entitled to it. The Regulation requires a prior court decision on the latter point.

Next a design may be declared invalid (on the application of the applicant for or the holder of the earlier right in the case of a Community design) if the design is in conflict with a prior design which has been made available to the public after the date of filing of the application or, if priority is claimed, the date of priority of the Community design, and which is protected from a date prior to the said date.

A design can also be declared invalid if a distinctive sign is used in a subsequent design, and Community law or the law of the Member State governing that sign confers on the rights holder of the sign the right to prohibit such use (see Case T–148/08 *Beifa Group Co. Ltd v OHIM* [2010] ETMR 42). Once more the Regulation requires that the application for the declaration of invalidity be made by the applicant for or the holder of the earlier right in the case of a Community design and the Directive leaves the Member States free to introduce or not to introduce this ground of invalidity into their design laws. This also applies for the following additional grounds of invalidity that are found in the Regulation.

It is also a ground for invalidity of a design if the design constitutes an unauthorized use of a work protected under the copyright law of a Member State (see Cases T–566/11 and 567/11 *Viejo Valle SA v OHIM (Établissements Coquet intervening)* EU:T:2013:549).

And the final ground for invalidity applies if the design constitutes an improper use of any of the items listed in Article 6*ter* Paris Convention, or of badges, emblems, and escutcheons other than those covered by the said Article 6*ter* and which are of particular public interest in a Member State.

A registered design that has been declared invalid shall be deemed not have had any effects from the outset (Article 26 of the Regulation).

19.7 Duration of the Registered Design Right

The design right is protected upon registration (assuming that means it meets all the relevant requirements), but the term of protection starts to run from the date of filing. The initial term of protection will run for a period of five years, but it can be extended by renewing the registration for further successive terms of five years. The maximum total term of protection is 25 years (Article 10 of the Directive/Article 12 of the Regulation).

In practice, the commercial life of a design will often be shorter than 25 years and it can be expected that many registered designs will be allowed to lapse, because their owners request no further renewal. Fashions do indeed exist in this area. Many features of appearance that were very popular around 2010 are no longer popular, so there is no need to renew the design registration. In doing so, one would incur a cost that could no longer be recuperated by profits through sales of items made to the design.

The application for renewal of the Community design must be made by the rights holder or a person authorized by the rights holder and such an application must be addressed to OHIM during the last six months of the previous five-year period. In the absence of such an application, the right will cease to exist upon expiry of the previous five-year period. The owner of the right is, however, given an additional six-month period during which he can renew the right, although a restoration fee will be payable on top of the normal renewal fee. If the right is restored, it shall be treated as if it had never expired (Article 13 of the Regulation). Most national legislation operates a comparable system.

19.8 International Commercial Exploitation

International exploitation of registered designs is facilitated by the fact that the Paris Convention 1883 covers this area. A design application in one of the Contracting States will result in a priority right, the term of which is six months, in relation to applications made in other Contracting States. But substantial problems relating to the international exploitation of a registered design are created by the tremendous international disparity in design protection systems. So, contrary to the EU system, many foreign systems do not provide for an examination, but operate a deposit system, which means that designs are entered into the register upon application, with a possibility for all interested parties to object to the validity of the design and to request its removal from the register. The latter option was also taken by the Contracting Parties to the Hague Agreement 1925,[14] which aimed at creating a unified registration system for designs, but this system never managed to attract much international support although now the EU has adhered to it in the context of the Community design right.

19.9 Community Design

We have indicated that the EU approach to registered designs has been based on two tracks. The first track consisted of the Directive, aimed at harmonizing national registered design laws. The second track consists of the Regulation, which puts in place a system under which a single Community (registered) design will be granted as a result of a central single application with the Community Design Office, which is located in Alicante as part of the existing OHIM structure. Once granted, the Community design will apply in the whole of the Community. The Community design is separate from any national design rights. Until now we have looked at what both tracks have in common. The time has come to look at two aspects that are different. The first one is the procedural

---

[14] The 1999 Act of the Agreement entered into force on 23 December 2003.

aspect. We cannot compare it to 26[15] somewhat different national procedures though, but let us at least look at the procedure for the Community design in OHIM. And secondly, the Regulation also puts in place an unregistered design.

19.9.1 Procedural Issues

In procedural terms, OHIM deals with the application for and registration of Community designs (Titles IV and V of the Regulation, respectively). It examines whether the formal requirements and the definition of a design have been met. Upon registration the design is published. Novelty and individual character are not examined, but third parties can bring invalidity proceedings before the Office if they consider that the design should not be registered validly, because of lack of such. Articles 45 and 47 of the Regulation indicate the limited scope of the examination and implicitly refer back to Articles 24 and 25 on the point of invalidity. The procedural aspect of raising invalidity is dealt with in Article 52 of the Regulation.

Appeals against a decision made by OHIM—such as a decision to refuse registration—can be brought before the Boards of Appeal, which form part of OHIM's structure but act as independent tribunals. A further appeal can then be brought before the CJEU, via the General Court and, ultimately, before the Court of Justice itself (Title VII of the Regulation). Invalidity can also be raised as a counterclaim before the national courts, which will also deal with infringement cases. Each Member State has selected, for this purpose, a limited number of Community design courts among its national courts, both at first instance and on appeal (Articles 80 and 81 of the Regulation).

19.9.2 The Community Unregistered Design Right

The Regulation also created a Community *unregistered* design right, which complements the registered right.

The need for an unregistered right had become apparent in those industries in which fashion changes every couple of months and for which the registration process will simply last too long. There are also many cases in which registration will be costly and in relation to which the applicant would rather test the market for the design first before deciding on registration.[16]

The Community unregistered design right addresses these concerns by providing for a three-year term of protection without registration or other formalities. In order to be protected, the design will need to meet the same requirements as its registered counterpart. In terms of novelty this means that no identical design must have been made available to the public before the date on which the (unregistered) design for which protection is claimed has first been made available to the public (Article 5(1)(a) of the Regulation). And the same date is also determinative for the examination of the individual character of the (unregistered) design and the overall impression made on the informed user (Article 6(1)(a) of the Regulation; and see, e.g., in France *SA Mod Ecran v SAS Babou*, Court of Appeal Paris, CA Paris pôle 5-2, 7 February 2014, case no. 13/10689, [2014] 63 Propriétés Intellectuelles 435 where the court struggled with the concept of the informed user). The three-year term starts to run on the date on which the design was first made available to the public by publication, exhibition, use in trade, or any other way of disclosing the

---

[15] The three Benelux countries in the EU, Belgium, the Netherlands, and Luxembourg have a single design, based on a single design law and a single office.

[16] See V. Saez, 'The Unregistered Community Design' [2002] *EIPR* 585.

design if it could be reasonably known in specialized Community circles (Article 11 of the Regulation). The latter should not be restricted to designers in the relevant field and can include traders or retailers in the field (Case C–479/12 *H. Gautzsch Großhandel GmbH & Co. KG v Münchener Boulevard Möbel Joseph Duna GmbH* [2014] ECDR 14 [30]). In this respect, again, there are important similarities with its registered counterpart. And when it comes to using the concept of availability to the public for the purposes of disclosure in the context of Article 7 (novelty and individual character) all will depend on the factual circumstances, but the CJEU was not prepared to rule out the conclusion that a design has not become available to the public as a result of a single demonstration of the design in the showroom of a manufacturer outside the EU (or on the basis of a mere registration in a design register in a country outside the EU), even when coupled with the delivery of a single copy of an article made to the design to a company in the EU (Case C–479/12 *H. Gautzsch Großhandel GmbH & Co. KG v. Münchener Boulevard Möbel Joseph Duna GmbH* [2014] ECDR 14 [36]). Returning to Article 11, one should also note that there is no presumption of proprietorship of the unregistered design to the benefit of the person who made the design available to the public. The normal rule applies and the designer will be entitled to the unregistered design (see the *Bolero* case, German Bundesgerichtshof I ZR 23/12 [2014] *IIC* 239).

Infringement of the Community unregistered design right occurs in the same way as infringement of the registered right, apart from the fact that, in the absence of registration, the claimant must also prove that the defendant copied the protected design (see, e.g., in France *SAS Sprintex v Sarl Bahadirlar Tekstil* Paris, Court of Appeal Paris, CA Paris pôle 5-2, 7 February 2014, case no. 13/07500, [2014] 63 Propriétés Intellectuelles 435). There will be no infringement if there has been independent creation by the alleged infringer if the latter may reasonably be thought not to have been familiar with the unregistered design that was disclosed to the public by its holder (Article 19(2) of the Regulation). It is up to the holder of the unregistered design to prove that the contested use results from copying that design. However, if a Community design court finds that the fact of requiring that holder to prove that the contested use results from copying that design is likely to make it impossible or excessively difficult for such evidence to be produced, that court is required to use all procedures available to it under national law to counter that difficulty (Case C–479/12 *H. Gautzsch Großhandel GmbH & Co. KG v Münchener Boulevard Möbel Joseph Duna GmbH* [2014] ECDR 14 [44]).

When proceedings are brought for the infringement or the threatened infringement of an unregistered Community design, the Community design court shall presume that the unregistered design right is valid if the holder produces proof that the conditions of Article 11 have been met and indicates what is the individual character of the design. It is up to the defendant to contest the validity by plea or counterclaim for a declaration of invalidity (Article 85(2) of the Regulation). The rights holder is not, however, required to prove that the design has individual character within the meaning of Article 6. A mere indication of what in its view are the elements of the design that give it its individual character will be sufficient (Case C–345/13 *Karen Millen Fashions Ltd v Dunnes Stores and Dunnes Stores (Limerick) Ltd* [2014] Bus LR 756 [47]).

In terms of invalidity the standard rules of the Regulation apply to the unregistered Community design right if a problem with its validity arises. The Regulation merely adds that such a design shall be declared invalid by a Community design court on application to such a court on the basis of a counterclaim in infringement proceedings (Article 24(3) of the Regulation).

The seamless connection with the registered right is assured by the provision that allows a one-year grace period between the publication and the application for the registered right (Article 7(2) of the Regulation). Novelty will, in other words, not be lost by publication giving rise to a Community unregistered design right. This allows the designer to test the market before deciding on an application, as long as that application for a registered design is launched before the end of the one-year grace period.

19.10 Conclusions

The Directive and the Regulation have put in place a coherent set of design law provisions. It will take the courts a while though to provide sharp definitions of concepts of novelty and individual character. In particular the concept of the informed user is currently causing problems. Infringement seems more straightforward, even if there is of course also in that context the issue that whilst the system is protecting designs it is necessarily allowing their registration for certain categories of goods and services. The influence that has on the operation of the system is another delicate point. And of course the troublesome issue of spare parts protection has still not been addressed to everyone's satisfaction.

What remains true, however, and what drives the development of the system is the fact that designs can be of tremendous commercial value. They do not amount to an invention and are not necessarily a trade mark; neither does copyright protect the idea behind the design, even if it can cover certain expressions of the design. So there is a very real need to register the design as a registered design. It is the only way in which to prevent competitors from cashing in on a good and valuable design by using one that is substantially identical. The Directive and the Regulation make a very real contribution in this respect.

Further Reading

CARBONI, A., 'Design Validity and Infringement: Feel the Difference' (2008) 30 *EIPR* 111

IZQUIERDO PERIS, J.J., 'Registered Community Design: First Two-Year Balance from an Insider's Perspective' [2006] *EIPR* 146

IZQUIERDO PERIS, J.J., 'OHIM Practice in the Field of Invalidity of Registered Community Designs' (2008) 30 *EIPR* 56

SAEZ, V., 'The Unregistered Community Design' [2002] *EIPR* 585

SCANLAN, G. AND GALE, S., 'Industrial Design and the Design Directive: Continuing and Future Problems in Design Rights' [2005] *Journal of Business Law* 91

PART V

Data and Information

20

Introduction to Rights in Data and Information

20.1 Moving Away from the Property Right

In this part of the book we deal with rights in data and information. There is a significant difference with the rights that we have dealt with up to now. Patents, trade marks, design rights, and copyright can be described as property rights, or at least rights that are similar to property rights. We are now moving away from these types of rights. There is no (property) right in a trade secret, even if its holder is entitled to see it protected against unauthorized divulgation. Privacy protection is again not giving rise to a property right in the information concerning one's private life. Once again the main element here is the provision of a remedy. Privacy has a close link with data protection. The latter offers protection when it comes to the processing of personal data concerning individuals. And data exclusivity does not provide a right in the data, but merely a period of exclusivity during which third parties who seek marketing authorization cannot rely on the data. The closest we come to a property right is when we look in the next chapter at the database right. Here a *sui generis* right is created, but it covers the structure of the database and does not affect the content of the database, i.e. the data.

Apart from moving away from property rights or rights similar to property rights, another key point is the emphasis on the fact that a remedy is made available. The availability of a remedy becomes the key component of the protection. This is a limitation. There is no transferable title or right. There is merely a remedy if the interests of the claimant are unfairly affected. This applies primarily to privacy invasions and the unauthorized divulgation of trade secrets, but there are also aspects of it in the protection that is provided when personal data are processed and data protection issues arise. The same can be said about data exclusivity. The first applicant is not exactly offered a remedy, but other applicants are stopped from relying on the data. The similarity may not be with damages as an example of a remedy, but with an injunction. The *sui generis* database right is again a bit of a case apart.

One should not underestimate the value of data and information, both in a commercial and in a private or personal setting. These 'rights' in data and information are therefore important and they make a significant contribution to the protection of valuable interests, either in combination with traditional IP rights or in their own right.

20.2 The Nature of Information and of the 'Rights' in Information

The real impetus for the creation of 'rights' in information is therefore not found in the fact that there is another form of human creativity that needs protection and that is not served by the existing IP rights such as patents and copyright. Instead the impetus is found in the financial investment in the gathering and the organization of the data and information. This area is entirely about the protection of investment against the ease of copying. The nature of what emerges is therefore also radically different from the traditional IP rights.

But let us focus in a first stage on the basic structure of our society. Our democratic system and our system of personal autonomy depend heavily on the free flow of information. Human beings need to absorb and digest lots of information during the process of their education to acquire the personal autonomy they need to function in society. And only educated people can make informed choices and real contributions to the functioning of our democratic system. Free access to information is therefore vital. The traditional IP rights fit in with the logic, as they merely protect original contributions to the wealth of human knowledge. In other words, they do not protect the information as such, but what people do with it. Patents protect inventions rather than mere discoveries and copyright is not granted for ideas but for individual original expressions of such ideas. Or to put it succinctly, IP rights protect added value. Added value in terms of creativity is not easily identified in the area of 'rights' in information. One can think of the structure of a database, but inevitably in a digital environment one also limits access to the data and the information if one protects the structure of the database. Access to the data and the information is only possible through the database. Data protection, with its link to personal data and privacy, may legitimately bring the protection of the fundamental rights of the individual to the fore, but again, and irrespective of the 'good' reasons for doing so, this also restricts the access to information. It is therefore of the essence to strike the right balance between the various interests involved. And to work out a system that guarantees access to information, whilst at the same time protecting the investment in databases in particular and structured access to the information in general.

This also fits in with the fundamental nature of information. Information as such is a public good. It is non-excludable and non-rivalled in nature. The fact that some does something creative with the information does not exhaust it. Others can use it again and the social cost of its use by many people, once it is produced, is zero. The non-excludability of the information makes it unsusceptible to appropriation, except by grant of exclusive right coupled with the threat of enforcement. But introducing the latter risks upsetting the fundamental order of things. It is therefore desirable that information be at least partially non-excludable, because that attribute permits free access to information by those who value it at its social cost—the value of their attention to it—but not enough to pay a positive price above that social cost.

Traditional IP rights such as patents, trade marks, and copyright are exclusionary rights, but they are transferable in nature. One can assign these rights. The only real exception are moral rights as an aspect of copyright. But in the area of 'rights' in information, non-transferability is the norm, rather than the exception. Suffice it to think here of the parallel between moral right, linked to the person of the author, and personal information in the context of data protection. 'Rights' in personal information are also not transferable. This is yet another element that contributes to the different conception of the 'rights' in information.

20.3 The Set-Up of the Various Chapters

With that in mind we will now turn to the protection of databases and the database right, as the one that is probably still most closely related to the traditional IP rights. But instead of the data being protected directly, in the same vein as the copyright work or the patented invention, these data themselves are not the object of protection. That protection is given to the database, as the organizational structure in which the data are placed and from which they can be retrieved. Any protection for the data is therefore of an indirect nature, mainly through the right to stop extraction and reutilization.

Be that as it may, data have become extremely valuable in our modern society and they are protected and used widely. Personal data are however amongst the most sensitive data and our society is much more worried about certain forms of use being made of them. It is therefore appropriate to consider next the special data protection regime that was put in place for these personal data.

This is one form of restriction placed on the use of certain kinds of data. But there are different types of restrictions. Public health considerations require applicants to publish research data on their new pharmaceuticals, but these data are extremely valuable and a lot of resources have gone into their creation. It would therefore be unfair to impose that burden entirely on one party and let subsequent parties free ride on that effort. Restrictions are therefore placed on the use of the data in these very specific circumstances. This is a narrow area, but one that is vital for pharmaceutical patents. Considering patents for pharmaceuticals without considering the complementary system of data exclusivity gives rise to a distorted picture and it is to this form of restriction that we therefore turn next.

Up to now the discussion has been about bodies of data that are, albeit with restrictions, available and often available in the public domain. In the final two chapters in this part we deal in more detail with data that one may wish to keep out of the public domain and at the legal tools that are available for that purpose. From a commercial perspective these data are referred to as trade secrets and there seems to be an increasing need to protect them against industrial espionage. From a private point of view we are concerned with the right to privacy.

21

Database Rights

21.1 Introduction

Databases became to be seen in the 1990s as valuable assets, but assets that on the one hand require substantial investment for their creation and that are on the other hand easy and straightforward to copy. Traditional IP protection, such as copyright, was often not able to protect databases as they lacked originality. Suffice it by way of example to refer to telephone directories. Their value is derived from their completeness and from their alphabetical listing of names and numbers. Yet, these very characteristics point irremediably to a lack of originality. Another tool was therefore created to protect the valuable investment in the creation of a database and to stimulate the development of a home-grown European database industry, even if IP does, at least historically, not merely protect investments. The Directive that emerged combined this *sui generis* right with copyright for the appropriate, be it somewhat rare, cases. What became known as the Database Directive is in terms of EU law European Parliament and Council Directive on the protection of databases [1996] OJ L 77/20.[1]

Long before the arrival of digital technology various forms of databases were around in analogue format, as for a database everything centres around placing information in a usable format. Telephone directories, divided by town or village, and with entries then organized alphabetically on the basis of the surname of the subscriber to the telephone service are a typical example, as are encyclopedias. The real value of a database lies in the comprehensive nature of the information it contains, rather than in the originality of the information itself. Digital technology opened up opportunities of scale in this area and made data easy to search. But at the same time it impeded the mere consultation or reading of the data, that are now hidden in a digital format. Earlier databases were in that respect more easily reconcilable with the right of access to information. This right is of concern to various categories of users as it may involve information in the public domain (e.g. an electoral register), information where the

---

[1] In the UK the Directive was implemented by means of the Copyright and Rights in Databases Regulations 1997, SI 1997/3032 and the regime came into force on 1 January 1998.

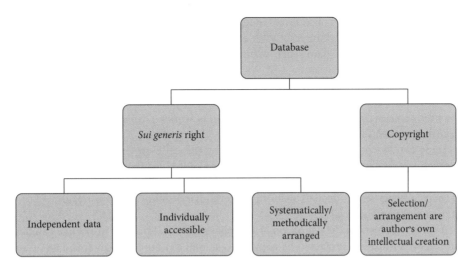

Figure 21.1 The database architecture system after the Database Directive

database constitutes the only available source of that information (e.g. a telephone directory), information pertaining to academic and scientific research and other public interest users such as consumers, the disabled, libraries, and information which is 'created' independently of any other activities where the primary purpose or principal activity is the creation of a database whether using own data or data acquired from another source. Granting an exclusive right in a collection of data or information, without any requirement of originality in relation to the data or information, not only risks interfering with the right of access to information, the exclusive nature of the right, i.e. granting it to a single entity, but also risks interfering with the freedom of competition, as the only workable access to information and data that are themselves in the public domain and freely available will now pass via the rights holder and its database. This may stifle some economic and business initiative by pushing up costs and by limiting access. The database right has therefore the difficult task of striking the right balance between the various interests involved and the Directive has been accused of putting in place the least balanced and most anti-competitive exclusive right in the EU. As will be seen later on though, the CJEU has addressed some of these issues in its case law. What remains clear is that the Directive has not managed to succeed in stimulating to any great degree the European database industry. Its effectiveness is therefore more limited than had been anticipated. Before we go into detail, the architecture of the system that emerged from the Directive can be summarized schematically as shown in Figure 21.1.

21.2 A Database

Whilst the Directive protects a database in any form, one still needed a legal definition of a database and the IT/database industry's definitions did not all point in the same direction. The Directive addresses this issue in its Article 1(2) and defines the term 'database' as 'a collection of independent works, data, or other materials, arranged in a systematic or methodical way, and are individually accessible by electronic or other means'. This definition can be summarized by means of a number of points, as follows.

A database has to be a collection of independent material. In practice, this means that separate items that do not interact with each other are stored in a database. The non-interaction rule excludes items such as film, in which the script, music, etc., interact to form the final work.

The items in a database must be accessible on an individual basis—that is, one must be able to retrieve them individually. This excludes numerous multimedia works in which the user necessarily gets access to a combination of works in different media at any one time during the use of the work.

These two key points were also highlighted by the CJEU in Case C–444/02 *Fixtures Marketing v OPAP* [2004] ECR I-10549 when the Court ruled that a database is 'any collection of works, data, or other materials, separable from one another without the value of their contents being affected, including a method or system . . . for the retrieval of each of its constituent material'.

A further element of the definition of a database is the fact that the works in a database can be works that are protected by copyright, as well as non-copyrightable data or any other materials. Copyright protection for these items, as such, is not required and a database can contain a mixture of different items: for example, a combination of copyright works and other data.

Both electronic and non-electronic collections or databases are included in the scope of the definition.

The independent works, etc., must be arranged in a systematic or methodical way. Putting random information and items in a box will therefore not create a database—but it can be argued that a newspaper is a database, because the articles in it (which are independent and individually accessible works) are arranged in a systematic way (grouped by home news pages, overseas news pages, etc.).

This final requirement creates specific problems in relation to electronic databases. Often, the information is fed into the system in a random way, while the software of the database organizes the information afterwards. The physical storage of the information in the memory of the computer (or on floppy disk, CD-ROM, etc.) is not even necessarily in the same or another systematic way. It is submitted that these collections nevertheless meet the arrangement criterion. A systematic or methodical arrangement exists and it is provided by an element of the database itself. The technical way in which this is achieved is irrelevant in this context. The facts of Case C–202/12 *Innoweb v Wegener* [2014] Bus LR 308 where the CJEU accepted that the database right in such a database existed fit this pattern and the Court therefore implicitly accepts that there is a database in the first place. The conclusion must be different when the arrangement is provided by an element outside the database itself. A clear example is the Internet, which forms a collection of independent and individually accessible materials. A systematic arrangement is missing, however, and the presence of search engines cannot change that. These search engines are external to the collection of materials and so is the arrangement of the materials that they provide. A collection such as the Internet is therefore not a database.

Article 1(3) of the Directive adds in this context that the Directive does not apply to computer programs used in the making or operation of databases accessible by electronic means. These need to be distinguished from the database and they are (at least potentially) covered by the Software Directive. The special regime of protection for the database does not affect either of these. The computer program will potentially be protected by copyright as a computer program, under the provisions that implement the Software Directive, if it meets the standard requirements for computer programs. Those items that are included in a database and which were works protected by copyright will continue to benefit from the protection afforded to them in that way. The rights of the owner of the copyright in these works will not change and neither will the ownership of that copyright.

21.3 Copyright Protection for a Database

Not only does the Directive not apply to computer programs used in the making or operation of databases, its copyright regime does not affect the data that are contained in the database either, i.e. its contents. Unprotected works, data, and other materials will not attract copyright through their inclusion in a database. And any pre-existing rights in the contents will not be affected. Article 3(2) of the Directive stipulates this clearly.

Second, the contents and the computer programs, and the copyright in them, need to be distinguished from the database and any potential copyright in the database. Any copyright in a database will have to be independent from the rights in the contents, etc., and will come on top of the existing rights. It may also be awarded to different owners.

Copyright in a database is thus confined to the selection and arrangement or structure of the materials that are contained in it. The originality criterion that applies to databases, according to Article 3(1) of the Directive, is the slightly higher originality criterion that is found in all European directives and that was declared of general application and explained by the CJEU in Case C–5/08 *Infopaq v Danske Dagblades Forening* [2009] ECR I-6569:

> [copyright exists in a database] which, by reason of the selection or arrangement of the contents of the database constitutes the author's own intellectual creation.

This originality criterion means that some intellectual judgment that is the author's own must have gone into the selection of the materials or into the method of their arrangement.[2] This approach will deny copyright protection to most modern databases: for example, because they aim at complete coverage of a certain topic, rather than at selecting material, or because they arrange their materials in an alphabetical or other standard way, rather than in an original way. This approach must be applauded, because the alternative would have involved the grant of multiple copyrights in standard and commonplace structures, and such a multitude of exclusive rights could have stifled competition in this area.

The limited scope of copyright protection on this point became even clearer when the CJEU ruled in Case C–604/10 *Football Dataco and Others v Yahoo! UK Ltd and others* [2012] 2 CMLR 24, [2012] ECDR 10 that the Directive's emphasis on the fact that the selection or arrangement of the data amounts to an original expression of the creative freedom of the author implies that any intellectual effort located, not in the selection or arrangement of the data, but in their creation, is irrelevant and cannot lead to copyright protection for the database. The focus on the originality in terms of selection and arrangement of the data also means that it is irrelevant whether or not that selection or arrangement includes the addition of important significance to the data and on its own the investment of significant amounts of skill and labour in setting up the database is also neither here nor there.

---

[2] Compare the US approach in *Feist Publications v Rural Telephone*, 499 US 330 (1991) (Supreme Court). Article 10 TRIPS Agreement also points clearly in this direction.

An 'original' database is subject to the normal copyright regime. Article 5 sets out the 'rights' part of that regime as follows:

> In respect of the expression of the database which is protectable by copyright, the author of a database shall have the exclusive right to carry out or to authorize:
>
> (a) temporary or permanent reproduction by any means and in any form, in whole or in part;
>
> (b) translation, adaptation, arrangement and any other alteration;
>
> (c) any form of distribution to the public of the database or of copies thereof. The first sale in the Community of a copy of the database by the rightholder or with his consent shall exhaust the right to control resale of that copy within the Community;
>
> (d) any communication, display or performance to the public;
>
> (e) any reproduction, distribution, communication, display or performance to the public of the results of the acts referred to in (b).

Additionally, a legitimate user of a database is allowed to do anything that is necessary for the purposes of gaining access to the database and for the use of the contents of the database, according to Article 6(1). We will discuss the proper exception to the right later in conjunction with the exceptions to the database right.

21.4 The Database Right

A new *sui generis* right to protect databases has been created in Chapter III of the Directive and that right operates irrespective of whether the database, or any of its contents, attracts copyright protection. The creation of this right was necessary because copyright was not the appropriate instrument to protect non-original databases, which are nevertheless valuable and have required substantial investment. Electronic databases especially are, in such a situation, extremely vulnerable and it was felt that some form of protection was needed to protect the valuable investment in these databases.

21.4.1 The New Right

The new database right has been defined as a property right and it is, according to Article 7 of the Directive, granted if there has been qualitatively and/or quantitatively a substantial investment in either the obtaining, verification, or presentation of the contents of the database. Once again, this right does not interfere with any of the existing materials and the rights in them. As a right in the database, it comes on top of any existing rights and its existence rewards, and is conditional on a substantial or sizeable investment either in collecting, in verifying, or in presenting the contents of the database. For example, the substantial investment requirement will not be met by simply putting different works together on a single support; such a collection will not be protected by the database right.

The CJEU turned its attention to the various types of substantial investment in Case C–203/02 *The British Horseracing Board Ltd & ors v William Hill Organisation Ltd* [2004] ECR I-10425. The Court held that 'obtaining' must be interpreted as referring to the resources used to seek out existing independent materials and to collect them in the database. The resources used for the creation of materials that make up the contents of the database are not covered. That latter important point was confirmed by the CJEU in Cases C–338/02 *Fixtures Marketing Ltd v Svenska Spel AB* [2004] ECR I-10549 and C–46/02 *Fixtures Marketing Ltd v Oy Veikkaus Ab* [2004] ECR I-10497. 'Verification', however, refers to the resources used with a view to ensuring the reliability of the information contained in the database, to monitor the accuracy of the material originally collected, as well as later on. Resources used to verify materials that are created for the database are not covered. It follows that investment in common data will not trigger the *sui generis* right. Databases that consist of created data, such as television listings or dates of sports fixtures, will thus remain unprotected.

The English decision in the *British Horseracing* case[3] offers the example of lists of riders and runners that were intending to run in a certain race. Without further verification as to who would actually be running, etc., there could not be a database right in simply listing existing independent material.

By excluding the creation of data from the concept of obtaining, the CJEU has significantly curtailed the potential scope of the database right and its impact on the right of access to information and on the freedom of competition. Including the creation of data would have locked everything away behind the exclusive right, whereas now the information and the data as such remain in the public domain. Only the collection of data and as a consequence often the most convenient and comprehensive way of accessing the data can be covered by the exclusive right. The data as such remain freely accessible to all competitors.

The first owner of the database right has been identified as the maker of the database, as Article 7 of the Directive provides the *sui generis* right specifically for that person. In the logic of Article 7 the maker of the database is, in turn, 'the person who takes the initiative in obtaining, verifying, or presenting the contents of the database and assumes the risk of investing in that obtaining, verification or presentation'. Recital 41 also goes in that direction. Making a database may involve more than one person. If several people act together in relation to the activities that have to be undertaken by the maker, they will be the joint makers of the database and the joint first owners of the right, as the Directive offers no tool or intention to prioritize a person involved in a specific activity listed in Article 7. The Directive does on the other hand offer no indication at all about ownership by employees. This is left entirely to Member States. In the UK a database made by an employee in the course of his employment will be considered to have been made by the employer, subject to any agreement to the contrary. In other words the copyright rule is applied to the *sui generis* right too, which makes sense as certain databases will attract both copyright and *sui generis* right protection. Applying the same ownership rules to both of these rights is then a logical way to proceed.[4]

The database right exists for a 15-year term. That term starts running from the end of the calendar year in which the database was completed, but that rule is displaced if the database is made available to the public before the end of that period. In that case, the right expires 15 years from the end of the calendar year in which the database was first made available to the public. Article 10(1) and (2) of the Directive sets out this two-step rule on term of protection and adds that protection will be available from the date of the completion of the making of the database.

Article 10(3) contains a significant addition to the rules on term of protection though. A substantial change to the contents of the database that can be considered to be a substantial new investment will lead to the grant of a new 15-year term of protection. Such a change may be the result of the 'accumulation of successive additions, deletions or alterations' to the database. Any sustained effort and investment to keep the database up to date will therefore automatically lead to permanent protection through the ever-renewed

---

[3] *British Horseracing Board Limited & ors v William Hill Organisation Ltd* [2005] RPC 35, [2005] ECDR 28.

[4] Copyright and Rights in Databases Regulations 1997, reg. 15(2).

database right in the latest version of the database. This is the case because, as Advocate General Stix-Hackl clarified in her opinion in Case C–203/02 *The British Horseracing Board Ltd & ors v William Hill Organisation Ltd* [2005] RPC 13, the concept of 'substantial change' to the contents of a database, which qualifies the database for its own term of protection, entails that the resulting database must be considered to be a new, separate database. This is of course a restriction on access and competition, especially as not all data and all aspects of the database will be updated. Also the non-updated elements will be locked up in a further exclusive right for the database as a whole, if the latter meets the criterion of Article 10(3).

21.4.2 Infringement of the Right

We now know what it takes to get a database right, who owns it, and what its term of protection will be. It is now time to turn to the content of the database right. Article 7 of the Directive gives the maker of the database right a right to prevent certain acts, which means that once again content and infringement of the right are two sides of the same coin.

The owner of the database right is granted the right to object to the extraction or reutilization of all, or a substantial part, of the contents of the database. The right in the investment clearly covers the use of the contents of the database. The right will be infringed by the unauthorized extraction or reutilization of all, or a substantial part, of the contents of the database, according to Article 7(1). And Article 7(5) adds that the threshold of a substantial part of the contents of the database can be passed through the repeated and systematic extraction or reutilization of insubstantial parts of these contents. A typical example of an infringement would consist of the taking out of a substantial part of the contents of the database and its reorganization by computer into a prima facie different database.

Let us look in more detail at these provisions using the *British Horseracing Board* case as an example. The case dealt with an issue involving information related to horseracing, which was originally contained in the British Horseracing Board's database, emerging on the website of the Internet betting service of William Hill Organisation and went from a first instance judgment by Laddie J[5] and the Court of Appeal for England and Wales[6] to the CJEU.

In this case, the information had been supplied to the claimant by an intermediary, but it was virtually certain that it had been derived from the claimant's website. The first essential point that arose was whether extraction and/or reutilization of a substantial part of the database had taken place. Laddie J rightfully pointed out that, while a systematic and methodical organization of the information was required for a database right to exist, extraction and reutilization as forms of infringement of such a database right were not linked to the arrangement of the database being used by the alleged infringer. Extraction and/or reutilization of the data as such was sufficient for there to be infringement of the database right. The CJEU followed up on this point by ruling that the terms 'extraction' and 'reutilization' must be interpreted as referring to an unauthorized act of appropriation and distribution to the public of the whole, or part, of the contents of a database. In the view of the Court, direct access to the database is not implied in this definition; the fact that the contents of the database were made accessible to the public by the maker of

---

[5] *British Horseracing Board Limited & ors v William Hill Organisation Ltd* [2001] 2 CMLR 12.

[6] The decision applying the CJEU's guidance is found at *British Horseracing Board Limited & ors v William Hill Organisation Ltd* [2005] RPC 35, [2005] ECDR 28.

the database or with its consent has no impact on the right of the maker of the database to prevent acts of extraction and/or reutilization of the whole, or a substantial part, of the contents of its database. It is therefore fairly certain that the question of whether the works, data, or other materials derived from the database have the same systematic or methodical arrangement and individual accessibility as in the original database is not relevant to the interpretation of the expressions 'a substantial part . . . of the contents of that database' or 'insubstantial parts of the contents of the database'.

Extraction of data from a database did not, according the Advocate General[7] (who agreed on this point with Laddie J), need to involve data being taken away from the database. Mere copying of data and their transfer to a new medium were sufficient, insofar as a substantial part of the database had been extracted.

The latter question depends, in essence, on a comparison between what has been taken (or used) with what has been left in the claimant's database, but the importance to the claimant of the data that had been extracted also had to be taken into account. Additionally, account has to be taken of the protection that the Directive affords for the investment made by the database owner in obtaining, verifying, and presenting the contents of the database. A substantial part can therefore be extracted and/or reutilized if the claimant relies upon, and takes advantage of, the completeness and accuracy of the information in the database. Qualitative considerations are therefore also to be taken into account.

The CJEU has since followed up this analysis in a few more cases and it has consistently taken the line that the concept of extraction is to be interpreted broadly. It involves any unauthorized act of appropriation of the whole or part of the contents of a database, irrespective of the nature and the form of the process used. It also covers, according to the judgment in Case C–545/07 *Apis-Hristovich EOOD v Lakorda AD* [2009] ECR I-1627, both a permanent and a temporary transfer and there is extraction as soon as material is taken and copied (stored) somewhere else. The distinction between permanent and temporary depends simply on the length of storage on the other medium.

One could argue that a selection process taking place when poems were taken from a database resulted in there no longer being extraction. The CJEU adamantly rejected this and held in Case C–304/07 *Directmedia Publishing GmbH v Albert-Ludwigs-Universität Freiburg* [2008] ECR I-7565 that critical assessment of the material that was transferred was irrelevant, as was in general the objective pursued by the transfer of the material. In the same vein subsequent changes to the material that is transferred and differences in structure between the database from which material is taken and the newly created database are irrelevant in deciding whether extraction took place. Similarities between both databases may, however, point in the direction of infringement. The latter point was made in the *Apis* case where further evidential rules were set out by the CJEU ([55]):

> The fact that the physical and technical characteristics present in the contents of a protected database made by a particular person also appear in the contents of a database made by another person may be interpreted as evidence of extraction within the meaning of art.7 of Directive 96/9, unless that coincidence can be explained by factors other than a transfer between the two databases concerned. The fact that materials obtained by the maker of a database from sources not accessible to the public also appear in a database made by another person is not sufficient, in itself, to prove the existence of such extraction but can constitute circumstantial evidence thereof.

---

[7] Opinion of Advocate General Stix-Hackl in Case C–203/02 *The British Horseracing Board Ltd & ors v William Hill Organisation Ltd* [2005] RPC 13.

And with that we return to *British Horseracing*. In the view of the CJEU, the term 'substantial part' refers to the volume of data extracted from the database and/or reutilized. It must be assessed in relation to the total volume of the contents of the database. The scale of the investment in obtaining, verifying, and presenting the content of the subject of the act of extraction and/or reutilization is to be taken into consideration as an important factor, irrespective of whether that subject represents a quantitatively substantial part of the contents of the database. An 'insubstantial part' of the database is simply defined by the Court as any part that does not fulfil the definition of a substantial part, evaluated both quantitatively and qualitatively.

That bring us to the reutilization point and as Laddie J had concluded that a substantial part of the database had been extracted along the lines of his analysis, he had already moved on to consider this point in the first instance decision. He ruled that any use by the defendant of a database through which the extracted data was transmitted or made available to the public amounted to reutilization, and that this included loading the information concerned onto the defendant's computers for the purpose of making it available on its website. The fact that some of the information was also available from another source was entirely irrelevant in this respect. The CJEU added that any unauthorized act of distribution to the public of the whole or a part of the contents of a database amounts to reutilization and that the term does not imply direct access to the database concerned.

An interesting question arose in that respect: a meta-search engine was made available, allowing users to search multiple databases through a single gateway. The CJEU ruled in Case C–202/12 *Innoweb BV v Wegener ICT Media and another* [2014] Bus LR 308 that this amounted to an act of reutilization where the dedicated meta-engine:

- provides the end user with a search form which essentially offers the same range of functionality as the search form on the database site;
- 'translates' queries from end users into the search engine for the database site 'in real time', so that all the information on that database is searched; and
- presents the results to the end user using the format of its website, grouping duplications together into a single block item but in an order that reflects criteria comparable to those used by the search engine of the database site concerned for presenting results.

Reutilization is therefore a very broad concept indeed in an Article 7 context.

The issue of the localization of the act of reutilization was addressed by the CJEU in Case C–173/11 *Football Dataco Ltd, Scottish Premier League Ltd, Scottish Football League and PA Sport UK Ltd v Sportradar GmbH and Sportradar AG* [2013] 1 CMLR 29. The defendants were providing information about football matches that found its origins in the claimants' database to betting websites and via these ultimately to the consumer. The hardware used was located in different countries and the question arose where the act of reutilization took place. The Court was not satisfied by the argument that the consumer can access the website anywhere, i.e. that is not enough for there to be reutilization in any of these places. The act also had to target persons in a certain territory for there to be reutilization in that territory. In the *Football Dataco* case there was reutilization in the UK, as the data related to English and Scottish football matches that would therefore be of interest to the public there. The use of the English language, i.e. the language of the target market rather than the language of the defendant, was also relevant, as was the fact that the contract between the defendant and the betting companies was tailored to the UK market. The Court concluded that an act of reutilization 'is located in the territory of the Member State of location of the user to whose computer the data in question is transmitted at his request, for the purposes of storage and display on screen'. The Court does not thereby exclude the act of reutilization also taking place upstream in the chain of communication and it specifically rejects the suggestion that the act of reutilization exclusively takes place in the territory of the Member State in which the web server from which the data is sent is located. Any application of the emission theory is therefore turned down by the Court.

Having defined the concepts of extraction and reutilization in *British Horseracing Board* and the cases that followed it, we return one last time to the initial *British Horseracing Board* case to consider the second essential point that arose, namely whether the defendant had engaged in 'repeated and systematic' extraction or reutilization of the contents of the database. The defendant's database was in constant evolution and was updated on a day-to-day basis. The defendant took information from it on a daily basis and this prejudiced the legitimate interests of the claimant, and amounted to repeated and systematic extraction or reutilization of the contents of the database in the view of the court. That point was never doubted in the further history of the case.

Finally, it should be remembered, too, that the threshold of a substantial part of the contents of the database can be passed through the repeated and systematic extraction or reutilization of insubstantial parts of these contents. In this respect, the CJEU held in Case C–203/02 *The British Horseracing Board Ltd & ors v William Hill Organisation Ltd* [2004] ECR I-10425 that the prohibition contained in Article 7(5) Database Directive refers to unauthorized acts of extraction or reutilization that have, as their cumulative effect, the reconstitution or the making available to the public of the whole or a substantial part of the contents of the database, in the absence of any prior authorization by the maker of the database. In being made available in this way, the unauthorized acts seriously prejudice the investment of the maker of the database.

21.4.3 **Rights and Obligations of the Lawful User**

Article 8(1) at first glance seems to give a right to the lawful user of a database. In fact, it merely restates an obvious point. As the exclusive right of the holder of the database right is limited to the extraction and reutilization of at least a 'substantial part' it is obvious that a lawful user is free to deal with 'insubstantial' parts of the contents of the database. The more interesting question is that of the definition of the concept of a 'lawful user', but the Directive does not offer such a definition. In a software context the CJEU has now offered a definition of the concept of a lawful user in its decision in Case C–128/11 *Usedsoft v Oracle International* EU:C:2012:407. It seems that the Court has gone beyond the restrictive approach that merely refers to a user who lawfully acquires the program (or the database) and that any user who relies upon exceptions by law or contract is also a lawful user. It would make sense to apply that definition also in a database context.

Paragraphs (2) and (3) introduce obligations. Paragraph (2) seems to impose a further restriction of what the lawful user can do along the lines of the three-step test. By definition, one is concerned in Article 8 with the use of insubstantial parts, but even in using (lots of) insubstantial parts the lawful user should not enter into conflict with the normal exploitation of the database or unreasonably prejudice the legitimate interests of the maker of the database. In practice, Article 8(2) is redundant though as a result of the CJEU's interpretation of the provision in Article 7(5) dealing with repeated and systematic extraction and reutilization. Paragraph 8(3) merely means that the lawful user must respect copyright and related rights when extracting and/or reutilizing protected subject matter that is part of the content of the database. This is a logical consequence of the strict separation between the database right and the rights in the content of the database, which forms one of the cornerstones of the Directive.

21.4.4 Exceptions to the Right

The exceptions to the database right are not numerous and they are also narrower in scope than their copyright counterparts. There is nevertheless a strong parallelism between them and we therefore discuss them here together. The Directive is basically anchored on three exceptions which the Member States may implement in their laws if they wish to do so.

First of all there is the right to private reproduction, in the copyright version in Article 6(2)(a), or extraction for private purposes, in the database right version in Article 9(a). There is no restriction as to where the act should occur, but there is an important restriction of the exception to non-electronic databases only.

The second exception deals with research and teaching and is subject to three cumulative conditions. There must be an illustration for teaching or scientific research, the source must be indicated, and the illustration for teaching or research must not be for a commercial purpose. The copyright exception in Article 6(2)(b) applies broadly to 'use', but its database right in Article 9(b) is limited to 'extraction'. This restriction is very significant as, in a context of teaching and research, communication to the public (a way of reutilization) is often vital and the exception does not seem to cover that aspect.

The third exception deals with use (copyright, Article 6(2)(c)) and extraction and/or reutilization (database right, Article 9(c)) respectively for the purposes of public security or an administrative or judicial procedure. There is an exact correspondence between the two versions.

In relation to copyright, and without prejudice to the exceptions in Article 6(2), Member States are also allowed to apply traditional copyright exceptions to the copyright in databases and the Directive explicitly subjects Article 6 and the application of the exceptions contained in it to the three-step test.

21.4.5 Qualification

There is also a qualification requirement that has to be met before the database right can be granted. The main principle of this is that an attempt has been made to require reciprocity in the sense that non-European Economic Area (EEA) persons will only be granted the right if their country offers a similar level of protection to that of the European makers of databases. Article 11 of the Directive puts this into practice by requiring that the maker or rights holder is a national of a Member State or has its habitual residence in the territory of the EU. For companies and firms the link with the EU is provided by the presence of their registered office, central administration, or principal place of business. They should also have been formed in accordance with the law of a Member State.

21.5 Conclusions

Database protection falls apart in two different and entirely independent rights. On the one hand there is copyright in a database which, by reason of the selection or arrangement of the contents of the database constitutes the author's own intellectual creation. Admittedly, few databases qualify for copyright protection as their most useful practical characteristics are completeness and logical organization, for example alphabetically by surname. This is exactly the kind of selection and arrangement method that is not the author's own intellectual creation, but a readily available standard form of selection and arrangement.

On the other hand there is the *sui generis* database right that protects a collection of independent works, data, or other materials, arranged in a systematic or methodical way, and are individually accessible by electronic or other means, if there has been qualitatively and/or quantitatively a substantial investment in either the obtaining, verification, or presentation of the contents of the database. This is in essence a form of investment protection and in that aspect it is fundamentally different from the traditional IP rights that require rather different elements, without directly protecting the investment of the author or inventor, to name just these two. By not requiring any form of originality in the data, there is a risk that the right of access to information and the freedom of competition are affected, but the CJEU has significantly curtailed the database right and the risks to these rights by excluding the creation of data from the concept of 'obtaining' and therefore also from the database right.

Further Reading

DERCLAYE, E., 'Database *Sui Generis* Right: What Is a Substantial Investment? A Tentative Definition' (2005) 36 *IIC* 2

DERCLAYE, E., 'The Court of Justice Interprets the Database *Sui Generis* Right for the First Time' (2005) 30 *European Law Review* 420

22

Data Protection and Data Exclusivity

22.1 Introduction

In the previous chapter we dealt with the protection of databases. In most cases the nature and the specific aspects of the data, as the content of the database, are not important factors in relation to the protection of databases. In this chapter we move away from the database in order to look at the data. We do so in the context of data protection in this chapter and in the context of data exclusivity, which will take up the next chapter. It will become clear from the outset that we are not concerned with any kind of data, only with specific types of data.

22.2 From Article 8 ECHR to Article 8 CFR

Data protection in Europe is rooted in Article 8 ECHR. The fundamental right that is protected by Article 8 is the right to respect for private and family life, home, and correspondence. It is easy to see how a right to the protection of personal data fits in this context and personal data is therefore covered by Article 8. A first point to pick up here is that data protection is not concerned with any kind of data. Its roots in Article 8 ECHR, i.e. rules on data protection as a means of putting Article 8 into practice, clearly point to the idea that data protection is concerned with personal data.

The European Court of Human Rights (ECtHR) has dealt over the years with a number of Article 8 cases in which data protection issues arose. The issue of the interception of communications arose in *Malone v United Kingdom* (No. 8691/79, 2 August 1984) and in *Copland v United Kingdom* (No. 62617/00, 3 April 2007). *Klass and others v Germany* (No. 5029/71, 6 September 1978) and *Uzun v Germany* (No. 35623/05, 2 September

2010) were concerned with various forms of surveillance, whilst in *Leander v Sweden* (No. 9248/81, 26 March 1987) and *Marper v United Kingdom* (Nos 30562/04 and 30566/04, 4 December 2008) the issue of the protection against the storage of personal data by public authorities took centre stage. These examples are particularly illuminating, as they show that in many personal data cases there are conflicting interests, such as public safety, involved. This will require a balancing of interests and inevitably a restriction on the right in Article 8 in a context of data protection.

In the context of the Council of Europe, a Convention for the protection of individuals with regard to the automatic processing of personal data (1981) has also been concluded. This Convention is commonly referred to as Convention 108 and it applies to all data processing carried out by both the public and the private sector, for example data processing by or on behalf of law enforcement agencies. The Convention protects individuals against abuses that may accompany the collection and processing of personal data and it also regulates the transborder flow of personal data. When it comes to the collection and processing of personal data the Convention deals with standards for the fair and lawful collection of data and their automatic processing, the storage of data for specific legitimate purposes, the prohibition of the use of data for ends that are incompatible with the purposes for which the data are kept, and with the issue of not keeping data for longer than is necessary. The Convention is also concerned with the point that data should be adequate, relevant, accurate, and proportionate. Sensitive data, such as data on a person's race, political views, health, religion, sexual life, or criminal record are not to be processed, in the absence of proper legal safeguards. But rights in the Convention need to be balanced with other interests and can be overridden when other interests such as state and public safety are involved. The individual also has the right to know that information is stored on him or her and to have that information corrected, if necessary. When it comes to the transborder flow of information, the Convention puts in place the principle of the free flow of information between the states that are parties to the Convention, but restrictions are imposed on the flows to states where legal regulation does not provide equivalent protection.

The EU Member States have all signed up to Convention 108, but there are more specific measures at the EU level. Article 16 TFEU gives the EU competence to legislate on data protection measures and the Charter of Fundamental Rights of the European Union (CFR) includes an Article 8 that establishes a right to data protection, on top of Article 7 that guarantees respect for private and family life. The key instrument with which we are concerned in this chapter is, however, Directive 95/46/EC of the European Parliament and the Council of 24 October 1995 on the protection of individuals with regard to the processing of personal data and on the free movement of such data (the Data Protection Directive [1995] OJ L 281/31). As the CJEU put it:

> In that context, it must be noted that Directive 95/46 is intended, as appears from, inter alia, recital 8 in the preamble thereto, to ensure that the level of protection of the rights and freedoms of individuals with regard to the processing of personal data is equivalent in all Member States. Recital 10 adds that the approximation of the national laws applicable in this area must not result in any lessening of the protection they afford but must, on the contrary, seek to ensure a high level of protection in the EU…Accordingly, it has been held that the harmonisation of those national laws is not limited to minimal harmonisation but amounts to harmonisation which is generally complete.…[1]

---

[1] Joined Cases C–468/10 and 469/10 *Asociación Nacional de Establecimientos Financieros de Crédito (ASNEF)* (C–468/10), *Federación de Comercio Electrónico y Marketing Directo (FECEMD)* (C–469/10) v *Administración del Estado* [2011] ECR I-12181.

The Directive is of course addressed to the Member States, but data protection also arises as an important issue for the institutions of the Union. Regulation (EC) No. 45/2001 on the protection of individuals with regard to the processing of personal data by the institutions and bodies of the Community and on the free movement of such data (EU Institutions Data Protection Regulation [2001] OJ L 8/1) deals with this point.

At the EU level the protection of personal data has now been enshrined in the CFR and more in particular in its Article 8. Article 8 has an exceptionally broad field of application, which goes well beyond the mere establishment of the single internal market. Where databases and therefore also the Database Directive were intimately linked to the establishment of the internal market, Article 8, and with it Directive 95/49/EC, go well beyond it, as the CJEU made clear in Case C–465/00 *Österreichischer Rundfunk* [2003] ECR I-4989. The Directive even applies to purely domestic operations of data processing, as Advocate General Kokott emphasized in her conclusions in Case C–73/07 *Satamedia* [2008] ECR I-9831 [53].

22.3 The Balancing of Rights Characteristic

It is in this legislative framework that we will examine data protection in more detail in this chapter. It is however worth emphasizing a crucial point before we do so. The protection for data protection is not absolute. It needs to be balanced with other interests and rights. Obvious candidates are the right to freedom of expression, protected in Article 11 CFR, which also includes a right of access to documents or information, the freedom of the arts and sciences, protected in Article 13 CFR, and the right to protection of property, in Article 17 CFR.

But let us start with a less obvious candidate. It is clear that the protection of personal data and Article 8 CFR have close links with Article 7 and the right to privacy. The latter, as we will see in more detail later on, has moved beyond its starting point as a right to be left alone. The modern and broader notion of privacy has a strong strand of self-determination in it. One could then link privacy and the right to data protection by introducing a notion of informational self-determination, which involves a right to control one's own personal information. The overlap between Articles 7 and 8 is however less important than it may seem on the basis of this notion of informational self-determination. The latter has the concept of consent at its heart, whereas the EU approach to data processing has created a system of checks and balances to ensure the lawful processing of personal data, in which consent is only one of the grounds for legitimate processing. The latter can also take place in certain circumstances without the consent of the person involved. It may not be entirely accurate to speak in terms of balancing of rights between Articles 7 and 8, but this key difference highlights that the balancing concept is firmly enshrined in EU data protection rules.

The balancing with the right to freedom of expression came to the fore in a case that was concerned with the freedom of the press. Tax data concerning 1.2 million people, obviously covered by data protection, had been disseminated. The CJEU argued that the dissemination of data from documents that are in the public domain may be classified as journalistic activities covered by the right to freedom of expression if their object is the disclosure to the public of information, opinions, or ideas, irrespective of the medium used to transmit them. If that is the case, the right to data protection may have to be restricted to accommodate the balance with the right to freedom of expression (Case C–73/07 *Tietosuojavaltuutettu v Satakunnan Markkinapörssi Oy and Satamedia Oy*

[2008] ECR I-9831). When asked for minutes of a meeting, the Commission blanked out the names of five individuals who attended the meeting. The party that requested access to the document objected, but the CJEU argued that the balance in this case fell on the side of data protection. The people attending the meeting had not given their consent and the applicant had not shown a necessity for those personal data to be transferred to it (Case C–25/08 P *European Commission v Bavarian Lager* [2011] 1 CMLR 1). Looking at it from a more theoretical perspective one can only agree with Herke Kranenborg's analysis that:

> The right to freedom of expression (Art 11 of the Charter) is about imparting and receiving information. The right to data protection has a dual relationship with this right. On the one hand, data protection rules aim to reach a harmonized level of data protection ensuring the free flow of information, including in the context of the free-dom of expression. On the other hand, data protection rules might require a restric-tion of the freedom of expression. In that respect, there is an obvious tension between the two rights. A balance between the underlying interests of both rights should be found.[2]

That balance is a matter which the CJEU leaves to the national courts. The CJEU does emphasize in this context that Article 9 of the Directive allows for the introduction of limitations and exceptions and that these limitations and exceptions should be seen as a tool for achieving the balance between the various rights and interests (Case C–101/01 *Lindqvist* [2003] ECR I-12971).

An example of the balancing with the freedom of the arts and sciences can be found in an ECtHR case, where Article 10 ECHR also covers Article 13 CFR. The case dealt with a collage comprising photos of the heads of public figures on bodies depicted in various sexual positions. The Austrian courts had given preference to data protection and injunc-ted the exhibition of the pictures at the request of a politician whose photo had been used. The Court argued that it was obvious from the collage that the aim was not to depict or even suggest reality and that a public figure must adopt a greater degree of tolerance in respect of criticism. On that basis the Court concluded that the injunction had been disproportionate and held that the balance of interest in this case favoured the freedom of the arts and sciences over data protection (*Vereinigung bildender Künstler v Austria* (No. 68345/01, 25 January 2007).

In relation to the right of property Case C–275/06 *Promusicae v Telefonica* [2008] ECR I-271 is an interesting example. In a copyright infringement case an associ-ation of rights holders asked an Internet provider to reveal the personal data of some of its clients, and alleged infringers. Telefonica refused and relied on data protection. Promusicae argued that it needed the data in order to be able to defend its right to prop-erty (in the copyright works). The CJEU insisted on the need to balance both rights and concluded that:

> Community law requires that, when transposing those directives, the Member States take care to rely on an interpretation of them which allows a fair balance to be struck between the various fundamental rights protected by the Community legal order. Further, when implementing the measures transposing those directives, the authori-ties and courts of the Member States must not only interpret their national law in a manner consistent with those directives but also make sure that they do not rely

---

[2] H. Kranenborg, 'Article 8' in S. Peers, T. Hervey, J. Kenner, and A. Ward, *The EU Charter of Fundamental Rights: A Commentary* (Hart Publishing, 2014) 231.

on an interpretation of them which would be in conflict with those fundamental rights or with the other general principles of Community law, such as the principle of proportionality.[3]

In this case the CJEU concluded that EU law does not require the Member States to oblige ISPs to communicate personal data to allow (intellectual) property rights holders to enforce their property rights. But such an obligation is not forbidden either if the right balance is struck between the protection of the property right and the protection afforded to personal data. The CJEU made that clear in Case C–461/10 *Bonnier Audio* [2012] 2 CMLR 42, when it held that Swedish law struck the right balance. Protecting the right of property through an obligation of the ISP systematically to filter files that transit through its network would however go too far and strike the wrong balance (Case C–70/10 *Scarlet Extended* [2012] ECDR 4).

22.4 Key Concepts

Data protection works with the concept of a person, who is the data subject. For the purposes of data protection, data are personal data if they relate to an identified person, or at least to an identifiable person (Article 2(a) Data Protection Directive). That person is known as the data subject. A person is identifiable if her identity can be established by obtaining additional information without unreasonable effort. The fact that a person is indirectly identifiable, for example Internet addresses can indirectly identify the person accessing copyright material on the Internet. Due to the link with the right to respect for private life, natural persons are the primary beneficiaries of data protection. The CJEU held in Joined Cases C–93/09 and 93/09 *Volker and Markus Schecke and Hartmut Eifert v Land Hessen* [2012] All ER (EC) 127 that

> legal persons can claim [protection] ... only in so far as the official title of the legal person identifies one or more natural persons.... [T]he right to respect for private life with regard to the processing of personal data ... concerns any information relating to an identified or identifiable individual...

The next concept that flows from this is the concept of personal data. We are concerned here with the nature of the data. Provided that it relates directly or indirectly to a person, any kind of information can be personal data. The concept of personal data therefore covers first of all information pertaining to the private life of the person concerned, but second it also covers information about her professional or public life. It is also clear that this concept is independent of the form in which the personal data is stored. The form of storage is not relevant when it comes to the applicability of data protection laws. Article 8 Data Protection Directive deals with special categories of personal data, that by their nature pose a risk to data subjects when they are processed. They therefore need additional protection and processing of these sensitive data can therefore only be allowed with special safeguards. In the list one finds personal data that reveal ethnic or racial origin, personal data that reveal political opinions or religious and other beliefs, personal data concerning health or sexual life, and personal data revealing trade union membership. Data on the other hand lose the personal data status once they have been anonymized (often for statistical purposes). This is the case if all identifying elements

---

[3] *Promusicae* [65].

have been eliminated from a set of personal data and there is no element left that would allow for re-identification.

The concept of data processing refers primarily to the automated processing of the data, but it also refers to manual processing in structured filing systems (Articles 2(b) and 3(1) Data Protection Directive). Processing includes any operation such as collection, recording, organization, storage, adaptation or alteration, retrieval, consultation, use, disclosure by transmission, dissemination or otherwise making available, alignment or combination, blocking, erasure, or destruction, performed on personal data. By way of example, the CJEU held in Case C–101/01 *Bodil Lindqvist* [2003] ECR I-12971 that:

> [t]he act of referring, on an internet page, to various persons and identifying them by name or by other means, for instance by giving their telephone number or information regarding their working conditions and hobbies, constitutes 'the processing of personal data wholly or partly by automatic means' within the meaning of article 3(1) of Directive 95/46/EC.

The concept of a (data) controller introduces the person who decides to process the personal data of others into the procedure and in that context determines the purposes and means of the processing of personal data (Article 2(d) Data Protection Directive). From being a controller flows a legal responsibility to comply with the obligations of data protection law. In practice the controller is either a natural or a legal person, or an authority in the public sector. The Directive does however exclude private individuals who process personal data in the course of a purely personal or household activity (Article 3(2) Data Protection Directive, last indent). In Case C–131/12 *Google Spain SL v Agencia Española de Protección de Datos (AEPD)* [2014] 3 CMLR 50 the CJEU held that a search engine is a controller of personal data, as it processes personal data. Google was unable to escape the application of the Data Protection Directive despite the fact its physical server is located outside the EU, as it has a branch or subsidiary in the EU. The latter is sufficient for the application of the Directive. A (data) processor on the other hand is defined as someone who processes personal data on behalf of the controller (Article 2(e) Data Protection Directive), with overall responsibility remaining with the controller. Once more legal obligation flows from taking on the capacity of processor.

Anybody who receives data from a controller is a recipient. A third party is someone who is legally different from the controller (Article 2(f) Data Protection Directive). Turning such a party into a recipient and disclosing legal data to them will require a specific legal basis. The employees of a controller or processor on the other hand may become recipients of personal data without further legal requirements if they are involved in the processing operations of the controller or processor.

A final key concept is that of consent. Consent is required as a legal basis for the processing of personal information and needs to be free, informed, and specific in order to be valid (Article 2(h) Data Protection Directive). The data subject must have been under no pressure when giving his consent. The data subject must have been duly informed about the object and consequences of his consent. And finally, the scope of the consent must be reasonably concrete. Consent can of course be given explicitly, but it can also be non-explicit if it can be derived from the circumstances. In any case, consent must be given in an unambiguous way. The processing of sensitive data always requires explicit consent though. The data subject can withdraw his consent at any time.

Figure 22.1 attempts to summarize the key concepts involved.

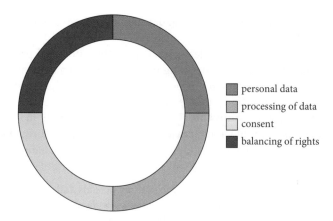

personal data
processing of data
consent
balancing of rights

Figure 22.1 Key data protection concepts

22.5 **Key Principles**

Article 6 of the Data Protection Directive lays out a set of key principles. They are not merely a starting point for the more detailed provisions that follow. All later data protection legislation will have to comply with these principles and they are the cornerstones of any interpretation (by the courts) of the provisions on data protection. Any exemption or limitation that national law can provide on the basis of Article 9(2) needs to be provided by law, needs to pursue a legitimate aim, and needs to be necessary in a democratic society, with the three requirements applying cumulatively.

The first principle is that of lawful processing. Similar requirements apply. The processing of personal data is only lawful if it is done in accordance with the law, if it pursues a legitimate purpose (a public interest or right or freedom of others), and if it is necessary in a democratic society in order to achieve the legitimate purpose.

From this follows the principle of purpose specification and limitation. In essence, this boils down to the rule that the legitimacy of processing personal data will depend on the purpose of the processing (Article 6(1)(b) Data Protection Directive). The controller needs to specify and make the purpose manifest before the processing of data starts and this must be done by a declaration or a notification to the appropriate supervisory authority, or at least by internal documentation which the controller makes available for inspection to the supervisory authorities and for access to the data subject. Each new purpose for the processing of data needs to have its own legal basis and cannot rely on the fact that the data were initially acquired or processed for another legitimate purpose. Legitimate processing is also limited to its initially specified purpose. Any new purpose of processing will require a separate legal basis. Disclosure of data will have to be considered carefully in this context, as it amounts to a new purpose. Disclosure to third parties will therefore require a legal basis that is distinct from the one for collecting the data. But the Directive adds specifically that further processing of data for historical, statistical, or scientific purposes shall not be regarded as incompatible with this principle if the Member State concerned provides appropriate safeguards.

There is also a set of principles concerning data quality. These must be implemented by the controller in all processing operations. The first one is the data relevancy principle. Only data that are 'adequate, relevant and not excessive in relation to the purpose for which they are collected and/or further processed' meet this principle (Article 6(1)(c) Data Protection Directive). Data need to be chosen as a function of the aim of the exercise. The data must be directly relevant for the specific purpose that is being pursued. Second, is the data accuracy principle. No information shall be used without taking steps to ensure with reasonable certainty that the data are accurate and up to date. And third is the limited retention of data principle. It is necessary to delete data as soon as they are no longer needed for the purpose for which they were collected. Any exceptions (e.g. for historical, statistical, or scientific use) need to be provided by law and need special safeguards for the protection of data subjects. Article 6(1)(e) Data Protection Directive limits the time during which identification of the data subjects is possible to a period no longer than is necessary for the purposes for which the data were collected or for which they are further processed. Storage of data without the data subject being identifiable remains an option.

The next principle is the fair processing principle, that primarily governs the relationship between the controller and the data subject. This principle requires transparency of processing, especially in the relationship with the data subject. Data subjects must be informed before their data are processed by the controller and the information provided must at least cover the purpose of the processing and the identity and address of the controller. Secret and covert processing of personal data is not allowed, unless it is specifically permitted by law. And data subjects have the right to access their data wherever they are processed.

Finally, Article 6(2) Data Protection Directive imposes a duty on the controller to ensure compliance with the data quality principles contained in its paragraph 1. That leads us to the principle of accountability. This involves the active implementation of measures to promote and safeguard data protection in their processing activities. Data controllers are responsible for compliance with data protection law in their processing operations. And they should be able to demonstrate such compliance to data subjects, supervisory authorities, and the general public at any time.

22.6 Data Protection Law Rules

Useful as they are, and let us not forget that they have to be complied with, principles are by definition of a general nature. Detailed rules are therefore needed in order to establish a working system of data protection. In the context of the single market a harmonized set of rules was needed. Twenty-eight very different data protection regimes would be a hindrance to the operation of the single market. The Directive therefore lays out a set of detailed rules on data protection.

22.6.1 The Rules on Lawful Processing

Moving on from the principles, Article 7 Data Protection Directive provides a set of criteria for making data processing legitimate. These work as alternative criteria, meaning that the processing will be lawful if one of the criteria has been met. As Article 8 contains special rules for sensitive data the latter are excluded from the scope of Article 7.

The first criterion (Article 7(a)) is that the data subject has given her unambiguous consent for the processing of the data. The second criterion refers to a contractual relationship the data subject has entered into or is about to enter into. Data processing can then take place if it is necessary for the performance of the contract or if steps need to be taken at the request of the data subject prior to the parties entering into the contract (Article 7(b)). For example, to conclude a loan with a bank the personal data of the data subject will need to be processed when drafting the contract in order to make the loan possible. Third, data processing may be necessary if the controller is to comply with its legal obligations (Article 7(c)). Airlines and ferry companies, for example, by law need to compile a passenger list for each flight or crossing. That requires the processing of the personal data of the passengers. The fourth criterion stipulates that the processing of personal data may be necessary to protect the vital interests of the data subject (Article 7(d)). One thinks here primarily about health data or any other data related to the survival of the data subject. The fifth criterion refers to a task carried out in the public interest or in the exercise of official authority. This task can be carried out by the authorities or by a third party on their behalf and therefore also covers the disclosure of data to third parties to enable them to carry out the task (Article 7(e)). Case C–524/06 *Huber v Germany* [2008] ECR I-9705 dealt in this context with legislation that set up a register of foreigners residing in Germany for more than three months and that was held to comply with Article 7(e) only if there was no other way of enforcing immigration and residence status rules. Finally, the sixth criterion establishes that processing of personal data may be necessary for the purposes of the legitimate interests of the controller or of the third party to whom they are disclosed. But those interests may be overridden by the fundamental rights and freedoms of the data subject (Article 7(f)).[4]

The processing of sensitive personal data involves substantially greater risks. Article 8 therefore sets out a special regime for sensitive data. The starting point is a clear prohibition on their processing:

The processing of special categories of data

1. Member States shall prohibit the processing of personal data revealing racial or ethnic origin, political opinions, religious or philosophical beliefs, trade-union membership, and the processing of data concerning health or sex life.

2. Paragraph 1 shall not apply where:

   (a) the data subject has given his explicit consent to the processing of those data, except where the laws of the Member State provide that the prohibition referred to in paragraph 1 may not be lifted by the data subject's giving his consent; or

   (b) processing is necessary for the purposes of carrying out the obligations and specific rights of the controller in the field of employment law in so far as it is authorized by national law providing for adequate safeguards; or

   (c) processing is necessary to protect the vital interests of the data subject or of another person where the data subject is physically or legally incapable of giving his consent; or

   (d) processing is carried out in the course of its legitimate activities with appropriate guarantees by a foundation, association or any other non-profit-seeking body with a political, philosophical, religious or trade-union aim and on condition that the processing relates solely to the members of the body or to persons who have regular contact with it in connection with its purposes and that the data are not disclosed to a third party without the consent of the data subjects; or

   (e) the processing relates to data which are manifestly made public by the data subject or is necessary for the establishment, exercise or defence of legal claims.

---

[4] Note that the Directive sets out an exhaustive list of criteria. Member States cannot add criteria, nor can they add conditions to any of the existing criteria. See Joined Cases C–468/10 and 469/10 *Asociación Nacional de Establecimientos Financieros de Crédito (ASNEF)* (C–468/10), *Federación de Comercio Electrónico y Marketing Directo (FECEMD)* (C–469/10) *v Administración del Estado* [2011] ECR I-12181.

3. Paragraph 1 shall not apply where processing of the data is required for the purposes of preventive medicine, medical diagnosis, the provision of care or treatment or the management of health-care services, and where those data are processed by a health professional subject under national law or rules established by national competent bodies to the obligation of professional secrecy or by another person also subject to an equivalent obligation of secrecy.

4. Subject to the provision of suitable safeguards, Member States may, for reasons of substantial public interest, lay down exemptions in addition to those laid down in paragraph 2 either by national law or by decision of the supervisory authority.

5. Processing of data relating to offences, criminal convictions or security measures may be carried out only under the control of official authority, or if suitable specific safeguards are provided under national law, subject to derogations which may be granted by the Member State under national provisions providing suitable specific safeguards. However, a complete register of criminal convictions may be kept only under the control of official authority.

   Member States may provide that data relating to administrative sanctions or judgements in civil cases shall also be processed under the control of official authority.

6. Derogations from paragraph 1 provided for in paragraphs 4 and 5 shall be notified to the Commission.

7. Member States shall determine the conditions under which a national identification number or any other identifier of general application may be processed.

In other words, there are cases in which one can depart from the prohibition to process sensitive personal data, but these are enumerated exhaustively. The obvious example is where the data subject explicitly consents to the processing of the personal data and as the existence of a contractual relationship is not in the list a separate explicit consent will have to be given before any processing of sensitive data can take place when a contractual relationship is in place or is being created. Consent will on the other hand not be needed if the data have manifestly been made public by the data subject. It is also not a surprise to find the criterion of the protection of the vital interests of the data subject in the list and a more restrictive approach to the legitimate interests of others. And obviously, the public interest is another criterion that can authorize the processing of sensitive personal data.

22.6.2 **The Rules on the Security of the Processing**

Data security is a vital component of any data protection framework. Personal data need to be processed in a safe environment and controllers and processors must have adequate measures in place to ensure data security. Article 17 Data Protection Directive imposes therefore appropriate technical and organizational measures to protect personal data against accidental or unlawful destruction or accidental loss, alteration, unlawful disclosure or access, and all other unlawful forms of processing. Implementing this provision requires internal organizational rules and training on top of adequate hardware and software. In addition to this provision of the Data Protection Directive, an obligation[5] has been put in place for providers of electronic telecommunications services to notify data breaches to likely victims and to the supervisory authorities in an attempts to

---

[5] Article 4(3) Directive 2002/58/EC of the European Parliament and of the Council of 12 July 2002 concerning the processing of personal data and the protection of privacy in the electronic communications sector [2002] OJ L 201, as amended.

avoid or limit damage resulting from such breaches, for example when usernames and passwords are stolen by hackers. And Article 16 Data Protection Directive introduces confidentiality of processing between the controller and the processor. Processing of the data should only take place on the instructions of the controller or when there is a legal obligation to do so.

22.6.3 **The Rules on the Transparency of the Processing**

The processing of personal data needs to happen in a transparent way in order to put the principle of fair processing into practice. This means that the controller proactively has to inform the data subject of its identity and of the purpose of the data processing before starting the process, unless the data subject already has this information (Articles 10 and 11 Data Protection Directive). On top of the duty to inform, the Directive imposes a duty to notify. This duty implies that the controller notifies the competent supervisory authority of their processing operations with a view to their publication by the authority. National laws implementing the Directive can alternatively provide that the controller needs to employ a personal data protection official who will keep a register of all processing activities carried out and who will make that register available to members of the public upon request (Article 18 Data Protection Directive).

22.6.4 **The Rules on Promoting Compliance**

The same personal data protection officials are also tasked with ensuring that the rights and freedoms of the data subject are unlikely to be affected negatively by any data processing operation. Having a specialist person in place will clearly promote compliance and minimize risks for the data subject. Article 20 Data Protection Directive adds to this by providing that Member States shall identify processing operations that present specific risks to the rights and freedoms of data subjects. For these data processing operations prior notification and prior checking shall be required. Compliance is also further enhanced by the encouragement of codes of conduct on data protection that can be established by sectors of industry and their representative bodies (Article 27 Data Protection Directive).

22.7 **The Rights of the Data Subject**

The data subject has a right of access (Article 12 Data Protection Directive). This means that the data subject can request from the controller confirmation of whether data relating to him or her are being processed and obtain information on the purpose of the processing, the categories of data that are being processed, and on the recipients to whom the data are disclosed. In a second stage the data subject can request that the data, as well as information regarding their source, be communicated to him or her in an intelligible form. In a final stage a request can be made to correct the data or to erase them or block their processing if the process is not in compliance with the Directive. Individuals have, under certain conditions, the right to ask that search engines, in their capacity of data controllers, remove links to information about them that is no longer relevant, for example when an auction notice in repossession proceedings of a home is still referred to on the webpage of a newspaper despite the fact that the proceedings have been resolved for a number of years and the debt has been repaid. This right to be forgotten applies when the information is inaccurate, inadequate, irrelevant, or excessive for the purposes of data processing, according to the CJEU's decision in Case C–131/12 *Google Spain SL v Agencia Española de Protección de Datos (AEPD)* [2014] 3 CMLR 50. The economic interest of the controller in providing a complete set of information cannot prevail, even if the right to be forgotten is not absolute and needs to be balanced against other fundamental rights, such as the freedom of expression and of the media. A case-by-case approach is in other words warranted and will need to take account of the type of information, its sensitivity for the private life of the data subject, as well as the interests of the public in having access to the information. The role the data subject plays in public life is also relevant. There are exceptions to the right of access, but the main grounds for these exceptions in Article 13 are national security, defence, and public security.

On top of the right of access the data subject is granted a right to object. This right exists first of all for automated individual decisions, i.e. decision that are taken using personal data processed solely by automatic means. In a banking context one can think of computer programs making decisions on the creditworthiness of clients. By way of a special safeguard the Directive provides in Article 15 that final decisions should not be made solely by automated systems. They can advise, but human intervention is required. And the data subject has a right to review the automated decision. It is on the other hand clear that the data subject has no general right to object to the processing of her personal data. Article 14 requires in this respect compelling legitimate grounds that relate to the particular situation of the data subject. If these are present in a particular case then the processing by the controller may no longer involve the affected data. Direct marketing forms an exception to this approach. The data subject can object to the use of her personal data for the purposes of direct marketing (Article 14(b) Data Protection Directive).

Independent supervision plays an important role in this context. Effective data protection, because of its sensitive nature involving personal data, needs independent supervisory authorities. We have already seen them mentioned in relation to a couple of provisions. These national authorities must act with complete independence and that independence must be reflected in their organizational structure (Article 28 Data Protection Directive).[6] The tasks of the authorities shall include the task to:

- promote and monitor data protection in the Member State concerned;
- advise data subjects and controllers, as well as the public at large and the government;
- hear complaints and assist the data subject in cases of alleged violations of rights;
- supervise controllers and processors;
- warn and if necessary sanction controllers and processors in the case of breaches of data protection law;
- order the correction, blocking, or deletion of data or impose a ban on their processing;
- refer matters to court.

In order for the rights of the data subject to be effective there is a need for remedies and sanctions. A breach of the right to data protection needs to lead to a remedy. Data protection rules start from the principle that one first approaches the controller, who must according to Article 12 Data Protection Directive reply without excessive delay. National implementation can also require that one approaches the national supervisory authority first, before going to court (Article 22 Data Protection Directive).

---

[6] See Case C–518/07 *Commission v Germany* [2010] ECR I-1885, Case C–614/10 *Commission v Austria* [2013] 1 CMLR 23, and Case C–288/12 *Commission v Hungary* [2014] 3 CMLR 42.

Article 24 deals with sanctions by imposing the principle, but leaving its implementation to national law:

> The Member States shall adopt suitable measures to ensure the full implementation of the provisions of this Directive and shall in particular lay down the sanctions to be imposed in case of infringement of the provisions adopted pursuant to this Directive.

22.8 Transborder Data Flows

The Data Protection Directive deals in a separate chapter with the transfer of personal data to third countries. This comes on top of the free flow of data between the Member States provided by Article 1(2). The transfer is to take place involving personal data which are undergoing processing or which are intended to be processed after transfer. The concern here is with a communication of personal data that is directed at a specific recipient. Mere publication of the data, for example on the Internet, is not sufficient according to the CJEU's decision in Case C–101/01 *Bodil Lindqvist* [2003] ECR I-12971. Articles of 25 and 26 Data Protection Directive subject such transfers to third countries to a set of conditions. First and most importantly, the third country needs to ensure an adequate level of protection. In practice it is up to the Commission to make an assessment whether the country involved has effectively implemented the main principles of data protection in its national law. A comparable level of protection is required, i.e. adequacy rather than equivalence. Alternatively transborder data flows may be authorized because the transfer is necessary in the specific interests of the data subject or because there are legitimate prevailing interests of others, which includes important public interests. This derogation is allowed by Article 26 Data Protection Directive on the following conditions:

(a)   the data subject has given his consent unambiguously to the proposed transfer; or

(b)   the transfer is necessary for the performance of a contract between the data subject and the controller or the implementation of precontractual measures taken in response to the data subject's request; or

(c)   the transfer is necessary for the conclusion or performance of a contract concluded in the interest of the data subject between the controller and a third party; or

(d)   the transfer is necessary or legally required on important public interest grounds, or for the establishment, exercise or defence of legal claims; or

(e)   the transfer is necessary in order to protect the vital interests of the data subject; or

(f)   the transfer is made from a register which according to laws or regulations is intended to provide information to the public and which is open to consultation either by the public in general or by any person who can demonstrate legitimate interest, to the extent that the conditions laid down in law for consultation are fulfilled in the particular case.

There is also a solution for the transfer of personal data to those countries that do not ensure an adequate level of protection. The controller is then required to subject the intended data flow to examination by the national supervisory authority. The controller will in the course of that process have to demonstrate that there is a legal basis for the transfer of the personal data to the recipient and that measures are in place to safeguard adequate protection of the data at the recipient's end (Article 26(2) Data Protection Directive). The latter can be put in place by contract or by binding corporate rules.

22.9 Data Exclusivity

22.9.1 **The Need for Protection**

The pharmaceutical sector is regulated heavily. Marketing authorization needs to be obtained before a new product can be released onto the market. Significant amounts of data need to be generated as part of this process. These data concern the efficacy and the safety of the product and are as such entirely separate, as is the marketing authorization, from the patent for the pharmaceutical product at issue. The major task in this respect falls on the first applicant for approval and the substantial body of data will also include the results of the pre-clinical and the clinical tests. It also represents a significant investment. Hence the idea to compensate the innovator company for that investment by granting it a period of data exclusivity, independent of any form of patent protection. Data exclusivity comes on top of any patent protection.

This needs to be seen against the background of a regulatory regime that permits generic companies that wish to gain their own approval for the same drug substance to rely on the information filed by the innovator company when it made its first application if they can show that their product has the same qualitative and quantitative composition. The aim is indeed to avoid costly duplication of work, but it would be unfair to put the entire burden on the innovator company. Hence the idea of a period of exclusivity.

22.9.2 **The Exclusive Right**

Data exclusivity is a form of product exclusivity right for medicinal products in Europe. The current regime has been put in place by Directive 2004/27/EC of the European Parliament and of the Council of 31 March 2004 amending Directive 2001/83/EC on the Community code relating to medicinal products for human use [2004] OJ L 136/34. The first applicant will enjoy a period of data exclusivity during which their pre-clinical and clinical trials data may not be referenced in the regulatory filings of other companies for the same drug substance. The period of data exclusivity runs for eight years from the date of first authorization in Europe. In the current regime there is an additional period of two years' market exclusivity. During that additional period a generic company may not market an equivalent generic version of the pharmaceutical product concerned. But it can use the period to have its application for marketing authorization processed. The combined data and market exclusivity normally comes to an end after ten years. Exceptionally one year can be added if the original applicant is granted marketing authorization for a significant new indication (the new Article 10 inserted in the amended Directive). The fact that a new marketing authorization for a significant new indication is required also emphasizes the point that data and market exclusivity relate to the active ingredient per se. Approval of new routes of administering the pharmaceutical product, new dosage forms, or even minor new indications do not give rise to new periods of data or market exclusivity.

22.9.3 **Outcome**

Data and market exclusivity protect the significant investment made by a first applicant for marketing authorization in generating the efficacy and safety data that are required and that rely on the outcome of pre-clinical and clinical tests. The first applicant is granted a period of eight years of data exclusivity, followed by two years of market exclusivity.

In exceptional circumstances one more year can be added. Data and market exclusivity are independent of any patent protection for the pharmaceutical product concerned and come on top of it. They cover different elements.

22.10 Conclusions

The essence of data protection is that one is concerned with the personal data of individuals and their, often automated, processing. The basic concept is that the processing of personal data involves almost by definition risks and that there therefore has to be a right to data protection. That right is by no means absolute and will need to be balanced with other fundamental rights, such as the right to property and the right to freedom of expression.

The two major players in the context of data protection are on the one hand the data subject and on the other hand the data controller. The data subject is the individual whose personal data are being processed. On quite a number of occasions the data subject's consent plays a vital role. Data protection law gives the data subject certain rights. One thinks primarily of the right of access to the data and the right to have them corrected if necessary. Case C–131/12 *Google Spain SL v Agencia Española de Protección de Datos (AEPD)* [2014] 3 CMLR 50 brought this right back into the spotlight and established that it contained a right to be forgotten on the Internet. The controller on the other hand is the person that will process the data. Such processing needs to be lawful and for a specific purpose. The quality of the data needs to be guaranteed by the controller and the processing must be fair. Security and transparency also play an important role.

A key element is the need for independent supervision. The Data Protection Directive addresses the need for independent supervision by putting in place in each Member State a national supervisory authority.

Inside the EU there is a free flow of personal data. With third countries there can also be a transborder flow of personal data, but this is subject to special conditions. In essence an adequate level of protection needs to be in place in the third country concerned.

Further Reading

CAREY, P., *Data Protection: A Practical Guide to UK and EU Law* (4th edn, OUP, 2015)

GUTWIRTH, S., LEENES, R., AND DE HERT, P. (eds), *Reforming European Data Protection Law* (Springer, 2015)

GUTWIRTH, S., LEENES, R., DE HERT, P., AND POULLET, Y. (eds), *European Data Protection Law: Coming of Age* (Springer, 2013)

23

Trade Secrets

23.1 Introduction

Database rights and data protection, which were dealt with earlier on in this part, are relatively new issues and rights in the IP arena. In this chapter we deal with a much older and more established issue in IP, the legal protection of trade secrets.

Traditionally, trade secret protection has been left to the national laws of the Member States. In part, this was due to the very varied national approaches. Only recently has there been a trend towards (minimal) harmonization at the EU level. There are also provisions in the international treaties that are relevant, but again these provisions have a rather narrow (harmonizing) scope.

23.2 Starting Points: National Laws and International Agreements

23.2.1 National Laws: Traditional Approaches

Defining exactly what amounts to a trade secret is not an easy task and there is no widely accepted definition of a trade secret. It is also important to note right from the start that the vast majority of countries in the EU offer a remedy in this area, rather than an (exclusive) right. Italy is the most notable exception, as the Italian intellectual property code specifically lists trade secrets as an IP right. Sweden has ad hoc legislation on trade secrets and Portugal and France (the latter only for manufacturing trade secrets) have specific provisions on the protection of trade secrets in their respective IP codes. Most other countries rely heavily on unfair competition law to offer a remedy for abuse of trade secrets. Austria, Belgium, Germany, Poland, and Spain are good examples. Yet other countries, such as the Netherlands and Luxembourg, rely on general principles of tort law to offer a remedy. On the common law side there is a strong reliance on breach of confidence, for example in the United Kingdom and in Ireland, but also in Malta.

All countries also rely heavily on contract law. Often there is also a (somewhat more limited) role for criminal law. Belgian law is a good example. Whereas trade secrets in general are protected by the law of unfair competition and the law of contract, there is special protection in criminal law for the more restrictive category of trade secrets known as manufacturing trade secrets.

What emerges from this patchwork is first of all that there exists no uniform definition of 'trade secrets' within the EU. Indeed, only ten Member States amongst the group that has specific legislation that covers the protection of trade secrets have a specific definition of what is a trade secret in their legislation. So even Member States that have specific provisions on civil redress and protection against the misappropriation of trade secrets, fail to provide a definition of what information may be protected as a trade secret. Often elements of the definition of a trade secret are spread over different pieces of legislation or are left to the case law. This frequently makes it difficult to reconcile all elements in a unique and clear concept. Add to that that each jurisdiction has adopted different eligibility standards for information to qualify as trade secrets and a complex and somewhat confusing picture emerges. One only finds specific statutory definitions in the Swedish trade secrets law, in the Italian and Portuguese Codes of Intellectual Property and in the unfair competition laws of Bulgaria, the Czech Republic, Greece, Poland, and the Slovak Republic. The civil codes of Hungary and Lithuania provide a statutory definition, whilst in Slovenia the latter is found in the Companies Act. The following countries turn to case law for their definition of trade secrets: Austria, Belgium, Cyprus, Denmark, Estonia, Finland, France, Germany, Ireland, Latvia, Luxembourg, Malta, the Netherlands, Romania, Spain, and the UK.

This somewhat discouraging and disappointing starting point should not, however, lead one to the conclusion that a form of unmanageable chaos reigns in the EU on this point. One has to admit, as do the authors of the Study on Trade Secrets and Confidential Business Information in the Internal Market, prepared for the Commission in 2013, that certain requirements that allow information to be qualified as a trade secret keep resurfacing in the national approaches:

(a) technical or commercial information has to be present that relates to the business;

(b) that information is secret in the sense that it is not generally known or easily accessible;

(c) that information has economic value in the sense that it confers a competitive advantage on whoever owns it; and

(d) reasonable steps have been taken to keep the information secret.

But once one moves away from this common core, additional requirements emerge and the picture becomes more and more diverse. On top of the commercial economic value of the information one sometimes finds a reference to the interest of the trade secret holder. In Bulgaria the latter is even used as an alternative requirement, whilst Hungarian law requires that the publication, acquisition, or use of a trade secret by an unauthorized person violates or imperils the financial, economic, or market interests of the owner of the information. Damage is another candidate for an additional requirement. By way of contrast the Swedish Trade Secrets Act requires the presence of 'competitive' damage, whilst the Slovak Commercial Code does not mention damage at all. The inclusion of the relevant legislation in the Companies Act in Slovenia means that information is deemed to be a trade secret if it is qualified as such by a corporate written resolution. And the Lithuanian Civil Code provides the option for the legislature to exclude specific types of information from the scope of trade secrets protection.

A second important point apart from the definition of a trade secret is the set of actions and remedies that are available. Once more there is no single approach that prevails. The actions and remedies that are available vary from Member State to Member State, as do the prerequisites for a remedy to become available. Logically speaking the claimant will need to show that he had a protectable trade secret, that there was an infringement of the latter, and that the misappropriation or use by the defendant was unlawful in nature. But if the national action is one in unfair competition one may also need to establish that the defendant had the intention of competing with the owner of the information. An action for breach of contract on the other hand will require evidence of the existence of an actionable contractual obligation and of a breach of the latter. Tort actions rely instead on the claimant proving the defendant's fault, the damage resulting from it, and the causal link between these two.

There is also no uniform approach to the question who can be the defendant in a trade secrets case. The defendant can of course potentially be at least any of the following: a recipient of the information in bad faith in a case of industrial espionage, a competitor, a licensee or other contractual partner, a current or a former employee, or an innocent recipient who receives the information in good faith. Countries such as Austria, the Czech Republic, Denmark, Estonia, Finland, Germany, Ireland, Latvia, Lithuania, and Portugal merely require that the defendant obtained the information. That also means that a recipient in good faith can be a defendant (even if damages may not be awarded easily against such a defendant). But in other Member States, such as Malta, which go down the contract route the trade secrets owner can only take legal action for breach of contractual obligations, which severely limits the number of potential defendants. It is also not clear that the Enforcement Directive (EC/2004/48) assists on this point. The Directive applies to IP rights, but national courts may not necessarily qualify trade secrets as (formal) IP rights.

On the list of remedies one finds injunctive relief, return/seizure/withdrawal/destruction of infringing goods or materials embedding trade secrets, restraint orders, penalties, and damages, but the remedies most commonly applied in Member States' court practice are injunctions and damages. In Bulgaria, Cyprus, Estonia, Finland, Luxembourg, and Malta the latter are the only remedies available.

23.2.2 National Laws rather than a Directive or a Regulation

What has become clear from these introductory comparative comments is that not only is there no exclusive right, leaving Italy to one side for a moment, but only a remedy based on different legal principles, there is also no EU instrument dealing with trade secrets. At present there is no harmonization directive or a Community trade secret based on a regulation. *De lege lata* the whole matter is left with the individual Member States. As we will see though, that may change in the near future (*de lege feranda*).

23.2.3 The Paris Convention and the TRIPS Agreement

There are however some international foundations on which this area of law and the various approaches in the Member States are built. Article 10*bis* Paris Convention obliges the Member States to provide effective protection and unfair competition. The appropriation of trade secrets without permission is probably one of the clearest examples of acts of unfair competition and, as was seen earlier, Article 10*bis* and the reliance on principles of unfair competition is reflected in the national laws of many Member States. Section 7 TRIPS Agreement then builds on this starting point and Article 39 TRIPS Agreement deals explicitly with the protection of undisclosed information. As all EU Member States are bound by the TRIPS Agreement and in the absence of an EU instrument dealing with trade secrets, the following provision is the common core of the national approaches to trade secret protection:

SECTION 7: PROTECTION OF UNDISCLOSED INFORMATION

Article 39

1. In the course of ensuring effective protection against unfair competition as provided in Article 10*bis* of the Paris Convention (1967), Members shall protect undisclosed information in accordance with paragraph 2 and data submitted to governments or governmental agencies in accordance with paragraph 3.

2. Natural and legal persons shall have the possibility of preventing information lawfully within their control from being disclosed to, acquired by, or used by others without their consent in a manner contrary to honest commercial practices so long as such information:

   (a) is secret in the sense that it is not, as a body or in the precise configuration and assembly of its components, generally known among or readily accessible to persons within the circles that normally deal with the kind of information in question;

   (b) has commercial value because it is secret; and

   (c) has been subject to reasonable steps under the circumstances, by the person lawfully in control of the information, to keep it secret.

3. Members, when requiring, as a condition of approving the marketing of pharmaceutical or of agricultural chemical products which utilize new chemical entities, the submission of undisclosed test or other data, the origination of which involves a considerable effort, shall protect such data against unfair commercial use. In addition, Members shall protect such data against disclosure, except where necessary to protect the public, or unless steps are taken to ensure that the data are protected against unfair commercial use.

Note: For the purpose of this provision, 'a manner contrary to honest commercial practices' shall mean at least practices such as breach of contract, breach of confidence and inducement to breach, and includes the acquisition of undisclosed information by third parties who knew, or were grossly negligent in failing to know, that such practices were involved in the acquisition.

A first important point in this Article is the definition that is offered of the concept of undisclosed information. That definition falls into three requirements. First of all, protection is, or should be, available if the information is secret. That is in turn defined as information that is not generally known among or readily accessible to persons within the circles that normally deal with the kind of information in question. Availability of the information in the public domain seems to be the bottom line here. Second, on top of that the aspect of secrecy must give or add commercial value to the information. And third, the person lawfully in control of the information must take reasonable steps to keep it secret. This is summarized in Figure 23.1.

The importance of this definition is, for example, also shown by the fact that the Italian Intellectual Property Code has copied it quasi verbatim when defining its trade secret right.

Whilst the focus is clearly on secrecy and the confidential nature of the information, there is virtually no restriction, apart from the element of 'commercial value', on the kind of information that can be protected. In practice a diverse range of information is covered. Technical knowledge, often referred to in this context as know-how, is the obvious

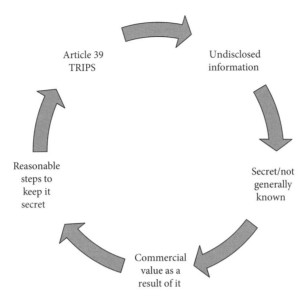

Figure 23.1 Undisclosed information as the cornerstone for the protection of trade secrets

example, but all kinds of commercial data such as information on customers and suppliers, business plans, market strategies, and market research are also included in the range of information that can be protected as a trade secret.

A second important point is the indication that is given as to what kind of dealings with trade secrets will entitle their holder to a remedy. Or if one wants to put it this way, what will amount to an act of unfair competition or when will a tort be committed in relation to a trade secret? On this point Article 39 TRIPS Agreement places the emphasis on the unauthorized disclosure, acquisition, or use by others without the consent of the holder of the undisclosed information in a manner contrary to honest commercial practices. The concepts of disclosure, acquisition, or use without the consent of the holder of the undisclosed information are rather straightforward and do not require additional clarification. The qualification that these aspects happen in a manner contrary to honest commercial practices is interesting though and goes beyond a mere reference to unfair competition. The note to Article 39 explains that for the purpose of that provision, 'a manner contrary to honest commercial practices' shall mean at least practices such as breach of contract, breach of confidence, and inducement to breach, and includes the acquisition of undisclosed information by third parties who knew, or were grossly negligent in failing to know, that such practices were involved in the acquisition. Especially the reference to third parties who know or who were grossly negligent in failing to know brings in a subjective element. There is on the other hand a strong tendency to keep this element to an objective test. Obliging the claimant to prove a subjective element in the mind of the defendant makes effective trade secret protection more burdensome and harder to achieve. There may not be a right in the information that forms the trade secret, but applying merely an objective test makes obtaining protection easier and seems to be more aligned to the practice in relation to IP rights. We will return to this debate later on in this chapter in the context of the proposed EU directive. Suffice it to say here that the Commission proposal included a subjective element, clearly based in the wording of Article 39 TRIPS Agreement and the note to it, whilst the Council prefers an objective test.

23.3 The Draft Directive

23.3.1 A Minimalist Approach is Proposed

Pushed to an extent by allegations of large-scale espionage by the United States, the European Commission proposed a 'Directive on the protection of undisclosed know-how and business information (trade secrets) against their unlawful acquisition, use and disclosure' in November 2013.[1] The Council has now issued its opinion (19 May 2014)[2] on the draft Directive, but the European Parliament is still debating the draft. There is therefore not yet a European instrument in this area, let alone one that has been implemented by the Member States, but the EU is clearly edging towards a degree of harmonization when it comes to the protection of trade secrets.

Whilst it is true that cybercrime and industrial espionage are challenges that companies in the EU are faced with every day, protecting the strategic assets of EU companies adequately against theft and misuse is only part of the background to the draft Directive. Small and medium-sized companies often find the patent system unduly complicated and expensive and they lack the in-house expertise to use it successfully and efficiently. They therefore often rely on the law of trade secrets. A single approach to the threat of the theft of trade secrets will not only simplify matters, it will also boost the confidence of businesses, creators, researchers, and innovators in collaborative innovation across the internal market. What will remain unchanged however is that the protection of trade secrets themselves, i.e. the foundation of the alternative to the patent system and of the additional protection that is available for trade secrets, will remain governed by 28 different national laws. These approaches are very different indeed and wholesale harmonization would have been extremely complex and hard to achieve. It is also not clear that there is a real need for such wholesale harmonization in the area of trade secrets. The idea behind the initiative is that the draft will cover the most urgent matters in detail and that in doing so confidence in trade secrets as a tool will increase and that the whole system, whilst still relying on 28 national laws, will become more effective.

The aim is therefore not to put in place a comprehensive EU regime for the protection of trade secrets. There will only be partial harmonization of the national laws of the Member States, focusing on the unlawful acquisition, disclosure, and use of trade secrets, and that harmonization will be of a minimalist nature in the sense that Member States may provide, in compliance with the provisions of the Treaty, for more far-reaching protection against the unlawful acquisition, use, or disclosure of trade secrets than that required in the Directive. The Council thought it wise to add that *expressis verbis* to Article 1 of the draft Directive. Whilst businesses will be able to rely on a minimal level of protection for their trade secrets in every Member State, they will still have to contend with 28 (slightly) different national laws rooted in different areas of law. The benefits of this harmonization will therefore be much more limited than the benefits in other areas of IP law, such as trade marks, design, and even copyright.

---

[1] See http://ec.europa.eu/internal_market/iprenforcement/docs/trade-secrets/131128_proposal_en.pdf.
[2] See http://register.consilium.europa.eu/doc/srv?l=EN&f=ST%209870%202014%20INIT.

23.3.2 **Definitions**

The Directive does of course need a definition of a trade secret. In this respect the draft sticks closely to Article 39 TRIPS Agreement. This is the version of Article 2 of the draft Directive:

> For the purposes of this Directive, the following definitions shall apply:
>
> (1) 'trade secret' means information which meets all of the following requirements:
>
> > (a) is secret in the sense that it is not, as a body or in the precise configuration and assembly of its components, generally known among or readily accessible to persons within the circles that normally deal with the kind of information in question;
> >
> > (b) has commercial value because it is secret;
> >
> > (c) has been subject to reasonable steps under the circumstances, by the person lawfully in control of the information, to keep it secret;
>
> (2) 'trade secret holder' means any natural or legal person lawfully controlling a trade secret;
>
> (3) 'infringer' means any natural or legal person who has unlawfully acquired, used or disclosed trade secrets;
>
> (4) 'infringing goods' means goods whose design, quality, functioning, manufacturing process or marketing significantly benefits from trade secrets unlawfully acquired, used or disclosed.

Whilst it is the generally accepted definition, it should not be forgotten that this definition is very wide in scope and covers an immense variety of technical and commercial information.

23.3.3 **The Scope of Unlawful Acquisition, Use, and Disclosure**

Article 3 then turns to the crux of the matter and defines the scope of violation of a trade secret. Redress is provided for the unlawful acquisition, use, or disclosure of a trade secret. The key concept here is that the relevant activity must be unlawful. In the Commission's proposal proving unlawfulness involved passing a threshold of intention or (at least) gross negligence. This subjective element might raise the burden of proof and is out of line with the traditional approach towards primary infringement of IP. The Council therefore proposed to replace it with a more objective approach that holds that any acquisition, use, or disclosure which is, under the circumstances, considered contrary to honest commercial practices will be unlawful. This is also a return to the text of Article 39 TRIPS Agreement, whereas the Commission had taken over the language of the final sentence of the note to that Article. Knowledge as a factor is then restricted to forms of violation that can be characterized as indirect or secondary. In the Council's version this results in the following provision:

> … 2. The acquisition of a trade secret without the consent of the trade secret holder shall be considered unlawful, whenever carried out by … unauthorised access to, copying or appropriation of any documents, objects, materials, substances or electronic files, lawfully under the control of the trade secret holder, containing the trade secret or from which the trade secret can be deduced [or] any other conduct which, under the circumstances, is considered contrary to honest commercial practices.

3. The use or disclosure of a trade secret shall be considered unlawful whenever carried out, without the consent of the trade secret holder by a person who is found to meet any of the following conditions:

   (a) have acquired the trade secret unlawfully;

   (b) be in breach of a confidentiality agreement or any other duty to not disclose the trade secret;

   (c) be in breach of a contractual or any other duty to limit the use of the trade secret.

4. The acquisition, use or disclosure of a trade secret shall also be considered unlawful whenever a person, at the time of acquisition, use or disclosure, knew or should, under the circumstances, have known that the trade secret was obtained directly or indirectly from another person who was using or disclosing the trade secret unlawfully within the meaning of paragraph 3.

5. The production, offering or placing on the market of infringing goods, or import, export or storage of infringing goods for those purposes, shall also be considered an unlawful use of a trade secret when the person carrying out such activities knew, or should, under the circumstances, have known that the trade secret was used unlawfully within the meaning of paragraph 3.

This provision gives the protection of trade secrets an extremely wide scope. And in certain circumstances such a wide scope of protection will not be appropriate and could trample on other rights. Article 4 tries to address that problem by putting in place a number of limitations. In a first step the Article holds the acquisition of trade secrets to be lawful if it is achieved by independent discovery or creation; through observation, study, disassembly, or test of a product or object that has been made available to the public or that it is lawfully in the possession of the acquirer of the information who is free from any legally valid duty to limit the acquisition of the trade secret; or any other practice which, under the circumstances, is in conformity with honest commercial practices. In all these circumstances there is no real obligation of secrecy and definitively no breach of any such obligation. There is in other words no clash or conflict with the protection of the trade secret. In a second step the Article has however to deal with those circumstances where there is a real clash with other rights or interests. One thinks here of the freedom of expression of investigative journalists, whistleblowers, workers' representatives, etc. The Council has made this distinction very clear by adding a sentence that inserts the principle that any acquisition, use, or disclosure of a trade secret will be lawful to the extent that it is required or allowed, not merely by EU law, but also by the national law of the Member State concerned. The reference to national law should not simply be seen as a sign of weak harmonization. National law still governs major issues in our society where trade secrets could potentially interfere with other rights and interests, for example in relation to criminal justice, press regulation, or certain elements of labour law and the representation of workers in companies. It is therefore important to state clearly that the Directive will not overrule those other legal provisions. The final paragraph of Article 4 illustrates that principle by ruling out any remedy for any alleged acquisition, use, or disclosure of a trade secret that was carried out:

(a) for making legitimate use of the right to freedom of expression and information;

(b) for the purpose of revealing a misconduct, wrongdoing or illegal activity, provided that the alleged acquisition, use or disclosure of the trade secret was necessary for such revelation and that the respondent acted in the public interest;

(c) the trade secret was disclosed by workers to their representatives as part of the legitimate exercise of their representative functions, provided that such disclosure was necessary for that exercise; ...

(e) for the purpose of protecting a legitimate interest recognised by Union or national law.

One should not underestimate the importance of Article 4. There was a clear need to protect other rights and interest, not all of which are in areas of (exclusive) EU competence. The version of the Article suggested by the Council goes a long way towards achieving the right balance between the interest of the holder of the trade secret and the various other rights and interests that count in our society. The remainder of the effort lies with the Member States and the courts when they implement and apply the Directive.

23.3.4 **Redress**

The draft Directive provides various form of redress, but the Commission's draft and, even more explicitly through the insertion of the word 'civil' in Article 5, the Council's draft make it very clear that the draft Directive is only concerned with civil redress. Criminal law is not affected, which, in combination with the minimalist approach of the draft Directive, also means that those national laws that do have criminal sanctions, for example for the violation of manufacturing trade secrets, will be allowed to retain these or to introduce additional criminal sanctions. The measures, procedures, and remedies that the Member States put in place by way of civil redress need to meet the general standards of fairness, equitableness, effectiveness, and dissuasiveness and need not be unnecessarily complicated or costly, nor entail unreasonable time-limits or unwarranted delays. This approach has been copied from the TRIPS Agreement and the Enforcement Directive. Similarly, any application of such measures, procedures, and remedies needs to be proportionate and provide safeguards against their abuse. There will also be a limitation period for claims based on the Directive's provisions, but whereas the Commission wants to work with a very short period of one to two years after the holder of the trade secret becomes aware of the breach, the Council prefers to leave this to the Member States and to impose merely a maximum limitation period of six years. Both approaches reflect the perceived need to deal quickly with these matters and to remove any uncertainty in the interests of all parties involved.

Legal proceedings concerning a trade secret and its allegedly illegal acquisition, use, or disclosure are of course in themselves a risk for the disclosure of a trade secret. It is therefore important that those involved in the proceedings can be given an obligation not to disclose the trade secret. That is what the Commission's draft did in its Article 8. The Council's draft takes a more cautious approach and requires a reasoned application by the interested party to install a secrecy regime in relation to information that the competent authorities have identified as confidential. However one deals with it, confidentiality of trade secrets in the course of proceedings is in certain cases necessary and a vital ingredient of any regime dealing with trade secrets.

Just as with many other types of IP, time is often of the essence. Secrecy is something that cannot be restored once it has been broken, making fast measures to prevent the acquisition, use, or disclosure of a trade secret vital. Once a violation has occurred it is imperative to stem the breach and avoid the consequences of the violation of the trade secret causing irreparable or widespread damage. The draft Directive addresses these concerns in its Article 9 by putting in place a system of interim and precautionary measures. The holder of a trade secret can apply to the court for an interim injunction that prohibits or orders the cessation of the use or the disclosure of the trade secret on an interim basis. The holder can also apply for interim measures that deal with allegedly infringing goods. These measure can take the form of an order prohibiting the production, offering, or placing on the market of the allegedly infringing goods and their importation, exportation, or storage for these purposes. Allegedly infringing goods can also be seized or their delivery up can be ordered to prevent their entry into the market or their circulation within the market.

Once a decision on the merits has been reached and the acquisition, use, or disclosure of the trade secret has been held to be unlawful, the draft Directive provides a range of possible measures in its Article 11. At the top of the list of measures one finds injunctions, essentially to order the cessation or prohibition of the use of the disclosure of the trade secret. A prohibition to produce, offer, place on the market, or use infringing goods that have benefited from the trade secret in any way, or to import, export, or store such infringing goods for those purposes may also be granted by the court by way of injunctive relief. On top of that the draft Directive proposes corrective measures with regard to the infringing goods. These infringing goods can be recalled from the market[3] or their infringing quality can be removed. The court can also order the destruction of the infringing goods or the destruction of all or part of any document, object, material, substance, or electronic file containing or implementing the trade secret or, where appropriate, the delivery up to the applicant of all or part of those documents, objects, materials, substances, and electronic files.

In addition damages can be awarded, either damages that are commensurate with the actual prejudice suffered or damages as a lump sum (e.g. on the basis of an estimate of royalties that could have become payable for the lawful use of the trade secret). The courts can also order the publication of the judgment.

23.4 **Conclusions**

Trade secrets play an important role in our modern economy and business environment. In the form of know-how they not only form an alternative to patent protection for an invention, but even if a patent is granted there is complimentary know-how, for example concerning the best way to exploit the patent, that is not included in the patent application. That know-how is then kept and protected as a trade secret. But also outside the area of technical information there are all kinds of elements of commercial information, for example about the market and (potential) clients, that are not available in the public domain at large, but that have great value, in part due to their confidential nature.

In the absence of an IP right that protects the trade secret, national laws have a long-standing tradition of protecting trade secrets by offering a remedy against their unlawful acquisition, use, or disclosure. These national regimes are rooted firmly in existing legal rules in the areas of unfair competition, tort, or breach of confidence. But there is diversity, rather than uniformity. The only uniform provisions *de lege lata* are found in the basic provisions of the Paris Convention and the TRIPS Agreement.

The EU draft Directive that is currently under consideration proposes to change that by imposing on Member States a minimal form of harmonization and uniformity. It would not impose a (Community) right in relation to a trade secret, but it works with a common basic definition of a trade secret, the principle that there needs to be redress for the unlawful acquisition, use, or disclosure of a trade secret, and a catalogue of measures and remedies. Its aims are therefore limited, but its adoption would mean some progress in this area.

---

[3] The holder of the trade secret can also request that the infringing goods are delivered up to it or to charitable organizations.

Further Reading

Aplin, T., 'A Critical Evaluation of the Proposed EU Trade Secrets Directive', King's College London Law School Research Paper No. 2014-25 http://papers.ssrn.com/sol3/papers.cfm?abstract_id=2467946

Aplin, T., Bently, L., Johnson, P., and Malynicz, S., *Gurry on Breach of Confidence: The Protection of Confidential Information* (2nd edn, OUP, 2012)

Van Caeneghem, W., *Trade Secrets and Intellectual Property: Breach of Confidence, Misappropriation and Unfair Competition* (Wolters Kluwer, 2014)

24

Privacy

24.1 Introduction

One might wonder how a chapter on privacy finds a place in an IP context. Privacy is traditionally a fundamental right that is limited to the right to be left alone, i.e. the individual has a right not to be interfered with by the authorities. Admittedly, the right has evolved a lot in recent years and has come a long way from its traditional origins. Be that as it may, there has always been an impact on IP. Copyright covers both pictures taken of private individuals (be they famous or not) and gives the copyright to the photographer, as well as articles written about aspects of the private life of individuals, again with the copyright being granted not to the individual concerned but to the author of the article. And in EU Member States such as the UK, breach of confidence has been used to protect both trade secrets and aspects of the private life of individuals. Taken together, these elements warrant a more in-depth analysis of the right of privacy in an IP context.

24.2 Starting Points

24.2.1 The Charter, the Convention, and National Law

When one looks at privacy from a European perspective there are two obvious starting points. The EU now has privacy as part of its Charter of Fundamental Rights of the European Union (CFR) and there is also a provision in the European Convention on Human Rights (ECHR). Article 7 CFR is entitled 'Respect for private and family life'. It puts forward what seems like a simple principle:

> Everyone has the right to respect for his or her private and family life, home and communications.

Article 7 CFR corresponds to Article 8 ECHR and it focuses primarily on individual autonomy. Article 8 ECHR uses the word 'correspondence' and the change to the word 'communications' must merely be seen as an attempt to take account of recent techno-logical developments. Communications are now covered irrespective of the means of communication that is used.

It is therefore correct to say that the Charter does not change or add anything and that it instead merely mirrors the right to privacy enshrined in the ECHR. One should add that most Member States also have a right of privacy as part of their constitutional provisions, be it in the constitution itself or in a separate Bill of Rights or Human Rights Act. Individuals can then enforce their right to privacy directly on the basis of the constitution, the Human Rights Act, or even on the basis of the ECHR, which has direct effect in many Member States. The UK is probably the biggest exception, with privacy being enforced by means of a breach of confidence action in the absence of a specific provision that can be directly invoked by individuals.

24.2.2 Application in a Broad Range of Situations and a Broad Scope

The right of privacy can arise in a large number of situations, as the Strasbourg case law shows well. But one should take into account in an IP context that this is not a property-style exclusive right. Instead the 'right' is an entitlement to see one's privacy respected. That 'right' will most often clash with copyright, for example where a press photographer has taken a picture of a scene in the private sphere of an individual (a celebrity or not) in which the photographer owns the copyright, the exploitation of which might clash with the right of the individual to see his privacy respected. The right of privacy covers matters as wide apart as a person's physical and mental integrity on the one hand and the sphere of intimate relationships on the other. It applies to the social sphere of the person, as it is intended inter alia 'to ensure the development of each individual in his relations with other human beings', as can be seen in *Botta v Italy* (No. 21439/93, judgment of 24 February 1998, [32] and [35]). But it can also apply in the professional sphere of a person and even touch upon the protection of the environment. Suffice it in this respect to refer to *Guerra and Others v Italy* (No. 14967/89, judgment of 19 February 1998, [57]). In this case the ECtHR ruled that the state has obligations to notify the affected residents of the risks associated with the operation of a fertilizer plant, due to the use of toxic substances and inflammable gases. Similarly, in *McGinley and Egan v UK* (Nos 21825/93 and 23414/94, judgment of 9 June 1998, [101]), the ECtHR found that the right of privacy has a role to play if government employees are exposed to radiation during tests of nuclear weapons in the course of their employment, as this may affect their health.

Let us now on a preliminary basis turn to the scope of the right to privacy. What does the right to privacy encompass? Obviously, an entitlement to privacy can be seen as 'the right to be left alone'. The other side of that coin is an obligation on states not to interfere. *Malone v UK* (No. 8691/79, judgment of 2 August 1984, [51]) makes it very clear that this is a cornerstone of the right to privacy. The individual person is entitled to freedom from unwarranted and arbitrary interference, in essence interference contrary to established legal principles, from public authorities or private actors or bodies independent of the state, such as private electronic databanks, into activities that society recognizes as belonging to the realm of individual autonomy and the private sphere of the person concerned. The ECHR counterbalances that with a right for states to interfere in the interests of national security and public safety or the economic well-being of the country, for the prevention of disorder or crime, for the protection of health and morals, or for the protection of the rights and freedoms of others.

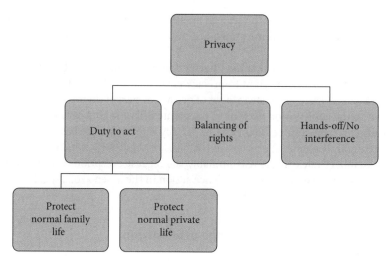

Figure 24.1 A summary of the key elements of privacy

These are in other words legitimate reasons to interfere with the private sphere of the individual.

But for states the right to privacy goes beyond the hands-off/no interference point. There is also a duty to act. That duty to act should have as its aim for the state to facilitate the normal development of family and private life. A typical example is the obligation of states to provide legislation that facilitates the integration of children born outside marriage into the family. Treating these children differently and granting them fewer rights was therefore a clear breach of the Convention according to the decision in *Marckx v Belgium* (No. 6833/74, judgment of 13 June 1979, [31]). And the combination of private life and home and family goes beyond the physical framework and also covers the person's philosophical, religious, or moral beliefs, as well as the person's emotional life. All these need to be respected (hands-off) and protected (active duty).

Figure 24.1 provides a summary of the key elements of privacy.

24.3 Respect for Private Life

Let us turn now in a bit more detail to each aspect of Article 7 CFR. First of all, the right of privacy entails respect for private life. That goes over a right to know which information is collected about you and your health to an entitlement to non-interference with one's personal life choices, and a typical example is found in *Von Hanover v Germany* (No. 59320/00, judgment of 24 June 2004) where respect for private life was held to mean that the publication of photos relating to the private life of Princess Caroline of Monaco, which did not occupy any official function, for example out shopping or horse-riding with family members, in a number of German magazines did not contribute to a debate of general interest. Only the latter could have outweighed the right to respect for the Princess's private life. The ECtHR therefore ruled that 'anyone, even if they are known to the general public, must be able to enjoy a 'legitimate expectation' of protection of and respect for their private life'. One clearly sees the interference here with the copyright of the photographer and the interests of the publishers of the magazines.

Personal integrity, and especially the non-disclosure of facts relating to one's health, must relate to respect for private life, as does the preservation of confidential and personal data, especially when held in public files. In the area of data security there is also important implementing legislation at the EU level in the form of Council Directive 2002/58/EC of the European Parliament and of the Council of 12 July 2002 concerning the processing of personal data and the protection of privacy in the electronic communications sector [2002] OJ L /201 37, which deals with the protection of individuals in connection with the treatment of personalized data. Its Preamble refers in paragraphs 11 and 24 explicitly to Article 8 ECHR. One finds a first specific reference to the right to privacy in Article 4, which obliges the provider of a publicly available electronic communication service to take appropriate measures to protect the security of its services. If there is a particular risk of a breach of the security of the network, which might put private information at risk, the provider must inform the subscribers of such a risk. Article 8(1) follows up on the privacy side by imposing the principle that, where caller identification is offered, the service provider must give the caller the opportunity to prevent identification. This must be available by the use of simple means and be free of charge. In terms of privacy this is important, as it protects the privacy of callers. And following the introduction of the Directive, the use of automatic calling machines, fax, or email for direct marketing purposes will only be allowed for subscribers who have given prior consent, in accordance with Article 13(1) of the Directive.

In general, when it comes to a person's communications states are obliged to take all necessary measures to restrict the unlawful obtaining of information by public authorities as well as by other private parties. A person's right to confidentiality in terms of her communications is the reflection of the right to privacy in this area. The recent mobile phone hacking cases in the UK demonstrate this clearly. *News of the World* journalists almost systematically hacked the mobile phones of celebrities and in doing so invaded their privacy. In quite a few cases the material that was accessed illegally, for example photographs, was protected by copyright, showing once more the interaction with IP rights (*Jeff Brazier v News Group Newspapers Ltd*; *John Leslie v News Group News Newspapers Ltd* [2015] EWHC 125 (Ch)).[1]

This is also an area where the risks have increased as a result of technological advances that have rendered mobile phones and email systems particularly susceptible to improper surveillance by state authorities. The Charter uses the term communications to encompass newer technologies, whereas the Convention still focuses on correspondence. The latter refers mainly to communications in writing and by telephone. Limitations on the right to confidentiality of correspondence, i.e. when letters are opened or withheld, must be justified under Article 8(2) ECHR. This interpretation of the provision was clearly stated by the ECtHR in *Silver and Others v UK* (Nos 5947/72, 6205/73, and 7052/75, judgment of 25 March 1983). In the view of the Court only letters which contain threats of use of violence or planning of criminal acts could legitimately be stopped in accordance with the requirements in Article 8(2).

Privacy also includes respect for a person's home. Often that is the family home and therefore closely linked to the family life aspect of the right to privacy, to which we now turn.

---

[1] In this case an early settlement, entered into before the full extent of the hacking and the amount of copyright material taken was known, was held to block a further action by the claimants.

24.4 Family Life

In a modern society reality consists of a diversity of family life and a multiplicity of con-
stellations may be included in this notion. It is clear that within different social, cultural,
religious, and geographical conditions as well as over time the concept of family life may
vary or change. Respect for family life as an integral part of the right to privacy therefore
means respect for that diversity.

The family as a unit needs first and foremost to be protected when respect for family
life is put into practice. What is protected is the actual living together (i.e. de facto family
life) of inter alia spouses and parents with their children or, if one prefers to put it that way,
the de facto family life is what is protected. In order to make a determination whether a
particular situation constitutes 'family life' the ECtHR has held that a number of factors
may be relevant. These include 'whether the couple live together, the length of their relationship and whether they have demonstrated their commitment to each other by having
children together or by any other means' (*X, Y and Z v UK* (No. 21830/93, judgment of
22 April 1997, [36]). In other words, the Court examines the degree of consanguinity
between individuals and the existence of effective family life between them.

The ECtHR has adopted an approach that shows that the respect extended to family
life varies and that the protection is related to a kind of hierarchy of relationships. Within
a heterosexual marriage there is always 'family life' and this is followed by the category
of cohabiting heterosexual relationships that gains some respect and protection under
Article 8 ECHR. In between, family relations also include the mother–child relationship,
and this is irrespective of the mother's marital status as was clearly demonstrated in the
Marckx case (*Marckx v Belgium* (No. 6833/74, judgment of 13 June 1979)), as well as, at
least to a certain extent the relationship between unmarried fathers and their children
(*Berrehab v the Netherlands* (No. 10730/84, judgment of 21 June 1988) and *Kroon v the
Netherlands* (No. 18535/91, judgment of 27 October 1994). Relationships between sib-
lings (*Moustaquim v Belgium* (No. 12313/86, judgment of 18 February 1991)) and in some
cases between grandparents and grandchildren (*Marckx*) present yet other dimensions
of family life.

Whilst this case law is no doubt also valid when it comes to the interpretation of
Article 7 CFR, the fact that same-sex couples are so far confined to the lesser protection
afforded under the 'private life' element only of the ECHR may cause problems in relation to the Charter. Article 19 TEU prohibits after all any form of discrimination on the
basis of sexual orientation. Article 7 CFR therefore requires an interpretation, which is
more in line with the contemporary legal developments and which also grants same-sex
couples protection for their family life if the factors used to determine whether there is
family life are present.

Finally, it is important to note that protection is provided for family life rather than for
the family itself as a unit, both in Article 7 CFR and in Article 8 ECHR.

24.5 Balancing of Rights and Interests

In the previous sections a picture has emerged of a right of privacy with many aspects and
a broad scope, but a right that can conflict with IP rights. It is also clear that the right is not
absolute in nature and will need to be balanced with other fundamental rights and with
other interests, including those arising from IP rights.

Returning to the link or conflict between IP and privacy, there are multiple areas where such a link or conflict can arise. We have already referred to copyright earlier on, but this remains the primary field where IP and privacy can enter into conflict. A photographer will own the copyright in a photo taken of a (famous) individual, a sculptor will own the copyright in a sculpture of an individual, and a painter will own the copyright in the portrait he painted of an individual. But when the copyright is exploited privacy concerns may arise. Suffice it to mention that the use of pictures in a publicity campaign or even merely on an artist's website to promote his business will necessarily reveal aspects of the individual that are covered by the right to privacy. One also reads frequently in recent times of certain images going viral on the Internet. This often involves derivative works or parodies on YouTube, for example on the basis of the wedding pictures of a couple, with added material from a different context or with added captions. Without the permission of the persons involved there is a clear conflict with their right to privacy. But there may also be a clash in other areas of IP, such as patent law. In recent times a sizeable number of patents have been awarded for genetic material or in cases where human genetic material was part of the raw material leading to the patented invention. In the process, elements of the genetic characteristics of the person involved are made available to the public and this clearly interferes with the person's privacy.

24.6 Conclusions

We have already touched upon aspects of privacy in Chapter 22 concerned with data protection and data security. In this chapter we looked in detail at the right of privacy. It is important to emphasize that the right of privacy is not an exclusive right or an IP right. Instead, as a fundamental right it has a higher status. It has a broad scope, but this also means it touches upon a range of other fundamental right, for example the right of freedom of expression (which has a copyright element to itself). There is therefore first of all a need to balance the right of privacy with other fundamental rights and in that exercise there are already elements of IP, mainly copyright, present. But there is also a balance to be struck with other legitimate rights and interests and there IP rights play a prominent role. Certain patents may, for example, facilitate the interception of private communications and if one reverses the perspective, copyright for photographers and journalists may have to give way if the content of the copyright work is an aspect of the private life of the individual concerned, who is entitled to a right of privacy in this respect.

Further Reading

APLIN, T., 'The Development of the Action for Breach of Confidence in a Post-HRA Era' [2007] *IPQ* 19

PEERS, S., HERVEY, T., KENNER, J., AND WARD, A., *The EU Charter of Fundamental Rights: A Commentary* (Hart Publishing, 2014) Article 7

PART VI

Enforcement and Remedies

25

Enforcement

25.1 Introduction

IP rights are private rights. One can debate whether they, or whether all of them, are property rights, or at least rights that are similar to property rights, but they are by no means public rights, they are squarely private rights. That means for our current purposes that it will be up to the rights holders to enforce their rights, i.e. private enforcement of private rights is the norm. Coupled with the idea that most IP rights are negative rights to stop other parties from performing acts, for example the copyright holder can stop third parties from reproducing their work or the patent holder can stop third parties from making the patented product, this means that the emphasis falls squarely on the (private) enforcement of private rights. The outcome of such enforcement will be remedies, with the aim of restoring the harm done by the infringement of the IP rights.

Leaving the unitary patent and the opposition procedures in the EPO and OHIM to one side, the enforcement (and the remedies) of IP rights in Europe remain a national matter, governed by national laws that are only partially harmonized by means of a directive. Contrast that with European patents, Community trade marks, and loads of parallel national IP rights, i.e. with IP rights that are exploited across borders and at a European (if not global) level and one clearly sees issues of private international law lurking around the corner. To take a simple example, which courts will have jurisdiction to deal with the matter, and which national substantive IP law will such court that has jurisdiction apply, if such cross-border exploitation allegedly infringes a set of parallel IP rights?

We will therefore look in this first enforcement and remedies chapter at the issue of private international law. The first issue will be to determine which court will have jurisdiction to deal with IP and IP-related cases. Once that is out of the way, we will need to look at the issue of how the court with competent jurisdiction will determine the law applicable to the matter before it. Chapter 26 will then turn to enforcement and remedies at a national level, i.e. the content of the applicable law determined by the court with competent jurisdiction, be it at a procedural or substantive level.

It is at this juncture important to note that 20 or so years ago most commentators would never have considered this topic to involve IP *and* private international law. Instead they might have argued that the debate was about IP *or* private international law. They were after all two entirely separate disciplines, or so it seemed at least. IP lawyers spoke about national treatment as the cornerstone of their 'international' IP system.[1] They argued that as a result there never was a 'conflict of laws'. Questions of jurisdiction and choice of law did not seem to arise. Private international law experts did not know what to make of national treatment. It did not fit easily with their jargon and with their concepts of jurisdiction and choice of law. IP seemed for them to be a weird and complex area and, as the IP experts argued that there was no private international law problem to be identified, they were more than happy to move on to more promising hunting grounds. How wrong could one be, though. Pandora's box is now wide open and complex private international law problems seem to emerge on an ongoing basis, in step with the rapid evolution that is taking place in the area of IP.

National treatment simply means that the foreign applicant for a patent or a trade mark, as well as the foreign author who wishes to rely on copyright protection for her work, will be treated as a national of the member state to the international convention that imposes the national treatment principle. It is easy to see how one derives the concept of territoriality from this principle. The international protection of IP and the international IP system seem to operate on a country-by-country basis. Hence the idea of a territorial patchwork of national IP regimes, rather than a truly international or cross-border international IP regime. But one should not lose sight of the idea that at the relevant time, i.e. the end of the 19th century, nationality was the key concept in order to operate a legal system. Treating the national of a foreign country as a national of one's own country then takes on a different meaning. It is essentially a non-discrimination clause and nothing more than that. The foreigner is granted access to the national IP law system. That makes perfect sense if one reads the conventions, as the national treatment clauses are followed by provisions that implement a minimal level of harmonization of the substantive IP law provisions. One does not find a supranational IP law and neither does one find detailed jurisdiction and choice of law rules. The international community was clearly not prepared to go that extra mile at the end of the 19th century. One could call it a lack of consensus, but there was also no real need for it, as IP was very much exploited on a country-by-country basis. Suffice it to mention the example of authors who often sought a different publisher in each country.[2]

Such a territorial, country-by-country system with predominantly local exploitation of the IP rights makes one lose sight of the potential international aspect of each case. Private international law is then easily overlooked and it seems perfectly acceptable to proceed on the basis that the national courts of each country will deal (on an exclusive basis) with the IP cases that arise. And in doing so the court will then 'logically' apply its own national IP law. But in reality there is nothing logical about it. In many cases it will be the outcome, but one needs to know on the basis of which rules courts take jurisdiction and which connecting factors will lead to the applicable law. Suffice it to say that in a nationality-driven environment the idea that the law applicable to copyright would in each country be the law of the nationality of the author seems entirely plausible. Nationality as a connecting factor (that treats all authors in the same way without discrimination) and a single law that applies globally to a copyright work make

---

[1] See, e.g., P. Goldstein and P.B Hugenholtz, *International Copyright: Principles, Law, and Practice* (2nd edn, OUP, 2010) 91–115.

[2] See J.J. Fawcett and P. Torremans, *Intellectual Property and Private International Law* (2nd edn, OUP, 2011) ch. 12.

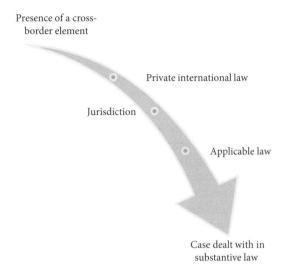

Figure 25.1 The streamline approach of private international law

sense..., or at least a strong defence of this approach is found in George Koumantos's legal writings.[3]

In short, jurisdiction and choice of law questions do arise in the area of IP and the international IP conventions have anything but complete answers to these questions.[4] Not all options are open as the system needs to comply with the national treatment idea, but it is a fair conclusion to say that the standard private international law instruments will cover IP and will need to determine which court has jurisdiction and which law applies. It will not always be a perfect fit. Territorially awarded exclusive rights are not the most straightforward topic in private international law. And things have not become easier when the paradigm of national country-by-country exploitation of IP rights was replaced by the paradigm of cross-border exploitation of IP rights. With that in mind, every case will proceed as set out in Figure 25.1.

25.2 Intellectual Property and Private International Law: Jurisdiction

Let us therefore look in a bit more detail at the application of the rules on private international law to IP and let us start with jurisdiction. In a European context one is therefore looking at the application of the Brussels I Regulation (Council Regulation (EC) No. 44/2001 of the European Parliament and of the Council of 22 December 2000 on jurisdiction and the recognition and enforcement of judgments in civil and commercial matters [2001] OJ L 12/1, replaced as of 10 January 2015 by the recast version Regulation (EU) No. 1215/2012 of the European Parliament and of the Council of 12 December 2012 on jurisdiction and the recognition and enforcement of judgments in civil and commercial matters (recast) [2012] OJ L 351/1) to IP cases, as they are after all civil and commercial

---

[3] [1979] *Il Diritto di Autore* 616 and (1998) 24 *Copyright* 415.
[4] See J.J. Fawcett and P. Torremans, *Intellectual Property and Private International Law* (2nd edn, OUP, 2011) ch. 12, p. 671.

cases and therefore fall within the scope of the Brussels I Regulation. Rather than try to summarize all aspects of the Brussels I Regulation that are relevant, let us look at a practical scenario that shows the often problematic link between the jurisdiction rules and IP.

25.2.1 **The Most Common Scenario**

The contrast between national IP rights, which are still granted on the basis of the territoriality principle, and which, as a consequence, logically produce on the one hand parallel rights in several countries and on the other hand the international exploitation of such rights, results in a scenario where similar violations, mostly performed by defendants with a mutual relationship between them, give rise to claims based on similar national provisions on IP. Article 4 (old Article 2) Brussels I Regulation allows for the separate prosecution of every defendant in the country where she resides, or in the words of the Regulation:

> persons domiciled in a Member State shall, whatever their nationality, be sued in the courts of that Member State.

There is no reason not to apply the basic rule of the Brussels I Regulation to cases involving IP. That basic rule is based on the link between the defendant and the jurisdiction. There is also a rule that is based on the link between the facts of the case and the jurisdiction and that can apply as an alternative at the choice of the claimant in cases to which the basic rule is applicable. Article 7(2) (old Article 5(3)) grants in this respect jurisdiction to 'the courts for the place where the harmful event occurred or may occur'. A long and well-established line of cases has held that this comprises both the place of the act leading to the damage and the place where the damage occurs (see Case 21/76 *Handelskwekerij G.J. Bier BV v Mines de Potasse d'Alsace SA* [1976] ECR 1735; Case C–68/93 *Fiona Shevill and others v Presse Alliance SA* [1995] ECR I-415; and Case C–523/10 *Wintersteiger AG v Products 4U Sondermaschinenbau GmbH* [2012] ETMR 31).

   Although Article 7(2) (old Article 5(3)) provides for an alternative solution, the standard scenario involves a multitude of claims submitted country by country, apparently as a logical consequence of the territoriality principle.[5] This has been re-enforced by recent decisions from the CJEU (see Case C–228/11 *Melzer v MF Global UK Ltd* [2013] QB 1112, [2013] 3 WLR 883, [2013] CEC 1023; Case C–170/12 *Pinckney v Mediatech* [2013] ECDR 15, [2014] FSR 18; and Case C–360/12 *Coty Germany v First Note Perfumes NV* [2014] ETMR 49) that stress the factual nature of the examination under Article 7(2) (old Article 5(3)) Brussels I Regulation. Whilst it is positive to avoid dealing with substantive law matters at the jurisdiction stage, as this could give rise to a second mini trial of the same issues, the reality is that the mere factual potential presence of an act leading to damage or damage in the jurisdiction is very easy to demonstrate in IP cases if one disregards the question whether or not the claimant even has a reasonable chance of winning the case on substance (e.g. is it at least arguable that the factual act or damage amounts to an infringing act in the jurisdiction in the light of substantive IP law and its territorial nature). Even hopeless cases will therefore pass the jurisdiction stage and this opens the door to harassment of a defendant by suing in multiple Member States, knowing that the defendant may not be able to afford to defend all these cases to the end of all the substantive trials. It is positive though that the CJEU limits these cases to local damage in each jurisdiction. In an even more recent case the Advocate General also suggested that the second lid of the provision, i.e. the (local) damage-based

---

[5] See ibid ch. 5.

provision, should not apply to cases of ubiquitous infringement (Opinion of Advocate General Cruz Villalón in Case C–441/13 *Pez Hedjuk v EnergieAgentur* EU:C:2014:2212). That could have avoided partial cases being brought in each and every Member State, but the Court decided not to follow the advice of its Advocate General and stuck to its approach despite the obvious risks associated with it.

25.2.2 **Multiple Defendants in a Single Forum**

IP has been the object of considerable harmonization over the years, on the basis of both international treaties and EU law. Without going into too much detail, it is obvious that the combination of territorial (national) IP rights and their exploitation beyond national boundaries raises questions related to the possible application of Article 8(1) (old Article 6(1)) Brussels I Regulation:

> A person domiciled in a Member State may also be sued:
>
> (1) where he is one of a number of defendants, in the courts for the place where any one of them is domiciled, provided the claims are so closely connected that it is expedient to hear and determine them together to avoid the risk of irreconcilable judgments resulting from separate proceedings;.

A *forum connexitatis* offers in fact the possibility of pursuing the infringement of what, from a commercial point of view, is often considered as a single right, rather than a bundle of parallel national IP rights. Thus, the patent infringement performed in a uniform manner, for example by the commercialization of a copy of the patented product by related defendants, is pursued as a single case before a single court. Article 8(1) (old Article 6(1)) offers therefore an interesting opportunity in a number of IP cases. However, Article 8(1) (old Article 6(1)) is principally targeted at defendants residing in different Member States acting with a common agenda (e.g. *Pearce v Ove Arup Partnership Ltd* [2000] Ch 403 and *Chiron Corp. v Evans Medical Ltd and Others* [1996] FSR 863), and this is in contrast with the most common scenario of IP rights infringement, which involves both parallel rights and defendants that act (individually) in a parallel fashion, whether or not they act within a group of companies.

One could therefore expect anything but a straightforward case when the Court looked for the first time at the potential application of Article 8(1) (old Article 6(1)) Brussels I Regulation in a case concerning IP rights in Case C–539/03 *Roche Nederland BV et al. v Frederick Primus and Milton Goldenberg* [2006] ECR I-6535. At the very least, one can state that this judgment is controversial.[6] In short, Primus and Goldenberg had filed an application for a European patent; and they had obtained a patent, according to the European Patent Convention (EPC), as a bundle of national patents. They claimed that the Roche group had infringed their European patent. In practice the infringement was performed in each country, every time by the local branch of the Roche group, but the case was handled and coordinated by the group's central unit. Therefore, it would have been useful for Primus and Goldenberg to have the whole case treated by a single court. This was also possible because Dutch courts had developed for the purposes of Article 8(1) (old Article 6(1)) the so-called 'spider in the web' doctrine in cases such as the Court of Appeal of The Hague's decision in *Expandable Grafts Partnership v Boston Scientific BV* [1999] FSR 352. The *Roche* case seemed to be a typical case. The spider's web of patent infringement had been woven, or at least

---

[6] Ibid paras 11.05 *et seq.* and A. Kur, 'A Farewell to Crossborder Injunctions? The ECJ Decisions *GAT v. LuK* and *Roche Nederland v. Primus and Goldenberg*' (2006) 37 *IIC* 844.

conceived, by the central unit of the group. The local branches merely carried out this strategy. Why not entrust the coordinated infringement of the European patent to a single court, the court of the spider, whose competence was recognized by Article 8(1) (old Article 6(1))?

Yet, was the existence of a spider at the centre of the web of patent infringement the right starting point? According to the text of Article 8(1) (old Article 6(1)), the presence of a spider implies a link between the claims, undoubtedly a close link. However, this is not what Article 8(1) (old Article 6(1)) requires. Article 8(1) (old Article 6(1)) requires that the cases are 'so closely connected that it is expedient to hear and determine them together to avoid the risk of irreconcilable judgments resulting from separate proceedings'. A risk of irreconcilable judgments is the *conditio sine qua non* to apply Article 8(1) (old Article 6(1)) which constitutes a derogation to Article 4 (old Article 2) and takes away one or more defendants from the forum of their domicile. Different judges can rule differently on a particular case, even if their decision is grounded on the same facts and on the same law. But Article 8(1) (old Article 6(1)) does not have the purpose of preventing such divergence. The only risk that needs to be averted is that of contradictory judgments that are incompatible. This risk exists only if two judges of two countries decide, on each side, on the same factual and legal situation, as was recognized by the CJEU in Case C–539/03 *Roche Nederland BV et al. v Frederick Primus and Milton Goldenberg* [2006] ECR I-6535 [26]. If we take an example from the field of IP rights, this risk exists if the defendant A, domiciled in X, together with the defendant B, domiciled in Y, manufactures in Z reproductions of an artwork by an author, without the author's authorization, and puts them on the market. If a judge in country X exerts her jurisdiction on the basis of Article 4 (old Article 2) Brussels I Regulation over defendant A, and another judge in the country Y does the same in relation to defendant B, both judges would decide the same dispute. In this case there is the risk that the same activity performed together in the country Z by the two parties (and to which the law of Z if probably applicable) is considered by one of the judges as an infringement and by the other judge as a perfectly lawful activity. These decisions would therefore be incompatible.

The Court of Justice has ruled, in *Roche Nederland* ([27]), that the condition of the same factual situation was not met. According to the Court each branch operated in a separate country and the details of the patent infringement were different in each country. The infringing activity was also performed in different countries by each defendant. In other words, there was no joint activity in a particular country, and there were no overlapping infringing activities or defendants. There were purely parallel factual situations, territorial and national. In addition, the Court argued that this case was not even subject to the same law, because the European patent consists of a number of national patents and is granted as such. Each of these patents is subject to national patent law and these patents are independent from each other. This is certainly the case when patent infringement is expressly covered by national law (*Roche Nederland* [29]–[31]).

If we are ready to follow the analysis of the Court on this point, there is no question of irreconcilable judgments. Every defendant must answer for her deeds in a specific factual and legal situation. There is no factual situation involving several defendants jointly, and every form of overlapping is avoided. The need for claims 'closely connected' cannot be demonstrated despite the similarities among national cases, and Article 8(1) (old Article 6(1)) is not applicable because the conditions required by the text of this Article are not met (*Roche Nederland* [33]).

The 'spider in the web' doctrine argues that there is a supplementary factor to be considered, in addition to the web of coordinated activities: the planning by the spider.

The *forum connexitatis* therefore is identified with the location where the spider is based. Given this additional factor, it is desirable to bring the cases before an individual judge because of the close link resulting from the coordination by the spider. However, in the analysis of the Court there is no room for this supplementary step. The Court is not able to go this far and it does not apply the 'spider in the web' doctrine because the requirements of the wording of Article 8(1) (old Article 6(1)) are not met (*Roche Nederland* [34]–[35]).

It is fair to say that there have been cases since *Roche Nederland* that indicate that this rather inflexible approach may not be the final word on the matter, but suffice it to say here by way of advance warning that the outcome and the way forward are not very clear at present. A first case to consider in the search for corrections to the *Roche Nederland* approach is Case C–98/06 *Freeport plc v Olle Arnoldsson* [2007] ECR I-8319.

To be honest, the *Freeport* case has nothing to do with IP rights. It was essentially about two connected cases against two defendants on the basis of different legal situations, namely the contractual responsibility on the one hand and the tortious liability on the other hand. And this was exactly the most criticized point of *Roche Nederland*. National patent law is largely harmonized and national rules on patent infringement are all translations in national law of Article 69 EPC and of the Protocol to this Article. The strict application of the territoriality principle to a case concerning the infringement of a European patent on the basis that this cannot be a single legal situation is perhaps a little too simplistic. The *Freeport* case has given the Court the opportunity to re-examine the requirement of the single legal situation, and therefore this judgment becomes of crucial importance for our analysis. The Court goes immediately to the point. The requirement of an identical legal situation is softened, one year only after *Roche Nederland*. The identity of the legal foundations of the claims, for example an identical provision on patent infringement in the national patent law, as in *Roche*, is not required. The emphasis is again on the risk of irreconcilable judgments. A simple divergence is not sufficient; and there must be a connection so close as to produce the risk of irreconcilable judgments. This requires an identical factual situation and a converging legal situation, even though the latter condition is equally satisfied if there is a different legal basis for each case. Moreover, the Court introduces some flexibility on this second condition. The national judge must consider every aspect, including an identical juridical basis, if that is the case, although this aspect is not decisive, and he must decide if there is a risk of irreconcilable judgments.

Also the rules of national patent law that are only partially harmonized are no longer an obstacle. The *Roche Nederland* approach is clearly softened on this point and Article 8(1) (old Article 6(1)) would certainly be applicable today if two branches of *Roche* would jointly infringe a patent by performing the same activity in two different countries. Even a different legal basis, as the infringement of a patent in country A and a case of unfair competition based on the infringement of an exclusive right in country B, would not make a difference.

Arguably, a next step, or if one wishes to view it that way a new correction, is taken in Case C–145/10 *Eva-Maria Painer v Standard Verlags GmbH et al.* [2011] ECDR 6. Here the *Freeport* doctrine is applied to a case concerning IP rights and the Court goes on to look at the requirement of a same factual situation.

The factual situation in *Painer* is relatively simple. Ms Painer was a photographer and she took pictures of children in schools. She kept her copyright on the images that she sold. In this capacity, she took a picture of Natascha Kampusch before her kidnapping. After the kidnapping the Austrian police used the picture of Natascha Kampusch in their search and therefore diffused the picture, which allowed a press photo agency to offer the picture to some newspapers after Natascha Kampusch's escape, at a time when new pictures were not yet available.

Ms Painer claimed that the publication in the German and Austrian newspapers infringed her copyright. She sued both German and Austrian newspaper publishers before an Austrian court, on the basis of Article 8(1) (old Article 6(1)) Brussels I Regulation. It needs to be noted that some German publishers were not active in the Austrian market, despite the fact that all publishers performed the same activity in relation to the picture, that is the publication of the picture obtained by the agency (retouched with the face-ageing software used by the police). From a *Roche Nederland* perspective neither the legal provisions nor the factual situation are in all scenarios identical.

The Court strongly emphasized that copyright law, which protected the picture at hand, has been harmonized by different European directives. It is as if the Court had sought to explain that the requirement of the same legal situation of *Roche Nederland* had almost been met. However, immediately afterwards the Court cited *Freemont*, with the purpose of dismissing some minor divergences between national copyright laws (of Germany and Austria), because an identical juridical basis was no longer necessary. The Court went for a discretional appreciation of the legal situation instead.

The Court then returned to the fact that the factual situation was not identical either in respect of each of the defendants and that there was no concerted practice amongst them. Again, the court no longer saw this as an insurmountable hurdle, but as factors to be taken into account in the discretional appreciation of the question whether a risk of irreconcilable judgments existed. Admittedly, the wording of the judgment is not always optimal, but one thing is clear: after *Painer*, neither the first nor the second condition established in *Roche Nederland* remains intact. If *Freeport* softened the second condition, *Painer* does the same thing to the first condition.

This is even more important if one considers that these two conditions are no longer followed by a separate evaluation (or prediction) of the danger of irreconcilable judgments in the specific case. The existence of a single factual situation and of a sufficient juridical concordance is on this point sufficient because it is only a question of a *risk* of irreconcilable judgments. This risk cannot be tested in absolute terms and therefore one needs to fall back on the two above-mentioned conditions as clear indicators of the existence of such a risk.

The litigation between Solvay and Honeywell appeared to provide an ideal opportunity to clarify the matter (Case C–616/10 *Solvay SA v Honeywell et al.* (12 July 2012)). Since both *Freeport* and *Painer* had departed from the guideline established by the Court in *Roche Nederland*, it was interesting to see the matter again considered in a case regarding a European patent, after a case with no relation to IP (*Freeport*) and another case concerning copyright (*Painer*).

In the Netherlands, Solvay sued a Dutch company of the Honeywell group for the infringement of a European patent. The infringement involved the sale in certain European countries of a product identical to the product protected by the patent. A similar activity had been performed in a number of European countries by two companies in the Honeywell group, based in Belgium. Solvay argued that the principal claim was directed against a Dutch company on the basis of Article 2 Brussels I Regulation and claimed that there was a close relation with the claims against the two Belgian companies, which were part of the same group and which performed the same activity. Solvay further stated that on the basis of such a close relationship Article 8(1) (old Article 6(1)) was applicable to determine the competence of the sole Dutch judge as a *forum connexitatis*.

The application of the *Freeport* approach regarding the condition of an identical juridical basis was foreseeable, because national rules on patents have been harmonized as much as—or even more than—copyright rules, whereas the directives have left more room for different national approaches. And the existence of the same facts is perhaps more plausible if one supposes that companies within the same group align their behaviour and perform the same infringing activity by selling the product concerned in different European countries. Thus, *Solvay* could have followed this line and extended the application of Article 8(1) (old Article 6(1)) to a scenario such as in *Roche*. It could have.

A first part of the ruling rehearsed the well-known arguments in relation to Article 8(1) (old Article 6(1)). One can recognize the softened approach of *Freeport*, as well as clear references to *Painer*. But then a paragraph that refers to *Freeport, Painer*, and *Roche Nederland*, in order to make the same points, took the Court back to *Roche Nederland*. The way in which a European patent is treated by *Roche Nederland* is simply repeated, without discussion. Thus, the Court chose the easier way by arguing that *Solvay* is an exception to *Roche Nederland*, on the basis of the specific factual situation of *Solvay*. Or, in common law terminology: '*Solvay* is distinguished from *Roche Nederland*'. The Court figured that the two Honeywell companies, Dutch and Belgian, were active on the Finnish market. If Article 8(1) (old Article 6(1)) were not applied, we would have two rulings relative to the same activity in Finland. This suggests that, according to the Court, there would be a real risk of irreconcilable judgments. The overlapping activities in Finland make the difference with the *Roche Nederland* scenario, where each company was only active in one country. And on the basis of the risk of irreconcilable judgments Article 8(1) (old Article 6(1)) applies to this exceptional situation.

Obviously, *Solvay* represents a revival of the *Roche Nederland* doctrine. The rulings in *Freeport* and *Painer* are clearly important, but the Court is not prepared to give up completely the *Roche Nederland* approach. In this sense, *Solvay* does not provide the clarifications one could have hoped for.

One of the interesting aspects of *Solvay* is that, despite the fact that only a limited part of the claims against each defendant refers to the same activity in the same country, the whole case was brought before a Dutch court on the basis of Article 8(1) (old Article 6(1)). Even the claims that were not irreconcilable were brought before the *forum connexitatis*. The emphasis appears to be put on the defendant. If there is a risk, all claims against the defendant are brought before the *forum connexitatis*. This obviously has the advantage of avoiding a fragmentation between different claims. Additional proceedings in the *forum connexitatis* for part of the claims are in fact not an ideal solution.

25.2.3 **Exclusive Jurisdiction**

Article 24(4) (old Article 22(4)) confirms the principle which is found in most jurisdictions that proceedings resulting in a decision by which the validity or registration of an IP right is affected must be brought exclusively before the courts in the state where the right is registered or is deemed to be registered. Where the provision applies, it prevails over all other heads of jurisdiction, including general jurisdiction and jurisdiction by prorogation. All other courts seized with the same subject matter must decline jurisdiction on their own motion.

Or, in terms of the Regulation:

The following courts of a Member State shall have exclusive jurisdiction, regardless of the domicile of the parties:…

(4) in proceedings concerned with the registration or validity of patents, trade marks, designs, or other similar rights required to be deposited or registered, irrespective

of whether the issue is raised by way of an action or as a defence, the courts of the Member State in which the deposit or registration has been applied for, has taken place or is under the terms of an instrument of the Union or an international convention deemed to have taken place.

Exclusive jurisdiction provisions have a long history in private international law instruments covering IP rights. The most convincing reason for their existence that is still valid today is that they touch on proceedings the outcome of which may require an intellectual property office to correct its registers. That link with national administrative procedures—where one can see a parallel to a national court using its own procedural law—militates in favour of such issues being handled on an exclusive basis by the courts of the country of registration. Moreover, as public authorities, intellectual property offices and national legislators may find it unacceptable if the grant of a registered right as 'an exercise of national sovereignty' is subject to review by a foreign court that is part of a foreign sovereign state. The decision whether or not to grant and register an exclusive right also touches upon the public policy, particularly the economic and cultural policy, of the state of protection.

However, having accepted that there are convincing arguments that justify the principle of exclusive jurisdiction and that militate in favour of retaining a ground of exclusive jurisdiction of some sort, it must nevertheless be restricted in order to remain within the boundaries of the justification given, and its limits must be circumscribed precisely and narrowly. A first restriction is due to the vital role played in this context by the registration. Without it the issues and arguments mentioned earlier do not arise. This is why the exclusive jurisdiction clause is restricted to registered rights. Registered rights in this context are understood as rights for which an application to register is obligatory and which only come into existence upon registration (in particular patents, registered trade marks, and registered designs). That definition excludes rights such as unregistered designs and unregistered trade marks as well as copyright that may be subject to voluntary registration. Without registration one cannot argue that the office incorrectly registered the right or that the procedure will result in an instruction being given to the office by a foreign court.

A second restriction is found in the link with registration and validity. The justification for exclusive jurisdiction is, as seen earlier, linked to the decision to grant and to register the right. This justification does not therefore cover every aspect related to the IP right, but is limited to the issues of validity and registration. Traditionally, this limitation has resulted in the use of wording such as disputes 'concerned with the validity and registration'. There are a number of basic elements involved. There may have been a problem with the grant of the right itself. The problem may also not be the grant as such, but the registration as the technical result that flows from it. And, finally, the essence may be invalidity, i.e. for one reason or another the right was not validly granted and registered and should never have existed. The registration can also be abandoned or may be revoked, for example as a result of being declared invalid. It is worth spelling these elements out as it clearly shows the limited number of scenarios that may give rise to exclusive jurisdiction.

Article 24(4) (old Article 22(4)) Brussels I Regulation was interpreted by the CJEU in Case C–4/03 *GAT v LuK* [2006] ECR I-6509. The decision concerned a dispute between two German firms over the infringement of a French patent. By way of objection, the defendant had argued that the patent was invalid. The question consequently referred to the CJEU was whether this triggered the application of Article 16(4) Brussels Convention. The Court came to the conclusion that the rule of exclusive jurisdiction laid down in Article 16(4) Brussels Convention (and, thus, also Article 24(4) (old Article 22(4)) Brussels I

Regulation) concerns all proceedings relating to the registration or validity of a patent, irrespective of whether the issue is raised by way of an action or a plea in objection. As soon as the validity issue is raised, irrespective of the stage at which this takes place, any court other than the court in the country of registration will have to declare itself incompetent.

The *GAT v LuK* decision has led to widespread criticism by commentators.[7] It has been argued that a broad interpretation of exclusive jurisdiction which includes mere defences is inconsistent with both the general trend to give a narrow reading to the rules on exclusive jurisdiction and the established principle that the court's jurisdiction must be established on the basis of the applicants' respective claims alone, without the defence later raised by a defendant being taken into consideration. Equally important, as a result of *GAT*, is that any infringement action in which the defendant contests the validity of the registered right falls, at least in principle, under the exclusive jurisdiction of the country of registration. This makes it highly unattractive to litigate registered rights outside the country of protection because any infringement action runs the risk of being thwarted by a later plea of invalidity, even if that defence proves to be unfounded or even abusive. As a final result, this leads to fragmented infringement actions which make the enforcement of European patents much more expensive and create the risk of diverging judgments on the different national parts of a European bundle patent. In a sense, the bankruptcy of the *GAT* approach is spelled out involuntarily by the UK Court of Appeal in its judgment in *Research in Motion UK Ltd v Visto Corporation* [2008] FSR 20, (2008) 15(11) LSG 23. The court acknowledges that there is nothing it can do against the undesirable situation in which opposition proceedings are coupled with revocation and negative declaration proceedings in the UK in relation to the UK (European) patent and with negative declaration proceedings in relation to European patents in another Member State. This is the inevitable result of the push towards country-by-country proceedings in the UK courts which the CJEU supported in *GAT*. Multiple proceedings at a high cost that can lead to divergent solutions are exactly what business does not need.

Additionally, *GAT v LuK* has left a number of questions unanswered, some of which have been referred to the CJEU in Case C–616/10 *Solvay SA v Honeywell et al.* (12 July 2012). The CJEU did not answer all of them, but its decision clarifies that the restrictive *GAT v LuK* approach does not apply to interim measures. Or in more detail and in the context of the case, Article 24(4) (old Article 22(4)) Brussels I Regulation is not applicable in proceedings seeking provisional relief on the basis of a foreign patent, such

---

[7] C. González Beilfuss, 'Nulidad e infracción de patentes en Europa después de "GAT" y "ROCHE"' (2006) *Anuario español de derecho internacional privado* 269, 273 *et seq.*; C.A. Heinze and E. Roffael, 'Internationale Zuständigkeit für Entscheidungen über die Gültigkeit ausländischer Immaterialgüterrechte' [2006] *GRUR Int* 787, 795; A. Kur, 'A Farewell to Cross-Border Inunctions? The ECJ Decisions *GAT v. LuK* and *Roche Nederland v. Primus and Goldenberg*' (2006) 37 *IIC* 844, 847 *et seq.*; A. López-Tarruella Martínez, *Litigios transfronterizos sobre derechos de propiedad industrial e intellectual* (Dykinson SL, 2008) 207 *et seq.*; Schlosser in B. Hess, P. Schlosser, and T. Pfeiffer (eds), *The Brussels I-Regulation (EC) No 44/2001—Application and Enforcement in the EU* (Beck, 2008) para. 668; D. Moura Vicente, 'La Propriété Intellectuelle en Droit International Privé' (2008) 335 *Recueil des Cours* para. 186; P. Torremans, 'The Way Forward for Cross-Border Intellectual Property Litigation: Why GAT Cannot Be the Answer' in S. Leible and A. Ohly (eds), *Intellectual Property and Private International Law* (Mohr Siebeck, 2009) 191–210; P. Torremans, 'Consolidation of Intellectual Property Litigation in Europe' in *Essays in Honour of M.P. Stathopoulos* (Ant. N. Sakkoulas, 2010) 2985–3007; CLIP, Exclusive Jurisdiction and Cross-Border IP (Patent) Infringement—Suggestions for Amendment of the Brussels I Regulation, http://www.ip.mpg.de/shared/data/pdf/clip_brussels_i_dec_06_final.pdf p 3 and [2007] *Praxis des internationalen Privat- und Verfahrensrechts* 284 and [2007] *EIPR* 194.

as a provisional cross-border prohibition against infringement, if the defendants in the main proceedings argue by way of defence that the patent invoked is invalid. This is so taking into account that the court in that case does not make a final decision on the validity of the patent invoked but makes an assessment as to how the court having jurisdiction under Article 24(4) (old Article 22(4)) of that Regulation would rule in that regard, and that the application for interim relief in the form of a prohibition against infringement shall be refused if, in the opinion of the court, a reasonable, non-negligible possibility exists that the patent invoked would be declared invalid by the competent court.

25.3 Intellectual Property and Private International Law: Choice of Law

25.3.1 Introduction

Of course, once jurisdiction has been established the question of the applicable law arises. Even a broad-brush approach, as is appropriate here, should make a distinction between the IP right as such, and its infringement, on the one hand and the contractual transfer of the IP right on the other hand. Not only may different laws, such as the *lex loci protectionis*/law of the country for which protection is sought on the one hand and the *lex contractus*/law of the contract on the other hand, apply, but important issues of categorization arise. Which issues are covered by which category and its respective connecting factor and applicable law? Let us once more proceed by taking one issue as an example and analyse it in a bit more detail. Transferability is such an ideal example. Is this an aspect of the IP right as such or is one here already dealing with the transfer of the IP right? The lead-in starts with the (copyright) as such.

25.3.2 The Right As Such

25.3.2.1 The Creation of the Right

The discussion of the right as such necessarily starts with the creation of the IP right. Most Copyright Acts do not contain any detailed guidance on the issue of the applicable law. One could argue that the creation of copyright leads to an exclusive right that restricts competition. It would, therefore, seem to follow that local public policy dictates that the creation of a copyright that will be exercisable in the country will be governed by the provisions of the local *lex loci protectionis*.

The Berne Convention also leads to the application of the law of the country for which protection is sought to issues related to the creation of copyright (see Judgment of 22 December of the French Cour de cassation, *Société Fox-Europa v Société Le Chant du Monde* (1960) 28 *RIDA* 120, annotated by Holleaux at 121 *et seq.* and more recently the judgment of the Oberlandesgericht Munich (6th Civil senate) of 10 January 2002, [2002] MMR 312, [2003] ZUM 141), as these issues form part of the non-contractual 'property' category. Contract is not involved here, rather this relates to the 'right as such'. Which issues, though, are related to the creation of copyright? One obviously thinks of the thorny issue of originality, but another good example are the types of works that will be protected. Article 2 Berne Convention restricts itself to stating the principle that 'literary and artistic works', which include 'every production in the literary, scientific and artistic domain', will be protected, and Article 2*bis* allows for certain limitations without obliging Member States to introduce them. The precise definition of the types of works that will be protected and the decision whether or not to introduce any limitation is left to the Member States and their domestic legislation. Even if they are not large, differences exist between the laws of the Member States. Whether a work comes within a category of works that will be protected and, if so, in which category of works will be determined by the law of the country for which protection is sought.

25.3.2.2 The Scope of the Right

Once copyright has been created it is important to know what the content of the exclusive right will be, i.e. what is the scope of the right. How far will the protection and the restriction of competition extend? Logically speaking, this issue is inextricably linked with the decision to grant copyright, as it determines what exactly is being granted. The issue should, therefore, be decided under the same applicable law. The law of the country for which protection is sought should apply (see *Novello & Co. Ltd v Hinrichsen Edition Ltd and Another* [1951] 1 Ch 595). The law of the place where the right is used has to decide whether the right exists and what its content is (see the judgment of 1 March 1989 of the Arrondissementsrechtbank (Dutch court of first instance) in Leewarden, *United Feature Syndicate Inc. v Van der Meulen Sneek BV* [1990] *Bijblad Indutriële Eigendom* 329). There is, however, no specific that deals with this issue in the majority of national laws.

This choice of law point is important, in practice, as the Berne Convention does not define the scope of protection in a rigid way. It rather sets minimum standards. While it is generally accepted that the copyright holder has the exclusive right to reproduce the work and make public representations of the work, certain national legislations add to this the exclusive right for the copyright holder to distribute copies of the work. The exact scope of the economic and moral rights granted depend on the national law and are different on a country-to-country basis. Hence the importance of determining the applicable law of the country for which protection is sought (see the *Spielbankaffaire* judgment of 2 October 1997 of the Bundesgerichtshof (German Supreme Court), [1998] GRUR Int 427).

Whether one sees moral rights as an integral part of copyright or as separate rights, the precise content of the moral rights that are granted is also determined by the law of the country for which protection is sought. Either they are just part of the scope of the copyright that has been granted, or, if they are seen as independent rights, they come into being automatically through the creation of the copyright. It is logical, in these circumstances, to accept that they are governed by the same rule, for reasons of uniformity. The applicability of the law of the country for which protection is sought is confirmed by Article 6*bis*(3) Berne Convention which states explicitly that the means of redress in relation to moral rights are governed by the law of the country for which protection is sought. The specific means of redress for each moral right are linked so strongly to the moral right concerned that it would make no sense to separate them in terms of the applicable law. Moral rights, i.e. their content and who can exercise them, before and after the death of the author, and how, are therefore governed by the law of the country for which protection is sought (confirmed by the French *Giacometti* case, *L.P. v B.G. and others*, Court of Appeal Paris (first chamber), judgment of 23 September 1997, (1998) 176 RIDA 418; confirmed by the judgment of 6 July 2000, Cour de cassation (first civil chamber), *Mrs Lisa Palmer v Roland Dumas q.q., B. Giacometti and others*, [2001] RCDIP 329).

A different approach could be suggested though. Moral rights could also be seen as personality rights that are linked to the person of the author of the work. From a choice of law point of view, they could then be classified as forming part of the personal law of the author. An alternative, in copyright terms, could be the law of the country of origin, because the latter is closely linked to the author. The common law approach to substantive copyright and moral rights, which is based on the commercial exploitation of the work rather than on the author, has never gone down this path. It is, therefore, submitted that this choice of law approach is to be rejected.

Moral rights are also a topic certain legal systems care a lot about and that bring us to consider public policy and overriding mandatory rules issues. We have argued elsewhere that moral rights should be seen as fundamental rights that protect the author against the abuse of her work.[8] From that point of view, the Belgian approach to moral rights should form part of its public policy. This would have important implications in a situation where the case is litigated in Belgium, but where the law of the country for which protection is sought is not the Belgian Copyright Act. Rather than applying the law of the country for which protection is sought, the court would be obliged to apply Belgium's provisions on moral rights, if the standard of moral rights protection in the law of the country for which protection is sought would be lower than the one in the Belgian Copyright Act. That could be the case if the *lex protectionis* is the UK or the US Copyright Act, which overall afford lower protection to moral rights. It needs to be stressed that this approach does not replace the choice of law rules and the law of the country for which protection is sought altogether. Public policy considerations, and eventually the application of the law of the forum, can only be considered at a later stage.

Overriding mandatory rules, however, operate in a slightly different way. These rules are directly applicable and the choice of law process is not followed at all. The provisions on moral rights of the forum are directly applicable, irrespective of the content of the law of the country for which protection is sought, if they are mandatory rules. This is the approach that was taken by the French Court de Cassation in the *John Huston* case (judgment of 28 May 1991, Cour de cassation, [1991] RCDIP 752). It is submitted that the nature of moral rights, as rights that come into operation only when the copyright work is used abusively, does not justify the latter approach. The traditional law of the country for which protection is sought, plus the public policy of the forum in exceptional cases, is far more suitable. The same law would then also be applied to all issues that form part of the scope of copyright.

25.3.2.3 Exceptions and Limitations

Restrictions placed on the exclusive right modify the content of the latter. So, if all issues relating to the content of the exclusive right granted by copyright are to be governed by the law of the country for which protection is sought, exceptions to the rights granted to the copyright holder form the next issue in this category. The precise scope of the rights granted is, indeed, only to be determined when these exceptions are also taken into account. For example, the rights holder's exclusive right to make copies of the work is restricted by the exceptional right of the user to make a copy for personal use. Further exceptions might exist for reporting current events, research and private study, etc. Important differences exist in this area from one national law to the other. This is therefore another point where the determination of the law of the country for which protection is sought has a real impact (see, e.g., the examples in the German and Italian case law: judgment of the Landgericht Hamburg (16th Chamber for Commercial Cases), 4 September 2001, [2002] NJW 623, [2002] ZUM 156 and judgment of 4 February 1997, Court of Appeal in Milan, [1998] GRUR Int 503). The same exceptions, obviously, also play a role as defences against copyright infringement.

---

[8] P. Torremans, *Holyoak and Torremans Intellectual Property Law* (7th edn, OUP, 2013) ch. 14.

25.3.2.4 **Transferability**

That brings us to the issue of the transferability of the right, i.e. the copyright including the economic right and the moral right. We are not concerned here with the actual transfer of the right. Before a transfer of a right enters the picture, there is a preliminary issue which needs to be addressed. This is the issue of whether the right can be transferred in the first place. Does the issue of the scope of the right which is granted also include the issue of whether the rights holder is able to transfer the right to another party? Once more, the statutory provisions of most countries remain silent on this point.

This transferability issue is linked with the grant of the right, rather than with the transfer of the right by means of a contract. Transferability and assignability are closely linked to the issue of what can be assigned, for example pecuniary rights and moral rights or pecuniary rights only, and with the scope of the right. It would clearly not be desirable to apply the law of the contract to it and allow the parties to choose a law which allows the transfer of the right at their convenience. It is, therefore, submitted that the issue of transferability should be governed by the law which governs the creation and the scope of the right. The choice of law rule should thus result in the application of the law of the country for which protection is sought. This solution has been approved in *Campbell Connelly & Co. Ltd v Noble* [1963] 1 WLR 252, 255. In this case, the proper law of the contract (English law) was de facto applied to determine whether the contract had validly transferred the copyright in a popular tune, but only after the assignability issue had been determined under the law of the country for which protection was sought (US law). Whether the US copyright could be assigned had to be decided as a preliminary point and that issue was governed by the law of the country for which protection was sought (see also the US case *Corcovado Music Corpn v Hollis Music*, 981 F2d 679 (2d Cir. 1993) for a similar result).

The issue of transferability assumes practical importance due to the fact that some legal systems allow for the transfer of the copyright itself, while others do not. For example, the UK's Copyright, Designs and Patents Act 1988 allows the transfer of copyright in section 90(1), whilst the German Urhebergesetz (Copyright Act) rules out any such transfer. The German Act only provides the opportunity to grant licences to carry out some form of activity which would otherwise have amounted to copyright infringement. In contrast, the view is held, almost unanimously, that moral rights are not transferable, and so no choice of law problem arises (see, e.g., section 94 Copyright, Designs and Patents Act 1988).

Up to now, we have been concerned primarily with the transfer of the right by contract during the lifetime of the rights holder. Similar problems arise though after the death of the author. These are of less practical importance in terms of private international law. This is because the rules in the various legal systems are very similar in this respect and allow for the transfer of copyright and moral rights by testamentary disposition. In the absence of a will, a statutory transfer regime is, generally, provided for. But once more a distinction is to be made between the transferability which is governed by the law of the country for which protection is sought (see the French *Giacometti* case, judgment of 6 July 2000, Cour de cassation (first civil chamber), *Mrs Lisa Palmer v Roland Dumas q.q., B. Giacometti and others*, [2001] RCDIP 329) and the will and actual succession issues that are classified differently and see the application of another governing law depending on the approach taken in each country.

In the final analysis, there is no reason not to apply the law of the country for which protection is sought to the issue of transferability of rights, regardless of the situation in which it arises. Several national courts have effectively adopted this approach (see in Germany the judgment of the Bundesgerichtshof of 2 October 1997 in the *Spielbankaffaire* case [1998] GRUR Int 427, Oberlandesgericht Munich (6th Civil Senate), judgment of 10 January 2002, [2002] MMR 312, [2003] ZUM 141; Oberlandesgericht Düsseldorf (20th Civil Senate), judgment of 24 April 2007, [2007] ZUM-RD 465; in the UK *Campbell Connelly & Co. Ltd v Noble* [1963] 1 WLR 252 and *Peer International Corp. v Termidor Musical Publications* [2004] Ch 212 (CA); in the United States *Corcovado Music Corpn v Hollis Music*, 981 F2d 679 (2d Cir. 1993); and in France *Anne Bragance v Olivier Orban and Michel de Grèce*, judgment of 1 February 1989, Cour d'appel de Paris, (1989) 142 RIDA 301).

The boundaries of the issue need to be taken into account, though. Assignability is restricted to the question whether or not the right can be assigned. Whether and under what conditions a transfer or assignment occurred is a matter for the law of the contract, if the law of the country for which protection is sought allows the principle of an assignment or a transfer of the right. This approach was followed by the Court of Appeal in Paris in *Anne Bragance v Olivier Orban and Michel de Grèce* (judgment of 1 February 1989, Cour d'appel de Paris, (1989) 142 RIDA 301). The contract between Anne Bragance, who had helped Michel de Grèce with writing his book, and the latter was governed by US (New York) law and included a transfer of all aspects of copyright to Michel de Grèce. This included both the moral and the pecuniary aspects of copyright. Due to the publication of the book in France, French law was the law of the country for which protection was sought. The French court ruled that moral rights are not assignable under French law and it was therefore impossible for the contract and the law of the contract to transfer these rights effectively. Pecuniary rights are, on the contrary, assignable under French law and the assignment was valid under the law of the contract. In practical terms, the outcome of the case was as follows. Anne Bragance gained the right to be identified as an author on every (French) copy of the book, but she did not gain any further pecuniary compensation, as she had effectively assigned all her pecuniary rights.

A very practical issue that is often ignored in private international law arises from the reality that the copyright in a work is often owned by more than one person. Collaboration in creative endeavours is the norm, rather than the exception, and as a result the copyright in a work is often held by more than one person. One could argue easily that these persons each own a share of the copyright and then the question arises whether these shares can be transferred from one person to another. Hence the need to determine which law applies to the transferability of shares (see the CLIP Principles http://www.cl-ip.eu/_www/en/pub/home.html at Article 3:402(2), European Max Planck Group on Conflict of Laws in Intellectual Property, *Conflict of Laws in Intellectual Property: The CLIP Principles and Commentary* (OUP, 2013)).

Transferability of the right itself is very much an aspect of the right as such. The issue with which we are confronted here is very much the same, apart from the fact that one person does not own the whole right, but various persons own a share of it. It is therefore logical to apply the same law to what is basically the same point of law, even if the situation in which it arises is different as the transferability of shares is not the same as the transferability of the right. The transferability of the shares of each co-owner will therefore be governed by the law of the state for which protection is sought.

It is of course clear that one needs to distinguish transferability from the actual transfer. Once the *lex protectionis* allows transferability of the right and makes a transfer possible the actual transfer can take place and in the standard scenario of a contractual transfer such a contract will then be governed by the *lex contractus*.

The fact that transferability is a question that needs to be separated from the (contractual) transfer and to which it is sensible to apply the *lex protectionis* becomes even clearer when one looks at non-contractual transfers. When one talks about a voluntary non-contractual transfer (i.e. donation of the right[9]), abandonment of the right, or waiver of the right there is no *lex contractus* or another applicable law in sight. But there is clearly a separate legal question whether one can effectively waive or abandon a right or operate an effective voluntary non-contractual transfer. These are issues of transferability and the question whether such transactions are possible is strongly linked to the right that was granted in the first place. Hence the choice in favour of the *lex protectionis*. Once it has been decided that such a transaction or such a way of dealing with the right is possible, the next question arises, i.e. what will be the effect of such a transaction or such a way of dealing with the right. In the absence of another candidate such as a *lex contractus* (as there is no contract involved) it is sensible to apply the *lex contractus* to this separate issue too. It is clear though that instances of waiver or abandonment will occur less frequently in relation to shares than in relation to the right as a whole.

The analysis above shows that the *lex protectionis* approach can accommodate the national rules that hold that moral rights are not transferable, as well as other transferability issues. It also highlights the need to distinguish between transferability and the actual transfer. There is therefore no need for an alternative *lex protectionis*-based approach that risks creating conflicts with public policy in each country. Very similar issues also arise in relation to the transfer of shares in copyright.

25.3.3 Infringement

25.3.3.1 *De lege lata*

IP rights are in essence negative rights, for example the right to stop anyone apart from the patent holder from making the patented product or the right to stop anyone apart from the copyright holder from reproducing the copyright work. There is therefore an extremely narrow link between the scope of the right and the infringement of the right. Following on from the previous discussion of the right as such and the application of the law of the country for which protection is sought to the issue of the scope of the IP right, it is therefore no surprise that Article 8 Rome II Regulation (Regulation (EC) No. 864/2007 of the European Parliament and of the Council of 11 July 2007 on the law applicable to non-contractual obligations [2007] OJ L 199/40) applies the law of the country for which protection is sought to the issue of IP right infringement (see the *Sonnenblende II* decision of 22 September 1998, Landgericht Düsseldorf [1998] Entsch LG Düss 75, the judgment of the 3rd chamber of the Tribunal de Grande Instance de Paris of 3 September 1997, *Didier Barbelivien and Gilbert Montagné v Sté AGAPES and others* (1998) 175 RIDA 343, and the judgment of 2 April 2003 of the 4th chamber of the Cour d'appel de Paris, *Antonio Martinelli and Roberto Meazza v Editions Gallimard and Sté APA* (2003) 198 RIDA 413). Or as the Regulation puts it:

Article 8

Infringement of intellectual property rights

1. The law applicable to a non-contractual obligation arising from an infringement of an intellectual property right shall be the law of the country for which protection is claimed.

---

[9] A classification problem might arise in this context. Common law systems tend to classify donation as non-contractual, whereas the majority of civil law systems classify donation as contractual. Donation is therefore not always a non-contractual example, but in all cases the transferability point arises.

2. In the case of a non-contractual obligation arising from an infringement of a unitary Community intellectual property right, the law applicable shall, for any question that is not governed by the relevant Community instrument, be the law of the country in which the act of infringement was committed.

3. The law applicable under this Article may not be derogated from by an agreement pursuant to Article 14.

The result is therefore a patchwork of national IP law that is applied on a country-by-country basis. This rule works well if the infringement of the IP right occurs in a single country (or in a couple of countries), but it works very badly in a situation where the infringement occurs in a lot of countries. It poses a tremendous burden on the rights holder to prove the content of all these national laws and the fact that its IP right was infringed under each of them, as well as on the court that has to apply all these different national laws to the infringement and remedies issues. Article 14 Rome II Regulation could have offered some assistance, as it allows the parties in certain circumstances and under certain conditions to agree on the applicable law, i.e. the parties choose the applicable law and choose a single law. But the legacy of territoriality was apparently so strong in the area of IP that Article 8 Rome II Regulation explicitly excludes Article 14 and its freedom for the parties to choose the applicable law in cases of the infringement of IP rights.

25.3.3.2 Ubiquitous Infringement

The Internet has made ubiquitous infringement a reality in far more cases than ever before. Copyright exists without registration and the combined effect of the national treatment provisions of the Berne Convention and the TRIPS Agreement result in many cases in a truly global copyright protection for the rights holder, each time under the provisions of the law of the country for which protection is sought in every single country. Such 'global' copyright can be infringed 'globally' in every single country if the copyright work is uploaded and communicated to the public through the Internet. The work is available everywhere without the consent of the rights holder. Such infringement, in practice copyright infringement on the Internet as patents and trade marks are never registered in every single country, allegedly happens in every single country in the world and is therefore ubiquitous.

Applying the existing legal rules and thus de facto every single copyright law in the world on a country-by-country basis as a result of the choice of law rule that relies on the law of the country for which protection is sought, leads therefore to an unworkable situation and in practice the IP right becomes unenforceable. One forces rights holders to pick a few countries in which they can then effectively enforce their rights and to forget about pursuing the infringement in all other countries. This is entirely unacceptable in a system that is based on private enforcement of what are in practice negative rights and it has elements of a denial of justice in it. There is no solution *de lege lata*, but the CLIP project, led by the Max Planck Institutes in Munich and Hamburg and leading European academics, has proposed a solution that consists of applying a single law, i.e. the law with the closest connection with the infringement in such cases. Or in full detail:

Article 3:603: Ubiquitous infringement

(1) In disputes concerned with infringement carried out through ubiquitous media such as the Internet, the court may apply the law of the State having the closest connection with the infringement if the infringement arguably takes place in every State in which the signals can be received. This rule also applies to existence, duration, limitations and scope to the extent that these questions arise as incidental questions in infringement proceedings.

(2) In determining which State has the closest connection with the infringement, the court shall take all the relevant factors into account, in particular the following:

   (a) the infringer's habitual residence;

   (b) the infringer's principal place of business;

   (c) the place where substantial activities in furtherance of the infringement in its entirety have been carried out;

   (d) the place where the harm caused by the infringement is substantial in relation to the infringement in its entirety.

(4) Notwithstanding the law applicable pursuant to paragraphs 1 and 2, any party may prove that the rules applying in a State or States covered by the dispute differ from the law applicable to the dispute in aspects which are essential for the decision. The court shall apply the different national laws unless this leads to inconsistent results, in which case the differences shall be taken into account in fashioning the remedy.[10]

25.3.3.3 *De Minimis* Rule

There is also a problem at the other end with the general rule. Websites can be accessed anywhere in the world and IP rights sued on them, such as trade marks may be owned by different people in different countries. This may lead to infringement claims despite the fact that the owner of the foreign website does not trade actively in the jurisdiction. The question that arises is whether mere accessibility is sufficient for a finding of infringement. Or, if we take trade marks as an example, does mere accessibility amount to using the trade mark in the course of trade?

The CLIP group suggested that the answer should be in the negative and that substantive IP laws should be interpreted in that sense. This resulted in the following suggestion for a rule:

Article 3:602: De minimis rule

(1) A court applying the law or the laws determined by Article 3:601 shall only find for infringement if

   (a) the defendant has acted to initiate or further the infringement in the State or the States for which protection is sought, or

   (b) the activity by which the right is claimed to be infringed has substantial effect within, or is directed to the State or the States for which protection is sought.

(2) The court may exceptionally derogate from that general rule when reasonable under the circumstances of the case.

It is encouraging to see that judges have started to follow this line of thought (*Euromarket Designs Inc. v Peters* [2001] FSR 20).

25.3.4 **Intellectual Property Contracts**

It is not our purpose to go into detail here, as we are concerned with enforcement and remedies. It is nevertheless useful to highlight that a different choice of law rule applies to contractual issues. IP contracts are in this context no different from other contracts. The same choice of law rule applies to all contracts. The main principle is very simple, the

---

[10] European Max Planck Group on Conflict of Laws in Intellectual Property, *Conflict of Laws in Intellectual Property: The CLIP Principles and Commentary* (OUP, 2013) 314.

parties have the freedom to choose the law applicable to their contract. This rule can be found in Article 3 Rome I Regulation (Regulation (EC) No. 593/2008 of the European Parliament and of the Council of 17 June 2008 on the law applicable to contractual obligations [2008] OJ L 177/6):

Article 3

Freedom of choice

1. A contract shall be governed by the law chosen by the parties. The choice shall be made expressly or clearly demonstrated by the terms of the contract or the circumstances of the case. By their choice the parties can select the law applicable to the whole or to part only of the contract.

The Regulation also has, in its Article 4, a rule for the scenario in which the parties have not chosen the applicable law, based on the characteristic performance principle:

Article 4

Applicable law in the absence of choice

1. To the extent that the law applicable to the contract has not been chosen in accordance with Article 3 and without prejudice to Articles 5 to 8, the law governing the contract shall be determined as follows:...

2. Where the contract is not covered by paragraph 1 or where the elements of the contract would be covered by more than one of points (a) to (h) of paragraph 1, the contract shall be governed by the law of the country where the party required to effect the characteristic performance of the contract has his habitual residence.

3. Where it is clear from all the circumstances of the case that the contract is manifestly more closely connected with a country other than that indicated in paragraphs 1 or 2, the law of that other country shall apply.

4. Where the law applicable cannot be determined pursuant to paragraphs 1 or 2, the contract shall be governed by the law of the country with which it is most closely connected.

25.4 Conclusions

IP rights are increasingly exploited across national borders. Parallel rights exist in many countries and exploitation and allegedly infringing activities also take place across borders. Enforcement of IP rights therefore also has to take account of the cross-border element.

In this chapter we addressed the preliminary aspect of private international law. Before enforcement actions can get off the ground one needs to know which court will have jurisdiction and which law that court will apply.

Jurisdiction is based on the domicile of the defendant as a basic rule, but alternative fora are available. The courts of the place of the harmful event may also have jurisdiction and there are special rules for multiple defendant cases. Validity cases are subject to exclusive jurisdiction rules. All these rules present specific problems in an IP context. In terms of choice of law, the law of the country for which protection is sought takes centre stage when it comes to IP. It is the law applicable to the IP right as such and it also applies to infringement. Contracts relating to IP are subject to the law of the contract, essentially the law chosen by the parties. But it is vital to distinguish properly between the various categories. Transferability is, for example, different from the actual transfer.

And ubiquitous infringement cases raise very specific problems, for which existing national laws are not very well equipped.

Further Reading

EUROPEAN MAX PLANCK GROUP ON CONFLICT OF LAWS IN INTELLECTUAL PROPERTY, *Conflict of Laws in Intellectual Property: The CLIP Principles and Commentary* (OUP, 2013)

FAWCETT, J.J. AND TORREMANS, P., *Intellectual Property and Private International Law* (2nd edn, OUP, 2011)

26

Remedies

26.1 Introduction

Throughout this book we have been concerned with rights, with IP rights that are private rights and in need of enforcement by the rights holder. In this part we are looking very specifically at the enforcement of IP rights. Such enforcement takes place in search of redress and that redress is obtained in the form of remedies.

We will look first of all at civil remedies. Civil proceedings brought by private parties are the norm in the enforcement of private rights. It therefore comes as no surprise that civil remedies and civil enforcement proceedings also take the lion's share of the enforcement and remedies effort in relation to IP rights, since the latter are very clearly private rights.

A rights holder can bring proceedings to stop the threatened infringement of its IP right, in essence to preserve the exclusive nature of its right. This is what is called a *quia timet* action. One tries to pre-empt the infringement of the IP right when one is aware that preparation for allegedly infringing activities are being made and one is afraid that infringing activities will take place if one does not pre-emptively bring proceedings. The form of redress sought is typically an (interlocutory) injunction. This will then be in essence an interdict prohibiting the planned infringing activity.

And the most obvious enforcement scenario is the one where the rights holder or its exclusive licensee goes after the alleged infringer of the IP right once the alleged infringement has taken place. Redress will then take the format of an action that aims at putting the rights holder back in the position in which it found itself before the infringement, i.e. with its exclusive right intact. One can think of a permanent injunction to stop the infringement, payment of damages by way of compensation, or an account of profits to hand the gains of the breach of the exclusive right over to the rights holder.

Enforcement and especially a final decision may take time. Interim measures can then be awarded to stop the damage from becoming too important. And there are also measures to obtain evidence or to make sure compensation can be paid at the end of the proceedings.

All this is part of the private enforcement of IP rights by the rights holders. On top of that there is also a much smaller public side to enforcement. Customs authorities often intervene as they conveniently act at the border, before shipments are distributed. And there are also criminal remedies at the end of criminal enforcement proceedings. State intervention of this kind is generally reserved for blatant cases, real acts of piracy, or repeat offenders. We turn to criminal remedies later in this chapter.

IP rights are often applied for in many countries. In such cases, many of these rights may be involved in a single infringement action or similar infringing acts may have been committed in the various jurisdictions. IP rights are also increasingly exploited internationally; that exploitation may also give rise to transnational litigation. The interaction between IP and private international law gives rise to complex issues, both at the jurisdictional level (which court will decide the case) and at the choice of law level (which law will that court apply). We dealt with these matters in the previous chapter. They are very much part of the enforcement of IP rights and when they arise they do so at a preliminary stage. That is, one only gets to what is discussed in this chapter once the competent court has been identified and once it has chosen the applicable law or laws. But once the preliminary stage has been dealt with it no longer has an influence on what is the topic of this chapter. We will therefore not deal with private international law matters in this chapter and act as if the infringement and the enforcement and the remedies are limited to a single country.

26.2 Civil Remedies

26.2.1 General Principles

Despite a slight reservation for breach of confidence, most IP rights can be characterized as property rights. The way in which that property right is affected in cases of infringement can consequently be described as tortious in nature. Essentially, what we are dealing with are torts committed against property. On top of that come the actions between assignors and assignees, and between licensors and licensees, some of which are contractual in nature, because the claim is not based on the infringement of the IP right involved, but on a breach of the contractual provisions that had been agreed. This can lead to actions for breach of contract.

Whilst enforcement and remedies are essentially governed by national law this area has now been partially harmonized by the Enforcement Directive (Directive 2004/48/EC of the European Parliament and of the Council of 29 April 2004 on the enforcement of intellectual property rights [2004] OJ L 195/16, which is in turn in compliance with the provisions of the TRIPS Agreement 1994). The Directive sets out its main principle by way of a general obligation imposed on Member States:

Article 3

General obligation

1. Member States shall provide for the measures, procedures and remedies necessary to ensure the enforcement of the intellectual property rights covered by this Directive. Those measures, procedures and remedies shall be fair and equitable and shall not be unnecessarily complicated or costly, or entail unreasonable time-limits or unwarranted delays.

2. Those measures, procedures and remedies shall also be effective, proportionate and dissuasive and shall be applied in such a manner as to avoid the creation of barriers to legitimate trade and to provide for safeguards against their abuse.

The emphasis is clearly on the fact that Member States are and remain free to organize their own enforcement and remedies system in their national law, but the Article imposes a number of criteria. Measures shall be fair and equitable, there shall be no unduly high costs or long delays, and the measures, procedures, and remedies shall also be effective, proportionate, and dissuasive. All qualities which every suitable and effective system of enforcement and remedies should possess. The Directive then follows up with more specific measures.

A preliminary point that has to be dealt with is the definition of the persons who are entitled to apply for the application of the measures, procedures, and remedies that are provided for in the Directive. The Directive takes a very wide approach to this issue in its Article 4 and includes in this group:

(a) the holders of intellectual property rights, in accordance with the provisions of the applicable law;

(b) all other persons authorised to use those rights, in particular licensees, in so far as permitted by and in accordance with the provisions of the applicable law;

(c) intellectual property collective rights-management bodies which are regularly recognised as having a right to represent holders of intellectual property rights, in so far as permitted by and in accordance with the provisions of the applicable law;

(d) professional defence bodies which are regularly recognised as having a right to represent holders of intellectual property rights, in so far as permitted by and in accordance with the provisions of the applicable law.

It is, however, extremely important to note that the Directive refers to the provisions of the applicable law for all categories. In other words, a licensee is only entitled to apply for procedures, measures, and remedies (in their own right and of their own initiative) if the provisions of the applicable law, as determined along the lines set out in the previous chapter, allow them to do so.

Thus whilst infringing acts may also give reason for concern to licensees of IP and whilst it is obvious that the owner of the right is entitled to bring an action against the alleged infringer, the same cannot be said about the licensee. It all depends on the applicable law. Let us by way of example assume that English law is the applicable law. The starting point then is, in what may look at first glance to be a contrast with the provisions of the Directive, that a licensee cannot sue for infringement and must rely on the owner of the IP right to bring the action. Exceptionally, an exclusive licensee can bring the action. This possibility is subject to a number of restrictions:

(a) It has only been made possible in relation to exclusive patent (Patents Act 1977, section 67), trade mark (Trade Marks Act 1994, section 31) copyright (Copyright, Designs and Patents Act 1988 (CDPA 1988), section 101), and unregistered design (CDPA 1988, section 234) licences. Registered design licences and know-how licences, etc., are not covered.

(b) The exclusive licence must be fully exclusive, in the sense that even the licensor cannot exploit the right in the area that has been allocated to the licensee.

(c) The licensor has to be joined as a party to the proceedings, normally as a claimant, or alternatively as a defendant.

By way of comparison, French law equally reserves the right to act to the exclusive licensee, but requires that the rights holder/licensor has first been asked to act and has failed to do so. That is coupled with a provision that every party to a licence agreement can intervene in the proceedings (Article L615-2 Code de la propriété intellectuelle—Patents; Article L716-5 Code de la propriété intellectuelle—TM).

Registered IP rights present in general no problems when it comes to identifying who is the holder of the IP right, thanks to the register and it is fair to say that every single applicable law starts from the principle that the rights holder is entitled to apply for measures, procedures, and remedies. But copyright is, in the absence of registration, different and there could be a discussion about who is the rights holder when someone tries to bring a case. Article 5 of the Directive solves this problem through the introduction of a presumption along the following lines:

Article 5

Presumption of authorship or ownership

For the purposes of applying the measures, procedures and remedies provided for in this Directive,

(a) for the author of a literary or artistic work, in the absence of proof to the contrary, to be regarded as such, and consequently to be entitled to institute infringement proceedings, it shall be sufficient for his/her name to appear on the work in the usual manner;

(b) the provision under (a) shall apply mutatis mutandis to the holders of rights related to copyright with regard to their protected subject matter.

On the defendant's side one finds the alleged infringer: this is normally the person who performed the restricted act. Anyone who collaborates with that person in common design can be sued as joint tortfeasor (see *Mölnlycke AB v Procter & Gamble Ltd* [1992] RPC 21, 29; *Unilever plc v Gillette (UK) Ltd* [1989] RPC 583, 608). An employer, but not someone who commissions a work, is vicariously liable for the infringement of IP that an employee committed in the course of her employment, just as this is the case for any other tort. Such an employer is quite often a company, but also the real person behind the company, such as a company director, can be personally liable for torts committed on behalf of the company if she has ordered or procured their commission (*MCA Records v Charly Records* [2002] FSR 401, [2002] EMLR 1 (CA)).

26.2.2 **The Gathering of Evidence**

The gathering of evidence is often a crucial issue in IP cases. In this section of the chapter, we will highlight the instruments that are used most often; an overview of all of the relevant aspects of the law of civil procedure is not envisaged. The Enforcement Directive also addresses the issues surrounding evidence.[1] The starting point is set out in Article 6 of the Directive:

Evidence

1. Member States shall ensure that, on application by a party which has presented reasonably available evidence sufficient to support its claims, and has, in substantiating those claims, specified evidence which lies in the control of the opposing party, the competent judicial authorities may order that such evidence be presented by the opposing party, subject to the protection of confidential information. For the purposes of this paragraph, Member States may provide that a reasonable sample of a

---

[1] Articles 6 and 7 Enforcement Directive.

substantial number of copies of a work or any other protected object be considered by the competent judicial authorities to constitute reasonable evidence.

2. Under the same conditions, in the case of an infringement committed on a commercial scale Member States shall take such measures as are necessary to enable the competent judicial authorities to order, where appropriate, on application by a party, the communication of banking, financial or commercial documents under the control of the opposing party, subject to the protection of confidential information.

In a UK court setting, most of these principles are readily implemented in our procedural rules. One thinks particularly of the rules on disclosure in an IP context, as it is of such vital importance. Infringing activity often takes place in private industrial or commercial buildings, making it difficult for the rights holder, for example, to prove that the defendant is using its patented process, and it is particularly in this context that one needs to appreciate the usefulness of the measures envisaged in Article 6 of the Directive. In other Member States procedural rules are also important in this respect, but attention should, for example, in France also be given to the *saisie-contrefaçon*, which we will discuss in the context of Article 7 of the Directive. Its very low level of prima facie evidence for the claimant in obtaining the order makes it an excellent tool for obtaining evidence by means of the description carried out by the bailiff. The Court of Appeal in Paris has held explicitly that a *saisie-contrefaçon* has both an evidentiary and a protective function (CA Paris, 4th Chamber, 22 February 2008, Jurisdata no. 2008-361186). The claimant may then have less need to rely on Article 6.

26.2.3 Measures for Preserving Evidence: Search Orders

This is then followed up in Article 7 of the Directive by rules on measures to preserve the evidence. In the UK system this refers to what is now known as the search order. Article 7 expresses it as follows:

1. Member States shall ensure that, even before the commencement of proceedings on the merits of the case, the competent judicial authorities may, on application by a party who has presented reasonably available evidence to support his/her claims that his/her intellectual property right has been infringed or is about to be infringed, order prompt and effective provisional measures to preserve relevant evidence in respect of the alleged infringement, subject to the protection of confidential information. Such measures may include the detailed description, with or without the taking of samples, or the physical seizure of the infringing goods, and, in appropriate cases, the materials and implements used in the production and/or distribution of these goods and the documents relating thereto. Those measures shall be taken, if necessary without the other party having been heard, in particular where any delay is likely to cause irreparable harm to the rightholder or where there is a demonstrable risk of evidence being destroyed.

   Where measures to preserve evidence are adopted without the other party having been heard, the parties affected shall be given notice, without delay after the execution of the measures at the latest. A review, including a right to be heard, shall take place upon request of the parties affected with a view to deciding, within a reasonable period after the notification of the measures, whether the measures shall be modified, revoked or confirmed.

2. Member States shall ensure that the measures to preserve evidence may be subject to the lodging by the applicant of adequate security or an equivalent assurance intended

to ensure compensation for any prejudice suffered by the defendant as provided for in paragraph 4.

3. Member States shall ensure that the measures to preserve evidence are revoked or otherwise cease to have effect, upon request of the defendant, without prejudice to the damages which may be claimed, if the applicant does not institute, within a reasonable period, proceedings leading to a decision on the merits of the case before the competent judicial authority, the period to be determined by the judicial authority ordering the measures where the law of a Member State so permits or, in the absence of such determination, within a period not exceeding 20 working days or 31 calendar days, whichever is the longer.

4. Where the measures to preserve evidence are revoked, or where they lapse due to any act or omission by the applicant, or where it is subsequently found that there has been no infringement or threat of infringement of an intellectual property right, the judicial authorities shall have the authority to order the applicant, upon request of the defendant, to provide the defendant appropriate compensation for any injury caused by those measures.

5. Member States may take measures to protect witnesses' identity.

It is once more up to the Member States to shape such a measure in detail in their national law. It would lead too far to examine this in detail in the 28 national laws of the Member States, but as the UK's search order was taken as an example during the drafting process of the Directive, let us look in more detail at that one by way of example, as it shows very well the problems that can arise in this context and which Article 7 also tries to address.

26.2.3.1 **The Origin of the Order in the UK**

The success of infringement actions and the effectiveness of remedies depend on the availability at the trial stage of evidence relating to the alleged infringement. It is vital that the claimant is given the opportunity to discover this evidence. It is relatively easy for a mala-fide defendant to alter or to destroy incriminating documents, to move goods, or to hide machinery and raw materials, once she has been served with a writ. The production of infringing copies of audio cassettes or CDs provides a good example: all that is needed are a number of cassette players or computer with CD drives and CD-burning software and blank tapes or CDs, plus some labels; all of this can be moved within a few hours and it can be hidden in any spare room or shed.

What is required, then, is a tool that would allow the claimant to discover the evidence without any advance warning being given to the defendant. This tool would involve an *ex parte* application to the court, which would then authorize the claimant and his solicitors to enter the defendant's premises, in order to discover the evidence and to seize or copy any relevant information. It would be a kind of civil search warrant.

Such a tool was introduced by the Court of Appeal in *Anton Piller KG v Manufacturing Processes Ltd* [1976] Ch 55, [1976] 1 All ER 779 and consequently became known as the 'Anton Piller' order'. Changes in the wake of the Civil Procedure Act 1997 led to that order being renamed the 'search order' (section 7; Civil Procedure Rules, rule 25; Practice Direction, para. 25.).

Lord Denning MR has described the order as follows:

Let me say at once that no court in this land has any power to issue a search warrant to enter a man's house so as to see if there are papers or documents there which are of an incriminating nature. But the order sought in this case is not a search warrant. It does not authorise the claimant's solicitors or anyone else to enter the defendants' premises against their will. It only authorises entry and inspection by the permission of the defendants. It does more, it actually orders them to give permission—with, I suppose, the result that if they do not give permission they are guilty of contempt of court.[2]

Applications for a search order are to be made *ex parte* to a patents judge in the High Court or to the patents county court. They can eventually also be made to a Chancery judge (Civil Procedure Rules, rule 25A; Practice Direction, para. 8.5).

26.2.3.2 The Order and its Expansion

The essential prerequisites for making such an order were set out by Ormrod LJ (*Anton Piller KG v Manufacturing Processes Ltd* [1976] Ch 55, 62; see also *Thermax Ltd v Schott Industrial Glass Ltd* [1981] FSR 289; *Columbia Picture Industries v Robinson* [1987] Ch 38, [1986] 3 All ER 338):

> First, there must be an extremely strong prima facie case. Second, the damage, potential or actual, must be very serious for the applicant. Third, there must be clear evidence that the defendants have in their possession incriminating documents or things, and that there is a real possibility that they may destroy such material before any application inter partes can be made.

The claimant's solicitor will be authorized to carry out the order as an officer of the court and the defendant is obliged to permit the inspection, otherwise he will face proceedings for contempt of court. This does not, however, deprive the defendant completely of the possibility of refusing to permit the inspection, but this option becomes very risky and needs to be combined with a swift application for discharge of the order. The applicant has a duty of full and frank disclosure of all relevant elements to the court, and the granting of the order is subject to the applicant making a cross-undertaking in damages.

It is the basis of the search order to preserve evidence that may otherwise be destroyed by the defendant. The real need meant that the order became an instant success, rather than the exceptional measure it was supposed to be. One of the first cases to extend the order slightly was *EMI Ltd v Sarwar & Haidar* [1977] FSR 146, 147 in which the defendants were also ordered:

> to disclose to the person serving the order, the names and addresses of the persons or companies responsible for supplying the defendants and to place into custody all invoices, books of sale, order books, and all other documents in their possession, power, custody or control relating to the acquisition, disposal or distribution of the infringing tape recordings.

This will enable the defendant to obtain full evidence regarding anyone involved in an infringement network on the basis of a single search order and it increases the value of the order substantially. It also became possible to obtain an order against a represented class of persons if there is a sufficient amount of identity of interest among the members of such a class. This extension allowed EMI Records to act against all persons dealing in a certain type of pirated audio cassette with one search order, because they all had an interest in preventing EMI from tracing the source of the pirated cassettes.

The expansion of the search order and its growing effectiveness came under threat when the House of Lords decided that orders requiring the defendant to make a disclosure that could be self-incriminating were contrary to the principle of privilege against self-incrimination (*Rank Film Distributors Ltd v Video Information Centre*

---

[2] *Anton Piller KG v Manufacturing Processes Ltd* [1976] Ch 55, 58.

[1982] AC 380, aff'd [1981] 2 All ER 76). The possibility for the defendant to withhold information on the basis that she would otherwise be incriminating herself reduces the potential and value of the order substantially. This conclusion, which had been reached by a reluctant House of Lords, was reversed by section 72 of the Supreme Court Act 1981 when the legislature stepped in to preserve the order. The self-incrimination defence will now no longer be available against the implementation of a search order (*Universal City Studios Inc. v Hubbard* [1984] Ch 225, [1984] 1 All ER 661), although the statements or admissions made at that stage will not be admissible as evidence in relation to any related offence.

26.2.3.3 Abuse of the Order and its Redress

26.2.3.3.1 Abuse

Not only did search orders become a frequently used tool, they also gave rise to abuses (see *Lock International plc v Beswick* [1989] 3 All ER 373, [1989] 1 WLR 1268 (Hoffmann J)), of which two forms can be identified. First, the courts became too flexible in granting the order (see the remarks in this sense by Whitford J in *Systematica Ltd v London Computer Centre Ltd* [1983] FSR 313) and it became fashionable to use them to go on a 'fishing expedition'. An order was, in such cases, granted on the basis of a mere suspicion of infringement, rather than on the basis of a very strong prima facie case, and was used simply to establish whether the infringement took place. Often the applicant also obtained very valuable commercial information on a competitor.

Second, the execution of the order was not always impeccable. The limits and restrictions imposed in the order were often exceeded, documents disappeared (*Universal Thermosensors v Hibben* [1992] 1 WLR 840, [1992] FSR 361), etc., and the orders were also used to harass the defendant and to drive him or her out of business (*Columbia Picture Industries v Robinson* [1987] Ch 38, [1986] 3 All ER 338). Orders were executed at impossible times (*Universal Thermosensors v Hibben* [1992] 1 WLR 840, [1992] FSR 361) or with a great deal of publicity. So much material was taken that the defendant could no longer operate properly and meet his contractual obligations (*Columbia Picture Industries v Robinson* [1987] Ch 38, [1986] 3 All ER 338) or improper publicity surrounding the order scared customers away from further dealings with the defendant (*BUPA v First Choice Health Care* [1993] 4 EIPR 87).

26.2.3.3.2 Towards a Solution

The urgent need to weed out these abuses, while at the same time preserving the search order as an extremely useful tool in certain circumstances, became clear and Sir Donald Nicholls V-C suggested a way to achieve this double goal in *Universal Thermosensors v Hibben* [1992] 1 WLR 840, 860–1. Most points of his advice were then incorporated in a new Practice Direction (Practice Direction [1994] 4 All ER 52, [1994] RPC 617) and further refinement followed in the wake of the Civil Procedure Act 1997.

Search orders will now only be given if the matter is urgent or if the order is otherwise desirable in the interest of justice (Civil Procedure Rules, rule 25.2(2)(b)). Search orders should also only be executed on working days during office hours and not at weekends, or early in the morning, or late at night (Practice Direction [1994] 4 All ER 52, 54, Annex 1; *Universal Thermosensors Ltd v Hibben* [1992] 1 WLR 840, 860 (Sir Donald Nicholls V-C)). This implies that the defendant should be in a position to use effectively his right to consult a solicitor and to obtain legal advice at the very moment that he is presented with an order before complying with it, without running the risk of being in contempt of court by delaying the execution of the order (*Universal Thermosensors Ltd v Hibben* [1992] 1 WLR 840, 860 (Sir Donald Nicholls V-C)). A woman should also be present when the order is to be executed by a male solicitor at premises that are likely to be occupied by an unaccompanied woman (Civil Procedure Rules, rule 25A; Practice Direction, para. 7.4(5)). Additionally, when the nature of the items that are removed makes this necessary, the applicant should insure them (Practice Direction [1994] 4 All ER 52, 53; CDPA 1988, section 3B(3)).

The Practice Direction contains a further range of provisions and also allows the judge more time to consider the application in more depth, but by far the most important change is that the claimant's solicitor should now no longer execute a search order. The role of the claimant's solicitor is reduced to securing the grant of the order and, afterwards, the execution is entrusted to a solicitor who does not act for the applicant. This *'supervising solicitor should be an experienced solicitor, having some familiarity with the operation of [search] orders, who is not a member or employee of the firm acting for the applicant'* (Practice Direction [1994] 4 All ER 52, 53; CDPA 1988, section 3B(1)(a)). The supervising solicitor must also explain the terms of the search order to the respondents in plain English and he must advise them of their rights (Civil Procedure Rules, rule 25A; Practice Direction, para. 7.4).

In the old situation, the claimant's solicitor was torn between the interests of his client, who was also footing the bill, and his neutral role as an officer of the court. This will now no longer be the case, although the risk of bias remains at the application stage due to the *ex parte* nature of the proceedings. The Practice Direction and the Civil Procedure Rules are also unsuccessful in solving the difficult problem of who may consent to entry to the premises, to the searching of these premises, and to seizure. In the absence of the obvious defendant, the Practice Direction gives this power to 'a responsible employee of the defendant' as well as to the more established category of 'person(s) appearing to be in charge of the premises' (Practice Direction [1994] 4 All ER 52, 54–5, Annex 1). The precise definition of these categories is bound to cause confusion, which may lead to incidents when a search order is executed under these circumstances.

It is nevertheless submitted that the Practice Direction and the new Civil Procedure Rules will be successful in eliminating the abuse, and in securing the survival, of the search order. In the new system, claimants who:

> wish to take advantage of this truly draconian type of order...must be prepared to pay for the safeguards experience has shown are necessary if the interests of defendants are fairly to be protected.[3]

26.2.3.4 *Saisie-Contrefaçon*

French law adopts a slightly different approach. The legal tool that is used is called '*une saisie-contrefaçon*'. The name refers to seizing goods in infringement cases, but that is slightly misleading. The primary aim of the tool is to arrive at a detailed description of infringing goods, facilities, documents, etc. Its secondary aim is to seize any of these, but this is not always included. In fact a lot of the *saisies-contrefaçon* are merely limited to the descriptive part (Article L615-5 Code de la propriété intellectuelle—Patents; Article L716-7 Code de la propriété intellectuelle—TM; Article L332-1 Code de la propriété intellectuelle—Copyright).

Any interested party may apply for a *saisie-contrefaçon*, but it can only be imposed by a court order. Such an application to the court is typically made on an *ex parte* basis. The order is typically applied for for the alleged infringer's place of business, but this is not necessarily the case. It may cover any place where the evidence may be found. What

---

[3] *Universal Thermosensors Ltd v Hibben* [1992] 1 WLR 840, 861 (Sir Donald Nicholls V-C).

is particularly interesting is the fact that the claimant has to present the court with very little in terms of evidence or a prima facie case. The claimant has to submit evidence of its exclusive right, i.e. a copy of the title, and of course one must indicate an alleged infringer and the place where one thinks evidence may be found. But French law shies away from requiring a strong prima facie case. In part this is linked to the fact that in most cases one is merely asking for a description of the situation. The court order is executed by a bailiff (*huissier de justice*), who may be assisted by the police. The legislation itself does not require the bailiff to be independent, but in practice courts may emphasize this aspect when granting the order. The rights holder may also be asked by the court to offer a warranty in case the alleged infringer suffers damage.

Often a request to seize goods is only made once the description has taken place. In any case, if the order is applied for before the case on substance is brought, French law requires that the case on substance is then brought within 15 days (Court of Appeal Paris, 25 March 2003, RG no. 2001/14909). Otherwise the effects of the *saisie-contrefaçon* are invalidated and the alleged defendant can ask for the return of any seized goods and documents.

Belgian law adopts a similar, but not quite identical, approach to the *saisie-contrefaçon*. Here the court will appoint an expert, who will draft a report. In this context the expert proceeds with a description, but she can take samples. In order to get an expert appointed the claimant will not merely have to prove its title to the court, but it will also need to show that there are indications that the IP right is or is likely to be infringed. Often by separate order, the court can also prohibit the alleged infringer from moving or destroying the goods or documents and exceptionally their seizure can be ordered (Article 1369*bis* Code Judiciare).

26.2.4 **The Right of Information**

The enforcement of IP rights through infringement actions often start when the owner of an IP right finds an infringing product at the end of the distribution chain; the goods may alternatively be in transit. It is vital for the rights owner that he is able to trace the source of the infringing product in order to be able to stop the infringement at its roots, because the person in whose hands the product is found may not even know that the product is a copy or an infringing product and may not be infringing himself. The person may also be unaware of the fact that others must have infringed any IP right. The only way for the rights owner to proceed successfully in such a case is to obtain the names and addresses of any consignors or consignees, and to track the infringing product all the way up to its manufacturers.

The Directive addresses this issue in its Article 8, that puts in place a right of information:

Right of information

1. Member States shall ensure that, in the context of proceedings concerning an infringement of an intellectual property right and in response to a justified and proportionate request of the claimant, the competent judicial authorities may order that information on the origin and distribution networks of the goods or services which infringe an intellectual property right be provided by the infringer and/or any other person who:

    (a) was found in possession of the infringing goods on a commercial scale;

    (b) was found to be using the infringing services on a commercial scale;

    (c) was found to be providing on a commercial scale services used in infringing activities; or

(d) was indicated by the person referred to in point (a), (b) or (c) as being involved in the production, manufacture or distribution of the goods or the provision of the services.

2. The information referred to in paragraph 1 shall, as appropriate, comprise:

(a) the names and addresses of the producers, manufacturers, distributors, suppliers and other previous holders of the goods or services, as well as the intended wholesalers and retailers;

(b) information on the quantities produced, manufactured, delivered, received or ordered, as well as the price obtained for the goods or services in question.

3. Paragraphs 1 and 2 shall apply without prejudice to other statutory provisions which:

(a) grant the rightholder rights to receive fuller information;

(b) govern the use in civil or criminal proceedings of the information communicated pursuant to this Article;

(c) govern responsibility for misuse of the right of information; or

(d) afford an opportunity for refusing to provide information which would force the person referred to in paragraph 1 to admit to his/her own participation or that of his/her close relatives in an infringement of an intellectual property right; or

(e) govern the protection of confidentiality of information sources or the processing of personal data.

National legislators can put this right of information in place as they wish.

26.2.4.1 The *Norwich Pharmacal* Order

In the UK the *Norwich Pharmacal* order has the same aim and such an order obliges the party against whom it is made to reveal the names and addresses of any consignors or consignees, and to track the infringing product all the way up to its manufacturer (Civil Procedure Rules, rule 31). In the original case (*Norwich Pharmacal v Comr of Customs & Excise* [1974] AC 133, rev'd [1974] RPC 101), from which the name of this disclosure order is derived, the Commissioner of Customs and Excise was obliged to reveal the names of the importers of a patented drug. Later cases obliged telephone operators, for example, to reveal the names of mobile phone users who were allegedly involved in passing off (*Coca-Cola Co. v British Telecommunications* [1999] FSR 518).

The order is discretionary in nature and as a starting point requires frank disclosure on the part of the applicant, as is also clear from paragraph 1 of Article 8 of the Directive.[4] The order will normally only be granted if it is the only way in which the claimant can get hold of the information, which in essence imposes a condition of necessity, and if it is demonstrated that the person against whom it is made is (unwittingly) facilitating the infringement or any other wrongful act. There is also a requirement of proportionality (*Golden Eye (International) Ltd v Telefonica UK Ltd* [2012] EWHC 723 (Ch) [83] and [117]; *Rugby Football Union v Viagogo Ltd* [2011] EWCA Civ 1585). The order will only go as far as is necessary to allow the rights to be asserted.

---

[4] e.g., withholding information about a revenue-sharing agreement between the rights holder and a third party will be held against the applicant, as will the indiscriminate practice of sending out threatening letters demanding £700 from persons whose Internet connection was used in a file-sharing activity, without properly pointing out the options available to these persons. See *Golden Eye (International) Ltd v Telefonica UK Ltd* [2012] EWHC 723 (Ch). But the presence of a revenue-sharing agreement did not dis-entitle a category of rights holders being granted a *Norwich Pharmacal* order. See *Golden Eye (International) Ltd v Telefonica UK Ltd* [2012] EWCA Civ 1740.

On the other hand, the order may also be extended to cover a prohibition to remove the infringing goods.

The *Norwich Pharmacal* order is often applied in tort—that is, infringement—cases, but it is not confined to tort. It can, for example, also arise in the context of breach of contract, such as breach of a licence contract, and in the context of breach of confidence (*Ashworth Hospital Authority v MGN Ltd* [2003] FSR 311 (HL); see also *Interbrew v Financial Times* [2002] EMLR 446). If it is applied in an infringement context, bringing proper infringement proceedings in a court is not a prerequisite for the order being granted (see *Golden Eye (International) Ltd v Telefonica UK Ltd* [2012] EWHC 723 (Ch) [53]; *British Steel Corp. v Granada Television Ltd* [1981] AC 1096).

Arguably the order goes further than is strictly required by Article 8 of the Directive. A national rule obliging ISPs to release personal information concerning clients who had committed copyright infringement online was held by the CJEU not to be imposed by European law. That is effectively what the result of a *Norwich Pharmacal* order would be though. But it did not breach European law either according to the Court's judgment in Case C–275/06 *Productores de Música de España (Promusicae) v Telefónica de España SAU* [2008] ECR I-271). UK courts too have held that the order complies with Article 8 of the Human Rights Act 1998 (the right to private life) and with the rules on data protection. This is another aspect of the requirement of proportionality. The court will not hold back from granting the order, but a proper balance with data protection rules and fundamental rights will be struck (*Golden Eye (International) Ltd v Telefonica UK Ltd* [2012] EWHC 723 (Ch) [117] and at the European level Case C–461/10 *Bonnier, Earbooks, Norstedts Förlagsgrupp, Piratförlaget and Storyside v Perfect Communication Sweden* [2012] 2 CMLR 42).

Bringing all these elements together Arnold J set out the following test in *Golden Eye*:

> In my judgment the correct approach to considering proportionality can be summarised in the following propositions. First, the Claimants' copyrights are property rights protected by Article 1 of the First Protocol to the ECHR and intellectual property rights within Article 17(2) of the Charter. Secondly, the right to privacy under Article 8(1) ECHR/Article 7 of the Charter and the right to the protection of personal data under Article 8 of the Charter are engaged by the present claim. Thirdly, the Claimants' copyrights are 'rights of others' within Article 8(2) ECHR/Article 52(1) of the Charter. Fourthly, the approach laid down by Lord Steyn where both Article 8 and Article 10 ECHR rights are involved in In re S [2004] UKHL 47, [2005] 1 AC 593 para 17 is also applicable where a balance falls to be struck between Article 1 of the First Protocol/Article 17(2) of the Charter on the one hand and Article 8 ECHR/Article 7 of the Charter and Article 8 of the Charter on the other hand. That approach is as follows: (i) neither Article as such has precedence over the other; (ii) where the values under the two Articles are in conflict, an intense focus on the comparative importance of the specific rights being claimed in the individual case is necessary; (iii) the justifications for interfering with or restricting each right must be taken into account; (iv) finally, the proportionality test—or 'ultimate balancing test'— must be applied to each.[5]

This test was subsequently endorsed by the Supreme Court, which added some refinement in *Rugby Football Union v Consolidated Information Services Ltd (Formerly Viagogo Ltd) (In Liquidation)* [2012] UKSC 55 [44] and [45]. The Supreme Court held that a *Norwich Pharmacal* order could be issued to oblige the operator of a website on which Twickenham tickets had been resold anonymously for highly inflated prices

---

[5] *Golden Eye (International) Ltd v Telefonica UK Ltd* [2012] EWHC 723 (Ch) [117].

against the RFU's policy to reveal the identity of those involved. The Supreme Court argued ([45]) that:

> [a]n 'intense focus' on the rights being claimed in individual cases does not lead to the conclusion that the individuals who will be affected by the grant of the order will have been unfairly or oppressively treated

but that suggesting that it would generally be proportionate ([46]):

> to make an order where it had been shown that there was arguable wrongdoing and there was no other means of discovering the identity of the arguable wrongdoers

would go too far.

According to the Supreme Court ([46]),

> [t]he particular circumstances affecting the individual whose personal data will be revealed on foot of a Norwich Pharmacal order will always call for close consideration and these may, in some limited instances, displace the interests of the applicant for the disclosure of the information even where there is no immediately feasible alternative way in which the necessary information can be obtained.

26.2.4.2 Other Member States

Belgian law contains a straightforward provision that allows the judge, at the request of the claimant in an infringement case, to order the defendant to provide the claimant with all the information in its possession concerning the origin of the goods and its distribution networks. The measure merely has to be justifiable and proportionate, leaving a large amount of discretion to the court. A similar order is available against persons found in possession of commercial quantities of the infringing goods, persons who were using infringing services on a commercial scale, or persons who were supplying on a commercial scale services that were used in infringing activities (Article XI.334 §3 Commercial Code). Article 101 of the German Copyright Act follows the same approach. France similarly has a right of information provision (e.g. Article L331-1-2 Copyright and Article L716-7-1 TM Code de la propriété intellectuelle). French law specifically adds that in cases of non-respect of the order the judge can order the payment of a daily amount until the order is complied with (*astreinte*), but this option is also open to his Belgian counterpart. The French provision needs to be invoked by the rights holder, but it can be invoked before the court has arrived at a finding of infringement (see the judgment of the Supreme Court, Cass. com., 13 December 2011, [2012] Comm. com. électr., comm. 14).

26.2.5 Freezing Orders

A right of information is fine, but later on in the procedure the successful claimant rights holder will need access to assets in order to satisfy any award of damages (and/or costs). In a number of situations the risk may arise that a dishonest defendant will dispose of its assets, or remove them from the jurisdiction. The Directive does not address this issue specifically, but Member States of course remain free to do so in their national laws. The UK did so many years ago and the freezing order provides a good examples of a useful tool which Member States can provide on top of the Directive. It also shows in practice how the partial harmonization of the Directive works.

Derived from the name of one of the parties in the oldest case in this area, *Mareva Cia Naviera SA v International Bulk Carriers SA* [1980] 1 All ER 213, [1975] 2 Lloyd's Rep 509, the so-called '*Mareva* injunction' was often called a 'freezing injunction', because this *ex parte* injunction freezes the assets of a party by restraining that party from removing them from the jurisdiction. In the wake of the Civil Procedure Act 1997, the order has now been renamed the 'freezing order'.

Lord Denning MR laid down the following guidelines in *Third Chandris Shipping Corp. v Unimarine SA* [1979] QB 645, *sub nom Third Chandris v Unimarine* [1979] 2 All ER 972:

(a) The claimant must make full and frank disclosure of all relevant information and materials.

(b) He must set out his claim and the grounds for it, as well as the arguments raised against this claim by the defendant. He must also give indications that the defendant has assets within the jurisdiction and that there is a risk that the assets will be removed from the jurisdiction.

(c) The claimant must give an undertaking in damages.

These guidelines were later supplemented by two further guidelines (*Ninemia Maritime Corp. v Trave Schiffahrtsgesellschaft mbH und Co. KG (The Niedersachsen)* [1984] 1 All ER 398):

(d) The claimant must show that his case has a certain strength.

(e) That strength needs to be balanced against all other relevant factors before the judge uses the discretion to grant a freezing order.

Banks and other third parties can be bound by a freezing order (see *Z Ltd v A-Z & AA-LL* [1982] QB 558, [1982] 1 All ER 556), which therefore becomes another useful tool in the war against untrustworthy defendants in IP infringement cases. Quite often a search order is combined with a freezing order (Civil Procedure Rules, rule 25(f)) and, while this offers a great deal of relief to the claimant, it must be clear that this can also be used quite effectively to put a defendant out of business (*CBS United Kingdom Ltd v Lambert* [1983] Ch 37, [1982] 3 All ER 237). This risk is especially present in cases brought by commercially powerful claimants against small innovative competitors, because the latter may go out of business before the case is fully argued in court. It can even be said that, on certain occasions, that has been the claimants' purpose, because it has been quite clear, on these occasions, that no infringement would eventually be found, and yet an application for a search order and a freezing order was nevertheless brought.

French copyright law also has a provision that amounts to a freezing order. Article L331-1-1 Code de la propriété intellectuelle provides as follows:

> If the applicant provides proof of circumstances that are likely to endanger the recovery of damages, the court may order the precautionary seizure of movable and immovable property of the alleged infringer, including the blocking of his bank accounts and other assets, in accordance with the general provisions of law. To determine the goods may be subject to seizure, it may order the communication of banking, financial, accounting or commercial documents or the access to relevant information.

26.2.6 **Injunctions**

The rights holder's first concern in cases of infringement is that the infringement of her right stops: the sooner this happens, the easier it will be to limit the damage to her trade, rights, and reputation. As an order of the court that directs a party—here, the alleged infringer—to do an act or to refrain from doing an act, the injunction is an excellent tool and remedy for that purpose, hence its frequent use in IP cases. The injunction will almost necessarily be prohibitory and will either stop the threatened commission of infringing acts or the continuation of infringing activities. The order is normally highly effective, partly because wilful non-compliance will amount to contempt of court and contempt is punishable by fine, imprisonment, or sequestration of assets (see, e.g., *A-G v Newspaper Publishing plc* [1988] Ch 333, [1987] 3 All ER 276; *Director General of Fair Trading v Smith's Concrete* [1991] 4 All ER 150).

26.2.6.1 Interlocutory Injunctions

If you discover that a rival trader is seeking to attack your market share by flooding the shops with counterfeit clothing, bootleg records, or stair-carpet grips made in breach of confidence, there is no time to waste. Allowing this trade to develop will obviously be harmful to you, yet the losses will be difficult to calculate precisely in a competitive capitalist society. So immediate action is necessary and the obvious legal route to take is to seek an injunction to prevent the allegedly illegal trade that is about to develop. In this respect, the usual delays of the civil justice system are not helpful and it is therefore necessary to expedite matters with the use of an interlocutory injunction in a quest to freeze the situation before damage can start to occur, pending a subsequent trial on the merits. Of course, the reality, in many cases, is that proceedings are subsequently abandoned or settled and thus the interlocutory stage is the only formal litigation that is ever recorded. This means that the basis of such proceedings must be examined closely.

The Enforcement Directive places a lot of importance on provisional and precautionary measures. In the UK these will come in most cases as interlocutory injunctions. The demands imposed by the Directive read as follows:

Article 9

Provisional and precautionary measures

1. Member States shall ensure that the judicial authorities may, at the request of the applicant:

    (a) issue against the alleged infringer an interlocutory injunction intended to prevent any imminent infringement of an intellectual property right, or to forbid, on a provisional basis and subject, where appropriate, to a recurring penalty payment where provided for by national law, the continuation of the alleged infringements of that right, or to make such continuation subject to the lodging of guarantees intended to ensure the compensation of the rightholder; an interlocutory injunction may also be issued, under the same conditions, against an intermediary whose services are being used by a third party to infringe an intellectual property right; injunctions against intermediaries whose services are used by a third party to infringe a copyright or a related right are covered by Directive 2001/29/EC;

    (b) order the seizure or delivery up of the goods suspected of infringing an intellectual property right so as to prevent their entry into or movement within the channels of commerce.

2. In the case of an infringement committed on a commercial scale, the Member States shall ensure that, if the injured party demonstrates circumstances likely to endanger the recovery of damages, the judicial authorities may order the precautionary seizure of the movable and immovable property of the alleged infringer, including the blocking of his/her bank accounts and other assets. To that end, the competent authorities may order the communication of bank, financial or commercial documents, or appropriate access to the relevant information.

3. The judicial authorities shall, in respect of the measures referred to in paragraphs 1 and 2, have the authority to require the applicant to provide any reasonably available evidence in order to satisfy themselves with a sufficient degree of certainty that the

applicant is the rightholder and that the applicant's right is being infringed, or that such infringement is imminent.

4. Member States shall ensure that the provisional measures referred to in paragraphs 1 and 2 may, in appropriate cases, be taken without the defendant having been heard, in particular where any delay would cause irreparable harm to the rightholder. In that event, the parties shall be so informed without delay after the execution of the measures at the latest.

    A review, including a right to be heard, shall take place upon request of the defendant with a view to deciding, within a reasonable time after notification of the measures, whether those measures shall be modified, revoked or confirmed.

5. Member States shall ensure that the provisional measures referred to in paragraphs 1 and 2 are revoked or otherwise cease to have effect, upon request of the defendant, if the applicant does not institute, within a reasonable period, proceedings leading to a decision on the merits of the case before the competent judicial authority, the period to be determined by the judicial authority ordering the measures where the law of a Member State so permits or, in the absence of such determination, within a period not exceeding 20 working days or 31 calendar days, whichever is the longer.

6. The competent judicial authorities may make the provisional measures referred to in paragraphs 1 and 2 subject to the lodging by the applicant of adequate security or an equivalent assurance intended to ensure compensation for any prejudice suffered by the defendant as provided for in paragraph 7.

7. Where the provisional measures are revoked or where they lapse due to any act or omission by the applicant, or where it is subsequently found that there has been no infringement or threat of infringement of an intellectual property right, the judicial authorities shall have the authority to order the applicant, upon request of the defendant, to provide the defendant appropriate compensation for any injury caused by those measures.

Let us now look at the position in the UK in more detail.

26.2.6.1.1 Two Basic Points in the UK
In order to obtain any injunction, two basic points need to be established:

(a) it must be clear that damages will not be an adequate remedy (*London & Blackwall Rly v Cross* (1886) 31 Ch D 354, 369 (Lindley LJ)), although this, as just explained, should not be too frequent a problem in an IP case. The matter must be urgent or the granting of an injunction must otherwise be desirable in the interests of justice (Civil Procedure Rules, rule 25.2(2)(b));

(b) it is important to remember that an injunction is an equitable right and is thus subject to equity's ever-present requirement of conscionability (see, e.g., *Leather Cloth Co. Ltd v American Leather Cloth Co. Ltd* (1863) 4 De GJ & Sm 137, aff'd 11 HL Cas 523).

26.2.6.1.2 American Cyanamid
The leading case on interlocutory injunctions remains the decision of the House of Lords in *American Cyanamid Co. v Ethicon Ltd* [1975] AC 396, [1975] 1 All ER 504. In this case, the claimants were the holders of a patent for absorbable surgical sutures and they were displeased to discover that the defendants were proposing to put on to the market a similar, and allegedly infringing, product. The House of Lords agreed with the judgment of the court of first instance and allowed the claimants an interlocutory injunction preventing Ethicon from proceeding with its plans.

The House of Lords, in the sole speech of Lord Diplock, took the opportunity to clarify the general approach to interlocutory injunctions (this approach was again confirmed by the Court of Appeal in *Dyrlund A/S v Turberville Smith Ltd* [1998] FSR 774). Lord Diplock pointed out in *American Cyanamid* that the general practice was to require the claimant to undertake to compensate the defendants for any losses incurred by them if the claimant failed to prove the case at full trial. This appeared to justify a generous approach to the award of interlocutory injunctions. It was necessary merely to show that there was a 'serious question to be tried' and that the balance of convenience as between the parties, having regard to the utility or otherwise of an award of damages to the claim-ant or an indemnity by the claimant, should then be considered. Both of these factors were found to be favourable to the claimants.

It should be noted therefore that there is not really, in most cases, an enquiry into the merits of a dispute, but rather simply a finding that there is a genuine issue at stake. This therefore carries a vitally important implication that has been alluded to frequently, but which needs to be spelled out clearly at this juncture. The decision to award an interlocu-tory injunction in, for example, a case of alleged passing off does not mean that a right has been infringed, merely that one might have been; there is a serious issue to be tried, in theory, at a future date. So, on the one hand, the court is answering 'maybe', rather than 'yes', to the question of whether a right exists. On the other hand, a refusal to award an interlocutory injunction is really rather damning: not only is an injunction refused, but the basis of the claimant's entire argument is regarded as quite unsustainable.

It is, however, more appropriate to examine the merits of the claims more closely in cases in which, as in those typical of passing off or trade mark infringement, the interloc-utory stage is likely, in fact, to be the only stage of the proceedings. The evident strength of the claimant's claim may assist in gaining injunctive relief (*Quaker Oats Co. v Alltrades Distributors Ltd* [1981] FSR 9) and this is a justifiable consideration if it is the only stage in the proceedings; the courts are prepared to make a preliminary assessment of the evi-dence in deciding whether or not the grant of an injunction is justified (*Rizla Ltd v Bryant & May Ltd* [1986] RPC 389).

26.2.6.1.3 Applications

Plenty of examples can be found of courts endeavouring to apply these general principles. In *BBC v Precord Ltd* [1992] 3 EIPR D-52, the defendants proposed to make a rap record featuring illicitly obtained extracts from an unbroadcast interview in which the then Opposition leader had famously lost his temper. This was an appropriate case for inter-locutory relief. Although a delay to the record might harm its sales at the peak Christmas season and there were arguable defences, the key point was that a clear property right had been infringed and this was the fundamental issue that merited protection.

In *Mothercare UK Ltd v Penguin Books Ltd* [1988] RPC 113, meanwhile, the complete lack of likely confusion meant that no interlocutory relief was permitted in the passing off claim and that the defendants were allowed to continue publishing a serious socio-logical study entitled *Mother Care/Other Care*. Likewise, the small and quantifiable harm to an established claimant, as compared with the very disruptive effects of an interloc-utory injunction on a new magazine with a similar title that was just in the process of being launched, meant that no injunction was awarded in *Emap Pursuit Publishing v Clive (t/a Matchday)* [1993] 2 EIPR D-40. On the other hand, an interlocutory injunction was granted to prevent an online children's game company from promoting an animated char-acter known as 'Lady Goo Goo' and its song on the YouTube website and from making it available on iTunes as there was a real risk of confusion between the character and the music artist Lady Gaga. Her associated trade mark would be tarnished and the substantial damage would be hard to quantify. The clear risk of confusion and substantial damages that are hard to quantify shift the balance in favour of the award of an injunction in this case (*Ate My Heart Inc. v Mind Candy Ltd and Moshi Music Ltd* [2011] EWHC 2741 (Ch)).

The courts do indeed seem prepared to look very carefully at where the balance of convenience lies and should 'take whichever course appears to carry the lower risk of injustice if it should turn out to have been "wrong"' (*Films Rover International Ltd v Cannon Film Sales Ltd* [1986] 3 All ER 772, [1987] 1 WLR 670, 681, 680 (Hoffmann J); see also *Dalgety Spillers Foods Ltd v Food Brokers Ltd* [1994] FSR 504). Thus in *Neutrogena Corp. & Neutrogena (UK) Ltd v Golden Ltd & L'Oréal (UK) Ltd* [1994] 6 EIPR D-157 (see also *Vollers The Corset Company Ltd v Cook and ors* [2004] ECDR 288), a dispute concerning possible passing off of the claimants' product 'Neutrogena' by the defendants' new 'Neutralia', Ferris J considered that an injunction would cause loss to the defendant through loss of sales, wasted preliminary expenditure, loss through having to compensate others, loss of opportunity to enter the market, and general disruption, and so, in the light of these factors, refused interlocutory relief. This case and the *Emap* case both show that the time of the actual launch of a rival product may well be too late to gain injunctive relief, given the commitments entered into by the defendant and the resultant shift in the balance of convenience. *Cowshed Products Ltd v Island Origins Ltd* [2010] EWHC 3357 (Ch) is another case that shows the mechanism clearly. Here the grant of an injunction would effectively destroy the defendant's business as they would be unable to enter the market as planned, whereas a refusal of an injunction would only see the claimant suffer modest damage in the period leading up to a speedy trial that would take place within months. But one should also not forget the need to show that the matter is urgent and that damages are no alternative.

In *Thane Direct Co. v Pitch World Ltd* Chancery Division, 27 February 2012, unreported, the court refused to grant an injunction enjoining the sale of an allegedly infringing five-function steam mop because the defendant had undertaken to stop selling the product within a couple of weeks and the damage was largely quantifiable.

Overall, the post-*Cyanamid* approach to the award of interlocutory injunctions[6] shows the courts able to invoke a range of potentially contradictory factors in a generally sensible way. In any event, the more cautious approach to their use in cases in which they may well be the final solution rather than a mere preliminary (*Peaudouce SA v Kimberly-Clark Ltd* [1996] FSR 680), which will be the case in many IP examples, goes some way to cushion the impact of *Cyanamid* in this particular area. They will thus remain a significant way of resolving IP disputes.

26.2.6.1.4 An Attempt to Summarize Matters

A lot of factors need to be considered and an attempt was made in *Series 5 Software Ltd v Clarke* [1996] 1 All ER 853, [1996] FSR 273 to summarize the matters that the court should take into account when considering whether or not to grant an interim injunction:

- the grant of an interim injunction is a matter of discretion and depends on all the facts of the case;
- there are no fixed rules as to when an injunction should or should not be granted—the relief must be kept flexible;

[6] The court now also has to take certain human rights aspects into account and, in cases in which the injunction may have an effect on the right to freedom of expression, no relief that restrains publication prior to trial is to be granted 'unless the court is satisfied that the applicant is likely to establish that publication should not be allowed': Human Rights Act 1998, section 12(3).

- because of the practice adopted on the hearing of applications for interlocutory injunctions, the court should rarely attempt to resolve complex issues of disputed fact or law.

Major factors that the court can bear in mind are:

- the extent to which damages are likely to be an adequate remedy for each party and the ability of the other party to pay;
- the balance of convenience;
- the maintenance of the status quo;
- any clear view that the court may reach as to the relevant strength of the parties' cases.

Helpful as it may be, it should, of course, be kept in mind that this summary stems from a first instance decision that is yet to be affirmed by a higher court.

26.2.6.1.5 Other Member States

In Belgium the claimant can use a procedure called '*Kort Geding*'. The president of the court will at short notice and often on the basis of an *ex parte* application hear the case. The key element is that there is urgency, which in practice means that unless interim measures are ordered the status quo will not be maintained and there is a risk that the damage may not be repairable in the case on substance. The court has a large degree of freedom when it comes to the measures it can impose. It often also imposes the payment of an amount of money per day the order is not implemented by the defendant (*dwangsom-astreinte*). The Dutch version of the '*Kort Geding*' is similar (see the emphasis on urgency in Articles 254–9 Wetboek van Burgerlijke Rechtsvordering), but often results in a mini-trial with both parties being present in court.

The French Code de la propriété intellectuelle also provides for interim measures in cases of urgency, in the sense that damage to the IP right is imminent, and here too the *astreinte* is present in a prominent way. The power given to the court, even on an *ex parte* basis, is extremely wide (Article L 716-6—TM and Article L 615-3 Patents). In patent cases and on condition that the alleged infringement amounts to an obvious case there is even the option to impose a provisional payment of damages on the defendant (Article L 615-3).

26.2.6.2 Final Injunctions

A final injunction can be granted as a remedy after a trial in which the infringement of the claimant's right was established. The injunction is, at that stage, granted to protect the proprietary right or interest of the claimant, but the court retains its discretion. An injunction is readily granted against the proven infringement of patents, designs, trade marks, and copyright. Otherwise the claimant would be unable to stop the continuation of the infringement and would be compelled to grant a de facto licence.

The Enforcement Directive approaches the issue as follows:

Article 11

Injunctions

Member States shall ensure that, where a judicial decision is taken finding an infringement of an intellectual property right, the judicial authorities may issue against the infringer an injunction aimed at prohibiting the continuation of the infringement. Where provided for by national law, non-compliance with an injunction shall, where appropriate, be subject to a recurring penalty payment, with a view to ensuring compliance. Member

States shall also ensure that rightholders are in a position to apply for an injunction against intermediaries whose services are used by a third party to infringe an intellectual property right, without prejudice to Article 8(3) of Directive 2001/29/EC.

A standard final injunction contains an order to cease the infringing activity. This is, for example, the cornerstone of Article XI 334 §1 Belgian Economic Law Code:

When the judge finds that there has been an infringement of a patent, a supplementary protection certificate, a breeder's right, a copyright, a related right, the right of a producer of databases or the right to a topography of a semiconductor product, he orders the termination thereof by any infringer. The judge may also issue an injunction against intermediaries whose services are used by a third party to infringe a right.

In France the provisions that allow an interim injunction are also of use for a final injunction. But in terms of final remedy the emphasis is firmly on damages and in practice the injunction is often part of a claim for damages. The idea that the defendant is merely ordered to cease the infringing activity is less widely accepted.[7]

In Germany the Copyright Act provides for final injunctions in Article 97:

Article 97 Right to require cessation of infringement and to damages

(1) Any person who infringes copyright or any other right protected under this Act may be required by the injured party to eliminate the infringement or, where there is a risk of repeated infringement, may be required by the injured party to cease and desist. Entitlement to prohibit the infringer from future infringement shall also exist where the risk of infringement exists for the first time....

In practice a lot of factors need to be taken into account in the exercise of the court's discretion. In the UK the courts provided a summary of how this will work, emphasizing that the complex mechanism will not stand in the way of the grant of injunctions in many IP cases, in *Cantor Gaming Ltd v GameAccount Global Ltd* [2008] FSR 4:

I therefore summarise the applicable principles as follows. First, an injunction may be granted pursuant to s. 37(1) of the Supreme Court Act 1981, whenever it is just and convenient to do so. Secondly, the grant of an injunction involves the exercise of the court's discretion, and the court should, in so doing, take account of all of the circumstances, one factor of which is the importance or triviality of the breach. Thirdly, there are certain kinds of case, of which intellectual property cases are examples, in which an injunction will normally be granted if a claimant has established infringement of its rights and there is a threat to continue (or at least no clear and unequivocal undertaking not to continue). Fourthly, where there is no threat to continue acts which have been held to be unlawful, because the defendant has clearly and unequivocally agreed not to do them before the action was brought, it is not right in principle to grant an injunction. Fifthly, there may, however, be situations where, even though a defendant may have agreed not to undertake the acts in question, an injunction may be just and convenient, having regard to all the circumstances. This may be, for example, because of the greater incentive for respect of a claimant's rights that an injunction would provide, and which, in particular cases, it may appear just to grant. Sixthly, the court may, in appropriate cases, take proportionality into account in granting or refusing injunctive relief.

An injunction remains a flexible remedy. Its terms can be amended at a later stage if the circumstances change, for example because the right that was infringed has since been

---

[7] A. Lucas, H.-J. Lucas, and A. Lucas-Schloetter, *Traité de la propriété littéraire et artistique* (4th edn, LexisNexis, 2012) 894.

invalidated by the court (*Adobe Systems Inc. v Netcom Online.co.uk Ltd and anor* [2012] EWHC 446 (Ch), [2012] 2 CMLR 41 [39]).

Recently there have been several attempts (in the Belgian courts in particular) to get an injunction against ISPs that would oblige them to monitor the information that is transmitted over their networks and to install a filtering system that would catch files that infringe copyright and particularly those that originate from peer-to-peer file sharing. The Court of Justice has however ruled that such a general obligation to monitor and filter all transmissions over a network goes beyond the scope of Article 11 of the Directive and is therefore illegal (Case C–70/10 *Scarlet Extended v Sabam* [2012] ECDR 4; Case C–360/10 *Sabam v Netlog* [2012] 2 CMLR 18). Article 11 is therefore limited to specific measures that prevent further infringement (Case C–324/09 *L'Oréal and ors v eBay* [2011] ETMR 52, [2012] EMLR 6, [2011] RPC 27).

The question then is what are these specific measures to prevent further infringement. Article 11 of the Directive provides for injunctions in relation to rights holders in its third and final sentence:

> Member States shall also ensure that rightholders are in a position to apply for an injunction against intermediaries whose services are used by a third party to infringe an intellectual property right, without prejudice to Article 8(3) of Directive 2001/29/EC.

The domestic problem in the UK is that that third sentence has not specifically been implemented, but be that as it may the CJEU ruled clearly in *L'Oréal v eBay* that the courts have the power to grant an injunction against an intermediary who is not an infringer itself as a result of the final sentence of Article 11 of the Directive (Case C–324/09 *L'Oréal and ors v eBay* [2011] ETMR 52, [2012] EMLR 6, [2011] RPC 27). ISPs which do not infringe IP rights themselves, but which do provide access to websites that carry or provide links to infringing material can therefore be confronted with an injunction. Judges in the UK, and in particular Mr Justice Arnold, have in recent times seen many applications brought by copyright holders in music and films against the main ISPs with a view to obtaining an injunction to block access to sites carrying or providing links to the infringing material. The list of websites can then also be updated at a later stage in case the infringing material moves. Such injunctions have now been granted on a number of occasions and the number of applications is growing. The applications have inevitably relied on section 97A CDPA 1988 and on section 37(1) Supreme Courts Act 1981. Or to summarize the position in the words of Arnold J:

> Over the last three years, a series of orders have been made requiring the ISPs to block, or at least impede, access to websites pursuant to s.97A of the Copyright, Designs and Patents Act 1988 ('the 1988 Act'), which implements art.8(3) of European Parliament and Council Directive 2001/29 on the harmonisation of certain aspects of copyright and related rights in the information society ('the Information Society Directive'). I have considered the principles to be applied to applications of that kind in a series of judgments: *Twentieth Century Fox Film Corp v British Telecommunications plc* [2011] EWHC 1981 (Ch); [2012] Bus LR 1471 ('*20C Fox v BT*'); *Twentieth Century Fox Film Corp v British Telecommunications plc (No 2)* [2011] EWHC 2714 (Ch); [2012] Bus LR 1525 ('*20C Fox v BT (No 2)*'); *Dramatico Entertainment Ltd v British Sky Broadcasting Ltd* [2012] EWHC 268 (Ch); [2012] 3 CMLR 14 ('*Dramatico v Sky*'); *Dramatico Entertainment Ltd v British Sky Broadcasting Ltd (No 2)* [2012] EWHC 1152 (Ch); [2012] 3 CMLR 15 ('*Dramatico v Sky (No 2)*'); *EMI Records Ltd v British Sky Broadcasting Ltd* [2013] EWHC 379 (Ch), [2013] ECDR 8 ('*EMI v Sky*'); *Football Association Premier League Ltd v British Sky Broadcasting Ltd* [2013] EWHC 2058 (Ch); [2013] ECDR 14 ('*FAPL v Sky*'); and *Paramount Home Entertainment International Ltd v British Sky Broadcasting Ltd* [2013]

EWHC 3479 (Ch); [2014] ECDR 7 ('*Paramount v Sky*'). Since the last of those judgments, Henderson J has considered the impact of the judgment of the Court of Justice of the European Union in *Svensson v Retriever Sverige AB* (C-466/12) [EU:C:2014:76] in *Paramount Home Entertainment International Ltd v British Sky Broadcasting Ltd* [2014] EWHC 937 (Ch) ('*Paramount v Sky 2*').[8]

All these cases make it clear that the imposition of an injunction requires that a number of requirements are satisfied:

i)   the relief must be necessary;

ii) the relief must be effective;

iii) the relief must be dissuasive;

iv) the relief must not be unnecessarily complicated or costly;

v)   the relief must avoid barriers to legitimate trade;

vi) the relief must be fair and equitable and strike a 'fair balance' between the applicable fundamental rights; and

vii) the relief must be proportionate.[9]

The *Cartier* case saw this copyright approach successfully transplanted to cases of trade mark infringement through websites selling fake and counterfeit items wearing the trade mark. And Arnold J set out the threshold conditions for the grant of an injunction succinctly:

> In my judgment, it follows that similar threshold conditions must be satisfied in order for a website blocking injunction to be granted in a trade mark case. First, the ISPs must be intermediaries within the meaning of the third sentence of art.11. Secondly, either the users and/or the operators of the website must be infringing the claimant's trade marks. Thirdly, the users and/or the operators of the website must use the ISPs' services to do that. Fourthly, the ISPs must have actual knowledge of this. Each of the first three conditions follows from the wording of art.11 itself. The fourth condition is not contained in art.11, but in my view it follows from art.15 of the E-Commerce Directive and by analogy with arts 13(1)(e) and 14(1)(a) of the E-Commerce Directive. If ISPs could be required to block websites without having actual knowledge of infringing activity, that would be tantamount to a general obligation to monitor. It is also difficult to see that such a requirement would be consistent with the requirements of art.3(1) of the Enforcement Directive. As to what constitutes "actual knowledge" in this context, I see no reason to interpret this requirement differently to the manner in which I interpreted it in the s.97A / art.8(3) context: see *20C Fox v BT* at [114]–[157].[10]

These developments show clearly how flexible the tool of the injunction is and that it can be exercised in new ways (see also *Samsung Electronics (UK) Ltd v Apple Inc.* [2012] EWCA Civ 1339, [2013] ECDR 2).

26.2.7 **Damages**

Damages are awarded with the aim of undoing the effects of the defendant's breach of contract or commission of a tort. The claimant is compensated for the harm that is caused

---

[8] *Cartier International AG, Montblanc-Simplo GmbH and Richemont International SA v British Sky Broadcasting Ltd, British Telecommunications Plc, EE Ltd, Talktalk Telecom Ltd and Virgin Media Ltd; Open Rights Group Intervening* [2014] EWHC 3354 (Ch), [2015] ETMR 1 [3].
[9] *Cartier* [158].   [10] *Cartier* [141].

by the tort or the breach of contract, but losses that are unforeseeably remote are excluded. Exemplary damages that exceed the amount needed for the compensation of the harm suffered may only be awarded in exceptional cases in which the defendant's conduct was calculated to make a profit that would exceed the damages that would have to be paid to the claimant (see *Rookes v Barnard* [1964] AC 1129, 1220–31).

Article 13 Enforcement Directive sets out the basics:

1. Member States shall ensure that the competent judicial authorities, on application of the injured party, order the infringer who knowingly, or with reasonable grounds to know, engaged in an infringing activity, to pay the rightholder damages appropriate to the actual prejudice suffered by him/her as a result of the infringement. When the judicial authorities set the damages:

   (a) they shall take into account all appropriate aspects, such as the negative economic consequences, including lost profits, which the injured party has suffered, any unfair profits made by the infringer and, in appropriate cases, elements other than economic factors, such as the moral prejudice caused to the rightholder by the infringement; or

   (b) as an alternative to (a), they may, in appropriate cases, set the damages as a lump sum on the basis of elements such as at least the amount of royalties or fees which would have been due if the infringer had requested authorisation to use the intellectual property right in question.

2. Where the infringer did not knowingly, or with reasonable grounds know, engage in infringing activity, Member States may lay down that the judicial authorities may order the recovery of profits or the payment of damages, which may be pre-established.

Most civil law systems leave a lot of discretion to the judge when it comes to damages and work with a very broad provision laying down the principle that damages are payable in infringement cases. A typical and recent example is found in Article XI 335 Belgian Economic Law Code:

§ 1. Without prejudice to paragraph 3, the injured party is entitled to compensation for any injury sustained due to the impairment of a right referred to in Article XI.334, § 1, paragraph 1.

§ 2. When the extent of the damage cannot be determined in any other way, the court may reasonably and fairly set a fixed amount as damages.

The judge may, by way of damages, direct delivery to the plaintiff of infringing goods, and, in appropriate cases, of the materials and implements predominantly used in the creation or manufacture of these goods that are still in the possession of the defendant. If the value of such goods, materials and instruments goes beyond the scope of actual damage, the judge sets the cash balance to be paid by the applicant.

In case of bad faith, the court may, by way of damages, order the transfer of all or part of the profit made as a result of the infringement and order that accounts be delivered up in this regard. Only costs directly related to counterfeiting activities concerned are deducted to determine the profit.

In the German Copyright Act the damages provision is Article 97:

Article 97 Right to require cessation of infringement and to damages

(1) …

(2) Any person who intentionally or negligently performs such an act shall be obliged to pay the injured party damages for the prejudice suffered as a result of the infringement. When setting the damages any profit obtained by the infringer as a result of

the infringement of the right may also be taken into account. Entitlement to damages may also be assessed on the basis of the amount the infringer would have had to pay in equitable remuneration if the infringer had requested authorisation to use the right infringed. Authors, writers of scientific editions (Article 70), photographers (Article 72) and performers (Article 73) may also demand monetary compensation for damage which is non-pecuniary in nature provided and to the extent that this is equitable.

The UK dealt with these issues almost entirely through case law.

In the UK, contrary to an injunction, damages are completely *res judicata* once the judgment has been granted and the defendant is estopped from raising the issue again. That means that the damages will stand and remain payable even if the right that was infringed has since been declared invalid by the court (*Poulton v Adjustable Cover & Boiler Block Co.* [1908] 2 Ch 430; *Coflexip* [2004] EWCA Civ 213; *Unilin* [2007] EWCA Civ 364; and *Adobe Systems Inc. v Netcom Online.co.uk Ltd and anor* [2012] EWHC 446 (Ch), [2012] 2 CMLR 41). The one exception is where there is still an appeal open on the calculation of damages. Only then can the judgment be undone according to the Supreme Court's decision in *Virgin Atlantic Airways v Zodiac Seats* [2013] UKSC 46. In civil law systems the damages could be reclaimed as they would amount to an unfair enrichment.

26.2.7.1 The Assessment of Damages

There is no standard rule for the assessment of damages in IP cases. Article 13 Enforcement Directive provides a number of factors which national courts are to take into account, but it does not go further than that.

In a first scenario, the claimant and the defendant may be competitors. If the claimant would have been willing to grant a licence if only the defendant had applied for one, the amount of damages will normally be calculated on the basis of the royalties and other costs that would have been payable under the licence (Article 13, paragraph 1(b) of the Directive and see *General Tire & Rubber Co. v Firestone Tyre & Rubber Co.* [1976] RPC 197, 212). If the claimant would not have been willing to grant a licence, the amount of damages is normally calculated on the basis of the losses suffered by the claimant through the defendant's competition. Lost profits, lost opportunities, and competitive position acquired by the defendant may all be taken into account (*Gerber Garment Technology Inc. v Lectra Systems Ltd* [1995] RPC 383).

In a second scenario, the parties do not find themselves in a competitive relationship. Damages are then calculated on the basis of a reasonable royalty for a licence for non-competing use. If neither of these scenarios suggests itself as the most appropriate way forward, the claimant is left with the choice between damages calculated on the basis of lost profits or damages calculated on a royalty basis. Even a combination of both can be envisaged in appropriate cases (Article 13, paragraph 1(a) of the Directive and see *Gerber Garment Technology Inc. v Lectra Systems Ltd* [1997] RPC 443, 486 (CA)).

In the UK the grounds on which damages need to be assessed have now been set out in the course of the implementation of the Enforcement Directive in reg. 3 Intellectual Property (Enforcement, etc.) Regulations 2006 (SI 2006/1028), in which it is stipulated that:

(1) Where in an action for infringement of an intellectual property right the defendant knew, or had reasonable grounds to know, that he engaged in infringing activity, the damages awarded to the claimant shall be appropriate to the actual prejudice he suffered as a result of the infringement.

(2) When awarding such damages—

    (a) all appropriate aspects shall be taken into account, including in particular—

        (i) the negative economic consequences, including any lost profits, which the claimant has suffered, and any unfair profits made by the defendant; and

        (ii) elements other than economic factors, including the moral prejudice caused to the claimant by the infringement; or

    (b) where appropriate, they may be awarded on the basis of the royalties or fees which would have been due had the defendant obtained a licence.

It is important to keep in mind though that the burden of establishing that the loss claimed is caused by the infringement is on the claimant. Let us turn to a couple of examples to see how this works in practice. If we take a patent infringement case as an example this means in practice that since the object of a patent is to confer a monopoly of profit and advantage, any infringement is likely to cause some loss or damage through loss of actual sales or chance of sales, or through the appropriation of something of value. So in a case where the patent belonged to a manufacturer who exploited the invention by selling products at a profit, the legal burden would be discharged by the inference that the effect of the infringement was to divert sales to the infringer (*Fabio Perini SPA v LPC Group plc, Paper Converting Machine Co. Italia, Paper Converting Machine Co. Ltd and LPC (UK) Ltd* [2012] EWHC 911 (Ch)). In those cases where the infringer is able to adduce evidence that shows that the usual inference is not to be drawn, the claimed loss is to be decided on the proved facts, and inferences properly drawn from those facts, using commercial common sense, taking account of all relevant factors, particularly the fact that the patent owner has a right to a monopoly in respect of the invention and that the infringer has destroyed that monopoly (*Coflexip SA v Stolt Offshore MS Ltd (formerly Stolt Comex Seaway MS Ltd) (No. 2)* [2003] EWCA Civ 296, [2003] FSR 41). The focus of any enquiry is then on whether the patent owner would or might have secured the infringer's contract themselves. In a copyright case where a newspaper without a licence issued a free CD containing songs of a concert in London by the Jimi Hendrix Experience in 1969 the claimants proved that the infringement had delayed the launch of their film of that concert by a year. Their damage was assessed on the basis of that loss and they were compensated accordingly (*Experience Hendrix LLC v Times Newspapers Ltd* [2010] EWHC 1986 (Ch)).

26.2.7.2 Account of Profits

Article 13, paragraph 1(a) Enforcement Directive specifically refers to the option for the claimant to recoup lost profits as a way of claiming damages. The claimant is thus entitled to reclaim the amount earned by the defendant by way of unjust enrichment through the infringement of the claimant's IP right. To achieve this, the claimant can use the remedy of an account of profits, which is restitutionary and equitable in nature. The court therefore has a discretion whether or not to grant this remedy, see *Sir Terence Conran v Mean Fiddlers Holding* [1997] FSR 856, in which an account of profits was refused in relation to a case in which the trade mark infringement was innocent, and in which the causal link between the profits and the infringement was hard to establish.

Rather than be compensated by damages, the claimant may opt to investigate the actual accounts of the defendant and to require that any profit that was made as a result of the infringement be handed over (in the UK see Patents Act 1977, section 61(2); CDPA 1988, section 96(2)). That profit may be the profit on each item that is sold and in which the protected subject matter is included (*Peter Pan Manufacturing Corp. v Corsets Silhouette Ltd* [1963] 3 All ER 402) or the increase in the defendant's profit made through the use, other than by inclusion in the defendant's products, of the protected subject matter (*United Horse Shoe v Stewart* (1888) 13 App 401, 3 RPC 139, 266–7).

It is clear that the exercise is to ascertain the net profits realized by the defendant on the basis of the infringing activity. The defendant is allowed to deduct from any profit only the overheads that are directly associated with the infringing activity. Taking into account (a proportion of) general overheads is not allowed. The claimant on the other hand cannot bring the amount of damage it suffered into the equation, when it opted for an account of profits rather than the award of damages (*Hollister Inc. v Medik Ostomy Supplies Ltd* [2012] EWCA Civ 1419).

In practice, it is often difficult to calculate the profit that is caused by the infringement, because the latter is often not the single cause of the profit. Often, only a part of a product is an infringement and, in all these cases, the courts face the difficult task of determining what part of the profit has been caused by the infringing acts (see *Celanese International v BP Chemicals* [1999] RPC 203). This remedy is therefore not used often, because it involves a lot of work and an expensive accounting procedure. The decision by the House of Lords that additional damages cannot be awarded in copyright or unregistered design cases in which the claimant opted for an account of profits is bound to make it an even less popular remedy (*Redrow Homes Ltd v Bett Bros plc & Nail Co.* [1999] 1 AC 197, [1998] 1 All ER 385, overruling *Cala Homes (South) Ltd v Alfred McAlpine Homes East Ltd (No. 2)* [1996] FSR 36). Nevertheless, the claimant could be well advised to consider the use of this remedy in those cases in which she could never have made the profits that were made by the defendant, because it may enable the claimant to obtain a higher amount by way of compensation.

26.2.8 **Abuse of Enforcement Proceedings**

Enforcement proceedings can also be abused. Such proceedings can, for example, be threatened in cases where on substance there is clearly no case to answer. Particularly in patent cases that are notoriously long and expensive such a tactic when applied by a party with deep pockets against a smaller less well-funded opponent can be particularly damaging. It therefore comes as no surprise that Article 41.1 TRIPS Agreement and Article 3(2) Enforcement Directive demand that states take appropriate measures against the abuse of enforcement proceedings.

In the UK this demand is met by section 70 Patents Act 1977, which deals specifically with groundless threats:

(1) Where a person (whether or not the proprietor of, or entitled to any right in, a patent) by circulars, advertisements or otherwise threatens another person with proceedings for any infringement of a patent, a person aggrieved by the threats (whether or not he is the person to whom the threats are made) may, subject to subsection (4) below, bring proceedings in the court against the person making the threats, claiming any relief mentioned in subsection (3) below.

(2) In any such proceedings the claimant or pursuer shall, subject to subsection (2A) below, be entitled to the relief claimed if he proves that the threats were so made and satisfies the court that he is a person aggrieved by them.

...

(3) The said relief is—

    (a) a declaration or declarator to the effect that the threats are unjustifiable;

    (b) an injunction or interdict against the continuance of the threats; and

(c) damages in respect of any loss which the claimant or pursuer has sustained by the threats.

(4) Proceedings may not be brought under this section for–

(a) a threat to bring proceedings for an infringement alleged to consist of making or importing a product for disposal or of using a process, or

(b) a threat, made to a person who has made or imported a product for disposal or used a process, to bring proceedings for an infringement alleged to consist of doing anything else in relation to that product or process.

Those threatened with groundless proceedings therefore get their own action for relief. It does not apply though to those that make or import the product (even if they also distribute or sell), but those parties can bring an action for a negative declaration (i.e. that they do not infringe) in case the patentee fails to follow the threats up with a claim form.

Another problem that seems to create injustice arises when a successful infringement action (leading to the award of substantial damages) is followed by a decision by the European Patent Office to invalidate the patent on which the action was based. Surely it cannot be just to award damages for the infringement of a patent that was not valid in the first place. Typically though the problem of invalidity arises once the infringement decision has become *res judicata*. English courts have in those cases bluntly refused to offer a remedy, arguing that it would be fundamentally wrong to tinker with the principle of *res judicata* leading to estoppel (*Unilin Beheer v Berry Floor and ors* [2007] FSR 25). The Supreme Court was however prepared to overrule that decision, at least if the procedure to assess damages is still open (*Virgin Atlantic Airways Ltd v Premium Aircraft Interiors UK Ltd* [2013] UKSC 46). The decision to award damages can no longer be reopened, however, once a final award of damages has been made and the damages have been paid, even if the Supreme Court seems to hold back from finally closing that door. Other legal systems offer a more constructive approach and hopefully the UK will be able to follow their example in the future. Injunctions present a different picture though, and can be modified or lifted.

26.2.9 **Dissemination of Information**

The Enforcement Directive also recognizes that there are circumstances in which the public and the trade need to be alerted. Its Article 15 allows therefore the judicial authorities to order appropriate measures for the dissemination of information concerning their decision. This is done at the request of the applicant and at the expense of the infringer and may include the publication or display of the judgment, for example in national newspapers or specialist magazines. This is one of the aspects of the Directive that was far less known in the UK before the adoption of the Directive. In other countries this tool has been present all along and has been used more frequently. In Belgium, for example, the relevant provision is Article XI 334 § 4 Economic Law Code and in Germany the relevant provision is Article 103 Copyright Act.

26.3 **Criminal Remedies**

Criminal proceedings do not play an important role in the area of IP. Some offences do, however, exist and these types of proceedings are specifically concerned with cases of infringement that are seen as particularly serious from a public policy point of view. Obvious examples are actions against copyright or trade mark pirates.

The Enforcement Directive specifically excludes 'criminal procedures and penalties' from its scope in Article 2(3). Subsequent efforts to draft and agree a separate directive on criminal enforcement failed and the matter is therefore entirely left with the national laws of the Member States. Those Member States are however bound by Article 61 TRIPS Agreement, which sets out minimum guidelines:

> Members shall provide for criminal procedures and penalties to be applied at least in cases of wilful trademark counterfeiting or copyright piracy on a commercial scale. Remedies available shall include imprisonment and/or monetary fines sufficient to provide a deterrent, consistently with the level of penalties applied for crimes of a corresponding gravity. In appropriate cases, remedies available shall also include the seizure, forfeiture and destruction of the infringing goods and of any materials and implements the predominant use of which has been in the commission of the offence. Members may provide for criminal procedures and penalties to be applied in other cases of infringement of intellectual property rights, in particular where they are committed wilfully and on a commercial scale.

Let us look in a bit more detail at the situation in the UK by way of example. The commission of the kind of acts that amount to secondary infringement of copyright now also leads to criminal liability in the circumstances that are described in section 107 CDPA 1988.[11] The Act also makes provision for orders for delivery up (CDPA 1988, section 108) and for search orders (CDPA 1988, section 109, as amended by Copyright, etc. and Trade Marks (Offences and Enforcement) Act 2002, section 2; the latter Act also expanded the search order system to unauthorized decoders by inserting section 297B into the CDPA 1988 in this context. Infringing goods can be disposed of (CDPA 1988, sections 114 and 204 in relation to illicit recordings) and can be forfeited (CDPA 1988, sections 114A (infringing copies), 204A (illicit recordings), and 297C (unauthorized decoders) inserted by Copyright, etc. and Trade Marks (Offences and Enforcement) Act 2002, sections 3–5).

In those cases in which both criminal and civil proceedings can be brought, the court cannot express a preference or make a choice. The rights owner makes his choice when bringing the case either via civil or via criminal proceedings (*Thames & Hudson Ltd v Designs & Artists Copyright Society Ltd* [1995] FSR 153). These offences can, in serious instances, be prosecuted summarily or on indictment (CDPA 1988, sections 107–10).

Counterfeiting of registered trade marks can also give rise to criminal liability. This will, for example, be the case if the trade mark, or a similar and confusing mark, is applied to goods or their packaging, if such goods are sold or offered for sale, or if such a sign is applied to packaging or labelling material (Trade Marks Act 1994, sections 92 and 93. The system of search warrants has also been added here as section 92A by Copyright, etc. and Trade Marks (Offences and Enforcement) Act 2002, section 6. Section 92 does, however, require use of the mark as a trade mark; descriptive use is not covered: see *R v Johnstone* [2003] FSR 748, [2003] 3 All ER 884 (HL). A defendant manning a market stall and found in possession of counterfeit clothing which he was offering for sale received on this basis a sentence of six months' imprisonment, suspended for two years (*R v Singh (Harpreet)* [2012] EWCA Crim 1855), whereas an offender who had been involved in the planning and organization of such an enterprise was given a sentence of two years' imprisonment (*R v Brayford (Richard Frederick)* [2010] EWCA Crim 2329). The goods to which the mark is applied can obviously be goods within the class for which the mark has been registered,

---

[11] For an example concerning a provision of German law on the basis of which a transporter was held liable for aiding and abetting the unlawful distribution of a work protected by copyright law (but not protected in the country where it was manufactured) see Case C–5/11 *Donner* EU:C:2012:370.

but other goods are also covered in cases of improper dilution (Trade Marks Act 1994, section 92(4)).

Other offences exist in relation to IP registers. It is an offence to make, or cause to be made, false entries in the Trade Marks Register (Trade Marks Act 1994, section 94); another offence covers the act of falsely representing a trade mark as registered (Trade Marks Act 1994, section 95). Both of these types of offence also exist in relation to patents (Patents Act 1977, sections 109 and 110; see also section 111) and registered designs (Registered Designs Act 1949, sections 34 and 35).

In more general terms, the crime of conspiracy to defraud can also be committed in relation to IP. This could, for example, be the case for those agreeing to try to bribe cinema employees into handing over copies of films that would subsequently be copied and released on video in an unauthorized way, because the conspirers seek to obtain a pecuniary advantage and they try to make others act contrary to their duties (see *Scott v Metropolitan Police Comr* [1975] AC 819). The crime also applies to cases in which the conspirers are proposing to acquire property, which could include IP, dishonestly. The outcome of the attempt to obtain an advantage, or to make others act against their duties, or to acquire property is not particularly relevant, because it is the conspiracy element that counts, and neither is the fact that the infringement of the right amounts to an offence as such.

These criminal offences are hard to prove: the defendant must be shown to be guilty 'beyond reasonable doubt', rather than 'on the balance of probabilities' as is the case in most civil cases, and the type of *mens rea* must be that the defendant knew, or had reason to believe, that she was committing an infringing act or another offence.

26.4 **Administrative Procedures**

Customs officers, trading standards authorities, and advertising standards authorities play an ancillary role in the enforcement of IP rights. Only the role played by customs officers is really of great significance in relation to the main IP rights.

The main instrument in this area is an EU regulation to stop the release into free circulation of counterfeit goods (Regulation (EU) No. 608/2013 of the European Parliament and of the Council of 12 June 2013 concerning customs enforcement of intellectual property rights and repealing Council Regulation (EC) No. 1383/2003 [2013] OJ L 181/13).

The EU Regulation lays out a set of rules that are aimed at facilitating the cooperation between rights holders and the customs authorities. The public policy aim is to stop counterfeit and pirated goods from entering the common market and prevent their marketing. In that sense the Regulation also implements Articles 51–60 TRIPS Agreement 1994. All the procedures are based on an application by the owner of the right—that is, a 'tip-off', including a description of the goods—but customs authorities can also act on their own initiative, for instance by means of random checks. The system in the Regulation falls apart in a phase where specific attention is being paid and preparatory measures are being taken on the one hand and a phase that is characterized by the actual intervention of the customs authorities on the other hand.

The first phase can of course be activated on the basis of information about a suspect shipment that is passed on to customs by the rights holder or one of its affiliates through what the Regulation calls an application, but often smaller and medium-sized companies do not necessarily have the means to gather that kind of information. Article 18.1 therefore provides a mechanism for the customs authorities to take action *ex officio*. This mechanism is triggered when during an action the customs authorities come to believe that there are sufficient grounds to suspect that goods they discover in the course of such action are infringing IP rights. The mechanism then provides for the suspension of the release or the retention by the customs authorities of these goods for four working days. The rights holders are notified of the intervention by customs and they are then given time to lodge an application for further action with the customs authorities.

In the application system the rights holder needs to provide according to Article 6:

(a) details concerning the applicant;

(b) the status, within the meaning of Article 3, of the applicant;

(c) documents providing evidence to satisfy the competent customs department that the applicant is entitled to submit the application;

(d) where the applicant submits the application by means of a representative, details of the person representing him and evidence of that person's powers to act as representative, in accordance with the legislation of the Member State in which the application is submitted;

(e) the intellectual property right or rights to be enforced;

(f) in the case of a Union application, the Member States in which customs action is requested;

(g) specific and technical data on the authentic goods, including markings such as barcoding and images where appropriate;

(h) the information needed to enable the customs authorities to readily identify the goods in question;

(i) information relevant to the customs authorities' analysis and assessment of the risk of infringement of the intellectual property right or the intellectual property rights concerned, such as the authorised distributors;

(j) whether information provided in accordance with point (g), (h) or (i) of this paragraph is to be marked for restricted handling in accordance with Article 31(5);

(k) the details of any representative designated by the applicant to take charge of legal and technical matters;

(l) an undertaking by the applicant to notify the competent customs department of any of the situations laid down in Article 15;

(m) an undertaking by the applicant to forward and update any information relevant to the customs authorities' analysis and assessment of the risk of infringement of the intellectual property right(s) concerned;

(n) an undertaking by the applicant to assume liability under the conditions laid down in Article 28;

(o) an undertaking by the applicant to bear the costs referred to in Article 29 under the conditions laid down in that Article;

(p) an agreement by the applicant that the data provided by him may be processed by the Commission and by the Member States;

(q) whether the applicant requests the use of the procedure referred to in Article 26 and, where requested by the customs authorities, agrees to cover the costs related to destruction of goods under that procedure.

In addition it is wise to give customs as much information as possible, for example to point out the differences between the authentic goods and counterfeit items that have been found or that are suspected to be in the shipment or information about the value and routing of the goods.

On the basis of the application and the information contained in it, customs then move to the second phase and may suspend the release of the goods and retain them, according to Article 17. The rights holder will be informed swiftly and has a ten-day period to confirm that in its view the goods are infringing. In the case of perishable goods a three-working-day period applies. The rights holder can also request the names and addresses of the consignee, the consignor, the declarant of the holder of the goods, and the origin of the goods.

The holder of the goods will also be informed. After the ten-day period the goods will be released, unless the holder of the goods agrees to their infringing nature and their destruction or unless customs have been notified of the initiation of proceedings to determine whether or not the goods are infringing. Article 23 sets out the relevant procedural steps.

That should give the rights holder enough information to decide on action during the suspension period of ten days. The rights holder can bring an action before the competent authority to determine whether the goods are counterfeited or pirated. If that turns out to be the case the goods will not be allowed to enter the common market or be released for free circulation.[12] Removal from customs, exportation, re-exportation, or placement under a suspensive procedure or in a free zone or warehouse will also no longer be possible.[13] The rights holder can also apply for the immediate destruction of the goods (even without there being a need to determine their infringing nature). This of course involves seeking the agreement of the holder of the goods or of their owner.[14]

In this whole system definitions of concepts such as counterfeit goods are essential. These are contained in Article 2:

   (1) 'intellectual property right' means:

      (a) a trade mark;

      (b) a design;

      (c) a copyright or any related right as provided for by national or Union law;

      (d) a geographical indication;

      (e) a patent as provided for by national or Union law;

      (f) a supplementary protection certificate for medicinal products as provided for in Regulation (EC) No 469/2009 of the European Parliament and of the Council of 6 May 2009 concerning the supplementary protection certificate for medicinal products;

      (g) a supplementary protection certificate for plant protection products as provided for in Regulation (EC) No 1610/96 of the European Parliament and of the Council of 23 July 1996 concerning the creation of a supplementary protection certificate for plant protection products;

      (h) a Community plant variety right as provided for in Council Regulation (EC) No 2100/94 of 27 July 1994 on Community plant variety rights;

      (i) a plant variety right as provided for by national law;

      (j) a topography of semiconductor product as provided for by national or Union law;

      (k) a utility model in so far as it is protected as an intellectual property right by national or Union law;

---

[12] Article 13 of the Regulation.   [13] Article 16 of the Regulation.

[14] Article 11 of the Regulation. See Case C–93/08 *Schenker SIA v Valsts Ienemumu Dienests* [2009] ETMR 35.

(l) a trade name in so far as it is protected as an exclusive intellectual property right by national or Union law;

(2) 'trade mark' means:

(a) a Community trade mark as provided for in Council Regulation (EC) No 207/2009 of 26 February 2009 on the Community trade mark;

(b) a trade mark registered in a Member State, or, in the case of Belgium, Luxembourg or the Netherlands, at the Benelux Office for Intellectual Property;

(c) a trade mark registered under international arrangements which has effect in a Member State or in the Union;

(3) 'design' means:

(a) a Community design as provided for in Council Regulation (EC) No 6/2002 of 12 December 2001 on Community designs;

(b) a design registered in a Member State, or, in the case of Belgium, Luxembourg or the Netherlands, at the Benelux Office for Intellectual Property;

(c) a design registered under international arrangements which has effect in a Member State or in the Union;

(4) 'geographical indication' means:

(a) a geographical indication or designation of origin protected for agricultural products and foodstuff as provided for in Regulation (EU) No 1151/2012 of the European Parliament and of the Council of 21 November 2012 on quality schemes for agricultural products and foodstuffs;

(b) a designation of origin or geographical indication for wine as provided for in Council Regulation (EC) No 1234/2007 of 22 October 2007 establishing a common organisation of agricultural markets and on specific provisions for certain agricultural products (Single CMO Regulation);

(c) a geographical designation for aromatised drinks based on wine products as provided for in Council Regulation (EEC) No 1601/91 of 10 June 1991 laying down general rules on the definition, description and presentation of aromatized wines, aromatized wine-based drinks and aromatized wine-product cocktails;

(d) a geographical indication of spirit drinks as provided for in Regulation (EC) No 110/2008 of the European Parliament and of the Council of 15 January 2008 on the definition, description, presentation, labelling and the protection of geographical indications of spirit drinks;

(e) a geographical indication for products not falling under points (a) to (d) in so far as it is established as an exclusive intellectual property right by national or Union law;

(f) a geographical indication as provided for in Agreements between the Union and third countries and as such listed in those Agreements;

(5) 'counterfeit goods' means:

(a) goods which are the subject of an act infringing a trade mark in the Member State where they are found and bear without authorisation a sign which is identical to the trade mark validly registered in respect of the same type of goods, or which cannot be distinguished in its essential aspects from such a trade mark;

(b) goods which are the subject of an act infringing a geographical indication in the Member State where they are found and, bear or are described by, a name or term protected in respect of that geographical indication;

(c) any packaging, label, sticker, brochure, operating instructions, warranty document or other similar item, even if presented separately, which is the subject of an act infringing a trade mark or a geographical indication, which includes a sign, name or term which is identical to a validly registered trade mark or protected geographical indication, or which cannot be distinguished in its essential aspects from such a trade mark or geographical indication, and which can be used for the same type of goods as that for which the trade mark or geographical indication has been registered;

(6) 'pirated goods' means goods which are the subject of an act infringing a copyright or related right or a design in the Member State where the goods are found and which are, or contain copies, made without the consent of the holder of a copyright or related right or a design, or of a person authorised by that holder in the country of production;

(7) 'goods suspected of infringing an intellectual property right' means goods with regard to which there are reasonable indications that, in the Member State where those goods are found, they are prima facie:

(a) goods which are the subject of an act infringing an intellectual property right in that Member State;

(b) devices, products or components which are primarily designed, produced or adapted for the purpose of enabling or facilitating the circumvention of any technology, device or component that, in the normal course of its operation, prevents or restricts acts in respect of works which are not authorised by the holder of any copyright or any right related to copyright and which relate to an act infringing those rights in that Member State;

(c) any mould or matrix which is specifically designed or adapted for the manufacture of goods infringing an intellectual property right, if such moulds or matrices relate to an act infringing an intellectual property right in that Member State;

(8) 'right-holder' means the holder of an intellectual property right;

(9) 'application' means a request made to the competent customs department for customs authorities to take action with respect to goods suspected of infringing an intellectual property right;

(10) 'national application' means an application requesting the customs authorities of a Member State to take action in that Member State;

(11) 'Union application' means an application submitted in one Member State and requesting the customs authorities of that Member State and of one or more other Member States to take action in their respective Member States;

(12) 'applicant' means the person or entity in whose name an application is submitted;

(13) 'holder of the decision' means the holder of a decision granting an application;

(14) 'holder of the goods' means the person who is the owner of the goods suspected of infringing an intellectual property right or who has a similar right of disposal, or physical control, over such goods;

(15) 'declarant' means the declarant as defined in point (18) of Article 4 of Regulation (EEC) No 2913/92;

(16) 'destruction' means the physical destruction, recycling or disposal of goods outside commercial channels, in such a way as to preclude damage to the holder of the decision;

(17) 'customs territory of the Union' means the customs territory of the Community as defined in Article 3 of Regulation (EEC) No 2913/92;

(18) 'release of the goods' means the release of the goods as defined in point (20) of Article 4 of Regulation (EEC) No 2913/92;

(19) 'small consignment' means a postal or express courier consignment, which:

   (a) contains three units or less; or

   (b) has a gross weight of less than two kilograms.

For the purpose of point (a), 'units' means goods as classified under the Combined Nomenclature in accordance with Annex I to Council Regulation (EEC) No 2658/87 of 23 July 1987 on the tariff and statistical nomenclature and on the Common Customs Tariff if unpackaged, or the package of such goods intended for retail sale to the ultimate consumer.

For the purpose of this definition, separate goods falling in the same Combined Nomenclature code shall be considered as different units and goods presented as sets classified in one Combined Nomenclature code shall be considered as one unit;

(20) 'perishable goods' means goods considered by customs authorities to deteriorate by being kept for up to 20 days from the date of their suspension of release or detention;

(21) 'exclusive licence' means a licence (whether general or limited) authorising the licensee to the exclusion of all other persons, including the person granting the licence, to use an intellectual property right in the manner authorised by the licence.

One of the main weaknesses of the previous versions of the Regulation was that the regime only applied to goods that were to be released for free circulation. Goods in transit and goods that were in customs terms subject to a suspensive procedure, such as customs warehousing, were not covered. The argument was that these goods were technically not in the country, and therefore cannot infringe a national IP right. The new Regulation solves that issue in its Article 1 and adopts a very wide scope:

1. This Regulation sets out the conditions and procedures for action by the customs authorities where goods suspected of infringing an intellectual property right are, or should have been, subject to customs supervision or customs control within the customs territory of the Union in accordance with Council Regulation (EEC) No 2913/92 of 12 October 1992 establishing the Community Customs Code, particularly goods in the following situations:

   (a) when declared for release for free circulation, export or re-export;

   (b) when entering or leaving the customs territory of the Union;

   (c) when placed under a suspensive procedure or in a free zone or free warehouse....

26.5 Conclusions

This second chapter in this part deals with enforcement and remedies proper, once jurisdiction and applicable law have been dealt with. It does so on the basis of a national case, as national law will apply. But in the EU there has been a degree of harmonization through the Enforcement Directive and that Directive therefore figured prominently in this chapter. Each time we took UK law as an example to demonstrate how national law has implemented the Directive and at times goes further than the minimum standard set out by the Directive. The palette offered by the Directive can be schematized as shown in Figure 26.1.

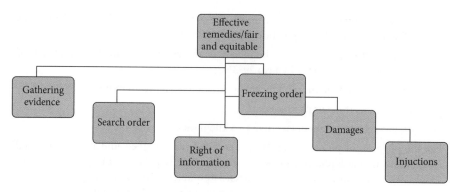

Figure 26.1 The Directive's enforcement palette

The main way of enforcing IP rights, as private rights, is through private enforcement proceedings in civil courts. Civil enforcement and civil remedies therefore took up the major part of the chapter. Criminal proceedings are reserved for blatant cases and real piracy. And they are entirely subject to national law in implementation of the minimum standard set out in the TRIPS Agreement. There is no European instrument that deals with them.

Customs also increasingly play a role in relation to the enforcement of IP rights and the new European Regulation sets out detailed rules and procedures that go further than ever before.

Further Reading

CONAGLEN, M., 'Thinking about Proprietary Remedies for Breach of Confidence' [2008] *IPQ* 82

CORNISH, W.R. ET AL., 'Procedures and Remedies for Enforcing IPRS: The European Commission's Proposed Directive' [2003] *EIPR* 447

HEATH, C., 'Wrongful Patent Enforcement: Threats and Post-Infringement Invalidity in Comparative Perspective' (2008) 39 *IIC* 307

HUNIAR, K., 'The Enforcement Directive: Its Effects on UK Law' [2006] *EIPR* 92

TREACY, P. AND WRAY, A., 'IP Crimes: The Prospect for EU-Wide Criminal Sanctions—A Long Road Ahead?' [2006] *EIPR* 1

PART VII

Future Trends

27

Future Trends

27.1 Introduction

This book is not only about ideas. That should have become clear by now! It is about ideas skilfully expressed in writing, in music, or in a sculpture. It is about the bright idea for an invention, the details of which have been worked out and which takes the form of a product or a process that can be applied industrially. It is also about a logo or name applied to products in order to distinguish them from other products in the same category and to indicate their origin. It is also about clothes and exhaust pipes made to a new design. IP is more than a reward for inventors and creators on the basis of a bright idea. If it wasn't, there would be no reason to keep IP rights. IP rights are practical tools that play a role in our society. They are all, or at least should be all, about added value. We argued earlier in the book that one cannot justify each and every rule of IP and that we keep the system, because abolishing it would be more difficult and costly than keeping it. In other words, it is by no means a perfect system, but one way or another it works and it fits into our society and the way it operates. It plays a role.

This role needs to be understood in the context of what we discussed in the first three chapters of this book. One cannot look at IP rights from a purely IP-centric technical perspective. IP is embedded in our socio-economic system and that in turn tries to take account of the sociological and psychological foundations and goals of our democratic free market society. In the three first chapters of this book we set out to offer a definition of IP, what its origins are, and, most importantly, what the purpose of the IP rules is. Our attempt to answer the question of the very purpose of IP required us to attempt to facilitate the critical reflection of the reader in this respect. We opened that reflection in Chapter 3 by explaining how the various theoretical approaches make a contribution to the understanding of the IP system, its structure, operation, and, above all, its purpose. With these building blocks to hand we invited the reader into the technical detail of the various rights and elements that make up the field of IP. For each of them the technical analysis at the European level was the key component of these chapters, but there was also space for critical reflection. Having acquired all that technical knowledge, the time has now come to return to the theory and to the question of the purpose of IP in order to complete the analysis and in order to reap the fruits of what we initiated in Chapter 3. We do so in a particular and practical context. This chapter offers an outlook to the future at the European level. The EU and its legal instruments primarily approach IP from a utilitarian free market perspective and that applies also to the way they look at the future. This chapter therefore also focuses primarily on that angle when it looks at how the European IP system could and should function in the future and which direction it is taking. In a sense we offer an opportunity for reflection and we try to enhance the reader's insight in, and understanding of, IP by wrapping the critical analysis of its technical rules up in a more theoretical analysis.

27.2 Outlook

The real idea behind this chapter is to provide an outlook. Or if one prefers the more lyrical version, let us stare at our crystal ball and see what the future holds. The construction of the European temple of IP rights is very much a work in progress. We are creating a unitary patent and its single patent court, we are perfecting the Community trade mark regime, and we are taking a fresh look at copyright at the European level... One could fill pages and pages by describing all these initiatives and by trying to predict their outcome. The former would amount to repetition, as we referred to these initiatives in the previous chapters of this book. The latter would be foolish, as the factor of political compromise that weighs heavily on these discussions also renders the outcome unpredictable to a large extent. Let us therefore move away from the detail and from the immediate future. Let us take a strategic view.

The European system that we have and that is being developed further day after day is based on the premise that, whilst the EU may not be in the best position to compete at global level on the point of labour costs and cheap raw materials, we are ahead in the competitive game when it comes to IP. That then translates into a need for an IP law system that offers a high level of protection for that IP. The recitals of the various European copyright directives spell this out *expressis verbis*. What makes things worse is that in general rights holders are better represented in the lobbying game than users. The development of EU policies is therefore tilted towards the direction of more is better. New initiatives have a tendency to strengthen IP rights. But one should not forget that one is not always the holder of the more and stronger patents. One also needs to take out the endless numbers of licences. An ever broader scope of protection for trade marks makes it more difficult to choose an alternative trade mark that works in a competitive environment without running the risk of infringement. And in a digital copyright environment users cut and paste when creating user generated content. Let us think of a YouTube clip that retains the music, for example of the Gangnam Style clip, but that adds new images. Surely one does not simply wish to qualify this as an infringement. There may even be a new copyright in there. Be that as it may, there is a balance to be struck between the rights of the rights holder and the interests of the user. That balance is inherent in the whole IP system.

From that perspective one should look critically at any initiative that aims to further strengthen IP protection. One needs to be sure that the IP system will in its amended form be even better at enhancing competition at the creative and innovation level, whilst not unduly restricting competition at other levels, such as that of the user. Let us call that a form of justifying IP law. There is a balance to be struck between enhancing competition at the level of creation and innovation. This balance is necessary if we believe that progress is inherently needed in our society, irrespective of whether or not we see it as our competitive strength, on the one hand and the need on the other hand merely to correct the risk of market failure and not to interfere with the principle of free competition in the absence of a risk of market failure. Free competition is after all the basic principle of our market economy and of our society. A theory that sees and justifies IP rights as an instrument to promote competition fits in well in this context. We will therefore return in essence to Michael Lehmann's theory, augmented with some elements of other theories. We have discussed these points already in some detail in Chapters 1 and 3, where the unfair competition approach is also analysed. It should be emphasized here that this theory is not the only valid theory or not even the 'best' theory (whatever that could mean). It is merely an approach that fits in well with the EU's utilitarian goal of safeguarding competition and of creating a single market for goods and services as a way to enhance competition. That contrasts with the survival of national territorial IP rights and the way they are to be fitted in with the single market concept. Since we are providing an outlook on further developments at the European level these elements are particularly relevant and are likely to influence these development, as a sudden radical and fundamental change in approach does not seem likely.

Let us therefore analyse in a bit more detail how IP rights, as property rights and exclusive rights, can and should function in this context. Once we have done this we will look at a couple of case studies that show the challenges for the future evolution and development of IP rights in the EU.

27.3 IP as a Mechanism to Promote Competition

27.3.1 Market Failure and Freeriders

So why are these intangible property rights created? Economists argue that, if everyone were to be allowed to use the results of innovative and creative activity freely, the problem of the 'freerider' would arise. No one would invest in innovation or creation, except in a couple of cases in which no other solution was available, because to do so would put them at a competitive disadvantage. All competitors would simply wait until someone else made the investment, because they would then be able to use the results without having invested that money in innovation and creation, and without having taken the risk that the investment might not result in the innovative or creative breakthrough at which it aimed. The cost of the distribution of the knowledge is relatively insignificant.

As a result, it is argued, the economy would not function adequately, because innovation and creation are essential elements in a competitive free market economy. From this perspective, innovation and creation are required for economic growth and prosperity. Property rights should be created if goods and services are to be produced, and used, as efficiently as possible in such an economy. The knowledge that they will have a property right in the results of their investment will stimulate individuals and enterprises to invest in research and development, and these property rights should be granted to those who will economically maximize profits.[1] It is assumed that the creator or inventor will have been motivated by the desire to maximize profits—either by exploiting the invention or creation herself, or by having it exploited by a third party—so the creator or inventor is granted the rights.

---

[1] M. Lehmann, 'Property and Intellectual Property: Property Rights as Restrictions on Competition in Furtherance of Competition' [1989] *IIC* 1.

This argument applies as well to intangible property rights such as patents, which determine the value of an item in a direct way, as it does to rights such as trade marks, which do so only indirectly through their use as a means of communication.

27.3.2 Exclusivity and Perfect Competition

But how does such a legally created, monopolistic, exclusive property right fit in with the free market ideal of perfect competition? At first sight, every form of monopoly might seem to be incompatible with free competition, but we have already demonstrated that some form of property right is required to enhance economic development: competition can only play its role as market regulator if the products of human labour are protected by property rights. In this respect, the exclusive monopolistic character of the property rights is coupled with the fact that these rights are transferable. These rights are marketable: they can, for example, be sold as an individual item. It is also necessary to distinguish between various levels of economic activity, as far as economic development and competition are concerned. The market mechanism is more sophisticated than the competition–monopoly dichotomy. Competitive restrictions at one level may be necessary to promote competition at another level.

Three levels can be distinguished: production, consumption, and innovation. Property rights in goods enhance competition on the production level, but this form of ownership restricts competition on the consumption level. One has to acquire the ownership of the goods before one is allowed to consume them and goods owned by other economic players are not directly available for one's consumption. In turn, IP imposes competitive restrictions on the production level: only the owner of the patent in an invention may use the invention and only the owner of the copyright in a literary work may produce additional copies of that work. These restrictions benefit competition on the innovative level. The availability of property rights on each level guarantees the development of competition on the next level.

Property rights are a prerequisite for the normal functioning of the market mechanism.[2] To take the example of patents: 'patents explicitly prevent the diffusion of new technology to guarantee the existence of technology to diffuse in the future'.[3] Trade marks, meanwhile, distinguish identical goods or services of different sources. They therefore allow the consumer to distinguish between such products and services, and grant the rights holder the exclusive right to apply the mark to the goods and services for which it has been registered. In doing so, trade marks enable competition between producers of identical goods or services. They therefore encourage the availability of a wider variety of goods and services between which the consumer can distinguish, by means of the trade mark, in terms of quality, price, etc.

This clearly demonstrates that it is not correct to see IP rights as monopolies that are in permanent conflict with the fundamental rule of free competition. Free competition can only exist, and a market economy can only flourish, when certain restrictions in furtherance of competition are accepted. IP rights are necessary to achieve this. The main problem is that this only justifies the existence of exclusive property rights as the result of innovative activity. The particular form that IP rights have taken in a particular national IP statute—and, even more, the way in which these rights are used and exercised—are not

---

[2] M. Lehmann, 'The Theory of Property Rights and the Protection of Intellectual and Industrial Property' [1985] *IIC* 525.

[3] R. Benko, *Protecting Intellectual Property Rights: Issues and Controversies*, (American Enterprise Institute, 1987) ch. 4, p. 19.

automatically justified by this theory. The restrictions on competition are only justified insofar as they are restrictions in furtherance of competition on the next level, which is either the production level or the innovation level; any restriction that goes further hinders the optimal functioning of the market economy. It is the task of the provisions on competition law to regulate this system in such a way that this optimal level of functioning is achieved and maintained. This coexistence of IP and the rules on free competition is a permanent balancing act, and one of the most challenging and interesting parts of the study of IP.

If we focus on patents for a moment, in order to go into a bit more detail, we have to start from the premise that the economic justification does not give us ready-made rules on every aspect of patent law. Instead, we are confronted with a constant, built-in dialectic tension between the protection of the patented—that is, already realized—innovation and the promotion of subsequent innovation. The strongest possible protection is therefore not only not a logical consequence of the economic justification, but would also unduly focus on one aspect of that tension. The promotion of subsequent innovation that builds on what has already been achieved would be harmed—and this would be all the more serious, because the tension is not restricted to the relationship between the patentee and its competitors. It does, indeed, influence the overall market's actual and potential competitive dynamics. What is needed, therefore, is a set of rules for a patent system that respects and enhances a rich dialectic interrelationship between the need to guarantee a differential return on activities and investments in research and development, on the one hand, and the need to safeguard the actual chance of third parties' subsequent innovation and the competitive fabric of the market as a whole, on the other. This balance will be struck in the rules on patentability—that is, that certain thresholds need to be passed before a patent is warranted—and in the scope of the patent and the limitations to the exclusive right, among others.

An ideal patent system that can be fully justified will not, therefore, simply involve rewarding inventors in order to stimulate them to invent more, or stimulating them to achieve, in turn, inventive steps. The finer points of the system set out here require that such a patent system will more specifically reward:

> the innovation already developed in such a way that the reward granted to the current inventor stimulates both the inventor to continue and third parties to develop a subsequent innovation which might compete with the preceding one, thus also spurring on the first innovator, in a virtuous pro-innovation and pro-competition dynamic process.[4]

Goods perish through use, while intangible property is—at least in theory—perpetual. But the socio-economic value of these rights is not so important that a perpetual restriction on competition is necessary and justifiable to enhance competition on other levels. Innovative activity will be sufficiently enhanced, without restrictions of competition on the production level that are too far-reaching, when the IP right is restricted in time. For patents, which grant the patentee extensive restrictive powers and the protection of which is wide in scope, the term of protection is relatively short (20 years). From now on, literary works are to be protected under copyright for a period of the life of the author plus 70 years, but the protection granted is weaker than that offered under patents: only the particular expression of an idea is protected; the idea as such is left unprotected. This attempt to get the balance between restriction on, and freedom of, competition right through the use of a fixed term can be seen as lacking precision and potentially unjust, but introducing a sliding scale would require the determination of the term of protection

---

[4] G. Ghidini, *Intellectual Property and Competition Law: The Innovation Nexus* (Edward Elgar, 2006) 24.

on the basis of the merits of each individual invention or creation. This would create massive administrative costs that outweigh the benefits derived from the system and, on top of this, it would create an undesirable climate of legal uncertainty.

27.3.3 A Duty to Exercise

Another way of getting the balance right is the duty to exercise and use, which is linked to patent and trade mark rights. Compulsory use and compulsory licences are an integral component of most IP legislations. The idea behind this is, first of all, that use of the IP right will provide an income to its owner and that this profit will encourage him to continue his innovative work. The only reason why a restriction of competition at the level of production is acceptable is the enhancement of competition on the innovative level, through the possibility for the owner of the right to realize a profit. This justification collapses if this right is not used, a defect that is remedied by the introduction of the duty to exercise and use. The weaker protection accorded under copyright law renders this restriction superfluous in that area; neither does such a duty exist for real and personal property. This can be seen as an important difference between intangible industrial property, and real and personal property.

A second reason for the obligation to use is the feeling that the grant of an exclusive right should be counterbalanced by the fact that the previously unavailable subject matter of the right is made available to society. The obligation to use is necessary because, due to the exclusive right, the owner of the IP right is the only one who makes it available. More specifically, for patents, there is the additional requirement to reveal the technical details and specifications of the invention, in order to bring them into the public domain. In exchange for the exclusive right, society has the right to share the development of technical knowledge, and, eventually, to use it for further research and further developments.

This represents an additional advantage of the patent system, because the alternative is to be found in the use of the secrecy system. Technological developments are, in the absence of a patent system, kept secret. Society is unable to share this new knowledge and the inventor can only use the invention in a way that does not reveal the technical functioning of it, because, once in the public domain, it can be used freely by all of the competitors. In that instance, the inventor is put in a very weak position. It has been demonstrated that a patent system that grants the inventor adequate property rights fulfils the task reserved for such a system in a market economy in a better way. The law of secrecy cannot replace the patent system fully; it can only be a useful addition to it.

27.3.4 Copyright Involves Other Factors Too

To this point, we have mainly been concerned with patents and trade marks. Historically, copyright developed on a very different basis, with a lot of emphasis on the link between the author and his work. An attempt was made to make sure that it was the author, rather than someone else, who would secure the benefits resulting from the work and its exploitation.

Over the years, however, copyright has increasingly been used to protect the commercial exploitation of the work and new, more technologically orientated, types of work have been protected by copyright. It is therefore submitted that the same economic justification theory can now be applied to copyright. Protection against the copying of the work, for example, will restrict competition between the rights holder and her exploitation of the work, on the one hand, and copyists, on the other. Such a restriction will encourage the rights holder to create more works, thus enhancing competition at the higher, creative level, because there is now more of a prospect of securing a return. This is no doubt not the only motivation for authors, but it is clearly an important factor.

But one additional problem arises in relation to the economic analysis of copyright. Copyright has to strike a balance between providing the incentives for authors, on the one hand, and the right of access to information of the public, on the other. In the words of the famous study by Landes and Posner:

> Copyright protection—the right of the copyright's owner to prevent others from making copies—trades off the costs of limiting access to a work against the benefits of providing incentives to create the work in the first place. Striking the correct balance between access and incentives is the central problem in copyright law.[5]

Cooter and Ulen focus on the same issue when they argue that: 'Put succinctly, the dilemma is that without a legal monopoly too little of the information will be produced but with the legal monopoly too little of the information will be used.'[6]

Let us analyse the implications of these specificities of copyright in a little more detail. The innovation and creation level interacts with the production level; this is a given. In the copyright sphere, we are dealing with works that are the expression of ideas. Starting from these ideas, one has to recognize that they are, by their nature, public goods, and can therefore freely be accessed and used by anyone. The way in which these ideas enter the public domain is through their expression by an individual author, because such expression is required for the transmission of the idea. From an economic point of view, it is also important to keep in mind that such access is non-exhaustive in nature: the consumption of the expression does not necessarily make the expression and its material support unsuitable or unavailable for further consumption. It is also the case that, in the light of modern (digital) technological advances, the costs of reproduction and distribution of the expression of the idea have become marginal, and that such reproduction and distribution is easily achievable and can be done in a minimum amount of time. There is therefore plenty of room for freeriders. The situation is therefore entirely in favour of competition at the production level; at the innovation and creation level, there is very little in terms of incentive to create. The creator may not be able to recoup the cost of production, because the cost of copying is lower and there is no tool to reap any substantial benefit from such creative activity. In economic terms, then, there is no efficient market of the authors' expression of ideas.

Copyright, therefore, is the tool that is created to give authors a right in their expression of ideas, hence securing for them appropriate profits derived from their act of creation. Copyright will lead to the creation of an immaterial property right in the expression of an idea by the author, a right that the author can use to secure appropriate profit from that act of creation on the market. This will enhance creation by providing an incentive, and therefore competition on the innovation and creation level will be stimulated, while any such right will inevitably limit competition at the production level, because competitors are no longer free to copy the copyright work. A restriction on competition is put in place in furtherance of competition.[7]

Copyright fulfils here the 'pro-competitive' regulating role filled by the property right when it comes to the consumption and the production level—but an important

---

[5] W. Landes and R. Posner, 'An Economic Analysis of Copyright Law' (1989) 18 *Journal of Legal Studies* 325, 326.

[6] R. Cooter and T. Ulen, *Law and Economics* (HarperCollins, 1988) 145.

[7] Lehmann (n 1) 1–15.

distinction must be drawn. Property rights are a legal recognition of a situation—that is, of the physical possession of and control over the goods—whereas copyright is not based on a de facto situation at all: it is rather an artificially created right, put in place by the legislator to regulate competition at the innovation and creation level, and to provide the much-needed incentive to create. This difference gives copyright a different standing. The legislator created it specifically as a tool through which to enhance competition.

Copyright plays therefore, *mutatis mutandis*, the same pro-competitive role in relation to literary and artistic works that patents play in relation to inventions. An important additional factor in the context of copyright, however, is the need to safeguard access to information and freedom of expression. This reflects itself in the basic rule that copyright will not protect ideas, but only their expression. The threshold for that expression to be protected will be the fact that it satisfies the originality expression that allows one to distinguish it from the mere idea. It has been said that copyright therefore protects 'independently achieved expressive results',[8] which applies both in a *droit d'auteur* tradition, with its 'subjective' notion of originality, and in an Anglo-Saxon copyright environment. In the *droit d'auteur* tradition, the author's personal expression is therefore protected as a creative work, irrespective of the mediocrity or otherwise, of the expressive results; copyright systems focus instead on the concept of independent creation. Protection by means of copyright, therefore, depends on the objective attainment of a result—again, irrespective of its mediocrity or otherwise in terms of creative effort—that arises from a contribution that is neither copied from anyone else, nor reproduced using known standard models.

Up until now, we have looked at 'traditional' copyright in literary and artistic works, such as books and sculptures. It is however necessary to add that copyright has developed in two ways in recent years that may have influenced the position: on the one hand, copyright has been expanded to protect the results of technological evolutions; on the other, we have seen an increasing emphasis on the economic interests of those who exploit copyright works, such as producers and publishers. It is important to note that, as a result, copyright is increasingly used to protect information goods and the investment needed for the creation of these goods. It is clear that, in these circumstances, the level of originality involved in the creation of such information goods is lower, and that the link with the author and his creativity, which makes the work his own individual creation, is weaker. This must also weaken the justification for strong copyright protection for these information works, because these elements were described as the basis for the economic justification of copyright. Another important element is the fact that, by their nature, information goods have a poor substitutability. This applies, to some extent, to all copyright works: for example, we are interested in a novel because of the way in which the author has expressed the idea and therefore the novel cannot be easily substituted by another novel in which another author expresses the same idea in her different own way. This factor is, however, more strongly present in relation to information goods.

27.3.5 A Special Type of Monopoly

It may well be that some additional remarks on the type of monopoly that is granted by IP rights are appropriate. That monopoly is, in no way, absolute and it is limited in time; it is also subject to competition with similar products, similar trade marks, etc. Inventions compete with substitute technologies, so that the profits based on the exclusive use of

---

[8] Ghidini (n 4) 54.

the invention are rarely monopolistic rents. The latter situation only arises in those rare situations in which an invention is such a radical step forward that there is a (temporary) absolute lack of substitutability. In copyright, meanwhile, only one particular expression of an otherwise unprotected idea is granted copyright protection.

IP rights do not give their owners an automatic profit: they are directly oriented towards demand. The reward that they provide for innovative activity depends upon the competitive structure of the market concerned. Only when the market appreciates the innovation on its merits will the owner be rewarded and make a profit: 'The ownership of intangibles in the sense of abstract property rights . . . is therefore limited to a temporary, ephemeral competitive restriction'.[9] IP rights confer exclusive rights, but they hardly ever confer a real monopoly, in the sense that the monopolist can act in an arbitrary way without being influenced by his competitors.

27.3.6 **Those in Favour and Those Against**

It has to be added that a number of economists have argued against the existence of IP rights and especially against the existence of patents. In their view, patents do not promote technological innovation—or there are more effective ways in which to do so. These critics are, however, unable to provide clear evidence that IP rights do not fulfil a useful economical function and none of their alternatives has ever been tested successfully in practice.[10] All they can demonstrate is that some features of the existing patent system cannot be justified economically and that the existing system does not always achieve a perfect balance between the various levels of competition. This is undoubtedly true, but the solution is not the abolition of the whole system. What is required might rather be described as 'fine-tuning' of the system.

There is also a substantial amount of empirical economic evidence that supports the economic justification for the existence of IP rights. Most of these studies deal with patents, and the causal relationship between the availability of patent protection and investment in research and development and in innovation.[11]

27.3.7 **Who Gets the Right?**

Thus economic theory provides a justification for the existence of IP rights. A related point is the issue of who gets these IP rights. It has been suggested that the economic theory proves that it is valuable to have IP rights, but is unable to guarantee that the enforcement of these rights will have valuable results in each individual case. The author and the inventor must obtain these rights to secure the best possible system—and this can only be accepted if one uses labour theory to justify the allocation of the property rights the existence of which the economic theory justifies.[12]

The Labour theory was formulated by John Locke[13] and is the combination of two concepts: the first is that everyone has a property right in the labour of his own body and

---

[9] Lehmann (n 2) 537.

[10] This is admitted by F. Machlup, 'An Economic Review of the Patent System', Study No. 15 of the Senate Judiciary Subcommittee on Patents, Trademarks and Copyrights, US Congress (1957), at the end of his study.

[11] e.g. A. Silberston, *The Economic Importance of Patents* (CUP, 1987).

[12] H. Spector, 'An Outline of a Theory Justifying Intellectual and Industrial Property Rights' [1989] 8 *EIPR* 270, 272–3.

[13] J. Locke, 'The Second Treatise of Government', Pt 27, reproduced in P. Laslett (ed.) *Two Treaties of Government* ([1690] CUP, 1970).

brain; the second adds that the application of human labour to an unowned object gives you a property right in it. When applied to IP rights, this might explain why it is the author who gets the copyright in the book and why it is the inventor who gets the patent in the invention.

The combination of the economic theory and the labour theory provides a full justification for the system of IP rights. This reference to the labour theory explicitly justifies the fact that it is the author or the inventor who should own the IP right—but it is submitted here that this is already implicit in the economic theory. An IP right, as a restriction on competition at the production level (because not everyone can produce the goods protected by the right), will not stimulate competition on the innovation level if the right is not given to the innovator, whether an author or an inventor. One will only be stimulated to innovate when one gets the IP rights in the innovation. This effect, which is the key element in the economic justification theory for IP, disappears when someone else gets the IP rights in the innovation. The actual exploitation of the right can be undertaken by the rights holder or by a licensee—this does not affect the justification at all.

27.4 Case Studies as a Way to Look at Future Trends

Having looked at one of the theories behind IP rights and how that theory and the specific role which IP rights play in a free market economy precondition the scope and shape of IP rights, as well as their future development, especially in an EU context with its emphasis on free competition on a single market that should not be partitioned by (the surviving) national territorial IP rights, the time has come to move away from this framework in which IP rights operate and function to look at some of the challenges faced by the rights that exist inside this framework and how they deal with the new challenges of accelerating technological change on the one hand and European integration on the other hand. We propose to do so by means of two case studies. The first one looks at the challenge posed by transformative works in a context of accelerating technological change in the area of copyright. The second one looks at European integration issues in the area of patents. The unitary patent was covered in earlier chapters, but with it also comes the need to integrate the court systems and to create a single patent court that coexists with national courts systems, at the very least during a seven-year transition period.

27.5 Copyright and the Transformative Works Conundrum

We have seen earlier on that EU copyright, at least for now, works with a closed list of limitations and exceptions. In the digital age this approach has increasingly come under pressure. There is the ease with which a perfect copy can be made. And such a perfect copy can be partial and form the basis of a properly original work (at least in terms of what is added) created by the 'copyist'. One of the many questions that arises is whether such a new work infringes copyright or whether it should receive its own copyright. And is there a role for limitations and exceptions in such a context? Our first case study looks at these transformative works, as a form of user-generated content, and the way in which copyright could accommodate them through the system of limitations and exceptions. We will try to argue that transformative works form a special case in the digital age and that they do not receive adequate treatment by the existing limitations and exceptions. By doing so we try to set out the possible future trends to accommodate transformative works and the ways in which copyright could evolve. We will, of course, also express a preferred way forward, backed by the analysis found in the preceding chapters.

27.5.1 The Concept of Transformative Works and Their Place in EU Copyright

Most, if not virtually all, copyright works have drawn inspiration from other works.[14] That is how our society works, how we educate ourselves, and how we are part of our own history. Copyright acknowledges that in the basic rule that ideas do not get protection, whereas (individual forms of) expressions do. The fundamental right of freedom of expression comes from the same background, but it seems to go further. One can also borrow bits of expression in the exercise of the freedom of expression.[15] But let us be honest, copyright goes further too than the basic rule could suggest. There will only be copyright infringement if a substantial part of the work is copied and cases such as Case C–5/08 *Infopaq International A/S v Danske Dagblades Forening* [2009] ECR I-6569 suggest that one needs to take the original contribution of the author to get over the threshold. Limitations and exceptions further assist in getting the balance right and allowing certain specific and limited uses of copyright works.[16] That brings us straight back to our topic.

The concept of transformative works is therefore not new. There is no transformative work if only the pre-existing idea is taken, but in the majority of cases something more will be taken, i.e. at least some element that is expression in a pre-existing work. In many cases copyright infringement rules suffice, as suggested earlier, to determine whether such taking is allowable. But the argument is that certain of these new works deserve special treatment. There are special circumstances that give them an added value and that may then in turn shift the copyright infringement balance. News reporting that serves the fundamental right to freedom of information comes in as an example and explains why copyright systems have special limitations and exceptions dealing with reporting current events. The more limitative concept of transformative works suggests that the added value lies in the transformative character of the new work. It transforms the original work. The new work has strong links with the original work, but the public will not confuse the two because of the transformation. The question that arises is whether the transformative character as such is a sufficiently strong element to go beyond normal copyright infringement rules and to offer additional freedoms to copy expression from the original through limitations and exceptions.

Before the arrival of the digital age, the processes described earlier necessarily, i.e. for technological reasons, involved imperfect copying and the resulting copied parts were often imprecise. That was even the case if the copying was related to one element only of a composite work, such as the music, but not the lyrics and the images, of a music video. With the arrival of the digital age all that has changed fundamentally. Perfect digital copies are possible. And if one sticks to the example of the music video one only needs to look at YouTube to appreciate that music videos with changed (parodied) lyrics and

---

[14] See A.C. Yen, 'The Interdisciplinary Future of Copyright Theory' in M. Woodmansee and P. Jaszi (eds), *The Construction of Authorship. Textual Appropriation in Law and Literature* (Duke University Press, 1994) 159–74.

[15] See D.F. Alvarez Amezquita, 'La libertad de expresion como resultado y garantia principal del derecho de autor' (2007) *Revista Iberoamericana de Derecho de Autor* 1(1).

[16] Yen (n 14) 159–74.

images, but with a perfect digital copy of the music, are big business. Whereas copyright infringement rules and their concept of substantial copying could perfectly handle matters in the analogue age, it is far less clear whether that conclusion is still valid in the digital age. Maybe one needs a limitation or exception here.

The *Infopaq* case law of the Court of Justice of the European Union (Case C–5/08 *Infopaq International A/S v Danske Dagblades Forening* [2009] ECR I-6569) has raised a further complication. The Court highlighted the principle that there is copyright infringement whenever the originality of the work, i.e. the personal contribution of the author, is copied without permission. In the *Infopaq* context the Court specifically said that that originality could also be found in small units. Flipping the coin over from infringement to copyright protection this must mean that small units of a larger work will also attract their own copyright protection if they meet the originality requirement. Infringing that kind of copyright is a lot easier. A perfect digital copy of a smaller part of a work or of one element of a composite work is much more likely to infringe copyright if originality is found in smaller units. The threshold for infringement goes down when the size of the work that can attract copyright goes down. Transformative works that contain by definition (small) parts of the expression of the pre-existing works are therefore by definition at risk of copyright infringement. But if we value the added value of the transformative nature of the work, limitations and exceptions need to be in place to overcome this hurdle and to allow valuable transformative works.

27.5.2 **The Parody Exception**

A first limitation and exception that comes to mind as a candidate is the parody exception. By its very nature a parody transforms the original work and, as a part of the original work is retained and copied, there is a risk of infringement. The exception allows in certain circumstances that one goes beyond what the normal copyright infringement rules would allow.

Directive 2001/29 of the European Parliament and of the Council of 22 May 2001 on the harmonisation of certain aspects of copyright and related rights in the information society provides Member States in its Article 5(3)(k) with the option to have an exception for parody in their copyright laws. Member States are however not under an obligation to have the exception as part of their copyright laws and, even more importantly, the Directive does not offer a definition of the concept of parody. The latter problem has now been addressed by the CJEU in the *Deckmyn* case, where the Court offered an autonomous interpretation of the concept of parody (judgment of the Grand Chamber of 3 September 2014 in Case C–201/13 *Johan Deckmyn and Vrijheidsfonds VZW v Helena Vandersteen, Liliana Vandersteen, Isabelle Vandersteen, Rita Dupont, Amoras II CVOH and WPG Uitgevers België* EU:C:2014:2132 [14] and [15]). Member States remain free to have or not to have the exception in their national laws, but if they decide to adopt the exception, i.e. take up the offer of Article 5(3)(k), the autonomous interpretation of the concept of parody will apply (see [16]). It is to be recalled here that the parody exception was already discussed in Chapter 13 in the wider context of copyright exemptions and limitations. The need to balance fundamental rights in that context was also discussed in that chapter and these points are entirely relevant for this more narrowly focused discussion.

What sounds like music to the ears of the makers of transformative works is that the CJEU has firmly established in *Deckmyn* that in order to benefit from the exception a parody needs to evoke the original copyright work of which it is allegedly a parody. There can only be a parody if there is a perceivable link with the original. Parody is by definition a 'treatment' of the original work, so the original work must be identifiable. At the same time, that 'treatment' needs to show itself and produce results. It is therefore logical that the CJEU requires at the same time that the alleged parody is noticeably different from the original parodied work (see [20]). Again, that works well from a transformative work point of view. An exception is needed, because the link with the original is necessarily achieved through a form of copying, which might transgress the substantial part barrier, but at the same time there needs to be transformation and added value and there the requirement that the parody be noticeably different fits in well. What is lacking at present though is a tool to delineate exactly what the exception permits and what not.

It is submitted that this is where confusion comes in as a delineating tool. The combination of evoking the original work, whilst becoming noticeably different is acceptable insofar as there is not creation between the original work (and its author) and the parody of the original work (and its author). The benefit for society of having a parody, or any other transformative work for that purpose, is the added value and more (cultural) diversity and for that purpose a degree of copying can be allowed as long as it does not interfere with the exclusive right in the original work. A parody or transformative work that is noticeably different to a sufficient degree will not cause confusion. As such it will not negatively affect the exploitation of the original work and it will not become an alternative for the original work. In other words, it leaves the exclusive right in the original work and its exploitation unaffected. That justifies that the exception goes beyond the normal contours of copyright infringement. The CJEU adds that the concept must enable the effectiveness of the exception and its purpose to be observed (see [23]). Coupled with the standard idea of a restrictive interpretation of exceptions that means that there is also a necessity criterion. One can only copy as much as is necessary to make the point of the parody (see the Court of Appeal in Amsterdam, Hof Amsterdam, 9 September 1982, [1983] Auteursrecht/AMR 91).

But the exclusive right and its exploitation are more than that. The work and its author are as a result of its exploitation positioned in a certain way in the market. They acquire a certain reputation, not necessarily in the moral rights sense, but more in a trade mark sense. That reputation sustains the continued normal exploitation of the copyright work and of future works of the same author. This is what comes to mind when the CJEU talks about balancing of rights and taking account of the legitimate rights of the author (*Deckmyn* [27]). In *Deckmyn* it is clear that the association with a discriminatory message can affect the legitimate interests of the author. It may simply prevent disgusted consumers and readers from buying more comic strips in the same series. That would affect the exclusive right of the author and goes beyond the mere moral rights aspect. It would therefore be simplistic to reduce the legitimate interest point in *Deckmyn* to a mere moral rights point.[17] The confusion tool is capable of getting that balance at least well under way. By way of comparison, Deckmyn's alleged parody ran into trouble because it puts itself in the same context as the original work, i.e. readers could be confused into thinking it is part of the original series of comic strips because the ingredient of the cover and the context are similar. On the other hand there is the example, also from Belgium, of a Danish painter[18] who parodied the Tintin persona by putting it in his paintings in an

---

[17] *Contra*, but arguable wrongly, see the IPKat opinion at http://ipkitten.blogspot.fr/2014/09/has-cjeu-in-deckmyn-de-facto-harmonised.html.

[18] Court of Appeal Brussels, 14 June 2007, [2007] TBH-RDC 687–93. See P. Torremans, 'Hay Vinculacion entre la Prueba de los Tres Pasos y la Interoperabilidad?' in ALAI Uruguay (ed.), *El Derecho de Autor en el sigle XXI: el lugar del autor ante los desafios de la modernizacion* (ALAI -IUDA-UM, 2011), 679–89. The decision was later overruled by the Cour de cassation in a much disputed and summary judgment (Cass. 18 June 2010, C.08.0247.F/1).

erotic context. Hergé, the original author, did not do paintings of Tintin and shied away from any amorous, let alone erotic, element in the comic strips. That rules out the element of confusion, at least for the reader with a basic knowledge. The uninformed potential future reader might still get the wrong end of the stick, but here the purely potential impact on the exclusive right is arguably *de minimis*.

The CJEU's concept of parody in *Deckmyn* also consists of a second element. The CJEU ruled out any other requirements, but it is clear that without being requirements some of these will often apply in practice. The judgment of the Grand Chamber in *Deckmyn* brings home that point ([21]) as follows:

> It is not apparent either from the usual meaning of the term 'parody' in everyday language, or indeed, as rightly noted by the Belgian Government and the European Commission, from the wording of Article 5(3)(k) of Directive 2001/29, that the concept is subject to the conditions set out by the referring court in its second question, namely: that the parody should display an original character of its own, other than that of displaying noticeable differences with respect to the original parodied work; could reasonably be attributed to a person other than the author of the original work itself; should relate to the original work itself or mention the source of the parodied work.

With that, let us come back to the second element that is required. According to the Court, the alleged parody must also constitute an expression of humour or mockery (*Deckmyn* [20], *in fine*). The Court does not offer more by way of an insight into what constitutes an expression of humour or mockery and leaves the matter to the national court. It is submitted that this gives the exception a particular and narrow focus. But one should maybe move away from the all too narrow idea that a parody must be funny and must make one laugh. Humour and mockery are no doubt broader than that. The confusion element already having ruled out undue damage to the legitimate interests of the author, but at the level of economic and moral rights, one could argue that this requirement of an expression of humour and mockery is met by the decontexualization of the elements of the original work that are retained. The consumer, reader, or viewer will in the absence of confusion spot that a party that is not the author puts the original work or elements of it in a context in which its author would not have put it. The responsibility for that action will be put on the shoulders of the author of the parody and the change in context will provoke the expression of mockery or it will at least be seen as humorous. Maybe it is sufficient that the observer thinks of the change as bizarre, absurd, or even weird but interesting. That could, for example, be the case in the Tintin saga to which we referred earlier. Putting Tintin in an erotic context is clearly an act of decontextualization and an observer would blame the Danish painter rather than the creator of Tintin for this weird but interesting impression which it creates.[19]

But even if humour and mockery are seen in such a wide sense it remains the case that this second requirement does not fit all forms of transformative works. There are a number of them that cause no confusion and add significant added value. They deserve protection too, but they fall outside the scope of the parody exception, as defined by the CJEU in the *Deckmyn* case. For these transformative works another solution is needed and it has been suggested that fair use would be a way forward.

But before we turn to fair use another outstanding problem should be highlighted. Music video parodies are a good example in this respect. Music videos are composite

---

[19] Court of Appeal Brussels, 14 June 2007, [2007] TBH-RDC 687–93, see Torremans (n 18) 679–89. The decision was later overruled by the Cour de cassation in a much disputed and summary judgment (Cass. 18 June 2010, C.08.0247.F/1).

works, composed of music, lyrics, and images, to name just these. Lots of parodies change the lyrics and the images, but keep the music. Arguably the parody criteria apply to the composite work and the parody benefits from the exception. But how does one deal with the exact digital copy of the music? That is after all a copyright work in its own right. Can the exception justify a 100 per cent copy if it happens in the context of a composite work? For now this is very much an open question and one with which the courts or a future transformative works exception should deal. And with that we look at fair use as another contender and maybe one with less problems associated with it.

27.5.3 **Fair Use, US Style**

27.5.3.1 **The Tool Explained**

The fair use clause has a long history in US copyright law. Having originally been shaped by the courts over a longer period it was eventually codified as § 107 Copyright Act. As such it has become the main limitation on the exclusive rights of the copyright holder in US copyright law (Copyright Law of the United States and Related Laws Contained in Title 17 of the United States Code, see http://www.copyright.gov/title17/). The codified version of the fair use clause reads as follows:

> **§ 107. Limitations on exclusive rights: Fair use**
>
> Notwithstanding the provisions of sections 106 and 106A, the fair use of a copyrighted work, including such use by reproduction in copies or phonorecords or by any other means specified by that section, for purposes such as criticism, comment, news reporting, teaching (including multiple copies for classroom use), scholarship, or research, is not an infringement of copyright. In determining whether the use made of a work in any particular case is a fair use the factors to be considered shall include:
>
> (1) the purpose and character of the use, including whether such use is of a commercial nature or is for nonprofit educational purposes;
>
> (2) the nature of the copyrighted work;
>
> (3) the amount and substantiality of the portion used in relation to the copyrighted work as a whole; and
>
> (4) the effect of the use upon the potential market for or value of the copyrighted work.
>
> The fact that a work is unpublished shall not itself bar a finding of fair use if such finding is made upon consideration of all the above factors.

A first major element to note is that the list of purposes for which fair use can be invoked (criticism, comment, etc.) is prefaced by the words 'purposes such as'. What follows are therefore mere examples and the list is open-ended. Use for other purposes than those listed in § 107 can also be fair use. This is a major difference with fair dealing. It completely changes the nature of the exception, whereas fair dealing starts (and ends) with evidence of specific purposes being present, for example research, and only then adds fairness as a subsequent requirement, in the United States the role of the purpose is of secondary importance. The key element is instead the concept of fairness.

That concept of fairness is then determined on the basis of essentially four factors that are listed in the Act. They are essentially four factors as again the list is not a closed one. But in practice one sees the four factors being determinative, with courts rarely addressing, let alone giving significant value, to other factors. It is important to note that a successful determination of fairness by no means depends on all four factors going in the same, positive, direction. This is in essence a balancing act in which, depending on the specific aspects of the case, each factor is given a certain weight before a final balance is achieved. The use can therefore be fair even if one or more of the factors go against such a determination. It all depends on the overall balance and the weight given to each factor.[20]

27.5.3.2 A Critical Analysis

The fact that the court can take into account all circumstances and facts gives it of course a large amount of flexibility and discretion. This not only means that in theory the court can 'get it right' in each particular case, it also means that the court has a flexible tool at its disposal to react to developing technological conditions (see, e.g., *Perfect 10 v Amazon, Inc.*, 487 F3d 701 (9th Cir. 2007) and *Field v Google, Inc.*, 412 F Supp 2d 1106 (D. Nev. 2006)). The other side of the coin is of course called 'uncertainty'. Fair use proceedings are costly and can be long. Before one engages in such proceedings some form of predictability and certainty is a bonus. But in practice the enormous flexibility of the fair use tool means that rights holders cannot in many cases predict the outcome with any degree of certainty and that same uncertainty pushes particularly the smaller defendants with less deep pockets to settle, take a licence, or change their behaviour, even in those circumstances where ultimately they had copyright law on their side in the sense that they did not step on the exclusive right of the copyright holder.[21] One could make the assessment worse by suggesting that in essence the court forms an (abstract) opinion on the fairness of the use and then works back from there with the four factors to build a reasoning that supports the conclusion that became the starting point. The four factors then become even less the drivers of the analysis and certainty and predictability become even more of an illusion.[22]

The very broad scope of the fair use exception, its high level of uncertainty, and unpredictability due to the case-by-case approach also raises questions concerning its compatibility with the three-step test and in particular with the first leg of that test.[23] The flexibility of the fair use test may be an asset and may encourage and facilitate the creative industries, but the uncertainty and unpredictability, coupled with the high cost of the almost inevitable litigation, make it a poisonous tool for small and medium-sized enterprises.[24] The latter rather dominate the UK and EU industry though and it is therefore doubtful whether the mere introduction of the fair use doctrine in Europe would really have a positive effect on copyright and the creative industries. Rather than the absence of a fair use tool the absence of funding may be a key problem politicians should address.[25]

---

[20] See J. Griffiths, 'Unsticking the Centre-Piece—The Liberation of European Copyright Law?' [2010] 1 *Journal of Intellectual Property, Information Technology and Electronic Commerce Law* 87, 91 [1].

[21] See N. Netanel, *Copyright's Paradox* (OUP, 2008) 66.

[22] See D. Nimmer, 'Fairest of Them All and Other Fairy Tales of Fair Use' (2003) 66 *Law & Contemporary Problems* 263, 281.

[23] See, e.g., H. Cohen Jehoram, 'Restrictions on Copyright and Their Abuse' [2005] *EIPR* 359.

[24] The Hargreaves Review in the UK also looked into these issues and decided against recommending the introduction of a fair use clause. 'Digital Opportunity: A Review of Intellectual Property and Growth' http://ww.ipo.gov.uk/ipreview-finalreport.pdf, [5.17] is particularly telling: 'Does this mean, as is sometimes implied, that if only the UK could adopt Fair Use, East London would quickly become a rival to Silicon Valley? The answer to this is: certainly not. We were told repeatedly in our American interviews, that the success of high technology companies in Silicon Valley owes more to attitudes to business risk and investor culture, not to mention other complex issues of economic geography, than it does to the shape of IP law. In practice, it is difficult to distinguish between the importance of different elements in successful industrial clusters of the Silicon Valley type. This does not mean that IP issues are unimportant for the success of innovative, high technology businesses. The Review's judgment is that they are of growing importance and that they merit serious attention from the UK Government.'

[25] See M. Senftleben, 'The International Three-Step Test: A Model Provision for EC Fair Use Legislation' [2010] 1 *Journal of Intellectual Property, Information Technology and Electronic Commerce Law* 67, 68 [1].

Rather than pursuing this policy line of argument though it is worth adding that fair use in the United States depends heavily on the judges. They have a lot of experience with fair use and they are used to the delicate balancing act it involves. On top of that, all of them have an identical background and starting point in US copyright. European judges on the contrary come from very different backgrounds in their home countries and they lack the years of experience with fair use and its balancing act. It would therefore be very difficult for them harmoniously to develop a fair use doctrine if it were to be introduced in Europe. The risk of diverging decisions pulling in different directions is enormous, which could make the whole system even more unpredictable and uncertain than in the United States.[26]

That brings us to an even more fundamental issue. Fair use fits in completely with the utilitarian approach to copyright that is adopted traditionally in the United States. US copyright law is only subsidiarily based on the idea that there exists an ongoing creative as well as economic relationship between the author and her work and that that relationship deserves, and is in need of, protection. Instead the utilitarian approach sees copyright fundamentally as a prerogative that is granted to enhance the overall welfare of society by ensuring a sufficient supply of knowledge and information. From that starting point one easily arrives at the idea that rights should in a utilitarian way only just be strong enough to achieve this aim. That leads to narrowly defined rights and the idea that all the rest is free. A broad and flexible exception such as fair use fits in well with this aim. The right is kept to the narrow basis that is needed from the utilitarian perspective and the exception allows anything else, any other use of the work is to be treated as fair and therefore unhindered by copyright. The European approach, both in the UK and in the civil law tradition, is fundamentally different and takes the ongoing creative, as well as economic, relationship between the author and his work as its main starting point. Rights then become broader in order to achieve this aim and exceptions become narrow and focused.

For all these various reasons fair use does not fit in easily in European copyright and merely copying the fair use doctrine may therefore not be suitable.[27] But that must not be the final conclusion. There may be other ways in which the fair use concept can form a useful addition to European copyright.

27.5.3.3 A Role for Fair Use in European Copyright

Doing away with the European system of exceptions and merely replacing it with the US fair use exception is therefore not a good idea. There may be a way though to use the concept of fair use inside a European copyright system organized along the lines with which one is currently familiar. Alternatively, one could customize the fair use clause for the European copyright system.

27.5.3.4 The Concept of Fairness

The main disadvantage of the European system of a closed list of narrowly and very specifically defined exceptions is that these exceptions are unable to adapt themselves to the changing and rapidly developing circumstances. For example, when they were drafted the concept of thumbnail (small format, low resolution) images on Internet search engines that lead to sites containing the original image was unheard of. That leaves open the question whether the search engine provider could be covered by an exception for

---

[26] See Griffiths (n 20) 87 [1].

[27] See M.-C. Janssens, 'The Issue of Exceptions: Reshaping the Keys to the Gates in the Territory of Literary, Musical and Artistic Creation' in E. Derclaye (ed.), *The Future of Copyright Law*, Series Research Handbooks in Intellectual Property (Edward Elgar, 2009) 317–48.

citation that was drafted with hard copies of literary works in mind (and reflected in its wording). On top of that courts tend to apply the three-step test in individual cases, i.e. on top of the specific exception. That means that even if one fits within the exception the three-step test may still rule out the application of the exception to the individual case before the court. Such a double-whammy approach is extremely restrictive and undesirable as it makes it even more unlikely that the exceptions can be applied to a new situation that arises as a result of new and developing technological circumstances. Hence the proposal in the literature to get rid of the three-step test as an additional negative constraint and to use the three-step test instead as a positive mechanism to bring new circumstances within existing exceptions insofar as the uses concerned do not conflict with the conditions of the three-step test. These uses that are acceptable are then in a sense seen as fair uses.[28]

In all cases one would need a 'similar' exception in the existing list of exceptions. That is an exception that addresses similar situations and similar uses in the environment in place before the technological evolution to which the legislature has not yet reacted took place. Second, the (new) use to which the exception is proposed to be extended does not conflict with the conditions of the three-step test. And third, the concept of fairness (not the US factors though) is used as a tool in operating the three-step test as an enabling tool. Fairness, particularly in the balance between the interests of the various parties concerned, becomes the ultimate yardstick. Or to put it in the words of the approach's main backer, Martin Senftleben:

> To allow new internet industries to develop and take advantage of their economic potential, sufficient breathing space for copyright limitations is indispensable . . . Given these challenges, the time seems ripe to turn to a productive use of the three-step test. Instead of employing the test as a straitjacket of copyright limitations, modern copyright legislation should seek to encourage its use as a refined proportionality test that allows both the restriction and the broadening of limitations in accordance with the individual circumstances of a given case. The adoption of a fair-use system that rests on the flexible, open criteria of a conflict with a normal exploitation and an unreasonable prejudice to legitimate interests would pave the way for this more flexible and balanced application of the test.[29]

This approach is radically different from a mere copying of the US fair use clause in European copyright law, but this imaginative use of the concept of fair use could not only be acceptable and useful, it could also introduce that very flexibility which European copyright law is so dearly in need of.

27.5.3.5 Fair Use, European Style

A more radical approach combines the US fair use clause and the European idea that there exists an ongoing creative, as well as economic, relationship between the author and his work and that that relationship deserves, and is in need of, protection.[30] That would involve introducing the broad fair use approach on the one hand and on the other hand expanding the set of factors to be taken into account in the fairness evaluation. These extra factors would address the specific importance in Europe of certain concepts. These would include the need to foster competition on secondary markets (derivative works),[31]

---

[28] See Senftleben (n 25) 67 [1].

[29] M. Senftleben, 'Fair Use in the Netherlands—A Renaissance?' [2009] *Tijdschrift voor auteurs, media en informatierecht* 1, 7.

[30] Griffiths (n 20) 87 [1].

[31] See the *Magill* case (Cases C–241/91 P and 242/91 [1991] ECR I-743), P. Torremans, *Holyoak and Torremans Intellectual Property Law* (7th edn, OUP, 2013) 355–9.

the protection of fundamental (human) rights,[32] the need to promote technical innovation, as well as the ongoing moral and economic interest of the author in her work.

That proposal would combine the best of both worlds, the US fair use doctrine with its open-endedness and flexibility and the respect of the fundamental principles of European copyright law. But admittedly, such a positive evaluation only applies to the broad concept of the combination. Drafting the exact terms of such a combined fair use clause will be a nightmare and as indicated earlier European courts will struggle to apply it.

Or to put it in the word of its main protagonist, Jonathan Griffiths:

> The idea floated here is beset with obvious difficulties. A number have been sketched above. The negotiation of the terms of any modified 'European fair use' clause would be highly contentious and there would also be little point in providing such a valuable instrument to judges if, as in the case of the Infopaq court, they seem determined to apply a rigid framework to the law. Nevertheless, it is worth investigating the development of such a doctrine. Any obstacles to the project should be viewed against the background of the dire situation in which we currently find ourselves.[33]

27.5.4 Licensing

A word should be said here too about licensing. Certain industry circles categorically reject the suggestion that a new limitation or exception for transformative works is warranted or needed and prefer the licensing strategy. For example, in the context of music video parodies YouTube now benefits from licences. But these seem to benefit only certain rights holders, whilst others receive nothing and one runs the risk of ending up with multiple layers of licences in combination with certain rights holders and authors who lose out. This is not desirable either.

Even more importantly, one can refuse to license. If our society really thinks that transformative works bring added value we should not leave them to the mercy of rights holders in other works, especially if they do not cause confusion and do not directly compete with the original work.

27.5.5 **A Way Forward**

The alternative approaches which have just been highlighted all have their problems. What is needed in an ideal scenario is a new limitation or exception for transformative works, based on the first leg only of the *Deckmyn* concept of parody, as explained earlier. Or one could amend the parody exception in that sense or operate a very wide concept of humour and mockery if one prefers not to tinker with the Directive. The CJEU's judgment in *Deckmyn* is flexible enough and leaves enough room to the national court to allow this.

The *Deckmyn* case also shows clearly that the exclusive rights of the copyright owner are by no means absolute and that a balancing act between rights and fundamental rights is required. Going back to the theory that we mentioned earlier on in this chapter, for copyright to play its role in enhancing competition the protection should not be absolute, as it would in our example stifle the development of derivate transformative works. By granting copyright one puts in place a restriction of competition, here in practice the reproduction right, but by adding a balancing act with other fundamental rights and by creating an exception for parody in our scenario, one avoids an undue restriction on competition at the creative level. The exception does not take away the essence of the copyright, but by allowing transformative works to an extent, it stimulates further creative

---

[32] See P. Torremans (ed.), *Intellectual Property and Human Rights* (Kluwer Law International, 2008).
[33] Griffiths (n 20) 93 [1].

efforts and the creation of more copyright works. One sees here the complex operation of copyright in our European society and the theory can help in explaining and understanding the system and the way in which it operates (or the way in which the CJEU tries to let it operate).

In order to end on a positive note, it is worth closing the circle and reverting to the idea of an autonomous interpretation of the concept of parody. One of the biggest dangers to the Directive's system of limitations and exceptions in the digital age would be a divergent interpretation of the various concepts such as parody in each Member State. Private international law cannot address that problem, as the applicable law would each time be the local *lex protectionis*.[34] The CJEU's strategy to go each time for a single autonomous interpretation of these concepts (*Deckmyn* [17]) is therefore very valuable and reduces the problems significantly, even if the Directive does not oblige the Member States to introduce certain exceptions and limitations.

27.6 Patents and the Unitary Patent Court Jurisdiction Conundrum

The most recent major development in European patent law is the creation of the unitary patent (Regulation (EU) No. 1257/2012 of the European Parliament and of the Council of 17 December 2012 implementing enhanced cooperation in the area of the creation of unitary patent protection [2012] OJ L 361/1). But it comes on top of national patents and on top of the existing European patent. And it comes in tandem with the Unified Patent Court (Agreement on a Unified Patent Court [2013] OJ C 175/1), that will essentially deal with all European and unitary patent-related matters. National patents remain a matter for the national courts and not all Member States will join the new system. And of course there are courts outside the EU that could deal with European and unitary patents if the defendant is from inside their jurisdiction. Couple that with the fact that the Unitary Patent Court (UPC) will have national, regional, and central divisions and a nice set of jurisdiction issues arises. How will one determine the jurisdiction of the various courts?[35] This is our second case study. EU integration policies give rise to a layered system in which national and supranational rights coexist. How does one unravel the jurisdiction conundrum that comes with it?

The EU is quite used to dealing with the jurisdiction of courts in civil and commercial matters (see the various versions of the Brussels Convention and the Brussels I Regulation that eventually resulted in Regulation (EU) No. 1215/2012 of the European Parliament and of the EU Council of 12 December 2012 on jurisdiction and the recognition and enforcement of judgments in civil and commercial matters [2012] OJ L 351), but in essence all that experience refers to national courts of single Member States. The Benelux Court (Verdrag betreffende de instelling en het statuut van een Benelux-gerechtshof (Treaty establishing a Benelux Court and its Statute) 31 March 1965, [1973] Belgisch Staatsblad—Moniteur belge 14062/the Court has been operational since 1974) has been in existence for quite a number of years as a court that is common to Belgium, the Netherlands, and Luxembourg, but at least until now, it has never operated at first instance level.[36] That removed the need

---

[34] See J.J. Fawcett and P. Torremans, *Intellectual Property and Private International Law* (2nd edn, OUP, 2011) ch. 15.

[35] This analysis relies heavily on P. Torremans, 'An International Perspective II: A View from Private International Law' in J. Pila and C. Wadlow (eds), *The Unitary EU Patent System* (Hart Publishing, 2015) 161–78 and is in fact an abridged version of it.

[36] The Benelux Court issues preliminary rulings at the request of national courts, e.g. concerning the Benelux trade mark. Negotiations are ongoing to allow the public direct access to the court in trade mark

to include it in the jurisdiction rules. So even if that picture may change for the Benelux Court, the UPC is the one that does not fit the mould. The UPC will be a (first instance) court that is common to a large number of Member States. On top of that, as we saw earlier, the UPC will have local and regional divisions, which again at least potentially raises issues of jurisdiction or at least of a division of labour.

It was not entirely clear from the outset how this would fit in with the European legal framework on jurisdiction. At least arguably, nothing needed to be done. A common court which a Member State shares with other Member States is, or at least fulfils the role of, a national court of the Member State concerned and if it deals with civil and commercial matters it comes within the scope of the Brussels I Regulation (Regulation 1215/2012). That gives one a set of international jurisdiction rules to play with and the rest is a matter to be dealt with in patent law and therefore with the Regulation and the UPC Agreement. But that would have created some uncertainty and also the need to establish jurisdiction rules for defendants that are not domiciled in a Member State, as a common court cannot rely on various national rules in this respect. The Brussels I Regulation does not deal with these cases. A proposal to change that was rejected when the Regulation was recast in 2012. The way forward that was chosen was therefore to have explicit rules and to amend the Brussels I Regulation (Article 89(1) UPC Agreement). That should have provided for legal certainty. But maybe one needs to emphasize the word 'should' here...

27.6.1 The Starting Point(s)

The UPC Agreement provides a first obvious starting point in its Article 31:

> **Article 31**
>
> International jurisdiction
>
> The international jurisdiction of the Court shall be established in accordance with Regulation (EU) No 1215/2012 or, where applicable, on the basis of the Convention on jurisdiction and the recognition and enforcement of judgments in civil and commercial matters (Lugano Convention[37]).

Article 31 is the first Article in Chapter VI of the UPC Agreement that is entitled 'International jurisdiction and competence'. Article 31 deals with the international jurisdiction, whilst the remainder of the chapter deals with competence issues. The international jurisdiction of the UPC is therefore governed by the Brussels I Regulation. The court should fit in with the existing system for civil and commercial matters, despite the fact that it is not a national court, but a court common to Member States and despite other aspects that do not fit straightforwardly into the mould of the Brussels I Regulation.

For a private international lawyer every court first needs to establish its international jurisdiction. This is where it all starts and without international jurisdiction a court cannot hear the case. Before the UPC can hear a case it has to establish that

---

matters. See the enabling Protocol 'Protocol tot wijziging van het Verdrag van 31 maart 1965 betreffende de instelling en het statuut van een Benelux-Gerechtshof, ondertekend te Luxemburg op 15 oktober 2012', Tractatenblad 2013, nr 12. Further changes to the relevant Benelux texts on IP are still required before the system can be put into action.

[37] Convention on jurisdiction and the recognition and enforcement of judgments in civil and commercial matters [2007] OJ L 339/3, signed between the EU on the one hand and Norway, Iceland, and Switzerland on the other hand in Lugano in 2007.

it has international jurisdiction to hear the case. Article 31 UPC Agreement imposes the Brussels I Regulation rules as the only rules by which the UPC can establish its jurisdiction. That was also made clear by the change of the word 'jurisdiction' to the word 'competence' for the other elements contained in Chapter VI. From Article 32 onwards one finds provisions on the internal distribution of labour inside the UPC and its various local and regional divisions and aspects of subject matter jurisdiction. International jurisdiction is a separate matter and one that comes first. Only once international jurisdiction has been established can one turn to the competence of the court, which means on the one hand the subject matter jurisdiction of the court as a common patent court that will deal roughly speaking with the infringement and validity issues surrounding European patents and European patents with unitary effect and on the other hand the division of labour inside the UPC, its central, local, and regional divisions.

A second starting point is found in Article 89(1) UPC Agreement:

Article 89

Entry into force

1. This Agreement shall enter into force on 1 January 2014 or on the first day of the fourth month after the deposit of the thirteenth instrument of ratification or accession in accordance with Article 84, including the three Member States in which the highest number of European patents had effect in the year preceding the year in which the signature of the Agreement takes place *or on the first day of the fourth month after the date of entry into force of the amendments to Regulation (EU) No 1215/2012 concerning its relationship with this Agreement, whichever is the latest.*[38]

Once more it is clear that the international jurisdiction of the UPC will be governed by the Brussels I Regulation. But the UPC does not fit the mould and therefore the Brussels I Regulation will be amended.[39]

When putting both these starting points together a clear approach emerges. The UPC Agreement itself contains no rules on the international jurisdiction of the common court. It refers the issue entirely to the Brussels I Regulation, as amended in due course. The Unitary Patent Regulation also offers no provisions on private international law. The UPC will therefore only be able to deal with those cases for which the Brussels I Regulation, as amended in due course, grants it jurisdiction. If such jurisdiction is forthcoming the other provisions in Chapter VI of the UPC Agreement, those on competence, will become relevant and will decide whether the subject matter of the case forms part of the subject matter for which the court has competence and which division of the court can deal with the matter.[40]

---

[38] Emphasis added.

[39] There is also the view that Article 89(1) is a clerical error. The negotiators had the idea that the unitary patent negotiations would be concluded first and then there would have been no point in starting the operations of the court with the 'old' Brussels I Regulation. One would wait for the recast that was also supposed to extend its rules to defendants that were not domiciled in a Member State, which is a crucial point for the UPC. As it happens, the Brussels I recast went ahead (in a different form) before the negotiations on the European patent with unitary effect were concluded and that should have meant that the requirement that the Brussels I Regulation be amended first should have been dropped. See M. Desantes Real, 'Hay que modificar el Reglamento Bruselas I bis de 12 de diciembre de 2012 para que pueda entrar en vigor el Acuerdo sobre un Tribunal Unificado de Patentes de 19 de febrero de 2013?' http://conflictuslegum.blogspot.be/2013/03/manuel-desantes-el-acuerdo-tup-no-exige.html.

[40] Along the lines of the civil procedure rules in civil law jurisdictions that decide whether the subject matter at hand is one for the civil court or for the commercial court to deal with and whether the civil or commercial court of judicial district X or Y will deal with the case.

But this is a second stage that merely comes into play once the jurisdiction issue is dealt with in favour of the UPC.

For our current purposes this implies that we should look first of all at the Brussels I Regulation and the amendments to it, before we turn to the competence rules in the UPC Agreement.

27.6.2 **The Process of Amending the Brussels I Regulation**

The European Commission set the process to implement Article 89(1) UPC Agreement and to amend the Brussels I Regulation yet again in motion on 26 July 2013, with a proposal for a regulation. Or to put it in the words of the Commission:

> Article 89(1) of the UPC Agreement provides that the Agreement cannot enter into force prior to the entry into force of the amendments to the Brussels I Regulation (recast) regulating the relationship between both instruments. The aim of these amendments is twofold. First, the amendments aim at ensuring compliance between the UPC Agreement and Brussels I Regulation (recast), and second, at addressing the particular issue of jurisdiction rules vis-à-vis defendants in non-European Union States.[41]

Ensuring compliance is of course vital if the Brussels I Regulation is supposed to provide the international jurisdiction rules for the UPC Agreement. Both instruments have to cooperate seamlessly and a perfect fit is required. And as the Brussels I Regulation does not contain uniform jurisdiction rules for defendants that are not domiciled in a Member State and instead relies on the national law of the Member States that point has to be addressed head-on, as the common court cannot apply several different national laws on this point.

The proposal seems to suggest that the compliance exercise is a minor one. Several elements point in that direction. The Commission constantly uses the term 'to clarify', which seems to hint at minor amendments that provide clarifications rather than changes of a fundamental nature. And no modification at all is proposed to the core of the Brussels I Regulation which is formed by its jurisdiction rules. Instead, the 'clarifications' are almost to be buried at the end of the Regulation in new Articles 71a to 71d, amongst the provisions that deal with other private international law agreements concluded by the Member States. This is hardly a place to which the attention of most readers is drawn and one does not expect to find there changes to the main jurisdiction rules of the Regulation, let alone changes that are of a fundamental nature. Nevertheless, the compliance operation is anything but a minor one and some of the changes are rather fundamental in nature!

The proposal was eventually adopted in a slightly modified version on 15 May 2014 as Regulation 542/2014 (Regulation (EU) No. 542/2014 of the European Parliament and of the Council of 15 May 2014 amending Regulation (EU) No. 1215/2012 as regards the rules to be applied with respect to the Unified Patent Court and the Benelux Court of Justice [2014] OJ L 163/1).

27.6.3 **The Insertion of a Common Court: A Mere Clarification**

But let us start with what is indeed little more than a mere clarification. A court common to several Member States does after all for each of the Member States concerned the work

---

[41] Proposal for a Regulation of the European Parliament and of the Council amending Regulation (EU) No. 1215/2012 on jurisdiction and the recognition and enforcement of judgments in civil and commercial matters, COM (2013) 554 final, 2.

of a national court, so it makes sense to treat it as such for the purposes of the Brussels I Regulation. If the common court is a court of the Member State then the Brussels I Regulation determines the international jurisdiction of such a court when it deals with civil and commercial matters, as defined in the Regulation. The Regulation clarifies this point for two common courts, the Benelux Court of Justice (for Belgium, the Netherlands, and Luxembourg, of which the Benelux consists) and the one that concerns us at present, the UPC:

In Chapter VII of Regulation 1215/2012, the following Articles are inserted:

Article 71a

1. For the purposes of this Regulation, a court common to several Member States (a 'common court') shall be a court of a Member State when, pursuing to the agreement establishing it, it exercises jurisdiction in civil and commercial matters within the meaning of this Regulation.

2. For the purposes of this Regulation, each of the following shall be a common court:

    (a) the Unified Patent Court established by the Agreement on a Unified Patent Court signed on 19 February 2013 (the 'UPC Agreement'); and

    (b) the Benelux Court of Justice established by the Treaty of 31 March 1965 concerning the establishment and statute of a Benelux Court of Justice (the 'Benelux Court of Justice Treaty').[42]

27.6.4 Uniform Jurisdiction Rules Regardless of the Domicile of the Defendant: Anything But a Mere Clarification

This is entirely uncontroversial, as one merely declares the UPC a court of a Member State, or at least the equivalent of one. But the controversy is not far away. Indeed, in the very first paragraph of the same Article of the draft Regulation one finds an addendum to recital 14 Brussels I Regulation. At first glance it brings a mere reference to the concept of the common court into the recitals of the Brussels I Regulation by stating that uniform jurisdiction rules are also required for the common court. Nothing is more logical and straightforward if the common court de facto operates for each of the Member States concerned as a national court for that Member State. The same need for uniform jurisdiction rules that gave birth to the whole Brussels I system arises after all if one integrates the common court into the landscape of national courts dealing with civil and commercial matters. But, almost inadvertently, a little phrase that refers to the second aim of the amendments to the Brussels I Regulation is slipped in. Article 1(1) therefore reads as follows:

> Uniform jurisdiction rules should also apply *regardless of the defendant's domicile* in cases where courts common to several Member States exercise jurisdiction in matters coming within the scope of application of this Regulation.[43]

It is indeed obvious that we need uniform jurisdiction rules that apply regardless of the defendant's domicile. We have already referred to it earlier. And the proposal that resulted eventually in the 2012 recast of the Brussels I Regulation contained an extension of the existing common jurisdiction rules that rely on the cornerstone of the defendant being domiciled in a Member State unless one is concerned with exclusive jurisdiction, to defendants that are not domiciled in a Member State. That extension would therefore have

---

[42] Article 1 (*partim*).   [43] Emphasis added.

replaced on that point the national private international rules of the Member State on jurisdiction. Suffice it to say that that extension did not make it into the final recast. The Brussels I regime is therefore still based on and limited to defendants that are domiciled in a Member State. Doing for patents what was turned down for all other cases is anything but a clarification of the application of the Brussels I Regulation. Burying the change at the end of the Regulation is potentially misleading and at least mildly controversial. In fact, what is introduced is a form of subject matter jurisdiction, irrespective almost of personal jurisdiction, and that remains a concept that is alien to the Brussels I system. The fact that the national jurisdiction rules tended to provide that solution and that patent lawyers are at ease with the concept does not change that. One is paying lip-service to Brussels I to do exactly the opposite of what the system stands for, which for sure is a weird type of clarification.

Article 1(1) did not survive in the Regulation, as adopted. But the principle has been retained and has instead been slipped in as part of recital 6 to the amending Regulation:

> As courts common to several Member States, the Unified Patent Court and the Benelux Court of Justice cannot, unlike a court of one Member State, exercise jurisdiction on the basis of national law with respect to defendants not domiciled in a Member State. To allow those two Courts to exercise jurisdiction with respect to such defendants, the rules of Regulation (EU) No 1215/2012 should therefore, with regard to matters falling within the jurisdiction of, respectively, the Unified Patent Court and the Benelux Court of Justice, also apply to defendants domiciled in third States. The existing rules of jurisdiction of Regulation (EU) No 1215/2012 ensure a close connection between proceedings to which that Regulation applies and the territory of the Member States. *It is therefore appropriate to extend those rules to proceedings against all defendants regardless of their domicile.* When applying the rules of jurisdiction of Regulation (EU) No 1215/2012, the Unified Patent Court and the Benelux Court of Justice (hereinafter individually referred to as a 'common court') should apply only those rules which are appropriate for the subject-matter for which jurisdiction has been conferred on them.[44]

This does not address the lack of clarity. On the contrary it aggravates it, as it will not be part of the amended version of Brussels I. The reader will now have to spot that part of the new jurisdiction rules in Article 71b are de facto based on the principle and the non-expert reader is therefore even more likely to overlook this point.

27.6.5 The New Rules on International Jurisdiction: Article 71b

27.6.5.1 Paragraph 1

Let us start with the straightforward element in the new international jurisdiction rules. In a situation where the Brussels I Regulation gives jurisdiction to the courts of a Member State that is party to the UPC Agreement and where the subject matter of the case comes inside the scope of the subject matter covered by the UPC Agreement (what we will discuss later as the 'competence' of the court) that jurisdiction is transferred from the national court to the UPC. This works well if the Brussels I jurisdiction is based on the domicile of the defendant in the Member State concerned, in application of what has now become Article 4 Brussels I Regulation (the old Article 2). And

---

[44] Emphasis added.

persons so domiciled can also be sued in the courts of the place where the harmful event occurred or may occur, in application of Article 7(2) Brussels I Regulation.[45] A domicile in a Member State remains the *conditio sine qua non*, unless the ground for exclusive jurisdiction in Article 24(4) applies, i.e. in cases dealing with the validity of the patent. Article 24(4) does not create problems at this stage and neither does Article 8(1) that allows the claimant to bring multiple defendants before a single court if certain circumstances are met.[46]

By using the words 'a common court shall have jurisdiction', Article 71b seems to suggest that the common court will merely also have jurisdiction. This is not the case. The UPC Agreement clearly works on the basis that the jurisdiction of the national courts will be transferred to the UPC and that the national courts lose their jurisdiction. It might have been better to spell this out *expressis verbis*. Especially in relation to Article 24(4) there can only be one court with exclusive validity jurisdiction and the UPC Agreement clearly sees the UPC in that role. But that can only happen if the Brussels I Regulation grants it exclusive jurisdiction. This is clearly intended, but it would have been clearer to spell it out at the level of the Brussels I Regulation.

This is even more so insofar as the seven-year transition period is concerned. During that period Article 83(1) UPC Agreement accepts that parties will be able to bring cases both before the national courts and before the UPC. This concurrent jurisdiction should ideally be spelled out in the Brussels I Regulation. Admittedly the current wording of Article 71b leaves this possibility open, but this is clearly not intended. The plan was not to leave it open and to again amend the Brussels I Regulation at the end of the seven-year transition period. Even worse, at least during the transition period there will be two courts with exclusive jurisdiction under Article 24(4). That means that the jurisdiction of the court excludes the jurisdiction of any other court. But how is that to work vis-à-vis another court with exclusive jurisdiction? Simply leaving Article 24(4) as it is provides no solution. One can only assume that the idea might have been to leave this matter to the *lis pendens* rules and to operate on the basis that the court first seized has priority, but that is not clear from the text. And if a national court deals with the validity of a single designation of a European patent the UPC should be able to deal (at least) with the validity of the other designations of the same patent, but its judgment covers by definition all designations (Article 37 UPC Agreement leaves no doubt on this point). Contradictory judgments which invalidate the patent in one designation and validate it for all designations, or vice versa, then become an option. This cannot be intended and is entirely undesirable and unacceptable, even during the seven-year transition period.

Far less controversial, but maybe unexpected, is the fact that Article 25 Brussels I Regulation may also apply. Parties to a licence agreement may agree that any infringement case amongst them will be brought before the UPC (parties are free not to treat the case as contractual, e.g. when the licensee allegedly goes beyond what is allowed in the licence contract). This may be particularly useful during the seven-year transition period, as it provides predictability and certainty.

---

[45] For a detailed analysis of the application to IP cases of the jurisdiction rules of the Brussels I Regulation see Fawcett and Torremans (n 34) ch. 5.

[46] Compare the evolution between Case C–539/03 *Roche Nederland BV et al. v Frederick Primus and Milton Goldenberg* [2006] ECR I-6535, Case C–145/10 *Eva-Maria Painer v Standard Verlags GmbH et al.* [2011] ECDR 6, and Case C–616/10 *Solvay SA v Honeywell et al.* (12 July 2012). And see P. Torremans, 'Intellectual Property Puts Article 6(1) Brussels I Regulation to the Test', CREATe Working Paper No. 8 http://www.create.ac.uk/wp-content/uploads/2013/09/CREATe-Working-Paper-No-8-v1.0.pdf.

27.6.5.2 **Paragraph 2**

Those drafting the proposed Article 71b clearly thought that paragraph 1 dealt in the most complete possible way with cases involving defendants that are domiciled in a Member State. As the 2012 Brussels I Regulation recast had rejected the extension of these jurisdiction rules to defendants that are not domiciled in a Member State the problem that remained was to deal with those defendants, as they may be the ones infringing European patents (with or without unitary effect) or as they may want to invalidate such patents or on the contrary be called upon to defend the validity of such patents. The solution that was retained in the proposal is exactly what was rejected in the recast. Let us do to patent cases what was not acceptable for all other cases and act as if the defendant was domiciled in a Member State even if this is not the case. The jurisdiction rules shall apply as if the defendant was domiciled in a Member State.

Admittedly, paragraph 2 needs to deal with pure subject matter jurisdiction to implement the 'regardless of the defendant's domicile' phrase. The language of the provision sounds horrific though. One cannot apply the solution to Article 4, as one cannot create a fake domicile and there is no impact on Article 24(4) either, but the language of the new provision clearly refers to them as they are cornerstones of Chapter II of the Brussels I Regulation. Effectively what one does is to remove the requirement that the domicile requirement in Article 4 is met before one can apply Article 7 in infringement cases, or for that purpose Article 8(1) in multiple defendant cases. The non-expert reader might find it very hard though to extract that simple message from the text. And applying both Articles as mere subject matter jurisdiction is not without its risks. They have been designed to apply with the added safeguard that the defendant is domiciled in a Member State, which guaranteed a strong link between the case and the Brussels I territory. Removing that safeguard without replacing it can give the UPC jurisdiction over defendants whose links with the Brussels I territory are extremely weak. Territorial patents are ideally suited to locate some damage in the jurisdiction and it is relatively easy to blame, for example, a foreign (parent) company for it. One may not succeed in substantive law, but harassing defendants by obliging them to defend the case becomes relatively easy.

It would be far clearer for the user of the system and from a legal perspective much more elegant, clear, and safe to provide Article 7-specific language. Hence the proposal to replace the current language by the following text:

> In disputes concerned with the infringements of intellectual property rights over which a court common to several member states exercises subject matter jurisdiction, a person may be sued in the common court if the alleged infringement occurs or may occur in any of the member states concerned, unless the alleged infringer has not acted in any of the member states concerned and his or her activity cannot reasonably be seen as having been directed to that state.
>
> In disputes concerned with a contractual obligation that comes within the subject matter jurisdiction of a court common to several member states, a person may be sued in the common court if the obligation in question is to be performed in any of the member states concerned.[47]

The second paragraph is irrelevant for the UPC, but is there to cover any other common court, since the proposal also covers the Benelux Court. Paragraph 1 clearly states what the mechanism is, place of infringement without domicile, but also builds in a safeguard

---

[47] Based on Articles 2:201 and 2:202 CLIP Principles; see European Max Planck Group on Conflict of Laws in Intellectual Property (CLIP), *Conflict of Laws in Intellectual Property: The CLIP Principles and Commentary* (OUP, 2013) 69–84.

mechanism. One does not want the common court to have jurisdiction over a foreign defendant that did not act or direct action in or towards the jurisdiction, such as a manufacturer of a patented product based in a country where there is no patent protecting the product whose independent distributor imports the product in the Member States (where a patent is in force). But as the safeguard applies cumulatively, any foreign parent company that directs the operations of subsidiaries, etc. will be caught without the need to rely on Article 8(1).

For reasons of clarity it is advisable to add a paragraph on Article 24(4):

> In disputes having as their object a judgment on the validity or revocation of intellectual property rights over which a court common to several member states exercises subject matter jurisdiction the common court will have exclusive jurisdiction.
>
> During the transition period provided for by Article 83(1) Agreement on a Unitary Patent Court the exclusive jurisdiction of the common court and the national court will be exercised concurrently. The relationship between the common court and the national court will be determined by Article 31.

Inside the common court the division before which validity is raised during infringement proceedings has the option to continue with the infringement case and to rule on validity too (Article 33(3) UPC Agreement). This effectively reverses that position taken by the CJEU in Case C–4/03 *GAT v LuK* [2006] ECR I-6509. As a result, it no longer makes sense to keep the strict current version of Article 24(4) Brussels I Regulation, as interpreted in *GAT v LuK*, for other registered IP rights[48] and for national patents. Not allowing the infringement court to rule *erga omnes* and to instruct a foreign patent office to change the register is sufficient. Hence the idea of adding the following paragraph to Article 24(4):

> Paragraph 1 does not apply where validity arises in a context other than by principal claim or counterclaim. The decisions resulting from such disputes do not affect the validity of those rights against third parties.

It would allow the defendant in an infringement case to raise the invalidity of the right as a defence, i.e. one cannot infringe an invalid right, without the infringement court having to stay the case. But it then remains an infringement case and the decision of the court will simply determine between the parties whether the defendant infringes the right of the claimant. Any decision on invalidity proper, i.e. one with effect *erga omnes* that will find its way onto the register, will still have to be brought in the court that has exclusive jurisdiction.

Article 8(1) Brussels I Regulation allows multiple defendants to be brought before a single court and can of course also be extended to defendants that are not domiciled in a Member State, but its application in patent cases (and in IP cases in general) is a mess. Case C–539/03 *Roche Nederland BV et al. v Frederick Primus and Milton Goldenberg* [2006] ECR I-6535 was unduly strict and without saying so the CJEU has been backtracking ever since. There was Case C–98/06 *Freeport Plc v Arnoldsson* [2007] ECR I-8319 and then Case C–145/10 *Eva-Maria Painer v Standard Verlags GmbH et al.* [2011] ECDR 6 and Case C–616/10 *Solvay SA v Honeywell Fluorine Products Europe BV, Honeywell Belgium NV and Honeywell Europe NV* [2012] All ER (D) 127. The latter two cases are simply incompatible with the strict *Roche Nederland* approach. One can leave it to the CJEU to sort out the mess and hope the Court will continue with the de facto more flexible

---

[48] As the rule was essentially there for (European) patents.

approach in *Solvay* and *Painer*. But Article 33(1)(b) UPC Agreement has very different language to offer:

> An action may be brought against multiple defendants only where the defendants have a commercial relationship and where the action relates to the same alleged infringement.

Admittedly, this provision cannot operate at international jurisdiction level, where Article 31 refers uniquely to the Brussels I Regulation, and its Article 8(1), and it therefore only operates at the competence level, i.e. once the UPC already has jurisdiction over each of the defendants. But it may not be wise to leave both versions in existence side by side, without any clarification for the non-private international law expert as to which one applies when. Be that as it may, there will be little scope for Article 8(1) if the defendant is not domiciled in a Member State. It will be very hard to find a defendant that one would nevertheless want to join to the case before the UPC, but that cannot be brought before the court on the basis of Article 7(2) if the domicile safeguard no longer applies. Any defendant against whom one has a realistic chance of success will at least contribute to the act causing the damage or be at least partially responsible for the damage. And once the jurisdiction point has been handled by Article 7(2) Brussels I Regulation the competence provision in Article 33(1)(b) will enable the claimant to centralize the claim against multiple defendants before a single division of the court. Article 33(1) does not expressly extend the application of its paragraph (b) to defendants that are not domiciled in a Member State, but this is clearly intended. The paragraph on defendants that are not domiciled in a Member State merely adds the option to sue them before the central division, without excluding anything.

Finally, the proposal makes Article 35 Brussels I Regulation applicable even if the courts of other Member States have jurisdiction as to the substance of the case. This gives the UPC an appropriately wide power to issue provisional measures.

27.6.5.3 Paragraph 3

Paragraph 3 was always intended to add to the basis on which jurisdiction can be taken, but what was proposed in the draft Regulation was very different from what made it into the Regulation that was in the end adopted. Let us look in turn at both versions.

Paragraph 3 of the proposal was intended to offer a further ground of jurisdiction over a defendant that is not domiciled in a Member State. The idea was simple. An additional ground of jurisdiction was provided as a safety net for those cases for which no other provision of the Regulation gives jurisdiction to a Brussels I Court. Whilst this may not only appear to be simple, but also reasonable if one considers the recast of the Brussels I Regulation, it is hard to see how this remains simple and reasonable if the massive expansion that results from paragraph 2 of Article 71b is also taken on board. Be that as it may, paragraph 3 did set out to grant the UPC jurisdiction over a defendant that is not domiciled in a Member State and that is not subject to the jurisdiction of the court on the basis of any other Brussels I provision if:

a) property belonging to the defendant is located in a Member State party to the agreement establishing the common court;

b) the value of the property is not insignificant compared to the value of the claim;

c) the dispute has a sufficient connection with any Member State party to the agreement establishing the common court.[49]

---

[49] Article 1(2).

The explanatory memorandum referred to the fact that various Member States have an asset-based ground of jurisdiction in their national jurisdiction rules, but that does not mean it is needed or useful in a patent context where paragraph 2 is already in place. The explanatory memorandum gave the example of a Turkish defendant, with assets in the EU one assumes, who infringes a European patent covering several Member States and Turkey. There is a slight problem with the example though. It is not covered by paragraph 3. Paragraph 2 does the job as an Article 7(2) without the domicile requirement will grant jurisdiction in respect of any of the Member States concerned as the infringement takes place there and Article 34 UPC Agreement makes sure that the judgment covers any designation of the European patent. One never gets to paragraph 3, as there is a ground of jurisdiction in the Regulation that applies.

In its version in the proposal paragraph 3 of Article 71(b) is the ultimate power grab! It could make sense as a limitation or check and balance on paragraph 2, but that is clearly not what it is. It is however very hard to see which case that would not already be covered by paragraph 2 would be covered by paragraph 3 and would be reasonable in terms of the jurisdiction of the common court. One can only assume that this is supposed to cover the foreign parent or holding company in a multiple defendants case in the absence of a working multiple defendants provision at international jurisdiction stage. As shown above, a properly worded paragraph 2 will do the job and a properly worded Article 8(1) provision can only help. Paragraph 3 is thus redundant and will only serve to (rightfully) infuriate foreign countries. It also undermines the criticism we always have when, for example, the Texas courts grab jurisdiction on such a basis. A case that comes to mind is *Rhapsody Solutions, LLC v Cryogenic Vessel Alternatives, Inc.* (US District Court, S.D. Tex., 5 March 2013), where it was held that a foreign company accessing software on a server in the United States, with the foreign company having a subsidiary and assets in the United States, is subject to the jurisdiction of the court in Texas. Even in the United States this case and the District Court for the Southern District of Texas's approach to jurisdiction is controversial, which makes it even harder to understand why the EU would want to adopt a similar approach. In its proposal version paragraph 3 is also entirely out of line with the very principles of the Brussels I jurisdiction.

As these criticisms were conveyed to the draftsmen, it is satisfying to see that the final version of paragraph 3 looks radically different. The starting point is now very clearly not an independent ground of jurisdiction, but a case where the common court already has jurisdiction on the basis of paragraph 2. In such a case damage inside the EU may be coupled with damage outside the EU in a third state. It may make sense for the common court to deal also with that latter damage and to avoid the need for there to be additional litigation in the third state. Article 7(2) Brussels I Regulation, even if applied without the domicile requirement as a result of paragraph 2, may not have covered damage in a third state and paragraph 3 serves a useful purpose on this point. Once that starting point has been established two of the factors that were also retained in the proposal return, but this time they operate as additional safeguards:

> Such jurisdiction may only be established if property belonging to the defendant is located in any Member State party to the instrument establishing the common court and the dispute has a sufficient connection with any such Member State.

27.6.6 *Lis Pendens*

The issue of *lis pendens* arises if we leave jurisdiction rules in the strict sense to one side. Several courts that deal with the same or a related issue between the same parties, the idea has never found favour for obvious reasons in private international law. The proposal has a simple solution to offer. The existing Brussels I Regulation rules on *lis pendens* would be expanded to cover two additional situations. On a permanent basis there is the situation where proceedings are brought in the UPC and in the national courts of an EU Member State that is not a party to the UPC Agreement and on a temporary basis there is the situation where proceedings are brought in the UPC and in the national courts of a Member State that is a party to the UPC Agreement during the transition period that is referred to in Article 83(1) UPC Agreement.

One has to ask the question though whether matters can be that simple. The Brussels I approach can be abbreviated to the concept that the court first seized is given preference. But that assumes that there is a single cause of action, i.e. the same (or a very related) case is brought in two or more courts. Patent cases fit badly with that idea. There are infringement cases, claims for a negative declaration, and (in-)validity claims, or counterclaims. They can arise in the same case or in separate cases, but the link between them is very strong. And until we are merely left with European Patents with Unitary Effect there are the various national designations of a European patent. Not all claims relate to all designations and the various claims do not necessarily refer to the same designations, even though there may (or may not) be an overlap on this point. Perhaps the easiest way forward is to look at a number of practical examples. And it will become clear very quickly that these complicating factors cause significant problems for the simple solution proposed by the Commission.

It needs to be clarified what the private international law role is of Article 34 UPC Agreement. How and when does it lead to a same cause of action? And the systematic preference for the court first seized in the Brussels I Regulation is not always the way forward in the patent-related cases. Maybe one ought to give preference to the UPC in a (large) number of circumstances. But can that be reconciled with the political comprise that underpins Article 83(1) UPC Agreement? This is clearly an area where the proposal is anything but satisfactory and where a lot of clarifying work remains to be done.

27.6.7 **Recognition and Enforcement**

Not all EU Member States will become parties to the UPC Agreement. There will therefore in practice be judgments from those Member States that did not join and judgments from the UPC. Each of these may require recognition and enforcement in the other area. The proposed Article 71d deals with this problem and applies the standard Brussels I Regulation mechanism. This does not give rise to major problems and is acceptable as a workable solution.

The focus changes of course if one is merely dealing with the recognition and enforcement of a judgment given by a common court in a Member State that is party to the instrument establishing the common court. The proposal did not address this issue, but the Regulation, as adopted, now adds the obvious solution, which is to apply any rules on recognition and enforcement in that instrument instead of the Brussels I rules. This is found in Article 1 (*in fine*), which will become the final paragraph of Article 71d Brussels I Regulation.

27.6.8 **Competence**

Once the international jurisdiction of the UPC has been established the second part of Chapter VI of the UPC Agreement comes into play.

Article 32 deals with the competence of the court and establishes the subject matter with which the court will deal. Article 33 then follows up with the internal distribution of cases between the various divisions of the court. Here one finds elements such as the flexible multiple defendant rule that was referred to earlier and rules on *lis pendens* and priority. There is also a rule that allows the transfer of a case that really covers most of the territory of the court to be transferred from the regional divisions to the central division if the infringement has occurred at least in the territories of three regional divisions, as well as further procedural rules.

And of course then follows the by now well-rehearsed rule in Article 34. Its role as a competence rule is uncontroversial and clear, but its wider implications in relation to jurisdiction are less clear and less uncontroversial. It would however lead too far to offer here a complete in-depth analysis of the competence rules. Suffice it to repeat that they are to be distinguished from the jurisdiction rules and that they play a different role.

It is slightly less obvious how this private international law development links back to the aspects of theory set out earlier in this chapter. No new exclusive right is created and so the question whether we did get the balance right to let the new right play its role in the promotion of competition does not arise. But the enhancement of competition question arises indirectly. A patent system that gets the balance right and that enhances competition must be a system that works smoothly and effectively in practice. It must be a system in which the rights holder can in an effective and not unduly burdensome and costly way enforce its rights and in which the alleged infringer can effectively and smoothly defend its position. This is the aim of these new rules and the analysis of their effectiveness and workability needs to be seen against that background.

27.7 Conclusions

Our two case studies were of course not chosen randomly. The introduction of the unitary patent will no doubt be a major evolution in IP in the EU and once it gets underway the establishment of the UPC and the development of its case law, during the seven-year transition period and afterwards, will become a major factor and future trend. Our case study demonstrated that private international law will play an important role in this context. This is also true in general. The cross-border elements in the practice of IP in the EU and beyond are taking on an increasingly important role and with it come transborder litigation and aspects of jurisdiction and applicable law. More and more such cases will arise and courts will increasingly deal with foreign IP rights and apply foreign IP laws.

Transformative works on the other hand are just one example of the issues that have arisen as a result of the digital revolution in copyright. That is not merely something that has taken place. It is also a future trend. Digital technology and the business models that it enables will continue to develop at a rapid pace. Applying the existing copyright rules to them and developing copyright to keep pace with them will be a major and ongoing challenge. The digital revolution is here to stay, also in copyright.

One could add a potentially endless list of additional future trends to these two. Suffice it to mention here that a major reform of the Community trade mark system is underway. The idea is to modernize the system and to take account of the at times tortuous case law of the CJEU. In the area of design law there is not yet a wealth of CJEU case law, but if the trade mark and copyright examples are anything to go by one will see an increasing number of cases soon, setting out an autonomous interpretation of the Community design system. And that brings us back to copyright. In this area too a major review of the *acquis communautaire* is underway. Whether that will merely result in directives being redrafted or directives being added, or whether the EU will attempt to push forward the grand but extremely complex (if not virtually impossible in combination with national copyrights) idea of a Community copyright that would replace the piecemeal approach of the directives, remains to be seen. And finally one should never forget the ongoing battle on the enforcement front. This will without doubt remain an important trend for the future. The European Observatory on Infringements of Intellectual Property Rights, now placed inside OHIM, will continue to play a major role in the EU's efforts against piracy. How effective these efforts will be remains to be seen.

Index

abuse of enforcement
proceedings 601–2
groundless threats, UK
addressing 601
account of profits 600–1
ascertaining net profits realized
by defendant 601
court's discretion 600
deductions from profits 601
difficulties with 601
restitutionary and equitable in
nature 600
administrative procedures
604–9
counterfeit goods,
preventing 604
definitions 606–9
rights holder's
application 605–6
wide scope of regulation 609
advertising, comparative and
misleading 460–2
AdWords 405–7, 415, 425–6
amending/correcting European
patents or applications 151–2
limits on amendments/
corrections that may be
made 151
pre-grant and post-grant
opportunities for
amendment/
correction 151–2
animal varieties see plant and
animal varieties
Anton Piller orders 580–5
abuse of the order and its
redress 583–4
conditions for issuing 583–4
expansion of order 582–3
Member States'
obligations 580–1
origins of 581–2
Practice Direction 583–4
Aromatised Wine
Regulation 480–1
content of applications for
protection 481
nature of aromatised
wine 480
assignment
design rights, of 497–8
trademarks, of 395

authorial works protectable by
copyright 269–84
assessing EU definition of
authorial works 280–4
conflating authorial works
and their parts 281–2
failing to reflect convincing
non-legal definition of
authorial work 282–4
'pros' and 'cons' of
definition 281
computer programs as
authorial works 278–9
copyright protection for only a
work's authorial aspects 302
databases as authorial
works 279–80
distinguishing authorial
(original) from non-authorial
(unoriginal) protectable
works 271–4
author's own intellectual
creations 271
expansive definition of
authorial works 272–4
ideas as not bounded
expressive works 271
individual words 271–2
simplicity no bar to
copyright 272–4
sporting events 271–2
failing to reflect convincing
non-legal definition of
authorial work 282–4
film props as authorial
works: Lucasfilm 283–4
people as authorial works:
Eva and Adele 282–3
films
authorial works, as 275
non-authorial films
protectable by related
rights 275–6
film scenes as authorial
works 275
perfumes as authorial
works 276–8
author's own intellectual
creation, as 276
divergent treatment of
perfumes by European
States 276

objections to treatment of
perfumes as authorial
works 276–7
photographs
authorial works, as 274–5
non-authorial photographs
protectable by related
rights 275–6
photographic scenes as
authorial works 275
photographs as authorial
works 274–5
statutory framework 269–71
European/EU
framework 270–1
international
framework 269–70
authors
balancing authors' claims for
protection with freedom of
third parties 15
commitment to individuated
concept of authorship 14–15
copyright ownership 292–3
works, copyright for see
authorial works protectable
by copyright

bad faith in trade mark
application 392
Berne Convention 31–2, 35
amendments to 33
biodiversity 86
biological processes see under
varieties/essentially biological
process exclusions
biopiracy 85
Biotech Directive 1998 129–30,
156–7
scope of patents: gene patents
granted in respect of EU
Member States 203–4
Art 9 Biotech Directive 203
meaning of Art 9:
Monsanto 203–4
significance of
Monsanto 204
biotechnology patenting case
study 101–7
judicial perspectives
on biotechnology
patenting 102–5